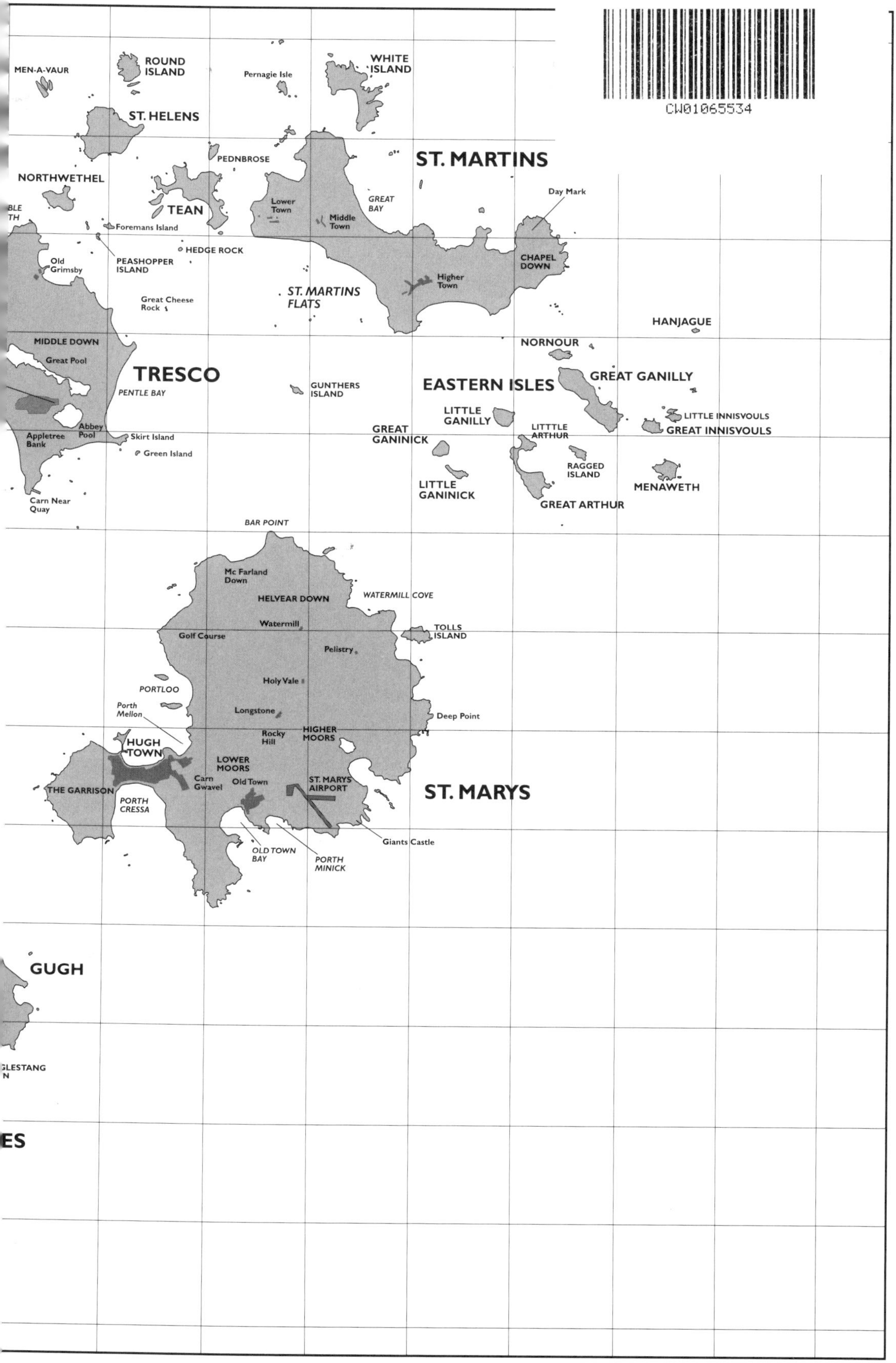
MEN-A-VAUR
ROUND ISLAND
Pernagie Isle
WHITE ISLAND
ST. HELENS
PEDNBROSE
ST. MARTINS
NORTHWETHEL
TEAN
Lower Town
Middle Town
GREAT BAY
Day Mark
Foremans Island
HEDGE ROCK
PEASHOPPER ISLAND
Old Grimsby
Higher Town
CHAPEL DOWN
ST. MARTINS FLATS
Great Cheese Rock
HANJAGUE
MIDDLE DOWN
Great Pool
NORNOUR
TRESCO
PENTLE BAY
GUNTHERS ISLAND
EASTERN ISLES
GREAT GANILLY
LITTLE GANILLY
LITTLE INNISVOULS
GREAT INNISVOULS
Abbey Pool
Appletree Bank
Skirt Island
Green Island
GREAT GANINICK
LITTTLE ARTHUR
RAGGED ISLAND
LITTLE GANINICK
MENAWETH
GREAT ARTHUR
Carn Near Quay
BAR POINT
Mc Farland Down
HELVEAR DOWN
WATERMILL COVE
Watermill
TOLLS ISLAND
Golf Course
Pelistry
Holy Vale
PORTLOO
Porth Mellon
Longstone
Deep Point
Rocky Hill
HIGHER MOORS
HUGH TOWN
LOWER MOORS
Carn Gwavel
Old Town
ST. MARYS AIRPORT
THE GARRISON
PORTH CRESSA
ST. MARYS
Giants Castle
OLD TOWN BAY
PORTH MINICK
GUGH

# The Birds of
# THE ISLES OF SCILLY

# *The Birds of* THE ISLES OF SCILLY

Peter Robinson

CHRISTOPHER HELM
LONDON

Published by Christopher Helm, an imprint of A & C Black Publishers Ltd., 37 Soho Square, London W1D 3QZ

Copyright © 2003 Peter Robinson
Illustrations © 2003 Andy Redden

ISBN 0-7136-6037-6

A CIP catalogue record for this book is available from the British Library

All rights reserved. No part of this publication may be reproduced or used in any form or by any means – photographic, electronic or mechanical, including photocopying, recording, taping or information storage and retrieval systems – without permission of the publishers.

A & C Black uses paper produced with elemental chlorine-free pulp, harvested from managed sustainable forests.

Printed in Slovenia on behalf of Compass Press Limited

Produced and designed by Fluke Art, Cornwall

10 9 8 7 6 5 4 3 2 1

www.acblack.com

# CONTENTS

| | |
|---|---|
| Acknowledgements | 7 |
| Introduction | 9 |
| Abbreviations | 10 |
| Scilly at a glance | 11 |
| Visiting Scilly | 15 |
| Scillonian fauna and flora | 18 |
| A background to the birds of Scilly | 21 |
| Birding in Scilly | 24 |
| Introduction to the Systematic List | 30 |
| Systematic List of the birds of the Isles of Scilly | 33 |
| Records of introduced or escaped birds | 579 |
| Bibliography | 585 |
| Index | 603 |

To the memory of

Edward Hearle Rodd 1810–1880
David Bassil Hunt 1934–1985
Peter James Grant 1943–1990

# ACKNOWLEDGEMENTS

The author is indebted to a large number of people for their help or advice, both whilst carrying out fieldwork during the period 1990–2000 and during preparation of this book. The Duchy of Cornwall was always most helpful and sympathetic to my demands, including the provision of land dimensions and advising on tenancies. Thus a great dept of gratitude is owed to both the present and former Land Stewards, Jeremy Pontin and Lt. Colonel Robertson, respectively. Particular thanks are also due to the Rogers family for allowing fieldwork on Lunnon Farm on St Mary's, whilst John Banfield (Holy Vale) and Barnesley Ward (Normandy) allowed similar activities on adjoining land. Noel and Angela Jenkins granted permission to catch and ring birds on adjacent areas of Carn Friars Farm.

The Isles of Scilly Environmental Trust granted access to uninhabited islands for various seabird survey and monitoring work and agreed to ringing work being carried out on sections of Higher Moors under their control, whilst the Council of the Isles of Scilly granted permission to utilise their water pumping facility in Higher Moors as a ringing centre. Mike Rogers gave encouragement and advice on Common Birds Census work from the outset and provided his own data for the years 1986–87. Roy Taylor provided much advice and encouragement on Song Thrush fieldwork and data handling; Will Wagstaff assisted with net-ride clearance and provided timber for nestbox construction, as well as contributing his own ringing data; whilst Stella Turk provided copies of her late husband Frank Turk's papers on Scillonian faunal fossil remains. I am also deeply indebted to Royal Society for the Protection of Birds Librarians Ian Dawson and Lyn Giddings for their prompt attention to my numerous queries, and similarly to Robert Prys-Jones, Effie Warr, Alison Harding and Mark Adams of the British Museum (Natural History) at Tring. My thanks also go to Paul McCartney of the Cornwall Wildlife Trust, Steve Ottery and Di Barnes at the Isles of Scilly Museum, staff of the General Zoology Library, South Kensington and Linda Birch of the Oxford University Zoological Libraries, all of whom provided access to their respective collections and responded sympathetically to my numerous enquiries. Johan Wallander provided details of the Swedish Ringed Plover. Nick Harrison-Ward of the Cornish Wildlife Trust provided details on the size of the Cornish landmass. Others who were generous with advice or encouragement include Steve Gantlett, Rosemary Parslow and Martin Scott. A particular debt of gratitude is owed to Bob Scott, who generously handed over the results of his previous researches into published early Scillonian records. Paul Griffiths of ADIT gave invaluable help and support during preparation of the maps. Much of the seabird information included here results from ongoing surveys organised by English Nature (formerly NCC) and/or the Isles of Scilly Environmental Trust, or, in the case of Seabird 2000, by the Joint Nature Conservation Committee. To assist with all of this survey work, English Nature generously provided sea-borne transport in the form of the launch *Melza*, together with their invaluable boatman Cyril Nicholas.

Numerous individuals and groups contributed to the Scillonian ringing effort, many of whom from earlier years are sadly unknown to the author. However, the following all contributed significantly during the 1990s and without their efforts our knowledge of bird movements, both within and outside Scilly, would be greatly reduced: Hayley Ashwell, Gordon Avery, Mark Barratt, Brian Bailey, Nigel Bray, Roy Bryher, John Cameron, Peter Clement, Dave Clugston, Greg Conway, Adam Cornish, Shani Course, Paul Derbyshire, Erin Down, Janine Dowrick, Carol Drage, Allen Drewitt, Graeme Dunlop, Maurice Durham, Graham Elliott, Stephan Elliott, Trevor Girling, Ray Gribble, Ken Hamblyn, Vickie Heaney, Andrew Holden, John Holmes, Jim Lennon, Mark and Lucy Love, Dave Mawer, Geoff Mawson, Phil Mitchell, Phil Mountain, Dave Murdock, Rebecca Nason, Ross Newham, Cyril Nicholas, Roger Peart, Ruth Points, John Sanders, Darryl Saunders, Hanne Tatchell, Colin Taylor, Roy Taylor, Luke Thomson, Will Wagstaff, Kester Wilson and Rob Young. Caroline Dudley made numerous corrections and suggested frequent improvements to my original text and George Reszeter and Steve Young very generously provided photographs for inclusion. Thanks are also due to Marianne Taylor at Christopher Helm, and to Julie Dando of Fluke Art who undertook the design and layout of the book.

I owe a particular debt of gratitude to my wife Susan, who as always endured without complaint the countless early morning disturbances and spoiled meals inevitably associated with long hours of fieldwork, plus of course the numerous hours of family inconvenience involved during the writing of what is a long overdue and much needed work on all the birds of Scilly.

# INTRODUCTION

Although the geographical position of the Isles of Scilly makes them one of the most important ornithological sites in western Europe, there has been a notable shortage of comprehensive publication on the birds of this isolated island group. As long ago as 1906, James Clark and Francis Rodd commented that although 'accidental visitors have from time to time received due recognition in the pages of the *Zoologist* and elsewhere, with the exception of a short appendix to Rodd's *The Birds of Cornwall and The Scilly Islands* (1880), and a compilation by the Reverend Smart in the *Transactions of the Penzance Natural History and Antiquarian Society* for 1885, no general account has yet been published of the birds of these islands'. The author of the *The Birds of Cornwall and The Scilly Islands* referred to was Francis's celebrated uncle E H Rodd of Penzance in west Cornwall. The *Zoologist*'s editor, James Harting, had already voiced much the same sentiments during his 19th century posthumous preparation of the elder Rodd's landmark 1880 publication.

True, Rodd also gave coverage to Scilly but this was often somewhat secondary to the main objective of providing an account of the birds of Cornwall, and his remarks often lacked important detail and were far from what might be described as comprehensive. Although also well researched and invaluable, Clark and Rodd's 1906 *Zoologist* paper was similarly lacking in detail, and, just like E H Rodd's publication in the previous century, Penhallurick's two volumes dealt mainly with mainland Cornwall, much of the information concerning Scilly being comparatively brief.

Whilst that situation perhaps remained tenable up until the mid-20th century, recent major advances in our knowledge of Scillonian, Eurasian and Nearctic ornithology argued for something more closely linked to the islands: a book on *The Birds of the Isles of Scilly* dealing with all species, not just the rarities, especially as some breeding species are of particular importance nationally. Nonetheless, rarities play a major part in raising Scilly to prominence as a major European birdwatching site and perhaps the most likely European site at which to encounter Nearctic migrants with any degree of regularity. Who among those involved, for example, will ever forget the excitement of the second week of October 1999, when the arrival of Britain's first Short-toed Eagle was followed over the next seven days by White's Thrush, Siberian Thrush and then a fine male Blue Rock Thrush (for scientific names of birds see the Systematic List).

Records dealt with in the following pages commence with those evident from bone remains unearthed at prehistoric sites within the islands, including two species, Great Auk and Black Grouse, not previously included in any list of Scilly's avifauna. The bulk of the information used in the text, however, comes from papers, letters and books originating from the 18th century onwards, the amount of material available for research understandably increasing into the 19th and 20th centuries, and the extent and volume of the research involved being readily apparent from the bibliography. At least 151 (52.6%) of the 287 full species considered by the British Birds Rarities Committee (BBRC) up until the end of 1999 have occurred at least once in Scilly, plus at least another two, Red-billed Tropicbird and Brown/South Polar Skua, that were added to the list since 1999. These 153 nationally rare species comprise 36% of the present possible Scillonian total of 425 species. This last figure puts the comparatively small island group on a par with far larger geographical areas, such as mainland Cornwall or Shetland, or the combined areas of 'Yorkshire', and ahead of the legendary Fair Isle. Indeed, these 424 species represent just under 75% of the total of 564 species on the British List up until autumn 2002. The situation remains fluid with Savi's Warbler and the 'Black-headed' form of Yellow Wagtail, both being considered for acceptance as a consequence of sightings during spring 2003.

# ABBREVIATIONS

## Abbreviations Used in the Systematic List and Elsewhere in the Text

| | |
|---|---|
| AOU | American Ornithologists' Union |
| BBRC | British Birds Rarities Committee |
| BOC | British Ornithologists' Club |
| BOU | British Ornithologists' Union |
| BOURC | British Ornithologists' Union Records Committee |
| CBWPS | Cornwall Birdwatching and Preservation Society |
| CBWPSAR | Cornwall Birdwatching and Preservation Society Annual Report |
| EN | English Nature |
| IOSBG | Isles of Scilly Bird Group |
| IOSBR | Isles of Scilly Bird Report |
| IOSSBG | Isles of Scilly Seabird Group |
| JNCC | Joint Nature Conservancy Council |
| NCC | Nature Conservancy Council |
| RSPB | Royal Society for the Protection of Birds |
| SABO | St Agnes Bird Observatory |
| SABOA | St Agnes Bird Observatory Annual Report |
| SRP | Scilly Records Panel |
| SVRG | Severn Vale Ringing Group |

## Abbreviations Used in Ringing Recapture Summaries

| | |
|---|---|
| 1stY | First-year (hatched that year) |
| 2ndY | Second-year (hatched the previous year) |
| AD | Ringed as an adult |
| AS | Aboard ship |
| BR | Breeding |
| CT | Controlled (intentionally captured and released) |
| F | Female |
| FD | Found Dead |
| FG | Full grown |
| FI | Found injured |
| FN | Entangled in commercial fishing net |
| FR | Field record (usually colour-ring or wing-tag sighting) |
| GP | Found in gull pellet |
| KC | Killed by cat |
| KW | Struck window |
| LO | Leg only found |
| M | Male |
| Ol | Found oiled |
| Pul | Ringed as a pullus |
| RT | Recapture (local) |
| SH | Shot |

# SCILLY AT A GLANCE

Drive west the six or so hours from London to the western tip of Cornwall's Land's End peninsula and stand on the clifftop looking west past the Longships Lighthouse in the direction of North America. If the weather is kind, and that is not always so in this part of Britain, you may perhaps see a cluster of tiny islands hugging the horizon away to the southwest. These are the Isles of Scilly, a low-lying archipelago, with nowhere more than 50 metres high, comprising two hundred or so small islands and lesser rocks situated 45 kilometres (28 miles) out into the North Atlantic.

Only the five largest islands are inhabited and although one, Tresco, is managed privately by the Dorrien-Smith family, all are in the ownership of the Duchy of Cornwall. The total resident human population is in the region of 2,000 souls, although this can and often does double during the summer holiday season. St Mary's, with a landmass of 629 hectares and a population of 1,200, is the largest of the five inhabited islands, the others being Tresco, St Martin's and Bryher, plus St Agnes and the partly attached Gugh. The Scillonian climate is significantly influenced year-round by the proximity of the Gulf Stream, with resultant mild winters and largely dry summers, the islands experiencing little seasonal variation in temperature. Winter months are marked by the near absence of frost, plus frequent strong winds and rain from off the North Atlantic. Most workable farmland is under individual tenancy agreement, with most untenanted land and the uninhabited islands managed under lease by the Isles of Scilly Environmental Trust.

The late 19th and early 20th century witnessed the growth of a thriving winter flower industry supplying eager mainland markets, with an associated decline in the extent of grazing land. Although *Narcissi*, in particular, thrive in Scilly's mild climate, frequent strong winds cause costly crop damage. To resolve this problem, high hedgerows of evergreen shrubs, e.g. *Pittosporum crassifolium, Escallonia macrantha, Olearia traversii, Euonymus japonicus*, Hedge Veronica *Hebe franciscana* or Tamarisk *Tamarix gallica*, now provide protection for numerous small fields, typically of about half a hectare. Tourism, flower farming and fishing (mostly shellfish) now form the basis of Scilly's economy. Tourism underwent a period of sustained growth during the mid-20th century but may now have stabilised and is in any event limited by several factors, including local housing demands, increasing transport costs and, at least until recently, a shortage of fresh water. Flower farming too may currently be experiencing a downturn, in part owing to improvements in mainland production capabilities but also owing to increased competition from world markets, the richly scented bunches of Soleil D'ors and similar flowers now competing on the florist's shelves with exotic blooms flown in daily from as far away as South America.

The islands were largely treeless until the start of the 20th century, with just a few wind-pruned elms *Ulmus* (probably Cornish Elm *U. stricta* (Coleman, M. 2002. British Elms. *British Wildlife* 13: 390–395)) and stunted willows *Salix* (probably Goat Willow *S. caprea*) thriving in low, mainly damp areas and with walled fields maintained mostly as grazing. A period of intensive tree planting during the early 1920s heralded the appearance of numerous shelterbelts on inhabited islands, primarily of introduced Monterey Pine *Pinus radiata*. Nowadays, substantial areas of Common Reed *Phragmites communis* occur around Tresco's Great Pool and around Porth Hellick and Lower Moors pools on St Mary's, having apparently been introduced during the mid- to late 19th century. These reedbeds are now perhaps the most significant west of Cornwall's River Tamar after those fringing the Marazion pools to the east of Penzance.

About 35 islands are suitable for breeding seabirds in addition to four of the five already mentioned. Largest of these are Samson, which until quite recently was inhabited, and the only slightly smaller Annet, which is the undoubted main seabird breeding site in Scilly.

Evidence of Scilly's historical past abounds, among the most obvious being stone-lined burial chambers on the summit of Samson's north and south hills, or above Gugh's eastern slopes. Most of these probably date from between 500 and 1,000 BC, whereas well-preserved remains of prehistoric buildings exist at Halangy Down on St Mary's and on Nornour in the Eastern Isles. Fly over the shallow waters linking the islands at low tide and in fine weather Bronze Age field walls become readily apparent still, five of the six largest islands having been joined until some time during the first millennium AD; the exceptions are St Agnes and the associated Western Isles, all of which seem always to have been separated by a deep-water channel. During exceptionally low tides it is still possible to walk (or wade) the several kilometres from Tresco east to St Martin's and then south across Crow Sound to Bar Point on the northern tip of St Mary's (pers. obs.), although not without proper preparation and not without ensuring others have been informed – spring tides may go out a long way, but they come in again rapidly!

## THE CONSERVATION IMPORTANCE OF THE ISLANDS

The Isles of Scilly comprise the final decayed stage of a once significant mountain chain known as the Armorican Mountains and they are now the sole European example of a Lusitanian semi-oceanic archipelago (UK Biodiversity Steering Group 1995). They have also been identified as an Important Bird Area (IBA) under European legislation and are proposed as a Special Protection Area (SPA) and a RAMSAR site. In addition, they are a designated Area of Outstanding Natural Beauty and a Heritage Coast site. A voluntary Isles of Scilly Marine Park encompasses almost all islands and operates out as far as the 50-metre depth contour, this Park being jointly acknowledged by the Duchy of Cornwall, Isles of Scilly Environmental Trust, local Sea Fisheries Committee, Isles of Scilly Council and English Nature.

Some 23 sites totalling just over 800 hectares or 50% of the total landmass, on both inhabited and uninhabited islands, have been designated as Sites of Special Scientific Interest (SSSI) by the Government's statutory nature conservation advisers, English Nature, either for their botanical or ornithological importance. Similarly, many buildings, fortifications and archaeological sites are managed by English Heritage.

The islands are the only published English Storm Petrel breeding site and more species of seabirds annually breed in the islands than at any other site in England or Wales. In addition, some passerine breeding densities may be greater in Scilly than anywhere else in Britain. The islands also hold nationally or perhaps internationally important numbers of a few species. Wintering Sanderlings, for example, reach levels of national importance (Lock 1999) and perhaps up to 3% of British Shag and 4% of Great and Lesser Black-backed Gull populations breed. Wintering numbers of these last two species, and perhaps of Little Egret and Greenshank, are probably also nationally significant, as may be some wintering wildfowl populations.

In addition to all of this, of course, the geographical position of the islands makes them extremely important to tired, disorientated migrant birds from places far removed from western Europe, as becomes abundantly evident from the following pages.

## ISLAND SIZE

Geographically the islands occupy an area about 18 by 10 kilometres, the actual area of landmass involved being far smaller. The following Table shows approximate island land areas as obtained from various sources. In the case of some smaller islands, areas shown are approximate but the landmass involved is small enough not to significantly affect overall figures.

**Estimated Land Areas for Individual Islands**

| Inhabited Island | Hectares | Acres |
|---|---|---|
| Bryher | 126.0 | 311.3 |
| St Agnes | 109.3 | 270.0 |
| (Gugh) | 38.6 | 95.3 |
| St Martin's | 221.7 | 547.8 |
| (White Island, St Martin's) | 15.4 | 38.0 |
| St Mary's | 628.7 | 1553.4 |
| Tresco | 297.4 | 734.8 |
| **Total** | **1437.1** | **3550.6** |
| **Central Isles** | | |
| Puffin Island | 0.5 | 1.23 |
| Samson | 39.0 | 96.3 |
| White Island, Samson | 1.54 | 3.8 |
| **Total** | **41.04** | **101.33** |
| **Western Isles** | | |
| Annet | 21.4 | 52.8 |
| Gorregan | 1.46 | 3.6 |
| Melledgan | 1.5 | 3.7 |
| Rosevean | 1.0 | 2.47 |
| Rosevear | 1.9 | 3.9 |
| **Total** | **27.26** | **66.47** |

| Northern Isles | | |
|---|---|---|
| Castle Bryher | 0.5 | 1.23 |
| Gweal | 6.0 | 14.8 |
| Illiswilgig | 1.21 | 2.9 |
| Maiden Bower | 0.5 | 1.23 |
| Men-a-Vaur | 1.21 | 2.9 |
| Mincarlo | 1.82 | 4.4 |
| Northwethel | 4.86 | 12.0 |
| Round Island | 3.8 | 9.3 |
| Scilly Rock | 1.21 | 2.9 |
| St Helen's | 19.9 | 49.1 |
| Tean | 16.0 | 39.5 |
| **Total** | **57.01** | **140.26** |
| **Eastern Isles** | | |
| Great Arthur | 3.64 | 8.9 |
| Great Ganilly | 2.64 | 6.5 |
| Great Ganinick | 1.8 | 4.4 |
| Great Innisvouls | 0.65 | 1.6 |
| Guther's Island | 0.2 | 0.5 |
| Little Arthur | 2.0 | 4.9 |
| Little Ganilly | 2.4 | 5.9 |
| Little Ganinick | 1.8 | 4.4 |
| Little Innisvouls | 1.54 | 3.8 |
| Menewethan | 2.4 | 5.9 |
| Middle Arthur | 1.6 | 3.9 |
| Nournour | 1.34 | 3.3 |
| Ragged Island | 0.6 | 1.4 |
| **Total** | **22.61** | **55.4** |
| **All-island Total** | **1585.02 ha** | **3914.06 acres** |

# EARLY SCILLONIANS

Little is known for certain about the origin of early Scillonian populations and even less about how and when the first settlers arrived in the islands. However, given the archipelago's geographical position, nautical background and amenable climate, subsequent communities seem likely to have comprised a mix of nationalities, cultures and religions, as indeed rather remains the case to the present day. First authoritative evidence of an apparent presence originates from about 2,250 BC, though brief visits and perhaps longer stays probably occurred throughout the late Neolithic to early Bronze Age periods, i.e. from as early as 4,000 BC (Thomas 1985). Such evidence as there is for a Roman presence spans the period AD 100–400. Following the Roman departure, little again is known of Scilly, save that Viking raiders maintained a base in the islands, until removed by King Athelstan around AD 928 (Vyvyan 1953). It was the latter who left in place the first of many garrison forces. In AD 938, Benedictine monks settled in the islands and are popularly thought to have built both Tresco Abbey and a convent in Holy Vale on St Mary's. From around AD 1040 the islands came under the control of Tavistock Abbey, this remaining very much the situation through until Scilly became Crown property upon Dissolution of the Monasteries in AD 1539.

From the point of view of what follows, the next most important milestone in Scillonian history was Augustus Smith's acquisition of the islands from the Duchy of Cornwall in 1835, under the impressive title of 'Lord Proprietor'. As a consequence, Augustus removed himself from his comfortable Hertfordshire country house and took up residence in Tresco Abbey, committing his considerable organisational skills towards improving the life on the islands for all, though such attentions were not universally welcomed. Following his death in 1872, Augustus was succeeded by his nephew Lieutenant Thomas Algernon (Algy) Dorrien-Smith. On Thomas's death in 1918, control of the islands in turn passed to his son, Major Arthur

Algernon Dorrien-Smith. With the exception of Tresco, the lease of all inhabited islands reverted back to the Duchy of Cornwall in 1920.

The geographical position of Scilly, within the Western Approaches, makes them strategically important to Britain's defence, a point not lost on successive monarchs and governments. Evidence of this prevails, for example in the form of extensive fortifications surrounding the St Mary's Garrison, in Cromwell's Castle on Tresco, and in that part of Hugh Town known as The Parade. However, since its conversion to a communal park the previous use of the last named has become rather less obvious, but early photographs exist showing this former military parade ground in its apparently original state. With a military presence of one kind or another in the islands throughout most of the last millennium, it would be truly surprising if that had not also left its mark in the genetic make-up of the community, to say nothing of the plethora of passing shipping, from lowly merchantmen to mighty man-of-war, many of which would have been forced to take shelter within the islands during bad weather. Today, the troops have gone and the only naval presence involves the occasional passing warship, crews of which seldom now enjoy the pleasures of shore leave in the islands.

# VISITING SCILLY

## TRAVELLING TO AND FROM SCILLY

Construction of the Great Western Railway commenced in 1835 and by at least 1845 the line extended from London to Totnes in south Devon, any journey to Scilly then involving onward travel by horse-drawn coach to Plymouth and then eventually to Penzance. From Penzance the only option was the weekly packet which, weather permitting, sailed from Scilly on Monday and left for the mainland again on Thursday. Crossings during bad weather involved perhaps 15 hours at sea.

Thankfully, the situation today is much improved, it now being possible to make a leisurely start from London, either driving or taking the train direct to Penzance and still be on the islands by late afternoon, although the final crossing is still subject to acceptable weather. There are three options for crossing the stretch of water between mainland Cornwall and the Isles of Scilly. The first of these involves the Isles of Scilly Steamship Company's RMV *Scillonian III*, which sails daily from Penzance throughout the summer, except on Sundays, the journey taking approximately two-and-a-half hours; the second a small fixed-wing aircraft operated by the Steamship Company flying from several departure points; and the third the frequent British International Helicopter service which leaves from Penzance. Most flights take from fifteen to twenty minutes and, like the boat, there are no Sunday services.

*Scillonian III* sails in most weathers, the limiting factor for this mode of travel perhaps being whether passengers might wish to endure the conditions. On the other hand, aircraft are quickly grounded by impaired visibility, 'the boat' usually then offering a somewhat slower and not always enjoyable alternative. Rare birds do not, of course, time their arrival according to company schedules, and various groups, but especially birdwatchers, occasionally have reason to get on, or off, the islands outside normal travel periods. In such cases, small mainland aircraft are normally available for private charter, though again flights are subject to weather conditions.

For those arriving by sea under their own power (or sail), there are normally ample moorings available for small to medium-sized craft, though some of the safest anchorages involve a mooring fee and can become crowded during a few weekends in the summer, when the islands may be visited by numerous French boats, among others.

Travel between the five inhabited islands is normally possible year-round, though this too may become temporarily impaired during bad weather. During summer, however, various inter-island launches cater for the needs of holiday visitors, at which time it is normally possible to land on some of the uninhabited islands, though seabird islands remain closed during the breeding season. Nonetheless, overnight stays, camping and the lighting of fires are not permitted.

## NAUTICAL SCILLY

No account of the Isles of Scilly, no matter how brief, would be complete without mention of the nautical side to island life. Water-borne craft of all shapes and sizes play in important role in any island community and whilst not all of Scilly's residents own a car, most have a boat. Indeed, many make their living on the water, either from fishing, from operating inter-island boat services, or by maintaining these various craft. In addition, one of Scilly's main links with mainland Britain remains the Isles of Scilly Steamship Company's daily passenger ship *Scillonian III*, or her sister ship, the cargo-carrying *Gry Maritha*.

Today, navigation between and around the islands is assisted by three local lighthouses, positioned on the exposed Bishop Rock to the west, on lofty Round Island to the north and on Peninnis headland on the southern end of St Mary's, as well as by the Seven Stones Lightship, positioned over ledges to the east of the islands. An earlier lighthouse, now a private dwelling, on St Agnes was the first lighthouse erected in either Cornwall or Scilly, having been commissioned in 1679 and extinguished in 1911, following its replacement by the Peninnis light. Although commenced around 1849, the impressive Bishop Rock Lighthouse was not completed until ten years later, having at least once been washed away by a winter storm during construction; this structure was later extended to its present height of 33 metres.

In addition to the four light stations, a daytime navigation aid, the Daymark, is positioned on the eastern end of St Martin's, plus a recent similar construction is sited on the northern tip of St Agnes. There are also a variety of moored and static channel markers. However, much navigation within the archipelago is by the use of landmarks, knowledge of which is often handed down from father to son. Nonetheless, submerged rocks and ledges abound and regularly account for the incautious navigator.

During the hundred years up until 1930, over 3,000 lives were saved in Scillonian waters, sailing pilot cutters and the local rowing gigs often going up to 160 km out to sea in order to perform a rescue. The Royal National Lifeboat Institution (RNLI) has maintained a lifeboat on St Mary's since 1837, with a second boat on St Agnes during the period 1890–1920, although today the RNLI's Severn Class boat in St Mary's harbour provides the only local cover. Introduced into service in 1996, the 41-tonne Severn Class vessels carry a crew of six, are capable of 25 knots and have a range of 250 nautical miles. Designed to carry up to 45 survivors inside, if necessary they can accommodate up to four times that number. Nowadays most call-outs involve small craft, e.g. yachts, but the St Mary's boat regularly heads out into stormy seas when all other sensible folk are already safely in harbour. Improvements in navigational aids, not least satellite-aware global positioning systems, have markedly reduced the number of serious incidents, though the 1990s alone saw several large vessels in need of assistance and one total wreck – the container ship MV *Cita* on Newfoundland Point on the southeast corner of St Mary's. The islands nevertheless remain critically vulnerable to any such incident, involving as they all do the potential for loss of substantial amounts of oil, plus of course any cargo the ship may be carrying.

Several past wrecks have left indelible marks on the islands and their inhabitants. Two of the most notable without doubt were the loss of much of Sir Cloudesly Shovell's navel fleet in 1707, including his flag ship, the *Association*, and the loss of some 2,000 lives; and the tragic loss of the transatlantic liner SS *Schiller* near the Bishop Rock on 7th May 1875. Sailing from New York and bound for her home port of Hamburg, she struck at night in thick fog and the wreck went undetected until the following morning, some 310 lives being lost.

Other wrecks referred to in the following pages include the grounding of the 13,500-tonne liner SS *Minnehaha* west of Bryher in the early hours of 18th April 1910. Apart from 230 head of cattle, 160 cattlemen and 66 passengers, the ship carried a live consignment of North and Central American bird species en route from the New York Zoological Society to the London Zoological Society. Before the ship was refloated three weeks latter the birds involved had been liberated and most of the cattle thrown over the side and taken ashore on nearby Samson. Liberation of the birds was publicised in *British Birds* 'so if any reports of their being shot should come to hand ornithologists will know their origin' (Seth-Smith 1910).

The SS *Castleford* was similarly loaded with cattle when she struck the Crebawethans in dense fog on 9th June 1887 whilst en route from Montreal to London. Reports suggest that between 250 and 450 animals were rescued and temporarily landed on Annet, at least some allegedly remaining on that island for ten days, though the need for fresh water would have demanded their urgent removal. Importantly, the presence of these animals on that island during June posed a substantial threat to breeding seabirds, particularly shearwaters and petrels breeding below ground. One contemporary report pointed out how 'They trampled everything to pieces, broke in all the Shearwaters' holes, probably destroying many birds, and made a ruin of everything' (Gurney 1889). Rescuers of the *Castleford*'s cattle reportedly received £2.00 per man, any live animals then being transported to Falmouth. However, welcome as the reward money undoubtedly was it probably failed to cover the cost of rebuilding the pilot gig *O & M* after a steer fell onto her bow from the deck of the stricken vessel. Drowned cattle from this incident later washed ashore on the Cornish mainland as far east as St Ives and Mount's Bays.

Finally, no nautical account of Scilly would be complete without mention of the infamous loss of the supertanker *Torrey Canyon* on Pollard's Rock among the Seven Stones ledges on the morning of 18th March 1967, particularly in view of the disastrous consequences of this incident for marine life over such a wide area of the Western Approaches. Built in the USA in 1959 to carry a cargo of 60,000 tonnes, her capacity was later increased to 120,000 tonnes of cargo plus 63,000 tonnes of fuel oil. Single engined, she had a cruising speed of 17 nautical miles per hour, manoeuvred extremely slowly and took five miles to stop. She was owned by a subsidiary of Union Oil, registered in Liberia, on charter to BP and carried an Italian crew.

On 19th February the ship left Kuwait fully loaded for the North Atlantic and whilst in the Canary Islands on 14th March was informed of her ultimate destination, Milford Haven in southwest Wales. Thus she had no opportunity to obtain detailed charts and in the event was badly informed about navigable waters in the area of Scilly. Owing to the vessel's great size and to tidal considerations, it was imperative the ship arrived at the entrance to Milford Haven at 18.00 hours on 18th March, any delay necessitating a wait to unload of a further six days. On the morning of 18th March, the captain awoke to find the Isles of Scilly visible on the ship's radar away to the northwest, i.e. on the left (port side), not the northeast (starboard side) as they should have been if the ship was to pass safely west of the islands. Mindful of the extra time involved in altering course at that juncture, the captain decided to take the vessel through the narrow, seven-mile-wide channel between Scilly and the Seven Stones ledges, a fatal decision as it turned out. Pushed eastwards by a combination of tide and a force 4 northwesterly wind, and having to move east in any event to avoid fishing operations in the narrow channel, the ship struck the ledges around 09.00 hours. Ultimately breaking in two, the wrecked vessel released 31,000,000 gallons of oil as it floundered around on the Seven Stones for the next few weeks, before finally being bombed from the air by the Royal Air Force. Although westerly winds meant Scilly escaped much of the ensuing oil pollution, beaches in Cornwall and further along the English Channel were seriously affected, as were those in northern France.

# SCILLONIAN FAUNA AND FLORA

## LAND AND SEA ANIMALS

Land-mammals are restricted to just five naturally occurring species: Rabbit *Oryctolagus cuniculus*, Brown Rat *Rattus norvegicus*, House Mouse *Mus musculus* and Wood Mouse *Apodemus sylvaticus* and the small but attractive Lesser White-toothed Shrew *Crocidura suaveolens*, which occurs mainly in central and southern Eurasia, east to Korea and breeds no closer to Scilly than the Channel Islands. In recent years the Hedgehog *Erinaceus europaeus* was introduced to St Mary's, where it has become widespread and seems destined to reach other inhabited islands in due course. When this happens, we may expect its predatory behaviour to adversely affect certain breeding seabirds, plus any other ground-nesting species, e.g. Pheasant. On the six inhabited islands (including Gugh), feral cats *Felis catus* have become a conservation problem for breeding seabirds, not least because they apparently target areas in the process of colonisation by Storm Petrels (P J Robinson 1999b), though there is also an incident on record of them taking both adult and unfledged young Kittiwakes (P J Robinson 1998).

Marine mammals and some large predatory fish occur regularly in Scillonian waters, though seldom in numbers approaching those observed up until the 1960s or 1970s and less seldom now between the islands. Formerly, it was normal to see schools of Harbour Porpoise *Phocoena phocoena* or Common Dolphin *Delphinus delphis* comprising 100 or more animals, even among the islands, but such sights have become something of a rarity in recent years. Even less frequent are both Bottle-nosed *Tursiops truncatus* and Striped Dolphins *Stenella coeruleoalba*. Basking Shark *Cetorhinus maximus* too is less common now, sightings of this impressive large fish being once regular during crossings to and from mainland Cornwall. Despite frequent suggestion of a tropical comparison, Scilly is not much troubled by lesser shark species, though Blue Sharks *Prionace glauca* up to two metres in length and 18 kilos in weight are regularly landed on rod and line during offshore fishing trips, the required 30-fathoms-plus depth being readily accessible off Scilly within half an hour's sailing, these fish seldom if ever being seen close inshore. Porbeagle Shark *Lamna lanus* too has been taken, but not in the huge sizes experienced within the species' normal range. Among non-predators, mention must also be made of the oddly structured sun fishes, probably Ocean Sun Fish *Mola mola*, from more southerly latitudes, individuals of which are not infrequently encountered waggling their laboured course between or around the islands.

The commonest and most regular sea mammal is the Atlantic Grey Seal *Halichoerus grypus*, numbers of which frequent the Northern, Western and Eastern Isles, annually giving birth there to their attractive white-coated pups. The smaller Common or Harbour Seal *Phoca vitulina* is perhaps unknown in Scilly. Whales are uncommon in or around Scilly, though the occasional Pilot Whale *Globicephala melaena* is encountered and there are equally infrequent and often unconfirmed claims of Killer Whale *Orcinus orca*. The most recent such sighting involved a group of four orcas ten kilometres south of the islands and two closer in, both during early May 2002. At the other extreme of the mammalian size range, and once quite common on Scilly, bats have become something of a rarity during the past few decades, the vast majority of recent reports are believed to involve one of the pipistrelle *Pipistrellus* species.

Marine turtle sightings are equally infrequent but usually dramatic, especially when that Chelonian colossus the Leatherback Turtle *Dermochelys coriacea* is involved. Up until 1989 there had been fifty or so Leatherback records from Cornwall and Scilly (Penhallurick 1990 – *Turtles of Cornwall, The Isles of Scilly and Devonshire*) and the remains of two animals were present on Samson during winter 1992–93. A two-metre long live individual was landed on Gugh as recently as 1983. Less frequent is the Common or Atlantic Loggerhead *Caretta caretta*, Penhallurick tracing some 15 records for the southwest during the same period. The most recent turtle record seems to be the immature Kemp's Ridley Turtle *Lepidochelys kempii* found on Porthloo Beach, St Mary's, on 19th February 1999, only the second Scillonian record of this now seriously endangered species since the first in 1925 and perhaps only the ninth for Cornwall and Scilly combined. There are two old, 1940s, claims of Hawksbill Turtle *Eretmochelys imbricata* from St Agnes, though Penhallurick thought these likely to have involved one of the above species.

As might be expected, invertebrates are limited in comparison with the mainland, butterflies, for example being restricted to a few common species, e.g. Small Tortoiseshell *Aglais urticae*, Speckled Wood *Pararge aegeria*, Small Copper *Lycaena phlaeas*, Common Blue *Polyommatus icarus* and Holly Blue *Celastrina argiolus*. But the absence of several familiar mainland species, e.g. Orange-tip *Anthocharis cardamines*, is ably compensated for by arrivals of migrant Painted Ladies, *Vanessa cardui*, sometimes in huge numbers, or European Clouded Yellows *Colias croceus*, plus the occasional autumn arrival of storm-blown Monarch *Danus plexippus* butterflies, which presumably originate from North America, although just possibly from colonising populations in the Canary Islands or Azores. In recent years, there has also been at least one claim of American Painted Lady *Vanessa virginiensis*.

Moths are clearly a more substantial subject, though autumn birders are showing increased interest in the larger species, included among which are the hawk-moths, e.g. Convolvulus *Agrius convolvuli* and Privet Hawk-moths *Sphinx ligustri*, and, more rarely, Spurge Hawk-moth *Hyles euphorbiae*, whilst the appearance of a feeding Hummingbird Hawk-moth *Macroglossum stellatarum* can usually be guaranteed to attract attention. Although migrants predominate among dragonflies, Southern *Aeshna cyanea* and Migrant Hawkers *Aeshna mixta*, Common *Sympetrum striolatum*, Yellow-winged *S. flaveolum* and Red-veined Darters *S. fonscolombii* all occur, plus there is a single record of Emperor Dragonfly *Anax imperator* from autumn 1992. Among the *Orthoptera*, most obvious is the Great Green Bush-cricket *Tettigonia viridissima*, with colonies on both St Mary's and Tresco. Less easy to find, though, is the Long-winged Cone-head *Conocephalus discolor*, small populations of which were recently discovered on St Martin's, St Mary's, Tresco, St Agnes and Gugh, the species having probably initially arrived in the islands from France. Even less obvious, and so far restricted in Scilly to St Agnes and St Mary's, is the closely related Short-winged Cone-head *C. dorsalis*.

## BOTANICAL SCILLY

Viewed from a botanical perspective, Scilly is something of a challenge, many plants encountered during a day's walk having escaped from local gardens, although perhaps originating from Tresco's world-famous Abbey Gardens. Nonetheless, there is an interesting mix of native plants, many of which, e.g. Corn Marigold *Chrysanthemum segetum*, a plant which often covers dormant flower fields, are no longer easily found on mainland Britain. Only a small sample are mentioned here and those wishing to further increase their knowledge are advised to consult the specialist literature.

Most obvious among escapes and introductions are probably the 3-metre high, blue-flowered Echiums *Echium* and the equally blue Agapanthus *Agapanthus* or Blue Nile Lily, the latter being extremely obvious where they occur amongst Tresco's sand dunes. Obvious too is the profusion of natural and exotic species to be found in cultivated fields once the winter flower crop is over. Three eye-catching examples are blood-red Whistling Jacks *Gladiolus byzantinus*, white garlic-scented Three-cornered Leeks *Allium triquetrum* and the extensive carpets of yellow Bermuda-buttercup *Oxalis per caprae*. The last named comes from southern Africa, not Bermuda. However, there is much more in these Scillonian flower fields apart from the obvious, including once widespread British plants such as Field Pansy *Viola arvensis*, Small-flowered (English) Catchfly *Silene gallica*, and Rosy Garlic *Allium roseum*. Those with time to search further will perhaps be rewarded with real Scillonian specialities, such as Spring Beauty *Montia perfoliata* from North America, or the low-growing Prickly-fruited *Ranunculus muricatus* and Small-flowered *R. parviflorus* Buttercups from southern Europe.

The commercial narcissus crop is picked mainly during winter and largely whilst the flowers are in bud, early varieties being available for marketing from perhaps late October, though the last of the crop endures through into February, or even March. Fields then remaing largely untouched until summer, following which the last season's vegetation is burned off, about 20% of the crop lifted, bulbs separated and the land generally readied for the coming growing season. The timing of all this conveniently accommodates both the natural plant communities and the farmland breeding passerines, and no doubt substantially contributes to the unusually high densities of both.

Away from the flower fields, roadside verges and wild corners are an array of Foxgloves *Digitalis purpurea*, Red Campion *Silene dioica*, Alexanders *Smyrnium olusatrum*, Common Mallow *Malva sylvestris* and perhaps Fennel *Foeniculum vulgare*. Although wetter areas are often dominated by luxuriant stands of the poisonous Hemlock Water Dropwort *Oenanthe crocata*, other interesting plants include Wild Angelica *Angelica sylvestris*, Greater Tussock-sedge *Carex paniculata* and Purple-loosestrife *Lythrum salicaria*, with beds of Common Reed *Phragmites communis* around any standing water. The somewhat restricted Balm-leaved Figwort *Scrophularia scorodonia* is present on sandy heathland, along with the orange-berried Stinking

Iris *Iris foetidissima* and, confined to Bryher's southern extremity, the diminutive Dwarf Pansy *Viola kitaibeliana*, which in Britain is restricted to Scilly.

Of interest too is that group of plants growing immediately above the reach of high tides, including Sea Bindweed *Calystegia soldanella*, Sea Holly *Eryngium maritimum*, Sea Beet *Beta maritima*, Sea Kale *Crambe maritima*, Sea Campion *Silene uniflora*, Sea Pea *Lathyrus japonicus*, Sea Rocket *Cakile maritima* and Rock Samphire *Crithmum maritimum*. In addition, four plants perhaps most associated in our minds with coastal southwest Britain occur: Thrift *Armeria maritima*, Common Scurvygrass *Cochlearia officinalis*, Tree Mallow *Lavatera arborea* and Hottentot Fig *Carpobrotus edulis*.

As with birds, of interest too are those plant species absent from the islands, such as Dog's Mercury *Mercurialis perennis*, Teasel *Dipsacus fullonum* and Cross-leaved Heath *Erica tetralix*, to name just three. The much-planted Tresco aside, trees are mainly restricted to elm *Ulmus* and willow *Salix*, though with prominent stands of introduced Monterey Pine, the last planted extensively as windbreaks since 1920. Interestingly, following the ravages of Dutch Elm disease throughout mainland Britain, the comparatively small areas of elm on the five main islands now assume national importance, this destructive disease never having reached the archipelago.

# A BACKGROUND TO THE BIRDS OF SCILLY

## RESIDENT SPECIES

Just 45 landbirds breed annually in the islands and a further four do so irregularly. In addition, there are three introduced gamebird species: Pheasant, Red-legged Partridge and Golden Pheasant, plus the reintroduced Grey Partridge. Seabirds are limited to 13 regularly breeding species plus two terns, Sandwich and Roseate, that are less regular, the latter perhaps now lost to the islands. Interestingly, this situation is partially reflected across the water in west Cornwall, where there is also a marked reduction in species abundance west of a line from St Ives to Marazion (Ryves & Quick 1946).

As with most island bird communities, it is interesting to consider which species are absent from Scilly, including as this does all breeding owls, woodpeckers and buntings, Nuthatch, Treecreeper, most warblers and four species of tit, i.e. Long-tailed, Marsh, Willow and Coal Tit, plus all but two waders. And whilst considering absence, we must also think in past terms, quite radical changes in Scillonian land management over the last one hundred or so years having left their perhaps inevitable mark on resident species. There were, for example, almost no trees on Scilly, other than on Tresco, until around 1920 (Inglis-Jones 1969), so that as recently even as 1946 Ryves and Quick were able to comment on the absence or extreme scarcity of species that today either breed commonly, or at least regularly in small numbers; these include Kestrel, Stock Dove, Carrion Crow, Chiffchaff, Willow Warbler, Blackcap and Blue Tit. Equally worthy of consideration are the likely effects on both resident and migrant species of the provision of exotic nectar-bearing trees and shrubs, such as Tresco's Australian banksias and eucalypts, or the beautiful South American puyas (Hunt 1969), or indeed semi-exotic evergreen windbreak hedgerows surrounding most flower fields. As further proof, if it were needed, that nothing in ornithology remains unchanged for long, breeding species recently lost to Scilly, e.g. Skylark, are perhaps about to be balanced by additions, as in the case of Little Egret, which may already have attempted to breed around Tresco's Great Pool. However, not readily apparent is the manner in which several Scillonian species assume importance in either a national or regional context. Thus, quite limited wintering numbers of Mute Swan, Gadwall, Shoveler and Pochard on both Tresco and St Mary's are, or were until recently, among the highest, if not actually the highest, in southwest England (Owen *et al.* 1986). The counties of Dorset and Avon contain the next nearest comparable numbers of Gadwall. Equally, farmland densities of breeding Song Thrush, Blackbird and Wren, at least, are almost certainly greater in Scilly than elsewhere in Britain. In addition, there are a number of prehistoric records, some species of which still breed within the islands, whilst others, e.g. Black Grouse, no longer do so.

Reed (1984) examined numbers of breeding landbirds in Scilly against selected environmental variables, and tried to determine if results were affected by landmass. He found numbers of species on each island to be influenced primarily by habitat diversity, rather than by the size of the island or its position within the archipelago. Understandably, there is an apparent tendency towards greater absence among those species that are less inclined towards geographical movement, e.g. Magpie.

Seabirds are no less intriguing, with around 4% of British Lesser Black-backed and Great Black-backed Gulls and 3% of British Shags breeding within the islands, and with more seabird species breeding or attempting to breed each year than anywhere else in England or Wales, albeit often in low numbers. Scilly also remains the only published English Storm Petrel breeding site, whilst Annet probably holds the single largest British breeding concentration of Great Black-backed Gulls. In addition, among prehistoric records is one for Great Auk, though it remains unclear whether the species bred in the islands.

## MIGRANT AND VISITING BIRDS

Despite its tiny geographical area and even smaller landmass, Scilly scored fifth among British County and Regional bird lists for total number of species recorded (*Birdwatcher's Yearbook* 2001: 139–141), outshining many substantially larger areas with the level of attraction it offers to migrant and vagrant birds alike, despite limitations in the number of resident species.

| County/Region | Species Total |
|---|---|
| Cornwall | 451 |
| Yorkshire | 428 |
| Shetland | 417 |
| Norfolk | 409 |
| Scilly | 407 |
| Devon | 405 |
| Kent | 398 |
| Dorset | 397 |
| Northumberland | 388 |
| Sussex | 380 |

**Top Ten British County or Regional Bird Lists (*Birdwatcher's Yearbook* 2001)**

In truth, though, Scilly should perhaps feature higher in the table, the possible 426 species recorded up until spring 2003 advancing the archipelago to perhaps third overall, though allowances must also be made for subsequent additions to other lists. Much of this prominence is attributable to the frequent arrival of migrants from areas far removed from southwest Britain.

Understanding reasons behind this high rarity level is no simple task, though regular adverse weather patterns and Scilly's geographical situation are clearly major considerations. Indeed, a substantial proportion of Nearctic species reaching the islands owe their appearance there and elsewhere in western Europe to the presence of fast-moving, severe late autumn anticyclonic depressions out over the North Atlantic. Often, though, there are additional, underlying factors, as in the case of Nearctic migrants, several of which apparently have western or central North American populations that first move east towards the coastal North Atlantic, before then heading south (Nisbet 1959; Brewer *et al.* 2000). This west-east autumn migration strategy carries a potential for overshooting all or a proportion of the North Atlantic. In addition, an as yet largely unknown percentage of Nearctic autumn migrants may take a transoceanic route out over the North Atlantic, through or east of Bermuda and down to the Caribbean, or even fly direct to northwest South America (Durand 1972; Cramp *et al.* 1977–94; Frankland 1989; Elkins 1999). Similarly, Nisbet (1963) previously pointed out that an alteration in the frequency of Nearctic migrants reaching western Europe post-1950 probably had its origins in changes to factors inducing reverse migration within eastern North America.

Less easy to interpret are factors influencing long-distance migrants reaching Scilly from Asia, especially from populations that breed no closer to Scilly than perhaps Tibet or China, and which winter solely within the Indian subcontinent, or even further east. Olive-backed Pipit, for example, breeds in northern Asia east of the Caspian Sea and winters from India eastwards, thus its near annual presence in southwest England seems unlikely. The suggestion often is that much of this 'migrant vagrancy' can be explained by reverse migration, though with unsettled weather doubtless playing an important role, the latter being readily apparent from the range of rare or scarce species so often arriving in the islands at the same time. Difficult to explain, too, are apparent simultaneous arrivals of species from two or more opposing points of the compass, such occasions offering a truly memorable birding experience, as in October 2000 when Common Nighthawk, Spectacled and Pallas's Warblers were all present within the islands at the same time. Most of the above applies largely to autumn, the pattern of spring arrivals being somewhat different. For one thing, several species involved breed mainly or wholly to the south of Scilly, e.g. Black-eared Wheatear, and Hoopoe, the timing of their arrival normally fitting known spring movements. Similarly, although Black-headed and Yellow-breasted Buntings both breed well to the east of Scilly, both also winter in southern Asia and are therefore liable to overshoot on return migration.

Which just leaves the issue of wintering birds from elsewhere, comparatively few of which occur by mainland standards. Scilly has little in the way of low-tide feeding areas and a shortage too of high-tide grazing, both of which perhaps help to explain the near absence of visiting waterfowl, except during unusually severe winter weather elsewhere in Britain or Europe, and the small number of wintering waders. Few Woodcock arriving in autumn remain throughout what passes for midwinter in the islands, whilst the limited area of mature woodland and low scrub rules out a further wide range of species. Only Chiffchaff and perhaps Goldcrest spring to mind as wintering in anything resembling large numbers, the often impressive autumn mixed thrush flocks having mostly moved on by the end of November.

Two additional issues are perhaps best discussed at this juncture. Firstly, the question of ship-assisted passage, opinions remaining divided over whether birds arriving in Europe wholly or partially as a consequence of having been ship-assisted should gain recognition. In the event, this remains very much a personal decision, although complicated substantially by uncertainties over exactly which individuals did land upon a ship during their crossing of the North Atlantic. However, Elkins (1979) suggested that an average crossing time for a vagrant might be two to three days, and if so then the odds seem substantially against a small bird remaining airborne in bad weather throughout that period. This being the case, we might reasonably expect most Nearctic landbirds reaching Scilly, or indeed western Europe, to have gained at least some degree of ship-assistance.

An equally interesting question concerns the extent to which numbers of Scillonian records are influenced by observer bias. On mainland Britain this mainly involves weekend bias (Fraser 1997) but in the enclosed environs of Scilly weekends are not an issue, although it is clear from the records that sudden additional influxes of observers, particularly during relatively quiet periods and even just for the day, can and sometimes do result in the discovery of additional rarities which we must assume would otherwise probably have remained unrecorded. It seems undeniable, however, that annual autumn birder concentrations produce a dramatic but nonetheless immeasurable increase in both the species involved and numbers of individuals recorded. Worse still, from a statistician's viewpoint, as the rarity level rises so the volume of birder input increases, as even more birders arrive from the mainland. In answer to the question, then, does Scilly receive more rarities than most areas of mainland Britain, the answer is probably yes, though many, perhaps most, might go unrecorded but for this high level of visiting birder interests. Certainly this must be so for the more retiring and difficult-to-find species, after all many hands make light work, in which case comparisons with Scilly should perhaps be confined to other similarly favoured sites, e.g. Fair Isle, or Kent's Dungeness.

# BIRDING IN SCILLY

Scillonian birding is separable into three main components – breeding landbirds, breeding seabirds and any migrants – the latter mainly concentrated into and most numerous during the months of September and, in particular, October. However, spring migrants, winter visitors and, presumably, vagrants may have been under-recorded in the past, primarily owing to the lack of birdwatcher coverage outside the recognised autumn period. Scilly also lies rather far west of main European migration routes. Consequently, most migrants passing through the islands are weather-affected flocks or individuals from either Britain, western Europe or, in many cases, much further away, including North America and eastern Asia.

The autumn 'Scilly Season' has become something of a tradition for many British and an increasing number of overseas birders, such that during particularly busy periods of migrant activity 1,000 or more visiting birders may be present on St Mary's, with lesser numbers on other main islands, but particularly St Agnes. The main flood of autumn migrants annually reaches the islands from around mid-September, the season coming to a close quite abruptly at the end of October, although it remains unclear exactly how much this last has to do with the seasonal closure of hotels and guesthouses, rather than an absence of migrants.

Few of Scilly's breeding landbirds seem likely to attract birdwatchers from mainland Britain, though some may be interested in the extreme densities involved. Seabirds, however, hold rather more interest, though most of these will have left the islands by the start of autumn migration. Winter in Scilly has little to offer the birdwatcher, involving as it does only small numbers of a quite limited range of species, even by comparison with nearby Cornwall.

All of this is in stark contrast to the situation in late September and October, when virtually any weather pattern is likely to bring migrants, many of which are likely to be extreme British rarities, with the constant possibility of something even rarer – perhaps a first British or European record.

## SPECIES SURVEYS

Organised and structured surveys, as opposed to random, unstructured counts, can be roughly divided into those involving breeding residents and summer migrants on the one hand, and wintering residents or winter visitors on the other. Most obvious among these have been various seabird surveys, commencing in 1974 with Robert Allen's all-island survey on behalf of the then Nature Conservancy Council, followed in 1983 and 1987 by repeat NCC surveys, the former by Paul Harvey, the latter by Mike Birkin and Andy Smith. From 1991, a series of near-annual general or species-specific seabird counts were carried out on behalf of either the NCC's successor, English Nature (EN), or the Isles of Scilly Environmental Trust (IOSET), mostly by the author but also by Will Wagstaff. Most recent of these was the two-year all-island, all-species counts forming part of the Joint Nature Conservancy Council's (JNCC) national Seabird 2000 survey. The end map shows the positions of the five inhabited islands plus Gugh, Samson and Annet and the position of those uninhabited islands holding breeding seabirds. Very occasionally seabirds breed elsewhere but only in small numbers.

In comparison with seabirds, the landbirds of Scilly have received scant attention. The earliest organised surveys seem to have been the series of counts of breeding birds carried out on St Agnes and Gugh during eight of the 22 years from 1957–78 (*IOSBR* 1979). Apparently the only other long-term breeding study is the author's ten-year Common Birds Census work on behalf of the British Trust for Ornithology (BTO) on the 16 hectare Lunnon Farm plot on St Mary's. More recently, however, the two-year Breeding Bird Atlas attempted an assessment of distribution and numbers of all non-seabird species present on all islands (Chown & Lock 2002). However, the choice of 1-km squares and small landmass involved rendered detailed plotting a near impossibility, though for some species, estimates of likely numbers allow rough calculations of all-island totals.

There have been even fewer winter surveys, perhaps the first on record having been carried out on Tresco during January–February 1965 and documented by King (1965). An important subsequent source of information on wader distribution within the islands was Kirby's excellent, unpublished, assessment during winter 1984–85 (Kirby 1988). In addition, Hale (1974) examined the status of waders roosting at two sites on St Agnes during winter 1994–95. More recently still, the RSPB organised three surveys of winter shorebird distribution, firstly during March 1996, again in January 1997 and finally during January 1998 (Lock 1999).

## SPECIES-SPECIFIC SURVEYS

Surveys or other fieldwork directed at particular species involved Lesser Black-backed Gull, Kittiwake, Roseate and Common Terns, Budgerigar, Song Thrush, Sedge, Reed and Willow Warblers and House Sparrow. Dealing with the last species, in the 1980s Roger Penhallurick (1993) took a personal interest in the newly discovered cliff-nesting House Sparrow population, and this behaviour has since been shown to occur quite widely within the islands. More recently, Oxford University's Edward Grey Institute examined the possibility of inter-island genetic differences in this species using DNA information (David Hole *in litt.*), although results of this potentially fascinating study were unfortunately not available at the time of going to press. Despite the scarcity of British free-flying Budgerigar populations, the Tresco birds of the 1970s apparently attracted little local attention, or if they did the results failed to appear in the *IOSBR*; fortunately we have Bernard King's informative 1978 *British Birds* paper to rely on.

A small number of Lesser Black-backed Gull pulli were annually colour-ringed by Will Wagstaff from the mid-1990s, though a protracted pre-breeding period means there is as yet a shortage of information on their subsequent British movements. However, the study has already shown just how far south down the coastal eastern Atlantic pre-breeding Lesser Black-backs penetrate. Terns were mainly looked at with a view to numbers, distribution and productivity and, therefore, these should perhaps be considered as general surveys. The exception is a multi-agency Roseate Tern recovery programme currently in operation within the islands and funded by English Nature as part of the JNCC's wider national programme (Robinson & Colombe 2001). As another part of this programme, the JNCC recently also funded research into the past and present status of all tern species in Scilly (P J Robinson 1999a). The author also conducted annual productivity studies of local Kittiwake colonies, which should perhaps more safely be treated as one population.

## RINGING

As with field observations of rarities and resident species, it is possible that ringers visited the islands in past years and information on species and numbers of individuals involved has subsequently been lost. However, known records up to and including 1999 are divided into birds ringed prior to 1970 and those ringed since that date, mainly to enable comparison between species and numbers ringed by the former SABO and those ringed subsequently. The latter exercise is enlightening for two main reasons. Firstly, because it apparently reveals an earlier culture of including extreme rarities among species targeted for ringing purposes, unlike the present day where the deliberate pursuit of rarities is discouraged by the BTO. But perhaps more importantly, the list highlights recent local declines in some breeding species involved, most notably Manx Shearwater, as well as recent increases, e.g. Fulmar, or the two common *Larus* species. Most SABO ringing activity seems to have taken place on St Agnes, or on Annet and in the nearby Western Isles, though with occasional forays to other main islands, e.g. Tresco.

Since 1970 the Severn Vale Ringing Group (SVRG) has annually worked on spring and autumn migrants, initially on St Martin's but more recently on St Agnes. Also on St Martin's, Mark and Lucy Love ringed near-annually during the 1980s and 90s in the area of Higher Town. In addition, during the 1990s, the Scillonian Seabird Group accounted for most if not all of the post-1970 seabird totals, directing particular attention towards Storm Petrel, Shag, Fulmar and Kittiwake. The only resident ringers recently appear to have been Will Wagstaff, who ringed migrant and resident species in the St Mary's Lower Moors area during the mid-1990s, plus the author, who concentrated on both residents and migrants in the Higher Moors, Lunnon Farm and Holy Vale areas of St Mary's throughout the whole of the 1990s. From time to time. other visiting individuals or groups have ringed in the islands, but the need, now, for specific prior BTO permission to ring in Scilly has removed the possibility of uncontrolled casual visits. As elsewhere, details of rings found on live or dead birds should be reported to the Ringing Office of the British Trust for Ornithology, The Nunnery, Thetford, Norfolk IP24 2PU, or as indicated on the ring itself. This includes details of birds ringed overseas.

During the late 1900s, the SVRG carried out specific ringing studies aimed at Willow Warblers passing through Scilly, and more recently the author concentrated much of his own ringing effort on Reed Warblers, Sedge Warblers and Greenfinches, whilst at the same time carrying out a more general Song Thrush study, focused largely on the Lunnon Farm study plot.

## SOME LEADING PARTICIPANTS IN SCILLONIAN ORNITHOLOGY

During the past two hundred or more years, a number of individuals enjoyed a period of prominence in Scillonian ornithology, some more so than others, but most of those listed below made significant contributions at some time. In a few cases that contribution was substantial, as in the case of Augustus Smith, E H Rodd, Augustus Pechell and Francis Rodd during the 19th century, or A A Dorrien-Smith, James Clark, Roger Penhallurick and David Hunt in the 20th century. Nonetheless, all of these, and indeed many more, had a part to play and most left a permanent mark in ornithological history. Even if, like the not always so fortunate Tresco gamekeeper David Smith, they are remembered as much for what might have been!

**Blair, Dr R H**
One-time Chairman of CBWPS and Editor of its annual report (*CBWPSAR*), prominent Cornish ornithologist of the early to mid-20th century and visitor to Scilly.

**Borlase, Dr William**
Born 1696 and died 1772, besides being rector of Ludgvan, near Penzance in west Cornwall, he was a prominent naturalist and antiquarian. He made several early observations on the birds of Scilly. Visited Scilly during summer of 1752, making several early observations on the birds of the islands. Indeed, his *Observations on the Ancient and Present State of the Islands of Scilly and their Importance to the Trade of Great Britain* was described by Johnson as 'one of the most pleasing and elegant pieces of local inquiry that our country has produced' (*Literary Magazine*, May 1756).

**Britton, George**
Butler to A A Dorrien-Smith. Like many on the islands, he was adept with a gun and shot Scilly's first and Cornwall's second White's Thrush in December 1886, though he thought it was a Mistle Thrush.

**Camden, William**
Wrote 1610 *Britannia* (first published 1607 in Latin), describing Scilly as 'near 145 islands covered with grass or greenish moss [lichen?], besides dreary rocks and innumerable crags, forming altogether a cluster about eight leagues from extremest point of Cornwall. Some of them yield plenty of corn, and all abound with rabbits, cranes [Cormorants?], swans, herons and seafowl.'

**Carew, Richard**
Born 1555 and died 1620, his valuable, if rather protracted, *Survey of Cornwall* was published in 1602. Many of his comments were concerned with birds and their culinary capabilities. Of the 'Puffin' he wrote that it 'hatcheth in holes in the Cliffe, whose young are thence ferreted out, being exceedingly fat, kept salted, and reputed for fish as coming nearest thereto in their taste'. He added that 'the eggs of diverse of these seafowl are good to be eaten'. These comments apparently applied to both Cornwall and Scilly in general.

**Clark, Professor James**
Native-born Scot with distinguished academic career, becoming Principal of Cornish Central Technical Schools from 1899–1908, when appointed Rector of Kilmarnock Academy. Wrote main element of ornithological entry for the *Victoria County History of Cornwall* (1906). Together with co-author Francis Rodd, researched and wrote landmark early 20th century *Zoologist* review of *The Birds of Scilly* (Clark & Rodd 1906). He visited the islands at least seven times from 1903 and spent much time examining the Tresco Abbey records.

**Couch, Jonathan**
Born Polperro, west Cornwall in 1789 and died 1870. After training as a doctor in London he returned to west Cornwall, later writing *The Cornish Fauna* of 1838, E H Rodd also making a substantial contribution to this work.

**Courtney, J S**
Mid-19th century author of *A Guide to Penzance and its Neighbours, including The Islands of Scilly* (1845),

which contains a list of local birds as observed in the collections of E H Rodd, Truro Museum and the Penzance taxidermist Vingoe.

### Dorrien-Smith, Lieutenant Thomas Algernon (T A)
Proprietor of Scilly 1874 to 1918. Nephew of Augustus Smith, born Thomas Algenon Dorrien, he changed his name to Dorrien-Smith following his uncle's death in 1872. He first set foot on the islands in 1865.

### Dorrien-Smith, Major Arthur Algernon (A A)
Born 1876, died 1955. Son of T A Dorrien-Smith and Proprietor of Tresco 1918 to 1955. A keen naturalist, founder member of CBWPS and regular subscriber to *British Birds* and *CBWPSAR*. Personally responsible for a number of major Scillonian bird records and at one time was the probable leading authority on several Nearctic species in Europe.

### George, Mr L R
No details, except that he lived on St Mary's during the late 19th and perhaps early 20th century, probably in the Holy Vale area of St Mary's.

### Harvey, Arthur William Hext
Born 1880 and died 1962, like E H Rodd he practised as a solicitor in Penzance. Author of several letters, short papers or similar on the birds of Scilly and west Cornwall.

### Heath, Robert
Mid-18th century sportsman, observer and one time army officer stationed in Scilly, he wrote *A Natural and Historical Account of the Islands of Scilly, with a Description of Cornwall* (Heath 1750). Heath was probably the Scillonian correspondent frequently quoted by Gilbert White of Selborne. Made reference to Gannet in Scilly but failed to say whether breeding.

### Hunt, David Basil
Born 1934 and raised in Devon, David was tragically lost in a fatal encounter with a Tiger *Panthera tigris* whilst leading a bird tour in India's Corbett National Park during February 1985. RSPB representative and one-time Recorder for Scilly and Editor of the *IOSBR*. David was a skilled musician and naturalist, an accomplished author and a major figure in late 20th century ornithology.

### Jackson, Mr F
No details other than that he lived on St Mary's, presumably during the mid- to late 19th century.

### Jenkinson, Reverend John H
Onetime mid-19th century vicar of St Mary's and of Reading in Berkshire; responsible for many shot bird specimens.

### King, C K
Early 20th century resident wildlife photographer and writer, provider of much useful information on distribution and numbers.

### Leleand, John
At the command of Henry VIII toured England some time after 1533 in search of its 'antiquities'. Described Scilly as 140 islets with, among others, 'Gulles and Puffinnes … with plenty of Conyes'.

### MacKenzie, Peter Zambra MBE
Born 1913, died 1977. After working as a veterinary officer in the Sudan from 1939 to 1955, he retired and took over a flower farm on St Mary's. He later set up Scilly's first veterinary practice and became personally involved in negotiating the loan of the Tresco Abbey skin-collection to the Isles of Scilly Museum. Among his other duties was that of Island Warden for the then Nature Conservancy Council (NCC). Most notable perhaps was his identification of Britain's first record of American Purple Gallinule.

### Millett
Mid-19th century Penzance collector and probable dealer in skins and eggs.

### Mitchell, D W
Mid-19th century Penzance collector and dealer in skins and eggs, and one-time secretary of the Zoological Society.

### North, Reverend Issac
Chaplain of St Mary's at least by 1847. Wrote *A Week in the Isles of Scilly* (1850), illustrated by Lady Sophia Tower of Berkhamsted, close friend of Augustus Smith.

### Parsons, A G
Hospital radiographer and prominent ornithologist of the early to mid-20th century. Visitor to Scilly and one-time Editor of *CBWPSAR*.

### Pechell, Augustus
Gentleman son of Reverend Horace Pechell and therefore cousin of Augustus Smith. Credited with obtaining many Scillonian bird specimens during the mid-1880s. Shot on the islands every autumn or winter from 1849 to 1870, most of his specimens going to E H Rodd before later passing into the hands of Rodd's nephew Francis. Frequently referred to in the early literature.

### Pechell, Reverend Horace
Rector of Bix, near Henley-on-Thames, uncle of Augustus Smith and father of Augustus Pechell. A 'sporting' man, he shot on Scilly during the early to mid-1880s.

### Penhallurick, Roger D
Author of *Birds of the Cornish Coast* (1969) and *The Birds of Cornwall and the Isles of Scilly* (1978, and until recently Curator of Natural History at Truro Museum.

### Quick, Hilda M
Born in Penzance in 1895, died on St Agnes in 1978. Hilda joined the CBWPS in 1931 and was long-term Editor of both the *CBWPSAR* and *IOSBR*. Co-author with Lt. Col Ryves, of *British Birds* paper *A survey of the status of birds breeding in Cornwall and Scilly since 1906* (Ryves & Quick 1946). Moving from Penzance to Priglis Cottage in 1951, she was responsible for the identification of a string of rarities, most notable perhaps being Britain and Ireland's second Blue-cheeked Bee-eater, though at the time it was believed to be the first.

### Rodd, Edward Hearle
Born 1810 and died 1880, some doubt surrounds his background. Penhallurick (1978) suggests that he was the son of the rector of St-Just-in-Roseland, west Cornwall, whereas Inglis-Jones (1969) thought him the son of the squire of Trebartha. Trebartha was also the home of his nephew Francis and therefore presumably the family estate. Whatever the truth, he later practised as a solicitor in Penzance, where he is known to have lived from 1833. During this time he also acted as Town Clerk, Superintendent Registrar and Head Distributor of Stamps in Cornwall. Author of *The Birds of Cornwall and The Scilly Islands* (1880) he was a good friend of Augustus Smith. Died during publication year of above, which was prepared for the publishers by James Harting, Editor of the *Zoologist*. Recipient of many specimens shot on Tresco and elsewhere in the islands and owner of important skin-collection comprising some 270 mainly Cornish specimens, which eventually went to his nephew Francis Rodd. A frequent and prolific contributor to the *Zoologist* on the birds of both Scilly and Cornwall, he certainly visited the islands, though perhaps not often. Perhaps no better tribute can be found than that included by James Harting in *The Birds of Cornwall and The Scilly Islands*; 'Owing to his zealous exertions, many a rare bird in Cornwall was rescued from oblivion, while several species, such as Spotted Eagle [*Aquila clanga*], Lesser Grey Shrike, Red-breasted Flycatcher, and American Stint [Least Sandpiper], were added to the list of British Birds entirely through his instrumentality'.

**Rodd, Francis Rashleigh**
Nephew of E H Rodd, born 1839 and died 1922. A sportsman and naturalist, he lived at the former Trebartha Hall on the eastern edge of Bodmin Moor. Made at least five lengthy visits to Tresco between 1859 and 1870, where he shot mainly Snipe and Woodcock. Credited with obtaining many important ornithological specimens in the islands. Co-author, with Dr James Clark, of the landmark early 20th century *Zoologist* review of 'The Birds of Scilly' (Clark & Rodd 1906). During preparation of his *The Birds of Cornwall and The Scilly Islands* (Rodd 1880), the elder Rodd relied heavily upon letters sent to him from Scilly by Francis; these E H Rodd included as a separate chapter entitled *A Few Leaves from the Journal of a Sportsman and Naturalist on the Scilly Islands* (pages 279–298). According to Penhallurick (1978), Francis inherited E H Rodd's important skin-collection, which was later destroyed in a fire in 1949, along with Trebartha Hall.

**Rogers, Michael J**
Short-term resident of Scilly during 1980s, former Recorder, Editor and joint Editor *IOSBR* 1981–89. Long-term Secretary of British Birds Rarities Committee (BBRC) and now resident in west Cornwall.

**Ryves, Lt. Col. Benjamin Hervey**
Born in India in 1875 and educated at Sandhurst, died 1961. Invalided out of the army in 1921, he settled in Mawgan-in-Pydar, west Cornwall. Founder member of CBWPS c. 1931 and subsequent long-term Editor or joint Editor of *CBWPSAR*. Having a particular interest in breeding biology, he frequently contributed to *British Birds*. Co-author, with Hilda Quick, of *British Birds* paper *A survey of the status of birds breeding in Cornwall and Scilly since 1906* (Ryves & Quick 1946). Author also of *Bird Life in Cornwall* (1948).

**Smith, Augustus John**
Son of James Smith and his second wife, the former Mary Isabella Pechell of Berkhamsted, his father owned estates in Berkhamsted. Born in Harley Street, London, in 1804, Augustus Smith died in the Duke of Cornwall's Hotel, Plymouth in the early hours of 1st August 1872. Proprietor of Scilly from 1834 until his death, he was known to the immediate family as 'The Emperor' and rather unkindly in certain London business circles as 'Scilly Smith'. He is buried in the churchyard at St Buryan, on mainland Cornwall but close to Land's End. Although Smith's precise ornithological capabilities remain unknown, he clearly had more than a passing interest, as seems evident from a passage in a letter to his long-time and dear friend Lady Sophia Tower of Berkhamsted, describing how two days of exceptionally calm May weather 'enabled me to begin pilfering the sea-birds' nests for you'. He went on to relate how two subsequent days of violent gales 'afforded me plenty of time to blow the said eggs with Mr Walter's apparatus for that purpose' (Inglis-Jones 1969).

**Smith, David**
Described by Clark and Rodd (1906) as a veteran Tresco ex-gamekeeper, collector of several important specimens. He is perhaps mostly remembered, however, for supplying the description of an alleged Rufous Bush Robin seen from a Tresco Abbey window during autumn 1883, whilst he was still 'too ill to hold a gun'. In fact, 1883 was a bad year for Smith, he being also remembered for the near miss of a Bridled Tern, plus a similar close encounter with Scilly's first Great Reed Warbler during the following year.

**Vingoe, W H**
Celebrated Penzance taxidermist and allegedly the most skilled in Cornwall. He also acquired specimens with the gun (as did his son Edward), but apparently never on Scilly.

**Wagstaff, William H**
Recent Recorder for the islands and joint Editor of the *IOSBR* 1988–89.

# INTRODUCTION TO THE SYSTEMATIC LIST

The following species accounts each have a broadly similar layout. They commence with a brief summary of world range, racial variation and main British, European or world status, followed by an historical island summary, an analysis of modern records and a brief summary of the timing and source, or possible source, of any arrivals.

For all rarities except the most frequent, e.g. Richard's Pipit, brief details of all records are listed in an accompanying Table which includes one or more published references for all species with around ten or fewer Scillonian sightings. For species that are nationally common but in Scilly appear only rarely, records of which are assessed by the Scilly Records Panel (SRP), references are normally included only for pre-1960 records.

No attempt has been made to categorise species according to frequency, e.g. very rare, rare, scarce, etc. This is mainly because the inclusion of all records for the majority of rarities suitably clarifies their status, whereas the text makes clear the situation regarding other species. All arrival dates for national and local rarities with more than one acceptable 20th century record are charted on a weekly basis, months being divided into four periods as follows: 1st to 7th, 8th to 14th, 15th to 21st, and 22nd to the month's end. Most of what many other publications consider as vagrants are treated here as migrants, e.g. Blackpoll Warbler, and Radde's Warbler, mainly because examination of long-term arrival dates reveals obvious annually repeatable seasonal patterns, plus a marked lack of random movement. In fact, examination of the relevant Charts shows that few rarities qualify as mere vagrants in Scilly.

For Palearctic species, the list follows the British Ornithologists' Union (BOU) *Checklist of Birds of Britain and Ireland*, 6th edition (Knox 1992), as periodically amended by the BOURC. Species names given at the head of individual accounts are those in general use, followed, where appropriate, by the BOU's recommended new name in parentheses. Nearctic species are dealt with according to the *Field Guide to the Birds of North America*, 3rd edition (National Geographic 1999), which takes into account recent taxonomic changes implemented by the American Ornithologists' Union (AOU). Species names are accompanied by a single letter signifying their BOU category (A–E), followed by Scillonian percentages of national rarity totals accepted by the BBRC since the committee's inception in 1958, up to and including 1999.

A small number of records within the Tables are enclosed by squared brackets and should be treated with caution, though normally some explanatory comment is incorporated into the text. In some cases, e.g. Red-eyed Vireo, and Cattle Egret, the bird in question was seen by several (even many) observers but the record was nevertheless not submitted, a not uncommon problem in Scillonian ornithology. Entries appearing in italics in the Tables involve records still to be considered by the appropriate committee at the time of writing. Unless otherwise stated, any analysis of records is for the period ending December 1999, even though subsequent records may be included in the appropriate Table up until spring 2003.

For breeding species, each account is accompanied by a map. For seabirds, these maps show overall breeding distribution during 1999 or 2000, the size of individual markers giving some indication of the relative size of breeding concentrations. In addition, seabird texts contain a Table listing numbers of pairs at all sites during fieldwork for the national Seabird 2000 survey. Non-seabird breeding distribution is depicted on a 1-km$^2$ basis only, using findings of the 2002 Breeding Bird Atlas (Chown & Lock 2002).

The recording area comprises all islands within the archipelago and all maritime waters up to the 200-nautical-mile UK Economic Exclusion Zone, as now recognised by the BOURC and BBRC. Any separation between mainland Cornwall, Ireland and France is assumed to involve the midway point. A few informative reports are also included from the UK weather station Kilo, positioned 800 kilometres southwest of Scilly in the Western Approaches (McLean & Williamson 1959), though no rarity records are involved. Also included are a small number of reports of birds seen on board or leaving ships at various positions in the North Atlantic (e.g. Halle 1960, Durand 1972), though none outside the 200-nautical-mile limit involves a direct link with Scilly.

## SPECIES INVOLVED

Discounting Wood Duck, Northern Bobwhite, Golden Pheasant, Budgerigar and Red-headed Bunting the Scillonian total stands at a possible 426 species. This includes prehistoric records of Great Auk and Black Grouse, plus American Bittern, Ivory Gull, Ruddy Shelduck, Pallas's Sandgrouse and Marsh Tit and the possibly now extinct Eskimo Curlew, none of which has occurred in Scilly within the past 50 years, though the late 20th century status of Ruddy Shelduck is disputed by many. Also included in the list are Brown/South Polar Skua, Little Swift, Brown Shrike, Savi's Warbler and Blyth's Reed Warbler, all of which first occurred after 1999 and some of which have still to be accepted by the BOURC or BBRC, but nevertheless seem likely to gain recognition. Wilson's Snipe, which by publication should have been split from Snipe (D Parkin pers. comm.), is also listed. Zino's/Fea's Petrel records are treated as those of a single species until the true situation becomes clearer and is considered generally acceptable. Some authorities, e.g. Wink (2002), consider the distinctive eastern forms of Stonechat, e.g. *maura*, as a full species, Siberian Stonechat *Saxicola maura*, though they are treated here as forms of Stonechat, awaiting their separation by the BOURC. Similarly, Black-headed Wagtail, *M. f. feldegg* is treated here as a form of Yellow Wagtail and not as a full species, *Motacilla feldegg*, as recommended by some authorities. Yellow-legged Gull, however, is viewed as distinct from Herring Gull.

Species appearing in squared brackets either ought perhaps to have occurred, i.e. Rock Dove; were introduced but so far have failed to sustain themselves, e.g. Northern Bobwhite; or claims of them having occurred were rejected, e.g. River Warbler and Pallas's Grasshopper Warbler. In addition, a few apparently valid records pre-date current vetting procedures and so are probably now lost, e.g. Sooty Tern and Rufous Bush Robin. These entries are included both to provide as comprehensive a picture as possible of Scillonian ornithology, but also to explain why records perhaps mentioned elsewhere fail to gain acceptance in these pages.

In general, category D species and other exotics or escapes appear separately at the end of the Systematic List under the heading 'Records of Escaped or Introduced Species', two obvious exceptions being Wood Duck and Red-headed Bunting, both of which feature in the main Systematic List owing to their possible future upgrading.

## SOURCES OF INFORMATION

The majority of available written information covers mainly the second halves of both the 19th and 20th centuries, the early part of the 20th century sadly representing something of a black hole in Scillonian ornithology. Generally speaking, the species analysis involves records only up until the end of 1999, though every effort has been made to include subsequent national rarities in appropriate Tables; any records still to be considered by the British Birds Rarities Committee appear in italics.

Earliest island records come from bone remains excavated from prehistoric sites on the islands of Nornour, St Martin's or Samson and date between mainly the 2nd and 7th centuries AD. These include at least two species subsequently unrecorded from the islands: Great Auk and Black Grouse. Following these there are a smattering of pre-19th century records, few of which are greatly specific, before the comparative wealth of information from around 1850 up until the first decade of the 20th century. Much of the latter is in the form of letters from E H Rodd to the *Zoologist*, backed by posthumous publication, in 1880, of Rodd's own *The Birds of Cornwall and The Scilly Islands*.

Equally pivotal to all that follows was the major *Zoologist* review of the *Birds of Scilly* by E H Rodd's nephew Francis and his co-author James Clark (Clark & Rodd 1906), without which any modern book on the subject would be difficult to contemplate. Early to mid-20th century sources are limited to mainly a small number of *Zoologist* letters and papers, plus an increasing volume of submissions to the emerging *British Birds*, none more so than from A A Dorrien-Smith. Although commencing its long-running history in 1931, the annual review of the Cornwall Birdwatching and Preservation Society (CBWPS) initially contained few reports from the islands, though this situation had changed greatly by the 1950s. Additional sources from this period include A A Dorrien-Smith's useful list of *Birds of Scilly as Recorded at Tresco Abbey* (Dorrien-Smith 1951). From the mid-1950s through to the mid-1960s, annual or biannual reports of the St Agnes Bird Observatory (SABO) provided a further rich source, even allowing for a period of duplicity between this and mainland publication. This last problem was resolved with commencement of the annual *Isles of Scilly Bird Report* (*IOSBR*) from 1969 through to at least 2000, this last journal providing the bulk of any post-1960s information.

Also much referred to in the following pages are Roger Penhallurick's two outstanding reviews of both mainland Cornwall and Scilly (Penhallurick 1969, 1978), both of which also suggest further sources of information. Around that same time, Bob Scott utilised staff lunch hours at the British Museum to compile a sizeable Scillonian directory of 19th century sources of species information, all of which proved invaluable in preparing the following accounts. Problematical throughout, however, has been the long-term shortage of reliable resident observers in the islands, and the low numbers of ornithologists and general naturalists visiting Scilly down through the years, but particularly during the 19th and early 20th centuries, The lack of any local journal at this time resulted in either no published reports or their appearance in other county journals, as in the case of J H Gurney's visit of 1889, the account of which appeared in the *Transactions of the Norfolk and Norwich Naturalist's Society* (Gurney 1889).

Numerous other publications were also consulted, a full list of which appears in the bibliography. Most notable perhaps are the nine volumes of *The Birds of the Western Palearctic* (Cramp *et al.* 1977–94), though some earlier volumes have already been overtaken by more recent work. Other vital sources include two national breeding atlases, *The Atlas of Breeding Birds in Britain and Ireland* (Sharrock 1976) and *The New Atlas of Breeding Birds in Britain and Ireland 1988–91* (Gibbons *et al.* 1993), plus the useful *The Historical Atlas of Breeding Birds in Britain and Ireland 1875–1900* (Holloway 1996) and *The Atlas of Wintering Birds in Britain and Ireland* (Lack 1986). In addition, the European Bird Census Council's *Atlas of European Breeding Birds* (Hagemeijer and Blair 1997) proved invaluable in adding a broader European perspective to any discussions on distribution. Any references to British national records mainly concern the BBRC's published list up to and including 1999. Whilst in commenting on Scillonian records in a national context, frequent use was made of *Rare Birds in Britain and Ireland* (Dymond *et al.* 1989), *First for Britain and Ireland 1600–1999* (Palmer 2000) proving a valuable source for initial British records.

Information on the known long-distance movements of Eurasian migrants was gleaned mainly from among the above, from species-specific publications or from the British and Irish *Migration Atlas* (Wernham *et al.* 2002). However, for many (perhaps even most) species occurring as rarities, too few individuals have been ringed or subsequently recovered to address many of the issues raised in the following pages.

Looking northwest from Bryher towards Castle Bryher and the Northern Isles; Thrift *Armeria maritima* in foreground. (*Peter Robinson*)

Round Island and its unmanned lighthouse from the western side of St Helens; Hottentot Fig *Carpobrutus adulis* in foreground. (*Peter Robinson*)

Menawethan in the Eastern Isles, from nearby Great Innisvouls. Until quite recently it held a small breeding population of Puffins. (*Peter Robinson*)

Isolated Hanjague in the Eastern Isles, seen from nearby Great Ganilly. (*Peter Robinson*)

Haycock rocks, Annet Head, Annet; with Thrift *Armeria maritimi* in foreground, May. (*Peter Robinson*)

Narcissus flower crop with shelter-belt of Monterey Pine *Pinus radiata*. Normally the flowers are picked before the buds open. (*Peter Robinson*)

A typical Scillonian scene – Higher Town St Martins with flower fields by the sea. The pink blooms are Belladonna Lilies *Amaryllis belladonna*. (*Peter Robinson*)

The rugged northern coast of St Martin's. (*Peter Robinson*)

Bronze Age community site at Bant's Carn St Mary's, from around the 5th century AD. Tresco visible to the left. (*Peter Robinson*)

Scillonian flower fields, typically enclosed by semi-exotic evergreen hedgerows. Middle Town, St Martin's. (*Peter Robinson*)

St Mary's Higher Moors and Porth Hellick Pool from Kitty Down – southern edge of the Lunnon Farm study plot. (*Peter Robinson*)

A rare sight – snow on Scilly. St Mary's looking towards Kitty Down and the Lunnon Farm study plot. (*Peter Robinson*)

Wood Mouse *Apodemus sylvaticus*, one of five naturally occurring land mammals in Scilly. This species is confined to St Mary's & Tresco. (*Peter Robinson*)

Grey Seal pup *Halichoerus grypus*, Rosevean in Western Isles. This is the only seal species to visit Scilly. (*Peter Robinson*)

Great Black-backed Gull *Larus marinus* nest, Annet. (*Peter Robinson*)

Great Black-backed Gulls *Larus marinus* on Rosevear, resting on the remains of the building used by constructors of Bishop Rock Lighthouse (Peter Robinson).

Kittiwake *Rissa tridactyla* breeding colony on Gugh, with Herring Gulls *Larus argentatus* below and Lesser Black-backed Gulls *L. fuscus* above. (*Peter Robinson*)

Kittiwake *Rissa tridactyla* breeding site, Samson; many Scillonian nests are only two to three metres above the boulder beach. (*Peter Robinson*)

A brood of Kittiwake *Rissa tridactyla* chicks, Gugh. Most Scillonian Kittiwake females lay two eggs per nest. (*Peter Robinson*)

Razorbill *Alca torda* Rosevean, Western Isles. (*Peter Robinson*)

Typical Scillonian Cormorant *Phalacrocorax carbo* nest; Ragged Island, Eastern Isles. (*Peter Robinson*)

Fulmar *Fulmarus galcialis* chick, Annet Head; a species currently expanding its breeding population in Scilly. (*Peter Robinson*)

Brood of Shags *Phalacrocorax aristotelis* Rosevear, Western Isles. (*Peter Robinson*)

Storm Petrel *Hydrobates pelagicus* chick, Annet August. (*Peter Robinson*)

Oystercatcher *Haematopus ostralegus* nest on Samson, with typical clutch of three eggs. (*Peter Robinson*)

Pre-season sanding of rocky ground used by nesting terns *Sterna* leads to increased predation by large gulls *Larus* spp. Green Island Tresco. (*Peter Robinson*)

Roseate Tern *Sterna dougallii* nest box; Green Island, Tresco. (*Peter Robinson*)

Remains of Storm Petrel *Hydrobates pelagicus* predated by domestic cat *Felis domesticus*, Gugh (Peter Robinson)

Laying bait for Brown Rat *Rattus norvegicus* on Samson's northern end; Puffin Island in middle distance (*Peter Robinson-Isles of Scilly Seabird Group*)

Juvenile Song Thrush *Turdus philomelos* with pollen on crown after feeding on South American Puya. (*Peter Robinson*)

Typical Scillonian brood of four Song Thrushes *Turdus philomelos*. (*Peter Robinson*)

Rock Pipit *Anthus petrosus* clutch with Cuckoo *Cuculus canorus* egg on the right, Tresco. (*Peter Robinson*)

Song Thrush *Turdus philomelos*, Garrison Wall, St Mary's; the sub-specific status of Scilly's Song Thrushes is unclear. (*Peter Robinson*)

Wreck of the MV Cita off Porth Hellick, St Mary's, after hitting Newfoundland Rocks at the entrance to the bay. (*Peter Robinson*)

RMV *Scillonian III* making her daily approach to St Mary's harbour. (*Peter Robinson*)

Visiting October birders disembarking from RMV *Scillonian III*. (*Peter Robinson*)

Birding information boards, displayed throughout autumn and updated daily. (*Peter Robinson*)

Death's Head Hawkmoth *Acheronia atropos*, one of several scarce immigrant Lepidoptera species which occasionally reach Scilly. (*Steve Young & George Reszeter*)

Adult female Little Bittern *Ixobrychus minutus*, Porth Hellick Pool, St Mary's, May-June 1995. (*Garry Cook*)

Male Black Duck *Anas rubripes* Tresco 1994; the fourth Black Duck to reach Scilly. (*Steve Young & George Reszeter*)

Glossy Ibis *Plegadis falcinellus* Tresco May 1996; the sixteenth individual Glossy Ibis on Scilly but only the ninth record - there are early records of a pair and a flock of seven. (*Garry Cook*)

Spotted Crake *Porzana porzana*; an annual autumn migrant to Scilly's wetter areas. (*Steve Young & George Reszeter*)

Spotted Sandpiper *Actitis macularia* in summer plumage, St Agnes, May 1996; a regular Scillonian Nearctic vagrant. (*Garry Cook*)

Baird's Sandpiper *Calidris bairdii*, St Agnes October 1995; the twelfth Scillonian record. (*Steve Young & George Reszeter*)

Dotterel *Charadrius morinellus*, St Agnes, October 1995; an annual autumn migrant in small numbers (*Steve Young & George Reszeter*)

Pectoral Sandpiper *Calidris melanotos*, another annual or near-annual autumn vagrant to Scilly. (*Steve Young & George Reszeter*)

Buff-bellied Pipit *Anthus rubescens*, the second record for Scilly, this bird was seen on various islands September-October 1996. (*Steve Young & George Reszeter*)

Eye-browed Thrush *Turdus obscurus*, St Mary's, October 1991. The sixth out of seven Scillonian records. (*George Reszeter*)

First-winter male Subalpine Warbler *Sylvia cantillans*, St Agnes, October 1995; a regular spring and autumn visitor to Scilly. (*Steve Young & George Reszeter*)

Radde's Warbler *Phylloscopus schwarzi*; up to eleven have occurred on Scilly during a single autumn. (*George Reszeter*)

Red-breasted Flycatcher *Ficedula parva*. The regular presence of this delightful flycatcher is a feature of autumn on Scilly. (*Steve Young & George Reszeter*)

Bluethroat *Luscinia svecica*, a scarce but regular migrant through Scilly; seven had been ringed up until 2000. (*Peter Robinson*)

Red-eyed Vireo *Vireo olivaceus*, Old Town, St Mary's, October 1995. A regular Nearctic vagrant. (*Steve Young & George Reszeter*)

First-winter male Black-and-white Warbler *Mniotilta varia* St Mary's 1996; four have reached Scilly. (*Steve Young & George Reszeter*)

Yellow-rumped Warbler *Dendroica coronata*, Tresco, October 1995; the fifth Scillonian record. (*Steve Young & George Reszeter*)

First-year male Northern Parula *Parula americana*, St Agnes October 1995; the sixth Scillonian record. (*Steve Young & George Reszeter*)

Apparent first-year Ortolan Bunting *Emberiza hortulana*; another annual to near-annual autumn migrant to Scilly. (*Steve Young & George Reszeter*)

Rustic Bunting *Emberiza rustica*, autumn 1994; yet another regular autumn migrant to Scilly. (*Steve Young*)

First-year Yellow-browed Bunting *Emberiza chrysophrys*, St Agnes, October 1994. The first record for Scilly and the fourth for Britain and Ireland. (*George Reszeter*)

Bobolink *Dolichonyx oryzivorus*, St Mary's, October 1996; 60% of British records are from Scilly. (*Steve Young & George Reszeter*)

## Red-throated Diver *Gavia stellata* A

**Scarce winter visitor and possible migrant, full written description required by the SRP.**

Circumpolar, breeds northern Scotland eastwards through northern Eurasia and arctic Canada to Greenland, from northern coasts south to southern Sweden, Lake Baikal and southern Quebec; including Greenland, Iceland. Monotypic. Dispersive and migratory, leaving freshwater breeding grounds and moving south in winter to inshore tidal waters. Included on Annex I of 1979 EEC 'Birds Directive'. Amber-listed in UK: recent 36% decline to 390 breeding pairs in main part of range; moderate decline in non-breeding population over past 25 years; unfavourable world conservation status (Gregory *et al.* 2002).

Perhaps slightly less frequent or numerous in Scilly than Black-throated Diver *G. arctica*, birds recently present in approximately three out of four years. Earliest mention of this species on Scilly seems to be E H Rodd's comment that it occurred during autumn and winter (Rodd 1880), the first published record involving a bird shot by Tresco gamekeeper David Smith in the spring of 1894 (Clark & Rodd 1906). As these last authors pointed out, however, it may well have been overlooked, particularly in view of its presence primarily during the winter months. In addition to which, of course, the finer points of the field identification of winter-plumage divers were still far from refined, even well into the 20th century. However, E H Rodd's general observations regarding the Cornish mainland are of interest, especially as he considered this the commonest of the three species known to visit the county (Rodd 1880).

The first 20th century mention concerns a comment that it was seen frequently during late March 1947 (*CBWPSAR* 17), though the next recorded sighting was not until 1958, when one was noted off the Gugh in October. Admittedly, this record coincided with the establishment of St Agnes Bird Observatory, but that alone seems unlikely to account for the obvious increase in the number of sightings from the late 1950s onwards, especially as the observatory was largely unmanned from late autumn until spring, and a greatly increased awareness of the seasonal presence of divers in Scillonian waters seems a far more logical explanation. Typically, birds appear from late September or October onwards, though some arrive earlier, and are then to be seen about the islands until as late as April or May. Very few records involve more than singles and few if any refer to birds in breeding plumage, even though some at least should have completed their pre-breeding moult by mid-April (Cramp *et al.* 1977–94). The extent, if any, to which migrant, as opposed to wintering, birds are involved remains unknown. The species is widely distributed around the coasts of Britain and Ireland in winter (Lack 1986) and regularly extends south and west at least as far as northwest France, not infrequently into the Bay of Biscay (Cramp *et al.* 1977–94). Scilly's Atlantic position, however, does not lend itself to the obvious coastal movements that make this and the other divers so conspicuous off mainland coasts of Britain during spring and autumn.

As with the two other common diver species, estimating exact numbers involved in any series of sightings is difficult and is not helped by the combination of regular heavy-sea conditions and daily tidal movements. Even so, a total of 20 or so birds occurred in seven of the ten years 1990–99, at an average of two per year; although in 1990 up to six individuals may have been present. One suggested explanation for the low numbers of birds present off Scilly may be the closeness of deep water around the islands and the relative lack of shallow feeding areas, particularly at low tide. Yet availability of suitable feeding areas seems unlikely to be an issue, given the continued presence in winter of a substantial proportion of Scilly's 1,200 pairs of breeding Shags, plus an unknown percentage of the past season's young Shags. Birds are also occasionally seen from the RMV *Scillonian III* during crossings to and from the mainland, though since the 1990s the service has been suspended from October through to Easter. Wintering Red-throated Divers reaching southern England originate from as far away as Greenland, Sweden and Finland, though most come from the Faeroes and northern Scotland. Small numbers reach at least northern France (Wernham *et al.* 2002).

## Black-throated Diver *Gavia arctica* A

**Scarce winter visitor and possible migrant, full written description required by the SRP.**

Circumpolar, similar breeding distribution to Red-throated Diver *G. stellata*, though extending further south in central Asia and Canada; absent from Greenland, Iceland, Spitsbergen and Franz Josef Land. Polytypic: nominate *arctica* occurs West Palearctic to east of Lake Baikal; *viridigularis* from east of Lake Baikal perhaps to eastern Alaska; *pacifica* (increasingly treated as separate species – 'Pacific Diver') North

America east to Hudson Bay and perhaps eastern Siberia. Dispersive and migratory, birds move to tidal waters and southwards in winter. As UK breeding species, confined to Scotland; mid-1990s population of 155–189 pairs. Included on Annex I of 1979 EEC 'Birds Directive'. Amber-listed in UK: 1994 population of no more than 189 breeding pairs; unfavourable world conservation status (Gregory *et al.* 2002).

Slightly more regular and numerous than Red-throated Diver, otherwise the same comments apply. E H Rodd thought this the least common off mainland Cornwall of the three regularly visiting diver species, pointing out that those he knew of had all been in immature plumage. However, most of these observations probably involved field sightings, and a summer-plumage individual from Looe in 1879 may have been the only 19th century specimen obtained in Cornwall (James Clark, in W Page 1906). E H Rodd's nephew Francis and co-author James Clark knew of no specimen obtained from Scilly in the 19th century, but did include a possible sighting in 1904 (Clark & Rodd 1906).

Following these early records, we have the familiar lack of information from the first half of the 20th century, and as a consequence a bird found dead at an unspecified location on 5th October 1951 prompted the comment 'rare here' (*CBWPSAR* 21). Like Red-throated Diver, Black-throated sightings continued intermittently during the 1960s and 1970s, but gradually increased in frequency and number to the point where it was present in autumn, winter or early spring during each of the ten years 1990–99, with approximately 41 individuals at an average of just over four per year recorded. Up to 12 in 1997 was probably the most in any year but, as with the other two regularly occurring diver species, arriving at precise counts is complicated by various factors, including heavy seas and daily tidal conditions. Birds either in or assuming/losing breeding plumage are on record, e.g. during April 1952, but most were seemingly in full-winter plumage. Although most come from within the archipelago, sightings are widely distributed about the islands and this may reflect observer coverage more than diver distribution, particularly in winter. Individuals are not infrequently present in and around St Mary's Harbour, as in January–February 1969.

Birds appearing briefly within the islands in September–October or April–May are often assumed to be migrants and though possibly correct, any evidence seems mainly circumstantial. Successions of sightings of single birds in broadly the same area, however, are normally assumed to involve just one wintering individual, but again, although perhaps correct, this is largely based on assumption, though it is easier to identify specific individuals where different plumage stages are involved. A bird of unknown age off St Helen's on the unusual date of 15th June 1989 is difficult to explain. Just four birds were recorded in Scilly during the Winter Shorebird Survey on 25th–26th January 1997: three off St Mary's and one off Tresco.

Black-throated Diver is far less widely distributed around the coasts of Britain and Ireland in winter than Red-throated, but, interestingly, is quite common off southwest Cornwall (Lack 1986). According to Parrack (in Lack 1986) the British Isles lie too far west to become involved in the main migration path and most Black-throated Divers in Britain and Ireland in winter may breed locally (Cramp *et al.* 1977–94). However, winter numbers may be too high to be attributed entirely to that source, in which case some may originate from northern Europe, possibly Norway. The east Palearctic form *viridigularis* and the now increasingly separated North American and east Siberian 'Pacific Diver' *G. pacifica* could occur in Scilly and this needs to be borne in mind when examining any supposed Black-throated Divers.

# Great Northern Diver *Gavia immer* A

**Regular winter visitor in small numbers, also possible spring and autumn migrant.**

Mainly confined to North America, in east extends to Greenland and Iceland, in west to Aleutian Islands, south to Great Lakes. Monotypic. Dispersive and migratory in western Europe, wintering south to Azores, Madeira and western Mediterranean. Included on Annex I of 1979 EEC 'Birds Directive'. Amber-listed in UK: 20% or more of European non-breeding population occurs in UK (Gregory *et al.* 2002).

Earliest evidence of this species in Scilly comes in the form of bone remains unearthed from the prehistoric site on Samson and dating from the 6th to 9th centuries AD (Turk 1973, 1984b), the author of the subsequent write-ups suggesting that this is an unusual find at any archaeological site. There is an early reference to the seabirds of the islands including 'Loons' (Heath 1750). However, though the species concerned is unknown, it seems most likely to have involved Great Northern, simply because it is the most frequent diver, at least it certainly has been over the past 150 years. E H Rodd, however, commented that by the late 1880s it was 'apparently much more common now than formerly'. He went on to suggest that this might (even by then!) be attributable perhaps to an increased interest in ornithology and a resultant growth in numbers of observers (Rodd 1880). Rodd made it clear that this species occurred mainly in immature plumage and, at least in west Cornwall, mainly in autumn; but he did describe receiving at least three specimens in summer plumage, all in October (Rodd 1866f). He also mentioned an unusually large influx into west Cornwall and Scilly in 1865, during which time he received no less than five specimens in two weeks and heard of many more having been obtained. Of particular interest is his description of Great Northern Divers becoming entangled in nets set for herrings *Clupea harengus* off the coast of Cornwall – perhaps one of the earliest of such accounts.

Dealing now with Scilly, although no specimen seems to have been obtained, there are specific references to it being present in the islands, for example, in E H Rodd's nephew Francis Rodd's account of visiting St Martin's on 7th November 1870 and observing that 'Great Northern Divers and some smaller divers had arrived'. However, the most useful early assessment comes from Francis Rodd and co-author James Clark (Clark & Rodd 1906), who described it as being seen singly and in small flocks in immature plumage during autumn and winter, occasionally in spring also. It was particularly common in flocks of six to ten birds during the winter 1901–02 and their mention of a bird off St Helen's on 20th May 1903 shows it occurred then in late spring, as indeed it still does. Further confirmation of 19th century Great Northern Diver presence in Scilly comes from Uren (1907), who, in a description of the island of Annet, lists this species among the 'occasionally rarer specimens' that might be met with, whereas Jesse (1887) quotes an earlier reference by Gilbert White to it being a 'winter resident' in the islands.

After the almost predictable lack of published records in the early 20th century, next mention is of a summer-plumage individual in St Mary's Harbour in mid-May 1932 (*CBWPSAR* 2). This was followed by singles reported in 1947 and 1957, but by the 1960s it was appearing in print almost annually and by the 1990s up to 40 sightings a year are on record. However, deciding precisely how many individuals are involved in these annual totals is no simple task and the true figure is more likely to be in the order of perhaps 10 to 15 birds annually. As with all seabird counts in Scilly, frequent rough seas and daily tidal changes influence the efficiency of counts. In addition, winter restrictions on inter-island boat traffic limit observations at that time of year and birds feeding outside the archipelago are unlikely to be recorded in any event. Occasional loose concentrations are to be seen, as in the case of 14 feeding off Annet on the evening of 2nd May 1995. A total of six individuals were recorded during the Winter Shorebird Survey on 25th–26th January 1997: one off St Mary's, four off Tresco and one off Samson.

Not so much in autumn, but certainly during April and May it is possible to encounter a bird in dazzlingly bold breeding plumage, though rarely, it seems, are such birds about the islands for long, giving weight to the view that they are perhaps en route to northern breeding grounds from wintering areas further south. Great Northern Divers in and around Scilly are likely to originate from Iceland or Greenland populations, which depart their breeding areas in September–October and winter along west European coasts south to the Azores and Mediterranean (Cramp *et al.* 1977–94). Birds return to the breeding areas from early May to mid-June, with pre-breeding individuals remaining in coastal waters further south, including Shetland. However, there are few, if any, summer records for Scilly. In mainland Cornwall, it occurs far more commonly, from October onwards, but greatest numbers are from January to March. In 1999 there were just under 600 reported Cornish sightings, with 141 in January being the highest monthly total; there were 6 June records plus a single individual in August.

## White-billed Diver (Yellow-billed Diver) *Gavia adamsii* A BBRC 0.5%

**Extremely rare migrant, full written description required by the BBRC.**

[1925 One (age and plumage unknown) off Toll's Island, St Mary's April]   Penhallurick 1969
1990 One (first-summer) off Bryher & Samson 6th May   *British Birds* 84: 452

Breeds Kola Peninsula and arctic Russia eastwards to arctic Canada, dispersing south in winter. Main West Palearctic wintering area believed to be off northern Norway. Monotypic.

An early report off Toll's Island, St Mary's, in April 1925 lacks supporting published information and

*Birds of the Isles of Scilly*

was rejected in a review of all past British records (Burn & Mather 1974), leaving the bird off Bryher and Samson in May 1990 as the sole accepted Scillonian representative of this much sought-after species (*IOSBR* 1990). In general, numbers of divers using Scilly are small, both on migration and in winter, probably reducing the chances of this species reaching the islands, but increasing the possibility of it being identified should it do so. Taking into account the Burn and Mather review, the BBRC list of accepted records for the period 1958–99 totals 199, and there were just 18 prior to that period.

Although not accepted by the BBRC, a claim of first one and then two White-billed Divers together off the western side of St Agnes in February 1965 is worth recounting. The first sighting involved what at first looked like a Great Northern Diver *G. immer* seen in Periglis Bay on 11th, but on closer inspection the bill was seen to be 'strikingly white' with an 'upper mandible that was horizontal, while the lower sloped up to it'. The second individual appeared on 19th, having a bill much the same shape and on 21st both were on view together (*CBWPSAR* 35). According to the editors of the Report, the record was rejected by the BBRC mainly on the grounds that it was 'almost impossible, then, to be certain of White-billed Diver in the field'. The BBRC also believed that shape and size of the bill and its colour were not considered decisive factors.

## Pied-billed Grebe *Podilymbus podiceps* A BBRC 5.4%

**Extremely rare migrant or winter visitor, full written description required by the BBRC.**

1994  One (adult) Tresco 11th November to 15th April 1995  *British Birds* 88: 497, 89: 485
1998  One Bryher, Tresco & St Mary's 28th October to 20th March 1999  *British Birds* 93: 515–516
2000  One (killed by Peregrine Falcon) St Agnes 25th October  *British Birds* 94: 455

Breeds North America, from Canada south through Central America and Caribbean into most of South America. Northern half of North American population moves south in winter but remains mostly within USA. Polytypic: nominate *podiceps* occurs North America; *antillarum* Caribbean; *antarcticus* South America. Central USA population recently 'boomed' and accounts for overall upward trend, though elsewhere, e.g. Canada, doing particularly badly (Bryant 1997).

It may seem surprising that this species was first identified on Scilly as recently as the 1990s and that three should then occur in the space of just seven years. However, this follows the national trend, as the first British record was itself as recent as 1963, though an earlier, 1880–81, record was subsequently rejected (Palmer 2000).

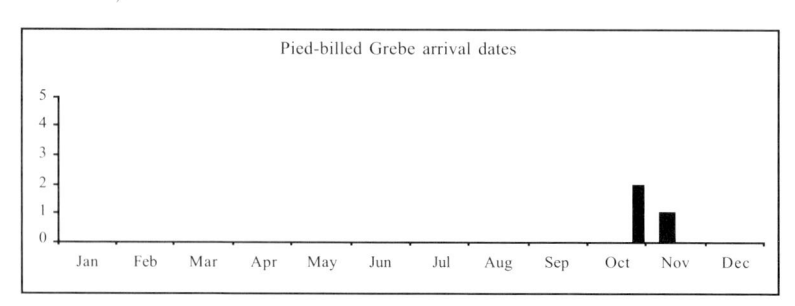

The 1994 individual arrived on Tresco's Abbey Pool and was seen sufficiently well and over a long enough period to safely eliminate any possibility of it being one of three hybrid young produced earlier the same year by a Pied-billed Grebe x Little Grebe *P. ruficollis* pair at Stithians Reservoir, Cornwall. Among other features, this possibility was ruled out on bill shape and overall structure. In addition, the possibility of the Stithians adult, a male, having relocated to Tresco in autumn could be discounted by the continued presence of that bird at Stithians to the year's end (*IOSBR* 1994; *CBWPSAR* 64).

The species' second appearance on Scilly came in October 1998, when a bird was found on Bryher Pool. It remained there until 1st November, then relocated to nearby Tresco Great Pool from 24th November and was seen at that site into 1999. One suggested explanation for its apparent November absence from Scilly was the appearance of a Pied-billed Grebe at Nanjizal on Cornwall's Land's End peninsula at this time. The latter bird (the fifth for Cornwall), however, was subsequently shown to be present after the reappearance of the Scilly individual (*IOSBR* 1998; *CBWPSAR* 68). The bird on Scilly remained on the Tresco pools until mid-March 1999 and was last seen during a brief two-day visit to Porth Hellick Pool, St Mary's, from 17th to 19th of that month. By the end of its stay it had moulted into breeding plumage and from its aggressive behaviour was thought likely to have been a male.

The most recent bird had a short but no less eventful stay, arriving on St Agnes on 25th October 2000 and being taken in flight the same day by one of the wintering Peregrine Falcons *Falco peregrinus*. During its brief presence on St Agnes, it was watched commuting between The Pool and the nearby sea, which of course contributed significantly towards its demise (*IOSRB* 2000). British records are widely distributed, from the Outer Hebrides, Dumfriesshire and Aberdeenshire, to Yorkshire, Norfolk, Dorset, Somerset, and of course Cornwall, plus Co. Wexford in Ireland. The BBRC accepted 37 records for Britain during the period 1958–99, with none previously, therefore the first two Scillonian individuals represent over 5% of the national total for the period.

## Little Grebe *Tachybaptus ruficollis* A

**Winter visitor in small numbers and possible migrant, does not breed.**

Breeds central and southern Eurasia from Atlantic to Pacific, Indonesia, northwest Africa and Africa south of Sahara. Polytypic: nominate *ruficollis* occurs Europe, northwest Africa, Israel and Turkey; *iraquensis* Iraq and Iran; *capensis* Caucasus, Armenia, Egypt, Africa south of Sahara and south Asia; at least six other forms further east. Mainly resident in West Palearctic, though some movement southwards or to coast, especially during severe weather. BTO Waterways Bird Survey showed 57% decline 1975–2000. Green-listed in UK: in need of basic conservation assistance (Gregory *et al.* 2002).

Little Grebe seems to have been generally accepted as a regular migrant or winter visitor to Scilly during the mid- to late 19th century, with E H Rodd describing it as a 'Periodic migrant, varying according to circumstances, in numbers and time of appearance' (Rodd 1878b). The same author later described it as not uncommon in winter, even mentioning the specific sighting of two on 19th December 1864 along with a noticeable arrival of other 'small Divers' (Rodd 1880). E H Rodd's nephew Francis Rodd and co-author James Clark went somewhat further, suggesting it was 'not infrequently found at Tresco during the autumn and winter', pointing out too that it had been seen on Tresco's 'Long Pool' (Great Pool) for several weeks in succession, whilst at the same time confirming it had never been known to breed in the islands (Clark & Rodd 1906). It bred at that time as far west in Cornwall as the Land's End peninsula, where E H Rodd described it as not uncommon (Rodd 1880), although according to Holloway (1996) it may always have been commoner there than in the remainder of the county. Certainly, it still bred in the Land's End area, only 45 km from Scilly, up until publication of the 1976 Atlas (Sharrock 1976), though it may since have ceased to do so (Gibbons *et al.* 1993).

The pattern with many species that occur either commonly in small numbers in Scilly is for them to disappear almost entirely from the records from the end of the 19th century until some time around the middle of the 20th century, and this indeed happened with the species under consideration here. However, part of the explanation for this and several other species may be their presence during late autumn or winter, thereby escaping the attention of early 20th century naturalists, who tended to visit in spring, summer or early autumn. We find, therefore, that mention of one in Periglis, St Agnes, from 4th to 13th October 1947 (*CBWPSAR* 17) is perhaps the first recorded Little Grebe to be present in Scilly since E H Rodd's December 1864 individuals. Lack of observer presence, however, cannot be the complete answer, as seems apparent from two 1940's records of coastal midwinter Black-necked Grebes *P. nigricollis*. So perhaps they were simply overlooked, or even considered unworthy of comment, though an even more likely explanation is editorial preference – Little Grebe quite suddenly making an annual appearance in the *CBWPSAR* from around 1962.

Certainly until around the mid-1980s, annual sightings were recorded routinely during the period mid- or late September through to late October or early November, with a marked absence of midwinter records, but with something of a reappearance during February or early March, implying a late winter or early spring passage. Examination of more recent records, however, reveals an increase in the frequency of midwinter sightings, suggestive perhaps of overwintering individuals having been previously overlooked, although none were recorded during the all-island Winter Shorebird Survey on 25th–26th January 1997.

Occasional birds arrive in the islands at other times of the year, as in August 1999 when three juveniles put in a brief appearance on Porth Hellick Pool, St Mary's. Recent annual totals hover around ten or less, but in some years may be as low as two or three and inter-site movement normally makes authoritative counting difficult in any event. Tresco's Great Pool rarely fails to attract overwintering birds, with the St Mary's Porth Hellick and lesser pools elsewhere rather less favoured, but many individuals also frequent inshore tidal waters at various locations, though usually away from shorelines most affected by bad weather. Normally, last spring sightings occur from mid- to late February but occasional individuals are to be seen as late as April, or even early May.

According to Cramp *et al.* (1977–94), autumn movement of British Little Grebes is limited, but there is some evidence, e.g. from ringing, that birds from northwest Europe migrate or disperse in a south to southwesterly direction, whereas those from central and southeast Europe are less predictable in direction, but do reach southwest Europe. Most movements are between England and Continental coastal areas from the Netherlands to the Cherbourg peninsula, but with two notable recoveries from Denmark and Latvia (Wernham *et al.* 2002). In Europe generally, birds begin vacating their breeding areas from July and commence reoccupying them from March to early May. Wintering Little Grebe distribution is widespread throughout England and Ireland, with ringing evidence showing that some reach France at least. Birds ringed in Germany, Denmark and the Netherlands have been recovered in England in winter and the marked winter increase along the English east coast may be indicative of a more general Continental immigration (Lack 1986). As with some other grebe *Podiceps* species using Scilly in winter, it is difficult to predict where Little Grebes originate from and their source could be Ireland, Britain or continental Europe.

# Great Crested Grebe *Podiceps cristatus* A

**Rare migrant and winter visitor.**

| | | |
|---|---|---|
| 1895 | One (shot) Scilly 14th February | Penhallurick 1969 |
| 1953 | One Tean Sound 16th September | Penhallurick 1969 |
| 1956 | One offshore St Agnes 5th February | *CBWPSAR* 26 |
| 1979 | One off Samson 12th to 15th September | |
| 1981 | One Old Grimsby, Tresco, & Periglis and Warna's Cove, St Agnes 10th to 26th May | |
| 1985 | One (near full summer plumage) Bar Point, St Mary's 2nd to 6th March | |
| 1986 | One St Mary's Harbour & Porth Cressa 15th February to 25th March | |
| 1986 | One Porth Cressa, St Mary's 18th to 23rd February | |
| 1987 | One Porth Cressa, St Mary's 19th to 22nd January | |
| 1987 | One Watermill, St Mary's 23rd October | |
| 1991 | One Bryher Quay 26th March | |
| 1992 | Two Tresco 19th March | |
| 1995 | One Higher Town, St Martin's 12th November | |
| 1996 | One Porth Cressa 31st January | |
| 1997 | Up to two, various islands 24th January to 13th March | |
| 1997 | One Tresco Channel 23rd August | |
| 1999 | One Peninnis, St Mary's 7th October | |

Breeds Eurasia, Africa, Australia and New Zealand. In West Palearctic, from Britain and Ireland east to Caspian Sea and from southern Finland and Sweden south to north Africa and Iraq. Dispersive and migratory, the northwest West Palearctic population winters south to limit of breeding range. Polytypic: nominate *cristatus* occurs Eurasia; *infuscatus* Africa; *australis* Australia and New Zealand. National 6% decline 1994–99 (Bashford & Noble 2000). Green-listed in UK: in need of basic conservation assistance (Gregory *et al.* 2002).

Despite its status as a widespread and moderately common breeding and wintering bird throughout much of Britain (Lack 1986; Gibbons *et al.* 1993), this species remains something of a rarity in Scilly. Indeed much the same can be said of its status on the Cornish mainland; according to Harrison & Hollom (1932) there were too few suitable nest sites in the southwest. It suffered severe persecution throughout the 19th and early 20th centuries and the total British breeding population was estimated to be in the range 31–72 pairs by 1860 (Harrison & Hollom 1932). Despite this severe decrease in numbers, a fairly rapid recovery followed introduction of national bird protection legislation, and by the end of the 19th century it was far more widely distributed, but nevertheless remained largely absent from the southwest (Holloway 1996).

Earliest reference to Great Crested Grebe in Scilly is probably Uren's comment that it was one of the rarer species to be encountered about the islands and outlying rocks, together with Great Northern Diver *Gavia immer* (Uren 1907). E H Rodd made no mention of it in Scilly but suggested that it was 'not very uncommon' in winter in mainland Cornwall, 'especially in the marsh pools in the Land's End district' (Rodd 1880). James Clark (in W Page 1906) goes slightly further, pointing out that in the Land's End district it was sometimes to be found in flocks of 12–15, but had only twice been obtained in breeding plumage.

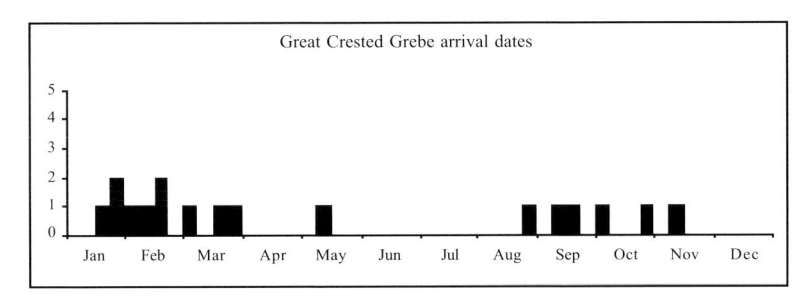

*Great Crested Grebe arrival dates*

The sole 19th century Scillonian record involved a bird reportedly shot in February 1895 and noted in the Tresco Abbey records (Penhallurick 1969). There are no records at all from the early half of the 20th century and it occurred in just 13 of the 50 years from 1950 to 1999, primarily as a migrant or winter visitor. Earliest recorded arrival date during the period was 12th September and the latest sighting was on 26th May, excepting the bird in Tresco Channel on the rather surprising date of 23rd August, 1997. All sightings involved birds on the sea off the coasts of various islands. According to Lack (1986), the normal wintering population of Britain and Ireland was in the region of 7,000 to 10,000 individuals by the early to mid-1980s, but with a substantial increase, to around 20,000, involving birds from continental Europe during particularly cold weather. Similarly, British and Irish birds tend to move south and west during very cold weather, into France and southwest Ireland. Like Little Grebe *Tachybaptus ruficollis*, most ringing recoveries were from England, nearby France and the Netherlands, but with two movements involving Denmark (Wernham *et al.* 2002).

## Red-necked Grebe *Podiceps grisegena* A

**Rare migrant or winter visitor, full written description required by the SRP.**

| | | |
|---|---|---|
| 1906–23 | One (shot) Scilly   Penhallurick 1969 | |
| 1965 | One St Mary's 23rd January | |
| 1966 | One St Agnes 9th October | |
| 1966 | One St Agnes 8th November | |
| 1981 | One Peninnis, St Mary's 13th October | |
| 1984 | One (first-year) Gimble Porth, Tresco & Old Town, St Mary's 19th September to 17th October | |
| 1985 | One (first-year) Porth Minnick, St Mary's 22nd October | |
| 1987 | One Samson 22nd October | |
| 1988 | One Watermill, St Mary's 21st October to 12th November | |
| 1990 | One Tresco 20th January | |
| 1990 | One off Telegraph, St Mary's 27th December | |
| 1994 | One Tresco 21st October | |
| 1995 | One St Martin's, Tresco & The Roads 14th to 27th October | |
| 1996 | One Tresco 25th February to 21st March | |
| 1996 | One Tresco 21st November | |
| 1997 | One The Roads 21st March | |
| 1997 | One Horse Point, St Agnes 4th October | |
| 1998 | One The Roads & Porth Cressa 1st to 17th October | |

Breeds Eurasia, south of arctic–alpine zone from Denmark east to Kazakhstan and from east of Lake Baikal to Kamchatka, and in North America from Alaska east to Great Lakes. Dispersive and migratory, in West Palearctic wintering in tidal waters from southern Norway south to eastern Mediterranean. Polytypic: nominate *grisegena* occurs West Palearctic; *holboellii* or 'American Red-necked Grebe' eastern Asia and North America. Amber-listed in UK: five-year mean of 2.6 breeding pairs; 50% or more of breeding population at ten or fewer sites (Gregory *et al.* 2002).

There are no early references to Red-necked Grebe in Scilly. E H Rodd thought it best described as the rarest of the grebes in Cornwall but nevertheless considered it almost as common as Great Crested Grebe *P. cristatus*, commenting that from time to time a specimen showing some red feathering was obtained in spring. In addition, James Clark and Francis Rodd's failure to mention the species in a Scillonian context may be taken as a reliable statement of its absence (or could alternatively mean that it had been overlooked) prior to publication of their landmark review (Clark & Rodd 1906). Penhallurick drew attention to the scepticism of some more recent writers regarding earlier statements of Red-necked Grebe near-abundance off Cornwall, using the absence of any Scillonian records as proof of its probable scarcity towards the end of the 19th century (Penhallurick 1969). Clark, though, seems always to have been reliable and adds weight to his suggestions of occasional frequent appearances by quoting years when it was considered plentiful in Cornwall, e.g. January 1891 and 1895 (in W Page 1906).

As with Slavonian Grebe *P. auritus* and Black-necked Grebe *P. nigricollis*, there are almost no records from the early part of the 20th century. Penhallurick (1969) quoted one shot some time between 1906 and 1923 but gave no further details. He also gave the date of the first modern record as 17th October 1965, mistakenly quoting from the preceding *CBWPSAR* entry relating to Red-throated Diver (*CBWPSAR* 35), whereas the correct date is as shown in the accompanying Table.

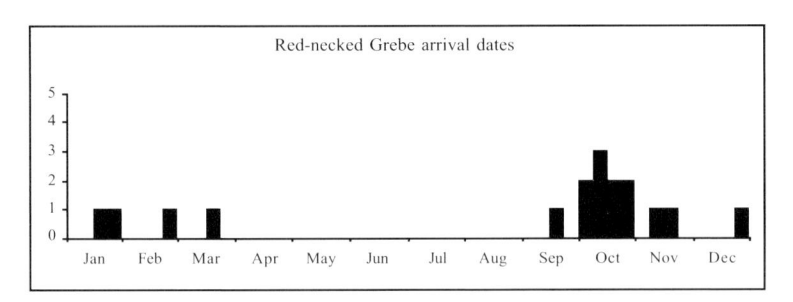

Red-necked Grebe arrival dates

Ignoring the earliest record, there have been a total of 17 sightings involving 17 individuals in 11 of the 35 years since 1965, at a rate of just over one every three years. The earliest arrival was 19th September and the latest 21st March, whereas the last date any bird was seen in the islands was also 21st March (2). Twelve birds stayed just one day, the others remaining for 29, 25, 23, 17 and 14 days. The average length of stay was seven days and there was no apparent relationship between arrival date and length of stay. The Chart comprises all known Red-necked Grebe arrival dates and shows the typical pattern for an autumn migrant and winter visitor, appearing mainly in October and with subsequent random winter sightings through to early spring.

According to Lack (1986) Red-necked Grebe winters down the British east coast from the Firth of Forth to Kent and then sparingly along the English south coast to Cornwall, but is absent from Ireland. In continental Europe it is found in winter as far west as northern France. Interestingly, Red-necked Grebe was not recorded in Scilly during the unprecedented invasion into Britain of this species and Black-necked *P. nigricollis* and Slavonian Grebes *P. auritus* during winter 1978–79, although it reached the Cornish mainland (Chandler 1981). Whether or not there has been a national redistribution since the 1980s seems unclear, but a recent RSPB survey found that 40% of the British wintering Red-necked Grebes are now found off the Cornish south coast (Geary & Lock 2001).

The form *holboellii* or 'American Red-necked Grebe' occurs in North America and the East Palearctic and could conceivably appear in Scilly, particularly during autumn or winter. It is noticeably larger than nominate *grisegena* with a bill some 20% longer and there is already at least one claimed previous British record, from Ross-shire, Scotland, in September 1925 (Gantlett 1998).

# Slavonian Grebe *Podiceps auritus* A

**Rare winter visitor and possible migrant, full written description required by the SRP.**

| | | |
|---|---|---|
| 1868 | One Tresco November | Penhallurick 1969 |
| 1902 | At least one November | Clark & Rodd 1906 |
| 1985 | Up to two Blockhouse Point, Tresco 28th to 31st January | |
| 1985 | One St Mary's Harbour 13th February | |
| 1985 | One Eastern Isles & St Martin's 9th to 29th April | |
| 1985 | One The Roads 19th & 20th October | |
| 1986 | Three south of St Helen's 9th February | |
| 1990 | One Porth Cressa 22nd December | |
| 1993 | Three off Tresco (east side) 13th February | |
| 1994 | One Tresco Channel 27th March | |
| 1994 | One Old Town & Porth Mellon, St Mary's 17th to 29th October | |
| 1994 | One The Roads 14th November | |
| 1995 | One Porth Cressa, St Martin's & Tresco 12th to 27th October | |
| 1996 | One Porthloo, St Mary's 16th to 19th January | |
| 1996 | Six Tresco 27th & 28th March | |
| 1996 | One Tresco 30th November | |
| 1996 | Up to five Tresco & Tean 24th December to at least 26th January 1997 | |
| 1997 | One St Martin's 12th to 19th November | |
| 1998 | Two The Roads 11th January | |
| 1999 | One The Roads, Bar Point, St Mary's & Eastern Isles 11th February to 20th March | |
| 1999 | One Bar Point, St Mary's & Tresco 28th October to 7th November | |

Circumpolar, breeds south of tundra from Iceland east through northern Scotland, Norway, central-northern Eurasia and Canada to north of Great Lakes. Some authorities treat as monotypic, though others recognise North American birds as *cornutus* (Gantlett 1998), using *auritus* for remainder (Cramp *et al.* 1977–94). Migratory or dispersive, most move from fresh water to inshore tidal waters, in West Palearctic withdrawing south along Atlantic coast as far as northwest France, also northern Mediterranean and Black Sea. Included on Annex I of 1979 EEC 'Birds Directive'. Amber-listed in UK: recent 36% decline to 40 breeding pairs; moderate decline in non-breeding population over past 25 years (Gregory *et al.* 2002).

The exact status of this species in both Scilly and mainland Cornwall during the 19th century remains unclear. E H Rodd described it as occasionally obtained but less commonly in Cornwall than either Red-necked Grebe *P. grisegna* or Great-crested Grebe *P. cristatus*, whereas in Scilly he thought it occurred 'occasionally in winter' (Rodd 1867a, 1880). Nevertheless, by the early 1900s it appeared in the islands sufficiently often for E H Rodd's nephew Francis Rodd and fellow author James Clark to describe it as an occasional autumn and winter visitor, appearing chiefly on Tresco and by no means rare (Clark & Rodd 1906), going on to point out that it last appeared in 1902. Penhallurick added mention of an earlier, 1868, individual in the Tresco Abbey records (Penhallurick 1969); though it seems surprising that Francis Rodd failed to mention this last bird, given the amount of time he spent shooting rarities on Tresco in the mid- to late 1880s.

There then followed a huge gap of 83 years before Slavonian Grebe was next recorded within the islands. On the face of it, this prolonged period of absence appears difficult to explain, but it is almost certainly more perceived than real and, as with so many other species in Scilly, almost certainly reflects a general breakdown in ornithological recording during the first half of the 20th century. But whatever the reasons for the former lack of information, the species reappeared in the records in a big way in 1985, when at least five birds were recorded. Furthermore, if the evidence of the final decade of the 20th century is to be believed, it seems now to have become an annual visitor. Ignoring the two old records, there were 19 arrivals in 10 of the fifteen years since its reappearance in the literature in 1985, involving at least 31 individuals. The earliest arrival was 12th October 1995 and the latest any bird was seen was 29th April 1985. Eight of the records involved single-day sightings but several individuals or groups are known to have moved about between the islands and the chances of such a small 'seabird' being recorded throughout its stay during winter must be low. The longest sustained presence involved the bird off the Eastern Isles and St Mary's for 38 days in February–March 1999 and the next longest were 21, 16 and 13 days, with no others reaching double figures. The average length of stay was just seven days. The Chart comprises all arrival dates since 1985 and shows a fairly broad spread across autumn, winter and spring. It is suggested in the literature that between-year arrivals on or around the same date may involve returning individuals, as is known to occur in Black-necked Grebe *P. nigricollis*. Unlike Black-necked, Red-necked and Great-crested Grebes, a feature of Slavonian Grebe's presence in the islands, as elsewhere (Chandler 1981), is the appearance of small groups of up to six individuals. Most *auritus* winter around the coast of Britain and Ireland and off Denmark and the Netherlands (Wernham *et al.* 2002).

Slavonian Grebe arrival dates

Gantlett (1998) rightly drew attention to the possibility of the slightly greyer North American form *cornutus* (not fully recognised by Cramp *et al.* 1977–94) occurring in Britain, in which case Scilly might be a likely recipient. Although Slavonian Grebe winters all around Britain and Ireland there is an obvious preference for the coast of southern and southwest England, from Hampshire to extreme west Cornwall (Lack 1986). In addition, birds winter in continental Europe as far as the coast of northwest France (Cramp *et al.* 1977–94; Chandler 1981). Peak autumn movement occurs October–November and, at least in western Europe, main departure from the wintering areas commences March–April, all of which fits the pattern of sightings within the archipelago (Cramp *et al.* 1977–94). Birds wintering off Scilly could originate from Iceland, Scotland, Norway, Sweden, northeastern Europe or Asia. Chandler (1981) documented three major influxes of Slavonian, Black-necked and Red-necked Grebes into Britain during winter 1978–79 in numbers unprecedented during the 20th century and suggested that they came from countries bordering the North Sea, from France to Denmark, and the western Baltic. None of these three species is on record as having occurred in Scilly around this time, even though Slavonian Grebes appeared as far west as Devon and mainland Cornwall, with at least 25 present on Devon's Exe Estuary (Chandler 1981).

## Black-necked Grebe *Podiceps nigricollis* A

Rare winter visitor, plus autumn or possible spring migrant, full written description required by the SRP.

1867    One Scilly November    Rodd 1880
1895    One (shot) Tresco 14th February    Clark & Rodd 1906
1947    Three (possibly shot) Scilly 2nd September    CBWPSAR 17; Penhallurick 1969
1949    Two St Mary's Harbour 15th December    CBWPSAR 19
1964    One St Agnes 22nd to 24th December
1968    One St Mary's Harbour October to April 1969
1969    One St Mary's Harbour 28th September to end of March 1970
1969    One Porth Hellick 6th October
1969    One Tresco 26th October
1970    One 20th September to year's end
1971    Two St Mary's Harbour September to April 1972
1972    Two St Mary's Harbour September to late March 1973
1973    One St Mary's Harbour 29th September, two from 18th October, both to March 1974
1974    One St Mary's Harbour 18th September to 24th March 1975
1975    One St Mary's Harbour 2nd October to 12th March 1976

1977 One Crow Sound 7th May
1979 One Gugh 28th August
1990 One Abbey Pool, Tresco 12th & 13th August
1996 One Tresco Channel 21st to 27th March
1997 One Eastern Isles 20th March
1997 Up to two (1st-year) Abbey Pool, Tresco 9th September into 2000
2000 One Tresco 20th February to 6th March

Breeds central and southern Europe, western Asia, Mongolia and central and western North America, with small isolated populations in eastern and southern Africa. Migratory and dispersive. West Palearctic population winters mainly along coasts, from British Isles to Iberia and around Mediterranean, Caspian, Adriatic and Black Seas. Polytypic: nominate *nigricollis* occurs Palearctic; *gurneyi* Africa; *californicus* North America (Cramp *et al.* 1977–94). Amber-listed in UK: five-year mean of 55.4 breeding pairs (Gregory *et al.* 2002).

E H Rodd's lack of comment regarding Black-necked Grebe in the 19th century demonstrates the care required when using his normally trustworthy and informative account of *The Birds of Cornwall and The Scilly Islands* (Rodd 1880). Although it gets no mention in either Rodd's main species accounts or his supplementary *List of Birds Observed in The Scilly Islands*, there is a comment among letter extracts from nephew Francis Rodd that an 'Eared Grebe' was observed in the islands during late November 1867. Francis Rodd and co-author James Clark later confirmed this particular sighting and added the additional record of a bird shot by a Joe White near Plump Rock (possibly Plum Island), Tresco, on 14th February 1895 (Clark & Rodd 1906).

As with so many species in Scilly, Black-necked Grebe then disappears from the records until three were reported at an unnamed location on 2nd September 1947 (*CBWPSAR* 17). This was followed by just 19 further sightings in 16 of the 54 years up to and including 2000, involving a likely 26 individuals reported throughout the whole of the 20th century. And even that may be something of an overstatement as the series of records from St Mary's Harbour during the early to mid-1970s seem likely to have involved the same one to two annually returning individuals (*IOSBR*; Lack 1986). Penhallurick suggested that the three 1947 birds were shot, but this information does not appear in the *CBWPSAR* and he gives no additional reference (Penhallurick 1969). Discounting the two 19th century records and those for which no specific dates are stated, the earliest reported sighting was 12th August and the latest arrival was 7th May, the latter date also being the latest any bird was seen in the islands.

Interestingly, according to Penhallurick, this species was far more common in winter in mainland Cornwall prior to 1959, in apparent marked contrast to Scilly, with flocks of around 15 seemingly normal in winter and with up to 52 present at one location in January 1948. However, in both Scilly and on mainland Cornwall it seems to be almost exclusively maritime in behaviour. Black-necked Grebe breeds sparsely in Scotland and England south as far as the Home Counties, but with very few pairs involved annually (Gibbons *et al.* 1993). In contrast, the wintering population seems rather larger and is distributed mainly along the southern coast of England, coastal Wales and extreme southern Ireland (Lack 1986). More recently, an RSPB survey found that 70% of British wintering Black-necked Grebes are now located off the Cornish south coast (Geary & Lock 2001). In Lack's view, the British breeding population accounts for only a small proportion of Black-necked Grebes wintering within the British Isles, which he presumed derive mainly from populations in western continental Europe and further east.

*Birds of the Isles of Scilly*

**Black-necked Grebe arrival dates**

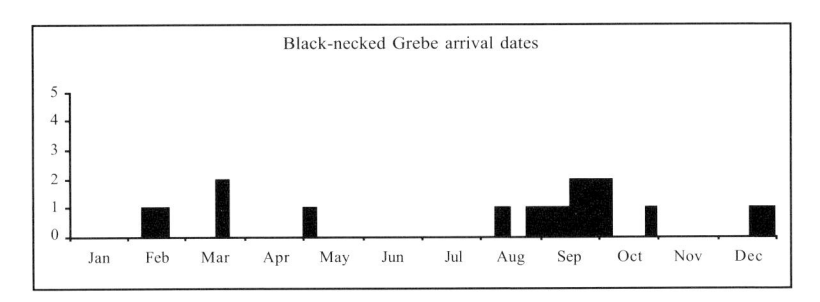

[Bar chart showing monthly counts: Feb 1, Mar 2, May 1, Aug 1, Sep 1, Sep 2, Nov 1, Dec 1]

In Europe, southwards dispersal commences mid-August and peaks around October, with most birds in their wintering areas November to March, whereas northwards return movement commences in March with most breeding lakes reoccupied by early May. The possibility of the subtly different North American form *californicus* reaching west-coast Britain must be kept in mind.

## Grebe *Podiceps*

Two birds thought to have been either Slavonian *P. auritus* or Black-necked Grebe *P. nigricollis* were seen in flight off Horse Point, St Agnes, on 6th October 1962 (*SABOAR* 1961–62).

## [Wandering Albatross *Diomedea exulans*]

**No acceptable British or Irish records, full written description required by the BBRC.**

Breeds Southern Hemisphere, occasionally straggling beyond equator into northern oceans. Polytypic: *exulans* occurs Tristan da Cunha and Gough Island; *chionoptera* elsewhere.

A claim of a Wandering Albatross off Scilly on 26th July 1962 was rejected by the BBRC/BOURC (BOURC 1968). Cramp *et al.* (1977–94) refer to a record of one off France around 1830, which was apparently accepted; unconfirmed reports of dead birds in Belgium: near Antwerp in September 1833 and Blankenberge in April 1887; an immature male killed Palermo, Sicily in October 1959; and a sighting of an immature about 80 km off Portugal in October 1963.

## Black-browed Albatross *Thalassarche melanophris* A  BBRC 8.0 %

**Extremely rare vagrant, full written description required by the BBRC.**

    1978    One (apparent adult) from Scillonian 8 km NE of St Mary's 20th September    *British Birds* 72:508
    1978    One (apparent subadult) from Scillonian II 5·5 km NE of St Mary's 16th October
                                                                              *British Birds* 72: 508

Breeds islands in Southern Ocean, dispersing widely in southern winter, reaching Antarctic pack ice and regularly wandering north to Tropic of Capricorn, occasionally further. Polytypic: *impavida* occurs New Zealand and adjacent islands; nominate *melanophris* elsewhere. Removed from great albatrosses *Diomedea* and placed with mollymawks *Thalassarche* by BOURC September 2002 (BOURC 2002b; Sangster *et al.* 2002a).

Given Scilly's geographical position, it comes as no great surprise to find there have been two accepted records of this oceanic wanderer, with just 25 British sightings accepted by the BBRC from 1958 up to and including 1999. What is perhaps surprising, though, is that both observations occurred within weeks of each other and that there was a third undescribed sighting six days after the October individual. Given the circumstances, it might seem tempting to suggest that just one individual was involved but the BBRC agreed that ages differed between sightings.

Both accepted records involved birds seen from the RMV *Scillonian II* in 1978, a probable adult on 20th September 8 km northeast of St Mary's and one 'showing subadult characters' 5.5 km northeast of the islands on 16th October (*British Birds* 72: 508). Extracts of the full descriptions were not published in the annual *IOSBR*, Black-browed Albatross having to compete that year with Black Duck *Anas rubripes*, Semipalmated Plover *Charadrius semipalmatus*, Pallid Swift *Apus pallidus* and Red-eyed Vireo *Vireo olivaceus*, so regrettably we have only very brief information. No age is given in the *IOSBR* for the unreported individual, which was claimed for Crow Sound, to the north of St Mary's, on 22nd October.

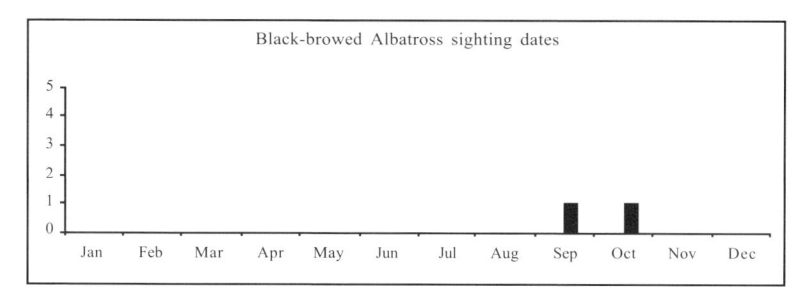

## Albatross *Diomedea/Thalassarche/Phoebetria*

**Extremely rare vagrants, full written description required by the BBRC in all cases.**

[1921   One off Golden Bar, St Mary's]   Penhallurick 1969
1986   One off St Mary's 19th October   *British Birds* 82: 508

Large oceanic seabirds breeding in the Southern Hemisphere and occasionally reaching northern oceans. Most likely to reach the North Atlantic are Black-browed *T. melanophris*, Yellow-nosed *T. chlororhynchos* Black-footed *P. nigripes*, Wandering *D. exulans* and Royal *D. epomophora*. Generic status of albatrosses reclassified November 2002 (Sangster *et al.* 2002).

An albatross seen initially off Jackie's Point and then off Giant's Castle, both St Mary's, on 19th October 1986 was thought probably to have been Black-browed, but owing to uncertainties over bill colour it was not assigned to a particular species by the BBRC (*IOSBR* 1986; *British Birds* 82: 508). This was preceded on the Cornish mainland by a similar record of an unidentified albatross near Marazion, just east of Penzance, on 23rd August 1964 (*CBWPSAR* 37). However, Penhallurick (1969) drew attention to a far earlier, 1921 sighting shown in the Tresco Abbey records as having involved an unidentified albatross off 'Golden Bar', probably what is now known as Golden Ball, between Tresco's northern end and nearby Men-a-Vaur.

## Fulmar (Northern Fulmar) *Fulmarus glacialis* A

Resident and possible migrant, breeds in noticeably increasing numbers.

Fragmentary breeding distribution, in North Atlantic from northwest France, Great Britain and Newfoundland northwards; in Pacific from Sea of Okhotsk north and east to southwest Alaska. Migratory and

*Birds of the Isles of Scilly*

dispersive, in West Palearctic wintering south to about limit of breeding range. Polytypic: nominate *glacialis* occurs North Atlantic; *rodgersii* north Pacific. Upgraded from Green to Amber-listed in UK 2002: 50% or more of breeding population at ten or fewer sites (Gregory *et al.* 2002).

The fact that within the North Atlantic by the mid- to late 19th century Fulmar was still confined to St Kilda and that it was not recorded breeding in Shetland until 1878, means that it played no part in the early ornithology of Scilly. Indeed, even at the time of publication of *The Handbook of British Birds* (Witherby *et al.* 1940) its authors were able to describe Fulmar only as present in Scilly and not yet shown to breed. First mention of it in *CBWPSAR* comes with the 1936 description of one seen 20 miles west-northwest of the islands on 11th June that year, with a second off the Western Rocks on 20th June the following year, local fishermen commenting on not having seen the species previously. In nearby Ireland, first recorded breeding, in Co. Mayo, occurred around 1907 (Witherby 1911), with the timing of similar events down the western coasts from St Kilda being well documented: Orkney 1891, Cape Wrath 1897, Barra Island 1899–1902, Handa Island 1900–01 and Flannan Isles 1902.

Certainly from the early 1940s onwards, Fulmars were seen about the islands annually, with birds observed going ashore, but breeding, or attempted breeding, not recorded until an egg was found on Bryher's Shipman Head on 24th June 1951 (*CBWPSAR* 21). In 1952, three to four 'pairs' were said to be 'sitting tight' on rugged Men-a-Vaur, plus three 'pairs' on Shipman Head, though breeding was not confirmed. Things clearly progressed at a pace, however, for by 1954 three eggs were located on Shipman Head and four pairs were site-sitting on Men-a-Vaur, with even a lone bird on remote Hanjague. The first recorded hatching on Scilly involved a pair on Shipman Head in 1955, whereas the first possible fledging was not until 1960, when a ready-to-fledge youngster was seen on Men-a-Vaur (*CBWPSAR* 30).

By 1974, there were some 14 breeding pairs at six sites incorporating the Northern, Western and Eastern Isles, i.e. Men-a-Vaur, Round Island, Hanjague, Castle Bryher, Great Innisvouls and Gorregan (Allen 1974). But as a measure of the continuing spread of Fulmars within the islands, by 1999 a total of 183 incubating birds were recorded on 15 islands, an increase of nearly 600% in 25 years, the greatest number at any one site being 32 on Round Island (Seabird 2000 data). The pattern of spread within the islands has been recognisably one of occupation by one to two pairs, with egg-laying perhaps by year two, but without productivity for several years. A few sites, e.g. Gugh's eastern side, were deserted after two to three years of trial occupation.

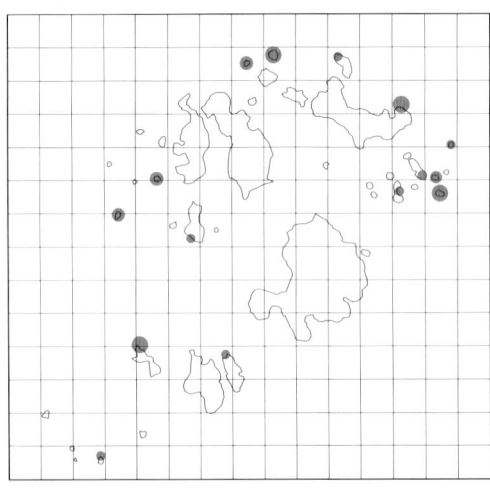

| Island | Nests |
|---|---|
| Annet | 21 |
| Gugh | 2 |
| Round Island | 32 |
| St Martin's Daymark | 32 |
| Menawethan | 27 |
| Men-a-Vaur | 16 |
| Mincarlo | 15 |
| Castle Bryher | 13 |
| Great Innisvouls | 7 |
| St Martin's White Island | 5 |
| Great Ganilly | 4 |
| Great & Little Arthur | 3 |
| Samson South | 2 |
| Gorregan | 2 |
| Hanjague | 2 |

**Distribution of 183 Incubating Fulmars – 1999 (Seabird 2000 data)**

Interestingly, the well-documented pattern of southward spread by breeding birds already referred to is further supported by a small number of birds ringed as nestlings in southern Ireland and found breeding in Scilly, the only known source of Scillonian birds so far. And whilst not surprising, the degree of site faithfulness among breeding birds revealed by retrap data is also worthy of note. For reasons already outlined, no Fulmars were ringed in Scilly up to 1970, although since then a total of 259 have been ringed, the majority as pulli (Scillonian Seabird Group – unpublished data). In France, Fulmars now breed as close to Scilly as Brittany (at least four sites) and Normandy (Guermer & Monnat 1980; Hagemeijer & Blair 1997) but it still remains to be established whether birds involved there were ringed originally in Scilly. In Britain, Fulmars breed as close to Scilly as west Cornwall, whilst in Ireland, Little Saltee, the origin already of three Scillonian breeding birds, remains the nearest site to the islands. On Scilly, good numbers of birds appear back at the breeding sites by the year's end.

| | | | | | |
|---|---|---|---|---|---|
| FV46967 | Pul | Little Saltee, Ireland 26th July 1980 | BR | Gorregan 2nd July 1993 | |
| | | | BR | Gorregan 20th July 1994 | |
| FS95116 | Pul | Little Saltee, Ireland 8th August 1981 | BR | Annet 7th July 1994 | |
| FR18177 | Pul | Little Saltee, Ireland 10th June 1990 | BR | Menawethan 4th June 1998 | |
| FA79563 | Ad | St Martin's 9th July 1996 | FD | Chale, Isle of Wight 16th February 2000 | |

**Fulmar Selected Ringing Recaptures**

## [Bulwer's Petrel                                                             *Bulweria bulwerii*]  A

One now rejected record involving an old skin specimen. Full written description required by the BBRC.

[1897   One 'near Scilly' 2nd October]   *Journal of Biological Curation* 1: 53–70; *Ibis* 134: 213

Oceanic species with limited, widely dispersed breeding distribution. Monotypic. Occurs equatorial and northern Atlantic, e.g. Cape Verde and Canary Islands, with other known populations in northern and central Pacific. Migratory, vacating North Atlantic in winter and moving south into tropical waters.

Bulwer's Petrel has a somewhat chequered history as a British species, with the circumstances of old records varying, dependent on the authority consulted. Palmer (2000) credited the earliest record to a bird found dead in County Durham in 1837, the skin of which was misplaced for some 50 years before being rediscovered and placed in the Yorkshire Museum. However, Morrison (1998) gave the finding location for this specimen as West Tanfield, Yorkshire. He credited the second British record to an undated bird from Scarborough, North Yorkshire, in 1849 but most authorities attribute the second record to a bird washed up dead near Scarborough on 28th February 1908, the skin of which is also in the Yorkshire Museum (Palmer 2000).

Neither Naylor (1996) nor Evans (1994) mentioned the specimen in Oldham Museum, marked 'Near Scilly, England 2 October 1897' (*J. Biol. Curation* 1: 53–70). This record was recently considered by the BOURC, who felt that although identification was not an issue there were 'elements of doubt surrounding the claimed circumstances of collection and the provenance of the specimen' (BOURC 1992a). The BBRC/IRBC accepted records involve an Irish sighting off Cape Clear Island in 1975 and one off Walney Island, Cumbria, in 1990. However, Morrison gives details of 13 'at sea' records from England, Scotland, Wales or Ireland, plus six inshore records presumably rejected by the two national committees and 11 at sea off France, Spain, Norway or Italy. As at January 2002, the BOURC were reviewing all past records of this species (BOURC 2002)

## [Matsudaira's Storm-petrel/Bulwer's Petrel
## *Oceanodroma matsudairae/Bulweria bulwerii*]

No accepted Scillonian record of either species.

[1988   One at sea (49.2°N 4.5°W) 48 km southwest of Scilly 3rd August]   Gantlett 1988; Swash 1988; Hume *et al.* 1997.

For details of Bulwer's Petrel distribution see that species. Matsudaira's Storm-petrel breeds Pacific islands off Japan, wintering off Southeast Asia and probably northern Indian Ocean.

A well-publicised bird seen from the MV *Chalice* 'the Chalice petrel', during a pelagic trip in sea area Sole, 45 km southwest of the islands, on 3rd August 1988 is thought to have been one or other of these two species (Gantlett 1988; Swash 1988; Hume *et al.* 1997). Although probably a moulting Bulwer's

Petrel, a final decision on this and three subsequent English records awaits the benefit of further research (Morrison 1998). Whether we should consider a bird seen so far out at sea among a list of the birds of Scilly is of course debatable, but presumably the BOU's proposed extended recording limit – out to 320 km – means that such records will now be included. But in the end, these things may largely be a matter of personal choice.

## Zino's/Fea's (Cape Verde) Petrel
### *Pterodroma madeira/feae* A BBRC 12.5%

Extremely rare vagrants or migrants, full written descriptions required by the BBRC.

| | | |
|---|---|---|
| 1996 | One 3.2 km southwest of Bishop Rock 18th August | British Birds 91: 460 |
| 1999 | One 1.5 km south of Bishop Rock 24th August | British Birds 95: 479 |
| 1999 | One 4.8 km south of St Agnes 31st August | British Birds 93: 345 |
| 1999 | One 5 km south of St Agnes 31st August | British Birds 94: 455 |
| 2001 | One 12 km south of St Mary's 8th July | British Birds 94: plate 221, 95: 479 |
| *2002* | *One between Scilly and mainland 14th August* | *Birding World 15: 311* |
| *2002* | *One south of St Mary's 8th September* | *Birding World 15: 355* |

Oceanic, breeding on islands in northern and subtropical Atlantic. Previously considered part of Soft-plumaged Petrel *P. mollis* superspecies complex, both now treated as full species. Zino's Petrel *P. madeira* occurs Madeira mainland, whereas Fea's Petrel *P. feae* occurs Bugio Island, Desertas and Cape Verde Islands. Among least known seabirds in North Atlantic, probably remaining close to breeding sites most of year. Zino's Petrel is restricted to two small colonies of perhaps no more than 50 pairs, whilst Fea's Petrel population limited to a few hundred pairs. Both currently treated as monotypic. (Cramp *et al.* 1977–94; BOURC 1992b; *Bull. Brit. Orn. Club* 103: 52–58).

Scilly's first record of any member of this complex group flew close to the local launch *Kingfisher* over the Poll Bank fishing ground, 3.2 km southwest of the Bishop Rock late evening on 18th August 1996, later being accepted by the BBRC as either Zino's or Fea's Petrel. The second, third and fourth records, during August 1999, were seen in greatly similar circumstances, when birds again flew close, near the site of the earlier individual, respectively 1.5 km, 4.8 km and 5 km south of St Agnes. One displayed its most important features to a stunned group of birders present in the boat as it banked steeply before leisurely drifting away to the west. At the time of going to press, the 2002 sighting still awaits BBRC approval.

Statistically, the chances of these sightings involving Zino's Petrel, rather than Fea's, must be slight, given the known imbalance in population numbers, though we understand little still about their movements at sea. In addition, separation of these two species at sea is still not fully acceptable to some authorities. Nonetheless those involved in the 2001 sighting photographed and filmed the bird close enough and long enough (12 minutes) to be satisfied that it was Fea's and many who have subsequently seen the pictures think similarly. The bird was seen from the launch *Kingfisher* at around 15.50 hours on 8th July, 12 km south of the islands, in a moderate, force 3–4, northwest wind, in a slight swell and with an overcast sky (Fisher & Flood 2001).

A second 2001 sighting claimed to have involved one or other of these two seen and filmed from the deck of RMV *Scillonian III* on her annual summer pelagic trip, about 100 km southwest of Scilly on 12th August (Lees 2001), but seems not to have been submitted to the BBRC by October 2002, though the consensus of opinion was in favour of Fea's. Although initially disappearing after just a few minutes, the

**Fea's/Zino's Petrel sightings**

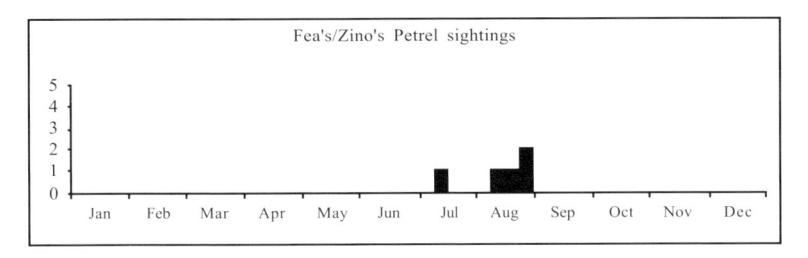

bird was soon refound and remained viewable to about 270 excited birders for some 80 minutes, affording useful comparison with nearby Gannets *Morus bassanus* and other seabirds in the process and raising the interesting question: are numbers of 'soft-plumaged petrels' present offshore from Britain increasing, or is increased awareness of their presence bringing its own rewards? For a review of the status and identification of Zino's and Fea's Petrels and related species in the North Atlantic, see Brinkley & Patterson (1998). The four earliest records represent 12.5% of the 32 BBRC-accepted records during the period 1958–99.

# Cory's Shearwater *Calonectris diomedea* A

**Scarce but regular offshore migrant or casual visitor, mainly during August and September. Treated by the BBRC as a national Scarce Migrant.**

Breeds islands in Mediterranean and subtropical eastern North Atlantic. Migratory, wintering mainly North Atlantic and eastern South Atlantic. Polytypic: nominate *diomedea* occurs Mediterranean; *edwardsii*, or 'Cape Verde Shearwater' (treated by some authorities as a full species), Cape Verde Islands; *borealis* remainder of subtropical eastern Atlantic. Removed from BBRC Rarities List January 1983 (Grant 1982b).

The earliest acceptable British Cory's Shearwater record involved a flock of 60 seen by V C Wynne-Edwards off south Devon as recently as September 1933 (Palmer 2000). During the 19th century, all large shearwater sightings in Scillonian waters, or off southwest England, were recorded as 'Great Shearwater' (*P. major*), but by the late 1930s it became increasingly accepted that Cory's also occurred, although probably in fewer numbers than Great Shearwater and with doubts remaining over the form or forms involved (Witherby 1940). Even to the present-day, few if any Cory's Shearwaters seen in or around Scilly are attributed subspecifically. Most though are likely to be *borealis* from the subtropical east Atlantic, but the smaller nominate Mediterranean *diomedea* and the more distinctive *edwardsii* (treated by some authorities as a full species) from the Cape Verde Islands are also possible and should be looked for (Gantlett 1998). The 'Great verses Cory's Shearwater in southwestern waters' debate came to a head in the 1930s, with a letter from an A Farrant to *British Birds* suggesting large shearwaters seen during a crossing to Scilly in August 1938 had been 'North Atlantic Great Shearwaters', i.e. Cory's (*P. kuhlii*) (Farrant 1938). This was followed by a letter from R S R Fitter confirming that birds seen on a similar crossing in September 1938 had also been Cory's, even suggesting the form involved, i.e. *P. k. borealis* (Fitter 1939). As the senior editor of *British Birds*, Harry Witherby was well aware of this correspondence, and in characteristic manner set about resolving the issue, as evident from the 1939 remarks of Tresco's A A Dorrien-Smith:

> Not being satisfied as to the species (of large shearwater) which is common about these Islands in the early autumn, I set out, at the suggestion of Mr H F Witherby, to get specimens. Owing to the War conditions I was unable to obtain more than one specimen, towards the end of August. This turned out to be *P. Gravis* the South Atlantic species, and is the same as that preserved in the Bird cases here (Tresco Abbey) (*CBWPSAR* 9).

The same writer expressed doubts that Cory's Shearwater occurred around Scilly, suggesting late October or November might nevertheless be an appropriate time to look for it. He further suggested that birds might be acquired by accompanying a fishing boat to the seas between Land's End and the Wolf Rock, where there were generally greater numbers of large shearwaters, and throwing a baited line on the surface, though 'if they are on passage they will not stop for any lure'. Witherby confirmed Dorrien-Smith's acquisition for him as a Great Shearwater, which was the same as an August 1899 skin already in the Tresco Abbey collection. He agreed, meanwhile, that Cory's did occur, but pointed out that up to that time there had only

*Birds of the Isles of Scilly*

been about four sightings, including those of Farrant and Fitter (Witherby 1940). The Witherby-Dorrien-Smith skin is still in the collection of the British Museum (Natural History) with Witherby's original label, marked '1944–11.9.68 shot Bishop Rock 24th August 1939 and shown to be a male'. It seems, though, that the debate was not entirely settled, for Dorrien-Smith wrote again to *British Birds* saying he had seen many large shearwaters off the Wolf Rock in 1941, all of which he identified as Greats (Dorrien-Smith 1941), whilst in 1946 H G Alexander threw his hat into the ring by suggesting he had seen both species within sight of Scilly. He added that there was perhaps slight evidence that Great was the only large shearwater formerly visiting the western English Channel but that Cory's had recently commenced visiting in autumn.

Numbers involved in Scillonian waters today vary greatly, though the species is almost annual, being recorded almost exclusively off the perimeter of the islands, or from the RMV *Scillonian III* on daily crossings to and from mainland Cornwall. Looking through all records from the mid-1970s, it was absent in about five years, and in three – 1989, 1998 and 1999 – was recorded in far greater numbers than normal. There is a clear tendency towards more sightings in recent years, doubtless in line with a greater interest in seawatching in Scilly. Excluding 1998–99, the mean numbers of birds seen annually during the 1990s was around 25, in the range one to 130 (though one of those annual totals includes 30 seen during the annual *Scillonian III* summer pelagic). The three recent big years involved 227 and 123 off St Agnes on 14th and 15th August 1989 (*IOSBR* 1989), 720 passing the same island on 6th September 1998 (*IOSBR* 1998) and an impressive 2,000 or so recorded throughout 1999 (*IOSBR* 1999). Most of the latter passed the islands during the first half of September, though as early as June, 255 were counted offshore. However, 1999 was a notable year for this species in the southwest generally, with 4,000 off southwest Ireland during late summer and 3,500 off Cornwall in the same period. Without doubt August and September offer the greatest chance of seeing this species in Scilly, but to be certain spend a day or two seawatching off the Cornish mainland before or after visiting Scilly, and travel on *Scillonian III*. Occasional unseasonal sightings involve individuals seen as early as June and it is increasingly being recorded in October.

According to Cramp *et al.* (1977–94), non-breeders become widespread across the temperate North Atlantic from May or June, from the Bay of Biscay to New England. The same authors describe 'occasional' large numbers off southwest Ireland between July and September. Non-breeders then move south to join birds from the breeding colonies before all depart to winter in the South Atlantic.

# Great Shearwater *Puffinus gravis* A

**Regular offshore migrant or casual visitor, mainly during August to October.**

Breeds islands in southern Atlantic, migrating to North Atlantic during southern winter. Monotypic.

Reports of large shearwaters off southwest England during the 19th century described them all as 'Great Shearwater' (*P. major*), otherwise known as 'Cinereous Shearwater', though both Great *P. gravis* and Sooty Shearwater *P. griseus* are now known to have been involved (Rodd 1880). At the time, it was thought that the darker Sooty was the young of the paler *gravis*, though Temminck earlier thought them male and female of the same species (Palmer 2000). Importantly, D W Mitchell (one-time secretary of the Zoological Society) obtained specimens of light individuals plus one dark bird from Mount's Bay, west Cornwall, during 1838–39, the last of which was used by Yarrell to (wrongly) illustrate young *gravis*; the fact that it was Britain's second record of Sooty Shearwater was only later appreciated (Palmer 2000). By the early 20th century, growing realisation that Cory's Shearwater *Calonectris diomedea*, also then known as 'North Atlantic' or 'Mediterranean Great Shearwater', may also have been involved led to a great deal of discussion and speculation (see Cory's Shearwater).

E H Rodd knew these large shearwaters as annual visitors to Cornwall and Scilly, where in the islands they went by the somewhat unusual name of 'Hackbolt'. He even appreciated that the timing of their arrival varied annually, as did the number of sightings 'in some years being tolerably common', and noting too that in some years they failed to appear at all (Rodd 1880). There is an early record from the Bishop Rock Lighthouse, involving a reported 20 large shearwaters seen by a lighthouse keeper 'sufficiently familiar' with Manx Shearwater *P. puffinus* to eliminate that species (Harvie-Brown *et al.* 1887).

In their commendable 1906 review of *The Birds of Scilly*, James Clark, and E H Rodd's nephew, Francis, described 'Great Shearwater' as a somewhat regular visitor in flocks during autumn and winter, concluding that it had probably never been seen within the islands (Clark & Rodd 1906), which largely remains the situation today. From about the late 1930s, however, large shearwaters in southwestern waters became a fashionable subject, surrounding the debate over whether or not Cory's also regularly occurred (Witherby 1940). For example, in 1941, A A Dorrien-Smith wrote to *British Birds* saying that he had seen many large shearwaters off the Wolf Rock – immediately southwest of Land's End – on 23rd–24th October, all of which, in his opinion, were Greats (Dorrien-Smith 1941).

More recently, the pattern has been one of single years, or a succession of years, without any sightings, a greater number of years with just a few birds seen and the occasional year with substantial numbers involved. However, long-term trends may previously have been obscured by a more casual approach towards recording, creating the impression, perhaps, that it was scarcer in Scillonian waters than was actually the case. Prior to the 1960s, most sightings came from crossings on the RMV *Scillonian* to or from mainland Cornwall and the first report of substantial numbers involved up to 240 off St Agnes in October 1967. From the mid-1970s onwards, first arrivals were noted as early as 24th July (1999), although mid-September usually witnessed the bulk of any passage, with late stragglers mostly having passed by early October. The only apparent contradiction involves a remarkable unseasonable bird off Tresco on 19th March 1989, though spring sightings are very occasional during April or May. None at all were recorded during the five years 1984–88, whilst, at the other extreme, good to exceptional numbers were noted in 1981 (peak of around 150), 1991 (peak of 60), 1998 (peak of 50) and 1999 (peak of 1,138). The latter year also saw substantially greater numbers elsewhere in the British Isles, with 230 off Porthgwarra, Cornwall, on 8th September, 500 an hour past Galley Head, Ireland, two days later and 700 past the same site on 18th September. Interestingly, although daily numbers normally fall short of those during good Great Shearwater years, both Cory's and Sooty Shearwaters are now more regular off Scilly, perhaps also reflecting increased local interest in seawatching.

Great Shearwaters depart the breeding grounds from April and May and move north along the eastern coasts of South and North America, before spreading out across the North Atlantic. Large numbers reach European coastal areas by August–October, most remaining well offshore but perhaps being driven inshore in large concentrations during adverse weather. The rapid return passage commences in August and most birds reaching European shores are thought likely to be non-breeders (Cramp *et al.* 1977–94).

## Sooty Shearwater *Puffinus griseus* A

**Scarce but regular offshore migrant or casual visitor, mainly singly and mainly August to October.**

Breeds islands off New Zealand, southern Australia and southern South America. Migratory, spending much time in the colder oceans of both hemispheres. Monotypic. Recent reports of global decline.

Until around the late 19th century, this species, also then known as 'Cinereous Shearwater', was thought to be the young of Great Shearwater (*Puffinus major*) (Palmer 2000). An individual was acquired by D W Mitchell – former Zoological Society secretary – in 1838, the bird having been obtained in Mount's Bay to the east of Penzance, west Cornwall. Yarrell used Mitchell's specimen to illustrate his *History of British Birds* (1843), some time elapsing before it was appreciated this was in truth Britain's second Sooty Shearwater – the first having been shot on the river Tees in August 1828 (Palmer 2000). In fact, the true second British record probably involved a bird presented to Couch in 1933, having taken a fisherman's bait, presumably in Cornwall. From Couch's description, there seems little doubt that this was a Sooty Shearwater, but credit now goes to Mitchell's bird (Penhallurick 1969).

First mention of Sooty Shearwater on Scilly involved a bird allegedly found exhausted on a St Mary's beach on 5th September 1952 and put back into the sea (*CBWPSAR* 22). Subsequent records involved singles off St Agnes in August and September 1961 and singles off the same islands on two dates in August and one in September 1962 (*IOSBR* 1961, 1962). From this time onwards it appeared almost annually in the records. In the ten years since 1990, it was recorded at an average of 43 individuals per year, in the range 10 to 68. Many sighting came from crossings on the RMV *Scillonian III*, e.g. eight on 21st September 1993, but birds were also to be seen around the edges of the archipelago, though seldom if ever between the main islands. Most sightings involve lone individuals, but highest daily counts for the ten years were the 58 noted on 18th September 1999, along with unusually large numbers of Great *P. gravis* and Cory's Shearwaters *Calonectris diomedea* (*IOSBR* 1999). Most were recorded between August and September, but two in June 1999 were particularly early and two on 16th–17th November 1997 were late. Like the two other large shearwater species, there has been a marked increase recently in the number of records, doubtless in line with the recent increased interest in seawatching in Scilly.

Sooty Shearwater occurs in greater numbers off mainland Cornwall, e.g. monthly totals of 165 and 206 in August and September 1999 respectively and an annual total of just under 500 for the same year (*CBWPSAR* 69).

## Manx Shearwater *Puffinus puffinus* A

**Summer visitor in decreasing numbers, currently known to breed on three uninhabited and three to four inhabited islands; all-island population may now be as low as 200 pairs (Heaney *et al.* 2002).**

Within West Palearctic, breeds Britain and Ireland, Iceland, Faeroes, France (Brittany), Madeira and Azores, also New Zealand and northwest North America, small presence northeast North America. Migratory or dispersive. Polytypic: nominate *puffinus* occurs eastern temperate North Atlantic; five additional forms sometimes considered separate species. Amber-listed in UK: 20% or more of European breeding population in UK, 50% or more at ten or fewer sites; unfavourable European conservation status (Gregory *et al.* 2002).

This species and Storm Petrel *Hydrobates pelagicus* are the two least known of Scilly's breeding seabirds, for perhaps obvious reasons, i.e. nocturnal and subterranean breeding biology, and pelagic lifestyle. According to Couch (in Rodd 1880), the provincial name for this species was 'Skidden' though it is not used now, or apparently not in Scilly. Earliest evidence of Manx Shearwater in Scilly comes from the skeletal remains of more than one individual unearthed from the prehistoric site on Nornour in the Eastern Isles (Turk 1971, 1984b). This species is seldom found at prehistoric sites in western European and its presence in Scilly doubtless reflects its earlier availability (Turk 1971). As early as the 2nd century it was common to make payment for land rental in the carcasses of young seabirds, generally referred to as 'puffins'. More recently, this has been interpreted as referring to the Atlantic Puffin *Fratercula arctica*, whereas the truth is rather different (Lockwood 1984). The term 'puffin', or 'puffling' was originally attached to cured carcasses of young Manx Shearwaters, an esteemed delicacy up until the 18th century, supplies of which came regularly from Scilly and the Calf of Man, in particular. As evidence of the origin of the word 'puffin', Lockwood cites the scientific shearwater name *Puffinus* used by early naturalists, the name Puffin only later being attached to *Fratercula arctica*, perhaps through the close association of these two species at breeding sites such as Annet. Several writers have commented over the years on the presence of both species often in the same burrow on Annet, e.g. Walpole Bond (1937).

To Scilly falls the distinction of being the first recorded site in Britain or Ireland involving payment in 'puffins'. Gurney (1921) suggested the earliest mention was 1337, when the islands were leased by Edward III (Earl of Cornwall) to Abbot Ranulphus of Blancminster, for the costly sum of 6 shillings and 8 pence, or 300 'Puffins' annually. However, Suffern (1939) drew attention to another document of 1337 or thereabouts, *Descriptive Catalogue of Ancient Deeds* (10 Edward III), contained in the Public Records Offices. This witnesses the subletting, by Ranulph de Blaunchminster (presumably the same Abbot Ranulphus), of all or most of Scilly to John de Allet by way of 'knight-service and by service of keeping Ranulph's castle in the said Isles for a certain time'. Indeed, the agreement apparently went even further, for we see too that 'the said Ranulph has released and quitclaimed for self and heirs, to John and his heirs the service of keeping the said castle for ever'. For his part, John appears to have agreed a (presumably annual) rent of 13 shillings and 4 pence, or 150 'pufforum' in the event of default, whereas John was granted the right to take 'poffonis' for his own use at a rate of one penny for three.

There are not too many 19th century estimates of numbers of breeding Manx Shearwaters on Annet, though Gurney thought there were no more than 200 pairs. He dismissed an apparent roosting two-mile-long (3.2 km) flock seen by a Captain White of St Mary's in August 1885, and thought to contain 'many thousands', as probably comprising birds from 'further north' (Gurney 1889).

Nevertheless, Manx Shearwater was clearly abundant enough in Scilly at the beginning of the 20th century for James Clark and Francis Rodd to remark that during the breeding season the sea was thick with them for half a mile (0.8 km) off northeastern Annet (Clark & Rodd 1906). And although there is disagreement now over likely numbers involved, Yarrell, in his *A History of British Birds*, described how Mitchell of Penzance regularly encountered flocks of at least 300 around Annet's northern end during June (Yarrell 1837–43; Rodd 1880). In addtion, Gilbert White estimated a July flock of at least 100,000 (in Jesse 1887) and H W Robinson (1911a) recorded local estimates of breeding numbers on Annet in the range 100,000 to 150,000: a far cry from Gurney's estimated 200 pairs.

Presumably Robinson was referring to individuals rather than pairs, but provides no additional information, other than confirming that the northern end of Annet was the species' stronghold in Scilly – although most now nest on the southern end (pers. obs.). Earlier, in 1904, Frohawk stayed overnight on Annet during early June, and based his estimate of 100,000 individuals on numbers observed (Frohawk 1908, 1915–16). The same author noted how the calls of so many shearwaters in one place obscured the noise of the sea washing onto the rocks just 30 metres away. Conversely, Walpole Bond (1937) visited the same island during daylight and so based his estimate of 'thousands' on the number of burrows seen, noting that of those they dug out, from an area of approximately two hectares, nearly all contained Manx Shearwaters, rather than Puffins. However, the most vivid account of being amongst Annet's shearwaters comes from C J King (1924), who described thousands of birds, such that 'one's face is constantly fanned by the wind from their wings, and one finds it wiser to sit down to avoid collision with them as they wheel about'. He also described the accumulated noise of thousands of wings and calls as 'perfectly deafening'. Indirect support for this number of birds in Scilly comes from reports from early day seawatchers in west Cornwall, some of whom counted up to 20,000 Manx Shearwaters passing during a single day in spring, on a northwesterly course in the direction of Scilly (Thorpe 1935; Trahair Hartley 1935). As an indication of numbers present on Annet even by the mid-20th century, on the night of 17th–18th April 1958 more than 400 were ringed, the session only ending when the supply of rings ran out (*SABOAR* 1958). By 1961, up to 500 were being recorded offshore (*SABOR* 1961–62) and again in 1971 (*IOSBR* 1971). Parslow thought the 1970's Annet population in the region of 2000 breeding pairs, pointing out, though, that lack of previous data made it impossible to say whether this represented an increase or decrease since the beginning of the 20th century (Parslow 1970), though a decrease was more in keeping with 'other evidence'.

Clearly, regular evening gatherings off northern Annet were well known even during the 19th century. North described how, in 1826, Millett, of Penzance, attempted a shot at the flock, having heard they were present nightly (North 1850). However, North omitted the outcome of Millett's efforts, unlike Mitchell, who described in detail how needing 'a few specimens more than I had dug out of the burrows, I ran my boat well up to them, and when they rose, got as many as I wished, besides a few unfortunate cripples who were only winged, and proved, by their agility, in swimming and diving, a good deal too much for my boatman' (in Yarrell 1937–43). Interestingly, Frohawk (in Trahair Hartley 1935) noted that on Scilly in the evening most returning Manx Shearwaters arrived from the southeast.

Too little information is available for us to assess the effects of collecting pressures on the local Manx Shearwater population. However, Gurney (1871) felt sufficiently concerned over numbers killed commercially on Annet to write to the *Zoologist* concerning 100 seen on sale at Leadenhall Market during late March 1871, which he felt were probably killed on Annet. This view was doubtless confirmed when, during a visit to Annet in mid-May 1887, Gurney found extensive evidence of 'a terrible robbery' of breeding shearwaters or eggs a few days before, the south end of the island having been 'dug over in all directions' (Gurney 1889). Various writers (e.g. Joy 1912) noted how the Dorrien-Smiths maintained Annet as a sanctuary, so we must assume commercial collecting was either unauthorised, or at least controlled. And as Gurney's 1887 visit to Annet was in Dorrien-Smith's own yacht there seems little doubt that at least the incident mentioned above was unauthorised.

We know that breeding Manx Shearwaters on Annet still fall victim to large gulls *Larus*. H W Robinson (1911a) suggested that both Great *L. marinus* and Lesser Black-backed Gulls *L. fuscus* were involved, but the former seems more likely (pers. obs.). Predation by large gulls has been an often-suggested main cause of shearwater decline on Annet, but there is no acceptable evidence to that effect and the true causes doubtless lie elsewhere. Parslow (1967a) concluded that there was no evidence gull predation had caused a serious depletion in any shearwater population. Nevertheless, there have been occasional incidents of gull nests, or even gulls themselves, being destroyed on Annet, presumably in response to these reports of predation. However, incidents such as the wreck of the *SS Castleford* on the Crebewethens on 8th June 1887, when, according to reports, at least 250 out of 450 head of cattle were rescued and temporarily landed on Annet, have the potential for substantially greater harm. Allegedly, these animals remained on Annet for some ten days, though the need for fresh water would have demanded their urgent removal. As Gurney put it when summarising his visit to Annet, 'there appeared to be a fatality on the poor Shearwaters in 1887, for before they had time to recover (from digging out)… five hundred head of cattle were saved from the ship (*Castleford*), and landed there. They trampled everything to pieces, broke in all the Shearwaters' holes, probably destroying many birds, and made a ruin of everything' (Gurney 1889). Interestingly, Gurney suggests that all 500 or so cattle were landed on Annet from the *Castleford*.

Other writers commented more recently on the threat posed by grazing animals to shearwater and petrel colonies (e.g. Batten *et al.* 1990) and 250 head of cattle on Annet represents about eleven animals per hectare. However, excluding Annet's substantial area of Thrift *Armeria maritima*, which today covers one-third to a half of the island, temporary grazing density from the *Castleford* was likely to have been perhaps nearer about 25 per hectare. Doubtless, large numbers of Manx Shearwater and Puffin burrows were destroyed during those ten days and an unknown number of birds trampled underground. Rescuers of the *Catleford*'s cattle cargo reportedly received £2.00 per head, the recovered animals then being transported to Falmouth. However, welcome as the reward money undoubtedly was, it probably failed to repay the cost of rebuilding the pilot gig *O & M*, after a steer fell onto her bow from the deck of the stricken vessel. Drowned cattle from the incident washed ashore on the Cornish mainland as far east as St Ives and Mount's Bays.

Further pressures on Annet's Manx Shearwater colony came in the form of frequent egg-collecting expeditions from mainland Britain. Examination of Manx Shearwater eggs in the collection of the British Museum (Natural History) shows they include 45 eggs taken by 14 individuals and one group, from Holloway College, during the period 1880–1936. Names on data cards read like a who's who of oology and icluded such luminaries as the Reverend F C R Jourdain, Charles Rothschild, F W Frohawk, Edgar Chance and J Walpole Bond. And doubtless, many more shearwater eggs taken on Annet still reside in the numerous private collections that stand as a memorial to this aspect of Britain's shadowy past (Cole & Trobe 2000). Most collectors apparently adopted a 'no nonsense' approach towards obtaining Annet shearwater eggs and just dug out the burrows (e.g. Bidwell 1889). Mitchell (in Yarrell 1837–43) describes hearing a chick calling from an egg, whilst preparing a skin late at night, two days after taking the egg from an Annet burrow. He was instantly reminded, so he claimed, of Asmodeus in the bottle! Frohawk even described digging out one burrow to a length of 7 metres before finding the incubating shearwater, with an adult Rabbit *Oryctolagus cuniculus* located a further 3.5 metres into the same burrow (Frohawk 1915–16). The same author noted that whenever Manx Shearwaters and Puffins shared the same burrow, the former's egg was always furthest below ground.

Various writers, e.g. Roberts (1929), described their visit to Annet without necessarily explaining why they were there. In addition, we know from other publications, e.g. Cole and Trobe (2000) that Annet figured high on the egg-collector's list of required visiting. One particularly interesting feature arising from examination of the British Museum collection was the discovery that A A Dorrien-Smith was issuing day permits to visit uninhabited islands as long ago as 1931. One case involved the Souter brothers (see Table), who on 24th May that year were granted written permission to land on 'any island except tern islands for up to one hour'. The permit, marked No. 3 and in what appears to be Dorrien-Smith's own hand, is still attached to the data card for the three Manx Shearwaters eggs taken by the brothers on Annet that same day. The question is, of course, did Dorrien-Smith know they were intent on taking shearwater eggs – or that they also took Storm Petrel *Hydrobates pelagicus* eggs? Not that it was necessarily illegal at that time and it may have been generally accepted that people going ashore on islands in Scilly would take eggs. However, the action seems violently at odds with the concept of maintaining Annet as a sanctuary.

Still on the subject of collecting, a Manx Shearwater skeleton in the British Museum, taken in Scilly on 1st July 1924, Reference 1924.7.4 is credited to H W Robinson, whereas one embryo and two adult spirit specimens taken in Scilly on 14th May 1928, Reference 28.5.9, and four skeletal specimens taken April 1926, Reference 26.4.30, are attributed to A A Dorrien-Smith.

Although Allen (1974) estimated the Scillonian Manx Shearwater population at 900+ pairs, he urged caution in using his figure, which was largely speculative. Allen's distribution was 800+ pairs on Annet, with 50 or more each on Round Island and St Agnes, and perhaps residual populations on Tresco and Bryher; breeding having only been proved on Round Island in 1961 (Beswetherick 1961). For Annet this represents a greater than 50% decrease on Parslow's 1967 figure, over a period of seven years. Between 1957 and 1964 the former St Agnes Bird Observatory ringed a total of 2,545 shearwaters, almost all on Annet, at an average of 318 annually. Certainly it would be difficult to ring even 100 in one year on the same island today, though there is a strong element of chance involved in ringing this species, much of which relates to weather conditions. There also appears to be between-year variation in numbers present within the islands, perhaps relating to local breeding conditions or to winter conditions at sea. In addition, SABO visits were apparently much earlier in the year and in greater numbers than in the 1990s.

Gurney (1889) mentioned Annet's long-standing freedom from rats *Rattus* and his suggestion that this perhaps holds the secret to Annet's long and successful relationship with Manx Shearwaters (and Storm Petrels) could be at least partly true. Although why this island should have been consistently and naturally rat-free is difficult to understand, it being probably the only well-vegetated island within the archipelago not known to have held rats at some time. Most islands lacking more than just token vegetation, e.g. Melledgan, or Mincarlo, are frequently inundated by winter seas, presumably making them untenable to rats. Although Annet appears capable of retaining a viable rat population, that is evidently not so, presumably because winter seas wash over Annet sufficiently to affect its suitability to these animals. At those sites where shearwaters and rats meet, e.g. Gugh, or St Agnes, numbers of shearwaters have either remained low or may even have disappeared altogether (pers. obs.). Until Samson was cleared of Brown Rats *Rattus norvegicus* in the early 1990s, these animals moved down to the shoreline during winter, the suggestion being there was insufficient food 'inland' to ensure their survival (P J Robinson unpublished data). Round Island has been rat-free since at least the 1990s, the probability there being that, if the island ever was infested, it was cleared by Trinity House staff whilst the light was still permanently manned.

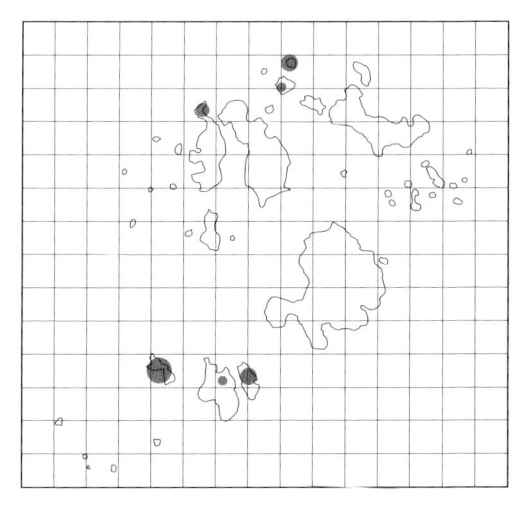

| Island | Burrows |
|---|---|
| Annet | 123 |
| Round Island | 34 |
| Shipman Head, Bryher | 12 |
| St Agnes | 5 |
| Gugh | 22 |
| St Helen's | 5 |

**Distribution of 201 Occupied (Responding) Manx Shearwater Burrows – 2000 (Heaney et al. 2002)**

More recently, an estimate of the Scillonian Manx Shearwater population was attempted using diurnal taped playback, as part of the Seabird 2000 national survey (Heaney et al. 2002). Results of the survey, corrected to take account of possible non-responding individuals, suggest something in the order of 200 apparently occupied burrows (see Table). For the islands as a whole, this represents a 90% decrease from Parslow's 1970's figure and a 78% decrease from Allen's 1974 assessment. For Annet, it represents an 85%

decrease on Allen's 1974 finding, though that island nonetheless remains the main breeding site for this species in Scilly. In recent years there have been attempts to assess the Annet shearwater population based on numbers involved in evening gatherings of the island's northern end. This may be an unreliable method, however, both because the number of non-breeders involved is unknown and because most evening observations are made in good weather, whereas numbers of shearwaters going ashore may be greater in bad weather.

There is little published information concerning the timing of Manx Shearwater breeding in Scilly, though birds seem to arrive offshore from late March and fledging young have been ringed on Annet in late August and September. This means that eggs would have been laid around late April (Cramp *et al.* 1977–94). Certainly as long ago as 1904, Frohawk noted that hatching occurred during the latter half of June, finding no young in any of the burrows examined in Scilly earlier in the month (Frohawk 1908). Apart from Puffins, Manx Shearwaters on Annet must often share nest burrows with Rabbits, which on this island are also largely nocturnal (pers. obs.) – presumably in response to probable predation by large gulls. Turk (in *CBWPSAR* 16, 1946) found there was variation in the amount of nest material used by Manx Shearwaters, plus a positive relationship between the amount of material and the number of nest parasites, which increased with the amount of material.

A minimum of 3,081 Manx Shearwaters have been ringed on Scilly, but only 152 of these since 1970. Undoubtedly the disparity in numbers between the two periods reflects the species' continued decline in Scilly, though there may also have been an imbalance of time spent on ringing. No shearwaters were ringed between 1970 and 1991, and since that time sessions have been restricted to one to two nights annually on both Annet and Round Island. The majority of shearwaters were ringed when full-grown and 25 were subsequently recovered elsewhere, all before 1970. Three (12%) moved south as far as Spain, though eleven (44%) reached south only as far as France (at least two of which were shot). A surprising number were subsequently recorded north of Scilly, four (16%) off the coasts of Wales or Ireland and one as far north as Cumbria. Five birds (20%) were recovered in Cornwall or Devon and two (8%) at sea 96 km and 152 km southwest of Scilly. Controls from elsewhere prior to 1970 involved birds from Lundy in Devon, Skokholm in Dyfed and one from Brittany. The only post-1970 control involved a bird ringed as an adult on Lundy Island, Devon, five years earlier.

There are two reports in the literature of Manx Shearwaters hitting the Bishop Rock Light. During August 1884 several struck the lantern between lighting up and 4 am but were not killed, whilst on 3rd September 1886 one struck and was killed some time after 11 pm (Harvie-Brown *et al.* 1885, 1887). Given the shortage in Scilly of suitably sized avian prey, e.g. Feral or Rock Pigeon *Columba livia*, or Jackdaws *Corvus monedula*, it seems surprising there are no recorded instances of Peregrine Falcons *Falco peregrinus* taking Manx Shearwaters in Scilly. In west Cornwall, Peregrines have been seen attacking shearwaters (B King 1965a) and Penhallurick (1969) mentioned the remains of a Lundy-ringed shearwater found in a falcon's (presumably Peregrine Falcon) eyrie at St Agnes, mainland Cornwall, in July 1948. In addition, at least one pair breeding beside Scotland's Loch Ness took several shearwaters (pers. obs.) – presumably birds using the Loch as a short cut between the Atlantic and the North Sea. Similarly, in west Wales Grey Seals *Halichoerus grypus* have been observed catching Manx Shearwaters on the surface (McCanch 1981) but there appears to be no record of this behaviour in Scilly, despite the regular presence of Grey Seals around several of the peripheral islands.

According to Cramp *et al.* (1977–94), breeding birds return to the colonies from late February to early May, with an influx of older immatures around May. Adults commence leaving the breeding areas from July and the young follow in September. Manx Shearwaters cross the mid-Atlantic to winter off coastal South America, probably returning to Europe northwards off the African coast. Dispersal of the young to the South Atlantic is rapid and young birds seldom visit the breeding colonies in their second calendar-year.

| Year & Month | Island | Eggs | Collection |
| --- | --- | --- | --- |
| 1880 May | 'Scilly' | 4 | Prof. Wood-Jones |
| 1880 May | 'Scilly' | 1 | Prof. Wood-Jones |
| 1890 May | 'Scilly' | 1 | FCR Jourdain |
| 1890 May | 'Scilly' | 2 | Radcliffe-Saunders |
| 1890 | Annet | 2 | Holloway College |
| 1890/91 May | 'Scilly' | 8 | Charles Rothschild |

| | | | | | |
|---|---|---|---|---|---|
| 1894 May | | Annet | 10 | | Edgar Chance |
| 1894 | | Annet | 1 | | W Borrer-Tracy |
| 1897 May | | Annet | 5 | | FC Selous |
| 1898 | | Annet | 2 | | W Borrer-Tracy (obtained from Williams, Penzance) |
| 1899 May | | Annet | 1 | | FW Proctor |
| 1904 May | | 'Scilly' | 2 | | FW Frohawk |
| 1905 June | | Annet | 1 | | EW Hounsom |
| 1913 June | | Annet | 2 | | J Walpole-Bond |
| 1936 May | | Bryher | 3 | | JAF & RMT Souter |

**Annet Manx Shearwater Eggs in the British Museum Collection**

| Island | Responses | Adjusted Figure |
|---|---|---|
| Annet | 73 | 123 |
| Round Island | 32 | 34 |
| Gugh | 20 | 22 |
| Bryher (Shipman Head) | 11 | 12 |
| St Agnes (Wingletang Down) | 5 | 5 |
| St Helen's | 5 | 5 |
| | 73 | 201 |

**Apparently Occupied Manx Shearwater Burrows – Year 2000 (Heaney et al. 2002)**

**Controls**

| | | | | | |
|---|---|---|---|---|---|
| ? | ? | Scilly 18th June 1912 | ? | | Finistere, France January 1914 |
| ? | Ad | Annet July 1949 | SH | | Cape Finistere, France July 1950 |
| ? | Ad | Annet July 1949 | SH | | Cape Finistere, France August 1950 |
| ? | ? | Annet 12th July 1952 | ? | | Pontervedrs, Spain 16th September 1952 |
| AT60322 | Ad | Annet 18th April 1958 | AS | | 96 km southwest of Scilly 13th August 1958 |
| AT60408 | Ad | Annet 9th April 1958 | CT | | Annet 25th August 1958 |
| | | | ? | | Bootle, Cumbria 22nd August 1962 |
| AT60284 | Ad | Annet 18th April 1958 | AS | | 152 km west-southwest of Scilly 16th April 1959 |
| AT43656 | Ad | Annet 17th April 1958 | ? | | Loire-Atlantique, France 31st May 1960 |
| AT61204 | Ad | Annet 16th August 1958 | ? | | Criccieth, Caernarvon 5th July 1960 |
| AT43636 | Ad | Annet 4th May 1957 | ? | | Fairbourne, Merioneth 28th July 1960 |
| AT57755 | Ad | Annet 27th April 1960 | ? | | Fuenterrabia, Guipuzoca, Spain February 1962 |
| AT58592 | Pul | Annet 4th September 1958 | FD | | Garretstown, Co. Cork 5th August 1963 |
| ? | ? | Annet 1st September 1960 | ? | | Cabode Lastres, Spain 10th March 1966 |

**Recoveries**

| | | | | |
|---|---|---|---|---|
| ? | Ad | Lundy Island, Devon 21st July 1949 | CT | Annet 4th June 1950 |
| AT40886 | Ad | Skokholm, Pembrokeshire 9th July 1956 | CT | Annet 9th April 1958 |
| | | | CT | Annet 25th August 1958 |
| FA2264 | Ad | Ushant, Finistere, France 30th July 1957 | CT | Annet 9th April 1958 |
| AT24735 | Pul | Skokholm, Pembrokeshire 23rd August 1954 | CT | Annet 17th April 1958 |
| AT49812 | Ad | Skokholm, Pembrokeshire 26th July 1957 | CT | Annet 17th April 1958 |
| 2024313 | Ad | Skokholm, Pembrokeshire 6th July 1959 | FD | Annet 22nd May 1961 |
| ? | Pul | Skokholm, Pembrokeshire 22nd August 1960 | FD | Annet 30th June 1970 |
| FC37618 | Ad | Lundy Island, Devon 23rd July 1992 | CT | Annet 30th June 1993 |
| | | | CT | Annet 12th August 1997 |

**Manx Shearwater Selected Ringing Recaptures**

# Balearic Shearwater *Puffinus mauretanicus* A

**Scarce but regular, migrant or vagrant; perhaps annual, though this is not yet reflected in the records, full written description required by the SRP.**

Breeds Balearic Islands. Migratory or dispersive, wintering Mediterranean and eastern Atlantic. Monotypic. Separated from Manx Shearwater *Puffinus puffinus* in 1991, as Mediterranean Shearwater *P. yelkouan*, comprising *P. y. yelkouan* and *P. y. mauretanicus* (BOURC 1991). However, in October 2000, *mauretanicus* elevated to full species status, along with Yelkouan Shearwater *P. yelkouan*, which breeds eastern Mediterranean islands (BOURC 2001; Sangster *et al.* 2002b). Of these two, up until January 2001, only Balearic Shearwater accepted as occurring in British waters, although there are claimed sightings of Yelkouan. The Balearic Shearwater breeding population may comprise less than 2,000 pairs.

The first British and Irish record of 'Mediterranean Shearwater' was killed by an E Hart in Christchurch Bay, now Dorset, in August 1859 (BOURC 2001), though according to Palmer the record may not be safe. If that is the case, the first British and Irish record probably involved a bird shot in the Firth of Forth, Scotland, in 1874 (Palmer 2000) – though it could of course have been Yelkouan Shearwater! Balearic Shearwater probably occurs annually off Scilly, mainly, if not exclusively, in autumn and all records both before and after the BOURC's split are assumed to have involved this species, rather than Yelkouan Shearwater. First mention comes with a report of three 'Balearic Shearwaters' off the southern end of St Agnes on 6th September 1957, followed by a further bird flying west at the same location five days later (*CBWPSAR* 27). Next was mention of 'one of the rare *mauretanicus*' off St Agnes in October 1963, following which numbers of reports increased, presumably in line with increased awareness that the form was out there to be looked for. On the Cornish mainland, especially large shearwater concentrations were recorded in autumn 1961, with flocks of up to 300–400 off the Lizard peninsula possibly all this species (Penhallurick 1969). The same increased presence was reflected in Scillonian waters that year, with 'Balearic' Shearwater noted during many autumn crossings to and from the islands on RMV *Scillonian II* (*SABOAR* 1961–62), with a maximum count of 65+ between Penzance and Land's End (outside the Isles of Scilly recording area).

Taking the ten-year period 1990–99, none were recorded during the first four years, regardless of the species' newly appointed status from 1991, apparently confirming that numbers in the eastern North Atlantic do fluctuate between years. Including *Scillonian III* or other pelagic trips to the west of Scilly, birds were recorded in each of the remaining six years, annual totals being 94 (9), 95 (2), 96 (12), 97 (32), 98 (22) and 99 (66). Earliest for the six-year period was one seen from *Scillonian III* on 16th May 1998, followed by one in St Mary's Sound on 29th May 1997, the only other spring record involving one off Peninnis, St Mary's, on 25th June, also 1997. The earliest autumn record was on 2nd July 1999 and the latest for any year was 8th December, also 1999. Monthly totals during 1999 were: July (11), August (10), September (39), October (4), November (1) and December (1). The most seen together within the period was six, whilst the highest day-counts were 29 on an unspecified date in October 1997 and 15 during strong winds on 18th September 1998.

There appears to be a recognisable tendency now for the number of records to increase over time, though whether that situation will be sustained remains to be seen. Care must also be taken to avoid confusion with either Manx Shearwater, which is common in Scillonian waters and breeds locally, or with the recently split and quite similar, but much rarer, Yelkouan Shearwater, which up to January 2001 had not been accepted as occurring in Britain, although it has been claimed. It may also be worth repeating the cautionary note appearing in the 1999 edition of the *IOSBR*, to the effect that not all 'brown' shearwaters are necessarily Mediterranean, the complexities of light and plumage sometimes giving a 'Mediterranean' feel to Manx Shearwaters.

Interestingly, numbers of Mediterranean Shearwater sightings also increased on the Cornish mainland during the second half of the 1990s, with an estimated 546 birds reported during 1999 (*CBWPSAR* 69), the vast majority of which occurred during the period August–October. Although of course the Cornish 'catchment area' is substantially greater, one theory is that Balearic Shearwater may remain within what can best be described as the outer English Channel, close to Cornwall, whilst moulting, seldom venturing out as far as Scilly (*IOSBR* 1999).

# Little Shearwater  *Puffinus assimilis*  A  BBRC 1.03%

Extremely rare migrant, full written description required by the BBRC.

1974   One off Horse Point, St Agnes 30th April   *British Birds* 68: 310

Fragmentary distribution in eastern North Atlantic. Occurs Azores, Madeira, Canary Islands and Cape Verde, with further populations in South Atlantic, Pacific and Indian Oceans. In east Atlantic, remains in or near breeding colonies all or most of year, though all populations dispersive to some extent after breeding. Polytypic: *boydi* occurs Cape Verde Islands; *baroli* remaining eastern Atlantic; seven additional forms elsewhere, including nominate *assimilis* in Lord Howe and Norfolk Islands in Pacific (Cramp *et al.* 1977–94).

Scilly's only acceptable record of this enigmatic shearwater was one seen passing Horse Point, St Agnes, at a range of about 350 metres about midday on 30th April 1974. It first attracted attention by its small size, short-winged appearance and distinctive flight pattern, progressing in an even series of short flat shears, soon re-passing the original observer at even closer range. The bird's flight was later described as a mixture of flaps and short glides, with the occasional bank, somewhat reminiscent of an auk (*Uria* or *Alca*). In comparison with Manx Shearwater, its flight appeared less rapid and apparently required more effort. In addition, whilst flying away the bird appeared to flap the whole of the wing, rather than just the wing-tip as in Manx Shearwater, which perhaps accounted for the auk-like appearance (*IOSBR* 1974; *British Birds* 68: 310).

Another claimed off Peninnis Head, St Mary's, on 18th September 1999 (*IOSBR* 1999) was rejected by the BBRC in 2002, after lengthy consultations (*British Birds* 95: 572), although, interestingly, two accepted 1999 records brought the Cornish mainland total to five (*CBWPSAR* 69). Gantlett (1998) drew attention to the possibility of the slightly differently coloured Cape Verde form, *boydi*, occurring off the Atlantic coast of Britain, in which case Scilly must rate as a prime contender. The single Scillonian record amounts to just over 1% of the 97 British sightings accepted by the BBRC during the period 1958–99.

The nearest breeding Little Shearwaters to Scilly are in the Azores, Madeira and the Canary Islands, most birds remaining in the mid-Atlantic during winter.

# Wilson's Petrel
# (Wilson's Storm-petrel)  *Oceanites oceanicus*  A  BBRC 18.1%

Recent annual offshore sightings in small numbers in summer but doubtless it is much more numerous. Most sightings currently originate from continental shelf sections of Western Approaches, though increasingly it is being found close to Scilly, i.e. 3–4 km south of the islands. According to Cramp *et al.* (1977–94) it avoids central tracts of open ocean, preferring offshore and even inshore waters. A full written description is required by the BBRC.

1995   One Poll Bank, 3–4 km south of St Mary's August   *British Birds* 93: 516
1998   One 5 km SSW of Bishop Rock 11th August   *British Birds* 92: 557
1999   One Poll Bank, 3–4 km south of St Mary's 7th July   *British Birds* 93: 516
1999   One Poll Bank, 3–4 km south of St Mary's 18th July   *British Birds* 93: 516
1999   Two Poll Bank, 3–4 km south of St Mary's 16th August   *British Birds* 93: 516
2000   One 5 km SW of Bishop Rock 5th July   *British Birds* 94: 455
2000   One 5 km SW of Bishop Rock 12th July   *British Birds* 94: 455
2000   One 5 km SW of Bishop Rock 16th July   *British Birds* 94: 455–456
2000   Two 5 km SW of Bishop Rock 17th July   *British Birds* 94: 456
2000   One 3–5 km south of St Mary's 28th August   *British Birds* 94: 456
2001   One 10 km south of St Mary's 7th June   *British Birds* 95: 479–480
2001   One 12–14 km south of St Mary's 13th July   *British Birds* 95: 479–480
2001   One 10 km south of St Mary's 21st July   *British Birds* 95: 479–480
2001   One 10 km south of St Mary's 22nd July   *British Birds* 95: 479–480
2001   One 11 km south of St Mary's 23rd July   *British Birds* 95: 479–480
2001   One 10 km south of St Mary's 29th July   *British Birds* 95: 479–480

2001  One 10–12 km south of St Mary's 3rd August   *British Birds* 95: 479–480
2001  One 10 km south of St Mary's 5th August   *British Birds* 95: 479–480
2001  One 12 km south of St Mary's 5th August   *British Birds* 95: 479–480
2001  One 12–14 km south of St Mary's 10th August   *British Birds* 95: 479–480
2001  One 10 km south of St Mary's 15th August   *British Birds* 95: 479–480
2001  One 12 km south of St Mary's 16th August   *British Birds* 95: 479–480
2001  One 10–13 km south of St Mary's 20th August   *British Birds* 95: 479–480
2001  One 11–13 km south of St Mary's 20th August   *British Birds* 95: 479–480
2001  One 16 km south of St Mary's 2nd September   *British Birds* 95: 479–480

Breeds Antarctic and subantarctic regions. Migratory, extending throughout southern oceans and into the North Atlantic during Antarctic winter. Polytypic: nominate *oceanicus* occurs subantarctic South Atlantic and Indian Ocean; *exasperatus* Antarctic; *maorianus* New Zealand.

It comes as something of a surprise to discover that E H Rodd and others in west Cornwall were familiar with Wilson's Petrel in the mid- to late 19th century, although Rodd mentioned just one Cornish specimen, a bird picked up dead in a field near Polperro in 1838, during what, from his own account, was quite obviously a mid-August petrel wreck (Rodd 1880). In the light of what follows here, Penhallurick's cautious 1969 comments make interesting reading. In particular, he quotes Gould's account of a sea journey off the southwest in May 1838, describing how 'immediately off the Land's End, Wilson's Storm Petrel was seen in abundance, and continued to accompany the ship throughout the Bay (of Biscay). The little Storm Petrel (*P. pelagicus*) was also seen, but in far less numbers; both species disappeared on approaching the latitude of Madeira' (Penhallurick 1969). According to Penhallurick, Gould's account was regarded with scepticism, presumably because few envisaged Wilson's Petrels in such numbers close to Britain.

Prior to the 1980s, there was the occasional inshore sighting of Wilson's Petrel off Cornwall and elsewhere, but the species remained a major rarity throughout Britain and Ireland. However, the discovery of birds within regular overnight, or even day-trip, range of southwest England meant it soon became available to all who wanted to see this species in British waters.

A mini boom in summer pelagic cruises soon developed in the southwest, culminating in an impressive 71 recorded Wilson's Petrel sightings during 1987 and a staggering 102 in 1988, the majority of which were classified as 'at sea' records. Inevitably, there is an element of luck involved in pelagic cruising, though some trips scored highly with this species, e.g. 16 on 18th August 1987 and 10th August 1988, plus 15 and 14 on 22nd and 15th August 1987 respectively. The earlier pelagic cruises commenced from mainland Cornwall, eventually bringing the RMV *Scillonian III* into the picture with an annual August day-trip from Penzance out to the continental shelf, whereas the fashion more recently is for short trips well within sight of the islands, e.g. 5 km, using Scillonian-based launches. A number of excellent photographs or video recordings of Wilson's Petrel and other species encountred are now available, which in many cases remove the need for lengthy deliberation. One by-product of these cruises has been the sighting of other difficult-to-see pelagic species, e.g. large shearwaters *Puffinus, Colonectris,* or Sabine's Gull *Larus sabini,* plus at least five sightings up to mid-2001 of Zino's/Fea's Petrels *Pterodroma madeira/feae*.

The Table lists only those records involving inshore sightings in Scillonian waters up to the year 2001, the five birds during the years 1958–99 representing just over 18% of all BBRC-accepted records for that period. More recently, i.e. by 2002, the species was known to be occurring sufficiently regularly for it to be reported in only general terms, e.g. 'two or more seen during pelagic trips from St Mary's on several dates between 4th and 30th (August), with at least six on 14th' (*Birding World* 15:311). On 14th and 15th, singles were also reported from the RMV *Scillonian III* during her routine crossing from mainland Cornwall.

Wilson's Petrels migrate north into all oceans, but the North Atlantic and Indian Oceans hold particular importance (Cramp *et al.* 1977–94). Breeders and non-breeders commence moving north from late February or March, mainly along the coast of South America, with some off Africa, most reaching the North Atlantic by June. By far the majority 'winter' in the Gulf Stream off North America but it is fairly numerous off Iberia and in the Bay of Biscay, with fewer north of 45°N (Bordeaux). Return to the South Atlantic commences in September, birds lingering longer on the eastern side of the Atlantic, with stragglers into November or even December. Both Gantlett (1998) and Cramp *et al.* (1977–94) draw attention to the possibility of the slightly smaller subantarctic nominate *oceanicus* occurring in the West Palearctic alongside the more likely *exasperatus*, in which case future observers should perhaps concentrate on trying to establish the presence of both forms in waters off Scilly.

# Storm Petrel (European Storm-petrel) *Hydrobates pelagicus* A

**Summer visitor in large numbers, known to breed on eleven uninhabited islands, with prospecting recently on several more, including at least three that are inhabited. The all-island breeding population is currently estimated in region of 1,500 pairs (Heaney *et al.* 2002). Main concentration is, and may always have been, on Annet, and Scilly is the only published English breeding site for this species.**

Breeds northeast North Atlantic, from Iceland, Faeroes, Britain and Ireland, Norway, France, Spain into western and central Mediterranean. Migratory and dispersive, wintering off South Africa. Monotypic, though some authorities treat Mediterranean birds as a separate form, *melitensis*, or 'Mediterranean Storm Petrel'. Included on Annex I of 1979 EEC 'Birds Directive'. Amber-listed in UK: 50% or more of breeding population at ten or fewer sites; unfavourable European conservation status (Gregory *et al.* 2002).

Probable first mention of Storm Petrel in Scilly comes in an early account of the archipelago (Heath 1750), where we read that among the birds 'in all the islands' were 'Pinnicks'. This is a Cornish name which, apart from pertaining to the Storm Petrel, was applied to a puny child or person of small appetite (Penhallurick 1969). More suitable perhaps is the old fisherman's name of 'storm-finch'. Storm Petrel was well known to 19th century writers, E H Rodd noting it as common in the summer months five or six miles (eight or nine kilometres) offshore in Mount's Bay, west Cornwall, though Rodd and doubtless others were probably wrong in thinking petrels flitting about above the waves were 'in pursuit of small insects' (Rodd 1880). Gilbert White recorded it as reaching Scilly in April and leaving in July (in Jesse 1887), but it is difficult to see how anyone might have arrived at such a conclusion at that time, given the apparent lack of information on local breeding behaviour.

Rodd quoted Penzance resident Mitchell's (the same who shot the 1840 Pectoral Sandpiper on Annet) pre-1880 correspondence with Yarrell recording that breeding Storm Petrels were confined to one unnamed island in the extreme southwest of the archipelago – 'where the steamer *Thames* ran ashore', pointing out too that in Scilly it is among the last seabird species to lay, an egg he took being freshly laid in mid-June. The difficulty with Mitchell's statement is that the *Thames* struck the Bishop Rock, a site clearly incapable of holding breeding petrels. However, part of the wreckage fetched up on nearby Rosevear, where Storm Petrels have been recorded breeding since at least 1863 (fairly common) and 1870 (tolerably common) (Allen 1974). There is a probable relationship between this mid-19th century awareness of breeding petrels on Rosevear and erection of the Bishop Rock Lighthouse, as construction crews lived on tiny Rosevear and could hardly have missed Storm Petrels calling from below ground. In fact, the remains of their stone houses still stand and are a regular nest site for two to three pairs of Storm Petrels even today (pers. obs.).

*Birds of the Isles of Scilly*

In their admirable early 20th century review of Scillonian bird life, James Clark and E H Rodd's nephew Francis thought Storm Petrels still bred on Scilly by the turn of the century, though 'in greatly diminished numbers' (Clark & Rodd 1906). The species bred, so they said, 'in chinks and under boulders in the Western Isles' and was 'fairly common' prior to 1863, though they thought only a few pairs bred by 1906. Clark and Rodd blamed increasing public knowledge of the main breeding colony (Rosevear) for this alleged decline, with 'one or two eggs' taken almost annually, concluding with the comment that birds had bred on Annet only since 1903.

The truth is, though, that probably no one during the 19th and early 20th centuries knew for certain where all the Scillonian Storm Petrel breeding sites were. The earliest reliable authority seems to be C J King (1924), who, between 1890 and the last-mentioned date, proved petrels bred in large numbers and on islands other than Rosevear. King also described how the Round Island Lighthouse keepers were mystified by the nightly appearance of black feathers in their living quarters, eventually discovering that among the Round Island residents, only the lighthouse cat *Felis catus* had been aware of the presence of Storm Petrels. Clearly, though, these were men of considerable environmental awareness, opting as they did to destroy the unfortunate feline in favour of the petrels. But as King pointed out, men had been resident on Round Island for many years without being aware of the petrels, until the lighthouse cat rashly disclosed the secret. In addition, it is worth noting that despite detailed annual reports on the breeding and migrant birds of Round Island, over several years, lighthouse keeper A T Beswetherick failed to mention Storm Petrel (e.g. Beswetherick 1961, 1968). King also mentioned having been ridiculed for suggesting that petrels bred on a particular island where those concerned had been 'walking over the birds all their lives without being aware of their presence'. Although this last description sounds suspiciously like Annet (but could have been St Agnes), unfortunately King was at pains to protect colonies from egg- and skin-collectors and therefore omitted site names – as indeed he also did for Peregrine Falcon *Falco peregrinus*. King concluded by saying he had little doubt there were 'many thousands' of Storm Petrels around the western coasts of Scilly. As with Manx Shearwater *Puffinus puffinus*, proof that King's fears about collectors were justified is contained in the collection of the British Museum (Natural History), where eggs taken by Mitchell and others are to be found (see Table), with doubtless many more Annet eggs in numerous private collections (Cole & Trobe 2000). Still on the subject of collecting, two skeletal specimens in the British Museum (Natural History), Reference No. 1924.7.4 and dated 1st July 1924 are credited to H W Robinson.

There were early 20th century concerns that predation by large gulls *Larus*, but particularly Great Black-backed Gull *L. marinus*, might be adversely affecting Scillonian Storm Petrel and Manx Shearwater populations (e.g. H W Robinson 1911a, Wallis 1923). These concerns were based, in the case of shearwaters, on numbers of corpses regularly found on Annet, in particular, and in the case of Storm Petrel, on numbers of gull pellets containing petrel remains – normally one petrel per pellet (pers. obs.). Parslow (1965c) felt there was a need for research aimed at determining whether gulls could reduce populations of these two species in Scilly, whilst at the same time seeing no alternative explanation for the 'extinction' of petrels from Rosevear, which coincided with an increase in Great Black-backed Gulls on that island. However, although some 95 pairs of Great Black-backs breed on Rosevear today, 57 pairs of petrels were estimated to be present in 2000 (Heaney *et al.* 2002). Realistically, however, the fact that construction workers and their families lived on tiny Rosevear for several years during the building of the Bishop Rock Lighthouse, in the mid-1800s, seems far more likely to have caused the Storm Petrel's desertion of that island. Besides which, there seems never to have been an early count of the Rosevear petrel population and estimates of its importance within the islands may have been arrived at prior to discovery of the far larger Annet colonies. Particularly interesting, however, is Parslow's estimate of at least 1,500 pairs of breeding petrels on Annet by the mid-1960s. Although there has been much discussion in recent years on likely number of pairs of Storm Petrels breeding throughout the islands, almost all estimates have been largely based on speculation. In fact, despite all the survey and productivity monitoring effort expended on seabird populations in Scilly over the past 25 years, Storm Petrel and Manx Shearwater remain the two least understood breeding species within the islands. Storm Petrel totals for Scilly suggested by various workers are shown in the Table, though it is not possible to draw many conclusions, primarily owing to uncertainties over the most effective means of surveying breeding petrels, or even to ascertain whether a survey's findings involve pairs or individuals.

Nothing is known about the origin of King's early estimate of breeding pairs, though Parslow's figure for Annet was arrived at using counts of 'singing' birds below ground over several years, combined with data from retrapped marked individuals (Parslow 1965c). In contrast, Allen's figure was based on sample counts of singing birds over three successive nights, extrapolated to incorporate all suitable breeding habitat, at an observed density of 0.33 singing birds per square metre. Robinson and Haw's findings utilised the diurnal taped playback census method (Ratcliffe *et al.* 1998) at two differently 'constructed' boulder beaches, producing density findings of 0.4 and 0.8 apparently occupied sites (AOS) per square metre, extrapolated to incorporate all suitable occupied habitat (Robinson & Haw – unpublished data). There is a measure of similarity between these three findings.

More recently, the author estimated the extent of suitable breeding habitat at all sites with a known history of Storm Petrel occupation, extrapolating possible total densities based on the 1998 Annet mean density of 0.6 AOS per m2 (P J Robinson 1999b). However, although the estimated total of between 9,800 and 17,000 pairs for Scilly as a whole was clearly excessive, diurnal playback remains untested as far as numbers of non-responding birds are concerned – or at least in boulder beaches, with a possible significant underestimate resulting. There is also significant between-colony variation in the probability of occupied nest sites being detected using diurnal playback (Ratcliffe *et al.* 1998). In addition, the Seabird 2000 finding of nearly 1,500 pairs for all islands (Heaney *et al.* 2002) seems at variance with numbers of birds present within colonies – with up to 600 trapped at individual sites in one night (IOSSBG – unpublished ringing data) – as it does with all recent independent assessments of apparent numbers on Annet.

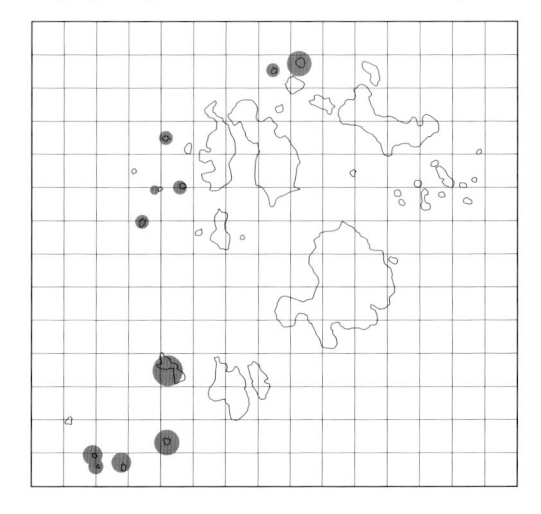

| Island | Occupied Nests |
| --- | --- |
| Annet | 938 |
| Round Island | 183 |
| Melledgan | 140 |
| Rosevear | 57 |
| Gorregan | 49 |
| Rosevean | 37 |
| Men-a-Vaur | 20 |
| Mincarlo | 17 |
| Castle Bryher | 17 |
| Scilly Rock | 14 |
| Illiswilgig | 3 |

**Locations of 1475 Occupied (Responding) Storm Petrel Nests – 2000 (Heaney *et al.* 2002)**

The Table and Map show the eleven islands currently known to hold Storm Petrels below ground, all of which are thought to be active breeding colonies. In addition, birds have been recorded coming ashore at night in recent years on at least five further islands, i.e. Gugh (Kittern Rock), St Martin's (Daymark), St Agnes (Burnt Island), Bryher (Gweal Hill) and St Mary's (Giant's Castle), all of which are inhabited islands and none of which have been shown to have active breeding sites, though birds are known to come ashore of their own volition. In some cases, e.g. Bryher, these involve extremely small and apparently unsuitable rocky outcrops. One habitat not yet explored on Scilly for the presence of breeding Storm Petrels is buildings; in the Channel Islands, Dobson (1952) recorded birds breeding in close proximity within the roofs of buildings. Although we might expect their nocturnal calling to give them away in any occupied structure, they could be present and remain undetected in barns or outlying farm sheds, particularly on the four smaller inhabited islands. There is an old record of a bird calling from a wall in Hugh Town, St Mary's (C J King 1924), the same author also mentioning birds 'among the ribs of an old ship'. Penhallurick (1969) refers to suspected breeding on The Garrison, St Mary's, in 1947 and on Peninnis, also St Mary's, in 1952. As the author gives no references in either case, it must be assumed that these were in boulder beaches or similar.

Regrettably, Scilly's history of Storm Petrel predation by cats is not confined to Round Island. On Gugh, St Agnes and Bryher the presence of cat-predated Storm Petrel remains (wings, legs, tails) are a main means of proving petrels come ashore at these sites (plus an additional source of ring recoveries, including one French-ringed individual). In addition, cats have been seen in the immediate vicinity of the St Martin's Daymark and St Mary's Giant's Castle sites during overnight petrel trapping sessions. Feral cats are believed to be mostly involved, although 'domesticated' individuals cannot be ruled out. Animals engaged in nightly petrel predation may later be identified by smell, with the possibility, even, of new breeding colonies being discovered by this novel means. Nevertheless, 'cat sniffing' has the potential for substantial public misunderstanding (pers. obs.) and must necessarily be carried with considerable circumspection.

The majority of Scillonian Storm Petrels breed beneath boulder beaches, most of which comprise small to medium-sized boulders (up to one metre diameter). Some, though, are in beaches comprising boulders of substantially greater volume, as on Gorregan, where some birds call from beneath many tonnes of granite. A smaller number of birds occupy isolated patches of boulder scree and, particularly on Annet, an even smaller number are in earth burrows, or fissures in isolated rocky outcrops. Although drystone walls are plentiful in Scilly they are, by tradition, loose affairs of limited depth and are apparently uninhabited by Storm Petrels. Boulder beaches used comprise both long-established, 'stable' and compacted structures above the reach of normal winter tides, or less stable storm beaches, as on Annet's western coast. Sampled diurnal playback from one each of these two beach types on Annet produced a 2:1 imbalance in favour of responses from the stable beach (Robinson & Haw – unpublished data). Reasons for this are unclear, but could involve the ability for breeding petrels to penetrate deeper into more substantial unstable storm beaches, thereby making any responses less easy for the human ear to detect.

Examination of inter-colony breeding phenology (Ratcliffe *et al.* 1998) showed significant national variation. On Annet, laying occurs around 25th June and hatching around the first week of August, young fledging from that island from September to mid-October (Cramp *et al.* 1977–94; Ratcliffe *et al.* 1998). However, the presence of fresh eggs on Annet as late as July suggests perhaps some unfledged young well into November. During the mid- to late 1990s, the biometry of a small number of young were examined annually on Annet (Robinson & Haw – unpublished data; Ratcliffe *et al.* 1998) and although young involved were ringed, none have yet been detected within the adult population.

A total of 7,869 Storm Petrels were ringed on Scilly up to and including 1999, 4,985 (63%) of those since 1970 and closure of the SABO (IOSSBG – unpublished data), making Storm Petrel the most ringed species in Scilly. This imbalance between the two periods is the reverse of Manx Shearwater *Puffinus puffinus*, where 95% of birds were ringed prior to 1970. Reasons for this recent increase in numbers of petrels available for ringing are unclear, but may perhaps be partly associated with an increased use of tape lures. Listed below are a selection of controls and recoveries, other than recaptures of locally ringed birds, within the islands, or those in either category within Cornwall (28, or 3.7% of all controls and recoveries), up to and including year 2000. Surprisingly there appear to be no recorded recoveries or controls for the period before 1970.

Thirty-five petrels ringed in Scilly were recovered beyond Cornwall, 22 (62.8%) qualifying as international recoveries (providing 12 in Ireland are included); nine (25.7%) were recovered in France or the Channel Islands. The most distant recovery involved a bird trapped on Fair Isle, Shetland, just over a year after having been ringed on St Martin's. At 24, rather fewer Storm Petrels were controlled on Scilly after ringing elsewhere, 20 (83.3%) qualifying as foreign; 12 of these (60%) from France and the Channel Islands, six (30%) from Ireland and two (10%) from Portugal. The most distant controls originated from Portugal (2) to the south and Tyne and Wear and Calf of Man to the north. Several features of these movements are noteworthy. Firstly, no Scillonian-ringed petrels were recovered further east in the English Channel than the Isle of Wight and the Channel Islands, though this may also reflect a lack of trapping effort in the eastern Channel and southern North Sea. The lack of a positive connection (other than the single Fair Isle recovery) with any of the northern colonies, e.g. Shetland Isles, Norway, Faeroes, is particularly noteworthy, especially considering the numbers of northern-ringed petrels controlled in Portugal (Harris *et al.* 1993; Fowler & Hounsome 1998).

One possible explanation for this lack of northern birds among Scillonian captures is that more northerly populations migrate further out into the Atlantic. Yet, even if the timing of migration for northern birds differed from the current Scillonian trapping timetable, this ought not to inhibit captures of wandering northern pre-breeders. Equally interesting is the single control of a bird ringed in the North Sea (Tyne and Wear) three years previously. However, especially obvious, and perhaps more easily explained, is the high proportion of controls and recoveries from the small number of colonies in Brittany, suggesting a regular mixing of birds from north and south of the Western Approaches. Eleven French controls were divided between Annet (6) and Round Island (5), the mean age of eight between-year controls being 3.3 years and of three same-year controls just 12.6 days. In comparison, disregarding the 'wrecked' inland individual (below), the mean age of four between-year recoveries in France was 7.5 years and three same-year recoveries 13 days. As noted by McKee (1982), there was a noticeable tendency for the percentage of controls to increase away from known breeding sites, as at St Martin's Daymark, where two Cape Clear birds were captured on the same night – out of eight controls and no local recaptures, or on Samson, where the only two captures of the night were controls. However, the most unusual record goes to the bird found on 7th January 2000 at Lussac les Chateaux, 150 km inland from the French west coast, having been ringed on Annet five-and-a-half years earlier.

Several writers have commented on Storm Petrels with missing toes, feet or tarsi (e.g. Bowey 1995; Stonehouse 1996) and something in the order of 1%–2% of birds trapped on Scilly fall within this category (pers. obs.). One possibility is that their manner of paddling across the sea's surface makes them vulnerable to predatory fish, particularly in tropical waters. However, Zonfrillo (1996) considers it more probably due to translucent gelatinous trematode worm larvae wrapping themselves around the leg of small petrels whilst at sea; when out of the water the larvae dry and shrink, forming a constriction above the toes.

In his review of changes of status among Britain's breeding birds, Parslow (1967a) thought too little was known about this species to make a constructive comment. Nevertheless, he considered that some measure of overall decline occurred towards the end of the 19th century, when it disappeared from several Scottish islands and 'decreased markedly at its main colony in the Isles of Scilly', though he also thought it possible that a degree of redistribution may have been involved. Cramp *et al.* (1977–94) confirm the presence of birds, possibly late migrants, in lower northern latitudes only very rarely in early winter, with winter individuals north to Mauritania more the norm. Uncertainty remains over whether Mediterranean birds (which some authorities consider a separate form, *H. p. melitensis*, or 'Mediterranean Storm Petrel', e.g. Amengual *et al.* 1999) leave the Mediterranean in winter, though apparently there are few winter records. Most birds have left British and Irish waters by November, returning to the area of the colonies from April onwards.

| Year | Scilly | Individual Islands | Reference |
| --- | --- | --- | --- |
| 1924 | Many thousands | | C J King 1924 |
| 1965 | | 1,500 (Annet) | Parslow 1965 |
| 1974 | | 1,800 (Annet) | Allen 1974 |
| 1983 | | 1,500 (Annet) | Harvey 1983 |
| 1992 | 1,000 | | Pritchard *et al.* 1992 |
| 1996 | | 1,640 (Annet) | Robinson & Haw – unpublished data |
| 1999 | 9,811–17,390 | | P J Robinson 1999b |
| 2000 | 1,475 | | Heaney *et al.* 2002 |

**Recorded Storm Petrel Totals (pairs)**

| Year & Month | Island | Eggs | Collection |
| --- | --- | --- | --- |
| Pre-1842 | 'Scilly' | 1 | DW Mitchell |
| 1904 June | Annet | 6 | Maj. FW Proctor |
| 1906 June | Annet | 2 | EW Hounsom |
| 1936 May | Annet | 5 | JAF & RMT Souter |

**Annet Storm Petrel Eggs in the British Museum Collection**

*Birds of the Isles of Scilly*

**Controls**

| | | |
|---|---|---|
| SA830120 | Ad Banneg Island, Brittany 8th August 1991 | CT Round Island 23rd July 1992 |
| 2301511 | Ad Focarrig, Cape Clear Island 27th July 1983 | CT Annet 4th August 1993 |
| SA776921 | Ad Banneg Island, Brittany 13th July 1989 | CT Annet 4th August 1993 |
| 2229232 | Ad Calf of Man 28th July 1982 | GP Round Island 28th June 1993 |
| 2255149 | Ad Great Saltee, Wexford 27th June 1983 | CT Round Island 6th July 1993 |
| SA779659 | Ad Banneg Island, Brittany 7th August 1989 | CT Round Island 26th June 1994 |
| DO12722 | Ad Algarve, Portugal 14th June 1994 | CT Annet 28th June 1994 |
| C38753 | Ad Alderney, Channel Islands 6th July 1985 | CT Annet 7th July 1994 |
| 2196184 | Ad Isle of Wight 2nd July 1995 | CT Burnt Island, St Agnes 5th August 1995 |
| DO16496 | Ad Algarve, Portugal 21st June 1995 | CT Annet 8th August 1995 |
| SA549953 | Ad Beniguet Island, Brittany 20th July 1997 | CT Annet 24th July 1997 |
| 2316836 | Ad Cape Clear Island 27th July 1998 | CT Daymark, St Martin's 15th July 1999 |
| 2513302 | Ad Abersoch, Gwynedd 24th July 1999 | CT Calf of Man 25th July 1999 |
| | | CT Menawethan 31st July 1999 |
| 2434811 | Ad Tynemouth, Tyne & Wear 20th July 1996 | CT Round Island 29th July 1999 |

**Recoveries**

| | | |
|---|---|---|
| 651008 | Ad Annet 25th May 1963 | CT Skokholm, Pembrokeshire 10th May 1965 |
| 652236 | Ad Annet 1st July 1965 | CT Burhou, Alderney, Channel Isles 2nd July 1966 |
| 2427048 | Ad Annet 29th June 1993 | CT Ballybranagan, Co. Cork 7th August 1993 |
| 2440391 | Ad Annet 7th July 1994 | CT Carnsore Point, Wexford 9th July 1994 |
| 2427275 | Ad Annet 7th July 1993 | CT Fair Isle, Shetland 29th July 1994 |
| 2427871 | Ad Round Island 26th June 1994 | CT Great Skellig, Co. Kerry 3rd July 1995 |
| 2440603 | Ad Annet 13th July 1994 | CT Sanda Island, Kintyre, Strathclyde 27th July 1996 |
| 2441284 | Ad Annet 8th August 1995 | CT Portland Bill, Dorset 1st July 1998 |
| 2441703 | Ad Annet 23rd July 1997 | CT Cape Clear Island, Co. Cork 7th July 1998 |
| 2473220 | Ad Round Island 29th July 1999 | CT Banneg Island, Brittany 21st August 1999 |
| 2427080 | Ad Kittern Rock, Gugh 4th July 1993 | BR Banneg Island, Brittany 7th June 2000 |
| 2473035 | Ad Daymark, St Martin's 15th July 1999 | CT Bridges of Ross, Loop Head, Co. Clare 28th June 2000 |
| 2473237 | Ad Menawethan 31st July 1999 | CT Plemont, Jersey, Channel Islands 1st July 2000 |
| 2427964 | Ad Annet 28th June 1994 | CT Eilaen nan Ron, Highland Region 16th July 2000 |

**Storm Petrel Selected Ringing Recaptures**

## Leach's Petrel (Leach's Storm-petrel)    *Oceanodroma leucorhoa*  A

**Scarce migrant, full written description required by SRP.**

Breeds headlands or islands North Atlantic, from British Isles to northeast USA, also north Pacific, from Russia to Japan and southwest USA (Morrison 1998). Migratory, North Atlantic population winters South Atlantic. Polytypic, with complex racial structure: nominate *leucorhoa* occurs North Atlantic and North Pacific from Japan to Alaska; at least three additional forms, perhaps more. Included on Annex I of 1979 EEC 'Birds Directive'. Amber-listed in UK: 20% or more of European breeding population in UK, 50% or more at ten or fewer sites; unfavourable world conservation status (Gregory *et al.* 2002).

The only 19th century mention of this species in Scilly was James Clark and Francis Rodd's observation that a 'specimen in poor condition' was picked up on St Agnes in late autumn 1869 and that it had not been noted in the islands since (Clark & Rodd 1906). There is, however, doubt over the timing of the first 20th century record. According to the *CBWPSAR*, it probably involved another dead individual, brought in by a Mr Anderson's cat on St Mary's on 22nd December 1955 (*CBWPSAR* 25), but Penhallurick (1969) referred to an entry in the Abbey Records of one found dead in October 1931, presumably on Tresco. In addition, the same source referred to information from John Parslow to the effect that one was found dead on 25th October 1952 (no site given), regardless of an entry in the *CBWPSAR* for that year stating none were found during the wreck at the end of October (*CBWPSAR* 22). This last autumn was noteworthy for the large wreck of small petrels that occurred in Britain and Ireland around the end of October, with Leach's Petrels picked up in every county of England and Wales except Rutland. Southwest England was particularly affected with around one-third of all casualties reported from Somerset's Bridgwater Bay, the Cornwall total being 34.

The first recorded live sightings for the islands concerned four off St Agnes on 12th October 1966 and another next day, plus an unspecified number of singles off the same island between 4th and 12th and two on 16th October the following year (*CBWPSAR* 36, 37). However, unlike some other pelagic species, there was no subsequent build-up in either numbers of reports or number of individuals as knowledge of their presence offshore spread – just nine being recorded in three of the eight years up until 1975. Instead, it remained a scarce and erratic migrant, as indeed it still does today. Taking the period 1990–99, birds were recorded in only six of those ten years, totalling 29 individuals, including 15 in 1997. Of these, no less than nine were seen from RMV *Scillonian III* during daily crossings to and from the islands. Earliest bird was on 3rd July, though mid-September was more normal, whilst the latest sighting was 28th October, though possibly this last reflects an absence of observers from that time of the year onwards as much as an absence of Leach's Petrels.

In 1999, two only were recorded during the big blow on 18th September, even though far greater than usual numbers of large shearwaters were noted. Similarly, none was recorded in Scilly during the substantial movement of Leach's Petrels into British coastal waters in mid-December 1989 and an even larger movement later that month, when birds were driven far up the English Channel and Severn Estuary. It could be, of course, that by definition Scilly's position 45 km out in the open Atlantic makes it too far offshore to be affected by birds storm-driven into British or Irish coastal waters, the same severe weather possibly having the effect of actually removing any birds that were in evidence about the islands.

Adult Leach's Petrels desert their young in September, while still in the nest, with maximum build-up of birds in October–November in the eastern North Atlantic, following which numbers decline as birds move south. Non-breeders depart the North Atlantic earlier and occasional late stragglers, of unknown status, may remain in the North Atlantic throughout the northern winter (Cramp *et al.* 1977–94). In Scilly, and no doubt at other breeding sites, young Storm Petrels *Hydrobates pelagicus* are still fledging well into September, or even October, some of which show a very obvious white panel in the upper-wing – formed by diffused broad white tips to the greater coverts (pers. obs.). The possibility of these newly fledged, wing-panelled young, which greatly outnumber any Leach's Petrels that may be present around the islands, being mistaken for that species needs bearing in mind by all observers during late autumn. Certainly, the presence of a pale wing-panel should not be viewed in isolation when considering the possibility of Leach's Petrel in Scilly at that time of year.

## [Swinhoe's Petrel (Swinhoe's Storm-petrel)        *Oceanodroma monorhis*] A

**Extremely rare vagrant, full written description required by the BBRC. No acceptable Scillonian record but three petrel sightings at sea off the islands are considered to have probably involved this species (Morrison 1998).**

[1991    One at sea 40 km southwest of Scilly 18th August]    Morrison 1998
[1993    One at sea between Scilly and Cornwall 9th August]    Morrison 1998
[1993    One at sea (sea area Sole) southwest of Scilly 15th August]    Morrison 1998

Breeds northwest Pacific on islands off China, Japan, Korea and Russia, wintering in Indian Ocean (Morrison 1998).

*Birds of the Isles of Scilly*

The first of these sightings was seen and described by several observers 40 km southwest of the islands during a pelagic trip in sea area Sole on 18th August 1991. The second was seen from the deck of the RMV *Scillonian III* on 9th August 1993, on a routine daily crossings between Cornwall and Scilly. The last was also seen from the deck of *Scillonian III*, but this time on a specially organised, day-long pelagic trip to the southwest of the islands on 15th August, also in 1993 (Morrison 1998). Although for all three records the possibility of confusion with Leach's Petrel *O. leucorhoa* cannot be entirely dismissed, the descriptions were considered more indicative of what is currently known about the identification of Swinhoe's Petrel in the North Atlantic, though any final decisions await the outcome of still further research (Morrison 1998). Morrison also listed some 15 other European at-sea or inshore sightings of large dark-rumped petrels with similar characteristics to the above three birds, in addition to 14 birds trapped and identified positively as Swinhoe's Petrel.

## Red-billed Tropicbird  *Phaethon aethereus*  A  BBRC 100%

Extremely rare vagrant or migrant, full written description required by the BBRC.

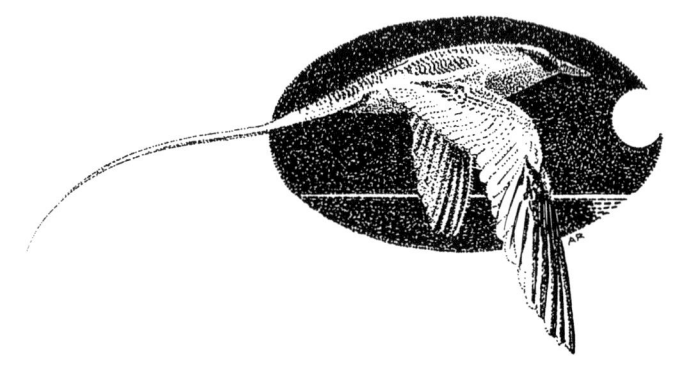

2001    One 32 km southwest of Scilly 7th June    *British Birds* 95: 480; BOURC 2003
2002    *One from* RMV *Scillonian III 6 km east of St Mary's 29th March*    *Birding World* 15: 90

Breeds Persian Gulf and Arabian and Red Seas, subtropical North and South Atlantic, including Cape Verde Islands and Azores, plus Caribbean and east Pacific. Resident or dispersive. Polytypic: *mesonauta* occurs Cape Verde Islands, coastal Senegal, Caribbean and east Pacific; *indicus* Arabian and Red Seas and Persian Gulf; nominate *aethereus* tropical South Atlantic. Substantial decline Cape Verde Islands to under 1,000 by 1977 (Cramp *et al.* 1977–94); perhaps now 150 pairs (BOURC Press Release 30th July 2002).

Until July 2002 there were no accepted British or Irish records, carcasses found in Worcestershire in 1854 and in Suffolk in 1993 having been rejected by the BOURC (Knox 1994). However, a report of a subadult off Prawle Point, Devon, during August 1999, plus same-day reports from Norfolk and the Channel Islands on 9th September 2001 (the latter a multi-observer sighting), all still await consideration by the two committees.

In 2001, a photograph was published on the internet of a Red-billed Tropicbird allegedly seen by four non-birders from a yacht 32 km south-southeast of Scilly on 7th June that year whilst en route to France, though no accompanying description appeared in the main ornithological journals. A great deal of disbelief was expressed about this record at the time, much of it doubtless born out of the lack of information. However, on 30th July 2002 the BOURC issued a press release announcing the committee's acceptance of the June 2001 individual and the consequent addition of the species to the BOU's Category A. Evidence in support of this record included a copy of the original film, showing pictures of the Isles of Scilly and France before and after the photographs in question, a copy of the vessel's log book and, of course, a full description. Although the bird could not be identified subspecifically from the photographs, the committee thought it likely to have been the form *mesonauta*, which breeds as close to Scilly as the Cape Verde Islands.

Meanwhile, five birders aboard the in-bound RMV *Scillonian III*, six kilometres east of Scilly late morning on 29th March 2002, were stunned by the appearance of an adult Red-billed Tropicbird, which flew in from the south and over the ship, level with her bridge, before then flying alongside about 40 metres away and then departing towards the northeast (*Birding World* 15: 90). This sighting handsomely compensated birders involved for their subsequent failure to see the reason for their presence off the islands at the critical time, namely an Alpine Swift previously on Tresco for some days. Up until at least August 2002, this last record was still subject to BBRC approval. Prior to acceptance of the June 2001 individual, the only acceptable European record involved a bird seen 162 kilometres west of Portugal in mid-August 1988.

## Gannet (Northern Gannet) *Morus bassanus* A

**Frequent and often numerous offshore outside and sometimes between the islands, though there appears to be no record of it even attempting to breed.**

Breeds North Atlantic, in Iceland, Faeroe Islands, Great Britain, northern and western Norway and northwest France, also Newfoundland and surrounds. Migratory or dispersive, winters northern and eastern North Atlantic, south down African coast north of equator. Monotypic. Amber-listed in UK: 20% or more of European breeding population in UK, 50% or more at ten or fewer sites; unfavourable European conservation status (Gregory *et al.* 2002). Within Sulidae, Gannets recently separated from Boobies, and placed in their own genus, *Morus* (BOURC 1991b)

Earliest evidence of Gannet presence in Scilly comes from bone remains unearthed from the prehistoric site on Nornour in the Eastern Isles, probably from the Iron or Bronze Ages (Turk 1971). We can reasonably expect any early Scillonian breeding site to have been exploited by the local people, e.g. for food, and the paucity of remains uncovered argues against the presence of a gannetry in Scilly prehistorically, though they are known to have previously existed in Cornwall and the southwest generally. Penhallurick (1969) pointed out that Gannets bred on Lundy, off north Devon, until 1909, at which time the site failed owing to long-term commercial exploitation. There are also early references to Gannets nesting near Padstow, on the Cornish mainland, from 1478, but this site probably ceased to function by the early 1600s (Penhallurick 1969). In any event, the nearest gannetries to Scilly now are Grassholm, Pembrokeshire, and 2–3 off the coast of Brittany (Hagemeijer & Blair 1997). The old Cornish name for Gannet, 'saithor', was apparently derived from the Cornish word saith, or arrow, though this seems not to be used now in Cornwall or Scilly (Penhallurick 1969).

Next mention of Gannet in Scilly was Heath's comment (1750) that it was included among all the seabirds of the islands. Gilbert White's comment that it was a spring visitor to Scilly (in Jesse 1887) conflicts with E H Rodd, who described it as a non-breeding visitor to Scilly and Cornwall, being well known in autumn out at sea (Rodd 1880). As usual, James Clark and E H Rodd's nephew, Francis, were particularly informative, describing this species as visible on the open sea around the islands at all times, but rarely in among them, except in very stormy weather (Clark & Rodd 1906), and recounting how one was captured in St Helen's Pool, east of Tresco, on 3rd May 1903, on the afternoon of an exceptionally calm day.

The first published 20th century record from the islands appears to be the 1937 comment that 'a good many' had been seen on journeys over from mainland Cornwall between 8th and 15th July that year (*CBWPSAR* 7). Following this record, the species gets fairly regular mention in the annual reports. Bringing things up to date, the situation today seems not much changed from the 19th century. Certainly, birds are still evident about the islands in greater or lesser numbers almost constantly, by far the majority being apparent adults. Regardless, however, of what early writers had to say, they are not at all uncommon in the western end of St Mary's Roads, between St Mary's and Samson to the east and St Agnes and Gugh to the west. They are often seen fishing in small groups immediately above and around tourist launches making their way to and from the Western Isles, though numbers can be expected to increase during bad weather further out to sea, or during autumn. Taking the ten-year period from 1990 as representative, mainly small numbers were to be seen during the early part of the year, with little indication of passage. There are small scale exceptions, however, as in the case of double-figures off St Agnes for two days in February 1997. More normally, there was a gradual build-up of moving birds throughout the summer, until up to 300 or more an hour were passing the islands on some days, with 717 heading south off St Mary's on 19th October 1995 being typical. From the end of October, reported numbers decrease considerably, e.g. 157

*Birds of the Isles of Scilly*

(mostly adults) past St Agnes on 28th November 1999, but this may also partly reflect a fall off in observer coverage once October is past.

Feeding congregations can sometimes be impressive, as in the case of 500+ feeding in association with dolphins *Delphinus, Tursiops, Lagenorhynchus* to the south of St Mary's in early September 1990, with 98 similarly employed on 9th October the same autumn. There were two late 19th century observations from the Bishop Rock Lighthouse, the first of which referred to large numbers of Gannets fishing on 5th October 1884 (Harvie-Brown *et al.* 1885). The other concerned autumn of the following year and records that birds were observed passing on 'passage' from the beginning of September until 2nd November, with 'scores' going west all day on 1st October (Harvie-Brown *et al.* 1886). There are also a few shore-based early counts of Gannets and other seabirds, though mostly it seems from mainland Cornwall. Thorpe (1935) observed a huge movement of Manx Shearwaters *Puffinus puffinus*, auks *Uria, Alca* and Gannets off Land's End in early April 1935, all of which headed steadily away southwest, in the direction of Scilly. Thorpe's estimate of 300 birds per minute for three hours included 5% Gannets and gives a total for this species alone of around 2,700. Trahair Hartley (1935) looked at autumn movements of the same species off Land's End for the years 1932–35, finding numbers involved and the direction of travel not dissimilar to Thorpe's results.

One Gannet was ringed in Scilly during the period before 1970, presumably involving an injured or oiled bird that was later released, although in fact very few injured or oiled Gannets are found around the islands. Recently, the question of whether or not Cape Gannet *M. capensis* occurs in European waters has been raised (Paterson & Riddiford 1990) and certainly the possibility should be borne in mind when dealing with the present species, in Scilly as elsewhere. In Gannet, migration is not clearly separable from dispersal or feeding activity, and in partial confirmation of Thorpe's and Trahair Hartley's earlier observation, conspicuous and large-scale offshore foraging and migratory movements are a feature around British and Irish coasts and off the Atlantic seaboard of western Europe and Africa (Nelson 1978). The same author drew attention to the regular heavy southwest passage off Cornwall, which 'seems totally unexceptional', whilst also confirming that first-years migrate south to African waters but then seldom go far south in subsequent years (Wernham *et al.* 2002). Birds moving south or north off Cornwall and Scilly could breed in Iceland, Faeroes, Norway, northern Britain, Wales or Ireland.

## Cormorant (Great Cormorant) *Phalacrocorax carbo* A

**Resident, breeds in small numbers, substantially less numerous than Shag *P. aristotelis*.**

Wide breeding range, including Greenland, Iceland, Great Britain, western Europe, central Asia, Africa, Indian subcontinent, Southeast Asia, Australia and New Zealand. Migratory or dispersive. Polytypic: nominate *carbo* occurs coastal North Atlantic; *sinensis* or 'Continental Cormorant' central and southern Europe east to Japan and Southeast Asia; *maroccanus* coastal northwest Africa; *lucidus* coastal west and southern Africa plus inland east Africa; *novaehollandiae* Australasia. National 5% decline 1994–99 (Bashford & Noble 2000). Upgraded from Green- to Amber-listed in UK 2002: 50% or more of breeding population at ten or fewer sites; 20% or more of European non-breeding population in UK (Gregory *et al.* 2002).

The small breeding population of around 50–60 pairs appears to have remained remarkably stable throughout at least the latter half of the 20th century (Harvey 1983; P J Robinson 1993), and is almost equally distributed between a small number of established sites in the Western, Northern and Eastern Isles. Earliest evidence of Cormorant on Scilly involves bone remains extracted from various levels of the prehistoric site on the island of Nornour, Eastern Isles (Turk 1971). However, the next earliest reference is probably Camden's comment that 'all the islands abound with … Cranes' (Camden 1610); this species apparently often formerly referred to as 'Crane' (Rodd 1880). In fact, Rodd had little to say on the Cormorant, describing it merely as breeding in the cliffs in Scilly, whereas Gilbert White considered it resident (in Jesse 1887). However, James Clark, and E H Rodd's nephew Francis were far more forthcoming, such that it would be remiss not to quote in full their excellent account for the three years 1901–03.

> Considerable numbers nest on the outer rocky islets, shifting their breeding stations more or less completely from year to year. In 1901 there was a large colony, for example, on

Inner Innisvouls, another on Mincarlo, a third on Melledgan and a fourth on Rosevean. In 1902 only three nests were found on Inner Innisvouls, but there was a big colony on Outer Innisvouls, another on Menawethan, and several nests on Hanjague. Mincarlo was deserted, but there was a group on Castle Bryher, a little cluster on Rosevean, and a new colony on Melledgan. In 1903 there was not a single nest on Menawethan, and none were noticed on Outer Innisvouls or Castle Bryher, and only five on Rosevean. Inner Innisvouls, however, was again thickly populated, and there was a large colony on Melledgan, and one of twenty-nine nests on Rosevear (Clark & Rodd 1906).

All that is missing from this otherwise informative description is a definition of what Clark and Rodd thought were 'considerable numbers', otherwise, it qualifies as a reasonable outline of the situation still today. Regrettably there is little in mid- to late 19th century published reports to help answer this question of overall population size, though even by 1937 Castle Bryher was still talked of in terms of 'large numbers' (*CBWPSAR* 7). The possibility remains, of course, that some early writers confused this species with Shag, though there is no evidence to that effect and certainly James Clark was above such an error. Nevertheless, by 1951 there were reportedly just two colonies, only one of which, on Great Crebawethan, was of apparent permanency, with the Illiswilgig colony down to half strength at just five nests (*CBWPSAR* 21), none of which suggests particularly large numbers of birds. Without explanation, Allen (1974) interpreted the early Clark and Rodd description as suggestive of at least 100 pairs, further suggesting that a decline clearly occurred during the first half of the 20th century, down to c. 60 pairs by 1945, though again he gives no reference. Allen speculated on likely causes of this decline, suggesting shooting by fishermen and dwindling flatfish availability. Several local boatmen have commented on the days, not too long past, when many Scillonian boats carried a loaded shotgun in case a Cormorant or Shag flew past, the carcasses often then used to bait fish traps (pers. comm.). In addition, comments in the 1960s (*CBWPSAR* 38; Parslow 1967b) refer to the destruction of Cormorant nests on Melledgan and Castle Bryher during 1967 – notices issued to local boatmen highlighting relevant provisions of bird protection legislation. Vyvyan (1953) also mentions 'Christmas cormorant-shooting parties' (possibly involving this species and/or Shag), which were later limited by the rising cost of cartridges.

Again, Allen's description of Cormorant breeding distribution and numbers for 1974 almost exactly describes the situation today, with an expected two occupied sites in both the Eastern and Northern Isles and one in the Western Isles, plus a marked between-year tendency to alternate between two or more preferred sites. However, occupation of White Island, Samson by two to three pairs since 2000 seems a totally new feature, perhaps resulting from removal of Brown Rats *Rattus norvegicus* from Samson and its satellite islands during the early 1990s.

Blair (in *CBWPSAR* 21) attributed low Scillonian Cormorant numbers to their apparent inability to adapt to Great Black-backed Gull *Larus marinus* predation, i.e. to utilise protected sites in the manner of Shags. However, there appears to be no apparent evidence of Cormorant nest predation by large gulls *Larus* in Scilly, other than when colonies are inexpertly disturbed. Allen found no evidence that Cormorant nest-site selection is affected by Great Black-backed Gull density or distribution, unlike Shag, which seems to be markedly influenced by the potential for Great Black-backed predation (P J Robinson 1992a). That said, breeding Cormorants in Scilly can suffer from predation of eggs and small young by large gulls whilst subject to human disturbance, particularly uninformed disturbance (*CBWPSAR* 21; Harvey 1983; pers. obs.), adults being quick to leave the colony and slow to return (pers. obs.).

A marked feature of this species in Scilly is the consistently early laying date, normally around the end of February but seldom confirmed first hand owing to weather and sea conditions at that time of year. Thus the timing of laying is usually extrapolated based on the age of young present in the colonies later (pers. obs.). This early laying is compatible with findings on Great Saltee in Co. Wexford, Ireland, some four degrees north of Scilly, where well grown young at the end of April were estimated to have hatched from eggs laid at the beginning of March (Goodbody 1947). In Ireland generally, however, 4th April was considered an exceptionally early first laying date (Kennedy *et al*. 1954), whereas on the Channel Islands, at roughly the same latitude as Scilly, eggs are unlikely before the latter half of May (Dobson 1952). Even as long ago as 1911, H W Robinson (1913) reported finding nearly full-grown young on 22nd May, from eggs that would apparently have been laid about the first week of March.

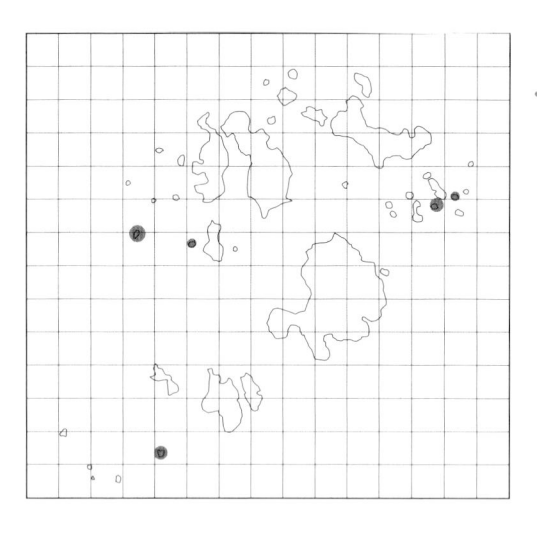

| Island | Nests |
|---|---|
| Melledgan | 16 |
| Mincarlo | 25 |
| White Island, Samson | 1 |
| Ragged Island | 12 |
| Great Innisvouls | 2 |

**Location of 56 Cormorant Nests – 1999 (Seabird 2000)**

More than one writer has commented on the number of late clutches found on visits to colonies during May or June, though reasons for this remain unclear. One possible explanation is replacement clutches for failed nests, but late-breeding subadults could also be involved. On Scilly, Cormorant nest losses are likely to occur as a consequence of gale force winds early in the year, particularly in view of the species' fondness for nesting on the upper extremities of bare rocky outcrops. As on Great Innisvouls and Ragged Island in the Eastern Isles, or on the summit of Mincarlo, Northern Isles (*IOSBR* 1994). A comment by A A Dorrien-Smith helps on several counts, pointing out that 21-metre high waves washed out Cormorant nests on the top of Mincarlo in early May 1943, by which date ten or twelve young were 'sufficiently feathered' to survive the tragedy (in *CBWPSAR* 13). Humphrey Wakefield is reported as later seeing repeat nests on Mincarlo, though they could have been late nests of other pairs. In addition, Dorrien-Smith commented that he had found Cormorants 'well advanced' in March and with unfledged young in September.

Stone *et al.* (1997) suggested a British population of 7,000 breeding pairs, in which case the Scillonian population may represent less than 1% nationally.

As with Shag, early Cormorant sample specimens from Scilly exist in the collection of the British Museum (Natural History), in the form of two spirit pulli collected by H W Robinson on 23rd and 25th June 1924, Reference 1924.6.25; plus skins of a juvenile and adult male taken by the same person on 4th December 1933, Reference 33.11.21 and 34.1.1; and two adult spirit specimens from 21st August 1933, Reference 33.8.17 and 4th December 1933, Reference 33.11.21.

Few modern accounts of Cormorants in Scillonian waters mention subspecific identification, it being normally assumed all are nominate *carbo*. However, the possibility of the central and southern European form *sinensis* occurring are real, particularly as it already breeds in southern England. Occasional individuals showing varying amounts of white about the head and neck have been seen over the years but it has not been considered safe to attribute any to *sinensis*.

A great deal of correspondence accompanied the discovery in Scilly, around 1905, of Cormorants with substantially white undersides, culminating in the acquisition of specimens on 30th June 1909 and 16th March 1910 (Frohawk 1910b). Several extremely experienced BOC members felt unable to accept that these were immature birds, C B Ticehurst even suggesting it was a previously unknown adult colour-phase (Frohawk 1910). Interestingly, only Ogilvie-Grant among those at the meeting felt certain it was a bird of the year, pointing out that there were already a number of similar specimens in the collection of the British Museum (Natural History). Publication of *The Handbook* (Witherby *et al.* 1940) clarified the issue, the authors emphasising the existence of young Cormorants with white underparts among the British population as a whole, the white sometimes even intensifying following the onset of post-juvenile moult (Cramp *et al.* 1977–94). Cramp *et al.* also noted that the amount of white on the undersides of young birds is variable between populations, averaging greatest in southern birds, though they apparently mean within the southern West Palearctic, rather than Britain. The existence of a small percentage of young Cormorants with white underparts, some substantially so, remains a feature of Scilly today.

Up to and including the year 2000, at least 161 Cormorants had been ringed in Scilly, 90 of these in the period since 1970 and presumably the majority as pulli, but certainly all those since 1970. Earliest recorded overseas recovery of a Scillonian-ringed Cormorant probably involved a nestling ringed on Melledgan in May 1911 and found in the mouth of the river Alberwack in Finnistere, France, in December the same year. It now seems obvious that first-winter Cormorant dispersal very much mirrors that for Shag, though a far greater percentage routinely go south as far as Atlantic coastal Portugal and Spain, some (at least) apparently remaining there during their second, or perhaps third calendar-year. Some clearly disperse very soon after leaving the nest, one youngster being recovered off the coast of France by mid-July. Compared with Shag, a higher proportion cross to coastal France and few seem inclined to wander north, Glamorgan being the furthest on record for Scilly. Five Cormorants ringed elsewhere have been recovered in Scilly, four from Ireland and one from southwest Wales. Of these, one was a rapidly moving first-year, three were in their second summer and the fifth had been ringed in Co. Antrim fifteen years before. Coulson and Brazendale (1968) found that British Cormorants do not migrate, though there is an extensive dispersal – finding too that dispersal rate in relation to distance travelled is constant for a particular colony. The comparatively few national recoveries or controls recorded between Britain and continental Europe east of the Netherlands mostly involved eastern England (Wernham et al. 2002). There appears to be a significant difference in the destinations of dispersing birds from the three Scillonian breeding groups (see Table), with 55% and 75% respectively from the Western and Eastern Isles reaching France, compared with only 25% from the Northern Isles. Only the Western Isles provided birds reaching Spain (28%), and Cornwall was the main destination for birds from the Northern Isles (37%). Only one bird moved north, to Glamorgan, and one moved east as far as Suffolk. There is a suggestion in all this that the three breeding groups may have become genetically isolated, though the question has not been addressed so far.

| Western Isles | | Northern Isles | | Eastern Isles | |
|---|---|---|---|---|---|
| France | 10 (55.5%) | France | 2 (25%) | France | 3 (75%) |
| Cornwall | 1 (5.5%) | Cornwall | 3 (37.5%) | Cornwall | 1 (25%) |
| Devon | 1 (5.5%) | Devon | 2 (25%) | | |
| Glamorgan | 1 (5.5%) | Suffolk | 1 (12.5%) | | |
| Spain | 5 (27.7%) | | | | |

**Source and Recapture Areas of Scillonian-Ringed Cormorants (excluding those recaptured in Scilly)**

## Controls
| ? | Pul | Sheep Is, Co. Antrim 17th June 1977 | FN | 'Scilly' 7th August 1978 |
|---|---|---|---|---|
| 5139709 | Pul | Tenby, Pembrokeshire 20th June 1987 | FD | Porth Hellick, St Mary's 5th May 1988 |
| 5084450 | Pul | Sheep Is, Co. Antrim 17th June 1977 | FD | St Mary's 31st May 1992 |
| 5195816 | Pul | Ardboline Is, Co. Sligo 12th June 1997 | FD | Hugh Town, St Mary's 25th August 1997 |
| 5191012 | Pul | Capel Is. Co. Cork 17th June 1997 | FD | Old Town, St Mary's 7th April 1998 |

## Recoveries
| ? | ? | Melledgan 22nd May 1911 | ? | Finistere, France 12th December 1911 |
|---|---|---|---|---|
| ? | ? | Melledgan 20th April 1914 | ? | Cotes du Nord, France 19th July 1914 |
| ? | ? | Melledgan 19th May 1914 | ? | Galicia, Spain 6th October 1914 |
| 5003150 | Pul | Melledgan 27th June 1962 | ? | Rhossili, Glamorgan 25th June 1963 |
| 5003138 | Pul | Melledgan 8th June 1962 | ? | Coruna, Spain 20th February 1964 |
| 5000499 | Pul | Mincarlo 31st May 1963 | ? | Ipswich, Suffolk 15th March 1964 |
| ? | ? | Melledgan 22nd June 1964 | ? | Colunga, Oviedo, Spain December 1964 |
| 5162905 | Pul | Ragged Island 12th May 1992 | SH | Guilers, Finistere, France 3rd March 1997 |
| 5170327 | Pul | Melledgan 25th May 1999 | FN | Pontevedra, Spain 8th March 2000 |

**Cormorant Selected Ringing Recaptures**

## [Double-crested Cormorant *Phalacrocorax auritus*] A

Full written description required by the BBRC. No acceptable Scillonian record, one claimed by Will Wagstaff at Porth Hellick Pool, St Mary's, during November 1990 having been rejected by the BBRC (*IOSBR* 1990, 1992).

[1990   One Porth Hellick Pool, St Mary's 1st, 2nd & 4th November]   *British Birds* 86: 539

Breeds North America, from Alaska east to Newfoundland and south to Gulf of California and Cuba. Migratory in north of range, particularly in east, wintering mainly within breeding range.

The possibility of this highly migratory species reaching Scilly from North America should be borne in mind. The only British record so far of this distinctive Nearctic species involved a bird in Cleveland, Tyne and Wear, from December 1988 to late April 1989, followed by one in Galway Harbour, Ireland, in 1995 (Palmer 2000). A bird also appeared in the Azores during October 1991 (Snow & Perrins 1998). For assistance on the identification of Double-crested Cormorant see Alstrom (1991).

## Shag (European Shag)   *Phalacrocorax aristotelis* A

Resident and breeds, young Shags disperse away from the islands during their first winter.

Confined to West Palearctic, breeds Iceland, Faeroes, Britain and Ireland, northern Norway, Sweden, Finland, northwest Russia, France, Iberia, Mediterranean and Black Sea. Dispersive. Polytypic: nominate *aristotelis* occurs north and west Europe; *riggenbachi* northwest Africa; *desmarestii*, or 'Mediterranean Shag' Mediterranean and Black Sea. Amber-listed in UK: 20% or more of European breeding population in UK, 50% or more at ten or fewer sites (Gregory *et al.* 2002).

One of the more obvious of the archipelago's breeding seabirds, although, unlike many other UK sites, Shags on Scilly breed almost exclusively beneath boulder beaches, or in holes in low cliffs, perhaps in response to unusually high densities of breeding Great Black-backed Gull *Larus marinus* (P J Robinson 1992). During the most recent count, for Seabird 2000, a total of 1,109 apparently occupied nests were recorded on 24 islands; including 209 on Annet, 117 on Rosevear and 105 each on Gweal and Melledgan (Seabird 2000 – unpublished data). Present Cornish breeding numbers are unclear, though in 1999 it was described as breeding in small colonies on all coasts (*CBWPSAR* 69). However, Penhallurick (1969) thought the then estimated Scillonian population of around 1,000 pairs was several hundred pairs more than in Cornwall. Taking the most recent UK estimate of 37,500 pairs (Stone *et al.* 1997), Scilly now holds some 2.9% of the national breeding total, though this figure may change once the national results of Seabird 2000 become known.

E H Rodd had little to say on the subject of the Shag in Cornwall and even less regarding Scilly, merely commenting that it bred in the cliffs (Rodd 1880). Fortunately, however, a number of other writers reported in more detail on its status around the end of the 19th and early 20th centuries. Gilbert White recorded it as a resident in the islands (in Jesse 1887) and those dependable observers of late 19th century Scillonian ornithology, James Clark and Francis Rodd, noted it as much more abundant than Cormorant *P. carbo*, breeding in 'great numbers on all outer rocks not washed by the sea, and also in small numbers on Annet'. The last comment is of particular interest in view of Annet's prominence now as the main Shag breeding site in Scilly. Of considerable surprise too is that people spent time ringing Shags and other seabirds on Scilly as early as 1910, the same people also taking time to record breeding details. From this information we know that by the end of May 1911, Shag nests were extremely numerous 'on all the islands' and that none had hatched eggs by that time, large numbers having one egg still (H W Robinson 1913). The same author also confirmed low numbers on Annet (H W Robinson 1911a). We also know from comments in various *CBWPSAR* that there was no apparent early 20th century period of decline, Mincarlo being described in 1937 as having every available 'crack and crevice' occupied by breeding Shags (*CBWPSAR* 7). Nonetheless some islanders still recall the time, not too long ago, when local boats kept a loaded shotgun beneath the foredeck in case a Shag or Cormorant flew past, the carcasses then being used to bait fish traps. Evidence of early scientific interest in this species in Scilly is evident today in the collection of the British Museum (Natural History), in the form of a nestling spirit specimen Reference 1924.6.25, collected 23rd June 1924 by H W Robinson, and the skin of an adult male, Reference 26.4.28, collected 24th April 1926 by A A Dorrien-Smith.

Parslow (1967a) found evidence of a, at times, marked increase in the British Shag population from the mid-20th century up until 1967. However, the earliest recorded modern count of Shags in Scilly is Allen's all-island 1974 survey for the then NCC, in which he recorded an estimated 850 breeding pairs on some 22 islands and lesser rocks (Allen 1974), two islands, Annet and Rosevear, vying for the highest total, with 95 on the former and 80–100 on Rosevear. Further NCC or EN all-island counts continued on an approximate five-yearly basis, with annual counts mainly confined to Annet (see Charts). For Shag, these surveys show a pattern of little overall change, though with some obvious redistribution between islands. Annet totals, for example, demonstrate the dangers inherent in assessing a species' overall status based on selective site surveys, although, at least on Scilly, Shags show no obvious periodic annual breeding failure, unlike large gulls *Larus* and Kittiwake *Rissa tridactyla*, for example. Thus, whatever the factors controlling population size, they apparently operate outside the breeding season – unless they involve predation of pre-fledged young, which is often quite marked at some main breeding concentrations, e.g. Annet.

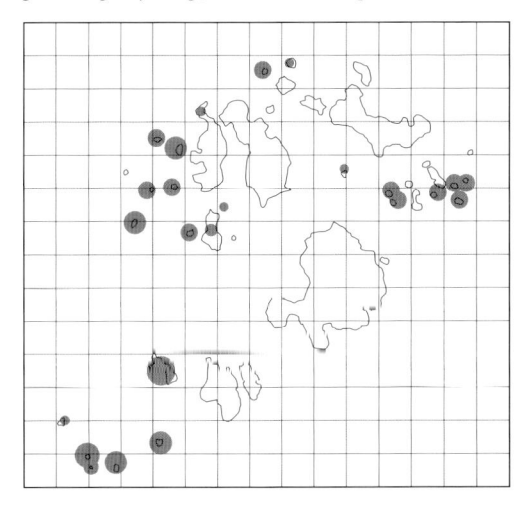

| Island | Nests |
|---|---|
| Annet | 209 |
| Melledgan | 105 |
| Gorregan | 74 |
| Rosevean | 30 |
| Rosevear | 117 |
| Great Crebawethan | 5 |
| Mincarlo | 82 |
| Illiswilgig | 25 |
| Scilly Rock | 39 |
| Castle Bryher | 22 |
| Gweal | 105 |
| Samson | 7 |
| White Island, Samson | 32 |
| Shipman Head, Bryher | 4 |
| Puffin Island | 4 |
| Men-a-Vaur | 24 |

| | | | |
|---|---|---|---|
| Round Island | 2 | Ragged Island | 39 |
| Guther's Island | 1 | Great Innisvouls | 69 |
| Great Ganinick | 23 | Little Innisvouls | 28 |
| Little Ganinick | 25 | Menawethan | 37 |

**Location of 1108 Shag Nests – 1999 (Seabird 2000 data)**

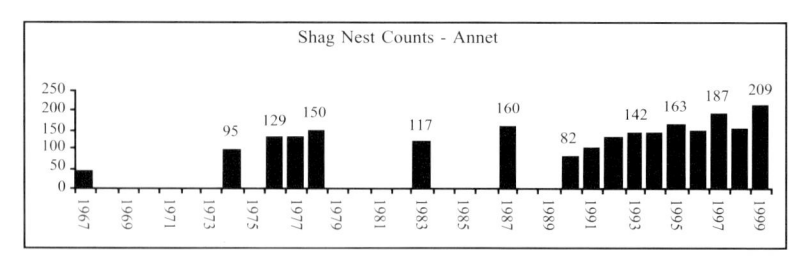

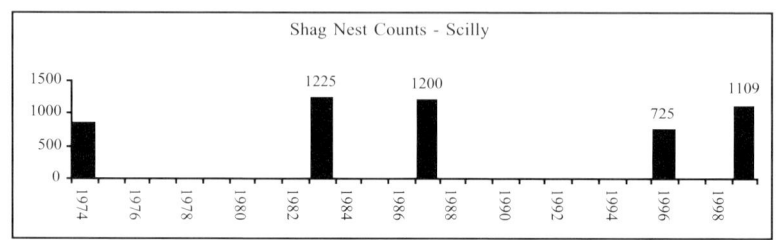

**Shag Nest Counts - Annet**

1967: (small value); 1973: 95; 1975: 129; 1977: 150; 1982: 117; 1986: 160; 1989: 82; 1991–1999: 142, 163, 187, 209

**Shag Nest Counts - Scilly**

1974: ~850; 1983: 1225; 1987: 1200; 1996: 725; 1999: 1109

Laying normally commences late April or early May (P J Robinson 1992b) and though late clutches of newly laid eggs are not uncommon, in the absence of colour-ringing it is difficult to know whether replacement clutches or late breeders are involved. Early nests are more limited, with the occasional clutch from mid- to late March. On Annet, mean clutch size for the years 1993–95 was in the range 2.46 – 2.92 eggs per active nest (P J Robinson 1998). There is a very pronounced likelihood of open nests in Scilly being predated (presumably by Great Black-backs), if not at the incubation stage then certainly once young are left unattended, giving rise to the possibility that availability of appropriate nest-site type may be the main controlling factor on Shag breeding numbers at some colonies, e.g. Annet. Since 1991 at least, there has been no apparent colonisation of new breeding sites, the one obvious exception being Samson, which was occupied immediately following the removal of Brown Rats *Rattus norvegicus* during the early 1990s (P J Robinson 1998) and which by 2000 held ten to eleven pairs (pers. obs.).

By the end of 1999, a total of 3,174 Shags had been ringed on Scilly, 1,739 (54%) of these prior to 1970; only Storm Petrel has a larger Scillonian ringing total. Most Shags are ringed as pulli, though in recent years adults have been increasingly ringed – in an effort to ascertain levels of local breeding recruitment using retrap data. Inevitably, much has been learned about the movement of Scillonian-reared Shags away from the islands, and not just during the mid- to late 20th century; a Shag ringed in Scilly in 1914 was recovered in Brest, France, in November 1928. It seems well understood now that many (at least) first-year birds leave the islands by late summer, spending their first winter in the English Channel and Western Approaches, as far south as northwest France and east to the Channel Islands and Isle of Wight (Wernham *et al.* 2002), with little or no regular northward movement (Parslow 1965a; IOSSBG – unpublished data). Parslow calculated a recovery rate of between 5% and 19% for first-year Scillonian Shags for six of the seven years 1957–63 (none in 1959) at an average of 10.5%.

Of 48 known first-year Shag recoveries during the period 1995–99, 21 (43.7%) came from the English south coast, between west Cornwall and Hampshire, 19 (39.5%) from coastal northwest France and one (2%) from the Channel Islands. A further seven birds were recovered north as far as Grampian Region, Scotland, including two in landlocked Warwickshire and one in Northamptonshire. A lesser number of older birds recovered away from Scilly during the same period involved five in their second calendar-year (Devon two, France two and Lothian Region one), one third calendar-year (Channel Islands), three fourth calendar-year (all France) and two fifth calendar-year (both Cornwall). Four second-calendar-year individuals were recovered April–May and could conceivably have returned to Scilly within the subsequent breeding season, though the fifth was recovered in Lothian in July. Less easy to explain, however, is the presence of three fourth-calendar-year birds in France (though all were outside the breeding season), unless of course they were breeding at one of about 20 Brittany colonies (Guermeur & Monnat 1980). In general, these findings were much in keeping with those of Parslow earlier (1965a), though the incidence of birds shot in France appear to have almost ceased. Nevertheless, a substantial proportion of all Shag recoveries still involve birds accidentally caught in fishing nets ('trap set for other species'). One obvious difference between Parslow's 1960s findings and the 1990s, however, are the two September 1962 Netherlands' recoveries. The most southerly Shag recovery involved a bird from Rosevear found in Spain in late 1965. Finally, there is a noticeable absence of recoveries in Scilly of Shags ringed elsewhere and almost nothing is known about the makeup of the wintering population within the islands.

The oldest known recovery of a Scillonian-ringed Shag appears to involve a ring found on a Kingsbridge estuary in south Devon in August 1994, from a bird ringed on Annet 27 years earlier. The ring number was still easily readable and had therefore not been detached from the bird for too long. The oldest provable recovery, however, may be the bird ringed in 1914 and recovered in northwest France in November 1928.

A notable feature of the Scillonian Shag population, at all times of year, are the mass gatherings of feeding birds, often involving up to five hundred, or even 1,000 (pers. obs.) individuals. Such flocks feed in a 'rolling' manner, with birds surfacing at the rear overflying the flock and plunge-diving at the head of the advancing mass (B King 1974). Very little information is available on food sources exploited by Shags in Scilly, though handled birds may disgorge partly digested remains of what appear to be Sandeels *Ammodytidae*, which would equate with the feeding method described above. Penhallurick (1969) refers to an early, 1930s, government examination of Cornish Shag food intake, concluding that only five individuals out of 188 tested had taken fish species 'of economic importance'. Whatever their true diet, however, local fishermen on Scilly have been known to make up their own minds on fish species involved and to take action to reduce numbers taken, as in 1967 when a post-Torrey Canyon breeding survey of Castle Bryher and Melledgan was adversely affected by a visit by fishermen to kill Shags and Cormorants (Parslow 1967b). As with Cormorant, little thought appears to have been given to assessing the subspecific status of Shags in Scillonian waters. However, the likelihood of individuals of *desmarestii*, or 'Mediterranean Shag', reaching Scilly has been raised by both Flumm (1993) and Gantlett (1998), the first of these two authors drawing attention to at least seven records of birds in southwest England showing features of this distinctive form, five of which were unsuccessfully submitted to BBRC. Although a few subadult Shags showing some features of *desmarestii*, but with notable white underparts, occur regularly in the Scillonian population, so far none have shown the distinctive pale upperwing-coverts to any degree; and no adults have been recorded in Scilly showing features of this distinctive form. It may be worth noting that extremely pale or even totally white (*IOSBR* 1992) juvenile or older Shags are not uncommon in Scilly and need keeping in mind when examining likely *desmarestii* contenders.

# Bittern (Great Bittern) *Botaurus stellaris* A

**Very rare migrant or cold-weather vagrant, possibly occurs more frequently than records suggest. Full written description required by the SRP.**

1864   One (shot) St Mary's 24th December   Rodd 1880
1867   At least one (shot) Scilly   Rodd 1868; 1880
1900   One (shot) Porth Hellick, St Mary's   Clark & Rodd 1906
1945   One St Mary's 25th January
1959   One Tresco 5th September   Tresco Abbey records
1962   One St Agnes 11th January (dead several days)
1979   One St Mary's 5th to 12th January
1996   One Porth Hellick, St Mary's 17th and 20th January, presumably same 3rd March
1998   One Hugh Town, St Mary's 9th February

Breeds Europe and central Asia, from the Atlantic to the Pacific, plus Africa; west European population extremely fragmentary. Unclear if species migratory or merely dispersive, the latter mainly in response to cold weather. Polytypic: nominate *stellaris* throughout Palearctic; *capensis* southern Africa. Included on

*Birds of the Isles of Scilly*

Annex I of 1979 EEC 'Birds Directive'. Red-listed in UK: long-term historical decline plus recent rapid 25-year breeding decline of 62% to 19 booming males, with 50% or greater range reduction over same timescale; 50% or more of non-breeding population at ten or fewer sites; unfavourable world conservation status (Gregory *et al.* 2002).

There may be early evidence of this species in the form of bone remains unearthed from 2nd to 7th century AD levels of the prehistoric site at May's Hill, St Martin's (Turk 1971); though identification is uncertain. E H Rodd and his contemporaries thought this a regular species in the southwest, Rodd even commenting that 'some years, as in the winter of 1867, a great many get shot' (Rodd 1880), whilst James Clark and Francis Rodd (1906) referred to six or seven obtained on Tresco and St Mary's. Francis Rodd's 1864 written account to his uncle, E H Rodd, of his Christmas Eve shooting of the St Mary's bird is a graphically inspiring description of his chance encounter with this normally elusive species. With obvious feeling Francis explained to his uncle how:

> The living bird was quite different to stuffed specimens. I particularly remarked the beautiful blue feathers on the head (these must be looked at by sunlight), and the colouring about the bill and legs. I shall write to Vingoe to have him set up, I think, in a standing position, with the feathers on the neck rather "rampant" than "couchant".

In fact so taken was Francis with this bird that he even thought necessary to mention how the 'colouring of the head and legs in Gould's plate is not overdone' (Rodd 1880). Sadly, details of only three of Clark and Rodd's stated six or seven individuals seem to have survived. In all, there are just nine documented occurrences of Bittern for Scilly, though we may safely accept another three or four from the 19th century. Without much doubt, the species is probably greatly unrecorded, as seems ably demonstrated by just three sightings of a bird that apparently occupied the Porth Hellick reedbed on St Mary's for a period of at least 46 days during winter 1996 – the same winter during which up to three were at Marazion in west Cornwall. The national declines and extinctions of the 19th century were well-documented, as is the more recent recovery, particularly in eastern England. Nonetheless, Bittern remains a rare bird throughout most of Britain, showing a clear tendency towards staying within the breeding areas as long as these remain unfrozen, according to Cramp *et al.* (1977–94) often preferring to starve rather than move away.

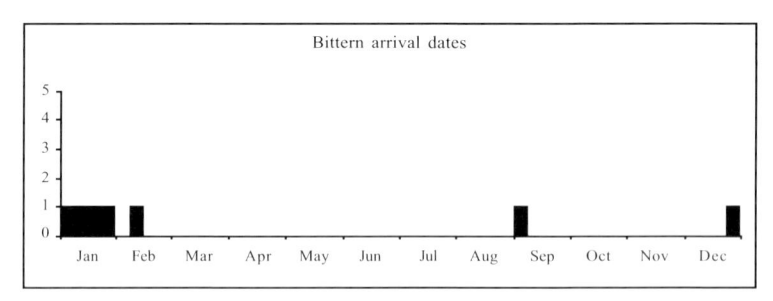

In fact, Cramp *et al.* found no evidence of emigration by British birds but did mention British winter recoveries of ringed birds from the Low Countries, Germany and Sweden. From this, it seems possible that birds visiting Scilly in winter could originate from mainland Britain, but equally probably from nearby continental Europe, where Bittern breeds as close as southern Brittany. The Chart incorporates arrival or first-sighting dates for the seven records where these are know and shows an apparent pattern of winter presence, which fits the theory of birds being forced west by hard weather elsewhere. However, in view of what has already been said about the likelihood of birds remaining undiscovered, this must be treated with a measure of caution. There were a total of 141 records of Bittern for mainland Cornwall up to and including 1999 (*CBWPSAR* 69).

## American Bittern *Botaurus lentiginosus* A  BBRC 0%

**Extremely rare migrant, full written description required by the BBRC.**

   1903   One Bryher 10th October (taken into captivity)   Pigott 1903; Clark & Rodd 1906

Breeds North America, from central Canada south to central USA, wintering western and southern coastal

USA, Central America and Caribbean. Monotypic. Recent population crash but slight increase since 1979 (Bryant 1997).

One old record of an exhausted and emaciated bird found on the western side of Bryher on 10th October 1903 and taken into care. It responded well once confined in an aviary on Tresco, where it remained until at least 1906 (Pigott 1903; Clark & Rodd 1906; Witherby & Ticehurst 1908). The mounted skin is on permanent loan from Tresco Abbey in the IOS Museum on St Mary's. Griffiths (1982) gave the capture date for this bird as the 19th.

The first British and Irish record involved a bird shot in Dorset in 1804, though it was not correctly identified until 1913 (Palmer 2000). There was a total of 50 American Bittern records for Britain and Ireland prior to 1958, but only 11 have been accepted by the BBRC since that time. There is an obvious risk of confusing this species with the more likely Bittern *B. stellaris* and quite clearly all bitterns seen on Scilly need careful examination. To date there are 17 records in total from southwest England.

American Bittern is a substantial wanderer in late summer and early autumn, presumably involving mainly post-fledging dispersal. Autumn migration occurs mainly in September–October but with some still moving south in November. Accidental transatlantic autumn migrants to northern Europe are thought likely to originate from among that part of the population moving through southeast Canada and northeast USA (Cramp *et al.* 1977–94). There are six records of American Bittern from mainland Cornwall up to and including 1999 (*CBWPSAR* 69).

## Little Bittern *Ixobrychus minutus* A BBRC 6.4%

**Rare migrant, full written description required by the BBRC.**

    1866  One (male) (shot) Tresco 10th June   Rodd 1866b
    1955  One (male) St Agnes 7th May    CBWPSAR 25
    1964  One (male) St Agnes & St Mary's 16th to 18th April
    1968  One (male) St Mary's 3rd June
    1970  One (female) Tresco 8th June
    1987  One (male) St Mary's 15th April to 3rd May
    1987  One (male) St Agnes 2nd May
    1988  One (male) St Mary's 1st April (moribund 3rd)
    1989  One (male) St Mary's 21st May to 7th June
    1992  One (female) St Mary's 20th April
    1992  One St Martin's 19th May
    1994  One (male) Tresco 5th to 8th May
    1994  One (female) St Mary's 8th to 17th May (remains found 31st)
    1995  One (female) St Mary's 23rd May to 4th June
    1997  One (female) St Mary's 3rd to 5th May

Breeds Eurasia, Africa and Australasia, West Palearctic birds winter mainly East African. Polytypic: *minutus* occurs Europe and western Asia; *payesii* Africa; plus another three forms further east.

There is one old 19th century record and then a further 14, including the first recorded 20th century sighting in 1955. The first arrival on Scilly involved a bird shot on Tresco on 10th June 1866. E H Rodd attributed the specimen to 'Mr Smith of Tresco' (Rodd 1866b, 1880) and we can probably safely assume that this was the Tresco gamekeeper David Smith, who obtained many rarities in his time. Rodd claimed it was shot on the 'large pool near the Abbey on Tresco' but it is unclear from this exactly which of the pools was involved. Fourteen of the 15 birds recorded were sexed, nine as males and five as females. The lack of any subadults is surprising and it remains possible that one or more of the claimed females could have been wrongly aged, but even so the preponderance of males is noteworthy, as of course is the fact that all were spring arrivals.

Obviously, as with any species that spends much of its time concealed in reedbed vegetation, some doubt surrounds the exact timing of arrival and departure. But bearing that in mind, the earliest known arrival date was 1st April and the latest 8th June, which was also the latest any bird was recorded in the islands. The shortest recorded stay was one day (seven individuals) and the longest 19 days, whereas the average recorded length of stay was 5.5 days; the bird shot in 1866 is omitted from these calculations owing to the lack of information on the date of first sighting. The Chart shows all arrival dates except the 1866 individual and assumes first sighting equals arrival date, which of course may not have been so. The spread of dates probably reflects the extent to which spring arrivals of, presumably, overshooting southern European herons are dictated by annually variable weather factors. Typically, birds took up temporary residence by one of the larger reed-fringed pools, such as Porth Hellick on St Mary's, or Tresco's Great or Abbey Pools, and even the St Agnes visitors managed to locate that island's relatively small pool.

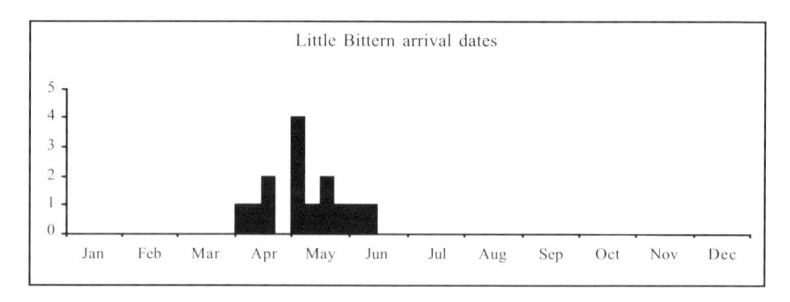

*Little Bittern arrival dates*

Little Bittern breeds as close to Britain as northern France (including Brittany), Belgium and the Netherlands. Return passage from the African wintering grounds occurs in the Mediterranean from mid-March, with central European breeding areas reoccupied by April or early May. Males normally precede females, with subadults arriving mainly from mid-May onwards. However, there seems to be no obvious sexual bias to arrival dates on Scilly. Scillonian arrivals are presumed to involve the European or western Asian form *minutus*, though the possibility of the African *payesii* also being involved cannot be ruled out entirely.

Although the migratory and very similar North American Least Bittern *I. exilis* remains unrecorded in Britain and Ireland, it has reached Iceland and the Azores (the latter more than once) and must be a prime contender for eventually being identified on Scilly. Certainly, all small bitterns encountered in the islands should be examined minutely. There are a total of 37 Little Bittern records for mainland Cornwall up to and including 1999 (*CBWPSAR* 69).

## Night Heron (Black-crowned Night Heron)
### *Nycticorax nycticorax*  A  BBRC 7.8%

**Rare migrant, full written description required by the SRP.**

1849   Two Tresco 15th May   Rodd 1849c; 1880
1925   One (shot) Scilly October   Penahallurick 1969
1944   One Scilly 6th May   *CBWPSAR* 14

| | | |
|---|---|---|
| 1955 | One immature St Mary's and Tresco 24th April (shot 28th)   Penhallurick 1969 | |
| 1961 | Three St Mary's: two adults 29th April then one adult and one juvenile 30th to 13th May; then four to 2nd June | |
| [1962 | One (subadult) Tresco Great Pool during May]   *CBWPSAR* 32 | |
| 1965 | One Tresco 26th March to 1st April | |
| 1970 | Up to three St Mary's 26th April to 6th June | |
| 1979 | One (adult) St Agnes 10th & 11th June | |
| 1980 | One (subadult) Tresco & Bryher 18th September | |
| 1981 | One (second-summer) St Mary's 22nd to 30th April | |
| 1985 | One (subadult) St Mary's 11th to 20th October | |
| 1985 | One (adult) St Mary's 13th October | |
| 1987 | One (adult) St Mary's 1st & 2nd April | |
| 1987 | One St Mary's 15th to 30th April | |
| 1990 | One (adult) St Mary's 17th March to 1st April | |
| 1990 | One (adult) St Martin's & Tresco 18th March to 9th April | |
| 1990 | One (adult) St Mary's 29th March to 4th April | |
| 1990 | One (adult) St Mary's 4th April to 2nd May | |
| 1990 | One (adult) St Mary's 9th April to 13th May | |
| 1990 | One (adult) St Mary's 19th to 24th April (dead 24th) | |
| 1990 | One (adult) St Mary's 24th April to 4th June | |
| 1990 | One (subadult) St Mary's 3rd May to 15th June | |
| 1990 | One (subadult) St Mary's 17th & 18th May | |
| 1994 | One (adult) St Mary's 2nd to 4th May | |
| 1996 | One (adult) St Mary's 21st & 22nd April | |
| 1997 | One (adult) St Mary's 11th June | |
| 1999 | At least six St Agnes & St Mary's 9th April to 6th June (four adults, one first-year & one second-year) | |
| 1999 | One (subadult) St Mary's 22nd September to 18th October | |
| 2002 | One Tresco 8th June | |

Breeds Eurasia, Africa and Americas; West Palearctic populations particularly fragmentary. European population winters Africa south of Sahara. Polytypic: nominate *nycticorax* occurs Eurasia and Africa; *hoactli* confined to Americas. Removed from BBRC Rarities List January 2002 (*British Birds* 94: 290).

E H Rodd was familiar with this species on the Cornish mainland, mostly it seems in spring, commenting too that birds were often encountered in apparent breeding plumage. Penhallurick (1969) referred to birds on the Lizard peninsula and in west Cornwall in or just prior to 1838 as the apparent first records for the county. The first recorded in Scilly, on 15th May 1849, suffered the unfortunate experience of being 'knocked on the head' by Tresco gamekeeper David Smith when he came across it resting in some bushes (Rodd 1849c, 1880). Rodd recorded that he received the carcass from Mr James, the Tresco Land Steward, commenting that 'Another example was seen at the same time, and I believe secured.' Interestingly, Moore (1969) mentioned eight shot on the river Erme in south Devon during May and June that same year.

The next mention of it on Scilly is contained in the Tresco Abbey records and concerns one shot, presumably on that island, in October 1925 (Penhallurick 1969), followed by a brief report of one somewhere in Scilly on 6th May 1944. The final pre-BBRC occurrence is of interest not so much for the record itself, as for the revelation that rarities were still liable to be shot on Scilly, even into the mid-1950s. The bird involved was identified in the field as a 'young male' and was seen on St Mary's by a Mr and Mrs Hayes on 24th April, though according to R Symonds it may have been about that island for the best part of a month beforehand (*CBWPSAR* 25). It is recorded as last sighted on Tresco on 28th April, the same date Penhallurick records one shot on Tresco; information presumably obtained from the Tresco Abbey records (Penhallurick 1969).

The Chart shows all known arrival dates, though in the case of some multiple arrivals, e.g. 1999, only the known earliest date was used. There is an obvious pattern of spring arrivals, which outnumber autumn arrivals by about 8:1. The earliest recorded spring arrival was 17th March and the latest 11th June, with the last recorded spring presence on 15th June. The earliest autumn arrival was 18th September and the

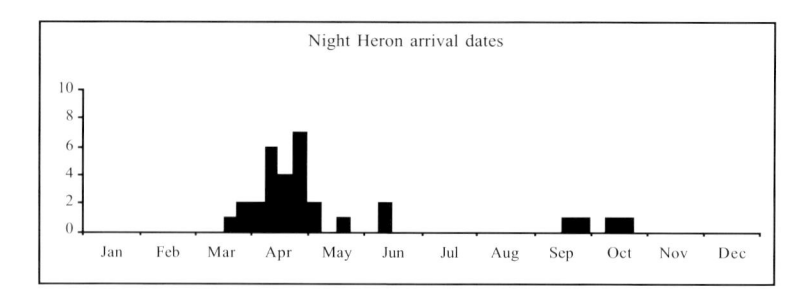

*Birds of the Isles of Scilly*

**Night Heron arrival dates** (bar chart showing peaks in March–April)

latest 13th October, with 20th October the last date any bird was seen on the islands. However, given Night Heron's preference for feeding during the early morning and late evening and its ability to hide itself away during the day, chances are that this species is greatly under-recorded on Scilly, as must surely be the case elsewhere. In addition, of course, totals given for multiple-arrival years are probably only minimum figures.

As with most other extralimital herons on Scilly, the pattern of spring arrivals suggests that birds are overshooting migrants from populations further south, e.g. central and coastal France (where it breeds as close as southern Brittany), failing which they may have been destined for breeding sites in nearby continental Europe, e.g. the Netherlands. Few if any Scillonian sightings have been attributed subspecifically but the predominance of spring arrivals supports the view they are European *nycticorax*. However, observers should be alive to the possibility of the slightly smaller North American form *hoactli* crossing the Atlantic, perhaps paying particular attention to any autumn arrivals (Gantlett 1998). Certainly, the opportunity should be taken to examine carefully any individuals found dead. In northeastern USA, Night Herons breed as far north as New Brunswick and Nova Scotia. Altogether, 39 Night Herons have been recorded on Scilly and the 34 post-1958 individuals represent 7.8% of the 435 accepted by the BBRC up to and including 1999. There were a total of 37 records for mainland Cornwall up to and including 1999 (*CBWPSAR* 69); thus the combined Cornwall and Scilly figure was 17.5% of the national total.

An unidentified small heron seen in the area of Abbey Farm beach, Tresco, at dusk from 19th to 21st October 1993 was also thought to have been this species (*IOSBR* 1993).

## Squacco Heron          *Ardeola ralloides*  A  BBRC 9.8%

**Rare migrant, full written description required by the BBRC.**

| | | |
|---|---|---|
| 1842 | One (shot) Scilly in autumn | Rodd 1843: 143; Penhallurick 1969 |
| 1849 | One (shot) Scilly May | Witherby & Ticehurst 1908; Clark & Rodd 1906 |
| Pre-1906 | One Scilly | Clark & Rodd 1906 |
| 1915 | One (shot )Tresco April | Penhallurick 1969 |
| 1970 | One St Mary's, Tresco & St Agnes 1st May to 3rd June | *British Birds* 64: 345, 68: 76 |
| 1977 | One (male – recently dead) Rosevear 17th June | *British Birds* 71: 489 |
| 1990 | One St Mary's 20th March to 9th April | *British Birds* 84: 454 |
| 1990 | One Bryher & St Martin's 15th May to 1st June | *British Birds* 84: 454 |
| 1994 | One various islands 3rd May to 6th June | *British Birds* 88: 499 |

Breeds southern Europe, Africa, Asia Minor and southwest Asia, fragmentary distribution doubtless reflecting specific habitat requirement. Eurasian and North African populations winter Africa south of Sahara, with a few irregularly further north. Monotypic.

E H Rodd was almost dismissive of this species in Cornwall (Rodd 1880), saying it occurred at intervals and had frequently been met with, always in spring. He also described a number he had received, which he said always lacked adult breeding plumes. The first bird on Scilly was described in Greenwood's letter to the *Zoologist* entitled *Note on the occurrence of the Squacco Heron near Penzance* and concerned a bird shot in autumn 1842 (A Greenwood 1843); about the same time others were in west Cornwall (Rodd 1843d, 1880). And whilst we find reference to the second, 1849, individual in Witherby & Ticehurst (1908), this individual too coincided with birds in Cornwall. Interestingly, E H Rodd's nephew, Francis Rodd, and his co-author James Clark claimed the first Scillonian record was 1849, but then mentioned birds killed on St

*Squacco Heron arrival dates* (chart)

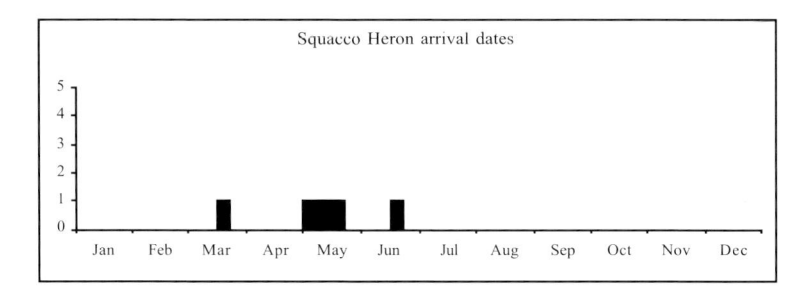

Mary's, Tresco and St Martin's, which is at least one more bird than was recorded earlier (Clark & Rodd 1906). The Tresco Abbey records also list one shot on that island in 1915 (Penhallurick 1969) and the mounted skin of one of these early Squacco Herons currently resides in the Isles of Scilly Museum on St Mary's.

There are five recent records, one of which was found freshly dead on Rosevear in the Western Isles. The earliest arrival date was 20th March, whereas the latest, 17th June, involved the dead bird, which probably arrived a day or so beforehand. Disregarding the dead bird, the shortest stay was 18 days and the longest 35, at an average of 27 days. The Chart incorporates the five most recent records and shows the typically protracted pattern for spring arrivals of heron species in Scilly, which perhaps reflects the extent to which the spring appearance of presumably overshooting southern-European herons is dictated by annually variable weather factors. Cramp *et al.* (1977–94) confirm overshooting migrants as the most likely explanation for the spring appearance of this species in countries bordering the North Sea. Though they also highlight the recent marked decline in the numbers of such records, i.e. 90 in Britain up to 1914 but around ten only in the period 1954–71. In fact, the BBRC accepted just 51 British records during the period 1958–99 inclusive, in which case the five Scillonian records represent almost 10% of the national total. There are 23 records of Squacco Heron for mainland Cornwall up to and including 1999 (*CBWPSAR* 69).

## Cattle Egret *Bubulcus ibis* A  BBRC 0%

**Extremely rare migrant, full written description required by the BBRC.**

2001   Up to two St Mary's, St Martin's, St Agnes & Tresco 16th to 19th May   *Birding World* 14: 179

Breeds Iberia, Near East, Africa, Indian subcontinent, Australasia, North and South America, Caribbean and Pacific Islands. Polytypic: *coromandus* occurs Australasia; nominate *ibis* elsewhere. Northern populations migratory and/or dispersive, much of current world distribution attributable to the species' dispersive nature, e.g. Africa to South America, and then South America to North America.

The first and second records for the islands arrived as recently as 2001, in the form of single birds on various islands from 16th to 19th May, though no more than two birds were thought to have been involved. Cattle Egret remains something of a major rarity in Britain and Ireland with just 107 records accepted by the BBRC during the period 1958–99 (BBRC 2000). According to Cramp *et al.* (1977–94), colonisation of new sites is mainly attributable to the species' dynamic dispersive tendency, though the timing of these Scillonian records seems more typical of spring overshoots. In any event, their arrival advances the total of *Ciconiformes* species in the islands to 14, at least four or five of which normally occur in Scilly as overshooting spring migrants. Assuming there are no further national records post-1999 then these two represent less than 2% of the British and Irish total. Amazingly, although these two birds were seen by numerous birdwatchers during their stay in the islands, only one sighting, on St Agnes on 16th and the following day, had been reported to the BBRC up until at least autumn 2002. Elsewhere, the BBRC accepted a total of eight records during the same year, all in England.

## Little Egret *Egretta garzetta* A

**Until recently a rare migrant, but now resident in small numbers and a likely breeding addition.**

Records pre-1990
   1955?  One (shot) Tresco?  Penhallurick 1969

| | |
|---|---|
| 1955 | One, St Agnes and St Mary's 13th May to 2nd June  *CBWPSAR* 25 |
| 1962 | One St Agnes 13th to 28th May |
| 1963 | One Old Town, Lower Moors and Porth Cressa, St Mary's 3rd to 30th April |
| 1966 | One Tresco 6th to 9th May |
| 1972 | One St Agnes & Bryher 21st to 27th May |
| 1976 | One St Mary's, St Agnes, Tresco & Annet 19th May to 30th October |
| 1985 | One St Mary's & Bryher 29th June to 2nd July |
| 1987 | One Tresco & St Mary's 15th & 16th April |
| 1989 | One St Mary's 1st to14th December |
| 1989 | One St Mary's & Bryher 1st to 9th December (dead 10th) |

Breeds southern Europe, Africa, southern Asia and Australasia. European population fragmentary and migratory, wintering southern Iberia, southeast Europe, Persian Gulf and Africa. Polytypic: nominate *garzetta* occurs southern Europe, south Asia, northwest Africa, Cape Verde Islands and East and West Africa; three further forms Southeast Asia and Australasia. Removed from BBRC Rarities List January 1991 (Lansdown & Rarities Committee 1990). Included on Annex I of 1979 EEC 'Birds Directive'. Upgraded from Green- to Amber-listed in UK 2002: five-year mean breeding population of 16.2 pairs (Gregory *et al.* 2002), though population increasing.

All records up to and including 1989 are shown in the Table, but from 1990 onwards it became increasingly difficult deciding exactly how many birds were present in the islands and whether they were resident or transient. The Chart shows annual minimum numbers of individuals present, based more recently on recorded maximum single-day counts. The timing of establishment of this apparently now resident population equates with the build-up elsewhere in Britain (Lock & Cook 1998), though the main influx into Britain occurred a year earlier than on Scilly (*British Birds* 83: 443–446; Combridge & Parr 1992). In Scilly, the main focus of Little Egret attention appears to be Tresco, which regularly hosts the largest roost, though birds feed in the tidal areas and, to a lesser extent, main freshwater areas of the six main islands year-round, e.g. the 1997 late January Shorebird Survey recorded it on five of the six largest islands. A marked feature, however, has been the lack of birds in adult breeding plumage, and though two on Tresco in May 1993 were reportedly observed 'mating' and stick-carrying there is no record of a true attempt at breeding. Little Egret has bred in southern England from at least 1996 (Lock & Cook 1998), however, and apparently suitable breeding habitat is present around Tresco Great Pool.

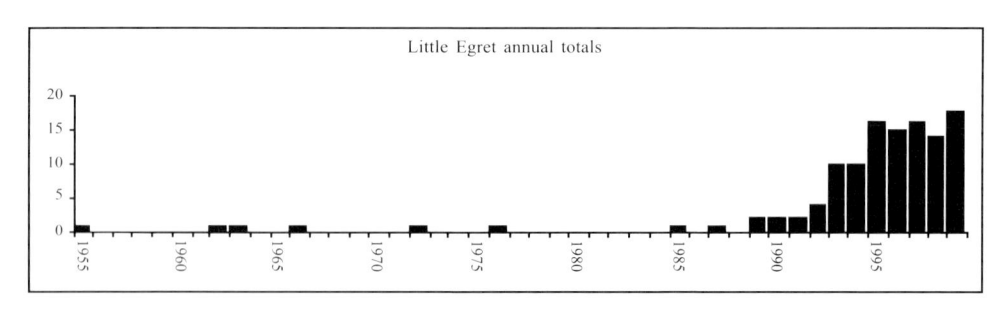

Little Egret annual totals

The first recorded Little Egret on Scilly arrived in 1955, with only nine more in the 44 years to 1989. The earliest recorded sighting involved a bird watched by Hilda Quick on 13th May as it flew in from the south and alighted by St Agnes pool. It then flew to the nearby beach and was promptly mobbed by gulls *Larus*, whereupon it flew to nearby St Mary's, where it was subsequently to be seen until 2nd June. Intriguingly, a mounted skin in the Isles of Scilly Museum, but from the Tresco Abbey collection, does not appear among the published records. However, Penhallurick (1969) apparently suggested it was shot in 1955, although he also suggested April, which in turn indicates that there were two individuals that year.

Prior to 1989, the pattern of arrival dates was very much what might be expected had the individuals involved been overshooting spring migrants from populations further south, whereas the presence now of birds year-round makes it virtually impossible to assess the timing of any additions. Certainly during the early years of colonisation, in the mid-1980s, there was more than a suggestion of seasonal fluctuations and the apparent underlying trend may still be one of lower numbers during summer, followed by an autumn build-up.

There seems little chance of these birds being anything other than the nominate *garzetta* from either Europe or Africa, though presumably the former. Nonetheless, observers should keep in mind the possibility of the quite similar Snowy Egret *E. thula* reaching European shores from North or even Central America; there are known incidents of Little Egrets making the crossing in the other direction, and Britain's first Snowy Egret appeared in Argyll in 2001. Like most European herons, Little Egrets undergo a random post-juvenile dispersal, mainly during the period July–September, e.g. there are records of Spanish birds moving 400 km northwards. Interestingly, Cramp *et al.* (1977–94) thought most West Palearctic birds were trans-Saharan migrants, with autumn departure of adults occurring from late August at least into October, but with a minority wintering within the Mediterranean Basin. Return migration occurs early, with many southern colonies reoccupied by February. Cramp *et al.* considered it prone to overshooting in spring (it now breeds as close as Brittany) and, as with Spoonbill *Platalea leucorodia*, late arrivals in Britain during May or June are presumably more likely to involve non-breeders.

The earliest record for mainland Cornwall apparently concerned a 'pair' allegedly taken at an unidentified site some time in either 1826 or the previous year (Penhallurick 1969), plus Couch (1838) made mention of it in the county. A bird subsequently spent some time on the Hayle Estuary, west Cornwall, in 1943–44 (*CBWPSAR* 13). Lock (1999) thought the Little Egret wintering population on Scilly represented a 'significant percentage' of the UK population at that time of year.

## Great White Egret (Great Egret) *Ardea alba* A BBRC 1.7%

**Extremely rare migrant, full written description required by the BBRC.**

1993   One Tresco 22nd & 23rd April   *British Birds* 87: 511
1995   One (photographed) Bryher mid-March   *British Birds* 89: 488

Breeding range almost cosmopolitan, although within Europe very local. Partial migrant and dispersive, most European breeders winter south only as far as Mediterranean Basin. Polytypic: nominate *alba* occurs Europe and northern Asia; *modesta* southern and eastern Asia, Australia and New Zealand; *melanorhynchos* Africa south of the Sahara; *egretta* the Americas. Recently reclassified from *Agretta* (BOURC 1997).

Just two, quite recent records of this impressively large white heron. The bird on Tresco on 22nd–23rd April 1993 fed around the Great Pool and roosted alongside Little Egrets *E. garzetta* and Grey Herons *Ardea cinerea* on the horizontal branches of a large tree at the pool's southwestern corner. From here it was viewable from boats in nearby Tresco Channel (*IOSBR* 1993; pers. obs.), though it was initially identified from inside the island's laundry. The second individual visited the islands briefly on 10th March 1995, where it was seen and photographed beside Bryher pool by just a single observer (*IOSBR* 1995).

Confusion may be possible with any wandering Nearctic or Neotropical Great White Egret *Ardea alba* should they occur, and Scilly must be a prime contender for such a visit, there having already been several British claims (Gantlett 1998). And although equally unlikely, the possibility exists nonetheless of confusion between Great White Egret and the white-morph North American Great Blue Heron *Ardea herodias*, the far more numerous blue morph having already occurred on the eastern side of the North Atlantic. There are seven Great White Egret records for mainland Cornwall up to and including 1999 (*CBWPSAR* 68).

## Grey Heron *Ardea cinerea* A

**Uncommon migrant or vagrant, present year-round in small numbers, does not breed.**

Breeds central and southern Eurasia from Atlantic to Pacific, plus Africa and Southeast Asia. Dispersive, migratory or partially migratory, in West Palearctic greatest movement in north of range. Polytypic: nominate *cinerea* occurs western and central Eurasia and Africa; *monicae* coastal northwest Africa; *jouyi* Japan, China, Southeast Asia; *firasa* Madagascar. National 14% increase 1994–99 (Bashford & Noble 2000). Green-listed in UK: In need of basic conservation assistance (Gregory *et al.* 2002).

Grey Herons can be encountered on an almost daily basis but tend to concentrate in any numbers at only a few known locations, e.g. Tresco Pools, or at Porth Hellick Pool on St Mary's. They also show a marked tendency to feed in tidal pools, where they can often now be seen alongside Little Egrets *Egretta garzetta*, and at a few favoured roosting sites, e.g. Puffin Island at Samson's northern end.

Bone remains of this species were unearthed from prehistoric sites at May's Hill, St Martin's and on Nornour in the Eastern Isles (Turk 1971, 1984a, 1984b). Those from St Martin's are thought to originate from between the 2nd and 7th centuries AD. Other than this, the earliest reference seems to be Camden's comment that 'all the islands abound with rabbits, cranes, swans, herons and seafowl' (Camden 1610). This is followed by Robert Heath's mention of 'Herons' among his list of 'Sea-Birds' recorded in the islands (Heath 1750). Unfortunately, neither author was more specific. The normally informative E H Rodd described the 'Common Heron' as quite often seen in mainland Cornwall, observing too that it spent much time feeding in creeks and estuaries (Rodd 1880). However, his only apparent mention of herons on Scilly are contained in his remarks regarding the Spoonbill *Platalea leucorodia* shot on Hedge Rock, south of Tean, in 1871, commenting that the site was 'frequented by herons', and in his supplementary list of *Birds Recorded in the Scilly Islands* in which he claimed it might breed on 'Stack Rock' (Rodd 1880) – presumably what we now know as Hedge Rock.

By comparison, E H Rodd's nephew Francis and his co-author James Clark had much to say (Clark & Rodd 1906), pointing out that even in the early 20th century it occurred year-round. They also confirmed its fondness for roosting on isolated tidal rocks, making particular mention of Guthers Island to the south of St Martin's, stating too that 20–30 birds were regularly to be seen at such roost sites and suggesting this could occasionally increase to 60. In addition, they suggested that where freshwater pools were used for fishing, as on Tresco, this was mostly at night. Particularly important is their observation that 'most, if not all, the birds are immature', as is their confirmation that none had been found breeding, or even attempting to breed. In this last respect they usefully highlighted a report from around 1900 that a pair had built a nest on what they described as 'Inner Innisvouls', presumably Great Innisvouls, confirming that no trace of a nest could be found.

Broadly speaking, nothing much seems to have changed in the past 100 years. Adult Grey Herons remain something of a rarity, or certainly adults in breeding plumage, and pretty much the same tidal rocks are still in use as roosts today. Birds seem mainly distributed between St Mary's and Tresco, doubtless in response to available areas of open fresh water and trees for roosting, though tidal feeding perhaps predominates. Because birds are so spread out among the islands, however, there are difficulties involved in getting anything like a meaningful count, though it seems clear there are seasonal fluctuations. An obvious build-up in numbers during late summer and early autumn is followed by a general decline towards winter, to perhaps as few as 10–15 individuals through to the following summer, at which time there may be a further decrease, to as little as five even, before the annual autumn influx.

However, it seems possible, indeed even inevitable, that some birds will get missed and so we can perhaps use two specific events to gauge the accuracy of what are otherwise mostly random counts. The first of these involved Porth Hellick Pool, which in 1990 dried out almost completely, exposing an apparently large number of Eels *Anguilla anguilla*, or perhaps mullet *Mugilidae*. One inevitable consequence of this was a rapid build-up of feeding herons, which increased from 22 on 10th September to a peak of 37 on 5th October, on which date 20 were seen roosting on Puffin Island in Tresco Channel. The second useful event concerned the RSPB-organised 1997 Winter Shorebird Survey, which recorded a total of 25 individuals. The survey also demonstrated how widely distributed birds are at this time of year, with nine around coastal St Mary's, two Tresco, seven Bryher, one St Agnes, two St Martin's and four Samson. Although these counts were limited to birds feeding around the coast, only St Mary's and Tresco seem likely to have held additional inland birds. The most often-counted roosts seem to be Puffin Island, between Samson and Bryher, where 15 or so birds appears to be normal, plus the roost tree at the southwest corner of Tresco Great Pool, which has held about the same number. Uninformed remarks by one or two visiting observers in the early to middle part of the 20th century to the effect that birds were breeding on this or that cliff are not supported by fact and seem mainly prompted by an unfamiliarity with the behaviour of this species in Scilly.

As with most European herons, post-fledging dispersal is entirely random, although south or southwest movement predominates. According to Cramp *et al.* (1977–94), the British population is non-migratory, unlike those in continental Europe, and young birds move on average only 150 km, though some reach Ireland, the Low Countries, France, Spain or even West Africa (Wernham *et al.* 2002). By comparison, Continental birds move greater distances, with recoveries of 300–400 km common and with an obvious association between time and distance: an average of 150 km in June increasing to 250 km in August. Some Norwegian birds migrate, mainly to winter in Britain and Ireland, and some central and eastern

European birds also migrate, mostly on a south or southwest heading, with those in the northeast showing the strongest tendency to move. Of all foreign-ringed British recoveries, 53% originated from Norway and were ringed as nestlings, though most Norwegian recoveries came from northern Britain or Ireland (Wernham *et al.* 2002). Return passage from wintering areas commences in February with most breeding sites reoccupied by March, though some non-breeders may remain. All of which fits the pattern of arrivals and departures from Scilly and suggests that the autumn build-up is composed mainly of dispersing juveniles, as evident from the lack of adults. Nevertheless, there may well be an element of migration involved, particularly in view of the first-year individual ringed in Norway in May 1994 and still present in Lower Moors, St Mary's on 23rd May 1995.

The distinctly different New World species, Great Blue Heron *A. herodias* (though still considered by some authorities as conspecific with Grey Heron), has reached western Europe on several occasions (King & Curber 1972) and could be confused with Grey Heron. It breeds throughout North America south into the Caribbean and Mexico, and northern populations are migratory, with a period of random post-fledging dispersal followed by southward migration from mid-September to late October (Cramp *et al.* 1977–94). Its possible presence in Scilly should constantly be kept in mind, particularly in autumn (regarding the possibility of confusing the all-white phase of Great Blue Heron with Great White Egret *Ardea alba* see that species).

**Recoveries**
271542   Pul   Rogaland, Norway 10th May 1994        FR   Lower Moors, St Mary's 23rd May 1995

**Grey Heron Ringing Recaptures**

# Purple Heron *Ardea purpurea* A

**Rare migrant, mainly in spring. Treated by the BBRC as a national Scarce Migrant, full written description required by the SRP.**

    1858   One (shot but not killed) Tresco 5th November   Clark & Rodd 1906
    1878   One (immature) (shot) St Mary's 30th August   Rodd 1878a; Clark & Rodd 1906
    1898   One (immature) Tresco & (shot) St Mary's April   Clark & Rodd 1906
    1944   One Scilly 25th April   *CBWPSAR* 14
    1945   Two (adult & subadult) Tresco 17th April   *CBWPSAR* 15
    1950   One St Martin's 3rd April (exhausted – died)   *CBWPSAR* 20
    1958   One (subadult) St Mary's & St Agnes 22nd to 24th April
    1961   One (subadult) Tresco 29th April
    1961   Up to three St Mary's 27th April to 23rd May
    1962   One (adult male) Porth Hellick, St Mary's 10th to 23rd May
    1966   One (subadult) St Mary's 1st to 30th May
    1966   One (subadult) Tresco 14th to 18th May
    1970   One (adult) St Mary's & St Agnes 26th Apr to 3rd June
    1970   One St Agnes 11th May
    1970   One Annet 23rd May
    1970   One (adult) St Mary's 30th May (found dead – previously ringed)
    1970   One (subadult) St Agnes 13th October
    1975   One St Mary's 23rd April to 22nd May
    1977   One St Mary's 26th April to 9th June
    1979   One (subadult) St Mary's 2nd October
    1981   One (subadult) St Agnes & St Mary's 9th to 11th April (found dead 14th)
    1981   One (adult) St Mary's & Tresco 3rd to 10th May
    1999   One (adult) Porth Hellick, St Mary's, Samson, Bryher & Tresco 25th April to 22nd May
    1999   One (subadult) Porth Hellick, St Mary's 26th April to 16th May
    2000   One (first-year) Tresco 23rd & 24th September

Breeds central and eastern Europe, southwest Asia, India, Southeast Asia and central and eastern Africa south of Sahara. West Palearctic population fragmentary, breeding coastal North Africa, including Cape

Verde Islands, and Iberia, north to the Netherlands and east to Caspian Sea. Migratory and dispersive; most European birds winter Africa south of Sahara. Polytypic: nominate *purpurea* occurs southwest West Palearctic to Caspian Sea and Iran, plus east and southern Africa; *bournei* Cape Verde Islands; further forms in Madagascar and Southeast Asia. Removed from BBRC Rarities List in January 1983 (Grant 1982b).

E H Rodd described three birds killed in mainland Cornwall prior to his receipt of a fresh specimen from Scilly on 2nd September 1878 (Rodd 1880). Other than that, he made no mention of this species on Scilly, but, fortunately, his nephew Francis Rodd and Francis's co-author, James Clark, fill in some of the gaps (Clark & Rodd 1906). According to these two, a Mr Fylton shot a heron on 5th November 1858 on Tresco, probably near where the Island Hotel now stands, knocking out a few feathers but not killing the bird. However, he took back a feather to the Abbey, where Augustus Pechell identified it as coming from this species. The same authors provided details of a bird seen initially on Tresco in April 1898 but eventually killed on St Mary's.

The earliest 20th century sighting concerned a bird seen in April 1944 and this was followed by two more sightings prior to the formation of the BBRC in 1958, after which all records were subject to full investigation by the national committee. The Chart includes arrival dates for all except the shot birds and shows a clear spring bias, with a late April peak. Dealing with records from 1958 onwards, a total of 21 birds arrived in ten (24%) of the 42 years up to and including 2000, with 5 in 1970 being the highest in any one year. The earliest spring arrival date was 3rd April and the latest 30th May, which was also the last spring date any bird was recorded. Earliest of the three autumn arrivals was 23rd September and the latest a one-day bird on 13th October.

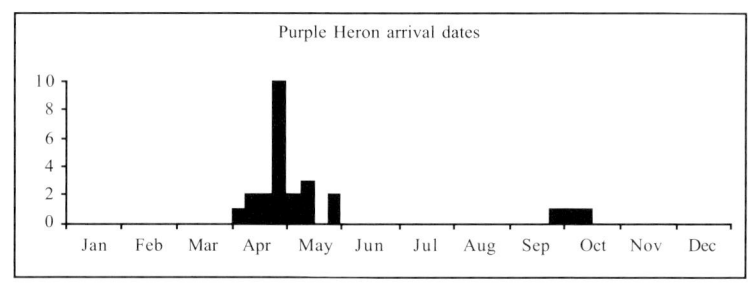

Purple Heron arrival dates

Spring passage commences early March, with the majority of birds reaching the breeding areas during April and May, though it is known to regularly overshoot during periods of southerly wind and make an annual appearance in Britain (Cramp *et al.* 1977–94). Presumably, the majority of birds involved were heading for breeding colonies in Iberia or France, where it breeds as close to Britain as southern Brittany. A bird found dead on St Mary's on 30th May 1970, however, had been ringed as a nestling at Noorden, Netherlands, in June two years earlier, suggesting that at least some Purple Herons reaching Scilly in spring may be off-course, rather than overshooting. There were a total of 29 records for mainland Cornwall up to and including 1999 (*CBWPSAR* 69). One interesting but difficult question to answer is what do large herons find to eat on Scilly, given the general lack of freshwater fish and amphibians. Part of the answer perhaps is that they adopt an opportunist approach to survival, as indeed did the Purple Heron seen to take and swallow an incautious Song Thrush *Turdus philomelos* that wandered too close to the motionless heron (*IOSBR* 1995). The mounted skin of one of three 19th century individuals is in the Isles of Scilly Museum on St Mary's.

Recoveries
8022276   Pul   Noorden, Netherlands 6th June 1968   FD   St Mary's 30th May 1970

**Purple Heron Ringing Recaptures**

# Black Stork *Ciconia nigra* A BBRC 1.7%

**Very rare migrant, full written description required by the BBRC.**
    1887   One (shot) Tresco September   Clark & Rodd 1906
    1890   One (shot) Scilly 8th May   Clark & Rodd 1906; *British Birds* 1: 350

1979    One (in flight) St Agnes 25th May    *British Birds* 73: 496
1985    One St Agnes 28th & 29th August    *British Birds* 79: 532
2001    One (in flight) St Agnes & St Mary's 27th August    *British Birds* 95: 483

Breeds central Europe east to Pacific, outlying population Iberia and southern Africa; central and southern European population fragmentary. European birds winter Africa. Monotypic.

Just five so-far accepted records, spanning a period of 114 years. Earliest was a bird reportedly shot on Tresco in September 1887, followed by one shot by A A Dorrien-Smith in May 1890, presumably also on Tresco (Harting 1890; Clark & Rodd 1906). More recently, one was watched flying west out to sea past Wingletang, St Agnes, on 25th May 1979 (*IOSBR* 1979). Understanding exactly where landbirds might be heading when observed taking a westerly course from the islands is difficult. Although one explanation here could be an overshooting spring migrant from further south attempting to correct the error. Another on St Agnes on 29th August 1985 was probably the 'huge black bird' reported over that same island the previous evening. It paid a brief visit to Samson but had left the islands by the following day (*IOSBR* 1985). The fifth, on the closely similar date of 27th August, was watched in flight by resident birders attending the island's annual summer carnival along the Strand in Hugh Town; this possibly being the same as that seen over south Devon from 28th to 30th (*Birding World* 14: 498).

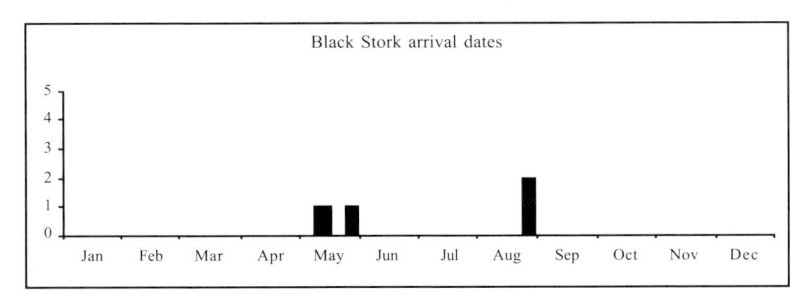

Black Stork arrival dates

There were 26 British and Irish records prior to 1958, mostly from the 19th century. More recently, the number of reports has increased, doubtless reflecting Black Stork's improved status in western Europe, with birds now breeding as close as northeastern France (Dymond *et al.* 1989; Hagemeijer & Blair 1997). Between 1958 and 1999 the BBRC accepted a total of 116 British records, of which the two Scillonian arrivals represent under 2%. Returning birds reach northern breeding areas from late March to late April and therefore the two in May could have been either overshooting or off-course migrants. The three late summer arrivals are less easily explained but possibly involved post-fledging dispersal prior to them moving south. The mounted skin of one or other of the two 19th century individuals is currently in the Isles of Scilly Museum on St Mary's. There are 11 records of Black Stork from mainland Cornwall up to and including 1999 (*CBWPSAR* 68). The Chart excludes the shot 1887 individual.

# White Stork                                                    *Ciconia ciconia*  A

**Very rare migrant. Treated by the BBRC as a national Scarce Migrant, full written description required by the SRP.**

1971    Two St Mary's, Samson & Tresco 11th to 16th April    *British Birds* 65: 327
1971    Two (ringed immatures) St Mary's 12th, 13th & 18th September    *British Birds* 65: 327
1976    One St Mary's & Tresco 10th & 11th April    *British Birds* 70: 415
1977    One Tresco, St Agnes & St Mary's 10th & 11th September    *British Birds* 71: 491
1978    One St Agnes 1st August    *British Birds* 72: 511

Breeds central and southern Europe, northwest Africa, central and eastern Asia. European population winters central and eastern Africa south of Sahara. Polytypic: nominate *ciconia* occurs Europe, North Africa and Middle East; *asiatica* central Asia; *boyciana* east Asia. Removed from BBRC Rarities List in January 1983 (Grant 1982b).

Bone remains excavated from the prehistoric site on Nornour in the Eastern Isles were identified 'with reasonable certainty' as being from this species (Turk 1971, 1984b). The remains are thought to represent three individuals and date from sometime between the middle of the second millennium BC and the end of the fourth century AD. Regrettably it is not possible to know in what context these birds were present in the islands and, although the species is understood to have been more widely distributed in Europe formerly, they could have been either on passage or breeding in Scilly.

However, there appears to be no mention of this species in the islands in a modern context until they were visited by two birds in April 1971, and then, amazingly, by two different individuals in September that same year. The April birds arrived on St Mary's on 11th but soon moved to Tresco, where they remained together until 15th, though with occasional excursions to St Martin's and St Mary's. They roosted together in a tree beside the Great Pool and were seen feeding behind tractors working nearby fields, one even swallowing the remains of a Rabbit *Oryctolagus cuniculus* killed by a rotary hoe. By 16th, only one was to be seen and by the following day it too had departed (*IOSBR* 1971).

The two September individuals appeared on St Mary's Church in Hugh Town on the afternoon of Sunday 12th, and, as they showed every intention of roosting overnight, the Chaplain kindly agreed not to ring the church bells for evensong. The pair left Hugh Town next morning and were eventually spotted gaining height at 16.00 hours, preparatory to leaving the islands. They then headed east and were later seen in Penzance, west Cornwall, before making a brief reappearance in Scilly on 18th (*IOSBR* 1971). Both were aged as juveniles and both carried rings on their legs, the numbers being read through a telescope. They were subsequently identified as coming from a brood of three ringed in Denmark in September, one of which fell down a Somerset chimney as the three siblings made their way west across the breadth of southern England (*British Birds* 65: 4–5). One of the two survivors was later sighted in Madeira, even further out in the Atlantic, on 21st of the month, though by now it was in rather poor condition. Interestingly, even from the point of departure from their Danish nest, the three followed a heading 90° west of the normal direction taken by migrant Danish White Storks, which normally head southeast towards the Bosphorus.

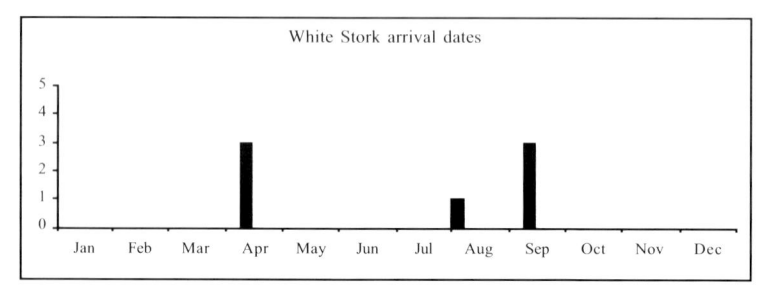

The remaining three records all involved brief visits of one to two days. The arrival dates of all seven birds are plotted on the Chart. There seems no reason to think that birds visiting Scilly are anything other than the nominate *ciconia*, which breeds as close as Spain, Portugal, France (recently in Brittany), the Low Countries, Germany and Denmark. There are 23 records of White Stork for mainland Cornwall up to and including 1999 (*CBWPSAR* 68).

**Recoveries**
DKC1351/52  Pul North Jutland, Denmark August 1971    FR  St Mary's 12th, 13th & 18th September

**White Stork Ringing Recaptures**

## Glossy Ibis  *Plegadis falcinellus*  A  BBRC 3.8%

**Rare migrant, mainly in autumn, full written description required by the BBRC.**

| | | |
|---|---|---|
| 1854 | One (shot) Tresco 19th September | Rodd 1854c; Clark & Rodd 1906 |
| 1866 | One (shot) Scilly 8th October | Rodd 1866c; Clark & Rodd 1906 |
| 1883 | One Tresco November | Clark & Rodd 1906 |
| 1902 | Two Tresco (one shot) 11th October | Clark & Rodd 1906; *British Birds* 1: 350 |
| 1932 | One 'Scilly' in autumn | Penhallurick 1969 |
| 1941 | Seven Tresco 18th to 31st October | Dorrien-Smith 1941 |
| 1978 | One Tresco 21st August to 17th September | *British Birds* 72: 512 |
| 1994 | One various islands 23rd to 27th September | *British Birds* 88: 500 |
| 1996 | One (subadult) Tresco & St Mary's 16th May to 12th June | *British Birds* 90: 460 |

Fragmentary breeding range, from southern Europe, central Asia and Africa east to India, Australasia, southern USA and Caribbean. Northern populations migratory with West Palearctic birds wintering south to Africa. Polytypic: *falcinellus* occurs southern Europe, North Africa, central Asia, southeast USA and Caribbean; *peregrinus* Madagascar, Indonesia and Australasia; status of other populations unclear.

E H Rodd was familiar with this species, emphasising that although it occurred occasionally in both Cornwall and Scilly this was always in autumn. He also pointed out that its appearance was all the more remarkable for the fact that it does not go further north to breed and concluded that there must be 'some other influence, at present unexplained, which brings them to our shores' (Rodd 1880). As with so many 19th century Scillonian records, the first for the islands involved a shot bird, an immature obtained on Tresco by John Jenkinson on 19th September 1854 (Rodd 1854c). This was followed 12 years later by another immature on 8th October 1866, again shot by John Jenkinson (Rodd 1866c). However, a bird present in November 1883 was more fortunate, being recorded as a sight record only.

The fourth record, on 11th October 1902, is of particular interest. It involved two birds seen flying towards Tresco from the west, one of which was shot by A A Dorrien-Smith near the Abbey, leaving the other to fly on over Pentle Rock, still heading east (Clark & Rodd 1906).

There is little information on the next sighting, in 1932, but the flock of seven in 1941, presumably on Tresco, were reported by A A Dorrien-Smith, whilst the 1978 bird, another immature, remained around Tresco's Great pool from 19th August and was last seen on 17th September. The 1994 individual, another immature, was first seen on the Hayle Estuary in west Cornwall, arriving on Samson on 23rd September before quickly moving to Bryher and then Tresco, visiting St Mary's the next day. However, it soon settled back on Tresco and was last seen leaving that island and flying away high to the northeast on 27th. The most recent to grace Scilly arrived in mid-May 1996 and visited all occupied islands before departing on 13th June. It spent much of its stay feeding in various meadows, including beside Tresco Great Pool and in the Parting Carn area of St Mary's, often attracting the attention of islanders.

According to Cramp *et al.* (1977–94), there has been a marked contraction in the Glossy Ibis breeding range in western and central Europe over the last 100 years, it having withdrawn from Spain, France, Italy and Austria, among others. Unsurprisingly, this has been reflected in a reduction in the numbers of sightings in Britain. The nearest breeding colonies are in the Balkans and therefore it is difficult to explain the presence of birds in Britain, though the species has a reputation for nomadic wandering (Cramp *et al.* 1977–94). In addition, juvenile post-breeding dispersal is extremely random, though first-years and others have commenced moving south by September, with most European birds probably crossing the Sahara. Northward passage commences late March, but with some still moving in early May. Interestingly, Dymond *et al.* (1989) found that for the period 1958–85 there were no spring arrivals nationally prior to 1975, though they stopped short of suggesting an explanation. The same authors thought an unknown percentage of records probably involved escapes, whilst also suggesting that the pattern of spring and autumn peaks points to most being genuinely wild individuals. The Chart includes all arrivals where a first date is known, and treats multiple arrivals as a single date. It compares favourably with the findings of Dymond *et al.* regarding the probability of genuinely wild birds being involved. The only spring arrival was on 16th May, remaining until 12 June. The earliest autumn date was 21st August and the latest autumn arrival some time in November, which was also the latest any bird was recorded in the islands. The mounted skin of one of the shot 19th-or early 20th century birds is in the Isles of Scilly Museum on St Mary's. T A Dorrien-

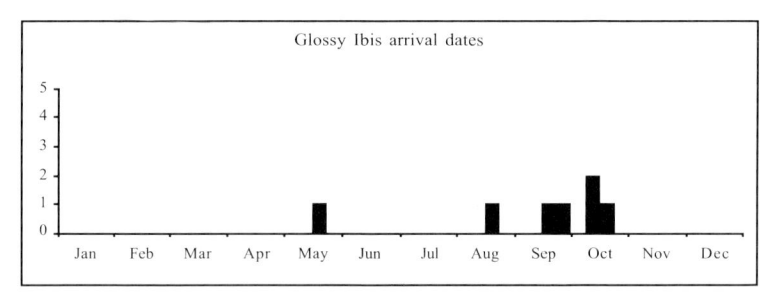

Smith attributed the pre-1950s individuals to the form *falcinellus*, perhaps correctly but without giving details (Dorrien-Smith 1951).

There were 78 records accepted by the BBRC during the period 1958–99, thus the three most recent Scillonian arrivals represent just under 4% of the national total. There were 36 records of Glossy Ibis for mainland Cornwall up to and including 1999.

## Spoonbill (Eurasian Spoonbill) *Platalea leucorodia* A

**Rare migrant, mainly in spring. Treated by the BBRC as a national Scarce Migrant, full written description required by the SRP.**

| | | |
|---|---|---|
| 1850 | One (adult male) shot Scilly 7th June | Rodd 1880; Clark & Rodd 1906 |
| 1860s | Three Abbey Pool, Tresco | Clark & Rodd 1906 |
| 1869 | One Tresco August | Anon 1869; Rodd 1880 |
| 1870 | One Abbey Pool, Tresco April | Rodd 1880 |
| 1871 | One (shot) Hedge Rock January | Rodd 1880 |
| 1871–72 | One (shot) Scilly | Rodd 1880 |
| 1898 | One Scilly 16th October | Clark & Rodd 1906 |
| 1909 | At least one Tresco October | Penhallurick 1969 |
| 1941 | Thirteen 2nd October, at least five to 13th, presumably Tresco | Dorrien-Smith 1941 |
| 1942 | Three 4th October to early December, two to 28th December | *CBWPSAR* 12 |
| 1943 | One Scilly November 8th for 'few days' | *CBWPSAR* 14 |
| 1945 | Two Scilly 15th November | *CBWPSAR* 15 |
| 1966 | One (subadult) St Mary's 23rd to 27th November | |
| 1966 | Seven St Mary's & Agnes 24th November | |
| 1974 | One various islands 28th May to 3rd July | |
| 1983 | One Great Pool, Tresco 22nd October | |
| 1988 | One Tresco and St Mary's 20th to 23rd October | |
| 1996 | Three Eastern Isles, Tresco, Bryher, St Mary's 24th & 25th May | |
| 1998 | Two St Martin's & Tresco 11th May (one ringed Netherlands) | |
| 1999 | One (adult) Great Pool, Tresco, 27th May to 5th June | |

Breeds central and southern Europe, central and eastern Asia, Red Sea and India. European population fragmentary and migratory, wintering Nile Valley and Africa north of equator. Polytypic: nominate *leucorodia* occurs Palearctic, India; *balsaci* Mauritania; *archeri* Red Sea and Somalia. Included on Annex I of 1979 EEC 'Birds Directive'. Upgraded from Green- to Amber-listed in UK 2002: five-year mean of 3.2 breeding pairs; unfavourable European conservation status (Gregory *et al.* 2002).

A total of at least 46 individuals involved in 20 sightings in 18 or 19 different years, 12 of these in the 20th century. Seven arrivals involved more than one individual, the largest flock being 13 in October 1941 (Dorrien-Smith 1941). After 150 years of speculation on where birds visiting Scilly originate, the answer probably came in 1998.

Between them E H Rodd (Rodd 1880), Rodd's nephew Francis and his co-author James Clark (Clark & Rodd 1906) documented at least seven occasions where one or more individuals were present in Scilly up to the end of the 19th century, at least three of which were shot. The first of these, in the unusual month of June, was a male in full breeding plumage (Rodd 1880). Being large, white and in any event distinctive, we can hopefully rely upon most reported sightings, although a bird that fed in shallow tidal waters around Hedge Rock, south of Tean, for some months in late 1870 was mistaken for a Great White Egret *Ardea alba*, until shot in January 1871 (Rodd 1880).

The Chart includes all known arrival dates (treating multiple arrivals as a single date) and shows a clear pattern of spring and autumn presence. The earliest spring arrival was 11th May and the latest 7th June, which was also the last date any bird was recorded in the early part of the year. The earliest autumn arrival was on 2nd October and the latest on 24th November, with more than one individual remaining almost into the following year.

One of two that visited the islands on 11th May 1998 carried a colour-ring combination identifying it as from the Netherlands' breeding population (*IOSBR* 1998). In itself the cluster of dates around May and early June are suggestive of overshooting or off-course migrants, the real point at issue being where from, or where to? However, there have now been enough international sightings of colour-ringed Spoonbills from Netherlands' breeding colonies to establish links with West African wintering areas, with individuals identified during winter in Senegal (pers. obs.) and Gambia (Cramp *et al*. 1977–94) and on passage in Morocco (pers. obs.) and Canary Islands (Cramp *et al*. 1977–94). Indeed, considering that the next nearest breeding populations to Britain after the Netherlands are in either southern Spain or eastern Europe, the Netherlands seems the most likely source of any reaching Scilly, though overshooting Spanish birds cannot be ruled out. The mounted skin of one or other of the three shot individuals is in the Isles of Scilly Museum on St Mary's.

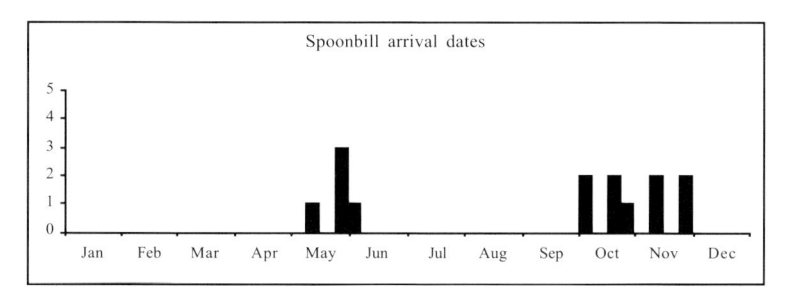

Spoonbill arrival dates

Some arrive back in the Netherlands by late February but the bulk return late March or April, with any later arrivals likely to involve non-breeders, which tend to wander in summer (Cramp *et al*. 1977–94). There is a brief period of, usually, short-distance post-fledging dispersal, with birds from the Netherlands reaching Germany, southeast England and the Azores. However, the main southward departure from European colonies occurs August–September, with few remaining into October. Especially in mild winters, individuals occasionally remain in Europe, including southwest England and Ireland. On this basis the May–June Scillonian spring sightings are suggestive of returning non-breeders from the Netherlands (Wernham *et al*. 2002). However, the source of the autumn arrivals, which are rather late, is less clear and could presumably involve wanderers from populations further east. A total of 202 Spoonbills were recorded on mainland Cornwall up to and including 1999 (*CBWPSAR* 69).

**Recoveries**
? ? ? Netherlands FR St Martin's & Tresco 11th May 1998

**Spoonbill Ringing Recaptures**

# Mute Swan *Cygnus olor* A & C

**Resident, breeds in very small numbers, birds from elsewhere may occasionally visit and even remain.**

Fragmentary breeding distribution across central Eurasia, with introduced population elsewhere, e.g. Australia, North America. West European populations now extensively dependent on humanly modified habitats. Monotypic. Birds in northern Europe largely migratory. BTO Waterways Bird Survey showed 76% increase 1975–2000. Upgraded from Green- to Amber-listed in UK 2002: 21.7% of European breeding population in UK (Gregory *et al*. 2002).

There is an early reference to all the islands of Scilly abounding with 'swans' (Camden 1610), but it remains doubtful which swans were involved, or indeed whether any swan species really was ever that numerous in Scilly. Significantly, E H Rodd (1880) made no specific mention of a Mute Swan presence in Cornwall or Scilly, other than to suggest, under his heading Whooper Swan *C. cygnus*, that a report of three of that species at Falmouth in 1851 probably involved escaped individuals of the present species, particularly as a nest was built 'on the sedge bank' and eggs laid. He pointedly asked, 'May not these have been escaped and partially wild examples of the Mute Swan, *Cygnus olor*, which is known only with us as a domesticated species?' In fact, Penhallurick (1969) referred to the area known as Swan Pool close to Falmouth and known to have contained domesticated swans at least until 1700.

So it fell to E H Rodd's nephew Francis and co-author James Clark to note that several Mute Swans were shot on Scilly during the winter of 1870–71 (Clark & Rodd 1906), though in view of the elder Rodd's earlier comments these records too may seem doubtful. However, Clark and Rodd referred to an arrival of 12 Bewick's Swans *C. bewickii* on Tresco's pools at Christmas 1890, some of which were shot and some of which flew away, whilst four remained among the 'tame' swans and other waterfowl, later associating with the four survivors out of a group of six Whooper Swans that arrived on 20th January.

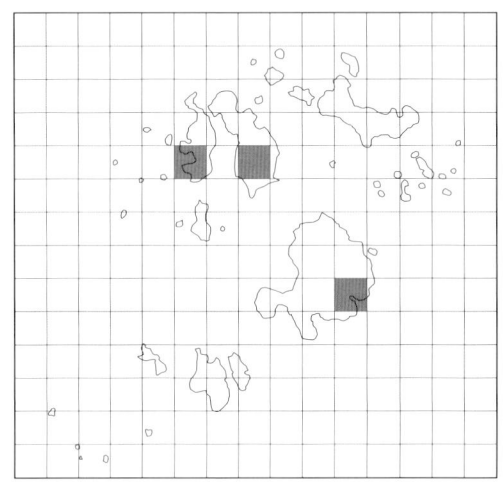

The same authors also mentioned the arrival of nine more Bewick's Swans about 1895, pointing out that they remained on Tresco for some five weeks before being 'driven away by the other swans'. Regrettably, the other swans are not named but Clark and Rodd's description seems highly suggestive of breeding Mute Swan behaviour.

Nonetheless, the true status of Mute Swans in Scilly throughout the 19th and first half of the 20th century remains obscure. In fact, the first 20t century record is probably an oblique mention, under the heading 'Whooper Swan', of an adult and then three subadults on St Agnes from July 1953 until April 1954 (*CBWPSAR* 23), this being followed by increasing mention of it in small numbers on St Agnes and elsewhere from around 1958. In its 1961–62 report, the St Agnes Bird Observatory noted 'more records than usual' on that island, i.e. up to nine, suggesting these had come from Tresco. This was soon followed by the SABO revelation that a pair

**1-km Mute Swan Breeding Distribution – 2000–01 (data Chown & Lock 2002)**

bred on Tresco in 1963 and two pairs in 1964, with a pair also on St Mary's in the latter year. Then, in fairly quick succession, we read of pairs breeding on Bryher (1970–71) and on Tresco again in 1973 (*IOSBR* 1970, 1971, 1973). From all of this we are led to believe that Mute Swans were probably present on Tresco as confined or feral breeders from perhaps the end of the 19th century, but probably went unrecorded until such time as they commenced appearing on other islands in the group. Certainly, by the mid-1980s up to 20 were noted in the islands in some years, though the drought of 1976 seems to have reduced them to just two pairs the following year.

Interestingly, the situation has not changed greatly, with reports for the ten years 1990–99 showing an overall presence of up to 35 birds annually, mainly on Tresco's two freshwater pools and on Porth Hellick Pool, St Mary's, plus occasionally the two smaller brackish pools on St Agnes and Bryher, but with a few birds also feeding in tidal waters around sheltered coasts. Within that same period one to two pairs bred annually on Tresco, though for reasons that are unclear this rose to around six pairs in 1995. Productivity appears to have been generally low, however. The only breeding recorded away from Tresco within the 1990s concerned a pair that raised three young from a clutch of seven eggs on Porth Hellick Pool, St Mary's, in 1992, having arrived at the site the previous autumn. The 2000 Breeding Atlas recorded Mute Swan in just three (4.4%) of the 67 1-km squares surveyed, with a count of five pairs and with breeding confirmed in just two squares (Chown & Lock 2002).

There are various suggestions in the published reports of at least occasional autumn influxes, or of birds leaving the islands, but evidence for this is unclear and these suggestions presumably rely on apparent increases in periodic all-island counts. Certainly, there seems to be no published account of birds seen arriving or leaving the islands and no sightings of birds from the *RMV Scillonian* between Scilly and mainland Cornwall. During winter wildfowl shoots on Tresco, Mute Swans – and other waterfowl – may temporarily vacate that island, boosting numbers feeding elsewhere. Allegedly, even at a level of up to 20 birds, the Tresco flock may qualify as the greatest concentration of Mute Swans in Cornwall (Owen *et al.* 1986).

## Bewick's Swan (Tundra Swan) *Cygnus columbianus* A

**Rare migrant or winter visitor.**

| | |
|---|---|
| 1890 | Twelve (four shot) Tresco Christmas to 23rd March 1891   Clark & Rodd 1906 |
| 1895 | Nine Tresco in winter for five weeks   Clark & Rodd 1906 |
| 1938 | At least thirteen 21st December to 4th January 1939   Witherby 1939 |
| 1956 | Three St Agnes & St Mary's 30th March to 1st April |
| 1962 | One Tresco 24th November |
| 1963 | Two St Agnes 14th to 20th January |
| 1963 | One St Mary's 30th November |
| 1968 | Two Tresco 22nd November to mid-December |
| 1971 | One (adult) St Agnes 2nd October |
| 1987 | One (very confiding) Lower Moors, St Mary's 21st January to 2nd February (dead 14th) |
| 1990 | Three St Mary's & Tresco 24th October to 17th December |
| 1991 | Four (two adults & two immatures) Great Pool, Tresco 21st November to 12th January 1992 |
| 1992 | One in flight Tresco 26th October |

Subarctic distribution, from Novaya Zemlya and adjacent mainland Russia east to northeast Siberia, plus North America. Polytypic: nominate *columbianus* or 'Tundra/Whistling Swan' occurs North America; *bewickii* elsewhere. Migratory, entire Eurasian population winters western Europe. Included on Annex I of 1979 EEC 'Birds Directive'. Amber-listed in UK: 20% or more of northwest-European non-breeding population occurs in UK, 50% or more at ten or fewer sites; unfavourable world winter conservation status (Gregory *et al.* 2002).

Apparently not common in Cornwall during the 19th century and perhaps mainly confined to captivity. E H Rodd's only reference in his *The Birds of Cornwall and The Isles of Scilly* was that it was for a long time confused with the larger Whooper Swan *C. cygnus* and that it 'may be included in the Cornish avifauna, and is represented in my collection by a specimen killed in this county' (Rodd 1880). However, his nephew Francis and co-author James Clark were more helpful, documenting the arrival of 12 on the Tresco pools at Christmas 1890. Four of these were shot and four (perhaps understandably) flew away, leaving four to subsequently take up company with four out of six Whooper Swans that arrived on 20th January, eventually becoming 'exceedingly restless' and departing the islands on 23rd March, two days after the Whoopers (Clark & Rodd 1906). They were watched by A A Dorrien-Smith as they flew out over the Eastern Isles in the direction of mainland Cornwall.

About 1895, four adult and five reported young Bewick's Swans appeared on Tresco (presumably in winter), staying for five weeks before being 'driven way by the other swans' (see Mute Swan *C. olor*); they are recorded as being 'remarkably tame' (Clark & Rodd 1906). There is a far earlier reference to all the islands abounding with 'swans' but it is not possible to say which species were involved, or even the time of year (Camden 1610).

There are just eleven 20th century records, involving a minimum of 32 individuals in ten different years, all of which appear to have been the Eurasian *bewickii*. The Chart includes all eleven known arrival dates and reveals a pattern similar to that of several other large waterfowl, of mainly autumn appearances but with others reaching the islands through into midwinter. Typically, birds arrive in ones or twos, but the three early appearances all involved small flocks, the 1938 group, which accompanied an arrival of Whooper Swans, representing part of a massive influx of Bewick's into Britain during winter 1938–39 (Witherby 1939). Within the British Isles, Bewick's Swans winter commonly in England west as far as the Somerset Levels, and small groups regularly penetrate into Cornwall (see below), whereas in Ireland it reaches the southern coast (Lack 1986). Any of these wintering populations could account for birds reaching Scilly.

*Birds of the Isles of Scilly*

Nevertheless, Bewick's Swans wintering in continental Europe regularly wander as far as northwest France, in which case there may be some movement between Britain and France. However, with little suitable feeding habitat available in Scilly, the species seems unlikely to occur commonly in the archipelago and it is probable that at least some arrivals are accidental. Most visiting swans settle either on the Tresco pools or at Porth Hellick Pool on St Mary's, but also occasionally visit the two smaller pools on either St Agnes or Bryher.

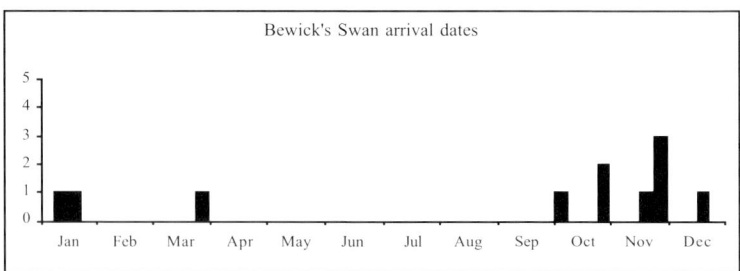

Bewick's Swan arrival dates

Some authorities treat the two forms as full species, Tundra Swan *C. columbianus* and Bewick's Swan *C. bewickii*, and observers should be alert to the possibility of the distinctive *columbianus* occurring in Scilly. Indeed, by the end of 1997, the BBRC had already accepted at least 13 sightings (Naylor 1998), including one individual as close to Scilly as mid-Somerset, though fewer than six birds may have been involved. On mainland Cornwall, Bewick's Swan occurs regularly in small numbers and has been annual since 1959, with a total of around 516 since 1930 (*CBWPSAR* 69).

## Whooper Swan                                                    *Cygnus cygnus* A

**Scarce migrant or winter visitor.**

Breeds northern and central Eurasia, from southern Sweden and northern Norway east to Pacific and south to Kazakhstan and Sakhalin, with a discrete population in Iceland. Monotypic. Most birds wholly migratory, in West Palearctic wintering British Isles, Norway, western continental Europe southeast to Caspian Sea. Included on Annex I of 1979 EEC 'Birds Directive'. Amber-listed in UK: five-year mean of 6.6 breeding pairs; 20% or more of northwest European non-breeding population occurs in UK, 50% or more at ten or fewer sites (Gregory *et al.* 2002).

There is a very early reference to all the islands of Scilly abounding with 'swans' (Camden 1610) but it is not possible to say which species was involved, or even the time of year in question. Nevertheless, it seems clear that when E H Rodd compiled his classic *The Birds of Cornwall and The Isles of Scilly* this was the commonest of the three swan species in Cornwall (Rodd 1880), even though it only appeared in winter, and even then generally only 'after a long continuance of hard frost, when it visits the harbours and estuaries as well as the larger rivers'. Rodd also mentioned a report of three Whooper Swans (which he alternatively referred to as 'Wild Swan') in Carrick Roads near Falmouth in 1851, one being shot by the captain of a French ship. The remaining pair allegedly built a nest on the sedge bank and Rodd suggests, probably correctly, that this incident involved escaped domesticated Mute Swans *C. olor*.

E H Rodd noted it as occurring on Scilly in severe winters (Rodd 1880), though the first factual mention of Whooper Swan in Scilly comes from James Clark and E H Rodd's nephew Francis (Clark & Rodd 1906), who documented seven seen on Tresco on 20th November 1858. Following this record, Francis saw five on the same island on 28th December 1870 and then on 31st watched 'a fine flock of 17 Wild Swans' fly around a few times and depart southwards (Rodd 1880). Clark and Rodd go on to list the appearance of from two to seven birds in at least six more years up until 1895. None are then on record until the winter of 1938–39, when probably nine Whoopers reached the islands in company with 13 Bewick's *C. bewickii*, all of which formed part of a huge influx of these two species into the British Isles that winter (Witherby 1939).

Throughout the whole of the 20th century, birds are recorded arriving in only 27 years, involving a total of 110 individuals at an average of 4.03 per arrival year. Twenty in 1956 was the largest 20th century group, but 2–5 was more usual, and in nine years only singles were present. Birds tend to arrive about mid-

October, suggestive perhaps of some level of intended migration, and leave before the end of the year, though a few remain until early spring. The fact that birds have arrived in every year since 1988 (44% of the 27 years birds were present) suggests a recent increased use of the archipelago by Whooper Swans, confounding E H Rodd's 19th century assertion that arrivals of this species were normally associated with periods of particularly cold weather further north. An outstanding arrival on 23rd October 2002, the largest on record, involved at least 33 individuals. A bird that arrived in October 1968 was later found with gunshot wounds, despite Whooper Swans being legally protected. As with the two other European swan species, most Whoopers soon found the Tresco freshwater pools or Porth Hellick Pool on St Mary's, but also occasionally used the two smaller pools on St Agnes and Bryher.

In England and Wales, Whooper Swans normally only winter as far south as Gloucestershire and perhaps Somerset (Lack 1986), though individuals and groups do penetrate further; it is annual in mainland Cornwall, over 500 having been recorded since 1930 (*CBWPSAR* 69). However, the Icelandic population winters commonly in Scotland and in Ireland south to the coasts of counties Wexford, Waterford and Cork, and, therefore, birds reaching Scilly would seem most likely to originate from Iceland. Birds in eastern and southern England are thought more likely to form part of the continental-wintering Russian population, which regularly occupies the Low Countries and perhaps occasionally reaches even further west, and this is largely borne out by ringing recoveries (Wernham *et al.* 2002). It is therefore possible that at least some of these Scillonian arrivals involve Russian and not Icelandic Whooper Swans.

# Bean Goose *Anser fabalis* A

**Very rare migrant or winter visitor, full written description required by the SRP.**

| | | |
|---|---|---|
| 1876 | One (shot) Scilly | Clark & Rodd 1906 |
| 1879 | Three on 9th December | Clark & Rodd 1906 |
| 1882 | Two 15th January | Clark & Rodd 1906 |
| 1890–91 | Common about the islands | Clark & Rodd 1906 |
| 1905 | At least one Scilly | Clark & Rodd 1906 |
| 1974 | Four Porth Hellick, St Mary's 27th to 31st October | |
| 1974 | One Maypole, St Mary's 1st & 2nd November | |
| 1981 | One (*fabalis*) Tresco & St Mary's 9th to 30th October | |
| 1983 | One (*rossicus*) Tresco 13th June | |
| 1995 | Two (*rossicus*) Old Grimsby, Tresco 31st December to 29th March 1996 | |

Breeds northern Eurasia, from Norway and central Sweden east to Pacific, south to extreme northern Mongolia. Migratory, West Palearctic wintering range fragmentary, south to Iberia and Italy. Polytypic: nominate *fabalis* or 'Taiga Bean Goose' occurs northern Europe east to Urals; *rossicus* or 'Tundra Bean Goose' Russian tundra east to Taymyr peninsula; *johanseni* western Siberia east to Yenisey and Lake Baikal; two more forms further east. Amber-listed in UK: 50% or more of UK non-breeding population at 10 or fewer sites (Gregory *et al.* 2002).

Early evidence of this species in Scilly comes in the form of bone remains unearthed from the prehistoric site at May's Hill on St Martin's and believed to date from the 4th or 5th centuries AD (Turk 1984a, 1984b). There are a handful of records from the 19th century and these are mostly summarised by Clark & Rodd (1906), who described at as a reasonably common winter visitor in Scilly up to the 1860s, from which time it put in only an occasional appearance. They also listed specific incidents of one shot in 1876, three on 9th December 1879 and two on 15th January 1882, pointing out that it was 'fairly common' in the winter of 1890–91 with several gaggles about the islands. However, it was not then recorded again until November 1905. The only other early reference to this species seems to be Gilbert White's comment (in Jesse 1887) that 'a few visit the islands at certain periods in winter, with east winds'. Although E H Rodd made no specific mention of this species on Scilly, he helps clarify the wider picture, pointing out that, in his view, 90% of wild geese visiting Cornwall (and therefore presumably Scilly also) up until at least 1880 were of this particular species (Rodd 1880), commenting that 'after a hard frost of long continuance in the north, we usually notice arrivals of Bean Geese, sometimes in considerable numbers'.

The more modern records amount to just five arrivals in four different years, involving just nine individuals. In the three most recent years, birds involved were attributed racially, with one in 1981 considered

*Birds of the Isles of Scilly*

Bean Goose arrival dates

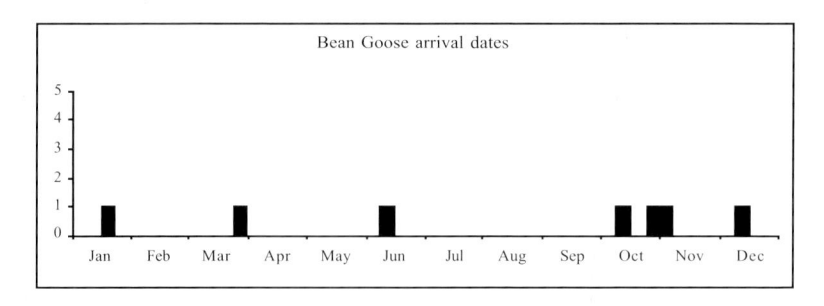

to have been nominate *fabalis*, the so-called 'Taiga Bean Goose', whereas birds in 1983 and 1995 were believed to have been *rossicus*, or 'Tundra Bean Goose'. *Fabalis* occurs from Scandinavia to central Asia and the somewhat smaller *rossicus* in northwest Asia (Cramp *et al.* 1977–94; Gantlett 1998, 2001). Future observers should concentrate on attributing any Bean Goose to a particular form. Given the date of the 1983 individual, its origins seem questionable, but the timing of the remainder appear much as might be expected. Unlike the other three grey geese, no 20th century Bean Goose records show birds as shot, though of course they may have been. According to Cramp *et al.* (1977–94), the British wintering population mostly comprises *fabalis*, which rarely appears before January. Therefore, considering the known Scillonian arrival dates, three of which are much earlier than January, plus the presence in at least two years of birds of the form *rossicus*, the suggestion is that these originated from continental Europe rather than Britain or Ireland. Interestingly, E H Rodd's observation that this was by far the commonest 19th century visitor no longer holds true for Scilly, with White-fronted Goose *A. albifrons* now much the most frequent of all geese.

On mainland Cornwall, the most recent sighting was of two in winter 1991–92, bringing the total number of individuals to around 20, most of which occurred in January (*CBWPSAR* 62).

## Pink-footed Goose *Anser brachyrhynchus* A & C

**Rare migrant or winter visitor, full written description required by the SRP.**

    1962   'Small party' St Agnes 5th October
    1972   Two St Agnes 23rd October
    1973   One Peninnis, St Mary's 1st & 2nd May
    1974   Fourteen (five shot) Annet, Tresco & St Mary's 27th September to 5th October
    1975   One St Agnes 11th October
    1981   One (shot) St Mary's & Tresco 22nd October to 1st November
    1988   One St Mary's & Tresco 27th April to 16th May
    1988   Six St Mary's 4th & 5th October
    1989   One Great Pool, Tresco 21st April to 30th May
    1990   Three Tresco 2nd November
    1992   One St Mary's & St Martin's 9th to 20th May
    1993   One Samson 24th October
    1994   Six St Mary's & St Agnes 29th September (one St Mary's & Tresco to 7th June 1995)
    1996   One over Hugh Town, St Mary's 6th October
    1997   One St Mary's & Tresco 7th to 29th May

Breeds Iceland, east Greenland, Spitsbergen. Migratory, populations from Iceland and Greenland winter Scotland, England and Ireland, those from Spitsbergen winter Germany, Denmark and Low Countries, occasionally Britain, Belgium, France. Monotypic. Amber-listed in UK: 100% of northwest European non-breeding population occurs in UK, 50% or more at ten or fewer sites (Gregory *et al.* 2002).

Surprisingly, there appear to be no records of this species in Scilly or on the Cornish mainland up to the end of the 19th century, regardless of it being the most abundant goose in Britain in winter. Penhallurick (1969) mentioned a James Clark letter recounting one seen in Scilly some time between 1906 and 1923. The next earliest record in the southwest is Penhallurick's own account of a single individual with 100 White-fronted Geese in west Cornwall in 1947.

[Chart: Pink-footed Goose arrival dates]

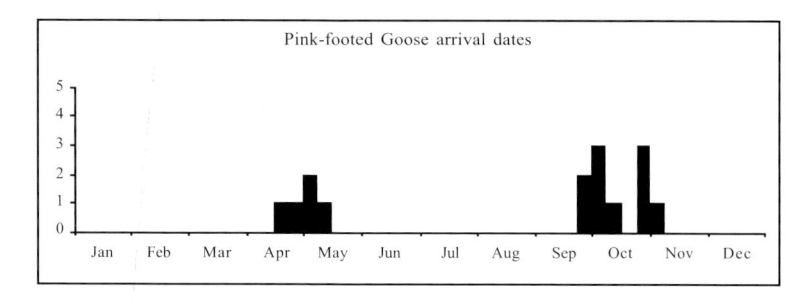

The earliest record on Scilly after Clark's bird was a small group seen and heard in flight over St Agnes in October 1962 and, whilst the next sighting was not until 1972, it had become almost annual by the 1990s. The Chart shows all arrival dates and perhaps the most obvious feature are the five spring records, which are perhaps accounted for by birds from the Spitsbergen population reaching as far south as France (Cramp *et al.* 1977–94). Analysis of the length of stay is equally interesting, with the nine autumn arrivals remaining for an average of only two days, whereas those in April and May spent an average of 19 days, perhaps putting on weight for the long flight back to their northern breeding grounds.

Up to and including 1999 the total for mainland Cornwall stood at around 85 individuals, the majority of which arrived in September and October (*CBWPSAR* 69).

# White-fronted Goose
# (Greater White-fronted Goose) *Anser albifrons* A

**Scarce migrant or winter visitor.**

- 1851–2  At least one Tresco   Clark & Rodd 1906
- 1854  'Two gaggles' October   Rodd 1854a; Clark & Rodd 1906
- 1859  At least three October   Clark & Rodd 1906
- 1879  October   Clark & Rodd 1906
- 1880  October   Clark & Rodd 1906
- 1890–01  In winter   Clark & Rodd 1906
- 1895  October   Clark & Rodd 1906
- 1950  Two Great Pool, Tresco 28th January (for few days)
- 1951  Three Lower Moors, St Mary's 9th to 11th November
- 1956  One (*flavirostris*) Tresco 26th to 29th February
- 1962  Five St Agnes February
- 1963  One (briefly) St Agnes 16th January
- 1964  One St Mary's 18th October
- 1964  Six (at least four shot) St Agnes & St Mary's 24th December
- 1966  Eight (all shot) St Mary's 25th & 26th October
- 1967  Two St Mary's 15th December
- 1968  One St Mary's 3rd November
- 1968  Five St Mary's 16th November
- 1972  Five Tresco 16th January
- 1972  One (*flavirostris*) St Mary's 24th October
- 1972  Twenty-four (twenty *flavirostris* and four *albifrons*) Tresco 24th & 25th October
- 1972  Twenty-five (20 *flavirostris*) Tresco 3rd to 5th November
- 1977  Two Eastern Isles 28th September
- 1977  Five (one *flavirostris* four shot) St Mary's 29th to 31st December, one to early January 1978
- 1980  One (*albifrons*) St Mary's Airport 17th & 18th October
- 1980  Thirteen (*flavirostris* – one shot) Tresco, Northwethel and nearby islands 22nd October to 19th April 1981
- 1981  Up to two (*albifrons*) St Mary's & Tresco 9th to 30th October

1982  One Blockhouse, Tresco 28th February to 14th April
1985  Four Tresco 22nd January
1987  Two St Mary's & St Agnes 8th October
1987  Up to two (*flavirostris*) St Mary's, Tresco & St Agnes 22nd to 30th October
1988  Three over Lower Moors, St Mary's 17th October
1989  Up to two (one *flavirostris*) St Mary's & Tresco 6th to 26th November
1990  Six (*flavirostris*) all islands 2nd November to 26th March 1991
1991  One (*flavirostris*) St Mary's & St Agnes 8th to 23rd May
1993  Two Tresco 14th October
1993  Up to two (*flavirostris*) St Mary's, Tresco & St Martin's 21st October
1998  One (*flavirostris*) Old Town, St Mary's 29th January
1998  One (*flavirostris*) St Martin's, St Agnes & Tresco 18th October to 20th February 1999
2002  One (*flavirostris*) St Agnes & St Mary's 21st to at least 27th October

Circumpolar subarctic breeding range, from Novaya Zemlya and adjacent mainland Russia east to arctic Canada and western Greenland. Polytypic: nominate *albifrons* or 'White-fronted Goose' occurs Kanin Peninsula and Novaya Zemlya east to Kolyma (eastern Russia); *frontalis* or 'Pacific White-fronted Goose' Kolyma east to central Canadian Arctic; *flavirostris* or 'Greenland White-fronted Goose' southwest Greenland; *gambelli* central northwest Canada; *elgasi* central-southern Alaska. Migratory, *albifrons* winters West Palearctic including Low Countries and France, but in British Isles is limited to southern England and perhaps South Wales; *flavirostris* winters Ireland, western Scotland and perhaps Wales; other forms winter further east (Cramp *et al.* 1977–94; Lack 1986). Amber-listed in UK: 20% or more of *flavirostris* non-breeding population occurs in UK, 50% or more at ten or fewer sites; moderate decline in numbers of *albifrons* wintering in UK over past 25 years (Gregory *et al.* 2002).

During the 19th century, White-fronted Goose was considered almost common in winter in both Cornwall and Scilly. E H Rodd described it as infrequently obtained in the Land's End area, but mentioned an account by Couch of a considerable invasion during winter 1829 (Rodd 1880). Referring specifically to Scilly, Rodd described it as 'not uncommon in winter'. However, Rodd's nephew Francis and co-author James Clark provided most of the information of value, listing birds seen or shot in Scilly in seven years during the second half of the 19th century. There was subsequently the familiar half century gap in the information before the first modern record, involving two on Tresco's Great Pool during midwinter 1950. There were a total of 33 arrivals in 23 (43%) of the years 1950–98. The Chart includes all arrivals for which the date is recorded, but omits the most recent, and shows a pattern very similar to that of Brent Goose *Branta bernicla*, i.e. an obvious concentrated autumn peak followed by a wider spread of winter arrivals. In 15 sightings where the racial identification of White-fronted Geese was determined, all but two involved *flavirostris*, or 'Greenland White-fronted Goose', which winters in western and northern Scotland and, more importantly, Ireland, with perhaps a few in Wales (Lack 1986), and this points the way perhaps to where most Scillonian White-fronts originate. It remains unclear, however, whether the obvious October–November peak involves overshooting birds from Ireland or birds intent on crossing to France, though the lack of a return spring passage perhaps favours the former. Interestingly, only three sightings involved the northern Eurasian *albifrons*, which winters as close to Scilly as southwest England, plus Belgium, Netherlands and France. Examination of arrival dates for both forms revealed no obvious differences, other than that all three *albifrons* fell within the marked October–November peak. There was no significant difference in the length of stay between autumn and winter and 14 arrivals remained for one day or less. A bird shot on 24th

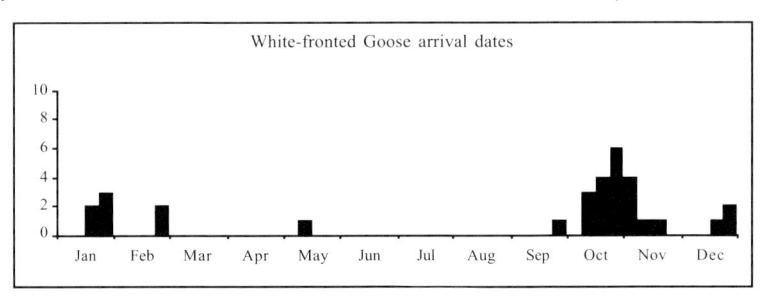

December 1964 on St Mary's had been ringed at Slimbridge, Gloucestershire, in March 1962, and, though the racial identity is uncertain, it was presumably *albifrons*, which shows a distinct tendency to reach southwest England (Wernham *et al.* 2002).

**Recoveries**
SWT575   Ad   (*albifrons?*) Slimbridge, Gloucestershire
                6th March 1962                                SH  St Mary's 24th December 1963

White-fronted Goose Ringing Recaptures

## Greylag Goose                                                    *Anser anser*   A & C

Rare migrant or winter visitor, full written description required by the SRP.

  1863   One (shot) Scilly November
  1870   At least one Abbey Green, Tresco October
  1885   At least two (shot) Scilly October
  1968   One St Mary's 3rd November
  1968   Two Castle Down, Tresco 5th to13th November
  1969   Two Tresco & Northwethel 28th April to 2nd May
  1974   Two St Agnes 28th March
  1975   One Tresco late November to 26th April 1976
  1978   One St Martin's & Tresco 10th October
  1983   One (*anser*) Tresco 30th April to 2nd May
  1983   One all islands 17th to 19th October
  1985   One Great Pool, Tresco 10th January to 8th April
  1986   One all islands 20th to 27th April
  1990   Three Tresco & St Mary's 27th October to 29th December
  1991   Two off St Agnes 16th April
  1993   One St Agnes & St Mary's 24th October
  1993   One (shot) St Mary's 25th October to 3rd November
  1993   Two Great Pool, Tresco 4th November to 7th April 1994
  1996   One Great Pool, Tresco 20th to 30th April
  1996   One St Mary's & Tresco 29th to 31st December to 18th March 1997
  1998   One Tresco 10th April

Breeds Eurasia, from Atlantic to Pacific, north to northern Norway and south to Mediterranean and Persian Gulf. Migratory or partially so, West Palearctic populations winter southern part of range to North Africa. Polytypic: nominate *anser* occurs west and northwest Europe; *rubrirostris*, or 'Eastern Greylag Goose' southeast and eastern Europe and Asia. Amber-listed in UK: 50% or more of UK breeding population at ten or fewer sites; 80% of northwest European non-breeding population occurs in UK, 50% or more at ten or fewer sites (Gregory *et al.* 2002). National 100% increase 1994–99 (Bashford & Noble 2000) includes introductions.

The probable earliest reference to wild geese in Scilly was by Robert Heath in his *Natural and Historical Account of the Island of Scilly – With a Description of Cornwall* (Heath 1750). Heath was an officer in the armed forces and served in the garrison on Scilly. Unfortunately, we have no way of knowing now which particular goose species were involved, or even whether they were resident or occurred only as migrants or winter visitors. However, there is a strong suggestion in what E H Rodd had to say later that this may have been the least likely of all the geese to have been recorded in southwest England during the 18th and 19th centuries (Rodd 1880). Rodd had not heard of it in Cornwall or the islands until one was shot in Marazion Marsh, just to the east of Penzance, and commented that 'it is evidently a much rarer bird with us then either the Bean (*A. fabalis*) or White-fronted Goose (*A. albifrons*), both of which occur almost every winter in varying numbers, according to the severity or mildness of the season'.

Rodd also provided us with the first definite record of Greylag Goose on Scilly, involving the carcass of a bird he received from the islands during the last week of November 1863, details of which were contained in a note to the *Zoologist* entitled 'Greylegged Geese near Penzance' (Rodd 1864a). Nonetheless, up until

*Birds of the Isles of Scilly*

the time of his death in 1880, Rodd knew of only three obtained in Cornwall or Scilly. And in fact, there were just two more records prior to the first 20th century sighting, namely one shot at and wounded by E H Rodd's nephew, Francis Rodd, on Tresco's Abbey Green in October 1870 and two killed at an unnamed location in October 1885 (Clark & Rodd 1906).

All traceable 20th century records are listed in the Table and all known arrival dates are charted, revealing an obvious pattern of mainly mid-spring and mid- to late autumn arrivals, similar to other geese, but with late birds continuing to reach the islands well into winter and often then remaining until spring. The latter presumably represents those cold-weather movements referred to earlier by E H Rodd. And as with Pink-footed Goose, spring arrivals remained for considerably less time on average (4.2 days) than those reaching the islands in the latter part of the year (51.9 days). The nominate form *anser* occurs generally throughout west and northwest Europe (though many British populations originate from introduced stock). Nevertheless, the possibility of the form *rubrirostris* or 'Eastern Greylag Goose' occurring should be considered when examining any birds in the field, even in Scilly.

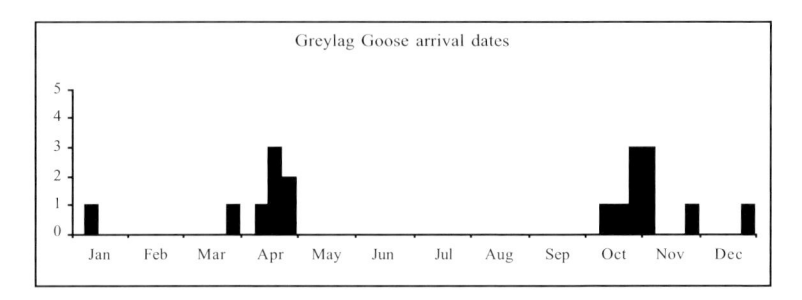

Greylag Goose arrival dates

In mainland Cornwall the total number of individuals recorded up to and including 1999 was 253, making it far more common than on Scilly, which of course lacks any feral breeding populations (*CBWPSAR* 69).

# Grey Geese                                                                  Anser

Unidentified large 'grey geese' were recorded as shown below.
   1982   One Lower Moors, St Mary's 9th October
   1996   One Tresco 22nd December
   1995   Six St Agnes 24th December

# Canada Goose                                                *Branta canadensis*   A & C

**Resident in small numbers and breeds, birds from elsewhere may visit.**

North American, breeds arctic Canada and USA, from Alaska and southern Rocky Mountains in west, eastwards to Quebec and Virginia. Withdraws to southern USA and parts of northern Mexico in winter. Widely established in Britain, probably from escapes rather than deliberate introductions. Birds in private collections from the 1700s and movements of escaped or feral birds well documented by mid-1800s, though wild birds from North America are known to reach Britain and Ireland (Batty & Low 2001). British populations thought to derive from within range of eastern form *canadensis*, with perhaps a few *interior* (Fitter 1959; J L Long 1981). National 18% increase 1994–99 (Bashford & Noble 2000).

This specied was first mentioned by James Clark & Francis Rodd (1906), who reported it being 'obtained at Scilly prior to 1863'. Francis Rodd's uncle, E H Rodd (1880), clarified that odd birds – 'genuine immigrants or escapes from captivity' – were occasionally obtained in mainland Cornwall in winter during this time, including a bird shot near Falmouth in January 1871. However, the failure of Ryves & Quick (1946) to mention Canada Geese appears to confirm its absence from Scilly as a breeding species up until that time.

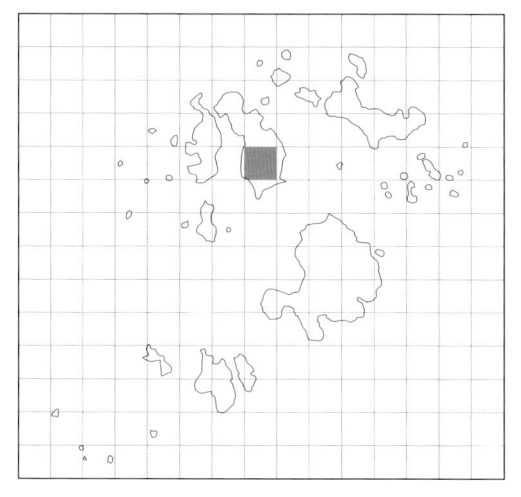

**1-km Canada Goose Breeding Distribution – 2000–01 (data Chown & Lock 2002)**

In fact, the species gets no further mention until one visited St Mary's for two days in January 1962 and for a single day in November 1963. Following these two records there was another long gap in records, until thirteen presumed visitors from elsewhere were seen in flight about the islands for one day in November 1968. However, from around 1969, various references to birds on Tresco appear in *CBWPSAR*, with the statement in 1979 that they had been in the collection there 'for many years'.

There are also entries relating to one to two Tresco pairs producing young in some years, but the population never seems to have exceeded 28 individuals (1980) and by the end of most years appears to have numbered just eight to ten. There is no explanation of what might have been limiting numbers, or, indeed, whether these Tresco birds were full-winged; certainly there seems to be a lack of records of Canada Geese visiting other islands. Indeed, the observer of the 1963 individual on St Mary's considered it unusual enough to have supported the sighting with a brief description (*CBWPSAR* 33).

Interestingly, there is one piece of reliable information supporting the suggestion of an earlier presence on Tresco, as concealed away in the vast skin collection of the British Museum (Natural History) is that of a hybrid Canada x Chinese Goose *Anser cygnoides* (Ref 1953.74), one of two hatched on Tresco in 1953. This means that the 1962 bird already referred to could perhaps have originated from that island.

The situation now is much as described above, with up to ten or so birds present on Tresco only, and with breeding being less than annual and involving few pairs. Of interest, though, is that single pairs occasionally nest on small isolated islands away from the relative safety of Tresco's freshwater pools. Such an example involves a pair which hatched a brood on tiny White Island, west of Samson, in 1994. Against all odds, and escaping the attentions of numerous large gulls *Larus*, at least four small young were safely escorted across the considerable tidal expanse of Samson flats and Tresco Channel to Tresco Great Pool. The 2000 Breeding Bird Atlas recorded three pairs and in just one (2%) of the 67 1-km squares surveyed (Chown & Lock 2002).

Seven birds behaving out of character by visiting St Agnes, in flight, on 10th May 1997 were thought to have been from outside the islands. However, caution is advisable as pairs of Tresco Canada Geese do occasionally move about the islands nowadays, particularly in spring, but rarely are more than two involved. The exception to this is perhaps if and when organised autumn duck shooting occurs on Tresco's Great Pool, whereupon many waterfowl temporarily vacate that island, particularly seeking refuge on Higher and Lower Moors on St Mary's.

Regardless of the likelihood of most visiting birds originating from the feral population in mainland Britain, the possibility of wild Canada Geese arriving on Scilly from North America should not be overlooked, especially since a bird ringed and colour-marked in Maryland, eastern USA, in February 1992 was present in Grampian, Scotland, from November that year until January 1993, at which time it was shot. The bird was thought to be from one of the smaller forms among the group often referred to as 'Lesser Canada Goose', which includes the forms *leucopareia*, *minima* and *taverneri*, often collectively lumped under the name *hutchinsii* (BOURC 1997; Gantlett 1998). According to Batty & Lowe (2001), Canada Geese reach Britain or Ireland from North America annually, normally occurring among flocks of Barnacle *Branta leucopsis*, Pink-footed *Anser brachyrhynchus*, Greylag *A. anser* or Greenland White-fronted Geese *A. albifrons flavirostris*.

## Barnacle Goose  *Branta leucopsis*  **A & E**

Rare migrant.

    1876   At least one   Clark & Rodd 1906
    1880   At least twelve (shot) September   Clark & Rodd 1906
    1884   Three Tresco January   Clark & Rodd 1906
    1895   Fifteen January   Clark & Rodd 1906
    1960   Five St Agnes 28th October
    1961   One Wingletang Down, St Agnes 2nd December
    1966   Twelve (at least eight shot) St Agnes 23rd & 24th October
    1967   Four St Agnes 17th October
    1968   Seven Annet and St Agnes 3rd November
    1969   Six St Mary's 29th September
    1972   One St Mary's 13th to 21st October
    1973   Five Tresco & Samson 17th October
    1978   Up to three St Agnes, St Mary's & Tresco 16th to 29th October
    1979   Three Porth Hellick 18th October
    1980   Seventeen Annet 17th October
    1981   One St Mary's 3rd October
    1987   Four St Agnes & Annet 8th October
    1988   One Watermill, St Mary's 4th to 17th October
    1990   Up to forty-two all islands 31st October
    1993   One Bant's Carn, St Mary's 6th October
    1994   One (presumed feral) Abbey Pool, Tresco 11th June
    1994   Four Eastern Isles 24th October
    1997   Two Tresco & St Martin's 13th October
    2002   Five St Mary's & Western Isles 17th to 21st October
    2002   Eleven Tresco & St Martin's 18th October

Limited world range, breeding eastern Greenland, Spitsbergen, Novaya Zemlya and Vaigach Islands. Monotypic, the three migratory breeding populations have distinct wintering areas. Greenland population migrates via Iceland to winter Scotland and Ireland; Spitsbergen population via Norway to Solway Firth; those from Novaya Zemlya and adjacent islands via Finland and Baltic to mainly the Netherlands. Included on Annex I of 1979 EEC 'Birds Directive'. Amber-listed in UK: 100% of northwest European non-breeding population occurs in UK, 50% or more at ten or fewer sites; unfavourable European winter conservation status (Gregory *et al.* 2002).

What must surely be the earliest reference to this species in Cornwall comes from the early 15th century, among a list of 'certaine flying Citizens of the ayre... who some serve for food for us' (Carew 1602). E H Rodd knew it as 'Bernicle Goose', commenting that small parties occasionally appeared in mainland Cornwall in hard winters, at which times 'their black and white plumage rendered them very conspicuous on the wing'. He referred to specimens obtained in marshes near Land's End, at Mount's Bay near Penzance and at Helford, but made no mention of Scilly (Rodd 1880). On the other hand, Clark and Rodd (E H Rodd's nephew Francis) listed one identified in Scilly in 1876, plus others seen or shot in three further years (Clark & Rodd 1906). This suggests a situation not too far removed from the present day, with birds arriving in four to five years out of every ten since the first 20th century record in 1960.

Nevertheless, the situation differs significantly from most other species of geese in that there are no recorded spring arrivals and none can be said to have overwintered, and, in fact, few stayed for more than a day or two. The Chart includes all known arrival dates for the period 1960–97 and shows a clear October peak; the single June individual was believed to be either feral or an escape. Discounting the June bird, the shortest stay in the islands was one day (14 birds, or 77% of arrivals) and the longest 14 days (two arrivals), whereas the average stay was just 2·9 days, all of which argues against E H Rodd's early theory of a cold-weather association and is in favour of a measure of regular migration, though where from or where too remains unclear. There is little evidence that the Spitsbergen population moves further south than the Solway Firth, but the timing of arrivals in Scilly might fit overshooting by birds from Greenland, which

*Swans, Geese and Ducks*

Barnacle Goose arrival dates

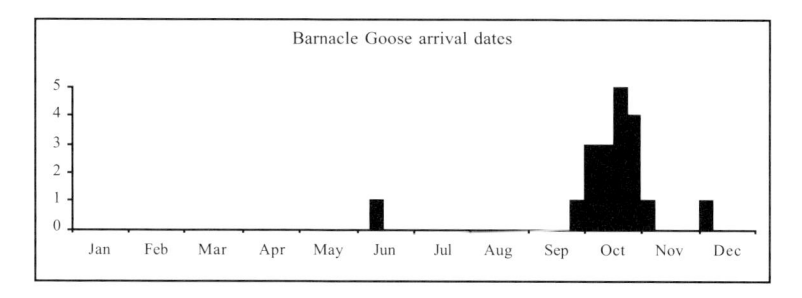

arrive in Scotland and, more importantly, Ireland from mid- to late October. Cramp *et al.* (1977–94) suggest that some birds from the northeastern population move on through continental Europe, reaching as far as northwest France, but usually only in severe weather; however, this is not fully supported by ringing recoveries (Wernham *et al.* 2002). In the latter case, however, we might expect these arrivals to occur in late autumn or winter and to be less co-ordinated, plus birds would probably remain for longer than three days.

Up to and including 1999, a total of around 283 individuals had occurred in mainland Cornwall; the highest monthly total being in October, though records were fairly evenly distributed from September to March.

# Brent Goose *Branta bernicla* A

**Scarce migrant and winter visitor.**

Circumpolar, breeding edge of arctic seas. Polytypic and highly migratory: nominate *bernicla* or 'Dark-bellied Brent' breeds Russian tundra region, wintering progressively south through western Europe, into the Netherlands, France and southeast and southern England; *hrota* or 'Pale-bellied Brent' breeds Spitsbergen, Franz Josef Land, Greenland and Canadian high and low arctic, birds from Greenland and Canadian high arctic winter in Ireland, those from northern Europe winter mainly Denmark and northeast England, whilst those from Canadian low arctic winter eastern North America; *nigricans* or 'Black Brant' (treated by some authorities as full species) breeds Siberia, Alaska and west Canadian Arctic islands, wintering coastal north Pacific (Lack 1986). Note, though, that a third, distinct and perhaps genetically isolated, but so far unrecognised, grey-bellied population 'Grey-bellied Brant' occurs in west Canadian high Arctic, north of *nigricans* and west of *hrota* (Garner & Millington 2001). Amber-listed in UK: 42.7% of northwest European non-breeding population occurs in UK, 50% or more at ten or fewer sites; unfavourable wintering world conservation status (Gregory *et al.* 2002).

E H Rodd thought it not uncommon in Scilly in winter, also noting that in west Cornwall it sometimes gathered in large flocks in Mount's Bay, near Penzance, but during severe weather remained 1–2 km offshore, at which times professional punt-gunners often recorded large kills (Rodd 1880). However, there are no records of such large accumulations in Scilly and no apparent mention of punt-guns being used against this or any other species within the archipelago. A bird shot by E H Rodd's nephew Francis in October 1860 was the only positive 19th-or early 20th century record, but the feeling at the time was that reports from local boatmen of flocks of 'sea-geese' probably involved this species, particularly in winter 1890–91 and in February 1902 (Clark & Rodd 1906). Further confirmation of its early Scillonian status comes from the comment that a few Brent Geese visit the islands at uncertain times in winter, usually during easterly winds (Gilbert White, in Jesse 1887).

As with so many other species, we hear nothing further of Brent Goose until well into the 20th century, when a flock of five paid a brief visit to Tresco on 18th February 1942 (Penhallurick 1969). Certainly in the case of this species, any lack of information must surely have to do more with recording failure than any genuine period of absence from the islands. The Chart comprises all known arrival dates and shows a pattern of autumn and winter arrivals similar to Greylag Goose *Anser anser*. However, examination of all records attributed specifically to either Pale-bellied or Dark-bellied Brent reveals that autumn and winter Dark-bellied arrivals are focused around a narrower timescale than those of its western relative. In addition, whereas both Dark and Pale-bellied remained on average for similar periods during autumn and early winter (8 days and 6.2 days respectively), late winter and early spring visits of Dark-bellied were significantly shorter than those for Pale-bellied (28 days compared to 49 days).

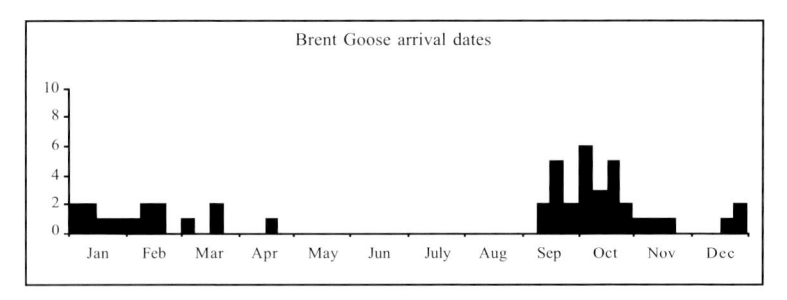

Brent Goose arrival dates

There is a well-defined separation of these two forms within the British Isles during winter, with Dark-bellied confined to England, from Northumberland south to Kent and west at least as far as Devon, plus nearby continental Europe as far as western France, whereas Pale-bellied is mainly confined to Ireland and Scotland, south into England as far as Northumberland, at which point the two forms overlap (Cramp *et al.* 1977–94; Lack 1986). Both are known to move south as far as France, though Pale-bellied only exceptionally, but the extent of any winter inter-site movement is very much related to weather conditions and food availability. Thus, it seems that Scillonian records of Pale-bellied Brent most probably involve wanderers or overshoots from Ireland, whilst arrivals of Dark-bellied birds could involve a westward extension of the regular continental European wintering population, or even birds from southwest England en route to or from France. Both Pale-bellied and Dark-bellied have been recorded in Scilly in only six years and only once, in 1983, did they form into a single flock.

Scilly lacks extensive areas of exposed tidal mud (as opposed to shell-sand) for feeding and is almost devoid of Eel Grass *Zostera*. The islands also lack extensive areas of undisturbed grazing and it is noticeable that both this species and Barnacle Goose show a greater tendency than other geese to head for the undisturbed island of Annet. In addition, strong tidal conditions and frequent heavy seas may create difficulties for flocks seeking a safe roosting area.

On mainland Cornwall, both Pale-bellied and Dark-bellied occur more commonly, with the greatest numbers during September and October (*CBWPSAR* 69). In addition to the two forms discussed above, observers should be aware of the possible occurrence in Scilly of the distinctive form *nigricans*, or 'Black Brant', which is treated as a full species by some authorities and which breeds in western North America but has occurred as far east in Britain as Norfolk. There is also a possibility of the occurrence of the thus far unrecognised, but perhaps genetically isolated 'Grey-bellied Brant', which breeds north and east of *nigricans* and is known now to occur in the north of Ireland in company with Pale-bellied Brents (Garner & Millington 2001).

## [Egyptian Goose *Alopochen aegyptiacus*] C

Breeds Africa, south of Sahara in west, north as far as upper Nile Valley in east. Introduced populations elsewhere, e.g. England, or the Netherlands. Partially migratory in Africa. Monotypic. Current British population in region of 750–800 individuals (early 1990s) (Snow & Perrins 1998).

There is an intriguing entry in the Appendix to E H Rodd's *The Birds of Cornwall and The Scilly Isles* (Rodd 1880). In which Rodd attributes to Courtney the statement that Egyptian Goose has become 'naturalised in the islands of Scilly, as elsewhere' (Courtney 1845). Thankfully, this is given clarification by Penhallurick's tireless research. This author pointed out that although claims of birds seen in the wild in 19th century Cornwall cannot be taken seriously, Augustus Smith (original Lord Proprietor of the Islands) introduced this species to Tresco between the mid-1830s and mid-1840s; he even exhibited them on the mainland. On 11th May 1845, Smith wrote to an unnamed recipient saying he had been reluctant to disturb the Egyptian Geese that year in case they failed to hatch young, which indeed proved to be the case (Penhallurick 1969). However, some slight uncertainty remains, particularly in view of James Clark and Francis Rodd's statement that Francis (nephew of E H Rodd) 'obtained' this species in Scilly prior to 1863

(Clark & Rodd 1906). Francis Rodd was a regular guest on Tresco, and shot many birds there and in the remainder of Scilly, including a numbers of rarities. He would have been extremely familiar with events in the island and it seems surprising that neither he nor his co-author made mention of any introductions or, more particularly, of this shot bird being from that source.

## Shelduck (Common Shelduck) *Tadorna tadorna* A

**Resident and breeds in small numbers, the destination of an annual late summer moult-migration remains unknown. Also a possible passage migrant in small numbers.**

Breeds northwest Europe, and in southern Europe east through central Eurasia to Mongolia. Migratory or dispersive, with additional, earlier, moult migration in some populations. Northwest European populations mainly moult German Waddenzee area, some of which return to winter in breeding areas. Small numbers of West Palearctic birds, mainly from areas east of the Waddenzee, winter south to North Africa, Nile Valley, Middle East. Monotypic. National 40% decline 1994–99 (Bashford & Noble 2000). Amber-listed in UK: 20% or more of northwest European non-breeding population occurs in UK, 50% or more at ten or fewer sites (Gregory *et al.* 2002).

Early evidence of Shelduck presence in Scilly takes the form of a fragment of humerus unearthed with other bone material from the archaeological site at May's Hill, St Martin's and originating from somewhere between the 2nd and 7th centuries AD (Turk 1984).

Although E H Rodd knew it almost exclusively as a winter visitor to Cornwall, where it seems to have been regular but common only during sever weather (Rodd 1880), there are few 19th century records from Scilly. E H Rodd's nephew Francis reported eight seen on one of the Tresco pools on Christmas Day 1864, though he mentioned it in terms suggestive of it perhaps occurring more frequently. Later still, Francis and co-author James Clark reported one shot on Tresco in 1876 and another, apparently shot at the same site, in 1895 (Clark & Rodd 1906). Penhallurick draws attention to an early account of Shelduck breeding in Cornwall (Carew 1602, in Penhallurick 1969) but there appear to have been no further breeding records for the county until about the turn of the 20th century (W Page 1906). Breeding subsequently became more widespread on the Cornish mainland, with a marked further increase and spread during the 1930s and early 1940s (Penhallurick 1969). The latter author also drew attention to the exodus of Shelducks from Cornwall around July, followed by a slow return from mid-November onwards.

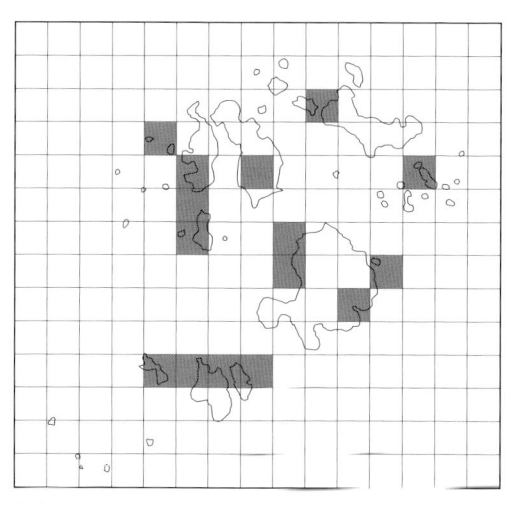

1-km Shelduck Breeding Distribution 2000–01 (data Chown & Lock 2002)

On Scilly, the first 20th century proof of Shelduck presence is probably mention by Wallis (1923) of it breeding around the Tresco pools. However, owing to the depredations of Great Black-backed Gulls *Larus marinus* he doubted they would rear a single duckling, but for the fact their eggs were dug out and hatched under domestic chickens *Gallus domesticus*. Clearly, though, this did not help establish a viable wild population as next mention concerned a one-day visit by a bird to St Agnes Big Pool on 15th January 1955. Doubtless the species occurred, if only rarely, during the period from 1900, and as likely as not the Scillonian increase mirrored the mainland situation; but few duck species are recorded regularly in early issues of the *CBWPSAR*, prior to about 1960. The second 20th century record was shown as frequenting tiny White Island, to the west of Samson, from 16th to 23rd January 1957, the impression gained thus far being very much of an occasional winter visitor. If this was the case, the bird entering a (presumably Rabbit *Oryctolagus cuniculus*) burrow on Samson in mid-May 1958 and a pair with young near adjacent Green Island in early July that same year, must be the first confirmed breeding record. A pair with ducklings was seen off Samson during mid-June of the following year, and by 1961 came reports of a pair with ducklings at the same site, plus 16 adults, 'mainly paired'. By 1962, the published reports spoke of a 'big increase in the breeding population' and by 1963 pairs were said to have also colonised the Eastern Isles. By the mid-1970s, up to eleven breeding pairs were believed present in Scilly. Indeed, Parslow (1967a) noted the spread to Scilly and west of Cornwall as having occurred 'in recent years'.

More recently, the picture has clearly become one of a breeding population of some 20 or more pairs, plus an obvious early autumn departure, with very few about the islands between late July and late October and with a noticeable return from early to mid-November. Several aspects, though, remain less clear. Firstly, understanding of the true size of the archipelago's Shelduck population is not helped by the lack of recent co-ordinated counts, which until very recently were limited to the single all-island winter shorebird count of 25th–26th January 1997, when a total of 45 individuals was recorded.

Secondly, understanding of the size of the breeding population is hindered by the species' secretive behaviour in the vicinity of its nest, plus of course its use mainly of underground sites, perhaps raising doubts that the observed 1958 breeding record was in fact the first. The majority of nesting areas are known, however, and include Samson, Tresco, Bryher, St Agnes, St Helen's, St Martin's, Annet and the Eastern Isles. One interesting failed attempt involved a deserted clutch of eggs found under dead bracken on White Island, on the north side of St Martin's, in the mid-1990s (pers. obs.). The 2000 Breeding Bird Atlas recorded a possible 32 breeding pairs in 15 (22%) of the 67 1-km squares surveyed, though breeding was confirmed in only five (Chown & Lock 2002).

Other unanswered questions concern the level of productivity and the involvement of birds in an annual moult migration. It seems generally accepted that predation by large gulls, i.e. Herring *L. argentatus*, Great Black-backed *L. marinus* and Lesser Black-backed Gulls *L. fuscus* takes a heavy toll of newly hatched Shelduck young in Scilly, particularly among pairs forced to take broods onto the open sea, e.g. from Samson, or St Helen's, or among those taking young to freshwater pools devoid of substantial cover, e.g. on Bryher, or St Agnes. Indeed, it seems possible that only those pairs breeding in the vicinity of Tresco's Great and Abbey Pools stand any substantial chance of rearing young to the flying stage. However, occasional broods of flying young encountered about the islands, e.g. on Samson, or Annet, may have been hatched either on Tresco or elsewhere. According to Cramp *et al.* (1977–94), immatures normally accompany adults on the moult migration, leaving any unfledged young in the care of a minority of adults. This perhaps partly accounts for the presence of a small number of reports during the period when most Shelducks are away from the islands, with the annual number of remaining birds dictated by productivity, or the lack of it. There is no information on the moulting area used by Scillonian birds. Most probably, though, it is on the Wadenzee, along with the majority of other west European Shelducks. But speculation persists that those from Scilly and the Cornish mainland join others in the Bridgewater Bay area (*CBWPSAR* 69), though some authorities still consider this merely a collecting point for birds en route to the Waddenzee (Penhallurick 1969).

Although in mainland Britain this is largely an estuarine species, in Scilly such habitat is lacking, and birds are mostly to be found feeding at low-tide on exposed sandy areas off Samson's east side (Samson Flats), or around Tresco, St Helen's and Tean. The nearest breeding Shelduck populations to Scilly are in England, Ireland, France (Brittany), Netherlands and Belgium, all of which underwent substantial increases around the mid-20th century (Cramp *et al.* 1977–94). In mainland Cornwall it is also viewed as a passage migrant, with a marked increase in numbers at the start of the year and a clear drop, by about 50%, in recorded numbers during April (*CBWPSAR* 69).

# Ruddy Shelduck *Tadorna ferruginea* B & D

**Extremely rare migrant, vagrant or escape from captivity. Treated by the BBRC as a national Scarce Migrant.**

1906–23   One Scilly   Penhallurick 1969
   [1994   Six St Mary's & Tresco 29th & 30th October]   *British Birds* 94: 91–92

Breeds southeast Europe and Asia Minor east across southern Asia to Mongolia and eastern China, also North Africa. Monotypic. Most populations migratory, wintering Indian subcontinent and Southeast Asia, but also northeast Africa in small numbers.

None of the pre-20th century writers refer to this species in either Scilly or mainland Cornwall, though

Penhallurick mentioned one obtained on Scilly some time between 1906 and 1923 (Penhallurick 1969), plus five on Cornwall's Camel Estuary in mid-July 1972 (Penhallurick 1978). More recently, six were observed in flight over St Mary's harbour on 29th October 1994, before being refound on Tresco the following day. Prior to this, six birds, presumably the same group, had been present in the Hayle and Drift Reservoir areas of west Cornwall from early October and five reappeared there soon after the Scillonian sightings (*CBWPSAR* 64). All these last records almost certainly involved the same birds, as the chances of two different groups of six Ruddy Shelducks being present in southwest England at the same time appear remote.

In 1992, the BOURC determined that most post-1946 records were likely to involve escapes from captivity (BOURC 1992a) with some also probably involving individuals from feral European populations, e.g. the Netherlands. However, following the recent multiple Scillonian and Cornish sightings, there was considerable speculation that birds involved might have been genuinely wild, but the point remains unresolved. Duff, for example, argued that despite numbers in western England being higher in 1994, there was no evidence for an increase in numbers in England overall. He further argued that the occurrence of one or more flocks, or of unapproachable individuals, is not necessarily evidence that genuine wild birds were involved (*British Birds* 94: 91–92). As at March 2002, the BOURC took the same view, deciding that no post-1950 British Ruddy Shelduck records were acceptable (Harrop, H. J. 'The Ruddy Shelduck in Britain': *British Birds* 95: 123–128), though the point remains contentious.

## [Wood Duck *Aix sponsa*] E

**Extremely rare migrant or escape from captivity.**

[1996   One Tresco 20th June to 2nd July]

Breeds North America, in east from southern Canada to Texas and Florida, in west from British Columbia south to California; two discrete populations. Withdraws from northern part of range during winter, extending into central northern Mexico. Widely encountered in captivity, small non-self-sustaining feral British populations thought to originate from escapes. No acceptable British record involving a bird of provable wild origin, but known to have reached the Azores naturally, possibly also Iceland.

A full-winged male of unknown origin was discovered on Tresco on 20th June 1996, where it remained until 2nd July the same year (*IOSBR* 1996). Two to three pinioned pairs are among the oddly assorted small 'captive' waterfowl collection at Porthloo Duck Pond on St Mary's, but few young are hatched and none from this well-watched area are known to have reached full-winged status. In addition, no captive or feral pairs or individuals are known to have frequented other suitable areas within the islands.

A bird shot in Worcestershire in 1848 was generally considered to be the first British record, but this and all subsequent records are currently treated as escapes (Palmer 2000). As of October 2000, the BOURC were reviewing all Wood Duck records for southwest England with a view to considering its eligibility for transfer from Category E to either A or D (BOURC 2001). Cramp *et al.* (1977–94) refer to a North American-ringed individual shot in the Azores in January 1985 and a likely further transatlantic migrant there in December 1963, plus up to three possibly from North America in Iceland up until 1992.

## Wigeon (Eurasian Wigeon) *Anas penelope* A

**Regular migrant or winter visitor in moderate numbers, does not breed.**

Breeds Eurasia, from Iceland and northern Britain east to Kamchatka and Sakhalin, south to Aral Sea and Lake Baikal. Monotypic. Migratory, in West Palearctic wintering south to coastal North Africa. Amber-listed in UK: 33.3% of northwest European non-breeding population occurs in UK, 50% or more at ten or fewer sites (Gregory *et al.* 2002).

Early writers make abundantly clear that Wigeon was no 19th century stranger to Scilly, first mention appearing to be Heath's comment that it featured among a number of 'landbirds' present in all the islands during winter (Heath 1750). However, more interesting, but not necessarily true, is Gilbert White's suggestion 'a few remain to breed' (in Jesse 1887). Such unsupported comments are reasonably common in the earlier literature and in this case could well have been based on the presence of captive birds among the Tresco waterfowl collection, though there is no evidence to that effect either. However, we can say that no other writer credits this species with breeding in the islands, e.g. Ryves and Quick (1946) made no mention of it in their review of Scilly's breeding birds. E H Rodd made various references to it and leaves no doubt that it appeared in winter in numbers of up to 150 on Tresco (Rodd 1880), and doubtless there were comparable gatherings in suitable habitat elsewhere, e.g. Porth Hellick, St Mary's. Unfortunately, unqualified references to 'large flocks', or birds shot in 'more or less numbers' do little to help clarify the situation. And the normally helpful James Clark and Francis Rodd were no more enlightening on this occasion, merely describing it as common in severe weather, at times in large flocks (Clark & Rodd 1906).

However, despite this alleged regular winter presence, and even though up to eleven other duck species get a mention in the interim, the first 20th century report of Wigeon is not until 1963, when up to three were about the islands between 2nd and 14th October. It was subsequently reported in small numbers most years, until the intriguing 1967 comment that up to four pairs were seen on Tresco in May. However, this was accompanied by the additional comment that up to two birds present on St Agnes that same month was unusual (*CBWPSAR* 37); and perhaps we should not take references to 'pairs' too literally in any event. Taking the ten years from 1990 as broadly representative, the first birds of the autumn normally arrive in September, with 7th August being the extreme arrival date. In most years, it is recorded as present until the year's end, but there is a dearth of information concerning early spring presence. Latest spring dates are far more protracted than autumn arrivals, varying as they do from January or February through to mid-June. Assessing total numbers involved is problematical, mainly owing to the lack of simultaneous all-island counts, although individual site maxima are in the range 13 to 60. Taking the data at face value, though, there appears to be a drop-off in numbers as winter progresses. This is evident from the late January 1997 all-island shorebird count, when one on St Mary's was the only evidence of its presence, although at least 28 had been counted the previous October. Of course, Scilly has very little suitable Wigeon feeding habitat and this may help determine winter numbers, so it is interesting that Lack (1986) suggested that maximum British and Irish numbers occur in January, following a midwinter influx of Continental birds.

By comparison, mainland Cornwall recorded an October 1999 total of over 2,300 birds, increasing to 2,800 by December with larger numbers in cold winters (*CBWPSAR* 69). Importantly, the site with the highest Cornish total, 1,700 in the Hayle/Copperhouse Creek area of west Cornwall in November, is also one of the Cornish sites closest to Scilly. One possible explanation for the contrast between recent small Scillonian totals and those in the 19th century could be recent climatic changes, with fewer resultant cold winters. Wigeon from several northern European countries, e.g. Iceland, Fennoscandia and western Siberia, winter south and southwest in Europe as far as Britain, France, Iberia and Ireland (Cramp *et al.* 1977–94; Wernham *et al.* 2002).

## American Wigeon *Anas americana* A

**Very rare migrant, full written description required by the SRP.**

1976   One (first-winter male) St Mary's 8th October   *British Birds* 70: 417
1985   One (first-winter) St Agnes, St Mary's & Annet 28th September to 24th October
*British Birds* 79: 534–535
1986   One (first-winter male) Tresco 8th to at least 31st October   *British Birds* 80: 526
1996   One (first-winter female) St Mary's 10th to 13th September   *British Birds* 90: 462

Breeds North America, from Alaska east to Nova Scotia, south to northern California, Colorado and (rarely) Pennsylvania. Monotypic. Migratory, wintering mainly south of breeding range, to southern Atlantic-coastal USA, Mexico and Pacific-coastal USA, though some reach West Indies, Venezuela and Columbia. Decline in Canadian population obscured by upward trend in central USA, but trend overall considered upwards (Bryant 1997). Removed from BBRC Rarities List January 2002 (*British Birds* 94: 290).

Although American Wigeon was accepted onto the British List by 1830 – after a dead male was purchased at London's Leadenhall Market (Palmer 2000) – E H Rodd made no mention of it in his epic *The Birds of Cornwall and The Scilly Islands* (Rodd 1880), and neither does Penhallurick in either of his two volumes (Penhallurick 1967, 1978). Therefore, the immature at Porth Hellick, St Mary's, on 8th October 1976 represented the species' introduction to both the islands and mainland Cornwall. The next, also a first-winter, remained on St Agnes Big Pool from 28th September until 24th October 1985, though it also visited nearby Annet and Porth Hellick on St Mary's. Scilly's third record, identified as a first-winter male, frequented Tresco's Great Pool from October 8th to 31st 1986 and the most recent visitant was a first-winter female that spent four days at Porth Hellick from 10th September 1996.

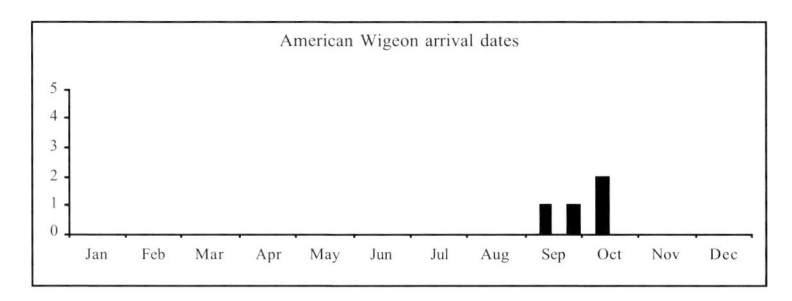

American Wigeon arrival dates

The Chart shows all four arrival dates, which, like Ring-necked Duck *Aythya collaris*, suggest a migration element. The average length of stay was 16 days, but none remained after October, and one individual was present for just one day. In North America, the species winters mostly south of the main breeding range, in Atlantic and Pacific coastal States and the Gulf of Mexico, but also south as far as Columbia, West Indies and Venezuela (Cramp *et al.* 1977–94). As with some wader species, those wintering in eastern USA include birds that migrated east from the central northern Canadian prairies by way of the Great Lakes, which, like some wader species, perhaps helps explain the high incidence of transatlantic autumn vagrancy. Autumn migration commences September and peaks during October to early November, some reaching Columbia by October (Cramp *et al.* 1977–94). The recovery of more than one ringed individual shows that at least some European records involve genuine transoceanic crossings. The first for mainland Cornwall arrived in 1981 and there had been 22 individuals in the country up until the end of 1999 (*CBWPSAR* 69).

# Gadwall *Anas strepera* A

**Resident and breeds in small numbers.**

Breeds central Eurasia, from British Isles, France and Spain east to Lake Baikal, plus central northern North America from Pacific to central States. Mainly resident, but migratory in north and eastern West Palearctic. Polytypic: nominate *strepera* occurs throughout range; one extinct form *couesi* Pacific. Amber-listed in UK: 50% or more of population breeds at ten or fewer sites; 20% or more of northwest European non-breeding population occurs in UK; unfavourable world conservation status (Gregory *et al.* 2002).

One of the archipelago's more interesting duck species, which also has a fascinating British history. Earliest record from Scilly involved a bird shot on Tresco pools on the very first day of the 20th century (Clark & Rodd 1906). According to Fitter (1959), all Gadwalls in England (though not necessarily in Scotland and Ireland) descend from a pair of trapped Continental migrants released in Norfolk around

1850. By 1875 a 'substantial' local population existed, though the possibility of migrants being involved in any sightings remained. Nevertheless, by the date of the first Tresco bird around 1,500 were thought to be breeding in Norfolk, with the first two pairs recorded in Scotland soon after, though breeding was not proven in Ireland until the 1930s (Holloway 1996). Looking westwards, among subsequent centres of Gadwall release were the former Severn Wildfowl Trust in Gloucestershire, plus Scilly in the 1930s (J L Long 1981). Neither of these sources accounts for the 1900 individual on Tresco, however, which may have been a genuine winter vagrant from either continental Europe or eastern England.

Regrettably, little information survives on the Scilly releases and Gadwall first appeared in the *CBWPSAR* for 1948 – two pairs on 26th April and one pair on Tresco on 30th. There was no suggestion of seven on Tresco Great Pool on 15th December of the following year being linked to the Tresco Abbey waterfowl collection. Unfortunately, the following few years include the period during which there are few if any reported duck records for Scilly, and the next mention of Gadwall involved ten on Tresco on 30th March 1956. There is subsequently a distinct improvement in reporting, but an obvious continued absence of any mention of Gadwall. The next record, then, concerned 55 (including a possible 20 pairs) on Tresco's Great Pool in September 1960 (*CBWPSAR* 30), accompanied by the suggestion that this represented the largest concentration for southwest England after 70 at Chew Valley Lake in Somerset. Published annual totals then remained in the region of 35–65, e.g. 65 on Tresco in late January 1965 (B King 1965b), with a clear inference that few occurred away from Tresco and with little suggestion of any seasonal variation in numbers.

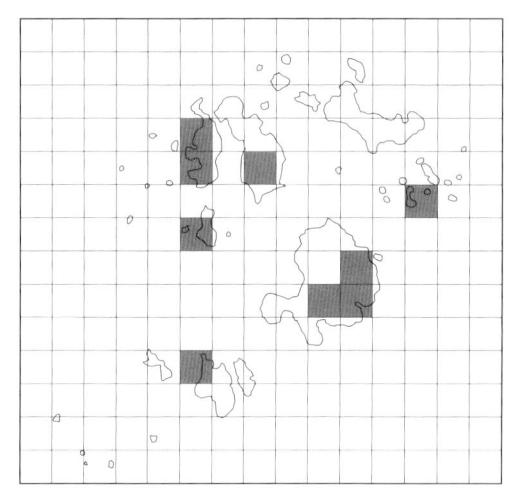

That largely remains the situation to the present day, with the main concentration centred upon Tresco, where maximum counts for the period 1990–99 varied from a low of four (May) to 50–60+ (October through to December or January). There is a strong suggestion among the random counts of a marked drop-off in numbers from March or April through to September, accompanied by comments such as 'presumed present all year'. Until very recently the only co-ordinated all-island count on record involved the late January 1997 Winter Shorebird Survey, when a total of 37 was recorded, though this count will have missed birds feeding on freshwater pools away from the shore. Certainly there is no suggestion of a breeding population compatible with stated earlier totals of 60 or more birds, with three or four breeding pairs more the norm, and no confirmed breeding at all during some years. Unlike other breeding ducks in Scilly (with the possible exception of Mallard *A. platyrhynchos*), unusually early or late broods are occasionally recorded, e.g. January 1995 and October 1997. Most breeding takes place on Tresco, with a small number of pairs at Porth Hellick, St Mary's, plus occasional isolated pairs on other main islands, e.g. St Agnes or Bryher. Several pairs are regularly to be seen feeding off Samson's eastern shore in summer and the probability is that breeding will take place there soon, if indeed it has not already occurred – regardless of the lack of freshwater pools. The 2000 Breeding Bird Atlas recorded up to 20 pairs in 9 (13.4%) of the 67 1-km squares surveyed, though breeding was confirmed in just four (Chown & Lock 2002)

**1-km Gadwall Breeding Distribution – 2000–01 (data Chown & Lock 2002)**

Surprisingly, first suggestion in local reports of successful breeding in the islands was contained in the brief 1973 reference to 'A small breeding population on Tresco' (*IOSBR* 1973). This was followed a year later by the suggestion that only two pairs actually bred on Tresco, though a pair may have attempted to do so on St Mary's. However, Fox (1988) helpfully clarified the situation, stating that Gadwall bred annually on Tresco from 1934, following the release there of a pinioned wild drake. He also quoted a figure of 12 pairs by the late 1960s.

Owen *et al.* (1986) commented on the 'marked feature' of 70–80 birds on Tresco, the next nearest concentrations being in Dorset and Gloucestershire. The closest breeding birds to Scilly now are in south

Devon (around four pairs) and then Dorset and Somerset (Gibbons *et al.* 1993), plus a small number in Brittany (Guermeur & Monnat 1980). Although the Scilly population apparently exceeds 2% of the estimated national total, it fails to meet the 50 pairs minimum requirement for national importance.

Small numbers of birds from Iceland and central Europe, from the Netherlands east to northwest Russia, winter in Ireland and Britain whilst those from Scotland move southwest into Ireland and, to a lesser extent, into England (Wernham *et al.* 2002). Whilst English breeders are mostly sedentary, recovery of a small number of ringed individuals from eastern England shows that some move south as far as Spain, Italy, Mediterranean, Netherlands and Atlantic coastal France. In addition, birds breeding in the Baltic region, Germany, Poland, Sweden and western Russia winter chiefly in the Netherlands and Britain (Cramp *et al.* 1977–94; Lack 1986). Therefore, there is a possibility that not all Gadwall encountered in Scilly are resident.

## Teal (Common Teal) *Anas crecca* A

**Winter visitor and autumn (possibly also spring) migrant, a few normally summer and a pair or two occasionally breed.**

Breeds Northern Eurasia, from Iceland, Great Britain, France east to Pacific and south to Mediterranean, Black Sea, Kazakhstan and Mongolia. Mainly migratory, West Palearctic populations winter south to North Africa, Nile Valley and Middle East. Polytypic: nominate *crecca* breeds throughout, except Aleutian Islands, where replaced by doubtfully separable *nimia*. Amber-listed in UK: 20% or more or northwest European non-breeding population occurs in UK (Gregory *et al.* 2002). Formerly included distinctive North American *carolinensis*, or 'Green-winged Teal', which from October 2000 has been treated as full species, Green-winged Teal *A. carolinensis* (BOURC 2001).

Earliest evidence of Teal in Scilly involves bone remains unearthed from the May's Hill prehistoric site on St Martin's and thought to date from between the 2nd and 7th centuries AD. Next mention was Heath's description of it among 'the landbirds of all the islands' (Heath 1750). E H Rodd and his nephew Francis Rodd made various references to it about the islands, first of which is Francis's 1864 account of unusually large numbers on 22nd December, followed by his shooting of three birds two days later. On Christmas Day, he reported making a tour of the Tresco ponds and noting a flock of 15, before shooting another, this time on St Mary's, on 4th January 1865. Francis referred to it again on 7th September 1870, presumably on Tresco, and recorded too that some were shot in December that same year. He also commented that between 23rd and 28th December he made four excursions to the snowy St Mary's Moors – in what was obviously a hard winter by Scillonian standards – and noted the presence of Teal, among others. And finally, for the winter 1878–79 season he recorded a total of 67 shot in the islands (Rodd 1880). In their normally helpful *Zoologist* paper 'The Birds of Scilly', James Clark and Francis Rodd were uncharacteristically brief, describing it simply as appearing every autumn and winter, sometimes commonly (Clark & Rodd 1906). Meanwhile, Gilbert White added a slightly different note, suggesting for the first time that a few pairs remained behind to breed (in Jesse 1887).

Interestingly, E H Rodd knew it as a sometimes common winter visitor to Cornwall, particularly in the west of the county, but had never heard of it breeding in either Cornwall, Devon or Somerset (Rodd 1880). Nephew Francis, however, later penciled a comment on one of his uncle's lists that 'a few still breed with us' (Penhallurick 1969), whilst Clark (in W Page 1906) thought pairs nested regularly on Bodmin and Goss Moors, sometimes further west. In his late 19th century review of Britain's breeding birds, Holloway (1996) shows it as rare in southwest Devon at that time, uncommon in Dorset and only probable in Somerset, but nonetheless absent from Cornwall. And as if to emphasise any uncertainties, in their 'Survey of the Status of Birds Breeding in Cornwall and Scilly Since 1906', Colonel Ryves and Hilda Quick considered it an increasingly rare breeder in Cornwall by the mid-20th century, although they thought it did so almost annually on Tresco (Ryves & Quick 1946).

Taking the ten-year period 1990–99, the picture was very much one of a small overwintering population, varying from around ten to perhaps no more than 30 birds in most years, followed by even smaller numbers during spring and an often complete absence during May and June, culminating in a noticeable build-up during October, when combined numbers on Tresco and St Mary's alone can reach 200 plus. However, as with other duck species, there is a marked lack of co-ordinated all-island counts – for all seasons – and the situation is worsened by a lack of observer coverage outside the busy autumn migration period. The sole co-ordinated count during the period under review involved the late January 1997 all-island winter shorebird count – when a total of 33 (including 28 off Samson) on 25th–26th January excluded birds on freshwater pools. Even so, whilst there is ample evidence that Scilly is involved in a regular autumn passage of Teal, what few published data there are do not support the additional suggestion (e.g. Penhallurick 1969) that there is also a regular spring passage. It could well be, however, that during the well-watched period of the St Agnes Bird Observatory these things were more easily determined.

During the same ten year period breeding was suspected but not proved in 1991 on Tresco's Great Pool and at Porth Hellick, St Mary's, and also at Porth Hellick in 1998. Reports of 'pairs' being present appear throughout the annual reports, e.g. two pairs at Porth Hellick and three on Tresco in 1978, but being unaccompanied by published accounts of identifiable breeding activity are of little value. In fact, there are no reportedly proven cases of breeding in Scilly for at least the last 25 years, the nearest documented evidence being the (nevertheless unsupported) statement that in 1975 'Several pairs nest on Tresco plus at least two pairs on St Mary's' (*IOSBR* 1975). However, there are reports of females with young, as in 1969 when a duck and seven ducklings were on Porth Hellick Pool (*IOSBR* 1969).

Penhallurick (1969) referred to 34 Teal ringed in continental Europe and shot on the Cornish mainland up until that time, two-thirds of which were ringed in the Netherlands or close by, plus 53 ringed in Britain. Doubtless, this is mainly a reflection of the greater number of shooters in Cornwall, compared to Scilly, but up until 2000 just two ringed Teal had been reported in the islands. Whereas most British and Irish breeders are sedentary, Icelandic Teal migrate to winter in Britain and Ireland. In addition, the greater majority of birds from the northern West Palearctic, east as far as western Siberia and northern Kazakhstan, winter in the area of Britain, France and the Low Countries (Cramp *et al.* 1977–94; Wernham *et al.* 2002). Although annual distribution within that broad area seems largely weather dependent, an immediate westward movement can be expected during cold spells, whilst in more severe weather many move on south into France and Iberia, some even reaching North Africa. It seems easy to see how Scilly might become involved in those movement patterns.

### Recoveries

| | | | | |
|---|---|---|---|---|
| 21801 | ? | Netherlands date unknown | SH | 'Scilly' 25th November 1947 |
| KP70655 | 1stY male, Abberton, Essex 5th September 1975 | | CT | Felixstowe, Suffolk 4th November 1975 |
| | | | SH | Tresco 15th December 1975 |

**Teal Ringing Recaptures**

## Green-winged Teal *Anas carolinensis* A

Rare migrant or winter visitor. Treated by the BBRC as a national Scarce Migrant.

- 1971 One (shot – ringed) St Mary's 2nd January 1971
- 1971 One Tresco 1st June onwards
- 1975 One St Agnes & St Mary's 1st to 22nd May
- 1979 One Porth Hellick, St Mary's 11th December to 16th January 1980
- 1985 One (first-winter) St Mary's 23rd October to 21st November
- 1993 One (male) Lower & Higher Moors, St Mary's 21st February to 25th March
- 1994 One (male) Great Pool, Tresco & elsewhere 4th December to 3rd April 1995
- 1995 Up to two (males) Tresco 11th November to 23rd March 1996
- 1996 One (male) Great Pool, Tresco 26th April to 8th May
- 1996 One (male) St Mary's, St Agnes & Tresco 24th December to 2nd May 1997
- 1997 One (male) Tresco & St Mary's 22nd October to 2nd May 1998
- 1998 One (male) Lower Moors & Porth Hellick, St Mary's 2nd December to 26th March 1999
- 1999 One (eclipse male) Porth Hellick, St Mary's 26th to 29th October
- 1999 One (male) Great Pool, Tresco 26th November to 11th December
- 1999 Up to four (three immature males & female) St Mary's & Tresco 4th November to 14th April 2000

Previously treated as distinctive form of Teal *A. crecca* but afforded species status by BOURC from October 2000 (BOURC 2001). Breeds North America, from Canada south to northern USA. Migratory, wintering USA, West Indies and Central America. Monotypic. Population appears static overall but Canada and eastern USA recently experienced big increase, followed by equally big decline of 95% in eastern US (Bryant 1997). Removed from BBRC Rarities List January 1991 (Lansdown and the Rarities Committee 1991).

Circumstances surrounding the shooting of a male 'Green-winged Teal' in Sussex about 1840 were not made known until 1880, at which point it became the earliest British record, replacing a Yorkshire specimen of 1851 (Palmer 2000). It seems hardly surprising, therefore, that E H Rodd and his 19th century contemporaries made no mention of it in either a Cornish or Scillonian context. Penhallurick (1969) details three birds in mainland Cornwall between 1962 and 1968, but by 1999 mainland Cornwall had hosted 38 individuals (*CBWPSAR* 69).

Scillonian records commenced with a bang (literally and metaphorically) when a first-year shot at Porth Hellick, St Mary's, on 2nd January 1971 was found to have been ringed in New Brunswick, Canada, the previous August. This was followed soon after by the archipelago's second, a male on Tresco's Great Pool in June the same year. In total, there were 19 birds in the islands in eleven of the 30 years 1970–1999 (equal to 50% of the Cornish total in 78% of the time and in a fraction of the land area). A probable six in 1999 indicated the likely scale of things still to come.

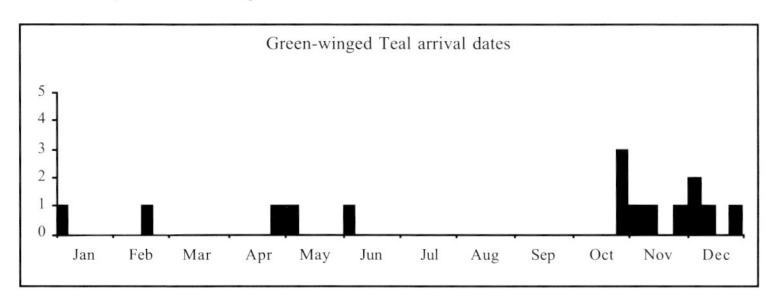

The Chart includes all known arrival dates and shows a very different pattern to that of American Wigeon *A. americana*, Blue-winged Teal *Anas discors*, Ring-necked Duck *Aythya collaris* or Surf Scoter *Melanitta perspicillata*. This is because, although there is a recognisable peak in autumn, it occurs later and arrivals are more protracted than for the previously mentioned four species, plus there are spring sightings and what appear to be random winter arrivals. There is also a strong suggestion of at least one returning wintering individual being involved from 1996. At 61.5 days, the average length of known stay (excluding the two 1971 individuals and multiple occurrences), it also differs from the other species mentioned. The shortest length of stay was just four days and then 16, but with the two longest 132 and 130. Predictably, records were concentrated at Tresco Great Pool and at Porth Hellick Pool on St Mary's. The most recently listed sighting, of up to four birds from early November 1999, involved a BBRC-accepted female, probably the first recorded in Britain.

Presumably, autumn migration in North America broadly mirrors that of Teal in Europe, where to some extent the bulk of the movement is weather related. It normally commences in July (probable failed breeders) but peaks October–November and with males tending to precede females (Cramp *et al.* 1977–94). There is also variation in the extent of short or long-distance moult migration among males.

### Recoveries
?     1stY New Brunswick, Canada   22nd August 1970    SH   St Mary's 2nd January 1971

### Green-winged Teal Ringing Recaptures

# Mallard                                               *Anas platyrhynchos*   A & C

**Common resident, migrant and winter visitor, breeds in small numbers on all six main islands, plus a few others.**

Breeds Eurasia, from Iceland, British Isles and Iberia east to Kamchatka, south to Mediterranean and China, plus North America, from Alaska east to Great Lakes, also Greenland. Mostly migratory, in West

Palearctic mainly wintering south to extent of breeding range. Polytypic: *conboschas* occurs Greenland; nominate *platyrhnchos* remaining Eurasia; plus three further forms North America and two Hawaiian Islands. Current status in North America unclear, though apparently holding its own, but with local population explosions (Bryant 1997). BTO Waterways Bird Survey showed national increase of 190% 1975–2000. Recent BOURC reclassification as both Category A and C reflects high level of UK introductions by wild-fowlers (BOURC 1993b). Green-listed in UK: in need of basic conservation assistance (Gregory *et al.* 2002).

Seasonal concentrations occur at Higher and Lower Moors on St Mary's and at Great and Abbey Pools on Tresco, with fewer numbers at St Agnes and Bryher Pools, whilst St Martin's lacks suitable fresh water areas. Also feeds commonly inshore in sheltered marine waters, notably Samson Flats and around Tresco, but may be encountered anywhere around the coasts. As elsewhere, often breeds some distance from fresh water and may more frequently breed adjacent to saltwater feeding areas than currently appreciated, though the presence of large gulls perhaps seriously limits productivity at these sites.

The earliest known evidence of this species in Scilly involves bone remains unearthed from the prehistoric site on Nornour in the Eastern Isles (Turk 1971, 1984b). Most early Scillonian references to 'wild ducks' or just 'ducks' doubtless involve this species, with what may be the first of such being the mid-19th century account of 'Ducks' being included among the 'landbirds of all these islands' (Heath 1750). E H Rodd's nephew Francis Rodd made various references to Mallard, in varying numbers and at various locations between 1864 and 1879 (Rodd 1880). Undoubtedly, E H Rodd obtained much of the island information for his *The Birds of Cornwall and The Scilly Islands* from Francis and it is probably to that source we can attribute the elder Rodd's brief reference to Mallard breeding on the 'pools and shores of Samson' (Rodd 1880). However, the comment perhaps tells us as more now about changes to Samson's hydrology than it does about Mallard breeding distribution within the islands. Gilbert White knew it as a winter visitor to the islands, 'a few remaining to breed' (in Jesse 1887). More informative, however, was the subsequent summary of Mallard status by Francis Rodd and James Clark, who helpfully described it as common in winter but breeding sparingly, with nests having been found in 1903 on Tresco, at Porth Hellick on St Mary's and among bracken on Samson, St Helen's and Tean (Clark & Rodd 1906).

Penhallurick quoted David Hunt, when suggesting that 25 or so pairs bred annually on Tresco, St Mary's and Samson combined up until the mid-1980s – this perhaps also included other islands mentioned by Clark and Rodd, e.g. St Helen's and Tean (Penhallurick 1969). Penhallurick also drew attention to the lack of published information on numbers of Mallard in Scilly at all times of the year, though he suggested an annual winter increase. One thing we can say, though, is that at least into the 1980s – and although winter flocks were not large by British standards – numbers present on Tresco were thought to be regionally significant, being 'appreciably larger' than on any of the Cornish lakes, with 260 regular and a maximum of 400 (Owen *et al.* 1986).

Taking numbers for the ten-year period 1990–99, there is a suggestion among reported counts of a reduction in autumn and winter totals on Scilly since the 1970s–80s. A total of 254 on Tresco in September 1995 was the highest autumn figure, but some back-end counts were as low as 50 or 60; and there was an average of 145 for the highest counts in seven different years combined. The only winter totals reported during this time were 121 on Tresco's Abbey Pool on 31st December 1993, 60 (probably on all islands) on 11th February 1996 and 139 around main island coasts during the two-day winter shorebird count of late January 1997. This last figure took no account of 'inland' birds on the majority of freshwater pools. There does appear to be support among published counts for the view that Mallards pass through Scilly on autumn migration, though not for the spring period. However, deciding exactly what level of numbers are involved during autumn passage, or what the true summer and wintering populations are requires a great deal more effort in the form of co-ordinated all-island counts, and even then it will be necessary to first compare the data with recent annual releases of captive-reared Mallard on Tresco, together with data on numbers of birds shot on that island during winter. But if nothing else, on Scilly Mallard provides an example of how easy it is to under-record a common species, published reports for the five years 1985–89 providing no counts other than random summer reports of females with broods. Islands mentioned in the recent literature where pairs are thought to have hatched broods include all those mentioned above, plus Bryher, St Agnes, St Martin's and Northwethel. The 2000 Breeding Bird Atlas recorded up to 64 pairs in 14 (20.8%) of the 67 1-km squares surveyed, with a population estimate in the range 30–60 pairs and with breeding proved in just five squares (Chown & Lock 2002).

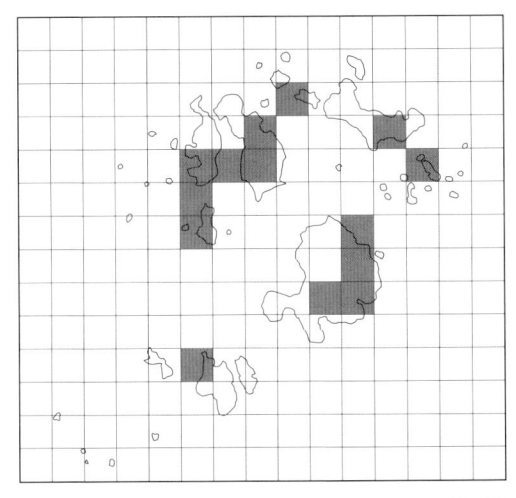

**1-km Mallard Breeding Distribution – 2000–01 (data Chown & Lock 2002)**

Wilson (*CBWPSAR* 69) provided reported annual Mallard totals for up to 24 sites in mainland Cornwall during 1999. October all-site totals peaked at 1,473 (from 21 sites), with the maximum number 219 at both the Hayle Estuary and Loe Pool, but were as low as four to six at some sites. In fact, 219 was also the highest mainland single-site count of the year. Mallard wintering in Britain originate from Iceland, Fennoscandia, northwest Russia, the Baltic States, Poland, Germany and Denmark, a few moving further south into Iberia (Cramp *et al.* 1977–94; Wernham *et al.* 2002). Interestingly, even by 1969 there had been fifteen Cornish mainland recoveries of British-ringed Mallards, ten originating from the Wildfowl and Wetlands Trust at Slimbridge and five from elsewhere in England, east to Norfolk, Northamptonshire and Buckinghamshire. In addition, there had been three recoveries of birds ringed in continental Europe: Netherlands (two) and Denmark (Penhallurick 1969). Up to and including 1999, however, there have been no Scillonian recoveries of marked individuals. Gantlett (1998) drew attention to the possibility of the larger, paler and greyer and smaller-billed migratory Greenland form *conboschas* reaching Britain, and it should be looked for in Scilly as elsewhere, especially as there is at least one record of a British Mallard being recovered in Canada (Cramp *et al.* 1977–94).

## Black Duck (American Black Duck)     *Anas rubripes*   A   BBRC 14%

**Extremely rare migrant or vagrant, full written description required by the BBRC.**

1969    One Tresco 4th September   *British Birds* 64: 368
1976    Up to two Tresco 27th October to winter 1983–84   *British Birds* 70: 416, 78: 537
1994    One (male) Great Pool, Tresco 1st April to 1st November 1997   *British Birds* 78: 537, 91: 466
2000    One (male) Tresco 2nd December to 25th February 2001 (dead 17th March)
          *British Birds* 94: 463

Breeds North America, from west of Hudson Bay east to Newfoundland and south to Virginia and North Carolina. Migratory and dispersive, wintering mainly within breeding range. Monotypic.

The first Black Duck record for Britain and Ireland involved a dead female discovered in a poulterer's shop in Co. Waterford in February 1954 (BOURC 1960), with a second seen alive in the same area until at least February 1961. However, the first Black Duck in Britain was discovered in Kent in March 1967 (Palmer 2000), whilst the first Scillonian record, and the fifth for Britain and Ireland, arrived on Tresco on 4th September 1969, being watched closely for an hour and a half by an observer familiar with the species in North America (*IOSBR* 1969). This was followed by the unexpected discovery of two together on Tresco's Abbey Pool on 27th October 1976, both probably present at the same site from 25th (*IOSBR* 1976). One of the two then departed on 1st November, leaving the remaining individual (a female, as became clear later) in long-term residence, being last seen during winter 1983–84. The third record for Scilly involved a male, again on Tresco, from 1st April 1994 until it was last seen at the same site in November 1997 (*IOSBR* 1994–97).

In North America, Black Duck hybridises extensively with Mallard *A. platyrhynchos*, therefore it was no great surprise that the 1976 female paired with a male Mallard in 1978, rearing at least four out of a brood of seven hybrid offspring, only one of which could be located by late December. The following year, three young were reared and in 1980 two downy young were seen in mid May but could not be refound later, though two full-grown hybrids were present in October. Much the same occurred in 1981, with small young seen in early June but just two full-grown first-year hybrids viewable latter, both of which were thought to resemble male Black Ducks. By spring 1982, two hybrid adults (apparently male and female) were in evidence about the Tresco pools and the original female was accompanied by four young in July, though the outcome remains unknown. In 1983, however, she apparently reared three young to the flying stage, before disappearing some time during the following autumn or winter. The exact number of hybrid young produced to maturity by this female Black Duck cannot be assessed with any accuracy, and numbers surviving to the following year may have been affected by autumn and winter wildfowl shooting on Tresco. Nevertheless, up to four adult hybrids were present in 1978, 1980 and 1983–89 inclusive. Coincidentally, perhaps, a female Black Duck appeared at Crowdy Reservoir, Cornwall, on 5th December 1985 (*CBWPSAR* 56).

The 1994 male appeared equally willing to fraternise with the local female Mallards, being paired before the end of April, though no offspring were recorded that year. In 1995, it briefly visited St Mary's in November but no earlier breeding activity was noted. In 1996, however, it was seen paired with an apparently pure-bred white Mallard, and observed escorting four downy ducklings on 1st July, though none could be found later. In 1997, the male Black Duck began exploring other islands, being seen on both Bryher and Samson, and was last recorded on 1st November. More recently, a male appeared on Tresco in early December 2000 and was eventually found dead on that island on 17th March 2001, having been last seen alive on 25th February.

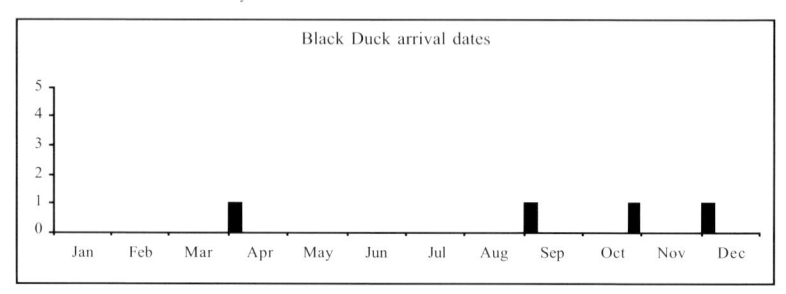

Black Duck arrival dates

Just 28 Black Duck records were accepted by the BBRC up to and including 1999, therefore, the four Scillonian individuals represent 14.2% of the total of this national rarity. In east-coast North America, a few Black Ducks winter north as far as Newfoundland but most move to coastal marshes as far south as South Carolina, some reaching Florida. Peak southward movement occurs November, though some depart from September. Apart from the British Isles, individuals have reached the Azores and Sweden, both during November. This may seem a somewhat unlikely transatlantic migrant or vagrant, but the presence of wintering birds as far north in the Atlantic as Newfoundland in some years may have something to do with its appearance on the eastern seaboard.

## Pintail (Northern Pintail) *Anas acuta* A

**Scarce migrant and winter visitor in very small numbers.**

Breeds Northern Eurasia, from Iceland and British Isles east to Kamchatka and south to Baltic and central Kazakhstan, with small isolated populations further south, also northern North America, from Alaska east to Newfoundland. Mainly migratory, in West Palearctic south to sub-Saharan Africa. Amber-listed in UK: five-year mean of 43.6 breeding pairs; 20% or more of northwest European non-breeding populations occurs in UK, 50% or more at ten or fewer sites; unfavourable world conservation status (Gregory *et al.* 2002).

E H Rodd's nephew Francis mentioned the first Pintail record for Scilly in a December 1870 letter, describing how an afternoon walk over the St Mary's Moors 'yielded twelve couples of Snipes, a Woodcock and a female Pintail' (Rodd 1880). Later still, James Clark and Francis Rodd clarified the situation, pointing out that Pintail appeared in the islands mainly during severe weather, as in 1870, 1879, 1886–87, 1890–91 and 1895, although mostly in small groups (Clark & Rodd 1906).

Penhallurick described its status in Cornwall as regular in winter in the west up until the early 20th century, following which it became scarce in the west but more numerous in the east of the county (Penhallurick 1969), with birds arriving during late October and departing again late February or early March. The same author suggested that although there is no recognisable passage movement, birds do appear outside the winter period, mainly during April or in August–September. He also described it as uncommon and by no means annual in Scilly up until the mid-1960s. This is still the case today, with birds arriving in nine of the ten years 1990–99 and with a low of two and a high of 16, the latter including one fly-over flock of 11 in 1990. Apart from this flock, plus a flock of 13 in 1991, all records involved groups of no more than four individuals. There was a noticeable autumn bias to arrival dates, with birds recorded from July to late November, the majority in late September and October. Winter and spring sightings were limited to a pair on 19th–21st February 1993, a male 21st–30th January 1994, a male in March 1996, six in January 1997 and seven in May the same year. However, care must be taken with island records, since the recent introduction of one or two pinioned captive individuals on Porth Loo pond on St Mary's.

Pintail breeds sporadically in Britain south as far as Kent, but the nearest substantial breeding population to Scilly is probably in Norway (Hagemeijer & Blair 1997), though it also occurs thinly in Spain and Denmark, among other European countries. It winters widely in Britain and Ireland and shows a clear preference for large estuaries, thus the closest winter concentrations to Scilly are in central southern England, the Somerset Levels and the Bristol Channel. Most birds in Britain in winter originate from western Siberia, Scandinavia and Iceland, numbers peaking around December in Britain and November or December in western Ireland (Cramp *et al.* 1977–94; Lack 1986; Wernham *et al.* 2002). The origin of large numbers of Pintail wintering in sub-Saharan Africa remains unclear, though British-ringed birds moving south to Iberia and northwest Africa in autumn and winter demonstrate the possibility that birds move south through Scilly.

# Garganey *Anas querquedula* A

**Scarce migrant in extremely small numbers, very occasionally breeds.**

Breeds northern and central Eurasia, from Great Britain east to Kamchatka and south to Mediterranean and Caspian Seas. Winters south to sub-Saharan Africa, Indian subcontinent and Southeast Asia. Monotypic. Amber-listed in UK: five-year mean of 115.2 breeding pairs; unfavourable world conservation status (Gregory *et al.* 2002).

Rather surprisingly, E H Rodd made no mention of Garganey in relation to Scilly, though he knew it well enough in west Cornwall, describing it as an occasional spring visitor. He also saw the occasional specimen for sale in Penzance poulterers, assuming they were killed locally (Rodd 1880). First direct reference to it in the islands comes from E H Rodd's nephew Francis and joint author James Clark, in their useful *Zoologist* paper on 'The Birds of Scilly' (Clark & Rodd 1906), in which they describe first a bird killed by gamekeeper David Smith on Tresco's Great Pool on 29th March 1881, followed by five shot in March 1883 and finally one at Porth Hellick, St Mary's, rather surprisingly around Christmas 1900.

Penhallurick considered it almost annual in appearance in Scilly, most typically between March and May, but also in September. He described a maximum accumulative count of at least 17 in the islands between mid-March and late May 1959 as 'especially numerous', with a further ten during a seven-day period in September that same year. Penhallurick also says a pair bred on Tresco in 1959 but gives no authority for this statement, suggesting too that it may not have been the first time breeding had occurrd on Scilly (Penhallurick 1969). However, there is certainly no mention of this breeding record in the annual report of that year (*CBWPSAR* 29; *SABOAR* 1959–60). The first 20th century confirmation of Garganey in Scilly comes with a reported 'pair' on St Agnes on a typical date of 29th March, 1957 (*CBWPSAR* 27), though doubtless the species continued to arrive in the islands between 1900 and then. Taking the period 1970–99, one or more birds occurred in 22 (73%) of the 30 years, up to a maximum of eight (1993) and at an average of 2.9 per year. The most recent blank year was 1995, and the longest period of absence was during the three years 1977–79. Spring arrivals were recorded in the months March to May, with the earliest on 19th March, whereas autumn arrivals were distributed from July to October, with the last sighting on 28th October. What were described as a 'pair' of birds were reported on perhaps ten occasions, most often in spring. There was also a tendency towards males being reported more often than females, though this may perhaps be attributable to females being less easily identified.

Garganey is highly migratory. Only small numbers winter in the Mediterranean region or further north and most cross into southern sub-Saharan Africa, some travelling even further. Huge numbers occur in West Africa, where aerial counts exceed the known European population, suggesting a major involvement of perhaps Russian breeders (Cramp *et al.* 1977–94). Birds ringed in the Senegal River delta have been recovered in France, Italy, Netherlands, former Yugoslavia, Poland and Russia. British breeders migrate south through France and Italy, where they are joined by migrants from further east, en route to West

Africa. Return migration commences February, nearly all birds having left Senegal by the end of March, though the main return passage through central Europe occurs March–April. Thus, birds arriving in Scilly in spring may be British breeders, or birds en route to northern Europe, as far east perhaps as western Siberia. In mainland Cornwall, it is described as a scarce passage migrant in fluctuating numbers, mainly in spring. It has bred there on at least six occasions, including 1981–83 (*CBWPSAR* 69).

## Blue-winged Teal *Anas discors* A BBRC 1.2%

**Rare migrant, full written description required by the BBRC.**

1977 One (female) Porth Hellick, St Mary's & Tresco Great Pool 24th August to 27th October
*British Birds* 71: 493
1982 One (female) Porth Hellick, St Mary's 9th to 20th September *British Birds* 76: 486
1989 One (juvenile or first-winter female) Porth Hellick, St Mary's 7th October
*British Birds* 83: 450, 477
[1999 One (female) Newford Duck Pond, St Mary's 26th October] *British Birds* 95: 527
2000 One (first-winter male) Tresco 10th to 27th October *British Birds* 94: 463

Breeds North America, from British Columbia east to Newfoundland and south to California, New Mexico, central Texas and Louisiana. Monotypic. Migratory, wintering south of breeding range, from Florida and southern Texas south to Chile and Argentina. Overall pattern of breeding population unclear, but significant 'downturn' in Canada in last 15 years (Bryant 1997).

A specimen obtained in Dumfriesshire in 1858 is the likely first British and Irish record (Palmer 2000) and no other occurred in Britain up to publication of E H Rodd's *The Birds of Cornwall and The Scilly Islands* (Rodd 1880), though by the early 20th century it was beginning to appear with more regularity in Ireland (Witherby *et al.* 1940).

First record for Scilly and the Cornish mainland was an immature female that mainly frequented the Porth Hellick area of St Mary's, having arrived on 24th August 1977. In the evenings it took to feeding along the shore before moving to nearby Tresco some time between 9th and 12th September, being then confined to the southern end of the Great Pool and last seen on 27th October. The next record was also of a female, this time at Porth Hellick for eleven days from 9th September 1982 (with another at Marazion, west Cornwall, on 18th), and the third, yet another female and again a probable first-winter, was viewable at Porth Hellick for just 7th October 1989. The supposed fourth record also involved a female, which was on view at Newford Duck Pond, St Mary's, on 26th October 1999 (*IOSBR* 1999); however, in October 2002 the BBRC finally rejected this record (*British Birds* 95: 527). The long-awaited male and the fourth record for the islands finally materialised in October 2000, in the form of a first-winter individual viewable for 18 days on Tresco.

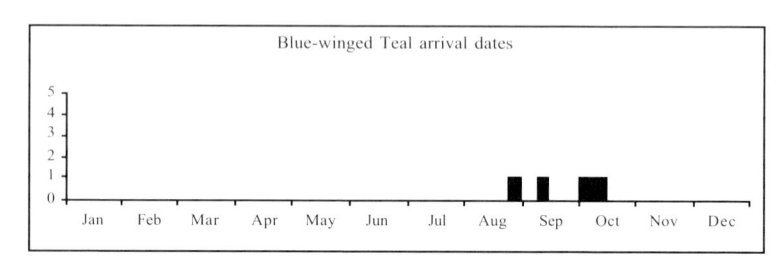

Blue-winged Teal arrival dates

The rejected 1999 individual was reported at the same time as, or within a day, of Green-winged Teal *A. carolinensis*, Lesser Scaup *Aythya affinis* and Surf Scoter *Melanitta perspicillata*. The Chart lists all four acceptable Blue-winged Teal arrival dates and shows yet another fairly obvious Nearctic migration pattern, similar to that for American Wigeon *A. americana*, Ring-necked Duck *Aythya collaris* and Surf Scoter *Melanitta perspicillata*. Average length of stay was just under 24 days, but is reduced to under eight if the 1977 individual is discounted. With 232 sightings accepted by the BBRC by the end of 1999, the first three Scillonian individuals represent 1.2% of the British total since 1958; prior to that time there were just 19 accepted national records (BBRC 2000).

A breeding concentration in the central North American prairies means that most migrants use the inland rather than Atlantic or Pacific flyways. Southward migration occurs from mid-August to October – fitting the Scillonian arrivals well – and, like Garganey *A. querquedula* in Europe, is particularly rapid: a ringed bird moving from Alberta to Venezuela in four weeks (Cramp *et al.* 1977–94). Cramp *et al.* consider the lack of known transatlantic crossings, compared with, say, Green-winged Teal, attributable to few Blue-winged Teals using the eastern Atlantic coast of North America. In support of this view they quote ringing evidence showing a possible eastern Canadian origin for European arrivals.

## Shoveler (Northern Shoveler) *Anas clypeata* A

**Uncommon migrant or winter visitor in small numbers, very occasionally breeds.**

Breeds northern Eurasia, from Iceland and Great Britain east to Kamchatka and south to Mediterranean and Caspian Seas, also northern North America, from Alaska east to Nova Scotia. Mainly migratory, in Europe wintering south to North Africa and Nile Valley. Monotypic. Amber-listed in UK: 20% or more of northwest European non-breeding population occurs in UK (Gregory *et al.* 2002).

Earliest mention of Shoveler in Scilly appears to be Francis Rodd's comment in a letter to his uncle, E H Rodd, to the effect that a few were on the pools in late December 1864 (Rodd 1880). Following this record was the suggestion that the weather in winter 1870 may have been particularly severe, Francis noting a flock of Shoveler on the sea (but out of gun-shot range) on 28th November and a 'large flock' somewhere in the islands on 21st December (Rodd 1880). Francis also recorded that this species appears among the list of 'game and wildfowl' shot, presumably mainly on Tresco, during winter 1878–79. Sadly, though, he noted it only as killed 'in more or less numbers'. However, in the main text of his *The Birds of Cornwall and The Scilly Isles*, E H Rodd (1880) noted only that Shoveler occurred occasionally in winter, though Francis and co-author James Clark later described it as a fairly frequent winter visitor to the islands, being most in evidence during hard frosts (Clark & Rodd 1906). E H Rodd's references to it in 19th century mainland Cornwall were equally brief, describing it as not at all uncommon in severe winters.

In the *Victoria History of Cornwall* (W Page 1906), James Clark thought it the most abundant duck in west Cornwall during some winters, whilst Penhallurick (1969) recorded it as occurring in mainland Cornwall mainly between mid-September and March, recalling no flock greater than 108. The latter author also confirmed that on Scilly smaller winter groups were the norm, but with more expected in hard weather, up to a maximum of 20. Nothing, then, appears to have changed in that time, with 20 off Samson in December 1995 being probably the greatest single flock count in the last 20 years. If anything, winter numbers have shown a decrease, with a total or near total absence in some years, but with a few birds present during summer in all years since at least 1980. Certainly, there is little now to support the earlier statement (Owen *et al.* 1986) that the wintering flock of up to 60 plus on Tresco Great Pool make the islands significant in terms of the southwest peninsula, even though mainland numbers remain appreciably low. In most years on Scilly, there are fairly distinct signs of passage, though more so in autumn than spring and always with the precise picture clouded by long-staying individuals.

Despite its poor representation in terms of numbers, Shoveler has bred in Scilly. The first record involved a clutch of ten eggs found on 17th May 1958 in a nest situated on a piece of raised moorland some 200 metres from a freshwater pool (*CBWPSAR* 28). Unfortunately, details of the island and site are not given, and although Penhallurick (1969) speculates on it being Tresco, the description could fit any one of a number of sites, on more than one island. Next mention of probable breeding involved at least two pairs on Tresco during summer 1973 (*IOSBR* 1973) and a further suspicion of breeding at the same site in 1974 and 1978. In comparison, the first recorded attempt at breeding on mainland Cornwall occurred in 1997 (*CBWPSAR* 67).

Shoveler breeds no closer to Scilly than perhaps east Devon and the Somerset Levels (Gibbons *et al.* 1993) and the British and Irish breeding population probably moves south as far as France and Spain, even North Africa. These breeders are replaced in winter by birds from as far east as western Siberia, and probably Iceland (Cramp *et al.* 1977–94, Wernham *et al.* 2002), some of which also move further south as winter progresses (Lack 1986; Wernham *et al.* 2002). The source of substantial numbers wintering in West and north-central Africa is unclear, but is though likely to involve European breeders (Cramp *et al.* 1977–94). British winter numbers formerly peaked February–March, but there is now an obvious November peak

(Lack 1986). There is a suggestion, too, that a succession of mild winters throughout the 1960s and mid-1970s obviated the need for returning migrants to stop off in Britain, with the habit then persisting (Owen *et al.* in Lack 1986). Whatever the truth, this current pattern of known movement fits the situation on Scilly.

## Red-crested Pochard *Netta rufina* A

**Extremely rare migrant or vagrant. Treated by the BBRC as a national Scarce Migrant, full written description required by the SRP.**

c. 1927   One Scilly 21st November   Penhallurick 1969
    1985   One (eclipse male) Tresco 30th August to 1st October & 28th October to 27th December

Breeds central Asia with small scattered populations in western and southern Europe, from Spain east to Caspian Sea and north to southern Baltic. Monotypic. Migratory, more so in north of range. Removed from BBRC Rarities List January 1963 (Harber & Swaine 1963)

E H Rodd was familiar with this species under the name 'Red-crested Duck' but his sole mention of it in his *The Birds of Cornwall and The Scilly Islands* concerns a bird shot at the Swanpool near Falmouth on mainland Cornwall in February 1845. He lamented the fact that rather than being preserved it was eaten, though this was fortunately not before it had been examined by a competent authority. Penhallurick's only contribution was mention of the 1927 individual, as listed in the Tresco Abbey records (Penhallurick 1969).

The only other record concerns the male in eclipse plumage that arrived in Scilly on southeasterly winds the day after a Black Stork *Ciconia nigra*. First found on Tresco, it remained until 1st October and then returned on 28th of that month, before finally departing on 27th December. During its temporary absence from the islands, what was presumably the same individual paid a visit to St Stithians Reservoir in nearby mainland Cornwall.

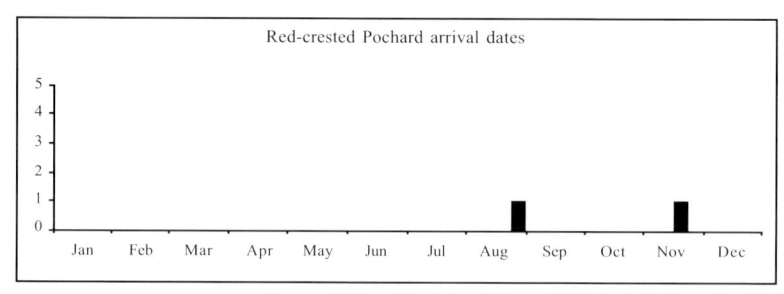

Red-crested Pochard arrival dates

The introduction of at least one pair of pinioned Red-crested Pochards on the St Mary's Porthloo Duck pond since the 1990s poses a potential problem to future identification of this species in Scilly, particularly should any progeny of these birds be left free-winged. In addition to this, of course, the status of most British sightings is clouded by the possibility of escapees or birds of feral origin, and Cramp *et al.* (1977–94) consider infrequent winter records in north or northwest Europe likely to include escapes. The main autumn migration in the west and east of its range occurs from late October to early November but earlier movements of moulting birds, which congregate at traditional sites in central-western Europe, obscure the picture.

## Pochard (Common Pochard) *Aythya ferina* A

**An annual migrant, winter visitor in small numbers and a recent breeding colonist.**

Breeds central Eurasia, from Iceland, British Isles and Denmark, south to Iberia, Nile delta and Turkey, east to Lake Baikal. Mainly migratory. Monotypic. Amber-listed in UK: 20% or more of northwest-European non-breeding population occurs in UK (Gregory *et al.* 2002).

E H Rodd was particularly brief in his description of the status of Pochard in the 19th century, describing it merely as a common winter visitor to Cornwall, particularly west Cornwall. He described it as 'one of the best wildfowl for the table', as a consequence of which 'professional gunners find a ready sale for all they can procure' (Rodd 1880). As regards Scilly, the elder Rodd merely listed it as occurring in winter, but his nephew Francis Rodd helps cast a little more light on the situation, noting that six were on the Tresco pools on 1st January 1865, and one was killed by overhead wires in the St Mary's Moors on 6th January 1871. He also commented, less helpfully, that it was shot 'in more or less numbers' in Scilly during winter 1878–79 (Rodd 1880). Francis and his co-author, James Clark, added little to this in their later review of Scilly's birds, simply describing it as an irregular autumn and winter visitor, either singly or in small flocks (Clark & Rodd 1906).

Unfortunately, the absence of published ornithological records for Scilly during the early 20th century leaves a serious gap in our knowledge of this and many other species in the islands. First mention then of Pochard after Clark and Rodd's earlier comment came with a report of 'several' on Tresco's freshwater pools in December 1957 (*CBWPSAR* 27). For a few years following this date it appeared only sporadically in published reports, but certainly from the late 1960s onwards featured almost annually in autumn, winter and spring. During the ten years from 1990, it was recorded in maximum winter numbers of from 16 to 67, at an average of just over 40. Latest spring sightings ranged from late March to mid-April, whereas first autumn arrivals were equally condensed, from late September to mid-October. There seems to be evidence among the random counts of a fall-off in autumn numbers around November, followed by a further build-up, to maximum winter totals in the period December–February. This is presumably because migrants are involved earlier in the autumn, followed by wintering individuals. However, as with several other species, distinguishing wintering individuals from spring and autumn migrants is difficult.

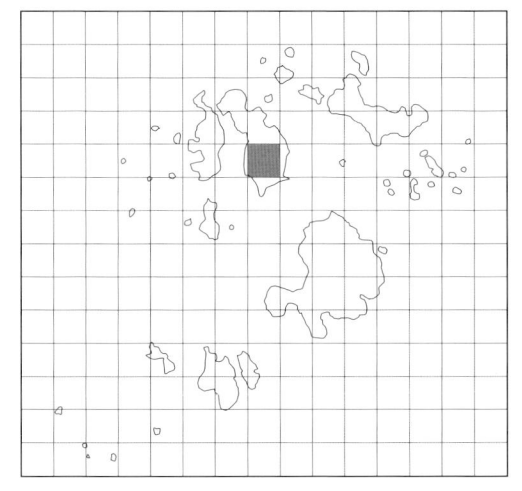

Penhallurick (1969) considered that most Pochard appeared on St Agnes, but more recently Tresco's freshwater pools predominate, with the lower numbers on St Mary's and St Agnes pools rarely mentioned. However, birds can appear on apparently unsuitable pieces of water, as did the female that spent two January days on the tiny Porthloo Duck Pond. The largest individual count involved 250 on Tresco on two dates in January 1978, though 175 were noted at the same site in January 1979 and 180 in 1981. Intriguingly, the 1978 birds were believed to have originated from Drift Reservoir in mainland Cornwall, though reasons for this assumption are unclear. Winter counts of this magnitude were not unusual during the 1970s and early 80s, prompting Owen *et al.* (1986) to comment that wintering numbers on Scilly were appreciably larger than on any of the Cornish lakes – but see above for more recent maximum winter counts.

**1-km Pochard Breeding Distribution – 2000–01 (data Chown & Lock 2002)**

Interestingly, two sites in mainland Cornwall recorded January totals in excess of 200 individuals during 1999 and the overall January county total exceeded 500 (*CBWPSAR* 69). Until very recently, there were no known or suspected breeding records for the islands, though at least two individuals had summered. The first, a probably injured male, remained on Tresco Great Pool from summer 1992 until last seen in September 1994, whereas a female with a damaged wing remained at the same site during summer 1999, being last noted in late October that year. However, the 2000 Breeding Bird Atlas recorded three to four broods on the Tresco pools during 2001, with up to four pairs believed present in that single 1-km square, though no young apparently fledged from these attempts (Chown & Lock 2002).

The exact pattern of migration among British breeding Pochards is unclear, though there is evidence that some at least move to southeast France (Cramp *et al.* 1977–94). Birds from Europe, as far east as western Siberia, certainly reach Britain and Ireland, particularly during hard weather (Wernham *et al.* 2002), as indicated by the Latvian-ringed individual shot on St Mary's in 1992. However, the main European and western Asian wintering concentration occurs quite far south, a substantial proportion reaching the Mediterranean and North Africa, with some even crossing the Sahara to coastal West Africa, or negotiating the Nile Valley into East Africa.

**Recoveries**
C71552      Pul Lake Engure, Latvia May 15 1990      SH Porth Hellick, St Mary's November 3,1992
**Pochard Ringing Recaptures**

## [Pochard/Ring-necked Duck *Aythya ferina/A. collaris*]

A bird showing the apparent characteristics of a hybrid between these two species remained on Tresco's Great Pool from 5th to 22nd March 1990 (*IOSBR* 1990).

## Ring-necked Duck *Aythya collaris* A

Rare migrant. Treated by the BBRC as a national Scarce Migrant, full written description required by the SRP.

1979    One (female or immature) Great Pool, Tresco 17th October to 1st November
1980    One (male) Great Pool, Tresco 30th September until at least 2nd January 1981
1982    Three (male & two first-winter) Porth Hellick, St Mary's 27th September
1985    One (first-winter male) Tresco 14th October to 17th November
1986    One (male) Great Pool, Tresco 29th October
1988    One (eclipse male) Great Pool, Tresco 21st October to 7th November
1989    One (male) Great Pool, Tresco 13th November
1990    One (male) Great Pool, Tresco 8th to 17th October
1993    One (eclipse male) Great Pool, Tresco 23rd September
1999    Two (first-winter males) Porth Hellick, St Mary's & Great Pool, Tresco 11th October to 2nd November
2000    Up to three (including adult drake) St Mary's & Tresco 14th to 23rd October
2001    One (immature) St Agnes 2nd to 15th October
2002    *One (first-winter) St Mary's & Tresco 9th October to at least 5th November*

*Birding World 15: 444*

Breeds North America, from British Columbia east to Newfoundland and south to Washington, Michigan and New York; breeding range recently extended to east of Great Lakes. Monotypic. Migratory, wintering mainly USA south of breeding range. Removed from BBRC Rarities List January 1994 (Lansdown and the Rarities Committee 1993)

As this species was not discovered in the wild in Britain until 1955 (Palmer 2000), when a bird was seen in Gloucestershire, its absence from Scillonian records prior to 1979 comes as no surprise. In fact, the second British record was not found until March 1977 (from the same site), and this being the case, Scilly has fared quite well, but perhaps no more than might be expected given the archipelago's reputation for hosting Nearctic migrants. Up until December 1993, however, when the species was removed from the BBRC's Rarities List, the number of accepted British and Irish records had grown to an impressive 379 (Palmer 2000).

There have been 11 records involving up to 16 individuals since the first arrival in Scilly and up until the end of year 2000. The Chart shows all 11 arrival dates and leaves little room for doubt that these birds were involved in some form of migration rather than being just casual wanderers, though exactly where they were coming from or going to remains open to discussion. Birds remained on average about 18 days, though this drops to around 10 days if the 1980 part-wintering individual is omitted, and six birds (four records) stayed for just one day or less.

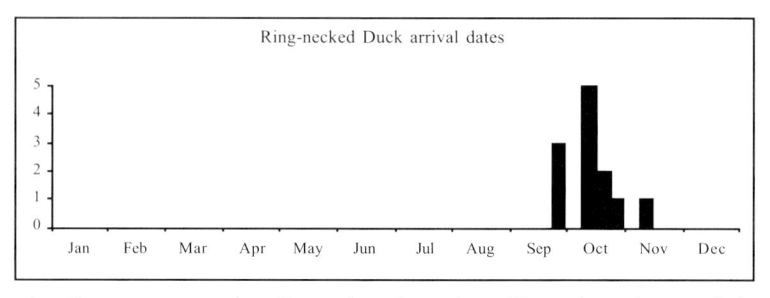

Autumn migration commences late September through to November, the population then being distributed over western, eastern and southern USA, south of the main breeding range as far as Mexico,

West Indies and Guatemala, extreme individuals reaching Venezuela. Spring passage commences late February with birds reaching the most southerly breeding grounds by late March (Cramp et al. 1977–94). It seems difficult to ignore the comparable timing of Ring-necked Duck's reported population increase east of the Great Lakes and its recent arrival in Britain and elsewhere in Europe. However, this in itself does not help explain the mechanism by which individuals cross the Atlantic. Some authorities, e.g. Cramp et al. 1977–94, still consider that at least some records involve escapes from captivity, but that theory seems wholly unsupported by the timing of arrivals in Scilly. Since preparing this account another individual was present on St Agnes.

## Ferruginous Duck                                                    *Aythya nyroca* A

**Extremely rare migrant or vagrant, full written descriptions required by the SRP.**

    1944   One (male) shot Scilly 15th January   *CBWPSAR* 14
    1997   One (female) Newford Duck Pond, St Mary's 18th to 27th May 1997

Breeds central Europe east to Kazakhstan and Aral Sea, wintering southern Europe and North Africa eastwards to Indian subcontinent. Monotypic. Migratory with pronounced movement out of northern part of range.

No early writer makes reference to this species in either Scilly or Cornwall, though it was known to occur in Britain by that time, *The Handbook of British Birds* (Witherby et al. 1940) describing it as a rare vagrant. There are, in fact, just two island records, the first of which is quite old and involves a male shot on 15th January 1944. The report appears in *CBWPSAR* 14, and, although the location is not given, the record originated from Major A A Dorrien-Smith, and thus seems likely to have been Tresco. The second individual was a female that arrived on St Mary's on 18th May 1997, spending time at both Newford Duck Pond and Porthloo before departing the islands on 27th.

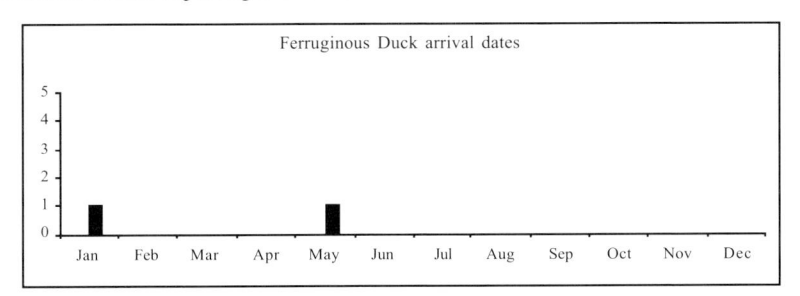

*Ferruginous Duck arrival dates*

The closest substantial breeding populations are in central-eastern Europe, e.g. Poland and Hungary, with smaller isolated populations in southern Spain, and with occasional breeding pairs in several other countries. Escapes and feral breeding groups, however, confuse the situation (Hagemeijer & Blair 1997). Ferruginous Duck maintains its solitary and secretive nature into the wintering areas and can occur in substantially greater numbers than are readily apparent (Cramp et al. 1977–94). Details of migration are still poorly understood, with no available data for large parts of its breeding range and there are few long-distance ringing recoveries. Nonetheless, a juvenile ringed in the former Czechoslovakia was recovered in Brittany the following March. Departure from the breeding grounds commences September and peaks by October, with return movement commencing early March and lasting well into May – the latter probably involving non-breeders.

## Tufted Duck                                                         *Aythya fuligula* A

**Scarce migrant and winter and summer visitor in small numbers, up to three pairs have bred in recent years.**

Breeds northern Eurasia, from Iceland east to Kamchatka and northern Japan. Predominately migratory, in West Palearctic wintering south to North Africa, Nile Delta and Iraq. Monotypic. National 9% increase 1994–99 (Bashford & Noble 2000), BTO Waterways Bird Survey showed 41% increase 1975–2000. Green-listed in UK: in need of basic conservation assistance (Gregory et al. 2002).

Tufted Duck first bred in Britain around 1849, in Yorkshire and Nottinghamshire, and even a brief glance at its historical distribution shows it was still thinly distributed in Britain and Ireland by the close of the 19th century (Holloway 1996), perhaps then breeding no closer to Scilly than Hampshire, Shropshire and southwest Ireland. Interestingly, E H Rodd knew it in Cornwall only as a winter visitor, 'on inland pools, and quiet, out of the way ponds – not in large flocks, but in parties of perhaps ten to twenty'. Perhaps significantly, he makes no mention of it in relation to Scilly and omits it from his appended *List of the Birds Observed in the Scilly Islands* (Rodd 1880). First mention of it in the islands, then, comes from James Clark and Francis Rodd, who described it as occasional during winter, either singly or in pairs, but less regular than Scaup *A. marila* (Clark & Rodd 1906). The first specific 20th century published reference of it, however, is probably the 1932 mention of a pair on Porth Hellick Pool, St Mary's, for three weeks in May (*CBWPSAR* 2).

Even as recently as the mid-1960s, Penhallurick (1969) felt able to describe it only as an increasingly common winter visitor to mainland Cornwall and an extremely scarce breeder, meanwhile noting a regular passage in spring and autumn. He also quoted it as an irregular visitor to Scilly's freshwater pools in parties of no more than ten, in all months, but particularly between December and May. The first specific 20th century mention of Tufted Duck in the islands appears to be the brief report of a single-day male on St Agnes Big Pool on 1st January 1955 (*CBWPSAR* 25), with another single-day sighting from Porth Hellick Pool, St Mary's, in September the following year. The first summer record involved a 1958 report of a 'pair' on Bryher on 28th May and a male, again at Porth Hellick, on at least four dates in July that same year. In fact, it seems to very quickly have become an annual visitor, both in winter and summer, appearing in the records in increasing numbers, almost annually from the mid- to late 1950s. The next mention of an apparent pair was in May 1970, again on Bryher, followed by a pair at Porth Hellick for two weeks in May 1972. Breeding was first confirmed by David Hunt in 1983, in the form of a pair on Tresco in June and a female with ducklings at the same site on 11th July. By this time, autumn or wintering numbers were occasionally reaching 25.

In total, up to three pairs have bred or attempted to breed in eleven years since 1963, only on Tresco and almost annually since 1988. Paradoxically, Tufted Duck remains something of a scarcity in Scilly. In general, greatest numbers occur in winter, and during the period 1990–99 the highest Tresco winter count was 60, followed by 52, but once less than ten. Over the same period, numbers on Tresco in summer range between five and eleven and for autumn ten to 20. Clearly there is a measure of seasonality involved and in at least some years birds may be absent from the islands for up to three months. Nevertheless, frequent inter-island movement and winter arrivals cloud the situation and this difficulty is magnified by a rapid dispersal of all duck species from Tresco's freshwater pools at the onset of any organised autumn shooting on that island. Suggestions of an annual summer moult-migration involving Scillonian Tufted Ducks (*IOSBR* 1999) may be correct, but if so have yet to be proved. Although Tresco remains the Tufted Duck's stronghold within the islands, individuals or small groups do appear at other sites, notably Porth Hellick Pool on St Mary's. Regardless of occasional published references to a 19th century wildfowl collection on Tresco, little information is available now on species and numbers involved, thus the possibility of breeding pairs having colonised Scilly from that source cannot be dismissed entirely.

Tufted Duck breeds as close to Scilly as mainland Cornwall, though only scarcely (Gibbons *et al.* 1993). However, regardless of mainland Cornwall's substantially greater landmass, numbers for the period October to March 1999 varied between 180 and 370, decreasing to just 17 in June (*CBWPSAR* 69). According to Cramp *et al.* (1977–94), Tufted Duck is primarily migratory, with birds from northern Britain moving mainly southwest into Ireland, though some apparently move as far as Iberia. Icelandic birds winter mainly in Ireland, with some reaching southern Britain, France and Iberia. Additionally, many from northern European populations as far east as western Siberia also reach Britain, particularly during hard weather, and there is now a small breeding population in Brittany (Guermeur & Monnat 1980). These various movements make it difficult to ascertain the origin of individuals visiting in the islands.

# Scaup (Greater Scaup) *Aythya marila* A

**Infrequent migrant and winter visitor.**

Breeds arctic Eurasia, from Iceland and Norway east to Kamchatka, also North America, from Aleutian Islands east to Hudson Strait, with outlying population Newfoundland. Polytypic: nominate *marila* occurs

Europe and northern Asia east to about 120°E; *mariloides* the remainder. Migratory, in West Palearctic wintering south to Black Sea, northern Mediterranean and central-western France. Amber-listed in UK: five-year mean of 1.4 breeding pairs; 20% or more of UK non-breeding population at ten or fewer sites; unfavourable world winter conservation status (Gregory *et al.* 2002).

Earliest evidence of Scaup on Scilly comes in the form of a complete femur found among debris excavated from the archaeological site at May's Hill on St Martin's. This is thought to originate from between the 2nd and 7th centuries AD (Turk 1984a, 1984b). E H Rodd knew it as a winter visitor to mainland Cornwall, mostly around the coast, though sometimes also at the mouths of larger rivers, but with no more than two or three killed each winter (Rodd 1880). He also recorded a shot adult female received from Scilly on 3rd November 1877 (Rodd 1877). Later still, James Clark and E H Rodd's nephew Francis described Scaup as appearing occasionally in the islands in winter, either singly or 'in pairs' and more regularly than Tufted Duck *A. fuligula* (Clark & Rodd 1906).

More recently, Penhallurick (1969) thought it occurred in Scilly more frequently in October than in winter, also noting the unseasonable record of a male on Tresco on 24th June 1964. He suggested that most birds stayed for little more than a day, citing an eleven-day stay as exceptional. Taking the ten years from 1990, the species continues to waver between scarce and uncommon, with a total of some 21 individuals recorded in seven of the ten years. Seven in 1994 was the most in any year and four, also in 1994, was the most together. Earliest arrival was 23rd August, though late October or early November was more usual, and the latest a bird remained was 17th May. Of particular note were the two males and two females first recorded on St Agnes on 28th April 1994, before relocating to Porth Hellick, St Mary's, where two males and a female stayed until 17th May. Regardless of Penhallurick's earlier findings, most Scaup remained in the islands for anything up to two months during the ten-year period, though there were a few single-day sightings. Most birds occurred on freshwater pools.

Scaup from both Iceland and northwest Europe winter in Britain and Ireland, the nearest main concentrations being around the coasts of southern England and south and southeast Ireland, but by comparison it is relatively scarce in southwest England (Lack 1986; Wernham *et al.* 2002). In mainland Cornwall during 1999, the highest monthly total was eleven, in February, though it was recorded in all months. The slightly smaller and more boldly marked North American and Asian *mariloides* might be expected to occur in Britain (Gantlett 1998), and given Scilly's attraction to Nearctic and East Palearctic vagrants it seems a likely place to look.

## Lesser Scaup *Aythya affinis* A BBRC 2.2%

**Extremely rare migrant or vagrant, full written description required by the BBRC.**

1999　One (eclipse male) Great Pool, Tresco 26th October to 11th November

*British Birds* 93: 523–524

Breeds western North America, northern populations migratory, wintering South America as far as Columbia. Monotypic. Population stable overall but with substantial increase in most easterly population, e.g. three-fold increase in central states since 1996 (Bryant 1997).

Despite a British and Irish total of 44 records in 13 years, and despite Scilly's known attraction for Nearctic migrants, an eclipse male Lesser Scaup found on Tresco's Great Pool on 26th October 1999 was the archipelago's first (*IOSBR* 1999; Vinicombe 1999), though the fact that ten of those 44 occurred in 1999 perhaps helps to put the species' previous absence from the islands into perspective. When first found the Tresco bird was accompanied by what appeared to be a juvenile but the presence of at least some white in the primaries meant doubt remained over this bird's true identification (*IOSBR* 1999).

The first Lesser Scaup for Britain and Ireland was discovered on Chasewater, Staffordshire, as recently as March 1987 and the second in Co. Down, Ireland, in 1988 (Palmer 2000). The first for Cornwall, a female at Drift Reservoir on 17th–18th November 1996, was followed in the county by a first-winter male at Argal Reservoir, Falmouth, in December of the same year (*CBWPSAR* 66).

An interesting earlier report concerned two 'small female Scaup' seen on the sea close inshore off St Agnes from 10th October 1954. The account is brief and open to interpretation but nevertheless quoted in full here for the purpose of completeness. The report, appearing in the annual *IOSBR* under the heading 'Scaup Duck', is attributed to Hilda Quick and reads as follows: 'Two females on Periglis Pool joined on

23rd by a similar, but larger bird. All had conspicuous white 'masks'. The larger bird remained for a month' (*CBWPSAR* 24). Sadly, we may never know the true identity of these two ducks!

A total of 44 Lesser Scaup records were accepted by the BBRC up until the end of 1999, when the single Scillonian occurrence represented just over 2% of the national figure (BBRC 2000). Although, nationally, the number of Lesser Scaup records continues to increase, the likelihood of either hybrid Scaup x Tufted Duck *A. fuligula*, or even hybrid Tufted x Pochard *A. ferina* being involved should be considered in all cases (*British Birds* 54: 49). In addition, the possibility of the slightly smaller North American and Asian *mariloides* form of Scaup being involved must also be kept in mind (Gantlett 1998)

## Eider (Common Eider) *Somateria mollissima* A

**Irregular winter visitor or migrant in small numbers, full written description required by SRP in all cases.**

Breeds northwest Europe from Iceland to Novaya Zemlya and south to Low Countries, including British Isles, plus northeast Asia, North America and Greenland. Partially migratory and dispersive. Polytypic: nominate *mollissima* occurs northwest Europe including Novaya Zemlya; *faeroensis* Faeroes; *borealis* arctic North Atlantic from Iceland to Frans Josef Land, Greenland and Baffin Island region; *dresseri* Atlantic North America; *sedentaria* Hudson Bay; *v-nigrum* northwest North America and arctic east Siberia. Amber-listed in UK: 50% or more of UK non-breeding population at ten or fewer sites (Gregory *et al.* 2002).

E H Rodd described Eider as perhaps rarer than Surf Scoter *Melanitta perspicillata* on Cornish coasts, recalling just a single Cornish-taken specimen, shot on the River Looe and preserved in Truro Museum. He suggested that it was best looked for either during or after severe winter weather (Rodd 1880). Surprisingly, E H Rodd made no mention of a male and female shot by Tresco gamekeeper David Smith in the 1870s and documented by Clark & Rodd (1906). The same authors gave details of a 'fine male' shot somewhere in the islands on 5th April 1882, following E H Rodd's death, plus three shot in Tean Sound on 18th December 1891, the latter having 'been under observation for six weeks'. The only additional 19th century report concerns Gilbert White's comment that one was shot on Tresco in 1881 (in Jesse 1887).

Penhallurick (1969) uncovered only two Scillonian records for the early 20th century, involving just three birds. These were followed by the first of the modern records, one off the Eastern Isles on the last day of 1961 (*CBWPSAR* 31), it clearly being scarce enough then in Scilly to warrant a brief description. There were subsequently occasional isolated reports, but it remained scarce, e.g. three reported sightings in the 1970s, involving single-day visits of five birds, including three males together off Bryher in April 1971. More recently, there are slight signs of an increase in both the number and frequency of reports, the 1990s producing a total of 14 birds in ten separate sightings in six of the ten years – being evenly distributed between spring (4), autumn (3) and winter (3). Interestingly, only eight out of these fourteen birds were reportedly in adult male or immature male plumage, suggesting that the species may not easily have been overlooked in the past and that these 1990's sightings represent a genuine improvement in its status in Scilly.

The situation in the islands seems to have been mirrored on mainland Cornwall, where there were just eight documented records prior to 1900 and a further eight from 1931 to 1951, since when it became annual (*CBWPSAR* 69). In 1999, fewer than 50 reports were spread over the period October to April, but with a clear November peak. In Britain, Eiders breed no closer to Scilly than Northern Ireland and northwest England (Gibbons *et al.* 1993), plus some breed in Germany and the Netherlands (Hagemeijer & Blair 1997). The British wintering population remains largely within or close to the breeding areas, it being only thinly distributed about southern England at that time, and the Baltic is the probable main source of birds wintering in England, or at least in eastern counties (Lack 1986; Wernham *et al.* 2002). Cramp *et al.* (1977–94), however, consider the Netherlands to be almost certainly the source of many wintering Eiders on coastal eastern and southern England, this population being partially migratory and wintering south to western France.

## Long-tailed Duck *Clangula hyemalis* A

**Scarce but regular winter visitor, normally singly.**

Circumpolar, breeds arctic Eurasia, arctic Canada, Greenland, Iceland, Spitsbergen, Novaya Zemlya and Franz Josef Land. Monotypic. Most populations wholly migratory, in West Palearctic winters south to

Baltic, North Sea and coastal Britain and Ireland. Upgraded from Green- to Amber-listed in UK 2002: 20% or more of UK non-breeding population at ten or fewer sites (Gregory *et al.* 2002).

Bone remains unearthed from the prehistoric site at May's Hill, St Martin's, originated from between the 2nd and 7th century AD and were identified as this species (Turk 1984a, 1984b). There are four 19th century records, the two earliest of which came from Tresco and St Mary's in 1852. E H Rodd described it as one of the rarest of Cornwall's winter visitors, its appearance usually preceding severe weather. In his normally comprehensive account of *The Birds of Cornwall and The Scilly Islands* he listed a bird shot in early November 1864 (Rodd 1880, 1864b) but made no mention of the previous island records. Fortunately, his nephew Francis and co-author James Clark provided more detail (Clark & Rodd 1906), pointing out that Augustus Pechell shot the two 1852 individuals, whilst a fourth was obtained by an unknown gunman from Tresco's Abbey Pool in October 1854. All four shot birds were immatures.

The next recorded sighting was not until 1960 and involved a bird that came down at night in a yard in Hugh Town, St Mary's, on 12th October (*CBWPSAR* 30). It died soon after and Peter MacKenzie sent the body to the Natural History Museum, where it remains (Spirit Specimen 1060.36). From the mid-1960s onwards, Long-tailed Duck records became nearly annual on Scilly, almost invariably in winter and usually singly – though with a three-year absence during 1986–88. However, there are notable exceptions, such as the flock of 16 viewable from the deck of RMV *Scillonian III* in October 1991, though normally three to four is a crowd. Also normal are apparent multiple short-term sightings which, when analysed, are frequently found to involve single but highly mobile individuals. One to three birds annually in the islands seem to be about the norm. Most arrivals remain on the sea, but a notable exception was the first-winter female, first seen on St Agnes Pool before switching its allegiance to, of all places, Porthloo Duck Pond, from 7th to 10th November 1998. A bird that frequented the St Mary's and St Agnes areas from 26th October 1990 was found dead on the latter island on 3rd November, whilst an oiled individual was off the south side of St Mary's briefly during October 1993. The lack of records for this and many other species during the early 20th century is partly explained by an absence of published annual reports, but is compounded by an apparent failure by some subsequent editors to report comprehensively, although, in their defence, they mainly rely upon what they are told by observers.

The closest Long-tailed Duck breeding populations to Britain are in central Norway and Iceland (Hagemeijer & Blair 1997) and the Baltic holds the greatest West Palearctic wintering concentrations; up to 250,000 per 100 km$^2$ (Cramp *et al.* 1977–94). However, despite what might otherwise be assumed, there is little or no evidence of Icelandic birds reaching Britain during winter, even though some from Iceland reach southern Greenland and some Greenland birds reach Iceland and continental Europe, e.g. Denmark. Long-tailed Ducks ringed in Russia have been recovered west as far as Denmark, and the Baltic area is thought to be used by most Russian and Siberian breeders. Nonetheless the origin of British and Irish winterers remains unclear.

# Common Scoter *Melanitta nigra* A

**Scarce migrant and winter visitor**

Breeds northern Eurasia, from Iceland, Scotland and central Norway east to Kamchatka, also two widely separated North American populations in western Alaska and northeast Canada. Polytypic: nominate *nigra* occurs northern Europe and northern Asia to 120°E; *americana* remaining northeast Asia and North America. Red-listed in UK: recent rapid 25-year, 50% or greater contraction of breeding range and moderate breeding decline; 1995 breeding population of 95 pairs; 50% or more of UK non-breeding population at ten or fewer sites (Gregory *et al.* 2002).

Early writers clearly knew Common Scoter as a frequent winter visitor to the coasts of mainland Cornwall, according to E H Rodd (1880) sometimes in large flocks. E H Rodd also knew that they were sometimes shot as they ventured up the various Cornish rivers, as well as falling victim to inshore fishing nets in Mount's Bay, west Cornwall. James Clark and Francis Rodd (E H Rodd's nephew) commented that an immature was shot behind Bryher (presumably on the island's west side) in 1854 and Francis saw one between Tresco and St Mary's around 1860. They also recorded six killed on the Tresco pools in March 1881, with at least two others on unspecified dates (Clark & Rodd 1906).

More recently, Penhallurick described it as common in Cornwall as a passage migrant and winter visitor in both the 19th and early 20th centuries, though always scarcer in Scilly (Penhallurick 1969). The most noted in the islands up to 1969 were 24 in Crow Sound in November 1957. However, during at least the last 20 years it occurred annually, more often in the second half of the year, although in some years as few as 15–20 individuals have been recorded in total. Even so, the early 1990s witnessed something of a purple patch, with the 195 recorded in 1991 representing a relative high for this species. Since then, however, numbers of sightings returned to around the 10 to 20 level annually. Birds more commonly remain on the sea but individuals or groups do occasionally visit freshwater pools on Tresco and elsewhere. Some 30–50% of sightings involved one to four birds and few flocks were noted that were greater than 20; a report of 60 seen from the RMV *Scillonian III* on 24th October 1990 perhaps involved more than one flock.

Common Scoter breeds no closer to Scilly than Scotland and northwest Ireland and the nearest Continental population is in southern Norway. All, though, are migratory or partially so, as indeed are populations breeding further afield. The wintering area of British and Irish birds remains unclear, but Icelandic birds are known to winter around coastal Britain and France, some reaching Spain and Portugal, with at least one individual reaching the Azores (Cramp *et al.* 1977–94). Lack (1986) commented on large flocks passing through the English Channel in spring and autumn, attributing them to populations in Russia and Fennoscandia, which winter in Britain and Ireland but also reach France and Iberia.

Autumn arrivals should be looked for from mid-September – one 1990's individual appeared on 24th August – but mid-October is a more likely date. Most Common Scoters vacate the islands by late November but birds regularly winter within the islands in very small numbers, though not annually. The latest 1990's spring sighting was 3rd June. According to Cramp *et al.* (1977–94), peak autumn passage in the North Sea occurs November to early December, though Icelandic birds move south earlier. Return passage commences late February to April in both the Atlantic and North Sea, with northern breeding grounds reoccupied from mid-May. As a consequence, it seems probable that birds reaching Scilly originate either mainly from Iceland, given the early arrival dates, or northern or northeast Europe.

With its more extensive coastline, mainland Cornwall fares rather better than Scilly, and monthly totals for 1999 peaked at 288, surprisingly in July, though recorded totals for three months were into three figures and no month had less than 30. The recognisable North American and northeast Asian form *americana*, or 'Black Scoter', winters in both the Pacific and western North Atlantic, from Newfoundland southwards. Black Scoter has occurred in Britain at least five times (Gantlett 1998) and in the Netherlands at least twice (Cramp *et al.* 1977–94) and Scilly's proven attraction for Nearctic migrants makes it a likely recipient.

## Surf Scoter *Melanitta perspicillata* A

**Rare migrant. Treated by the BBRC as a national Scarce Migrant, full written description required by the SRP**

    1865   One (exhausted male) St Mary's 22nd September   Rodd 1865h
    1867   One (first-winter male – shot) Tresco October   Rodd 1867d
    1975   One (first-winter) Tresco & Round Island area 5th to 23rd October
    1976   One (first-winter) St Mary's 19th October
    1984   One (female) St Mary's 2nd October
    1994   One (first-winter female) various locations 21st to 26th October
    1998   One (female or first-winter) off Horse Point, St Agnes 27th October
    1999   One (adult female) off St Mary's, Tresco & St Martin's 27th to 31st October
    2002   One (immature female) off various islands at least 25th to 29th November

Breeds North America, from Alaska east to Labrador and south to northern British Columbia. Monotypic. Migratory, winters coastal Atlantic south to Florida and coastal Pacific south to Baja California. Removed from BBRC Rarities List January 1991 (Lansdown & the Rarities Committee 1990).

There are two surprisingly early Scillonian records of this North American rarity. The first is E H Rodd's reference to a moribund adult male found by a boy on the beach near Carn Thomas, St Mary's, on 22nd September 1865 (Rodd 1865g, 1880), the carcass of which was sent over to Penzance by boat for preservation by local taxidermist Vingoe, who immediately showed it to Rodd. E H Rodd's classic description is well worth repeating here: 'From the intense black of its plumage, the strongly developed tubercular enlargements on each side of the posterior part of the upper mandible, the definite division of white between these, and the brilliant orange-coloured anterior portion of the upper mandible, terminating in a pearl-grey nail, I took it to be a very old bird; the legs and feet were tile red, with the interdigital membrane black.' Two years later, in October 1867, E H Rodd's nephew Francis Rodd shot an immature male at Skirt Point on Tresco's southeast corner, the body reaching E H Rodd in Penzance on 28th (Rodd 1867d, 1880). However, these two Scillonian records were preceded on mainland Cornwall by a mutilated body found on a beach near Pendennis Castle in 1845, following a winter gale (Rodd 1880; Penhallurick 1969).

There are seven 20th century records for the islands, the first of which occurred over 100 years after Francis Rodd's shot Tresco individual. All but one were discovered in October between 2nd and 27th and all were either female or first-winter. The Chart shows all but the most recent modern arrival dates and belies any suggestion that these were wandering vagrants; indeed, what is perhaps most interesting about these records is the suggestion of onward autumn passage, but without any indication of a return. Three birds stayed one day or less and the average duration of stay was just 5.5 days.

Although it spent much time on the sea, the 1975 individual visited Tresco Great Pool on most days of its stay. The 1994 individual was initially viewable off St Mary's and St Agnes, and then off Tresco and Bryher on 21st, before being refound in poor condition off Great Parr, Bryher, on 24th–26th. The arrival of the 1998 bird coincided with one on Quessant, Brittany, the previous day, two in Ireland, plus three arrivals in mainland Cornwall between 13th and 29th October, the last of which remained until 25th November. These three birds took the Cornish mainland total to ten, all of which occurred since 1983 (*CBWPSAR* 68). The sixth of Scilly's 20th century records remained feeding in shallow waters south of St Helen's and Tean for five days, during which time it was visited by several boatloads of birders seeking close-up views.

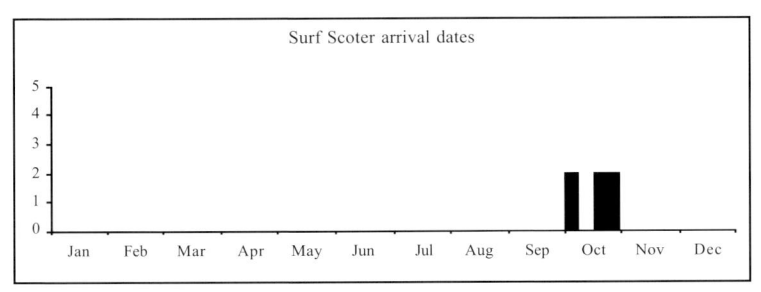

*Surf Scoter arrival dates*

This is the commonest scoter species off the Atlantic coast of North America in autumn, moving south from late September to early December and peaking off the New England coast during mid-October. It is the most frequent Nearctic duck in Europe, having occurred, among other countries, in Sweden, Finland, Netherlands, Belgium, France, the Mediterranean and even the former Czechoslovakia (Cramp *et al.* 1977–94). The route by which it reaches Europe in such numbers is unclear. The possibility exists that it may have been overlooked in the past, though in Scilly, numbers of all three scoter species are small and it therefore seems unlikely.

# Velvet Scoter *Melanitta fusca* A

**Rare migrant or winter visitor, full written description required by the SRP**

    1911   One Bishop Rock 23rd March   Penhallurick 1969
    1957   Two Crow Sound 28th November
    1959   One St Agnes 8th November
    1962   Two (male & female) Eastern Isles 19th December
    1972   One Horse Point, St Agnes 17th October
    1975   One (male) off Tean 20th September
    1978   Three off St Agnes 28th October
    1991   Two (adult & immature) south end of Tresco 24th December
    1996   One (female) south end of Tresco 23rd November
    1998   Two (male & female) south of St Mary's 8th May
    1999   One (female or immature) Crow Sound 24th October to 11th November

Breeds northern Eurasia, from Norway east to Kamchatka, also North America from Alaska east to Hudson Bay. Polytypic: nominate *fusca* occurs Eurasia east to Yenisey; *stejnegeri* Yenisey to Kamchatka; *deglandi* or 'White-winged Scoter' North America. Migratory in West Palearctic, wintering coastally as far south as English Channel. Amber-listed in UK: 50% or more of UK non-breeding population at ten or fewer sites; unfavourable world winter conservation status (Gregory *et al.* 2002).

Velvet Scoter clearly occurred in west Cornwall during the 19th century as E H Rodd mentioned a specimen obtained near Land's End in 1856 and two prior to 1880, plus one from the Helford area in December 1850 (Rodd 1880). However, although Penhallurick (1969) adds an initial Cornish record from 1808, the first account of Velvet Scoter in Scilly involved one in the vicinity of the Bishop Rock Lighthouse on 23rd March 1911 (Ogilvie-Grant 1912c).

There were just ten 20th century records, involving 16 individuals, in only ten of the 43 years since two were reported in Crow Sound, between St Mary's and St Martin's, for one day in October 1957. This makes this species almost as scarce in Scilly as Surf Scoter *M. perspicillata*. The Chart includes all arrival dates and shows a perhaps expected pattern of late autumn or early winter records, but with one very obvious spring sighting involving a male and female in flight past Giant's Castle, St Mary's, in May 1998. Discounting the 1911 record, which probably qualifies as an 'at sea' sighting, nine of the remaining ten involved single-day observations, with an average stay of just 2.8 days per record if the nineteen-day 1999 birds are included. This strongly suggests that most were migrating, though deciding where to or where from is more problematical. In mainland Cornwall today, it is described as a rare passage migrant and winter visitor, with 450 records in the period 1930–99, though interestingly these mainly occurred between November and February; there were nine in 1999 (*CBWPSAR* 69). In Europe it breeds as close to Britain as Norway and Sweden (Hagemeijer & Blair 1997), and Lack (1986) showed it to winter thinly around much of Britain, including southwest England, with a small number in Ireland and the Channel Islands. Cramp *et al.* (1977–94) make the point that wintering birds tend to stay well offshore, raising the possibility of it being under-recorded. The same authors give details of a pronounced passage in the Baltic region during October–November, presumably involving birds from north and east of there, with a build-up in Danish waters before a continued westerly movement, and with North Sea and English Channel numbers peaking as late perhaps as January. Spring passage is somewhat later than for Common Scoter *M. nigra*, peaking in Swedish waters in mid-May.

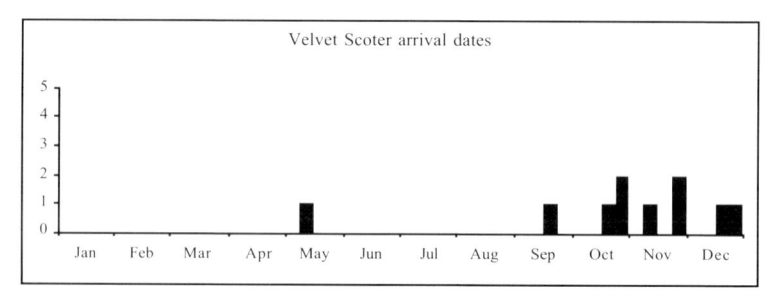

At least one adult male of the distinctive Nearctic *deglandi* or 'White-winged Scoter' has been reported in Scotland (June–July 1994) and the even more distinctive northeast Asian form *stejnegeri* might also be expected to occur in Britain (Gantlett 1998). Both should perhaps be kept in mind when examining Velvet Scoters in Scillonian waters.

## Bufflehead *Bucephala albeola* A BBRC 0%

**Extremely rare migrant, full written description required by the BBRC**

1920   One (female – shot) Tresco 7th January

*British Birds* 14: 67, 94: 61–73; *Bulletin of the BOC* 40: 155

Breeds North America, from Alaska east to Ontario and south to northwest USA. Withdraws south in winter, as far as Florida, Gulf States, Mexico, southern California. Monotypic. Population generally on increase, but with a stabilisation in southern Canada and reasonable rise in northern United States (Bryant 1997).

There is just one Scillonian record, a female or immature shot by Miss Dorrien-Smith on Tresco on 7th January 1920 (Langton 1920). The specimen is retained in the Tresco Abbey collection and is currently in the Isles of Scilly Museum on St Mary's.

Until recently the first acceptable British or Irish Bufflehead record involved a bird allegedly obtained from Great Yarmouth, Norfolk, in 1830, the skin of which is in Norwich's Castle Museum (Palmer 2000; BOURC 2001). However, the BOURC recently reviewed 16 pre-1950 records, plus the first two after that date, rejecting all but the Tresco individual, which becomes the first acceptable record for Britain and Ireland, though placed on Category B (BOURC 2001; *British Birds* 94: 61–73).

The committee concluded that although circumstances surrounding the first two post-1950 records made them acceptable for Category A, since that time numbers of captive Buffleheads had increased substantially – to at least 900 by 1991, in which case the likelihood of birds at liberty now being escapes was high. Nevertheless, the Tresco bird pre-dated all known imports of live birds by 16 years, thereby eliminating the possibility of it having been an escape. Other European records involve Iceland and the Netherlands.

# Goldeneye *Bucephala clangula* A

### Uncommon winter visitor and possible autumn and spring migrant

Breeds northern Eurasia and northern North America, from Norway east to Kamchatka and from Alaska east to Newfoundland. Recent successful introduction programme central Scotland. Migratory, in West Palearctic wintering south to northern Mediterranean. Polytypic: nominate *clangula* occurs Eurasia; *americana* North America. Amber-listed in UK: five-year mean breeding population of 87.8 pairs; 50% or more of UK non-breeding population at ten or fewer sites (Gregory *et al.* 2002).

Bone remains of this, or perhaps a similarly small duck species, were identified from among animal remains extracted from the prehistoric site on Nornour in the Eastern Isles (Turk 1971).

Although Francis Rodd and James Clark described it as a frequent winter visitor to the islands, particularly during winter 1890–91 (Clark & Rodd 1906), there is nothing in the early literature to suggest it was ever common. Francis's uncle, E H Rodd, made only two references to it up until his death in 1880 (Rodd 1880). The first of these involved a female seen on the Tresco pools on 1st January 1865, and the second recorded Francis's comment that Goldeneye was included among wildfowl shot 'in more or less numbers' in the islands during winter 1878–79. Penhallurick (1969) considered it a regular winter visitor to Cornwall and Scilly in small numbers, further suggesting that its status had probably not changed since the 19th century.

On Scilly it occurs mainly singly but can be seen in groups of perhaps up to four, usually between October and March and normally for only one to two days, though slightly longer in winter. Taking the ten-year period from 1990, it occurred in all but one year (1995), the earliest sighting being 28th September and the latest 19th May, most reports apparently involving females or immatures.

Most Goldeneyes wintering in Britain originate from Scandinavia, the Baltic States and western Russia (Wernham *et al.* 2002), though the wintering site of the small Scottish population is so far unknown. There is an apparent suggestion of autumn and spring passage in the Scillonian arrival dates, six out of 15 records falling within what might be considered winter, but with three in spring and six in autumn. However, this also fits the pattern of early, mid and late winter arrival peaks described by Lack (1986), though some northern European birds move on south as far as west-coast France (Cramp *et al.* 1977–94). Gantlett (1998) drew attention to the possibility of the slightly smaller, longer-billed North American form *americana* occurring in British waters, and, given Scilly's potential for attracting Nearctic vagrants, all visiting Goldeneyes should perhaps be examined carefully.

## Smew
## *Mergus albellus*  A

**Rare winter, late autumn or spring visitor**

- 1869  One (shot) Newford, St Mary's December   Clark & Rodd 1906
- 1891  Three (two immature males – shot) Higher Moors, St Mary's 23rd January   Clark & Rodd 1906
- 1954  One ('redhead') St Agnes 9th March
- 1957  One (in flight) Tresco 28th November
- 1959  One Tresco Channel 11th December
- 1980  One (female) Bryher & Tresco 3rd November
- 1985  One ('redhead') Great Pool, Tresco 19th January

Breeds northeast West Palearctic and northern Asia as far as Kamchatka. Monotypic. Migratory, West Palearctic population winters central-western and southern Europe, including Britain and Ireland, east to Kazakhstan; Asian populations Southeast Asia. Included on Annex I of 1979 EEC 'Birds Directive'. Green-listed in UK: in need of basic conservation assistance (Gregory *et al.* 2002).

A total of seven documented occurrences involving eight individuals, plus a handful of undocumented early records make Smew scarcer on Scilly than national rarities such as Red-eyed Vireo *Vireo olivaceus* or Solitary Sandpiper *Tringa solitaria* and about as rare as Surf Scoter *M. perspicillata*. E H Rodd made no mention of it in relation to Scilly in the 19th century, describing it as an occasional winter visitor to the Cornish mainland, even omitting it from his supplementary *List of the Birds Observed in the Scilly Islands* (Rodd 1880). This is surprising since his nephew Francis Rodd and co-author James Clark detailed several acquired or seen in the islands, one of which was well within the period of the elder Rodd's writings (Clark & Rodd 1906). The latter individual was shot at Newford Pool (now known as Newford Duck Pond) at Trenoweth, St Mary's, in late December 1869. In addition, two immature males were obtained out of three that visited Higher Moors, also St Mary's, on 23rd January 1891, eleven years after E H Rodd's death. Clark and Rodd also pointed out that several others 'seem to have been obtained at various unrecorded times by Pechell and others, but no (adult) male has ever been identified'.

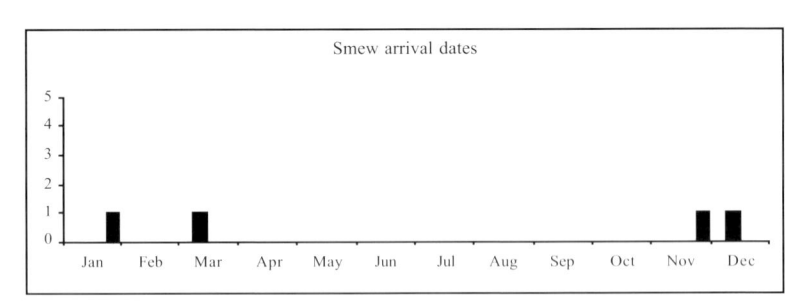

*Smew arrival dates* (bar chart showing single records in Jan, Mar, Nov, Dec)

Three of the five 20th century records involved are stated to have been 'redheads' (females or immatures) and we must assume that had the remaining two been otherwise the fact would have been recorded. Thus, Scilly still awaits a visit from one of the handsome adult males. Lack (1986) showed a mainly easterly bias to the winter distribution of this species in England, plus a near total lack of records in Cornwall, also drawing attention to a marked reduction in wintering numbers since the 1950s. There is a recognised tendency for immatures and adult females to move further south in winter than adult males, a feature apparent even among the British wintering population, where adult males make up a progressively smaller percentage of the total towards the south and west (Lack 1986). There is also a recognisable tendency for winter numbers in southwestern Europe to increase during periods of severe weather, in which case the absence of Scillonian records during winters 1962–63 and 1946–47 is noteworthy. Cramp *et al.* (1977–94) suggest that whilst most birds wintering in Britain probably arrive from Fennoscandia, some may have their origins in northwest Russia.

# Red-breasted Merganser *Mergus serrator* A

Scarce migrant and winter visitor

Breeds northern Eurasia, northern North America and Greenland; in West Palearctic including Iceland, Faeroe Islands and Novaya Zemlya, south regularly to Denmark and northern Poland, plus Wales and, increasingly, Devon. Migratory or partially so. Monotypic. Green-listed in UK: in need of basic conservation assistance (Gregory *et al.* 2002).

Red-breasted Merganser seems always to have been reasonably common around the coasts of mainland Cornwall in winter, certainly more so than Smew *M. albellus* or Goosander *M. merganser*. E H Rodd pointed out that it shared the local name of 'Dun Diver' with Goosander (Rodd 1880). However, it fell to James Clark and E H Rodd's nephew Francis to point out that it was reportedly a rare winter visitor to Scilly during the 1850s and 60s, though fairly common subsequently (Clark & Rodd 1906). Interestingly, Penhallurick mentioned a late 19th century report to the effect that it was common in Scilly in winter (Penhallurick 1969). In their summary, Clark and Rodd suggested it occurred only in immature plumage, but it seems possible that observers confused females and immatures. Nonetheless, Penhallurick pointed out that adult males were scarce off Cornwall in winter and much the same remains true of Scilly still.

The first recorded 20th century sighting involved a bird on the sea off Tresco on 2nd April 1947 (*CBWPSAR* 17), although, as for most other species, lack of earlier information is primarily due to an absence of any published reports. It continued to be rarely reported, getting scarcely a mention in the 1950s, though by 1960 it featured more frequently and certainly by the 1980s had become annual in the records. As with most other marine ducks, deciding precisely on the number of individuals involved in between-island or between-date sightings is difficult, though examination of annual reports suggests that around 41 individuals occurred during the ten years 1980–89. Broken down into seasons, 17 of these (41.5%) were in winter, three (7.3%) in spring and 21 (51.2%) in autumn. Similarly, a minimum of 80 were noted in the 1990s, at an average of eight per year; 29 (36.2%) in winter, six (7.5%) in spring and 45 (56.2%) in autumn. Of those 80, as few perhaps as three are recorded as males. Attempts to determine spring arrival dates are confused by the presence of lingering winter individuals, but late March through to April or early May appears reliable, with most remaining only briefly. In autumn, arrivals are fairly obviously confined to October or early November, though, again, separating autumn migrants from intended winterers is problematical. Taking the 1990s as the current norm, autumn arrivals were recorded in nine out of ten years, whereas obvious spring arrivals occurred in just five years. Multiple sightings seldom exceed four to five individuals.

Within the British Isles, Red-breasted Merganser breeds regularly no closer to Scilly than north Wales and southwest Ireland (Gibbons *et al.* 1993), and in continental Europe breeds south regularly only as far as Denmark and northern Poland (Hagemeijer & Blair 1997). Lack (1986) showed it to be wintering around the southern coast of Ireland, south Wales and southern England, west as far as Lyme Bay, Devon and Dorset, and with only scattered records for Cornwall. However, winter numbers are increasing in Cornwall and the total of 641 recorded in that county in 1999 was more than double the figure for 1992 (*CBWPSAR* 69), with the highest numbers occurring in midwinter and, unlike Scilly, comparatively few in autumn.

The British and Irish population probably winters close to the breeding areas, with most wintering off eastern and southern England thought likely to be of Scandinavian origin (Lack 1986), some of which also reach France (Cramp *et al.* 1977–94). Some Icelandic birds also winter south to at least Britain and Ireland (Cramp *et al.* 1977–94). Most northern populations vacate the breeding areas from mid- or late October, with a clear tendency for females and immatures to move earlier and further than males (Cramp *et al.* 1977–94). Return spring passage may commence as early as February.

# Goosander *Mergus merganser* A

Scarce winter visitor

    1851   One (shot) 22nd December   Clark & Rodd 1906
    1853   One (female – shot) Tresco late December   Clark & Rodd 1906
    1855   One (shot) November   Clark & Rodd 1906
    1870   Several (female – shot) Tresco 28th November   Clark & Rodd 1906

1884  One (shot) 5th January   Clark & Rodd 1906
1934  One (immature male – shot) Tresco 22nd December   Penhallurick 1969
1963  One (shot) St Mary's 1st January
1963  Four off Porth Cressa, St Mary's 4th January
1963  One Tresco Channel 18th December
1975  One (adult male) St Mary's harbour 28th December
1979  Two Porth Hellick, St Mary's 5th January
1980  One (female) St Mary's Harbour, early December to 2nd January 1981
1985  Four (male and three 'redheads') January 16th to 23rd
1992  One (male) off Eastern Isles 2nd January
1994  Two flying past St Agnes 27th February
1996  One (immature) Tresco 31st January to 4th February
1996  One ('redhead') Great Pool, Tresco 22nd December
1997  One Porth Cressa, St Mary's 4th January

Breeds northern Eurasia, from Iceland and Britain to Kamchatka, plus Tibet and surroundings, also northern North America, from Alaska to Newfoundland. Polytypic: nominate *merganser* occurs Eurasia; *comatus* Tibet and surrounds; *americanus* or 'Common Merganser' North America. Migratory or partially so, in West Palearctic wintering south to central France, northern Mediterranean and Black Sea. Green-listed in UK: in need of basic conservation assistance (Gregory *et al*. 2002).

E H Rodd made a mid-19th century reference to this species in Scilly, writing that in December 1853 he received an adult female specimen from Augustus Smith, the then Proprietor of the Islands (Rodd 1854b). In November 1870, his nephew Francis Rodd wrote from Tresco to the effect that he had shot another female, but although 'some good old males' had been seen they had not been obtained (Rodd 1880). Much later still, Francis and co-author James Clark noted that others had been killed on Scilly, on 22nd December 1851, November 1855 and January 5th 1884 (Clark & Rodd 1906). As far as 19th century mainland Cornwall is concerned, the elder Rodd described it as making an appearance at uncertain intervals, almost always in winter and rarely in adult plumage (Rodd 1880).

Penhallurick (1969) described an increase in the number of mainland records since 1955, with on average one to four sightings annually, the largest involving a flock of eleven and with an expected increase during winter 1962–63. He also mentioned a bird listed in the Tresco Abbey records as killed on that island in 1934. Other than that, there were twelve records involving 20 individuals in nine of the years after 1935, with the apparent slight recent increase in sightings perhaps explained by improved observer coverage. The Chart shows all 19th- and 20th century arrival dates, all of which, interestingly, fall in the period November to February, leaving no doubt that in Scilly Goosander is exclusively a winter visitor. However, most birds made only brief stays and, ignoring shot individuals and undated records, remained for an average of 2.1 days, with eight of the ten present for one day only. This suggests that they were birds passing through the islands rather than being winter visitors in the true sense. There has never been more than four together and never more than six in any one year.

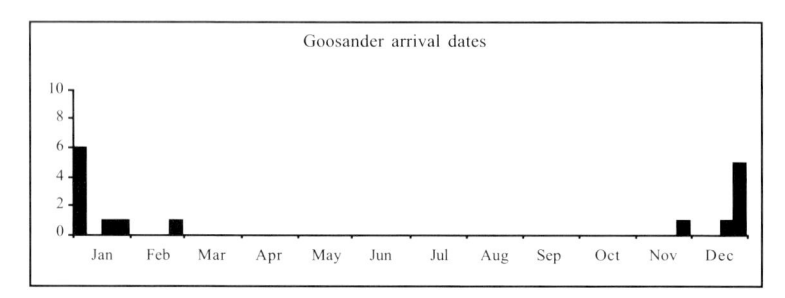

Goosander arrival dates

In Britain, main concentrations of wintering Goosanders occur in Scotland, northern and central-eastern England and Wales, with virtually none in Ireland and few in southwest England. However, hard weather can cause a substantial redistribution, with a resultant influx of birds from countries bordering the North Sea, or even further afield, e.g. Scandinavia, or Russia (Lack 1986).

The arrival in west-coast Britain of birds of the distinctive North American form *americanus*, or 'Common Merganser' remains a distinct possibility, in which case all individuals in Scilly should be examined carefully (Gantlett 1998), particularly in view of the archipelago's record for hosting off-course Nearctic migrants.

## Ruddy Duck                                          *Oxyura jamaicensis*  C

Rare migrant or winter visitor, full written description required by the SRP

    1979   One St Mary's & Tresco 5th to 26th January
    1980   One (female or immature) St Mary's late November to 4th May 1981
    1991   One (female) Tresco Great Pool 24th December to 26th January 1992
    1996   One (male) Great Pool, Tresco 15th to 29th October

Breeds North, Central and South America, introduced England and spread to much of Britain, plus Ireland. Polytypic: nominate *jamaicensis* occurs North and Central America plus British Isles; *ferruginea* South America. North American population migratory, withdrawing from north of range in winter.

There are just four records of what in Scilly amounts to a major rarity. Only the most recent record involved a known adult and information on age and sex of the 1979 individual went unreported. Two remained in the islands for some time and none of the four appeared in a hurry to leave. By 1991 the British breeding population extended as far south and west as Somerset and Dorset (with a small number in Ireland) (Gibbons *et al*. 1993) but birds were absent from Devon and Cornwall. Although the native North American population is largely migratory, British birds show no such tendency, though there is a pattern of short-distance seasonal movement (Cramp *et al*. 1977–94). Within the breeding areas, small pools are exchanged for large reservoirs and similar in autumn and by midwinter large accumulations occur, remaining intact until March or April. Cramp *et al*. consider that at least some wanderers are likely to be prospecting immatures, which if true perhaps puts Ruddy Duck on the list of possible future breeding species for the islands. The amount of suitable breeding and feeding habitat appears severely limited, however.

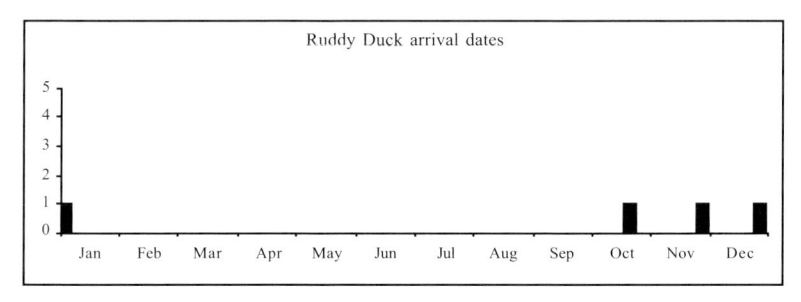

It remains to be seen if the current UK programme of culling Ruddy Ducks has any effect on the recent growing number of Scillonian records. Rationale behind the cull concerns the likely effect of encroachment by the growing UK population on the small Spanish population of the closely related White-headed Duck *O. leucocephala*. If this is the case, Scilly could be hosting birds moving south. However, up until at least March 2001, none of the ten or so known UK Ruddy Duck ringing recoveries (out of some 300 UK-ringed individuals) involved a bird crossing the English Channel (*British Birds* 94: 149).

## Honey Buzzard  (European Honey-buzzard)       *Pernis apivorus*  A

Scarce migrant, does not breed. Treated by the BBRC as a national Scarce Migrant, full written description required by the SRP.

    1866   One (immature – shot) Tresco 18th October   Rodd 1880
    1958   One (shot) Tresco 9th September Tresco
    1970   One Tresco, Bryher & St Agnes 23rd to 28th September
    1971   One St Agnes, Bryher & Tresco 23rd to 28th September
    1971   One St Mary's 14th October

1973   One Abbey Pool, Tresco 17th October
1976   One Scilly 29th May
1976   At least three various islands 26th September to 9th October
1979   One Telegraph, St Mary's 1st June
1980   One St Mary's 15th October
1982   One (subadult) St Agnes 26th May
1982   One St Mary's 27th August
1982   One (immature) various islands 2nd & 3rd October
1982   One St Mary's 29th October
1986   One Tresco & Bryher 1st May
1987   One St Mary's 30th August
1987   One St Agnes 5th September
1987   One St Agnes 18th September
1988   One St Agnes 19th July
1989   One St Agnes 4th July
1990   One Tresco & Tean 25th to 27th September
1991   One St Martin's & Tresco 1st & 2nd September
1992   One Eastern Isles & St Mary's 30th May to 1st June
1992   One St Mary's & Tresco 13th August
1993   One St Mary's, St Agnes & Tresco 12th & 13th May
1993   One St Martin's 30th May
1993   One Tresco 5th September
1993   Two Tresco 14th & 15th September
1993   One St Mary's & St Agnes 11th October
1996   One in off sea Porth Hellick, St Mary's 4th June
1997   One St Mary's 30th May
2000   Up to nine various islands 23rd September to 3rd October

Breeds West Palearctic and central-western Asia, east to northern Mongolia. Entire population migratory, wintering western and northern-central subequatorial Africa. Monotypic. Included on Annex I of 1979 EEC 'Birds Directive'. Amber-listed in UK: maximum of 61 breeding pairs during year 2000 (Gregory *et al.* 2002).

Although E H Rodd had much to say on the subject of Honey Buzzard, surprisingly little of it concerned Scilly, what there was being limited to several references to a bird shot by John Jenkinson on Tresco on 18th October 1866 (Rodd 1866a, 1880). He described this specimen, which was sent over to him on the steamer, as a chocolate-coloured bird of the year and the only instance of the species on Scilly to his knowledge. It is also notable that James Clark and E H Rodd's nephew Francis Rodd mentioned only the above bird in their otherwise informative review of the birds of Scilly (Clark & Rodd 1906). E H Rodd commented on the very real possibility of this species being mistaken for Buzzard *Buteo buteo*, suggesting that it may have been under-recorded during the 19th century.

The earliest 20th century record involved a bird reportedly shot on Tresco on 9th September 1956 (Parslow, in Penhallurick 1978), by which time one would have hoped that such activities might have ceased. But as this incident gets no mention in the annual *CBWPSAR* we must assume John Parslow learned of it from a local source. The Chart incorporates all arrival dates, including all nine in 2000 but omitting the two early, shot individuals, for which we have only imprecise information. There were a total of 36 records involving a minimum of 41 birds in 18 out of the 42 years 1959–2000. All records fell in the period from 1st May to 31st October with an obvious condensed spring peak at the end of May and early June and an equally obvious but more protracted autumn peak from late August to late October.

Of the 36 arrivals included in the Chart, 27 (75%) involved single-day sightings. The nine spring birds remained an average of 1.4 days, whereas the 32 autumn birds were present for 1.9 days. Inevitably, most if not all sightings involved birds seen passing overhead. Honey Buzzards leave their breeding areas from mid-August onwards and most have departed Europe by mid-October, though a few juveniles may linger into November. Return passage in central Europe commences mid-April with most reaching the breeding grounds during the second half of May, or late May to June in the north. Although large concentrations

Honey Buzzard arrival dates

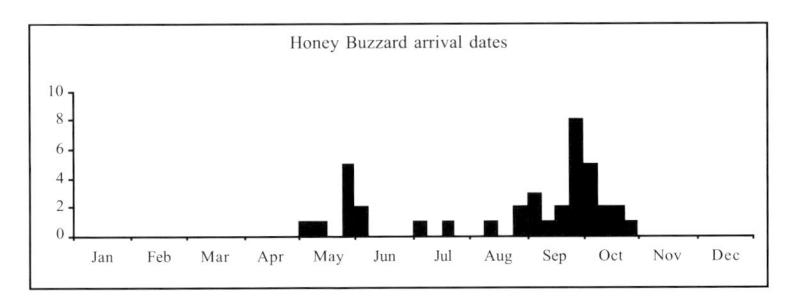

occur at narrow sea crossings, e.g. Strait of Gibraltar, Honey Buzzard is capable of sustained flight over large expanses of open water (Cramp *et al.* 1977–94). Ringing recoveries show that birds from as far east as central Europe use the Strait of Gibraltar, which suggests the possibility of those same birds reaching Scilly. Nevertheless, the origin of birds recorded in Scilly remains unknown.

# Black Kite *Milvus migrans* A BBRC 2.7%

**Very rare spring or autumn migrant, full written description required by the BBRC.**

1938   One (juvenile) Tresco from 6th September, shot 16th   A A Dorrien-Smith 1938
1942   One Tresco 28th to 30th May   A A Dorrien-Smith 1942
1966   One Tresco 23rd April   *British Birds* 60: 315
1970   One Tresco 4th June   *British Birds* 66: 355
1986   One St Mary's 31st August   *British Birds* 80: 531
1990   One Bryher, Tresco, St Agnes & St Mary's 13th May to 4th June
        *British Birds* 84: 464–465, 86: 466
1990   One St Mary's 13th & 14th July   *British Birds* 84: 464–465, 86: 466
1994   One St Mary's & Tresco 22nd to 24th May   *British Birds* 88: 504
1996   One St Mary's, St Agnes, Tresco & Bryher 22nd to 29th April   *British Birds* 90: 466
1999   One Tresco 23rd April   *British Birds* 95: 489
2001   One St Agnes, Gugh & St Mary's 15th and 19th–20th December   *British Birds* 95: 489
2002   One Scilly 23rd September   *British Birds* 95: 603

*Birds of the Isles of Scilly*

Breeds central and southern Eurasia, south to North Africa, Nile Valley, India and Southeast Asia, also Africa south of the Sahara, Indonesia and Australia. Polytypic: nominate *migrans* occurs Europe and North Africa; *lineatus* or 'Black-eared Kite' East Palearctic and China; *aegyptius* Egypt, East Africa and Arabia; *parasitus* Africa south of the Sahara; with two additional forms further east. European birds winter principally in tropical Africa.

Early writers make no mention of this species in either Scilly or mainland Cornwall and the first reference to it in the archipelago involves a bird shot by one of the Tresco gamekeepers on that island on 16th September 1938, the bird having reached Scilly a few days beforehand. The carcass was sent to the British Museum where it was identified as the nominate *migrans* (A A Dorrien-Smith 1938a). This represented the third British record, the previous two having come from Alnwick, Northumberland in May 1866 and Aberdeenshire in April 1901 (Palmer 2000). The skin of the 1938 Tresco individual remains in the collection of the British Museum (Natural History), catalogue number 3/305-12. Tresco also provided the next three Scillonian records, the 1942 arrival being seen by the same gamekeeper responsible for shooting the 1938 individual (A A Dorrien-Smith 1942), whilst the 1966 sighting involved a 'fly-over' moving from west to east across the island. Two in 1990 was quite exceptional. As is only to be expected with large raptors, three of the arrivals made tours of the islands, the 1996 individual appearing over St Mary's, Tresco, Bryher and St Agnes in the space of eight days.

The Chart shows all eleven arrival dates up to and including the 2001 bird, seven of which (64%) were in spring, the earliest, by one day, being 22nd April, with the last spring sighting on 4th June (two). Earliest autumn arrival was 13th July and the latest 15th December (until 20th). Discounting the shot 1938 individual, average length of stay was 4.1 days, or 2.3 days if the 1990 long-staying individual is ignored. Four birds were present on one day only.

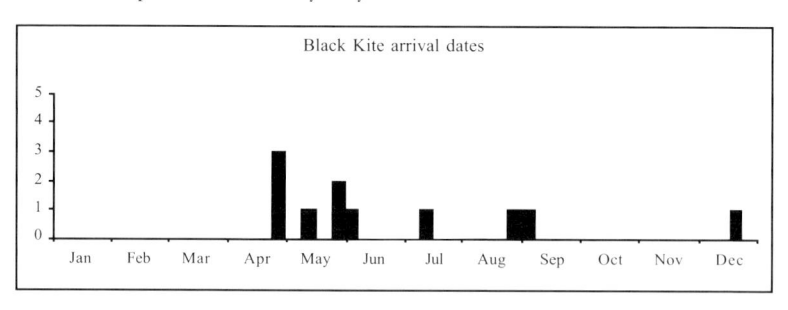

Black Kite arrival dates

The most likely explanation for the spring arrival of Black Kites in Britain is birds overshooting whilst en route to Iberia, southern France or Germany, the greater majority of Black Kites from the West Palearctic population crossing to and from Africa by way of the Strait of Gibraltar (Cramp *et al.* 1977–94). However, the western European population has undergone a substantial expansion since the mid 20th century and some authorities predict that Black Kite may breed in Britain before long (Dymond *et al.* 1989). Nationally, it occurs in Britain between April and November, but with the vast majority arriving in the early part of the year, between April and June. At least up until 1990, some 50% of all records came from southeast England, and Scilly might therefore be expected to receive few individuals. A total of 290 Black Kite records were accepted by the BBRC for the period 1958 to 1999, with Scilly accounting for just 2.7% of these. Nevertheless the two earlier Scillonian records must be viewed against just five nationally. The 2001 individual was presumably the same as that at Nanjizal and nearby Sennen, west Cornwall, on 16th and 17th. Confusion with the following species is perhaps most likely in the case of individuals of the East Palearctic *lineatus*, or 'Black-eared Kite' reaching Europe, as seems perhaps more likely during autumn, or in the case of rufous variant individuals of the present species.

## Red Kite *Milvus milvus* A & C

**Very rare autumn migrant or vagrant, full written description required by the SRP.**

    1890   One (shot) Tresco 9th September   Clark & Rodd 1906
    1968   One Tresco 22nd & 23rd November
    1971   One Annet, St Agnes & St Mary's 22nd to 27th October
    1975   One various islands 26th November to 1st December

Breeds southwest Europe, from Iberia, North Africa, Italy and Sicily through France and Germany to Sweden and as far as eastern Black Sea area. Polytypic: *fasciicauda* occurs Cape Verde Islands; nominate *milvus* elsewhere. Birds in northern and central Europe mainly migratory, resident or dispersive elsewhere. Included on Annex I of 1979 EEC 'Birds Directive'. Downgraded from Red to Amber-listed in UK 2002: historical population decline, but with doubling of population in past 25 years (Gregory *et al.* 2002), in part due to introductions away from traditional breeding areas. Removed from BBRC Rarities List January 1963 (Harber & Swaine 1963).

Like its near relative Black Kite *M. migrans*, Red Kite received no specific mention by the earlier writers in relation to Scilly, though Heath (1750) comments on 'the Kite' being found in the islands year-round and it seems generally accepted now that he was referring to this species. E H Rodd maked brief mention of it as a rare breeder on the Cornish mainland, stating that it bred prior to 1880, following which it was encountered only occasionally and the last bird he had knowledge of was shot on his brother's estate near Launceston, in December 1867 (Rodd 1880). In fact, the debate over whether or not, and if so the extent to which Red Kite bred in Cornwall during the 19th century continues to this day and opinions vary greatly. First mention of Scilly, however, comes with the bird shot on Tresco in September 1890 (Clark & Rodd 1906).

An almost inevitable gap in reports during the early 20th century coincided with the lengthy period of inadequate recording, which in the case of this present species ended with a bird observed flying around Tresco for two days in November 1968. This was followed three years later by a bird seen flying from St Agnes to neighbouring Annet in October 1971, before crossing back to St Agnes and then moving on to St Mary's. The fourth and final record involved a very brief report of one seen over St Mary's, Tresco and then St Agnes between 26th November and 1st December 1975.

All four records pre-date recent English and Scottish reintroduction schemes. Interestingly, all four arrived in the islands during autumn (see Chart), thereby eliminating the possibility of their having been European overshoots, as occurs in some years along coastal southern England (pers. obs.). Adults from the long-standing Welsh population remain close to the breeding area in winter, but birds-of-the-year are known to wander extensively and were thought to account for at least some winter sightings in southern England prior to the commencement of reintroductions (Cramp *et al.* 1977–94), and presumably still do. Nevertheless, birds from continental Europe have been proved to reach Britain during winter (Cramp *et al.* 1977–94; P Lack 1986) – five Red Kites ringed in Germany or Denmark were recovered in southern England (Wernham *et al.* 2002) – making it difficult to judge where these Scillonian visitors originated. Interestingly, five of the recently released, wing-tagged Scottish birds reached Ireland and one made it as far as west Cornwall, though English birds are less inclined to wander (Wernham *et al.* 2002).

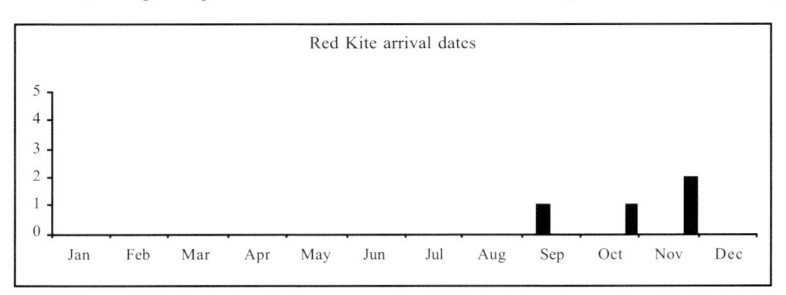

Red Kite arrival dates

Most European migrant Red Kites winter north of the Mediterranean, though some cross the Strait of Gibraltar into North Africa, usually in October or November. Return movements through Europe commence in February, though some birds arrive back on the northernmost breeding grounds by late March (Cramp *et al.* 1977–94). See the previous species for the possibility of confusion between the two.

# White-tailed Eagle *Haliaeetus albicilla* A & E  BBRC 0%

**Extremely rare autumn or spring migrant, full written description required by the BBRC.**

1835 'Traditional' belief of one in Seven Stones area   Clark & Rodd 1906
1909 Two, one shot Gugh 11th November   Frohawk 1909; Anon 1910
1924 One Tresco & St Helen's area November for about one week   H W Robinson 1926

1943   One high over Scilly (c. 300 m) 11th September   *CBWPSAR* 14
1947   One (adult) various islands 21st April to December   *CBWPSAR* 17

Breeds northern Eurasia, from Norway, Germany and Balkans northeast to Pacific, plus Greenland, Iceland and eastern China. Recently reintroduced to northwest Scotland. Monotypic. Migratory or dispersive in north, dispersive or resident in south. Included on Annex I of 1979 EEC 'Birds Directive'. Red-listed in UK: historical population decline; recent five-year mean of 19.6 breeding pairs; unfavourable world conservation status (Gregory *et al.* 2002).

Controversy and doubt surrounds the earliest suggestion of White-tailed Eagle presence in or close to Scilly: a so-called 'tradition' of one having been seen near the Seven Stones, northeast of Scilly in 1835 (Clark & Rodd 1906). For, according to these two extremely reliable authors, a note appeared in the hand of an unidentified person in a copy of *The Survey of Cornwall* (Carew 1602), in the possession of a W J Clyma of Truro, to the effect that:

> My boatmen and two other fishermen saw a few years ago a very large bird of prey at the Seven Stones, which they speak of as a Golden Eagle, but I feel satisfied myself that it was a Sea-Eagle, and their description has left no doubt in my mind that this was the bird they saw.

It is not clear how Clark and Rodd arrived at the year 1835 for this record, unless they have not quoted the remarks in full. H W Robinson (1926) drew attention to the position of the Seven Stones, an area of normally submerged ledges some 10 km northeast of the archipelago, concluding that there must have been some mistake. However, the above sighting is not impossible, as evident from the report of a fine adult seen by a Mr William Taylor of Edgbaston, now West Midlands, within 150–200 m of a yacht at a position midway between Scilly and Brest, northwest France, in August 1877 (Rodd 1880). Intriguingly, this may well have been the same adult seen on the north Cornish coast by a Mr Pike in autumn that same year (Rodd 1880). E H Rodd describes White-tailed Eagle as almost as rare as Golden Eagle (of which he knew but two records) in Cornwall, being only occasionally met with along the coast.

The first confirmed record of White-tailed Eagle in Scilly comes from Frohawk (1909), who documented the remarkable appearance of probably two individuals in late 1909, one of which, with a wingspan of 7 feet 6 inches (229 cm), was shot on Gugh in November that year (Frohawk 1909; Anon 1910), though the presence of a second bird was not fully confirmed. The next records came from H W Robinson (1926), who recorded the presence of one in the area of Tresco and St Helen's for about a week during November 1924; and, in September 1943, Dorrien-Smith reported a bird seen high over Tresco on 11th September, which 'as far as I could judge' was this species (*CBWPSAR* 14).

Quite remarkable, though, was an adult that frequented the islands from April 1947 until last seen on 21st December that year (*CBWPSAR* 17). According to the records, this bird developed into a creature of habit from around May onwards, e.g. most evenings it was to be seen flying from the Bar Point area in northeast St Mary's, over Porth Mellon and Hugh Town in the direction of The Garrison, which took it on a rough heading for Gugh, where it was thought to roost. Between July and September, it was seen only every two weeks or so, before returning to its old haunts for a while and becoming elusive again. The only record of any prey item refers to it seen eating a European Shag *Phalacrocorax aristotelis*. This individual was very probably the same one seen for a short time near Land's End, on the Cornish mainland, earlier in the year (*CBWPSAR* 17). The arrival of this bird in the southwest coincided with the particularly severe weather throughout much of Europe that winter, which of course may help explain its presence. Interestingly, although according to the records Tresco gamekeeper Wardle was among many who had a 'marvellous close-up view in flight', the bird nevertheless survived in the islands for some nine months, presumably demonstrating the extent to which earlier local attitudes towards rarities, and the need for them to be shot, were already undergoing a marked change. It is interesting to note, too, that so large a bird as this could disappear for two weeks at a time within an archipelago of busy boat activity and just 16 x 10 km in extent, and we are left to wonder whether it roamed even further afield during its stay, back to the mainland perhaps, or to France or Ireland. Intriguingly another, or perhaps even the same, adult was present briefly near Land's End, Cornwall, in June 1948 (Penhallurick 1978).

Extinction of the Scottish breeding population around 1916 and subsequent reductions in Iceland and Scandinavia resulted in a decline in British records, to the point where two in 1961 represented the only

British sightings for the 15 years 1958–72 (Dymond *et al.* 1989). However, since this last date, birds have begun to reappear, but this has not been reflected in Scilly, where there have been no records of birds from the Scottish reintroduction programme. Dymond *et al.* attribute the recent increase in wintering birds in Britain, mostly in southeast England, to a parallel increase in numbers wintering in the Low Countries and northern France. This, in turn, they attribute to recent increased breeding numbers in northwest Europe. According to Cramp *et al.* (1977–94), Russian birds north of approximately 60°N are wholly migratory, whereas most West Palearctic birds are strictly resident, though juveniles and immatures are inclined to wander extensively, mainly in a south to southwesterly direction. Norwegian immatures probably move the least, however, and there is no proof so far that birds bred in Iceland leave that country. Taken at face value this suggests that adults reaching southwest Britain are perhaps most likely to originate from northern Russia, whereas younger birds may originate from much closer.

## Short-toed Eagle *Circaetus gallicus* A BBRC 100%

**Extremely rare migrant, full written description required by the BBRC.**

1999   One (juvenile) various islands 7th to 11th October   *British Birds* 93: 526; *Ibis* 143: 171–175

Breeds northwest Africa, Spain and France east across Europe into Russia as far as Lake Baikal, with additional populations India and Southeast Asia. Monotypic. Migratory, eastern birds winter mainly in India, western birds in subtropical Africa south of the Sahel. Western population (at least) suffered recent declines resulting from agricultural changes and persecution (Cleaves 1999)

   The first and only British and Irish record up until at least autumn 2001 involved a juvenile seen arriving low over St Agnes from the west and heading on over the Gugh towards St Mary's at midday on 7th October 1999 (Cleeves 1999; BOURC 2001). Quickly making landfall on St Mary's by way of The Garrison, it then drifted east over Telegraph and was watched by open-mouthed birders all along its route as it again headed out over the sea, this time towards St Martin's. Spending time on White Island on the north side of St Martin's, it then drifted back over the east end of St Mary's to eventually land and roost overnight on Great Ganilly in the Eastern Isles. It remained mainly in the area of Great Ganilly until 11th, being last seen drifting away high over the sea toward the southeast. This bird arrived in an already rarity-packed week that had seen both Siberian Thrush *Zoothera dauma* and White's Thrush *Zoothera sibirica* on Scilly and with Blue Rock Thrush *Monticola solitarius* about to burst upon the scene!

Identity of the bird and the probability of it being anything other than a genuine wild individual were never an issue. Plumage-wise it was a typical juvenile and in apparently perfect condition. The primary diet of Short-toed Eagle is snakes and other reptiles, which in Scilly are wholly absent. However, the literature lists a variety of alternative prey items, including other birds, rabbits, rats and even invertebrates. Although the bird was not seen to feed throughout its five-day stay, there is suitable alternative food available in Scilly, in the form of Rabbits *Oryctolagus cuniculus*, Brown Rats *Rattus norvegicus* and various invertebrates; indeed several of the Eastern Isles are seriously plagued with Brown Rats. In addition, there are of course numerous large seabirds, of which the most likely victim might be Shag *Phalacrocorax aristotelis*. It has been suggested that the bird may not have fed throughout the period of its stay. This seems unlikely (as well as unnecessary), however, given that the bird had undertaken a sea crossing of at least 160 km to reach the islands and subsequently had to cover the same distance on leaving them (assuming mainland Britain was not involved in its journey).

Of course, the question of how many kilometres the bird flew on its way to and from Scilly is unanswerable without knowing from where it started, or, equally, where it went to after it left. Certainly, had it made landfall in west Cornwall it must surely have been seen, especially considering the number of birdwatchers touring west Cornwall in October. The bird's departure on 11th was accompanied by high pressure and resultant clear skies, and it was seen going to a considerable height, perhaps enabling it to soon gain early sight of northern France, 160 km to the south.

However, deciding where a migrant eagle went to from northern Europe in mid-October is a comparatively simple task compared with that of ascertaining the route by which it reached Scilly. As Cleeves (1999) pointed out, Short-toed Eagle is no stranger as a vagrant to northwest Europe, with some sixty or more records from Sweden, one from Norway and ten from the Netherlands, plus twenty-five from Germany between 1976 and 1996. Some of these records also include overshooting spring migrants. The most northerly breeding site in France lies some 100 km south of Paris, but summering birds have been recorded recently as close to Scilly as central Finistere, and numbers of records in northern France are apparently increasing (Cleeves 1999). Therefore, the bird on Scilly may have very quickly corrected a fairly simple navigational error. This view is perhaps given additional support by the coincidental appearance in southwest Britain on 25th October that year of Booted Eagle *Hieraaetus pennatus*, another West Palearctic summer migrant and with a remarkably similar breeding and wintering distribution. Alternatively, for the Short-toed Eagle to have arrived in Scilly by way of Ireland would have involved a sea crossing of around 240 km. Though it is clear that birds of prey are quite capable of making such sea crossings, e.g. Red-shouldered Hawk *Buteo lineatus* (Durand 1972), or Goshawk *Accipiter gentilis* and Snowy Owl *Nyctea scandiaca* (Witherby 1927b), we should perhaps also ask ourselves by what route do those Short-toed Eagles that pass through Sweden eventually find their way south into Africa?

## Marsh Harrier (Eurasian Marsh Harrier)     *Circus aeruginosus*   A

**Regular migrant and occasional winter visitor in small numbers, does not breed.**

Breeds central Eurasia from West Palearctic to Pacific, also coastal North Africa, Australasia and Madagascar. Polytypic: nominate *aeruginosus* occurs West Palearctic east to Lake Baikal; *harteri* coastal North Africa; *spilonotus* occurs east of *aeruginosus*, with some interbreeding within overlap; additional forms further east and south. Some authorities, e.g. Fefelov (2001) treat at least *aeruginosus* and *spilonotus* as full species, 'Western' and 'Eastern Marsh Harrier'. Included on Annex I of 1979 EEC 'Birds Directive'. Downgraded from Red- to Amber-listed in UK 2002: historical population decline, but more than doubled in past 25 years; five-year mean of 141.4 breeding pairs (Gregory *et al.* 2002).

A quick glance at the writings of E H Rodd (1880), and of James Clark and F R Rodd (1906) suggests that numbers of 19th century Marsh Harrier reports for Scilly were greater than for several other birds of prey species, e.g. Osprey *Pandion haliaetus*, or Montagu's Harrier *C. pygargus*. However, this conflicts somewhat with E H Rodd's opening comment that it was regarded as rare in Cornwall and Scilly by 1880 and becoming rarer every year. His first mention of it in Scilly concerns an October 1849 sighting, by Augustus Pechell, of a 'large buzzard-like bird, with a yellow head, which will prove, I have no doubt, to be a Marsh Harrier' (Rodd 1849b). This record was followed by his descriptions of an adult female shot, together with several Short-eared Owls *Asio flammeus*, after a severe gale in autumn 1863 (Rodd 1863b), plus a specimen obtained from St Mary's in October 1871 (Rodd 1871e). James Clark and E H Rodd's nephew Francis Rodd then add to the picture, detailing one killed by Joe White on Tresco in April 1886 and concluding with mention of an immature watched hunting over Tresco's Abbey Pool reedbeds on 12th October 1903; 'the afternoon of the day on which the great flight of Larks came to an end' (Clark & Rodd 1906).

First mention of this species on Scilly after Clark and Rodd's early 20th century review concerned a bird reportedly frequenting the Porth Cressa area of St Mary's up until mid-March 1949, though no arrival date is given. It subsequently becomes almost annual in occurrence, prompting the 1951 comment against the report of a large wintering female that it was now becoming a regular feature (*CBWPSAR* 21). The following year's comment that birds seen in spring and autumn usually roosted in kale patches is interesting now more for the fact that kale is entirely absent from the islands as a field crop.

Throughout the 1970s and 1980s, it occurred at the rate of from one to about three birds annually and was absent in perhaps only one year. Although occasional birds remain in winter, the pattern is very much one of spring and autumn passage, and in the period 1990–99 spring arrival dates ranged between late March or early April through to late May or early June, with 22nd June exceptional. First autumn arrival date was 16th August (two) with a fairly obvious cut-off around the last week of October. Single individuals spent all or part of winters 1991 and 1992 in the islands, whilst in the latter year a male and female frequented various parts of the islands from 10th to 26th May, but are not recorded as showing any breeding intentions.

An immature that stayed for 13 days in September 1984 was seen to take a Gadwall *Anas strepera* from one of the Tresco pools (*IOSBR* 1984).

Although a few individuals overwinter north to the British Isles, the main wintering area for the West Palearctic population of nominate *aeruginosus* is from the Mediterranean basin south into Africa, many crossing at the Strait of Gibraltar into North or even West Africa (Cramp *et al.* 1977–94; Wernham *et al.* 2002). In Europe generally, young birds disperse randomly, though most, including those from Britain, head south to southwest, whereas autumn adults show a stronger tendency to move in the latter directions. This is shown by ringing recoveries, with those from countries bordering the North Sea moving mainly through France and Iberia (Wernham *et al.* 2002), together with a few from Finland. Juveniles commence dispersing from early August, whilst adults move south during September–October, some even remaining into November. Birds begin moving north from February or March into late May, though with later records perhaps involving mainly immatures.

# Hen Harrier *Circus cyaneus* A

**Scarce but annual migrant or winter visitor in small numbers, does not breed.**

Breeds northern Eurasia from Atlantic to Pacific, also northern North America and southwestern South America. Polytypic: nominate *cyaneus* occurs West Palearctic east to Pacific; *hudsonius*, or 'Marsh Hawk', North America; *cinereus* South America; Falkland Island *histronicus* thought possibly extinct. In West Palearctic, northern and eastern populations migratory, largely sedentary or dispersive further south. Included on Annex I of 1979 EEC 'Birds Directive'. Red-listed in UK: historical population decline and still heavily persecuted in game-management areas; unfavourable world conservation status (Gregory *et al.* 2002).

E H Rodd had little to say about this species, implying that it was always rather scarce in Cornwall and Scilly and making clear that by the mid 19th century it was encountered less often than Montagu's Harrier *C. pygargus* (Rodd 1880). However, he is unclear if this mainly resulted from an increase in the latter species, although Hen Harrier certainly underwent a national decline during the final quarter of the 19th century and Holloway (1996) showed it as entirely absent from Cornwall at that time. Watson (1977), though, listed it as breeding in Cornwall up until 1939, though probably not in any numbers, or even annually, and by 1948 it was known only as a winter visitor.

E H Rodd recorded a ring-tail shot in Scilly on 30th October 1879 and sent to him in Penzance, which he described as the last coming 'under his observation' in Cornwall or Scilly (Rodd 1879b; Rodd 1880). Clearly, there were others from the islands, however, as James Clark and E H Rodd's nephew Francis mentioned a male shot pre-1875 (Clark & Rodd 1906). The last two authors also confirmed the late 19th century decrease in Scillonian sightings, listing birds shot in May 1888 and seen in June 1902 as the sole known records since the 1879 individual mentioned by the elder Rodd.

There then follows the unfortunate early 20th century gap in Scillonian ornithological records before two were reported by A A Dorrien-Smith in autumn and winter 1946 (*CBWPSAR* 16), presumably mainly on Tresco but probably elsewhere too. Even though these were followed by a reported single for a few days in late October 1949, there were no more confirmed records until a ring-tail on 1st May 1965, representing an absence of records for a further 17 years. However, from that time on it became almost annual in occurrence and in more recent years anything up to around eight individuals may be recorded during a single year, as in 1999 when two wintered and four probably passed through in spring and three in autumn. However, and as with most visiting birds of prey, arriving at a reliable count is constantly frustrated by the high mobility of birds involved and a distinct lack of winter observer coverage. Interestingly, there was a short run of unidentified Harrier sightings in the years 1963–65, which with hind-sight seem likely to have involved this present species, though Montagu's Harrier was also occurring at that time. Without doubt, 'ring-tails' (immatures or adult females) predominate, but adult or identifiable subadult males occur on average every three to four years. Most birds give the appearance of being on passage, but the presence of lingering, or even wintering individuals some years makes certainty difficult, and at least a few arrivals no doubt involve winter wanders. Final spring sightings normally occur during the period late March to mid-May, whereas first autumn arrivals are reported from around early October, rarely sooner.

Unsurprisingly, almost no information is available on the diet of visiting Hen Harriers, though Rabbits *Oryctolagus cuniculus* are assumed to figure largely, and an immature male on St Agnes for two days during October 1970 was seen to take a Song Thrush *Turdus philomelos* (*IOSBR* 1970). A first-winter bird on St Agnes from 22nd October 1982 until 7th June 1983 was confirmed as *hudsonius*, the slightly longer-winged and larger-billed North American 'Marsh Hawk' (Wallace 1998). Other individuals of this distinctive form have been identified elsewhere in Britain, and the possibility of further occurrences in Scilly means that all visiting Hen Harriers should be scrutinised thoroughly (Gantlett 1998). Indeed, a particularly orange-toned ring-tail on St Agnes and nearby Gugh during late March 1989 was also considered a likely contender for *hudsonius*, but a description seems not to have been submitted to the BBRC (*IOSBR* 1989).

Northern and eastern European Hen Harrier populations are largely migratory (moving mainly south or southwest), whereas those further south are sedentary or dispersive. Birds ringed in Scotland, the Netherlands, Belgium and Finland have been recovered in eastern or central England (P Lack 1986; Wernham *et al.* 2002). Lack also points out that an increase in numbers of wintering birds in eastern England post-1970 coincided with a breeding increase in the Netherlands, suggesting too that cold-weather movements must surely bring birds from eastern Europe. That aside, the extraordinary presence of at least four wing-tagged Scottish birds in Scilly during October 1993 is noteworthy (*IOSBR* 1993) and suggests a strong link between the islands and the Scottish breeding population, which winters as far south as Iberia. Hen Harrier also breeds in Ireland, France and Spain. No Hen Harriers have been trapped and ringed on Scilly, but given below are details of the four 1993 wing-tagged individuals. Mead (2000) gave the European population as 9,500 pairs and the British population during 1988–91 stood at 630 pairs in 498 10-km squares (Gibbons *et al.* 1993), with 180 pairs in Ireland in 123 10-km squares for the same period. Thus, Britain and Ireland hold some 9% of the European total.

## Controls

| | |
|---|---|
| Pul  wing-tagged southwest Scotland summer 1993 | FR  1stY/M St Agnes, St Mary's & Samson 17th to 19th October 1993 |
| Pul  wing-tagged Oban, Scotland summer 1993 | FR  1stY/M Tresco & St Agnes 19th to 22nd October 1993 |
| Ad/F wing-tagged eastern Scotland summer 1992 | FR  St Martin's 21st October 1993 |
| Pul  wing-tagged Pitlochry, Scotland summer 1992 | FR  1stY/M St Agnes October 25th 1993 |

## Hen Harrier Ringing Recaptures

# Montagu's Harrier *Circus pygargus* A

Scarce migrant, more frequent in spring than autumn, does not breed. Full written description required by the SRP.

| | | |
|---|---|---|
| 1852 | Several (three shot) Scilly April   Rodd 1852c; Rodd 1880; Clark & Rodd 1906 |
| 1868 | Obtained Scilly   Clark & Rodd 1906 |
| 1903 | One St Martin's 9th April   Clark & Rodd 1906 |
| 1951 | Two (female & immature) early September to end November   *CBWPSAR* 21 |
| 1956 | One (adult male) Bryher & Tresco 9th & 10th September |
| 1958 | One (female) St Agnes & St Martin's 22nd April and most of May |
| 1958 | One (immature) 5th September |
| 1960 | One (adult male) St Agnes 29th & 30th April |
| 1962 | One (female) St Mary's 24th to 27th April |
| 1964 | One (found dead – ringed) Tresco 31st May |
| 1971 | One (male) Bryher & Tresco 7th to 10th May |
| 1973 | One (immature) St Mary's & Tresco 6th to 8th October |
| 1974 | One (ring-tail) Daymark, St Martin's 26th May |
| 1977 | One (female) Tresco 15th & 16th May |
| 1980 | One (female) St Mary's 11th to 14th May |
| 1982 | One (immature) Great Pool, Tresco 12th May |
| 1982 | One (ring-tail) Bryher 3rd October |
| 1983 | Up to two (immature male & possible female) St Mary's & Bryher 7th & 8th May |
| 1986 | Up to two (adults – male and female) St Mary's 1st to 8th May |
| 1986 | One (female) Gugh 7th May |
| 1989 | Up to three (female, adult male, immature male) St Martin's 2nd to 5th May |
| 1989 | One (female) Giant's Castle, St Mary's 15th to 18th May |
| 1990 | Up to three (male & two females) St Martin's 3rd April |
| 1990 | One (male) all inhabited islands 4th to 13th May |
| 1991 | One (immature) Tresco 25th & 26th August |
| 1993 | One (male) in off sea at Porth Hellick, St Mary's 20th April |
| 1993 | One (female) Tresco 23rd May |
| 1993 | One (female) Bryher & Tresco 27th & 28th May |
| 1994 | One (ring-tail) St Mary's 14th May |
| 1994 | One (ring-tail) all inhabited islands 15th to 18th May |
| 1997 | One (immature male) St Mary's 7th to 9th May |

Breeds south-central West Palearctic and central-eastern Asia. West Palearctic populations winter Africa, Asian populations Indian subcontinent. Monotypic. Included on Annex I of 1979 EEC 'Birds Directive'. Amber-listed in UK: moderate (36%) contraction of breeding range over past 20 years; five-year mean of 10.6 breeding pairs (Gregory *et al*. 2002).

There are several mid- to late 19th century records and one just past the turn of the century. Subsequent sightings all cover the period of the more recent Montagu's Harrier decline throughout Britain and Europe, in view of which all Scillonian records are listed. Two things are immediately apparent: firstly that many more birds occurred in spring than autumn, and secondly that, if anything, the number of sightings increased as the population decreased. The first of these issues is discussed below, under the subject of population movements, whereas possible explanations for the second are either increased observer coverage or improved identification capabilities, or even a combination of these two. Disregarding earlier reports, there were a total of 28 records in 20 of the years during the period 1951–99, involving a minimum of 35 individuals. Of these, 22 records (78%), involving 28 birds (80%), occurred in spring. There is no particular tendency for one sex or age group to predominate, though an additional feature worth mentioning is the multiple arrivals of up to three individuals at any one time.

E H Rodd described a mid- to late 19th century increase in Montagu's Harrier in mainland Cornwall (where it was formerly 'very rarely met with') in parallel with a decline in Hen Harrier *C. cyaneus*. This was to the extent that by 1880 Rodd considered it far commoner than Hen Harrier, breeding every year in the

## Birds of the Isles of Scilly

area of the Lizard peninsula (Rodd 1880). Rodd also described various localities from where specimens had been obtained, including Scilly in April (presumably the 1852 specimens shown in the Table). James Clark and Francis Rodd (1906) mentioned a subsequent lack of specimens from Scilly until one was obtained in 1868, following which immatures and adults allegedly occurred almost annually during the 1870s, chiefly in spring. The same two authors also mentioned the bird seen on St Martin's in 1903.

E H Rodd also comments on melanistic plumage types encountered in the southwest. In particular, he describes a skin seen by him in September 1859 and shown by dissection to have been an 'old male', the whole of the plumage being a dark chocolate brown with some lighter coloration near the base of the tail, resembling in his view a diminutive Marsh Harrier *C. aeruginosus*. He also referred to two uniformly sooty-black individuals, both obtained in the Lizard area in May 1870 (Rodd 1880; Cramp et al. 1977–94).

Rodd makes some useful observations on food sources utilised by migrant Monatagu's Harriers in Scilly and Cornwall. For example, whilst skinning a bird shot in Scilly in April, Penzance taxidermist Vingoe noted what appeared to be egg yolk adhering to the sides of the bill. Similarly, a second specimen obtained from the same locality (Rodd gave no date) was apparently shot in the act of swallowing a Song Thrush *Turdus philomelos* egg, pieces of shell from which were still present in the bird's throat. Rodd also mentions a gamekeeper, George Williams, from a Lizard estate, who very effectively employed dead Adders *Vipera berus* as bait for his gin traps, 'when other dainties in the shape of small birds, eggs, etc. had failed to attract'. In 1874, the same George Williams sent Vingoe several Montagu's Harriers for preservation, the crops of which contained several lizards and what appeared to be a young sparrow *Passer*. Yet another specimen, the brown individual referred to earlier, contained a portion of Hare *Lepus capensis*, which in Rodd's view was probably taken as carrion, such behaviour being not unusual in a range of bird of prey species, e.g. Marsh Harrier *C. aeruginosus*, Gyr Falcon *Falco rusticolus* and Peregrine Falcon *F. peregrinus* (pers. obs.).

The Chart includes all know arrival dates for the period 1951–99, and reveals what seems to be a classic pattern of northward movement in April and May, with a marked peak during the first week of May, but with far fewer records in autumn. Of the 20 spring records where first and last date is recorded, 18 (90%) remained four days or less and the total combined average spring stopover time was just 2.9 days. Autumn passage was similarly hurried, with the five known-date visits lasting from one to three days, at an average of just 1.8 days. All of this perhaps suggests intentional rather than 'casual' migration. Up to and including the final quarter of the 19th century, Montagu's Harrier bred rarely in Cornwall, and perhaps Devon, plus central-southern England, Kent and East Anglia (Holloway 1996). By publication of the first of two modern national Breeding Atlases (Sharrock 1976), that situation had changed little, except for the addition of previously unrecorded small populations in central-northern England, southwest Wales and an even smaller one in southwest Ireland. However, by publication of the second Atlas (Gibbons et al. 1993), it had disappeared from Ireland, Wales, southwest and central-northern England, and by the end of the 20th century the sole British breeding population comprised a handful of pairs in central-southern England (Mead 2000).

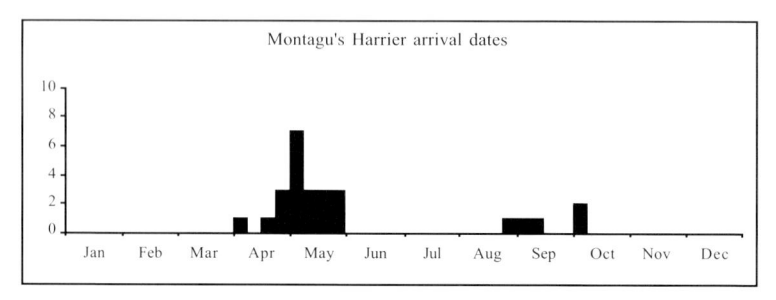

Montagu's Harrier arrival dates

The whole of the West Palearctic population is migratory, wintering in Africa from the northern grasslands down through East Africa. Interestingly, according to Cramp et al. (1977–94) autumn movement of West Palearctic birds is mainly in a southwesterly direction, presumably accounting for large concentrations at the Strait of Gibraltar, whereas in spring they move northeast, which ought perhaps to provide more Scillonian sightings in autumn than spring. One likely explanation for the pronounced concentration of records during late April and May could of course be overshooting by birds returning to the still comparatively healthy breeding populations in Iberia and France, regardless of any outward appearances of intentional migration. No Montagu's Harriers have been trapped and ringed in Scilly, but there is a record of a twelve-year-old bird found dead on Tresco on 31st May 1964, having been ringed as a nestling in the New Forest, Hampshire, in July 1952, perhaps throwing additional light on the origin of birds visiting Scilly. In total, 76.3% of the 38 British and Irish recoveries were attributable to death from human intervention, e.g. shot, trapped or poisoned (Wernham *et al.* 2002).

AD4456   Pul   New Forest, Hampshire July 1952       FD   Tresco 31st May 1964
**Montagu's Harrier Ringing Recaptures**

# Harrier *Circus*

Unidentified Harrier Records
    1963   One over Holy Vale, St Mary's 16th April
    1964   One (ring-tail) Tresco & Annet October–December
    1965   One (ring-tail) Tresco 24th to 27th January
    1965   One (ring-tail) Bryher 6th April
    1967   One Tresco 9th October
    1992   One flying east past Tresco & Bryher 3rd September
    1996   One (ring-tail) St Martin's 3rd May

Unidentified individual Hen Harriers *C. cyaneus* or Montagu's Harriers *C. pygargus* were recorded as shown in the Table. The first five of these coincided with either a period of increased Hen Harrier presence in the islands, or an increase in awareness of its likely presence (perhaps both), and for that reason seem more likely to relate to that species than Montagu's. More than one observer, however, thought that the 1964 bird was a Montagu's. The 1992 record involved a brief sighting of an at-sea fly-by and insufficient information is available on the 1996 individual for any comment.

# Goshawk (Northern Goshawk) *Accipiter gentilis* A & C

**Extremely rare migrant, full written description required by the SRP.**
    1935   One (adult *atricapillus*) shot Tresco 28th December
                                            Frohawk 1936; Anon 1936; Alexander & Fitter 1955
    1951   One St Agnes 10th September   *CBWPSAR* 21
    1969   One (immature male) Tresco 6th October
    1975   One Great Pool, Tresco 5th October
    1989   One (adult male) St Agnes 23rd October

Breeds northern Eurasia, from Iberia, France and Britain east to Pacific plus Mongolia, Japan and North America. Polytypic: nominate *gentilis* occurs much of West Palearctic, including North Africa; *buteoides* northern Sweden east to northern-central Siberia; *arrigonii* Corsica and Sardinia; *atricapillus* or 'American Goshawk' North America; with at least three other forms in Asia and North America. In western West Palearctic breeds Iberia, France and Britain south to the Mediterranean and north to Finnish Lapland and northeast Russia. Migratory or partially so in extreme north of range, but movements sometimes greater in years of prey shortage. Green-listed in UK: in need of basic conservation assistance (Gregory *et al.* 2002). Removed from BBRC Rarities List January 1963 (Harber & Swaine 1963).

    The earliest mention of Goshawk in relation to Cornwall seems to be E H Rodd's comment in the appendix to his *The Birds of Cornwall and The Scilly Islands* (Rodd 1880) that it may be added to the list of Cornish birds on the authority of Bellamy, who stated that a young bird was shot near Falmouth in August 1838 (*Natural History of South Devon* 1839). According to Penhallurick (1978), Bellamy claimed breeding in the country on the strength of this record but the evidence is insufficient to show this was anything other than an immature migrant or vagrant.

    There are just five records for Scilly, one of which is entirely beyond question and relates to the North American form *atricapillus* or 'American Goshawk'. It involved a bird shot on Tresco on 28th December

1935 (Anon 1936; Alexander & Fitter 1955), the mounted skin of which is now in the Tresco Abbey collection. Although there are no longer any other acceptable British records of this distinctive form, there are at least five for Ireland, one of which involved a bird shot in Co. Galway five days before the Tresco individual (Alexander & Fitter 1955). The most recent Irish record was in November 1969 (Naylor 1998), whereas there are only some 25 Irish records of *gentilis* (Palmer 2000).

The September 1951 record from St Agnes pre-dates formation of the BBRC, though Hilda Quick's description appears to conform with that of juvenile Goshawk (*CBWPSAR* 21), whilst the three remaining sightings post-date removal of Goshawk from the BBRC's Rarities List. D I M Wallace's graphic account of a large *Accipiter* with streaked under-belly soaring over the Tresco woods and chasing Wood Pigeons *Columba palumbus* out of the tree-tops makes fascinating reading (*IOSBR* 1969). In contrast, there is a lack of published detail concerning the 1987 Tresco individual. The only remaining sighting involved an alleged adult male on St Agnes in October 1989, and though precise details of this last bird too failed to appear in print, the claim will nevertheless have been scrutinised by the SRP. The Chart includes the late December *atricapillus* record.

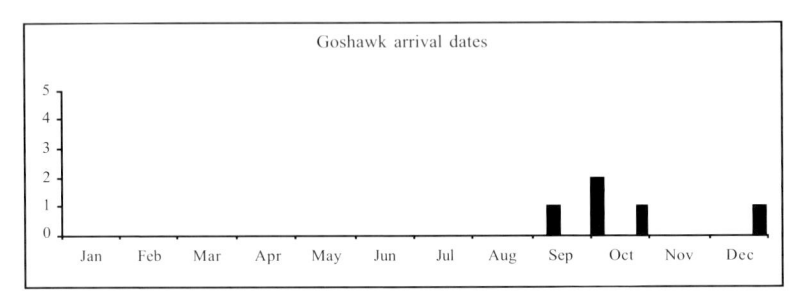

Goshawk arrival dates

It should perhaps be noted that only the two most recent records occurred within the period of the late 20th century British population increase, which was at least partially attributable to escapes and releases of a mixed European racial origin. Late summer post-fledging dispersal is random throughout most of its range, but by October movements are mainly southwards. The mean recovery distance for all 111 British Goshawk recoveries was 21 km (Wernham *et al.* 2002), and although a bird ringed in southwest Norway was recovered in Lincolnshire, there is no evidence that West Palearctic populations migrate regularly to southwest Europe. Birds seen crossing the Strait of Gibraltar and other main Mediterranean migration points are thought likely to represent extreme dispersal (Cramp *et al.* 1977–94). As a consequence, it is difficult to decide where birds reaching Scilly are likely to have originated from, except of course for any *atricapillus*. Even then the extent to which captive individuals of various geographic origins are kept in Britain advises extreme caution in determining the apparent origins of any Goshawks in the wild, and all individuals should be examined closely for indications of a captive source.

Griffiths (1982) listed a second *atricapillus* on Scilly during October 1982, but gave no precise date and no additional information, plus the record is not mentioned in the *IOSBR* or any official statistics.

## Sparrowhawk (Eurasian Sparrowhawk)   *Accipiter nisus*   A

**Regular spring and autumn migrant or winter visitor, in small numbers, does not breed.**

Breeds West Palearctic and North Africa, also northern-central and southern Asia. In West Palearctic, northern population migratory, wintering south to Mediterranean, North Africa and Middle East, remainder partially migratory or dispersive. Asian population wholly migratory, wintering south to Indian subcontinent and Southeast Asia. Polytypic: nominate *nisus* occurs West Palearctic east to western Siberia; *nisosimilis* central and eastern Siberia; *punicus* North Africa; with three more forms Mediterranean, Madeira and Canary Islands, and in central and southern Asia. National 1% increase 1994–99 (Bashford & Noble 2000). Green-listed in UK: in need of basic conservation assistance (Gregory *et al.* 2002).

The earliest reference to Sparrowhawk in Scilly seems to be North's statement that 'Some of the common British Hawks are permanently resident on the Isles, such as the Sparrow-Hawk and Kestrel' (North 1850). Writing in relation to Cornwall generally, E H Rodd described this as the commonest small bird of prey after Kestrel, being present year-round and usually found nesting in thick fir trees in or near plantations. E H Rodd's nephew Francis Rodd spent a great deal of time on Tresco in the mid-1850s in company with his friend Augustus Pechell. Between them, they accounted for a large number of important rarities, many of which they shot. On 5th January 1865 Francis wrote to his uncle pointing out that the previous day his friend – presumably Pechell – shot a female Sparrowhawk, one of 'a pair' chasing Starlings *Sturnus vulgaris* going to roost in the island's reedbeds. And he wrote again in early October 1870 to say that a 'pair' of Sparrowhawks arrived on the islands in company with the first Redwing *Turdus iliacus* and Starling flocks.

In a later review of Scilly's birds, Francis and co-author James Clark clarified the situation, suggesting that Sparrowhawks arrived in company with autumn flocks of species such as larks, e.g. *Alauda*, or *Lullula*, and Starlings, and more frequently in November than October (Clark & Rodd 1906). Nevertheless, E H Rodd described it as only an occasional visitor in his *List of the Birds Observed in the Scilly Islands* (Rodd 1880) and Clark and Rodd considered it unusual in winter. All specimens handled by Clark and Francis Rodd were immatures, as were all birds seen well by them in the field.

We then hear no more of Sparrowhawk in Scilly until the 1947 comment that it is always present except during the breeding season, numbers increasing in autumn and reducing again in December (*CBWPSAR* 17). This same report put the number normally present in the islands at around six and suggested a slight increase in spring, 'when migrants pass through'. That very much reflects the situation still today, although, as with other wintering birds of prey, arriving at an accurate count is hampered by problems of high mobility, brief views and low observer coverage. In addition, inconsistencies in recording during the mid-20th century make comparisons with more recent years unsafe. Another important point is that most mid-20th century reports originate from St Agnes and thus record migrants passing through that island, but not necessarily wintering birds, primarily because St Agnes Bird Observatory went largely unmanned during winter

During the ten years 1990–99 the earliest autumn sighting was 9th July, but in two years birds went unrecorded before early October. This may perhaps be exceptional but fits what Clark and Rodd had to say about late arrivals. In spring there was a pattern of last sightings during the period April to early May, but with late birds on 18th May plus 2nd and 18th June, the assumption being these last were also migrants.

Sparrowhawks were abundant throughout western England and Wales at the end of the 19th and into the early 20th centuries (Holloway 1996) – though less so in Ireland – and remained relatively common there up until the first national Breeding Atlas survey (Sharrock 1976), despite substantial pesticide-related declines in eastern England during the 1950s and 60s. But, ironically, by the time of the repeat atlas survey (Gibbons *et al.* 1993), numbers in the southwest had actually declined in comparison with, for example, those in central-southern England. This was a situation apparently reflected along the whole of western Britain and in Ireland, in contrast to the re-establishment of healthy populations in eastern England. Nevertheless, it seems hardly surprising that dramatic reductions in eastern England had no apparent effect on numbers recorded in Scilly; and though it went unrecorded in several years of maximum decline, this also occurred both earlier and later.

Northern birds of nominate *nisus* winter south into western Europe at least as far as the Mediterranean, with Continental birds moving predominantly south to southwest and with immatures having a stronger urge to migrate than adults. According to Cramp *et al.* (1977–94), all countries in western and southwestern Europe are visited in autumn and winter by migrants from further north and northeast, birds reaching as far as Iberia from both sides of the Baltic, Denmark, Germany and the Low Countries. British and Irish populations are wholly resident, but with some random post-breeding dispersal: 78% of birds ringed as pulli move less than 20 km and just a few greater than 100 km (Wernham *et al.* 2002). The Siberian *nisosimilis* winters almost wholly within Asia, a very small number of records from the eastern North Sea area being thought to involve this form (Cramp *et al.* 1977–94). There appear to be no claims of breeding for Scilly, despite North's early report of a year-round presence. Ryves and Quick (1946) also make no mention of it in their historical review of the breeding birds of Cornwall and Scilly, and it seems unlikely that evidence of breeding would go unnoticed in such a small geographical area. But should it ever occur, both Tresco and St Mary's, with their greater tree cover, seem most likely to be involved.

One Sparrowhawk was trapped and ringed on Scilly prior to 1970, but there are no recaptures.

# Buzzard (Common Buzzard) *Buteo buteo* A

Scarce but regular migrant or vagrant, usually singly and mainly in autumn.

Breeds central Eurasia, from Atlantic to Pacific, wintering East and southern Africa, Middle East, Indian subcontinent and Southeast Asia. Polytypic: nominate *buteo* occurs West Palearctic as far east as Poland, Romania and Turkey, but excluding Scandinavia and southernmost Atlantic islands; *vulpinus* or 'Steppe Buzzard' remaining area of Eurasia north and east of *buteo* from Swedish Lapland and Finland; *menetriesi* Crimea and Caucasus east to Iran; *rothschildi* Azores; *insularum* Canary Islands; *bannermani* Cape Verde Islands; *arrigonii* Corsica and Sardinia. National 29% increase 1994–99 (Bashford & Noble 2000). Green-listed in UK: in need of basic conservation assistance (Gregory *et al.* 2002).

Although badly broken, bone remains unearthed from the archaeological site on Nornour in the Eastern Isles were thought to have involved this species, though identification was uncertain (Turk 1971, 1984b). However, an early account of Buzzard as a 'regular passing migrant in autumn, usually in pairs but sometimes singly' (Clark & Rodd 1906) stands the test of time. although nowadays the species shows a tendency to appear singly. In fact, so familiar was E H Rodd's nephew Francis Rodd with Buzzard's autumn arrival in Scilly that in the winter of 1870–71 he wrote to his uncle remarking on its absence until January (Rodd 1880). In addition, Francis, who in December 1879 wrote to his uncle pointing out that during a particularly cold spell of weather one appeared on Tresco on 15th December, again highlighted the unpredictable nature of Buzzards arrival in Scilly. This bird was soon followed by two more, both of which departed after a few days, leaving the original bird feeding on Abbey Hill's Rabbit *Oryctolagus cuniculus* population and roosting in the island's fir trees (Rodd 1880).

The first 20th century mention of Buzzard in the islands was of a bird reported on Tresco by Richard Fitter on 9th September 1938 (*CBWPSAR* 8). This was followed soon after by A A Dorrien-Smith's description of a large bird of prey, which may have been either this species or an Osprey *Pandion haliaetus*, frequenting Tresco in early October 1942 (*CBWPSAR* 12). Unfortunately, some slight uncertainty also attaches to the next record, concerning as it does a report of two Buzzards on Tresco on an unspecified date during 1946. However, from 1958 onwards, reports become both more reliable and almost annual, though with some years of absence nevertheless and with a clear pattern of from one to three birds annually. In fact, there is no convincing record of four or more birds having arrived during any year. Most seem to have been on passage, arriving either in autumn or spring and often being seen for one day only. Earliest autumn arrival was 7th July, over Tresco Channel in 1966, and the earliest obvious spring migrant was probably 3rd April 1958, on St Mary's. The latest spring migrant may have been a bird seen flying between Tresco and Bryher on 30th May 1994, but enough birds either overwintered or remained long enough about the islands to make identification of true spring migrants problematical.

The Chart shows all known or presumed arrival dates, excluding four or so birds for which too little information is available. There is a clear autumn passage, from mid-September to mid-November, but with other birds arriving throughout the remainder of the year and with March, June and August the only blank months. Nominate *buteo* breeds in Europe east to Sweden, Poland and the Balkans and is largely migratory in the north of its range, wintering from the Baltic and southern Scandinavia south to at least the Mediterranean (Cramp *et al.* 1977–94). Uncertainties over whether *buteo* crosses the Strait of Gibraltar into North Africa are in part due to the number of intermediate *buteo/vulpinus* making the crossing and the existence of an unknown percentage of *vulpinus* lookalikes. British and Irish populations are mostly sedentary in winter and few move more than 30 km (Wernham *et al.* 2002), though a Hampshire individual is known to have crossed to France – as perhaps did two others (Wernham *et al.* 2002). However, Norwegian, Swedish and Danish birds, particularly immatures, follow a southwesterly heading, reaching Germany, Netherlands, Belgium and France, some even reaching Spain. A percentage of central European birds also move southwest, some also reaching Iberia – all of which, though, is confused by initial random dispersal among juveniles. Scandinavian migrants commence departing from September, whereas in central Europe they begin later and continue into November. Although the vast majority of *vulpinus* move south into eastern and southern Africa, some birds from Finland and Swedish Lapland move southwest, presumably accounting for some known crossings of the Mediterranean at the Strait of Gibraltar (Cramp *et al.* 1977–94).

Gantlett (1998) highlighted the possibility of the slightly smaller, long-distance migrant *vulpinus*, or 'Steppe Buzzard' reaching Britain, pointing out that there have already been several claimed sightings, but the risk of confusion with the extremely variable *buteo* means it is not safely separable in the field. Nonetheless there is one generally accepted record, involving a bird shot near Everleigh, Wiltshire, in September 1864, the skin of which is in the collection of the British Museum (Natural History) (Palmer 2000). Various subsequent claimed sightings have been rejected, including one from St Ives, on the Cornish mainland, in late October and early November 1975 (Palmer 2000). A bird described by observers as particularly small remained in Scilly from 17th January to 11th May 1990, mainly on St Mary's and St Martin's (*IOSBR* 1990).

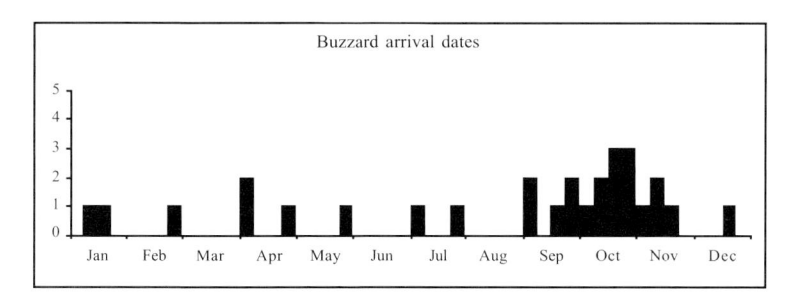

## [Red-shouldered Hawk                              *Buteo lineatus*]

No acceptable British or Irish record, full written description required by the BBRC.

[1961   One left ship when close to Scilly 22nd October]   Durand 1972

Breeds North America, in east from Great Lakes south to Gulf of Mexico and Texas, also California south into Baja California. Migratory or partially so, withdrawing from northeastern states in winter and extending into Central America. Polytypic, with two widely separated populations: nominate *lineatus* widespread in north and east; *alleni* occurs southeast; *extimus* southern Florida; *texanus* central Texas; *elegans* California.

Whilst in mid-Atlantic en route from New York to Southampton on 20th October 1961 an immature Red-shouldered Hawk was seen to arrive aboard RMS *Queen Elizabeth*. It left the ship on 22nd October when 'near' to Scilly (Durand 1972) and throughout its three-day stay fed exclusively on Leach's Petrels, and perhaps other petrel species.

Durand also mentions a Red-shouldered Hawk boarding RMS *Mauritania* on 5th September 1964 (together with a Baltimore Oriole *Icterus galbula*), while still only two days out from America. However, this individual did not stay the full duration of the transatlantic crossing, departing the ship when some three-quarters of the way towards Ireland. This bird too fed on Leach's Petrels. A Scottish record of one obtained at Kingussie, Speyside, on 26th February 1863 was not found acceptable by the BOURC (Evans 1994).

## Rough-legged Buzzard                              *Buteo lagopus*  A

Rare migrant mainly in autumn. Treated by the BBRC as a national Scarce Migrant, full written description required by the SRP.

1965   One Tresco & St Mary's 13th to 20th November
1966   One St Mary's and St Agnes late October to early November
1968   One St Mary's & St Agnes 28th October to 28th November
1981   One St Martin's, St Mary's & Bryher 25th to 28th May
1984   One (probable *sanctijohannis*) various islands 2nd to 10th October
1988   One Tresco, Bryher & St Martin's 9th to 18th October
1990   One Tresco 16th May
2001   One (probable *sanctijohannis*) various islands 1st October to month's end

Circumpolar, breeds northern landmass, range withdrawing south to central European, North American and Asian latitudes in winter. Polytypic: nominate *lagopus* occurs West Palearctic eastwards; *menzbieri* northern Siberia; *sanctijohannis* or 'Rough-legged Hawk' North America. In Britain occurs as a winter visitor, at which time confined primarily to the extreme eastern counties of England and Scotland. Like some other northern species, subject to occasional food-related irruptions.

It seems clear from his brief comments that E H Rodd (1880) knew very little about the status of this species in Cornwall and neither he nor his nephew Francis Rodd and co-author James Clark (Clark and Rodd 1906) make any reference to it in Scilly. No references can be found among any other literature either. There are in fact just eight recorded sightings for the islands, with the first not until 1965 and with nothing between 1990 and 2001 (*CBWPSAR* & *IOSBR*). The scarcity of this species so far west is surely not surprising, given its general easterly wintering distribution in England: 39% of all records for the ten years to December 1967 were in Suffolk, Norfolk and Lincolnshire (Sharrock 1974). However, wintering birds wander a good deal, in Britain reaching a number of counties in Wales and western England, though in very low numbers. Winter 1966–67 involved an exceptional influx, with 40% of all British and Irish records for the ten-year total to December 1967 occurring in that one season. The breeding grounds are normally reoccupied by late April and May, which makes the presence of birds in Scilly during mid-May 1981 and 1990 noteworthy.

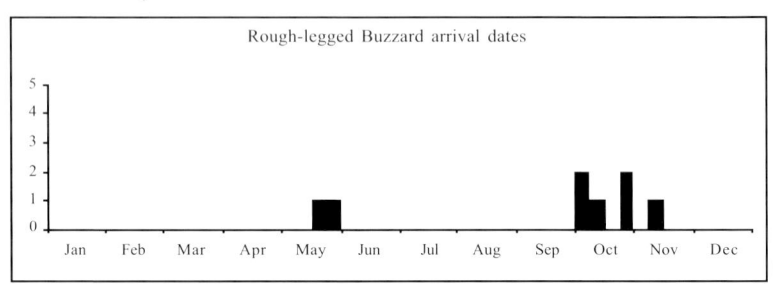

The Chart shows the pattern of arrival dates for the seven earliest individuals and lacks the winter and late spring element so obvious among the national data (Sharrock 1974). Earliest autumn arrival was 2nd October and the latest a bird remained was 28th November. The two May records were between 16th and 28th. Taking the six birds up until 1990 for which exact arrival and departure dates are known, the average length of an autumn stay was just over 14.5 days, whereas the two May individuals remained an average of only 2.5 days.

Gantlett (1998) draws attention to the possibility of the slightly larger and paler eastern Siberian form *menzbieri* and the slightly smaller and typically darker North American *sanctijohannis*, or 'Rough-legged Hawk' reaching Britain as migrants or winter vagrants. And, in fact, a bird on various islands in Scilly from 2nd to 10th October 1984 was thought by many observers to be a genuine contender for *sanctijohannis*. This theory was given added weight by the fact that its arrival on Scilly coincided with that of Surf Scoter *Melanitta perspicillata*, Blackpoll Warbler *Dendroica striata* and Common Yellowthroat *Geothlypis trichas*. The only other reported Rough-legged Buzzard at that time being one in Ireland on 13th–14th October; although both sets of records could just possibly have involved the same individual. Whatever the truth, the feeling of many seems to be that the North American form may be involved more frequently in sightings in western Britain than is currently appreciated, for, as the *IOSBR* for 1994 points out, of Ireland's 29 Rough-legged Buzzard sightings up until that year, the only two occurring on Cape Clear Island were in October 1963 and 1980.

Since preparing the above account, a seemingly prime contender for 'Rough-legged Hawk' frequented various islands throughout October 2001, appearing as it did in western Britain at the same time as other Nearctic landbirds, e.g. Grey Catbird *Dumetella carolinensis* and with the only other October Rough-leg in Britain in northeast Scotland. It also showed size and structural similarities in keeping with *sanctijohannis* and in further support of that probability, a bird thought to be *sanctijohannis* was present in the Azores from 11th to 20th October the same year (Millington 2001).

# Osprey                                                                    *Pandion haliaetus*  A

**Scarce migrant, mainly in autumn, full written description required by the SRP.**
Breeds primarily Northern Hemisphere, wintering south of equator. Birds from the West Palearctic winter mainly Africa south of equator. Polytypic: nominate *haliaetus* occurs Palearctic from Britain to Japan; *carolinensis* and *ridgwayi* North and Central America; *melvillensis* and *cristatus* Australasia. Included on

Annex I of 1979 EEC 'Birds Directive'. Downgraded from Red- to Amber-listed in UK 2002: historical population decline, but more than doubled in past 25 years; five-year mean of 118.2 breeding pairs; unfavourable world conservation status (Gregory *et al.* 2002).

In Scilly, first indication of the presence of one of these magnificent birds is often the noisy reaction from the local gull population as it drifts silently overhead. First mention of this species in the islands came in 1849 in a note by E H Rodd to the *Zoologist*, pointing out that a specimen had been procured towards the end of September that year (Rodd 1849d). E H Rodd's nephew Francis and co-author James Clark provided additional details for this bird, including that it was shot by Augustus Pechell, who noticed it came to roost every evening on a flag mast on Tresco's Castle Down (Clark & Rodd 1906). The same two authors credit the shooting in 1852 of an immature to John Jenkinson, and describe the sighting of an adult male on St Mary's in September 1902, a week before a bird was seen on the nearby Cornish mainland. The earliest 20th century record involved a bird that, according to A A Dorrien-Smith, spent early October 1942 fishing for Tench *Tinca tinca* on Tresco's Great Pool, having arrived a few days earlier (*CBWPSAR* 12). At the same time, poor views were had of a second large bird of prey, thought to be either another Osprey or a Buzzard *Buteo buteo*, probably the latter. Even into the late 1980s, Osprey seems to have remained something of a scarcity in Scilly in both spring and autumn, but with a marked increase in sightings from around 1990 possibly linked to increased observer coverage, although perhaps also genuinely reflecting recent growth in the size of the Scottish breeding population. Since 1990 there have been almost twice as many records in autumn (23) as in spring (12), with a total absence throughout 1992 and during spring 1994 to 1996. Arrivals ranged between one and three birds annually in spring and between one and five in autumn, with only very occasionally two birds present in the islands at the same time. A typical year was 1997, with the earliest of three spring records on 18th March and the last of three autumn visitors noted on 1st November, and with a mid-year absence from 24th June to 17th August.

Western European Ospreys leave their breeding grounds from mid-August, adults preceding juveniles and all moving on a broad front, but with variation in the direction of travel between populations. Swedish birds move consistently south-southwest, whereas most Finnish birds head initially south-southeast (Cramp *et al.* 1977–94). Most birds moving southwest reach the Mediterranean by September–October, following which Ospreys becomes scarce in Europe; the immature arriving in Scilly on 2nd October 1982 and remaining until at least the end of the year being unusual.

First birds commence arriving in Africa from mid-September to early October, many first-years remaining in the wintering areas or in the Mediterranean region during their second calendar summer. A bird fledged in central England reached West Africa in 20 days and one from Scotland in 39 days (Wernham *et al.* 2002). Adults commence their return journey from March and most recross the Mediterranean by the end of that month, the majority reaching the breeding grounds during April. According to Cramp *et al.* (1977–94), returning second-summer birds follow the experienced adults about one month later. There is no indication which breeding population birds reaching Scilly originate from, but observers should be alert to the possibility of the recognisable North American form *carolinensis* reaching west-coast Britain, and therefore Scilly, particularly during periods of severe North Atlantic weather. At least one bird reaching the Azores (in 1926) is thought likely to have crossed the Atlantic (Cramp *et al.* 1977–94; Gantlett 1998).

Typically, those birds that linger in the islands are to be seen fishing the main freshwater pools on Tresco and St Mary's, or patrolling shallow waters between the islands. Nonetheless it is difficult to say how many pass by Scilly without stopping, as perhaps was the case with the bird seen from one of the island launches 10 km south of the islands on 14th September 1993.

## Lesser Kestrel *Falco naumanni* A BBRC 0%

**Extremely rare migrant, mainly in spring, full written description required by the BBRC.**

    1891   One shot Tresco 3rd March   Jenkinson 1891
  [1925   One Tresco 23rd May]   Penhallurick 1978
    1926   One Scilly 24th February   Penhallurick 1978
  [1971   One St Agnes 28th October]   *British Birds* 65: 331; 88: 505
  [2001   One (in flight) St Mary's 27th August]   *Birding World* 14: 312
    2002   One St Mary's 16th to 26th May   *Birding World* 15: 180, 201–208

Breeds southern Eurasia, from Iberia east to Lake Baikal and Mongolia, with small numbers in North Africa. Monotypic. All populations winter sub-Saharan Africa.

A mid- to long-distance migrant breeding as close to Britain as northern Spain and southern France, there have been recent massive declines in the European population (Cramp *et al.* 1977–94). Earliest mention of Lesser Kestrel in mainland Cornwall involved the remains of a female shown to E H Rodd on 14th November 1876 (Penhallurick 1978), just nine years after Britain's first record, from North Yorkshire (Palmer 2000). The first for Scilly was a male shot on Tresco on 3rd March 1891 (Jenkinson 1891) and now among mounted skins in the Tresco Abbey collection and on loan to the Isles of Scilly Museum, St Mary's. Interestingly, another was shot at Shankill, Co. Dublin, some 15 days prior to the killing of the Tresco bird (*Zoologist* 1891: 152). The Tresco specimen was set up by the taxidermists Burton of London.

According to the Tresco Abbey records, a second bird was seen on that island on 23rd May 1925 and a third either there or elsewhere in Scilly on 24th February the following year (Penhallurick 1978). The first of these records is not considered acceptable and is show here in brackets.

The next Scillonian record concerned a bird described as an immature male seen by D I M Wallace and R J Johns on St Agnes on 28th October 1971 (*IOSBR* 1971). The record was originally accepted by the BBRC but later removed from the list for want of adequate documentation (*British Birds* 88: 505-506).

The dynamics of Lesser Kestrel migration have long occupied the minds of researchers. Surprisingly few are seen on autumn migration and it is thought to probably cross the Middle East, Mediterranean and Sahara regions, a journey of some 2,400 km, non-stop and at great height (Cramp *et al.* 1977–94). In contrast, spring passage is a high-profile affair with sometimes extremely large flocks involved, often at low altitude. Departure and arrival dates suggest that birds from more easterly breeding populations penetrate furthest south into Africa in winter. Some other species breeding in eastern Asia and wintering wholly or mainly in Africa, e.g. Black-headed Bunting *Emberiza melanocephala*, show a tendency towards late spring vagrancy in western Europe. However, that does not seem to occur with Lesser Kestrel and numbers reaching Britain seem evenly distributed between spring and autumn (Dymond *et al.* 1989). Just six records were accepted by the BBRC for the whole of Britain during the period 1958 to 1999 inclusive, whereas there were 11 prior to that time, with the three acceptable Scillonian records amounting to 27% of the total.

Since this text was prepared, two more Lesser Kestrels were reported on Scilly. The first involved a fly-over sighting by a few observers of a bird over Hugh Town and the nearby harbour area on 27th August 2001 and seems not to have been submitted. The second, a first-summer male, was first reported on 16th May 2002, within seven days of the claimed 1925 individual. Initially frequenting the St Mary's Peninnis area, by the following day it was being viewed by numerous visiting birders as it commuted between there and the Golf Course (*Birding World* 15: 201). At the time of going to print, this record remains subject to acceptance by the BBRC. The Chart includes arrival dates for the two acceptable early records plus the two yet-to-be accepted 2002 record. At least two birds occurred on one day only, though the arrival date of the shot Tresco individual is unclear.

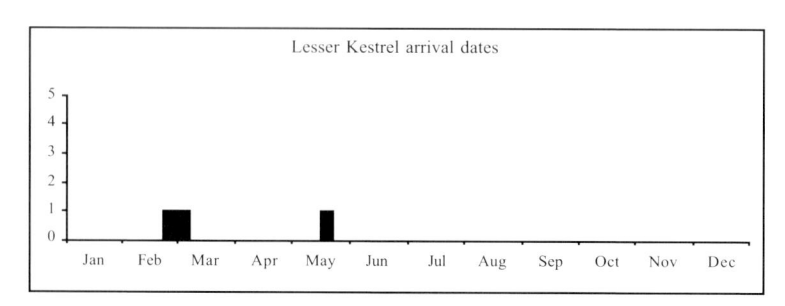

Lesser Kestrel arrival dates

There is evidence of a distinct northerly post-fledging (i.e. pre-September) dispersal among Spanish-reared Lesser Kestrels, movements on average being 210 km and greater than distances travelled by most other raptors, though similar to those covered by European Kestrel *F. tinnunculus*. This is hypothesised as forming part of the 'mental map' process in this strongly migratory species (*Bird Study* 48: 110-115), although of the Scillonian arrivals only the claimed 2001 individual apparently fits that timescale.

# Kestrel (Common Kestrel)            *Falco tinnunculus*   A

**Breeding resident in small numbers and probable annual migrant.**

Breeds Eurasia, Arabia, Indian subcontinent, Southeast Asia and Africa. Northern and eastern populations migratory, remainder migratory or dispersive. Polytypic: nominate *tinnunculus* occurs West Palearctic east to northeast Siberia and Mongolia; *canariensis* and *dacotiae* Canary Islands; *neglectus* and *alexandri* Cape Verde Islands; *ruficolaeformis* Egypt and Arabia; perhaps five other forms Asia and Africa. Amber-listed in UK: moderate (28%) breeding decline over past 25 years; unfavourable world conservation status (Gregory *et al.* 2002). National 40% decline during 25 years to 1996 and 30% decline 1994–99 (Bashford & Noble 2000).

The earliest reference to Kestrel in Scilly is North's comment that 'some of the British Hawks are permanently resident on the Isles, such as Sparrow-Hawk and Kestrel' (North 1850). Though E H Rodd's *List of Birds Observed in The Scilly Islands* showed Kestrel as a resident cliff breeder in the islands, he sadly does not mention numbers involved (Rodd 1880). By the turn of the century his nephew Francis Rodd and co-author James Clark could provide little additional information, merely describing it as evident year-round, though adding that islanders often confused it with Peregrine Falcon *F. peregrinus* (Clark & Rodd 1906). Then, like so many species, it apparently disappears from the records throughout the early half of the 20th century, until A A Dorrien-Smith's assertion that it was 'now only an occasional breeder' in the islands (Ryves & Quick 1946). This was followed by a 1948 report by Dorrien-Smith that it was 'well represented on autumn passage' (*CBWPSAR* 18); although identical comments appear in the same issue beside Peregrine, Hobby *F. subbuteo*, Merlin *F. columbarius* and Sparrowhawk *Accipiter nisus*.

Nonetheless, suggestions of a good autumn passage contrast starkly with the single bold statement that one arrived on St Mary's on 9th September 1952 (*CBWPSAR* 22). Equally enlightening is R Symons's comment that a nest with three young on St Mary's in 1956 was the first in Scilly in his experience, adding that a J Gibson recalled seeing a nest c. 90 years beforehand. The St Mary's pair bred again the following year, this time fledging an impressive six young, whilst three fledging on St Agnes that same season were recorded as the first bred on that island within living memory (*CBWPSAR* 27). Taken at face value these reports suggest either that earlier observers were mistaken and that Kestrel did not breed frequently in the mid-19th century, or that it ceased doing so some time in the late 19th or early 20th centuries, before reappearing around 1956. Sadly, trying to discover the true situation is often not helped by an apparently haphazard approach towards recording effort for this species.

Gradually, however, a pattern emerges of one to two breeding pairs each on St Mary's and St Martin's, with single pairs on St Agnes, Tresco and Bryher, and with occasional pairs on uninhabited islands, e.g. Samson and St Helen's, perhaps coinciding with temporary absence from more established sites. The highest annual all-island number of pairs is probably seven in 1993. Interestingly, then, the 2000 Breeding Bird Atlas recorded up to six pairs in six (8.9%) of the 67 1-km squares surveyed (Chown & Lock 2002). Nests are mostly situated on low coastal cliffs, with occasional use of rocky outcrops away from the shore. A pair that occupied Samson following removal of Brown Rats *Rattus norvegicus* in the early 1990s successfully utilised a cliff recess for two years. They then moved to a clifftop Rabbit *Oryctolagus cuniculus* burrow on the island's southern end, where they successfully reared young in two further years, despite the site's close proximity to a large Lesser Black-backed Gull *Larus fuscus* colony (pers. obs.).

Kestrels are fairly obvious birds and difficult to overlook, providing sufficient observers are present. Nevertheless, references to numbers of individuals present are often confusing, e.g. reports of small autumn influxes were often seemingly based on apparent increases in overall numbers on just one island, e.g. St Agnes, or Tresco. The pattern that emerges, though, is one of low summer numbers followed by a noticeable increase by October, but rarely to more than 20 birds island-wide. This is followed by a small but equally noticeable reduction in numbers by November and with few then present throughout winter and spring. However, it is unclear whether these estimates take account of post-fledging increases and an autumn total of 20 birds could represent the resident population plus the annual productivity from just one or two pairs. But a regular autumn passage would help explain frequent reports of reduction in numbers at the end of October – though so too might post-fledging dispersal, and this suggestion is supported by the ringing records listed below. In addition, there are occasional reports of birds seen flying out to sea, as in 1976 when lone birds were observed flying south out from St Mary's on 6th October and southwest of the

*Birds of the Isles of Scilly*

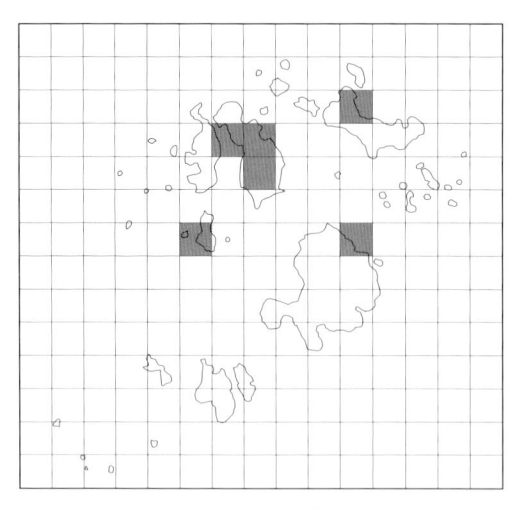

| Island | Pairs |
|---|---|
| St Mary's | 1 |
| St Martin's | 1 |
| Tresco | 3 |
| Samson | 1 |

**Kestrel 2000 Breeding Bird Atlas**

1-km Kestrel Breeding Distribution – 2000–01
(data Chown & Lock 2002)

Bishop Rock Lighthouse four days later. Another record involves a bird witnessed arriving in off the sea at Great Bay, St Martin's, on 22nd October.

A total of 50 Kestrels were ringed on Scilly as adults or pulli, 25 both before and after 1970, and there have been three recoveries plus one control. The bird ringed as a nestling in Glen Trool, southwest Scotland, on 30th May 1991 and recaptured on Samson the following October was presumably involved in normal first-winter random dispersal (Wernham *et al.* 2002), as presumably were the August–September recoveries of two Samson siblings in Devon and Ireland within 18 days of each other. A study of Kestrel ringing records (Landsborough Thomson 1958) showed a mixture of random dispersal for first-years of up to 150 miles and a more definite tendency towards mainly southerly migration, with some individuals reaching Belgium, France and Spain by midwinter. In addition, Kennedy *et al.* (1954) recorded evidence of migration in the north of Ireland, mainly in the form of a reduction in numbers, but including two birds recovered from lighthouses (one each in spring and autumn), plus one ringed as a pullus in northern England and recovered in Wexford. It has also been suggested (*Bird Study* 48: 110–115) that juvenile Kestrels and Lesser Kestrels *F. naumanni* have a greater displacement ability just after leaving the nest compared with other raptors.

Less easy to explain is the adult female found dead in France the summer after she reared a brood on Samson, though Kestrels breed commonly throughout Brittany (Guermeur & Monnat 1980). Nevertheless, recovery of the two Samson siblings within such a short timespan and the later recovery of the maternal female are of particular interest. There is also one interesting record from the ocean weather reporting station 'Kilo' positioned in the Western Approaches 800 km southwest of Scilly, involving a female Kestrel that appeared with easterly winds at 17.35 hours on 30th April 1958 and circled the ship until dusk, at which time it roosted on the balloon shed. It remained aboard ship or thereabouts until 13.40 hours the next day, but was not seen to take the food and water provided (McLean & Williamson 1959).

Given the lack of available small mammal species, it seems hardly surprising that passerines apparently figure in the diet of Kestrels on Scilly (though no study has been carried out); the choice of non-avian prey is limited to Wood Mouse *Apodemus sylvaticus*, House Mouse *Mus domesticus*, Lesser White-toothed Shrew *Crocidura suaveolens* and perhaps smaller individuals of Brown Rat. In addition, there is perhaps the occasional opportunity to take Common Frog *Rana temporaria*, though few apparently now survive in Scilly. Bird species observed being taken or pursued by Kestrels in Scilly include adult House Sparrow *Passer domesticus* but the potential list includes unfledged young of terns, Ringed Plover *Charadrius hiaticula* and Oystercatcher *Haematopus ostralegus* and perhaps even young gulls. A second-year male Kestrel attempting to catch newly fledged Song Thrushes *Turdus philomelos* in a St Mary's meadow became 'trapped' in the long grass, from which the vociferous young thrushes were calling (pers. obs.). There is at least one record of a Kestrel seen eating large beetles on the wing (*CBWPSAR* 32) but large insects too are in short supply compared with mainland Britain. Occasional reports of Kestrels found dead, e.g. in November (*IOSBR* 1989), presumably fit the normal pattern of post-fledging, first-winter mortality and could have involved local birds or winter visitors.

**Controls**
EK57796  Pul  Glentrool, Dumfries & Galloway
                30th May 1991                              CT  St Martin's 20th October 1991

**Recoveries**
ES21306  Pul   Samson 30th June 1993         FD  Tresco 11th February 1994
ES61406  Pul*  Samson 24th June 1998         FD  Blessington, Co. Wicklow
                                                                    27th August 1998
ES61409  Pul*  Samson 24th June 1998         FD  Budleigh Salterton, Devon
                                                                    13th September 1998
ES61416  Ad/F* Samson 24th June 1999         FD  Cosqueville, Manche, France
                                                                    24th November 2000

**Kestrel Ringing Recaptures (*female and siblings)**

# Red-footed Falcon  *Falco vespertinus*  A  BBRC 0.9%

**Rare migrant, mainly in spring, full written description required by the BBRC.**

   [1951   One Lower Moors, St Mary's, 27th October]  *CBWPSAR* 21
    1961   One (first-summer male) St Agnes 27th May to 4th June  *British Birds* 55: 571
    1970   One (female) Tresco 15th May  *British Birds* 64: 348
    1989   One (female) St Mary's 7th May to 5th June  *British Birds* 83: 457–458, 480
    1991   One (female) St Martin's 29th May to 2nd June  *British Birds* 85: 520
    1992   One (first-summer female) St Martin's & St Mary's 18th to 23rd May
                                                            *British Birds* 86: 466–469, 87: 519–520
    1995   One (female) Tresco 6th June  *British Birds* 90: 467

Breeds central Eurasia, from Poland and Hungary east to Mongolia. Monotypic. Migratory, entire population winters southern Africa.

E H Rodd was no stranger to Red-footed Falcon on the Cornish mainland, having himself acquired a specimen shot just over the county border in Devon and knowing of two others obtained within Cornwall prior to 1880, referring to it under an alternative name of 'Orange-legged Hobby' (Rodd 1880). In view of these three records, it is surprising to discover that there is no mention of this species in Scilly until the possible sighting of a bird on Lower Moors, St Mary's, on 27th October 1951 (*CBWPSAR* 21). Unfortunately, the published description by Hilda Quick is brief and lacking in detail, plus the date is rather suspicious compared with that of subsequent arrivals, and as the sighting pre-dates the formal BBRC vetting procedure, it must remain in slight doubt.

The Table shows the six BBRC-accepted records, all of which fit the classic pattern of spring arrivals. Like several other Asiatic species wintering in Africa, Red-footed Falcon demonstrates a tendency for northwest European vagrancy in spring. Nationally, all but two of the 284 records during the years 1958–85 occurred in the period April to November, with 75% in spring and a clear peak in the latter half of May (Dymond *et al.* 1989). National records are well scattered throughout England, with most in the east and south and with few birds making it to the southwest. Even so, apart from the individuals mentioned above, a bird reached Cornwall in 1935, and given Scilly's justifiable reputation for attracting extralimital spring and autumn migrants the lack of any reported sighting prior to the mid-20th century is surprising. Interestingly, none reached Scilly during the exceptional influx into Britain during 1973, although the 1992 individual coincided with a marked invasion of Britain and Ireland, when some 120 birds north to Shetland and southwest as far as Cornwall were matched by huge influxes in countries bordering the English Channel and North Sea (Nightingale & Allsop 1994). The Chart shows arrival dates for the six most recent records and typically these span a five-week period during May and early June. The earliest recorded arrival date was 7th May and the latest a bird was seen was 6th June. The average length of stay was 8.6 days, though two were present for one day only. Five of the six were recorded as female.

*Birds of the Isles of Scilly*

**Red-footed Falcon arrival dates**

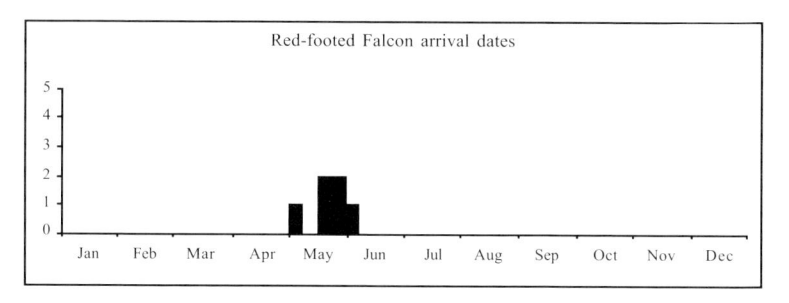

Red-footed Falcon is a broad-front autumn migrant, lacking concentrations at narrow sea crossings that are so much a feature of most migrant Eurasian raptors. Birds from more easterly breeding populations pass north of the Caspian and Black Seas in autumn before joining European birds and moving south towards Africa. Spring movement north out of Africa is orientated in an even more westerly direction, with substantial numbers crossing the Mediterranean from Algeria eastwards during mid-April to mid-May; consequently many reach western Europe in late spring (Cramp *et al.* 1977–94).

# Merlin *Falco columbarius* A

**Regular spring and autumn migrant, also winter visitor in small numbers.**

Circumpolar, breeds northern Eurasia, Alaska and Canada, withdrawing south in winter. In West Palearctic occupies area from British Isles and southern Sweden south to Mediterranean and east to Black Sea. Polytypic: *aesalon* occurs northern Europe east to central Siberia; *insignis* northern Asia; *subaesalon*, or 'Icelandic Merlin' Iceland; darker nominate *columbarius* northeast North America. Included on Annex I of 1979 EEC 'Birds Directive'. Downgraded from Red- to Amber-listed in UK 2002: historical population decline, but more than doubled in past 25 years (Gregory *et al.* 1996).

E H Rodd considered Merlin not uncommon in winter in Cornwall where moorland and cultivated land met, pointing out that specimens had been obtained from various mainland sites and from Scilly (Rodd 1880), but he made no mention of it breeding in the southwest. Earlier, Rodd wrote to the *Zoologist* describing a sighting on Scilly in December 1859 (Rodd 1860b; Couch 1838) and then again concerning a male obtained and sent over to Penzance by boat from Scilly in early November 1866 (Rodd 1867c). E H Rodd's nephew Francis and co-author James Clark later reviewed the birds of Scilly and confirmed Merlin as a regular autumn and winter visitor, chiefly on St Mary's Moors, 'where it was very active in the pursuit of snipe' (presumably Snipe *Gallinago gallinago* and/or Jack Snipe *Lymnocryptes minimus*) (Clark & Rodd 1906). He went on to claim that in all cases where descriptions were obtained, birds involved had been immature, from which we should assume E H Rodd's 1866 male was a subadult.

First 20th century mention of Merlin on Scilly involves A A Dorrien-Smith's 1948 suggestion that it was 'well represented on autumn passage' (*CBWPSAR* 18), though it seems to have been recorded annually from 1957 onwards. Winter numbers are normally difficult to assess, primarily owing to the amount of inter-island movement involved plus the species' natural high mobility. Nevertheless, it seems unlikely that more than four to five birds are present at any time during most winters, perhaps increasing to eight or so during October, but seldom, if ever, appearing to reach double figures. During the ten years 1990–99 there was an obvious early autumn peak in arrivals, between late August and late September, with the earliest the 26th July; followed by an apparent reduction in numbers before a marked October influx, as also noted by Penhallurick for mainland Cornwall (Penhallurick 1978). Clark and Rodd's failure to mention a spring movement is particularly interesting and Penhallurick picked up on this same point in the mid-20th century, describing the Cornish spring passage as indiscernible and suggesting that what little movement there is in mainland Cornwall is consistent with the departure of wintering birds. However, that may not be true of Scilly, where there was an obvious late-season spate of short-stay sightings during the 1990s, from around early April to as late as May 25th.

Penhallurick also speculated that some Merlins wintering in Cornwall may originate from Iceland, pointing out that individuals of the larger *subaesalon* ringed on Fair Isle have been recovered in continental Europe, e.g. Belgium and France (Cramp *et al.* 1977–94; Penhallurick 1978). These last authors give the winter range for *subaesalon*, or 'Icelandic Merlin' as mainly Ireland and western Britain (which is supported by ringing data – Wernham *et al.* 2002), with a minority reaching southern Europe. It therefore came as no great surprise that an immature female strongly showing characteristics of *subaesalon* was trapped and ringed on St Martin's on 28th October 1990 (M & L Love; P J Robinson).

Penhallurick refers to an isolated 1954 Cornish breeding record and pairs occasionally nest elsewhere in southwest England, e.g. Devon, but the nearest substantial breeding populations are now in Wales and Ireland (Gibbons *et al.* 1993). Adult British and Irish birds generally winter well within 100 km of their breeding areas, any movement being mainly southwards, with a few individuals reaching as far as western France (Wernham *et al.* 2002). And although birds from the Fennoscandian populations also reach southern Europe (mostly France), there is little evidence to suggest they cross to Britain (Wernham *et al.* 2002). This suggests that birds reaching Scilly come either from Britain, Ireland or Iceland, although, as Cramp *et al.* point out, in the absence of any ringing data little is known about the movements of the central Asian *insignis*, even though they are thought to perform the longest movements of any Eurasian Merlins. Cramp *et al.* also give the commencement of autumn *subaesalon* movement through Fair Isle as mid-August, peaking early October, with a cessation of movement by the end of that month, which of course fits the picture on Scilly.

However, Fair Isle experiences only a slight spring movement, which according to Cramp *et al.* suggests Icelandic Merlins move north via a more westerly route. P Lack (1986) showed a broad-based winter distribution throughout Britain and Ireland, suggesting 2–3 individuals per 10 km² is the norm, with anything greater than ten considered a very high density. The Scillonian archipelago measures roughly 16x10 km, much of which, however, is sea. Therefore, a winter density of around six birds within the archipelago appears close to the UK norm, but may in fact be excessive once the actual landmass area is taken into account. Stone *et al.* (1997) gave a UK population best-estimate of 1,330 pairs for the early 1990s.

Little or no information is available on prey exploited by visiting Merlins on Scilly. But Odin (1992) watched Merlins hunting at Dungeness, Kent, between February and April 1988, noting that of 34 birds coming in off the sea most were either chasing or carrying prey. He ascertained these were not arriving migrants, but birds going out to sea to hunt passerines (presumably migrants). No such behaviour seems to have been recorded in Scilly, which in general lacks any obvious diurnal passerine migration; the probable obvious exception being Swallow *Hirundo rustica*, though other species do move between islands. There are just two Merlin ringing records for Scilly: one before 1970 and the 1990 immature Icelandic female already referred to.

## Hobby (Eurasian Hobby) *Falco subbuteo* A

**Scarce spring and autumn migrant, does not breed.**

Breeds Eurasia, from Britain and Iberia east to Kamchatka, Sakhalin and China. Migratory, West Palearctic populations winter Africa south of equator, Asian birds in Indian subcontinent and southern China. Polytypic: nominate *subbuteo* is replaced in China by *streichi*. Green-listed in UK: in need of basic conservation assistance (Gregory *et al.* 2002).

E H Rodd had surprisingly little to say about this species on the Cornish mainland and even more surprisingly made no mention of it in relation to Scilly, other than to describe it in his supplementary *List of Birds Observed in the Scilly Isles* as occurring in spring and autumn (Rodd 1880). However, James Clark and Francis Rodd were far more forthcoming in their landmark review of the birds of Scilly (Clark & Rodd 1906), describing it as a spring and summer migrant which perhaps often escaped attention, specifically referring to a specimen shot by John Jenkinson in either Higher or Lower Moors on St Mary's in 1863, another found dead on St Mary's near 'the telegraph wire' on 29th April 1897 and one shot somewhere in the north of that same island in May 1899, concluding with mention of one seen by Clark and one other observer on 11th July 1903.

The first 20th century record appears to have involved a rather late bird on St Mary's in October 1947 – Penhallurick (1978) gave the date as 29th. In any event, it rather surprisingly remained in Scilly until shot early the following year (*CBWPSAR* 17), a wintering Hobby being exceptional in Britain (Cramp *et al.* 1977–94). Hobby subsequently got fairly frequent mention in the annual reports, with regular references to autumn passage, though as Penhallurick pointed out, reports of it being 'well represented' or 'numerous' on autumn passage seem best treated with caution (Penhallurick 1978). Equally intriguing is the May 1964 reference to a male 'displaying' over St Mary's for some 20 minutes, though sadly the nature of the alleged display is not described (*CBWPSAR* 34). The records suggest a not altogether surprising annual increase in numbers of reports as the level of observer coverage and standard of reporting improved. However, as for birds of prey generally, determining exactly how many individuals are present at any one time is problematical, as also is deciding whether several sightings from different islands involved the same individual.

Taking the ten years 1990–99, minimum numbers of birds recorded per year was in the range nine to 13, though in some years twice that many individuals could have been involved, depending on the approach adopted towards multiple observations. Earliest annual spring arrivals were in the range 21st March to 15th May, with mid- or late April nearer the norm, whereas last spring sightings occurred mid-June, with the latest on 22nd. First autumn arrivals occurred early July, though early September was more usual, and none was seen after October. The small number of July and August arrivals are difficult to interpret, suggested explanations ranging from wandering non-breeders to day-tripping birds from mainland Cornwall. A small, apparently dark falcon at Borough Farm, Tresco, on 4th October 1999 was reportedly wearing falconry type 'jesses' on its legs. It was seen well as it went to roost and was thought to be of this species (*IOSBR* 1999). Hobby is kept in captivity in Britain, but not commonly, and the possibility of this bird being one of various medium-sized falcons, or hybrids, commonly kept in captivity in the UK cannot be discounted entirely.

Hobby breeds as close to Scilly as Cornwall and Devon (Gibbons *et al.* 1993). Autumn and spring migration of the western European population takes place on a broad front without concentrations at main Mediterranean crossing points (Cramp *et al.* 1977–94). Birds from northern and central Europe move south in a broad arc, with ringed individuals recovered in various countries including France, but only once in Britain or Ireland (Wernham *et al.* 2002); the clear suggestion here is that that birds reaching Scilly originate from the English population. Autumn passage commences late August with most birds moving through Europe in September and with few left by mid-October. Return movement commences in March, most recrossing the Mediterranean between mid-April and mid-May, most European breeding areas being reoccupied during this time. All of this fits the pattern of arrivals and departures experienced on Scilly.

## Gyr Falcon *Falco rusticolus* A BBRC 3.8%

**Rare migrant or winter visitor, full written description required by the BBRC.**

 1895 One (adult male '*islandus*' – shot) St Martin's 15th January
  Clark & Rodd 1906; *Field* 26th Jan 1895
 1903 One (adult male – shot) Tresco 27th March Clark & Rodd 1906; *British Birds* 1: 320
 1913 One Tresco 15th March Ogilvie-Grant 1914
 1964 One (immature) Tresco 6th November to 5th January 1965 *British Birds* 59: 301
 1968 One (white phase) between Tresco & St Mary's 30th September *British Birds* 62: 466
 1972 One (white phase) Bryher 14th April *British Birds* 66: 339
 1972 One (white phase) St Mary's & St Martin's 6th to 10th May *British Birds* 66: 339
 1985 One (white phase) various islands 2nd January to 7th April *British Birds* 79: 541, 87: 520
 2002 One (dark phase) various islands December

Circumpolar, breeds northern Eurasia, from Iceland and Scandinavia east to Pacific, also North America from northern Alaska east to Baffin and Queen Elizabeth Islands, plus coastal Greenland. Monotypic. Migratory in extreme north of range, seldom extending beyond central Eurasia or North America in winter.

With so many large gulls present about the islands, it is always possible that white-phase Gyr Falcons may be overlooked and the potential for this impressively large falcon to be present in Scilly should be kept constantly in mind. Individual populations, e.g. from Greenland, or Iceland, were formerly afforded subspecific status, based on variations in size and plumage, but these features are now generally considered insufficient for taxonomic separation (Cramp *et al.* 1977–94).

E H Rodd mentioned two 'Greenland Falcons' obtained in mainland Cornwall sometime before 1880, plus the capture of an immature female 'Iceland Falcon' near Padstow in 1870. He also gave details of a letter from a Major Fisher describing three large imports of falcons from Iceland direct to falconers, mostly in South Wales. Based on this information, Rodd thought it wise to relinquish his claim on the Padstow bird as a 'true British and Cornish specimen' (Rodd 1880). Among other things, this incident demonstrates that the problem of escapes clouding any judgements on rarity claims is nothing new!

Earliest mention of Gyr Falcon in Scilly was E H Rodd's nephew Francis Rodd and James Clark's account of an adult male 'Iceland Falcon' shot near St Martin's Daymark on 15th January 1895 (*Field* 26th January 1895; Clark & Rodd 1906). The last two authorities also claimed that three or four other individuals were present in Scilly around the same time, but as they gave no qualifying information it must surely be possible that these additional reports referred to the above-mentioned bird, particularly in view of the high mobility of these large falcons. This was followed some eight years later by the shooting of a 'superb' male 'Greenland Falcon' on Tresco on 27th March 1903 (Clark & Rodd 1906). And that same year two more Gyr Falcons were obtained in west Cornwall, one at Mousehole in March and the other also near Penzance, date unknown, whilst another was obtained on Lundy Island, Devon, on 13th March (Penhallurick 1978). A bird on Tresco in March 1913 was documented in the *Bulletin of the British Ornithologists' Union* (Ogilvie-Grant 1914), but this sighting was followed by a substantial gap in time before a succession of records commencing in the mid-1980s. These started with a large pale immature recorded on numerous occasions in the Tresco area from November 1964 until last seen being mobbed by a Kestrel *F. tinnunculus* on 5th January 1965 (*CBWPSAR* 34; Penhallurick 1978). According to Penhallurick, this was very probably the same individual that frequented the Marazion Marsh and St Michael's Mount area of west Cornwall for two weeks from 15th January (presumably 1965).

The remaining four arrivals all involved white-phase birds, two of which occurred in the same year and two of which were seen on single days only. Although separated from each other by just three weeks, the 1972 sightings are believed to have involved two different individuals. The first was a brief fly-over on Bryher on 14th April, and the other was seen on St Mary's and St Martin's over a period of five days, having been first discovered on St Mary's Golf Course feeding on a freshly killed Whimbrel *Numenius phaeopus*. These two 1972 arrivals coincided with a small but marked influx into Britain that year (Dymond *et al.* 1989). The next Gyr Falcon to reach Scilly was an immature, tentatively identified on St Agnes on 2nd January 1985 and present for certain on Tresco from 6th of that month. It remained mainly in the area until 12th February, but perhaps also accounted for the sighting of a bird matching its description in the Dartmoor area of Devon on 18th–20th February. Its unexpected reappearance on Tresco on 6th April initially kindled thoughts of a second individual, but this was subsequently discounted. It was last noted on 7th April.

The possibility of escaped birds, either from falconers or captive-breeding schemes, being involved must be borne in mind, but no observers of the modern sightings noted features leading to that conclusion. Gyr Falcons now occur in Britain at the rate of only three or so per year but were formerly more frequent and are far more likely to occur in western Britain or Ireland. Most records involve white-phase birds, presumably from Greenland or arctic Canada, but the possibility of some level of visual bias should perhaps be considered, though there seems no doubting that sightings of white-phase individuals predominate. Nationally, records are fairly evenly spread over the period September to May, with a slight but nonetheless noticeable increase during March–April, and with another obvious peak in mid-December (Dymond *et al.* 1989). Since preparation of this text, a dark phase individual appeared in the islands briefly during mid-December 2002 and is not included in the above analysis.

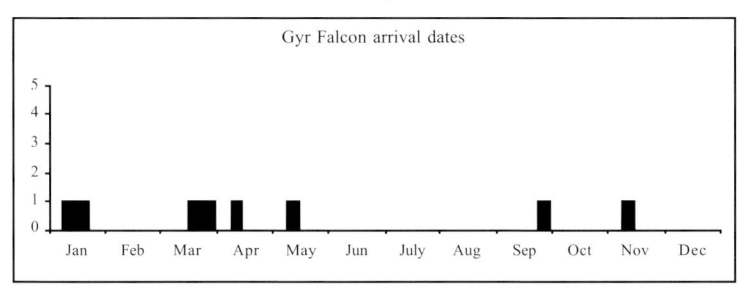

Gyr Falcon arrival dates

All Scillonian records fit the pattern noted by Dymond *et al.* (see Chart). Six of the eight records fall in the early half of the year and the earliest autumn arrival was 30th September and the latest any bird was seen was 10th May. Ignoring the two shot birds, average length of stay was 27.3 days, but the two long-stayers distort the true picture. Viewed separately the three spring birds (March–May) remained on average just 2.3 days and two of these were present on single days only. A total of 131 Gyr Falcon records were accepted by the BBRC during the period 1958–99 with the five Scillonian birds representing 3.8% of these. In his useful account of birds recorded at Tresco Abbey, T A Dorrien-Smith (1951) lists both 'Iceland Falcon' and 'Greenland Falcon' as having occurred up until that time.

# Peregrine Falcon *Falco peregrinus* A

**Scarce migrant or winter visitor and a former breeding resident, a single pair returned to breed in the 1990s.**

Global breeding distribution, occurring all continents. In Northern Hemisphere most northerly populations highly migratory. Polytypic: nominate *peregrinus* occurs West Palearctic east to Yenisey and south to Mediterranean and Ukraine; *brookei* southern West Palearctic; *anatum* North America except arctic tundra, where replaced by *tundrius*. Extensive and particularly marked reduction in many populations during 1950s and 60s resulting from widespread use of agricultural pesticides. Populations largely back to near former status. Breeds throughout much of British Isles, with exception of central lowland areas and sections of eastern and southeast coast. Breeds Cornwall and Devon. Included on Annex I of 1979 EEC 'Birds Directive'. Amber-listed in UK: unfavourable world conservation status (Gregory *et al.* 2002).

Unusually for E H Rodd (1880), his only contribution on the status of Peregrine Falcon was to point out that it was not uncommon in Cornwall and that the species bred on Scilly as elsewhere. First useful mention of Peregrines in the islands came from James Clark and E H Rodd's nephew Francis Rodd in their classic 1906 review of the birds of Scilly (Clark & Rodd 1906). Here they suggested that one, and in some years, two pairs nested on uninhabited islands, probably every year 'since the birds of Scilly first received systematic attention', with those on rocky Gorregan, in the Western Isles, in 1841 probably being the first documented incidence of breeding. Young were allegedly taken from a nest on isolated Hanjague in the Eastern Isles soon after that date, but main regular breeding sites were Round Island, Man-a-Vaur and Castle Bryher, with a pair breeding on Annet's Carn Irish in 1901. Ratcliffe (1980) agrees that Scilly once had at least two 'breeding places' but points out that because of the large number of islands involved Peregrine history is likely to be extremely patchy.

Heatherly (1913) spent the three years 1910–1912 meticulously observing and photographing Peregrines at the nest in Scilly. His record, far ahead of its time in terms of detail and conservation perspective, gives valuable insight into prey items taken during summer, whilst also confirming the presence of at least two breeding pairs (simultaneous clutches on two different islands) in 1911. He also confirmed that egg-collectors were at work in Scilly then, as elsewhere, taking a clutch of Peregrine eggs from one of his study nests. As a consequence, Heatherly sadly omits the names of sites involved. He also documents the apparent loss in 1910 of a female with young, which he presumed was shot, plus, even more importantly, the male's efforts in keeping the brood alive and her rapid replacement by another adult female; behaviour later described by Derek Ratcliffe in his epic work on Peregrines (Ratcliffe 1980).

A recent feature has been the recolonisation of Scilly by a single pair of Peregrines after an absence of some 66 years (*IOSBR* 1994). But more interesting still is their failure to increase beyond a single pair, despite apparently fledging young most years; a feature also of the long-standing single Raven *Corvus corax* pair. The most likely explanations for this are either a lack of suitably sized prey items, or low prey abundance during winter, especially considering the absence from Scilly of species such as Jackdaw *Corvus monedula*, together with low numbers of waders, e.g. *Charadrius*, and few resident Woodpigeons *Columba palumbus* or Stock Doves *C. oenas*. In this respect, then, Heatherly's account is of particular importance, recording as it does Peregrines with young regularly bringing to the nest Blackbird *Turdus merula*, Song Thrush *T. philomelos*, Razorbill *Alca torda*, Puffin *Fratercula arctica*, Curlew *Numenius arquata*, and even Dunnock *Prunella modularis* and Rock Pipit *Anthus petrosus*. The last two species are quite surprising given their small size and the relative abundance, at that time, of Puffins and other seabirds. E H Rodd's nephew Francis Rodd adds to the picture, graphically describing an immature Peregrine taking a Moorhen *Gallinula chloropus* in flight by Tresco's Abbey Pool in October 1863 (Rodd 1880).

Equally interesting among the prey items mentioned by Heatherly, considering neither would have been taken in flight, were nestling Shag *Phalacrocorax aristotelis* and even domestic fowl *Gallus domesticus*. However, this may not be too unusual, as Treleaven (1981) recorded a Cornish coastal female taking a 4–6-day-old Herring Gull *Larus argentatus* chick from a nest and feeding it to her young, whilst Tatum (1981) witnessed another coastal Peregrine catching large sand eels *Ammodytes* from the sea's surface off British Columbia, Canada. Though Peregrines have not thus far been reported fishing in Scilly, this last observation does demonstrate their ability to exploit a range of available prey items. It seems surprising, therefore, that no one in Scilly has recorded them taking Manx Shearwaters *Puffinus puffinus*, which breed locally. Peregrines have been seen attacking shearwaters off St Ives in west Cornwall (B King 1965a), and at least one pair breeding beside Scotland's Loch Ness are known to take shearwaters (pers. obs.), presumably birds using the Great Glen as a short cut between the Atlantic and North Seas. However, perhaps the most unusual, and certainly the rarest, item of prey known to fall victim to a Peregrine in Scilly was the Pied-billed Grebe *Podilymbus podiceps* taken in flight near St Agnes Pool in October 2000 (*IOSBR* 2000).

C J King (1924) largely confirmed Heatherly's earlier accounts, but Penhallurick (1978) was helpful with numbers for mainland Cornwall, suggesting probably no more than thirty or so pairs throughout in the 19th century and around 20–25 pairs by the 1930s. Penhallurick also suggested a single pair in Scilly from the 1840s, although also acknowledging the possibility of an occasional second pair.

The Peregrine's ability to reoccupy former nest sites after an absence of several decades is well documented, so it was no great surprise that the newly returned 1994 pair raised young on a ledge high above the southeast corner of Round Island, the same island in fact that Augustus Smith took eggs from in 1854 (Penhallurick 1978). Since then the new pair have raised young from at least two sites in the Eastern Isles, neither of which is previously referred to in the literature. With this being the case, and given the continued existence of illegal egg-collecting, it may be prudent not to mention them here. According to Penhallurick, breeding may have continued until 1928 on Men-a-Vaur, with the Castle Bryher site occupied by Cormorants from 1922. Thus, the absence of Peregrines from Scilly throughout the period of the Second World War meant that the islands were immune from the Government's temporary efforts at culling birds said to have been threatening message-carrying homing pigeons (Ratcliffe 1980).

In recent years, even during their absence as a breeding species, Peregrines were regularly recorded as adults or juveniles both on passage and during winter, with perhaps three to four sightings annually during autumn and winter and with the occasional bird outside those periods. Certainly away from the breeding season and early autumn this very much remains the case today, though it is still unclear to what extent the local breeding pair or their progeny are involved in any winter sightings, plus the Peregrine's high mobility urges caution in deciding exactly how many birds are present. According to Ratcliffe (1980) we might expect the breeding pair to remain in or close to Scilly during winter but the young to disperse in autumn, with birds from elsewhere either wintering or passing through. A juvenile found dead in 2001, and allegedly one of the local 2000 progeny, was found to have a small piece of wood embedded in its breast, presumably the result of some form of accident (IOSBG 2000).

The only Peregrines ringed in Scilly were two pulli handled by the author, Will Wagstaff and Graham Elliot at the Round Island site in 1994. The only recapture involved a bird ringed as a nestling at an undisclosed site in Cumbria in 1994 and found dead at Trenoweth, St Mary's, in late November the same year, a distance of some 400 km. This is a presumed case of random first-year dispersal, though somewhat further than the norm, mean travel distance of 554 British- or Irish-ringed Peregrines being just 45 km, with first-years tending to move least (Wernham *et al.* 2002). However, ringed birds from Sweden and Norway are recovered in southern England and therefore may reach Scilly. Over 98% of recovered ringed birds were found dead, 29% due to natural causes, and post-mortem examination of the Cumbria bird found no evidence of human intervention. As Ratcliffe pointed out, young birds of prey are on a very steep learning curve, with many failing to survive their first winter.

At most inland and coastal breeding areas the range of prey taken reflects local conditions, e.g. Jackdaws in cliff areas and, according to Ratcliffe (1980), only at seabird stations does it differ greatly from most inland eyries. Pigeons are predominant prey items (Rock and Feral Pigeons, with fewer domesticated birds) and in Cornish studies formed 90% by frequency of all prey species (Ratcliffe 1980). Reference has already been made to prey recorded by Heatherly in the early 20th century, but very little subsequent information is available. During various survey work about the islands, the author came upon what were considered to be remains of Peregrine kills. Included among these were Curlew and Whimbrel *Numenius phaeopus* (the latter only 'in season') but the author also found tern remains (probably Common *Sterna hirundo* but just conceivably Roseate *S. dougallii*) at the 1994 Round Island eyrie. In October 2000, a juvenile female was seen to take both the Pied-billed Grebe and Leach's Petrel *Oceanodroma leucorhoa* in flight in the area of St Agnes. Rock Doves *Columba livia* are not mentioned as ever having been present on Scilly and there are no feral birds filling that gap. In addition, local collections of domesticated birds are limited to two to three small groups of white 'fan-tails' *Columba* or similar. Nevertheless, quite substantial numbers of lost or tired homing pigeons *C. livia* are regularly about the islands during summer, the apparent by-product of races between France and Ireland, and during such times there is ample evidence of the resident Peregrine pair exploiting this temporary availability.

The probability exists of one or other of the Old or New World forms reaching Scilly, as elsewhere in Britain, though good views may be necessary to confirm that. Birds of one or other of the two North American forms were shot in Leicestershire in 1891 and caught in Lincolnshire in 1910 (Gantlett 1998). Nevertheless, the origin of birds wintering or passing through the islands remains largely unknown, the only real indicator being the ringed individual from Cumbria, which pretty much fulfilled expectation.

Controls
GF02230   Pul   Cumbria (site withheld) 4th June 1994   FD   Trenoweth, St Mary's 24th November 1994
**Peregrine Falcon Ringing Recaptures**

# Black Grouse *Tetrao tetrix* A

**Known from a single bone specimen from the Iron Age site on Nornour, Eastern Isles (Turk 1971, 1984b).**

Sedentary species of boreal, subarctic and arctic-alpine zones and mostly northern European lowlands with relict mid-latitude mountain populations, e.g. Alps. Typically inhabits transitional zone between woodland and open heath and presence of trees considered essential. Occurs broadly eastwards from Scandinavia and eastern Europe nearly to Pacific. Polytypic: nominate *tetrix* occurs continental Europe, southern Siberia east to Kolyma River and south to Lena River; *britannicus* Britain; *viridans* southeast Russia. Previously more widespread in Britain but confined mainly now to north, with outlying population North Wales. Red-listed in UK: rapid, greater than 50% breeding decline and moderate range retraction over past 25 years; unfavourable world conservation status (Gregory *et al.* 2002).

Known from a single bone specimen from the Iron Age site on Nornour, Eastern Isles (Turk 1971, 1984b), this is the only such specimen found within Scilly or Cornwall and is a rare find apparently in any Iron Age context. It is believed to originate from near the end of the prehistoric period. The find is particularly interesting for what it suggests about the nature of Scilly at that time, offering as it does the distinct probability of extensive tree cover, even though perhaps greatly stunted by maritime conditions, but in stark contrast, nonetheless, to the near total lack of tree cover know to have existed in Scilly by around the turn of the 20th century. No past writer makes mention of this species on Scilly and we must assume it was absent by at least the 18th or 19th century.

Black Grouse is known to have occurred in Cornwall west as far as Camborne until at least the mid-1800s (Penhallurick 1978) and E H Rodd (1880) clarify that it was found throughout the Cornish mainland until the early 1900s. The latter documented its subsequent decline to that of an extremely rare breeder and as being unrecorded by him in west Cornwall beyond 1868. Thus, by the late 19th century, Black Grouse was reduced to the level of a rarity throughout Cornwall and much of Devon (Holloway 1996). Nevertheless, it persisted in Cornwall until as recently as 1920, was still present on Dartmoor until 1959 and by the mid-1960s could still be found on Exmoor (Parslow 1967a), whereas the closest breeding population to Scilly now is in central Wales and that too may be in decline (Gibbons *et al.* 1993). Parslow blamed its disappearance from most areas on deliberate destruction, i.e. shooting, and loss of habitat and that seems likely to have been at least partly the case on Scilly, though the latter feature may have been driven by climate change.

## [Northern Bobwhite                                    *Colinus virginianus*] E

Formerly introduced to Tresco in small numbers, now no longer present.

Breeds North America east of Rocky Mountains from Canadian border south into Mexico, Guatemala and Cuba. Within New World, introduced western USA and Caribbean islands (Cramp *et al.* 1977–94). Introduced extensively worldwide, e.g. Hawaiian Islands, South Africa, New Zealand, Madeira, Canada, several European countries, including Britain – though not always successfully (J L Long 1981). Introductions England, Scotland, Wales and Ireland, but none persisted beyond about ten years, except perhaps population in east Suffolk, where still present to about 1980. Polytypic: precise origin of British populations unclear. Not yet admitted to any European national list.

According to both Cramp *et al.* (1977–94) and J L Long (1981), Northern Bobwhites were introduced to Tresco in 1964 and 1965 (six birds in each year). Although issues of the *CBWPSAR* suggest that introduction did not take place until 1966. Either way, it is clear from subsequent reported observations that it very quickly became established on the island, with perhaps a few making it as far as nearby Bryher to the west. Breeding occurred on Tresco from at least 1967, with 45–50 individuals in 1975 the maximum annual count, although in 1976 it was just 35. Numbers appear to have declined from around 1979 and it ceased to be mentioned in annual reports after seven were recorded on Tresco in 1980. Predation by cats was one suggested likely cause of the decline. Birds were therefore present on Tresco for at least fifteen years.

## Red-legged Partridge                                    *Alectoris rufa* C

Introduced for shooting purposes, mainly on Tresco, where it now breeds in small numbers; far less often seen on nearby islands, e.g. Bryher, Samson. Introduced in small numbers to St Mary's from the 1990s and may since have bred. More recent attempts at reintroduction to St Martin's are probably inconclusive.

Confined to West Palearctic, breeds western Europe, from Britain south to Iberia and east to northern Italy. Polytypic: nominate *rufa* occurs central and southern France, northwest Italy, Corsica and Elba; *hispanica* northern and northwest Spain, northern and central Portugal; *intercedens* eastern and southern Spain, perhaps also southern Portugal. Nominate *rufa* introduced Britain around 1670s, now large-scale releases of captive-reared birds for organised shooting. Status of British 'wild' population obscured by releases, but at between 90,000 and 250,000 thought to be in decline (Tapper 1999). National 16% increase 1994–99 (Bashford & Noble 2000).

Between 1875 and 1900 it was absent from southwest England generally, the nearest population being Dorset, where it was rare (Rodd 1880; Holloway 1996). Earliest mention of Red-legged Partridge on Scilly came from James Clark and Francis Rodd, who provided a detailed account of the introduction of both this and Grey Partridge *Perdix perdix* some time in the 1850s, but sadly without differentiating between the two (Clark & Rodd 1906). Partridges were first put down on St Martin's but most reportedly then flew out to sea, and, whilst those that remained are said to have bred, all very soon disappeared, allegedly never having been shot at. 'Hordes of cats' were largely considered responsible for this failure but no further details are given. 'A more determined effort' at introduction was made from 1866 onwards, but although 20–30 birds were shot annually on Tresco it never became common and had disappeared from this island by about 1879. Subsequent 19th century attempts on Tresco involved up to 150 birds being released, but once paired off, at the start of the year, they allegedly migrated east to St Martin's, where they were last seen.

The first 20th century reference to one or other partridge species involved mention of a covey on Samson in June 1956 (*CBWPSAR* 26). This was then followed by a long wait before it was said to be present and breeding on Tresco in 1995, after further reintroduction to that island by Tresco Estates in 1993 (*IOSBR* 1995). By the following year, at least one breeding pair had reached Bryher, and by 1997 there were still at least two pairs reportedly on Tresco. It was also introduced to St Mary's either in 1997 or the preceding year. As a consequence, by the end of 1998, birds were present in small numbers on Tresco, Bryher and St Mary's, and were presumably breeding on all three, though confirmation of that is lacking, despite at least one calling male being present on Lunnon Farm, St Mary's, during spring (pers.

*Birds of the Isles of Scilly*

obs.). Much the same situation existed during 1999, when numbers were still low but with obvious activity on St Mary's in the vicinity of the Trewince, Telegraph and Normandy areas.

The 'natural' spread of birds, first from Tresco to Bryher and then from Tresco or Bryher to Samson, is of particular interest, for although, at its narrowest, the crossing from Tresco to Bryher involves about a third of a kilometre, reaching Samson involves a minimum of one kilometre of open water. This gives support to earlier claims of released birds heading off to St Martin's, though reaching the latter involves only comparatively short crossings, via Northwethel, St Helen's and Tean. Nevertheless, whilst considering this species' ability to cross large stretches of open water, it is worth noting that there is slight past evidence of occasional immigration into eastern and southeastern England (Witherby *et al.* 1940), presumably from France.

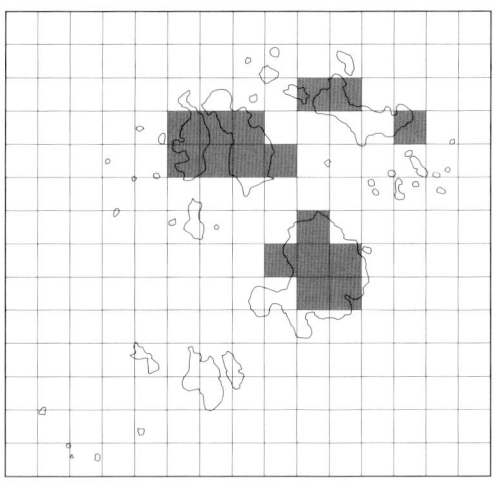

1-km Red-legged Partridge Breeding Distribution – 2000–01 (data Chown & Lock 2002)

Penhallurick suggested that rainfall may be a key factor in the successful colonisation of this species, with introductions to southwest England faring badly. Tapper (1999) also mentioned limitations posed by cold or wet conditions, whilst pointing out that large-scale releases of captive-reared birds were obscuring our understanding of the 'wild' population. Optimum Red-legged habitat requirements seem to be areas with 50% tilled land and a July temperature of at least 19°C, which under conditions of modern agriculture produces expected densities of around four pairs per km$^2$. And whilst it seems arguable that any agriculture on Scilly qualifies as 'modern', or at least in the sense implied by Tapper, applying his criteria to Tresco suggests an upper level of 12–16 pairs. Admittedly, Tapper went on to suggest that suitable habitat management can increase expected densities to eight pairs per km$^2$, with active keepering even extending this to 12 pairs per km$^2$. However, it seems doubtful there is scope for the required level of habitat manipulation on Scilly, plus of course most predators seen to be in need of control in mainland Britain are already absent from the islands. However, feral cats *Felis catus* and Brown Rats *Rattus norvegicus* may be in need of control, as eventually may the recently introduced Hedgehog *Erinaceus europaeus* on St Mary's – which seems bound to reach other islands in due course. Interestingly, the 2000 Breeding Bird Atlas recorded up to 34 pairs in 16 (23.8%) of the 67 1-km squares surveyed, though breeding was proved in just five (7.4%) (Chown & Lock 2002), birds being present throughout much of St Mary's, Tresco, Bryher and about half of St Martin's. However, not recorded by the above survey is the presence of two birds on Samson during spring 2001 (pers. obs.).

In the circumstances then, it seems unlikely that Red-legged Partridge will ever reach the point of self-sustainability in Scilly, given the geographical, climatic and habitat limitations, plus the high level of rough shooting on inhabited islands during winter. Since 1992, the release of hybrid Red-legged x Chukar Partridge *Alectoris chukar* has been prohibited by law, in which case recent Scillonian releases should all have involved pure Red-legged Partridges.

## Grey Partridge *Perdix perdix* A & C

**Introduced to Tresco, and perhaps Bryher, for shooting purposes, though exact number and timing of introductions unclear. May currently breed on Tresco in small numbers, but results of recent small-scale releases on St Mary's are unclear.**

Breeds central and southern Europe, central-western Asia and discontinuously across North America, where introduced late 19th century (J L Long 1981). Mainly sedentary western Europe. Polytypic: nominate *perdix* occurs northwest Europe, including Scandinavia, British Isles, northern France south to Greece and Bulgaria; *armoricana* Brittany, northern France north to Arden; *sphagnetorum* northern Netherlands, northwest Germany; *hispaniensis* Pyrenees, northern Spain, northern Portugal; at least three further forms to the east. Massive 20th century agriculturally related declines – 80% in 40 years post 1945 (Tapper 1999). Wild population Red-listed in UK: rapid 50% or greater breeding decline over past 25 years; unfavourable world conservation status (Gregory *et al.* 2002). National 80% decline during 25 years to 1996, 43% 1994–99 and 39% 1998–99 (Bashford & Noble 2000).

Unlike Red-legged Partridge *Alectoris rufa*, there is reason to suppose that Grey Partridge formerly occurred naturally on Scilly, evidence of which is contained in bone remains unearthed from the prehistoric site on Nornour in the Eastern Isles (Turk 1971). Turk made the point that Grey Partridge remains are unusual in an Iron Age context, perhaps for the reason Tapper (1991) gave, namely that it only arrived in Britain naturally after the last Ice Age.

Evidently, this species did not remain in the islands, however, for Borlase (1756) described how they were introduced to Scilly around 1752, having been 'brought over lately to increase and stock the islands [and] have answered that purpose well'. Unfortunately, like so many authorities (even to this present day) Borlase refers only to 'partridges', without distinguishing between the two species. At that time, however, Grey Partridge was increasing in Britain generally and was common on adjacent mainland Cornwall by the late 1800s (Holloway 1996), and therefore seems the more likely species to have been involved. Penhallurick (1978), perhaps rightly, thought it present in Scilly during historic times only when introduced, quoting the Reverend Woodley as having seen birds still present on Scilly in 1822, presumably from the 18th century introduction.

As already dealt with under Red-legged Partridge, James Clark and Francis Rodd provided a detailed account of the introduction of both this species and Red-legged, either together or separately, some time in the 1850s (Clark & Rodd 1906). The first attempt was on St Martin's, by Augustus Smith, but most birds allegedly flew out to sea, those that remained failing to breed and disappearing by 1864. From 1866 onwards 'more determined' efforts were made to introduce 'partridges' to Scilly but they had disappeared again by about 1879. Some time between then and 1906, up to 150 birds were put out in some years, but these tended to head east towards St Martin's in spring, on a 'genuine migration', from which island they were always last seen (Clark & Rodd 1906). Comments such as this last make it doubly regrettable that it is not now possible to say how they apply to these two species. It may also be the case that among the five or six main islands, St Martin's alone has the amount of suitable habitat required by both partridge species. Other writers made reference to this movement of released partridges towards St Martin's, e.g. Cornish (1883), though perhaps repeating what had already been said.

There are no apparent references to Grey Partridge on Scilly during the first half of the 20th century, though this is not necessarily proof of absence. In any event, the first published account involved 'a covey' seen on Samson by a Mrs Evans on 10th June 1956. The report gives no indication where these may have originated from, but the absence of any expression of surprise suggests they were occurring somewhere close by at that time, presumably on Tresco or Bryher. Similarly, two birds on Peninnis Head, St Mary's, on 20th April 1984 may not have been quite as unexpected as the report suggested, birds having been reared and released on Bryher, and subsequently shot on St Mary's the same year. Next mention appeared just before the turn of the present century and involved a bird at Trewince, St Mary's, late October 1999, thought to be a leftover from a few released on that island during winter 1997–98, all of which were previously believed to have been shot. Within that same timescale, autumn releases of captive-reared Grey Partridges are believed to have occurred on Tresco, along with Red-legged Partridges.

According to Tapper (1999), agricultural land with the potential to hold Grey Partridge can be identified by the presence of more than 10 hectares of tilled farmland and less than 10 hectares of woodland per km$^2$, with optimum habitat assessed on grounds of 50% or more tilled land and no more than 10 hectares of woodland per km$^2$. Under modern agricultural conditions, around four pairs per km$^2$ can be expected in optimum habitat and two pairs per km$^2$ on sub-optimum ground, with the proviso that these figures may perhaps be doubled in the face of intensive predator control, or through suitable habitat management. Certainly on Tresco and St Mary's, the percentage of what might reasonably be described as 'woodland' may be rather greater than 10%. In addition, a huge proportion of what might otherwise be described as agricultural land is given over to production of winter bulb flowers, and is therefore largely untilled. Any comments regarding the percentage of land under bulb-flower production applies equally to both Bryher and St Agnes, which are quite small by comparison. Although St Martin's perhaps qualifies on its relative lack of woodland, it too has extensive bulb-flower areas, though it also has perhaps 40% or more of open heath. Consequently, it seems unlikely that Tresco, for example, may ever be capable of holding more than in the region of 12–16 pairs of Grey Partridge. In addition, it seems doubtful whether a population that small could be self-sustaining. Its presence in Scilly will, therefore, probably continue to rely upon periodic releases of captive-reared birds, although these will not help conserve existing 'wild' stocks (Tapper 1999). Gamekeepering too is unlikely to increase survival rates in Scilly, simply because most mainland avian and mammalian predators are already absent, though feral cats *Felis catus* and presumably Brown Rats *Rattus norvegicus* may be problematical.

In the case of Grey Partridge, Witherby *et al.* (1940) suggested a sustained flight capability of around 1.6 km, quoting examples of birds flushed out over the water and coming down on its surface. Cramp *et al.* (1977–94) point out that only 10% of marked birds left a study area of 259 hectares, with just two venturing further than 8 km. This perhaps suggests that overcrowding may account for movements of released partridges on Scilly, with St Martin's attracting the bulk both because it contains the most habitat and because it is most easily accessed by short sea crossings.

## Quail (Common Quail) *Coturnix coturnix* A

**Regular migrant in decreasing numbers, more frequently in spring. Most often detected by its call. It has bred but there are no recent records.**

Widely distributed, breeds Eurasia from Britain, Denmark, Sweden, France and Iberia east to Lake Baikal and south to North Africa and northern India. Also eastern and southern Africa and Madagascar. Strongly migratory throughout Eurasia, West Palearctic populations winter Africa north of equator. Polytypic: nominate *coturnix* occurs West Palearctic except for Cape Verde Islands and Azores, plus Asia east to Lake Baikal; *conturbans* Azores; *inopinata* Cape Verde Islands; *erlingeri* East and northeast Africa; *africana* southern Africa and perhaps Madagascar. Red-listed in UK: historical population decline; unfavourable world conservation status (Gregory *et al.* 2002).

North (1850) thought Quail was only occasionally seen in the islands, though various other 19th century authors suggested it occurred more frequently, mainly on passage but, in some years, perhaps even regularly, a few pairs remaining to breed. Writing to his uncle E H Rodd in Penzance in the summer of 1870, Francis Rodd stated that Whimbrel *Numenius phaeopus* and Quail had been observed on 8th August, the latter having 'probably bred as usual on the islands'. He later pointed out that a careful inspection of St Mary's on 3rd October the same year yielded little of interest except 'the last Quails' (Rodd 1880). Interestingly, though, E H Rodd added a comment to his supplementary *List of the Birds Observed in the Scilly Islands*, to the effect that Quail sometimes stayed during winter, although without providing any confirmation (Rodd 1880). Later still, James Clark and Francis Rodd made mention of a 'bevy' seen and shot at by John Jenkinson prior to 1863, suggesting that by 1906 it had been recorded at least 12 times, usually in groups in autumn (Clark & Rodd 1906). The same authors suggested it bred at least twice on Tresco and once on St Mary's, Francis Rodd apparently changing his mind slightly on the frequency of breeding in Scilly since his earlier letter to his uncle, though it seems likely that any nests may have been easily overlooked.

Quail got regular mention in the 20th century annual *CBWPSAR* and *IOSBR*, though these were preceded by an account of one aboard ship midway between Scilly and Land's End on 30th September 1920. In 1938, a St Mary's farmer cutting rough herbage later found a deserted nest containing 12 eggs, two or three of which had been broken by the machinery; the eggs were later confirmed as being of this species (*CBWPSAR* 8). In the following year, one of the Tresco keepers caught a young bird, which he released alive without ever having seen the adults (A A Dorrien-Smith 1939a), and in 1958, eggshells thought to be from this species were found on St Martin's. From 1938 until 1970, it was recorded in almost exactly one out of every two years, with breeding suspected or confirmed in just four. Records of breeding in 1970 coincided with a large-scale increase in migrant and summering birds throughout Britain. Many calling individuals were heard on St Mary's, St Martin's and St Agnes during May and June that year, with at least four pairs remaining to breed. Deserted nests with eight and four eggs were discovered on St Mary's and a pair with twelve young were seen on Tresco. There was something of a reduction in sightings during the 1970s, with perhaps a slight tendency towards an increase in autumn sightings, though this may partly reflect a tendency for more observers to be present now within the islands at that time of year. There was another exceptional showing in 1989, the first individual of which arrived on 15th May, followed by one which was killed by a cat on St Agnes the next day, and by 17th as many as 30 may have been present on St Agnes, plus ten on St Mary's (*IOSBR* 1989). Individuals and small groups remained about the islands until the end of June, with one still calling in Holy Vale, St Mary's, until 4th July. In contrast, just four were recorded in the islands that autumn. The most unusual record for the islands concerned a bird killed by a cat on St Mary's on 4th February 1961, the body being sent to the British Museum (Natural History) for confirmation of the identification.

Bringing the review up to the present time, between 1990 and 1999 it occurred in all ten years during spring, at an average of 3.9 per year. In comparison, it was recorded in autumn in only six years, at an average of 2.1 per year of presence, or 1.3 for the ten years as a whole. Earliest recorded was 3rd March (1995), though early to mid-May was more usual and the latest any bird was seen was 10th November, though again mid-October was more the norm. One Quail has been ringed on Scilly: a bird trapped by St Agnes Bird Observatory on 24th May 1961.

Parslow (1967a) concluded that there had been a 'very marked and widespread decrease' by the mid-1970s, attributing this primarily to changes in agricultural methods. He also drew attention to an increased level of between-year fluctuations in numbers from about 1942. The migratory behaviour of this species sets it apart from all other Palearctic Phasianidae, though many questions remain about this and other aspects of its life history. Cramp *et al.* (1977–94) confirm its occasional winter presence in Britain and Ireland. Main autumn crossing of the Mediterranean region occurs late August to October, peaking mid-September, with a return from March to mid-May, males preceding females. The known pattern of movement through Scilly fits the broader picture for Britain, Ireland and nearby continental Europe (Gibbons *et al.* 1993; Hagemeijer & Blair 1997) and there seems little reason to suppose that birds reaching the islands belong to populations from further afield.

## Pheasant (Common Pheasant) *Phasianus colchicus* C

Introduced Tresco, Samson, perhaps other islands during 19th century. Population remains small and is supported by subsequent periodic releases. Birds currently occur on at least Tresco, St Mary's and Bryher.

Breeds China and Japan east to Black Sea. Sedentary. Introduced widely elsewhere, including Britain, allegedly by Romans. Polytypic: British and European populations complex mix of racial introductions. Widely exploited as game bird, in Britain involving annual release of at least 20 million captive-reared birds annually, plus annual take of at least 12 million individuals. National 1% increase in 'wild' population 1994–99 (Bashford & Noble 2000).

In their extremely useful early 20th century review of Scilly's ornithology, James Clark and Francis Rodd described this species as successfully introduced to Tresco over half a century before, i.e. prior to 1850 (Clark & Rodd 1906). They went on to say that it 'had been preserved in the usual semi-domesticated state ever since' and that it found 'convenient shelter in the furze'. At the same time, Cornish (1883) thought they had taken to the islands in a 'very kindly manner, but do not grow to any size'. The only published account of numbers involved in these early Tresco Pheasant introductions may be contained in Francis Rodd's letters to his uncle, E H Rodd of Penzance, listing 390 birds killed in Scilly during winter 1878–79 (Rodd 1880).

More recently, Penhallurick (1978) quoted useful correspondence from Tresco gamekeeper F Wardle, who also provided shooting data from the Tresco game books for the period 1875 onwards. Apparently, serious Pheasant rearing – presumably in the traditional 19th century 'rearing field' style, with hatching eggs and broody hens – and shooting commenced from about 1875, with few birds shot during earlier years. Wardle provided shooting totals for 29 of the 36 years from 1875 to 1910. Over this period, 8,668 birds were shot, at an average of 299 per reported year, or 241 overall – though Wardle suggested an average annual kill of about 450. Highest annual kill was 664 (1896) and the lowest 57 (1875), though the next lowest was 133 (1886 & 1887). Since the early 1960s, emphasis has switched to the annual purchase of 500 day-old chicks, which are liberated from release pens at around eight weeks of age, as is normal elsewhere in Britain. Around 450 are subsequently shot annually, the whole surviving population being shot and renewed each spring, this being the least costly way of maintaining shooting stocks on

Tresco. In the years following 1960, birds were also released on Samson, though rats *Rattus* and large gulls *Larus*, particularly Great Black-backed Gulls *Larus marinus*, proved problematical. About 25 birds were shot annually on Samson on average, though Wardle mentions killing 70 in one day on that island. Wardle went on to suggest that Pheasants would do well on Scilly generally, were it not for cat *Felis catus* predation and agricultural accidents, the latter presumably involving young birds or incubating females.

Releases of young captive-reared Pheasants continue on Tresco to the present day, as evident from comments in annual *IOSBR*. At least from 1996, many birds involved were of the distinctive form described as 'Michigan Blue-backs' (pers. obs.; S Parks pers. comm.). Pheasants allegedly bred on Samson in 1976 from birds released the previous year. Certainly by the 1990s, however, Samson releases had ceased and Pheasants are a rare sight on that island now, though Red-legged Partridges *Alectoris rufa* recently arrived from either Tresco or Bryher. Small numbers of Pheasants have also been introduced on St Mary's, in at least 1975 and again in 1990, though the species remains scarce still, perhaps owing to the pressure of winter rough-shooting on that island. Pheasants reportedly bred on St Mary's in 1996 and 1997, though by 1998 this may have ceased (*IOSBR* 1996, 1997, 1998).

The annual release of 500 Pheasants on an island as small as Tresco perhaps sounds excessive. However, Tapper (1999) pointed out that stocking densities of 10–12 birds per hectare should not cause significant conservation problems, with even greater numbers possible in suitable habitats, but with a ceiling of perhaps 20 individuals per hectare. An annual release of 500 birds gives a Tresco stocking density of just 1.6 Pheasants per hectare, which seems well below the 'negative ecological effects' threshold cautioned by Tapper and thus ought not to impose environmental problems, always assuming the overall situation remains stable between years. The possible 88 'pairs' recorded by the 2000 Breeding Bird Atlas (Chown & Lock 2002) in 12 of the 67 1-km surveyed squares may provide no true indication of the size of the breeding population, if in fact such exists on an annual basis, it being at best difficult to determine what percentage of managed gamebirds present on a shoot during summer were released the previous

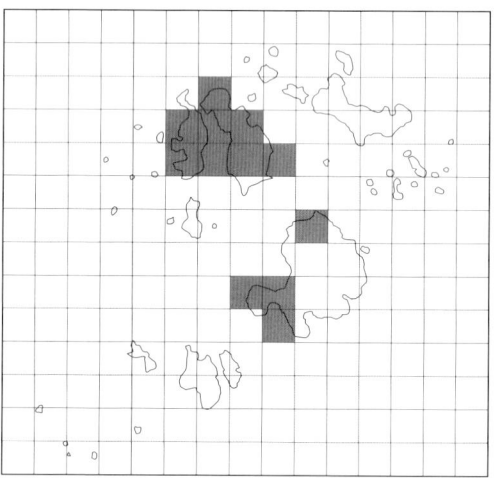

1-km Pheasant Breeding Distribution – 2000–01 (data Chown & Lock 2002)

autumn. This is particularly so in the case of Pheasant, which adopts a territorial harem defence breeding system in which groups of females select a territorial male and where not all males succeed in attracting females.

Normal conservation conflicts associated with gamebird rearing include the thorny question of avian predator control, though the lack of avian predators, other than Carrion Crows *Corvus corone* (which may legally be controlled) means this is not normally an issue on Scilly. Most predator-game-rearing conflicts on the islands are presumably limited to Brown Rat *Rattus norvegicus* and feral cat *Felis catus*, though it seems probable that the recently introduced Hedgehog *Erinaceus europaeus* on St Mary's will eventually reach Tresco and other islands.

## [Golden Pheasant *Chrysolophus pictus*] C

**Introduced to Tresco about 1975 and present still on that island in very small numbers, possibly sustained by occasional further releases. Presumably breeds but this seems not to have been proved.**

Breeds central China, introduced successfully Britain 20th century, less successfully elsewhere, e.g. North America (from 1780s), France (early 20th century) (J L Long 1981). Sedentary. Monotypic (BOURC 1992a).

First published mention of Golden Pheasant on Scilly came in 1990, at which time a minimum of four males and three females were believed to be present on Tresco (*IOSBR* 1990, 1991). By 1993 this had been adjusted to at least seven males and eight females, all centred round the Great Pool. For such a spectacular species, surprisingly little is known about Golden Pheasant on Tresco and there are no subsequent reliable counts, other than two males and a female on 2nd February 1999. This of course is mainly attributable to its preference for remaining concealed beneath Tresco's lush woodlands, particularly around the Great Pool. Nevertheless, given the amount of noise emitted during spring by calling males it seems difficult to accept that nobody has so far taken up the challenge of conducting a population survey. The Tresco Golden Pheasants seem ideally suited to a study using radio telemetry, being confined to a limited geographical area but nonetheless seldom seen.

Most recent sightings have come from the vicinity of the fenced horse paddocks, along the southern side of the Great Pool, which are viewable from along Abbey Road west of the Abbey itself. The 2000 Breeding Bird Atlas record of two 'pairs' (Chown & Lock 2002) in just one of the 67 1-km squares surveyed presumably refers to two males, in what is a bigamous species, with the upper pair estimate being three to four 'pairs', all on Tresco. In spring, males advertise their presence from beneath Rhododendron *Rhododendron* bushes with a distinctive 'sneezing' call, obviously a pheasant but lacking the boisterous explosiveness of its larger relative. Females are normally evident from their barred, rather than spotted plumage. The nearest established Golden Pheasant populations to Scilly are probably those in West Sussex and on the South Downs in Hampshire.

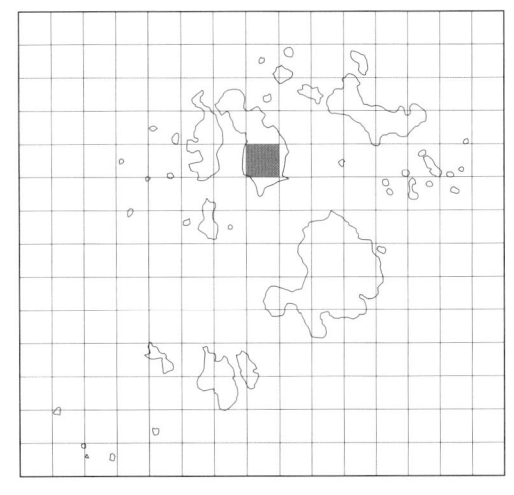

1-km Golden Pheasant Breeding Distribution – 2000–01 (data Chown & Lock 2002)

## Water Rail *Rallus aquaticus* A

**Reasonably frequent and widespread migrant and winter visitor, mainly in the region of pools, ditches and similar wet areas. It possibly breeds occasionally but documented confirmation is lacking, despite past reports of it having done so around Tresco Great Pool (Penhallurick 1969).**

Fragmentary breeding distribution across central Eurasia, from British Isles and Iberia east to Pacific, south of northern forests and south to Black Sea and western China. In West Palearctic, occurs mainly as summer migrant in eastern half. In western West Palearctic, e.g. British Isles, Iceland, Iberia, resident or partial migrant. Polytypic: nominate *aquaticus* occurs Europe; *korejewi* southwest and central Asia; *hibernans* Iceland; *indicus* further east. Amber-listed in UK: moderate contraction in breeding range over past 25 years (Gregory *et al.* 2002).

E H Rodd (1880) described it as common in the islands in autumn and winter and that remains the situation today. The fact that Water Rail was so commonplace probably accounts for the scarcity of any mention of it in the early literature. E H Rodd's nephew Francis shot one on St Mary's on 24th December 1864, making a tour of Tresco on Christmas Day and seeing Water Rails in among the flocks of Coots *Fulica atra* and Moorhens *Gallinula chloropus* (Rodd 1880). In November 1870, Francis visited the St Mary's Moors on 8th accompanied by his gun dog, and later recounted in a letter to his uncle how he saw some Snipe *Gallinago gallinago* and a great many Jack Snipe *Lymnocryptes minimus*, however 'the Water Rails were a positive nuisance, scuttling about in all directions and bothering my old dog terribly'. This is a description anyone who has been deep into the less visited areas of Higher or Lower Moors during October can instantly relate too. James Clark and Francis Rodd summarised the ornithological situation on Scilly up until the end of the 19th century (Clark & Rodd 1906). Like E H Rodd, they described Water Rail as common in autumn and winter, though absent as a breeding species, pointing out that in some years, e.g. 1863, 1869 and 1886, it is 'extraordinarily abundant on the exposed Moors of St Mary's, St Martin's and Tresco. In thick furze everywhere, in the orchards at St Mary's, and on the trees in the Abbey Gardens.' And even today, much the same applies during periods of abundance, at which time reports are received of birds on garden bird tables, in garden fishponds and in a host of other unusual places, and there is often an associated increase in reports of birds killed by the island cats *Felis catus*.

In truth, Scilly must be one of the best places in Britain to see this species, for in autumn one need not sit too long in one of the Tresco or St Mary's hides before one of these noisy, tail-flicking occupants of waterside vegetation creeps stealthily out onto the marginal mud, or scuttles rapidly, head down across a gap in the towering reeds *Phragmites australis*. Indeed, walk in among the reeds, Purple Loosestrife *Lythrum salicaria* and other aquatic growth in some years, particularly during October, and you are immediately aware of numerous unseen rails, which do indeed scuttle in all directions, and out of apparent sheer cheek, even run between the legs of people engaged in extracting Sedge *Acrocephalus schoenobaenus* and Reed Warblers *A. scirpaceus* from mistnets!

Earliest 20th century mention of Water Rail came in 1948 (*CBWPSAR* 19), when it was described as very numerous in Lower Moors during winter, five or six being visible at any one time. In December that year a bird was watched climbing in willows *Salix* to a height of three metres. In fact there was, and no doubt still is, a bias against the recording of this species in Scilly, simply because far fewer observers are present in winter, when Water Rails are still likely to be numerous. In this same context, Penhallurick (1969) made the important point that it may appear far more numerous during periods of low freshwater levels, when larger expanses of mud are exposed. Penhallurick also pointed out that there is little evidence of a marked spring passage, which remains true of Scilly. However, it is debatable whether migration, rather than dispersal, is involved at all with this species in either Cornwall or the islands but if migrants are passing through, they may originate from quite a way east in Europe. Undoubtedly, though, cold-weather movements are also a factor, and probably involve birds from continental Europe – Penhallurick quotes a record of an individual ringed in the Friesian Islands and killed by a dog near Wadebridge, Cornwall, in January 1962.

Numbers involved throughout the 1990s were too numerous to deal with individually, but fell into the expected pattern of autumn arrivals followed by a probably smaller wintering population. October probably remains the busiest month and, although estimating overall numbers is hugely problematical, the all-island count for October 1998 was thought to be in the region of 40–50 individuals, though it seems likely that this may still have been an underestimate. In most years, a few obvious wintering birds are still present up until the end of March, followed normally by five or so scattered sightings up to mid-May, though it remains unclear whether these are spring migrants or dispersed individuals returning to mainland or Continental breeding areas. More obvious is the arrival of autumn birds, which commences anywhere from early July until mid- or late August. By October, numbers present have increased noticeably, even allowing for the parallel increase in observers, and this is followed

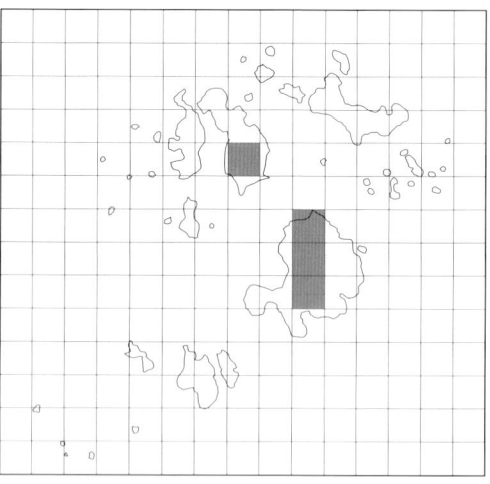

**1-km Water Rail Summer Distribution – 2000–01 (data Chown & Lock 2002)**

by a marked reduction towards late month, or in early November. Certainly by December combined totals from the most-watched sites, e.g. Tresco and the St Mary's Moors, are likely to be in the region of ten, though this too could be an underestimate.

Breeding has been suspected and even claimed (Penhallurick 1969), but appears to lack any documented evidence, regardless of very occasional references to birds present throughout the summer (*CBWPSAR* 21), whereas on mainland Cornwall it breeds in low numbers. The 2000 Breeding Bird Atlas recorded a possible eight 'pairs' in four (5.9%) of the 67 1-km squares surveyed: six pairs on St Mary's and two on Tresco (Chown & Lock 2002), though these apparently involved mostly single-bird sightings, or the presence of calling individuals.

Interesting incidents include the bird trying to land on a passenger's head during a crossing of the RMV *Scillonian III* on 19th October 1990, plus the bird observed carrying a White-toothed Shrew *Crocidura suaveolens* on 4th October 1991. In fact, Water Rail has something of a reputation for opportunistic exploitation of abnormal food sources, including small bird species, but one watched killing a Snipe at Porth Hellick on 29th September 1989 was possibly exceptional (*IOSBR* 1989). Equally bizarre was the bird chased indoors by a St Agnes cat in 1983, where it was subsequently fed bananas.

According to Cramp *et al.* (1977–94), although it supposedly remains in Iceland during winter, it has certainly been collected then in the Faeroes and is recorded as a migrant in the Scottish islands, plus it is a known winter visitor to Ireland. All of this points to some level of migration, possibly from further north, e.g. Iceland or Norway, in which respect October–December vagrants to Greenland are noteworthy. In fact, there is little evidence that British-bred birds migrate, but as already suggested, birds reaching Scilly in spring, autumn or winter could originate from populations further east in continental Europe. In support of this, there are British and Irish ringing recoveries to or from Sweden, Poland and the former Czechoslovakia (Wernham *et al.* 2002). Gantlett (1998) drew attention to the possibility of the slightly more well marked *hibernans* occurring in Britain, some of which could reach Scilly. Twenty Water Rails have been ringed in Scilly, seven since 1970. However, there are no controls or recoveries.

# Spotted Crake *Porzana porzana* A

Scarce but almost annual migrant in small numbers, it may just possibly have bred in 1903. Treated by the BBRC as a national Scarce Migrant, full written description required by SRP.

Breeds Europe and western Asia, from Iberia, France, Britain (rarely) and Norway east to Lake Baikal and south to Mediterranean, Iraq and Kazakhstan. Migratory, wintering southern Europe, Mediterranean, north Africa, some (perhaps many) crossing Sahara. A few winter temperate Europe. Monotypic. Included on Annex I of 1979 EEC 'Birds Directive'. Amber-listed in UK: 1999 population of 73 singing males (Gregory *et al.* 2002).

James Clark and Francis Rodd provided an accurate summary of the 19th century situation, noting that the first Spotted Crake recorded on Scilly was in autumn 1849, followed by one seen by Francis Rodd in Tresco's Abbey Gardens in 1860, the same observer having 'met with it in a few instances' in 1863 (Clark & Rodd 1906). Francis also shot one on 8th October 1870, though his uncle E H Rodd of Penzance was less clear later about the date (Rodd 1880), which Penhallurick (1969) gives as 1880. However, we may be sure of the identification, Francis having shot four Spotted Crakes in four hours on mainland Cornwall two years before, plus three on 30th September 1860 (Penhallurick 1969). Clark and Rodd concluded with the information that, at the end of May 1903, a Spotted Crake was flushed on two successive days from 'a likely nesting spot in the Higher Moors on St Mary's'. In his *List of the Birds Observed on the Scilly Islands* (Rodd 1880), the elder Rodd noted it as occurring occasionally in winter, whereas in his *Zoologist* review of British Spotted Crake records, Alpin mentioned the 1870 individual shot by Francis Rodd, usefully giving the location as St Mary's, further remarking that it was to be encountered on Scilly in both autumn and winter (Alpin 1890).

Although not referred to during the early 20th century, Spotted Crake gets regular mention during the latter half, commencing with one found dead on St Mary's on 19th April 1956 (*CBWPSAR* 26) and followed quickly by another, trapped and ringed by Chris Perrins on Tresco on 19th April 1957 (*CBWPSAR* 27). During the ten years from 1961, a total of 16 birds were reported in six years, including two together, though the most in any year was five in 1969. Fifteen individuals arrived in September (earliest 2nd) or in October; no date was given for the remaining bird. This compares with a minimum of 54 birds during the ten years from 1990, featuring in every year except one, though only three years in spring, involving four birds. The earliest in spring, killed by a cat *Felis catus*, was on 27th January 1992, followed by singles on 23rd February and two on 27th March. The February bird was believed to be a migrant, arriving on the islands with Hoopoe *Upupa epops* and Red-rumped Swallow *Hirundo daurica*, though it seems possible that the January bird may have been wintering. Autumn Spotted Crakes arrived at an average of 5.5 a year for the nine years it occurred, the earliest on 1st August and the last seen on 29th October – four (8%) were first seen on 18th October. At least three birds were found dead, although possible causes are not given. The most likely explanation for the apparently higher rate of occurrence in the 1990s is an increase in levels of observer coverage, particularly during September and October.

Understandably, most birds occur by freshwater pools bordered by dense vegetation and exposed mud, such as Tresco's Great Pool, the Porth Hellick and Lower Moors Pools on St Mary's, or St Agnes

Pool, though individuals can and sometimes do turn up almost anywhere. Other than Clark and Rodd's May 1903 suggestion for Higher Moors, which lacks supporting information, there appears to have been no suspicion even of attempted or possible breeding. Three Spotted Crakes have been trapped and ringed in Scilly: on Tresco on 19th April 1957 and 11th September 1968, and by the author in Higher Moors, St Mary's, on 15th October 1995.

Spotted Crake remains a rare breeding bird in Britain. A maximum 34 pairs were acknowledged by the Rare Breeding Birds Panel in England, Scotland and Wales during 1999, the highest yearly total since at least 1988 (*British Birds* 93: 376). Precise breeding locations were withheld, but two Somerset localities, involving up to two pairs, were probably the closest British breeding birds to Scilly. However, in France it breeds as close as southwest Brittany (Guermeur & Monnat 1980) and the Cherbourg peninsula (Hagemeijer & Blair 1997), thus any spring arrivals could conceivably involve overshoots. According to Cramp *et al.* (1977–94), a few individuals overwinter in countries bordering the North Sea. Autumn dispersal is complicated by early-moving birds interrupting their journey for two to three weeks during August to moult, during which time they are flightless. But from late August or early September the southward movement becomes more pronounced, the majority having at least reached the Mediterranean by November. Spring movement north commences early, few being found in northeast Africa after March and with European breeding grounds reoccupied by April.

## Sora Rail (Sora) *Porzana carolina* A BBRC 57%

**Extremely rare autumn migrant but nevertheless more frequent than Little Crake *P. parva*. Full written description required by the BBRC.**

1973 One (first-winter) trapped St Agnes 26th September to 9th October *Ibis* 116: 578
1982 One (adult) St Mary's 27th September *British Birds* 76: 490
1983 One (first-winter) Tresco 19th to 20th October *British Birds* 77: 520
1991 One (first-winter) St Mary's 15th October (probably since 4th) to 1st November
*British Birds* 85: 107

Breeds North America, from British Columbia east to Newfoundland and south to a line from Baja California east to West Virginia. Migratory, wintering southern North America south to Ecuador, Peru, Columbia, and Venezuela. Monotypic. Recent 'sharp' increase, mainly central populations, with those in east static and with slight recent increase in Canada (Bryant 1997).

Four records of this transatlantic migrant. The first for Scilly, fifth British record and the first since 1920 involved a first-year male trapped on St Agnes in 1973 and present on that island from 26th September for 14 days (Wallace 1976b). On the strength of this record, the species was reinstated to category 'A' of the British List after a gap of 50 or more years (BOURC 1974). The lucky few birders on St Agnes on 9th October were offered the unique opportunity to view Sora Rail and Little Crake in the same field of vision (*IOSBR* 1973). The 1973 individual was followed by two birds in successive years: an adult on St Mary's for one day only in September 1982 and another first-year, this time on Tresco, for two days in October 1983 (Vinicombe 1985). The latter represented the ninth British record. The 1982 individual, at Porth Hellick, St Mary's, was seen only fleetingly, unlike the bird on Tresco the following year, which showed itself well to almost everyone present.

For many Scillonian rarities there is a story to tell and the 1991 Sora Rail, again at Porth Hellick, was no exception. From around 4th October, reports had been flowing of a Spotted Crake *P. porzana* viewable from the two hides on the west side of Porth Hellick pool and identification was not questioned. However, late afternoon on the already action-filled 15th October, pandemonium erupted following reports of both Spotted Crake and Sora Rail viewable from the more southerly of the two hides. Doubts immediately arose concerning earlier identification in at least some cases, suspicion growing that the Nearctic species may have been present before 15th. This view was upheld when a photograph on the wall of the Porth Cressa Inn and taken several days before the 15th was found to depict Sora Rail, and not Spotted Crake as the caption suggested.

Locally abundant in suitable breeding areas, Sora Rails commence leaving their breeding sites from late summer or early autumn, often first assembling in large numbers around suitable marshes and ponds (Cramp *et al.* 1977–94). The timing of southward migration appears greatly dependent upon the onset of autumn frosts, normally during September or October. At this time birds move on a broad front over land and sea, and in strong winds are liable to easterly navigational drift, with birds regularly arriving in Bermuda. First birds arrive in Panama as early as October, leaving there for the north from around mid-March.

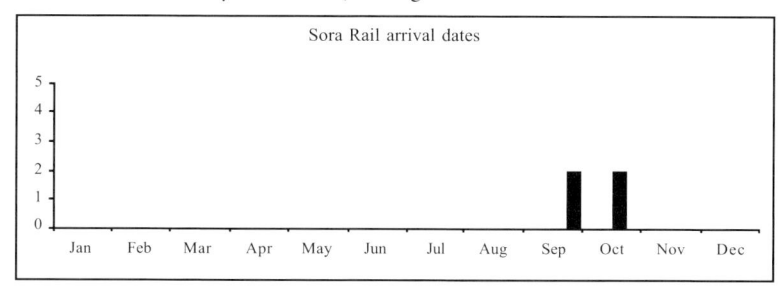

*Sora Rail arrival dates* (bar chart showing values approximately 2 in September and 2 in October; all other months zero)

A total of just seven Sora Rail records were accepted by the BBRC during the period 1958 to the end of 1999, in which case Scilly has accounted for 57% of the national total. There were five national records prior to 1958, the first of which was shot on the River Kennet, Berkshire, in 1864 (Palmer 2000). There is also a report of one captured in Greenland, though the time of year is omitted, plus two aboard a yacht in the Atlantic in 1897, at least one of which reached England. The only Sora Rail ringed in Scilly was the individual captured in 1973 and there are no recaptures.

## Little Crake                     *Porzana parva*  A  BBRC 3.1%

**Extremely rare autumn migrant, full written description required by BBRC.**

  1850s   One (shot) Scilly   Clark & Rodd 1906
  1973    One (adult male) St Agnes 9th October   *British Birds* 67: 320
  [1996   One Great Pool, Tresco 10th October]   IOSBR 1996; 1997

Breeds central West Palearctic, from Iberia and France east to Caspian Sea, isolated smaller populations western Asia, east to Lake Baikal. Migratory, most winter East Africa, with smaller numbers Nile delta, West Africa and northwest India, though range imperfectly known. Monotypic.

Just two acceptable Scillonian records, one of which is old. James Clark and Francis Rodd (1906) referred to one mentioned in 'Rodd's 1863 notes' – presumably those of Francis's uncle E H Rodd and author of the landmark *The Birds of Cornwall and The Scilly Islands* (Rodd 1880). It seems surprising, however, that E H Rodd did not include this in the main text of his normally comprehensive volume, especially as he devoted much space to a Little Crake killed by a cat *Felis catus* at St Diminick on mainland Cornwall in March 1878. The E H Rodd bird, referred to by Clark and Francis Rodd as 'Lesser Crake', was reportedly shot by Augustus Pechell and later seen by E H Rodd. However, Clark and Francis Rodd pointed out that there is no entry relating to this species in the Tresco game books since their inception in 1856, or in a list of birds killed in 1849, when Augustus Pechell first visited Scilly. Thus, the shooting must presumably have occurred between those dates, i.e. the early 1850s.

The remaining record involved a bird seen following a Sora Rail *Porzana carolina* across the mud of the St Agnes freshwater pool on 9th October 1973, being possibly seen at the same site the previous day and possibly also later on 9th (*IOSBR* 1973). A claim of one seen by three observers near the David Hunt Memorial Hide, on the eastern side of Tresco Great Pool (*IOSBR* 1996), failed to gain acceptance by the BBRC (*IOSBR* 1997). In addition, Penhallurick (1969) mentioned one claimed on St Agnes on 25th September 1966, but this was also not accepted by the BBRC.

Very little precise information is available on the size or distribution of the Little Crake population, though it may be less affected by land drainage and reclamation than other small European *Porzana* (Cramp *et al.* 1977–94). Scarce in Britain as a migrant, some individuals possibly overwinter. Apparently moves south from late August through to September or October, returning late March through to April, possibly even February to mid-May. The closest known regular breeding populations to Scilly are in Poland and Hungary (Hagemeijer and Blair 1997). A total of 32 Little Crake records were accepted by the BBRC during the period 1958–1999, therefore the single Scillonian individual represents just over 3% of the national total.

Between 22nd and 25th April 2000 a small unidentified crake was seen very briefly at various times by several observers in the area of the Lower Moors south hides on St Mary's. Although the general consensus of opinion was in favour of this species the record was not submitted and must remain undecided (IOSBG 2000).

## [Baillon's Crake *Porzana pusilla*] A

[1971   One Gugh 4th November]

Main breeding range central Eurasia, from eastern Europe to China and Japan, with outlying populations western Europe, southern Africa, and Australasia. In western Europe, breeds sparsely Iberia, France, Low Countries, Hungary etc. Migratory, but least known of Palearctic Rallidae, European birds probably winter northeast Africa, alongside resident population, though birds of unknown origin winter Middle East and Iraq (Cramp *et al.* 1977–94). Polytypic: *intermedia* occurs western, southern and central Europe and north Africa; nominate *pusilla* eastern Europe, from southern Russia east to Japan and south to India, China and Indonesia; four additional forms southern Africa and further east.

A claim of a bird flushed from beneath a stone wall at close range on Gugh on 4th November 1971 (*IOSBR* 1971) seems either not to have been submitted to the BBRC, or to have been withdrawn by the observers. Just 13 Baillon's Crake records were accepted by the BBRC during the period 1958–1999, whereas prior to 1958 there were reportedly 'many' (BBRC 2000). In any event, any individual of this species that does condescend to show itself in Scilly should be scrutinised carefully for features indicative of the distinctive eastern European and Asian form *intermedia* (Gantlett 1998).

## Corncrake (Corn Crake) *Crex crex* A

**Scarce migrant, bred in small numbers until 1960s. Full written description required by SRP.**

Breeds central Eurasia, from Britain and Ireland, France and Norway east to Lake Baikal, from 60°N south to Pyrenees, Black Sea and western Mongolia. Long-distance migrant, all populations believed to winter East Africa, from Lake Victoria to South Africa. Monotypic. Included on Annex I of 1979 EEC 'Birds Directive'. Globally threatened and Red-listed in UK: historical population decline and 79% contraction of UK breeding range over past 38 years; 50% or more of UK breeding population at ten or fewer sites (Gregory *et al.* 2002).

First reference to Corncrake in the islands appears to be North's comment that it was found every summer in suitable localities in the 18th century (North 1750). However, by the late 19th century, E H Rodd was describing it as occurring in spring and autumn, with a few pairs probably breeding (Rodd 1880), although it seems clear from other contemporary reports that these remarks understated the situation, or certainly in some years, as the events of autumn 1857 bear witness. Augustus Pechell wrote to E H Rodd from Tresco, around the first week of October that year, describing a huge fall of Corncrakes on Scilly. So large in fact was the number involved that Pechell managed to shoot 18 birds ('nine couples') in one day, two of which he failed to recover. According to Pechell, nearly every tuft of grass in 'the swamps and morasses' held two or more birds (Rodd 1857b, 1880). In 1879, E H Rodd's nephew Francis, fellow sportsman of Pechell, also wrote to his uncle, pointing out that among the list of game killed on Scilly during winter 1878–79 was the entry 'Landrails 3' (Rodd 1880). The only other specific date from the early records mentioned in relation to this species appears to be Francis Rodd's comment, again in a letter to his uncle, that a walk on St Martin's on 7th November turned up a single 'Landrail' in a gorse bush (Rodd 1880).

As usual, James Clark and Francis Rodd provided a clear and succinct summary of the situation by the start of the 20th century, pointing out that Corncrake apparently bred on the islands every year, though were most evident on passage during spring and autumn (Clark & Rodd 1906). Referring to Pechell's 1857 achievement with the gun, they pointed out that this was exceptional and that normally only a pair or two were encountered in the course of a day's shooting in Scilly. Interestingly, they believed it commoner in spring than autumn. They also mentioned that in 1903 it bred on St Mary's and Bryher, and that Pechell's record bag was taken in the St Mary's Lower Moors.

The only other early information involves birds reportedly striking the Bishop Rock Light, all in

September. The first of these was on 20th of that month in 1884, when one struck between 2 am and 5 am (Harvie-Brown *et al.* 1885). On 28th in 1907 'several were killed' (Ogilvie-Grant 1907) and on 3rd in 1910 a single bird was killed at 3 am (Ogilvie-Grant 1910).

Probably the next published 20th century report is that referring to single legs found in Peregrine Falcon *Falco peregrinus* and Great Black-backed Gull *Larus marinus* nests (H W Robinson 1923), whilst at least one pair bred on St Agnes and in a St Mary's garden in 1922 (H W Robinson 1923), and again on St Mary's in 1944, though detail is lacking (*CBWPSAR* 14). During the 1940s and 50s it figures only occasionally in the records, but by the 1960s it was being mentioned almost annually. Taking the ten years to 1969, it was seen on the islands in nine of those years and bred in at least three, i.e. 1966, 67 and 69. The greatest number recorded in a single year was also in 1969, when ten supposed migrants plus at least one breeding pair were noted. The earliest recorded date was 2nd May, but the presence of known or supposed summering birds made it difficult to gauge the end of spring passage. The last date a bird was seen in the islands was 25th October, though six of the seven known final dates fell in the preceding 16-day period. Certainly, there is no evidence from the 1960's annual reports to support Clark and Rodd's earlier suggestion that spring passage was more numerous than autumn passage, in fact quite the reverse. It is possible perhaps that the presence of breeding birds made it appear more numerous in the early period. The 1969 breeding effort on St Martin's failed, with the young reportedly drowned, and sadly this was the last breeding attempt recorded in the islands (*IOSBR* 1969).

Considering the 1990s next, no noticeable change seems to have occurred, other than the obvious absence of even suspected breeding activity. Birds were recorded in all ten years, at an average of 3.2 per year, with five in 1995 the highest annual number. Once again, spring records were fewer, this time noted in four of the ten years, all four first sightings falling within the period 17th April to 25th May. Final sighting dates for all ten years fell in the period 5th to 31st October, though to some extent this may have been influenced by the recent increase in October observer coverage.

Parslow (1967a) concluded that there had been a very marked and widespread decrease in the British and Irish Corncrake population, attributing this to changed methods of agriculture, particularly those associated with hay cutting, the decline perhaps even increasing after the 1950s. He also pointed out that the Scottish Western Isles and western Ireland were least affected, the species having withdrawn westwards. The timing of this decline was difficult to estimate, though it may have been well advanced even before the 1940s. In southeast England and eastern and central Scotland the decline commenced perhaps as early as the second half of the 19th century, but was matched in the rest of Europe by a similar decrease after 1920. Thus, the decline may have been affecting numbers of birds using Scilly even before regular records existed, whereas the substantial gap in recording during the early 20th century further detracts from our ability to assess long-term patterns in Scilly.

The long-distance nature of Corncrake migration belies its weak-winged appearance, though it is vulnerable to vagrancy during high winds, e.g. at least 20 Greenland records and nearly as many from North America. In Europe, southwards migration commences August, intensifying in September but continuing into November, with birds occasionally overwintering in Europe (Cramp *et al.* 1977–94). Return migration commences February or March and is less protracted than that in autumn, with birds crossing the Mediterranean from late March to mid-May. According to Cramp *et al.* numbers of birds recorded in East and Central Africa may not account for the estimated world population, giving rise to suspicions that more than are currently known winter in West Africa, perhaps including the now depleted northwest European populations. Although logic suggests that birds in Scilly may be passing to or from populations further north, e.g. Scottish Western Isles, it may not be unreasonable to think that long-distance migrants from central Asia could also be involved, as is the case with some other east-west Asiatic migrants.

## Moorhen (Common Moorhen) *Gallinula chloropus* A

**Resident and breeds in modest numbers, mainly around larger areas of fresh water. Also a probable migrant.**

Breeds all main landmasses except Australia, including most of West Palearctic except north, but only patchily in northern Africa. In western Europe, mainly resident or dispersive. Polytypic: nominate *chloropus*

*Birds of the Isles of Scilly*

occurs Eurasia east to Japan and south to Sri Lanka and Indonesia, northern Africa and adjacent Atlantic islands; 11 or more forms elsewhere. National 18% increase 1994–99 (Bashford & Noble 2000) although BTO Waterways Bird Survey showed 10% decline 1975–2000. Green-listed in UK: in need of basic conservation assistance (Gregory *et al.* 2002).

Earliest evidence, perhaps, of Moorhen presence in Scilly comes from what may be bone remains of this species found in the 2nd to 7th century AD levels of the prehistoric site at May's Hill, St Martin's (Turk 1971). Much later, E H Rodd briefly mentioned Moorhen on Scilly, describing it merely as resident and breeding (Rodd 1880), though in the same volume his nephew Francis described walking around Tresco pools on Christmas Day 1864 and noting a large flock. However, as is frequently the case, it fell to James Clark and Francis Rodd to provide the full picture (Clark & Rodd 1906). Apparently, it became conspicuous in Scilly during the early 1850s, at which time reeds – presumably the now-present Common Reed *Phragmites communis* – were planted around Tresco's freshwater pools. Prior to that time it had been noted on autumn migration only, just one being killed in April or May 1841. Evidently, they soon settled into the islands, being quickly described as common, and by 1860 or earlier breeding regularly on Tresco and sometimes on St Mary's. According to Clark and Rodd, by 1903 they were breeding freely around the Abbey Pools and in some numbers on St Mary's, with two nests even on Tean.

Examining the situation closer to the present time, precise information on numbers and even on distribution within the islands is hard to find. Penhallurick (1969) quoted David Hunt as suggesting about 20 breeding pairs on Tresco, apparently during the 1960s, whilst also pointing out that a pair or two may have bred annually on St Agnes from 1950. However, breeding concentrations remain centred around prominent freshwater areas, e.g. Great and Abbey Pools on Tresco, Higher and Lower Moors and Porthloo and Newford Ponds, all on St Mary's, plus St Agnes and Bryher Pools. Nevertheless, pairs are encountered away from these main sites from time to time, making it difficult to assess the true size of the Scillonian breeding population, and the problem is not necessarily solved by counts of autumn or winter assemblies, e.g. on Tresco, or at Porth Hellick Pool on St Mary's, both of which probably include an unknown percentage of migrants or wintering birds. Certainly there seems always to be an excess of birds over supposed numbers of breeding pairs, as on St Agnes in 1964, with a single breeding pair but counts of up to 15 individuals, though this reduced to three during winter. Similarly, Tresco counts of 130–150 during autumn 1963 and 1964 must be seen against a background of perhaps 20 breeding pairs on that island. Clearly, too, these are not all-island gatherings on Tresco, as smaller autumn accumulations exist elsewhere, though particularly at Porth Hellick on St Mary's.

A reasonable current estimate of breeding pairs might be 20–25 on Tresco, 10–12 on St Mary's, one to two each on St Agnes and St Martin's and perhaps one on Bryher, giving an all-island maximum of 42 pairs, though numbers doubtless vary annually. Interestingly, then, the 2000 Breeding Bird Atlas (Chown & Lock 2002) recorded up to 21 pairs in eight (11.9%) of the 67 1-km squares surveyed, with breeding confirmed in four squares

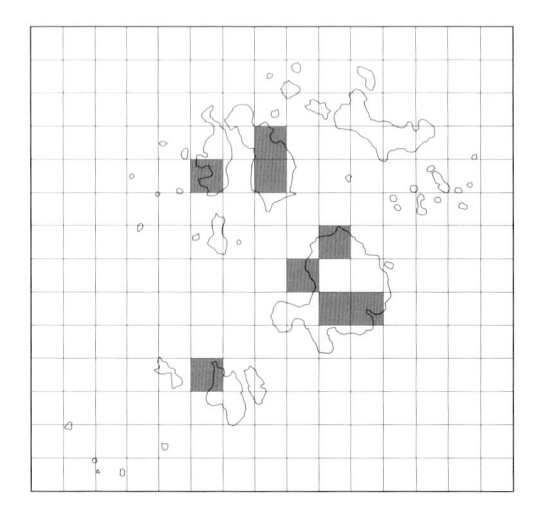

| Island | Pairs |
| --- | --- |
| Bryher | 1 |
| St Agnes | 1 |
| St Mary's | 12 |
| Tresco | 7 |

**2000 Breeding Bird Atlas – Moorhen (Chown & Lock 2002)**

1-km Moorhen Breeding Distribution – 2000–01 (data Chown & Lock 2002)

Deciding whether, and if so how many, migrant Moorhens are involved on Scilly is no easy task, particularly in the absence of ringing data. However, there are frequent references in the annual reports to a noticeable influx around September or early October, followed by an equally marked and rapid decline during early November, as demonstrated at Porth Hellick Pool in 1990, where 21 birds on 5th September increased to 27 next day and 35 by the month's end, with 39 still present by late October but less than four by late November. Regrettably, regular recent annual counts are lacking for the main Tresco Moorhen sites, though there is a suggestion among those we do have that former totals in the mid to low hundreds are perhaps no longer being achieved. There is also a marked absence of regular winter counts, though there is mention of 30 on St Mary's and up to 19 on Tresco in February 1982. One of the few comments relating to the age composition of Scillonian Moorhen groups is the 1983 observation that autumn counts included a 'high proportion' of first-year birds of various ages'. It is unclear here whether the writer is implying a good breeding season, as with the 1986 observation that 14 (50%) out of 28 birds present at Porth Hellick were immatures.

Occasionally, birds are encountered away from the main islands and in circumstances that are difficult to explain, like the individual found hiding beneath a boulder on the bare, seabird-inhabited island of Illiswilgig in the Northern Isles, or the bird found wandering around on Annet. And given the lack of suitably wet areas on Tean, certainly in the present day, the presence of two breeding pairs on that island during the very early 20th century seems exceptional.

Western European Moorhens are mainly sedentary, birds from northern Scandinavia and other northern European countries wintering south as far as Iberia and the Mediterranean, though many from these areas move southwest, some from Sweden, Denmark, Germany and France wintering in Britain and Ireland (Wernham *et al*. 2002). There is little or no evidence that British or Irish Moorhens migrate and recoveries over 20 km are considered unusual. The extent to which migrant Moorhens penetrate into North Africa remains unclear but it seems common in winter south at least to west Senegal (Cramp *et al*. 1977–94). Autumn migration follows a brief flightless period, most moving south during September–November. It therefore seems tempting to suggest that Moorhens passing through Scilly in autumn possibly originate much further east in Europe, though the lack of any evidence of a similar spring passage is particularly interesting.

Less than 20 Moorhens have been ringed on Scilly and none were recovered away from the islands, though two from St Agnes and one from Tresco were later recovered on St Mary's (Penhallurick 1969). Similarly, there are no Scillonian controls of Moorhens ringed elsewhere.

**Local**
?       1stY St Agnes 21st September 1963       FD St Mary's 17th April 1964

**Moorhen Ringing Recaptures**

# American Purple Gallinule     *Porphyrula martinica*   A   BBRC 100%

**Extremely rare migrant, the single-island arrival involving the first British or Irish and only the second European record. Full written description required by the BBRC.**

1958    One (first-winter female) Hugh Town, St Mary's 7th November (died 9th)
*British Birds* 53: 145–149

Breeds North, Central and South America. Monotypic, in North America occurs southwards from Texas, Tennessee, Mississippi, Louisiana and South Carolina. Population in USA largely migratory, birds flying directly across Gulf of Mexico to Central America. Stronger on wing than might be imagined from appearance and noted for numerous instances of long-distance vagrancy (Cramp *et al*. 1977–94). Drastic population decline 1966–79, more recent increase, though still to achieve former level (Bryant 1997).

A first-winter bird was discovered lying in the gutter of Hugh Town's main street on St Mary's late on 7th November 1958. It was found by a Miss Margaret Hughes on her way to work at the local telephone exchange, to where she took the bird and cared for it before contacting local ornithologist Peter Mackenzie the following evening. Mackenzie commenced feeding the bird on earthworms, which it readily accepted, but its already emaciated condition resulted in the bird dying on 9th November. The carcass was sent to the British Museum (Natural History), where its identification was confirmed and it was sexed as an immature female. The skin resides in the Museum collection at Tring, Hertfordshire, Reference No. 1958.2.7 (BOURC 1960; Anon 1960; Nisbet 1960; Parslow 1982a).

Nisbet drew attention to the preponderance of rail species on remote oceanic islands, arguing that this alone testifies to their powers of long-distance flight and their adaptability towards new environments. He also pointed out that several other, closely related, species are on record as having crossed the Atlantic from east to west, including Corncrake *Crex crex* and Spotted Crake *Porzana porzana*. Nisbet also recounted incidents of storm-bound North American autumn migrant American Purple Gallinules being blown north as far as Newfoundland, further pointing out that a storm of some magnitude occurred in the Gulf of Mexico on 4th–5th November 1958, before tracking northeast and blowing itself out in the Atlantic. The Hugh Town bird's emaciated condition points to it being newly arrived and thus the time of its discovery fits what might be expected had its presence on the wrong side of the Atlantic been attributable to this particular storm. Nisbet also made the point that such a feat of endurance and survival greatly exceeds that normally thought possible for passerines and perhaps helps to account for the presence of so many rail species on remote islands where other landbirds are scarce, though surely their capacity to rest on the water also plays a part.

The earliest known transatlantic crossing involved a 1883 record from Kristiansand, Norway (Mjos pers. comm.), making the St Mary's bird the second known to have completed a full crossing. The Scilly individual was preceded by a male which made it as far as the Azores on 26th November 1957. Since the arrival of the St Mary's bird, others have been recorded: at sea off the Azores in April 1961 and, surprisingly, in Switzerland in December 1967 (Cramp *et al.* 1977–94).

## Coot (Common Coot) *Fulica atra* A

**Resident, migrant and winter visitor, breeds in modest numbers.**

Breeds central and southern Eurasia, from Britain, Ireland, France and Iberia east to Sakhalin and Japan, also India and Australasia. Except for western Europe, mainly migratory in north, in West Palearctic wintering south to North Africa, Nile Valley and Iraq. Polytypic: nominate *atra* occurs Eurasia, North Africa and India south to Sri Lanka; three further forms southeast. National 33% increase 1994–99 (Bashford & Noble 2000), with BTO Waterways Bird Survey showing 61% increase 1975–2000. Green-listed in UK: in need of basic conservation assistance (Gregory *et al.* 2002).

E H Rodd described the status of Coot on the Cornish mainland in the mid- to late 1900s, considering it less numerous than Moorhen *Gallinula chloropus* and occurring on larger areas of water than that species (Rodd 1880), being particularly attracted by thick reedbeds, which Rodd thought provided it with 'plenty of concealment'. Rodd also mentioned large flocks seen gathered on the ice during cold weather, though he made no mention of the possibility of winter influxes from outside Cornwall.

First direct mention of this species on Scilly comes from E H Rodd's nephew Francis, who spent much time shooting on the islands. When touring the Tresco ponds on Christmas Day 1864, Francis noted a large flock of Coots (Rodd 1880). He commented that Coots arrived on Tresco during the night of 7th–8th November 1870, such that there were 'considerable numbers' on the latter date. However, his added comment that 'the reeds having been eaten by cattle on St Mary's, the flock on the ponds there disappeared the next day' makes it unclear whether migration or just a local movement was involved (Rodd 1880).

Later still, James Clark and Francis Rodd clarified Coot's 19th century status (Clark & Rodd 1906), describing it as a former scarce and irregular winter visitor and noting how, in the autumn of 1859, it arrived in such numbers that as many as 100 could be seen on the Tresco pools at any one time. Subsequently, two to three pairs bred in 1860, with a 'few' pairs present annually from then until at least 1906. They also noted that it was annually common during winter and frequently observed coming in off the sea in autumn on St Mary's. Interestingly, however, an unconfirmed source thought it did not breed in Scilly in 1885 and Smart (in Penhallurick 1969) also mentioned its absence as a breeding bird that same year. The latter suggested that only the occasional, possibly disabled individual remained throughout the summer. Surprisingly, Clark & Rodd made no mention here of reed *Phragmites communis* planting around the Tresco pools during the 1850s, yet, in the case of Moorhen *Gallinula chloropus*, they suggested this landmark event may have been at least partly responsible for establishment of a breeding population on Scilly. Coot seems equally likely to have benefited from the planting – certainly E H Rodd thought there was a link between Coots and mainland reedbeds. Penhallurick thought no more than 20 pairs nested in the islands by the mid-1960s.

Most counts of Coots on Scilly, at any time of year, come from Tresco, which also probably holds the greatest numbers of breeding pairs of any island. However, such counts are mainly random in nature and tend to concentrate on autumn, creating difficulties detecting seasonal changes in numbers, regardless of comments such as 'no spring passage noted'. The near absence of early spring and summer counts is particularly unfortunate, removing as it does the possibility of determining the dynamics of the apparent autumn build-up. This situation is further complicated by uncertainties over the extent of seasonal inter-island movements, there being evidence from St Agnes, at least, that the occasional breeding pair or two on that island are 'summer visitors' – presumably from Tresco. Nevertheless, some counts from the 1970s reveal an apparent autumn build-up, at least on Tresco, with numbers then holding through the winter, together with evidence of a decline by March. For example, on Tresco during 1986, a count of 29 on 16th August increased to 44 on 22nd September and peaked at 52 by the end of October, when counts ceased. Similarly, a count of 52 on the same island on 31st January 1987 contrasted with just seven by 3rd May, 28 on 24th August being attributed to a successful breeding season. In recent years, there seems to be evidence of an increase in wintering numbers on Tresco from about 1995, with the norm of 50s and 60s of earlier years replaced by counts of up to 170. The one obvious earlier exception was 150 counted on Tresco in late January 1965 (B King 1965b).

Even so, and as with Moorhen, there always seems to be a surplus of non-breeding individuals. There is also surprisingly little mention of the number of breeding pairs involved, though one to three on St Agnes and a similar total for St Mary's, mainly at Porth Hellick with the occasional pair at Porthloo, appears to be the norm for those islands. Possibly, the manner in which Coots hide their nest within reedbeds creates difficulties when counting Tresco's breeding pairs, though this seems seldom if ever to have been attempted, as evident from the 1980 comment 'as usual no count made on Tresco', or, in 1982, again in relation to Tresco ' no breeding season data being known'. This provides additional evidence, if it were needed, of past and present disinterest in recording details of resident breeding birds compared to the amount of attention directed at rarer visitors. The 1984 annual report got about as close as we might hope to providing an answer to the Tresco question, since it suggested one pair with young on 6th June, plus two pairs with nests and one to two further pairs, a total of five breeding or possible breeding pairs.

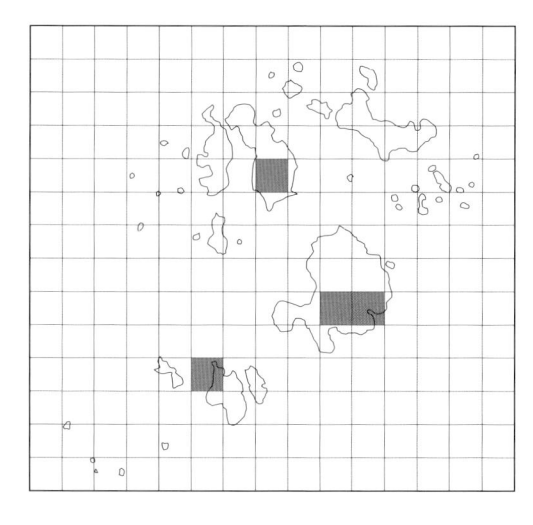

| Island | Pairs |
| --- | --- |
| St Mary's | 5 |
| Tresco | 10 |
| St Agnes | 1 |

**2000 Breeding Bird Atlas – Coot (Chown & Lock 2002)**

1-km Coot Breeding Distribution – 2000–01 (data Chown & Lock 2002)

*Birds of the Isles of Scilly*

This gives a likely annual total for the islands in the region of up to 11–12 pairs and less than the 20 pairs suggested by Penhallurick for the 1960s. More recently, the 2000 Breeding Bird Atlas recorded up to 16 pairs in four (5.9%) of the 67 1-km squares surveyed (Chown & Lock 2002), with breeding confirmed in three.

Ringing data show a general south or west movement of Coots throughout Europe during autumn, moving into France, Iberia or even West Africa, south at least as far as Senegal (Cramp *et al.* 1977–94), with Coots wintering in Britain and Ireland originating from as far away as the Baltic countries, though most ringing recoveries come from France, Germany or Denmark (Wernham *et al.* 2002). British and Irish birds are mainly sedentary, though some reach northern Spain. Wing moult commences from early July, most birds having completed by mid-September. Birds in eastern Europe begin moving south earlier than populations further west, perhaps from September, compared with October and early November in the west, though winter cold-weather movements can occur at any time and confuse analysis of ringing recoveries. Just two Coots have been ringed in Scilly, both prior to 1970. The single control gives some indication of where at least some birds involved in the autumn build-up may originate. The possibility of the closely similar American Coot *F. americana* reaching Scilly should be kept constantly in mind, particularly during autumn, even though only three records had been excepted by the BBRC up until the end of 1999.

**Controls**
H439153  Ad   Ratzeburg, Schleswig-Holstein, Germany
                26th December 1953                    FD  Tresco 22nd January 1957

**Coot Ringing Recaptures**

## Crane (Common Crane) *Grus grus* A

**Extremely rare migrant. Treated by the BBRC as a national Scarce Migrant, full written description required by the SRP.**

   1881   One shot Tresco 13th April   Clark & Rodd 1906
   1989   One (in flight) Tresco 3rd July
   1995   One St Mary's, St Agnes & Tresco 4th April to 6th May

Breeds central Eurasia, from northern Germany and Scandinavia east almost to Sea of Okhotsk and from edge of northern forests south to Turkey, Iran and southeast Kazakhstan. Strongly migratory in West Palearctic, northern European birds use two distinct western and eastern routes, wintering southern Europe south into North Africa. Polytypic: nominate *grus* occurs Europe east to Urals; *lilfordi* Turkey, west-central Siberia, etc. eastwards. Removed from BBRC Rarities List January 1988 (Lansdown and the Rarities Committee 1987). Amber-listed in UK: five-year mean of 3.8 breeding pairs; unfavourable world conservation status (Gregory *et al.* 2002).

Early references to 'Crane' in southwest England often relate to other species, e.g. Camden's (1610) account of Cranes in Scilly was in fact directed at Shag *Phalacrocorax aristotelis*. There are just three records of this unmistakable species in the islands, the first of which 'a fine example' was shot by Tresco gamekeeper David Smith on the north side of the Great Pool on 13th April 1881, after he watched it fly in from the southwest (Clark & Rodd 1906). The mounted skin is currently in the Isles of Scilly Museum on St Mary's. There was subsequently a very long wait before the second Scillonian record was watched flying over Tresco on 3rd July 1989. Last of the trio remained on the islands for most of April and into early May

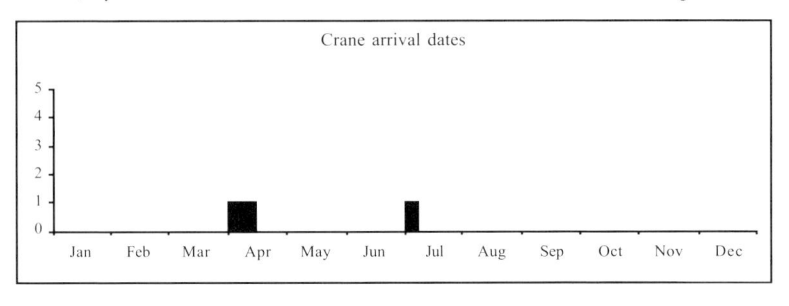

Crane arrival dates

1995, being first seen over St Mary's Airport on 4th. During this time, it also visited St Agnes and then Tresco, before settling in the Pelistry area of St Mary's, where it was a novel addition to the author's Lunnon Farm Common Bird Census totals.

Unlike some other large migrants, e.g. White Stork *Ciconia ciconia*, Crane readily crosses large expanses of open water. Nevertheless, northern European birds use two widely separated eastern and western routes, which avoid the central Mediterranean area (Cramp *et al.* 1977–94). The southwestern route involves part of the Scandinavian population, at least some from the Baltic and possibly even some from western Russia, with birds moving southwest over the Netherlands, Belgium and central France down into southern Spain and Portugal, a few crossing into North Africa. Birds reaching Britain, and therefore Scilly, are most likely to be associated with this source and thus may originate as far east as western Russia. In his useful booklet *Birds of Scilly as Recorded at Tresco Abbey*, T A Dorrien-Smith appeared to attribute the two early records to the nominate form (T A Dorrien-Smith 1951). There was a total of 28 records for mainland Cornwall up to and including 1999 (*CBWPSAR* 69).

## Little Bustard *Otis tetrax* A  BBRC 5.5%

**Extremely rare migrant, full written description required by the BBRC.**

[1881 One St Mary's]   Clark & Rodd 1906
1918 One killed St Agnes March   Penhallurick 1978
1921 One shot St Agnes 24th May   Penhallurick 1978
1975 One St Agnes, Gugh & St Mary's 29th October to 3rd November   *British Birds* 69: 334
*2002 One St Agnes 22nd March*   *Birding World* 15: 96; *Birdwatch* 119: 51

Breeds southwest and southern Europe, e.g. Iberia, France, Italy, Hungary, plus central Eurasia, from Black Sea east to Kazakhstan. More northerly populations migratory, west European birds wintering within southern part of range, e.g. Iberia. Monotypic.

There is a possible 19th century record, involving a bird flushed several times on the St Mary's 'Moors' during winter 1881 and thought to be this species (Clark & Rodd 1906). Clark and Rodd added that it was about the right size and rose like a Curlew *Numenius arquata*. Unfortunately, this appears to be the only published reference to this probable record, although in truth there seems little reason to doubt it was Little Bustard, particularly as Penhallurick (1978) listed no less than 23 on mainland Cornwall, mostly shot, between 1751 and the end of the 19th century. At least two of these were found hanging in a poulterer's shop labelled as 'Silver Pheasant'. Indeed, this is one of those species that formerly occurred in Britain in sizeable numbers, but has since failed to show itself often, following marked range declines during the late 19th and early 20th centuries (Cramp *et al.* 1977–94).

Penhallurick (1978) quoted information received from J L F Parslow concerning a bird shot on St Agnes in March 1918, followed soon after by another shot on the same island by J H Hicks, on 24th May 1921. The skin of the latter bird is now in the Isles of Scilly Museum in Hugh Town, St Mary's. More recently, a bird flushed from Wingletang, again on St Agnes, by Tim Inskipp on 29th October 1975, flew to nearby Gugh, before recrossing to St Agnes and then being discovered at Trenoweth, St Mary's on 2nd November. Later the same day, it was relocated near Telegraph, still on St Mary's, and was last seen in that same area on the 3rd (*IOSBR* 1975). On three occasions when the bird was flushed, St Mary's observers distinctly heard the 'startling whistle of the wing beat', from which it was suggested the bird was a male. The reasonably detailed description suggested it was larger than Mallard *Anas platyrhynchos*, perhaps equal

*Birds of the Isles of Scilly*

to Brent Goose *Branta bernicla* in size, with broad, rounded and mostly white wings, but with conspicuous black primary tips. The bill was short, head, neck and mantle grey/brown, and tail short and dark. It flew with stiff wings and powerful beats. Its size eliminated any possibility of Great Bustard *Otis tarda*, whereas the mode of flight and extent of white in the wing ruled out Houbara *Chlamydotis undulata* and the recently separated Mcqueen's Bustard *C. macqueenii*. It should be noted, too, that T A Dorrien-Smith appeared to attribute all three early records to the formerly *orientalis*, or recognised 'Eastern Little Bustard' (T A Dorrien-Smith 1951).

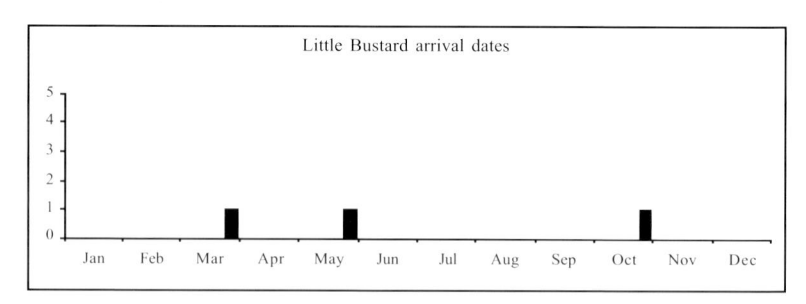

Little Bustard arrival dates

The BBRC accepted just 18 Little Bustard records during the period 1958–99, compared with 92 recorded sightings before that time (BBRC 2000). Therefore, the single Scillonian record within that time period represents 5.5%. In western Europe, all breeding populations now occur south or southeast of Britain and Ireland, in which case we would expect overshooting arrivals to be more likely to occur in spring than in autumn. There is a strong breeding population as close to Scilly as western and central France (Hagemeijer and Blair 1997). French birds commence flocking and moving south from August through to October, but with small-scale movements noted in northeast France into November and early December – though the origin of these birds is unclear (Cramp *et al.* 1977–94). French birds return to their breeding areas from mid-March to April. Prior to the general decline, birds from eastern populations, e.g. western Russia, moved southwest in autumn, regularly reaching the Balkans, some of which could conceivably reach Britain. By 1999 there had been a total of 19 Little Bustards reported from mainland Cornwall, including the 19th century records (*CBWPSAR* 66). Since preparing this text a bird was flushed from Punch Bowl, St Agnes on 22nd March 2002, and this record is seemingly likely to gain BBRC approval.

## Oystercatcher *Haematopus ostralegus* A

**Resident and obvious, especially whilst breeding. Widely but thinly distributed around the shore during summer, also probable migrant and winter visitor.**

Breeds Eurasia, fragmentarily from Iceland, Britain and Ireland, France and Norway east to Kamchatka, south to Mediterranean, Iraq and central eastern China. Migratory, though mainly resident in western Europe; France to Iberia. Polytypic: nominate *ostralegus* occurs Europe to western Russia, *longipes* central Russia east to western Siberia; *osculans* eastern Asia. Amber-listed in UK: 20% or more of European breeding population in UK; 20% or more of East Atlantic Flyway non-breeding population in UK, 50% or more at ten or fewer sites (Gregory *et al.* 2002). National 18% decline 1994–99 (Bashford & Noble 2000).

Bone remains from the Bronze and Iron Age up to the 7th century AD have been found for a range of species that currently occur in Scilly, plus several that no longer occur, e.g. Black Grouse *Tetrao tetrix* (Turk 1971). And as it seems reasonable to assume early local people exploited those species that were most readily available, the absence of Oystercatcher among these remains is worth noting.

Heath (1750) made probable first mention of this species in Scilly, listing 'Se Pies' among the 'seabirds on all the islands', whilst by the mid-19th century North (1850) was able to confirm it as a permanent annual breeding resident. Interestingly, the normally well informed E H Rodd seems to have been slightly less certain of its status, suggesting it was met with only occasionally in Scilly, though he agreed it bred (Rodd 1880). Inevitably, it fell to James Clark and E H Rodd's nephew Francis to clarify the situation (Clark & Rodd 1906). They confirmed that this species was abundant around the coasts and on rocky islands year-round and that it bred in 'considerable numbers', also describing how it flocked with other species, e.g. Curlew *Numenius arquata*, on low rocky islets, until pushed off by the advancing tide – quoting 200 as the upper limit for flock size.

Moving to the 20th century, H W Robinson (1911a) pointed out that a few pairs bred annually on Annet, whilst according to the 1937 report (*CBWPSAR* 7) a 'large number of nests' were found on Samson, an island it still particularly favours. From that point onwards, various authors and annual reports made passing reference to Oystercatcher, mostly suggesting it was common, though there are few if any reliable counts. Some of these references mention nests or apparent breeding pairs seen on specific islands, all of which hold one or more pairs to the present day, e.g. three nested on tiny Guther's Island in 1946 (*CBWPSAR* 16).

Nevertheless, as with several common species in Scilly, in most years up until, and in some years after, publication of the St Agnes Bird Observatory Reports, Oystercatcher gets no mention at all. Even by the 1970s, little information was available annually on the size of the breeding or wintering population and most annual reports contain an unstructured and often confusing list of random flock counts for various sites. Only in the case of St Agnes do we have any long-term breeding population data, in the range 5–16 pairs during the period 1957–78 (*SABOAR* 1979). And even what we might expect to be worthwhile sources of information usually prove disappointing, as with the post-1906 review of breeding birds of Cornwall and Scilly (Ryves & Quick 1946), which merely stated that it still bred abundantly in Scilly. The truth is that a dedicated full survey of breeding Oystercatchers seems never to have been carried out prior to the recent 2000 Breeding Bird Atlas (Chown & Lock 2002), the nearest to a full-island survey perhaps being the 1974 estimate of 109 pairs obtained during an all-island seabird count (Allen 1974). The only alternative is to rely upon occasional published island estimates, such as the suggested minimum four pairs on St Agnes, six on Tresco, 18 on Samson and five on Gugh in 1997. However, using these occasional published estimates plus the author's personal experience, it may be reasonable to think in terms of an annual all-island total of at least 100 pairs, particularly once we consider that some 30 smaller islands, e.g. Illiswilgig, Rosevear and both Green Islands, annually hold at least one pair each. Penhallurick (1969) quoted Parslow as suggesting 100–150 pairs, presumably by the mid-1960s, though no further information is given. Therefore, it comes as no surprise to find that the 2000 Atlas survey located up to 152 pairs in 45 (67%) 1-km squares surveyed, with breeding confirmed in 23 (34.3%). The Table shows the distribution of pairs on main islands. In the light of undoubted increased human visitor pressure since 1974, the lack of major reductions is worth noting, as is the fact that nearly 62% of pairs now nest on uninhabited islands, half of which are on Tean, Annet, Samson and St Helen's (Chown & Lock 2002).

The two most reliable indicators of wintering Oystercatcher numbers in Scilly are the winter 1984-85 (Kirby 1988) and January 1997 Winter Shorebird Surveys, the latter a sequel count to that of March 1996 (Lock 1996). Kirby located a total of 583 Oystercatchers (20% of a total of 2,825 waders counted) during five days of fieldwork between 15th December 1984 and 28th January 1985. Distribution was as shown in the Table. The 1997 survey, which arrived at the similar result of 619 individuals (an increase of about 15% over the previous figure) was conducted over two consecutive days at the end of January. However, several islands counted in 1984–85 were not visited during the more recent survey, e.g. Tean, Gweal and Northwethel, which earlier produced a combined 48 individuals. Explanations for the apparent increase between surveys are unknown, but could be attributable to differences in timing and methodology, e.g. two consecutive days verses six weeks, plus the less complete coverage already referred to.

*Birds of the Isles of Scilly*

| Island | Pairs |
|---|---|
| Bryher | 14 |
| Great Ganilly | 3 |
| St Agnes | 12 |
| St Helen's | 7 |
| St Martin's | 7 |
| Annet | 11 |
| St Mary's | 12 |
| Gweal | 4 |
| Tresco | 13 |
| Great & Little Arthur | 4 |
| Samson | 17 |
| Toll's Island | 4 |
| Tean | 12 |
| Great Ganinick | 3 |
| White Island, St Martin's | 4 |
| Others | 28 |

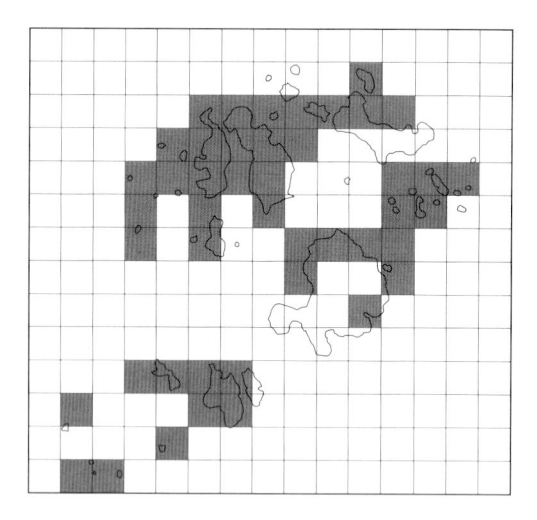

1-km Oystercatcher Breeding Distribution – 2000–01 (data Chown & Lock 2002)

2000 Breeding Bird Atlas – Oystercatcher (Chown & Lock 2002)

Although it already seems apparent that there are more Oystercatchers present in Scilly during winter than can be accounted for by the likely maximum of 150 breeding pairs, the question of how many migrants pass through Scilly during spring or autumn remains unanswered. Monthly count totals scattered throughout annual reports vary in quality and appear more numerous for October, but nevertheless suggest an apparent pattern of between 620 to 860 October individuals annually (e.g. *IOSBR* 1984, 1994, 1999), with the proviso of course that count dates are often not given and thus the extent of any inter-site movement remains unknown. Unfortunately, there are only limited data for September, though what few there are suggest an apparent increase in numbers around that period. But the near total absence of November data makes it impossible to tell whether these apparent late summer arrivals pass on through the islands, or remain to form the winter population. Similarly, the dearth of data for the early spring period creates difficulties deciding when any wintering individuals depart, or even whether comments such as 'small spring passage' are justifiable at all. Lock (1996), however, recorded at least 529 still present in Scilly by March 16th–19th 1996. Penhallurick (1969) quoted flocks of several hundred on migration in Cornish estuaries in spring and autumn, although at the same time pointed out that few figures had been published. One important piece of information may come from the analysis of winter wader roosts on St Agnes (Hale 1994), where the Oystercatcher totals for Burnt Island and nearby Browarth remained fairly static between October and January (in the range 129–165; mean of 142), but declined to 84 by February, 52 by March and 29 by April. Hale concluded that these reductions were most probably attributable to natural mortality and a deterioration in the weather on Scilly during December that year, in contrast to mild weather beforehand. He surmised that birds moved to other, more sheltered roosts, either in Scilly or on the Cornish mainland. Closer examination of the data showed that most of the reduction occurred from the Burnt Island site.

Typically, on less disturbed islands Oystercatcher nests are sited among small boulders or on sandy areas immediately above high tide, whereas on those islands experiencing increasing human disturbance during summer, e.g. Tresco, they tend to be placed further back from the water, often on raised banks at the edge of sand dunes, or at the base of low cliffs. Three eggs are the norm, with fewer clutches of two and very occasionally four. Examples of five eggs mentioned in the literature (e.g. *IOSBR* 1965) seem more likely to be the product of more than one pair, or involve eggs remaining from an earlier clutch. Individual pairs vary considerably in their response to human disturbance. Many seem content to slip quietly off the nest and move down to the water, such that only the experienced observer will be aware of a nest, though this may change with the presence of young, whilst others react in the most noisy fashion from the very outset. On some of the smaller islands, e.g. Bryher's Shipman Head, nests may be situated away from the shore and, in any event, often at a greater altitude.

At sites where a pair or two breed among Common Terns *Sterna hirundo*, the question recently arose of whether adult Oystercatchers kill young terns or damage their eggs, as recorded in some other areas (e.g. Tickle 1965). This seems to have occurred on Green Island off Samson in 1995, when some of 50 clutches of Common Tern eggs were believed to have been damaged by a breeding pair of Oystercatchers (P J Robinson 1995a).

Oystercatchers from Iceland, Faeroes, Norway, Sweden and the Netherlands winter in Britain and Ireland (Wernham *et al.* 2002) and arrive on their wintering grounds mainly during August–September. British birds show a tendency to move south or southwest, adults mainly as far as western France, birds up to their third or fourth winter reaching Iberia and North Africa (Wernham *et al.* 2002). Birds arrive back on the breeding grounds from January to April, though perhaps not until early May for some eastern European populations. A total of 43 Oystercatchers have been ringed in Scilly, 27 prior to 1970. There are no controls or recoveries.

| St Mary's | St Agnes & Gugh | St Martin's | Samson | Bryher | Tresco | Tean, Gweal & Northwethel | |
|---|---|---|---|---|---|---|---|
| 147 (121) | 111 (36) | 74 (98) | 44 (97) | 50 (126) | 109 (141) | 48 (?) | Totals 583 (619) |

Oystercatcher Wintering Numbers 1984-85* & 1997 (*from Kirby 1988; 1997 figures in parentheses)

## Black-winged Stilt *Himantopus himantopus* A BBRC 4.5%

Rare migrant or winter visitor, full written description required by the BBRC.

- c. 1905 Two (shot) St Agnes   Penhallurick 1969
- 1951 One St Mary's & Tresco 12th January to 7th February   *CBWPSAR* 21
- [1987 Seven (in flight) St Mary's 27th April]   *IOSBR* 1987
- 1990 One Tresco 18th March to 16th April

Breeds sporadically southern Eurasia, from Iberia and France east to Mongolia, also Africa, Americas and Australasia. Northern populations migratory, West Palearctic population winters trans-Saharan Africa. Polytypic, some authorities treat extralimital forms as full species: nominate *himantopus* occurs Eurasia east to Mongolia and Africa south to South Africa. Amber-listed in *Bird Species of Conservation Concern* (Gibbons *et al.* 1996).

There are no 19th century reports from Scilly of this unmistakable wader, though Penhallurick (1969) listed three shot on the Cornish mainland prior to 1900. Therefore, two shot on St Agnes in 1905 and mentioned in the Tresco Abbey records were the first for the islands (Penhallurick 1978). The mounted skins of these two are now in the Isles of Scilly Museum in Hugh Town, St Mary's. The third island record was viewable on the beaches of St Mary's between 12th and 16th January 1951 and the Tresco sighting of 7th February seems likely to have involved the same individual (*CBWPSAR* 21). Difficult to explain is the report of seven allegedly seen in flight over St Mary's in late April 1987. The record fails to appear in the BBRC annual reports as either accepted or rejected (*IOSBR* 1987; *British Birds* 81: 554–555 & 594), from which we may perhaps assume it was not submitted – as unfortunately still happens with far too many claimed rarities on Scilly. The most recent record concerned a bird present on Tresco from 18th March to at least 16th April 1990 and seen well by numerous observers.

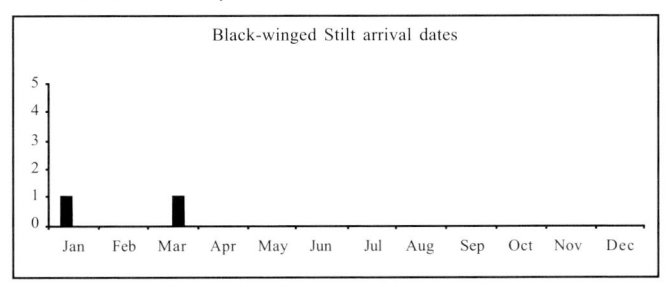

Black-winged Stilts breed as close to Scilly as northwest France (Hagemeijer and Blair 1997) and more commonly south into Iberia and southern Europe, and both the 1987 and 1990 records appear to fit the probability of spring overshoots, as, according to Cramp *et al.* (1977–94), return passage to the southern European breeding sites occurs mainly during March and April, perhaps extending into May. Also, the same authority highlights the tendency for irregular northward spring movements beyond the normal breeding range, perhaps associated with anticyclonic conditions and sometimes resulting in extralimital breeding, including in Britain. Up to and including 1999 there were a total of 21 Black-winged Stilt records in mainland Cornwall from the 20th century and before (*CBWPSAR* 63). The 22 records accepted by the BBRC for Britain during the period 1958–99 mean that the single Scillonian arrival represents 4.5% of the total, although that increases if the 1987 flock is included.

## Avocet (Pied Avocet) *Recurvirostra avosetta* A

**Rare migrant or winter visitor.**

| | | |
|---|---|---|
| 1970 | One St Mary's, St Agnes, Bryher & Tresco 15th to 20th May |
| 1971 | One Porth Hellick, St Mary's 28th to 30th August |
| 1973 | Two (in flight) Bryher 27th April |
| 1980 | One St Martin's 4th April |
| 1981 | One Great Pool, Tresco 6th April |
| 1985 | One St Martin's, St Mary's & Tresco 17th to 22nd January |
| 1987 | One Porth Hellick, St Mary's 24th January to 1st February, again 24th February |
| 1992 | Up to 20 Abbey Pool Tresco 14th to 15th November |
| 1997 | One Bryher & Tresco 25th January to 25th February (dead on last date) |
| 1998 | One Abbey Pool, Tresco 5th to 9th June |

Fragmentary breeding distribution across southern Eurasia, from Iberia, France and Britain east to Mongolia, also Africa. Migratory in north, West Palearctic populations winter south to trans-Saharan Africa, substantially more birds remain in north of range during mild winters. Monotypic. Included on Annex I of 1979 EEC 'Birds Directive'. Amber-listed in UK: 50% or more of UK breeding and non-breeding populations at ten or fewer sites; unfavourable world winter conservation status (Gregory *et al.* 2002).

There were no published references to Avocet in Scilly until one of these dainty waders arrived in mid-May 1970. Although the way in which Avocets re-established themselves in eastern England during the mid-20th century is well documented, Penhallurick (1969) drew attention to a parallel increase in numbers of wintering birds on the Tamar estuary in mainland Cornwall, also pointing out that the unexpected breeding of a pair in Ireland in 1938 coincided with sightings of single birds in west Cornwall during that and the following year, with another in 1943. All this and similar activity elsewhere in Britain culminated of course in breeding pairs in Essex and then Norfolk during the 1940s.

A minimum of 30 Avocets have appeared in Scilly on ten occasions in ten years, with 20 the most seen together; all records appear in the Table. Six records (60%) were in spring or summer and the remaining four are perhaps best classified as either late autumn or winter arrivals. Interestingly, there is a clear tendency towards later arrival dates and longer stays, with the six early season arrivals present just 2.8 days, compared with 15.4 days for autumn–winter arrivals. This perhaps suggests that early season birds are migrants and end-of-year individuals part of Cornwall's growing wintering population. The bird on Bryher in 1997 was found dead on 25th February, whereas the bird on St Martin's Flats on 4th April 1973 was watched flying away towards the northeast.

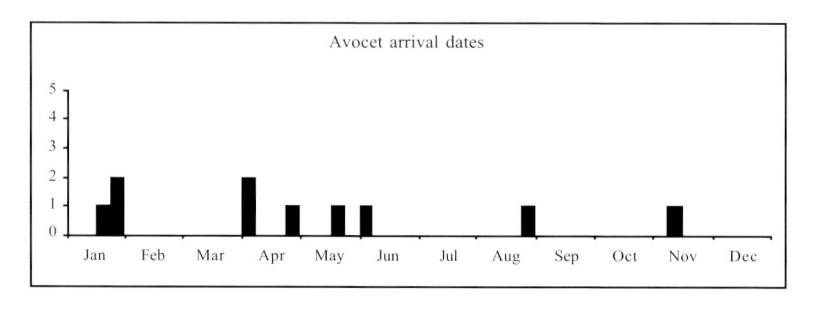

The Cornish wintering flock commenced its build-up from the winter of 1947–48 and has now expanded to include other nearby sites, e.g. the Lynher Estuary and St John's Lake. In 1999 up to 460 birds were involved. In addition, a wintering flock can now be found further east on Devon's Exe Estuary, where as many as 660 may be present. The Exe, however, may also be used as a staging post by Cornish birds and the full extent of inter-site movement in southwest England may not yet be fully understood. What is clear, though, is that overall numbers involved in southwest England are increasing, from which we may anticipate an increase in Scillonian sightings. Up until the mid-1960s, Penhallurick (1969) found that the first Avocets in Cornwall arrived during the last week of October or into early November, departing again during March, with few present after 20th. All of this fits the pattern of recent end-of-year and winter arrival and departures on Scilly. After eastern England, the next nearest regularly breeding Avocets are in the Netherlands and then western France (Hagemeijer & Blair 1997). The English population now probably exceeds 500 breeding pairs and in the Netherlands there are at least 2,700. Although the more northerly west European breeding populations are migratory, significant numbers remain in countries bordering the North Sea during mild winters, particularly perhaps in Britain and the Netherlands. However, in western Europe, the largest wintering numbers are in France and Iberia, which perhaps helps to explain its occurrence in Scilly during spring.

## Stone Curlew (Stone-curlew) *Burhinus oedicnemus* A

**Scarce spring migrant, allegedly more frequent in the early 19th century. Full written description required by the SRP.**

| | | |
|---|---|---|
| 1878 | One (shot) December | Clark & Rodd 1906 |
| 1879 | One (shot) Scilly | Clark & Rodd 1906 |
| 1890 | One (shot) 10th May | Clark & Rodd 1906 |
| 1946 | One St Agnes 4th May | *CBWPSAR* 16 |
| 1961 | One St Mary's 12th May | |
| 1968 | One St Martin's 29th July | |
| 1977 | One (in flight) between Samson and Tresco 25th May | |
| 1979 | One Tresco & Tean 21st May | |
| 1981 | One St Agnes & Annet 9th & 14th April | |
| 1982 | One Porthloo and Porth Hellick, St Mary's 6th–7th February | |
| 1986 | One St Agnes 25th April | |
| 1988 | One St Agnes 30th April | |
| 1988 | One St Agnes 13th May | |
| 1994 | One St Agnes & Tresco 24th to 28th April | |
| 1995 | One Peninnis, St Mary's 3rd March | |
| 1995 | One Wingletang, St Agnes 9th to 12th May | |
| 1996 | One Porth Killier, St Agnes 27th March | |
| 1997 | One St Agnes & St Martin's 28th to 29th May | |
| 1998 | One Pentle Bay, Tresco 10th April | |
| 2001 | St Mary's 19th & 20th October | |

Breeds southern Eurasia, from Iberia, France and Britain to eastern Kazakhstan, India and Southeast Asia. Northern populations migratory, in West Palearctic winters south from within breeding range to equatorial Africa. Polytypic: nominate *oedicnemus* occurs northwest Europe east to southern Russia and south to Iberia, Italy, Balkans and Caucasus; *saharae* smaller Mediterranean Islands, Turkey, Greece, North Africa, Middle East, Iraq and Iran; *insularum* eastern Canary Islands; *distinctus* western Canary Islands; *harterti* southeast Russia, central Iran and eastwards; *indicus* India and Southeast Asia. Included on Annex I of 1979 EEC 'Birds Directive'. National decline of 42% during 20 years to 1996. Red-listed in UK: rapid, 56% decline in breeding range over past 28 years; year 2000 breeding population of 254 pairs; unfavourable world conservation status (Gregory *et al.* 2002).

Early evidence of Stone Curlew in Scilly comes in the form of a few bones of a single individual found in a room of one of the houses at the Nornour prehistoric site in the Eastern Isles (Turk 1971). The same author suggested that these may even perhaps have been associated with some form of medicinal cure, e.g. for jaundice.

Far more recently, 19 Stone Curlews have been recorded arriving in Scilly in 17 different years, three prior to the 20th century and all but one dated record in spring. All records are shown in the Table. In two years, two different individuals were recorded. First for the islands involved a bird shot on Bryher in December 1878 and listed in the Tresco game books as 'Norfolk Plover'. This was followed quickly by another shot at an unknown location some time during 1879 and then the third, shot by Joe White on 10th May 1890, again at an unspecified location (Rodd 1880; Clark & Rodd 1906). The initial 20th century record was watched at close range on Burnt Island, St Agnes, whilst it was 'investigating the luncheon bag' (*CBWPSAR* 16).

A brief glance at the Chart leaves no doubt this is a spring migrant in Scilly, with just a single summer individual and one winter record from the 19th century. Commenting on the 1946 record, A A Dorrien-Smith thought Stone Curlew was formerly more common in the islands, though this apparently conflicts with the records. However, as Penhallurick (1969) pointed out, prior to the last quarter of the 19th century it was almost annual in mainland Cornwall, E H Rodd reporting three he knew of in 1858 (Penhallurick 1969). There may have been at least one additional record for the islands, according to the 1968 comment in *CBWPSAR* 38 suggesting a previous unsupported claim of a bird in St Martin's in an earlier year. The arrival on St Mary's on 6th February 1982 was claimed at the time to be the earliest ever in Britain by six days (*IOSBR* 1982).

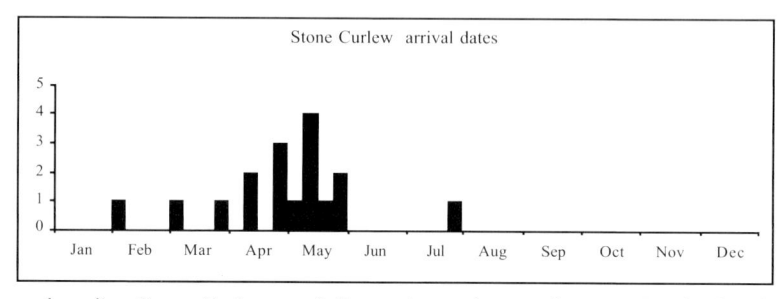

Stone Curlew arrival dates

The closest breeding Stone Curlews to Scilly are in southern and eastern England and in northeast, central and western France (Gibbons *et al.* 1993; Hagemeijer & Blair 1997). Most European Stone Curlews migrate, though a few remain in southern England and further south, e.g. southern France, during winter (Cramp *et al.* 1977–94). Substantial numbers also cross the Mediterranean to winter in Africa north of the equator (Wernham *et al.* 2002). Return passage occurs mainly in March but continues into April, British breeding sites being re-occupied by late March or early April, though, eastern European birds arrive back later. Consequently, it is difficult to decide whether birds arriving in Scilly are overshooting southern European migrants, birds returning to breeding sites in southern or eastern England or birds from populations further east. Since this text was prepared a further individual appeared on St Mary's on the 19th and 20th October 2001.

## Collared Pratincole *Glareola pratincola* A BBRC 1.9%

**Extremely rare spring migrant, full written description required by the BBRC.**

1990   One St Agnes 3rd & 4th April (died 4th)   *British Birds* 85: 552
2000   One St Mary's, Tresco & St Martin's 21st to 29th April   *British Birds* 94: 469

Breeds southern Eurasia, from Iberia to eastern Kazakhstan, also tropical and southern Africa. Migratory, West Palearctic populations thought to winter south to subtropical Africa north of equator. Polytypic: nominate *pratincola* in north of range; *erlangeri* northeast Africa; *fuelleborni* remainder of Africa.

There are just two Scillonian records of this much sought-after species, the first of which was found sheltering behind a St Agnes woodpile on 3rd April 1990, before being seen flying weakly and then found dead the following day. The second and most recent was discovered flying about in the Parting Carn area of St Mary's on 21st April 2000, before making a brief appearance on Tresco and then settling on St Martin's for two days.

The closest Collared Pratincole breeding populations to the islands are in southern Spain, Portugal and France. All are migratory or partially so and these island records fit the hypothesis of overshooting

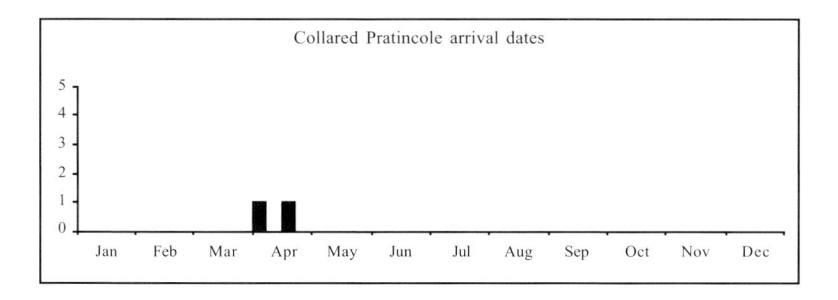

*Collared Pratincole arrival dates* (chart showing bars in Mar and Apr)

spring migrants. The BBRC accepted 52 Collared Pratincole sightings during the period 1958–99, in which case the single Scillonian record within that same timespan represented less than 2%. Prior to 1958 there were 31 recorded sightings (BBRC 2000).

## Pratincole *Glareola*

Unidentified Pratincole Records
   1971   One St Agnes 10th October   *IOSBR* 1971

A pratincole watched in typical 'tern-like flight' over St Agnes and also heard calling on 10th October 1971 was not identified specifically, though statistically it seems more likely to have been the last-mentioned species.

## Little Ringed Plover (Little Plover) *Charadrius dubius* A

**Scarce spring and autumn migrant, full written description required by SRP.**

Breeds lowland Eurasia, from Atlantic to Pacific, western populations fragmentary, contiguous central Europe eastwards. Most populations migratory, especially in north, West Palearctic birds winter northern tropical Africa and perhaps Persian Gulf, others India, Southeast Asia and perhaps Africa. Polytypic: *curonicus* occurs Scandinavia, Britain, northwest Africa east to China and Japan; nominate *dubius* India, Philippines, New Guinea and Southeast Asia.

    A bird shot by Francis Rodd beside Tresco's Abbey Pool in October 1863 caused a great deal of excitement, it being generally believed to be one of only two or three obtained in England, whilst E H Rodd was adamant it was the first record for the islands (Rodd 1863a). However, Morris (1851–57) mentioned an immature shot by a J B Ellman of Lewis, Sussex, by Abbey Pool in September 1851, preceding the aforementioned individual by at least six years. As with some other accounts of the circumstances surrounding 19th century British rarities in Scilly, Francis Rodd's 1863 description of his Little Ringed Plover discovery throws light on the level of field skills displayed by these early collectors (Rodd 1880). In this case, the information is contained in a letter from Francis to his uncle E H Rodd in Penzance, graphically describing finding the bird on the Abbey Pool's mud and instantly realising it 'was something rare'. He noted that as it rose its call was a 'single sharp whistle, not unlike that of the Common Ringed Plover, and shorter in duration', with a 'remarkably stint-like flight'. The younger Rodd's frequent companion, the equally experienced Augustus Pechell, watched the bird through a telescope (not the calibre of instrument in use now, but doubtless a long brass draw-tube) and decided the bird agreed exactly with Yarrell's description (Yarrell 1837–43).

    Exactly how many Little Ringed Plovers were obtained in Britain prior to Francis Rodd's bird is unclear now, if indeed it ever was known. Palmer refers to a bird from Sussex prior to 1853 as the claimed first, with others from the same area during that decade, whilst pointing out that these are not now generally accepted. This apparently ignores the alleged 1851 individual on Tresco in any event. However, assuming the early Sussex records are now unacceptable then one or other of the early Tresco specimens seems a strong contender for the first British record. Certainly the next record listed by Witherby *et al.* (1940) after the Sussex claims is Francis Rodd's 1863 Tresco individual, followed by two in the old county of Middlesex in August 1864. In the most recent *Birds of Sussex*, James (1996) mentions four records prior to the first attempted county breeding record in 1948, but unfortunately omits details.

All 20th century annual records are charted, revealing no obvious long-term increase after the first in 1971. The pattern of spring and autumn arrival dates is as might be expected for Britain as a whole, but with perhaps a more pronounced peak during spring. Again ignoring the two earliest records, there were a total of 43 birds in 21 years (1.4 per year of presence) over the 30-year period since 1971, with four in 1974 and 1989 the highest in any year. The earliest recorded date of arrival was 17th March (1990) and the latest arrival October 26th (1974). Spring arrivals accounted for 69% of all arrival dates

As far as can be ascertained now, no Little Ringed Plovers are recorded as having been ringed on Scilly. Nonetheless the *IOSBR* for 1971 shows the bird on the Gugh Bar, St Agnes, on 20th April as having been trapped and it seems unlikely it would not then have been ringed. Indeed, considering this was the first record for over 100 years it comes as a surprise to see no other comments accompanying this particular entry.

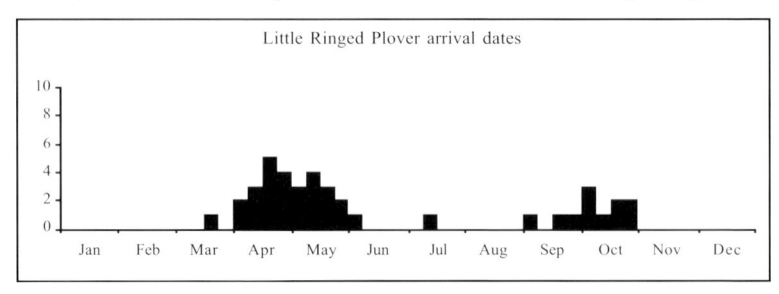

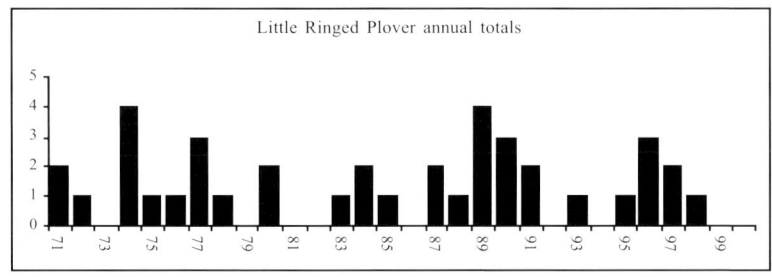

Little Ringed Plover commenced breeding in Britain around 1944 and by 1976 was still restricted to the eastern half of England (Sharrock 1976), since when it increased its range to include southern England west as far as Dorset and, more importantly, Wales (Gibbons *et al.* 1993). Several other west European countries have also experienced marked increases. Therefore, whilst the Scillonian spring peak could perhaps be explained by overshooting Continental breeders, that ought not to account for any autumn records, though birds moving to and from Welsh breeding areas might offer a more logical explanation for recent spring and autumn movements. Ringing data show that British Little Ringed Plovers winter south as far as the Mediterranean, some though reaching West Africa almost to the equator (Wernham et al. 2002). Interestingly, Penhallurick (1969) lists twice as many records (22) for Kentish Plover *C. alexandrinus* for mainland Cornwall and Scilly up until 1968 than for Little Ringed Plover (11) (Penhallurick 1969), whereas by 1999 there was an all-time total of just 57 Kentish Plovers for mainland Cornwall but 275 Little Ringed Plovers (*CBWPSAR* 69). In his useful booklet *Birds of Scilly as Recorded at Tresco Abbey*, T A Dorrien-Smith appears to attribute all island records up until 1951 to the form *curonicus* (T A Dorrien-Smith 1951). However, the basis for this is not given and it remains uncertain whether there were other records between 1863 (1851?) and 1971.

# Ringed Plover *Charadrius hiaticula* A

**Resident, migrant and winter visitor. Breeds on main islands in moderate numbers.**
Circumpolar, breeding primarily around northern edge of landmasses, including British Isles, Greenland, Iceland, Spitsbergen, Nova Zemlya. Polytypic: nominate *hiaticula* occurs northwest Europe from southern Scandinavia and Baltic south to western France, Iceland, Greenland and Spitsbergen; *tundrae*, or 'Tundra Ringed Plover' coastal and tundra Lapland and Russia (Cramp *et al.* 1977–94). Amber-listed in UK:

moderate decline in non-breeding population over past 25 years; 20% or more of East Atlantic Flyway non-breeding population in UK (Gregory *et al.* 2002). UK breeding population not monitored, but known spread inland perhaps associated with recent increase in numbers of gravel-pits and reservoirs (Gibbons *et al.* 1993).

Earliest mention of this species seems to be Heath's mid-18th century listing of it among the landbirds of the islands, using the local name of 'Cawilly' (Heath 1750). A century later, North (1850) confirmed that it bred annually in the islands. However, E H Rodd was almost dismissive of it on mainland Cornwall, stating only that it was generally distributed along the shore, where it bred rather earlier than other shore birds (Rodd 1880). He also pointed out that it was often seen in autumn among flocks of Dunlin *Calidris alpina*, with eggs found from the third week of April on Scilly. In fact, Rodd was so impressed with this last point that he wrote to the *Zoologist* in a letter entitled *Note on the early breeding of the Ring Plover* (Rodd 1843a). The only other 19th century observation appears to be that of E H Rodd's nephew Francis Rodd, who on Christmas Day 1864 noted the presence of large flocks of Ringed Plovers around the Tresco Pools (Rodd 1880).

Early in the 20th century, Francis Rodd and James Clark reviewed the status of Scilly's bird life (Clark & Rodd 1906), concluding that Ringed Plover was abundant on most beaches 'year-round' and bred in 'considerable' numbers. This assessment is of particular interest as by no feat of the imagination can it be described now as breeding in considerable numbers. True, some stretches of beach still hold one to two pairs, but no island probably holds greater than 6–8 pairs and perhaps the all-island total is in the region of 50 breeding pairs or less. Interestingly, then, Ringed Plover's mid-20th century decline in mainland Cornwall was at least partly blamed on increased tourism and a resultant lack of available breeding beaches (Penhallurick 1969). The same author made a comparison between the Cornish decline and the continued breeding presence in Scilly. Nevertheless, it seems difficult to equate the situation Penhallurick described in the mid-1960s with the account given by Clark and Rodd 50 years beforehand, unless of course the suggested 7–14 pairs on St Agnes qualified as 'abundant'. The suggestion is, of course, that even in Scilly Ringed Plover has not gone entirely untouched by increased tourism in the latter half of the 20th century. Penhallurick also described autumn concentrations on St Agnes of from 80 to 100, or even 160 birds. Wintering groups on that island were largely comparable, although up to 200 were recorded during the extremely cold weather of late 1963. The same author quotes evidence of a smaller spring passage, with up to 65 birds the highest recorded daily total.

Up until the 1960s, information on numbers present in Scilly tended to reflect the situation on St Agnes, rather than the islands as a whole. More recently that has changed and we now know rather more about numbers of Ringed Plovers present at various times of the year, although a view of the fuller picture is still largely denied by the recent lack of co-ordinated all-island counts. Taking the ten years from 1990, random site-counts from the late winter period varied between 40 and 188, though more enlightening was the two-day late January 1979 all-islands Winter Shorebird Survey. This survey recorded a total of 284 Ringed Plovers on the six main islands. A similar count during December–January 1984–85 (Kirby 1988) located 312 Ringed Plovers within broadly the same area, though some of the smaller Northern Isles were also included.

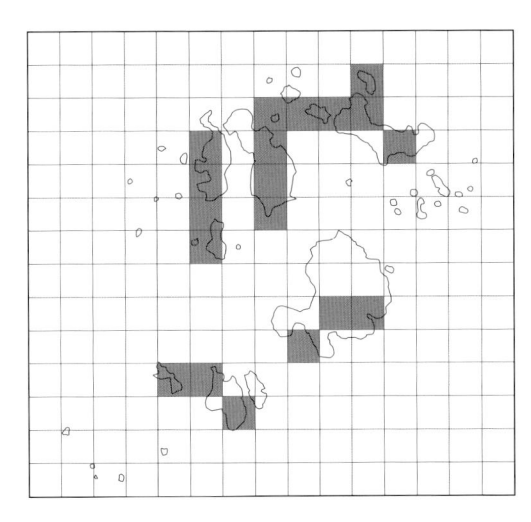

| Island | Pairs |
|---|---|
| Bryher | 4 |
| St Agnes | 5 |
| St Martin's | 5 |
| St Mary's | 3 |
| Tresco | 4 |
| Tean | 7 |
| St Martin's, White Island | 2 |
| Annet | 1 |
| Others | 1 |

**2000 Breeding Bird Atlas – Ringed Plover (Chown & Lock 2002)**

1-km Ringed Plover Breeding Distribution – 2000–01 (data Chown & Lock 2002)

*Birds of the Isles of Scilly*

In marked contrast, the four-day mid-March 1996 all-island Wader Count (Lock 1996) found just 79 birds within roughly the same area, suggesting that a marked decrease occurs by early spring. Despite Penhallurick's earlier suggestion of spring passage, none of any consequence was noted during the 1990s, four birds on St Agnes showing the characteristics of *tundrae*, or 'Tundra Ringed Plover' on 29th May 1998 being the only apparent recorded movement. Autumn passage, or winter arrival, commenced from early August, random site-counts producing totals of up to around 150 and although there are no co-ordinated autumn counts, all-island totals exceeding 400 appear the norm, with numbers remaining at that level until at least November, to be followed by an apparent further increase in numbers during December, e.g. 272 on St Martin's alone on 19th December 1994.

Breeding numbers show a marked reduction from the 1960s, e.g. the 7–14 pairs on St Agnes (H P K Robinson 1974a) reduced now to just 3–4 pairs. Most Ringed Plovers breed, or attempt to breed on sandy beaches, though a few pairs use suitable areas up to 50 m inland and there seems little doubt that the increased level of tourist activity during the latter half of the 20th century has limited the number of Ringed Plover pairs that can now breed in the islands. More recently, the 2000 Breeding Bird Atlas located up to 39 pairs in 19 (28.3%) of the 67 1-km squares surveyed, with breeding confirmed in eleven of these (Chown & Lock 2002). This represents a 10% reduction on Allen's 1974 figure of 35 pairs (Allen 1974; Chown & Lock 2002).

British and Irish Ringed Plovers are either mainly sedentary or in winter move south as far as western France, whereas Britain and Ireland are used as a wintering area or as a stopover by birds from Greenland, Iceland and northern Europe. In addition, large numbers from Denmark and the Baltic countries winter in England and Ireland (Wernham *et al.* 2002).

One of the most interesting records for the islands involved a colour-ringed female Ringed Plover, SVS3372197, from a study programme on Getteron Island, Sweden (57.08°N 12.13°E), which returned for at least four successive years to winter on St Mary's; mainly in the area of Hugh Town but with one sighting from Tresco. This bird had been first ringed as an adult breeding female on Gretton Island on 8th June 1996. Particularly noteworthy are the speed with which she moved between breeding and wintering grounds, the early date of arrival back in Sweden and the obvious site-faithfulness in her chosen wintering area. All Scillonian records of this distinctively colour-ringed individual involve field sightings and all known details of this bird's movements are shown below. We know that in 1996 her chicks were taken by a Common Gull *Larus canus* whilst still only days old and that she left the breeding site in early July. In 1997 she paired with the same male as in the previous year but again failed to rear any young, being last seen in Sweden on 29th July, just 24 days before she was seen by the author chasing other Ringed Plovers in apparent territorial defence opposite the Mermaid Public House in Hugh Town.

Lock (1999) was of the opinion that Scilly might hold nationally important numbers of wintering Ringed Plovers, though he thought too little information might currently be available on British numbers to allow proper assessment. Gantlett (1998) advised that the smaller and darker *tundrae* or 'Tundra Ringed Plover' might be expected to occur in Britain. Although little information is available on the racial identification of Ringed Plover sightings in Scilly, details of four apparent *tundrae* on St Agnes in spring are given above. A total of 102 Ringed Plovers have been ringed on Scilly, 91 of these prior to 1970. One control and one recovery are shown below. In addition, Penhallurick (1969) lists two Ringed Plovers ringed in Essex, one in October 1958 and one in July 1959, both being found dead in Cornwall during January 1963.

**Controls**

SVS3372197  Ad  Getteron Island, Sweden 8th June 1996
            FR  Getteron Island July 1996
                                            FR  St Mary's Quay 14th October 1996
                                            FR  Pentle Bay, Tresco 16th October 1996
                                            FR  Porth Hellick, St Mary's 16th October 1996
            FR  Getteron Island 28th February 1997
            FR  Getteron Island 29th July 1997
                                            FR  St Mary's Quay 22nd August 1997
                                            FR  Town Beach, St Mary's 5th October 1997

|   |   |   |   |
|---|---|---|---|
|   | FR Getteron Island 17th February 1998 |   |   |
|   |   | FR | Porthloo, St Mary's 1st to 29th October 1998 |
|   | FR Getteron Island 20th July 1999 |   |   |
|   |   | FR | St Mary's Quay 15th August 1999 |

**Recoveries**

| 60395X | 1stW St Agnes 5th September 1960 | ? | Laredo, Santander, Spain 3rd October 1960 |
|---|---|---|---|

**Ringed Plover Ringing Recaptures**

## Semipalmated Plover  *Charadrius semipalmatus*  A  BBRC 50%

**Extremely rare migrant, full written description required by the BBRC.**

1978   One St Agnes 9th October to 9th November   *British Birds* 72: 520

Breeds North America, from Alaska east to northern Newfoundland and Nova Scotia. Migratory, wintering coastal South America from Patagonia north to Central America, West Indies and coastal southern USA. Monotypic.

The record of a female obtained at Rye, now East Sussex, on 8th April 1916 became embroiled in the infamous Hastings Rarities scandal and was consequently deleted from the British List in 1962 (Witherby *et al*. 1940; *British Birds* 55 – August 1962). Therefore, the first British and Irish record involved a first-year individual identified by Paul Dukes and present on St Agnes from 9th October to 9th November 1978 (Dukes 1980, 1982; BOURC 1980). This occurred on the same beach as Britain's first Spotted Sandpiper *Actitis macularia* in September 1965. The bird was first noticed when Dukes and local birder-farmer Frances Hicks heard an unusual call from an apparent Ringed Plover *C. hiaticula* as it flew towards them on 9th October. But it was soon lost to view and could not be relocated among up to 100 Ringed Plovers present locally until 11th, at which time clear views were obtained of the webbing between the bird's toes. The report and description in *IOSBR* 1978 record the bird as present until 12th November, but the BBRC apparently accepted the sighting only up until the 9th.

Observers apparently agreed that the call was perhaps the bird's most distinguishing feature, being described as 'chewee' and said to resemble a subdued version of the 'chuit' flight call of Spotted Redshank *T. erythropus*. However, the palmations were also surprisingly easy to see, particularly when the bird stood on boulders, or on flat sand, being more extensive between the outer and middle toes. It was also recognisably smaller than Ringed Plover, at times recalling Little Ringed Plover *C. dubius*, though Dukes thought the smaller 'Tundra Ringed Plover' *tundrae* might be closer in size, although none were available for comparison. Once familiar with the individual, it could readily be picked out from among accompanying Ringed Plovers. During its stay the bird became inclined to defend an area of beach from Ringed Plovers, at which times it was heard to emit a Sanderling *Calidris alba*-like 'chip-chip' anxiety call, which often drew attention to its precise whereabouts.

A subsequent claim of this species in southern Ireland was not accepted and so the only other British and Irish record up to 2000 was the long-staying individual at Dawlish Warren, Devon, from mid-April 1997, thought to have been in first-summer plumage. The lack of ringing recoveries between northeastern North America and the West Indies suggests the species opts for the long transoceanic crossing of the North Atlantic, direct to the West Indies or northeast South America (Cramp *et al*. 1977–94). As with several other North American species, this particular migration strategy should be conducive towards periodic transatlantic vagrancy, in which case we might expect more European and North African arrivals than the two in Britain and one or two in the Azores, one of which was ringed in North America (Yesou 1982). So perhaps birds are being overlooked. For further reading on the identification of this species see Mullarney (1991).

## Killdeer *Charadrius vociferus*   A   BBRC 19%

**Rare spring or autumn migrant or winter visitor, full written description required by the BBRC.**

| | | |
|---|---|---|
| 1885 | One (female) shot Tresco 14th January | Cornish 1885; Clark & Rodd 1906 |
| 1957 | One St Agnes 12th December | *CBWPSAR* 27; *British Birds* 51: 398 |
| 1963 | Up to two St Martin's 19th Nov to 16th January 1964 | *British Birds* 59: 300 |
| 1976 | One Samson 30th March to 7th April | *British Birds* 70: 420 |
| 1979 | One Bryher & St Mary's 8th to 16th November | *British Birds* 73: 505, 74: 466–467 |
| 1979 | Up to three Bryher & St Mary's 11th December to 7th February | *British Birds* 73: 505, 74: 466–467 |
| [1980 | One St Agnes 15th to 27th December] | Griffiths 1982 |
| 1982 | One (probable juvenile) St Martin's & Tresco 21st to 31st October | *British Birds* 76: 491–492 |
| 1989 | One St Mary's 15th to 26th November | *British Birds* 83: 461 |
| 2002 | One (first-year) St Agnes 4th to 8th November | *British Birds* 95: 667 |

Breeds North America, from central Alaska and Canada south through Central America. Migratory, wintering coastal and central-southern USA south to Chile. Polytypic: nominate *vociferus* occurs North America south to Florida and Mexico; *ternominatus* Bahamas and West Indies; *peruvianus* South America. North American population peaked late 1970s and early 1980s, with Canadian population crashing since 1983, though with slight recent recovery (Bryant 1997).

James Clark and Francis Rodd refer to 'a fat and hearty female' obtained at the western end of Tresco's Great Pool on 14th January 1885. It was shot by F Jenkinson (son of the Reverend J H Jenkinson) after frequenting the same area for several days and the skin was mounted by Penzance taxidermist Vingoe (Cornish 1885; Clark & Rodd 1906). Prior to this, a bird had been obtained by one of the Vingoe family in December 1884 from a site near St Columb in mainland Cornwall (Cornish 1885). As with so many species, we hear nothing more of it until one was found by St Agnes resident Lewis Hicks on 12 December 1957, following a severe westerly gale. Although obviously tired, the bird was nevertheless still wary and on being approached flew off in the direction of St Mary's. What was generally believed to have been the same bird was later shot near St Columb Major, Cornwall, on Boxing Day, 14 days later (*CBWPSAR* 27). Equally puzzling is the lack of any comment within the published report regarding the species' absence from Scilly for the past 70 years.

There have been a total of seven 20th century arrivals up until 1999, involving 10 individuals. Particularly noteworthy were the two multiple arrivals but also the unusually high percentage of winter records compared with other transatlantic migrants. The Chart shows all but the most recent, 21st century arrival date and these fit the national pattern well, with winter occurrences normal and birds in early spring and late autumn (Dymond *et al.* 1989). According to Cramp *et al.* (1977–94) Killdeer is unique among North American waders in sometimes being carried north up Atlantic coastal North America by late autumn and winter storms, with some even reaching Newfoundland. Birds reaching Scilly also remain longer than many other vagrants or migrants, the average length of stay being 25.4 days; the two longest 77 and 59 days, the shortest just one day. A bird at Godrevy in mainland Cornwall on 20th November 2002 was thought likely to have been the individual on St Agnes until the 8th.

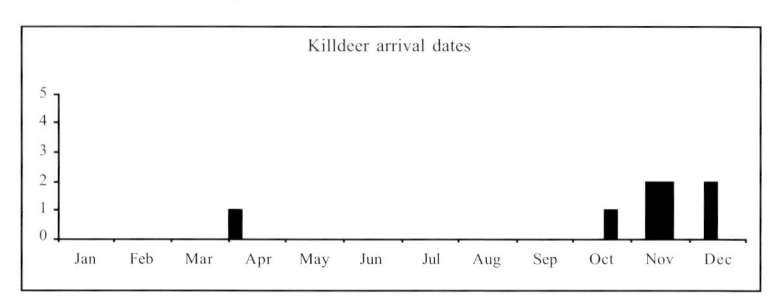

**Killdeer arrival dates**

The nine post-1958 Scillonian individuals represent 19% of the 48 British records accepted by the BBRC up to and including 1999.

# Kentish Plover *Charadrius alexandrinus* A

**Extremely rare spring and autumn migrant. Treated by the BBRC as a national Scarce Migrant, full written description required by the SRP.**

- 1854 One (killed) Scilly October   Penhallurick 1973
- 1881 One Tresco September   Clark & Rodd 1906
- 1965 One St Agnes 29th March to 10th April
- 1965 One St Mary's Airport 10th October
- 1966 One St Agnes 18th to 24th October
- 1992 One (female) Periglis, St Agnes 17th & 18th May
- 1994 One Great Bay, St Martin's 20th-21st May

Fragmentary breeding range across central Eurasia, south to northeast Africa, Sri Lanka and Taiwan, plus western and southern North America, Caribbean and west-coast South America. Migratory in north of range, generally dispersive in south. Polytypic: nominate *alexandrinus* occurs Eurasia, northern Africa south to Mauritania and west to India and Mongolia; *tenuirostris* or 'Snowy Plover' southeast USA and Caribbean; *nivosus* also known as 'Snowy Plover', western and central USA; *dealbatus* Japan, eastern China and local islands; with further two forms in western South America and Sri Lanka. Removed from BBRC Rarities List January 1963 (Harber & Swaine 1963).

E H Rodd was familiar with Kentish Plover from three specimens obtained near Penzance in 1852, 1858 and 1871 (Rodd 1880). Earliest reference to it on Scilly is Penhallurick's mention of one shot in 1854 and recorded in a Couch manuscript (Penhallurick 1978), followed by one seen by Tresco gamekeeper David Smith beside the Abbey Pool in September 1881 (Clark & Rodd 1906). Smith's initial reaction was that it might have been Little Ringed Plover *C. dubius* but Clark and Rodd's comment throws considerable light on the level of identification skills demonstrated by these apparently gun-happy men on their isolated islands. For according to Clark and Rodd, Smith 'was particularly struck with its black legs, which corrected his first impression that it might be a Little Ringed Plover (*C. dubius*)'. And this from a man who, as far as we know, had never seen Kentish Plover before and who probably last saw a Little Ringed Plover on Scilly twenty years beforehand (Rodd 1863a).

A period of 84 years elapsed before the next reported sighting of this species in Scilly, involving a bird seen on a St Agnes beach in October 1965. It was soon followed, however, by one on St Mary's Airfield in October that same year and by another the following year, again on St Agnes. The bird on St Agnes in May 1992 was an unexpected addition to the annual sponsored birdwatch, and the last of six Scillonian records came from the north side of St Martin's in 1994. There seems no easy explanation for the substantial gap between the first Tresco individual and the two in 1965 or, for that matter, the general paucity of records, given Scilly's reputation for harbouring migrant waifs and strays from continental Europe. Nevertheless, it seems reasonable to suggest that some may have been overlooked during the 19th and early 20th centuries. And, although early issues of the *CBWPSAR* often lacked basic information (as with Ringed Plover *C. hiaticula*, which failed to get a mention in many years), such omissions more often involved common species. We might therefore expect any Kentish Plover sightings to have been recorded. The Chart includes all five 20th century records, earliest of which was 29th March and the latest any bird was seen was 24th October. The shortest stay was just a single day and the longest 13 days, with an average stay of 4.8 days per individual.

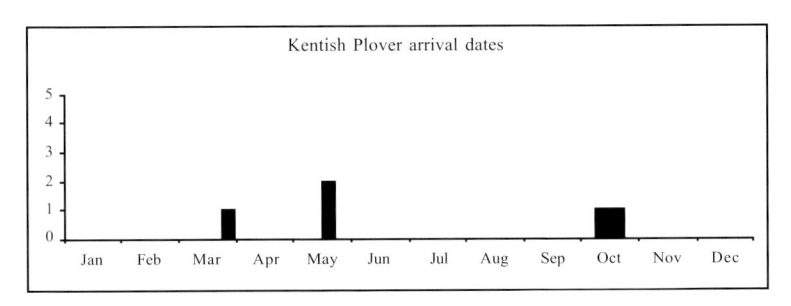

Kentish Plover arrival dates

The closest to Scilly that Kentish Plover breeds is France (including Brittany and the Cherbourg peninsula), Belgium, Netherlands, Germany and Denmark. All those populations are mainly or partially migratory, wintering either within the breeding range or south into northern tropical Africa (Cramp *et al.* 1977–94). However, the pattern and extent of migration is obscured by the presence of wintering individuals, though main northwards movement occurs during March to April, whereas the main autumn movement occurs during August and September. The two recognisably different North American forms of 'Snowy Plover' might be expected to occur in Scilly, as elsewhere in western Britain and Ireland.

Up until 1968, there were 22 Kentish Plover records for Cornwall and Scilly combined, compared with 11 for Little Ringed Plover (Penhallurick 1969). However, that situation has changed markedly, with just 57 Kentish Plover records all told up until 1999, but with the Little Ringed Plover total up around 275 by the same year.

## Caspian Plover *Charadrius asiaticus* A BBRC 50%

**Extremely rare migrant, full written description required by the BBRC.**

1988   One (male) St Agnes 21st May   Pellow 1990; *British Birds* 82: 522, 83: 549-551; *Ibis* 133: 218

Breeds central Asia, east from Caspian Sea into Kazakhstan, northern Iran and possible northwest China. Long-distance migrant, winters northeast Africa to South Africa. Monotypic.

Prior to the arrival on St Agnes in 1988, the BOURC had downgraded the species to category B, following 50 or more years since the first British record of two in Norfolk in May 1890 (BOURC 1991; Palmer 2000). The skin of one of the Norfolk birds is now in Norwich museum. The St Agnes bird arrived following several days of light to moderate southeasterly winds and was discovered by Keith Pellow as he walked across Wingletang Down. Immediately impressing him with its conspicuous orange-chestnut breast, which brought immediate thoughts of one of the two sand plovers *C. mongolus* or *C. leschenaultii*. However, after a more careful examination of the bird it became obvious it was a summer-plumage male Caspian Plover. The bird was seen by a few local and visiting birders and was seen going to roost that evening, but regardless of that could not be found next day and was not seen again. This was to the greater misfortune of several hundred birders who had crossed from the mainland early on 22nd in the hope of adding it to their British life list (Pellow 1990).

During its brief stay, the bird frequented the dry Wingletang area and was watched feeding in a typically plover-like fashion, with little short runs before stopping to pick up prey items from the ground. It was quite confiding, allowing observers to approach to about 10 m, preferring then to run rather than take flight. And on the two occasions when it did take flight it moved only short distances before continuing feeding; both times it called and this was described as a sharp 'chirrit' and an even sharper 'trit' (Pellow 1990).

Another, or even the same bird, was present at Aberlady Bay, Lothian, from 12th to 13th July that year, representing possibly the second British and Irish record (*British Birds* 82: 522). Acceptance by the BBRC of these two records was made easier by the species' scarcity in captivity and, in the case of the first record, by a photograph of the bird (Pellow 1990). A long-distance migrant, in spring Caspian Plover moves on a northeast axis to reach its breeding grounds; other species demonstrating this same pattern show a tendency towards spring appearances in Britain. Nevertheless, these remain the only British or Irish records up to and including 1999.

## Dotterel (Eurasian Dotterel) *Charadrius morinellus* A

**Regular spring and autumn migrant in small numbers.**

Breeds extreme northern Eurasia, from Scotland east to Bering Sea, also central Asia with small isolated populations central-southern Europe. Migratory, wintering mainly Middle East and North Africa. Monotypic. Included on Annex I of 1979 EEC 'Birds Directive'. Amber-listed in UK: 50% or more of UK breeding population at ten or fewer sites (Gregory *et al.* 2002).

This seems to be one of the few species almost entirely missed by the 19th century naturalists on Scilly. For mainland Cornwall E H Rodd was uncharacteristically brief, taking the view that it seldom appeared in the county, and then mainly on the open moors near the sea and usually in autumn (Rodd 1880). Rodd's first specific mention involved a bird procured near Helston on the Lizard peninsula in September 1868. There appears to be just a single 19th century record from Scilly, concealed in the pages of the *Royal Cornwall Gazette* for 1863 and involving a bird killed in early November that year (Penhallurick 1969). It was not subsequently reported from the island again until a group of three and then two more were recorded on Bryher during September 1956 (*CBWPSAR* 26). From that time it was reported almost annually, leaving little room for doubt that it had previously been overlooked in the islands. Summarising the situation on Scilly up until the mid-1960s, Penhallurick pointed out that most subsequent records had come from well-watched St Agnes and all in autumn between the dates of 27th August and 7th October, apart that is from one on St Mary's on 29th April 1962 and three over Tresco on 21st April 1967.

Looking at the ten years from 1990, a total of 25 Dotterels appeared during spring and 31 during autumn. Spring arrivals occurred at an average of 2.5 per year, in the range 1–9. The earliest arrival was 4th April (1997) and the latest any bird remained was 28th May. Autumn birds occurred at an average of 3.1 per year, in the range 1–7, though there may have been duplication in some years involving inter-site movement. The earliest autumn arrival was on 3rd September and the latest any bird was seen was 30th October. As might be expected, birds tended to frequent areas of open, short-vegetation heathland, often, but by no means always, on what on Scilly passes for 'high ground', e.g. Tresco's Castle Down, Bryher's Shipman Head Down or Giant's Castle on St Mary's, though short-grass areas such as St Mary's Airport and the Golf Course were also favoured. The greatest number of birds recorded together was five, on 5th May 1993, though singles predominated, with two together in ten out of the 40 or so sightings. A bird in the Giant's Castle area in mid October 1991 for five days was briefly accompanied by a Buff-breasted Sandpiper *Tryngites subruficollis*.

Dotterel breeding in northeast Siberia are long-distance migrants, wintering at least as close to Britain as Iran. Ringing evidence points to European birds, from as far north as Finnish Lapland, wintering in North Africa, where they are joined by at least some individuals from central-southern Europe, e.g. the Austrian Alps (Cramp *et al.* 1977–94). Little appears to be known about the movements of birds from further east in Europe and Asia, though a bird ringed in Ireland in winter was recovered in Siberia the following June. Dotterel may differ from most other wader species in showing a low between-year site-tenacity, a Scottish-ringed chick having been recovered in Denmark in autumn the following year and a Finnish-ringed chick in Siberia three years later. Examples such as these, plus the absence of any subspeciation, despite a widespread and fragmentary breeding range, perhaps have their origins in this lack of between-year site-tenacity; assisted perhaps by extensive intermixing within the wintering range. If this is the case, birds passing through Scilly could arrive from, or be heading for, breeding areas as far away as eastern Siberia, but seem most likely to involve the British population, an imaginary line drawn from the Scottish breeding and Moroccan wintering areas passing directly through Scilly (Wernham *et al.* 2002).

In Siberia, females commence departing the grounds from July, though they do so later in western Europe, e.g. early August in Scotland. Migration is overland on a broad front, often via traditional staging points, first birds arriving in their winter quarters by September. Importantly, perhaps, many from further east pause to moult in the Caspian area, presumably accounting for late autumn sightings on migration. Spring passage through western Europe occurs mainly during April and May, birds reaching northern European breeding grounds by late May to mid-June (Cramp *et al.* 1977–94). The closest breeding Dotterel populations to Scilly are in Scotland and southern Norway (Hagemeijer & Blair 1997).

Parslow (1967a) reported on a widespread 19th century decline in northern Scotland, allegedly due to shooting and egg-collecting, but with an increase by the 1960s to between 60 and 150 pairs. This perhaps helps to explain the lack of 19th century records from Scilly and the obvious improvement since the mid-20th century.

## American Golden Plover *Pluvialis dominica* A BBRC 12.8%

Scarce migrant, mainly in autumn, full written description required by the BBRC. Birds arrived in 22 (73%) of the 30 years 1971–2000.

    1962    One St Agnes 30th September to 10th October
    1971    One (adult) Tresco 6th to 14th September
    1972    One St Mary's 2nd to 7th August

1973 One St Mary's 20th to 25th September
1973 Two St Mary's & St Agnes 28th September to 15th October; one to 20th
1975 One St Mary's 18th & 19th September
1977 One St Mary's 9th to 13th May
1977 One (immature) St Mary's 14th to 23rd September
1978 One St Agnes 25th to 27th October
1979 One (juvenile) St Mary's, St Agnes & Gugh 12th September to 16th October
1982 One (juvenile) St Mary's 31st October to at least 14th November
1984 One (adult) St Agnes 13th September to 4th October
1984 One (first-winter) St Agnes & St Mary's 31st October to 1st January 1985
1985 One (adult) St Mary's 3rd to 22nd August
1985 One (juvenile) St Agnes & St Mary's 7th to 16th October
1987 One (juvenile) St Mary's 7th October
1989 One (juvenile) St Mary's & St Agnes 23rd September to at least 2nd October
1990 One (juvenile) Tresco & St Martin's 11th to 17th October
1991 One (juvenile) St Agnes & St Mary's 26th September to 16th October
1992 One (first-summer) Tresco 26th May to 7th June
1993 One (juvenile) St Mary's & St Agnes 14th October to 4th November
1994 One (juvenile) St Mary's 19th September
1995 One (adult) Tresco 23rd to 25th August
1996 One (adult) Tresco 5th August
1996 One (adult) St Agnes 9th September
1996 One (juvenile) St Mary's & St Agnes 13th September to 2nd October
1997 One (adult) St Mary's & Tresco 20th September to 12th October
1997 One (adult) St Martin's, Tresco & St Mary's 21st to 24th September
1998 One (juvenile) St Agnes & St Mary's 21st September to 17th October
1998 One (juvenile) St Agnes 11th to 17th October
2000 One (first-summer) St Mary's 30th May to 5th June
2000 One (juvenile) Tresco 1st November

Breeds arctic North America, wintering South America. Monotypic, occurs Alaska east to Baffin Island. Formerly considered conspecific with Pacific Golden Plover *P. fulva* (BOURC 1986).

Although the BOU did not separate American and Pacific Golden Plovers until the mid-1980s, earliest identification of the former species on Scilly occurred on St Agnes on 30th September 1962. The first for the Cornish mainland did not arrive until October 1986. Up to and including year 2000, a total of 33 American Golden Plovers arrived in Scilly, the only multiple arrival involving two on St Agnes in late September 1973. The graph includes all 33 arrival dates and shows a very obvious main peak around the third week of September, with a smaller, separate concentration in late October plus three May records. The earliest spring arrival was 9th May and the latest on the 30th, giving a spring arrival window of just 22 days; the latest any bird was present during spring being 7th June. The earliest autumn arrival date was 2nd August and the latest was 1st November, whilst the latest any bird remained during the latter half of the year was 14th November. There were just five single-day records, one each in August, October and November and two during September. Other than that, the shortest individual stay was two days and the longest 35 days, the average length of stay being 12.9 days. Birds arriving during spring or in August remained less time, i.e. 7.6 days for spring and 7.5 for August, compared to October and November arrivals, which remained significantly longer: 14.2 and 16.1 days respectively. During the 1990s, American Golden Plover occurred in all years except 1999, making it a near annual migrant.

As with some other wader species, newly arrived American Golden Plovers typically announced their presence by aerial calling as they carried out an immediate tour of the main islands. Birds were surprisingly catholic in their choice of habitats on Scilly, being seen feeding or roosting on grassy areas, e.g. St Mary's Golf Course, short-vegetation dry heathland, ploughed fields and both sandy and rocky beaches. Birds frequently moved between sites, one consequence of which was that most sightings were multiple-observer. Birds also showed a marked tendency not to associate with any Golden Plovers *P. apricaria* also present in the islands. The two birds that frequented St Agnes during early October 1998 were last seen on St Mary's Airport on 17th, following which two appeared together at Sennen on mainland Cornwall on the 18th. The individual on Tresco on 5th August 1996 was first found by birders searching for the Lesser Crested Tern *Sterna bengalensis* discovered in the same area three days before. A bird at Porth Hellick, St Mary's, for 20 days from 29th August 1976, was initially identified as this species, but after further review was accepted as Pacific Golden Plover some 20 years after it departed (*British Birds* 70: 420, 80: 534, 90: 469–470). Interestingly, this *fulva* record pre-dated the arrival of all American Golden Plovers on Scilly by five days.

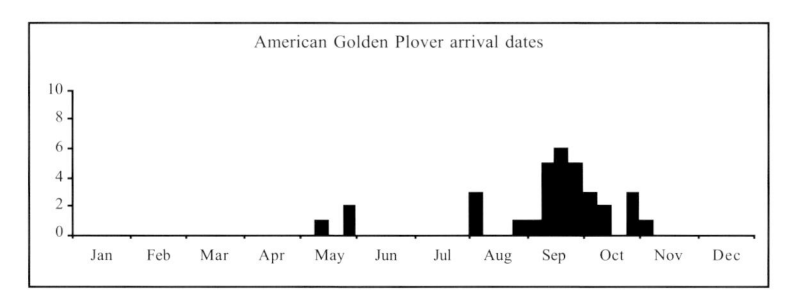

American Golden Plover arrival dates

In North America, birds move south during September and early October, most juveniles negotiating interior Canada and the USA. However, most adults and a proportion of juveniles first move east through the breeding areas before making a transoceanic flight out over the North Atlantic direct to northern South America (Cramp *et al.* 1977–94). Predictably, and as with most other species using this high-risk strategy, individuals are at risk of an involuntary transatlantic crossing when encountering severe weather in the mid-Atlantic. American Golden Plovers have occurred in a number of other European countries, including Iceland, France, Netherlands, Germany, Spain, Portugal and even as far east as Turkey and Ukraine. Return spring passage is via the central North American flyway, thereby accounting for the lack of European arrivals at that time of year. It remains debatable whether birds arriving in Britain in spring are same-year transatlantic migrants or wandering birds from a crossing in a previous year.

A total of 250 claimed American Golden Plover sightings were accepted by the BBRC during the period 1958–1999, therefore the 32 birds sighted on Scilly during that same period represent over 12% of the British total.

## Pacific Golden Plover *Pluvialis fulva* A BBRC 2.2%

**Extremely rare autumn migrant, full written description required by the BBRC.**

1976   One (adult) St Mary's 29th July to 17th August   *British Birds* 70: 420, 80: 534, 90: 469–470

New and Old World long-distance migrant, breeds north and northeast Asia and western Alaska, wintering southern Asia and Australasia. Monotypic. Formerly considered conspecific with American Golden Plover *P. dominica* (BOURC 1986).

The sole Scillonian record involved an adult present at Porth Hellick, St Mary's, from 29th July to 17th August 1976. However, the bird was not officially acknowledged as this species until twenty years later, following a BBRC review of golden plover records (*British Birds* 70: 420, 80: 534, 90: 469–470). For a useful paper on identification of Pacific and American Golden Plovers *P. dominica* see Golley and Stoddart (1991). A total of 45 Pacific Golden Plovers have now been accepted by the BBRC and this single individual represents just over 2%. It is worth noting that this record pre-dated all American Golden Plover arrival dates in Scilly by five days.

Many birds head south or southeast on a transoceanic route out into the Pacific, using Hawaii as a major staging post, and therefore make huge sea crossings. Birds commence leaving their tundra breeding grounds in late July or early August (Cramp *et al.* 1977–94).

## American/Pacific Golden Plover  *Pluvialis dominica/fulva*

Four birds currently fall into the unidentifiable category, only the last of which appears to have been accepted by the BBRC as one or other of these two species.

Unidentified non-*apricaria* Golden Plover Records
  [1962   One St Agnes 30th September to 10th October]   *CBWPSAR* 32
  [1971   One Tresco 6th to 14th September]   *IOSBR* 1971
  [1972   One St Mary's 2nd to 7th August]   *IOSBR* 1972
   1982   One (adult) Gugh & St Mary's 17th August to 10th September   *British Birds* 76: 492, 90: 469

Both long-distance migrants. American Golden Plover breeds North America from central Alaska east to Baffin Island and winters South America, whereas Pacific Golden Plover breeds north and northeast Asia and western Alaska, wintering southern Asia and Australasia. Formerly considered conspecific (BOURC 1986).

The majority of non-*apricaria* golden plovers arriving in Scilly are eventually attributed to *P. dominica*. A few, however, are either seen too briefly for a positive identification, or for one reason or another are considered beyond safe identification, e.g. abnormal plumage features, or inadequate descriptions.

## Golden Plover (European Golden Plover)   *Pluvialis apricaria*  A

**Annual migrant in moderate numbers during spring and autumn. It also winters in varying numbers.**

Breeds northern Europe, including Iceland, plus northwest Asia, wintering south to North Africa, Middle East and southern Caspian Sea. Monotypic, though early authorities, e.g. Witherby *et al.* (1940), recognised two forms: *apricaria* or 'Southern Golden Plover' and *altifrons* or 'Northern Golden Plover'. Downgraded from Amber- to Green-listed in UK 2002 (Gregory *et al.* 2002). National 18% decline 1994–99 (Bashford & Noble 2000).

Golden Plover seems to have been well known to the 19th century naturalists and sportsmen on both the Cornish mainland and on Scilly, if only because of its former status as a quarry species. E H Rodd thought it generally distributed on the Cornish moors and heaths in spring but it seems not to have bred (Rodd 1880; Holloway 1996), although more recently, at least, a few pairs are known to have bred on Devon's Dartmoor (Gibbons *et al.* 1993). First specific mention of Golden Plover on Scilly is probably E H Rodd's nephew Francis's description of apparently newly arrived birds flying about restlessly on St Mary's on 22nd December 1864. This was followed by his description of one among a mixed bag of Snipe *Gallinago gallinago*, Teal *Anas crecca*, Water Rail *Rallus aquaticus*, Rabbit *Oryctolagus cuniculus* and one Bittern *Botaurus stellaris*, all shot on the St Mary's Moors on Christmas Day 1864 (Rodd 1880). In 1870, the same observer noted first arrivals of the year on 30th September, presumably on Tresco, whereas by 11th October they had become plentiful. From 23rd to 28th December that same year, Francis made four excursions to St Mary's in that winter's snowy weather, finding 'plovers' – almost certainly this species. The Tresco game books show that included among the list of game and wildfowl killed in Scilly during winter 1878–79 were 84 Golden Plovers. All of the above led the elder Rodd to describe this species as a 'periodical migrant, varying according to circumstances, in numbers and times of appearance' (Rodd 1880).

By comparison with most other species, James Clark and Francis Rodd had much to say about Golden Plover in their early 20th century review of Scilly's birds (Clark & Rodd 1906). They confirmed that it arrived in September but 'was not well established until the latter half of October' and pointed out that in a normal winter numbers were 'remarkably uniform', though considerable influxes occurred whenever the mainland experienced severe weather. However, without, unfortunately, commenting on the mainland weather at the time, these two point out that on 30th January 1872 F Jenkinson (son of the Reverend J H Jenkinson) shot 17 Golden Plovers on the wing on Tresco's Appletree Banks beach, using one shot from a 12-bore shotgun and number 7 shot. Similarly, the same authors describe a flock of 40–50 on Castle Down, Tresco, during winter 1903–04, with 30–40 on St Martin's and 20 on St Mary's, but without making clear whether these were exceptional or normal numbers. They did, however, explain that birds normally left the shore areas at high tide to roost on the 'downs'. Clark and Rodd's comment that Golden Plover remain until May concluded their observations on this species, though under Lapwing *Vanellus*

*vanellus* they made clear that on 13th February 1900 huge numbers arrived among a flock of Lapwings three miles long.

Much later, Penhallurick (1969) mentioned an earliest arrival date of 5th August, also clarifying the numbers situation by mentioning flocks of 20–50 on most main islands during normal winters. He suggested, however, that these figures were 'considerably augmented' during hard weather, birds sometimes arriving several hundreds at a time and, as in February 1900, often in company with Lapwings. Penhallurick also felt confident enough to suggest most wintering birds left the islands by March, at which time passage flocks were most common, the latest date being 26th May.

During the ten years from 1990, the overall picture was much as described by previous writers, though in general numbers of wintering birds were low, most often in single figures but in other years involving several flocks of up to 70 birds. The only co-ordinated winter counts were those of December–January 1984–85, when just 25 were recorded on the main islands (Kirby 1988), and the late January 1997 two-day Shorebird Survey, when a single individual was found. Interestingly none were recorded during a four-day mid-March 1996 Wader Survey (Lock 1996). Spring flocks could be surprisingly high, as on 25th April 1994 when 108 were on St Mary's Golf Course and 26 on Tresco, with at least 150 on the islands on 26th–27th, reducing to just one by 28th. The single obvious reference to the presence of birds of the so-called *altifrons* form, or 'Northern Golden Plover', involved birds passing through St Agnes in spring 1999, when up to 20 were present on various dates between 20th April and 6th June, these said to represent a 'high percentage' of those present on the island (*IOSBR* 1999).

There are two 19th century lighthouse records, both from St Agnes. At noon on 4th October 1880, an unspecified number arrived in rain during a moderate east-southeasterly gale, whilst another flock, again of an unspecified number, moved southwest at 4 pm on 10th January 1881 (Harvie-Brown *et al.* 1881). British and Irish Golden Plovers are both sedentary and migratory, some moving south as far as Iberia or Morocco (Wernham *et al.* 2002). Wintering Icelandic birds are confined almost exclusively to Ireland, few going further south, whereas birds from eastern populations winter from Britain and Ireland south into Iberia and Morocco. The majority of Continental birds migrate southwest during autumn (Cramp *et al.* 1977–94), eastern populations departing their breeding areas from July, those reaching Morocco doing so from November onwards. Migrants passing through the Netherlands originate from as far away as Russia and are known to move east into mainly southeast and southern England (Wernham *et al.* 2002). Return movement from North Africa occurs from February, breeding areas in the far northeast being reoccupied by early June.

One Golden Plover has been ringed on Scilly, since 1970, but it was not recovered and there are no controls. However, Penhallurick listed four controls for mainland Cornwall up until 1969, two of which were ringed in Iceland (one chick, one adult) and shot in west Cornwall the same autumn. Both of the remaining two were ringed in the Netherlands during early spring, one being shot on Bodmin Moor three years later, the other in west Cornwall later the same year. Those ringed in Iceland will most likely originate from that country, whereas those ringed in the Netherlands were presumably on passage from further north or east when ringed.

# Grey Plover *Pluvialis squatarola* A

**Annual migrant in small to moderate numbers, with fewer in spring and with winter numbers varying between years. A former alleged preference for Samson no longer appears to hold true.**

Breeds extreme northeast West Palearctic, Asia and North America. Migratory, wintering coastally on all continents and main islands, from about 40°N south to Antarctic Ocean. Monotypic. Amber-listed in UK: 20% or more of East Atlantic Flyway non-breeding population in UK, 50% or more at ten or fewer sites (Gregory *et al.* 2002).

E H Rodd was rather circumspect in his initial 19th century account of Grey Plover, describing it as a 'Periodical migrant, varying, according to circumstances, in numbers and time of appearance' (Rodd 1878b). Later, however, he revised his earlier comments and described it as 'not uncommon in winter' (Rodd 1880). In fact, we can be more positive now, in the knowledge that it arrives annually in the islands from around August or early September. Winter numbers perhaps depend to some extent on the severity of the weather elsewhere and few are seen much after May. Earliest mention of it in the islands is probably E H

*Birds of the Isles of Scilly*

Rodd's nephew Francis's report of a few on Scilly's beaches on 19th December 1864 (Rodd 1880). The same observer recorded that in 1879 it became plentiful in the islands by 11th October. By the turn of the 20th century, Francis Rodd and co-author James Clark were able to confirm that it was indeed not uncommon in autumn, though casual in winter, sometimes singly and sometimes in parties of three to four, and was rarely seen anywhere but on the beaches and with a decided preference for Samson (Clark & Rodd 1906). The elder Rodd also referred to specimens obtained near Penzance, in west Cornwall, in apparent full-breeding plumage (Rodd 1880), and though he gives no dates these were presumably passage individuals nevertheless.

Penhallurick (1969) considered this one of Europe's 'most renowned' migrants, breeding as it does in extreme northern Asia and North America and being found in winter south as far as the Antarctic seas. The same author confirmed earlier thoughts on its movements through Scilly, arriving mostly from mid-September and leaving the islands annually by 5th May. The most he could find recorded together was nine, in September 1959, with up to five on St Agnes during winter, though he thought greater numbers might be present on other islands, e.g. Samson. Penhallurick also thought it less frequent in spring, occurring as it did in only three of the years from 1957.

Comparing the above figures for the period up until the mid-1960s with those for the ten years commencing 1990, we find that a greater depth of knowledge of Grey Plover movements throughout the year enables a fuller picture to emerge, although still with the familiar difficulties in distinguishing late wintering individuals from any genuine spring migrants. Quite small numbers were present within the islands at the start of some years, with sometimes just singles on each island, compared with 63 in the St Agnes wader roost alone during winter 1993–94. The only co-ordinated all-island winter count during the period was the two-day late January 1997 Winter Shorebird Survey, when 76 were recorded on the six main islands; including 46 (60%) on Bryher and only two on Samson (*IOSBR* 1979). This compared with 111 recorded over a slightly larger area during winter 1984–85, including 30 on Bryher, 29 on Tresco and 16 on Samson (Kirby 1988).

The latest spring individual was usually reported during late April or May, but up to five birds apparently present throughout June and July in some years rather confused the picture. Interestingly, a co-ordinated four-day non-breeding wader survey during mid-March 1996 (Lock 1996) located just 24 Grey Plovers on all main islands, ten of which were on Bryher with none on Samson. The events of spring 1994 appeared not unusual, passage in the period being confined to six on Tresco on 25th March and two on nearby Bryher on 13th May. Return passage was evident from around late August or September but the presence in July of apparent summering individuals may have clouded the picture. Autumn counts varied substantially both within and between years and lacked any co-ordinated all-island effort. Therefore, we have only the benefit of random spontaneous site counts. Highest flock count seems to have been 20 that arrived on 1st September 1991, though the dispersed nature of feeding Grey Plovers perhaps created difficulties deciding exactly what constituted a flock. There may be some evidence among the counts that numbers decrease after the initial early autumn flush of arrivals.

Grey Plovers wintering in the West Palearctic originate from at least northern Russia, the most easterly recovery of a bird ringed in Europe being 80°E in western Siberia, on a line roughly midway between Novaya Zemlya and Severnaya Zemlya (Cramp *et al.* 1977–94). Some individuals passing through the West Palearctic move on south as far as southern Africa, though those on the western seaboard perhaps go no further than the equator. Many wintering in South Africa, however, apparently reach there via more easterly routes. There is compelling evidence from museum skins that the majority, perhaps up to 90%, of birds wintering in tropical Africa are female, whereas most remaining in temperate European latitudes, again around 90%, are male (Cramp *et al.* 1977–94). A similar situation apparently applies in both the Americas and Asia. Most birds commence leaving the breeding grounds in August, adults preceding juveniles and with the latter passing through the White Sea area during September to mid-October. Birds commence arriving in Britain from July onwards, arrivals continuing well into winter. In central Europe, peak numbers occur during early to mid-September and in eastern England during late August. Although return passage from southern Africa commences from February, some birds wintering within Europe also depart this early, though the bulk of spring migration through Europe occurs rather later, i.e. April to late May in eastern England. According to Cramp *et al.*, non-breeding birds, presumably one-year-olds, commonly remain within the wintering areas, including England, during summer. This presumably accounts for those troublesome Scillonian summer records which probably also involve known northerly movements of birds within the wintering range during spring. There is also substantial evidence that individuals reoccupy the same winter feeding areas between years. Finally, one early 20th century indication of migratory movement on Scilly involved a bird killed striking the Bishop Rock light on the night of 21st–22nd October 1908 (Ogilvie-Grant 1910). No Grey Plovers have been ringed in Scilly and there are no controls.

## Lapwing (Northern Lapwing) *Vanellus vanellus* A

**Scarce migrant or winter visitor; sometimes appearing in moderate to large numbers during cold weather.**

Breeds central Eurasia, from Iberia, France, Britain and Ireland east to China. West Palearctic birds winter south to North Africa, Nile Valley and Middle East. Monotypic. Amber-listed in UK: moderate (41%) breeding decline over past 25 years; 29.7% of East Atlantic Flyway non-breeding population in UK (Gregory *et al.* 2002). National 20% decline 1994–99 (Bashford & Noble 2000), though BTO Waterways Bird Survey recorded 165% increase 1975–2000.

Typically, Lapwing arrivals on Scilly are associated with unpleasant weather elsewhere in Britain or continental Europe, and are often accompanied by noisy flocks of Redwings *Turdus iliacus* and Fieldfares *T. pilaris*. They are always difficult to miss as they move about the islands in tight groups with their distinctive 'flap-wing' flight and are often identifiable as new arrivals by their initial restless behaviour (Rodd 1880). Outside these periods of cold weather, most arrivals may be the product of post-fledging or post-breeding dispersal.

By far the earliest evidence of Lapwing on Scilly comes in the form of a portion of tibia unearthed from Bronze or Iron Age levels of the prehistoric site on Nornour in the Eastern Isles (Turk 1971). Nineteenth century writers knew it as a largely winter visitor, Gilbert White going as far as to suggest it arrived around Christmas (in Jesse 1887). In truth, however, it often arrived in autumn, though seldom in the kind of numbers involved during midwinter. Indeed, most specific early references to it apparently involve winter arrivals, by far the most dramatic of which is James Clark and Francis Rodd's account of events on 13th February 1900 when a great flock of Lapwings, three miles long, passed over the islands from the northwest. The rearguard, with followers and stragglers, settled, and next day the islands were alive with an extraordinary assortment of Lapwings, Golden Plovers *Pluvialis apricaria*, Starlings *Sturnus vulgaris*, Song Thrushes *Turdus philomelos*, Mistle Thrushes *T. viscivorus*, Blackbirds *T. merula*, Redwings and Fieldfares. However, these quickly passed on, leaving many dead behind. The authors concluded by pointing out that it was seldom present after mid-April and had never nested in the islands, numbers normally remaining remarkably constant, as indeed did those of Golden Plover. Not long after 1900, Witherby (1919) revealed details of a far more remarkable incident, involving a transatlantic crossing of large numbers of Lapwings, very probably in excess of 1,000, during midwinter. One feature of which was a Cumbria-ringed individual shot in Newfoundland on 27th December. Not unexpectedly, this Atlantic crossing was associated with most unusual weather conditions.

There are three late 19th century records of Lapwings noted passing St Agnes Lighthouse, all from the same source. The first was on 4th October 1880, when birds were seen at noon in a moderate east-southeast gale (Harvie-Brown *et al.* 1881). The next involved birds seen at 4 pm on 11th January 1881 (Harvie-Brown *et al.* 1882) and the last birds passing at 9 am on 22nd February, also 1881 and again in a strong east-northeast breeze (Harvie-Brown *et al.* 1882).

The earliest 20th century mention of Lapwing on Scilly seems to be the account of an 'enormous influx' of this and many other species during the severe weather of early 1947 (*CBWPSAR* 17). Reportedly, this included 'thousands' of Lapwings, plus Fieldfare, Redwing, Snipe *Gallinago gallinago* and Woodcock *Scolopax rusticola*, plus many others, mortality being described as very heavy. On the same page there appears an account of how, shortly after the onset of the bad weather, Lapwings, Golden Plovers and Mistle Thrushes completely disappeared from Cornwall, reappearing in mid-March once the situation had improved. The severe weather in winter 1961–62 prompted similar reports (Milne 1963), Lapwings allegedly arriving on St Agnes in their thousands, later suffering heavy mortality and being picked up dead in nearly every field.

Looking at the more recent period, things appear not to have changed, with 1981–82 being typical years. In the first of these two years 36 Lapwings were present on St Mary's on 5th February, with one on Tresco 23rd–27th April the only spring record. In autumn, one at Porth Hellick on 5th August increased to four by 10th, various numbers remaining about the island through September and October, up to a maximum of 22 in mid-October. Two December sightings involved 14 on St Mary's on 14th and five on 27th. By contrast, a flock of 25 were semi-resident on St Mary's during January and February 1982, though on 11th January a further 180 cold-weather refugees arrived from the mainland. By late February, however, only one could be found, with a single also subsequently noted on St Agnes and Tresco up until 9th May. By 29th July, post-breeding dispersal brought five back to St Mary's briefly, none being seen then until late September. Highest autumn count was 39, with eleven left by the year's end. Interestingly, Lapwing response to improvement in weather conditions elsewhere can be particularly rapid, as in 1985, when 750 to 1,000 arrived on St Mary's in late January, with 100–200 on St Agnes, all but 14 of which had departed by mid-February following a mainland thaw.

The remarkably vicious spell of cold weather that gripped most of mainland Britain during early 1963 was not experienced quite so severely on Scilly, though its effects in terms of cold-weather bird movements was very noticeable. On Scilly, this particular year provides a useful demonstration of difficulties involved in relying upon local published bird reports to review long-term, or national trends in bird populations. For neither Lapwing nor Golden Plover appear in the report's systematic list, which nonetheless was sufficiently detailed to mention a single Golden Oriole *Oriolus oriolus* and the presence of up to three Rooks *Corvus frugilegus*. However, we learn from the report's introduction that worst sufferers of what cold weather Scilly did have were, unsurprisingly, Lapwings and Golden Plovers, corpses of which 'littered the ground' (*CBWPSAR* 33).

Lapwings occasionally summer in Scilly or they are believed to do so, as in the case of one on Samson in late June 1986. Slightly more frequent are occasional summer wanders, including two on St Agnes for two days during early July 1987 and on St Mary's briefly later that same month. Less easy to explain though was the flock of about 100 watched flying southwest along the line of the Northern Isles on 15th July 1997. This was a surprisingly early date for such a large flock, especially as they appear not to have made landfall in the archipelago and were on a course taking then straight out into the Atlantic. Not that it is particularly unusual to see Lapwings or several other species heading out to sea in numbers, however. On 31st December 1961 a group of 30 Lapwings were watched heading southwest from St Agnes until they disappeared from view and Rooks *Corvus frugilegus* and Jackdaws *C. monedula* have been seen to do likewise; though are usually seen returning later.

Britain, Ireland, France and Iberia form the main European Lapwing wintering areas, a high proportion of birds in Britain originating from Scandinavia, the Netherlands and German populations (P Lack 1986). In this respect, the Norwegian individual shot on Tresco is of particular interest. British-bred Lapwings also winter within Britain, though many move south or east to continental Europe, or move west to Ireland. According to Lack, autumn movements into Britain may commence as early as June, but are unlikely to be easily separable from post-breeding dispersal of British birds. No Lapwings are recorded as having been ringed in Scilly, though there is the one Norwegian recovery.

**Controls**

?　　　　?　　Bryne, Jaeren, Norway 25th May 1941　　SH　Tresco 12th February 1945

**Lapwing Ringing Recaptures**

# Knot (Red Knot) *Calidris canutus* A

**Scarce migrant, annually in small numbers.**

Breeds discontinuously around edge of arctic seas outside West Palearctic, mainly northeast Canada, also Greenland, coastal northern Siberia and northern Alaska. Migratory, in West Palearctic wintering coastally south to North Africa and west-coast southern Africa. Polytypic: nominate *canutus*, or 'Siberian Knot' occurs central Siberia; *islandica*, or 'Greenland Knot' eastern Canadian high arctic and Greenland; *rufa* Canadian eastern low Arctic; *rogersi* northeast Siberia; identity of birds breeding Canadian central high arctic unclear. Amber-listed in UK: 20% or more of East Atlantic Flyway non-breeding population in UK, 50% or more at ten or fewer sites; unfavourable world winter conservation status (Gregory *et al.* 2002).

Probable earliest evidence of Knot in Scilly involves bone remains unearthed from the prehistoric site on Nornour in the Eastern Isles, where a humerus, tibio-tarsus and other smaller fragments were thought likely to be from this species (Turk 1984b).

Earliest 19th century mention of it is Francis Rodd's account of a bird shot in September 1857, this being the only known island record up until at least 1863 (Clark & Rodd 1906). However, that situation seems to have quickly altered, Francis's uncle, E H Rodd, publishing his nephew's account of five shot in Scilly between 5th and 8th September 1870 (Rodd 1870h, 1880). However, it must be borne in mind that the weather during winter of 1870–71 was particularly bad and apparently involved some unusual bird movements. For example, five Pectoral Sandpipers *C. melanotos* were shot about the same time as the five Knot. Nonetheless, by the early 20th century, James Clark and Francis Rodd thought Knot had probably become a regular visitor in small flocks during August and September, though it had still never been recorded in spring (Clark & Rodd 1906). Penhallurick (1969) identified the fact that largest flocks on mainland Cornwall up until that time, c. 1,000, were recorded in the east of the county, 35 being the maximum west as far as the Land's End peninsula. The same author pointed out that 45 was the largest flock recorded on Scilly. He also noted that mainland autumn passage commenced during late July and peaked in August, birds departing again before early April, those observed after this date assumedly on passage.

Examining the Scillonian data for the ten years from 1990, it is clear that Knot remains mainly a passage migrant and like several other wader species, e.g. Green Sandpiper *Tringa ochropus*, appears far more frequently in autumn. It was recorded in each of the ten years, though in only eight during spring. Autumn migration was a very recognisable affair, first arrivals being recorded between 6th and 31st August and the last sighting on 17th November, though mid- to late October was more usual. By comparison, spring arrival dates were more protracted, birds recorded from early February through to mid-April, apparently departing early May to early June. Outside of these dates birds were noted on 1st January 1997 (6) and behind St Mary's Quay on 3rd December 1993 (1). The largest flock reported during the ten-year period concerned twelve on Tresco on 26th August 1995. Unfortunately, there was the anticipated shortage of co-ordinated all-island counts during the period under review. These were confined to the two-day late January 1997 Winter Shorebird Survey, which recorded just one Knot (on Samson), and the similar four-day mid-March 1996 wader count, which recorded none. An earlier all-island midwinter wader survey (Kirby 1988) located ten wintering Knot on St Martin's during the period December–January 1984-85.

Birds of the form *islandica*, known as 'Greenland Knot', winter in western Europe (Wernham *et al.* 2002), whilst those of the nominate *canutus*, or 'Siberian Knot', pass through western Europe to winter in West Africa and either seems likely to occur in Scilly. There is at least one claimed British record of the pale form *rufa*, from the Canadian low Arctic (Gantlett 1998) and this too should presumably be looked for in Scilly, as elsewhere. Eight Knot have been ringed on Scilly, all prior to 1970; there are no controls or recoveries.

# Sanderling *Calidris alba* A

**Regular annual migrant in moderate numbers, by far the most numerous in autumn.**

Breeds arctic Canada and arctic central Asia, wintering coastal central and southern Europe, coastal and inland Africa, around the Indian Ocean, Southeast Asia and Australasia, also coastal North and South America. Monotypic.

Sanderlings are an obvious feature of Scilly's sandy beaches, where combined flocks totalling 300–400 individuals may be present during some years. E H Rodd provided little information other than that it occurred in the islands in both autumn and winter, though he also quoted from his nephew Francis Rodd, who in 1870 recorded its arrival around 20th August (Rodd 1880). In their useful end-of-century review, James Clark and Francis Rodd made clear that it appeared mainly in autumn, exceptionally, as in November 1902, in flocks of several hundreds (Clark & Rodd 1906). They further pointed out that it was remarkably tame when it first arrived. Occasionally flocks arrived during winter and, according to Clark and Rodd, the species was 'not infrequently seen in May'. The same authors suggested that these spring individuals were mostly immatures, although several on 29th of May 1903 were reportedly in breeding plumage.

Penhallurick gives the local Cornish name for Sanderling as 'towillees', allegedly after the flight call (Penhallurick 1969). In Scilly up until the mid-1960s, Penhallurick thought Sanderlings were to be seen in any month of the year, suggesting that on mainland Cornwall, however, it very much conformed to the pattern of autumn and spring migrants generally. Nevertheless, a quick glance at current data shows that even in Cornwall it is to be found in reasonable numbers year-round, or that is certainly the case now (*CBWPSAR* 69). In fact, Penhallurick thought it uncommon on Scilly only during the period mid-June to late July, although in some years first autumn birds appeared during late August. Peak site counts were in the region of 150–200 during autumn and 80 in spring, with a quoted winter count of 40 on St Agnes in late December.

Looking at the *IOSBR* for the ten years from 1990, there is an obvious pattern of mid- to late winter numbers in the range 150–350, at an average of 187, but with as few as 16 in 1999. The late January 1997 co-ordinated all-island Winter Shorebird Survey found a total of 309 individuals, with 134 (43%) on Tresco, 75 on St Mary's, 60 St Martin's and 40 St Agnes. Interestingly, an earlier count, during December and January 1984–85, recorded a very similar figure of 326 birds, most of which, 168 (51%), were on St Mary's, with Tresco holding the next highest numbers of 105 (32%) (Kirby 1988). As a consequence of these counts, Lock (1999) concluded that Scilly holds nationally important numbers of Sanderling, ranging between 13% and 19% of the UK wintering population.

There was a noticeable reduction in numbers during March, although the change from wintering birds to spring migrants was blurred, an all-island Non-Breeding Wader Survey of 256 during mid-March 1996 (Lock 1996) being difficult to interpret. And, although earliest spring arrival dates were impossible to determine, last spring sightings fell in the period 12th to 30th May, or at least for the four years where these were given. Apart from the 1996 survey, there are no co-ordinated all-island spring wader counts, maximum annual individual site counts falling in the range 40–142, at an average of 100. Since perhaps just one summering individual was present in most years, first autumn arrivals were more easily ascertained, dates for at least nine of the ten years falling within the surprisingly compact 29-day window of 1st to 29th July. Again, there is a lack of co-ordinated all-island counts during the autumn period, random individual site counts falling in the range 105–250, with an average of 196. However, the close proximity of inter-island site counts for early October 1999 suggested a minimum of 473 birds present in the islands, with a Tresco count of 300 later that same month. As with the early period, however, the conclusion of autumn passage merged into the winter period.

Along with Knot *C. canutus*, Sanderling is one of the major migrant travellers, breeding as it does on the edge of the Arctic Ocean and wintering south as far as the Cape of Good Hope and Cape Horn. In Europe, it winters regularly north at least as far as Denmark, being confined almost exclusively to tidal waters. Birds passing through the West Palearctic are believed to originate from two discrete areas, Russia and Greenland, though doubts remain over the precise wintering areas used by these two populations. Some authorities believe that one moults and winters in Europe, whilst the other merely stops off in Europe to regain fat deposits required for the remainder of their flight to Africa, though ringing returns suggest at least some individuals from both populations reach southern Africa. Adults depart Greenland breeding areas from mid-August, juveniles from early September, returning to Greenland from late May or early June, or Russia from early June.

Migration is by means of long flights using substantial fat deposits, up to 60% of lean weight, with birds departing South Africa carrying enough 'fuel' for estimated non-stop flights of 5,000 km (Cramp *et al.* 1977–94), and with spring fat deposits in eastern England perhaps adequate for a direct flight to Greenland. Importantly, like Knot, Sanderling uses a limited number of stopover sites of major importance. A total of 20 Sanderlings have been ringed in Scilly, 17 in the period before 1970. A bird ringed on Tresco's Abbey Pool in September 1967 was controlled in Lancashire in June the following year and Green (1978, in Cramp *et al.* 1977–94) refers to a bird colour-ringed in Greenland and recorded in Scilly during four subsequent autumns. Presumably this was the bird ringed in 1974 and mentioned as present in Scilly in July 1977 and in August 1978. More recently, up to three birds colour-ringed in southwest Iceland in May 1989 were present in the islands from September 1989 until at least the end of 1990, indicating perhaps that Sanderlings using Scilly originate from Greenland rather than from northern Russia.

**Controls**

| ? | ? | Iceland 21st to 28th May 1989 | FR | Up to three St Mary's 27th September 1989 to end of 1990 |

**Recoveries**

? 1stY Abbey Pool, Tresco 16th September 1967   CT   Southport, Lancashire 4th June 1977

**Sanderling Ringing Recaptures**

## Semipalmated Sandpiper  *Calidris pusilla*  A  BBRC 7.7%

**Rare autumn migrant, full written description required by the BBRC.**

1970  One Tresco 27th September   *British Birds* 67: 341, 72: 265
1984  One (juvenile) Tresco 30th September to 7th October   *British Birds* 78: 545
1986  One (juvenile) St Mary's & St Agnes 30th September to 24th October
    *British Birds* 80: 32, 356, 555
1986  One (juvenile) St Mary's 3rd to 5th October   *British Birds* 80: 32, 356, 555
1993  One (adult) Tresco 20th to 22nd August   *British Birds* 86: 624, 87: 525
1995  One (adult) St Agnes & Annet 29th August to 18th September   *British Birds* 89: 499
1996  One (juvenile) Tresco 1st to 6th September   *British Birds* 90: 471
1996  One (juvenile) Tresco & St Agnes 27th September to 14th October   *British Birds* 90: 471

Breeds North America, from arctic coasts south to Hudson Bay. Winters coastal South America south to Peru and Uruguay, a few individuals north to West Indies and Pacific-coastal Central America (Cramp *et al.* 1977–94). Monotypic.

Up to and including year 2000 there were eight BBRC-accepted Scillonian records of this rare North American wader. In addition, a bird seen and photographed by David Hunt on Tresco early morning on 19th August 1969 (*IOSBR* 1969) was first accepted as this species by the BBRC (*British Birds* 63: 277). However, it was later rejected following further review (*British Birds* 71: 500) and in 1984 was reidentified from original photographs as a moulting adult Western Sandpiper *C. mauri*.

Not unexpectedly, there is a clear autumn slant to arrival dates, all of which are shown in the Chart. Earliest arrival was 20th August and the latest 3rd October, within an overall arrival window of 45 days. The longest stay in the islands was 25 days (1986), with the average 10.6 days. Of the seven individuals that were aged, five were considered to be juveniles.

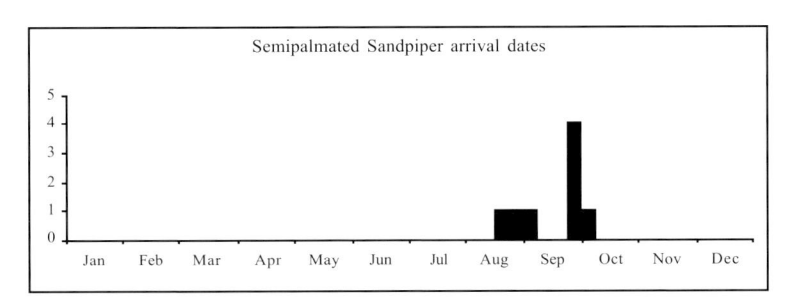

According to Cramp *et al.* (1977–94), previous assertions that Semipalmated Sandpiper wintered in southern coastal USA were incorrect, it having been confused with Western Sandpiper *C. mauri*. At least some central and eastern Canadian populations make transoceanic crossings of the North Atlantic directly to the Caribbean and, as with other species adopting this particular strategy, this renders them liable to involuntary transatlantic crossings during bad weather. Peak adult autumn passage in the Gulf of St Lawrence is around mid-July to mid-August, with juveniles still moving south into September. Interestingly, then, the two birds identified as adults both arrived in Scilly in August, whereas no juvenile arrived before September. A total of 103 Semipalmated Sandpiper records accepted by the BBRC during the period 1958–99 mean that 7.7% occurred in Scilly.

## Western Sandpiper *Calidris mauri* A BBRC 12.5%

**Extremely rare autumn migrant, full written description required by the BBRC.**

1969   One (adult) Tresco 19th August   *British Birds* 63: 277, 71: 500, 78: 546

In North America breeds Alaska and in Asia northeast Siberia, wintering mainly South America south to Peru, Central America, West Indies and southern USA. Monotypic.

One record of what remains a difficult bird to see on the eastern side of the North Atlantic involved a bird seen and photographed by David Hunt on Tresco early morning on 19th August 1969. This was first accepted by the BBRC as a Semipalmated Sandpiper *C. pusilla* (*British Birds* 63: 277) but then rejected after a review of all past records of this species by D I M Wallace (*British Birds* 71: 500). However, in 1984 it was identified as Western Sandpiper following re-examination of the original photographs and in the light of up-to-date knowledge (*British Birds* 78: 546), the BBRC then considered it a classic moulting adult.

As its name suggests, Western Sandpiper is mainly confined as a breeding species to the northwest corner of North America, though it also breeds in northeast Russia, from where birds are believed to cross to Alaska in autumn and migrate south with the bulk of the population. Some, perhaps most, southward movement is via the Pacific coastline, though with birds also recorded inland through mountain valleys. Nevertheless, it remains an extreme rarity in northeastern Canada and USA. Cramp *et al.* (1977–94) quote just three records from eastern Canada up to 1983, but point out that it occurs regularly on the North Atlantic coast in autumn from Massachusetts southwards, concluding from this that there is an element of east or southeast movement involved in autumn migration.

Given the marked difference between the transoceanic North Atlantic route of at least some autumn Semipalmated Sandpipers and the terrestrial strategy and western bias of migrant Western Sandpipers, we might expect a greater number of transatlantic records of the former. So it is interesting to see that Wallace (in Cramp *et al.* 1977–94) commented on the similarity in numbers of these two recorded in Britain and Ireland up until at least the mid-1980s. However, following various record reviews, as of year 2000 the totals stand at 103 Semipalmated and just eight Western. Undoubtedly this turnaround is mainly accounted for by improved knowledge on important identification features of these two, lack of which Wallace blamed for the previously similar totals. And neither have difficulties in separating these two been confined to Europe, with wide-scale former misidentification of wintering birds in the southern USA accounting for the previous false belief that Semipalmated Sandpiper wintered there commonly (Cramp *et al.* 1977–94), all but one of the winter-taken skins previously identified as Semipalmated in museums in four southeastern States being found to be of Western Sandpiper.

For further reading see Jonsson and Grant *Identification of stints and peeps* (*British Birds* 77: 293–315) and Grant *Four problem stints* (*British Birds* 79: 609–621).

## Little Stint *Calidris minuta* A

**Regular migrant in small numbers, annual in autumn but less frequent in spring.**

Breeds northern Eurasia, from Finland east to Laptev Sea. Migratory, wintering trans-Saharan Africa, Persian Gulf and around Indian Ocean. Monotypic.

Surprisingly, there is perhaps less 19th century information on this species than for the much less frequent Temminck's Stint *C. temminckii*. First mention of Little Stint in Scilly seems to be E H Rodd's letter of 15th September 1851 to the *Zoologist*, to the effect that two were shot within the previous week (Rodd 1851a). Next, E H Rodd (1880) and his nephew Francis Rodd and co-author James Clark (Clark & Rodd 1906) all make mention of two shot in Scilly in September 1857. The latter authors referring to the initial misidentification of the birds as Temminck's Stints (see that species). Lastly in the 19th century, E H Rodd quoted nephew Francis in reporting the arrival of 'Common Stints' in Scilly on 14th September 1870 (Rodd 1880). From the above, it is obvious that September figured prominently in the 19th century for Little Stint arrivals.

Penhallurick reported that small numbers visited Scilly annually up until the 1960s, mostly singly, though he also quoted groups of six and four. Earliest date was 24th August and the latest 18th October, arrival dates for four spring individuals being 29th April, 1st May (2) and 2nd June (Penhallurick 1969). Taking the ten years from 1990, birds occurred during autumn in all years, but in only three during spring.

Earliest autumn arrival was 3rd August but all arrivals fell in the intervening period up until 11th September; six (60%) in the ten days 3rd to 12th August. Last sighting dates were in the range 25th September to 10th November. All three spring arrivals occurred during May. Numbers of birds involved annually were difficult to calculate. Daily variation in numbers involved at specific sites being possibly attributable to inter-site movements or a genuine daily turnover of birds present within the islands, or simply because such a small wader is not easily counted accurately on a day-to-day basis. The most recorded as present on all islands at any one time was 60, in 1996, but numbers approaching that magnitude may have been present in 1990, 1993 and 1998. However, in 1999 just six were recorded, with seven in both 1991 and 1994 and eight in 1997. The most recorded at any one site was probably the 12 on Tresco on 21st September 1993, with one there the previous day and five on 23rd.

Little Stint is a broad-front migrant, in the West Palearctic occurring from the Atlantic seaboard eastwards and commencing its annual moult from the Mediterranean southwards. Birds moving through western Britain and Ireland, and therefore through Scilly, are most likely to originate from the Norwegian population, Swedish and Finnish birds mainly moving south through central Europe (Cramp *et al.* 1977–94). There is also an assumption that birds using the westerly route down into West Africa are mainly juveniles, perhaps from populations further east, East African wintering populations being found to comprise mainly adults. Like the closely related Temminck's Stint, the centre of gravity of spring passage shifts eastwards, thereby accounting for the comparative lack of birds in western Britain at that time. Little Stints begin leaving the breeding areas from July or August, peak passage through Britain occurring late July through to October. Return passage from Africa commences from around May, earliest returning birds being present in the breeding areas from late May or June.

# Temminck's Stint *Calidris temminckii* A

**Rare migrant, formerly in autumn but during late 20th century exclusively in spring. Treated by the BBRC as a national Scarce Migrant, full written description required by the SRP.**

    [1857  Two (shot) Scilly September]   Rodd 1857c
     1863  More than one Scilly early September   Rodd 1863d
     1864  One (shot) Scilly   Clarke & Rodd 1906
     1868  One (shot) early September   Rodd 1868c
     1868  At least one Scilly following October gale   Rodd 1880
     1945  One Scilly 18th August   Penhallurick 1969
     1981  One Porth Hellick, St Mary's 14th to 17th August
     1987  One St Agnes and Porth Hellick, St Mary's 28th to 30th April
     1991  One Abbey Pool, Tresco 17th May
     1994  One Great Pool, Tresco 4th to 7th May
     1996  One Bryher Pool 17th May
     2000  Two Abbey Pool, Tresco 2nd to 5th September

Breeds extreme northern Eurasia, from Scotland and Norway east to Bering Strait. Migratory, wintering south to sub-Saharan Africa, Persian Gulf, around Indian Ocean and Southeast Asia. Monotypic. Amber-listed in UK: five-year mean of 2.8 breeding pairs (Gregory *et al.* 2002).

The mid- to late 19th century records contain a surprising number of references to this species. The earliest seems to be E H Rodd's letter to the *Zoologist* stating that Augustus Pechell shot two on Scilly during the first week of October 1857 (Rodd 1857c). The same author wrote again on 10th September 1863 saying 'this little Tringa has made its autumn appearance at the Scilly Isles', presumably during early September (Rodd 1863d), and then again in 1868 pointing out that one was shot on Scilly during the week preceding 15th September that year (Rodd 1868c). Referring to its appearance in the islands following an October gale, again in 1868, Rodd describes Temminck's Stint as 'one of the smallest and the rarest of the Tringa' (Rodd 1880). In this last volume he noted that all specimens he had examined, from Scilly or mainland Cornwall, were killed in autumn.

Meanwhile, on mainland Cornwall, E H Rodd described it as far from rare in the saltmarshes of west Cornwall, local taxidermist Vingoe managing to shoot three out of a flock of at least 12 prior to 1873 (Penhallurick 1969).

Early in the 20th century, E H Rodd's nephew Francis could remember only that Pechell shot several prior to 1863. At the same time he commented on the remarkable tameness of Temminck's Stint and on it being found by the edges of the freshwater pools (Clark & Rodd 1906). Clark and Rodd stated that the first specimen they could trace had been shot in October 1864, and concluded with the comment that several had been shot in autumn by Pechell and John Jenkinson since then, mostly by Newford Pool, St Mary's. These two authors also drew attention to the shooting of two Little Stints *C. minuta* on 19th September 1857, pointing out that they were initially misidentified as Temminck's, causing 'some confusion in the record'. Interestingly, Penhallurick interprets this as discrediting Pechell's 1857 birds, but the text of E H Rodd's *Zoologist* letter suggests that Pechell's birds may have been shot before the 19th. Nevertheless, although the same authors acknowledge that Pechell obtained several Temminck's Stints prior to 1863, in the interests of caution the 1857 records are square-bracketed in the Table.

Penhallurick cites a bird seen on 18th August 1945 as the first 20th century Scillonian Temminck's Stint record (Penhallurick 1969). However, it should be borne in mind that few records were published for any species on Scilly for the first three to four decades of the 20th century and that this is not necessarily proof of absence. The Chart shows arrival dates for all seven 20th century published records (eight birds). Interestingly, all records or reports prior to and including 1981 occurred during autumn, whereas four of the five subsequent records occurred in spring, though with such a small sample it may be unwise to try and interpret reasons. However, increased observer coverage during the early part of the year might be a tempting explanation, except that this increased coverage is even more pronounced during autumn.

Putting this species in perspective, Temminck's Stint was slightly less frequent in its 20th century appearances in Scilly (7) than Semipalmated Sandpiper *C. pusilla* (8). In addition, it was over twice as scarce as Baird's *C. bairdii* and Pectoral Sandpipers *C. melanotos* (13 each) and over four times as scarce as White-rumped Sandpiper *C. fuscicollis* (26). As Clark and Rodd observed nearly one hundred years ago, Temminck's Stints are to be looked for around the edges of freshwater areas, such as the Tresco Pools, or the pools in Higher and Lower Moors on St Mary's. However, there seems no reason why it might not still occur around the smaller ponds, such as Newford Duck Pond, where Augustus Pechell and John Jenkinson shot them in the mid-19th century. All four recent spring arrivals were squeezed into a narrow 20-day window. Three of the seven 20th century records remained for just one day and the longest stay was four days (two birds), whereas the average length of stay was just over two days.

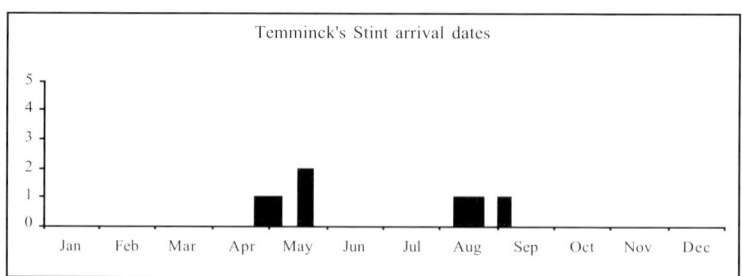

Temminck's Stint arrival dates

Temminck's Stint migrates overland through Europe on a broad front, numbers being lowest in countries bordering the Atlantic and North Sea. It occurs mainly in small groups, adults leaving the breeding areas from early to mid-July, abandoning the young before they are fully fledged (Cramp *et al.* 1977–94). Juveniles follow from around August. Departure from the wintering areas occurs during March and April, European breeding grounds being reoccupied from the second half of May, later in Siberia. It may be decreasing in at least some parts of its range. No Temminck's Stints have been ringed in Scilly and there are no recaptures.

## Least Sandpiper *Calidris minutilla* **A** BBRC 3.2%

**Extremely rare autumn migrant, full written description required by the BBRC.**

1962   One St Agnes 4th October   *British Birds* 56: 400, 57: 124–125

Breeds North America, from Alaska and British Columbia east to Newfoundland and Nova Scotia, south to southern Hudson Bay. Winters extreme southern USA, Central America, West Indies and northern South America. Monotypic.

E H Rodd knew it as 'American Stint', quoting two birds shot in southwest England prior to 1880: one near Penzance, Cornwall, on 10th October 1853 (shot by local taxidermist Vingoe) and one near Bideford, Devon, in September 1870 (Rodd 1880). The earlier of these two records being the first known European record. A third 19th century record from the southwest involved one shot near Mousehole, west Cornwall, in September 1890 (Penhallurick 1969). There is one Scillonian record of what remains an extreme national rarity, involving a bird that spent just over an hour on St Agnes on 4th October 1962, this being the 9th British and Irish record (*CBWPSAR* 32; Wallace 1964).

A claim by David Hunt of one keeping company with Little Stints *C. minuta* and Dunlins *C. alpina* by Tresco's Great Pool for half an hour on 24th August 1965 was rejected by the BBRC (*CBWPSAR* 35). This last individual was exceptionally confiding, allowing observations down to three metres and prior to its discovery the weather had been unsettled, with northwesterly gales. It was rediscovered on nearby Abbey Pool early the following afternoon in company with numerous small waders, though by now it was noticeably less confiding, and after being watched for just under an hour it flew to the far side of the pool and was not seen again.

Autumn migration occurs on a broad front, commencing from mid-July but with the bulk of the movement throughout August and September, with some still in evidence into October. Up until mid-August most birds are adults, with some evidence that females precede males, though juveniles predominate from then on. There is also evidence that some Least Sandpipers make the long transoceanic journey out over the North Atlantic from northeast USA to the Caribbean and perhaps northeast South America, it also being regular in Bermuda in autumn. And, just as with other species using this demanding route, individuals are liable to involuntary transatlantic crossings when encountering severe weather. Sample autumn adult weights in the Gulf of St Lawrence, Quebec, showed body fat levels sufficient to sustain a flight of 2,600–2,900 km, with some considered capable of achieving 3,600 km. The first birds reach northeastern South America by mid-July.

On this basis, we might expect the St Agnes individual to have been a juvenile. A total of 31 British records accepted by the BBRC up to and including 1999 mean this bird represents just over 3% of the national total.

## White-rumped Sandpiper  *Calidris fuscicollis*  A  BBRC 6.5%

**Rare autumn migrant, full written description required by the BBRC.**

| | |
|---|---|
| 1854 | One shot St Mary's 11th October   Rodd 1854a; Clark & Rodd 1906 |
| 1870 | One shot St Mary's 10th October   Rodd 1870l; Clark & Rodd 1906 |
| 1962 | One trapped St Agnes 2nd & 3rd October |
| 1964 | One St Agnes 22nd to 29th September |
| 1965 | One Tresco 6th to 28th September |
| 1966 | One Tresco 10th to 17th September |
| 1967 | One Tresco 6th to 20th September |
| 1970 | One St Mary's 6th October |
| 1970 | One Bryher 7th to 9th October |
| 1978 | One (adult) St Mary's 18th June |
| 1978 | One Bryher, St Agnes, St Mary's & Tresco 22nd to 26th October |
| 1983 | One St Mary's 14th October |
| 1983 | One Bryher 24th October |
| 1987 | One (juvenile) St Agnes 17th October |
| 1990 | One (adult) St Mary's 29th August |
| 1990 | One (juvenile) St Agnes 17th September |
| [1993 | One (first-winter) St Mary's 12th to 13th & 17th & 18th September] |
| 1999 | One (adult) Tresco 30th September to 6th October |
| 1999 | One (first-winter) 24th to at least 30th October |
| 1999 | Up to four (adult & three first-winters) 24th to 29th October |
| 1999 | Up to three (first-winters) St Mary's 22nd October to 2nd November |
| 2000 | One (adult) St Agnes 28th September to 5th October |

2000   One (juvenile) Bryher 24th October
2002   One St Agnes 27th to 29th August

Breeds North American, from arctic Canada and Baffin Island west to Banks Island and, irregularly, Alaska. Winters South America east of Andes, from Paraguay southwards, including Falkland Islands. Monotypic.

E H Rodd knew it as 'Schinz's Sandpiper', describing the first Cornish record involving a male and female shot at Hayle, west Cornwall, in October 1846 (Rodd 1880). In mid-October 1854 Rodd learned from John Jenkinson that Augustus Pechell had shot one on Tresco on 11th (Rodd 1854a), to be followed by another shot on the same island in 1870, this time on 10th October. This last individual was killed by E H Rodd's nephew Francis while it was feeding beside a freshwater pool on St Mary's. Francis sent his uncle the body, which the elder Rodd recorded as moulting from summer into winter plumage (Rodd 1870l). Interestingly, E H Rodd described how Penzance taxidermist Vingoe received a specimen acquired on Cornwall's Lizard peninsula on 29th October that same year, and Rodd claimed to know of four others shot elsewhere during that same month.

As with so many bird species on Scilly during the 20th century, we hear no more of White-rumped Sandpiper until one was trapped on St Agnes in early October 1962 and it subsequently appeared in the islands in a further 12 years, the most recent being 2002. In all a total of 29 individuals are on record as having visited the islands, the shortest stay being just one day (eight birds) and the longest 23 days, with an average stay of 5.7 days. For reasons that are unclear now, the bird seen on St Mary's over a six-day period in 1993 does not feature among the BBRC totals, so was presumably not submitted, though the record's validity seems hardly in doubt. With the notable exception of the adult on St Mary's in mid-June 1978, there is a marked autumn bias to arrival dates, all of which are charted except for the 2002 record. Ignoring the June individual, earliest arrival date was 29th August and the latest 2nd November.

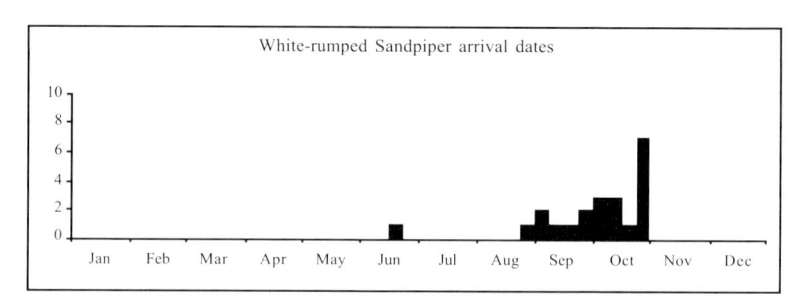

White-rumped Sandpiper arrival dates

Autumn migration begins from July but with the bulk of the movement during September, or even October into November, with adult males probably first to leave. There is also evidence of a major southeast movement across Canada towards coastal northeast USA, with perhaps most birds then taking the Atlantic coastal route (Cramp *et al.* 1977–94). However, like some other North American waders and some passerines, there is evidence that many White-rumped Sandpipers take a transoceanic route out over the North Atlantic and south to the Caribbean, or even fly direct to northeast South America. This is shown by the absence of same-autumn ringing recoveries in mid-eastern and southern States, by the regular autumn falls in Bermuda and by the marked number of autumn arrivals in Britain and elsewhere in Europe. For, like other species adopting this transoceanic strategy, individuals are at risk to involuntary transatlantic crossings when encountering extreme weather. Evidence for this is provided by the BBRC total of 442 accepted British White-rumped Sandpiper records during the period 1958 to 1999 – of which the 27 Scillonian individuals represent 6.5%. The timing of autumn arrivals in Scilly comfortably fits the migration pattern described here. Spring passage is noted in the USA from late April to May with breeding territories reoccupied by early June, which could also fit the timing of the sole spring arrival.

One White-rumped Sandpiper was trapped and ringed in Scilly. The total number of sightings for mainland Cornwall up to and including 1999 was just 16 (*CBWPSAR* 69).

# Baird's Sandpiper *Calidris bairdii* A BBRC 5.9%

**Rare autumn migrant, full written description required by the BBRC.**

1965   One St Agnes 25th September
1966   One Tresco 26th August to 12th September
1966   One St Agnes 19th to 30th September
1967   One Bryher 19th to 20th August
1967   One Tresco 9th to 28th September
1977   One Tresco 31st August to 12th September
1977   One Tresco 3rd to 8th October
1977   One St Mary's 24th September
1987   One (juvenile) St Agnes 2nd to 4th October
1987   One (juvenile) St Mary's 27th October
1995   One (juvenile) St Agnes 18th to 28th September
1995   One (juvenile) St Agnes 10th to 14th October
1997   One (juvenile) Bryher & Tresco 30th August to 12th September

Breeds North America and Asia, from northeast Siberia east to Alaska, arctic Canada and Baffin Island, also breeds northwest Greenland. Winters South America, mainly Andes from southern Ecuador to Tierra del Fuego. Monotypic.

First mention of this small wader in a Cornish or Scillonian context comes with the discovery of one on Wingletang Down, St Agnes, in September 1965. This was the 9th record for Britain and Ireland in what was obviously a notable autumn for North American waders in Scilly, with both Least *C. minutilla* and White-rumped Sandpipers *C. fuscicollis* also present. All told, there were 13 Baird's Sandpipers in Scilly in seven different years; all five individuals that were aged were judged to be juveniles. The earliest arrival date was 19th August and the last was 27th October, giving an overall arrival window of 70 days. The shortest stay was just one day (3 individuals) and the longest 20 days, with an average of 8.2 days. The Chart includes all 13 arrival dates and reveals a pattern typical of transatlantic autumn waders in Scilly.

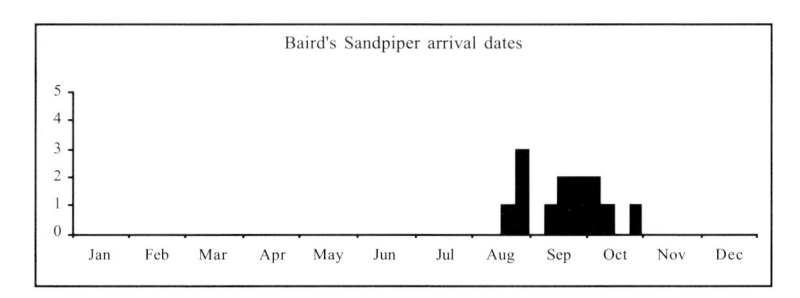

Birds breeding in northeast Russia cross to North America before moving south in autumn. Most autumn migration is via the central prairies with adults the first to move, on a narrower front than later juveniles. Adults mainly make a direct, non-stop flight to the South American Andes, with many, perhaps most, taking a circular transoceanic route of some 6,000 km out over the Pacific, bypassing Central America. Most adults have left North America by the end of August. Juvenile migration is more leisurely than that of adults and on a broader front, with peak passage in the USA occurring during the second half of August and with birds regularly reaching the Atlantic coast. At least a minority of birds reaching eastern coastal USA are believed to use the North Atlantic transoceanic route to reach South America, perhaps explaining European arrivals of what is essentially a central and western North American species.

These 13 individuals represent just 5.9% of the 219 records accepted by the BBRC in Britain during the period 1958–99. The total for mainland Cornwall up to and including 1999 was 22 (*CBWPSAR* 69).

# Pectoral Sandpiper                                     *Calidris melanotos*  A

A rare spring and autumn migrant. Treated by the BBRC as a national Scarce Migrant, full written description required by the SRP.

    1840   One (shot) Annet 27th May   Clark & Rodd 1906
    1840   One Annet 28th May   Clark & Rodd 1906
    1960   One Bryher 8th May   *CBWPSAR* 30
    1971   One Tresco 7th & 8th June   *IOSBR* 1971
    1974   One Tresco 19th May   *IOSBR* 1974
    1980   One Tresco 27th May   *IOSBR* 1980

Breeds North America and Asia, from northeast Siberia, Taimyr peninsula and Bering Strait east through Alaska to Hudson Bay. Winters southern South America to Falkland Islands and South Georgia, few Australia and New Zealand. Monotypic. Removed from BBRC Rarities List January 1963 (Harber & Swaine 1963).

Pectoral Sandpiper is probably the commonest transatlantic wader species reaching Britain and was well known in Scilly during the latter half of the 19th century. As early as 1840, D W Mitchell of Penzance shot one on Annet's rocky foreshore on 27th May, seeing another on the same island next day. Of particular note, though, were five shot during September 1870, two by John Jenkinson on Tresco and St Mary's and three more on St Mary's by Augustus Pechell. Three of these individuals found their way into the hands of E H Rodd in Penzance. Rodd later claimed one of the five had been shot 'from among a flock', though he omitted to say whether just Pectoral Sandpipers were involved (Rodd 1843b, 1870i, 1880; Clark & Rodd 1906). Tresco gamekeeper David Smith shot one in 1880, another was obtained from an unknown location in 1883 (Cornish 1883) and A A Dorrien-Smith shot one on Tresco during September 1891 (Clark & Rodd 1906).

The first recorded 20th century arrival involved a bird on Tresco for a few days from 12th September 1943, followed by one in 1951 and two in 1957. From 1960 it occurred almost every year and the Chart shows annual totals from then until 2000, birds occurring at a rate of 2.4 per year for the 41 years, or 3.1 per year of arrival. Also charted are all known arrival dates from the time of Mitchell's first Annet bird in May 1840. There appears to have been a slight reduction in numbers in recent years, regardless of any parallel increase in the number of observers. There have been just six spring records (Table), two of which involved the 1840 Annet individuals.

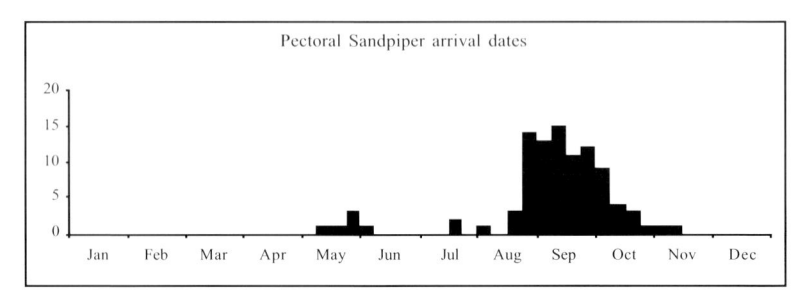

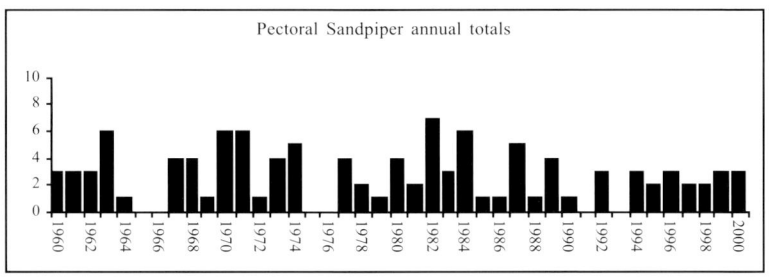

An analysis of records for the twenty years 1980–99 showed a minimum of 55 birds at an average of 2.7 per year. The most recorded ever in Scilly were the seven in 1982 and none was recorded in 1991 and 1993. The earliest arrival ever was on 12th July 1994 and the latest on 10th November 1997. Most birds, though, arrived from late August to late September, with an abrupt commencement of activity around the end of August (*IOSBR* 1998).

The North American population winters in South America with autumn migration mainly overland through the interior, though many reach the Atlantic coast. Main southward movement through the USA occurs from late July to September. Those reaching the northeast coast are then believed to take the transoceanic route out over the North Atlantic and head south direct to Bermuda, the Caribbean and northeast South America (Cramp *et al.* 1977–94). First arrivals occurr at the last named by early August, though continuing into November. The frequency of European arrivals is thought to be linked to involuntary weather-assisted vagrancy among birds using this transoceanic route, perhaps aided by a strong southeast autumn movement across Canada beforehand, many thought to overshoot the eastern seaboard of North America into the path of North Atlantic depressions. Nevertheless, debate continues over whether individuals from the northeast Asian population reach western Europe overland from the east, or indeed, whether some autumn western European sightings involve transatlantic vagrants from previous autumns.

Five Pectoral Sandpipers have been ringed on Scilly, all prior to 1970 and all probably on St Agnes. There are no controls or recoveries. On mainland Cornwall, a total of 227 had been recorded up to and including 1999 (*CBWPSAR* 69).

## Sharp-tailed Sandpiper *Calidris acuminata* A  BBRC 5%

**Extremely rare autumn migrant, full written description required by the BBRC.**

1974   One St Mary's 20th to 29th September   *British Birds* 68: 318

Breeds northern Siberia from Lake Baikal east to Bering Sea, wintering southern Pacific from New Guinea to Australia and New Zealand. Monotypic.

The sole Scillonian record of this rare wader species involved a bird accompanied by three Pectoral Sandpipers *C. melanotos* in a boggy field at Porth Hellick, St Mary's, for ten days from perhaps 20th September 1974 (Flumm 1974; Britton 1980). Although the bird was subsequently believed to have been present from 20th it was only on 24th that it was publicly discussed as a possible Sharp-tailed, after many observers had allegedly already accepted it as Pectoral Sandpiper. However, in the view of others it was easily distinguishable from the accompanying Pectorals by its greyer appearance and, more importantly, by its lack of a pectoral band (Flumm 1974). For an interesting paper on the possibility of confusing these two species see Britton (1980).

Autumn migration occurs on a broad front, from Lake Baikal east to the Bering Sea and continues out over the Pacific with a few even occurring as migrants in western North America. Southward movement begins July and peaks August to September, but with some still well up into northern latitudes by October or even November (Cramp *et al.* 1977–94). Suggestions of west European arrivals resulting from presumed westward migration across Eurasia from Siberia conflict with the fact that some Sharp-tailed Sandpiper arrivals coincide with those of wader species with a known transatlantic origin.

Just 20 British Sharp-tailed Sandpiper records were accepted by the BBRC up to and including 1999, therefore this single bird on Scilly represents 5% of the national total. There were no records from mainland Cornwall up to and including year 2000.

## Curlew Sandpiper *Calidris ferruginea* A

**Scarce migrant in small numbers, apparently far less numerous now than in the 19th century.**

Breeds northern central Asia, wintering sub-Saharan Africa, coastal Indian Ocean, Southeast Asia and Australasia. Monotypic.

Mid to late 19th century comments concerning this species bear little similarity to the situation we see today. In his epic *The Birds of Cornwall and The Scilly Isles* E H Rodd mentions flocks of Curlew Sandpipers arriving in the islands on (surprisingly) south to southwesterly winds between 1st and 15th September 1870 (Rodd 1880). According to Rodd, the species was particularly plentiful on Bryher, the same author pointing out that specimens were obtained during autumn 1865 (Rodd 1865a). In 1870, Rodd wrote to the *Zoologist* noting that since 1st September that year migrants arriving in the islands included 'flocks' of Curlew Sandpipers (Rodd 1870h). Early in the 20th century James Clark and E H Rodd's nephew Francis thought it 'not infrequently seen in the early autumn, with Dunlins and other shore birds, more especially on Samson and Bryher'. These two authors concluded with the observation that several females in breeding plumage were shot by Pechell (presumably Augustus) in 1865 (Clark & Rodd 1906). Assumedly these last were the 'specimens' mentioned by E H Rodd, but Clark and Francis Rodd make no mention of how they may have been sexed. The only obvious additional early mention of this species is in E H Rodd's appended *List of Birds Observed in The Scilly Islands* (Rodd 1880), where he again refers to it occurring in flocks during autumn.

Regrettably, there is no more early 20th century Scillonian information on this species than there is for most others. Therefore, next mention of Curlew Sandpiper is probably the 1952 comment that one was at Porth Killier, St Agnes, from 13th September until 23rd, when joined briefly by a second (*CBWPSAR* 22). Penhallurick, too, thought it may have been more frequent, and more numerous, during the 19th century, drawing attention to early reports of flocks of 50 to 100 on mainland Cornwall and pointing out that in the 1890s it was considered the second most common migrant wader in north Devon.

Any change in frequency and abundance, in both Cornwall and Scilly, seems to have occurred around the end of the 19th century. Clark's mention of a flock of 30 on the Camel Estuary in September 1900 (in W Page 1906) was perhaps the largest 20th century flock reported in Cornwall (Penhallurick 1969). The same author noted the absence of January and February records from the county and commented on its scarcity on spring passage, whilst at the same time describing autumn passage in Scilly as involving just ones and twos and quoting an earliest arrival date of 26th August and a latest sighting of 17th October. Within Scilly, comparatively large numbers occurred in 1959, up to 18 together, and in 1967 up to ten together, the single Scillonian spring record involving a bird on St Mary's on 24th February 1963. Stanley and Minton (1972) documented an unusually large influx of Curlew Sandpipers into Britain and Ireland, and elsewhere, in autumn 1969. This was reflected in Scilly by the presence of what was described as 'More than usual' but in fact involving only small parties of up to eight in many places during September and October (*IOSBR* 1969).

Taking the ten years from 1990, the picture appeared to be still much as Penhallurick described it. Curlew Sandpiper appeared in all ten years, though its appearance during spring in five of those years was perhaps surprising. The most seen in spring was four together, on 28th April 1993, plus two on 22nd April 1998 and one 6th–11th May 1990 and another on 18th May 1992. The earliest autumn arrival was 10th August, although late August or even early September was more normal. Last birds were generally recorded around mid- to late October, although one at Porth Hellick on 1st December 1996 was exceptional. The most recorded together was 16, though it mostly appeared on ones or twos. Trying to reach an agreement on annual totals involved in the islands is hindered by a lack of co-ordinated inter-island counts, though between 6–7 and 30, or perhaps 40, seems realistic. Unusually, one was seen from the RMV *Scillonian III* on 17th September 1998. Typically, Curlew Sandpipers frequent the sandy tidal areas at low tide, such as Samson Flats or the Tresco beaches.

Curlew Sandpiper is a long-distance migrant, some birds flying from the Arctic Ocean to as far as the Southern Ocean, although in the West Palearctic many go no further than northwest Africa, the Middle East or Iraq. Cramp *et al.* (1977–94) outlined three main West Palearctic migration routes to the African wintering areas: (a) Baltic and Norwegian coast direct to West Africa, (b) eastern Europe and the Mediterranean across the Sahara to West Africa, and (c) Russia via the Black and Caspian Seas to eastern and southern Africa. Importantly, spring migration of birds wintering in West Africa is mainly via route (b), thus accounting for smaller numbers visible on the Atlantic and North Sea coasts at that time. Birds using route (a) are mainly thought to comprise both adults and juveniles from more westerly populations, plus, in some years, large numbers of mainly juveniles displaced by the weather from populations further east (Cramp *et al.* 1977–94). Autumn passage commences from late August, adults moving first, juveniles during August or September, with breeding areas reoccupied from early June. Migration is rapid, returning birds accumulating sufficient fat deposits for a non-stop northward journey of nearly 4,000 km. In the West Palearctic, autumn moult commences from North Africa southwards. No Curlew Sandpipers have been ringed in Scilly and there are no controls.

# Purple Sandpiper *Calidris maritima* A

**Annual winter visitor in moderate numbers and probably migrant.**

Breeds edges of arctic seas and on Arctic islands, from 105°E, west through Franz Josef Land, Novaya Zemlya, Spitsbergen, Norway, Iceland, Greenland to northeast Canadian Arctic. Migratory or partially so, maritime outside breeding season. Southward movement dependent upon extent of winter ice, winters south in West Palearctic to coastal Britain, Ireland, France and Iberia. Monotypic. Amber-listed in UK: five-year mean of 2.0 breeding pairs; 20% or more of East Atlantic Flyway non-breeding population in UK (Gregory *et al.* 2002).

Earliest published mention of Purple Sandpiper in Scilly seems to be E H Rodd's account of it having been seen in November 1859 (Rodd 1860). This was followed later by his nephew Francis's description of a confiding individual unusually sitting on a stone by a freshwater pool on St Mary's on 8th November 1870, then an equally confiding group on rocks at Lizard Point, Tresco, on 27th December that same year (Rodd 1880). At the close of the 19th century, James Clark and Francis Rodd described it as generally present during winter, either singly or in small flocks, normally around Bryher's Shipman Head, Men-a-Vaur and Round Island, usually disappearing from the islands about the beginning of April, sometimes earlier, although casual groups might appear outside that period, as in May 1877 when a flock visited Annet (Clark & Rodd 1906).

Penhallurick (1969) thought the status of this species had remained unchanged since the 19th century in both mainland Cornwall and on Scilly. He pointed out that most reports came from St Agnes and that it was infrequently observed on St Mary's, but rarely on Tresco, suggesting too that it was probably more widespread on some of the rocky islands. As on mainland Cornwall, wintering birds arrived in the islands from late October, with what were assumed to be passing migrants from as early as late July or August. Penhallurick quoted spring accumulations on St Agnes of from 75, typically, up to a maximum of 150, mainly during April and May.

An all-island survey of waders during winter 1984–85 recorded a total of 106 Purple Sandpipers, at that time just short of the number required for national importance (Kirby 1988). The survey took place between 15th December and 28th January, most Purple Sandpipers being recorded on the west and east coasts of Samson and on St Agnes's north coast, at a density of 6–12 birds per kilometre. Elsewhere, wintering density was low with Purple Sandpipers showing a clear preference for boulder beaches rather than bedrock. These 106 Purple Sandpipers comprised just 3.7% of the 2,852 waders recorded during the survey. However, and as the author himself pointed out, it is important to appreciate that, particularly in the case of Purple Sandpiper, this figure probably represents a minimum estimate, due both to difficulties associated with counting waders on rocky shores at low tide and gaps in coverage with known favoured sites on Annet and in the Western Isles being omitted from this 1984–85 survey. In this respect, the author drew attention to a previous estimate of 250 wintering Purple Sandpipers in Scilly (H P K Robinson 1976, in Kirby 1988), which, if correct, placed the Scillonian wintering population well within the limits of national importance.

Similarly, just 65 Purple Sandpipers were recorded during the two-day Winter Shorebird Survey in late January 1997, principally because counts were confined to the five uninhabited islands plus Samson. Interestingly, none was recorded on Samson this time, or on Tresco and Bryher. At 34, St Mary's held the greatest number, followed by 21 on St Agnes and ten on St Martin's. As such then, the 1997 survey fails to tell the full story of Purple Sandpiper winter distribution or numbers in Scilly. Similarly, a four-day shorebird count during March 1996 covered those islands just mentioned, plus Tean and others in that immediate area, and, as with the 1997 results, perhaps little should be read into the total of 26 Purple Sandpipers recorded.

Examination of *IOSBR* for 1990–99 shows a pattern of small numbers during late winter, followed by an apparent spring passage, commencing early April and ending sharply within the period 17th–31st May. This is followed by an apparently far more protracted period of autumn arrivals, commencing any time from late July onwards. Birds are then viewable about the islands to the year's end, with varying numbers reported from a variety of sites. The highest number recorded, at different sites but within roughly the same timescale, was 127 during January–February 1999: 65 on St Mary's, 43 on St Agnes and 19 on Tean. This is somewhat greater than the midwinter total recorded by Kirby in 1984–85.

*Birds of the Isles of Scilly*

Whilst is seems beyond doubt that Purple Sandpipers using the islands depart during the second half of May and return again from late July onwards, the case for a distinct spring, or even autumn, passage remains unclear. An alternative possibility is that birds appearing in flocks during April or May could have wintered in more peripheral areas of the islands, e.g. the Western or Northern Isles, which remain mostly uncounted during winter. The truth, however, probably lies somewhere in between. Ringing data show that Purple Sandpipers using Britain in winter originate from Greenland, Iceland, Spitsbergen and Fennoscandia (Wernham *et al.* 2002). On average, shorter bill lengths among birds wintering in eastern Scotland and northeast England suggest that populations from Norway are mainly involved at these sites, whereas longer bill measurements elsewhere in Britain suggest that birds from populations other than Norway are mainly involved (Wernham et al. 2002).

Lack drew attention to the species' marked winter site tenacity, both within and between years, and considered between-year site movements of over 5 km rare. He also mentioned a difference in the timing of winter arrival between populations, those from Norway reaching eastern Scotland from July and prior to their moult, whereas those reaching northern and western Scotland did so in October or November, following their moult (P Lack 1986). In spring, birds depart their more southerly wintering areas during April or May. Fifteen Purple Sandpipers have been ringed in Scilly, 14 prior to 1970. There are no recoveries or controls.

# Dunlin *Calidris alpina* A

**Regular spring and autumn migrant in moderate numbers, a few winter but it is not recorded as having bred.**

Circumpolar, breeds western Greenland, Iceland, northern Britain and Norway east through northern Eurasia and Alaska to Hudson Bay. Migratory, West Palearctic birds winter south to North Africa, Red Sea and Iran. Polytypic: nominate *alpina*, or 'Northern Dunlin' occurs northern Scandinavia and northwest Russia east to Sea of Okhotsk; *schinzii*, or 'Southern Dunlin' southeast Greenland, Iceland, Britain and Ireland east to Baltic and north to southern Finland, Sweden and Norway; *arctica*, or 'Greenland Dunlin, northwest Greenland; *sakhalina* northeast Siberia; *pacifica* western Alaska and northeast Canada; *articola* northern Alaska; *hudsonia*, or 'American Dunlin' northern Canada. Amber-listed in UK: moderate decline in non-breeding population over past 25 years; 50% or more of breeding population at ten or fewer sites; 20% or more of East Atlantic Flyway non-breeding population in UK, 50% or greater at ten or fewer sites; unfavourable world winter conservation status (Gregory *et al.* 2002).

There is surprisingly little mention of Dunlin in Scilly by early writers. E H Rodd noted that it occurred in autumn and winter, including July 1870 (Rodd 1880), whereas Clark and E H Rodd's nephew Francis considered it common among flocks of other small 'shore birds' during winter, several times being noted in May. They ended with the observation that it did not breed. E H Rodd considered it the commonest 19th century small wader on mainland Cornwall in winter, also breeding west in Cornwall at least as far as Bodmin Moor. He observed, however, that more were present during winter than could be accounted for by the local breeding population and concluded that the surplus came from further north.

In his review of this species, Penhallurick (1969) suggested that the earliest arrivals in Cornwall were from July, birds being more frequent on autumn passage than in winter or spring, with midwinter flocks of around 1,000 in mainland Cornwall and with very few inland at this time. Importantly, Penhallurick found little evidence of a marked spring passage, considering the situation on Scilly similar to that on the mainland, although with far fewer birds involved. As on the mainland, autumn passage commenced from July, with 15 recorded between early April and early June considered 'spring stragglers'. Migrants moved quickly through the islands, 85 on St Agnes on 12th July being present for just the single day. The same author thought 180 on St Agnes, on 21st May, was the largest recorded spring concentration in the islands up until that time, i.e. 1969, with wintering numbers normally assessed in tens rather than in hundreds.

Looking at the period 1990–99, little seems to have changed since Penhallurick's earlier review. Spring passage occurred around late April and May, with few birds involved most years, though a 1993 all-island summary produced a count of 117 on 10th May. Autumn passage was evident from late June or July, with greatest numbers apparently passing through the islands early and with regular combined counts of around 50 individuals into September–October. Highest combined count was 91 (1994), though a flock of the same number was present for one day only in 1997. Numbers apparently declined markedly from around August. Winter counts were mostly in the order of ten to 40, although the 70 recorded during the late January 1997 all-island Winter Shorebird Survey was probably more realistic. Thirty of these last were located on Tresco, 15 on St Mary's and 14 on St Agnes. The only remaining midwinter all-island count was the 1984–85 Wader Survey (Kirby 1988), when 118 were recorded as follows: Tresco 58, Samson 36 and Bryher 24. Interestingly, the mid-March 1996 Wader Count found only 9 Dunlin (Lock 1996).

Examining ringing returns up until the mid-1960s, Penhallurick found evidence that Dunlins passing through mainland Cornwall originate from northern Europe, i.e. either *alpina*, *arctica* or *schinzii*, individuals recovered having been ringed in Denmark, Iceland, Norway and Sweden (2). Similarly, there was evidence of onward passage, two birds ringed in Cornwall and Scilly being recovered in West Africa and Atlantic-coastal France respectively.

Little effort seems to have been made to assign Dunlins in Scilly to any geographical origin, even though it seems very probable that several different forms use the islands. Gantlett (1998) assessed the options for Britain as a whole, concluding that nominate *alpina* or 'Northern Dunlin' and *arctica*, or 'Greenland Dunlin' from northeast Greenland were both likely to be encountered in Britain, alongside the resident *schinzii* or 'Southern Dunlin'. Gantlett also pointed out that the Canadian *hudsonia*, or 'American Dunlin' and the Siberian *sakhalina* might also be expected to occur as vagrants. At least some Dunlins passing through the islands in spring 1998 and 1999, and in autumn 1999 were recorded as showing plumage and bill features indicative of *alpina* (*IOSBR* 1998, 1999), whilst rather earlier, T A Dorrien-Smith listed both *schinzii* and *alpina* as having occurred on Tresco, but without further explanation (T A Dorrien-Smith 1951).

Dunlins from the western West Palearctic winter in northwest Africa south to Senegal, and whilst some move by comparatively short stages, others make long flights between main stopover areas, utilising substantial fat deposits in the process. A major difference between Palearctic and Nearctic populations is that the former mostly moult on the wintering grounds, although a few commence their moult further north and then complete it later (Cramp *et al.* 1977–94). In the West Palearctic, Dunlins commence leaving the breeding areas from July, returning during April and May. *Arctica*, *alpina* and *schinzii* all pass through Britain and Ireland, where they are joined by local birds of *schinzii*, on passage to northwest Africa. A few *schinzii* are believed to winter in southwest England, some of this form originating as far east in Europe as the Barents Sea. In spring, most *arctica* pass through western Britain and Ireland, whereas, except for the Icelandic element of the former, fewer *schinzii* or *alpina* reach Britain at this time, and this presumably accounts for the less marked spring passage through Scilly. There was one interesting offshore record from the ocean weather station 'Kilo' positioned in the Western Approaches 800 km southwest of Scilly. It involved two summer-plumage individuals that circled the ship for about 15 minutes from 08.40 hours on 30th April 1958, in light easterly winds (McLean & Williamson 1959). At the end of the 15 minutes, one then disappeared and the other landed aboard ship, before being flushed by a passing Arctic Skua *Stercorarius parasiticus* and it too disappearing. Presumably a different Dunlin then circled the ship for 35 minutes around midday on 30th.

**Recoveries**
60479X   Ad   St Agnes 1st October 1960          SH   Esnandes, Chasrente-Maritime, France
                                                        20th October 1960

**Dunlin Ringing Recaptures**

# Buff-breasted Sandpiper *Tryngites subruficollis* A

Rare early autumn migrant. Treated by the BBRC as a national Scarce Migrant, full written descriptions required by the SRP.

Breeds North America but range restricted and still poorly understood. Perhaps mainly confined to northwest arctic Canada and northeast Alaska, some possibly west into Russia. Winters South America, in central Argentina and Paraguay (Cramp *et al.* 1977–94). Monotypic. Removed from BBRC Rarities List January 1983 (Grant 1982b).

Buff-breasted Sandpiper's remote breeding range and non-stop trans-continental migration strategy make it a rare bird throughout most of North America. Typically, birds arrive in Scilly with the first of the autumn's westerly gales and are then to be found on the short-grass areas, e. g. the Golf Course, or St Mary's Airport, though seldom in typical wader habitats. Notable features too are their confiding behaviour and tendency to occur in small groups. Indeed, Scilly may be the most reliable site in Europe at which to see this species, and the southern end of St Mary's Airport's main runway is the key site in Scilly.

This is another of those intriguing transatlantic migrants that appeared with certainty in the 19th century but then, if the records are to be believed, shunned the islands until well into the 1900s. E H Rodd referred to three specimens obtained up to 1880, the first of which was shot on the beach between Penzance and Marazion, west Cornwall, whilst keeping company with Dunlins *Calidris alpina* and Ringed Plovers *Charadrius hiaticula*, 'several of which fell at the same discharge'. The second, obtained in Cornwall in 1860, was set up by Penzance taxidermist Vingoe, and the third record for the southwest involved one shot by Augustus Pechell beside Bryher Pool on 16th September 1870 (Rodd 1870d, 1880; Clark & Rodd 1906). Rodd's description of this last bird as a male (Rodd 1870a) was presumably based on a post-mortem examination.

We hear nothing further of this species until the 1944 entry from A A Dorrien-Smith (*CBWPSAR* 14) referring to his sighting of a 'Red-breasted Sandpiper' (presumably on Tresco) on 12th September the preceding year (1943). Unfortunately, even though T A Dorrien-Smith later used this name in his list of *Birds of Scilly as Recorded at Tresco Abbey* (T A Dorrien-Smith 1951), it remains unclear exactly which species was being referred to in relation to the 1943 record, mainly because other entries in the earlier local literature referred to one or other dowitcher *Limnodromus* species under the old name of 'Red-breasted Snipe'. Penhallurick (1969) gives no additional reference but nevertheless appears to accept the 1943 record, though he may have relied upon *The Handbook* (Witherby et al. 1940), which listed four records for Cornwall and Scilly up until 1943. As no records except those discussed here are known, we must assume too that these distinguished authors also accepted the 1943 claim. Nonetheless, caution seems advisable in relation to this record, particularly as an unidentified dowitcher, or 'Red-breasted Snipe' was shot on 17th September 1943 (Nisbet 1961), just six days after the 'Red-breasted Sandpiper' sighting. Penhallurick credits this 1943 individual as the first British record since 1906.

Following the supposed 1943 sighting, there are no Scillonian Buff-breasted Sandpiper records until three were found together on St Mary's Airport on 9th September 1962, some ten years after the establishment of a well-organised all-island recording system on St Agnes. But whilst it seems tempting to suggest that birds were overlooked, as indeed some may have been, it seems almost too simplistic an explanation for the apparent 20-year absence of such an obvious and confiding species, especially considering its almost annual appearance in the islands from 1962 onwards. Intriguingly, the first on the Cornish mainland after the 19th century records was a bird near Land's End in 1963 (Penhallurick 1969).

Disregarding the two earliest records, a minimum of 132 Buff-breasts arrived in Scilly during the years 1962 to 1999, in 30 (79%) of the 38 years involved and at an average of 4.4 birds per arrival year, or 3.4 per year overall. The maximum in any single year was 14 (1975) with 11 in both 1970 and 1980. Just three birds arrived in spring: two on St Agnes on 4th June 1971 and a more recent individual on St Agnes and then at St Mary's Airport from 8th to 13th May 1985. The June 1971 record appears not to have been accepted by the BBRC but would certainly be acceptable under the current system of vetting; it was possibly rejected because it was the first spring record. Disregarding the two May and June records, the earliest arrival date was 20th August and the last 29th October, which was also the last date any bird was present (two on St Agnes for one day in 1972).

## Buff-breasted Sandpiper arrival dates

## Buff-breasted Sandpiper annual totals

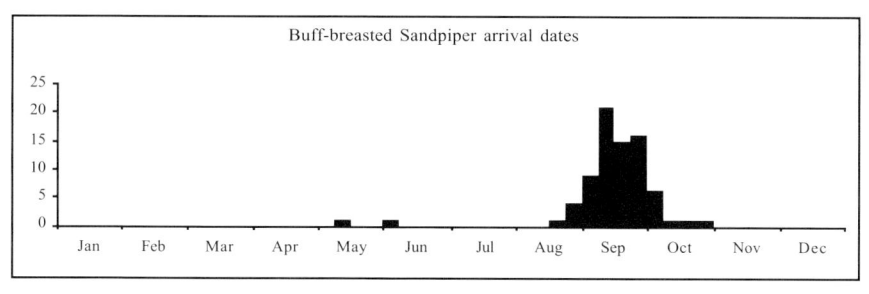

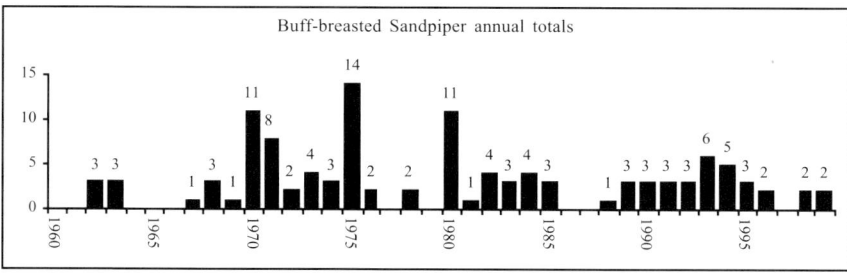

One of the three birds on St Agnes in 1992 was found dead on 26th September, and a bird that arrived on 3rd October 1998 was very probably the individual seen at Sennen, west Cornwall, from 12th September to 2nd October. The Charts show all accepted arrival dates (including the 19th century record, but exclude the bird found dead on St Agnes in 1992), plus annual recorded totals from 1960 to 1999. The former reveals the typical pattern of autumn transatlantic migrants on Scilly. A few obviously acceptable pre-1983 records seem never to have been submitted to the BBRC, as in the case of one at Pentle Bay, Tresco on 26th August 1974 and two on St Mary's Airport from 27th to 29th of that month (*IOSBR* 1975).

Birds commence leaving the breeding areas from mid-July to mid-August, with the bulk of the USA passage occurring during August–September (Cramp *et al.* 1977–94). Most move south through central North and South America, but an unknown (but possibly small) percentage move southeast across Canada south of Hudson Bay. These then either take the transoceanic route out over the North Atlantic and south to the Caribbean, or fly directly to northeast South America. Like other migrant wader species using this route, Buff-breasted Sandpiper is at risk of involuntary transatlantic vagrancy, in fact substantially more so judging from the numbers reaching Scilly. Return spring passage is thought to mirror autumn passage, and though lacking the transoceanic element, nonetheless involves overflying the USA north of the Gulf of Mexico. The breeding grounds are reoccupied from late May to mid-June. Birds arriving in Scilly in spring may be northward-bound remnants of previous autumn arrivals, rather than newly arrived transatlantic migrants. By 1999 the Cornish mainland all-time total stood at 96.

# Ruff *Philomachus pugnax* A

**Spring and autumn migrant, most occur during the latter period though the largest groups pass through in spring.**

Breeds northern Eurasia, from Britain, Netherlands and Norway to eastern Siberia north of Kamchatka. Migratory, wintering mostly equatorial and southern Africa, also east into Indian subcontinent. Monotypic. Amber-listed in UK: five-year mean breeding population of 3.2 pairs; 50% or more of UK non-breeding population at ten or fewer sites (Gregory *et al.* 2002).

Early evidence of this species in Scilly comes in the form of bone remains unearthed from the prehistoric site on Nornour in the Eastern Isles (Turk 1971, 1984b). There are three late 19th century records of Ruff on Scilly, involving birds shot by John Jenkinson in autumn 1864, on Tresco by T A Dorrien-Smith in September 1878, and John Jenkinson again in March 1885 (Rodd 1880; Clark & Rodd 1906). The 1878 individual appears in the Tresco Abbey records under the list of 'game' shot during winter 1878–79. In mainland Cornwall during the 19th century, E H Rodd knew it as an occasional visitor on autumn passage, all specimens he knew of having been acquired in first-winter plumage. He knew of no instance where an adult male in breeding or part-breeding plumage had been seen or obtained (Rodd 1880).

Moving to the 20th century, first mention may have been the report of three by Bryher pool during September 1920 (Boyd 1924) but the species gets a mention about every other year from the commencement of the *CBWPSAR*. These occurred either as singles or in groups of up to three or four, the very obvious exception being a flock of 50 reported by A A Dorrien-Smith on 4th June 1944 (A A Dorrien-Smith 1942), presumably on Tresco. By the mid- to late 1960s Penhallurick (1969) felt able to describe it as an annual autumn and less frequent spring migrant, autumn birds normally arriving by late August, an early date being 5th July. He also pointed out that late dates for autumn migrants would be around 10th to 17th October and drew attention to the lack of any winter records. Penhallurick thought spring migration commenced as early as mid-February, though in his view the main passage was more likely to occur during the period late March to late May, with 8th June considered exceptionally late. If this was the case, Dorrien-Smith's 1944 flock of 50 were very late spring migrants. Penhallurick also noted that, although spring migration is lightest, there is a clear tendency for larger groups of birds to arrive during this season, with 14 in late March 1965 the next highest after the 1944 flock.

In general, that situation persists, though with slight modifications, such as the individual present on St Agnes from mid-December 1981 until 27th, or the bird on Tresco for three days in mid-January 1985 – in total there have now been about six winter records. The cut-off date for late spring migrants has been pushed back to perhaps 27th June and for autumn birds to late November, but with the tendency for larger spring groups maintained. In addition, pleasant relief was provided by the presence of breeding-plumage males on grassy St Mary's Airport on 6th May 1986 and on Tresco 24th–27th June 1990.

The closest breeding Ruffs to Scilly are in eastern England (few) and the Netherlands, with even greater concentrations further north and east (Hagemeijer & Blair 1997). Although birds from some eastern populations move south into India, by far the majority of Ruffs winter in Africa, including some from northeast Siberia. Autumn movement through Europe occurs on a broad front (Cramp *et al.* (1977–94) and there is a clear south to southwest tendency, although most Ruffs moving through Britain and Ireland may originate from Scandinavia and western Europe and winter in Britain, western France and the Mediterranean south into West Africa, where roosts of almost one million have been recorded. Males migrate earlier than females, perhaps from late June or early July, with females and juveniles moving from July onwards. The first males reach Senegal in West Africa as early as mid-July, whereas return passage out of Africa commences from mid-February, although birds from northeast Russia perhaps return to their breeding grounds as late as mid-June. Just one Ruff was been ringed in Scilly, during the period prior to 1970, but it was not recovered and there are no controls. There is an interesting mid-20th century report of Ruffs seen at sea from ocean weather station 'Kilo', 800 km southwest of Scilly in the Western Approaches. On 30th April 1958, four different groups of Ruffs arrived in the vicinity of the weather ship, three of which (involving four, three and eight birds) arrived between 10.35 and 12.28 hours and all circled the ship before moving on (McLean & Williamson 1959). All three groups briefly settled on the water and one of the eight became waterlogged and was taken by a Lesser Black-backed Gull *Larus fuscus*. The last arrival, at 14.45 hours involved just two individuals, both of which were clearly exhausted and both of which died aboard ship. After post-mortem examinations, one weighed just 56 grams, rather than the expected 100 to 180 grams.

# Jack Snipe *Lymnocryptes minimus* A

**Regular migrant in small numbers, occasionally overwinters. Formerly shot on Scilly in substantial numbers.**

Breeds northern Eurasia, from Sweden east to 150°E in Siberia. Migratory, West Palearctic population winters discontinuously Britain and Ireland, southern coastal North Sea, France, Iberia, Mediterranean and trans-Saharan Africa north of equator. Monotypic.

Well known to the 19th century Tresco sportsmen, these early observers were under the impression that it generally occurred in areas where Snipe *Gallinago gallinago* were less numerous (Clark & Rodd 1906). First mention of Jack Snipe in the islands comes from Francis Rodd, in correspondence to his uncle E H Rodd in Penzance (Rodd 1880). Here he described how, during one of many shooting visits to

## Sandpipers, Snipes, Godwits, Curlews and Phalaropes

Tresco in 1870, he recorded the first Jack Snipe arrivals of that year on 20th September, he and others shooting no less than 50 during the period 1st to 12th November. He further observed that numbers around the Tresco pools on 2nd December made it clear that there had been an arrival the previous night, and similar numbers on the following night allowed '12 couples' (24 birds) to be shot on the St Mary's Moors on 3rd.

Frustratingly, early writers often referred to 'snipe', making it difficult to now decide which species were involved. However, in the cases mentioned above, Francis Rodd leaves no room for doubt, by making specific reference to Jack Snipe. Various additional reports from around the same period help to make it clear that this species was more frequent then in autumn and winter, e.g. 14 shot in one day in January 1879 and 73 in total during autumn/winter 1878–79. Clark and Rodd also mention the total of 364 Snipe and Jack Snipe shot during the 'really fine Snipe year' of 1858 (Clark & Rodd 1906). The only remaining 19th century Jack Snipe record involved a bird killed by striking the Bishop Rock Light at 20.00 hours on 10th November 1885 (Harvie-Brown *et al.* 1885).

As Penhallurick was able to point out even by the mid-1960s, Jack Snipe no longer occurred in Scilly in such numbers (Penhallurick 1969). Penhallurick analysed the records up to and including the 1960s, noting that most birds normally arrived during the first half of October, with additional arrivals into November and with singles reported into December in some years. Most birds remained only one to two days, though exceptions remained viewable for up to three weeks. Five at any one time seems to have been the expected upper limit and Penhallurick could find details of just four spring arrivals, all between 10th March and 13th May and all involving lone individuals.

Taking the ten years from 1990, although birds were present in spring and autumn in all years, arriving at reliable totals for numbers of individuals involved is problematical, owing primarily to the probability of inter-site movement but also to the species' unobtrusive habits and the presence, often, of up to six individuals at favoured sites, e.g. Porth Hellick Pool on St Mary's and Tresco's Great Pool. On Tresco in 1990, a count of six on 1st October dropped to five by 3rd and three by 9th, with 2–3 daily from then until six again on 15th and seven next day, but with a subsequent two then increasing to ten by 22nd. For the same year, the minimum all-island count was probably in the region of 27 birds, but could have been higher. Earliest obvious spring arrival for the ten-year period was 5th April 1990, though all known spring arrival dates were squeezed into the 23-day period ending 27th. The first returning migrant was recorded on 10th September and, like spring dates, autumn arrivals appeared remarkable consistent, within a 26-day window ending 5th October. Normal autumn departures appear slightly less condensed, within the 48-day period from 2nd November to 18th December.

In at least 1997 and 1998, birds lingered on into winter and in four years – 1990, 92, 95 and 99 – one or more were present at the start of the year. Four Jack Snipe have been ringed in the islands, three prior to 1970 and one by the author at dawn in an area of wet grassland in Higher Moors on 9th April 1995. There are no recoveries and no controls. Typically, these diminutive little waders, with their characteristic bouncing approach to life, are encountered among the low vegetation out in front of the two Higher Moors' hides, or the two hides in Lower Moors. And, whilst they also occur around the Tresco Pools, they are more difficult to see at the long ranges involved. It is also worth remembering just how well camouflaged they are and that a prolonged and thorough search of an even closely viewable area of mud and marginal vegetation will often reveal several individuals in full view, and where there were previously thought to be none.

The closest breeding Jack Snipe to Scilly are in southern Sweden. Although they winter throughout western and southern Europe and well down into Africa, the majority of Jack Snipe probably go no further than the western maritime countries, e.g. Britain, Ireland, France and Iberia (Cramp *et al.* 1977–94; Wernham *et al.* 2002). There is strong ringing evidence of a broad-front autumn movement southwest across Europe, which, at least up until 1983, involved birds ringed as migrants in Norway, Finland, Denmark and western Russia. Whatever the full extent of the movement involved, Jack Snipe passing through Scilly in spring and autumn must originate from at least southern Sweden and may come from a great deal further east.

# Snipe  *Gallinago gallinago*  A

**Common migrant and winter visitor, numbers vary annually. Does not breed, though it may possibly have done so in the past.**

Breeds northern and central Eurasia, from Iceland, Faeroes, Britain and Ireland east to Pacific, other populations South America and southern Africa. Northern populations migratory or partially so, in West Palearctic wintering south to Mediterranean, North Africa and Middle East, many reaching northern subtropical Africa. Polytypic: *faeroeensis*, or 'Faeroe Snipe' occurs Iceland, Faeroes, Orkney and Shetland; nominate *gallinago* elsewhere in West Palearctic; at least four more forms South America and southern Africa. Amber-listed in UK: moderate to high (67%) breeding decline over past 25 years (Gregory *et al.* 2002). National 7% increase 1994–99 (Bashford & Noble 2000).

A small bone sample from the prehistoric site at May's Hill, St Martin's, was identified as being from this species and probably dates from the period between the 2nd and 7th centuries AD (Turk 1984a). Next earliest mention of this species in Scilly is probably Heath's 18th century observation that winter landbirds on the islands included 'Snipes' (Heath 1750), an observation confirmed soon after by another 18th century commentator, who noted that 'Wildfowl of all sorts, from the Swan to the Snipes, are to be shot, and most of them in great plenty in the winter time' (Borlase 1756).

There is a great deal of 19th century information concerning the sporting status of this species, occasionally referred to as 'full Snipe', much of it stemming from the activities of Tresco Abbey shooting parties. However, it may be sufficient to say that large numbers fell to the guns during most winters. James Clark and Francis Rodd give the most informative overview (Clark & Rodd 1906), perhaps devoting more space to this species and Woodcock *Scolopax rusticola* than to any other. They begin by making clear that Snipe did not breed in the islands, though so-called family parties were reported from time to time – though unfortunately no additional information is given. Clark and Rodd go on to point out that at any time during autumn or winter the slightest hint of easterly wind would bring Snipe, their numbers increasing with the severity of the wind. They also observed that numbers varied between years, and that in favourable conditions more Snipe could be shot in Scilly on a single day than throughout an entire winter of 'contrary winds'. As evidence of this they described a single day during winter 1878–79 when an island-record bag of 93 Snipe were obtained from an area of St Mary's favourable for this species; in all, 545 Snipe and 73 Jack Snipe *L. minimus* fell to the guns that winter (Rodd 1880). Clark and Rodd contrast this with the winter of 1868–69, when just 14 Snipe were shot during an entire winter dominated by westerly winds. Very clearly, numbers involved on the islands could be truly impressive, as can be seen in Clark and Rodd's account of the events of 1858, when a total of 364 Snipe or Jack Snipe were killed, 93 falling to the gun of the Reverend John Jenkinson in two days. And as if to show these were not chance happenings, they also provided figures for 1857, when 299 Snipe were shot, including 101 in three days.

In letters to his uncle E H Rodd of Penzance in west Cornwall, Francis Rodd provides two first-hand accounts of mid-19th century Snipe movements on Scilly. The first involved birds watched arriving from the east on the morning of 22nd December 1870, as Francis walked over some high ground on St Mary's. He described precisely how 'about three o'clock Snipes began to appear from somewhere; it was difficult to tell the direction they came from, as they descended from a great height in wisps of four or five to perhaps 20'. He then went on to describe how 'some settled on the high land, but it was difficult to tell whether the birds remained or only rested for a few minutes, and the fields around the moors were at dusk perfectly alive with both (snipe) species in a very disturbed state' (Rodd 1880). The following day, 23rd, Rodd started for the moors immediately after breakfast and found 'the snipes were actually leaving the islands at that time, as those put up did not settle in again, but went straight away westwards'. Francis ended his account with the information that during a heavy snowstorm that same evening 36 Snipe were shot. It seems clear from information Francis Rodd gave in respect of this and some other species that the winter of 1870–71 was particularly severe by Scillonian standards, in which case it is of interest to note that these birds headed west after leaving the islands and not east in the direction of mainland Cornwall.

Frances's uncle E H Rodd also makes frequent reference to the appearance of large numbers of Snipe annually in the islands, on several occasions writing letters to the *Zoologist* to that effect. Included among these were *Snipe-shooting at St Mary's, Scilly* (Rodd 1871f), *Sport at the Scilly Isles* (Rodd 1860b) and *The Great Autumnal Migration of Birds* (Rodd 1864c). All of these dealt specifically or in part with the movement of Snipe through the islands during autumn and winter. As expected, most 19th century accounts refer to occasions when Snipe were present in obvious numbers, but there is very little information available now regarding periods of their absence. Francis also gave some indication of the timing of these autumn arrivals, describing 20th August 1870 as somewhat earlier than normal, although making it clear that birds were often to be met with later in that month.

Still in the 19th century, but in a slightly different context, there is a single report of a Snipe being killed striking the lantern of the Bishop Rock Lighthouse around 8 pm on 10th November 1885 (Harvie-Brown *et al.* 1886).

Together with many other species, we hear little of Snipe through the early half of the 20th century, although there is the odd later reference. For example, there is a 1943 report that A A Dorrien-Smith went to investigate claims of Snipe drumming over part of Higher Moors on St Mary's, spending two hours on 25th June watching the site but seeing no Snipe (*CBWPSAR* 13). Equally interesting is the comment made in 1944 that even by 17th December no Snipe had appeared in the islands, for the fourth year in succession. The author of the report suggested that 'the great frosts of 1940–41 nearly wiped out Snipe from western Europe, and the great droughts of 1938 and 1939 also took a heavy toll' (*CBWPSAR* 14). Indeed, regardless of the veracity of the above claim, the records apparently support the view that numbers were greatly reduced by this time, compared with the previous century, with almost no reference to Snipe from then until the mid-1960s, when the comment that 30 were flushed from the narrow centre of Annet appears, but with little information regarding the species' normal annual status. Even by the mid-1970s it seems to have been far from abundant, being described in the 1975 *IOSBR* as occurring in very small numbers in spring and autumn, with first arrivals around 28th August and with one to ten on major islands considered normal.

Examining the situation up to the present time, and taking the year 1990 as broadly representative, at least 50 were present collectively on the main islands at the start of the year. But with an obvious fall-off in numbers by April, at which time perhaps no more than eight were to be found, with the last sighting of the spring in Lower Moors, St Mary's, on 29th May. First of the autumn were three recorded on St Agnes on 23rd July, numbers increasing slightly from then on but with a further detectable influx from early October, numbers on St Mary's peaking at 46 on 28th. The year ended with perhaps the same number present as in January. And whilst it seems clear that numbers do increase around the expected times of migration, putting any sort of figure on exact numbers involved is hindered by the usual problem of inter-site movement. There are no confirmed reports of breeding having occurred in Scilly, though it is rumoured to have done so. Occasional birds remain during summer and as recently as late May 1991 a bird was reported 'displaying' in Lower Moors on St Mary's (Chown & Lock 2002).

Snipe continue to be shot on Scilly during winter, or at least on inhabited islands. However, in the St Mary's Lower Moors there is a recent shooting ban in force, although perhaps most Snipe frequent the Higher Moors and Porth Hellick area, which is still shot. As with many species, there is a dearth of co-ordinated all-island winter counts, three recent potentially useful surveys, i.e. Kirby (1988), Lock (1996) and the January 1997 Winter Shorebird Survey (unpublished data) concentrating on tidal and adjacent waters, thereby failing to address this mainly freshwater species.

A few Snipe winter in northern Europe, as far north as Norway, Iceland and the Faeroes but most move south, western European populations spending the winter from Britain and Ireland south to the Mediterranean. Many also reach Africa, some crossing the Sahara as far as the Gulf of Guinea (Cramp *et al.* 1977–94). However, Cramp *et al.* consider that the lack of European ringing recoveries from West Africa during winter suggests that birds involved may have a largely eastern European origin. Autumn passage commences during July, peaking in central Europe during September–October but with most in their wintering areas by November. Return migration starts from February or March, most Snipe reoccupying their breeding grounds by April or May (Cramp *et al.* 1977–94).

A total of 21 Snipe had been ringed in Scilly up until 1999, eleven since 1970. A bird ringed in Iceland in July 1954 was found dead on Tresco the following February and one ringed on St Agnes in October 1957 was shot on St Mary's two months later.

## Controls
85256    Pul   Fnjoskadalur, Iceland 3rd July 1954    FD  Tresco 17th February 1955

**Local**
V21258  Ad  St Agnes 11th October 1957                SH  St Mary's 15th December 1957

Snipe Ringing Recaptures

## Wilson's Snipe  *Gallinago delicata*  A  BBRC 100%

[1997:   One St Mary's 19th October]   *British Birds* 94: 504, 95: 528
[1998:   One Lower Moors, St Mary's 9th October into 1999]   *British Birds* 94: 504, 95: 528

Breeds North America from Alaska east to Newfoundland, wintering southern USA southwards though Central America. Steady decline viewed as significant in eastern population (Bryant 1997).

Gantlett (1998) highlighted the earlier limited presence in Britain of the distinctive North American form of Snipe *delicata*, or 'Wilson's Snipe', which by the appearance of this book should have been split from Snipe *G. gallinago* by the BOURC. Gantlett drew attention to the first British and Irish record shot in Ireland in October 1991, plus an earlier but now rejected Meinertzhagan specimen allegedly shot in Lancashire in September 1957, plus one from the Outer Hebrides in October 1920, which was also rejected (BOURC 1999; Palmer 2000). Hardly had the print dried on Gantlett's paper before a snipe apparently meeting all plumage and physical requirements was discovered at Lower Moors, St Mary's, on 9th October 1998 (Bland 1998; Bland 1999; Leader 1999), being subsequently well watched by numerous birders and remaining in Scilly until the year's end. What was assumed to be the same individual reportedly reappeared at the same site for five days during April 1999, although whether a bird allegedly also showing Wilson's Snipe characteristics at nearby Porth Hellick during September 3rd–8th 1999 was the same or a different individual remains unclear.

Up until at least October 2002, the long-staying 1998 Lower Moors individual and an earlier claim of one on St Mary's on 19th October 1997 remained under consideration by BOURC/BBRC (*British Birds* 95: 528) but seemed likely to gain acceptance (D Parkin pers. comm.), based partly on clear differences in drumming between this species and Snipe (BOURC 2002a).

## Great Snipe  *Gallinago media*  A  BBRC 3.6%

Rare migrant or winter visitor, full written description required by the BBRC.

    1877  One (shot) Great Ganilly January   Clark & Rodd 1906
1877–79  One (shot) 'Scilly'   Clark & Rodd 1906
    1940  One St Mary's 5th January   Penhallurick 1969
    1958  One St Agnes 26th October   *British Birds* 54: 176
    1962  One St Agnes 27th to 30th April   *British Birds* 56: 399
  [1963  One St Mary's 27th January]   *CBWPSAR* 33
  [1968  One Tresco 3rd October]   Penhallurick 1978
    1970  One St Mary's 6th October   *British Birds* 64: 350
  [1973  One St Agnes 13th October]   *IOSBR* 1974
    1973  One St Martin's 21st October   *British Birds* 67: 321, 68: 335
  [1976  One Great Pool, Tresco 9th to 15th October]   *IOSBR* 1976
  [1976  One Holy Vale, St Mary's 6th November]   *IOSBR* 1976

Breeds upland and arctic Norway, eastern Europe and western Asia, from Poland east to Kazakhstan. Winters Africa south of equator. Monotypic.

A feature of this species, formerly known as 'Solitary Snipe', is its scarcity in Scilly over the last 25 years, following a period during which it occurred with some regularity. E H Rodd described it as rare in Cornwall but made no mention of it in a Scillonian context (Rodd 1880). However, his nephew Francis Rodd and co-author James Clark referred to two birds shot in Scilly in the 19th century, one by Tresco gamekeeper David Smith on Great Ganilly, Eastern Isles, in January 1877, the other between that date and 1879. Although precise details of the second specimen had become lost by 1906, the skin was preserved (Clark & Rodd 1906). Next mention of Great Snipe in Scilly is a bird listed in the Tresco Abbey Record Books as seen on St Mary's on 5th January 1940 (Penhallurick 1969).

Great Snipe arrival dates

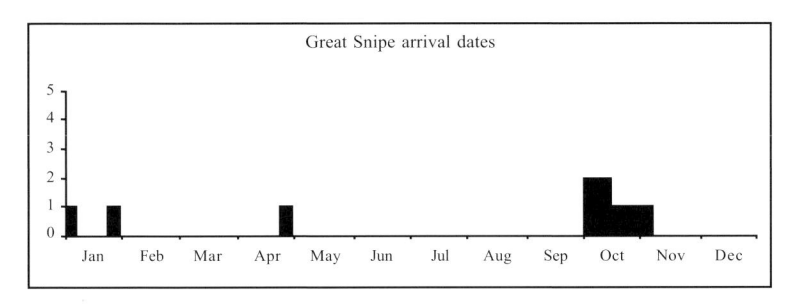

From the BBRC's inception until 1976 there are four accepted records for the islands and a further five claims of birds seen and described, at least one of which was not submitted to the Committee (St Agnes 13th October 1973). All but one of the unaccepted or unsubmitted claims appear to have involved multiple-observer sightings. They should also be viewed against the subsequent near total lack of any claims during the last quarter of the 20th century.

Cramp *et al.* (1977–94) discussed the marked decline in European range and numbers during the 19th and early 20th centuries. They pointed out that though underlying causes are unclear they probably involve a combination of climatic and habitat factors, plus perhaps excessive hunting. Most of the reduction in both range and numbers appears to have taken place in western and northwestern Europe, which perhaps explains the loss of migrant birds from Scilly.

## Long-billed Dowitcher *Limnodromus scolopaceus* A BBRC 4.3%

**Very rare migrant or winter visitor, full written description required by the BBRC.**

1857 One (juvenile) shot St Mary's 3rd October   Nisbet 1961
1966 One St Agnes 23rd October   *British Birds* 60: 317, 61: 362
1967 One Tresco 27th September to 22nd October   *British Birds* 61: 339–340
1968 Two Porth Hellick, St Mary's 21st to 22nd September   *British Birds* 62: 468
1975 One St Mary's 5th to 13th October   *British Birds* 69: 335, 72: 523
1977 One St Agnes & St Mary's 28th September to 19th February 1978
                                              *British Birds* 71: 502–503, 72: 523–524
1978 One (juvenile or first-winter) St Mary's & Tresco 13th to 15th September
                                              *British Birds* 72: 523, 73: 508, 76: 496
1978 One (juvenile) St Mary's & St Agnes 3rd to at least 29th October
                                              *British Birds* 72: 523, 73: 508, 76: 496
1985 One (juvenile) Porth Hellick, St Mary's 19th to 24th December   *British Birds* 79: 548

Breeds extreme northeast Siberia, St Lawrence Island and northern and western Alaska. Migratory, winters southern USA and Central America. Monotypic.

There were no recorded Scillonian dowitcher sightings between the mid-19th and mid-20th centuries, following one shot by Augustus Pechell in Higher Moors, St Mary's, on 3rd October 1857 (Rodd 1857a; Clark & Rodd 1906; Nisbet 1961). In his epic *The Birds of Cornwall and The Scilly Islands* E H Rodd refers to this record, under the heading 'Red-breasted Snipe *Macrorhamphus griseus*', as the only Cornish or Scillonian record up until that time (Rodd 1880). However, all early dowitcher records must be treated as indeterminate unless subsequently re-examined, as happened with the 1857 record. In his comprehensive review of British and Irish dowitcher records, following their separation, Nisbet (1961) unconditionally accepted the identity of the 1857 St Mary's individual as Long-billed. However, because the mounted skin of a dowitcher shot on Tresco on 17th September 1943 had not been examined up until Nisbet's review, he was unable to attribute this individual to either species. As far as is known this specimen still awaits examination and therefore appears in the following section.

Inexplicably, although there were eight Scillonian sightings involving nine Long-billed Dowitchers between 1966 and 1985, none were reported during the subsequent 15 years, a feature that is perhaps difficult to explain. The story of the 1966 arrival began with the appearance and trapping of a winter-plumage dowitcher on the Hayle Estuary, west Cornwall, on 30th October 1966. However, the finer points of dowitcher identification were still to be defined and the observation went into the records as indeterminate. But the bird remained in the area until 22nd April 1967, by which time it had assumed summer plumage, which simplified its identification as Long-billed (*British Birds* 60: 317, 61: 339–340 & 362). The bird on St Agnes, on 23rd October 1966 was also confirmed as Long-billed and in any event was generally considered to be the Hayle individual. Interestingly, in view of the more recent dowitcher absence from Scilly, the arrival of the 1966 Hayle individual coincided with the appearance of indeterminate dowitchers in Ireland on 29th September and 2nd October, plus an alleged Short-billed *L. griseus* on 8th.

Clearly, even by 1967 the niceties of dowitcher identification were becoming more generally understood, David Hunt and B R Dean's description of that year's individual including details of call, undertail-coverts and length of wings and bill (*CBWPSAR* 37). Consequently, the record was accepted as Long-billed. Perhaps surprisingly, there seems to be no published reference to the two 1968 arrivals prior to notification by the BBRC of their acceptance the following year (*British Birds* 62: 468). Although plumage features helped confirm identification of these two, much reliance appears to have been placed upon descriptions of their call, described as a 'monosyllabic *keek*' and heard by all three observers. The 1977 individual was widely considered to be the same as the bird present on the Hayle Estuary until May 1978 (shades of 1966). Whereas the individual on St Mary's and Tresco in mid-September 1978 was another originally thought by the BBRC to be indeterminate but then later accepted as this species (*British Birds* 72: 524, 73: 508). The only winter arrival in Scilly involved the bird at Porth Hellick, St Mary's, from 19th December 1985 for six days, following what was described at the time as a 'vigorous Atlantic depression' (*IOSBR* 1985).

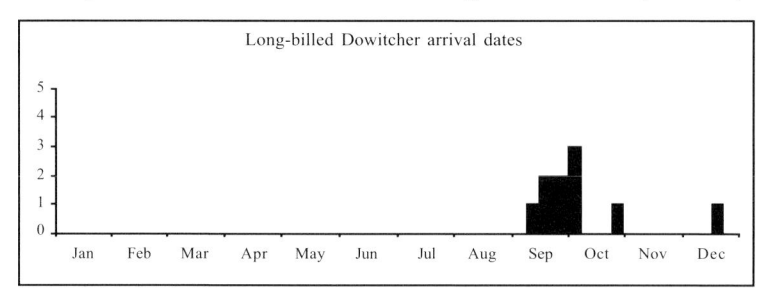

Long-billed Dowitcher arrival dates

All Scillonian Long-billed Dowitcher arrival dates are shown in the Chart, revealing a marked concentration around late September and the first week of October. Regrettably, the comprehensive review of rare birds in Britain and Ireland by Dymond and others (Dymond *et al.* 1989) only covered the period up to 1985, making it difficult to know whether the more recent absence of Long-billed arrivals is a Scillonian or a national trend, though the latter seems probable. Long-billed Dowitcher breeds in northern and western Alaska and northeast Siberia, but occurs in western Europe more frequently than Short-billed, which breeds in central and eastern Canada. This is generally thought attributable to a southeastern departure from the breeding grounds by some individuals of Long-billed Dowitcher, bringing overshooting birds into the path of mid-Atlantic depressions, as happens with several other migrant Nearctic wader species (Nisbet 1959). In Alaska, autumn migration occurs mainly during July–September, the majority passing through western states. A substantial proportion, however, move southeast of the Rocky Mountains through central states, leaving a probably smaller proportion to pass east over the Great Lakes and then south through the Atlantic coastal states. Birds using the central and eastern flyways winter mainly in New Mexico, central Texas, the Gulf coast and Florida, south into eastern Mexico and possibly the West Indies. It is possible that females move south before males (Cramp *et al.* 1977–94).

A total of 206 Long-billed Dowitcher records were accepted by the BBRC during the period 1958–99, in which case the nine Scillonian sightings represent just 4.3%. No dowitchers have been ringed on Scilly and there are no recaptures from elsewhere.

# Dowitcher *Limnodromus* A

Unidentified dowitcher Records
   1943   One (first-winter – shot) Tresco 12th to 17th September
                                         *CBWPSAR* 14; Nisbet 1961; *British Birds* 54: 343–356

[1944   One Tresco August]   Penhallurick 1969; Griffiths 1982
[1953   One Tresco August]   Penhallurick 1969; Griffiths 1982
[1971   One St Agnes 28th September – claimed as Short-billed]   IOSBR 1971
[1977   One St Mary's & St Agnes 1st to 3rd October]   Griffiths 1982

See monotypic Long-billed Dowitcher *L. scolopaceus* for distribution of that species. Polytypic Short-billed Dowitcher *L. griseus* breeds central and eastern Canada and southern Alaska: nominate *griseus* occurs eastern Canada, *hendersoni* central Canada and *caurinus* Alaska. Migratory, Alaskan birds winter California south to Peru, central Canadian birds use central flyway, wintering southern and southeast USA, Caribbean and South America to Brazil; nominate eastern birds use Atlantic route and winter much the same areas as those from central Canada.

The skin of a dowitcher shot on Tresco on 17th September 1943 and now in the Tresco Abbey collection could not be attributed to one or other species owing to a lack of prior examination (Nisbet 1961). Seemingly, this skin still awaits full identification. Two dowitcher sight records from the islands, in 1944 and 1953, seem not to have been published and are referred to only in the Tresco Abbey records (Penhallurick 1969). Finally, a bird seen well by Dr R J Rains on St Agnes on 28th September 1971 was claimed by him as Short-billed, on the strength of its call. The observer first heard what he recognised as a dowitcher call and immediately imitated it, whereupon the bird circled above him giving clear views and allowing a detailed description to be prepared (*IOSBR* 1971). Nonetheless the record appears not to have been submitted to the BBRC.

## Woodcock (Eurasian Woodcock) *Scolopax rusticola*  A

**Regular migrant in moderate numbers, fewer during winter.**

Breeds northern and central Eurasia, from Atlantic east to Sakhalin and northern Japan, also limited area of southern Asia, in West Palearctic wintering south to North Africa. Monotypic. Amber-listed in UK: moderate breeding decline and moderate range contraction over past 25 years; unfavourable world winter conservation status (Gregory *et al.* 2002).

Robert Heath's mid-18th century observation that 'Woodcocks' were included among a list of landbirds found on Scilly seems the earliest published reference to this species (Heath 1750), though Heath fails to clarify the time of year involved. Following this, there are numerous 19th century Woodcock or, to give it its Cornish name, Kevelek (Penhallurick 1969), reports, many of which refer to shooting bags, involving some quite impressive totals. The majority of such reports originate from the pen of E H Rodd and recount events witnessed by his nephew Francis Rodd, who spent much time shooting and observing on Tresco (e.g. Rodd 1860b, 1861a, 1867a, 1864c, 1874).

Most noteworthy perhaps were the events of winter 1878–79, when 415 Woodcock, 545 Snipe *Gallinago gallinago*, 73 Jack Snipe *G. minimus*, 390 Pheasants *Phasianus colchicus*, 84 Golden Plover *Pluvialis apricaria*, 67 Teal *Anas crecca* and 10 Curlew *Numenius arquata* fell to the guns on Scilly. And apart from 2,045 Rabbits *Oryctolagus cuniculus* listed in the Tresco game book, there were additional entries for Purple Heron *Ardea purpurea*, Stone Curlew *Burhinus oedicnemus*, Ruff *Philomachus pugnax* and Wood *Tringa glareola* and Green Sandpipers *T. ochropus*, as well as more recognisable wildfowl species, e.g. Wigeon *Anas penelope* and Goldeneye *Bucephala clangula*. The previous greatest annual Woodcock total for the islands was 223 in 1860. During October 1855, Captain Tower, friend of Augustus Smith, shot 39 Woodcock in a single day, whilst in November 1859 the all-island shooting total included 90 Woodcock and 150 Snipe (Rodd 1856).

Gilbert White (in Jesse 1887) recorded a large 18th century influx of Woodcock on St Mary's during the night of 10th–11th November, as informed by an unnamed correspondent, though according to Penhallurick (1969) the latter may have been the Robert Heath previously referred to. So many Woodcock were allegedly involved that just within the walls of The Garrison area the writer was able to shoot '26 couples, besides three couples which were wounded, but did not give himself the trouble to retrieve'. It is highly surprising that the wind was from the west at the time, the writer himself pointing out that easterly or northerly winds were normally far more conducive in bringing this species to Scilly, going on to suggest that perhaps birds involved on this occasion originated from Ireland. Equally surprising seems to have been that these birds left the island during the following night and on the same westerly wind, the writer assuming they left towards mainland Cornwall. So numerous were the Woodcock on this occasion that in nearby Hugh Town birds were said to have landed in the streets and to have run into houses and outbuildings (Rodd 1880). There are similar reports of mass arrivals on mainland Cornwall, Penhallurick (1969) recounting a report of Woodcock drowning in the sea in vast numbers before making landfall, and a story of youths catching them alive in the streets of Polperro around 1881 by the use of a bent pin and a live worm as bait.

However, it seems clear from other reports that events such as those described above were not necessarily the norm and James Clark and Francis Rodd usefully summarised Woodcock's status at the start of the 20th century. These authors pointed out that it sometimes arrived in the islands by the second week of October, with the greatest influxes usually occurring towards the end of that month. They also made it clear that by mid-January it usually became quite scarce, as in 1865 when Francis Rodd managed to shoot just one on 4th January. Nevertheless, severe mainland weather could dramatically alter this situation, as in winter 1880–81, when 'considerable numbers' arrived during late January, nearly 100 being killed at a time when the writers thought normal shooting should have ceased. It also seems clear that, like now, birds sometimes did not arrive until later in the year, as in 1864 when the first indication of autumn Woodcock migration involved eight killed on the Eastern Isles during easterly winds on 15th December (Rodd 1880). According to Clark and Rodd, the last reported date for 'a stray specimen' of this species in Scilly was mid-March, although they failed to say whether there was any indication of spring passage.

Courtney (1845) quoted Paris (*Guide to Mount's Bay* 1816), who thought Woodcock arrived earlier in Scilly than in 'any other part of England', though without further elaboration. He described them as most often accompanied by northeasterly or northwesterly winds and often being so exhausted that they could be caught in great numbers. For example, at St Agnes Lighthouse, to which they were attracted by the light's beam, some were killed by striking the glass. There are three additional published lighthouse observations from the late 19th and early 20th centuries. The first of these involved a report of Woodcock appearing at the St Agnes light at 8.30 am in a fresh east to southeast breeze on 11th October 1880 (Harvie-Brown *et al.* 1881). The others refer to single birds 'taken' at the Bishop Rock Lighthouse on the nights of 2nd–3rd and 7th–8th November 1907 (Ogilvie-Grant 1909), plus one killed at the same light on the night of 22nd–23rd October 1908 (Ogilvie-Grant 1910).

Penhallurick suggested that more recent under-reporting of Woodcock presence on mainland Cornwall may have created the impression it became scarcer during the mid- to late 20th century and certainly that may also be true of Scilly. Indeed, Penhallurick went as far as to suggest that numbers might even have increased in Cornwall, quoting bag increases on at least one Cornish estate showing a steady upward trend, the estate owner suggesting that most birds arrive immediately following October, November and December full moons.

Penhallurick (1969) agreed that little is known still about spring Woodcock migration in Scilly and Cornwall, other than it seems less marked than in autumn. The same author drew attention to birds seen in Scilly as late as 19th March on St Mary's (1964) and 20th March on St Agnes (1962), compared with 17th March on mainland Cornwall. The single obvious island exception up until that time was a bird A A Dorrien-Smith saw fly in from the south on 12th April 1946, land on a boat in Porth Cressa and, when flushed, continue northwards (*CBWPSAR* 16). Penhallurick also points out that in other parts of Britain spring migration continues into April or May.

Examination of the annual bird reports for the mid-1900s reveals a somewhat unenthusiastic approach to Woodcock recording, often with simple comments such as 'Frequently seen in suitable cover from mid-October, on all islands' (*IOSBR* 1973), or 'One found freshly dead on 4th November and another seen on 13th' (*SABOAR* 1959) being broadly representative. Indeed, in some years it gets even less mention. Nevertheless, the *SABOAR* for 1963 was rather more forthcoming, dealing as it did with the effects of the severe mainland weather conditions early that year, and usefully describing how 'exceptional numbers' of Woodcock occurred in the islands, with at least 50 shot on St Agnes alone during two weeks and possibly in excess of 1,000 killed in the islands generally at this time. Daily counts on St Agnes during the period 12th to 22nd January produced totals in the range 20–60, but with just three single sightings on that same island throughout the remainder of 1963 – two in October and one in December. Similarly, 200 were reportedly shot in the islands during the severe weather of winter 1961–62 (*SABOAR* 1961–62).

Looking at the ten years commencing 1990, there is a clear pattern of small numbers present at the start of the year and with last spring sightings during March or earlier, although a single on 21st April appears exceptional. First autumn arrivals for all ten years occurred during the 31 days 9th September to 9th October. For most years, there was no noticeable increase in numbers during October or November, irregular counts involving loosely associated roosting groups of up to 4–5 birds and individual site counts of about ten. Exceptions to this were 100 shot on Tresco on 12th January 1996, though few were recorded on that island subsequently, and 20th November 1998, when 25–50 were counted on St Agnes and up to two were thought present in most fields. In most years, small numbers remained at the end of the year, but sadly there are no co-ordinated winter counts.

Autumn Woodcock migration commences during the first half of October in the north of its range, e.g. Finland, although later further south, the exact timing being partly related to the onset of frost. Most birds reach their wintering areas by late November, but with possible subsequent cold-weather movements tending to confuse the wider picture. Return passage commences from early March, Scandinavian breeding grounds being re-occupied by April, although by mid-May further north, and again somewhat related to weather conditions. The majority of Woodcock wintering in Britain and Ireland originate from northwest Europe, east as far as western Russia, though at least one Irish-ringed recovery came from western Siberia (Wernham *et al.* 2002). But whilst British and Irish birds are largely sedentary, 70% of birds ringed in Scotland or northern England moved less than 80 km, many go south as far as northern Iberia. A total of nine Woodcock have been ringed on Scilly, all since 1970. Apart from the Perthshire control, two Scillonian-ringed individuals were shot locally during the same winter.

Interestingly, three out of four Woodcock ringing recoveries from the Cornish mainland up until 1969 involved birds ringed in Perthshire (2) and Cumberland, the one additional record involving a bird ringed in Friesland in the Netherlands.

Although Cramp *et al.* (1977–94) make no mention of geographical size or plumage variations, there are several Scillonian references to birds with apparently differing size and plumage features arriving in the islands, as in autumn 1948 when a 'large number' of the smaller and darker birds weighing from nine to ten-and-a-half ounces (255–297 g) were noted among those shot (*CBWPSAR* 18). This is almost exactly the same description that Clark and Rodd earlier applied to most birds reaching the islands, although on Christmas Day 1864 a small influx on Tresco involved 20 killed of the, mostly, heavy light-coloured birds (Clark & Rodd 1906).

## Controls
AP6261   ?   Ardoch, Perthshire 2nd July 1933   SH   St Mary's 20th December 1933

## Local
EP59675   1st Y   St Martin's 27th October 1993   SH   St Martin's 20th November 1993
EP59674   Ad   St Martin's 27th October 1993   SH   Lower Moors, St Mary's 10th January 1994

**Woodcock Ringing Recaptures**

# Black-tailed Godwit *Limosa limosa* A

**Scarce migrant in small numbers, occasionally occurs during winter months but does not overwinter.**

Black-tailed Godwit 19th and early 20th century Records
  1849   One (shot) Scilly   Clark & Rodd 1906
  1864   One (shot) Scilly September   Clark & Rodd 1906
  1870   One (shot – in summer plumage) April   Rodd 1870
  1871   One (shot – in summer plumage) St Mary's April   Clark & Rodd 1906
  1873   One (shot – in summer plumage) Tresco   Clark & Rodd 1906
  1903   One St Mary's 8th to 12th April   Clark & Rodd 1906

Breeds Eurasia, discontinuously from Iceland, Britain and France east to north of Kamchatka. Migratory, west European population winters southern Europe and North Africa, but mainly trans-Saharan Africa. Polytypic: *islandica*, or 'Icelandic Black-tailed Godwit' occurs Iceland, Scotland and northern Norway; nominate *limosa* England and remainder of western Europe, east to Yenisey River; *melanuroides* remainder of Siberia eastwards. Red-listed in UK: historical population decline; moderate breeding decline over past 25 years; five-year mean of 45.2 breeding pairs; 20% or more of East Atlantic Flyway non-breeding population uses UK, 50% or more at fewer than ten sites; unfavourable European winter conservation status (Gregory *et al.* 2002).

Bone remains of two humeri and an ulna were unearthed from the prehistoric site on Nornour in the Eastern Isles and identified as from this species (Turk 1971, 1984b). Additional bone remains from the same source were identified as merely from a godwit *Limosa* species. Although clearly always far from common in Scilly there are nevertheless a number of records from the latter half of the 19th century, all of which are listed in the Table.

It seems somewhat surprising that James Clark and Francis Rodd omitted the 1870 individual from their outstanding end-of-century review of 'The Birds of Scilly', as Francis's uncle E H Rodd mentions it in at least three separate publications, and therefore the record would appear beyond question. Perhaps the 1871 entry was a duplication of this as both birds were shot in April in complete or almost complete summer plumage. Whatever the truth, Francis spent a great deal of time observing and shooting on Tresco and it seems unlikely he would have been unaware of a bird having been shot in 1870 and passed to his uncle in Penzance. E H Rodd described Black-tailed Godwit as an occasional spring and autumn migrant in Cornwall and much rarer than Bar-tailed *L. lapponica* (Rodd 1880).

By the 1960s, Penhallurick (1969) felt confident enough to describe it as a migrant and winter visitor in Cornwall, drawing attention to an apparent increase in Cornish sightings from the 1920s onwards, wintering birds first being noted on mainland Cornwall during the mid-1930s. Up until the mid-1960s, Penhallurick knew of just two instances of Black-tailed Godwits in Scilly during winter, involving four birds in December–January 1956–57 and 1–2 on St Mary's in February 1965. Penhallurick also mentioned parties of up to 34 on Tresco and 25 on St Agnes, both in March 1966, with 20 his maximum recorded autumn gathering. Earliest spring arrival date up until that time was 2nd March and the latest sighting on 14th November, though mid-October was more usual (Penhallurick 1969).

Examining the data for the 1990s, things seem not to have changed greatly. Black-tailed Godwits occurred in all ten years up until 1999, though only eight years in spring. The maximum recorded in any year was 40, in 1992, followed closely by 38 in 1991. The least number recorded annually was five, in 1993, with 10 and twelve respectively in 1998 and 1997 the next highest. The greatest number recorded together was 19, which was short of Penhallurick's earlier figures. Earliest spring migrant date was 12th February and the latest 9th June, whilst the earliest autumn migrant was noted on 7th July and the last on 30th October. No Black-tailed Godwits were recorded wintering, though birds were present briefly during winter in three years, as follows: Tresco 15th November to 12 December 1991, Tresco 19th to 25th December 1993, Tresco 14th to 20th December 1998. Not enough detailed information is available to enable an analysis of arrival dates.

The closest breeding Black-tailed Godwits to Scilly are in Atlantic coastal France, Somerset and eastern England, followed by the Netherlands (Hagemeijer & Blair 1997). The overwhelming ringing evidence for migrants wintering in Britain and Ireland involves birds of the form *islandica*, or 'Icelandic Black-tailed Godwit', often as part of an onward movement to France, the Netherlands and Denmark, or south into Iberia (Wernham *et al.* 2002). By comparison, most British and European birds winter south as far as Sierra Leone.

Autumn migration commences mid-June, though most depart during July, passing through central Europe mid-July to September and most having completed by October. Return movement begins February, with most moving through central France during that month and during March, with breeding sites occupied mid-March to mid-April.

# Bar-tailed Godwit *Limosa lapponica* A

**Regular migrant and winter visitor in small to moderate numbers, far more frequent than the preceding species.**

Breeds northern Eurasia, from Norway east across Bering Strait to western Alaska. Migratory, in West Palearctic winters south coastally to Iberia, North Africa and Senegal. Polytypic: nominate *lapponica* occurs Europe and northern Asia east to 80°E; *baueri*, or 'Eastern Bar-tailed Godwit' remainder of northern Asia east to western Alaska. Included on Annex I of 1979 EEC 'Birds Directive'. Amber-listed in UK: 20% or more of East Atlantic Flyway non-breeding population in UK, 50% or more at ten or fewer sites whilst on passage; unfavourable world winter conservation status (Gregory *et al.* 2002).

Bone remains unearthed from the prehistoric Eastern Isles site on Nornour were identified positively as those of the previous species, Black-tailed Godwit *Limosa limosa* (Turk 1984b). However, additional bones from the same site could be attributed specifically no closer than 'godwit', in which case Bar-tailed cannot be excluded entirely.

Comments from at least two sources make it clear that Bar-tailed Godwit appeared regularly in Scilly during the 19th century. Relying on correspondence from his nephew Francis, E H Rodd recorded that it was more common than normal in the islands during 1870, at least four being shot that autumn (Rodd 1880). James Clark and Francis Rodd thought it regular in autumn and winter, occasionally in flocks, less occasionally in May and at least twice in June, though never in full breeding plumage (Clark & Rodd 1906). The Tresco Abbey game book entry for winter 1878–79 listed just one among the game and wildfowl killed that season (Rodd 1880). Penhallurick (1969) pointed out that E H Rodd's mention of it in Scilly pre-dated any similar note for the Cornish mainland, also drawing attention to Francis Rodd's description of a late 19th century flock on the islands into April. The same author highlighted the fact that more recently it was particularly abundant on Scilly during 1964, up to 35 being reported on most days in spring between mid-March and late April. The autumn maximum was 30 on 1st September, whereas 16 present still by the year's end remained into the following spring.

Examination of the situation for the ten years ending 1999 shows it remains mainly a passage migrant and in most years a winter visitor, though in small numbers. In most years, too, a few are encountered from January onwards, but with a notable passage usually during April and May. Occasional summering ones or twos are to be encountered, but in most years autumn passage commences from August, peaking during September and continuing through into October or November. The records suggest that in most years there is an absence of birds following the end of autumn passage, although evidence that this cannot be entirely true comes in the form of those individuals early in the year. There is some suggestion among the records that larger numbers are involved in spring than autumn, or certainly larger flocks, as in 1990, when flocks of 44 and 20 were present on St Martin's and Samson respectively on 4th May; autumn flocks are normally closer to the latter figure.

Fully co-ordinated winter wader or similar counts are sadly lacking in Scilly but two help throw light on numbers at that time of year. In the first, Kirby (1988) counted all wader species present on main islands during the period 15th December 1984 to 28th January 1985. Visits were carried out at or close to low tide, but the extent, if any, of between-site movement is unknown. A total of 55 Bar-tailed Godwits were recorded as follows: 40 Tresco, nine Samson, three St Agnes and Gugh, two St Martin's and one St Mary's. The only other co-ordinated winter count was the January 25th–26th Winter Shorebird Survey of 1997, when an all-island count of just 22 was recorded: 21 around the ever-popular Samson and one on St Martin's (*IOSBR* 1997).

According to Cramp *et al.* (1977–94) all records of Bar-tailed Godwits reaching Britain are likely to involve the nominate *lapponica* from northern Europe and northwest Asia, which winters coastally south to Iberia and North and West Africa. However, the possibility of the Siberian and western Alaskan *baueri*, or 'Eastern Bar-tailed Godwit', also reaching western Europe cannot be entirely dismissed, even though it normally winters in Southeast Asia and Australasia, and it should be looked for among flocks of Bar-tails visiting Scilly.

# Eskimo Curlew *Numenius borealis* B  BBRC 0%

**Former extremely rare migrant, possibly now extinct.**

Former common North American summer migrant, probably now extinct. The species' confiding nature allegedly made it an easy target, with 'massive' numbers shot on migration between South American wintering areas and western Canadian, and probably Alaskan, breeding grounds. Although this no doubt contributed substantially to its demise, changes in both breeding and wintering habitat, primarily to grazing and wheat production are also thought responsible. A population slump was noted from around 1870, with no large flocks reported after the mid-1880s. Infrequent and apparently reliable reports of one to two birds from areas of its former range, as recent even as 1977s, provide slim hope perhaps of recovery (Cramp *et al.* 1977–94).

Just a single 1887 Tresco record of what had by then become an extremely rare bird. It fell to the gun of Tresco's T A Dorrien-Smith on 10th September and represents the last authenticated record out of a total of only eight British and Irish occurrences of this elegant and perhaps now extinct species (Cornish 1887; Evans 1994). At the time of writing the mounted skin remains in the Isles of Scilly Museum on St Mary's and is a prime contender for Scilly's rarest bird ever. According to Griffiths (1982), the Tresco bird was in breeding plumage, though the date seems rather late.

## Whimbrel *Numenius phaeopus* A

**A common migrant in both halves of the year, with newly arrived spring passage flocks a marked feature. A few may now winter.**

Circumpolar with fragmentary distribution, breeding northern Eurasia and North America. Polytypic: nominate *phaeopus* occurs Iceland and northern Europe, including northern Scotland and Faeroe Islands, to western Siberia and winters Afrotropical region; *variegatus* and *alboaxillaris* further east; *hudsonicus*, or 'Hudsonian Whimbrel' North America, wintering South America to Chile and Brazil. Some authorities treat birds from Iceland as a separate race, *islandicus* (Cramp *et al.* 1977–94; Bosanquet 2000). Amber-listed in UK: 50% or more of breeding population at ten or fewer sites; 50% or more of UK non-breeding population at ten or fewer sites whilst on passage (Gregory *et al.* 2002).

E H Rodd (1880) refers to its local name of 'May-bird', from the timing of its spring migration, but makes no reference to it in a Scillonian context, other than that it occurred in spring and autumn, whilst in the same volume nephew Francis Rodd records its arrival on 8th August 1870. However, Clark and Francis Rodd (1906) are more forthcoming, describing it as 'fairly plentiful' in early autumn during the 1840s, such that it warranted a separate column in the Tresco game book, but going on to suggest a fairly rapid decline, down to 'very scarce' and with just four shot during the whole of the period 1856–67 compared with fourteen shot in 1843 alone. It is interesting to note, though, that Clark and Rodd thought it more probably a spring migrant, describing 'several hundred' on St Mary's in May 1903.

The situation today remains much the same, with spring flocks seen arriving from the south throughout April and early May but with often just a daily trickle during autumn. Most move on within a day or so and some may pass straight through the islands. Taking records for the final quarter of the 20th century, earliest spring arrival and departure dates appear to be 12th March and 7th July, with equivalent autumn dates being 20th July and 8th November. Numbers in spring grossly outweigh the autumn period, with single-day maximum counts up around 300–350 in 1981 and 1985, but with lows of 25–40 in some years, with an average of around 100. This compares to average maximum daily figures of just 10 in autumn. However, deciding exactly which are first and last dates for migrant Whimbrel is often confused by the presence of one to two apparently summering or wintering birds. The latter give the appearance of becoming more frequent in recent years; according to Cramp *et al.* (1977–94) few winter in Europe and then only irregularly north to Denmark.

We might expect most Whimbrel occurring in Scilly on spring or autumn passage to be *phaeopus*, or the putative '*islandicus*', though some Icelandic birds probably take a direct autumn sea route to Africa (Glutz *et al.* in Cramp *et al.* 1977–94; Wernham *et al.* 2002), with the outside chance perhaps of *variegatus* or *alboaxillaris*. Equally likely as an autumn vagrant on Scilly, however, is the distinctively darker *hudsonicus*, or 'Hudsonian Whimbrel', which is treated by some authorities as a full species. For, as Gantlett (1998) points out, there have already been records of *hudsonicus* in Britain, namely on Fair Isle (May 1955) and Shetland (August 1974) and more recently (May 2000) at the Gwent Levels Wetland Reserve in South Wales (Bosanquet 2000), plus one in Ireland in 1980. In addition, singles have reached the Azores (1985) and Cape Verde Islands (1991). Most certainly all autumn Whimbrel flocks on Scilly should be checked for the possible presence of this form.

Two Whimbrels were trapped and ringed prior to 1970, one of which, ringed on 24th April 1960, was shot in France on 20th April 1963, presumably whilst returning north. There are three records from the ocean weather station 'Kilo' in the Western Approaches 800 km southwest of Scilly (McLean & Williamson 1959), the first two of which involved flocks of unspecified numbers that appeared during easterly winds on 29th April 1958. Both flocks circled the ship and momentarily landed, before departing, one northwards and one to the east-northeast. The third record concerned an extremely tired individual that appeared aboard ship on 1st May and was not easily disturbed. At 17.30 hours on 2nd April, it fell into the sea and was drowned.

It is not that uncommon, particularly in late autumn, to find the remains of Whimbrels that have clearly fallen victim to avian predation, apparently by Peregrine Falcons *Falco peregrinus* (pers. obs.). Predation is usually attributable to a raptor, rather than large gulls, by the distinctive 'notched' bite marks along the sternum edge (pers. obs.). The only plausible alternatives to Peregrine on Scilly are Merlin *F. columbarius* and Kestrel *F. tinnunculus*, both of which seem unlikely culprits.

Recoveries

3026451  FG  At Agnes 24th April 1960         SH  Pointe de la Coubre, Charente-Maritime,
                                                   France 20th April 1963

Whimbrel Ringing Recaptures

## Curlew (Eurasian Curlew) *Numenius arquata* A

**Migrant and winter visitor, a small number of non-breeders summer, mostly in the area from Samson east to Tean and St Martin's.**

Breeds northern Eurasia, from Britain, Ireland and France east to northern Mongolia and southeast Siberia, south to Mediterranean, Black Sea and Mongolia. Mainly migratory, though some resident west of range; complexities of wintering areas poorly understood. In West Palearctic may winter mainly south to Mediterranean and North and West Africa, possibly southern Africa. Polytypic: nominate *arquata* occurs western Europe east to western Siberia; *orientalis*, or 'Eastern Curlew' central and eastern Asia, although with substantial intergrading. Amber-listed in UK: 30.2% of European breeding population in UK: 44.7% of East Atlantic Flyway non-breeding population in UK; unfavourable world winter conservation status (Gregory *et al.* 2002). National 12% decline 1994–99 (Bashford & Noble 2000).

The earliest recorded presence of Curlew in Scilly may involve bone remains extracted from the prehistoric site on Nornour in the Eastern Isles (Turk 1984b), which were identified as being those of a large wader, believed almost certainly to be this species. This was followed some considerable time later by Robert Heath's reference to 'Curloes' featuring during winter among all the landbirds of the islands (Heath 1750). Though there seems to have been a measure of disagreement among 19th century observers as to its true status. North (1850) considering it 'a constant resident', whereas Rodd (1880) thought it common in autumn and winter, whilst also clarifying that it did not breed. Like many other species, it put in a strong appearance during autumn and winter 1870, Francis Rodd reporting a flock of 200 to 300 birds in the vicinity of Hedge Rock, south of Tean, on 1st November (Rodd 1880), Curlews having been first noted from the end of July that year. Francis also recorded going out into the snows during late December this particular winter and encountering Curlews feeding on the St Mary's Moors. In addition, ten Curlews are included among the list of game and other wildfowl appearing in the Tresco game book as killed during winter 1878–79. However, as so often happens, the final 19th century word on the subject goes to James Clark and Francis Rodd, who noted it as evident year-round. They described it as appearing in winter in 'large flocks' on beaches and on rocks by the shore and also on farmland, where 'it seems to be continually turning over sheep's droppings in search of beetles', and concluded with the observation that it was 'by no means uncommon' in summer, particularly in the area of Tean, but nevertheless did not breed (Clark & Rodd 1906).

The situation today appears unchanged, with small-scale scattered numbers reported at the start of most years during the 1990s, perhaps up to 50. The only 1990's structured all-island counts during the early part of the year involved a total of 61 during a four-day shorebird count in mid-March 1996 and 113 during a similar Winter Shorebird Survey of 25th–26th January 1997. The January 1997 individuals were quite evenly distributed about the main islands as follows: St Mary's 21, Tresco 25, Bryher 19, St Agnes 8, St Martin's 24 and Samson 16. A somewhat greater number of Curlews was recorded during the 1984–85 Winter Wader Survey (Kirby 1988), which recorded a total of 181 individuals between 15th December and 28th January. Distribution was both widespread and quite even, 44 being found in the vicinity of

Samson, 34 St Helen's, Tean and Northwethel, 25 Tresco, 23 St Martin's, 20 each St Mary's and Bryher, and 15 St Agnes and Gugh.

Any wintering presence is followed by visible evidence of spring passage, from around April, with flocks of perhaps up to 30 on record. Meanwhile, the presence of a summering flock of around 50 individuals remains a notable, although still not fully explained, feature, though counts of 100 by August or early September doubtless included early autumn migrants. Autumn passage may commence from as early as July, with occasional flocks of up to 60–100 birds recorded from various sites through to November, at which time there is a marked decrease in Curlew presence throughout the islands. It seems unclear, however, whether the all-island total is ever very great, and may not reach 500 individuals.

The closest breeding Curlews to Scilly are in Cornwall, Devon, central southern England and Wales (Gibbons *et al.* 1993), followed by northern France, Ireland and the Low Countries (Hagemeijer & Blair 1997). Within Britain, there is a tendency among those that do move during winter to head southwest into Ireland and southwest England, whereas those vacating southern England reach France and even Iberia (Cramp *et al.* 1977–94; Wernham *et al.* 2002). However, birds from Scandinavia and even western Russia reach Britain, and the 1930 discovery of a bird wearing a Swedish ring confirmed that birds from Scandinavia also reach the islands. One Curlew has been ringed in Scilly, prior to 1970, but it was not recovered.

There are three early mentions of this species from Scillonian lighthouses. The first, from the Bishop Rock during the period 13th–25th January 1881, reported large flocks passing during periods of snow. Then at St Agnes at 09.00 hours on 22nd February the same year, birds were noted passing east-northeast in a 'strong breeze' (Harvie-Brown *et al.* 1882). The remaining report again involved the Bishop Rock light, when six or seven were recorded on 3rd September 1886 between 23.00 hours and daylight (Harvie-Brown *et al.*1887).

Gantlett (1998) draws attention to the possibility of the paler, longer-legged and longer-billed form *orientalis*, or 'Eastern Curlew', occurring in Britain. However, it may be difficult to identify, if only because of the extent of intergrading that occurs where populations overlap (Cramp *et al.* 1977–94). Nonetheless Scilly would be as good a place as any to commence searching.

### Controls
B2209     Pul    Mariestad, Skaraborg, Sweden 10th June 1930     ?     St Mary's 8th August 1930

**Curlew Ringing Recaptures**

## Upland Sandpiper *Bartramia longicauda* A BBRC 36%

**Rare migrant, full written description required by the BBRC.**

- 1883   One (shot) Scilly October 12th or before   Penhallurick 1978
- 1922   One shot Tresco 22nd September
  Kinnear 1922; *British Birds* 17: 289, 22: 47; *Bulletin BOC* 43: 76
- 1960   One St Mary's 18th to 28th November   *British Birds* 55: 566
- 1968   One Tresco & St Mary's 26th September to 12th October   *British Birds* 62: 486
- 1968   One St Mary's & Tresco 4th October   *British Birds* 62: 468
- 1972   One St Mary's 7th to 28th October   *British Birds* 66: 340
- 1982   One (juvenile) St Agnes & St Mary's 18th to 31st October   *British Birds* 76: 497
- 1983   One (juvenile) St Mary's 15th to 24th October   *British Birds* 77: 38
- 1984   One St Martin's 23rd to 27th October   *British Birds* 78: 550
- 1986   One St Mary's 22nd October to 17th November   *British Birds* 80: 34
- 1990   One (juvenile) St Mary's, St Agnes & Tresco 10th to 24th October   *British Birds* 84: 471
- 1993   One (juvenile) St Mary's & Tresco 6th October to 6th November   *British Birds* 87: 527
- 1995   One St Mary's 12th October   *British Birds* 89: 502
- 1999   One (juvenile) St Mary's Airport 7th to 31st October   *British Birds* 93: 533
- 1999   One (juvenile) St Martin's & St Mary's 10th to 31st October   *British Birds* 93: 533

Breeds North America, from Alaska east through Canada to interior USA south to Oklahoma, and then northeast to southern Quebec. Winters South America, mainly Brazil, Paraguay, Uruguay and Argentina;

though perhaps more frequent northeast South America than currently appreciated (Cramp *et al.* 1977–94). Monotypic. Considerable population increase 1966–79 followed by subsequent slow decline (Bryant 1997).

E H Rodd knew of just one record involving one individual shot in a turnip field on the Lizard peninsula in mainland Cornwall in November 1865 and sold to a game shop (Rodd 1880).

There are 15 Scillonian records, all involving single birds, but in two years two birds arrived. Earliest known arrival date was 22nd September (1922) and the latest 18th November (1960); this last individual stayed until 28th November and thus provided the latest date for any Upland Sandpiper on Scilly. A particular feature with this species was the length of time birds stayed in the islands, the longest being 32 days, four more over 20 days and five of ten or more days, with just two single-day sightings. The average length of stay was 15.5 days, the two shot birds having been excluded from this calculation. As with Buff-breasted Sandpipers *Tryngites subruficollis*, a notable feature of many individuals was their confiding behaviour, often allowing close approach, at least one taking food from an observer's hand (*IOSBR* 1983). Birds also behaved like Buff-breasted Sandpipers in naturally gravitating to short-grass areas; the two 1999 individuals eventually got together on St Mary's Airport for some twenty days.

The 1883 individual was mentioned by Yarrel (Penhallurick 1978), whilst the skin of the 1922 Tresco individual was exhibited to members of the British Ornithologists' Club in London (Kinnear 1922). The 1960 bird, however, set a pattern for the future, arriving on St Mary's Airport in the wake of severe westerly weather and showing a marked disregard for human approach throughout its 11-day visit. Typical of several early rarity sightings, the *CBWPSAR* for that year failed to mention that this was the first Upland Sandpiper to reach Scilly for nearly 40 years and only the third ever for southwest England. The bird on St Mary's on 12th October 1995 was seen heading back towards the mainland around midday and was possibly the bird found at Polgigga, Cornwall, on 21st.

The 13 birds on the islands since 1958 represent over one-third of all British records accepted by the BBRC up to and including 1999. This compares with just seven records on mainland Cornwall for the same period. In total, Scilly and Cornwall together have hosted over half the birds recorded in the British Isles since 1958.

According to Cramp *et al.* (1977–94), juveniles begin 'wandering' within the breeding range from mid-July but full migration commences in August, with northern breeding areas vacated later that month or by early September. The bulk of the southward movement occurs through central North America, though there is evidence that at least some individuals adopt the transoceanic strategy used by several other wader species and fly out over the North Atlantic from eastern Canada or northeast USA direct to the Caribbean, or even to northeast South America. As with all species using this route, individuals are at risk to involuntary transatlantic vagrancy, which presumably explains the appearance of Upland Sandpiper in Britain and Ireland and on Scilly in particular.

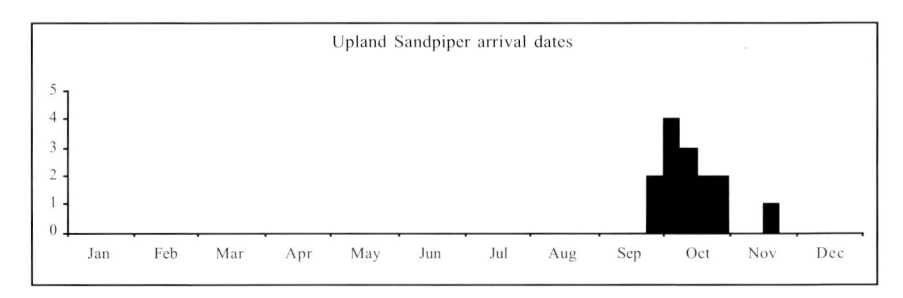

## Spotted Redshank *Tringa erythropus* A

**Scarce migrant in small numbers, annually but not always in spring. Has wintered.**

Breeds northern Eurasia, around edge of Arctic Circle from northern Norway east in Siberia almost to Bering Sea. Migratory, in West Palearctic wintering sparingly south to Mediterranean, greater numbers crossing Sahara to winter in Africa north of equator. Monotypic. Upgraded from Green- to Amber-listed in UK 2002: 20% or more of East Atlantic Flyway non-breeding population in UK (Gregory *et al.* 2002).

Earliest reference to this species in Scilly is E H Rodd's 1963 letter to the *Zoologist* entitled *The Spotted Redshank (Totanus fuscus) in Cornwall* and concerning a bird seen in the islands during early September that year (Rodd 1963g). Two years later one was seen on Tresco on 12th October by the Reverend John Jenkinson, who also shot a bird on nearby Bryher on 26th August 1870 (Clark & Rodd 1906). This last specimen went to E H Rodd in Penzance (Rodd 1880).

By the mid-1960s Penhallurick (1969) felt able to describe it as almost exclusively an autumn migrant in Scilly – quoting a single spring record from St Agnes on 7th April 1967. He also pointed out that, unlike mainland Cornwall, there were no winter records. There seems, therefore, to have been something of a change in the pattern of Spotted Redshank's use of the islands since that time. This commenced with a quite exceptional series of winter records, though possibly involving the same individual, present on St Agnes from autumn 1973 until April 1974 and on St Mary's during the four winters from autumn 1975 through to April 1979. In at least four of the five years concerned, the bird(s) departed the islands between 16th and 20th April. Interestingly, however, there have been no subsequent winter sightings.

Spring sightings may also have become more frequent since Penhallurick's review, although they are still far from annual and birds were recorded during this season in four of the ten years from 1990, in the range 1–4 individuals. Spring arrival dates fell in the period 4th April to 3rd May and the latest a bird was present was 11th May. Autumn arrivals were surprisingly well spaced, the earliest being 26th July and the latest 5th September, though mid- to late August was more normal. Autumn final departures were even more predictable, falling as they did in the period 4th to 24th October. Indeed, the sole November sighting of a passage bird in the last 25 years at least appears to have been the 1974 individual on Tresco on 9th. Arrivals of 1–2 birds seems the norm, though the greatest recent number was probably the party of nine seen in flight over St Agnes on 22nd October 1979. Intriguingly, few if any reports refer to birds in summer plumage, even during May. Typically, Spotted Redshanks in Scilly frequent the larger freshwater areas, e.g. Great Pool on Tresco, or the St Mary's Porth Hellick Pool. Few birds remain for even a full day, though occasionally they are still viewable three or four days after arrival and the bird on Tresco for eight days in October 1998 was a positive long-stayer by comparison.

In Europe, Spotted Redshank migration is characterised by continuous long-distance flights between traditional staging areas, which also have importance for the onset of moult. And in view of recent Scillonian wintering records, it is interesting to note that Cramp *et al.* (1977–94) cite evidence of increased wintering in Britain. Males are first to leave, departing the breeding grounds from about June and being followed by females and juveniles from mid-July and August. All remain for some time at main staging areas, for moult and fat deposition, before moving on south, most reaching West Africa by October. Return movement through Europe takes place during April and May. No Spotted Redshanks have been ringed in Scilly and there are no controls.

## Redshank (Common Redshank) *Tringa totanus* A

**Regular migrant in small numbers mainly in autumn, winters but does not breed.**

Old World species, breeds Iceland, Iberia, France, Netherlands, Denmark, Norway and Sweden east through Russia, eastern China and Tibet. Polytypic: nominate *totanus* occurs British Isles east to Russia; *ussuriensis* and *terrignotae* further east; *robusta*, or 'Icelandic Redshank' Iceland and Faeroes. Largely migratory. Amber-listed UK: moderate to high (63%) breeding decline over past 25 years; 70.9% of East Atlantic Flyway non-breeding population in UK; unfavourable European conservation status (Gregory *et al.* 2002), British 36% decline 1994–99 (Bashford & Noble 2000).

Bone remains unearthed from the prehistoric site on Nornour in the Eastern Isles come either from this species or Greenshank *T. nebularia* (Turk 1971, 1984b). Redshank never seems to have been particularly numerous on Scilly, generally arriving during late summer or early autumn, with far less evidence of a spring passage. There are apparently no published references to its presence in the islands before E H Rodd's various 1870 accounts of it 'appearing on its southern or autumnal migration' (Rodd 1870e; 1870l; 1880); at least one bird was shot at this time. James Clark and E H Rodd's nephew Francis described its status by the start of the 20th century as frequently seen from early autumn to midwinter, usually in small parties of up to 12 or 15 on Tresco's freshwater pools and concluded with the observation that it had been obtained on St Mary's during Christmas week (Clark & Rodd 1906).

By the late 1960s, Penhallurick (1969) was confident that Redshank had become more numerous in Cornwall during winter since the early 19th century, in addition quoting a small number of proven or suspected mainland breeding records. He also pointed out that very small numbers were to be found on Cornish estuaries, even during summer, and noted that first returning autumn individuals were evident from mid- to late June, with substantial numbers being present by late July, peak totals on at least two estuaries, Tamar and Lyner, in the region or in excess of 1,000. He further suggested that Continental birds might be involved in Cornwall. However, Penhallurick suggested that comparatively few birds were involved in Scilly, whilst at the same time pointing out that adequate information was lacking. Nevertheless, he quoted a maximum flock size of 25 on St Agnes from 24th to 28th November 1963, with ten on that island in late December the same year the only winter record. Apparently, however, he overlooked the reported 45–50 on Samson Flats on 16th November 1958 (*CBWPSAR* 28).

Redshank was often poorly recorded during the mid-1900s, even failing get a mention at all in some years, and any information that was published often lacked important detail, as in 1973, when there were: 'Small numbers most seasons, usually scattered over flats, with up to 30 in late July to August, in Samson area' (*IOSBR* 1973). However, by dint of careful interpretation, we may assume it was more numerous than most records show, e.g. up to 55 present on St Agnes during both winter 1960 (*SABOAR* 1960) and August 1961 (*SABOAR* 1961–62).

Referring to published reports for the ten years from 1990, the picture that emerges is one of small numbers present at the start of the year with an all-island total of 20–25 individuals distributed between six main islands. Last spring sightings were squeezed into a narrow period from 16th to 24th May but with uncertainties remaining over whether spring passage was involved. First returning birds were evident about the islands from mid- to late June, e.g. 11 around Samson on 27th June, increasing slightly into July and with a further increase around September or October. Yearly totals varied, as too did end-of-year counts, at which time from 15 to 50 seemed the norm. Interestingly there was no clear picture of an autumn decline in some years.

Several recent surveys addressed the question of wintering Redshank numbers in Scilly, the earliest of which recorded 49 individuals during December–January 1984–85 (Kirby 1988), birds being distributed as follows: 15 St Agnes and Gugh, 10 Tresco, 8 each St Mary's and Samson, 5 Tean, St Helen's and Northwethel and 3 Bryher. More recently, the two-day January 1997 Winter Shorebird Survey recorded 69 birds, the majority of which were on Samson (27) and Tresco (24) (*IOSBR* 1997), whereas the three-day mid-March Wader Count of 1996 managed to locate just 24 Redshank, 15 of which were around Tresco (Lock 1996). All of this fits nicely into the generally accepted pattern of winter Redshank presence on Scilly, as do the findings of a St Agnes wader roost study during winter 1994–95, when up to 25 Redshank were present at two adjacent St Agnes wader roosts – Browarth and Burnt Island – from November 1994 through to the following March (Hale 1994), when often exactly the same number were recorded feeding nearby as were later present within the two roosts.

Although most Redshanks migrate, a few in western Europe are sedentary. Those from Fennoscandia move furthest, to West Africa, whilst most Icelandic birds move no further than Britain or Ireland, those from central-western Europe wintering south to France, Iberia and the western Mediterranean (Wernham *et al.* 2002). Although within the West Palearctic the overall direction of movement is southwest to south-southwest, there is little indication of the geographical origin of Redshank visiting Scilly. Most, though, are presumably nominate *totanus* but with the obvious possibility of the larger *robusta*, or 'Icelandic Redshank' from both the Faeroes and Iceland, being involved. However, the possibility of *ussuriensis* from western-central Asia reaching the islands may be difficult to prove in the absence of any ringing recoveries. Two Redshanks were ringed on St Agnes prior to 1970 but were not recovered subsequently and there are no controls of birds ringed elsewhere. However, Penhallurick (1969) listed a small number of controls for mainland Cornwall, which possibly also shed light on the origin of birds reaching Scilly. These included two ringed as nestlings, in Cumbria and Warwickshire, two as juveniles, in Westmorland and Cheshire, and one as an adult in Lancashire.

## Marsh Sandpiper *Tringa stagnatilis* A BBRC 1%

**Extremely rare migrant, full written description required by the BBRC.**

1999   One (juvenile) Great Pool, Tresco 22nd to 25th July   *British Birds* 93: 101, 533–534

Breeds central Europe east to central southern Russia and northern Mongolia, but range poorly understood. Winters Africa mainly south of equator, Middle East (few), southern and Southeast Asia, Australia (Cramp *et al.* 1977–94). Monotypic.

The only record of this charming wader concerns one that arrived on Tresco's Great Pool on 22nd July 1999, where it remained until 25th. The bird was initially seen by a visiting birdwatcher, who tentatively identified it as this species, though this was not confirmed until the last day of the bird's stay. Marsh Sandpiper's addition to the Scilly list brought the total number of wader species to 60, including Terek Sandpiper *Xenus cinereus* (which was recorded for the first time earlier the same year) and the probably now extinct Eskimo Curlew *Numenius borealis*; and if 'Wilson's Snipe' *Gallinago delicata* is treated as a full species the total increases to 61.

The European and a minority of the Russian Marsh Sandpiper population winters in Africa, the latter crossing eastern Europe and the Middle East on a southwest heading, which is reversed in spring. Rare in western Europe generally, exactly 100 British records were accepted by the BBRC during the period 1958 to 1999 inclusive. Therefore, the lone Scillonian record represents 1% of this total. There has been a probable decrease in range and numbers in the West Palearctic, perhaps associated with habitat loss Cramp *et al.* 1977–94).

## Greenshank (Common Greenshank) *Tringa nebularia* A

**Regular migrant in small to moderate numbers, a few remain during winter.**

Breeds northern Eurasia, from northern Scotland and Norway east to Kamchatka. In West Palearctic winters Africa south of Sahara, though few remain north on Mediterranean and Atlantic-coastal North Africa. Monotypic. Downgraded from Amber- to Green-listed in UK 2002 (Gregory *et al.* 2002).

Bone remains unearthed from the prehistoric site on Nornour in the Eastern Isles come either from this species or Redshank *T. totanus* (Turk 1971, 1984b). E H Rodd made first mention of Greenshank in Scilly, describing in a letter to the *Zoologist* how two shot during the second week of December 1845 later reached him in Penzance (Rodd 1846). The same author quoted the presence of flocks of up to 30 on the Tresco pools during late October 1870, with further arrivals on Samson during early November that year

(Rodd 1870h, 1880). James Clark and E H Rodd's nephew Francis later describedg it as present in parties of from three to 12 in autumn, flitting restlessly over the surface of the Tresco pools, or crowded together beside the water's edge. They mentioned how tame they were when they first arrived (Clark & Rodd 1906) but, interestingly, failed to mention the elder Rodd's flocks of up to 30 birds.

Moving to the mid- to late 20th century, the picture seems very similar to that of Redshank *T. totanus*. Penhallurick thought that on mainland Cornwall autumn migration commenced from the second half of July, 27th June being extreme, and with peak numbers viewable from late August or early September, although significant numbers could also occur during October, the largest counts being in the region of 40 (Penhallurick 1969). As in the case of Redshank, Penhallurick considered there had been a recent increase in numbers of wintering Greenshank, these leaving by late March and being replaced by small numbers of spring migrants through into late May. Penhallurick went on to point out that although few figures were available for Scilly, maximum flock counts of about 20 seemed exceptional, quoting an early arrival date of 18th June. In Penhallurick's opinion, wintering numbers were low, e.g. up to 17 on Tresco, though he suggested that more may occur than records indicated.

Taking the most recent period, the ten years up to 1999, the pattern was one of winter counts of 10–15 followed by an obvious decrease before a small spring passage, last individuals being noted around late May. The occasional one to two noted during June may have been migrants or summering individuals, but autumn passage became obvious from late June or early July, numbers rising to all-island highs of up to 40 during October, before decreasing again to the winter level of 10–15 individuals. As with most species, there is a marked lack of co-ordinated summer Greenshank counts, but the species was recorded during recent winter wader or shorebird surveys, as in winter 1984–85 when a total of eight were recorded during the Winter Wader Count on all main islands between December and January (Kirby 1988). These were quite evenly distributed with two each in three islands, St Mary's, Samson and St Martin's and one each on Bryher and Tresco. Slightly more were noted during the two-day January 1997 Winter Shorebird Survey, when 13 were counted, including six on Tresco and three each on St Mary's and Bryher. The three-day March 1996 coastal Wader Count recorded only seven, however, distributed between St Mary's, Tresco and Bryher. It should be borne in mind, though, that in Scilly Greenshank is as much a bird of freshwater pools, in which case these figures are probably not truly representative of numbers present within the islands at those times.

Greenshank is a broad-front migrant, although, especially in western Europe, the largest numbers pass through coastal sites (Cramp *et al.* 1977–94). Although many western European birds reach West Africa south at least as far as the Gulf of Guinea (Wernham *et al.* 2002), a small percentage also stays north in winter as far as the Mediterranean and Atlantic-coastal North Africa. Birds depart their breeding areas from late June or July, with main passage from mid-July into October. Return passage through Europe occurs April and early May, being both more direct and without the concentrations noticeable in autumn.

No Greenshanks have been ringed on Scilly and there are no controls. However, a bird colour-ringed at Farlington Marshes, Hampshire, on 8th August was present on St Agnes from the following day and then on St Mary's from 25th of that month until early September. Lock thought the Greenshank wintering population on Scilly might represent a 'significant percentage' of the UK population at that time of year (Lock 1999).

# Greater Yellowlegs *Tringa melanoleuca* A BBRC 4.0%

**Very rare migrant, full written description required by the BBRC.**

1906 One (shot) Tresco 16th September   Griffith 1906; Clark & Rodd 1906; *British Birds* 1: 16
1927 One Tresco 23rd to 28th August
                          Witherby 1927; A A Dorrien-Smith 1939b; *British Birds* 21: 162
1939 One Tresco 7th May   Dorrien-Smith 1939b; *British Birds* 33: 113
1952 One Tresco 30th September   CBWPSAR 22
1975 One Tresco 24th August to 3rd September   *British Birds* 69: 336

Breeds North America, from Alaska and northern Canadian provinces east to Quebec, Labrador, Newfoundland and Nova Scotia. Winters southern USA, West Indies, Central America and South America south to Patagonia. Monotypic.

Slight caution is needed when dealing with earlier records of this and the following species in order to guard against confusion. However, E H Rodd makes no specific reference to this species and so the bird shot near Tresco Abbey by A A Dorrien-Smith in September 1906, and agreed and described by W Ogilvie-Grant, seems generally accepted as the first record for Europe (Griffith 1906; Ogilvie-Grant 1906; Saunders 1907; Palmer 2000). The next record was of one watched closely by Dorrien-Smith and others, again on Tresco, from 23rd to 28th August 1927 (Witherby 1927a; A A Dorrien-Smith 1939b). And amazingly, Dorrien-Smith briefly saw and heard a third bird on Tresco's Abbey Pool on the evening of 7th May 1939 (A A Dorrien-Smith 1939b), by which time he must have become a leading authority on this species in Europe.

The two more-modern records involve a bird first seen associating with Oystercatchers *Haematopus ostralegus* on Tresco Flats (between Tresco and Samson) on 30th September 1952 (*CBWPSAR* 22), followed by a confiding individual on Great Pool, Tresco, from 24th August until at least 3rd September 1975; on 28th August this bird visited Porth Hellick on St Mary's and was eventually found dead on 6th September. When seen in the field, this last bird gave the appearance of being rather small, and with no other species present for comparison seemed about the size of a slim Redshank *T. totanus*, though post-mortem measurements showed this impression to be false (*IOSBR* 1975).

Autumn passage is prolonged, commencing from mid-July but with birds still present into November, even in the northern part of its breeding range. Most birds probably move south through interior USA but a proportion are thought to arrest moult. Like several other wader species, Greater Yellowlegs takes the transoceanic route from eastern Canada or northeast USA, out over the western North Atlantic south to the Caribbean, or even directly to northeast South America (Cramp *et al.* 1977–94). Therefore, like other species using this particular migration strategy, individuals are at risk of involuntary transatlantic vagrancy when encountering Atlantic weather depressions. Return spring passage apparently involves overflying northern South America, with northward movement mainly then through central USA, although it is not uncommon on the Atlantic coast at this time. Most breeding grounds are reoccupied by late April. Autumn arrivals in Scilly fit the pattern of transoceanic migration but the single spring individual is less easy to explain, though it could involve a displacement from a previous autumn. Nevertheless, it is worth drawing attention here to the closeness of the three spring yellowlegs arrival dates, i.e. Greater Yellowlegs 7th May 1939, Yellowlegs sp. 11th May 1958 and Lesser Yellowlegs 11th May 1974 – a quite remarkable 5-day window involving a spread of 35 years.

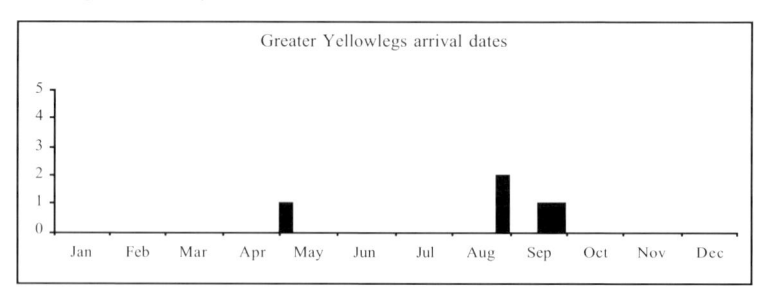

Greater Yellowlegs arrival dates

The Chart shows all five Greater Yellowlegs arrival dates, suggesting a rather earlier autumn presence than for most other North American waders on Scilly. The earliest arrival date was 23rd August and the latest 30th September, which was also the latest date a bird was known to be present. The shortest stay was two days (two individuals) and the longest 11 days, with an average of 4 days, the shot bird being omitted from this calculation. The single post-1958 record represents 4% of the total of 25 British records accepted by the BBRC up to and including 1999. Prior to 1958 there were twelve records, 33% of these on Scilly.

## Lesser Yellowlegs *Tringa flavipes* A BBRC 2.0%

**Rare migrant, full written description required by the BBRC.**

1920  One (female) shot Tresco 7th September   A A Dorrien-Smith 1939b
1921  One Tresco 19th August to 17th September   Witherby 1927a
1967  One St Mary's 26th to 29th October   *British Birds* 61: 469

| | | |
|---|---|---|
| 1973 | One Tresco 2nd to 17th September | *British Birds* 67: 322 |
| 1974 | One Porth Hellick, St Mary's 11th–18th May | *British Birds* 68: 317 |
| 1980 | One (juvenile) Tresco 20th September to 6th October | *British Birds* 74: 471–472 |
| 1980 | One (first-winter) St Mary's & Tresco 7th October to 4th November | *British Birds* 74: 471–472 |
| 1992 | One (juvenile) St Mary's 26th August to 22nd September | *British Birds* 86: 484 |
| 2001 | One Tresco 30th August to 28th September | *Birding World* 14: 316; 14: 360 |

Breeds North America, from Alaska and central Canada east to Hudson Bay, wintering southern USA (few), Central America, West Indies and South America south to Chile and Argentina. Monotypic. Population apparently decreasing (Bryant 1997).

E H Rodd described this species from an adult male specimen shot by Edward Vingoe at Marazion saltmarsh, east of Penzance, in September 1871. Although he referred to it as 'Yellow-shanked Sandpiper' he used the scientific name *Totanus flavipes* (Rodd 1880). However, neither E H Rodd nor his nephew Francis and co-author James Clark (Clark & Rodd 1906) mention either yellowlegs species on Scilly. This being the case, the female shot by A A Dorrien-Smith on Tresco on 7th September 1920 was the first record for the islands (A A Dorrien-Smith 1939b). This was followed closely by another on Tresco the following year, this time present from mid-August to mid-September (Witherby 1927a).

Seven subsequent records (one very recent) all post-date formation of the BBRC in 1958 and, as with Greater Yellowlegs *T. melanoleuca*, there is a single spring arrival. The first of these records, in October 1967, was discovered feeding beside Newford Duck Pond on the northeast corner of St Mary's (*CBWPSAR* 37). Two in one year made 1980 worth remembering, but it would have been even more memorable if they had not missed each other by just one day. The second of these two was driven off Porth Hellick Pool by rising water levels in late October, from whence it moved to Tresco. The eighth individual arrived in Lower Moors, St Mary's, in 1992 on the early date of 26th August and remained at the same site until last seen on 22nd September, though it occasionally commuted to Porth Hellick.

The earliest autumn arrival date was 19th August and the latest 26th October, whilst the latest any bird remained was 4th November. The average length of stay was 16 days, with the shortest just one day and the longest 30 days. The Chart includes all but the most recent arrival date. In North America autumn migration commences earlier in this species than in Greater Yellowlegs, from early July, but peaks mid-July to mid-September, numbers decreasing in the USA by October. As with Greater Yellowlegs, most move through central states but many nevertheless use the Atlantic coastal route, having crossed eastern Canada and northeast USA on a southeasterly heading. A few of these latter birds, at least, apparently opt for the transoceanic route out over the North Atlantic and south to the Caribbean, or even direct to northeast South America, having arrested their moult in readiness (Cramp *et al.* 1977–94). Like other species adopting this strategy, Lesser Yellowlegs is at risk to involuntary transatlantic crossings when encountering mid-Atlantic weather depressions. Some though may cross the Atlantic accidentally, having overshot the eastern seaboard and encountered severe weather. According to Cramp *et al.*, this initial southeast element of Lesser Yellowlegs autumn migration may account for the greater frequency of European records compared with Greater Yellowlegs.

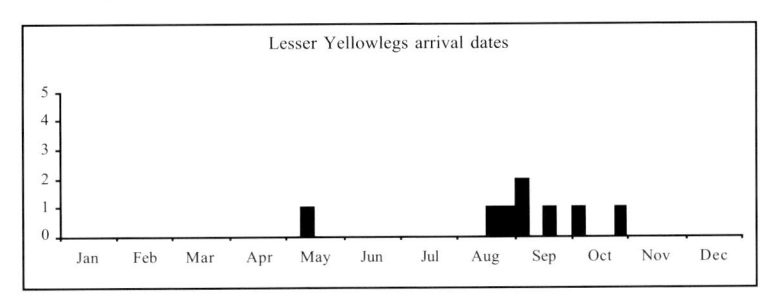

Main return migration is through central USA, with fewer following the Atlantic coast and with southerly breeding grounds reoccupied by early May. As with its larger relative, the timing of migration fits Scillonian arrival dates but the May individual could equally have been an off-course spring migrant or a leftover from a previous autumn's displacement.

## Yellowlegs *Tringa melanoleuca/flavipes*

Unidentified Yellowlegs Records
- 1943   One Scilly September 12th to at least 28th   *CBWPSAR* 14; Griffiths 1982
- 1958   One Bryher 11th May   *CBWPSAR* 28

For general status see Greater Yellowlegs *Tringa melanoleuca* and Lesser Yellowlegs *T. flavipes*.

There are two records of birds that cannot be attributed safely to one or other yellowlegs species. The first involved a 1944 report from A A Dorrien-Smith of a bird seen the previous year, presumably on Tresco, and described by the *CBWPSAR* editors merely as 'Yellowshank'. It was first found on 12th September and was present until at least 28th (*CBWPSAR* 14). The other, also described by the editors as 'Yellowshank', was watched at close range on Bryher for half an hour on 11th May 1958 (*CBWPSAR* 28). The editorial comment 'Satisfactory details supplied' suggests that perhaps the editors were aware which species was involved, but if so they omitted to include that information.

## Solitary Sandpiper *Tringa solitaria* A BBRC 34.7%

**Rare migrant, full written description required by the BBRC.**

- 1882   One shot Lower Moors, St Mary's 21st September   Cornish 1882c; Clark & Rodd 1906
- 1974   One Rosevear, St Mary's & Tresco 23rd to 25th July   *British Birds* 68: 316
- 1974   One Tresco 8th to 11th September   *British Birds* 68: 316
- 1975   One Tresco 12th September   *British Birds* 69: 336
- 1983   One (juvenile) various islands 19th September to 23rd October   *British Birds* 77: 527
- 1984   One (juvenile) St Mary's & Tresco 8th to 19th October   *British Birds* 78: 66
- 1985   One St Mary's 30th August   *British Birds* 79: 550
- 1987   One (juvenile) Tresco 28th September to 5th October   *British Birds* 82: 526
- 1988   One (juvenile) Bryher & St Mary's 1st to 10th September   *British Birds* 82: 526
- 2000   One (juvenile) St Mary's & Tresco 22nd September to 21st October   *British Birds* 93: 346, 94: 475

Breeds North America, in Canada and Alaska north to near tree-line, wintering Central America, West Indies and South America south to Argentina and Uruguay. Polytypic: nominate *solitaria* occurs northeast USA and central and eastern Canada; *cinnamomea* northwest Canada and Alaska.

Just nine birds since what turned out to be the second British and Irish record was shot by Joe White on Lower Moors, St Mary's, on 19th September 1882 (Cornish 1882c; Clark & Rodd 1906). This followed one shot on the River Clyde in Scotland prior to 1870 (Palmer 2000). All ten birds arrived in late summer or autumn, with 23rd July by far the earliest arrival and with the latest arrival 8th October and the latest sighting 23rd October. All attempts at ageing appear to have involved juveniles. Excluding the shot bird, the briefest stay was just one day (two individuals) and the longest 33 days, with an average stay of 11.3 days.

Autumn migration occurs on a broad front with main passage in the USA occurring early August to early September, though with some still moving into October. According to Cramp *et al.* (1977–94) most birds move south overland, the western *cinnamomea* via central USA and nominate *solitaria* through the Atlantic states. Unlike a number of other North American wader species reaching Europe in autumn, Cramp *et al.* make no mention of either transoceanic crossing south out over the North Atlantic, or of southeasterly drift from Alaskan or northern Canadian populations. It would seem difficult, therefore, to explain autumn arrivals in Britain and Ireland. However, Nisbet (1959) looked at wader migration in North America and its relationship to transatlantic wader vagrancy and found that: (a) there were few records of American east-coast species in Europe and that some vagrants reaching Europe are rarities on the American east coast, (b) species from inland American habitats are more frequent transatlantic vagrants, (c) species from western arctic America are much more frequent than those from eastern arctic America and, finally, (d) transatlantic vagrancy occurs mainly in species in which part of the population has an extensive west-to-east movement within North America. Therefore, we might perhaps expect at least some British sightings of Solitary Sandpiper to involve the slightly larger *cinnamomea* (Gantlett 1998).

*Sandpipers, Snipes, Godwits, Curlews and Phalaropes*

*Solitary Sandpiper arrival dates*

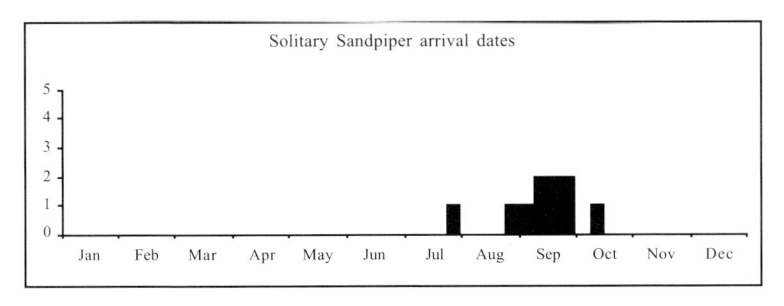

The eight Solitary Sandpipers recorded in Scilly between 1958–1999 represent 34.7% of the 23 British records accepted by the BBRC up to and including 1999.

## Green Sandpiper *Tringa ochropus* A

**Scarce spring and autumn migrant, either singly or in small groups.**

Breeds northern Eurasia, from Norway and northern Germany east to Pacific, south to 45°N. Migratory, wintering tropical Africa, Middle East, India and Southeast Asia. Monotypic. Upgraded from Green- to Amber-listed in UK 2002: five-year mean of 1.4 breeding pairs (Gregory *et al.* 2002).

This is another of those species where the present situation appears not to have changed much from that described by 19th century commentators. Clark and Rodd (1906) gave the first recorded date as 1857, in which year Augustus Pechell shot one somewhere in Scilly. They also described it as occurring in the islands as 'an occasional visitor on migration or in early autumn, but like most of the early autumn birds of passage, does not figure much in the Tresco game-book'. Another shot individual appears in the Tresco records for winter 1878–79 (Rodd 1880). Along with most other wader species, Green Sandpipers put in an appearance in Scilly prior to the apparently exceptionally bad weather of winter 1870. E H Rodd recorded his nephew Francis's observation that they commenced arriving in the islands some time between 10th and 20th July, noting its arrival too during August that same year (Rodd 1870e, 1880).

Writing in the mid-1960s, Penhallurick drew attention to the fact that records for Cornwall and Scilly for the period early May to mid-June were almost entirely absent up until that time (Penhallurick 1969). He described autumn passage as commencing from about late June or early July and peaking during August or early September. The same writer noted that Scillonian maxima of up to six at any site at any one time fell short of counts on mainland Cornwall, where loose accumulations of up to 20 had been reported.

Moving to the present time, little seems to have changed since the 19th century. Taking the ten years commencing 1990, Green Sandpiper appeared in all years, though only nine years in spring and with far fewer during the earlier half of the year. None was recorded in winter, thus this is clearly now limited to a spring and autumn migrant in Scilly, if not previously so. Earliest spring sighting was 3rd March (1990), though late March to mid-April was more typical, whilst latest reported spring sightings all fell in the period 17th April to 16th May. Ignoring a bird on St Mary's for three days on the unusual dates of 25th–27th June (1993), all reported autumn arrival dates (eight years) fell in the narrow 15-day window of 5th to 19th July, whereas latest autumn sightings were similarly condensed, into the 23-day period 29th September to 21st October. The most recorded in spring was ten (1990), with seven in two years and none in 1998.

Calculating autumn totals is complicated by inter-site movements and the reappearance of individuals at sites following periods of apparent absence. Up to 15 on Tresco on 2nd August 1998 seems to have been the highest collective single-island count, with numbers on that island decreasing by 9th, at which time the St Mary's total had climbed to ten. Most are discovered around the muddy margins of the Tresco or St Mary's main pools, therefore two flushed from an algae-covered puddle on the exposed upper level of bare Scilly Rock on 19th July 1994 (pers. obs.) were presumably new arrivals. The closest breeding Green Sandpipers to Scilly are in Norway, Sweden, Poland and possibly Denmark (Hagemeijer & Blair 1997; Cramp *et al.* 1977–94). A broad-front migrant wintering on freshwater areas, a few Green Sandpipers remain north as far as southern Scandinavia in mild winters. Green Sandpipers commence autumn migration particularly early, often departing their breeding grounds by mid-June in northern Scandinavia and reaching main west European wintering areas by late month, although the main passage occurs during July–August. Return spring passage commences from March or early April and is almost complete by mid-May. Little is known about the breeding origin of birds occurring in Britain on passage, though Norway or Sweden seem most probable (Wernham *et al.* 2002). No Green Sandpipers have been ringed on Scilly and there are no recaptures.

## Wood Sandpiper *Tringa glareola* A

**Regular spring and autumn migrant in small numbers.**

Breeds northern Eurasia, from Britain, Norway and Denmark east to Kamchatka. Migratory, wintering equatorial and southern Africa, India, Southeast Asia and Australasia. Monotypic. Included on Annex I of 1979 EEC 'Birds Directive'. Amber-listed in UK: five-year mean of 8.8 breeding pairs; unfavourable world conservation status (Gregory *et al.* 2002).

James Clark and Francis Rodd described Wood Sandpiper in the late 19th century as a rare autumn casual in immature plumage, having occurred on both St Mary's and Tresco (Clark & Rodd 1906). That account was apparently based on just one published Scillonian report, involving a bird shot on Tresco a day or two prior to 2nd September 1878 and quickly passed to E H Rodd in Penzance (Rodd 1880), although doubtless Clark and Francis Rodd relied on Francis's extensive experience of shooting and observing in the islands, along with such others as Augustus Pechell and the Reverend John Jenkinson on St Mary's.

Interestingly, E H Rodd knew it as both a spring and autumn migrant in mainland Cornwall. He also mentioned that as many as seven first-year individuals were shot in one day near Land's End and that it occasionally wintered (Rodd 1880). Therefore, it seems likely that Wood Sandpipers also passed through Scilly in the 1800s in spring, as now, but presumably there were then too few observers available at this time of year. Penhallurick thought it scarce in Scilly in the mid-1960s compared with mainland Cornwall (Penhallurick 1969), pointing out that only a few were reported in most years, normally in autumn but also during May. He also noted that the largest group recorded up until then was nine on St Agnes in 1952. Taking the ten years from 1990, Wood Sandpipers were recorded in all except one of those years, but in only six during spring. Annual combined spring and autumn totals ranged from five to 23, at an average of about nine, though spring totals of from one to four averaged 2.3 individuals for the six years. Earliest arrival was 30th April and the last spring sighting 22nd June, whereas the earliest autumn bird appeared on 8th July and the latest was recorded on 15th October, although mid-September was more usual. Typically, these dainty little waders appear around the edges of the main freshwater areas, such as Porth Hellick and the Lower Moors pools on St Mary's, or Great and Abbey Pools on Tresco. However, birds also often appear at smaller ponds, e.g. at Porthloo on St Mary's, or on St Agnes.

The nearest breeding Wood Sandpipers to Scilly are a handful of pairs in northern Scotland, then Denmark and then northern Scandinavia (Hagemeijer & Blair 1997). A small number of birds winter in coastal Morocco and the coastal Mediterranean but most from western Europe move south as far as the Afrotropical region (Cramp *et al.* 1977–94), being numerous south of the Sahara in winter. They traverse Europe on a broad front, being scarcest but nonetheless regular in Britain and Ireland, though there is, nevertheless, a slight south-southwest bias in the direction adopted by birds from northern Scandinavia. No Wood Sandpipers have been ringed in Scilly and there are no controls.

## Terek Sandpiper *Xenus cinereus* A BBRC 1.8%

**Extremely rare migrant, full written description required by the BBRC.**

1999   Porth Hellick Beach, St Mary's 11th to 23rd April   *British Birds* 93: 535

Breeds northeast Europe and Siberia, wintering Africa, Arabian Peninsula, India, Southeast Asia and Australia. Monotypic.

The long-awaited first record for Scilly was discovered at Porth Hellick, St Mary's, on 11th April 1999, providing excellent views to all who came to admire it. Typically for Scilly, the bird presented a unique British birding experience, it being possible at one point during its stay, and without moving position, to watch a singing male Sardinian Warbler *Sylvia melanocephala*, two or more Night Herons *Nycticorax*

*nycticorax* and Little Egret *Egretta garzetta*, as well of course as the main object of attraction. The bird finally departed on 23rd April.

This was the earliest British record by a long way, pre-dating the previous earliest, in Kent in 1998, by 25 days and also being the first recorded in April. For a photograph of the Porth Hellick bird see *British Birds* 92: plate 383. According to Cramp *et al.* (1977–94) the main breeding concentration is in Siberia and the largest numbers winter in India, although a significant minority cross the West Palearctic on a southwest heading to winter in Africa. In addition, of course, birds breeding in Europe west as far as Finnmark must move directly south into Africa. The timing of arrival of the St Mary's bird fits the pattern of other species from northeast Europe and northwest Asia know to winter in Africa. A total of 54 British Terek Sandpiper records were accepted by the BBRC during the period 1958–99 inclusive, with the St Mary's bird representing less than 2%.

## Common Sandpiper *Actitis hypoleucos* A

**Annual migrant in small to moderate numbers. In spring it arrives in April and leaves by May, in autumn arriving in July and leaving by October.**

Breeds Eurasia, from Spain, France, Britain and Ireland east to Pacific. Migratory, in West Palearctic small numbers winter coastally south to Mediterranean but majority cross Sahara into tropical and southern Africa. Monotypic. National 29% decline 1994–99 (Bashford & Noble 2000).

Up until at least the final quarter of the 19th century, Common Sandpiper was considered something of a rarity in Scilly, Francis Rodd and Augustus Pechell knowing of only one sighting, in 1857 (Clark & Rodd 1906). However, by the turn of the 20th century the same authors thought it was occurring occasionally during August and early September, either singly or in small flocks. Francis apparently forgot that he had written to his uncle E H Rodd in 1870 informing him that Common Sandpipers arrived by the end of July that year (Rodd 1880), and that he wrote again in early September to say more had arrived during the past fortnight (Rodd 1870e).

Interestingly, there appears to be no 19th century mention of it occurring in spring. However, by the mid-20th century Penhallurick felt able to confirm that it arrived in the islands singly or in small parties from early April through to the end of May, and similarly from mid-July through to mid-October (Penhallurick 1969). He quoted first and last dates as 29th March and 24th October respectively, plus the first Scillonian winter record, involving two on St Agnes up until 21st December 1964. Evidently, the situation differed somewhat on mainland Cornwall where substantial numbers remained at some sites during summer, e.g. up to 25 on the Camel Estuary in 1965. Parties of up to six were common on passage and noisy compact flocks of up to 35 were on record. In this last connection, Penhallurick omitted to mention a report of 22 in flight off St Mary's on 25th July 1958 (*CBWPSAR* 28).

Taking the last quarter of the 20th century, 22 on Tresco on 3rd May 1978 was the highest individual island count, whilst a loose flock of 13 seen by the author in Porth Conger, between St Agnes and Gugh, on 28th July 1992 was probably the greatest number recorded feeding together in Scilly. Taking the ten years from 1990, arrival and departure dates for the nine years where these are recorded were impressively regular, all spring arrivals falling within the 17-day window commencing 6th April. Similarly, spring departures were restricted to the period 2nd to 31st May and autumn birds were no less regular, all arrivals being restricted to the 14-day period 29th June–12th July and departures to the period 2nd–29th October. The only published records later than October for the last quarter of the 20th century involved singles on 13th and 14th November in 1977 and 1988 respectively and there still appears to be no instance of genuine wintering from the islands.

Typically, birds occur singly or in loosely associated groups but arriving at meaningful all-island Common Sandpiper counts is problematical, although up to ten on each of the six main islands during peak passage may not be an unreasonable suggestion, with the proviso that birds are always likely to be present somewhere within the islands between the above dates. One further difficulty in trying to compare daily counts is the random manner in which records are received for most of the uninhabited islands, e.g. St Helen's, Annet, Tean, each of which may hold one or more birds. Some are to be found by the edges of the freshwater pools, e.g. Tresco's Great Pool, Porth Hellick and Lower Moors pools on St Mary's, or St Agnes pool, but perhaps most frequent rocky shorelines. Interestingly, there appears to be no suggestion in the published accounts of either high-tide roosting congregations or increases in numbers around fresh water during high tides.

That Common Sandpiper is a mainly freshwater species is reflected in its behaviour on passage, with European birds crossing the Continent on a broad front, although with a marked southwest autumn bias (Cramp *et al.* 1977–94). This direction is reversed in spring, and birds move singly or in small groups. There may be a clear winter separation between northwest European breeding birds, those from western Russia migrating mostly to East Africa, and those from the Baltic area and further west wintering mainly in West Africa (Wernham *et al.* 2002). Some of the latter pass through Britain. The small percentage of European birds leaving the breeding grounds during late June is though likely to involve failed breeders. Most birds move south from early July and passage is normally almost complete by the end of October. In spring, trans-Saharan passage commences from late March or early April, the first birds reaching Europe during early April, with the bulk of European passage visible mid-April to mid-May. All of this seems to fit the pattern of movements in Scilly. Just four Common Sandpipers have been trapped and ringed in Scilly, all prior to 1970. There are no controls or recoveries.

## Spotted Sandpiper *Actitis macularia* A BBRC 19%

**Rare autumn and even rarer spring migrant, full written description required by the BBRC.**

1965   One (trapped) St Agnes 23rd September to 28th October   *British Birds* 59: 288
1966   One (trapped) Tresco 3rd September to 1st October   *British Birds* 60: 318
1966   One (trapped) St Agnes 23rd to 25th September   *British Birds* 60: 318
1967   One St Agnes 6th to 21st September   *British Birds* 61: 341
1968   One St Agnes & Tresco 18th September to 2nd October   *British Birds* 62: 469
1969   One St Mary's 4th to 25th October   *British Birds* 63: 276
1971   One St Agnes & Gugh 10th October   *British Birds* 65: 332
1974   One St Mary's 27th August to 11th September   *British Birds* 68: 317
1976   Two St Mary's 9th to 26th October, one to 2nd November   *British Birds* 70: 421
1978   One (juvenile) St Agnes 15th to 29th August   *British Birds* 72: 524, 76: 498
1978   Two (juveniles) Tresco 20th to 23rd August   *British Birds* 72: 524, 76: 498
1978   One (juvenile) St Mary's 8th to 30th September   *British Birds* 72: 524, 76: 498
1978   One (juvenile) Tresco 17th to 21st September   *British Birds* 72: 524, 76: 498
1978   One (juvenile) Tresco 7th to 14th October   *British Birds* 72: 524, 76: 498
1979   One (adult) Tresco 23rd September to 9th October   *British Birds* 73: 510
1982   One (probable juvenile) Tresco 6th October   *British Birds* 76: 498
1983   One (juvenile) Tresco 16th to 19th September   *British Birds* 79: 550
1985   One (adult) Tresco 4th to 21st October   *British Birds* 79: 550
1987   One (juvenile) Tresco 13th September to 6th October   *British Birds* 81: 560
1989   One (juvenile) Tresco 18th to 24th August   *British Birds* 83: 464
1993   One (juvenile) St Martin's 21st October   *British Birds* 87: 529
1996   One St Agnes 6th to 12th May   *British Birds* 90: 481
2002   One St Agnes & Gugh 11th to 23rd October   British Birds 95: 667, 96: 155

Breeds North America, from Pacific to Atlantic coasts, south of Canadian Arctic as far as California and Arizona in west and Maryland in east. Winters West Indies and South America south to Chile, Bolivia and Argentina. Monotypic. Increasing reduction in breeding population in last decade, particularly in eastern States (Bryant 1997).

This species seems to have gone unrecorded in Scilly and Cornwall in the 19th and early 20th centuries, chances being though that it was present but not identified. There are a number of claims from around the country dating back to a bird allegedly shot in Essex in 1757 but this and most others seem to have been surrounded by controversy (Palmer 2000). Perhaps the best contender for the first British record was one shot at Whitby, North Yorkshire, in 1849 and later mounted by York taxidermist Graham. However, whatever the truth, a bird found on St Agnes on 23rd September 1965 and trapped and ringed next day was only the second British record since the establishment of the BBRC in 1958. It remained on the island until 28th October (*CBWPSAR* 35; *British Birds* 59: 288). The first BBRC record came from Whiteland, Carmarthenshire, in May 1960.

As if to prove Spotted Sandpiper had almost certainly occurred before but been missed, birds were present on Scilly for five out of the next six years. In 1966 there were two, the first of which, on Tresco, was watched by various observers from 3rd September as it fed around the Great Pool and on nearby beaches. On 21st it was trapped and the identification confirmed, it being last seen on 1st October. The second for that year was present on St Agnes for three days from 23rd September (*CBWPSAR* 36).

The presence of six on Scilly in autumn 1978 was quite exceptional, especially as elsewhere in Britain there was just a single individual. Birds in spotted adult plumage were present on Great Pool, Tresco, in October 1985 and in the Browarth area of St Agnes in May 1996. A colour photograph of the latter was reproduced in *IOSBR* (1996), and this bird is the sole spring record of this species in Scilly so far.

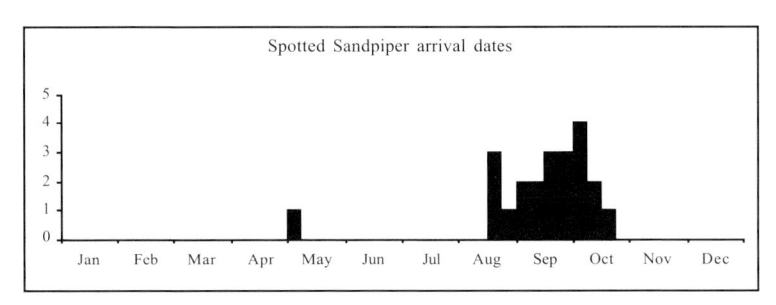

The Chart includes all 24 arrival dates and shows a pattern typical for North American migrant waders in Scilly, though perhaps one which is slightly more protracted. Disregarding the single spring individual, the earliest arrival date was 15th August and the latest 21st October, with 28th October the last date any bird was seen. The shortest stay was just a single day (three individuals) and the longest 36 days, with an average length of stay of 13.2 days. A total of 124 British records were accepted by the BBRC during the period 1958–99, the 24 Scillonian records representing just over 19% of all birds recorded during the same period. Autumn migration occurs on a broad front, mainly via inland freshwater habitats. Some at least of the more northerly breeding birds show a southeast bias in their direction of travel and are believed to use the transoceanic strategy, flying direct from eastern Canada or northeast USA out over the North Atlantic to the Caribbean, or even direct to northeast South America (Cramp *et al.* 1977–94). Towards the north of its range, migration commences around July, with adults moving first and juveniles evident mainly in August. Of the 11 Scillonian records that were aged, ten were thought to have been juveniles. A pair made a breeding attempt in the Highland Region of Scotland in 1975 but did not return in subsequent years. The initial three Spotted Sandpipers in Scilly were trapped and ringed, but there are no recoveries.

## Turnstone (Ruddy Turnstone) *Arenaria interpres* A

**Common passage migrant and winter visitor, most numerous wintering wader, outnumbering even Oystercatcher. Small numbers normally present during summer.**

Circumpolar breeding distribution, around edge of arctic seas, including eastern Greenland but excluding Iceland. In West Palearctic, includes Norway, Sweden, Finland, Spitsbergen and Novaya Zemlya. In West Palearctic, winters Mediterranean and Atlantic coasts, south into southern Africa. Polytypic: nominate *interpres* occurs throughout, except for arctic Canada, where replaced by *morinella*. Amber-listed in UK: 20% or more of East Atlantic Flyway non-breeding population in UK (Gregory *et al.* 2002).

The limited summer presence led some early observers to assume it bred in Scilly. For example, North (1850) commented that although Turnstone had not been proved to breed 'its appearance in the summer months would seem to indicate a probability that such is the case'. The same author described it as a constant resident. However, in their invaluable *Zoologist* summary of *The Birds of Scilly*, James Clark and Francis Rodd point out that it was evidently a rare bird on Scilly in May 1841, drawing attention to a comment by an unidentified writer to the effect that a Turnstone was brought to him on the very unusual date of 20th May that year. However, from their subsequent remarks it seems clear that by the mid-19th century it was commonly encountered in the islands during autumn and winter, some also remaining for the summer (Clark & Rodd 1906). This leaves us to wonder if the 1841 writer meant it was unusual for them to be shot in May, as opposed to being seen.

James Clark and Francis Rodd also addressed the question of whether Turnstone bred in Scilly. Clark, an extremely experienced and reliable ornithologist, believed it had done so 'lately', partly basing this on three eggs and part of a shell contained in local collections, but also citing skins of two 'young' shot in the islands in July, though it seems unclear whether these were unfledged, or merely in first-winter plumage. In addition, however, Clark referred to sightings of birds in adult plumage during early July, further suggesting that eggs had been taken by C J King and a Mr Jackson. Nonetheless, Clark decided to reserve final judgement until he himself found a nest, though there is no record of him ever having done so (Clark & Rodd 1906). Penhallurick subsequently discovered a letter Clark wrote to King in 1923 saying he received one Turnstone's egg from Jackson and another from a Miss Hicks of Truro, but formerly of St Agnes, whilst he found a third badly broken in the collection of L R George of St Mary's (Penhallurick 1969). Somewhat mysteriously, King later claimed a mistake by local boatmen, arguing that Ringed Plover *Charadrius hiaticula* eggs had been involved (C J King 1924). However, it seems most unlikely that Clark could have confused eggs of the two species. Clark also doubted that the three eggs in question could have been 'introduced' to the islands, from which it is assumed he meant acquired from other collectors. Whatever the truth, however, early claims of Turnstone breeding in Scilly remain in doubt and, interestingly, the species does not figure in the mid-20th century review of the breeding birds of Scilly and Cornwall (Ryves & Quick 1946). There was, nonetheless, a claim of a pair with downy young at an unnamed site in Cornwall in May 1950 (Penhallurick 1969).

We now know of course how regularly Turnstones arrive in Britain in summer in breeding plumage, often accompanied by birds still in first-winter plumage. In fact, several early accounts made this very point about Scilly, e.g. Gurney (1868) and Francis Rodd himself (in Rodd 1880), but contemporary observers apparently misread the situation. Penhallurick (1969) summarised the status of Turnstone on Scilly up until the mid 1960s, birds reaching their lowest numbers between mid-June and mid-July, by which time flocks of 20–40 were still to be found on 'many islands'. On St Agnes, main passage was noted from mid-August onwards, with up to 300 present in November and a wintering population of about 150. At the other end of the year, spring flocks on St Agnes regularly reached 200, and in May 1963 peaked at 373. Penhallurick suggested this annual St Agnes pattern was probably typical of most islands, which does seem to be the case. Although co-ordinated all-island late spring and autumn counts are lacking, there is a statement of up to 2,000 present during peak passage in the 1990s (*IOSBR* 1992). However, this figure may not have been achieved annually and there may have been a reduction in numbers of birds present in recent years (*IOSBR* 1999), as seems to be supported by results of the following surveys.

A total of 936 Turnstones recorded throughout the islands during a full shorebird count in winter 1984–85 represented just over 2% of the British wintering population and exceeded requirements for international importance. These 936 birds also represented 33% of all 2,825 waders found during the survey. Counts took place during December–January and, in general, birds avoided the harder substrata types, much preferring sandy beaches (Kirby 1988). Distribution of individuals was as follows: St Mary's 219, St Agnes and Gugh 148, Samson 149, Bryher 138, Tresco 198, St Martin's 45 and Tean, St Helen's and Northwethel 39. Linear densities (individuals per kilometre of beach) varied widely, in the range 4.6 to 40.3, at an average of 18.9. Samson (40.3) held over twice the densities of other islands, with the exception of Bryher (30.7).

There were two additional co-ordinated counts, the first of which involved the 1996 four-day, mid-March wader survey, which located 346 Turnstones on the five islands visited – St Mary's, St Agnes and Gugh, Samson, Bryher and Tresco (Lock 1996). Similarly, the late January 1997 two-day Winter Shorebird Survey recorded just 238 individuals, but although St Martin's was included on this occasion the survey nevertheless still lacked complete coverage. Additionally, a count of 110 on St Agnes seven days later indicated that birds had either been overlooked or had moved within the islands subsequent to the survey, or there had been a ensuing influx from outside the islands.

A total of 69 Turnstones have been ringed in Scilly, all but nine prior to 1970. Unlike many species, there is ringing evidence suggesting where Turnstones reaching Scilly originate, two ringed on St Agnes having been subsequently recovered in Greenland during summer. In addition, a bird ringed in Iceland in late May was controlled on St Agnes in early May the following year, and as the species does not breed in Iceland was presumably en route to Greenland when ringed. Most Turnstones using west-coast Britain can be expected to originate from either northeast Canada or Greenland and winter south into Europe and Africa as far as the Gulf of Guinea (Cramp *et al.* 1977–94; Wernham *et al.* 2002). Birds moving south reach western Europe from late July onwards, whereas main spring passage occurs April–May, though there is evidence of a pre-migration northwards drift within Britain. Birds from Fennoscandia and western Russia move mainly south down the coasts of continental Europe to winter in Morocco and West Africa, though some reach Britain, particularly those from Finland.

The slightly smaller and brighter plumaged *morinella* from arctic Canada has reached Britain at least once before and its possible presence should be kept in mind when dealing with any group of Turnstones in Scilly (Gantlett 1998). The current estimated UK winter Turnstone population is in the order of 64,000 individuals (Stone *et al.* 1997).

**Controls**
711083   Ad   Midnes, Iceland 25th May 1960        CT   St Agnes 10th May 1961
**Recoveries**
73939S   1stY   St Agnes 30th September 1963       SH   Kuvdlorssuak, Upernavik, Greenland (4th) 16th June 1967

60463X   FG   St Agnes 30th September 1960         FD   Station Dye (Greenland icecap), Greenland (6th) 28th July 1968

Turnstone Ringing Recaptures

# Wilson's Phalarope *Phalaropus tricolor* A BBRC 2.8%

Very rare autumn migrant, although there is also one spring record, now slightly more frequent in Scilly than Red-necked Phalarope *P. lobatus*. Full written description required by the BBRC.

[1963   One Tresco 8th October]   *SABOAR* 1963–64
1964   One Porth Killier, St Agnes 22nd & 23rd June   *British Birds* 58: 361
1971   One St Mary's 29th August to 7th September   *British Birds* 65: 335
1977   One Tresco 5th to 12th September   *British Birds* 71: 504

1977 One Tresco 3rd to 9th October  *British Birds* 71: 504
1981 One (juvenile) Tresco & St Mary's 15th to 26th September  *British Birds* 75: 505
1988 One St Mary's 2nd September  *British Birds* 89: 504
1995 One (juvenile) St Agnes 3rd October  *British Birds* 89: 504
1995 One (adult) Tresco 5th October  *British Birds* 89: 504

Breeds North America, in west from central Canadian prairies south to Colorado, in east limited to small area east of Great Lakes. Migratory, wintering south to Paraguay and Argentina. Monotypic. Apparent recent decline in breeding population (Bryant 1997).

Although the first BBRC-accepted Scillonian record came from St Agnes in 1964, a bird seen on Tresco the previous year was at the time thought likely to have been this species (*SABOAR* 1963–64). Little information other than date and location is available for most of the eight accepted local sightings, the single obvious exception being the 1971 individual on Porth Hellick Pool, St Mary's. Discovered by a Mr M Twist on 29th August, his provisional identification was confirmed by David Hunt the following day. The latter noted that the bird's 'pallid appearance alongside other waders' was always conspicuous (*IOSBR* 1971). The Chart shows all arrival dates. Earliest autumn arrival was 29th August and the latest sighting 9th October. Average length of stay was 5.4 days, in the range one to 12 days.

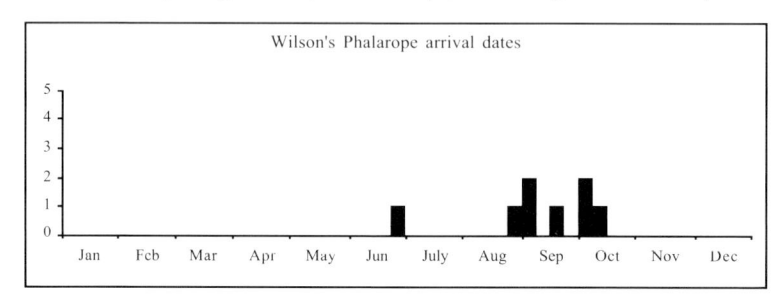

Wilson's Phalarope arrival dates

Importantly, Wilson's Phalarope differs from the two other phalarope species in its inland aquatic habits. Indeed, Cramp *et al.* (1977–94) quote just a single truly pelagic observation, involving a bird between Galapagos and Easter Island in February 1926. It is also a trans-equatorial migrant. Birds commence leaving the breeding grounds from late June or early July, females being the first to depart. Peak movement through the USA occurs during August, tailing off by late September (Cramp *et al.* 1977–94). The western population moves south through interior USA, most then by-passing Central America via direct transoceanic flight to Columbia and Ecuador, some vagrants reaching the Galapagos Islands and even Australia. Cramp *et al.* point out that European records commence from the mid-1950s, about the time expansion into southeastern Canada also commenced. Therefore, birds reaching Europe may be either the product of extreme eastwards migration or vagrancy involving individuals from western North America which perhaps then embarked upon a transoceanic crossing from east-coast North America, or birds from southeast Canada or northeast USA, autumn movements of which are still unclear. Interestingly, six of the seven Scillonian records occurred at a time that fits the requirements of autumn migration well.

# Red-necked Phalarope *Phalaropus lobatus* A

**Formerly scarce, now very rare autumn migrant and even rarer in spring. Slightly less frequent now than Wilson's Phalarope *P. tricolor*. Treated by the BBRC as a national Scarce Migrant, full written description required by SRP.**

1954 One St Agnes 17th September to 6th October
1957 One Warna's Cove, St Agnes 9th September
1959 One St Agnes 8th September
1959 Up to four St Agnes 23rd–24th October
1959 One St Agnes 24th October
1962 Two Kallimay Point, St Agnes 30th October
1962 One Eastern Isles 2nd November

1963   One from RMV *Scillonian II* 28th September
1965   One St Agnes 8th September
1975   One (long dead) Wingletang, St Agnes 5th October
1976   One Great Pool, Tresco 13th & 14th September
1981   One (female) Great Pool, Tresco 17th June
1989   One at sea 28th September
1997   One (female) Crow Sound 28th May

Circumpolar breeding distribution, around edge of arctic seas from Iceland, Britain and Norway east through Eurasia and North America to Greenland. Migratory, in West Palearctic winters mainly in northwest Indian Ocean. Monotypic. Included on Annex I of 1979 EEC 'Birds Directive'. Red-listed in UK: historical population decline; five-year mean of 22.8 breeding males (Gregory *et al*. 2002).

James Clark and E H Rodd's nephew Francis Rodd summarised the Scillonian records up to the close of the 19th century by quoting individuals killed on Tresco's Abbey Pool (by Francis) in 1860, another in 1863 (no location) and by the Reverend John Jenkinson on Bryher in October 1866 (Rodd 1860a; 1866e; Clark & Rodd 1906). E H Rodd noted too that it occurred less commonly in mainland Cornwall and the islands than Grey Phalarope *P. fulicarius*, usually in autumn and most often in October (Rodd 1880).

The Table lists all recorded Scillonian 20th century sightings, all except two of which were in autumn. Penhallurick (1969) drew attention to the tendency for this species to occur in Cornwall and Scilly at the same time as Grey Phalarope, invariably, he thought, following westerly gales. He also highlighted the lack of spring sightings compared with eastern England. However, one thing immediately apparent from the Table is the reduction in Scillonian sightings since the mid-1960s, as a consequence of which this species is now slightly less frequent in the islands than the nationally rare Nearctic Wilson's Phalarope. The Chart shows all known 20th century arrival dates, omitting the 1975 St Agnes individual, which had been dead an estimated two months, and omitting the bird seen from RMV *Scillonian*. The Chart shows an obvious two-phase autumn arrival, the explanation of which is unclear. Ignoring the long-staying 1954 individual, there was no appreciable difference in the length of stay between months.

Red-necked Phalaropes migrate mainly overland but are primarily pelagic during winter (Cramp *et al*. 1977–94). The main known West Palearctic wintering area is the Arabian Sea, Scandinavian birds moving southeast across Europe via the Black and Caspian Seas, probably largely non-stop. Icelandic, Faeroes and Scottish populations are also believed to utilise the Arabian Sea, with perhaps some suggestion of British east-coast arrivals being weather-related accidentals. Despite what are considered to be irregular winter records from Iberia and African countries, the winter destination of northwest European populations nevertheless remains unclear.

The bulk of the North American population moves southwest in autumn, to winter off northwest South America. A lesser percentage, possibly involving birds from Greenland and Iceland, apparently move south off eastern USA, and although this may involve congregations of up to 250,000 off southeast Canada in May and August, routes involved remain unclear, as does their ultimate destination (Cramp *et al*. 1977–94)

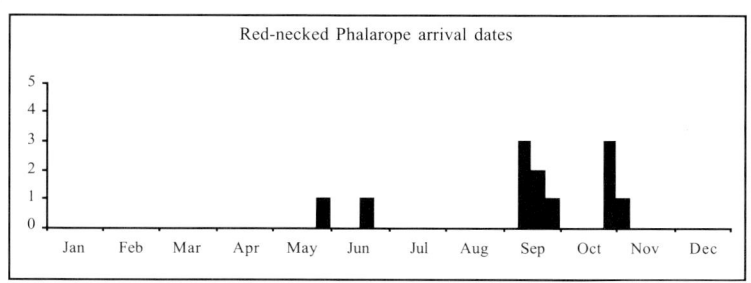

Red-necked Phalaropes depart the breeding grounds from late June, females preceding males and juveniles, most having left by early September and with passage through North Sea countries mainly confined to July–October. Most European Red-necked Phalaropes leave the Arabian Sea from April, reoccupying their breeding grounds from mid- to late May. No Red-necked Phalaropes have been ringed in Scilly and there are no controls.

## Grey Phalarope *Phalaropus fulicarius* A

**Autumn or early winter migrant in small numbers, recently annual and occasionally in greater numbers. Treated by the BBRC as a national Scarce Migrant. The commonest of the three phalarope species in Scilly.**

Circumpolar, breeds edge of arctic seas, from east Greenland and Iceland east through Spitsbergen, Novaya Zemlya, northeast Siberia, Alaska and arctic Canada to western Greenland. Migratory, most oceanic of three phalarope species, almost exclusively using sea routes. Occasionally occurs inshore in substantial numbers during severe weather. Monotypic.

First mention of Grey Phalarope in the islands may be James Clark and Francis Rodd's account of singles obtained on 13th and 23rd October 1857, plus birds on 14th September 1870, 7th January 1893 and 6th December 1902 (Clark & Rodd 1906). The same authors recounted a substantial wreck along Cornwall's south coast in December 1866, at which time 70 appeared off Tresco's northern end, plus a party of five off Old Town, St Mary in November 1905. Frances's uncle E H Rodd apparently mentioned at least one in Scilly during October 1860, also adding to the above records a flock of 13 reported to him by Francis during the latter half of October 1870 (Rodd 1880).

Penhallurick summarised records for Cornwall and Scilly up until the mid-1960s, pointing out that most occurred between October and early November, although not infrequently from September through to early December, extreme dates being 10th August and 30th December. There were just seven winter or spring sightings, the latest of which was May 1878, involving a bird in almost complete summer plumage. Significant Grey Phalarope wrecks occurred in Scilly during several years, including three in rapid succession in 1957, 1959 and 1960, all of which Penhallurick described in great detail. However, an entry in the 1951 *CBWPSAR* (21) demonstrates the difficulties involved in analysing past records, referring as it does to 'A large flock resting on the sea off Samson' on 28th September that year.

The 1957 arrivals formed part of a far wider influx into Britain and Ireland that autumn, though Scilly received very few by comparison (Sage & King 1959). Sage and King suggested that a maximum of 15 individuals may have been involved between 11th and 24th September but with no more than four together. Parties of six and seven were also seen between Scilly and Land's End. The 1959 influx was a much more noticeable affair and commenced with at least 28 on the sea off St Agnes on 9th October but only small numbers then until 23rd, when a flock of 350 appeared off Horse Point on the same island. Fewer were visible next day, around 100, but the impression gained was that most had moved further offshore, where they could not be seen. However, by the 25th all had departed and the next record was not until 7th November, when 20 were off St Agnes. The 1960 influx was even more impressive and besides Scilly involved Cornwall, Devon and Dorset plus Pembrokeshire and southern Ireland, although Scilly and Cornwall received most birds. First indication of what was to follow on Scilly involved 110 seen from RMV *Scillonian II* on 13th September plus 150, also off the boat, on 15th, with at least 1,000 off St Agnes on the last date. From 1st October through to 25th there followed an extraordinary sequence of records involving flocks off various islands of up to 500, the latter total featuring off both St Mary's and St Agnes on 2nd. A few dead birds were in evidence 'on the cliffs' on 23rd October (*CBWPSAR* 30). In all, some 2,300 Grey Phalaropes were believed to have been involved off St Agnes alone, this figure perhaps doubling once birds seen from other islands and from *Scillonian II* were taken into account (*SABOAR* 1959–60; Milne 1960). Around this same time 500 to 1,000 were present in St Ives Bay, north Cornwall, with 700 in Tor Bay, Devon (Cramp *et al.* 1977–94).

The only subsequent years involving larger-than-normal numbers were 1981, 1982 and 1984. During the first of these years, there were substantially more sightings than normal during September and October, with maxima of 200 off Bryher on 23rd September and 125 off Tresco's northern end on 8th October, although most records involved far fewer individuals, e.g. 13 north of Tresco on 3rd October. During 1982, birds were evident between late September and late October. Largest counts involving 72 in flight south of St Mary's during a gale on 5th October, 85 in the same area next day and 90 west of Scilly on 11th. Many other sightings involved fewer numbers. In 1984, Grey Phalaropes were reported on 23 dates between 5th September and 24th October, involving a total of 145 individuals. Of these, 93 were recorded between 1st and 5th October, either from the *Scillonian* or around the islands.

Examining the situation for the ten years from 1990, a total of 199 Grey Phalaropes were recorded at an average of just under 20 a year. Highest numbers occurred in 1991 (66) and 1995 (53), the next largest annual totals being ten in 1990 and eleven each in 1992 and 1997. The lowest annual figures were just two in both 1993 and 1994. Most records came from around the islands, though at least 25 were seen during regular crossings of *Scillonian III*. The earliest recorded date was 18th August and the last was 14th December. Interestingly, a bird on Tresco's Great Pool on 28th February 1993 was apparently the first ever Scillonian record for that month. Care is required when using T A Dorrien-Smith's useful booklet *Birds of Scilly as Recorded at Tresco Abbey*, as the author transposed the scientific names of this species and 'Red-breasted Snipe' (dowitchers) (T A Dorrien-Smith 1951).

The full extent of Grey Phalarope wintering range is still poorly understood, though many occur off western Africa, among other areas. Departure from the breeding grounds is staggered, adult females leaving before males and juveniles, most birds moving well offshore and reaching the wintering grounds by late November. Few are believed to enter the North Sea. The later-moving juveniles are possibly more susceptible to weather-related displacements and thus perhaps account for the majority of European coastal wrecks (Cramp *et al*. 1977–94). Even less is known about return spring movement, though birds off western Africa are thought to commence moving north from March, northern European breeding grounds being reoccupied by late May. According to Cramp *et al*., the presence of so many Grey Phalaropes across the North Atlantic during autumn may be indicative of a southeast movement of Nearctic populations to winter in the food-rich waters off western Africa, since few are recorded in the western Atlantic south of New England latitudes during autumn. Nine Grey Phalaropes were ringed in Scilly prior to 1970 but there are no controls or recoveries.

Since preparing the above text, a notable influx occurred in the islands during October 2001, involving 153 past Tresco on 1st, at least 200 off St Agnes on the 6th and around 100 during a local pelagic trip on the 12th. During the same period, 75 were seen past Pendeen, west Cornwall, on the 8th (*Birding World* 14: 403). An unseasonal individual was also seen during a mini-pelagic on 11th July 2002.

# Phalarope *Phalaropus*

Unidentified Phalarope Records
- 1958 St Mary's 19th September
- 1966 One St Agnes 20th October
- 1966 One St Agnes 27th November
- 1967 Two St Agnes 1st October
- 1967 Three St Agnes 7th October
- 1971 One St Agnes 10th October
- 1971 Two St Agnes 27th October

For details of world distribution of Red-necked *Phalaropus lobatus*, Grey *P. fulicarius* and Wilson's *P. tricolor* Phalaropes see those species.

Most phalarope sightings within the islands are now likely to involve Grey Phalarope, with the chance of Red-necked or Wilson's being involved then about equal. Unidentified phalaropes were recorded as follows, the first of which was thought likely by the observer to have involved Red-necked, which occurred far more frequently at that time.

# Pomarine Skua *Stercorarius pomarinus* A

**Scarce, mainly offshore migrant, mostly in autumn, full written description required by the SRP.**

Cosmopolitan, in northern Eurasia breeds from eastern Barents Sea to Bering Sea and in northern North America from eastern Alaska to Baffin Island, plus western Greenland. Migratory, in eastern Atlantic wintering south as far as coastal South Africa. Monotypic, but also polymorphic.

The sole 19th century mention of this species in or around Scilly seems to be James Clark and Francis Rodd's account of a bird seen in September 1895 and fed briefly with bait at close range (one to two metres) by T A Dorrien-Smith from a boat over 'Pawll Bank' (Clark & Rodd 1906). This was probably the area now known as Poll Bank, just to the south of St Agnes. The bird was feeding in company with four

Great Shearwaters *Puffinus gravis*. On mainland Cornwall the leading 19th century Cornish authority, E H Rodd, thought it occurred at 'irregular and uncertain intervals', mostly off the coast but it occasionally entered harbours and estuaries (Rodd 1880). Rodd nevertheless considered it 'one of our rarer seas birds', the only four specimens he knew of having been obtained at Penzance, Land's End, Mount's Bay and from Falmouth Harbour. The first British record of Pomarine Skua involved two skins sold at auction in 1819 in what is now East Sussex, and obtained in Sussex and Kent some time beforehand (Palmer 2000).

More recently, Penhallurick (1969) pointed out that although figures were never published this species was more abundant off the Cornish coast during autumns 1879 and 1891 than during any year up until at least the late 1960s. Penzance taxidermist Vingoe was allegedly offered many immatures during the earlier of these two years, whereas birds were noted off Cornwall annually between 1900 and 1906 (Clark, in W Page 1906). Nevertheless, Penhallurick drew attention to the apparent absence of any further records from Cornwall or Scilly until a possible sighting off St Mary's in May 1925, as mentioned in the Tresco Abbey records (Penhallurick 1969). The same author pointed out that up until the 1960s most southwest sightings came from either St Ives Bay in west Cornwall, from sea crossings between Land's End and Scilly, or from seawatches on St Agnes, with 80% of sightings during the period 1955–67 occurring between early September and late October, in the range 14th August to 16th November. Sightings in other months were exceptional. Most sightings involved single bird-days, though 12 or more accompanied 200 other skuas off St Agnes during a three-hour seawatch during mid-October 1958. In general, light-phase birds are apparently in the minority.

For a more recent comparison, data were examined for the 13-year period 1977–89 and the 10-year period 1990–99 (*IOSBR*). During the former period, birds were recorded in three years during spring and 12 years in autumn, at a mean annual rate of 0.3 and 4.9 respectively. The most recorded together were four off Peninnis, St Mary's, in 1985. In autumn 1985, from six to 19 individuals may have been involved in sightings over an 18-day period during October, but for analysis purposes this was treated as an arbitrary 12. During the ten years to 1999, birds were recorded in three years in spring, involving four birds, and nine years in autumn, involving 34 birds. Mean annual autumn numbers were 3.7 and the most recorded together was three in 1997, with none at all in 1993.

Earliest spring sighting dates for the two periods were 29th and 24th April respectively and the latest 22nd May (2) and 5th June. Earliest autumn sighting for the first period was on 2nd August and the latest 2nd November, comparable dates for the later period being 21st July and 28th November. Whilst it may be tempting to suggest that there was a change in the pattern of Pomarine Skua movements past Scilly during the final decade of the 20th century, a far more plausible explanation may be a general increase of interest in seawatching in the islands, as well as the obviously greatly increased birdwatcher presence. To some extent, annual numbers of sightings may be dictated by weather conditions further out to sea, as was possibly the case in 1985 when as many as 19 Pomarine Skuas may have passed the islands, with numbers of Arctic Skuas *S. parasiticus* similarly greater than normal.

As with Long-tailed Skua *S. longicaudus*, details of wintering distribution are still imperfectly known and, as for that species, this is not helped by difficulties involved in separating juveniles and non-breeding adults at sea. However, it seems clear that the timing of autumn Pomarine Skua movements off Scilly are somewhat later than for both Long-tailed and Arctic Skuas, as evident from the four recent November sightings. According to Cramp *et al*.. (1977–94) the majority of Pomarine Skuas using the Atlantic Ocean during winter remain north of the equator, which may help explain their later migration pattern. However, there is some uncertainty over the timing of the start of autumn movement, though at least one authority suggests September, in which case July or August North Atlantic sightings may involve non-breeders. Undoubtedly, though, main passage through the North Sea and the temperate North Atlantic occurs during September and October, with adults preceding juveniles and with a small number still evident into early December. Finally, although it seems widely accepted that most birds passing Britain and Ireland originate from northern Eurasia, the possibility of individuals with a Nearctic origin, e.g. Greenland, seems to have been less explored. Return passage commences during April and peaks in the North Atlantic during May, birds being noted in British and Irish waters from April through to June. All of which admirably fits the pattern of observed movements past Scilly. No Pomarine Skuas have been ringed on Scilly and there are no recaptures from elsewhere.

# Arctic Skua *Stercorarius parasiticus* A

Annual migrant in small numbers, mainly in autumn with fewer in spring, occasional during early winter.

Circumpolar, breeding edge of Arctic Ocean, in Eurasia from eastern Greenland, Iceland, Faeroes, Scotland, Norway and Sweden east to Bering Sea and Sea of Okhotsk. In North America, from Bering Sea east to Baffin Island and western Greenland. Migratory, largely pelagic away from breeding areas, south in eastern Atlantic during winter as far as Antarctic Ocean, also enters Mediterranean. Monotypic but polymorphic.

Some measure of doubt surrounds the status of this species and the closely related Long-tailed Skua *S. longicaudus* in Cornish and Scillonian waters during the 19th century, early writers apparently confusing the two species as skins if not in the field. E H Rodd mentioned 'Richardson's Skua', the former name for Arctic, as something of a rarity in Cornwall, being unable to refer to any specimen he had seen and mentioning just one he knew to have been obtained, a bird shot at Rosemullon Head. But he suggested, nevertheless, that it was 'met with at sea during the autumn and winter months', though he was also of the opinion that it seldom if ever occurred in any numbers (Rodd 1880). Under the heading 'Buffon's Skua', the former name for Long-tailed, Rodd discussed difficulties caused by the early attachment of the name 'Arctic Jager' [sic] to Long-tailed (Couch 1838); at least one of three alleged Cornish Long-tailed specimens Rodd knew of was thought by Yarrell in fact to have been what we now know as Arctic Skua (Rodd 1880).

That aside, the only 19th or early 20th century mentions of Arctic Skua in a Scillonian context involved a bird seen over Guther's Island, south of St Martin's, by Jenkinson (presumably the Rev. J H) in June 1852 and one shot on St Mary's on the unusual date of Christmas Day 1901 (Clark & Rodd 1906). Interestingly, Penhallurick (1969) also drew attention to the rarity of Arctic Skua in Cornwall up until at least the 1940s, pointing out that Ryves (1948) knew of only three records up until that time: one off Penzance in July 1924, one off Lelant in October 1936 and one in the Camel Estuary, also in 1936. Since the 1950s, however, Arctic Skua has become regular off the Cornish mainland, several hundreds occurring during some years according to Penhallurick. The same author thought the balance of light- and dark-phase Cornish birds varied between records and that spring sightings were comparatively rare, though perhaps annual since 1961, with most sightings at this time of year being recorded during April. The earliest spring sighting Penhallurick knew of involved a bird seen between Scilly and Land's End on 25th March, birds apparently then occurring in all months through to December and being last noted on 5th.

Penhallurick also summarised the situation on Scilly, where he thought Arctic Skua formerly very sporadic, occurring in only five years between 1852 and 1958. The truth perhaps being, though, that it very probably occurred in other years, there being a lamentable lack of records of most species in Scilly during the early 20th century, although doubtless it remained scarce throughout that time. Certainly Walpole Bond mentioned seeing one during his crossing to the islands on an egg-collecting trip during May 1937 (Walpole Bond 1937). However, things changed from 1958, in which year it was noted in considerable numbers off St Agnes, the first being logged on 16th September, whilst on 18th October at least 180 passed west off the southern side of that same island in just three hours (*SABOAR* 1958). From 1963 onwards it became annual in the islands.

Taking the ten years from 1990 as representative of the current situation in Scilly, Arctic Skua was recorded in all years but in only eight during spring. For the purposes of this analysis birds seen in June were treated as spring sightings and those in July as autumn sightings. Most first annual records for the latter period occurred between 9th and 29th July (six years). The earliest spring sighting was 18th February (1997) and the latest 27th June (1998), whereas the last published autumn record was on 20th December 1996 – two pursuing a Gannet *Morus bassanus* in The Roads. Far fewer birds occurred in the early half of the year, the greatest number of spring sightings being four in 1998, involving seven birds. Autumn numbers were significantly greater but the presence of some individuals for more than one day, or off more than one island, made accurate recording difficult, as in 1999, when 17 September sightings were thought to involve just six individuals. There was also the expected between-year variation in overall numbers, from perhaps nine in 1990 to the 80 sightings in 35 days during autumn 1999, which was probably nearer the norm. Very few published records mention the colour-morph involved, though most that do refer to light-phase individuals during spring. The impression gained is that dark, or apparently dark, individuals predominate and that only light birds warrant specific mention. Some records involved birds seen from the RMV *Scillonian* during routine crossings to and from mainland Cornwall, or from *Scillonian III* or other boats participating in pelagic cruises beyond Scillonian seas, as on 18th September 1994 when seven were recorded from the *Scillonian* 18 km southwest of the islands during a pelagic, with nine from the same source on 24th.

Although it is not possible to precisely explain causes of the upswing in Arctic Skua records from the mid-1950s onwards, undoubtedly this was at least partly due to an increased awareness among those visiting the former St Agnes Bird Observatory that skuas were present offshore if looked for. Nevertheless, Parslow's review of the species' British status up until the mid-1970s concluded that an overall increase of the breeding population had occurred following a 19th century decrease due to human disturbance (Parslow 1967a).

Arctic Skuas commence leaving their breeding grounds from early August and immediately begin moving south, though autumn passage remains evident off British and Irish coasts well into October (Cramp *et al*. 1977–94). Many use mid-Atlantic routes but some pass south through the North and Baltic Seas; first-years go as far as southern Africa (Wernham *et al*. 2002) and mostly remain in the South Atlantic during their second year. Return passage commences from April, being most evident throughout the North Atlantic during May, breeding adults reoccupying Scottish colonies from late April. Recoveries of ringed Scottish and European Arctic Skuas show a preponderance of records from countries bordering the North Sea, with no first-year individuals recovered in western Britain or Ireland.

## Long-tailed Skua *Stercorarius longicaudus* A

**Rare mostly offshore migrant, mainly in autumn. Full written description required by the SRP.**

1925   One 4.8 km east of Scilly 26th May   H W Robinson 1925a
1963   One off St Agnes 7th & 20th October
1967   One off Peninnis, St Mary's 16th October
1974   One (juvenile) 8 km off Eastern Isles 10th September
1976   Two (juveniles) off Tresco 7th October
1981   One off Tresco 3rd October
1981   One (juvenile) off St Agnes at least 9th October
1981   One off St Mary's 12th to 14th October
1985   One (adult) 7th October, found dead Porth Hellick, St Mary's 9th
1988   One (juvenile) Hugh Town & Porth Cressa, St Mary's 7th October
1990   One during *Scillonian III* pelagic 12th October
1994   One (adult) Eastern Isles 16th September
1994   One 18 km southwest of Scilly 18th September
1997   One off Peninnis, St Mary's 8th October
1997   One (adult) St Mary's & St Agnes 17th October
1999   One (juvenile) off Horse Point, St Agnes 23rd October

Cosmopolitan, breeds northern Eurasia and northern North America, plus east and west Greenland, Spitsbergen, Novaya Zemlya and Kamchatka peninsula. Migratory, in eastern North Atlantic wintering south to coastal southern Africa. Polytypic: nominate *longicaudus* occurs Scandinavia east to approximately 120°E; *pallescens*, or 'American Long-tailed Skua' remainder of range.

Long-tailed Skua was known to E H Rodd under its old name of 'Buffon's Skua' (*Lestris parasiticus*), though he failed to make any mention of it on Scilly and knew of only three instances of it occurring in Cornwall (Rodd 1880). The first of these concerned a bird mentioned by Couch (1838) as having been taken on a baited hook, the second involved one found inland at St Buryan on the Land's End peninsula in September 1861, though according to Rodd, Yarrell thought it a probable Arctic Skua *S. parasiticus*, and the third was sent to Penzance taxidermist Vingoe from the Falmouth area during early October 1874. Penhallurick (1969) made no mention of the last two records, though he added a further two for mainland Cornwall and drew attention to comments by D'Urban and Mathews (*The Birds of Devon* – 1892) regarding 'a large flock' driven ashore off southwest England during an October gale, apparently in 1879.

The first Scillonian record involved a bird observed 4.8 km east of Scilly on 26th May 1925 (H W

Robinson 1925a), following which there was a gap of 38 years before one was noted off St Agnes on two dates during October 1963 (*SABOAR* 1963–64). Disregarding the initial bird, there were a total of 16 sightings in eleven different years during the latter half of the 20th century, all involving singles apart from two off Tresco during October 1976. The Chart shows all 17 arrival dates, all but the first of which were in either September or October and all within a narrow 44-day window, leaving little doubt these birds were on passage. The earliest autumn arrival was on 10th September and the latest was 23rd October, this also being the latest sighting date. Disregarding the individual later found dead, all but two birds were seen on one day only. There were also several claimed sightings unsupported by written descriptions and therefore not accepted by the SRP, e.g. one allegedly seen from the deck of the RMV *Scillonian III* on 5th October 1991 (*IOSBR* 1991).

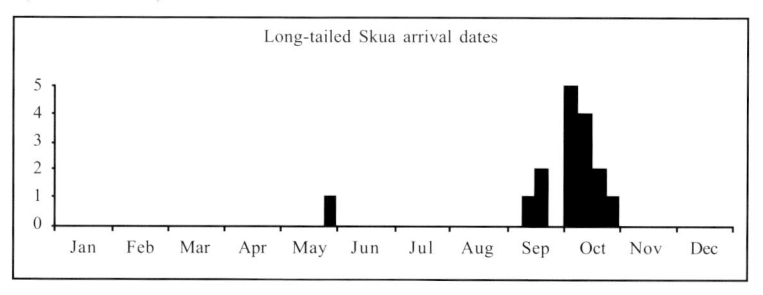

Long-tailed Skua arrival dates

The full complexities of Long-tailed Skua migration have yet to be unravelled, a situation not helped by the fact that difficulties in identifying juveniles and winter adults create a probable bias towards spring sightings. This point is, perhaps, of particular interest given the preponderance already of autumn records in Scilly. It is only rarely encountered in the Northern Hemisphere during winter and is the earliest of the three smallest West Palearctic skuas to commence its migration. Departure from the breeding grounds is co-ordinated and comparatively rapid, commencing during August and with most having left by early September. Return spring migration involves birds reappearing in the North Atlantic by April and into May, whilst also being more protracted than in the latter part of the year. Although little seems to be known about the summer distribution of non-breeding subadults, at least some are believed to be present in the North Atlantic (Cramp *et al*. 1977–94). No Long-tailed Skuas have been ringed in Scilly and there are no captures from elsewhere.

## Great Skua *Catharacta skua* A

**Annual migrant close inshore in small numbers but probably more numerous further out.**

Breeds Iceland, Faeroes, northern Scotland and northern Fennoscandia. Migratory, wintering throughout Atlantic to perhaps Antarctic Ocean. Monotypic. Formerly considered conspecific with *antarcticus* 'Great Skua' group, e.g. Brown Skua *C. antarcticus*, and still so by some authorities; the BOURC recently reclassified the status of the 'Great Skua' complex, moving them from the genus *Stercorarius* to *Catharacta* (BOURC 1997). Amber-listed in UK: 20% or more of European breeding population in UK, 50% or more at ten or fewer sites; (Gregory *et al*. 2002).

The sole early mention of this species close to Scilly appears to be E H Rodd's brief comment that in 1863 considerable numbers were observed near the Wolf Rock off the tip of mainland Cornwall (Rodd 1870a). The same authority agreed that to see them it was normally necessary to go a few kilometres offshore and that fishermen sometimes caught them using a baited hook (Rodd 1880).

Penhallurick's mid-1970s review showed it occurred in Cornwall and Scilly in all months, though not all years, including at least one June record between Scilly and Land's End. Records also reveal a slight but significant spring passage, around mid-April, followed by a more obvious autumn movement centred on September–October, but commencing from late August. The most seen in one day in Scillonian waters was eleven off St Agnes during October 1967, but with occasional sightings well into December, most involving single birds and with a high proportion between mainland Cornwall and Scilly. The same author perhaps rightly surmised that sightings outside these periods involve non-breeding wanderers.

More recent reports show it is now annual with a pattern, on average, of one spring sighting and with autumn passage sometimes evident from July, with up to 150 individuals recorded throughout the autumn period. October normally witnesses the main movement, e.g. 127 during 17th–30th October 1986, the latest date in recent years being 11th November. Outside passage periods, single individuals are occasionally recorded during winter or summer. The recent demand for summer pelagic cruises has given rise to an increase in summer skua records, as in mid-August 1998 when 36 Greats were recorded from RMV *Scillonian III* southwest of the islands.

Great Skua is pelagic outside the breeding season, moving south at least as far as the mid South Atlantic (Wernham *et al.* 2002), though the southern limit of its range is clouded by the presence of lookalike South Atlantic *Catharacta* species. Most Great Skuas migrate south out to sea west of Scilly, rather than travelling via the North Sea and English Channel route (Cramp *et al.* 1977–94). By the end of August some first-years may already have reached coastal West Africa, greatest dispersal being achieved by three-year-olds, though birds of five years and upwards remain mostly within European latitudes (Wernham *et al.* 2002). Much has been written in recent years about different plumage types of the *Catharacta* species and the possible presence of southern species in North Atlantic waters, all of which should be borne in mind when attempting to identify any large skua off Scilly, and indeed elsewhere in Britain (Jiguet 1997; Newell *et al.* 1997; see also Brown/South Polar Skua). No Great Skuas have been ringed in Scilly.

# Brown/South Polar Skua *Catharacta lonnbergi/antarctica* A

**Extremely rare migrants or vagrants, full written description required by the BBRC.**

2001   One St Agnes/Gugh 7th October (taken into care, released January 2002)

Breed southern oceans. Most authorities agree on separation of Great Skua *C. skua* as a full species but opinions vary on classification of southern *Catharacta* skuas. Many authorities recognise only three species, treating *antarctica*, or 'Falkland Skua', *hamiltoni*, or 'Tristan/Hamilton's Skua' and nominate *lonnbergi* all as forms of polytypic Brown Skua *C. antarctica*, plus monotypic South Polar Skua *C. maccormicki* and monotypic Chilean Skua *C. chilensis* (Gantlett & Harrop 1992). Whereas Sibley & Munroe (*Distribution and Taxonomy of Birds of the World* – 1990) recognise four species: monotypic Brown Skua *C. lonnbergi*; monotypic Chilean Skua *C. chilensis*; monotypic South Polar Skua *C. maccormicki*; and the polytypic Southern Skua *C. antarctica*, comprising *C. a. antarctica*, or 'Falkland Skua', and *C. a. hamiltoni*, or 'Tristan/Hamilton's Skua' (King & Parkin 1997). Up until preparation of this text (December 2002) the BOURC has still to decide which of these species/forms it recognises.

An apparently small, mainly dark brown and injured skua recovered by Paul Dukes from the sandbar between St Agnes and Gugh on 7th October 2001 was taken into care on St Mary's and received veterinary attention for a substantial breast wound of unknown origin. By January 2002, the bird was ready for release, but not before lengthy discussions regarding its likely identity and not before feather samples were obtained for molecular analysis (M Scott 2002; Votier *et al.* 2002); the latter process eventually confirmed the bird as one of the Brown Skua forms: *lonnbergi, antarctica or hamiltoni* (Newell *et al.* 2002). The record remained under consideration by the BOURC during preparation of this text but hopefully seemed likely to gain acceptance as the first confirmed southern *Catharacta* skua for Britain and the North Atlantic. Quite amazingly, a further southern *Catharacta* claim, from Aberavon, Glamorgan, South Wales, during February 2002, also involved a bird taken into care and was also awaiting consideration (Moon & Carrington 2002), molecular tests suggesting a similar outcome to the St Agnes individual, but with biometric data further suggesting 'Falkland Skua' *C. a. antarctica* (no biometric data were obtained from the St Agnes bird). Meanwhile, processes leading up to identification of these two individuals threw doubt on some past British records, e.g. the bird at West Bexington, Dorset, during January 1996, and others; the Dorset individual was believed at the time to be a contender for Britain's first South Polar Skua (Millington 2000). Meanwhile, a bird at Dungeness, Kent, in mid-February 2002 may yet prove to be another southern large skua.

The presence of large dark skuas which are not Great Skuas in waters off coastal West Africa has been known for some years, but until recently these were thought to probably involve mainly South Polar Skua. However, there is growing awareness of the possible presence of other lookalike species and several Brown Skua claims have been rejected or remain under consideration for North America's eastern seaboard (Jiguet 1997). The appearance of the above two individuals in UK waters during winter 2001–02 is yet further evidence that more attention directed towards large skuas in the North Atlantic seems likely to bring rewards.

# Mediterranean Gull *Larus melanocephalus* A

**Scarce but now annual migrant, mainly in autumn but with the occasional spring sighting, though extremely rare in winter. Full written description required by the SRP.**

Disjunct breeding distribution limited to West Palearctic, through central and southern Europe from southern England to Caspian Sea. Migratory, wintering North Sea and Atlantic coast from Denmark and Britain south to North Africa and throughout Mediterranean and Black Seas. Monotypic. Removed from BBRC Rarities List January 1963 (Harber & Swaine 1963). Included on Annex I of 1979 EEC 'Birds Directive'. Amber-listed in UK: three-year maximum of 89.0 breeding pairs (Gregory *et al.* 2002).

The first British or Irish record involved an immature allegedly shot at Barking, in what is now East London in 1866, but not identified until examined in the British Museum collection in 1871 (Palmer 2000). In contrast, the second was obtained during a Boxing Day shoot on Norfolk's Breydon Water in 1886, being identified by J H Gurney in combination with two others within hours of it being killed. According to Penhallurick (1969) the earliest on mainland Cornwall involved a first-summer individual at St Ives for about a month from 7th March 1960, followed by two more at the same locality before the year's end. However, the only Scillonian record Penhallurick could quote up until that time concerned one on Tresco on 21st June 1964 (*CBWPSAR* 34). This was one of only two June records for either Cornwall or Scilly that Penhallurick knew of, with none at all during May. However, the same author made the point, surely with justification, that the presence of this species must doubtless have been previously overlooked.

Since 1964, both the annual number and frequency of records have increased on Scilly, the three years 1997–99 producing the greatest annual totals with six in each year. The Chart incorporates all records up until 1999 except for the first and second in 1964 and 1969 respectively. Disregarding the June 1964 individual, only three birds occurred in the first half of the year, one on 3rd January 1993 and the others in April 1989 and 1997. First autumn dates advanced over time, progressing from late September or October during the 1970s to July or August by the 1990s, though it remains clear most if not all records involved migrant individuals. Most annual last-sighting dates fell within October, with two in November and one extremely late individual on 1st December. The first-winter individual off St Mary's on 3rd January 1993 was not known to have wintered, the last of autumn 1992 being noted on 12th September.

The recent increase in the number and frequency of birds reaching Scilly during autumn broadly fits the establishment of new European breeding colonies and population increases, mainly in the Mediterranean region from the 1950s but including France from 1968 and southern Britain from 1976 (Hagemeijer & Blair 1997). Even by the mid-1990s the Mediterranean held several thousand breeding pairs and western

*Birds of the Isles of Scilly*

**Mediterranean Gull annual totals**

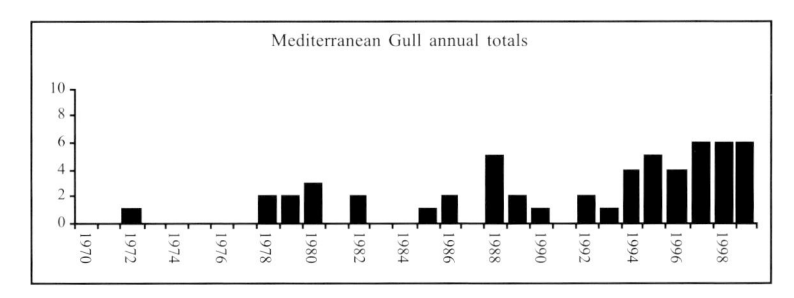

and central Europe some 200 pairs, about half of which were in Belgium and the Netherlands and this population is known to be rapidly increasing, including in southern England. Ringing evidence shows a marked lack of between-year site-fidelity among breeding adults. Birds commence leaving the breeding colonies from late June or July, juveniles initially dispersing randomly, adults returning from March onwards (Cramp *et al.* 1977–94). Ringing recoveries provide evidence for the autumn movement of birds from eastern European colonies (including most of the Hungarian population) to several Baltic countries and these are thought to at least partly explain the presence of birds along the west European seaboard at that time (Wernham *et al.* 2002). No Mediterranean Gulls have been ringed in Scilly and there are no captures from elsewhere.

## Laughing Gull *Larus atricilla* A BBRC 1%

**Extremely rare migrant or vagrant, full written description required by the BBRC.**

   1967   One St Agnes 31st October   *British Birds* 61: 344, 65: 79–80
   [1974   One (first-year) Gugh 22nd October]   *IOSBR* 1974
   1986   One (first-winter) St Mary's 26th October   *British Birds* 80: 541
   [1998   One Tresco 20th June]   *IOSBR* 1898
   2000   One (adult) St Mary's 7th to 20th January   *British Birds* 94: 476

Breeds North America, from Nova Scotia south to Florida, Gulf of Mexico, southern California, Mexico, West Indies and Venezuela. Migratory, on Atlantic coast wintering from North Carolina south to northern South America, though many stay within southern breeding range; rarely wanders inland. Polytypic: *megalopterus* occurs North America; nominate *atricilla* remainder of range.

Wallace described the first Scillonian record of this attractive American gull, an immature watched passing Horse Point, St Agnes, from the south on 31st October 1967, following severe overnight gales (Wallace 1972a). However, Landsdown's description of a bird in immature plumage off St Agnes on 22nd October 1974 was reportedly rejected by the BBRC (*IOSBR* 1974, 1975), though it appears to get no mention in the annual BBRC report. Subsequently, a first-winter individual was seen briefly as it passed over Hugh Town, St Mary's, heading west on 26th October 1986 and this record was found acceptable by BBRC. Another individual reportedly seen and heard as it overflew Tresco late evening on 20th June 1998 was not submitted, and the most recent sighting for the islands involved an adult viewable on St Mary's for two weeks during January 2000. The Chart shows arrival dates for the three accepted records.

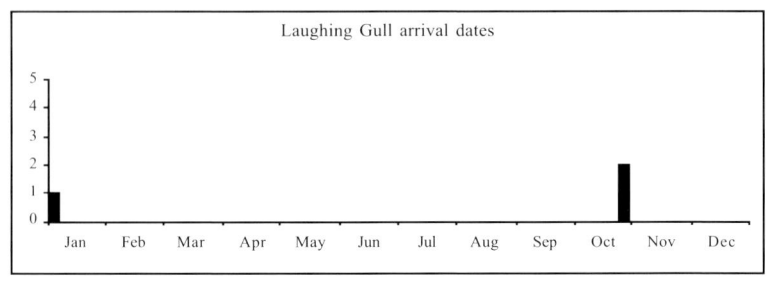

**Laughing Gull arrival dates**

The BBRC accepted a total of 100 Laughing Gull records during the period 1958–99 inclusive, so the single Scillonian record for the period represents just 1% overall. Other European records involved Iceland,

Faeroes, France, Belgium, Netherlands, Germany, Austria, Norway, Sweden, Hungary, Spain, Morocco, Azores and Madeira (Cramp *et al.* 1977–94; Snow & Perrins 1998). There were eight accepted records of this species on the nearby Cornish mainland up until 1999, the most recent in January 1998 (*CBWPSAR* 68). Birds begin leaving the breeding sites from late July or August and disperse initially randomly, before gradually moving southwards (Cramp *et al.* 1977–94). Large numbers of presumably southward-moving birds may be pushed north as far as Newfoundland by hurricanes off the eastern seaboard of North America in autumn, and this same feature is thought likely to account for the high incidence of European autumn vagrancy. However, at least some of those present in Europe outside the main migration period are thought likely to have crossed the North Atlantic during a previous season, which would of course help explain the June individual on Tresco (Cramp *et al.* 1977–94).

# Little Gull                                                                                                   *Larus minutus*  A

**Scarce but now annual migrant, mainly in autumn, though one or two may remain during winter.**

Three distinct central Eurasian breeding populations, in West Palearctic from Netherlands and Denmark (small numbers) to northwest Russia. A disjunct population breeds in western Siberia, northern Mongolia and eastern Siberia. Migratory, in West Palearctic wintering mainly coastally, including Baltic, Mediterranean, Black and Caspian Seas. Since 1962 also breeds in small numbers northeast North America, wintering on the east coast. Monotypic. Downgraded from Amber- to Green-listed in UK 2002 (Gregory *et al.* 2002).

E H Rodd knew it as one of the rarer gulls, quoting specimens obtained from Penzance and Land's End, among other Cornish sites, but made no mention of Scilly. This being the case, James Clark and E H Rodd's nephew Francis Rodd's comment that it had apparently been overlooked within the islands is the first mention of it in a Scillonian context. These two pointed out that it was thought to have been seen on St Mary's during October 1905, with a specimen obtained during Christmas week that same year, though they gave no location (Clark & Rodd 1906).

Penhallurick (1969) could trace only 15 Cornish records up until 1905, at least three of these prior to 1838 (Couch 1838) though the earliest dated record involved one from Land's End in December 1844. Penhallurick also thought it probably not as rare previously as published records suggested, pointing out that from 1947 it was noted annually in the county, being rare only during May–July when it was recorded in only three of the 21 years to 1967. Penhallurick also found that most sightings involved single individuals, though two or more parties of up to eight birds were on record.

The first confirmed 20th century island record concerned one on St Mary's on 18th October 1947, followed by singles on 15th and 18th September 1963. It was subsequently recorded almost annually in increasing but still small numbers. During the 13 years 1977–89, it occurred in spring in just seven years, involving 13 birds at an average of one per year, whilst a total of 32 appeared during autumn in all 13 years, at an average of 2.46. This compares favourably with the ten years 1990–99 when 20 were recorded in six years during spring, at an overall rate of 2 per year, whereas 25 appeared in all but one year during autumn, at an annual rate of 2.5 per year. The most seen together was two, on perhaps no more then three occasions and few remained more than 1–2 days. Records appeared to involve a mixture of adults and first-winter birds, though Cramp *et al.* (1977–94) considered the latter something of a scarcity in northwest Europe during winter, although not on passage.

Dates throughout the whole of the 23 years for which they were examined in detail suggest a pattern of wandering winter individuals, followed and preceded by what appeared to be spring and autumn migrants. Earliest recorded date was 1st January and the latest 29th December; however, there were just two May sightings and a single June appearance, with none at all during July. During the ten years from 1990, four of the six last spring sighting dates fell in the period 1st April to 4th May, five of the earliest autumn sightings occurreing in the period 15th August to 21st September.

Some 75% of autumn sightings in coastal England and Wales occur during August–November, peak passage past northern France being noted from October to early November (Cramp *et al.* 1977–94). Immatures mainly precede adults, apparently because many adults stop off to moult in central Europe en route. Return spring passage is evident off northern France (Cape Gris Nez) from late March to late April, fewer passing during May. Off the coasts of Britain, spring migration follows much the same timing as in northern France, but with substantially fewer birds involved than in autumn. Birds from the west Siberian population are believed to migrate through Kazakhstan and the Caspian Sea to winter in the Black Sea and Mediterranean area, some therefore mixing with birds from more western populations. No Little Gulls have been ringed on Scilly and there are no recaptures from elsewhere.

# Sabine's Gull *Larus sabini* A

**Scarce autumn migrant, almost annual, though in some years all or most sightings are from outside Scillonian waters, e.g. pelagic cruises, or from routine crossings of the RMV *Scillonian*. Treated by the BBRC as a national Scarce Migrant, full written description required by the SRP.**

Circumpolar but patchy breeding distribution, incorporating much of arctic North America, Greenland and central and northeast arctic Asia, though the only known West Palearctic breeding site is Spitsbergen. Migratory, in eastern Atlantic reaching Southern Ocean. Monotypic. Removed from BBRC Rarities List January 1963 (Harber & Swaine 1963).

Sabine's Gull was known to 19th century Cornish naturalists, E H Rodd describing it as sometimes met with in immature plumage in mainland harbours and estuaries, though irregular and uncertain in its appearances (Rodd 1880). The same author went on to say that he had never encountered a specimen in adult plumage, though he acquired an immature from Mount's Bay, west Cornwall, where a particularly confiding individual was knocked out of the air with an oar. On Scilly it just managed an appearance before the start of the 20th century, one being shot by Joe White in autumn 1893, presumably on Tresco (Clark & Rodd 1906) and a summer plumage adult was seen near the Wolf Rock in September 1894 (Penhallurick 1969).

There were perhaps sixteen 19th- or very early 20th century records from mainland Cornwall between 1860 and 1902 (Penhallurick 1969), the last involving an inland bird shot near Lostwithiel, west Cornwall. The next from Cornwall was noted in 1951, all sightings from then until the mid-1960s occurring during autumn, birds usually arriving during weather patterns suggestive of a North American origin. According to Penhallurick, the earliest sighting up until the mid-1960s concerned a bird, exceptionally, on 22nd July, whilst the latest was 25th December.

It may be no coincidence that the run of modern records in both Scilly and Cornwall commenced with birds that arrived during 1957 (Penhallurick 1969; *CBWPSAR* 27). In Scilly's case this involved one in The Roads on 12th September and then a first-year four days later between Tresco and St Martin's. Since that time it appeared increasingly and apparently always during autumn, apart from the exceptional record of a bird seen from *Scillonian III* on 23rd June 1990 (*IOSBR* 1990). During the 25 years 1975–99, it was recorded in all but four, numbers varying from one to a possible 18 in 1982, although, as with most seabird species, keeping track of individuals proved problematical. The greatest number reported on any day, however, concerned 14 off Tresco on 11th October 2000, during a month when 75, all allegedly juveniles, were reported in Britain and ten in Ireland (*Birding World* 13: 394). Sighting dates largely fell within the period late August to late October, with the apparent bias towards October perhaps reflecting the species' vulnerability to easterly drift during severe Atlantic weather.

Too few published records involve aged individuals to make analysis of age groups practical, but a significant proportion of sightings reportedly involved adults. However, reading the reports it seems clear that Sabine's Gull presents substantial problems in assessing the validity of reports. This apparently results from a combination of factors, foremost of which may be the tendency for birds to arrive in the least favourable viewing conditions, plus the preponderance of similarly plumaged first-winter Kittiwakes *Rissa tridactyla* about the islands during autumn.

Outside the breeding season, Sabine's Gulls are primarily pelagic, in the eastern Atlantic wintering south to the Southern Ocean, most using this route originating from Greenland and Canada, whilst those from Alaska and Siberia winter in the Pacific (Cramp *et al.* 1977–94). Greenland and Canadian birds reach the coast of western Europe via a transoceanic crossing of the North Atlantic, arriving on the eastern side between France and Morocco, and consequently it is largely a west-coast species in Britain. Breeding areas are deserted from August or early September, adults mainly departing before juveniles and the appearance of Sabine's Gulls in British and Irish inshore waters is largely associated with severe Atlantic weather systems, birds arriving from mid-August to mid-November. Cramp *et al.* suggest that 72% arrive in September–October, with 31% of adults but only 4% of juveniles recorded prior to 3rd September. Off

Africa, return passage is mainly evident during early May (Wernham *et al.* 2002), with the absence of Sabine's Gulls from European inshore waters presumably reflecting differences in North Atlantic weather patterns at this time of year. No Sabine's Gulls have been ringed in Scilly and there are no recaptures from elsewhere.

## Bonaparte's Gull *Larus philadelphia* A  BBRC 0.94%

**Extremely rare migrant or vagrant, full written description required by the BBRC.**

1944 One (shot) Scilly 16th December  *British Birds* 38: 358
1990 One St Mary's & St Martin's 21st March to 14th October  *British Birds* 86: 489

Breeds North America, from Alaska through northwest and central Canada south to central prairies. Migratory, wintering central coastal USA south to West Indies and Mexico. Monotypic.

Details of the first record for Scilly are contained in a brief note describing one shot whilst feeding on worms exposed by a plough at an unspecified site within the islands on 16th December 1944 (*CBWPSAR* 14). This was followed after a gap of 46 years by another, this time present at various sites throughout the islands during 1990, from 21st March until last seen off Innisidgen, St Mary's, on 14th October. When first found this individual was still in first-winter plumage but during its protracted stay progressed first into adult and then adult-winter plumage. It mostly frequented St Mary's but during April spent time on St Martin's. The first recorded date of the earlier individual is unknown, therefore arrival dates are not charted.

There were a total of 40 Cornish records up to and including 1999, the most recent of which was a first-year at Drift Reservoir, west Cornwall, in November that year. All sightings occurred between October and June, with 11 in March being the highest combined monthly total. The BBRC accepted 106 national records during the period 1958–99 and there were just 11 known records prior to that period (BBRC 2000). Given Scilly's geographical position we might perhaps be forgiven for expecting to see rather more of this species about the islands.

In autumn, Bonaparte's Gulls move south to the Pacific coast or southeast through the Great Lakes to Atlantic coastal USA, smaller numbers utilising the central flyway. Autumn passage is protracted, most moving south during September–October, though later along the Atlantic coast (Cramp *et al.* 1977–94). And as with several North American migrant passerines, the high incidence of autumn European vagrancy in this species is thought to be largely attributable to an extension of the initial southeast heading out of the central prairies and towards Atlantic coastal northeast North America, with some birds presumably either overshooting or taking a transoceanic route out into the path of any autumn Atlantic depressions.

## Black-headed Gull *Larus ridibundus* A

**Regular migrant and winter visitor, one or more very old and probably unsuccessful breeding attempts.**

Breeds northern and central Eurasia, from Iceland, Britain and Ireland, France and Iberia east to Kamchatka and Sakhalin, from tree-line south to Mediterranean and northern Mongolia. Migratory in north and east, partially so or dispersive remainder of range, in western Europe wintering south at least as far as Mediterranean. Monotypic. National 36% decline 1994–99 (Bashford & Noble 2000). Upgraded from Green- to Amber-listed in UK 2002: moderate breeding decline over past 25 years; 50% or more of breeding population at ten or fewer sites (Gregory *et al.* 2002).

One glance at the 19th century literature in respect of this species and we are into the realms of uncertainty. E H Rodd's combined account of Black-headed Gull in his *Birds of Cornwall and the Scilly Islands* (Rodd 1880) was short and to the point, describing it as occurring in winter and perhaps being the commonest gull, particularly on the sands at Hayle, though these comments were primarily directed at the Cornish mainland. He went on to say, however, that it might be observed in almost any month and that he was unaware of it having bred in any part of Cornwall, 'although it used to do so formerly at Scilly'. Regrettably, Rodd gave no authority for this last claim but we are able to glean a little more information from the comments of other writers and against this species in Rodd's appended list of birds observed in the island there appears the comment 'used formerly, to breed in some of the islands, but has now ceased to do so'.

James Clark and co-author Frances Rodd, nephew of E H Rodd, drew attention to a note in the margin of the elder Rodd's copy of Montagu's *Dictionary of Birds* (1802–13) (though not in Rodd's own hand) stating that Black-headed Gull bred in Scilly in 1845 (Clark & Rodd 1906). These last authors also stated that 'An unknown naturalist who visited Scilly in 1841 speaks of two nests of Black-headed Gull he saw on St Mary's', though unfortunately they too fail to provide any reference. Much later, H W Robinson (1925c) described finding a nest with two eggs in the midst of a Common Tern *Sterna hirundo* colony on 2nd June that year, though he too omitted the location. By 29th the nest was still intact and Robinson assumed it had been deserted, but by 12th July it had disappeared. This, he explained, occurred after a gap of some eighty years but the incident seems not to have been repeated as there was no mention of Black-headed Gull breeding in Scilly by the time of a mid-20th century review of breeding birds (Ryves & Quick 1946).

Returning briefly to the 19th century, Clark and Rodd considered it annually common in winter, occasionally appearing in flocks during late spring, also describing a flock of 14 on Tresco's Abbey Green on 25th May 1903, none of which were in breeding plumage. The sole remaining 19th century reference to what may have been this species comes from E H Rodd, who quoted his nephew Frances's report of a strange gull he was unable to identify on the Tresco pools on Christmas Day 1864, the younger Rodd describing it as rather larger than Kittiwake (*Rissa tridactyla*) with very pointed, white-bordered, tern-like 'blue' wings and very rapid flight: 'it might have been a skua, but I do not know'. E H Rodd suggested Black-headed Gull, but it seems apparent that some doubt remains, particularly as Francis must surely have been familiar with this species.

Penhallurick added nothing further to the Scillonian debate but reference to the *IOSBR* for the ten years from 1999 shows a pattern of varying early year numbers, of from just a few to 200-300, most departing by mid-March and leaving just scattered singles until late May. At this time there was normally evidence of a small spring passage, though seldom with more than small groups involved. June was usually marked by the occasional sighting of one to two birds before a noticeable return passage got under way in July, numbers at this time rapidly increasing from small to medium-sized groups to nearer 100. In some years numbers continued to increase into October, by which time individual flock counts in the mid-hundreds are on record. The only co-ordinated all-island counts involved 232 recorded during the two-day late-January 1997 Winter Shorebird Survey, 101 (43%) of which were on Tresco and 90 (39%) on St Mary's (*IOSBR* 1997). Little information is available on Black-headed Gull feeding behaviour in the islands, but on 31st July 1992 a swarm of emerging ants attracted a feeding flock of 150 or more over Hugh Town, St Mary's (*IOSBR* 1992).

In western Europe, Black-headed Gull winters from Iceland, Faeroes, southern Scandinavia and the western Baltic southwards, some reaching Senegal or even the Gulf of Guinea (Cramp *et al.* 1977–94). However, many British birds move only as far as Iberia and are probably replaced in winter by birds from central Europe and the Baltic states (Wernham *et al.* 2002). No Black-headed Gulls have been ringed on Scilly and there are no Scillonian recaptures of birds ringed elsewhere. However, even by the mid- to late 1960s Penhallurick (1969) listed 35 individuals found in Cornwall having been ringed elsewhere in Europe. Countries involved included Latvia (3), Estonia (1), Lithuania (1), Finland (5), Sweden (6), Norway (1), Denmark (3), Germany (7), Netherlands (4) and Belgium (4). This leaves little doubt that Black-headed Gulls reaching west Cornwall, and presumably also Scilly, originate substantially from, or at least pass through, a number of countries to the north or east of Britain. Most birds were recovered between September and March, but included were individuals in June, July and August.

# Ring-billed Gull *Larus delawarensis* A

**Until recently an extremely rare migrant or vagrant, now almost annual. Treated by the BBRC as a national Scarce Migrant, full written description required by the SRP.**

[1981 One (second-winter) St Mary's 25th November (possibly from early November) until at least 15th February 1982]
1982 One (first-year) St Mary's 18th October
1987 One (first-year) Porth Hellick, St Mary's 12th & 13th November
1990 One (adult) Porth Hellick & Golf Course, St Mary's 10th February to 31st March
1990 One (first-year) Porth Hellick & Golf Course, St Mary's 11th February until 8th October

1990  One (second-winter) St Mary's 22nd October to 20th December
1990  One (second-winter) St Mary's, & Tresco 22nd October to 20th December
1991  One Garrison, St Mary's 20th September
1996  One (first-winter) St Mary's & Tresco 12th November until perhaps 15th June 1997
1997  One (first-summer) Tresco 6th to 10th May
1998  One St Mary's Golf Course 19th to 22nd April
1998  One (first-winter) Porth Killier, St Agnes 23rd April
1999  One (first-winter) St Mary's 2nd to 8th November

Breeds central-northern North America, from British Columbia, Washington and Oregon east through Great Lakes to Gulf of St Lawrence. Two discrete populations, one western interior, the other Great Lakes through St Lawrence River area to coastal New Brunswick. Northerly populations migratory, wintering south into Mexico. Monotypic. Population increasing (Bryant 1997). Removed from BBRC Rarities List January 1988 (Lansdown and the Rarities Committee 1987).

Despite its presence on the islands for some three months, a second-winter individual seen by many observers and well described failed to gain acceptance by the BBRC (*IOSBR* 1981, 1982, 1984). In the light of what followed over the next two decades, however, this record is perhaps now worthy of reconsideration. At first glance, the apparent indiscriminate nature of the 12 accepted arrival dates and the proportion of individuals that remained more than a day or two suggest that these were not migrants. However, closer examination reveals a fairly obvious pattern of October–November autumn arrivals and an equally obvious sprinkling of spring individuals during April and May. In this respect it is interesting to note that Cramp *et al.* (1977–94) considered that the occurrence of long-staying summering individuals probably masked the true pattern of British and Irish arrivals. In any event there seems little doubt this species is destined to become an annual visitor to the islands, if indeed that is not already the case. Interesting, too, was the mix of ages involved in these 12 sightings, although only one was an apparent adult.

A rather different situation exists on mainland Cornwall with an impressive 280 birds recorded since the first sighting in 1979 (*CBWPSAR* 69), at an annual average of 14 over the 20 years. As a consequence, it seems difficult to resist comparing the recent sightings in Scilly and Cornwall with the suggested recent North American population increase (Bryant 1997). Most birds in North America winter in coastal states, though the two populations remain largely separated. In the east it winters from New England south to the West Indies, fewer going as far as Columbia (Cramp *et al.* 1977–94). In autumn, birds commence leaving the breeding grounds from mid-July, initially dispersing randomly across the Great Lakes. And although by September few have reached further south, the intensity of true migration then increases, most having left the Great Lakes by December. Interestingly, in view of the two late-winter Scillonian arrivals, evidence in the form of ringing recoveries suggests that arrivals in southern USA peak during January–February.

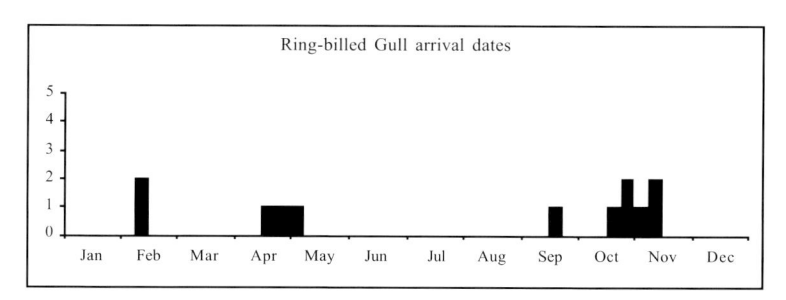

Ring-billed Gull arrival dates

A clear indication of the recent level of increase in British and Irish sightings can be gained from Cramp *et al.*, who by 1983 were able to draw on a sample of just 29 records, whereas by the late 1990s Snow & Perrins (1998) cited over 600 such records. The last authors also drew attention to the pattern of late-autumn or winter arrivals in coastal USA and commented that this same pattern of late-year arrival was evident among the 600 or so British and Irish records. However, they too thought the presence of long-staying summering individuals could be masking the fuller picture.

# Common Gull *Larus canus* A

**Migrant and winter visitor in small to moderate numbers.**

Breeds northern Eurasia, from Iceland, Britain and Ireland east to Kamchatka and Sakhalin, plus northwest North America. Mainly migratory, in West Palearctic wintering south to France, Baltic Sea and Iran. Polytypic: nominate *canus* occurs northwest Europe to White Sea; *heinei*, or 'Russian Common Gull' western-central Siberia; *kamtschatschensis* northeast Siberia; *brachyrhynchus* or 'Mew Gull' northwest North America. Amber-listed in UK: moderate breeding decline over past 25 years; 50% or more of breeding population at ten or fewer sites; unfavourable European conservation status (Gregory *et al.* 2002). National 4% decline 1994–99 (Bashford & Noble 2000).

There is some confusion in the 19th century Scillonian literature between this species and Lesser Black-backed Gull *L. fuscus*, Gilbert White apparently confusing the two, whereas W H Heaton though it might breed in the islands. The former stated similarly under both species (in Jesse 1887) that 'a few remain all the year round, the greater number leaving in the autumn and returning to their breeding grounds in April'. These remarks are now ideally suited to Lesser Black-backed but somewhat unsuited to Common Gull. Heaton, on the other hand, wrote to the *Zoologist* in 1876 claiming to have Common Gull eggs supposedly taken on Annet that same year and posing the question 'Does the Common Gull breed in the Scilly Islands?' (Heaton 1876). The journal's editor responded robustly remarking that Common Gull was not found in the islands during summer. He also pointed out that it was less common there in winter than several similar species and that Penzance taxidermist Vingoe and 'Mr Rodd', presumably E H Rodd, were equally certain it did not breed in the Land's End district. In fact Vingoe's remarks were based on at least one visit to Annet during the breeding season, at which time no Common Gulls had been observed. E H Rodd had very little to say about this species in Cornwall generally and nothing at all in relation to Scilly, describing it as by no means so plentiful as Kittiwake *Rissa tridactyla* or Black-headed Gull *L. ridibundus*, although going on to state that it was nevertheless not a rare bird in Cornwall and was not infrequently observed inland following the plough (Rodd 1880). Reasons behind Heaton's belief that his Common Gull eggs might have been taken on Annet are unknown, but we do know that enough experienced egg-collectors visited the islands during the 19th and early 20th centuries for them to have noticed this species had it been present. No other commentator apparently makes mention of it and certainly Penhallurick says nothing of even suspect nesting on the Cornish mainland. Similarly there is no mention of it the mid-20th century review of the breeding birds of the islands (Ryves & Quick 1946). The sole remaining early comment comes from James Clark and E H Rodd's nephew Frances Rodd, who thought small winter parties seemed not uncommon, though 'great numbers' appeared during autumn 1863 (Clark & Rodd 1906).

Penhallurick too thought it both a regular passage migrant and winter visitor to the Cornish mainland, believing its status little changed since the previous century (Penhallurick 1969). Nonetheless, the same author found further analysis frustrated by the lack of published numerical data, though it clearly had a rather patchy distribution throughout Cornwall, being seen in numbers of from one or two to as many as 250 or even 600, though a count of 2,400 at St John's Lake, Plymouth, in mid-January was presumably exceptional. Interestingly, Penhallurick found the situation on Scilly rather different, it being far less common, with smaller numbers involved on migration and just single individuals remaining during winter.

Examining the records for the ten years since 1990, we find it was present in every year, arriving in autumn between late July (earliest 24th) and 6th October. Although difficult to prove, there was some evidence of a slight early autumn passage, apparent in 1999 from 13th August until late October, after which it became scarce and only three wintered. This last, though, was unusual and in several winters single-site counts of up to 13–14 were recorded, e.g. 14 on Samson on 5th February 1996 and 13 on Tresco on 25th January 1997. In spring some lingered on until as late as June (one in 1999) though most departed by February or March. A favoured location for this and other gull species is the Morning Point sewerage outlet on St Mary's, where small accumulations of feeding Common Gulls are to be expected under the right conditions. The only all-island survey likely to have recorded this present species was the 1997 two-day late January Winter Shorebird Survey, which nevertheless failed to locate a single individual and only one Common Gull was recorded on St Agnes throughout the whole of 1999, along with one Ring-billed Gull *L. delawarensis*. A mounted skin in the Isles of Scilly Museum on St Mary's forms part of the on-loan Tresco Abbey collection and was presumably shot locally.

No Common Gulls have been ringed on Scilly and there are no recaptures from elsewhere. However, Penhallurick quoted ten Cornish recoveries up until the mid-1960s of Common Gulls ringed overseas, from Sweden (5), Norway (3) and Denmark (2) (Penhallurick 1969). But whilst this suggests a Scandinavian origin for at least some Common Gulls wintering in Scilly, this is clearly not the full picture, as evident from a bird ringed as a nestling in Co. Mayo, Ireland and recovered in Cornwall the following winter.

Nominate *canus* winters primarily in the eastern-coastal North Atlantic, as far as northern and western France but including the North and Baltic Seas, smaller numbers reaching the Mediterranean, particularly during severe winters (Cramp *et al.* 1977–94). Southward movement of autumn adults commences from July with most reaching the Baltic and North Seas by August or September, young birds initially dispersing randomly and moving south later than adults; main return movements occurr during March. In discussing winter ringing recoveries of European Common Gulls Cramp *et al.* thought a higher proportion of Swedish than Finnish birds reach Britain and Ireland and that most Norwegian individuals head for the same destination. In contrast, fewer numbers of Danish birds reach Britain and Ireland, a feature apparently borne out by the small sample identified by Penhallurick for mainland Cornwall. British and Irish birds seldom migrate, though 'extensive internal dispersals' can be expected, primarily in a south or southwest direction (Wernham *et al.* 2002). Little is known, still, about the seasonal movements of the larger and darker *heinei* from western-central Siberia; although most are believed to winter from the Caspian and Black Seas south to Iraq and Iran, a few perhaps reaching the Mediterranean, Baltic or further west. However, as Gantlett (1998) points out, its status in western Europe is clouded by the difficulty of certain identification. The North American *brachyrhynchus* winters mainly in the western Pacific and on the face of it seems an unlikely visitor to Britain.

## Lesser Black-backed Gull *Larus fuscus* A

**Summer visitor, migrant and possible winter visitor.**

Breeds mainly coastal western Europe and northwest Asia. Mainly migratory, wintering eastern Atlantic south to equator and West Africa – increasing tendency to winter in Britain. Polytypic: *graellsii*, or 'Western Lesser Black-backed Gull' occurs British Isles, Iceland, France, northwest Spain; *intermedius*, or 'Continental Lesser Black-backed Gull' Denmark, Netherlands, southern Norway; nominate *fuscus*, or 'Baltic Lesser Black-backed Gull' northern Norway, Sweden; *heuglini* and *taimyrensis* further east, as far only as about 100°E. Amber-listed in UK: 20% or more of European breeding population in UK, 50% or more at ten or fewer sites (Gregory *et al.* 2002).

There are currently around 3,600 breeding pairs on about 26 islands, though the bulk of these are on just five islands. Unlike the other two large gull species in Scilly, Lesser Black-backed Gull appears to be maintaining its numbers.

There is some apparent confusion in the 19th century Scillonian literature between this species and Common Gull *L. canus*, Gilbert White apparently confused the two and commented similarly (in Jesse 1887) under both species that 'a few remain all the year round, the greater number leaving in the autumn and returning to their breeding grounds in April'. These remarks suitably describe Lesser Black-backed Gull but are somewhat unsuited to its smaller relative. The only other significant early remark concerning this species seems to be that of James Clark and E H Rodd's nephew Francis who thought it abundant year-round and that it bred in numbers on most of the uninhabited islands (Clark & Rodd 1906). Early 20th century accounts include that it bred in large numbers among other gulls on Annet (H W Robinson 1911a), whilst by 1936 it was noted that outside the islands Lesser Black-backs were more numerous than Herring Gulls *L. argentatus* 'in the escort of drifters', whereas inside the islands their numbers swiftly decreased (*CBWPSAR* 6). This last comment almost certainly reflects the situation still today, Lesser Black-backs feeding mainly out at sea and being by far the least common of the three large gulls around St Mary's. This last journal remarked the following year that Samson held a 'huge' colony breeding amongst the Bracken *Pteridium aquilinium*, with a smaller colony on Bryher's Shipman Head (*CBWPSAR* 7), whilst by the mid-1940s Ryves & Quick (1946) were describing it as a common breeder on all suitable islands.

Very few Scillonian records make reference to racial characteristics of individuals involved, though local breeding birds should be *graellsii*, as should passing migrants from Iceland. A goodly percentage of migrants should also include *intermedius* and *fuscus*, with the possibility even of birds from further east occurring. Difficult to interpret, however, is the 1940's allegation that 'a considerable proportion' within a 'very large breeding colony' on St Helen's in 1946 were 'Scandinavian Lesser Black-backed Gulls' (*CBWPSAR* 16), presumably referring to the form *fuscus*. Two years later a comment appears in the same source (*CBWPSAR* 18) noting that about 400 Lesser Black-backed Gulls were examined – though presumably not in the hand – during 24th–25th July, approximately 5% of which were considered to have mantles darker than *graellsii*. However, according to the author, A G Parsons, the appearance of the spread wing ruled out 'Scandinavian Lesser Black-backed Gull', though a similarity with the 'Danish strain' remained. This remark was presumably intended to attribute these birds to the form *intermedius*, which today breeds in southern Norway, Denmark and the Netherlands. Certainly, no such assertion appears to have been published subsequently and doubt must be attached to these particular records.

The recent marked national trend towards overwintering within Britain is not reflected in Scilly, it being scarce in the islands during winter, first returning birds becoming evident from perhaps late February, though it is unclear if these are local breeders or on passage. Despite initial impressions of chaos, there is a great deal of order within Scillonian gull colonies. Herring Gulls being primarily confined to boulder beaches plus some rocky outcrops, with Lesser Black-backed Gulls occupying areas above the beach and further inland, a feature noted by E H Rodd back in the mid-19th century (Rodd 1880). Only in a few notable exceptions does this order break down and Lesser Black-backs extend down amongst the Herring Gulls, as on Gugh south of Cuckolds Carn, or at Tresco's Gimble Porth.

| Islands | Nests | Islands | Nests |
| --- | --- | --- | --- |
| St Martin's | 58 | Gweal | 4 |
| Tresco | 29 | White Island, Samson | 27 |
| Shipman Head, Bryher | 50 | Puffin Island | 108 |
| St Agnes | 2 | Round Island | 1 |
| Gugh | 1123 | St Helen's | 530 |
| Samson | 1062 | Tean & Pednbrose | 24 |
| Annet | 517 | Northwethel | 13 |
| Gorregan | 1 | White Island, St Martin's | 28 |
| Rosevean | 2 | Great Ganinick | 2 |
| Great Crebawethan | 1 | Great & Little Arthur | 1 |
| Mincarlo | 2 | Great Ganilly | 9 |
| Maiden Bower | 5 | Nornour | 1 |
| Scilly Rock | 2 | Menawethan | 6 |

**Locations of 3608 Lesser Black-backed Gull Nests – 1999 (Seabird 2000 data)**

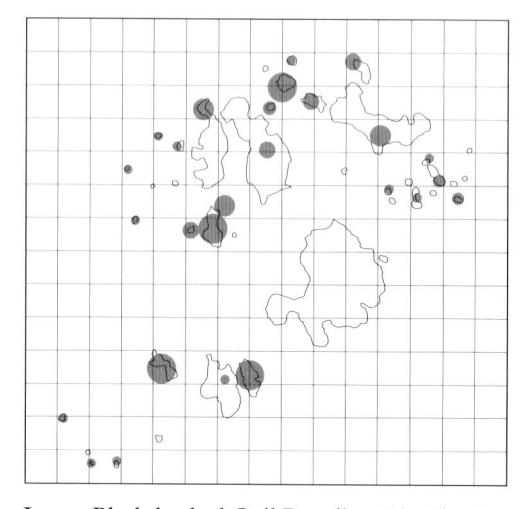

**Lesser Black-backed Gull Breeding Distribution – 1999 (data Seabird 2000)**

For a gull that spends most of the day out of sight of land, Lesser Black-backs show a remarkable preference for nesting within, or even beneath dense ground cover, frequently deep inside tangles of bramble *Rubus* and bracken *Pteridium*. Indeed, one surprising feature revealed by the Seabird 2000 count of 1999 was Lesser Black-back's recent withdrawal from areas where vegetation had become suppressed by weather or other actions, as on Annet, and their accumulation now on islands where vegetation has increased, with the consequence that 75% of the population (2,715 pairs) now nests on the three islands Samson, Gugh and St Helen's. Interestingly, of all islands utilised by this species, these three encounter by far the highest levels of human disturbance, but Lesser Black-backs seems unconcerned, being more than capable of deterring the occasional wandering human! As with several seabird species, Lesser Black-backed Gulls are absent from apparently suitable breeding sites in the Eastern Isles and though reasons for this have still to be determined they may be related to recent levels of Brown Rat *Rattus norvegicus* infestation, which seems certain to at least partially account for their recent desertion of Tean and St Martin's White Island.

Birds begin defending nest sites early in the year but egg-laying is normally delayed until well into May, and can be delayed even further in the event of cold easterly winds, the same feature sometimes resulting in the desertion of newly laid clutches. In normal years there is a gap of around three weeks between the mean laying date for Herring Gulls and Lesser Black-backs. Clutch size is two to three eggs, with a mean of around 2.8. In most years the majority of eggs laid hatch but in years of serious food shortage, for whatever reason, chicks die either soon after hatching or subsequently. As with other large gulls, estimating productivity for Lesser Black-backed Gulls in Scilly is hampered by high chick mobility soon after hatching, particularly in dense cover and the most beneficial method may be counts of large young around the time of fledging.

Lloyd *et al*. (1991) gave 205,000 Lesser Black-backed Gull pairs for Europe (apparently excluding the two most eastern forms) and 64,400 coastal breeding pairs for Britain and Ireland. In comparison, Stone *et al*. (1997) estimated the UK population at 83,000 pairs, which is close to the Gibbons *et al*. (1993) figure of 83,500 pairs for Britain. However, the British population increased by 46% during the period 1994–99 (Bashford & Noble 2000), in which case it may now be in the order of 93,000 to 120,000 coastal pairs. Though a reliable up-to-date figure will only become available once national Seabird 2000 results have been published.

However, using the Lloyd *et al*. 1991 figure of 64,400 pairs, the 1999 Scilly Seabird 2000 all-island count of 3,608 pairs represents 5.6% of the British and Irish population, use of the Gibbons *et al*. 1993 figure suggests 4.3%, whilst the possible current upper limit of 120,000 pairs still means Scilly holds 3%. Either way it seems clear that Scilly holds a measurable proportion of the British breeding total. Gibbons *et al*. also suggested that Lesser Black-backed Gull is fast disappearing as a breeding species in north Norway, in which case any recent British increases seem likely to be balanced by losses elsewhere in Europe. Calculations based on the figure of 230,000–250,000 pairs (Heath *et al*. 2000) for all European countries, indicate Scilly may hold some 1.5% of the overall European breeding population.

Numbers of breeding Lesser Black-backed Gulls recorded during various all-island surveys and on Annet are shown in the Charts, Annet totals are mainly based on nest counts whereas all-island counts were an alleged between-year mix of nests and pairs. Between-year variation in numbers on Annet is perhaps difficult to explain, but may partly relate to vegetational changes, as in 1976, when a two-thirds reduction in breeding pairs over two years was mainly thought attributable to a temporary loss of tall plants, e.g. Bracken, resulting from two particularly dry summers (Allen 1976). The more recent, late 1990s reduction is perhaps explained by a redistribution of pairs either to Samson, Gugh or St Helen's, again apparently attributable to a loss of tall vegetation caused by winter wind and salt damage (pers. obs.) and was not mirrored by comparable reduction in the all-island total. Looking at the all-island situation, it seems obvious that Lesser Black-backed Gull is maintaining its status within Scilly, regardless of marked declines in Herring and Greater Black-backed Gulls *L. marinus*.

The most recent winter count involved the two-day late January 1997 Winter Shorebird Survey (Lock 1999), when 636 were recorded throughout the main islands. Of these, 328 (51%) and 283 (44%) respectively were on Samson and Tresco. Lock suggested that the January 1997 figures might be internationally significant, the individual site criterion having since been set at 400 individuals. However, the timing of the 1997 survey means some early returning birds may also have been involved.

A total of 1,423 Lesser Black-backed Gulls had been ringed on Scilly up until 1999, 719 prior to 1970 and 704 since then. Perhaps more than any species involved in local ringing programmes, Lesser Black-backed Gull demonstrates the value of such work in helping to answer difficult but nonetheless important questions on long-term population dynamics. For example, birds ringed by St Agnes Bird Observatory volunteers as pulli on Annet in 1966 are known to have been alive and presumably breeding on the same islands until at least 1995, almost 30 years later. More recently, young from several islands, identifiable by engraved coloured plastic rings, have demonstrated a marked and quite rapid first-winter dispersal to the coasts of Portugal and Spain, some arriving before the end of August, at least one first-year moving on down to coastal Morocco by November. Some, however, apparently go no further south than Brittany and there is even a strong suggestion many young birds, perhaps even most, spend their first full summer around the coast of northern France. However, one problem with colour-ringing in Scilly is the relative absence of any intensive gull-watching effort during summer, plus obvious difficulties associated with trying to prove the presence of rings on birds breeding in deep vegetation.

So far, birds up to three years of age have been sighted in Spain, Portugal and Morocco in winter, though fewer of greater age from the study are available yet for reporting. In recent years, limited attention has been paid to July and August accumulations of Lesser Black-backed Gulls on Annet's west coast, with a number of colour-ringed adults originating from the Bristol Channel colonies, presumably involving birds moving south. Of considerable interest are the number of recoveries resulting from birds ringed in Scilly during the early 20th century, first of which was a bird ringed on Rosevear in July 1914 and shot in Portugal in December that same year.

Western European populations, i.e. *graellsii* and *intermedius*, winter coastally south to the equator, a few also enter the western Mediterranean, whereas nominate *fuscus* moves mainly south or southeast, overland to the Black Sea and eastern Mediterranean, some continuing into eastern Africa. Western European birds begin leaving the breeding colonies from late July, some reaching Iberia by August, though most movement occurs during September. There is a marked tendency for British and Irish first-winter birds to move further south than adults, and some 80% of African recoveries involve this category (Cramp *et al.* 1977–94; Wernham *et al.* 2002). This no doubt explains how adults are able to commence reappearing in Scilly from at least mid-February. Interestingly, Baker (in Cramp *et al.*) suggested that adults undertaking a long migration are perhaps disadvantaged in their competition for nesting territories and are therefore wintering closer to the breeding sites. The BOURC is investigating reports of British *fuscus* records based on recoveries of birds ringed in Scandinavia (BOURC 2002a).

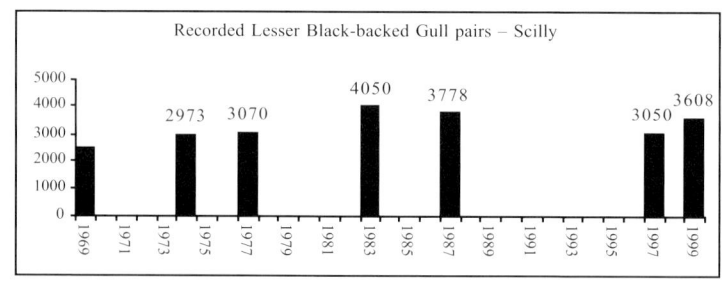

**Data Sources**: 1969 = Lloyd *et al.* 1991; 1974 = Allen 1974-77; 1977 = Allen 1974-77; 1983 = P Harvey 1983; 1987 = Birkin & Smith 1987; 1997 = Wagstaff 1997; 1999 Seabird 2000 – unpublished data.

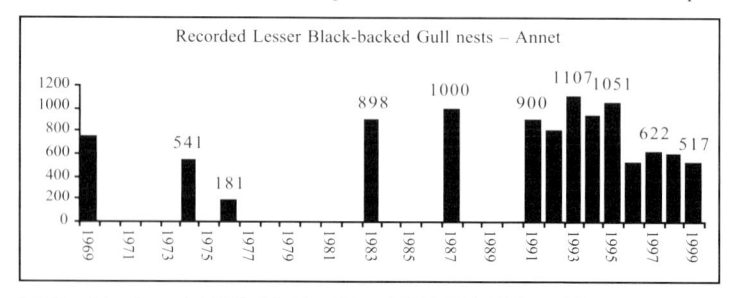

**Data Sources**: 1969 = Lloyd *et al.* 1991; 1974 = Allen 1974-77; 1976 = Allen 1974-77; 1983 = P Harvey 1983; 1987 = Birkin & Smith 1987; 1991 = W Wagstaff pers. comm.; 1992 = P J Robinson 1992b; 1993 = P J Robinson 1993; 1994 = P J Robinson 1994; 1995 = P J Robinson 1995a; 1996 = Wagstaff 1996; 1997 = Wagstaff 1997; 1998 = P J Robinson 1998; 1999 = Seabird 2000 – unpublished data.

**Controls**

| | | | |
|---|---|---|---|
| GK15863 | Pul | Skokholm, Pembrokeshire | |
| | | 9th July 1975 | FD Annet 13th April 1982 |
| GG24625 | Pul | Skomer Island, Pembrokeshire | |
| | | 4th July 1987 | FD Annet 25th May 1993 |
| CR | Pul | Skomer Island, Pembrokeshire 1985 | FR St Agnes 11th June 1996 |

| | | | | | |
|---|---|---|---|---|---|
| ? | Pul | Skomer Island, Pembrokeshire 1986 | FR | St Agnes 11th June 1996 | |
| | | | FR | Annet 17th July 1996 | |
| ? | Pul | Skomer Island 1984 | FR | Annet 18th July 1996 | |
| ? | Pul | Skomer Island 1990 | FR | Gull Point, Gugh 28th July 1996 | |

**Selected Recoveries**

| | | | | |
|---|---|---|---|---|
| ? | ? | Rosevear 16th July 1914 | SH | Fao, Minho, Portugal December 1914 |
| ? | ? | Annet 21st June 1923 | ? | Caperica, Lisbon, Portugal 28th September 1924 |
| ? | ? | Gugh 8th July 1924 | SH | Aiguillon sur Mar, Vendee, France 9th May 1925 |
| ? | ? | Samson 2nd July 1959 | SH | Olhao, Algarve, Portugal 12th January 1961 |
| AJ68046 | Pul | Annet 26th June 1962 | FI | Linea de la Concepcion, Cadiz, Spain 10th January 1963 |
| GM13817 | Pul | Annet 4th July 1966 | FD | Annet 14th May 1992 |
| GM13987 | Pul | Annet 7th July 1966 | FD | Annet 6th June 1995 |
| GF23896 | Pul | Samson 4th August 1993 | FD | Sale, Morocco 16th February 1996 |
| GA07232 | Pul | Gugh 9th July 1996 | FR | Viana Do Catelo, Minho, Portugal 20th October 1996 |
| | | | FR | Figueira Da Foz, Beira Litoral, Portugal 7th October 1997 |
| GF41318 | Pul | Gugh 4th July 1994 | FR | Casablanca, Morocco 25th February 1997 |
| GA07214 | Pul | Gugh 9th July 1996 | FR | Ille de Re, France 30th June 1997 |
| | | | FR | Portes de Re, France 30th June 1997 |
| | | | FR | Ille de Re, France 11th September 1997 |
| | | | FR | Ille de Re, France 15th July 1998 |
| | | | FR | Les Portes de Re, France 18th July 1998 |
| GA07233 | Pul | Gugh 9th July 1996 | FR | Marrais D'Olonne, Vendee, France 28th May 1998 |
| | | | FR | Marrais D'Olonne, Vendee, France 4th June 1998 |
| | | | FR | Figueia da Fos, Portugal 19th October 1998 |
| GF41308 | Pul | Gugh 4th July 1994 | FR | Beira Literal, Portugal 5th November 1999 |

Lesser Black-backed Gull Ringing Recaptures

# Herring Gull *Larus argentatus* A

Breeding resident plus probable migrant and winter visitor. A full written description is required by the BBRC in the case of all *smithsonianus* records.

*Smithsonianus* Records
1997 One (first-summer) St Mary's 18th December 1997 to at least 6th April 1998
*British Birds* 91: 479

2002 One various islands 30th January to 17th February  *Birding World* 15: 52
2002 One various islands from 6th February, dead Tresco 28th  *Birding World* 15: 52
2002 One various islands 25th to 28th February  *Birding World* 15: 52
2002 One (first-winter) Bryher 29th November  *Birding World* 15: 446

Circumpolar, breeding coastal West Palearctic through central Asia to 120°E, also northeast Asia, Canada and northeast USA. Dispersive, northern birds move south in winter. Polytypic: nominate *argentatus*, or 'Scandinavian Herring Gull' occurs Denmark and Scandinavia; *argenteus* Iceland, Faeroes, British Isles, western France and North Sea coasts to western Germany; *smithsonianus*, or 'American Herring Gull' (a probable pending split), North America and northern Siberia. Until recently Herring Gull was widely accepted as comprising three groups, i.e. '*cachinnans*', '*armenicus*' and nominate '*argentatus*' (Cramp *et al.* 1977–94; Collinson 2001b). Increasingly, however, authorities have treated *cachinnans* and *armenicus* groups as a full species, 'Yellow-legged Gull', but more recently this group too is being split even further (see Yellow-legged Gull). The form s*mithsonianus* is undergoing consistent North American population decline (Bryant 1997), as are western European forms. Amber-listed in UK: probably greater than 50% breeding decline over past 25 years; 50% or more of breeding population at ten or fewer sites (Gregory *et al.* 2002). National 17% decline 1998–99 (Bashford & Noble 2000).

About 900 pairs currently breed on 34 islands, making this the second most widespread breeding seabird in Scilly after Great Black-backed Gull *L. marinus*. Nevertheless, it has undergone a 60% decrease in Scilly generally since 1974 and an eleven-fold decrease on Annet since 1960. Numerous bone remains unearthed from the prehistoric site on Nornour in the Eastern Isles were thought to include those of young gulls *Larus* (Turk 1984b). And though they could not be identified specifically these presumably involve one or other of the three large gulls currently breeding in Scilly.

Herring Gull was not often referred to by early writers, E H Rodd's only contribution being mention of his nephew Francis seeing a large flock on Tresco's freshwater pools on Christmas Day 1864 (Rodd 1880). Gilbert White thought a few remained all year, though the greater number left during autumn and returned to their breeding grounds in April (in Jesse 1887), a comment White nonetheless applied to several gull species, not all of which bred in Scilly. However, by the start of the 20th century, James Clark and Francis Rodd considered it abundant year round and breeding in great numbers on most uninhabited islands (Clark & Rodd 1906). First published breeding account apparently involved H W Robinson's 1911 observation of a nest with five eggs on Melledgan on 22nd May (H W Robinson 1911b). This was followed some years later by a note of 'a few' breeding on Bryher's Shipman Head, plus 'a large colony' on what was described as Stony Beach, Samson (*CBWPSAR* 7). Nonetheless, by the mid-1940s it was being described as an abundant breeder (Ryves & Quick 1946).

According to Lloyd *et al.* (1991), numbers of Herring Gulls breeding in Britain increased by an estimated 10–13% annually from at least the 1940s until the mid-1970s, and Parslow (1967a) noted that it had increased widely, especially during the preceding 20 years. However, between the national surveys of 1969–70 and 1985–87, many populations decreased by more than 50%, this being reportedly more pronounced in western Scotland and western England. Unfortunately, there is only one pre-1974 Scillonian Herring Gull count, though the decline from that point on fits the national picture. Reasons for these late 20th century declines are complex but are mainly thought attributable to changes in the disposal of human waste, and to changes within the fishing industry, though Lloyd *et al.* thought that human persecution may also have played a role. Overall, though, numbers of Herring Gulls breeding in Britain and Ireland fell by around 40% between the two national surveys (Lloyd *et al.* 1991). However, without knowing more about the movements of adult Herring Gulls, particularly during winter, it may be difficult determining what the controlling factors are in relation to the Scillonian population. Yet, although local changes in waste disposal seem an unlikely cause, recent changes to the Cornish fishing industry may perhaps be relevant.

During the Seabird 2000 survey, 903 pairs of Herring Gulls were found breeding on 34 islands or rocks in 1999. Main concentrations were on Samson (184 – 20.3%), Gugh (159 – 17.6%) and Tresco (102 – 11.2%), the least number encountered being single nests on bleak Maiden Bower and precipitous Castle Bryher. Lloyd *et al.* (1991) concluded that the Scillonian Herring Gull population comprised some 16% of the total for southwest England, but that percentage may now have decreased.

As observed under Lesser Black-backed Gull *L. fuscus*, despite initial impressions of chaos there is a great deal of inter-specific order within Scillonian gull colonies. Herring Gulls are primarily confined to boulder beaches, or occur on some rocky outcrops extending inland from the beaches, whilst Lesser Black-backs mainly occupy areas above the beach and further inland. Even so, a few Herring Gull pairs are often found mixed with Lesser Black-backs away from main Herring Gull concentrations, as on Annet, St Helen's or Samson, where there is perhaps one pair of Herring Gulls in every two or three hundred Lesser Black-back pairs. This feature is easily accommodated during any survey once observers are familiar with differences in the calls of Herring and Lesser Black-backs, or with subtle differences in eggs of the two species.

During the early 1990s, productivity checks were carried out in the Herring Gull colony at Gull Point, Gugh. Mean clutch size was found to be in the region of 2.7 eggs, whilst during an average year pairs fledged about 0.53 young per total number of nests, or just over one chick per successful nest (P J Robinson

| Island              | Nests | Island                   | Nests |
|---------------------|-------|--------------------------|-------|
| St Mary's           | 2     | Round Island             | 8     |
| St Martin's         | 18    | St Helen's               | 64    |
| Tresco              | 102   | Tean & Pednbrose         | 62    |
| Shipman Head, Bryher| 23    | Northwethel              | 10    |
| St Agnes            | 25    | Foremans Island          | 5     |
| Gugh                | 159   | Crow Island              | 3     |
| Samson              | 184   | Plum Island              | 6     |
| Annet               | 42    | White Island, St Martin's| 34    |
| Rosevear            | 2     | Guther's Island          | 18    |
| Mincarlo            | 6     | Great Ganinick           | 2     |
| Illiswilgig         | 8     | Little Ganinick          | 6     |
| Maiden Bower        | 1     | Great & Little Arthur    | 8     |
| Castle Bryher       | 1     | Ragged Island            | 9     |
| Scilly Rock         | 10    | Great Ganilly            | 13    |
| Gweal               | 15    | Nornour                  | 3     |
| White Island, Samson| 15    | Great Innisvouls         | 3     |
| Puffin Island       | 31    | Menawethan               | 5     |

Locations of 903 Herring Gull Nests – 1999 (Seabird 2000 data)

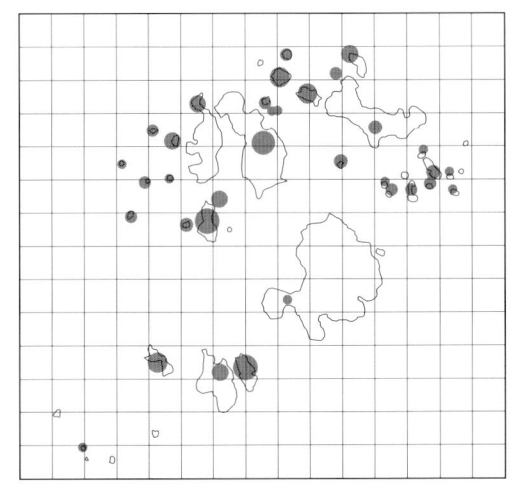

Herring Gull Breeding Distribution – 1999 (data Seabird 2000)

unpublished data). From this it was assumed that causes of any decline in Scilly were probably unconnected to breeding success. Since at least 1995, up to three or four pairs of Herring Gulls have been nesting or showing obvious signs of doing so, e.g. copulating, undergoing site selection, and rudimentary nest building, on rooftops in Hugh Town on St Mary's, and young have been fledged in at least two years, very possibly more (Wagstaff 1996; P J Robinson 1998). The level of such activity seems certain to increase within Hugh Town, as indeed it has at numerous other rooftop colonies throughout Britain. The closest such sites to Scilly are in St Ives, Newlyn and Penzance, all in west Cornwall, in which area large gulls were first recorded nesting on rooftops from about 1950 (Cramp 1971).

As with Lesser Black-backed Gull, little seems to have been published on the racial status of Herring Gulls involved in Scillonian sightings, except that a number of reports in recent years have referred to the appearance in the islands of yellow-legged individuals, treated here as a full species (see Yellow-legged Gull). Away from the colonies, co-ordinated counts have been few and in recent years were confined to the two-day late January 1997 Winter Shorebird Survey, when a total of 1,765 would have omitted Herring Gulls feeding away from tidal areas (Lock 1999). The species was fairly evenly distributed over four islands, Bryher, St Mary's, Tresco and Samson, these accounting for 443, 392, 366 and 352 respectively, whereas St Martin's and St Agnes scored 108 and 104 respectively. Other than this, counts have typically been random, as in 1994 when 100 plus were in Porth Cressa during January, with 300 on St Agnes and 265 on Tresco during October, the St Agnes figure reducing to 200 by mid-November. The greatest number recorded in one place, at least in recent years, probably involved 500 or so attending a trawler in The Roads for two days during December 1995. Although such figures may not be particularly helpful in determining the size of the non-breeding population, the species received even less attention in some years, to the point even of not being mentioned at all.

Little, too, has been published on the feeding behaviour of Herring Gulls in Scilly, though a report of them eating swedes during the severe weather of early 1963 perhaps demonstrates their adaptability

(*CBWPSAR* 33). By mainland standards, rubbish disposal sites are difficult to come by in Scilly now most human waste on St Mary's is incinerated, a factor reflected in the small number of Herring Gulls now frequenting 'The Dump' area. A few though still utilise the sewage outfall at Morning Point, St Mary's and up to about 50 regularly frequent the Hugh Town area in search of food provided by islanders and visitors alike. However, the vast majority of Herring Gulls in Scilly continue to feed along the intertidal zone and in adjacent areas and therefore seldom come into direct contact with humans. Young (1987) described an individual Herring Gull that specialised in feeding on Rabbits *Oryctolagus cuniculus* inside Jersey Zoo, but this behaviour seems not to have been recorded in Scilly, despite the presence of a widespread Rabbit population, including on some islands frequented by breeding gulls. However, it is noticeable that on islands with high concentrations of breeding gulls, e.g. Annet, or Samson, Rabbits seem disinclined to show themselves during daylight, although if this is a consequence of gull predation then Lesser and Great Black-backed *L. marinus* offer a more probable explanation.

An unusually dark first-winter *smithsonianus* or 'American Herring Gull' frequented St Mary's from 18th December 1997 until at least 6th April 1998 (see Table). It remained mainly in the Porth Mellon and Dump areas and because its presence in Scilly coincided with the discovery in Hugh Town of a putative Spotless Starling *Sturnus unicolor*, it was seen by many birders. The *smithsonianus* record was accepted by the BBRC as the fourth for Britain, the subspecies having been added to the BOU's Category 'A' on the strength of a bird in Ireland during November–December 1986 (BOURC 1992) and onto the British list via a bird in Cheshire during February–March 1994 (*Ibis* 139: 197). During February 2002, three reported first-winter *smithsonianus* frequented Scilly, one of which was found dead on Tresco (*Birding World* 15: 51, 106–110). First-winter 'American Herring Gull' plumage is normally distinctive, but less obvious individuals are nonetheless liable to be overlooked and Millington & Garner (1998) emphasised the likelihood of adult *smithsonianus* being overlooked among flocks of mixed-age large gulls *Larus*. The northern *argentatus*, or 'Scandinavian Herring Gull' must surely pass through the islands, or even winter, but if so the topic seems to have received little attention.

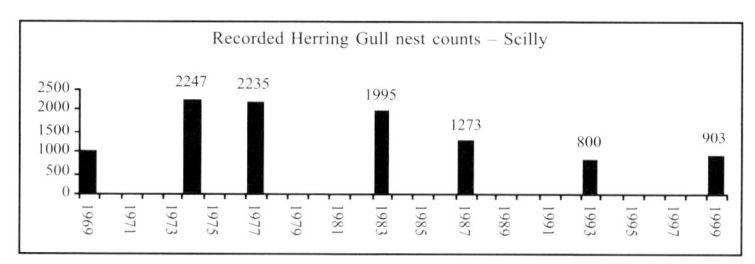

**Data Sources**: 1969 = Lloyd *et al.* 1991; 1974 = Allen 1974–77; 1977 = Allen 1974–77; 1983 = P Harvey 1983; 1987 = Birkin & Smith 1987; 1993 = P J Robinson 1993; 1999 Seabird 2000 – unpublished data.

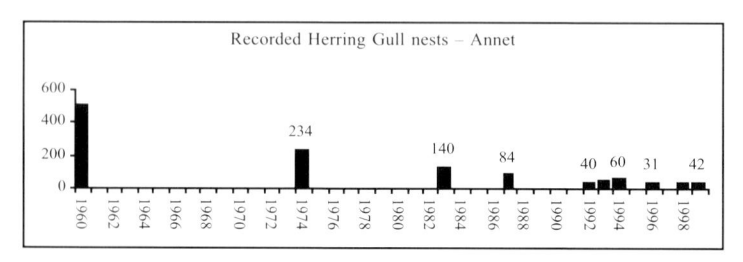

**Data Sources**: 1960 = Allen 1974–77; 1974 = Allen 1974–77; 1983 = P Harvey 1983; 1987 = Birkin & Smith 1987; 1992 = P J Robinson 1992b; 1993 = P J Robinson 1993; 1994 = P J Robinson 1994; 1996 = Wagstaff 1996; 1998 = P J Robinson 1998; 1999 Seabird 2000 – unpublished data.

The current national status of the Scillonian Herring Gull population will only become clear following publication of the Seabird 2000 results. However, at the time of the 1987 estimate of 190,900 British and Irish pairs (Lloyd *et al.* 1991), Scilly held less than 1% of the national population, whereas using Stone's UK figure of 180,000 pairs produced a very similar result (Stone *et al.* 1997). In Britain, Herring Gulls are widely distributed both coastally and inland during winter, ringing studies revealing that a large percentage of birds wintering south as far as the Home Counties are *argentatus* from northern Europe (Wernham *et al.* 2002). Within Britain, birds gravitate towards main gull wintering areas (mostly coastal) after breeding, with some southward drift among more northern populations (P Lack 1986). Ringing data show a clearly increased tendency for birds from southwest England to reach northwest France during winter than those from elsewhere in England or Ireland (Wernham *et al.* 2002). A total of 1,073 Herring Gulls had been ringed in Scilly up to the end of 1999, the 854 (79%) prior to 1970 doubtless reflecting its greater availability at that time. The Table, which shows a selection of known Scillonian-ringed controls and recoveries but omits local movements, suggests a south and east movement of Scillonian birds, though only as far as Cornwall or France, the single control from France involving a bird ringed in northwest Brittany the previous autumn. Some of the controls support the known southward movement of more northerly birds, though the Scillonian-ringed individual in Norfolk three years later is noteworthy.

**Controls**

| | | | | | |
|---|---|---|---|---|---|
| ? | Ad | Brest, France 17th October 1956 | FD | Scilly 17th April 1957 |
| AJ2025 | Pul | Lundy, Devon 14th June 1958 | ? | St Mary's 17th February 1963 |
| AJ96961 | Pul | Bodorgan, Anglesey 5th July 1963 | FD | St Agnes (spring) 1964 |
| ? | Pul | Isle of May, Firth of Forth 1967 | ? | Porth Cressa, St Mary's 28th September 1977 |
| GF41209 | Pul | Sanda Island, Kintyre 30th June 1994 | FR | Porth Cressa, St Mary's 8th October 1994 |

**Recoveries**

| | | | | | |
|---|---|---|---|---|---|
| AF3237 | Pul | Scilly 6th July 1952 | FD | Piriac, Penistin, Morbihan, France 23rd April 1954 |
| AJ68060 | Pul | Annet 26th June 1962 | FI | La Barra de Monts, Vendee, France 3rd December 1962 |
| AJ68275 | Pul | Gugh 24th June 1963 | ? | Newlyn, west Cornwall 2nd December 1963 |
| AJ88102 | Pul | Gugh 1st July 1964 | ? | St Ives, west Cornwall 26th September 1964 |
| AJ88123 | Pul | Annet 12th July 1964 | FI | La Turballe, Loire-Atlantique, France 1st November 1964 |
| ? | ? | Annet 30th June 1963 | | Old Great Yarmouth, Norfolk 27th February 1966 |
| GF4129- | Pul | Gugh 3rd July 1994 | FR | Par Sands, Cornwall 20th February 1995 |
| GF41212 | Pul | Gugh 27th June 1994 | FI | Hayle, west Cornwall 16th June 1995 |
| GA09929 | Pul | Gugh 29th June 1998 | FD | Plymouth, Devon 19th February 1999 |

**Selected Herring Gull Ringing Recaptures**

# Yellow-legged Gull *Larus michahellis* A

**Rare migrant or winter visitor, full written description required by the SRP.**

Still considered by some authorities as part of the Herring Gull *L. argentatus* complex, this largely recognisable group is increasingly viewed as a species in its own right (Collinson 2001b) and may perhaps soon be further split. Breeds West Palearctic from France south and eastwards through Mediterranean and Black Sea, migratory or dispersive. Polytypic: *atlantis* occurs Azores, Madeira and Canary Isles; *michahellis*, or 'Western Yellow-legged Gull' western France, western Iberia, Morocco and into Mediterranean; *armenicus*, or 'Armenian Gull' Armenia, eastern Turkey and western Iran. Opinions vary on wisdom of also including *cachinnans*, or 'Caspian Gull' and perhaps three additional forms of large white-headed gulls (Cramp *et al.* 1977–94; Collinson 2001b).

A small number of darker-mantled Herring Gull-type large gulls with yellow or yellowish legs are reported most years and are normally accepted as *michahellis*, or what is now generally referred to as 'Western Yellow-legged Gull'. Nevertheless, assessing numbers of individuals involved is often confused by long-stayers plus inter-island movements, for example a total of about twenty sightings during 1999 were thought to have involved perhaps just four individuals. However, it should also be borne in mind that a minute percentage of Herring Gulls do have yellow legs (Garner *et al.* 1997; Jonsson 1998). A typical year for Yellow-legged Gull sightings was 1996, commencing with one at the Tresco rubbish dump for two days during early January and another at nearby Gimble Porth on 24th March. These were followed by an adult at Lower Town, St Martin's, on 2nd April, this same individual possibly accounting for sightings from St Agnes and then Tresco's Great Pool on the 8th. Four more Tresco reports followed, on 27th April, 7th and 16th July and finally on 12th October, though the actual numbers of birds involved was impossible to ascertain. The form *cachinnans* is also a rare visitor to Britain most winters and so could occur in Scilly (Gantlett 1998). A presumed *michahellis* was seen apparently paired with a Herring Gull on Gugh early in spring 1992 (pers. obs.) but was not relocated subsequently. Early Scillonian records of Yellow-legged Gull in Scilly include one to two on St Mary's during late September and mid-October 1972 and what was presumably one of these two from 21st to 31st October.

# Iceland Gull *Larus glaucoides* A

**Regular migrant or winter visitor, full written description required by the SRP.**

| | | |
|---|---|---|
| 1852 | One (first-winter – shot) Bryher Rodd 1852b |
| 1884 | Oliver's Castle, Tresco 1884 Clark & Rodd 1906 |
| 1885 | One Tresco infant school 25th February Clark & Rodd 1906 |
| 1890 | One 'Scilly' 1st December Clark & Rodd 1906 |
| 1923 | One St Mary's wintered until 9th May Penhallurick 1969 |
| 1951 | One (adult) St Mary's 28th April |
| 1965 | One Tresco 12th February |
| 1967 | One (first-winter) St Mary's 3rd November |
| 1969 | One (adult) St Agnes 8th October |
| 1974 | One (first-year) Harbour, St Mary's February to mid-summer 1975 |
| 1974 | One (second-year) Harbour, St Mary's February to end of May |
| 1974 | One (adult) St Agnes 27th & 28th October |
| 1980 | One Porth Hellick, St Mary's 3rd February |
| 1981 | One (second-winter) Harbour, St Mary's 29th January |
| 1981 | One (second-year) Burnt Island, St Agnes 24th May |
| 1982 | One (second-winter) Bant's Carn & Porthloo, St Mary's 6th to 8th February |
| 1982 | One Porth Cressa, St Mary's 'end of year' |
| 1983 | One (second-year) St Mary's 6th to 27th February |
| 1984 | One (first-year) St Mary's 19th to 21st January (dead 22nd) |
| 1987 | One (first-winter) St Agnes & St Mary's 16th October |
| 1990 | One (first-winter) Porth Cressa, St Mary's 2nd & 3rd February |
| 1990 | One (first-winter) Porth Hellick & Porthloo, St Mary's 30th & 31st December |
| 1990 | One St Martin's & Tresco 30th December to 10th February 1991 |
| 1991 | One various islands 16th to 20th October |
| 1992 | One (first-winter) Annet 14th May |
| 1993 | One from RMV *Scillonian III* 13th October |
| 1994 | One (first-winter) Tresco & St Mary's 15th January to 16th May |
| 1994 | One Hugh Town, St Mary's 4th to 27th April |
| 1996 | One (first-winter) Porth Hellick, St Mary's 16th January to 4th March |
| 1996 | One (second-summer) St Agnes & Tresco 22nd May |
| 1997 | One (first-winter) Porth Cressa, St Mary's 12th to 16th February |
| 1997 | One (adult) St Mary's 18th February to 30th March |
| 1997 | One (first-winter) Daymark, St Martin's 6th March |
| 1998 | At least one (first-winter) St Mary's 2nd January to 8th May |
| 1999 | One (adult) Porth Mellon & Porthloo, St Mary's 8th February |
| 1999 | One (second-winter) Rocky Hill, Airport and Porth Cressa, St Mary's 1st to 6th December |

'Kumlien's Gull' Records
1994    One St Mary's 30th March to 4th June   IOSBR 1994
1998    One (possibly two) St Mary's 2nd February to 19th March
IOSBR 1998; *Birding World* 11: 86

Breeds south and west Greenland and northeast Canada. Migratory or dispersive, moving south in Atlantic during winter to line from British Isles to Carolinas in eastern USA. Polytypic: nominate *glaucoides* occurs Greenland and, recently, Novaya Zemlya; *kumlieni*, or 'Kumlien's Gull' northeast Canada. Some authorities treat closely related Thayer's Gull *L. thayeri* of central-northern Canada as form of Iceland Gull *L. g. thayeri*, whilst some also consider *kumlieni* a hybrid population between *glaucoides* and *thayeri* (e.g. Boertman – *British Birds* 94: 547–548).

First published mention of Iceland Gull in Scilly came in E H Rodd's letter to the *Zoologist* of 1852, entitled 'Occurrence of Iceland Gull (*Larus Islandicus*) at Scilly', in which he drew attention to the shooting of a specimen in the islands during the latter part of May or beginning of June that year (Rodd 1852b). He later mentioned that the bird had been in immature plumage and was shot by the Rev J H Jenkinson, describing the upperparts as 'dull white, with occasional broccoli-brown markings, the smaller webs of the quill feathers being also of a pale brown; the rest of the plumage being entirely white' (Rodd 1880). On mainland Cornwall Rodd described it as reasonably frequent in occurrence, though he knew of only four or so specimens obtained up until 1880. Clearly though, the situation changed on Scilly towards the close of the 19th century, James Clark and E H Rodd's nephew Francis mentioning three more in the islands by 1890 (Clark & Rodd 1906), also clarifying that Jenkinson's 1850's individual had been obtained on Bryher. First of the additional Scillonian records was shot by Tresco gamekeeper David Smith near Oliver's Castle at the northern end of Tresco Channel in 1884 and the next near Tresco infants school on 25th February 1885, whilst the last, a probable adult, was seen at an unnamed location on 1st December 1890.

Checking through earlier records, Penhallurick (1969) found just four 20th century Scillonian records up until the mid-1960s and only 10 for mainland Cornwall, suggesting, with apparent justification, that in Cornwall it was far scarcer than Glaucous Gull *L. hyperboreus*. Of the two Scillonian birds that were aged, one was an adult and one a first-year, and only one of the four possibly overwintered.

Taking the ten years from 1990, Iceland Gull was recorded in all except 1995, with the majority of sightings falling in the second winter period. However, during the 15-year period prior to the 1990s it arrived in only six years and in substantially fewer numbers. The Table shows all published Iceland Gull records up until 1999 and clearly demonstrates how much more frequent it has become since about 1980. Reasons for this increase are unclear and it may be more apparent than real, among other things perhaps reflecting increased observer coverage, apart from which it may also reflect an increased interest in gull identification in Britain generally. The Chart incorporates all 31 recorded arrival dates plus the two 'Kumlien's Gulls'.

The not always so easily identifiable 'Kumlien's Gull' from northeast Canada has been identified at least twice (possibly involving three individuals) in Scilly since 1994 (see Table), the first British record dating from 1869 and involving a bird killed in Shetland in late November (BOURC 1997; Palmer 2000). In addition, the closely related North American Thayer's Gull, which some authorities, e.g. Snow & Perrins (1998), treat as a form of Iceland Gull, *L. g. thayeri*, has occurred in Ireland (McGeehan & Millington 1998). So it is certainly worth bearing in mind the possibility of these two forms/species when confronted by any *glaucoides*-type individual. For useful reading on the identification of Kumlien's Gull see Garner *et al.* (2000).

Greenland populations of the low-arctic breeding nominate *glaucoides* are mainly migratory, the majority of eastern birds probably wintering along Iceland's northern coasts, where they arrive from late September, and depart again for their breeding grounds by late April (Cramp *et al.* 1977–94). However, each winter small numbers reach further south, including the Faeroes, Britain and Ireland, a few subadults remaining in more southerly latitudes after the adults depart in spring. The Canadian 'Kumlien's Gull' winters along the coasts of northeast North America, from Hudson Bay to at least Long Island and inland as far as the Great Lakes. Recent stragglers have been noted in Britain, Ireland, Denmark and Sweden (Snow & Perrins 1998). Thayer's Gull, which also bears some resemblance to Herring Gull *L. argentatus*, breeds in northwest Greenland and arctic Canada and winters primarily in west-coast North America south as far as California, though some can be found annually in mid-western and eastern coastal states south to Texas and Florida. Interestingly, Thayer's Gull breeds closer to Britain than Franklin's Gull *L. pipixcan*, for which there were 40 British records up until 1999 (McGeehan & Millington 1998). Thus all populations are likely to come in contact

*Birds of the Isles of Scilly*

Iceland Gull arrival dates

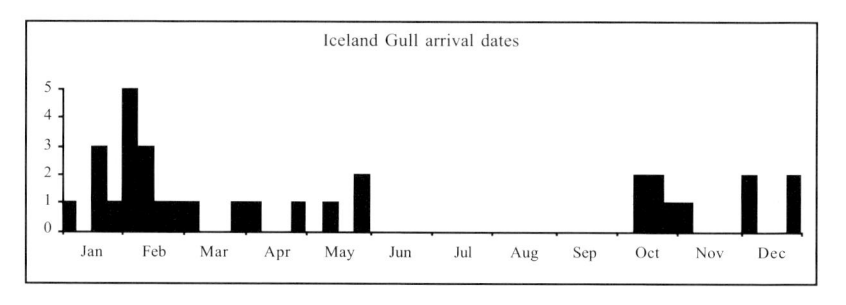

with each other at some time. For further reading on the identification of first-winter Kumlien's Gull see Garner *et al.* (2000). No Iceland Gulls have been ringed on Scilly and there are no recaptures from elsewhere.

## Glaucous Gull *Larus hyperboreus* A

**Scarce annual migrant or winter visitor, full written description required by the SRP.**

Circumpolar, breeding edge of the Arctic Ocean from southern Barents Sea east through extreme northern Asia, Alaska and Canada to Greenland, including Iceland, Spitsbergen and Novaya Zemlya. Polytypic: nominate *hyperboreus* occurs Eurasia and North America; *barrovianus* Alaska; *pallidissimus* eastern Siberia. Classification of paler Icelandic and Greenland birds questionable, perhaps as separate *leuceretes* or 'Greenland Glaucous Gull' (Gantlett 1998).

E H Rodd made no mention of Glaucous Gull in the islands but knew it as an occasional visitor to mainland Cornwall at irregular intervals, pointing out that a 'fine large bird of this species' in his collection was obtained in Mount's Bay, west Cornwall, during early April 1872 (Rodd 1880). According to James Clark and E H Rodd's nephew Francis, first and second Scillonian records involved a young female shot at Pentle Bay, Tresco, by veteran gamekeeper David Smith in 1874, and one shot by T A Dorrien-Smith at Carn Near, also Tresco, in 1885 (Clark & Rodd 1906).

Surprisingly, Penhallurick (1969) could trace only ten records of this species on Scilly up until 1967, latest dates being 16th May and 16th June. Unlike mainland Cornwall, where all records at least until the mid-1960s involved single individuals, on Scilly up to three birds had been recorded as being loosely associated, as on Tresco in May 1924. The most recorded in any one year appears to have been seven during early 1967, the earliest being an immature on St Mary's on 20th January and the last two seen off the Western Isles on 29th March.

Since the mid-1970s, Glaucous Gull has become almost annual on Scilly, though occurring during spring in just six of the ten years since 1990, though in two cases birds still present from the previous autumn were involved. In autumn, it appeared in seven years since 1990, with 14 birds occurring at an average of 1.4 per year for the full ten years. The latest obvious spring departure date was 10th May, though a first-winter individual on St Helen's for one day in mid-June 1999 was also presumably moving through the islands. The earliest autumn arrival date was 26th September, though in some years none arrived until December. Interestingly, three out of four that arrived during December were the only individuals remaining into the following year – 30th December on St Martin's until 10th February, 31st December in Tresco Channel until 25th January, and 14th December in The Roads until 31st January. Only one individual was reported from the RMV *Scillonian III* during routine crossings to and from Cornwall, this involving an unaged bird seen on 12th September 1992. Out of the total of 22 birds, 73% were aged as first-year or first-winter, 4.5% as first-summer and 14% as second-summer (see Chart). An adult was found dead on Tresco on 12th March 1995 and two remain unclassified, including the bird seen from *Scillonian III*. The June 1999 individual was not unique, with at least two other June sightings involving birds in flight over St Mary's Quay on 16th June 1947 and over Lower Moors, St Mary's on 16th June 1977; the similarity of these dates is noteworthy. Nevertheless, at least two of these June individuals were aged as first-year or first-winter, which if true would have involved a fairly rapid departure from the natal area and therefore the possibility of incorrect ageing remains.

In the West Palearctic, most Glaucous Gulls winter south only as far as limits set by winter sea-ice, or food availability allow, though vagrants are known to reach the Mediterranean, Caspian and Black Seas.

**Glaucous Gull recorded ages**

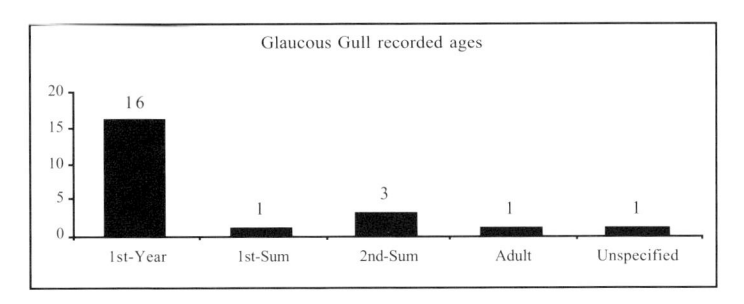

| 1st-Year | 1st-Sum | 2nd-Sum | Adult | Unspecified |
|---|---|---|---|---|
| 16 | 1 | 3 | 1 | 1 |

Adults leave the breeding areas before juveniles, the former commencing their departure by September. This marked delay in the departure of first-years calls into question the ageing of the two recent June Scillonian sightings (see above), whereas many non-breeders remain south of the breeding grounds during summer, some as far as the British Isles.

Gantlett (1998) suggested that paler birds from Iceland and Greenland, sometimes referred to as *leuceretes*, or 'Greenland Glaucous Gull', probably occur in Britain as vagrants and that the darker and longer-winged Alaskan *barrovianus* might also occur. However, no observer appears to have commented on the likelihood of hybrid Glaucous x Herring Gull *L. argentatus* occurring in Scilly, though they certainly occur elsewhere in Britain and Ireland and the possibility needs bearing in mind when examining any *hyperboreus*-type gulls in Scilly. Nevertheless, Dean (1984) drew attention to apparent regional differences in the abundance of these hybrids within Britain and it may be that Scilly falls outside their expected 'range'. A comment appears in *CBWPSAR* 17 regarding the shooting of four Glaucous Gulls during winter 1947, though no details are provided and it is unclear whether the early or late winter period was involved. A mounted and cased skin in Tresco's Island Hotel presumably involves either one of these four or one of two shot on Tresco during 1874 and 1885. No Glaucous Gulls have been ringed on Scilly and there are no recaptures of birds from elsewhere.

# Great Black-backed Gull *Larus marinus* A

**Breeding resident plus probable migrant and winter visitor.**

Breeds coastal North Atlantic, from northern France through Britain, Ireland, Fennoscandia, Spitsbergen, Iceland and Greenland to northeast North America. Mainly migratory in north but dispersive in south, to about 40°N. Monotypic. National 22% decline 1994–99 (Bashford & Noble 2000).

About 800 pairs currently breed on 38 islands, making this the most widespread, though not the most abundant breeding seabird in Scilly. It has experienced a 50% decline since a mid-1970's peak of nearly 1,600 pairs; large breeding concentrations, particularly on Annet, are an important feature of this species in Scilly.

Earliest mention of Great Black-backed Gull in the islands seems to be North's (1850) observation that it annually bred on the high rocks of Gorregan in the Western Isles, though he provided no information on numbers. Next mention was E H Rodd's comment that it was generally seen singly or in pairs (Rodd 1870a) and by the early 20th century James Clark and Rodd's nephew Francis felt able to describe it as 'resident but in limited numbers'. Their additional comment, however, suggested that it may in fact have been extremely limited: 'Eleven nests found in 1903, including eight on Menawethan, one on Great Ganilly, one on Little Ganinick and one on Inner

Innisvouls. Several birds were frequenting the Western Islands, but no nests were noticed' (Clark & Rodd 1906). By 1999 the first of these four islands alone held 63 pairs, with 20 on Great Ganilly, 32 on Little Ganinick and 50 on Great (Inner) Innisvouls. Noticeably, Clark and Rodd made no mention of Annet, which at around 140 pairs now holds the greatest local concentration.

It also seems clear from what E H Rodd had to say that it was not frequent on mainland Cornwall during the mid-19th century, i.e. 'not a common species on the Cornish coast, one or two may be seen at almost any season of the year about the cliffs and the open sands'. He added that, unlike most other gulls, it was usually observed singly or in pairs (Rodd 1880), and to further emphasise its precarious status, noted it only at Hayle, Marazion and Land's End in west Cornwall, plus Scilly, specimens also being procured in Falmouth Harbour.

According to Parslow (1967a), Great Black-backed Gull underwent a very marked and widespread increase in Britain from about 1880, involving an almost threefold increase in some island populations between 1930 and 1956, though the same author (Parslow 1965c) thought this a possible underestimate. He also suggested that the Scillonian increase commenced from 1890, whilst earlier C J King (1924) thought the 200 pairs in the 1920s compared with just 20 in 1890. This last author mentioned two colonies of over 50 nests each and suggested that there were few islands by that time where Great Black-backs did not now mix with other gulls *Larus* during the breeding season. And certainly by the mid-1940s, Ryves & Quick (1946) thought it bred abundantly.

Published all-island count data for Scilly as a whole are charted, showing an increase from 1924 up until 1974, though with huge gaps in the data. However, from a peak of 1,600 pairs in 1974, the population underwent a 50% reduction by the late 1990s, though Annet counts showed a post-1974 decrease in the order of 64%; presumably indicating that losses here were greater than for Scilly generally, or that there was a redistribution of pairs to other colonies. Interestingly, therefore, in 1978 the then Nature Conservancy Council carried out a control of Great Black-backed Gulls on Annet, the number of breeding pairs being reduced by some 35% on the preceding year (*IOSBR* 1978). It seems unlikely, however, that this action was primarily responsible for the subsequent long-term reduction in counts on that island, though at least one unauthorised control was carried out subsequently. In comparison, Lesser Black-backed Gull *L. fuscus* numbers on Annet actually increased between 1974 and the early 1990s. Lloyd *et al.* (1991) listed just eight British or Irish Great Black-backed Gull breeding sites in excess of 300 pairs, of these only Scilly sites were south of the Scottish northern coastline. Importantly, the 1999 Scillonian population of 808 pairs represents something in the order of 4% of the recent UK estimate of 20,000 pairs (Stone *et al.* 1997) and 3.4% of the total recorded during the 1985–87 British and Irish survey (Lloyd *et al.* 1991). In European terms, the Scillonian population comprises in the order of 0.5% or less overall (Heath *et al.* 2000).

| Island | Nests | Island | Nests |
|---|---|---|---|
| St Martin's | 3 | Northwethel | 18 |
| Shipman Head, Bryher | 13 | Foremans Island | 1 |
| Gugh | 3 | Hedge Rock | 2 |
| Samson | 5 | Peashopper Island | 1 |
| Annet | 137 | Crow Island | 3 |
| Melledgan | 28 | Half-tide Rock | 1 |
| Rosevean | 1 | Pernagie Island | 11 |
| Rosevear | 95 | White Island, St Martin's | 2 |
| Mincarlo | 23 | Guther's Island | 29 |
| Illiswilgig | 12 | Great Ganinick | 21 |
| Maiden Bower | 1 | Little Ganinick | 32 |
| Castle Bryher | 2 | Little Ganilly | 20 |
| Scilly Rock | 1 | Great & Little Arthur | 34 |
| Gweal | 62 | Ragged Island | 18 |
| White Island, Samson | 39 | Great Ganilly | 32 |
| Puffin Island | 2 | Nornour | 6 |
| Round Island | 5 | Great Innisvouls | 50 |
| St Helen's | 6 | Little Innisvouls | 10 |
| Tean & Pednbrose | 16 | Menawethan | 63 |

**Locations of 808 Great Black-backed Gull Nests – 1999 (Seabird 2000 data)**

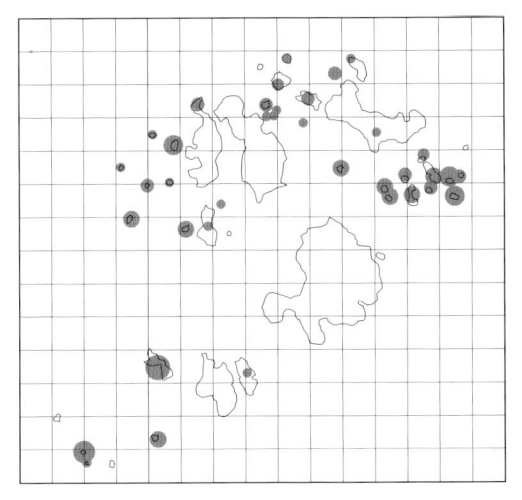

**Great Black-backed Gull Breeding Distribution – 1999 (data Seabird 2000)**

Although a few pairs still breed on what E H Rodd described as the highest rocks, as on the east side of White Island, St Martin's, most are now concentrated close to sea level, e.g. the 100-plus pairs on Annet. Most Great Black-backed Gull nests on Annet are currently distributed around the edges of that island's northern portion, particularly the western section south of Carn Irish, though formerly many more were spread out across the Thrift *Armeria maritima* carpet of the slightly more elevated northern plateau (C Nicholas pers. comm.).

C J King discussed Great Black-backed Gull feeding behaviour in the vicinity of other breeding seabirds, graphically describing how 'It makes havoc amongst the Puffins (*Fratercula arctica*) and the Shearwaters (*Puffinus puffinus*), and at the end of the nesting season leaves the whole district in a repulsive condition, strewn with the dead bodies of birds which it has slain and partly consumed' (C J King 1924). He also described how, apart from Great Black-back's normal behaviour with prey, he had witnessed them dropping recently captured Puffins onto rocks from 'a couple of hundred feet (60 m)'. The same authority quoted local lobster fishermen as having watched them attacking and taking Razorbills *Alca torda* from the surface of the water, though he could not claim to have seen this himself. Likewise, the author has never seen or heard of this happening within the islands more recently. However, a noticeable feature of Annet and Rosevear during late summer are the remains of large numbers of young Shags *Phalacrocorax aristotelis* killed by Great Black-backed Gulls, birds of even this size being turned inside out with apparent ease. Nevertheless, perhaps only a few 'specialist' gulls are involved as the predation usually appears confined to discrete groups of Shag nests. And in any event, on Annet, as elsewhere in Scilly, Shags have apparently adapted to black-backed gull predation, the vast majority now breeding within the boulder beaches, or in holes at the base of Scilly's low cliffs. These nest sites usually have only a single entrance, which the adult Shags appear more than capable of defending against attempted gull predation, most losses seemingly involving mobile or unattended young close to fledging.

Various writers besides King commented on Great Black-backed predation of Puffins, Manx Shearwaters and Storm Petrels *Hydrobates pelagicus* on Annet, most expressing concern over possible adverse effects on local populations of these three species. Interestingly, although Gurney, who visited Annet in May 1887, commented at length on the shearwater population, he made no mention of Great Black-backed Gull predation, regardless of his attention to all other details. In contrast, several early 20th century commentators, e.g. H W Robinson (1911a), Wallis (1923, 1924) and Walpole Bond (1937) all remarked at length on what they saw as the undesirable consequences of observed levels of Great Black-backed predation should it be allowed to continue.

Parslow pointed out that Great Black-backed Gulls were first recorded killing petrels on Annet in June 1914 (*Wildlife* 8: 269–279), observers finding a small number of petrel remains among a far greater number of Puffin and Manx Shearwater (Parslow 1965c). Parslow also suggested a direct correlation on Annet between an increased number of gull pellets containing Storm Petrel remains and the increase of breeding Great Black-backed Gulls on that island, noting in particular its spread to the southern half of Annet during the mid-1960s, adjacent to some of the main petrel breeding beaches. Although Parslow thought there was no evidence that Great Black-backed Gull predation caused the extinction of petrels from the small island of Rosevear, 'no other possible explanation comes to mind or fits the facts so well' (Parslow 1965c). However, early data on number of petrels on Rosevear were never obtained, or if so were not published, and the 19th century concept of this as the main Scillonian breeding site may have been formulated amidst a lack of appreciation that substantial numbers of petrels bred on Annet. In addition, construction crews from the Bishop Rock Lighthouse lived on Rosevear for some ten years during the mid-1980s and seem bound to have had an adverse effect on any breeding petrels. Therefore, arguments that Great Black-backed Gulls caused declines in any breeding seabird species in Scilly have yet to be established, although this has not prevented the occasional individual or group visiting the breeding islands and carrying out impromptu culls. Organised egg-pricking 'parties' were another regular feature of the not-so-distant past, with an apparent high proportion of the human population of the islands also involved in the collection of eggs for domestic use (Vyvyan 1953). Species involved including the other two large *Larus* gulls and perhaps even other seabirds.

A 1976 Great Black-backed Gull winter count produced a total of 1,200–1,500 individuals (*IOSBR* 1976). However, the only recent co-ordinated all-island non-breeding season count involved the two-day late January 1997 Winter Shorebird Survey, when 656 were recorded, most being fairly evenly distributed between Tresco, Bryher and Samson, at 186, 185 and 158 respectively. St Mary's had the next highest total with 84, whilst St Martin's held 38 and St Agnes just five. Importantly, in examining the significance of wintering wader populations in Scilly, Lock (1999) suggested that populations of wintering Great and Lesser Black-backed Gulls might also be nationally important, the individual site criterion for Great Black-backed Gull having more recently been set at 500. And in the absence, yet, of the national Seabird 2000 results, the current breeding season total of around 800 Great Black-backed Gull pairs amounts to over 4.2% of the stated British population of 18,900 pairs quoted by Lloyd *et al.* (1991). However, if account is taken of a more recently estimated 22% British decline (Bashford & Noble 2000), the Scillonian figure advances to perhaps 5.4%. Similarly, the figure of 19,000 pairs suggested by Stone *et al.* (1997) for the UK as a whole also suggests that Scilly may hold something in the order of 4.2% of breeding UK Great Black-backed Gulls.

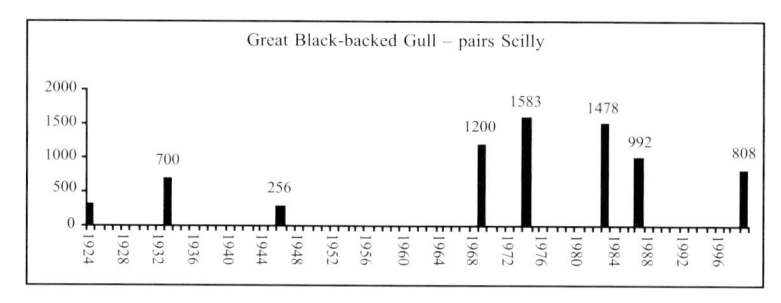

**Data Sources**: 1924 = Allen 1974–77; 1933 = Allen 1974–77; 1946 = Penhallurick 1969; 1969 = Lloyd *et al.* 1991; 1974 = Allen 1974–77; 1983 = P Harvey 1983; 1987 = Birkin & Smith 1987; 1999 Seabird 2000 – unpublished data.

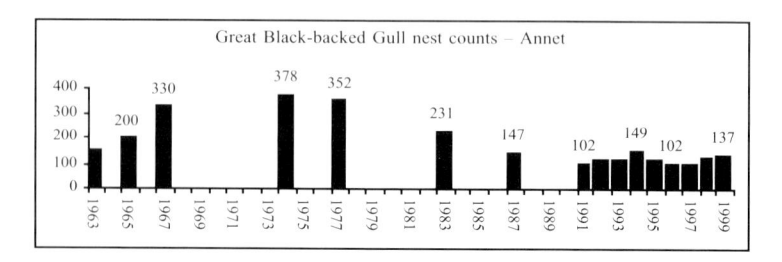

**Data Sources**: 1963 = Allen 1974–77; 1965 = Allen 1974–77; 1974 = Allen 1974–77; 1977 = Allen 1974–77; 1978 = *IOSBR* 1978; 1983 = P Harvey 1983; 1987 = Birkin & Smith 1987; 1990–92 = P J Robinson 1992b; 1993 = P J Robinson 1993; 1994–95 = P J Robinson 1995a; 1996 = Wagstaff 1996; 1997 = Wagstaff 1997; 1998 = P J Robinson 1998; 1999 Seabird 2000 – unpublished data.

Great Black-backed and the two other British large gulls breed on buildings as close to Scilly as Newlyn and St Ives, both in west Cornwall, but although some 3–5 pairs of Herring Gulls *L. argentatus* now do so regularly on St Mary's, no Great Black-backs have yet bred there. Nevertheless, 1–2 pairs have recently shown signs of doing so in the near future, e.g. in the vicinity of the Town Hall (pers. obs.). A pulli spirit specimen in the British Museum (Natural History) collection, reference 1924.6.25 and dated 25th June

1924, is attributed to H W Robinson, who carried out work on this and other seabird species in Scilly during the very early 20th century. Compared to the other two large gulls occurring regularly in Scilly, the likelihood of confusion with other species is limited. Nevertheless, Pineau *et al. (Birding World* 14: 110–111) drew attention to the presence in coastal North Africa of the closely similar Kelp Gull *L. dominicanus*, a southern species which now breeds in West Africa north at least as far as Senegal and which is thought capable of penetrating well into the West Palearctic. This species therefore has an outside chance of reaching Scilly and should be kept in mind.

A total of 1,254 Great Black-backed Gulls had been ringed on Scilly up until 1999, 856 prior to 1970 and most as pulli. There are no controls from elsewhere but the Table shows eleven recoveries of Scillonian-ringed birds, involving a fairly random dispersal of first- or second-winter individuals, as far as Spain (1), France (5), Kent (1) and southwest Ireland (2), plus two more locally. In the absence of any ringed individuals from elsewhere, there is little to indicate whether all birds within the islands belong exclusively to the local population, or whether mixed-age wintering or summering flocks include birds from other areas. Northerly populations are more migratory than those further south, birds reaching as far as the coasts of Spain and Portugal, young birds tending to travel furthest (Cramp *et al.* 1977–94). In the more northerly colonies, post-fledging dispersal commences from August, adults moving south from September or October, and although return passage occurs from March or April, many, perhaps most, immatures summer coastally between wintering and summering areas. Like Herring Gull, this species shows a clear tendency for more birds from southwest England to reach western France during winter than from elsewhere in England and Ireland (Wernham *et al.* 2002). A proportion of birds wintering in western England and Ireland are thought likely to originate from the Faeroes or Iceland, whereas many, perhaps most, wintering in eastern England come from arctic Norway and extreme northwest Russia (Wernham *et al.* 2002).

**Recoveries**

| | | | | | |
|---|---|---|---|---|---|
| AJ32280 | Pul | Rosevear 30th June 1961 | ? | St Guenole, Finistere, France 21st December 1961 | |
| 417873 | ? | Rosevear 28th June 1962 | ? | Minster, Isle of Sheppey, Kent 20th February 1963 | |
| 425680 | ? | Rosevear 22nd June 1964 | ? | Ile de Sein, Finistere, France 2nd October 1964 | |
| 425744 | Pul | Annet 27th June 1964 | ? | Penmarch, Finistere, France 15th October 1964 | |
| 425687 | Pul | Rosevear 22nd June 1964 | FD | St Guenole, Finistere, France 4th November 1965 | |
| HW00680 | Pul | Rosevear 29th June 1966 | FD | Le Lock, Finistere, France 19th January 1967 | |
| HW00791 | Pul | Annet 4th July 1967 | SH | Fuenterrabia, Spain 6th January 1968 | |
| HT54298 | Pul | Annet 7th July 1994 | FD | Praa Sands, Cornwall 9th January 1996 | |
| HT62044 | Pul | Annet 12th June 1996 | FD | North Slob, Wexford, Ireland 13th October 1996 | |
| HT62125 | Pul | Gweal 20th June 1996 | FD | Raven Wood, Wexford, Ireland 16th April 1998 | |
| HT62101 | Pul | Illiswilgig 19th June 1996 | FR | Newlyn, Cornwall 1st May 1998 | |

Great Black-Backed Gull Ringing Recaptures

# Kittiwake (Black-legged Kittiwake) *Rissa tridactyla* A

**Summer visitor, migrant and winter visitor.**

Breeds North Atlantic, in Iberia, France, Britain and Ireland, Russian Arctic islands, Greenland, northeast Canada, Newfoundland and Gulf of St Lawrence, also North Pacific. Dispersive in winter, occupying North Atlantic south to about 30°N, plus North Pacific, pre-breeders largely pelagic. Polytypic: nominate *tridactyla* occurs North Atlantic; *pollicaris* North Pacific. Upgraded from Green- to Amber-listed in UK 2002: 50% or more of breeding population at ten or fewer sites (Gregory *et al.* 2002).

Less than 300 pairs currently breed on five islands, three of which are inhabited, birds are also seen in varying numbers at other times.

Surprisingly, E H Rodd made no mention of Kittiwake breeding in mainland Cornwall, though he considered it did so 'in numbers' on Scilly's cliffs. Nevertheless, he thought it the commonest seabird on the Cornish coasts after Black-headed Gull *Larus ridibundus*, both adults and subadults entering harbours and estuaries during autumn (Rodd 1880).

Far more helpful is the summary by James Clark and Rodd's nephew Francis (Clark & Rodd 1906), who pointed out that since 1901 it failed to breed in the islands, though it formerly did so commonly. They also drew attention to former large breeding numbers on Menawethan in the Eastern Isles, as detailed in a letter from Jenkinson (presumably the Reverend J H) of 1852, before birds gradually relocated to exposed Gorregan in the Western Isles. This last remained the favoured breeding location in Scilly until just three nests could be found in 1900, up to 100 having been previously recorded there, though numbers steadily diminished from the 1870s. Interestingly, Clark and Rodd were nonetheless of the opinion that small flocks were seen from time to time during summer, suggestive perhaps of breeding elsewhere, ending with the comment that it was often seen during winter but that at all times of the year it seemed commoner between Land's End and Scilly than within the islands.

Earlier doubts over the presence of breeding Kittiwakes in mainland Cornwall seem to have been unjustified. Penhallurick (1969) pointed out that even by the late 1830s Yarrell knew of active colonies, whilst by the 1880s Lord Lilford knew of sites on the south coast. And it appears to have been present in the county ever since, with an estimated 515 pairs at three or more sites in 1999 (*CBWPSAR* 69).

Exactly when Kittiwake recommenced breeding on Scilly remains unclear, though in 1938 G H Harvey and others observed six nesting pairs on rugged Man-a-Vaur in the Northern Isles, noting too that at least one nest contained eggs. By 1949 birds were present at three sites on Gorregan plus a party of non-breeding Kittiwakes were observed on isolated Hanjague at Scilly's eastern extremity, where they had not previously been recorded (*CBWPSAR* 18), though nothing seems to have come of this last incident. By the mid-1950s, birds were nesting annually on both Gorregan and Men-a-Vaur and we have the benefit of one full count on Men-a-Vaur, Ron Simmons recording 258 nests in early July 1958, usefully pointing out too that although none contained three eggs, about one third did so the previous year (*CBWPSAR* 28). In 1959 came a report of a new site on the north face of St Helen's, facing nearby Men-a-Vaur, nests on Gorregan being seemingly down in number that same year. With the notable exception of Gorregan, most pairs up until the mid-1960s were concentrated in the north of the island group, followed by a period during which colonies were spread throughout the islands, before the Kittiwake centre of gravity shifted to the middle of the archipelago.

# Gulls

| | 38 | 39 | 40 | 41 | 42 | 43 | 44 | 45 | 46 | 47 | 48 | 49 | 50 | 51 | 52 | 53 | 54 | 55 | 56 | 57 | 58 |
|---|---|---|---|---|---|---|---|---|---|---|---|---|---|---|---|---|---|---|---|---|---|
| Gorregan | | | | | | | | 25 | 47 | F | | P- | | | 36 | | 55 | P | | | |
| Men-a-Vaur | 6 | P | | | | | | P | | | | | | | P- | P | P- | P- | | P | 258 |
| St Helen's | | | | | | | | | | | | | | | | | | | | | |
| Daymark | | | | | | | | | | | | | | | | | | | | | |

| | 59 | 60 | 61 | 62 | 63 | 64 | 65 | 66 | 67 | 68 | 69 | 70 | 71 | 72 | 73 | 74 | 75 | 76 | 77 | 78 | 79 |
|---|---|---|---|---|---|---|---|---|---|---|---|---|---|---|---|---|---|---|---|---|---|
| Gorregan | 50 | | | P | | 66 | | P | 91 | | | | | | P | 112 | | | | | |
| Men-a-Vaur | | 200 | | | P | | | | | + | 100 | | | | | P | 166 | | | | |
| St Helen's | 12 | 21 | 45 | P+ | 60 | 82 | 100 | - | 120 | | | | 60 | 80F | P | 43 | | | | | |
| Annet | | | | | | 2 | | P | | 28 | | | | | P | | | | 15 | 20 | |
| Daymark | | | | | | | | P | 20 | | | | | | 43 | | 104 | | | | |
| Rosevean | | | | | | | | | 1 | | | | 14 | | | 22 | | | | | |
| White Island** | | | | | | | | | | | | | | | | 51 | | | 74 | 75 | |

| | 80 | 81 | 82 | 83 | 84 | 85 | 86 | 87 | 88 | 89 | 90 | 91 | 92 | 93 | 94 | 95 | 96 | 97 | 98 | 99 |
|---|---|---|---|---|---|---|---|---|---|---|---|---|---|---|---|---|---|---|---|---|
| Gorregan | | | 124 | F | | | | 32 | | | | 5 | 14 | 10 | 18 | 3 | | | | |
| Men-a-Vaur | | | 128 | | | | F | | | | | 1 | 30 | 1 | | | | P | | |
| St Helen's | | 65 | 85 | | | | | 2 | | | | | | | | | | P | 7 | |
| Daymark | | 349 | | 292 | F | | 26 | 124 | D | D | | 46 | 56 | 13 | 17 | 10 | 6 | 3 | 10 | 27 |
| Annet | | | 46 | | | | | 27 | | | 43 | 36 | 29 | 8 | | | | | | |
| White Island | | 42 | 49 | | | | | 63 | D | | | | 8 | 1 | | | | | | |
| Shipman Head | | | 137 | | | | 10 | 84 | | 392 | | P | P | 31 | 19 | 9 | | | | |
| Gugh | | | | | | | 100 | 206 | P | | 115 | 110 | 109 | 125 | 118 | 119 | 145 | 182 | 136 | 155 |
| Samson South | | | | | | | 8 | 46 | P | 68 | 116 | F | 82 | 57 | 43 | 39 | 25 | 21 | 13 | 10 |
| Samson North | | | | | | | | | | | | | 8 | 13 | 32 | 22 | 37 | 23 | 28 | |
| Tresco Gimble Porth | | | | | | | | | | | | 3 | 8 | 20 | 35 | 42 | 56 | 48 | 54 | |

**Numbers of Reported Kittiwake Nests in the 20th Century by Island/Year. P present; F site failed; D colony deserted, + no published count but reported increase; - no published count but reported decrease; ** White Island, St Martin's**

Note: lack of data reflects a lack of annual published information and does not necessarily imply absence from the site.

As apparent from the Table, most Scillonian breeding sites lack long-term stability and though reasons for this are unclear it seems largely linked to annual site success or failure. New site occupation normally follows complete failure of an existing site and is seemingly triggered by the same-year relocation of failed breeders, some apparently building basic replacement nests, reoccupation of the new site the following spring being almost guaranteed, normally accompanied by the near or total abandonment of the failed site. Nevertheless, a lack of colour-marked individuals within the Scillonian population creates difficulties determining whether post-failure nest structures are in fact 'frustration nests' built by failed adults, or the efforts of pre-breeders.

Reasons for annual site failures vary, but are perhaps mostly due to weather and/or food-related causes. However, also involved have been nest predation by Brown Rats *Rattus norvegicus* (P J Robinson 1992b), Great Black-backed Gull *Larus marinus* (P J Robinson 1993), cats *Felis catus* (P J Robinson 1998) and, allegedly, Carrion Crows *Corvus corone* or Ravens *C. corax* (*IOSBR* 1984, 1986). In addition, a contributing factor at some sites may be their geological unsuitability. Another factor blamed for breeding failure is disturbance by birdwatchers and photographers, which allegedly facilitates predation by Herring Gulls *L. argentatus* (*IOSBR* 1971), although, interestingly, during the nine years 1991–99 not a single known incidence of Herring Gull interaction was recorded at any Scillonian Kittiwake nest. Nevertheless, there were a small number of incidents of Great Black-backed and, possibly, Lesser Black-backed Gull *L. fuscus* predation of both eggs and young. Known cat predation of Kittiwake nests during the ten years from 1991 was confined to Gugh, where one or more animals gained access to the upper ledges of the colony during 1998 (P J Robinson 1998) and perhaps 1999.

Kittiwakes can be seen occupying their breeding ledges from February onwards, particularly during good weather. The Gugh site suffers serious rat predation during some years, a situation not helped by the ease with which these animals can gain access to the numerous earth and rock ledges. In an attempt to limit rat access and to also test the feasibility of providing Scillonian Kittiwakes with additional, or alternative, less accessible nest sites, a small number of artificial ledges were excavated by the author on a vertical earth cliff in the Gugh colony during early 1992 and 1993. One of these ledges was occupied by a prospecting pair of Kittiwakes in July 1992 and over the following three years all were occupied by pairs that subsequently reared young.

The Chart incorporates all known Kittiwake counts and reveals a clear long-term increase from its reappearance in the islands in the 1900s up until the late 1960s, followed by a more rapid decline, to around 300 pairs by 1999. Reasons for these Scillonian changes are still poorly understood, but Lloyd *et al.* (1991) considered the long-term national increase attributable to a cessation of both human hunting pressures and egg-collecting, though they thought food supplies undoubtedly also played a part and suggested links with the parallel expansion of the fishing industry around Britain and Ireland during the 1940s. However, the same authors drew attention to the problems of over-exploitation of British sandeel *Ammodytes* stocks since the 1980s, which they knew to have resulted in widespread and greatly reduced Kittiwake productivity, particularly in northern Britain. On the other hand, reductions in the number of breeding Kittiwakes in southeast Ireland from the 1970s were thought attributable to declines in local Herring *Clupea harengus* stocks (Lloyd *et al.* 1991) and each of these theories fits the timing of the Scillonian Kittiwake increase and decline. The 1987 total of 585 pairs/nests amounted to approximately 10% of the population of southwest England (Lloyd *et al.* 1991).

Since 1991, a proportion of Scillonian Kittiwake nests have been individually marked for comparative study using numbered plastic labels, mostly on Gugh, Samson and Tresco. All Scillonian Kittiwake nests are positioned on the relatively low earth and boulder cliffs and perhaps for related geological reasons are mostly positioned above boulder beaches, which in turn are mostly above the reach of high spring tides. These same boulder beaches also usually accommodate breeding Herring or, less often, Lesser Black-backed Gulls. Owing to the limited height of Scillonian cliffs almost all nests are accessible for annual inspection, most without the use of a ladder. Indeed, nests are often positioned just a metre above the surface of the boulder beach and not infrequently the same distance from the nearest Herring Gull nest.

Approximately 80–90% of nests are positioned on protruding boulders, rather than earth ledges, presumably because they provide a more suitable support and whilst most are constructed substantially of seaweed, there are at least two recorded sightings of birds visiting Tresco's freshwater pools to gather nest material. The first of these was in June 1958 when Hilda Quick saw four to five individuals around the edge of Abbey Pool apparently plucking weed, though they were not seen to fly away with it (*CBWPSAR* 28). The second incident occurred two years later, the observer witnessing 'much carrying of mud from Abbey Pool' involving 'quite a noticeable traffic' (*CBWPSAR* 30). Although the Kittiwake colony or colonies involved were not stated, only nearby St Helen's and Men-a-Vaur and the much more distant Gorregan were recorded as active breeding sites that year (see Table). Eggs are laid in the majority of nests that are built.

In the single observed incident of Great Black-backed Gull predation, a subadult was observed removing eggs from nests in the Samson South colony (P J Robinson 1993), though large gulls were also suspected of predating small to medium-sized Kittiwake young at a Samson site in two years. In 1991, most nests, already containing well-grown young, were washed off the cliffs by torrential overnight rain during July. Samson has been rat-free since the removal of these animals during winters 1991–92 and 1992–93 (P J Robinson 1992c). However, on Gugh, which throughout the 1990s held the greatest Kittiwake breeding concentration, Brown Rats were kept in check by the limited application of proprietary rat poison (warfarin). Any absence of both adults due to difficulties in obtaining adequate food supplies apparently leaves even quite large young vulnerable to predation.

First-laying date varies between years, perhaps advancing during a run of successful years, or being earlier at larger colonies. Coulson & White (1958) suggested a figure of 70% two-egg clutches for their study colony and, as most Scillonian females lay two eggs, that may not be far off the Scillonian figure, mean clutch size being around 1.6 to 1.9 (P J Robinson 1993; P J Robinson unpublished data). The remaining 30% comprised a mix of one and three-egg clutches, the latter being something of a rarity.

During the ten years 1991–99, three-egg clutches were not recorded until 1993, one each on Gugh and Samson (P J Robinson 1993), with none in 1994 and never more than seven in any year. Coulson and White found three-egg clutches were laid by older, more experienced females, the percentage involved being used to measure the 'health' of a breeding colony. The same authors pointed out that although the average clutch size laid by any given species normally results in maximum productivity, three-egg Kittiwake clutches produce 1.5 times more young, regardless of their scarcity. The apparent anomaly is explained by the fact that only experienced female Kittiwakes lay three eggs, whereas both experienced and inexperienced individuals lay two. Interestingly, even in the 1950s, Hilda Quick thought that Scillonian Kittiwake laying dates were much later than on mainland Cornwall, e.g. at Morvah (*CBWPSAR* 22) and others have expressed similar views (e.g. J Coulson *in litt.*). There is, too, wide variation in the annual level of productivity, both between years and between sites (P J Robinson 1993, 1994, 1995), from close to or perhaps even complete failure, to approaching one young per total number of nests involved. Any between-year variation in productivity tends to reflect events during the nestling phase as most eggs hatch in most years.

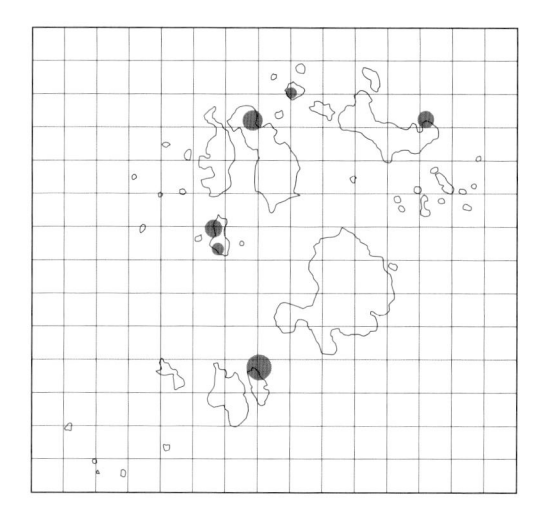

| Island | Nests |
| --- | --- |
| St Martin's | 27 |
| Tresco | 54 |
| Gugh | 155 |
| Samson | 38 |
| St Helen's | 7 |

**Locations of 281 Kittiwake Nests – 1999 (Seabird 2000 data)**

**Kittiwake Breeding Distribution – 1999 (data Seabird 2000)**

Post-fledging dispersal commences from July–August, ringing data revealing that the extent of autumn dispersal from coastal European waters increases with age up to three years, though birds remain mostly within the north Atlantic and adjoining waters. Birds move 1,200 km on average during their first autumn but reach 2,800 km by year three, then drop to 800 km by year four, comparable with adult dispersal. Birds first enter the breeding colonies from around year three, most males returning to the natal colony, and more females than males move to new breeding sites, though established breeders rarely if ever move to a new colony (Wooler & Coulson 1977, in Cramp *et al.* 1977–94).

A total of 1,282 Kittiwakes had been ringed on Scilly up until 1999, 1,154 (90%) since 1970, mostly as pulli and most since 1991, largely explaining just two pre-1990 recoveries. The six controls and nine recoveries provide an interesting overview of Scillonian Kittiwake movements, with several patterns detectable. Most obvious is the exchange of birds with colonies in northwest France, four hatched in Scilly being later found breeding in Finistere, one for perhaps at least two years, whilst three hatched in Finistere were discovered in Scilly, one of which was apparently breeding. Similarly, two birds ringed as pulli in the Northumbrian Farne Islands were later found breeding in Scilly, one on White Island, St Martin's, in 1975 and one on Annet in 1991. In addition, two colour-ringed individuals seen briefly in colonies during the late 1980s or early 1990s were believed to have originated from Norway (pers. obs.).

Prime contender, however, for Scilly's most unfortunate Kittiwake was the bird ringed on Tresco by the author in June 1999 and found entangled in fishing line in St Peter Port, Channel Islands, two months later. Having been released from this predicament its remains were eventually found in a marten's *Martes* nest in the roof of a Danish bungalow. Amazingly, Scilly's second Danish Kittiwake record came in August that same year. Given Kittiwake's tendency to wander widely outside the breeding season the recovery of birds in eastern Scotland, southwest Ireland, Denmark and off the west coast of North Africa are not unexpected, even the first of these, way back in 1939. The most southerly Scillonian record came from aboard ship between southern Morocco and the Canary Islands and on the face of it seems rather far south for this largely North Atlantic species. However, Cramp *et al.* (1977–94) point out that there is both a north-south and age-related North Atlantic distribution, birds reaching their southernmost limits during their first year, with British birds showing a more southerly distribution. Although British and Irish-reared Kittiwakes disperse randomly outside the breeding season, as far as Greenland, Newfoundland, Iberia and the North Atlantic islands, such movements are more marked among immatures (Wernham *et al.* 2002). In addition, British or Irish-reared birds have been recovered in subsequent breeding seasons from northern Norway and through Denmark south as far as northwest France.

Quick (*CBWPSAR* 22) remarked on the presence of at least one shot individual among several dead Kittiwakes noted on Gorregan during 1952 and the annual destruction of an unknown number of seabirds is known to have been a problem formerly, though hopefully this is no longer so. Worthy of mention, too, is the occasional presence in Scilly, as elsewhere, of Kittiwakes displaying red legs and thought to involve first-summer individuals (J Greenwood 1963). At least one such bird is mentioned in the literature (P J Robinson 1991b), though David Hunt reportedly also saw one about 1980 (W Wagstaff pers. comm.). Both Kittiwakes and Little Gulls *L. minutus* have been recorded feeding in company with Razorbills *Alca torda* (R E Scott 1972; Jones 1975). Scott gained the impression that Little Gulls were taking advantage of small fish driven to the surface by the feeding auks. In Scilly, one to two Kittiwakes are occasionally seen associating with feeding Razorbills, but it is difficult to know whether they are intent on robbery, or are merely feeding off the 'by-catch' (pers. obs.). R Harding (1959) described Kittiwakes apparently attacking feeding Grey Seals *Halichoerus grypus*, but despite a healthy Grey Seal population in Scillonian waters, no such Kittiwake behaviour has been noted.

Outside the breeding season, Kittiwakes occur in and around the islands in greater or lesser numbers, single-day autumn, winter or spring counts normally remaining around 100 or less, though this can vary tremendously, as in early April 1978 when 3,500 to 5,000 were recorded (*IOSBR* 1978), or in mid-January 1998 when about 1,000 presumably storm-blown birds were in The Roads (*IOSBR* 1998). However, reports of 100 per hour passing various vantage points, e.g. in October 1984, could have involved even greater numbers had the duration of the seawatch been stated.

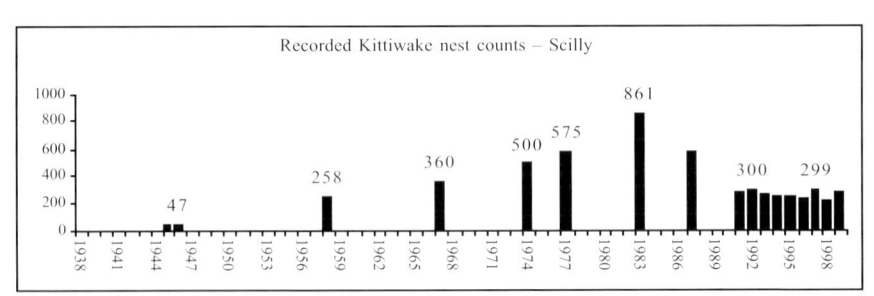

Recorded Kittiwake nest counts – Scilly

**Data Sources**: 1945–46 = Penhallurick 1969; 1958 = Penhallurick 1969; 1967 = Penhallurick 1969; 1974 = Allen 1974–77; 1977 = Allen 1974–77; 1983 = P Harvey 1983; 1987 = Birkin & Smith 1987; 1990–92 = P J Robinson 1992b; 1993 = P J Robinson 1993; 1994–95 = P J Robinson 1995a; 1996–98 = P J Robinson 1998; 1999 Seabird 2000 – unpublished data.

**Controls**

| | | |
|---|---|---|
| ED75271 | Pul | Farne Islands 5th July 1969 |
| EB91984 | Pul | Farne Islands 4th July 1980 |
| FT85755 | Pul | An Aoteriou, Finistere, France 17th June 1983 |
| EJ26864 | Pul | Farne Islands 16th June 1984 |
| FS19015 | Pul | Cape Sizun, Finistere, France 9th July 1991 |
| ? | ? | Brittany 1998 |

FR White Island, St Martin's 4th April 1975
FR Annet 28th June 1991

FR Samson 24th May 1990
FR St Agnes 25th May 1988

FR Daymark, St Martin's 13th July 1992
FR Men-a-Vaur 8th June 1999

### Recoveries

| | | | | | |
|---|---|---|---|---|---|
| ? | Ad | 'Scilly' 22nd May 1938 | FD | St Andrews, Fife 11th August 1939 | |
| EN58921 | Pul | Gugh 31st July 1986 | FR | Cape Sizun, Finistere, France 14th April 1990 | |
| ES19828 | Pul | Samson 4th July 1995 | FD | Glenbeigh, Co. Kerry, Ireland 19th August 1995 | |
| ET10665 | Pul | Gugh 30th June 1997 | AS | El Laâyoune, Western Sahara 14th April 1998 | |
| ES21279 | Pul | Gugh 2nd July 1993 | FR | Point du Raz, Plogoff, Finistere, France 9th July 1998 | |
| | | | CT | Point du Raz, Plogoff, Finistere, France 26th June 1999 | |
| | | | FR | Point du Raz, Plogoff, Finistere, France 11th March 2000 | |
| | | | FR | Point du Raz, Plogoff, Finistere, France 27th January 2001 | |
| ET44251 | Pul | Tresco 8th June 1999 | FI | St Peter Port, Guernsey, Channel Islands 17th August 1999 | |
| | | | FD | Sommerland, Nissum Fjord, Jylland, Denmark 15th February 2000 | |
| ET10598 | Pul | Gugh 9th July 1996 | FR/BR | Karreg Korn, Goulien, Finistere, France 28th May 2000 | |
| | | | FR/BR | Karreg Korn, Goulien, Finistere, France 20th June 2001 | |
| | | | FD | Nr Douarnenez, Finistere, France 1st August 2001 | |
| ET10533 | Pul | Gugh 25th June 1996 | FR | Bulbjerg, Jylland, Denmark 19th August 2000 | |
| ES19816 | Pul | Samson 4th July 1995 | FR/BR | Point de Raz, Plogoff, Finistere, France 30th June 2001 | |

**Kittiwake Ringing Recaptures**

## Ivory Gull *Pagophila eburnea* A BBRC 0%

**Extremely rare vagrant, full written description required by the BBRC.**

1917    One (shot) Scilly January    Penhallurick 1969

Breeds high Arctic, in Greenland, Spitsbergen, Russian Arctic islands and central Canadian Arctic. Despite perhaps deserting breeding areas in winter, remains largely within confines of pack ice. Monotypic.

There is just the single old record involving a bird shot on Scilly in January 1917 (Penhallurick 1969). It was sexed as a male, presumably on dissection, and the mounted skin placed in the Tresco Abbey collection, though it is currently in the Isles of Scilly Museum on St Mary's. The BBRC accepted a total of 44 British and Irish records during the period 1958–99 but there were 76 prior to that time. Therefore, this classic arctic gull appears to have become less frequent as a winter visitor to Britain during the latter half of the 20th century.

Although the complexities of the winter movements of Ivory Gulls in waters north of the Eurasian landmass are still poorly understood, there is growing support for the theory of southward autumn migration off eastern Greenland involving birds from the Eurasian Arctic islands, these perhaps going on to Labrador in northeast North America, as apparently also happens with other seabird species, e.g. Kittiwake *Rissa tridactyla*, Brünnich's Guillemot *Uria lomvia* or Little Auk *Alle alle*. This same movement is considered at least partly responsible for the high incidence of Ivory Gull records in the Faeroe Islands and in Britain and Ireland, in contrast to its rarity elsewhere in Europe (Cramp *et al*. 1977–94).

## Gull-billed Tern *Sterna nilotica* A BBRC 1.8%

Very rare migrant, full written description required by the BBRC, a mid-19th century claim of it having bred in Scilly seems unsupportable.

    1852   One (adult – shot) Tresco May or June   Rodd 1870a; Clark & Rodd 1906
[1967   One Tresco 3rd June] Accepted by BBRC but subsequently withdrawn   *British Birds* 76: 500
    1980   Two Tresco 16th May   *British Birds* 74: 475
    1980   One St Agnes 17th May   *British Birds* 74: 475
    1994   One Gugh 3rd May   *British Birds* 88: 520
    2000   One Lower Moors, St Mary's 10th April   *British Birds* 94: 478
    *2001*   *One St Mary's 3rd September*   *Birding World* 14: 360

Widespread around central latitudes, European populations winter Africa. Polytypic: nominate *nilotica* occurs Europe, North Africa and Middle East to Manchuria; *arenea* and three additional forms North America. Formerly classified as single-species genus *Gelochelidon*, but reclassified as *Sterna* by BOURC July 1996 (BOURC 1997).

In his *A Week at the Land's End*, Blight (1861) named this as one of several tern species the eggs of which could be found 'in other places, and generally in the sand or herbage about the shore'. However, no other 19th century writer suggested that Gull-billed Terns bred in Scilly and the circumstances described by Blight seem wholly unacceptable, as does his claim that Whiskered Tern *Chlidonias hybrida* also bred. Of the five pre-1999 records, one is very old and one was withdrawn by the observer after acceptance by the BBRC.

First mention of Gull-billed Tern in Scilly is contained in E H Rodd's short note to the *Zoologist* entitled 'Occurrence of the Gull-billed Tern (*Sterna Anglica*) at Scilly' (Rodd 1852a). In this he credits the shooting of the bird to the Reverend John Jenkinson, near Tresco Abbey, either at the end of May or the beginning of June 1852. Rodd later aged the bird as an adult (Rodd 1878b) and later still James Clark and Rodd's nephew Francis gave the month as May (Clark & Rodd 1906). E H Rodd also mentioned one shot near St Just, west Cornwall, on or about the 11th July 1872. Next on Scilly, however, and over one hundred years later, was a bird seen over Old Grimsby, Tresco, in June 1967. This was described by David Hunt (*CBWPSAR* 37), but although his description was accepted by the BBRC, David later withdrew the record, even though no explanation was published (*British Birds* 76: 500).

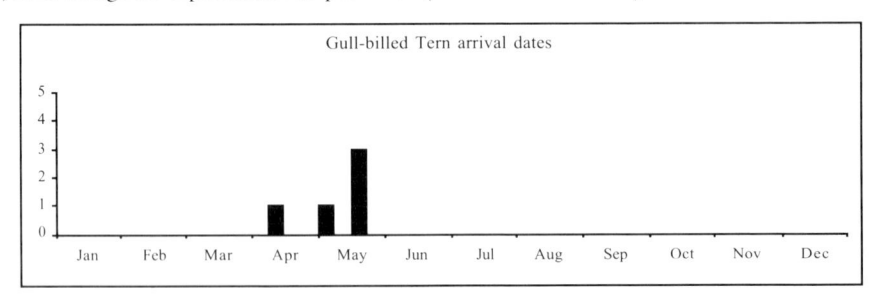

Gull-billed Tern arrival dates

The four remaining arrival dates for accepted records up until 2000 (five birds) were all in spring and disregarding the 19th century incident, for which there is no information, all Scillonian arrivals were present for just one day. These occurred too early for post-breeding dispersal and seem likely to have involved either overshooting migrants from French or Iberian populations or displaced migrant central-European individuals, presumably of the nominate *nilotica*. According to Cramp *et al.* (1977–94), migration routes are still poorly understood but spring passage is believed to be rapid and to involve a broad-front crossing of the Sahara, with 25% of European birds passing north through the Iberian Peninsula. Peak passage in central Europe occurs during April or May. As Gantlett (1998) pointed out, the slightly smaller North American *arenea* might be expected to occur in Britain, in which case Scilly seems a likely place to look for it. A total of 216 Gull-billed Tern records were accepted by the BBRC during the period 1958–99, with 52 prior to that time, the four accepted Scillonian individuals therefore represent 1.8% of the national total. As of summer 2002, the report of a Gull-billed Tern seen briefly on St Mary's on 3rd September 2001, the potential first autumn sighting for the islands, was still under considered by the BBRC. The nearest breeding colonies are in Denmark, Germany, southern France and Spain.

## [Caspian Tern                                      *Sterna caspia*]   A

**No accepted records, full written description required by the BBRC.**

[1962     Two off Tresco]

Cosmopolitan breeding distribution except for South America, West Palearctic populations winter coastally south to Africa north of equator and east through Iran to India and Bangladesh. Monotypic.

The only documented account likely to have involved this species is contained in *CBWPSAR* 32 for 1962 and is repeated here in full:

> July 22nd. My sister and I saw two large red-billed terns hawking off Tresco, which we identified as Caspian from their heavy build and flight, shortish forked tail and all-red, noticeably heavy bill. *Common Terns* were also present, so we were able to compare the size, build, etc. The Caspians flew lower over the water than the Commons, and quartered the area very methodically, diving with less of a splash than the smaller birds, and at a slant, not straight down.

The report, from a Miss Blount, is accompanied by no editorial comment and is not in squared brackets, but was presumably never submitted for scrutiny. However, the editors were all knowledgeable ornithologists and appeared to accept the record, in their introduction listing ten species new to the islands in 1962, excluding Caspian Tern, followed by nine 'Other records of interest' including Caspian Tern. From all of this it appears perhaps that not only did the report editors accept the two Tresco birds, but were also of the opinion Caspian Tern had previously occurred in Scilly. Penhallurick also seems to have accepted the record (Penhallurick 1969). However, Miss Blount's description fails to mention some obvious features and in any event perhaps fails to eliminate the possibility of other large, red- or orange-billed terns having been involved.

A total of 231 British Caspian Tern records were accepted by BBRC during the period 1958–99, whilst there were just 30 prior to that period.

## [Royal Tern                                            *Sterna maxima*]   A

[2000      Various islands]

Breeds coastal Pacific and Atlantic North America plus Caribbean Islands and northern coastal South America, also coastal West Africa. Migratory or dispersive, wintering coastally in Americas, Caribbean and western Africa. Polytypic: *albididorsalis* occurs West Africa; nominate *maxima* elsewhere.

A large orange-billed tern seen by various observers at a number of locations around the islands during year 2000 was reportedly believed to be this species by observers obtaining the best views (IOSBG 2000), though none saw it adequately enough to convince the BBRC that it was indeed a Royal Tern. The northwest African population is migratory, most wintering south coastally as far as Angola. Five records accepted by the BBRC up until 1999 could have involved African or Nearctic individuals.

## Lesser Crested Tern                    *Sterna bengalensis*   A    BBRC 12.5%

**Extremely rare migrant or vagrant, full written description required by the BBRC.**

1996    One (adult) Skirt Island, Tresco 2nd to 4th August    *British Birds* 90: 487

Breeds coastal North Africa, Red Sea, Persian Gulf and Indian Ocean east to coastal Australasia, migratory or partially so. Polytypic: nominate *bengalensis* occurs Red Sea, East Africa and eastern India; *torresii* North Africa, Persian Gulf, Pakistan, New Guinea and Australasia.

One confirmed record of this attractive and elusive tern involved a bird keeping company with Sandwich Terns *S. sandvicensis* in the area of Skirt and Green Islands, Tresco, from late evening on 2nd to mid-morning on 4th August 1996. One feature noted whilst the bird stood amongst the Sandwich Terns was the manner in which it periodically held its bill pointing vertically downwards, as if displaying to the other birds, though if this was the case no response was detected. The call was noted as quite distinct from that of Sandwich Tern, falling rather between that species and Common Tern *S. hirundo*.

Given the similarity of dates involved, it may be no coincidence that an unidentified medium-sized, orange-billed tern was seen on two or three occasions between St Mary's and Tresco for a few days from 28th August 1994 (*IOSBR* 1994). However, without the benefit of adequate views the possibility of hybrid Lesser Crested x Sandwich Tern could be discounted (Steel & McGuigan 1989), or even the possibility of Elegant Tern *S. elegans*. A total of just eight records of Lesser Crested Tern were accepted by the BBRC during the period 1958–99, though it is conceivable that as few as two individuals may have accounted for all or most of these (Palmer 2000), thus the Tresco bird represented at least 12.5% of the recorded national total. For a useful account of the problems involved in separating Lesser Crested from similar tern species see Dubois (1991). The North African *torresii* population vacates the Mediterranean basin during autumn to winter in coastal West Africa, possibly providing an explanation for vagrant Lesser Crested Terns seen in Britain and Europe.

# Sandwich Tern *Sterna sandvicensis* A

**Formerly up to perhaps 100 pairs bred but now less than annual and becoming scarce, though annual and sometimes numerous on passage during spring and autumn.**

Breeds central West Palearctic and eastern Central America. West Palearctic populations winter southern Europe east to Caspian Sea and south through Africa to Antarctic Ocean. Polytypic: nominate *sandvicensis* occurs coastal western Europe through Mediterranean to Caspian Sea; *acuflavida*, or 'American Sandwich Tern' North and Central America; *eurygnatha*, considered by some authorities as separate species, South America. Included on Annex I of 1979 EEC 'Birds Directive'. Amber-listed in UK: 50% or more of breeding population at ten or fewer sites; unfavourable European conservation status (Gregory *et al.* 2002).

Earliest reference to Sandwich Tern in Scilly seems to be in E H Rodd's *List of the Birds of Cornwall* in the *Zoologist* (Rodd 1870a), in which he pointed out that 'a few pairs' were observed in the summer months and that it bred annually on some islands. He wrote again to the *Zoologist* in 1879 having heard from T A Dorrien-Smith that there were now 'heaps of Sandwich Terns on their eggs and nests' on various islands, though naming Guther's Island in particular (Rodd 1879c). However, just a year later he commented on how only a few pairs might now be annually observed and not in such numbers as formerly (Rodd 1880).

As with many species on Scilly, it fell to the ever reliable James Clark and E H Rodd's nephew Francis to succinctly describe Sandwich Tern's status at the close of the 19th century, these two pointing out that in 1841 more than 100 pairs reportedly bred among the islands (Clark & Rodd 1906). They quoted A A Dorrien-Smith to the effect that up to 40 nests were annually found on the southern end of Annet's northern half, though this site seems to have been deserted from around the mid-1880s. Clearly, though, Dorrien-Smith could not have come by that information first hand as he was born in 1876 and it seems likely this description of the early Annet Sandwich Tern colony was handed down, presumably from his father, T A Dorrien-Smith. During the 20 or so years from the 1880s, just single nests were to be found about the islands in some years, though in 1903 two pairs unsuccessfully attempted to breed on Guther's. Nonetheless, at least one brood was successfully hatched in 'a less frequented spot' that same year. Penhallurick (1969) added to the picture by mentioning Saunders' failure to find evidence of breeding during the 1880s, likewise noting that H W Robinson found no such evidence during 1911.

Bringing the situation nearer the present time, Penhallurick made mention of up to 40 on passage off the Cornish mainland during the 1960s, though he considered four together nearer the limit for Scilly, with 13th October the latest recorded date. There appears to be no mention of even attempted breeding during the early to mid-1900s and certainly Allen found none during his comprehensive seabird surveys of 1974 and 1976, although in 1978 six to seven pairs were said to have bred successfully on Green Island, Samson (Birkin & Smith 1987). It then continued to breed up until 1981 and again from at least 1987, when 20 pairs were again present on Green Island. Birkin and Smith attributed any Green Island breeding failures to possible disturbance from passing tripper boats but gave no additional information. However, more recently inundation by spring tides has proved problematical for breeding terns at this last site (pers. obs.) and seems a far more likely explanation for past failures. Subsequent to 1987 the most successful year was 1991, when 15 pairs laid eggs among Common *S. hirundo* and Roseate Terns *S. dougallii* on the summit of Samson's North Hill, though this activity was brought to a conclusion by the attentions of Brown Rats *Rattus norvegicus* (P J Robinson 1992b), the only subsequent known breeding attempts involving three pairs in 1993, again on Samson's Green Island and a single pair there in 1998, both of which failed.

Sandwich Terns annually pass through the islands on passage to and from Atlantic-coastal Africa (Wernham *et al.* 2002), creating difficulties in spring determining whether birds are intent on breeding. Likewise, late summer adults may appear with and be seen feeding young seeming hardly capable of sustained flight, though the absence of local breeding evidence suggests these originate from colonies much further afield, e.g. southern Ireland. Cramp *et al.* (1977–94) commented on the rapid dispersal of young from the breeding colony, quoting sightings of birds 65 km from the colony three days after fledging, whilst Fernandez-Cordeiro and Costas commented on Sandwich Terns feeding juveniles in migration off the coast of Spain (Fernandez-Cordeiro & Costas 1991).

Earliest birds appear from early to mid-March and they are rarely seen after late October, though extreme dates during the period 1990–99 were 20th February and 14th December, both in 1997. Autumn passage substantially outnumbers spring passage and normally commences from early to mid-July. Determining numbers of birds present at any one time is confused by inter-island movement, but roosts of up to 60 or more were recorded post-1990, plus at least one feeding concentration of over 100 individuals over St Martin's Flats in 1992. More usually, though, daily totals of 10–40 birds occur during autumn with fewer in spring. Main roost sites include Samson's Green and Stony Islands, Tean's rocky shoreline and, sometimes, Green Island, Tresco. All these sites are situated within the shallow-water areas to the south of St Martin's and Tresco and east of Samson which are so much favoured by feeding *Sterna* terns in Scilly. Importantly, Sandwich Terns ringed as pulli in Britain and Ireland are regularly found breeding in other British, Irish or Continental colonies (Wernham *et al.* 2002), thus proving the potential for eventual recolonisation of Scilly.

There is already one British record of the slightly smaller North and Central American *acuflavida*, involving a dead ringed individual in Hertfordshire in 1984 (Gantlett 1998), so it may be worth examining birds in Scilly with this possibility in mind, particularly perhaps during autumn, though field identification may be problematical. Initial dispersal of European breeding adults and fledged young appears to be random, though by late September most are moving south, with return migration commencing as early as February.

# Roseate Tern *Sterna dougallii* A

**Summer visitor and passage migrant.**

Fragmentary world breeding range, including southwest Europe and Azores, East Africa, Western Atlantic, southern India and Australasia. European birds winter coastal West Africa south to Equator. Polytypic: nominate *dougallii* occurs Atlantic Ocean and Caribbean; *bangsi* Arabian Sea, coastal East Africa and Central Pacific; *korustes* Bay of Bengal east to Burma; *gracilis* Australia and South Pacific. Included on Annex I of 1979 EEC 'Birds Directive'. Red-listed in UK: rapid, greater than 50% decline over past 25 years and greater than 50% range retraction within same timescale; 50% or more of breeding population at ten or fewer sites; unfavourable world conservation status (Gregory *et al.* 2002).

Allegedly bred commonly up until the early to mid-19th century but then declined rapidly, since when it has remained either scarce, rare or absent. Roseate Tern did not breed or attempt to breed in Scilly from 1994 until at least 2001, though a multi-agency recovery programme is now in place.

According to James Clark and Francis Rodd (1906), Roseate Tern bred in considerable numbers when Penzance resident D W Mitchell visited the islands in May 1840. E H Rodd explained Mitchell's presence in Scilly as 'investigating the ornithological resources of the islands during the nesting season', though Mitchell was nevertheless able to obtain as many eggs as he required (Rodd 1880). Unsurprisingly, perhaps, numbers (and indeed those of other tern species in the islands) then very soon declined, to the point where Jenkinson (presumably the Reverend J H) found only one or two pairs of Roseate breeding by 1854 (Clark & Rodd 1906). Clark & Rodd pointed out that in 1867 Francis Rodd, or his esteemed uncle E H Rodd, 'saw a few in their former breeding haunts' but that was the last recorded presence in the islands up until at least 1906. Surprisingly, Clark & Francis Rodd make no mention of the breeding sites involved in the 19th century, though the elder Rodd named Annet in at least two sources (Rodd 1870a, 1878b). Interestingly, though, the latter's reference to additional breeding sites merely as 'a Scilly rock and some other locations' hints at some effort on his part to conceal their exact whereabouts away from Annet (Rodd 1878b), perhaps in response to egg-collecting.

*Birds of the Isles of Scilly*

Roseate Terns returned to the islands in 1920 after an absence of 60 years, at which time C J King (1924) knew of at least two pairs among Common Terns *S. hirundo*, though Penhallurick later put the number at 3–4 pairs (Penhallurick 1969). Something of a chequered history followed, birds probably being present almost annually through to the early 1990s, though with never more then 20 pairs involved and frequently less. The Table and Chart show minimum recorded numbers of pairs, the former including records up until 1949 and the Chart showing the subsequent situation; records of a 'few' were taken to imply a minimum of three pairs and high and low estimates were averaged to the nearest half pair. As with most breeding species in Scilly, Roseate Tern recording suffered from a lack of dedicated long-term interest, which reveals itself through the lamentably inadequate dataset on the number, distribution and success of breeding pairs.

Within the islands there is a clear history of Roseate Terns breeding within Common Tern colonies, a situation that persisted right up until the final few pairs during the early 1990s. However, reasons for this association are by no means clear and Roseates were undoubtedly disadvantaged in Scilly by the near annual fragmentation of the Common Tern breeding population, most Roseate nests being situated towards the edge of Common Tern colonies, often but by no means always within or under peripheral vegetation, e.g. low Bracken *Pteridium aquilinum* (Blair 1950). British and Irish Roseate Terns winter off the West African coast south as far as the Gulf of Guinea (Wernham *et al.* 2002) and though the precise spring return route through the western approaches is unclear, birds from sites in eastern Ireland seem likely to pass close to Scilly, as may those from any North Sea locations.

| Year | No. Pairs | Site | Reference |
| --- | --- | --- | --- |
| 1840 | 'common' | Annet? | Clark & Rodd 1906 |
| 1854 | 'few' | Annet? | Clark & Rodd 1906 |
| 1920 | 3–4 | Green Island, Samson – Guther's Island | C J King 1924; Penhallurick 1969 |
| 1921 | 1 | ? | Penhallurick 1969 |
| 1923 | 1 | ? | Penhallurick 1969 |
| 1924 | 1 | ? | Penhallurick 1969 |
| 1940 | 'recolonisation' | ? | Penhallurick 1969 |
| 1943 | 5 | Green Island, Samson – Guther's Island | *CBWPSAR* 13 |
| 1946 | 1 | Annet | *CBWPSAR* 16 |
| 1947 | 3 | Annet – Green Island, Samson? | *CBWPSAR* 17 |
| 1948 | 2–5 | Two unnamed sites | *CBWPSAR* 18 |
| 1949 | 1–3 | Two unnamed islands | *CBWPSAR* 19 |

**Numbers of Recorded Roseate Tern Pairs – Scilly pre-1950**

Commencing with the 1991 breeding season, timber nestboxes were deployed at a selection of tern breeding sites known to have previously held Roseates, e.g. Samson's North Hill, Merrick Island, Apple Tree Banks, Tresco and nearby Green Island, Tresco. At the last of these, up to two pairs utilised boxes in 1993, one laying a clutch of two eggs inside a box, whereas two chicks from an exposed clutch moved into a box as soon as they hatched (P J Robinson 1993). Nevertheless, the eventual loss of breeding Roseates from Scilly was probably mainly attributable to frequent failure of the more numerous Common Tern colonies, which in turn was attributable to a variety of factors, not all of which operated at the same time. However, there is some evidence that Roseate Terns may be more site-faithful to historical sites in Scilly than are Common Terns. By the start of the 21st century, a multi-agency Isles of Scilly Roseate Tern recovery programme was underway, aimed at establishing a viable multi-species tern colony at the much-favoured site on the summit of Samson's North Hill, this particular site being beyond the reach of even the highest tides, with at least some protection from the attentions of large gulls *Larus*, plus a controlled visitor presence, but perhaps most importantly, on an island now cleared of Brown Rats *Rattus norvegicus*.

The basis of the recovery effort, part of the National Roseate Tern Species Recovery Programme, is the pre-season provision of both nestboxes and artificial Common and Roseate Terns, supported by the constant playback of mixed-tern colony calls using a portable CD player powered by a miniature solar panel. Up until 2001, Common Terns were responding well, with a minimum of 25 pairs laying eggs at the site and a lesser number of young reared (Robinson & Colombe 2001).

The reported rapid decrease in the Scillonian breeding population during the early 19th century corresponds with the known national decline, just as the early 20th century recolonisation reflected a national improvement in the species' distribution and numbers (Parslow 1967a). However, interestingly, even by 1968 Parslow thought the national population was beginning to decline again, a view since confirmed in the eastern Atlantic, where the number of British breeding pairs fell from 700 to 64 during the 30 years 1970–99 (Batten *et al*. 1990; *British Birds* 94: 369). Caution may nonetheless be required in interpreting reported Roseate Tern breeding numbers in Scilly, as evident, for example, from the *IOSBR* claim of no successful breeding in 1969, whereas Cramp *et al*. (1974–77) quoted a figure of 20 breeding pairs. Similarly, although the *IOSBR* lists as few as two pairs for the five years 1969–73, Lloyd *et al*. (1975) produced a figure of 20 pairs for each of these years. In addition, throughout the 1960s and 70s only very scant information was published on even the presence of birds within the islands. The St Agnes Bird Observatory mainly reported only what was viewable from that island, thus the *SABOAR* mainly mentions only birds breeding in the vicinity of Annet. There also appears to be some confusion within the various reports over the difference between failed breeding and the absence of any attempted breeding. It must be appreciated, too, that whilst gaps in the Table or Chart show the absence of published information, this may not necessarily prove an absence of breeding Roseate Terns.

Estimating numbers of Roseate Terns present in and around the archipelago is frustrated by feeding movements and, similarly, calculating precisely how many breeding or potential breeding pairs may be present is complicated by the apparent inter-site movements of failed pairs, as is also true for Common Terns. Nevertheless, there seem to be few recorded counts involving more than the local Roseate Terns, with two to three roosting flocks of 20 during the early 1980s the apparent highest counts. Indeed, the suggestion that few Roseate Terns from elsewhere may pass through the islands on passage gains support from the fact that recorded sightings decreased in line with the recent reduction and eventual loss of breeding birds, to the point where just two and four birds were seen during the whole of 1998 and 1999 respectively.

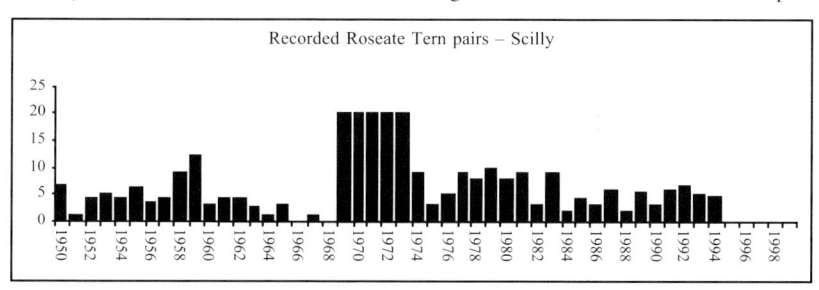

Recorded Roseate Tern pairs – Scilly

**Data sources**: mainly *CBWPSAR* and *IOSBR*

# Common Tern *Sterna hirundo* A

**Annual summer visitor and migrant, 100 breeding pairs or less represents a 50% decrease on the early 1990s.**

Breeds mainly south of Arctic Circle, from central and southern Europe through central Asia to Kamchatka and Bering Sea, also central northern North America. Migratory, wintering on coasts of most landmasses south to Southern Ocean. Polytypic: *longipennis* occurs eastern Siberia south to northern China; *tebetana* central-southern Asia; nominate *hirundo* remainder of range.

North (1850) recorded Common Terns in Scilly along with Sandwich *S. sandvicensis*, Arctic *S. paradisaea* and Roseate Tern *S. dougallii*, all of which he said bred on sand, shingle or grassy banks on various islands, though especially on Annet. By present standards, late 19th century assessments of the status of Common Tern status in the islands seem surprising, E H Rodd considering it less numerous than either Roseate or Arctic (Rodd 1878b), though he did agree it was an annual breeding visitor, as was also the case in mainland Cornwall (Rodd 1880). Even by the early 20th century, Rodd's nephew Francis and James Clark thought it 'not nearly so abundant as formerly, though it is still well represented in the breeding season' (Clark &

Rodd 1906). Sadly, however, they attached no population estimate and we still have no real idea how many Common Terns, or other tern species, were breeding in Scilly during the 19th and early 20th centuries.

However, some things clearly have not changed, Clark and Rodd lamenting that Common Terns were inclined to nest at sites frequently inundated by spring tides. In their assessment of terns generally, these two thought they had been much more abundant fifty years beforehand, noting too that even by 1854 Jenkinson (presumably the Reverend J H) thought terns had all diminished in numbers over the previous four years, i.e. 1850–54. There seems little doubt, though, that things were in a quite rapid state of change, for although E H Rodd considered Arctic more numerous than Common during the 1880s, by 1906 Clark and Rodd thought Arctic was greatly outnumbered by Common Tern. The only other reports prior to the mid-20th century are contained in the *CBWPSAR* for 1937 (No. 7), from which we see that only Common Terns bred in the islands that year, in colonies situated on Bryher (four sites) and Green Island, Tresco.

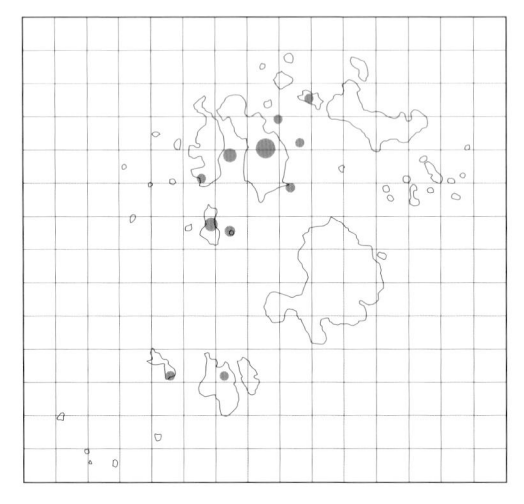

Common Terns have a chequered 20th century breeding history in the islands, characterised by years of extreme successes or extreme failure. Cataloguing this occupies much space and in the event proves little, save to show how adaptable the species is in the face of combined adversity. Similarly, a list of islands formerly or currently holding breeding terns would be unnecessarily extensive and in itself would prove little. However, it would reveal an obvious preference for the shallow sandy waters surrounding Tresco, Bryher and Samson, with mostly small gatherings or isolated pairs elsewhere, e.g. on St Agnes, or St Martin's. Typical years were 1945–46, when birds bred or attempted to breed at 15 locations from Annet east as far as Guther's Island and White Island, St Martin's. If all-island counts were conducted prior to 1969 they apparently went unrecorded, although such counts were carried out in 13 of the 31 years to 1999. The Chart shows that since at least 1973, numbers rose to over 200 in the early to mid-1980s, before declining to an end-of century level of under 100 pairs in 1999.

**Common Tern Breeding Distribution – 1999 (data Seabird 2000)**

| Island | Nests | Flush Count | Count Date | Extra Birds Involved |
|---|---|---|---|---|
| St Agnes – Killimay | 2 | 3 | 31/5 | |
| St Agnes – Browarth | 1 | 2 | 31/5 | |
| Peashopper Island | 1 | 2 | 7/6 | |
| Great Cheese Rock | 5 | 27 | 10/6 | 17 |
| Old Man of Tean | 1 | 2 | 10/6 | |
| Samson – Green Island | 7 | 48 | 14/6 | 34 |
| Merrick Island | 13 | 31 | 15/6 | 5 |
| Tresco – Apple Tree Banks | 39 | 80 | 22/6 | 2 |
| Tresco – Green Island | 1 | 3 | 22/6 | 1 |
| Annet | 1 | 2 | 23/6 | |
| Bryher – Colvel Rock | 1 | 2 | 24/6 | |
| Tresco – Castle Down | 13 | 15 | 25/6 | |
| Samson – North Hill | 11 | 60 | 7/7 | 38 |
| **Total Number of Nests** | **96** | | | |

**Distribution of Scillonian Common Tern Nests – 1999 (Seabird 2000 data)**

Causes of this recent decline are untested but would seem to be probably related to poor productivity, although driving forces behind recent colony failures are varied and not always associated. Foremost among them, however, is the inability of Scillonian Common Terns to agree on a preferred breeding site, the resultant fragmentary attempts leaving small, isolated breeding groups vulnerable to predation of eggs by Carrion Crows *Corvus corone*, or of small young by gulls *Larus*. Other causes of failure include high spring tides, disturbance by humans, predation by Brown Rats *Rattus norvegicus* or loss of eggs during heavy rain. More recently, the Scillonian Roseate Tern recovery programme is calling for the establishment of a single Common Tern colony on the summit of Samson North Hill, a site long favoured by terns but much troubled by Brown Rats until their recent removal from that island. This site is beyond the reach of high tides and has at least some protection from the attentions of large gulls, plus human access can be controlled, though it is still too soon to assess results.

The Table and Map show the distribution of 96 Common Tern pairs recorded during fieldwork carried out in 1999 as part of the national Seabird 2000 survey. Also shown are flush-counts (*Seabird monitoring handbook for Britain and Ireland* 1995) and numbers of additional or 'spare' birds believed to have been present at each site. Interestingly, both Samson's North Hill and Samson's Green Island scored highest in terms of additional birds and it has long been suspected that these two locations attract birds from failed sites elsewhere in the islands, the difference between them being that Green Island is susceptible to tidal flooding, whereas Damson North Hill is not. Several small rocky sites, e.g. Merrick Island, Tresco's Green Island or Great Cheese Rock, are devoid of vegetation or other cover and so are vulnerable to various causes of failure. Efforts during the mid-1990s aimed at reducing clutch losses by pre-sanding these sites proved extremely successful, numbers of pairs increasing from five up to 40. However, the resultant increased numbers of young, combined with the lack of suitable protection attracted the attentions of large gulls and it was considered safer not to encourage use of what are, in reality, only peripheral breeding sites. Up until the end of the 20th century, the recently introduced Hedgehog *Erinaceus europaeus* was confined to the main island of St Mary's, where terns and other seabirds do not breed. However, the potential spread of this active ground predator to other islands, e.g. St Agnes, Tresco or Samson, represents a serious threat to terns and other ground-nesting seabirds in Scilly.

The closest breeding Common Terns to Scilly are on Chesil Beach in south Dorset, along Ireland's southern coastline and in northern Brittany in northwest France, all of these being at a distance of at least 160 km. Penhallurick recorded evidence of Common Tern passage through west Cornwall in spring from mid-April to late May, and found it to be always lighter than in autumn, though a single-day count of over 500 was recorded off St Ives. Although autumn numbers were higher, 3,000 off St Ives during a gale was nevertheless exceptional and several hundred per day seemed more usual (Penhallurick 1969). On Scilly, any Common Tern passage is clouded by the presence of local birds and so the situation is less easily assessed. Consequently, Common Tern movements have mostly been poorly recorded and for many years the suggestion is of little or no movement through the islands at either end of the year. And certainly what data there are give a slight hint of a greater passage in spring than autumn. In nine of the ten years 1990–99, first sightings occurred between 5th and 29th April, the exception being 20th March. But whilst final sightings ranged between 1st and 26th October in nine out of ten years, a bird on 17th December (dead on 20th) proved the exception. Maximum single-day spring counts were in the range 70–100, but whilst autumn totals were broadly similar, there was a high of 200 on 27th July. The only report of birds showing '*portlandica*'-type plumage features during the ten-year period involved two in Tresco Channel on 1st July 1993.

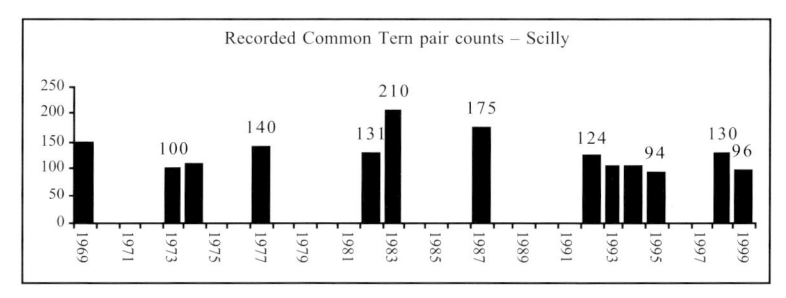

Recorded Common Tern pair counts – Scilly

The majority of the West Palearctic population winters off coastal West Africa, smaller numbers staying north as far as Iberia (Cramp *et al*. 1977–94). More northerly populations move furthest south and British

*Birds of the Isles of Scilly*

and central European birds winter mostly off West Africa, with ringing data showing that birds from the Baltic states also pass through Britain (Wernham *et al.* 2002). A total of 229 Common Terns were ringed in Scilly during the late 20th century, 145 (63%) since 1970. The only two recaptures are shown below, both of which fit the West African pattern. However, it is worth recording that as long ago as 1911 H W Robinson ringed 191 young terns on one island in Scilly (Penhallurick 1969). A pulli spirit specimen prepared by Robinson on 23rd June 1923 resides in the British Museum (Natural History) reference number 1924.6.25.

**Recoveries**

SX06437   Pul   Merrick Island 3rd July 1991        CT   Cape Three Points, Ghana
                                                          2nd December 1991

SX37862   Pul   Merrick Island 13th July 1992       AS   Offshore, Guinea Bissau
                                                          3rd January 1994

**Common Tern Ringing Recaptures**

# Arctic Tern                                          *Sterna paradisaea*  A

**Scarce migrant and former summer visitor, reportedly bred as recently as 1973.**

Breeds edges of Arctic Ocean, extending into North Atlantic as far as Britain and Ireland and extreme northeast USA, and into North Pacific to Sea of Okhotsk, Aleutian Islands, Alaska and northwest Canada. Long distance migrant, wintering south into Antarctic Ocean. Monotypic. Included on Annex I of 1979 EEC 'Birds Directive'. Amber-listed in UK: moderate population decline over past 25 years (Gregory *et al.* 2002).

According to E H Rodd, Arctic Tern was the commonest migrant tern in Cornwall and Scilly up until at least the 1880s, the same authority noting that although it bred in Scilly it did so in far fewer numbers than previously (Rodd 1870a, 1880). In a similar vein, by the early 20th century James Clark and Francis Rodd were lamenting the fact that although it had greatly outnumbered the Common Tern 20–25 years beforehand, it was now in the minority (Clark & Rodd 1906). Unsurprisingly then, by the mid-20th century Arctic Tern was believed to have disappeared from the islands as a breeding species (Witherby *et al.* 1940; Ryves & Quick 1946), the last recorded breeding perhaps having occurred in 1924. Nevertheless, in his review of changes among British breeding species Parslow found no evidence of wide-scale declines during the late 19th and early 20th centuries, though local fluctuations were known to have occurred (Parslow 1967a).

Most subsequent references to Arctic Tern in Scilly involve random sightings of what were assumed to be passage birds, mostly in very small numbers, e.g. four together on one of the two Green Islands on 6th June 1947. Nonetheless, the possibility of it lingering to breed remained, as evident from A A Dorrien-Smith's 1948 report that 'a few pairs attempted to breed' (*CBWPSAR* 18). However, far more frequent were comments such as 'heavy spring passage, but no evidence of nesting'. In fact, in 1961, an observer, having located a single Arctic Tern on Tresco on 16th August, saw the need to provide a description for what was indeed the only individual record in the islands that year.

During the ten years from 1990 it was recorded in all but 1994, but in surprisingly low numbers – though doubtless the odd individual escaped identification among the far greater number of Common Terns. A total of 67 passage Arctic Terns were recorded during the nine years, two-thirds of these in autumn and at an annual mean of 7.4. Sixteen in 1997 was the most in any one year, 15 of those in autumn, and two in 1993 was the lowest annual total.

All of this makes it difficult to understand claims that 30 pairs of Arctic Terns bred on Annet in 1945 (*CBWPSAR* 15), plus 12 pairs on the same island in 1963 and 40–60 pairs the following year (*SABOAR* 1963–64), with the further suggestion that a few pairs may have bred on Tresco during 1973 (*IOSBR* 1973) and 1977 (*IOSBR* 1977). Reactions to such claims are mixed, many taking the view that birds involved were incorrectly identified Common Terns. However, during the late 1960s and early 1970s, Arctic Terns bred in Dorset and around Ireland's southern coastline, with other outlying groups in Kent, Suffolk and Norfolk, a situation that persists to the present time (Sharrock 1976; Gibbons *et al.* 1993). In addition, some of the observers involved in Scilly were particularly reliable, the 1963–64 Annet pairs being seen by observers from the St Agnes Bird Observatory. But in any event, such issues are not easily reassessed at this distance in time and much reliance must be placed upon the integrity of both the observers involved and any editorial and vetting staff. More recently, a single Arctic Tern was witnessed among Common Terns above Green Island, Samson during a survey by the author and W H Wagstaff on 15th June 1995, though no nest could be attributed to this bird and it was not recorded subsequently (*IOSBR* 1995).

Much Arctic Tern passage occurs offshore, presumably explaining the paucity of Scillonian sightings of a migrant species that breeds in substantial numbers in Ireland, northern Britain, Fennoscandia, northwest Asia and adjacent Arctic islands. Ringing recoveries show that many birds from both shores of the Baltic Sea routinely pass through Britain (Wernham *et al.* 2002). No Arctic Terns are recorded as having been ringed on Scilly and there are no recaptures from elsewhere.

## Bridled Tern *Sterna anaethetus* A  BBRC 5.5%

**Extremely rare vagrant or migrant, full written description required by the BBRC.**

1991   One Tresco & Crow Sound 6th July to 13th August   *British Birds* 85: 107, 531

Fragmentary distribution, breeds Caribbean, Central America, tropical West Africa and Indian and Pacific Oceans. Migratory or highly dispersive, mainly offshore. Polytypic: *melanoptera* occurs West Indies and West Africa; *nelsoni* Central America; *antarctica* Red Sea, Persian Gulf and western Indian Ocean; nominate *anaethetus* eastern Indian Ocean and southeast Pacific (Cramp *et al.* 1977–94).

Just one occurrence of what remains an extreme rarity throughout the whole of the British Isles, with the BBRC accepting just 18 British records within the period 1958–99 and with only three records prior to that. The appearance of the 1991 individual, an adult, coincided with the arrival of an extreme low-pressure weather system, which remained centred over the islands for two days during early July and was marked initially by a prolonged period of extremely heavy rain. During its 39-day stay the bird mainly frequented the shallow water and sandy beaches around the southern ends of Tresco and St Martin's, and towards the end of its stopover occasionally visited Common Tern *S. hirundo* colonies (*IOSBR* 1991). During at least one such occasion it was heard to called repeatedly as it flew back and forth low over the colony on Tresco's southeast corner (pers. obs.).

Birds reaching the British Isles seem most likely to originate from West African, Caribbean or Central American populations (Cramp *et al.* 1977–94), though as Gantlett (1998) pointed out, the BOURC currently assumes all records are *antarctica*, based on a bird found dead in Kent in 1931. Dymond *et al.* (1989) showed that most, if not all, birds arrived in Britain and Ireland between mid-April and the last week of October, with a very obvious concentration in southwest England.

## [Sooty Tern *Sterna fuscata*] A

**Extremely rare vagrant or migrant, full written description required by the BBRC.**

[1883   One Tresco]   Clark & Rodd 1906

Fragmentary distribution, breeding Atlantic, Caribbean, Indian Ocean, Persian Gulf, tropical and southern Pacific. Migratory or dispersive, movements poorly understood. Polytypic: nominate *fuscata* occurs Caribbean and Atlantic; *nubilosa* Red Sea, Persian Gulf and Indian Ocean; with five more forms in Pacific.

Like the previous species, there is just a single claimed record, but in this case it is quite old and perhaps not as reliable as we might wish, originating as it does from a time when the only certain rarity was a dead one. James Clark was certainly sufficiently cautious about this record in his list of *The Birds of Cornwall* to enclose the entry in squared brackets (Clark 1902). The incident occurred after publication of E H Rodd's landmark *The Birds of Cornwall and the Scilly Islands* (Rodd 1880) and is summarised by James Clark and E H Rodd's nephew Francis Rodd in their normally dependable *Zoologist* review of 'The Birds of Scilly' (Clark & Rodd 1906). Here they explain that in 1883 veteran Tresco gamekeeper David Smith saw a strange bird hawking flies over the freshwater pools. Because he was still recovering from a severe illness, Smith asked a friend to shoot the bird, but the shot missed and the bird flew off and was never seen again. Smith was subsequently 'shown the plates in Gould', whereupon he allegedly identified the bird as Sooty Tern. The only pre-1883 Gould publication containing a Sooty Tern plate appears to be his 1848 *Birds of Australia*, which also contains a plate of Bridled Tern *S. anaethetus* (E Warr *in litt.*), thus demonstrating that Smith had a clear choice between these two look-alike species. However, in preparing the *Zoologist* text, Clark appeared slightly less cautious about this record than he did years earlier. Nevertheless, the record is square-bracketed here in view of the known possibility of confusing these two species, plus the lack of any known written description. It does not appear in the 1971 BOU Checklist (Snow 1971). A total of ten British Sooty Tern records were accepted by the BBRC during the period 1958–99, with 16 prior to that period, perhaps suggesting that the species has become less likely to be seen in the British Isles than formerly, allowing for the increased number of obsevers. European records attributed subspecifically are thought to have involved *fuscata* (Cramp *et al.* 1977–94). Clark and Rodd make no mention of the timing of the Tresco incident, and although Penhallurick (1969) gave it as autumn he too provided no additional information. In their review of 20th century British and Irish Sooty Tern records, Dymond *et al.* (1989) found that all occurred between late May and mid-August, though several older records fall within the period March or April through to October (Witherby *et al.* 1940). These last authors also made no mention of the claimed Tresco sighting.

## Little Tern *Sterna albifrons* A

**Scarce migrant, mainly now in spring. There seems no reason to doubt a claim that single pairs bred in 1908 and 1919.**

Breeds Caribbean, Central and North America, central and southern Europe, central and eastern Asia and Australasia. Migratory, west European population winters coastal West Africa to equator, perhaps further south. Polytypic: nominate *albifrons* occurs Europe to central Asia and south to North Africa, Iran and India; *guineae* West and central Africa; at least five additional forms elsewhere include the North and Central American *antillarum* or 'Least Tern'. Included on Annex I of 1979 EEC 'Birds Directive'. Amber-listed in UK: moderate population decline over past 25 years; 50% or more of breeding population at ten or fewer sites; unfavourable world conservation status (Gregory *et al.* 2002).

E H Rodd knew it as 'Lesser Tern *Sterna minuta*' and described it as far from rare along the Cornish coast, though as far as he knew it did not occur in Scilly during summer (Rodd 1880). Nonetheless, James Clark and Rodd's nephew Francis made mention of one in immature plumage shot on Guther's Island on 14th September 1857, the latter having also seen seven between Tresco and Samson in October 1863, three of which were shot. One also spent several weeks in the area of Tresco's Great Pool in July 1877 and another was present in the Bryher area in April 1904 (Clark & Rodd 1906). These records apparently were the sum total of published Little Tern reports up until the start of the 20th century.

Penhallurick reviewed the status of Little Tern up until the mid-1960s, pointing out that according to C J King, he and F W Frohawk found a Little Tern nest on Tean in 1908, King also making mention of a nest at Pelistry, St Mary's, in 1919 (Penhallurick 1969). However, Penhallurick also drew attention to King's confession that he once mistook an exceptionally small clutch of Common Tern *S. hirundo* eggs for those of Little Tern (C J King 1924) and on that basis suggested King's records were perhaps suspect. However, King was quite clear this misidentification took place on Guther's Island in 1923 whilst he was accompanied by his son, not by Frohawk and the error was corrected at the time, therefore there seems nothing in these remarks to cast doubt on the earlier record, though, unfortunately, King provided no additional information on the St Mary's record. Penhallurick considered Little Tern a scarce migrant in the islands at least by the 1960s, mainly in autumn, and drew attention to the fact that the earliest published 20th century account of it after Clark and Rodd's mention of one on Bryher in 1904 concerned a bird moving southwest past St Agnes on 20th August 1952 (*CBWPSAR* 22). Sightings ranged between mid-August and early October with eight the most seen together and there were just two spring records.

Examining the situation for the ten years from 1990, we see a slightly different situation to that described by Penhallurick, with 33 Little Terns arriving in eight years in spring, whereas just 21 appeared in five years during autumn. However, the spring figure is inflated by an excessive 16 during 1991 and once that count is disregarded overall totals for the two periods are similar. Some authorities suggest a fall-off in numbers in recent years, but the situation described differs little from the 13 preceding years, when none were recorded in at least two years, but with 19 in 1983 described as 'more than usual'.

The closest breeding Little Terns to Scilly are in Dorset and southeast Ireland (Gibbons *et al.* 1994) and in northwest France (Guermeur & Monnat 1980). In western Europe, post-breeding movement commences from early July and continues through into October, some travelling in family groups, which presumably accounts for a juvenile seen being fed by adults in Pentle Bay, Tresco, on 13th August 1995. Most passage south to the West African wintering areas (Wernham *et al.* 2002) occurs along the coasts and is sometimes rapid, return spring movement being less well documented but thought to commence from April, most passing north off European coasts during April and May (Cramp *et al.* 1977–94). Gantlett (1998) identified the possibility of the perhaps recognisable East African form *guineae* occurring in Britain and there are already British claims of the North and Central American *antillarum*. No Little Terns have been ringed in Scilly and there are no recaptures from elsewhere.

## Whiskered Tern *Chlidonias hybrida* A BBRC 0%

**Extremely rare migrant, full written description required by the BBRC. An early claim of breeding is unsupported by published detail and seems extremely improbable in any event.**

1851   One (immature – shot) Tresco 2nd August   Rodd 1851d; Clark & Rodd 1906

Fragmentary southern Eurasian breeding distribution, from Iberia and France east to China and south to East Africa, Madagascar, India and Australia. Migratory, European populations winter mainly tropical West Africa. Polytypic: nominate *hybrida* occurs Europe, North Africa, Middle East, northern India and southern Siberia and China; two further forms eastern and southern Africa plus Australia (BOURC 2002b)

In his *A Week at the Land's End*, Blight (1861) names this as one of several tern species the eggs of which were to be found 'in other places, and generally in the sand or herbage about the shore'. However, no other 19th century writer suggested that Whiskered Tern bred or even occurred in Scilly apart from the one obtained specimen and the circumstances described by Blight seem wholly unsatisfactory for what is principally a marshland species.

The single old Scillonian record involved a bird shot on Tresco in August 1851. In a note to the *Zoologist* entitled 'Occurrence of Whiskered Tern at Scilly' and dated 2nd September that same year, E H Rodd reported that 'a bird which I have no doubt is an immature specimen was shot near Tresco Abbey a few days since' (Rodd 1851d). Rodd later reconfirmed the record in his classic *Birds of Cornwall and the Scilly Islands*, pointing out too that as far as he knew it was still the only record for Cornwall and Scilly (Rodd 1880). In preparing the latter book, either the printer or James Harting (who was charged with completing the publication following Rodd's untimely death) mistakenly gave the year as 1857. Certainly James Clark and Francis Rodd knew of no other on Scilly by the time of their own review, commenting that a 'fine example in immature plumage' was shot on Tresco by Augustus Pechell on August 2nd 1851 (Clark & Rodd 1906).

However, whilst the record is not in doubt the precise date remains questionable, primarily because E H Rodd is unclear on the point. In their 1906 review Clark and Francis Rodd gave the date as 2nd August and it must be assumed they were quoting from the Tresco Abbey records, with which Francis would have been familiar and which ought to have been reliable. However, although E H Rodd's *Zoologist* letter of 1851 supports the view that it was shot in August, in later years he appeared to settle on an unspecified day in September (Rodd 1870a, 1878b, 1880).

A total of 107 records were accepted by the BBRC during the period 1958–99, compared with just 20 prior to that time. Birds reaching the British Isles are presumably of the form *hybrida* and certainly T A Dorrien-Smith (1951) made that assumption in the case of the Tresco individual.

## Black Tern *Chlidonias niger* A

**Scarce migrant in small numbers, mostly in autumn and not annual.**

Breeds southern Europe and central western Asia east to Kazakhstan, plus central North America. Migratory, Eurasian populations winter coastal West Africa south to Namibia and upper Nile Valley. Polytypic: nominate *niger* occurs Eurasia; *surinamensis* North America.

*Birds of the Isles of Scilly*

Black Tern was known to E H Rodd as a rare autumn visitor to mainland Cornwall, where it mainly occurred over rivers and freshwater pools. In April 1866 he received three summer-plumage specimens shot on a large pond near Land's End and he knew of others seen or obtained near Falmouth during October (Rodd 1880). Although Rodd made no mention of Scilly, his nephew Francis and co-author James Clark put right that situation soon after the start of the 20th century, pointing out that it was 'Seen every now and then on the pools of Tresco in immature plumage in the autumn, and sometimes in August'. They also mentioned an adult obtained some time during April 1877, whilst on 10th April 1903 a flock of seven were watched feeding over Porth Hellick Pool on St Mary's, and on 26th April 1905 four were similarly feeding over Tresco's Great Pool (Clark & Rodd 1906). The inference is that these last were exceptional records and that autumn birds were more frequent. Interestingly, Clark (in W Page 1906) thought there had been a slight increase in Cornish numbers or frequency post-1901, though the only prominent early 20th century report concerned two seen feeding over Porth Hellick Pool for seven days from 12th April 1925 (H W Robinson 1925b).

Scilly is largely positioned outside the main migration path of this species, though numbers annually pass through the Somerset Levels to the east. Examination of records for the ten years from 1990 supports earlier suggestions that this species was more frequent in Scilly during autumn, though spring arrivals are not unusual. Autumn records involved 39 birds in 25 sightings in all but one year, at an average of 4.3 per year, whereas 30 birds in spring involved eleven sightings in only five years. But although this last suggests an annual spring occurrence of six birds per year, 21 of these arrived during spring 1994 (groups of 15 and 6), giving an annual arrival rate of just 2.2 for the remaining four years. The great majority of sightings (90%) involved birds recorded on just a single day, the earliest spring arrival being 30th April (four years) and the latest 18th June, whilst the earliest in autumn was on 7th August and the latest the rather extreme date of 2nd October. The latest ever recorded in the islands may have been the bird found dead on St Mary's on 26th November 1967.

Black Terns breed regularly no closer to Scilly than the Netherlands, with other populations in Denmark, northwest Germany, central and northeast France and Spain (Hagemeijer & Blair 1997). Within the West Palearctic, autumn migration commences from late June or earlier, most adults moving before juveniles; initial juvenile movements taking the form of random dispersal (Cramp *et al.* 1977–94). The Netherlands has been identified as the probable prime autumn staging post for all northern and eastern European populations, plus possibly those in western Siberia, most birds then continuing south through France and Iberia (Cramp *et al.* 1977–94). As evident even from Scillonian records, the volume of between-year passage through Britain and other southwest European counties varies, being exceptionally heavy in some years. Return spring migration begins from late March, most birds passing through southern and central Europe during May. A substantial percentage of birds pass through the Strait of Gibraltar and follow the Atlantic coast northwards to reach Britain, Ireland and even Iceland.

The BOURC recently admitted the North American *surinamensis* to the British List on the strength of a juvenile at Weston-super-Mare, Avon, 3rd–11th October 1999 (BOURC 2002a; *Birding World* 12: 416–418). Consequently, and given the relative scarcity of Black Tern in Scilly, any bird found should be examined with care, especially perhaps during autumn (Gantlett 1998). T A Dorrien-Smith seems to have attributed all pre-1951 records to *niger* (T A Dorrien-Smith 1951).

## White-winged Black Tern
## (White-winged Tern)        *Chlidonias leucopterus*    A    BBRC 0.13%

**Extremely rare migrant, full written description required by the BBRC.**

1882   One (adult – shot) Great Pool, Tresco 14th May   Cornish 1882b; Clark & Rodd 1906
1933   One Great Pool, Tresco 17th April   *CBWPSAR* 3 (A A Dorrien-Smith)
1995   One (juvenile) St Agnes & Tresco 17th October (Hayle, Cornwall 18th)   *British Birds* 89: 50

Breeds intermittently west and central Europe but more consistently eastwards through central Asia to Mongolia and south to Iraq. Migratory, West Palearctic populations winter Africa south of Sahara, where probably joined by birds from further east. Monotypic.

The first of three acceptable Scillonian records involved a bird in full summer plumage shot by gamekeeper David Smith on Tresco's Great Pool on 14th May 1882 (Cornish 1882b, Clark & Rodd 1906). The skin of this individual is allegedly now in the Tresco Abbey collection. The next, again on Tresco Great Pool but some fifty years later, was reportedly seen in flight in April 1933 and unusually for Scilly up until that time, was not shot (*CBWPSAR* 3). Most recent was a first-winter individual initially seen on Tresco on 17th October 1995, before relocating to Periglis, St Agnes and leaving the islands later the same day. Interestingly, what was almost certainly the same bird was present in the Hayle Estuary, west Cornwall, on the 18th (*CBWPSAR* 65), before leaving in an easterly direction and very possibly also accounting for the sighting of a first-winter individual at Greater Westhay Moor, Somerset, from 23rd to 27th (*CBWPSAR* 65). The nearest recorded breeding colonies are in Poland and Hungary (Hagemeijer & Blair 1997).

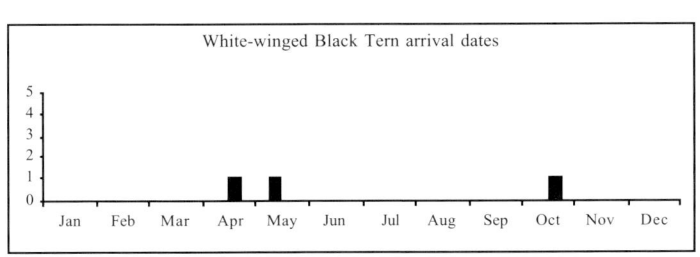

*White-winged Black Tern arrival dates*

An unusual 'marsh-tern' seen feeding off Tean on 24th June 1969 could have involved this species but the description left room for substantial doubt that something more exotic may have been involved, for according to the observer the bird was jet-black with white shoulders and white tail, reddish legs, yellowish bill and was watched flying low over the water and feeding by dipping rather than with the splash of a Common Tern *S. hirundo* (*IOSBR* 1969).

## Guillemot (Common Guillemot) *Uria aalge* A

**Summer visitor, breeds in small numbers at a few 'ancestral' sites, smaller numbers are evident in Scillonian waters during winter.**

Breeds northern edge of Atlantic and Pacific Oceans, in North Atlantic mainly Britain, Ireland, Norway, Iceland and Newfoundland. Dispersive, northwest Atlantic populations winter south as far as coastal Iberia. Polytypic: nominate *aalge*, or 'Northern Guillemot', occurs North Atlantic south on eastern seaboard to northern Scotland; *albionis*, or 'Southern Guillemot', remainder of Britain, plus Ireland south to Iberia; *hyperborea*, or 'Arctic Guillemot', northern Norway and adjacent Arctic islands; *californica* and *inornata* North Pacific. Amber-listed in UK: 20% or more of European breeding population in UK (Gregory *et al.* 2002).

Earliest evidence of Guillemot presence in the islands came from archaeological sites on Samson, May's Hill on St Martin's and Nornour in the Eastern Isles (Turk 1973, 1984a, 1984b). Bone remains at May's Hill originated from between 1700 and 1000 BC and the 3rd and 4th centuries AD, whilst a tibio-tarsus fragment from Samson dated from around 1200 BC. Unusually in a British context, Razorbill *Alca torda*, Guillemot and Puffin *Fratercula arctica* are the commonest bird species (in that order) found at archaeological sites in Scilly, although Guillemot remains were not found at the Halangy Down site on St Mary's, despite the presence there of Great Auk *Alca impennis* bones (Ashbee 1999).

Nineteenth- and early 20th century accounts of Guillemot on Scilly are as much concerned with plumage type as with numbers or location, Besley's Handbook (Anon, 19th century undated) describing both 'Common and Bridled Guillemot' as common in Cornwall during summer and breeding in Scilly. E H Rodd considered it a well-known seabird either singly or in small parties around coastal Cornwall, where, 'especially at Scilly', it resorted to the cliffs in May 'for the purposes of nidification' (Rodd 1880). Rodd also acknowledged that the bridled form, 'obtained occasionally on the Cornish coast', was generally now regarded as 'merely a variety of the common species'.

More informative, however, was James Clark and Francis Rodd's early 20th century account, these two pointing out that Guillemot was never as abundant in Scilly as Razorbill, though it formerly 'nested in great profusion' (Clark & Rodd 1906). They also noted that during the late 19th century it had 'sadly diminished', so much so that on Scilly Rock in 1903 only a single (broken) egg could be found, whilst on Gorregan, described by Clark and Rodd as one of its 'recent strongholds' only three eggs were discovered. Meanwhile, on Mincarlo, in the Northern Isles, no nests were found, even though King had described nine or ten eggs three years beforehand. However, it was still breeding on Men-a-Vaur in small numbers and was also thought to do so on Hanjague in the east. Clark and Rodd concluded with the observation that it was 'nowhere prominent'. Sadly, we have no means now of knowing just what Clark and Rodd meant when they described Guillemot as formerly nesting in 'great profusion', though the inference elsewhere is that perhaps not many were involved. In addition, although breeding Guillemots persist still at three or more of the above-mentioned sites, many pairs are what can best be described as subterranean, though we have no means now of assessing whether this was formerly the case, or, if so, whether these went unrecorded by early visitors to these remote sites. Importantly, Smart (1885–86) named only Men-a-Vaur, Hanjague and Scilly Rock as breeding sites, putting the total population even at that time at thirty pairs or less.

Penhallurick (1969) noted that precise details on early distribution and numbers of breeding Guillemots in Cornwall were lacking and though it clearly bred at fewer sites than Razorbill, overall numbers of these two were believed to be similar. The same author highlighted what appeared to have been substantial Cornish Guillemot reductions during the first half of the 20th century, though the timing of publication of his *Birds of the Cornish Coast* made it difficult to assess any effects of the 1967 *Torrey Canyon* disaster. On Scilly, King thought Razorbills outnumbered Guillemots by about 20:1 during the early 20th century and suggested perhaps five known breeding sites (C J King 1924). However, some early 20th century reports only confuse the overall picture; for example, according to Penhallurick, Harvey saw few on Mincarlo in 1938 where, again according to Penhallurick, Wallace had found many in 1923. In addition, whereas Ryves (1948) found good numbers on nearby Men-a-Vaur in 1938, Penhallurick also quoted an unnamed source who found that in 1946–47 numbers on Men-a-Vaur and Gorregan were 'too large to estimate'. Nonetheless, no co-ordinated early to mid-20th century all-island count appears to have been carried out, though by the late 1960s Penhallurick suggested a total of c. 50 pairs, with 25 on Men-a-Vaur, 8 on Scilly Rock and 17 on Gorregan. He further suggested that breeding may have ceased on Mincarlo and Hanjague and that by then most Scillonian Guillemots nested beneath boulders, whilst confirming this behaviour had not been recorded prior to 1923. Nonetheless, some still apparently bred on Mincarlo up until 1952, at which time the island was visited from the mainland by active egg-collectors (Cole & Trobe 2000).

The fragmentary distribution of breeding Guillemots in Scilly, the isolation of sites and relatively brief period when birds are present at colonies, plus difficulties involved in gaining access, all severely limit count data. Certainly since 1990, no Guillemots have bred on Hanjague in the Eastern Isles and the only indication of possible breeding on Mincarlo involved a single bird seen leaving the site during the Seabird 2000 count. Therefore, the current known Scillonian breeding sites are limited to Gorregan, Scilly Rock and Men-a-Vaur, plus possibly Mincarlo. Despite earlier observations of breeding on Rosevean in the Western Isles, none have been noted ashore there since 1974.

The Table shows all-island Guillemot survey totals plus associated individual site counts together with sources of information. The loaded oil tanker *Torrey Canyon* struck the Seven Stones reef to the east of Scilly on 18th March 1967, but regrettably there are no all-island count data for years prior to that time. However, results of a post-*Torrey Canyon* survey of Scilly and the Cornish mainland during summer 1967 revealed less-than-expected reductions in most mainland auk colonies. However, at least one Scillonian Guillemot site, Gorregan, was believed to show a marked reduction, based partly on the known (small) number of birds previously ringed at this site, plus the percentage found oiled during 1967 (Parslow 1967b), but also upon the knowledge that an estimated 50 breeding pairs had been present at this site five years beforehand. The Chart shows the pattern of all-island Guillemot count totals since 1967 and reveals either a recovery from the losses of 1967, or even a possible increase, and whilst the true island situation remains unclear the national population is known to be increasing.

Survey methods used in past all-island Guillemot counts are not always entirely apparent but the 1999 counts involved all birds leaving the main area of the breeding colonies but not adjacent 'roost' areas, these results then being multiplied by 0.67 (Walsh et al. 1995) to give the figure shown. It should also be noted, however, that there was strong evidence, in the form of birds counted away from the colonies, that 1999 represented a better than average year for this species in Scillonian waters.

|      | Total | Gorregan | Scilly Rock | Men-a Vaur | Mincarlo |                    |
|------|-------|----------|-------------|------------|----------|--------------------|
| 1967 | 50    | 17       | 8           | 25         |          | Parslow 1967b      |
| 1974 | 36    | 10       | 6           | 20         |          | Allen 1974–76      |
| 1983 | 104   | 27       | 20+         | 57         |          | P Harvey 1983      |
| 1987 | 109   | 20–40    | 20–40       | 40+        |          | Birkin & Smith 1987|
| 1999*| 130   | 26 (39)  | 26 (39)     | 78 (117)   | 1 (1)    | P J Robinson 1999c |

**Guillemot Breeding Distribution by Island (\*Seabird 2000 data [adjusted figures, full-count data in brackets])**

Numbers of wintering Guillemots in Scillonian waters are far less well understood, as demonstrated by the fact that the only birds recorded during the two-day late January 1997 Winter Shorebird Survey were two off St Mary's. Doubtless most individuals remain further out to sea and are therefore less visible from the islands. Although most observations seem likely to involve birds passing the islands during migratory or weather-related movements, most go no further south than the Bay of Biscay (Wernham *et al.* 2002). Examination of records for the ten years from 1990 reveals little reference to winter sightings, most of which in any event involve oiled individuals, up to a maximum of 10–15 per winter. Indeed, outside the breeding season there are just a few random sight records, the two very obvious exceptions being reports of up to 50 an hour passing the islands between 5th and 27th October 1997 and 45 past Peninnis, St Mary's, on of 22nd October 1998 (*IOSBR* 1997, 1998); neither account stating the direction of travel.

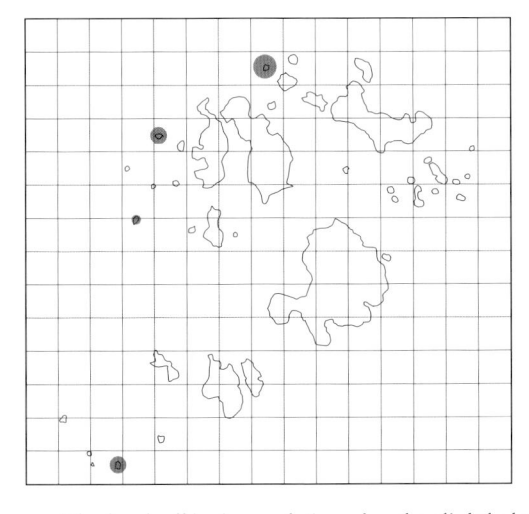

| Island      | Pairs |
|-------------|-------|
| Gorregan    | 39    |
| Scilly Rock | 39    |
| Men-a-Vaur  | 117   |
| Mincarlo    | 1     |

**Guillemot Breeding Distribution – 1999 (Seabird 2000 data)**

**Guillemot Breeding Distribution – 1999 (data Seabird 2000)**

The local *albionis* population plus the slightly larger and darker nominate *aalge* seem most likely to account for any winter Guillemot sightings in Scillonian waters. However, although the more northerly *hyperborea* mostly moves no further south than coastal Fennoscandia, some are known to reach southwest England and although perhaps not readily identifiable in the field all tide-line corpses should be examined carefully (Cramp *et al.* 1977–94; Gantlett 1998). Parslow attributed declines at Guillemot colonies in southern England to oil pollution, though he thought predation from large gulls *Larus* and food-related factors also played a part. A small number of (mainly dead) oiled Guillemots are washed ashore in Scilly each winter and as breeding adults mostly remain close to their colonies at this time that particular form of mortality has the potential to seriously deplete local breeding numbers. It is also interesting that 'cavity' nesting among local Guillemots reportedly commenced from the mid-1920s, which correlates closely with the colonisation and spread of Great Black-backed Gull *Larus marinus* in Scilly. Indeed, both Shag *Phalacrocorax aristotelis* and Razorbill now similarly nest almost exclusively beneath large boulders. Fogden & Greenwood (1965) found Guillemots breeding inside a natural chamber on Cape Clear Island, Ireland, in 1965, and pointed out that they knew then of just one other such example, in Norway, and attributed this behaviour to natural necessity brought about by the local geology at both sites, concluding that 'adaptive radiation has produced a wide range of nest-sites in the auk family'.

A total of 107 Guillemots have been ringed in Scilly as adults or pulli, 60 prior to 1970. The small number of recoveries shown here demonstrates that at least some local first-winter birds move south to the near limit of Guillemot's winter range in the eastern North Atlantic, whilst not all adults remain close to the islands outside the breeding season. In addition to those shown, two out of four ringed as breeding adults on Gorregan in 1962 were recovered in April 1967 as a consequence of the *Torrey Canyon* incident, one on St Mary's the other on the Cornish mainland. There was a marked difference in the mean age of recovered Guillemots, compared to Razorbills, the mean age of the four Scillonian recoveries being one year and eight months – or just over three months if the single long-lived individual is discounted, whereas the mean age of the seven Scillonian-ringed Razorbills was three years seven months, only one of which died in its first winter.

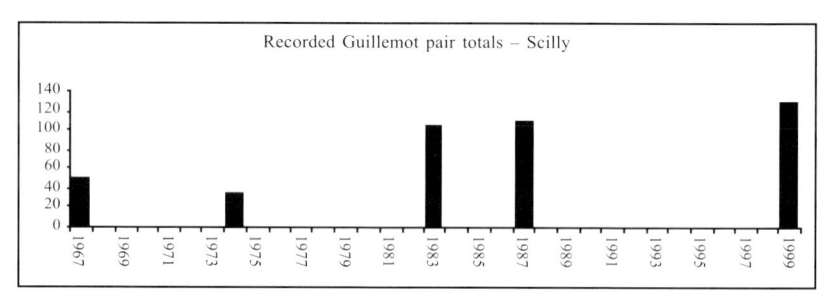

Recorded Guillemot pair totals – Scilly

**Data sources**: 1967 = Parslow 1967b; 1974 = Allen 1974–77; 1983 = P Harvey 1983; 1987 = Birkin & Smith 1987; 1999 = Seabird 2000 – unpublished data

### Controls
AT18601  Ad  Lundy Island, Devon 9th July 1954    FD  St Mary's 11th February 1955

### Recoveries
?         Pul  Men-a-Vaur 4th July 1958           SH  Pasajes, Guipuzcoa, Spain
                                                      20th November 1958
?         Ad   Scilly Rock 30th June 1960         ?   Fort-Bloque, Mobihan, France
                                                      23rd August 1960
AJ32243   Pul  Gorregan 29th June 1961            SH  Off Pasajes, Guipuzcoa, Spain
                                                      7th November 1961
?         Ad   Men-a-Vaur 4th July 1958           FI  Rade de Brest, Finistere, France
                                                      18th April 1964

**Guillemot Ringing Recaptures**

# Razorbill *Alca torda* A

**Summer visitor, breeds on about 14 uninhabited islands and in greater numbers than Guillemot *Uria aalge*. Probably fewer than at the start of the 20th century, smaller numbers are evident in Scillonian waters during winter.**

Breeds northeast and northwest North Atlantic, from northern France, Britain, Ireland and Fennoscandia west through Faeroes, Iceland and western Greenland to Newfoundland and Nova Scotia. Migratory in north of range, dispersive in south, in eastern Atlantic wintering south to coastal North Africa and Mediterranean. Polytypic: nominate *torda*, or 'Northern Razorbill' occurs north and west; *islandica* Iceland, Faeroes, Ireland, Britain and Brittany. Amber-listed in UK: 20% or more of European breeding population in UK, 50% or more at ten or fewer sites (Gregory *et al.* 2002).

Like Guillemot, earliest evidence of Razorbill in Scilly came from bone remains unearthed from archaeological sites on Nornour in the Eastern Isles, at May's Hill on nearby St Martin's and on Samson (Turk 1973, 1984a, 1984b). Bone remains at the May's Hill site date from between the Early Christian period and 1700, whilst on Nornour it was the commonest bird species unearthed and was found in almost all levels. Unusually in a British context, Razorbill, Guillemot and Puffin *Fratercula arctica* are the commonest bird species (in that order) found at such sites in Scilly, for though Razorbill remains are commonly found in kitchen middens in northern Scotland, they are seldom found at English sites (Turk 1984a). Interestingly, Carew (1602) mentions the use of 'murres' as food in Cornwall, this term being applied to both Razorbill and Guillemot in the county, though in west Cornwall more probably to Razorbill (Penhallurick 1969).

There are few early reports of this species in Scilly, E H Rodd briefly describing it as common in the late 19th century, 'sometimes appearing in small parties in Mount's Bay, and all round the coasts, especially at Scilly' (Rodd 1880), whilst elsewhere in the same volume he mentioned that it bred in Scilly's cliffs. However, as so often is the case, the most descriptive comments came from James Clark and E H Rodd's nephew Francis, who at the start of the 20th century observed that it 'Breeds in extraordinary numbers, especially in the Western Islands, and those to the north of Bryher' (Clark & Rodd 1906). Whilst it may be tempting to think there was perhaps a measure of exaggeration involved, the same authors described how 41 Razorbill eggs were found on the eastern section of isolated Scilly Rock in less than half an hour on 20th May 1903. These remarks must be viewed against a total of perhaps 15 surveyed pairs at the same site in 1999, Clark and Rodd's inference being that not all eggs were found in 1903.

Few published accounts provide an insight into the whereabouts of this species in Scilly during the late 19th and early 20th centuries. The Reverend Smart (1885–86) noted that it bred 'in countless numbers' on various rocks, specifically naming Hanjague in the Eastern Isles, Men-a-Vaur in the Northern Isles and all the Western Isles. F W Frohawk described climbing 'one of the loftiest stacks' on 30th June 1909, and upon reaching the 140-feet (42-metre) summit found himself in the midst of a Razorbill colony (Chatfield 1987). From the description this sounds very much like lofty Men-a-Vaur, which remains a main Razorbill stronghold today. H W Robinson and Uren both included this species among lists of seabirds found breeding on Annet (Uren 1907; H W Robinson 1911a) and there is more recent mention of a few on Bryher's Shipman Head, though on Mincarlo in the Northern Isles it was said to occupy 'Every available crack and crevice' (*CBWPSAR* 7). Finally, hundreds, or more, were said to be breeding on Rosevear up until at least 1914 (H W Robinson 1923) and a mid-20th century account of birds breeding on Mincarlo comes from two mainland egg-collectors who visited in 1952 and saw both breeding Razorbills and Guillemots (Cole & Trobe 2000).

Penhallurick (1969) demonstrated that in mainland Cornwall Razorbill is almost exclusively a bird of the north coast, though occurring in similar numbers to Guillemot. This situation is noticeably different from Scilly, where Razorbill currently outnumbers its close relative by about 3:2, rather less than the earlier suggested ratio of 20:1 (C J King 1924). The Chart includes counts from all-island 20th century surveys, though it should be borne in mind that counting methods varied between surveys and that periodic single-year counts run the risk of encountering either successful or poor breeding seasons. Distribution is noticeably different from that of Guillemot, birds being recorded breeding on at least 14 islands in 1999, but with Men-a-Vaur, Mincarlo and Gorregan between them holding about 80%. No Razorbills are currently known to breed on any of the five inhabited islands.

Razorbills in Scilly breed exclusively beneath boulders and most sites are inaccessible, making it extremely difficult basing a survey on numbers of apparently occupied nest sites, and though chicks can be quite vocal, determining numbers of adults involved using this feature is fraught with difficulties. Most counts, then, are based either on numbers of birds exiting from below ground, or on numbers of birds in the immediate vicinity. As with Guillemot, the 1999 Razorbill count formed part of the Seabird 2000 national survey, and, like Guillemot, counts involved all birds leaving the breeding colonies but not adjacent 'roost' areas, multiplied by 0.67 to produce the figure shown, to the nearest pair (Walsh *et al*. 1995). The 1969 total of 400 pairs represented in the order of 25% of the southwest England population (Lloyd *et al*. 1991).

Parslow (1967a) recorded marked and widespread decreases at Razorbill colonies in southern and southwest England, commencing from about the early 1940s and continuing until at least the mid-1960s. Various writers have attributed these declines to oil pollution, but doubtless other factors, e.g. food availability, also played a part. More recently, populations appear to be increasing (Mead 1993), though the lack of previous all-island counts create difficulties deciding whether this is also the case in Scilly. Gantlett (1998) drew attention to the possibility of the slightly larger nominate *torda* occurring in coastal Britain during winter, pointing out that there were already a few ringing recoveries, mostly from Norway, in which case particular attention should perhaps be paid to tideline corpses in Scilly, as elsewhere.

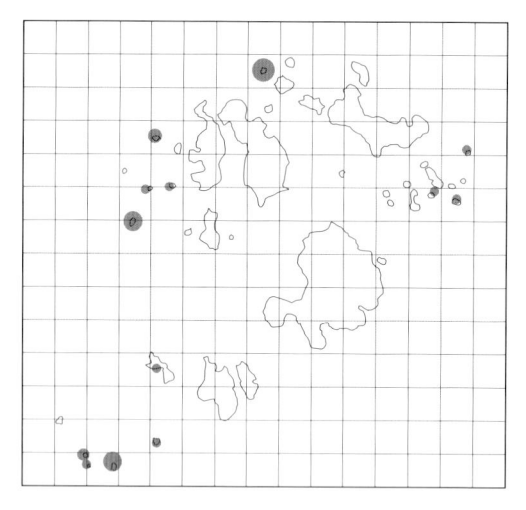

| Island | Nests/Pairs |
|---|---|
| Annet | 3 (4) |
| Melledgan | 4 (6) |
| Gorregan | 43 (64) |
| Rosevean | 3 (4) |
| Rosevear | 7 (11) |
| Mincarlo | 47 (70) |
| Illiswilgig | 5 (7) |
| Castle Bryher | 3 (4) |
| Scilly Rock | 15 (22) |
| Men-a-Vaur | 68 (101) |
| Ragged Island | 1 (1) |
| Menawethan | 1 (1) |
| Hanjague | 1 (1) |

**Distribution of 201 Razorbill Pairs – 1999 (Seabird 2000 data [adjusted figures, full-count data in brackets])**

**Razorbill Breeding Distribution – 1999 (data Seabird 2000)**

A total of 298 Razorbills had been ringed in Scilly up to the end of 1999, 243 prior to 1970. Of the eight recaptures, at least four were recorded as oiled and perhaps as many as six died from this cause. The bird recovered in Norway is notable, partly because it was shot but more importantly because it was so far north, though long-range displacements are not unusual in first-year Razorbills of the southern *islandica* form (Cramp *et al.* 1977–94). Significantly, the mean age of the seven Scillonian recoveries was three years and seven months, unlike Guillemot where the mean age of the four recoveries was just one year and eight months – or just over three months if the single long-lived individual was discounted. However, as Cramp *et al.* point out, this and other Alcidae may be under-represented by ringing data in the southern parts of their range and over-represented in areas where they are still shot, or entangled in fishing nets. It comes as no surprise, therefore, to find the majority of first-year Razorbills winter south as far as coastal Morocco and the western Mediterranean, most remaining well south of Britain during their first summer; whereas most adults remain close to the breeding areas during winter (Wernham *et al.* 2002).

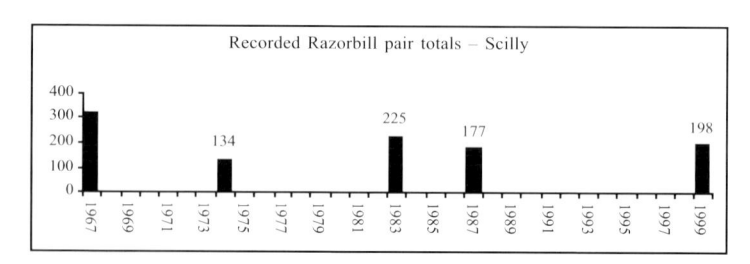

Data sources: 1967 = Parslow 1967b; 1974 = Allen 1974–77; 1983 = P Harvey 1983; 1987 = Birkin & Smith 1987; 1999 = Seabird 2000 – unpublished data

**Controls**
AT84988   Ad   4th July 1962 Skomer, Pembrokeshire   Ol   Tresco 5th February 1963

**Recoveries**
AT69151   Pul   Annet 22nd June 1961

AT69150   Ad    Annet 18th June 1961

?         Pul   Men-a-Vaur 4th July 1958

SH   Scottning Lighthouse, Hordaland, Norway 5th October 1962

Ol   Pendower, Veryan, Cornwall 16th February 1964

FD   Siouville, Manche, Normandy, France 20th June 1964

AT69186  Ad  Annet 9th July 1961              FD  Katwijk, Zuid-Holland, Netherlands
                                                    7th February 1965

?         Ad  Annet 30th June 1960             FD  Muzillac, Morbihan, Brittany, France
                                                    17th September 1966

M82451    Ad  Mincarlo 13th June 1996          Ol  Chesil Beach, Weymouth, Dorset
                                                    21st February 1997

M82455    Ad  Gorregan 17th June 1996          Ol  Sarzeau, Morbihan, France
                                                    31st December 1999

**Razorbill Ringing Recaptures**

## Great Auk                                                        *Pinguinus impennis*  B

**Now extinct, may have bred historically.**

Occurred boreal to subtropical latitudes in east and west Atlantic, breeding Newfoundland, Iceland, Scotland (St Kilda, possibly Orkney) and probably Faeroes, possibly Calf of Man; extinct since c. 1844. Prehistoric evidence of presence south to Mediterranean and coastal Florida probably indicates limit of winter range. Last British record probably 1840 on St Kilda (Fisher & Lockley 1954; Cramp *et al.* 1977–94).

Some 12 or so bones from among 105 excavated from the Halangy Down archaeological site, St Mary's, were identified as from this species, having been uncovered between 1950 and 1977 (Ashbee 1999). The Halangy Down site comprises a cluster of stone structures on a steep, west-facing slope at the northwest corner of St Mary's, it being deemed largely impossible to attribute bones and other artefacts to particular historical periods owing to the unstratified nature of the material under examination. However, the site dates from before 400 BC and a third of the bones were from 3rd century AD midden deposits, with the remaining 70% from disturbed levels. Great Auk remains appeared to originate from at least two individuals, one of which was only just full-grown. Similarly, an as yet unidentified large avian bone excavated on Samson during 1970–71, perhaps involving a 6th to 9th century AD site (Turk 1973), could conceivably be of this species.

Although the discovery of a past Great Auk presence in Scilly was a surprise, it ought not to have been wholly unexpected given Scilly's position 45 km out into the Atlantic. In addition, of course, there would have been an obvious incentive for early island occupants to exploit whatever resources were available locally. It seems generally accepted that the last sighting of this species within the British Isles came from St Kilda in 1840 (reputedly killed as a witch!) and there are reports prior to that of birds in Ireland in 1834 (Irish Rare Birds Committee 1998). Yet these are still very recent compared with the bones found on Scilly and the fact that the latter now represent the most southerly British and Irish records should pose no barrier to their acceptance, particularly as Great Auk remains have been found even into the Mediterranean (Fisher & Lockley 1954). However, not too much can be read into the apparent recent fledging of one of the Halangy birds, mainly because young Great Auks most probably left the nest site early in the fledging process, as with Guillemots *Uria aalge* and Razorbill *Alca torda* still. Therefore, a quite recently fledged young Great Auk off Scilly could have originated from a site further north; Fisher and Lockley thought that the most southerly former breeding site may have been the Calf of Man, though there is nothing to prevent us believing that Great Auk may once have bred in Scilly. Another explanation, however, was given by Ashbee who raised the possibility of carcasses or bones having been brought to the islands in connection with trade.

## Black Guillemot                                                  *Cepphus grylle*  A

**Extremely rare migrant or winter visitor.**

    1947   One St Mary's & Eastern Isles 4th March to 4th June   *CBWPSAR* 17
    1976   One St Martin's 14th April
    1994   Two (summer plumage) St Agnes 6th April
    2001   One (summer plumage) south of Samson 20th February

Circumpolar, breeds coastal northern latitudes south in West Palearctic to northern England, Ireland and Denmark. Less dispersive and less oceanic than other Palearctic Alcidae, with northerly populations showing most movement. Polytypic: nominate *grylle* occurs Baltic Sea; *arcticus* North America, southern Greenland, British Isles, Sweden, Denmark, Norway and White Sea; *faeroeensis* Faeroes; *islandicus* Iceland; *mandtii* arctic North America, west and east Greenland, and remaining Arctic islands east to Siberia and northern Alaska. Amber-listed in UK: unfavourable European conservation status (Gregory *et al.* 2002).

This remains a prime requirement species for most birder's Scilly list, just four records ever demonstrating the extreme rarity of this species so far south. The presence of the 1947 individual, plus its unexpected three-month stay, may well have been connected with the exceptionally cold European weather during early 1947, which had obvious profound effects on so many bird species throughout Cornwall and Scilly (*CBWPSAR* 17). We know little about the 1976 individual other than it was seen off St Martin's on 14th April. The third arrival involved a surprising two together in summer plumage off Horse Point, St Agnes, on 6th April 1994. More recently, a summer-plumaged individual, the fifth for Scilly, surfaced briefly next to the boat during a crossing to Samson in early 2001 (pers. obs.).

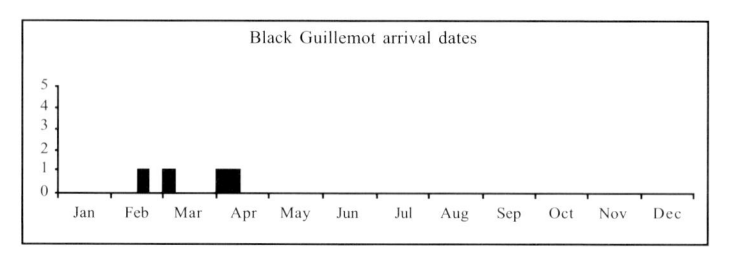

Black Guillemot arrival dates

These four sightings (of five individuals) represent extreme movements of this relatively sedentary species, the British and Irish population being least inclined to move among those in the West Palearctic (Cramp *et al.* 1977–94). Wernham *et al.* (2002) showed a small number of Fair Isle and Irish ringing recoveries to have moved south as far as Essex and southern Ireland. However, fewer birds from Iceland or the Faeroes seem likely to have been ringed and these areas may be under-represented among ringing data. As Gantlett (1998) suggested, *iclandicus* and *faeroeensis*, both of which are smaller than *arcticus*, might be expected to occur off the British Isles in winter but it seems unwise to speculate on where these Scillonian records may have originated.

# Little Auk *Alle alle* A

**Scarce winter migrant or vagrant, full written description required by the SRP.**

High-arctic species breeding Greenland, Arctic islands north of Eurasia and Ellesmere Island. Migratory and dispersive, regular south to British Isles in small numbers but more during major irruptions, perhaps then reaching western Mediterranean. Polytypic: nominate *alle* occurs Ellesmere Island, Greenland, Iceland, Jan Mayen, Bear Island, Spitsbegan and Novaya Zemlya; *polaris*, or 'Franz Josef Land Little Auk' Franz Josef Land. Racial identity of birds in northeast Asia and North Pacific unclear.

E H Rodd mentioned Little Auk as a winter visitor to Cornwall in parties of ten or so, which soon broke up and dispersed, single individuals then finding their way into harbours and estuaries. The same authority noted that birds were occasionally picked up some distance from the sea after strong winds, though he made no specific mention of Scilly (Rodd 1880). However, James Clark and Rodd's nephew Francis mentioned Little Auk in their subsequent *Zoologist* review of 'The Birds of Scilly', drawing attention to a single record of a bird found dead on St Agnes in midwinter 1900, though they thought the species perhaps overlooked in the islands (Clark & Rodd 1906).

The next mention of Little Auk in Scilly apparently came in 1963 and involved one picked up unharmed in a St Agnes garden on 20th December; the bird was ringed and then released. Following this, the very obvious pattern was of either no birds at all or only one to three per year through until the 1990s, though reasons for the apparent dramatic increase in records from that time are perhaps difficult to explain. Part of any explanation may be that earlier Bird Reports were often quite selective in what they contained, the auk species sometimes getting no mention at all in some years. In addition, of course, some earlier reports dealt only with St Agnes and its surrounds and in any event there were then fewer observers. However, quite a few Little Auks came to attention because of the unusual circumstances involved, like the bird in a garden in Hugh Town in February 1973, or one swimming in a puddle at Porthloo, St Mary's, in February 1988. Some too were found dead, or discovered in an emaciated condition and died later, though one record that stands out is the summer-plumaged individual found long dead on Tresco in June 1972.

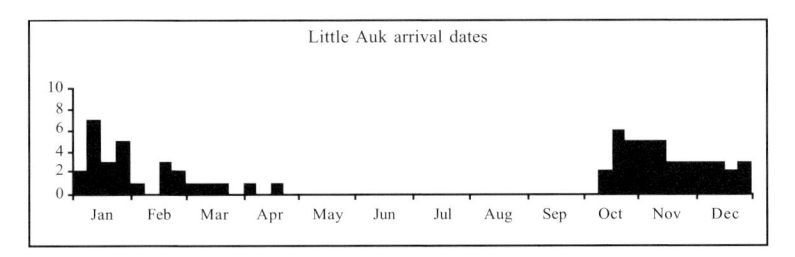

*Little Auk arrival dates*

The years 1991, 1996, 1997 and 1998 were especially productive, particularly the last with 12 sightings of up to 42 individuals, including one flock of 17. Examination of all published records shows a broad spread of first-sighting dates spanning the winter period, the earliest during the second week of October but with most birds having departed by early March, though two lingered into April. Given the normally quite severe winter weather and the limited amount of pre-arranged inter-island boat movement at that time of year, a surprisingly high percentage of sightings fell in the period November–February, though it nevertheless seems reasonable to suggest that many more went unrecorded. In addition, there may also be a more recent bias towards October sightings resulting from the increased interest in autumn birdwatching on Scilly. The Chart shows all recorded annual first-sighting dates. Gantlett (1998) suggested paying attention to tideline corpses in case individuals can be attributed to the larger *polaris*, or 'Franz Josef Land Little Auk'.

## Puffin (Atlantic Puffin) *Fratercula arctica* A

**Summer visitor breeding on eight or so uninhabited islands, in the range 100–200 pairs.**

Breeds northern North Atlantic, from France, Britain and Ireland north and west through Norway, Novaya Zemlya, Spitsbergen, Iceland, Greenland, Newfoundland and Nova Scotia. Dispersive, in eastern Atlantic wintering south to Azores, Canary Islands and western Mediterranean. Polytypic: nominate *arctica*, or 'Northern Puffin' occurs Iceland, central and northern Norway, Bear Island, southern Novaya Zemlya, southwest Greenland and northeast North America; *grabae* France, southern Norway, Britain, Ireland and Faeroes; *naumanni* Spitsbergen, northwest and eastern Greenland and northern Novaya Zemlya. Amber-listed in UK: 50% or more of breeding population at ten or fewer sites; unfavourable European conservation status (Gregory *et al.* 2002).

Scilly holds the distinction of being the first recorded Puffin breeding site in Britain. Gurney (1921) suggested that earliest mention was in 1337, when the islands were leased by Edward III (as Earl of Cornwall) to Abbot Ranulphus of Blancminster, for the costly amount of six shillings and eight pence, or 300 'Puffins'. Suffern (1939), however, drew attention to another reference, also for 1337 or thereabouts (10 Edward III) and contained in the Public Records Offices' *Descriptive Catalogue of Ancient Deeds*. This document apparently witnesses the subletting by Ranulph de Blaunchminster (presumably the same Abbot Ranulphus) of all or most of Scilly to John de Allet, by way of 'knight-service and by service of keeping Ranulphus castle in the said Isles for a certain time'. However, the agreement appears to have gone even further, for we also find that 'the said Ranulph has released and quitclaimed for self and heirs, to John and his heirs the service of keeping the said castle for ever'.

For his part, John appears to have negotiated a rent of thirteen shillings and four pence, or 150 puffins ('pufforum') in the event of his default, whilst also being granted the right to take puffins ('poffonis') at a rate of one penny for three. Payment of land rental in the carcasses of young seabirds, generally referred to as 'puffins', was quite commonplace as early as the 2nd century AD. More recently, entries such as these have been interpreted as referring to the Common or Atlantic Puffin *Fratercula arctica*, whereas the truth is that the term 'puffin, or 'puffling' was originally used to describe cured carcasses of young Manx

Shearwaters *Puffinus puffinus* (Lockwood 1984), a considered delicacy up until as late as the 18th century; supplies coming from Scilly and the Calf of Man, in particular. As evidence of the origin of the word 'puffin', Lockwood cites the shearwater's scientific name *Puffinus*, the name Puffin only later being attached to *Fratercula arctica*, perhaps through the close association of both species at breeding sites such as Annet, where both frequently occupy the same burrow (Walpole Bond 1937). However, there may be some doubt over the exact timing of the above historical events as Penhallurick (1969) described an official inquiry of 30th November 1300 (during the reign of Edward I) concerning rent of six shillings and eight pence, or 300 'puffons' payable by Scillonian tenants to Launceston Castle on mainland Cornwall. However, Penhallurick (1973) thought it reasonable to assume that such rents had been paid to all the earls of Cornwall beginning with Richard in 1225, or as early even as a Richard de Dunstanville in 1141.

Earliest physical evidence of Puffin in Scilly is contained among bone remains unearthed from the Bronze Age to Early Christian period at archaeological sites on Nornour in the Eastern Isles and at May's Hill on nearby St Martins (Turk 1984a, 1984b). Unusually among British archaeological sites, Razorbill *Alca torda*, Guillemot *Uria aalge* and Puffin were the three most frequently encountered species (in that order) among Scillonian bone deposits (Turk 1984a). Penhallurick (1969) speculated on when the culture of eating seabirds may have ended on Scilly, pointing out that an 1818 inquiry into the hardships of off-island life revealed no evidence of it continuing.

Given what has already been said about this species in Scilly during the 14th century, it comes as no surprise to find a large amount of early historical information available. In his writings of about 1470, Botoner noted its present on Tresco (Botoner 1478), and around 1533 Leland (Hearne 1710) thought it abundant about the islands, whilst, interestingly, in the 18th century, Heath (1750) was perhaps mistaken in listing it among species occurring in Scilly during winter. Borlase visited Scilly in 1752 and recorded the Puffin situation in considerable detail (Borlase 1756), noting they were 'very numerous', that they 'build upon the deserted rocks, and are of a fishy taste', though he personally saw 'but few' and assumed they were 'hatching or attending their young'. He also remarked, logically, that as Crown Rent had been paid in Puffins from as early as Edward I there must have 'been great numbers of them formerly, and very easily to be got at', though he was perhaps wrong in assuming they were valued more for their feathers than their flesh.

One hundred years later, E H Rodd thought it only occasionally observed on the Land's End cliffs in west Cornwall, pointing out that its favourite haunts were what he described as some of the precipitous rocks of Scilly (Rodd 1880). Predictably, the early 20th century *Zoologist* account of 'The Birds of Scilly' by James Clark and Rodd's nephew Francis paints the clearest picture (Clark & Rodd 1906), stating that on Annet it bred in 'thousands' alongside Manx Shearwaters and providing a graphic account of an island so riddled with burrows of both species 'that in walking across one sinks to the knee every two or three steps through the caving in of the roofs'. Clark & Rodd also pointed out that on Scilly Rock in the Northern Isles and on Men-a-Vaur in the Eastern Isles, it normally laid its egg on the bare rock. In addition, they also listed a number of other sites where Puffin bred up until at least the late 19th century, i.e. Rosevear and Melledgan in the Western Isles, Mincarlo, Castle Bryher and Round Island in the Northern Isles and Great Ganinnick and one or other of the Innisvouls in the Eastern Isles. Others noting the presence and abundance of Puffins around this time, but particularly on Annet, include F A Walker (1871), Uren (1907) and H W Robinson (1911a).

Numbers of Puffins declined dramatically in Britain during the early to mid-20th century, greatest reductions occurring in England during the period 1920–50. Parslow (1967a) considered the Annet decline in the range of from 100,000 birds in 1908 to below 100 by the mid-1960s. This same situation was reflected in other areas, e.g. on Lundy Island in North Devon they decreased from 'incredible numbers' in 1890 to just 93 pairs by 1962. Parslow blamed introduction of Brown Rats *Rattus norvegicus* for much of the British decline, particularly at island colonies, though he thought oil pollution and increased gull *Larus* predation also partly responsible, whilst other authorities thought reductions in food availability may have played a major role. Certainly in Scilly, the huge numbers of pilchards *Sardinops* formerly caught inshore during the 1880s were no longer apparent by the early to mid-1920s, though the timing of their decline may have preceded that of Scillonian Puffins.

According to various reports, numbers of Puffins varied during the early to mid-20th century, one account being the 1938 mention of breeding pairs on Annet, Mincarlo and Men-a-Vaur, though only in 'small numbers' (*CBWPSAR* 8), an estimated 20 pairs being present on the first of these three islands seven years later (Blair 1945). However, by 1946 it was being described as 'greatly diminished', with a 'small colony' still on Annet but only one or two pairs on Men-a-Vaur. Nevertheless, by 1959 'good numbers' were reportedly evident around Annet, and during June and July could be seen sitting in rows at their burrow entrances, several also breeding in the Eastern Isles. By 1961 numbers in the islands were 'well maintained' and for the first time we hear of an increasing colony on St Helen's, whereas their recent absence from Round Island was thought attributable to the presence of one or more lighthouse cats *Felis catus*. Particularly helpful is the 1965 account of 'a few pairs' of Puffins breeding on Menawethan and Great Innisvouls in the Eastern Isles and on Castle Bryher, Mincarlo and St Helen's in the Northern Isles, though the Annet colony allegedly amounted to more than all of these put together.

Following closely behind the 1967 wreck of the MV *Torrey Canyon*, just to the east of Scilly, came the results of the first structured all-island Puffin survey, which confirmed between 90 and 140 pairs on nine islands (Parslow 1967b). The lack of precise earlier data created difficulties deciding whether spilled oil from the *Torrey Canyon* caused further local Puffin reductions, but Parslow thought 1967 numbers may have been down by 10–20% on past years. However, no local birds were proved to have died as a result of the oil spill and 1967 could conceivably have been a naturally poor breeding season.

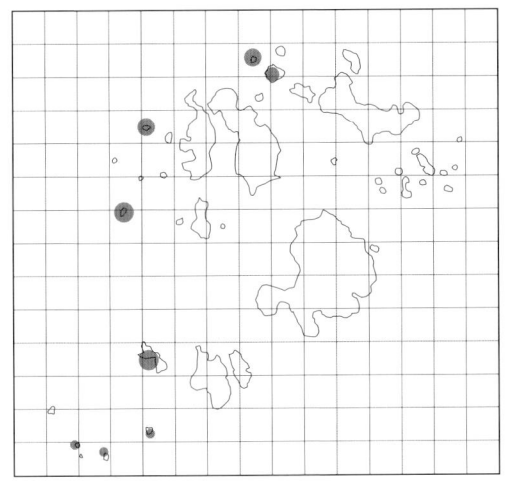

**Puffin Breeding Distribution – 1999 (data Seabird 2000)**

| Western Isles | 1967 | 1974 | 1983 | 1987 | 1999* |
|---|---|---|---|---|---|
| Annet | 50–100 | 53–57 | 55–79 | 60 | 47 |
| Rosevear | 1 | 3 | 2–4 | 3 | 3 |
| Melledgan | | | 1 | 1 | 2 |
| Gorregan | | | | | 1 |
| **Northern Isles** | | | | | |
| Castle Bryher | 2 | 2 | 2 | 2 | |
| Mincarlo | 12 | 11 | 10–20 | 4 | 53 |
| Scilly Rock | 4 | 2 | 6–10 | 4 | 25 |
| Men-a-Vaur | 1 | 6 | 6–10 | 6 | 25 |
| St Helen's | 8 | 8 | 9–14 | 12 | 11 |
| **Eastern Isles** | | | | | |
| Great Innisvouls | 5 | | | | |
| Menawethan | 8 | 2 | 2 | | |
| **Total Pairs** | 91–141 | 87–91 | 93–142 | 92 | 167 |

**Recorded Puffin Pair Totals – Scilly (Seabird 2000 data)**

The Table shows estimated numbers of Puffin pairs from main all-island surveys and it should be noted that the species no longer breeds in the Eastern Isles, Harvey's suggestion that Brown Rats were primarily responsible (P Harvey 1983) perhaps being borne out by more recent work (pers. obs.). As a consequence, an eradication programme is now in place on Menawethan and several other islands in the eastern group. There is some suggestion of an increase in overall numbers in Scilly since 1974, though the 1999 Seabird 2000 count (see Table and Map) probably coincided with one of the recent best breeding seasons. Nevertheless, it seems Annet may now have been replaced by Mincarlo as the main Puffin breeding site in Scilly, with apparent substantial increases also on Scilly Rock and Men-a-Vaur. Lack of data from other sites creates difficulties assessing the regional importance of the Scillonian population, though the islands recently appear to have held 50% or more of the southwest's Puffins (Lloyd *et al.* 1991).

Of the eight islands holding breeding Puffins in 1999, all but St Helen's are known to be naturally rat-free, birds on this last island being confined to a group of six to ten holes in a vertical low earth cliff. Some of these holes may be inaccessible to rats but others are clearly not, and in an attempt to improve productivity a series of new holes were recently manufactured in the sheer face, at least some of which are now in use, whilst a St Helen's rat-clearance programme is also in place.

Some observers, e.g. A A Dorrien-Smith (*CBWPSAR* 16), blamed early 20th century Scillonian Puffin and Manx Shearwater declines on the concomitant increase in Great Black-backed Gulls *Larus marinus*. However, more recent declines in other species, e.g. Herring Gull *L. argentatus* have been matched by reductions in Great Black-backed Gulls, and direct evidence that this species caused declines in any other species in Scilly is lacking still. Early observers may have failed to differentiate between good and bad breeding seasons, and the report of an evening raft of 95 Puffins off Annet in July 1950 suggested that there were perhaps greater than 20 pairs (*CBWPSAR* 20), birds also being noted that year on Men-a-Vaur after an alleged absence the previous season. One additional factor worth considering in relation to Annet's Puffins is the likely impact of the wreck of the SS *Castleford* on nearby Crebawethan on 8th June 1887, when, according to reports, at least 250 out of 500 head of cattle on board were rescued and temporarily landed on Annet. Although reportedly these animals only remained on the island for some ten days 'They trampled everything to pieces, broke in all the Shearwaters' holes, probably destroying many birds, and made a ruin of everything' (Gurney 1889). Undoubtedly, Puffins would have been similarly affected and, interestingly, unlike other writers, Gurney suggested that all 500 or so cattle were landed on Annet.

Limited information is available on Puffin return dates, but an early report from the Bishop Rock Lighthouse recorded them as first noted from 3rd March in 1886 (Harvie-Brown *et al.* 1887), and, similarly, in 1911 they were recorded returning to their nesting grounds from 22nd March (Ogilvie-Grant 1912c). During most of the ten years from 1990, first birds were present from between 19th and 28th March, last colony sightings occurring between 25th July and 8th August. Sightings outside the breeding season during this same period were restricted to a handful of October observations and the even more occasional winter report, e.g. one off St Mary's Quay on 27th December 1993. The slightly larger *arctica* occurs in Britain during winter but is mainly identified from tideline remains, and therefore attention should be paid to any dead individuals found in Scilly. As much as anything, the seven Puffins ringed in Scilly up until the end of 1999 testify to the level of 20th century reductions in the Scillonian population, with five of these having been ringed prior to 1970. There are few recaptures, the only notable record involving a bird from northern France found apparently breeding on Annet during May 1936.

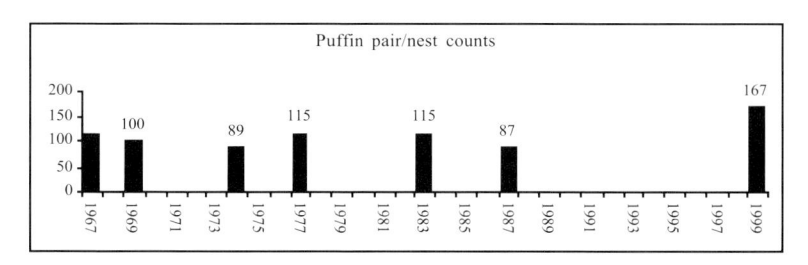

**Data sources**: 1967* = Parslow 1967b; 1969 = Lloyd *et al.* 1991; 1974* = Allen 1974–77; 1977 = IOSBR 1977; 1983 = P Harvey 1983; 1987 = Birkin & Smith 1987; 1999 = Seabird 2000 – unpublished data
* averaged total

## Controls
D2682     Ad Sept Illes, Core du Nord, France 6th July 1934     BR Annet May 1936

**Puffin Ringing Recaptures**

## Pallas's Sandgrouse                    *Syrrhaptes paradoxus*  A   BBRC 0%

**Extremely rare vagrant, full written description required by the BBRC.**

  1863   One (dead male) St Agnes 23rd June   Rodd 1863c; Rodd 1880; Clark & Rodd 1906
  1863   Small flock Scilly June 1863   Rodd 1863c
  1888   Eight to ten St Martin's 15th May   Clark & Rodd 1906

Breeds central Asia, from Kazakhstan east to Manchuria and China. Mainly sedentary but subject to irregular migration and irruptions, sometimes of considerable magnitude, reaching western Europe and sometimes leading to temporary range extensions. Northern populations more inclined to migrate, probably in response to extent of winter snow. Monotypic.

A dead male of this highly irruptive and extremely attractive species was found on St Agnes on 23rd June 1863 and described by E H Rodd in the *Zoologist* (Rodd 1863c). Its discovery coincided with the appearance of a small flock in Scilly (Clark & Rodd 1906), which presumably formed part of the big invasion of Britain that year (Newton 1864; Rodd 1880). The skin of the St Agnes male was preserved by Penzance taxidermist Vingoe, who reported that it was in 'a highly developed condition'. Rodd also recorded a female shot near Land's End, Cornwall, in the second week of June the same year, this too being sent to Vingoe for preservation. This bird was also in good condition and had a well-developed ovary, from which

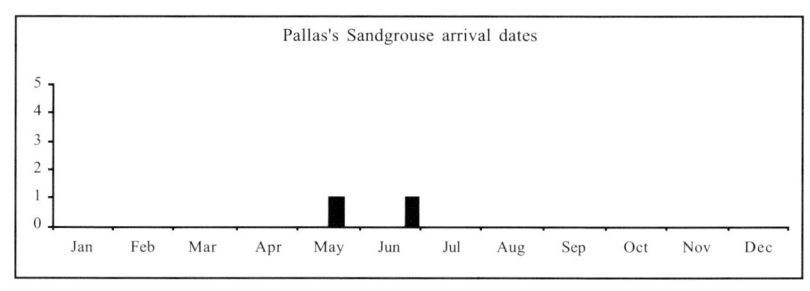

Rodd concluded Pallas's Sandgrouse might have bred in southwest England 'had they been allowed to remain unmolested' (Rodd 1880).

The only other Scillonian record coincided with the exceptional and well-documented invasion into Britain of 1888 and involved a flock of eight to ten seen 'feeding and evidently quite at home' on the west side of St Martin's on 15th May that year (Clark & Rodd 1906). Birds were also recorded in Cornwall around this time, some of which were shot (Penhallurick 1978). The only other exceptional influx into western Europe occurred in 1908–09 but appears not to have affected southwest England. A flock of 16 sandgrouse seen in flight in Cornwall in 1972 were thought by the observer to have been this species, but they evidently did not make it as far as Scilly (Penhallurick 1978). Pallas's Sandgrouse reaching Scilly must originate from at least east of the Caspian Sea.

## [Rock Dove                                                              *Columbia livia*]   A

**Does not occur in Scilly, but may possibly have done so historically.**

Widely distributed throughout the world, extent of original distribution masked by long history of domestication and escape. In West Palearctic breeds almost continuously except northern Fennoscandia and inland deserts of North Africa. Resident and mainly sedentary. Polytypic, large number of recognisable forms; nominate *livia* occurs western Europe including Canary Islands and central North Africa east to Kazakhstan.

Although Scilly regularly hosts lost to exhausted racing or wandering feral pigeons, there is no evidence suggesting a possibly wild Rock Dove presence in Scilly later than the very early centuries AD. Turk (1984a, 1984b) assessed bone remains unearthed from the Bronze Age to Early Christian periods at prehistoric sites on Nornour in the Eastern Isles and at May's Hill on nearby St Martin's, those from the latter site were thought to originate from around the 4th century AD. Both sites were thought to contain bones of truly wild Rock Doves, though the possibility of some level of domestication or transportation cannot be discounted entirely.

In their early 20th century review of the birds of Scilly, James Clark and Francis Rodd found that Rock Dove had 'been reported several times, but, so far as can be discovered, no Scillonian specimen has ever been seen by a competent ornithologist' (Clark & Rodd 1906). James Clark also made a similar comment in the *Victoria History of Cornwall* (in W Page 1906). Interestingly, even though Ryves & Quick (1946) noted it as 'Believed to be extinct in Cornwall and Scilly', T A Dorrien-Smith (1951) included Rock Dove in his list of *Birds of Scilly as Recorded at Tresco Abbey*, which appears to have been largely based upon skins in the Abbey collection. This list is preceded by the comment 'Birds not represented in the collection are either marked by an asterisk or are resident in the islands'; as this Rock Dove entry is not marked with an asterisk we might perhaps assume that it was either resident in the islands by 1951 (regardless of any lack of mention in the literature) or that a vagrant individual was recorded at some time. In either case, the possibility of confusion with domesticated individuals arises, particularly in the absence of a well-documented account. As an example, then, of how such confusion might arise, reference to a bird on Annet under the heading 'Rock Dove' during spring 1923 concluded with the words: 'The bird rose from ground riddled with the burrows of the Manx Shearwater (*Puffinus puffinus*). It had a pure white rump, and some white on its secondaries. What a tame pigeon was doing there among a thousand gulls I do not know' (Wallis 1923). However, a claim allegedly involving genuine pure Rock Doves concerned up to three individuals seen by D I M Wallace and others on St Agnes between 4th and 13th October 1971 (*IOSBR* 1971), even though the next nearest pure breeding population of this normally sedentary species would have been in western Ireland (Parslow 1967a; Sharrock 1976).

Penhallurick reviewed domestic pigeons and dovecotes in Cornwall from the 13th to 18th centuries and considered it unlikely that pure strains of Rock Dove could have survived in the county into the 19th century (Penhallurick 1978). Even so, according to other authorities 'pure Rock Doves' were thought to have possibly survived on remote parts of Cornwall's rugged north coast until as recently as 1997 (*CBWPSAR* 67). Importantly, however, there are no such published records for Scilly for any period, although very obviously lost or exhausted racing pigeons, mostly en route back to Ireland, are occasionally to be seen on one or two of the uninhabited islands – notably Round Island, where the presence of buildings may be a main attraction. Similarly, groups of visiting racing pigeons annually arrive and remain evident in the area of Hugh Town, St Mary's, where they seek food among litterbins and similar sources of human food waste, or at garden feeding stations. On the outer islands, their numbers seem to be quickly reduced by natural wastage – at least partly now through Peregrine Falcon *Falco peregrinus* predation, although on St Mary's and perhaps other inhabited islands they persist for rather longer.

## Stock Dove (Stock Pigeon) *Columba oenas* A

Resident and spring and autumn migrant, breeds in small numbers.

Breeds Europe south to extreme northwest North Africa and east to central and southern Asia, from Britain and Ireland to Kazakhstan and western Mongolia. Mainly resident or dispersive, migratory or partially so in colder areas. Polytypic: nominate *oenas* occurs Europe and North Africa east to Kazakhstan; *yarkandensis* further east and south. Amber-listed in UK: 36.7% of European breeding population in UK (Gregory *et al.* 2002). National 10% increase 1994–99 (Bashford & Noble 2000).

Earliest published mention of Stock Dove in Scilly may be North's observation that it had twice been obtained in the islands (North 1850), though this was followed soon after by E H Rodd's report of it having been seen during the last week of November 1867 (Rodd 1867a). However, Rodd was clearly unsure of its status, mentioning the presence of 'some' during September 1870 and also that one was obtained during early October the same year, all of which creates the impression it was far from frequent in the islands. Nevertheless, Rodd then rather clouded the issue by announcing it was 'common in flocks during winter' (Rodd 1880). As usual, though, it fell to James Clark and Rodd's nephew Francis to put the record straight, these two concluding it 'May be constantly seen during the autumn months on most of the larger islands, including Tean and St Helen's, both singly and in flocks', closing with the observation that 'It seems to have been quite as common in 1863 as it is now' (Clark & Rodd 1906).

In Cornwall and throughout most of Devon until the 1880s, it was known only as a winter visitor, breeding in the former county being first recorded in 1888 (Penhallurick 1978). However, by the early 20th century it had become well established on the Cornish mainland and by the end of that century bred throughout the county, though it is by no means numerous now. One extremely interesting report mentioned by Penhallurick concerns Stock Doves allegedly breeding alongside Swifts on one or two of Bodmin Moor's granite tors, as Penhallurick pointed out, a habitat not known to be occupied today.

Surprisingly, on Scilly even up until the mid-1970s Penhallurick still considered Stock Dove's status very much as in the late 19th century, it reportedly occurring in groups during most autumns and less occasionally during October and early November (Penhallurick 1978). The same author pointed out that

*Birds of the Isles of Scilly*

flocks larger than six or so may have been more frequent than records suggested, although he thought 200 moving north-northeast over St Agnes in early November 1959 clearly exceptional. Penhallurick also quoted 13th November 1959 as the latest recorded date for the islands, and summering seems not to have been recorded up until that time, Penhallurick noting few spring records all and these mainly between March and late April, with none after 1st May.

Ironically, progress towards the present small but apparently resident breeding population commenced almost as Penhallurick was going to press and appears to have developed from a greater-than-usual influx during winter 1975. The largest October single-island count that year was 25 on Bryher but some were still present on St Mary's to the year's end. Subsequently, one to two individuals annually remained later into summer, until, on Tresco, two to three pairs were present and for the first time song was heard during summer 1982. By 1985, song was also evident in the Holy Vale elm *Ulmus* woods on St Mary's with two pairs also believed to be present on Tresco, whilst by 1987 there was probably also a pair on Bryher. However, perhaps there was a total of no more than five to six pairs even by the late 1990s: up to three each on Tresco and St Mary's, though with the occasional summer individuals on other islands. On the 16-hectare Lunnon Farm study plot on St Mary's, a single pair was recorded by the 1987 CBC and one to two pairs annually from 1991. But although various published reports of breeding having occurred on both Tresco and St Mary's appeared during the 1980s and 1990s, proof was not forthcoming until the author located a nest with a single egg in Holy Vale during 1998. The nest site was an elm cavity near the northern edge of the Lunnon Farm plot, this pair successfully fledging one chick and using the same site to fledge two more the following year.

The limited tree cover in Scilly and the generally stunted nature of trees involved make it possible that nest-site availability may be at least partly limiting Stock Dove occupation, particularly given the intolerance shown by this species towards human disturbance and the distinct shortage of alternative nest sites in the form of suitably isolated farm and other buildings. The 2000 Breeding Bird Atlas recorded up to 17 pairs in eight (11.9%) of the 67 surveyed 1-km squares, though the authors thought the likely total less than ten pairs (Chown & Lock 2002).

The situation during autumn and winter remains much as described by Penhallurick, except that many more birds may now be involved. Most years commence with reports of less than ten each on St Mary's and Tresco with perhaps odd individuals or groups on other islands, decreasing to numbers commensurate with the believed breeding population

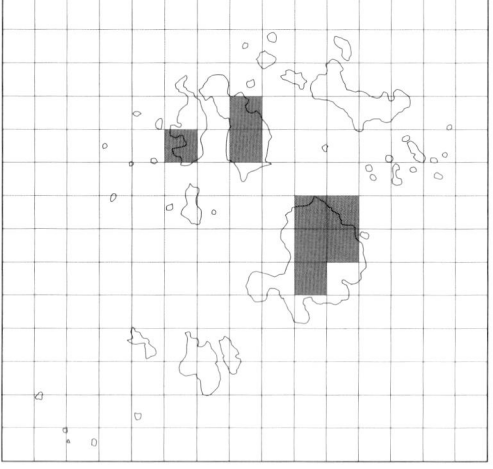

**1-km Stock Dove Breeding Distribution – 2000–01 (data Chown & Lock 2002)**

by late April. Last evidence of any spring movement is usually recorded during April or early May. During late summer, groups of 12 or more possibly involve local birds, but by late September flocks of 25 or so are in evidence, increasing to 40–50 by late October. By November, however, numbers are already decreasing and by the year's end perhaps only the local population remains. By far the largest flock recorded at any time remains the 200 seen over St Agnes on 4th November 1959.

Parslow (1967a) documented late 19th century increases throughout Britain, with birds colonising southwest England. These increases were followed, however, by marked reductions in many counties of England and Scotland during the mid-20th century, though Parslow considered the decline may have halted by the mid-1960s. Most authorities equate earlier increases to expansions in arable farming and the later reductions to the increased and widespread use of organochlorine pesticides, e.g. Marchant *et al.* (1990). Significantly, the colonisation of Scilly correlates well with subsequent further British population expansion following reductions in the level of organochlorine use, recovery commencing during the 1960s and smoothing out some time during the 1980s. Interestingly, Marchant *et al.* also point out that during the period of pesticide-induced declines Stock Doves withdrew into coastal areas.

Within Britain, Stock Doves are mainly resident, juveniles being only slightly more likely to disperse than adults, with no southerly tendency apparent within either age group. However, largely migratory populations from Fennoscandia eastwards and south into central and southern Europe are mainly orientated towards the southwest during autumn, most wintering in southern France and Iberia. Most depart Fennoscandia during late September and October and ringing data show few from northern Europe cross the North Sea to Britain (Cramp *et al.* 1977–94; Wernham *et al.* 2002). Return passage commences from February and increases in intensity throughout March, northern European birds reaching the breeding grounds by late March or April. The inference from all this is that birds reaching Scilly during spring and autumn are either off-course migrants breeding in northern or eastern Europe, or a minority of those same populations that do cross the North Sea and southern Britain on their way to and from France or Iberia. Without doubt the timing of Scillonian movements supports the theory that these are migrant birds.

Just four Stock Doves have been ringed in Scilly, all since 1970. Three of these were young ringed by the author in the 1998–99 Holy Vale nests and the fourth an adult trapped and ringed by the author in the Higher Moors section of the Lunnon Farm study plot on 21st June 1998. The are no recaptures. The very much scarcer but recognisably different and largely migratory Yellow-eyed Stock Dove *C. eversmanni* has a far more limited world range but could come into contact with Stock Dove in Kazakhstan during summer. Thus the possibility of it then reaching western Europe as a migrant is real and, given Scilly's reputation for attracting Asian migrants, all apparent passage Stock Doves should be viewed critically.

## Woodpigeon (Common Wood Pigeon)  *Columba palumbus*  A

**Spring and autumn migrant, sometimes in substantial numbers, also resident and breeds in small numbers.**

Similar breeding range to Stock Dove *Columba oenas*, but including Faeroes, Madeira, Azores and slightly more of North Africa. Like Stock Dove largely migratory in north and east, increasingly less so in south and west. Polytypic: nominate *palumbus* occurs Europe and North Africa east to western Siberia, Iraq and Turkey; *azorica* Azores; *iranica* Iran and southern Turkmenistan (former Turkmeniya); *casiotis* further east and south. No population change 1994–99 (Bashford & Noble 2000).

There are few 19th century Woodpigeon records and E H Rodd's brief comment that it was generally distributed throughout Cornwall wherever copses and plantations occurred was wholly unhelpful as far as Scilly is concerned (Rodd 1880). However, in their dependable early 20th century *Zoologist* review *The Birds of Scilly* James Clark and Francis Rodd (1906) drew attention to a letter written by Francis in 1863, presumably to his uncle E H Rodd. In this Francis described Woodpigeon as 'very rarely observed' in Scilly and made specific mention of one present on Tresco for several days during autumn 1863, this or another perhaps killed by a bird of prey. E H Rodd's only mention of the islands in relation to this species concerned a letter written by Francis in early November 1870, which pointed out that he had shot one and heard of another being seen, and concluded with the comment 'they only appear in winter and not often then'. Clearly though, its status in Scilly changed rapidly, for Clark and Rodd went on to describe it as a 'fairly common winter visitor by 1873, in which year the first nest was found on Tresco'. However, they unfortunately left doubts as to whether this was the first nest for Tresco or for the islands as a whole, though their observation that it became established as a resident around 1876 suggests the former, making it clear that it increased greatly in the islands since that time. These two authors concluded their account with a description of 400–500 arriving briefly in the Tresco woods during April 1888, allegedly causing a great deal of damage to trees

As with Scilly, there appears to be little information on the early status of this species in mainland Cornwall (Penhallurick 1978), though it was widespread and perhaps even abundant during summer by the mid-20th century (Sharrock 1976), and autumn saw an annual influx of large numbers of passage and wintering birds. Penhallurick quoted 7,446 killed in the Truro area during 1912, 2,323 of these between 5th and 12th February. The same author suggested a connection between the Woodpigeon's colonisation of Scilly and tree planting on Tresco, although the main programme of tree planting on Scilly occurred in the early 20th century and it seems unlikely that their introduction to just one island would have influenced Woodpigeons to that extent. Nevertheless, by the 1920s Wallis (1923) mentioned seeing a pair or two on Tresco and Penhallurick accepted this as proof of breeding, though no more provable after all this time is the report of breeding on St Mary's in 1959 (Penhallurick 1978). Similar, subsequent allegations of breeding on various islands, e.g. 20–30 pairs on St Mary's, four on St Agnes and two on St Martin's during 1974, are doubtless reliable but the fact remains there is no published evidence of a nest being found prior to the 1990s.

Certainly during the ten years from 1990, passage through the islands was mainly confined to autumn, being hardly noticed at all in spring during six years and negligible during the remaining four, the maximum recorded spring flock being 24 during April 1997. Autumn numbers were far more impressive – up to a maximum of 1,000 birds per day through St Mary's on 16th November 1998 – with lesser numbers on that island and elsewhere in Scilly at other times. Autumn movements commenced from as early as July but were normally most evident during October or November, though with perhaps little more than the local breeding population remaining by the year's end. There is surprisingly little mention of Woodpigeons becoming involved in cold-weather movements in Scilly, even during the particularly severe winters of 1961–62 and early 1963, perhaps because most had passed through the islands and were already wintering elsewhere.

A more realistic assessment of the current breeding population was provided by the 2000 Breeding Bird Atlas (Chown & Lock 2002), which recorded an estimated 133 pairs in 24 (35.8%) of the 67 surveyed 1-km squares, though the report's authors thought the true total was anywhere between 100–150 pairs. Of these, 52–70 were on St Mary's in year one of the survey, with the next highest, 8–17, on Tresco and nearly similar numbers, 5–10 and 5–12, on St Agnes and Bryher respectively. However, such surveys rely substantially on individual assessments and so inevitably suffer variations in observer skill and experience levels, in which case the unimpressive 4–5 pairs for the comparatively larger St Martin's could be an underestimate. This same survey suggests a St Mary's density in the range one pair to every 5.5 to 8.5 hectares. However, on the 16-hectare Lunnon Farm study plot on the same island, CBC results of between one and seven pairs for the eight years 1991–98 produced densities of one pair every 2.2 to 16 hectares. However, between-year variations in annual totals of from one to seven pairs produced a mean of 4.74 hectares and once allowance is made for greater observer familiarity with both the species and the Lunnon Farm study plot the two mean figures may not be very different. From two to five nests were found annually on the Lunnon Farm plot, the majority situated in the predominant elm *Ulmus* or willow *Salix*.

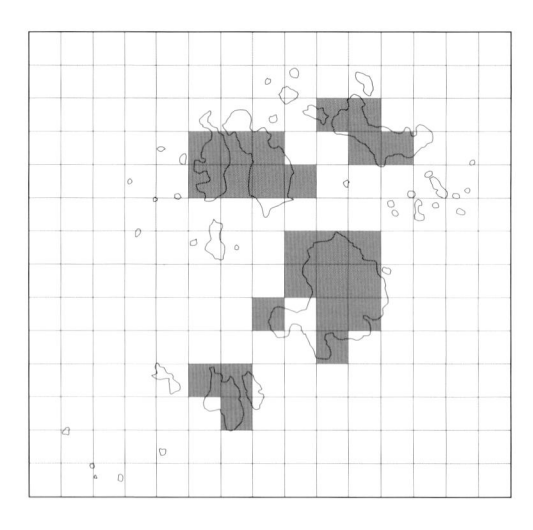

| Island | Pairs |
| --- | --- |
| Bryher | 14 |
| St Agnes | 7 |
| St Martin's | 7 |
| St Mary's | 70 |
| Tresco | 35 |

2000 Breeding Bird Atlas – Woodpigeon (Chown & Lock 2002)

1-km Woodpigeon Breeding Distribution – 2000–01 (data Chown & Lock 2002)

Northern and eastern European Woodpigeon populations move southwest down the eastern North Sea in autumn, most departing mid-September through to November and most wintering in southwest France or Iberia (Cramp *et al.* 1977–94). Ringing recoveries show clear evidence of movement between northern European countries, east as far as Austria, Poland, Finland and European Russia, and southwest France. Any occasional arrivals in eastern England are believed to be attributable to westerly drift during appropriate weather conditions, these quickly moving on either southwest or directly west into Ireland. There is also limited evidence of presumed westerly cold-weather movements into England and Ireland of birds ringed in the Low Countries. Birds from partially migratory western and southern European populations also demonstrate a marked tendency to head southwest in autumn, but do not penetrate as far, and many fewer reach Iberia. British populations are mainly resident, some 85% of adults and 65% of first-years being recovered within 40 km of where they were ringed and slightly more than 2% moved greater than 100 km, as far as southern France (Wernham *et al.* 2002).

Just 12 Woodpigeons were ringed on Scilly up until the end of 1999, all by the author on the St Mary's Lunnon Farm study plot during the three years 1997–99: ten as pulli and two as adults. The single recovery involved a bird ringed as a nestling on St Mary's and shot on Tresco ten months later.

Local
FC77661   Pul   Holy Vale, St Mary's 4th August 1997   SH   Borough Farm, Tresco 17th April 1998

Woodpigeon Ringing Recaptures

## Collared Dove (Eurasian Collared Dove)     *Streptopelia decaocto*   A

**Colonised during late 1950s, now a common breeding resident and perhaps vagrant or further colonist.**

Disjunct Eurasian breeding range, occurring central West Palearctic through Middle East and Indian subcontinent to eastern China. Mainly sedentary, altitudinal movements in mountainous regions. Polytypic: nominate *decaocto* occurs Europe and Middle East to Afghanistan and northern India; *stolickzae* southeast Kazakhstan and northwest China; *inercedens* southern India and Sri Lanka; one additional form further east. National 18% increase 1994–99 (Bashford & Noble 2000).

First mention of this species in Scilly concerned a bird seen in flight and at rest on St Agnes on 30th August 1957 (*SABOAR* 1957), whereas two years later a first-year frequented the same island from 30th September to 11th October (Penhallurick 1978). The next record was of one to two seen from 7th to 11th October 1961, again on St Agnes (*CBWPSAR* 31). The following year saw a mini invasion of Scilly, including the first spring record, a St Agnes adult on 31st May, plus others between June and October, involving perhaps five on St Agnes and the first for St Mary's, whilst the first for Tresco arrived in 1963 – two on 5th June.

Since early colonisation, numbers of Collared Doves on Scilly increased substantially, though the extent to which recorded flocks involve residents or alleged 'migrants' remains unclear. This frequent use of the term migrant in relation to Collared Doves on Scilly doubtless confuses the issue and takes no account of the fact that adults are largely sedentary, whilst only a proportion of immatures make pronounced dispersive movements (Cramp *et al.* 1977–94). Particularly more recently, though, published reports are punctuated by reference to 'no visible (spring or autumn) migration', from which it must be assumed that any counts involved only resident birds. Seasonal between-islands, or between-site increases or decreases are difficult to interpret and most recent allegations of 'passage' movement appear based wholly on these local fluctuations. However, two flying east past the Bishop Rock Lighthouse seven miles southwest of St Mary's on 21st May 1990 suggests at least unusual behaviour, as perhaps did 13 flying east past the RMV *Scillonian III* on 1st June 1985, or even singles among seabirds on Rosevean in the Western Isles on 4th May 1975 and on Gorregan, also Western Isles, on 1st June 1994. One aboard *Scillonian II* near the Wolf Rock Lighthouse during her daily crossing on 28th April 1975 is perhaps more easily explained, unlike seven watched arriving aboard the *Scillonian* from the east on 28th April 1984 and departing southwards after half an hour.

Earlier reports of apparent 'passage' involved immatures moving even further west, as in the case of 18 seen leaving westwards from Bryher on 5th May 1986 and it seems impossible to say when that type of movement might have ceased in Scilly, if indeed it has. Particularly impressive was the sheer ferocity of Collared Dove's colonisation of Scilly, where even by 1966 – ten years after its arrival – up to 60 gathered where they were fed regularly (*CBWPSAR* 36), with 30 on Bryher and up to nine seen daily on St Agnes. Taking the ten years from 1990, the highest count involved 95 at New Grimsby, Tresco, on 24th September 1996, followed by 89 at Porth Cressa, St Mary's, on 27th August 1999, though 150 on St Mary's during May 1977 seems to have been the all-time high. Collared Doves show a clear tendency to congregate at regular feeding sites, e.g. chicken coups, or where food is provided, as near the St Mary's launderette, being quick to commute between these last two sites (*IOSBR* 1982; pers. obs.). Some indication of minimal numbers may be gained from autumn 1994, when 45–55 were regularly present at the launderette site, whilst 15–25 were at three other sites on the same island, plus up to 30 on nearby St Agnes. This makes a total of up to 160 at just five feeding sites, to which must be added an unrecorded number of birds at various additional feeding sites on Tresco, Bryher and St Martin's, plus elsewhere on the first two islands. Interestingly, year one of the 2000 Breeding Bird Atlas (Chown & Lock 2002) recorded an estimated 44–80 Collared Doves in eight 1-km squares on St Mary's during summer 2000. However, this is a surprisingly secretive species when breeding, and unfamiliarity with such census work on the part of several observers involved almost certainly means this was an underestimate.

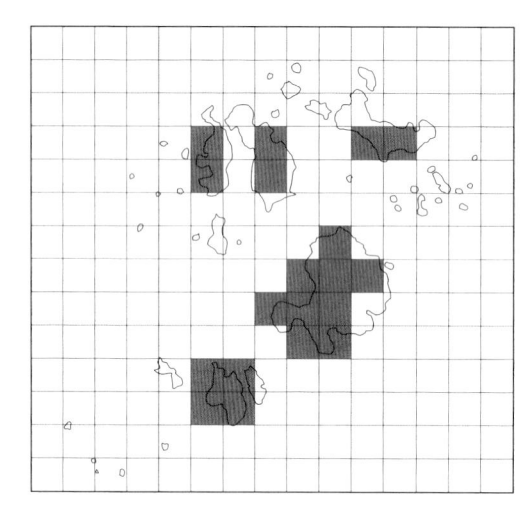

| Island | Pairs |
|---|---|
| Bryher | 7 |
| St Agnes | 8 |
| St Martin's | 4 |
| St Mary's | 33 |
| Tresco | 8 |

**2000 Breeding Atlas – Collared Dove (Chown & Lock 2002)**

**1-km Collared Dove Breeding Distribution - 2000–01 (data Chown & Lock 2002)**

Breeding was first discussed in print in 1965, at which time possibly as many as ten to twelve pairs were present on St Mary's in June, with a settled colony of four pairs at Normandy and two at The Garrison (*CBWPSAR* 35), whilst on St Agnes a pair displayed during early June but not subsequently. Penhallurick (1978) thought birds may have bred in the Normandy areas of St Mary's in 1964 but gave no reference, *CBWPSAR* 34 stating only that they were present. However, by 1966 they probably bred at six locations on Tresco, and by 1973 were thought to do so on all main islands (*IOSBR* 1973). However, by 1978 there was talk of a 'considerable decrease', followed by a 'further marked decrease' in 1979, with the accompanying suggestion it could become extinct in Scilly within the following five years (*IOSBR* 1978, 1979). These comments were made with apparent justification in view of totals for 1981, when 20 or fewer were on St Mary's during February and similar numbers in St Agnes and St Martin's in spring, whilst just six were on Tresco during mid-October. And although the reports are punctuated by reference to this species having bred on various islands, few, if any, prior to 1990 make specific reference to a nest being seen. Nevertheless, at least one nest was seen and documented by the author on the Higher Moors section of the Lunnon Farm study plot on St Mary's during the early 1990s and others were recently described elsewhere on the same islands, including Hugh Town as recently as 2001. For the islands as a whole, the 2000 Breeding Bird Atlas recorded up to 60 pairs in 19 (28.3%) surveyed squares, in the likely range 30–60 (Chown & Lock 2002).

On mainland Britain, Collared Doves were first reported in 1952, from Lincolnshire, and were breeding in Norfolk by 1955 (Richardson *et al.* 1957), the same year it first bred in Norway (Hudson 1965). The initial record for mainland Cornwall involved a bird discovered on the evening of 10th June 1959 near Land's End (Penhallurick 1978). The same authority suggested that subsequent colonisation of Cornwall may have involved birds breeding on St Mary's from the 1960s. Adults are largely sedentary and most colonisation is largely accomplished through post-juvenile dispersal – for further reading on the Collared Dove's colonisation of Britain and Ireland see Hudson (1965, 1972). Interestingly, the flow of ringed birds between Britain and nearby continental Europe reduced substantially after the 1970s (Wernham *et al.* 2002).

A total of 27 Collared Doves had been ringed on Scilly up until the end of 1999, for obvious reasons all since 1970. There are no recaptures, but Penhallurick (1978) mentioned a bird ringed in Westfalen in the former West Germany in July 1961 and recovered in Cornwall in June the following year (reportedly the first foreign-ringed British recovery), plus two ringed in Gloucestershire in 1966, one of which was recovered the following month, the other fourteen months later. An apparent hybrid Collared x Turtle Dove *S. turtur* was present on St Mary's during early October 1983 (*IOSBR* 1983).

## Turtle Dove (European Turtle Dove) *Streptopelia turtur* A

Until the 1980s a regular and common migrant, more frequent in spring than autumn but now scarce at any time. Bred during the early to mid-20th century, very probably earlier.

Breeds central and southern Eurasia east to Mongolia and Afghanistan, plus North Africa north of Sahara and east to Iran. Populations migratory with possible exception of North African desert, winters in African Sahel and adjacent savannah. Polytypic: nominate *turtur* occurs Europe, Canary Islands and most of eastern range; *arenicola* Balearic Islands and northwest Africa east to Iran; *rufescens* Egypt and northern Sudan; *hoggara* central Sahara. Red-listed in UK: rapid, 69% breeding decline over past 25 years; unfavourable world conservation status (Gregory *et al*. 2002). National 50% decline during 25 years to 1996 (Bashford & Noble 2000).

Earliest reference to Turtle Dove in Scilly is probably North's observation that it was common during summer (North 1850). Then in the early 1900s, James Clark and Francis Rodd summarised their own and E H Rodd's observations, pointing out that it occurred 'rarely in autumn, sometimes in winter and frequently in spring' (Rodd 1871d; Clark & Rodd 1906). They also noted that in May 1871 a flock of 34 was recorded and in May 1903 a flock of 19, concluding with the statement that it had nested at least once on Tresco.

Some early 20th century reports apparently belie previous suggestions that Turtle Dove was at times common in the islands, as does the 1943 comment 'Not seen by us but Major Dorrien-Smith told us he had seen two this year' (*CBWPSAR* 13). There are also many years when it failed to get any mention. Nevertheless, entries such as that in the *CBWPSAR* number 17 for 1947 help greatly in outlining the fuller picture, with up to six pairs breeding on St Martin's between 1940 and 1947, often fairly close together, but in 1947 just a single pair bred. The young reportedly left the island annually soon after fledging, though a flock of five was present on St Mary's on 1st July 1947, plus other small flocks during September and October that year. In confirmation of Clark and Rodd's earlier mention of Tresco, there is brief reference to Turtle Dove having occasionally nested there at least into the mid-1940s (Penhallurick 1978). Similarly, for 1951 there appears the comment 'Had an excellent breeding season and is now common: a number of non-breeding birds were present' (*CBWPSAR* 21), whilst as further evidence of its summer status it appears under the heading of breeding species in a list of migrant dates for 1959. However, this may be the last indication of Turtle Dove breeding in the islands, for since 1959 there is either frequent mention of it not having bred, or a lack of any evidence of it breeding. And whilst summering birds were to be seen and heard in subsequent years, these too were lost to the islands after summer 1993.

Early evidence of migration through the islands comes in the form of reports from the Bishop Rock Lighthouse seven miles southwest of St Mary's. On the night of September 27th–28th 1907 'a few' were recorded at the light (Ogilvie-Grant 1909) and at least one was noted at the same location on 15th May 1911 (Ogilve-Grant 1912c), whilst one was also killed at the Bishop Rock light at 3 am on the night of 27th–28th September 1910 (Ogilve-Grant 1912b). Earliest arrival dates fall around mid- to late April, though there is one old record of a bird on 28th February 1913 (Witherby *et al*. 1940). However, during the 1990s most moved on by the end of May or, a few, by the first week of June. Return passage occurs from about mid-September through to late October, though there are a few older records into mid-November. Numbers involved are variable but at least 100 were on St Agnes on 1st May 1962, whilst on 21st September 1968 a flock of 80 rested briefly on St Mary's. More common, though, were flock sizes in the range 10–30, although in recent years even 30 might be considered exceptional, with single-figure counts now the norm. Penhallurick (1978) made the point that large flock sizes formerly experienced in Scilly were not reflected on the Cornish mainland. During winter 1992–93, a bird with a damaged wing overwintered on Bryher, where it spent a great deal of time feeding with the local chickens (*IOSBR* 1993). An apparent hybrid Turtle x Collared Dove *S. decaocto* was present on St Mary's during early October 1983 (*IOSBR* 1983).

Turtle Dove is notable for the disparity between the size of its widespread Eurasian breeding distribution and its concentrated African wintering range north of the equator. Birds commence leaving their European breeding grounds from late July through to September or even October, return passage commencing late March or early April, with European breeding areas reoccupied during May (Cramp *et al.* 1977–94). Parslow (1967a) detected a slight decrease prior to the mid-1960s, together with a range contraction in English counties bordering Wales. However, from the mid-1970s, a more recognisable decline occurred linked to widespread changes in agricultural practices, particularly on grasslands (Marchant *et al.* 1990). Although ten Turtle Doves had been ringed in Scilly up until the end of 1999 there were no subsequent recaptures.

## Rufous Turtle Dove (Oriental Turtle Dove) *Streptopelia orientalis* **A** BBRC 33.3%

**Extremely rare migrant or vagrant, full written description required by the BBRC.**

1960   One St Agnes 2nd to 6th May   *British Birds* 53: 445–446, 54: 188

Breeds central Asia and Siberia east to China, Southeast Asia, India and Japan. Polytypic: nominate *meena* occurs central Asia and Siberia east to Altay mountains and south to Himalayas and Nepal, rarely straggling to western Europe; *orientalis* central Siberia, Southeast Asia, eastern Himalayas and northern Vietnam, also rarely straggling to western Europe; *agricola* Nepal to Bangladesh, Burma and eastern China; *erythrocephala* India; two more forms beyond these. Migratory in north, involving *meena* and northern populations of *orientalis*, Palearctic migrants winter Indian subcontinent, Indochina, Japan and Southeast Asia.

The only Scillonian record involved a bird on St Agnes on 2nd May 1960, where it remained until last seen on 6th (Elvy *et al.* 1960), which represented the third for Britain and Ireland of this extremely rare visitor. Rumours of a strange dove on St Agnes were circulating on 2nd May, following a substantial influx of about 25 Turtle Doves *Streptopelia turtur* on the night of 30th April, but the bird concerned was not seen well until the following day, when St Agnes resident Herbert Legg noticed an unusual dove flying with Turtle Doves over Wingletang Down, particularly noting the larger size and darker colour. It was quickly relocated and kept under observation for around an hour, even though extremely wary and difficult to approach, and eventually the bird's true identity became clear. Observers noted that although sometimes difficult to separate from accompanying Turtle Doves whilst on the ground, it was obviously different once in the air, being indeed recognisably larger and darker and lacking the conspicuous white outer tail of the commoner species.

The record was accepted by the BOURC and the BBRC plus other authorities, Naylor including it in his well-researched list (Naylor 1996) and Hirschfeld (1992) referred to it in his authoritative paper on Rufous Turtle Dove identification; nevertheless, Evans considered it unacceptable (Evans 1994). Away from their normal range, Rufous Turtle Doves are somewhat catholic in their habitat preferences, in Europe frequently appearing in urban areas and sometimes associating with Collared Doves *Streptopelia decaocto*. Scandinavia has fared much better than Britain and Ireland in numbers of vagrant Rufous Turtle Doves, most arriving during autumn or winter. European arrivals involved the migratory *meena* and *orientalis*, though with the latter predominating. The St Agnes individual was not attributed to a particular form but is likely to have been one of these two. Some other West Palearctic species wintering in India, e.g. Black-headed Bunting, reach western Europe as spring overshoots and this may explain the occurrence of the St Agnes Rufous Turtle Dove, but perhaps not European autumn and winter arrivals.

The first British and Irish example concerned a bird from Scarborough, North Yorkshire, in October 1889, the skin of which is now in the Yorkshire Museum (Evans 1994). The second involved a female *orientalis* shot at Castle Rising, Norfolk, in January 1946. This was followed by the St Agnes bird. One on Shetland during 1974 was closely followed by a record only recently recognised involving a moulting juvenile *meena* at Spurn, Humberside, on 8th November 1975 (BOURC 2002a). The latter was the first acceptable British and Irish record of this form. Claims of two individuals in Cornwall, at Land's End during October 1973 and St Ives during May 1978 were not accepted by the BBRC.

# [Budgerigar *Melopsittacus undulatus*] E

**Former, short-term feral breeding population on Tresco, some visited other islands.**

Restricted to Australia, where widely distributed away from coastal areas. Abundant and nomadic. Monotypic. Widely kept and bred in captivity worldwide, various colour mutations have been developed but wild populations predominantly green and yellow.

Probably the most detailed and almost the only worthwhile account of the presence of this species in Scilly comes from a short *British Birds* paper by Bernard King (B King 1978), providing as it does a prime example of why even the most insignificant ornithological events require documenting whilst still fresh in our minds, for without King's erudite summary much of what follows would have been lost.

In 1969, four pairs were acquired from Windsor Lodge by the Dorrien-Smith family and introduced into an aviary on Tresco. During autumn 1970, a further six pairs were added and some 16 nesting boxes provided, all of which were occupied by the following year. From 1972, the aviary was left open and pairs commenced breeding at liberty on Tresco, but with birds returning to the aviary for food, or for shelter during bad weather. Some were observed taking food put down for introduced geese Anatidae, or domestic chickens, and birds were also observed feeding on wild plant seeds.

First nests discovered away from the aviary were located in palms *Palmacaea* and cordylines *Cordyline*, according to King in 'holes', though on Scilly the trunks of these trees do not appear naturally holed. However, in an earlier note, preceding the Budgerigar introduction, King referred to House Sparrows *Passer domesticus* excavating holes in the trunks of palms on Tresco and quoted Viv Jackson as having seen the same on St Martin's (B King 1978). This being the case, the Tresco Budgerigars may have utilised holes previously made by House Sparrows and in any event were presumably capable of excavating their own. Equally, some nests may have been situated among dense accumulations of dead vegetation often associated with both plant species, as indeed is the case with Starlings *Sturnus vulgaris* still today on Tresco. Subsequently, nests were found in cavities in elms *Ulmus*, sycamores *Acer pseudoplatanus* and other trees in and around the Abbey Gardens, though it is not known now if these were natural holes or excavated by the birds themselves, or perhaps a combination of both. Although small flocks were observed visiting the other four main islands (Sharrock 1976), there is no account of nests being found other than on Tresco, and even then only around the Abbey and Abbey Gardens. According to King's assessment, some 35 nests were in use outside the aviary by 1974 with at least a further 30 non-breeding birds present. During summer the birds separated into two discrete flocks, one of which regularly fed with Starlings, accompanying these as and when they took flight and landing with them again subsequently. A feature of these birds whilst at liberty was the ease with which they apparently adapted to life in the wild, to the point even of the flock briefly seeking refuge in bushes before returning in small groups to feed on the ground.

Natural food plants King recorded as being utilised included Annual Meadow-grass *Poa annua*, Toad Rush *Juncus bufonius*, Slender Sandwort *Arenaria leptoclados*, swine-cress *Coronopus* and pearlwort *Sagina* (possibly Annual Pearlwort *S. apetala*). King also watched birds removing pieces from the leaves of Navelwort *Umbilicus rupestris* growing on the Abbey walls, which he thought might have some extra nutritional objective, whilst also observing birds apparently ingesting grit from off the ground.

Additional food was provided until 1974, at which time it ceased. By April 1975 King noted the population was already greatly reduced and during a ten-day stay in October that year he failed to see any Budgerigars on Tresco. Confusingly, however, the *IOSBR* for 1975 gives a population of 100 birds, including 35 breeding pairs, though it seems probable this was out-of-date information, the same reports suggesting possibly just one bird by December 1976 and none at all in 1977, which accords with what the BOU had to say (BOURC 1978). Reasons for this rapid decline are unclear, but have been blamed primarily on the withdrawal of artificial feeding (B King 1978).

Interestingly, despite the obvious level of Budgerigar breeding activity on Tresco over the period 1972–74, the editors of the *IOSBR* seem not to have adjusted to the situation, the species getting no mention other than the above.

## Ring-ringed Parakeet *Psittacula krameri* C

Extremely rare vagrant.

1985   One Lower Moors, St Mary's 29th December

The world's most widely distributed Psittacine, main breeding range African savannah region south into dry forest, plus Indian subcontinent; widespread in captivity and widely introduced. In Britain, main feral populations centred Greater London, Kent, Greater Manchester and Liverpool but could occur anywhere. Continental feral populations Low Countries.

A bird was briefly present at Lower Moors, St Mary's, on 29th December 1985; however, no further details were provided and it is surprising that such a noisy and obvious species was not seen elsewhere in the islands. Presumably the possibility of this having been a local escape cannot be entirely ruled out, although there was no information to that end. Main breeding concentrations are in southeast England, though the species has increased its range since 1988–91 (Gibbons *et al.* 1993; Butler 2002), a few Ring-ringed Parakeets now breeding as close to Scilly as Dorset, and birds have been encountered at many British and Irish locations far removed from any known breeding sites (Wernham *et al.* 2002).

## Great Spotted Cuckoo *Clamator glandarius* A   BBRC 8.5%

Extremely rare migrant, full written description required by the BBRC.

1971   One St Mary's 21st to 29th April   *British Birds* 65: 338
1979   One (subadult) Bryher 13th April   *British Birds* 73: 514–515
1993   One St Martin's 11th March to 1st April   *British Birds* 87: 536

Breeds southern Europe, Middle East and Africa. Polytypic: nominate *glandarius* occurs throughout range except Africa southwards from Zambia and southern Tanzania, where replaced by *choragium*. Migratory in northern Europe and southern Africa, northern birds winter North Africa, Egypt or Arabia, possibly also south of Sahara.

There are three records of this typical southern European spring overshoot, first of which was found feeding on burnet moth *Zygaena* larvae in long grass on headland slopes below St Mary's Airport on 21st April 1971. Briefly seeking protection in nearby flower fields when disturbed, it was confirmed as still present in the same area on 29th April, though a claim it was seen elsewhere on St Mary's on 31st May was not accepted (*IOSBR* 1971). Little information is provided on the next individual other than that it was judged to be in its second summer and was found on Bryher on 13th April 1979, the two observers being David Hunt and Bill Oddie. The third was discovered on St Martin's on the early date of 11th March 1993, where it remained until last seen on 1st April.

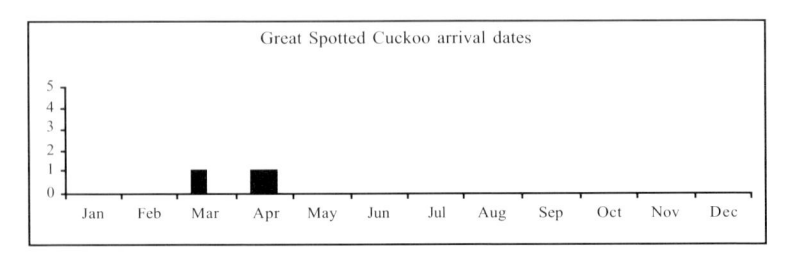

Great Spotted Cuckoo arrival dates

The BBRC accepted 35 Great Spotted Cuckoo records during the years 1958–99, these three individuals representing 8.5% of the total for that period. Return spring migration commences early, some reaching southern Spain by February, though the main passage occurs March to mid-April (Cramp *et al.* 1977–94). Nonetheless, whilst it appears to be accepted that most Great Spotted Cuckoos reaching northern Europe during spring are overshoots, return migration commences as early as June or July and raises doubts over the status of birds arriving at northern European sites during late spring or summer. Mean duration of stay of the three Scillonian arrivals was 10.6 days, though this figure is perhaps distorted by the long-staying 1993 individual.

# Cuckoo (Common Cuckoo) *Cuculus canorus* A

Summer visitor in small numbers but can appear more numerous, breeds on five inhabited plus main uninhabited islands, e.g. Samson, Annet, Round Island, St Helen's, Tean. Also a spring and autumn migrant but again in small numbers.

Extensive Eurasian breeding range, from Britain, Ireland, Iberia and North Africa east to Bering Sea, Japan and China. Large overlap with Oriental Cuckoo *C. saturatus* in eastern and central Asia. Migratory, two distinct wintering areas in southeast Africa and Southeast Asia; West Palearctic populations winter Africa, together with many from Asia. Polytypic: nominate *canorus* occurs Atlantic to Pacific and south to France, Italy, Turkey, Kazakhstan and Sakhalin; *bangsi* Iberia, Balearic Islands and northwest Africa; *subtelephonus* and *bakeri* further east and south. Upgraded from Green- to Amber-listed in UK 2002: moderate (31%) breeding decline over past 25 years (Gregory *et al.* 2002). National 27% decline 1994–99 (Bashford & Noble 2000).

The only 19th century comment appears to be E H Rodd's observation that it occurred in autumn (Rodd 1880); therefore, it fell to his nephew Francis and co-author James Clark to outline the true situation (Clark & Rodd 1906). According to these two, it arrived in 'fairly large numbers at the time of spring migration', nine allegedly being seen at once from a Holy Vale window on St Mary's. Clark and Rodd also gave the earliest 'authenticated' sighting as 29th March 1904, when it was seen by A A Dorrien-Smith, being observed also on 2nd April that same year. However, they suggested that a more normal date would have been mid-April. These two authorities concluded their summary with the interesting observation that it was commoner on Scilly during the breeding season than anywhere else in Cornwall.

This is a difficult species to census and, understandably, reports of distribution and numbers within the islands vary between years, but points that need to be kept in mind are the small land area involved and the difficulties of deciding the scale of duplication between reports. Suggestions in published reports of up to 16 calling individuals on one island are almost certainly overestimates. Birds are highly mobile and seem capable of covering a good proportion of St Mary's during a few hours (pers. obs.) and it is this feature that almost certainly gives rise to these inflated figures. During the 1990s, a realistic 'guesstimate' of the average numbers of pairs on each inhabited island was probably 3, perhaps 4 each on St Mary's and St Martin's and 2–3 maximum each on Tresco, Bryher and St Agnes. Very possibly the pair evident on Samson most years may have been resident there, but birds or pairs recorded on Annet or various uninhabited islands were either patrolling a larger area or visiting from a main island. Therefore, the pair total for Scilly in an average year may be in the range 14–19 and even this could represent a substantial overestimate. The 2000 Breeding Bird Atlas recorded a possible 49 pairs in 28 (41.7%) of the 67 surveyed squares (Chown & Lock 2002), though the report's authors thought 20 pairs a more likely estimate.

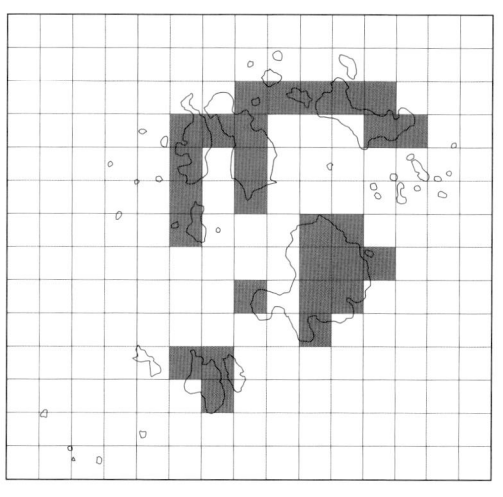

1-km Cuckoo Breeding Distribution – 2000–01 (data Chown & Lock 2002)

During the 1990s, the earliest date for foster parents feeding fledged young was 14th June. Unlike mainland Britain, on Scilly Cuckoos have little choice in their range of host species and by far the majority of pairs utilise Rock Pipits *Anthus petrosus*, which is the commonest coastal passerine. Quick (1964) referred to Meadow Pipit *A. pratensis* as a host species in Scilly, but this seems never to have been a numerous breeding species, or at least not in the 20th century. For although Clark & Rodd (1906) referred to it as an 'abundant resident' during the 19th century, an entry in the *IOSBR* for 1971 pointed out that two young Meadow Pipits being fed by adults on St Agnes on 5th June represented the first modern breeding record for the islands.

Surprisingly, perhaps, the next most frequently mentioned host species after Rock Pipit is Wren *Troglodytes troglodytes*, adults having been recorded feeding young Cuckoos on Tresco in 1985, St Mary's and St Martin's in 1989 and on Bryher in 1994. But whilst the possibility exists that these Wrens were coerced into feeding food-begging fledgling Cuckoos, the author recorded a Cuckoo's egg in a Wren's nest on the edge of the Lunnon Farm study plot on St Mary's during the 1990s. Similarly, a Cuckoo's egg was discovered in a Blackbird's *Turdus merula* nest on the Lunnon Farm plot during the same period, but the nest was predated before hatching.

During the mid-1990s the author watched a female Cuckoo eject a newly hatched Dunnock *Prunella modularis* brood from a nest on the Lunnon Farm plot, the female having sat watching the area long enough to have seen the adult Dunnocks taking food to the nest. It seems well accepted now that adult female Cuckoos will remove the eggs or young of breeding passerine pairs, thereby extending the laying period available to them through the need for the host to rebuild and relay (Cramp *et al.* 1977–94). A bird on St Agnes on 11th May was watched carrying what might otherwise have been described as nest material, apparently as part of some display. Cramp *et al.* make the point that male Cuckoos will occasionally fly down and pick up grass or similar, before returning to the female and presenting it to her, whilst also continuing with the display. In general, female Cuckoos are believed to be host-specific and the lack of a suitably abundant alternative to Rock Pipit perhaps rules out the regular use of any additional species.

Although the earliest recorded arrival date during the 1990s was 30th March (1997), just one day later than A A Dorrien-Smith's 1904 individual, most arrived between 6th and 17th April. Annual last sighting dates for the same period were more variable, in the range 14th June to 29th October, though it is probably under-recorded at this time of year. Penhallurick (1978) quoted 28th October as the latest date up until the mid-1970s. The migratory strategy of northern European Cuckoos is still poorly understood, though they begin departing from early August and most have gone by late September. Early returning birds reach Europe by late March and then throughout April and into May. First-summer individuals normally return to the natal area, arriving later than adults and on Scilly perhaps helping to explain those apparently excessive breeding season counts.

Given the known tendency for some southern European migrants to find their way north at least as far as southern England, the possibility should be borne in mind of the slightly smaller, shorter-winged Iberian and northwest African *bangsi* reaching Scilly. Similarly, the smaller and more finely barred eastern form *subtelephonus*, which breeds as close to Britain as the Caspian Sea, might just make it to Scilly (Gantlett 1998), especially as both winter in Africa alongside *canorus*; British ringing data suggest a marked southeast movement after leaving Britain and Ireland, birds apparently crossing to Africa via the central Mediterranean (Wernham *et al.* 2002). A total of 17 Cuckoos had been ringed on Scilly up to the end of 1999, 13 of them prior to 1970; the only recaptures involve two fairly old records of birds ringed and retrapped in Scilly.

Recoveries
1527?   Pul   Peninnis Head, St Mary's 1954     CT   St Agnes 17th May 1957
278982   Ad   St Agnes 12th May 1957     CT   Gugh 27th April 1958
                                                                           CT   St Agnes 18th May 1958

Cuckoo Ringing Recaptures

# Black-billed Cuckoo     *Coccyzus erythrophthalmus*   A   BBRC 44.4%

**Very rare vagrant, full written description required by the BBRC.**

     1932    One (immature) dead Tresco 27th October    Witherby 1933; *British Birds* 27: 111–112
     1982    One (juvenile) St Agnes 29th August (dead 30th)    *British Birds* 76: 502–503
     1982    One St Mary's 21st to 23rd October (dead 24th)    *British Birds* 76: 502–503
     1985    One (first-year) moribund St Mary's 12tth October    *British Birds* 79: 558
     1990    One St Mary's 10th October (dead 11th)    *British Birds* 84: 478

Breeds North America east of Rocky Mountains, from southern Canada south to Carolina, Tennessee, Arkansas and Wyoming. Migratory, wintering northwest South America to Peru. Monotypic. Recent undulating population levels, overall trend downwards with substantial decline last 15 years, though eastern populations less affected (Bryant 1997).

The BBRC accepted a total of just nine Black-billed Cuckoo records during the period 1958–99, thus the four Scillonian arrivals represent slightly less than half of all British records. Sadly, but nevertheless typically for this species, three out of the four were either found dead (one) or died within a day or so of arrival. If the extremely early August 1982 individual is discounted, all arrival dates fall within a narrow 18-day window, whilst mean length of stay was just 1.4 days.

The first for Britain and Ireland died after reportedly colliding with a stone wall on Tresco on 27th October 1932 and the mounted skin is allegedly the one in the Tresco Abbey collection, currently on loan in the Isles of Scilly Museum on St Mary's. Typically, birds frequent areas of elm *Ulmus* after their arrival in the islands and the combination of species rarity and the probability of birds soon dying usually results in large crowds of birdwatchers gathering within a short time, as on St Mary's in October 1985 when a moribund individual discovered in the Sunken Garden at the junction of Porthloo Lane and Telegraph Road quickly attracted a suggested crowd of over 500 observers. The 1982 experience of two in one year in such a small geographical area seems quite exceptional, particularly as they were sufficiently separated in time for them perhaps not to have been associated with the same transatlantic weather system. The arrival of the first coincided with the arrival of other Nearctic passerines elsewhere in Britain, whereas the second initially proved elusive but eventually took up residence in Hugh Town on the last day of its stay, where it was seen by most birdwatchers present in the islands.

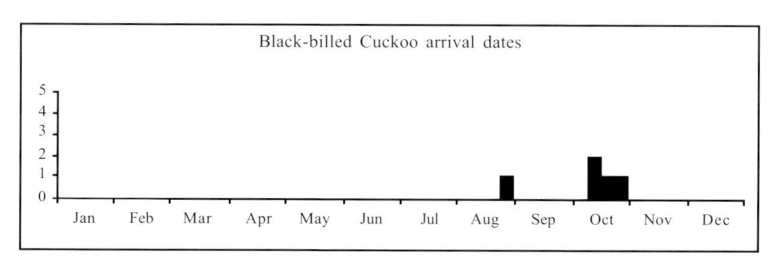

Black-billed Cuckoo arrival dates

The first British and Irish record came from Co. Antrim, Ireland, in September 1871. Black-billed Cuckoo is common in eastern North America and on average breeds further north than Yellow-billed Cuckoo *C. americanus*, extending into Canada. Nevertheless, its appearances on the eastern side of the North Atlantic are less frequent than those of Yellow-billed, a feature thought attributable to differences in migration patterns, Black-billed Cuckoos from northeast North America adopting a south to southwest route towards their wintering area in northwest South America, though some overfly the Gulf of Mexico. Post-breeding movements commence during late July to early August among more northerly populations but with the majority moving from mid-August to mid-September and with some still on the move into October (Cramp *et al.* 1977–94). Black-billed Cuckoo came seventh in Robbins' statistical review of expected transatlantic vagrancy among 31 Nearctic migrant passerines and near-passerines recorded in Britain or Ireland during 1947–76, the five accepted autumn records as good as equalled the predicted relative likelihood of 5.21 individuals (Robbins 1980). No American cuckoos have been trapped and ringed on Scilly, and none of the birds found dead had been previously ringed.

## Yellow-billed Cuckoo    *Coccyzus americanus*  A   BBRC 19.5%–24.3%

**Very rare migrant, full written description required by the BBRC.**

| | | |
|---|---|---|
| 1921 | One shot St Mary's November   Witherby 1924; *British Birds* 15: 242, 48: 7 | |
| 1940 | One (dead) Tresco 6th November (A A Dorrien-Smith 1941)   *British Birds* 34: 181 | |
| 1965 | One St Agnes & Gugh 28th October   *British Birds* 59: 291 | |
| 1970 | One St Mary's 4th October   *British Birds* 65: 351 | |
| 1980 | One (first-year) St Agnes & St Mary's 1st to 12th October (died)   *British Birds* 74: 478 | |
| 1981 | One St Mary's 23rd & 24th September   *British Birds* 75: 551 | |
| 1985 | Two to four various islands 12th to 23rd October   *British Birds* 79: 11, 558–559, 565 | |
| 1995 | One St Mary's 19th October   *British Birds* 89: 509, 587 | |
| 1999 | One Tresco 12th to 20th October   *British Birds* 92, 93: 345 | |

Breeds North America, from southern Canada to Mexico and Caribbean. Polytypic: nominate *americanus* occurs east of Rocky Mountains south to southeast Mexico and Caribbean; *occidentalis* western North America south to northwest Mexico. Migratory, broad-front autumn movement to winter South America east of Andes south to Argentina. Population undulating but with overall downward trend and 30% reduction in east since 1985 (Bryant 1997).

Scilly has recorded more Yellow-billed Cuckoos than any other European locality, including 19.5%–24.3% of the 41 accepted by the BBRC for Britain during the period 1958–99. According to Witherby (1922), the 1921 individual on St Mary's was shot off a cottage chimney. This bird was followed 19 years later by one found dead on Tresco on 6th November 1940 (A A Dorrien-Smith 1941). No details are provided for the first modern record, except that it was seen first on Gugh on 28th October 1965 before flying towards St Mary's (*CBWPSAR* 35). Similarly, the 1970 individual gets no mention in the relevant *IOSBR* and the relevant *British Birds* rarities review states merely that the BBRC was awaiting a submission. Though the record eventually did appear in the *British Birds* Rarity Report for 1971, we know only that it was found exhausted on St Mary's. The 1980 individual was initially present on St Agnes from 1st to 11th October, including during a severe westerly gale on 7th, before being found in a moribund state in Hugh Town, St Mary's, on 12th and eventually succumbing on the night of 13th–14th, although according to Griffiths (1982) this bird was last seen alive on 14th October. When handled, the corpse was extremely emaciated and observers were impressed by the small size of the bird, it being thought comparable to Blackbird *Turdus merula*. During its stay, this bird appeared to feed primarily on caterpillars and remained largely in the tree canopy, where it moved about in a somewhat 'noisy and clumsy fashion' (*IOSBR* 1980). Like the two earlier modern records we know little about the bird in 1981, other than that it was seen in the Porth Hellick and Salakee areas of St Mary's on 23rd–24th September.

On Scilly, autumn 1985 was exceptional for North American migrants, including a Black-billed Cuckoo *C. erythrophthalmus*. The number of Yellow-billed involved was extremely impressive, with as many as four about the islands during October, mostly on St Mary's but including a single-day visit to St Agnes and two separate sightings on both St Martin's and Tresco. None of these seems to have been subsequently found dead, but sadly this was not the case with the 1995 arrival, which was already in a moribund condition when first discovered near Harry's Walls, St Mary's, on 19th October, before being rediscovered and last seen at nearby Rocky Hill the same day (*IOSBR* 1995). The most recent arrival involved a bird frequenting the eastern side of Tresco's Great Pool from 12th to 20th October 1999, becoming more elusive towards the end of its stay (*IOSBR* 1999).

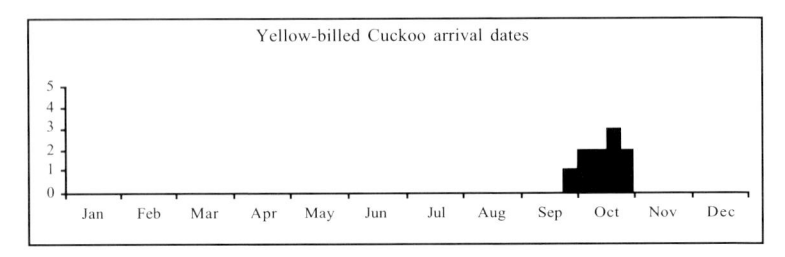

Discounting the two earliest records, all arrival dates fell within the 36-day window of 23rd September to 28th October. Again discounting these same two individuals plus the multiple 1985 arrivals an average stay of 4.3 days is suggested, with at least one of these bird subsequently dying. There have been five records for mainland Cornwall, all during October, the most recent also in 1999. There is increasing evidence that at least some of the eastern North American population may undertake a transoceanic autumn passage, from southeast Canada or northeast USA direct to the West Indies or South America (Cramp *et al.* 1977–94). If true, this would greatly increase the possibility of storm-blown transatlantic vagrancy, involving as it does an oceanic flight of between 2,000 and 3,000 km to the West Indies, or 4,000 km direct to South America. In northeast USA, autumn passage occurs from early August to mid-October, with the bulk of the population on the move from late August to September. All of this appears to explain the presence of Yellow-billed Cuckoo in Scilly during autumn. Yellow-billed Cuckoo came second in Robbins' statistical review of expected transatlantic vagrancy among 31 Nearctic migrant passerines and near-passerines recorded in Britain and Ireland during 1947–76. The 18 accepted autumn records greatly exceeds the predicted relative likelihood of 6.26 individuals (Robbins 1980). It seems unlikely that birds reaching Britain will be other than the race *americanus* and certainly T A Dorrien-Smith attributed the two earliest individuals to that form (T A Dorrien-Smith 1951). Papps (*Birdwatch* October 2002) attributed the high incidence of deaths among European vagrant Yellow-billed Cuckoos to poisonous unnamed green caterpillars, resembling those forming part of the species' normal diet. However, no reference is given for the statement and this is not mentioned by Cramp *et al.* 1977–94), who suggest deaths resulting from transoceanic stress.

## Barn Owl *Tyto alba* A

**Rare migrant or vagrant, full written description required by the SRP. Either the light-breasted *alba* or dark-breasted *guttata* might be expected to occur.**

1858  One (shot) Scilly  Clark & Rodd 1906
1962  One Gugh for two days February
1966  One (dead) St Mary's 2nd October
1975  One St Agnes 25th October
1976  One St Mary's early January
1977  One (*guttata* – freshly dead) Tresco 19th or 20th October
1979  One Porth Hellick, St Mary's 18th October
1981  One Garrison, St Mary's off RMV *Scillonian* 6th November
1988  One (*guttata*) Holy Vale, St Mary's 12th October to 2nd November
1991  One Garrison, St Mary's 2nd January

Cosmopolitan breeding range, West Palearctic populations isolated from remainder. Polytypic: within West Palearctic nominate *alba* occurs British Isles, France, southern Europe, including Canary and Balearic Islands, Sicily, Malta, Greece and former Yugoslavia; *guttata*, or 'Dark-breasted Barn Owl' central Europe, east to western Russia, with some grading into nominate *alba*. Primarily sedentary in West Palearctic though some random post-fledging dispersal, which in some years may become irruptive (Cramp *et al.* 1977–94). Amber-listed in UK: moderate (31%) contraction of breeding range over past 30 years; unfavourable world conservation status (Gregory *et al.* 2002).

The earliest evidence of a presence on Scilly comes from the bones of a single individual found among other excavated material from the prehistoric site at Halangy Down on the northwest corner of St Mary's (Ashbee 1999). This site dates from around 2000 BC, but owing to previous site disturbance it is not possible to date most of the various skeletal remains. In a more modern context, E H Rodd made no mention of Barn Owl on Scilly, though he made it clear that it was less common in west Cornwall than in the east of the county (Rodd 1880). This being the case, the earliest known reference is the remark by James Clark and E H Rodd's nephew Francis that one was shot by Jenkinson (presumably the Reverend J H) on November 13th 1858 (Clark & Rodd 1906).

Since then there have been nine records, all involving single birds and including two dark-breasted *guttata*. T A Dorrien-Smith's mention of only the nominate form in his 1951 list of *Birds of Scilly as Recorded at Tresco Abbey* suggests that the 1858 individual was of this form (T A Dorrien-Smith 1951). However, the unexplained 1951 comment that 'in spite of being unmolested, this bird cannot thrive on the islands and is frequently found dead or dying up to about a month after arrival' (*CBWPSAR* 21) perhaps suggests that some earlier arrivals went unrecorded. In February 1962, a Barn Owl roosted in a shed on the Gugh for two days and in 1966 a dead individual was found in an emaciated state on St Mary's

*Birds of the Isles of Scilly*

during early October. Next were two in quick succession, in October 1975 on St Agnes and in January the following year on St Mary's, followed by the freshly dead dark-breasted Tresco individual and then one at Porth Hellick, St Mary's, in October 1979.

These were followed by one of the more bizarre of Scillonian records, a Barn Owl seen flying off the RMV *Scillonian* and towards the nearby Garrison as the ship docked at St Mary's on 6th November 1981, having presumably flown aboard somewhere en route from Penzance. The remaining two sightings involved the second Scillonian dark-breasted individual, which remained in Holy Vale, St Mary's, from 12th October to 2nd November 1988 and finally a bird disturbed from its roost on The Garrison during early January 1991.

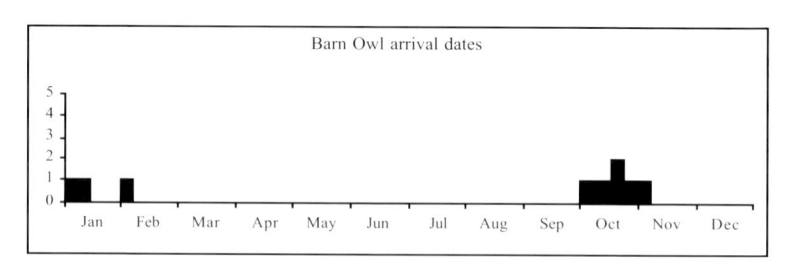

*Barn Owl arrival dates*

Within the West Palearctic, Barn Owls are largely sedentary, though juveniles are prone to disperse widely. The Chart comprises all nine 20th century arrival or discovery dates and shows a small but very obvious pattern of October arrivals, with a smaller but nonetheless equally obvious group of arrivals around midwinter. Whilst the latter could involve birds displaced by either British, Irish or Continental weather systems, autumn arrivals seem likely to involve post-fledging dispersal. It may also be relevant that the two dark-breasted individuals both arrived during October. According to Cramp *et al.* (1977–94), the range of post-juvenile dispersal is greater during irruption years, which in turn follow good breeding years, and involves more individuals. Under these conditions the dark-breasted central European *guttata* can reach Britain and there are records of birds doing so from the Netherlands and Belgium. Most ringing recoveries are within a range of 300 km, but during irruption years Barn Owls recovered in Spain originated from Germany, Netherlands, Switzerland and France, some having moved up to 1,650 km. Within Europe the bulk of post-fledging dispersal takes place September to November and is largely random, although, interestingly, movements greater than 300 km tend to be in a south or southwesterly direction. In Northern USA the declining, often dark-breasted Nearctic *pratincola* is partially migratory, adults as well as young moving south up to 2,000 km during autumn. Although large expanses of water normally act as a barrier to Barn Owl movement, Cramp *et al.* point out that its breeding presence on many oceanic islands is significant. If this is the case, *pratincola* could occur in Scilly during autumn, if only as a ship-assisted migrant, though its presence there or elsewhere in the West Palearctic would probably only be identifiable through ringing evidence. No Barn Owls have been ringed on Scilly and there are no recaptures from elsewhere.

## Scops Owl (Eurasian Scops Owl)   *Otus scops*   A   BBRC 11%

**Very rare migrant, full written description required by the BBRC.**

    1847   One (male – 'killed') Tresco 13th April   Rodd 1847; Clark & Rodd 1906
    1969   One St Agnes 29th September   *British Birds* 63: 281
    1976   One Old Town, St Mary's 5th to 14th April   *British Birds* 70: 427
    1989   One Tresco 3rd April   *British Birds* 83: 470

Breeds central West Palearctic and central western Asia, south to northwest Africa and east to Iran, Pakistan, Siberia and Mongolia. Northern populations migratory (some long-distance), others less so. All migration believed to involve birds moving to and from wintering areas in Africa north of equator. Polytypic: nominate *scops* occurs France, Sardinia and Italy east to Volga and south to Greece; *mallorcae* Iberia, Balearic Islands, perhaps northwest Africa; *cycladum* southern Greece, east through Asia Minor and south to Israel and Jordan; *cyprius* Cyprus; *turanicus* Iraq and Iran east to Afghanistan; *pulchellus* further east.

Earliest mention of this species in a Scillonian context was E H Rodd's letter to the *Zoologist* entitled *Occurrence of the Scops Eared Owl at the Scilly Islands* and detailing an exhausted bird captured by a Christian

Halliday on Tresco in April 1847 (Rodd 1847). The body, which lacked any obvious marks of injury, was sent to Rodd on 12th April by Tresco Steward Mr James and according to Rodd had been captured some time the previous week (Rodd 1880). The skin subsequently figured in Gould's *Birds of Britain* and was placed in the collection of Rodd's nephew Francis Rodd at his home at Trebartha Hall in east Cornwall. Apart from James Clark and Francis Rodd's brief reference to the above specimen (Clark & Rodd 1906), there is no further mention of Scops Owl until well over one hundred years later, when one was found on St Agnes on 29th September 1969. Interestingly, this record gets no mention in the *IOSBR* for that year but is listed in the BBRC report of accepted rarities (*British Birds* 63: 281), it being only the fourth British record in 12 years. The third Scillonian record involved a bird at Old Town, St Mary's, from 5th to 14th April 1976 (*British Birds* 70: 427). And finally, a bird on Tresco on 3rd April 1989 was first located via the sound of small birds mobbing something in bushes along the north side of the Great Pool.

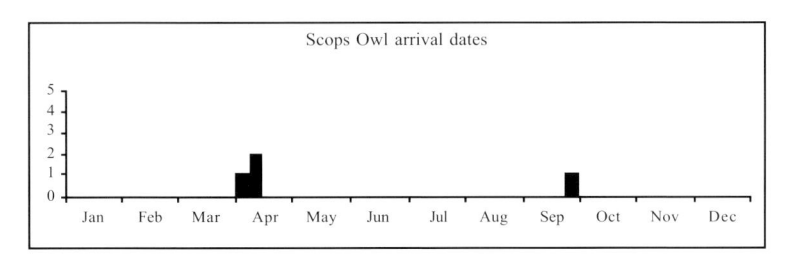

Scops Owl arrival dates

A total of 27 Scops Owl records accepted by the BBRC during the period 1958–99 compares with 68 documented records prior to that time, the three 20th century Scillonian sightings representing 11% of records for the later period. Although overshooting spring migrants of the nominate form *scops* is the most likely explanation for the three spring records, the possibility of the Iberian and northwest African *mallorcae* occurring, presumably also as overshoots, cannot be totally dismissed (Gantlett 1998). Nevertheless, eastern Eurasian populations, e.g. Siberia and Mongolia, also winter in Africa and thus are long-distance migrants along a northeast to southwest axis and some other species with similar migration patterns, occur regularly in western Europe during spring or autumn. The Chart shows all four arrival or discovery dates. A mounted skin in the Tresco Abbey collection and now on loan in the Isles of Scilly Museum on St Mary's is allegedly from the 19th century record. No Scops Owls have been ringed in Scilly and there are no recaptures from elsewhere.

## Snowy Owl                                           *Nyctea scandiaca*   A   BBRC 1.3%

**Very rare vagrant, full written description required by the BBRC.**

- 1905   One shot St Martin's September   Clark & Rodd 1906; Witherby & Ticehurst 1908
- 1913   One 'taken' St Mary's 25th October   Penhallurick 1978
- 1964   One St Agnes, Tresco, St Mary's & Tean 10th October to 10th March 1965
- 1972   One (adult male) St Martin's, Tresco, St Mary's & Gugh 8th March to 27th April

Circumpolar in low tundra, mostly north of Arctic Circle. Migratory or nomadic, sometimes irruptive, withdrawing south in winter, in West Palearctic normally only as far as southern Scandinavia. Monotypic.

On the face of it this is an extremely unlikely visitor to Scilly but the species is known for its tendency to penetrate south into Europe during some winters, movements doubtless often influenced by weather conditions further north. It is presumably unlikely to remain overlooked for long in Scilly, even on somewhere like the Eastern or Northern Isles. E H Rodd mentioned a specimen obtained in Cornwall (Rodd 1880) and Penhallurick (1978) gave the date as 1838. But first mention of Snowy Owl in a Scillonian context is reference to one shot on St Martin's during September 1905 (Clark & Rodd 1906), followed soon after by a bird taken on St Mary's on 25th October 1913 (Penhallurick 1978).

More recently, a bird arriving on St Agnes during October 1964 soon moved to Tresco's Carn Near, where it was watched catching rabbits *Oryctolagus cuniculus*. It remained in and about the islands until mid-March the following year, also visiting St Mary's Golf Course and uninhabited Tean. It was last seen on either 10th or 13th March 1965, having become something of a celebrity during its five-month residency.

*Birds of the Isles of Scilly*

Last of the four arrivals involved a fine adult male that appeared on St Martin's on 8th March 1972. It remained in Scilly until at least 27th April and during its stay visited Tresco, St Mary's and Gugh, plus St Martin's White Island.

According to Cramp *et al.* (1977–94), periodic irruptions are more regular among Snowy Owl populations in North America and Greenland, which, unlike many in Europe, are substantially dependent on Lemming *Lemmus, Dicrostonyx* cycles. However, European irruptions are as likely to be triggered by cold weather as by rodent populations and seem likely to involve birds from either Greenland or northern Europe. Interestingly, then, Witherby (1927b) documented a large North American movement of Snowy Owls and Goshawks *Accipiter gentilis* in the North Atlantic during November 1926, many of the owls being recorded aboard ships and with some captured and brought to Britain. The large majority of these sightings occurred in the western North Atlantic and only one came aboard ship off northern Scotland. Witherby pointed out that during the same year a Snowy Owl appeared in Chichester, Sussex, around the end of November and remained for three weeks. Unfortunately the lack of racial variation means the presence in Europe of birds from Greenland or North America is normally only likely to be established via the recovery of a ringed individual. However, a similar European influx of ship-assisted Snowy Owls occurred during autumn 2001, these arriving ashore in England, Netherlands, Belgium and Sweden. At least 17 Snowy Owls flew aboard three ships, two off southeast Canada and one off southern Greenland, in severe weather during October and at least six reached western Europe. Another Snowy Owl was found aboard a fourth vessel when it docked in Sweden in late October (Anon 2002).

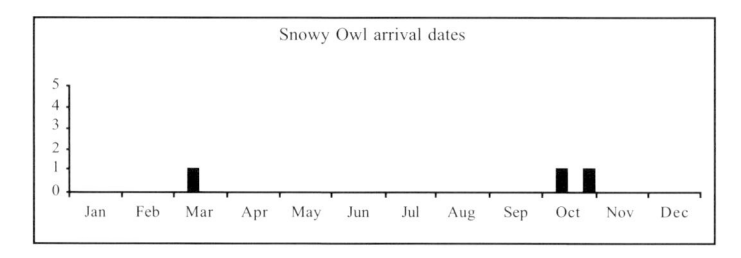

Snowy Owl arrival dates

The appearance of the 1972 bird on Scilly coincided with the temporary colonisation of the Shetland Isles (1967–75) and the 1964 individual only just preceded that period. Cramp *et al.* also refer to a 20th century Palearctic decline. Two mounted Snowy Owl skins from the Tresco Abbey collection, and currently on loan to the Isles of Scilly Museum on St Mary's, are allegedly from the 1905 and 1913 individuals. No Snowy Owls have been ringed in Scilly and there are no recaptures from elsewhere.

## Little Owl *Athene noctua* A

**Extremely rare vagrant or migrant, full written description required by the SRP.**

[1947 Adult with young Garrison, St Mary's] *CBWPSAR* 17
1960 One Bishop Rock Lighthouse 18th June Penhallurick 1978

Breeds western Europe to northeast China, naturally absent from British Isles and absent still from Ireland. Early British records may have involved escapes but structured introductions occurred from perhaps 1840s, by which time it may have been impossible to differentiate between released birds and Continental vagrants (Holloway 1996). Individuals reached Devon by 1911 and Cornwall by at least 1918 and breeding occurred in central Cornwall by at least 1922 and in Penzance area by 1923, whilst by the 1940s nesting pairs were commonly and widely established in central and western Cornwall (Penhallurick 1978). Polytypic: *vidalii* introduced Britain and occurs Iberia to Netherlands and east though Denmark and Baltic. National 8% decline 1994–99 (Bashford & Noble 2000).

Just two claimed records, at least one of which lacks adequate supporting information. The sighting at the Bishop Rock Lighthouse occurred at 10.35 pm on 18th June 1960 and involved lighthouse keeper A T Beswetherick, who lived at St Mawgan-in-Pydar on the Cornish mainland and was already familiar with this species in that area (Penhallurick 1978). Penhallurick also mentioned slight evidence of autumn Little Owl movements in west Cornwall around this same period, birds having been seen on Cornish cliffs during September. Interestingly this first report for the islands does not appear in the *CBWPSAR* for 1960.

A 1947 report of an adult with young on The Garrison, St Mary's (*CBWPSAR* 17), remains of extreme interest but is perhaps not now acceptable without additional supporting information; unfortunately *CBWPSAR* 17 provides no information in addition to that already shown here but this was not uncommon at that time. However, The Garrison record is not too far removed in time from the Bishop Rock sighting and would have been in keeping with Cornish mainland breeding range extension occurring at that time (Penhallurick 1978), Little Owls having become common in much of the county by the 1920s and early 1930s and with Beswetherick contributing information on a subsequent local scarcity of birds during the 1940s (Penhallurick 1978). Penhallurick's 1978 assessment of it was 'a little known bird, certainly less common than twenty to forty years ago'.

That further reductions occurred subsequent to that period is self-evident from the decrease from 19 occupied 10-km Cornish squares in the 1968–72 National Atlas (Sharrock 1976), to just three by the time of the 1988–91 survey (Gibbons *et al.* 1993). In other words, we should not allow our assessment of earlier records to be coloured by the very different present-day situation and must consider carefully before rejecting the Bishop Rock Little Owl sighting, or perhaps even the St Mary's breeding claim. Nevertheless, whether to accept or reject the above remains a matter of personal choice. No Little Owls have been ringed in Scilly and there are no recaptures from elsewhere.

## Tawny Owl *Strix aluco* A

**Extremely rare vagrant, full written description required by the SRP.**

    1965    Up to three Tresco 24th to 26th January
    [1993   One reported Porthloo, St Mary's 16th October]
    [1994   One reported Garrison, St Mary's 5th October]
    1997    One Carn Friars, St Mary's 23rd October

In West Palearctic breeds Britain, France, Iberia and coastal North Africa through Middle East to northern Iran and Kazakhstan. Mainly resident, post-fledging dispersal occurs August-November, subsequent movements mainly weather-induced. Polytypic, racial distribution complex: nominate *aluco* occurs Low Countries south to Alps and northern Italy and east to central European Russia, Ukraine and Crimea; *sylvatica* Britain, western France, Iberia, Turkey, southern Italy and Greece; *siberiae* Ural mountains and western Siberia; *mauritanica* northwest Africa; other forms further east. National 11% increase 1994–99 (Bashford & Noble 2000).

There appear to be no specific early references to this species in Scilly; Heath (1750) spoke of 'owls' being common in the islands but could have been, and probably was, referring to Long-eared *Asio otus* or Short-eared Owls *A. flammeus*. E H Rodd (1880) mentioned Tawny Owl as generally distributed throughout Cornwall in suitable habitat but without specific reference to Scilly, whereas Clark & Rodd (1906) made it clear that there was no record from the islands up until that time. Ryves & Quick (1946) also fail to mention it in their review of the breeding birds on Scilly.

First mention of Tawny Owl, then, comes in the report of the *Bird Census, Tresco, Isles of Scilly* January–February 1965 (B King 1965b), which, because of the species' rarity within the islands, is worth summarising in detail. First indications of Tawny Owl presence during the survey came in the form of a bird heard giving the well-known 'kiweak' call in Abbey Woods after dark on the 24th January, two were then seen briefly at dusk the following evening as they flew low over a field adjacent to Abbey Farm, north of the Great Pool. However, on the night of the 26th, at least three were watched in flight over fields close to Abbey Farm, from 17.35 hours for about ten minutes, being observed in flight directly overhead and all at the same time. The team of five observers, including Bernard King and Robin Prytherch, all agreed on the identification. Features noted included short rounded wings with thickset body and all-brownish colour, with quick wing-beats and flying on a more or less level plane, occasionally alighting on nearby conifers. The height of flight was estimated at up to 80 feet, although averaging around 20 feet, and was never particularly low. Also on the night of 26th, one was again heard repeating the 'kiweak' call but at a distance. Importantly, the annual report for 1965 (*CBWPSAR* 35) makes no mention of these records, though it does contain details of a Long-eared Owl heard calling ('in typical oo-oo-oo manner') on Tresco on the evening of 24th. The presence of this calling Long-eared Owl was also noted by King, who fully accepted the additional presence of this other species; a Long-eared Owl was later photographed in the Abbey chicken-house – though its purpose there went unrecorded.

There are also claimed single observations of birds on St Mary's during October 1993 and 1994, neither of which were described in writing and therefore were found unacceptable by the SRP. Consequently, the only other documented report of Tawny Owl on Scilly involved an individual seen by several observers at Carn Friars, St Mary's, on 23rd October 1979. A description was submitted by the observers and accepted by the SRP, though sadly a summary of the record was not included in the *IOSBR* for that year.

The spread of dates involved in the last three reported sightings is worth noting, falling as they do within the 19-day period commencing 5th October. But whilst the January 1965 Tawny Owl sightings would not draw a second glance on mainland Britain, the presence of not just one but three birds is difficult to explain. Nonetheless, if any short-term breeding is to be overlooked in Scilly, an owl is as likely as any species to have been involved, though the absence of any reported 'hooting' perhaps argues against breeding having occurred on this occasion. And despite there being no indications in *CBWPSAR* 34 that Tawny Owls may have arrived during autumn 1964, a Snowy Owl *Nyctea scandiaca* did arrive in the islands on 10th October that year and remained until mid-March 1965. It must also be noted, however, that Long-eared Owls occur regularly on Scilly during autumn, some at least remaining into the winter months. And certainly they can show a tendency towards roosting together in close proximity (pers. obs.), though whether or not they also hunt in loose groups seems not to have been explored on Scilly.

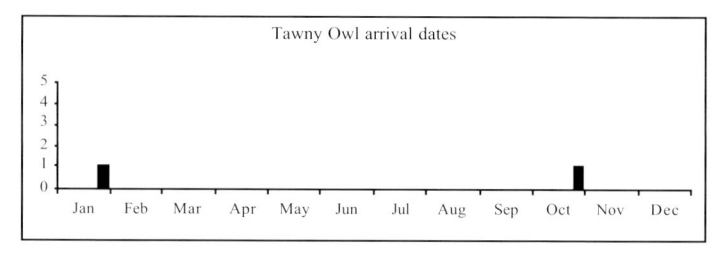

Breeding adult Tawny Owls are largely sedentary. Post-fledging juvenile dispersal follows a protracted period of parental dependence and occurs up until November, being random in direction and involving high mortality; those failing to replace lost breeding adults are likely to die by late autumn (Cramp *et al.* 1977–94). The probable sole reason for any additional movement is cold weather. Cramp *et al.* give average dispersal distances for birds as far north as Lapland, 68% of which moved less than 20 km and only 4% further than 100 km (Wernham *et al.* 2002). Interestingly, however, central European birds apparently move further and in a westerly direction, a Swiss-ringed nestling appearing 280 km away in France and a Belgian nestling travelling 450 km, also to France. In northern Russia, Tawny Owls were recorded participating in small-scale irruptions in at least 1960 and 1963, though distances involved were not stated. Tawny Owls breed as close to Scilly as mainland Cornwall and in France are common as close as Brittany (Guermeur & Monnat 1980), though they are naturally absent from Ireland. No Tawny Owls have been ringed on Scilly and there are no recaptures from elsewhere.

# Long-eared Owl *Asio otus* A

Regular autumn migrant in small numbers and perhaps occasional winter visitor. This is one of those species showing an apparent increase in records in Scilly during the latter half of the 20th century, to the point where written descriptions are no longer considered necessary (*IOSBR* 1996).

Breeds Europe, extreme North Africa and central Asia, from North Atlantic to Pacific Ocean, plus North America from Atlantic to Pacific. Migratory in north, mainly resident or dispersive further south, northern populations winter within southern range. Polytypic: nominate *otus* occurs Eurasia and North Africa to eastern Mediterranean, including Azores; *canariensis* Canary Islands; *abyssinicus* Ethiopia; *wilsonianus* eastern North America; two additional forms western North America and central and eastern Africa.

The earliest specific mention of Long-eared Owl in Scilly seems to be E H Rodd's *Zoologist* account of several seen in the islands during November 1859 (Rodd 1960b). The same author reported that it appeared to be 'almost gregarious' during November and that it was usually plentiful in winter, sometimes 'in small flocks' (Rodd 1880). Rodd also made specific reference to a bird frequenting bushes on St Martin's on 7th November 1870 and to the arrival of one or two on 15th December 1864. In addition, among letters from his nephew Francis Rodd is an account of five flushed from a bush in Holy Vale, St Mary's, on 8th November 1870 and several others elsewhere, plus the observation that 'The occurrence of this bird in the neighbourhood of Scilly is very frequent' (Rodd 1880). In describing the situation in mainland Cornwall, the elder Rodd thought the species especially common in west Cornwall (Rodd 1880).

In their informative *Zoologist* review of *The Birds of Scilly*, James Clark and Francis Rodd described it as common during autumn and winter, 'often in small parties in which both this and the Short-eared Owl (*A. flammeus*) not infrequently occur together' (Clark & Rodd 1906). They pointed out too that it apparently preferred Tresco and that four or five might occasionally be flushed from a single tree.

But despite these early claims of an obvious presence, up until 1974 Penhallurick (1978) could find only eight 20th century records – four each for Scilly and the Cornish mainland. And in Penhallurick's own words, 1975 was an exceptional autumn, particularly on Scilly where at least eight were recorded between 17th October and the month's end: five on St Mary's and one each on Tresco and Gugh, plus one on remote Rosevear in the Western Isles. One of these or another was found dead near Higher Moors, St Mary's, on 28th December and others were known to be present until the end of the year. There were perhaps four at Porthgwarra, west Cornwall, during that same October. However, despite this 1975 prominence, only 19 or so were recorded in the 14 years to 1989, at an average of 1.35 per year, whereas up to 110 were logged during the ten years 1990–99, at an annual average of 11. This increase in Scillonian records contrasts with a reported British decrease this century (Cramp *et al.* 1977–94) but could, at least in part, be attributable to increased observer coverage, many recent sightings involving roosting individuals found by birdwatchers peering into dense cover during autumn.

Regardless of the causes, this dramatic increase commenced with ten birds during 1990, the 19 reports during 1996 being the best showing for any single year and two in 1995 the lowest. Most regular sites were in wooded Holy Vale on St Mary's and in the Tresco woodlands, at both of which three or more regularly roosted in close proximity from October, sometimes through to the following late winter period. A bird roosting in Holy Vale on 27th April 1984 was the first apparent spring record for the islands, although one was still present on the Lunnon Farm study plot on 16th May 1992 and it was becoming evident that birds at least occasionally remained to the following spring. One seen by lighthouse keepers on the Bishop Rock on 25th October 1992 was presumably a migrant, and a far older record of a 'brown owl' from the same location, on the night of 4th–5th November 1909 (Ogilve-Grant 1911), presumably involved either this species or Short-eared Owl.

Establishing what migrant predators eat whilst present in the islands is always a challenge and two entries in the reports help throw light on this as far as Long-eared Owl is concerned. In the first, a Long-eared Owl roosting in Middle Town, St Martin's, for part of November and December 1991 was considered to be killing Collared Doves *Streptopelia decaocto*, judging from feathers found at the roost site (*IOSBR* 1991). In the other, a bird roosting quite publicly on St Agnes during the busy 1999 White's Thrush *Zoothera dauma* period was seen to take a Blackbird *Turdus merula* as it ventured too close to the apparently sleeping owl (*IOSBR* 1999).

Long-eared Owls from Fennoscandia and western Russia move mainly south or southwest in autumn, in some winters even reaching Iberia, whilst in central Europe passage is evident from September through to December. Birds ringed or recaptured in Britain moved to or from countries as far east as western Russia and the former Czechoslovakia (Wernham *et al.* 2002), whereas first-years from all populations undertake a random post-fledging dispersal, some British-ringed individuals moving up to 340 km, including one recovered in Finland (Cramp *et al.* 1977–94; Wernham *et al.* 2002). Nevertheless, Long-eared Owls ringed as nestlings in Switzerland were recovered the following winter as far away as Spain and Sardinia. Consequently, it is difficult to determine the source of Long-eared Owls visiting Scilly during autumn in the absence of ringing recoveries, though at least some could originate from eastern Europe. Of relevance, though, may be their apparent absence on spring passage, which on North Sea coasts is evident from early March through to early June. Clark & Rodd commented that this species and Short-eared Owl *A. flammeus* often occurred together on small parties and it is interesting that autumn 1975 also saw greater numbers of this last species than normal.

Gantlett (1998) considered that the differently marked, migratory or dispersive North American form *wilsonianus* could possibly occur in Britain during autumn, and if so Scilly would be as good a place as any to commence searching, particularly as there is already evidence of larger and equally unlikely North American species or forms reaching the islands, e.g. Goshawk *Accipter g. atricapillus*, 'Marsh Harrier' *Circus c. hudsonius* and 'Rough-legged Hawk' *Buteo l. sanctijohannis*. It may be the case that one or more of Scilly's visiting Snowy Owls *Nyctea scandiaca* originated from that part of their range (Witherby 1927b).

## Short-eared Owl *Asio flammeus* A

**Spring and autumn migrant in small numbers, also winters in some years. Probably fewer now than formerly, full written description now required by the SRP.**

Less widespread in Europe than previous species, absent from most of southern Eurasia but reaching Bering Sea, also North and South America. Migratory to partially migratory, European populations winter western and southern Europe and North Africa, a few reaching Afrotropics. Breeding distribution and winter range may vary between years in response to local factors. Polytypic: nominate *flammeus* occurs Eurasia and North America; eight additional forms elsewhere. Included on Annex I of 1979 EEC 'Birds Directive'. Amber-listed in UK: unfavourable world conservation status (Gregory *et al.* 2002).

Early writers thought Short-eared Owl occurred annually during autumn and winter. However, North (1850) considered it did so 'periodically', appearing with Woodcock *Scolopax rusticola* in autumn. The earliest specific reference concerns the arrival in the islands of several following a severe south-southeast gale during mid-October 1863, some of which were shot along with a female Marsh Harrier *Circus aeruginosus* (Rodd 1863b, 1880). E H Rodd described a 'considerable' arrival during December the following year, his nephew Francis having noted seven or eight on 24th of that month (Rodd 1880). In contrast, however, in autumn 1870 Francis recorded that Short-eared Owls seemed 'to have missed the islands altogether', observing that their place seemed to have been taken by Long-eared Owls *A. otus*. In their typically concise but reliably descriptive early 20th century review, James Clark and Francis Rodd described it as common during autumn and winter, often in small parties in which both this and Long-eared frequently occurred together (Clark & Rodd 1906). They pointed out too that they seemed to occur on all islands 'where the bracken patches are large enough to supply convenient shelter', E H Rodd's description of it on mainland Cornwall at this time being very much the same (Rodd 1880).

Penhallurick (1978) commenced his 1970's countywide review by pointing out that there were no 19th- or early 20th century breeding records for Cornwall, Scilly or Devon until at least one pair bred on the edge of Bodmin Moor during the 1930s and at nearby Wadebride in the 1940s. The only subsequently recorded summer presence in Cornwall involved a displaying pair on the Lizard in 1963, though breeding was not proved. Penhallurick drew attention to substantial Cornish and Scillonian autumn influxes during 1975, birds arriving on Scilly from 22nd September with at least 16 recorded up until 9th November and one evident on Tresco still by 23rd December. He concluded with the comment that 'one or two probably winter regularly in the islands' but that up to six were on Samson alone in 1962–63.

Examination of the records for the 23 years 1977–99 reveals an annual presence during autumn and spring for all years except 1993, though not always during winter. The number of annual sightings fell in the range 4–23, though high between-site mobility means much duplication may have been involved. There was also a strong suggestion among the data of an increase in sightings during the last ten years, some of which may have been attributable to increased autumn observer coverage. Certainly for the most recent ten years, autumn arrival dates varied from late August through to October and spring arrivals occurred during March–May, suggesting strongly that migrants rather than late winter wanderers were involved. Autumn sightings outnumbered those in spring by about two or three to one. During the full period under consideration at least five Short-eared Owls were found dead, or with broken wings, and whilst it is difficult to adequately explain this apparent high injury ratio, the possibility of illegal or accidental shooting remains high.

In Europe, the volume and extent of autumn passage varies between years but mainly occurs during August–October, with return spring passage evident during March–April. Birds from as far north as Finland and south to Germany reach France and Iberia in at least some years and at least some Icelandic birds are believed to reach Britain. Although a percentage of birds from northern Britain winter in Ireland, others have reached Spain and Malta (Wernham *et al.* 2002). Variations in wintering numbers may also be attributable to presence or absence at various European locations of breeding concentrations during years of vole abundance; thus there is no clear indication of where Short-eared Owls passing through Scilly might originate, though some apparently come from Norway and Finland (Wernham *et al.* 2002). A record of a 'brown owl' at the Bishop Rock Lighthouse in company with Woodcock *Scolopax rusticola*, Skylark *Alauda arvensis*, Starling *Sturnus vulgaris*, Black Redstart *Phoenicurus ochruros* and several thrush *Turdus* species on the night of 4th–5th November 1909 (Ogilvie-Grant 1911), presumably involved either this species or Long-eared Owl. One Short-eared Owl had been ringed in Scilly up until the end of 1999 but it was not subsequently recovered and there are no recaptures from elsewhere.

## Nightjar (European Nightjar) *Caprimulgus europaeus* A

Scarce but regular and almost annual migrant, formerly bred in small numbers. Full written description required by the SRP.

Breeds Europe and North Africa, east through central and southern Asia to eastern Siberia and Mongolia, excluding northern Norway and Sweden. Polytypic: nominate *europaeus* occurs central and northern Europe and northern Asia east to Lake Baikal; *meridionalis* southern Europe, North Africa and Asia Minor north to Pyrenees, central Italy, former Yugoslavia, Hungary, Crimea and east to Iran; additional forms further east. All populations believed to winter Africa south of Sahara. Included on Annex I of 1979 EEC 'Birds Directive'. Red-listed in UK: rapid, greater than 50% contraction of breeding range over past 25 years; 50% of breeding population at ten or fewer sites; unfavourable European conservation status (Gregory *et al.* 2002).

E H Rodd (1880) seemed quite familiar with Nightjar on mainland Cornwall but made no reference to it in Scilly, and given his close connection with those who regularly shot rarities on Scilly during the 19th century, it is tempting to think that Nightjar was absent at that time. Nevertheless, Clark & Rodd (1906) described it as 'by no means uncommon in autumn', qualifying this by pointing out that it had never been known to breed. Indeed, it was sufficiently well known on Scilly by 1906 for them to quote its 'favourite haunts', namely Abbey Hill, Castle and Middle Downs, all on Tresco, Higher Downs (presumably Higher Moors) on St Mary's and Samson's Bryher Hill. One intriguing report concerned a 'large flock' allegedly seen on Annet by A A Dorrien-Smith during August 1901. Ryves & Quick (1946) widened the picture by quoting B W Tucker's personal memories of finding a nest with two eggs on Tresco during June 1914, whilst still a boy. In addition, Wallis (1923) claimed to have heard Nightjar churring on Tresco during midday and confirmed that C J King had photographed this species on the nest. Although King made no mention of this in his *Some Notes on Wild Nature in Scillonia* (C J King 1924), Penhallurick (1978) later confirmed that King photographed eggs and young on St Mary's during 1918. Penhallurick also attributed a pre-First World War report of a nest with eggs to A A Dorrien-Smith and suggested that this may have been the nest found by Tucker, whilst Ryves and Quick claimed that Dorrien-Smith thought it a regular breeder in Scilly up until their report.

As with so many species, we hear little more of Nightjar on Scilly until well into the 1940s, other than the occasional passing comment, such as the reference to it arriving on 8th May (Ogilvie-Grant 1912c), or that in 1937 it was seen and heard on Bryher from 19th June onwards (*CBWPSAR* 7). One or two of the latter reports also mention first arrival dates, e.g. 9th May 1944, 17th May 1945 and 11th May 1946, which, if not proving breeding, suggest it passed through the islands regularly and probably in some numbers.

Nightjar's status in the islands now is purely that of migrant, there being just 35 acceptable reports for the forty-three years 1957–99, though it must surely always have been under-recorded on Scilly, as elsewhere. The pattern is seemingly one of 0.8 reported sightings per year on average, though with up to three in any one year and with 12 (34%) of records occurring during spring (May–June). The Chart includes all 31 of the 20th century records where the date of arrival or discovery is known and shows a clear spring peak during late May and a less abrupt autumn peak, from mid-September to early October. No records fell outside the period May to mid-October. As recently as 1987, a Nightjar was found shot on Tresco, though enquiries failed to identify the individual responsible (*IOSBR* 1987).

*Birds of the Isles of Scilly*

Nightjar arrival dates

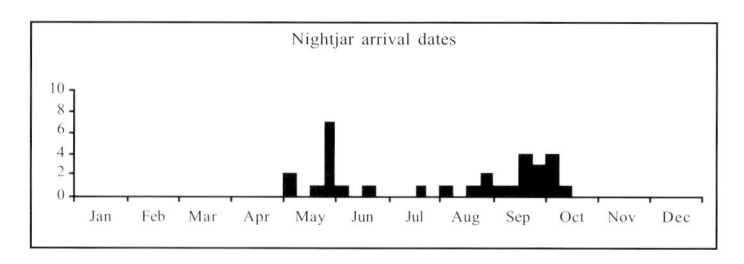

All British-ringed overseas recoveries involved birds moving directly south, the single exception being a bird recovered in northern Germany, and there is no ringing evidence to suggest that Continental birds pass through Britain on passage (Wernham *et al.* 2002). Gantlett (1998) drew attention to the possibility of forms other than the nominate *europaeus* reaching Britain and for this species the possibility of extralimital migrants occurring seems distinctly possible, either as spring overshoots of *meridionalis* from southern Europe, or any of the eastern forms – given the obvious western or southwestern involvement of birds leaving eastern Siberia and Mongolia (Cramp *et al.* 1977–94). Scilly has a proven record of providing temporary shelter for several other eastern migrants, so the possibility of encountering these forms on the islands should be borne in mind. Two Nightjars were ringed by SABO prior to 1970 but there are no recaptures.

## Common Nighthawk          *Chordeiles minor*  **A**  BBRC 66%
**Very rare migrant, full written description required by the BBRC.**

1927  One (female – shot) Tresco 11th September   Lowe 1927; *British Birds* 22: 98–100, 48: 8
1955  Two (female & juvenile) St Agnes 28th September to 5th October   *CBWPSAR* 25: 35–36
1971  One (immature) St Agnes 12th & 13th October   *British Birds* 65: 302–302, 338
1976  One (female) dead St Mary's 14th October   *British Birds* 70: 427
1976  One (female) dead St Mary's 25th October   *British Birds* 70: 427
1981  One St Mary's 12th to 14th October   *British Birds* 75: 511
1982  One (immature) St Agnes 20th October to 4th November   *British Birds* 76: 503
1989  One (juvenile) Tresco 16th to 22nd September   *British Birds* 83: 470, 471, 479
1998  One (male) St Agnes 9th to 13th September (died 14th)   *British Birds* 92: 170
1998  One (female or first-year) St Mary's 12th to 20th September   *British Birds* 92: 170, 585
1999  One Coastguard Cottages, St Agnes 22nd September   *British Birds* 93: 345, 541
1999  One Fraggle Rock, Bryher 23rd to 30th October   *British Birds* 93: 345, 541

Breeds North and Central America, from southeast Alaska and southern Canada south to Panama. Diurnal and nocturnal migrant in loose flocks, winters South America south to Argentina. Polytypic: nominate *minor* occurs southeast Alaska, Canada and northeast USA east of Great Plains south to Georgia and Virginia; *chapmani* southeast USA south of *minor* and south to Florida and Louisiana east of Great Plains; seven further forms south-central Canada south to Central America and Florida Keys (Cramp *et al.* 1977–94). Steady decline throughout, worst in eastern North America, i.e. 65% since 1966 and 45% during last 15 years (Bryant 1997).

As with Yellow-billed Cuckoo *Coccyzus americanus*, Scilly is undoubtedly the premier spot in the West Palearctic for encountering this much sought-after species from across the North Atlantic, 13 individuals having occurred on the islands up to and including year 2000. In fact, with just five other records accepted by the BBRC during 1958–99 an impressive 66% of all sighting for that period came from Scilly. The Chart incorporates all known Scillonian arrival dates, making it abundantly clear that for those who still need Common Nighthawk on their British list, late September and October hold the greatest promise.

The first European record of this enigmatic species came from Scilly: a bird shot on Tresco during September 1927 (Lowe 1927; Witherby 1928). However, like the two American cuckoos *Coccyzus*, Common Nighthawks seem particularly unfortunate once they make landfall in the islands, for of the 13 individuals involved on Scilly, one was shot (albeit a long time ago) and three were either found dead, or died soon afterwards. In addition, we have no way of knowing how many birds recorded alive subsequently succumbed, a fate not at all unlikely once we consider the particularly stressing circumstances of their arrival.

The 1927 individual, reportedly an exhausted female, was shot by Major A A Dorrien-Smith and mounted and held in the Tresco Abbey collection. Very noticeable, however, is the absence of any earlier records from the islands compared with the number of other extreme rarities obtained or seen during the 1800s. Nonetheless, it seems difficult unlikely that Common Nighthawks did not occur at that time and equally tempting to think this species, perhaps above all others, may have been overlooked by those otherwise extremely vigilant and ever-eager men with their trusty guns. Most initial sightings of live Common Nighthawks appear to have involved individuals feeding low over open areas at dusk, e.g. Lower Moors or the Airport, both St Mary's, or Tresco's Castle Down. Most sightings were fairly evenly distributed between St Mary's and St Agnes, but with two on Tresco and one, the most recent, on Bryher. The 1955 St Agnes record may currently be under review by the BBRC, presumably to ascertain whether or not there were two birds involved.

The 1998 St Agnes individual, an adult male, was first briefly watched hawking insects outside the Turk's Head public house on the evening of 8th September, before disappearing until midday on 9th. It was then rediscovered by resident farmer and birder Francis Hicks, as it roosted on the ground in one of his ridged flower fields, Francis having seen the species before on St Agnes. The bird stayed several days and Francis kindly allowed access so that visiting mainland birders could see it as it continued to roost in his field by day. However, at some time during the morning of the 14th, the bird died, giving rise to speculation that some birders may only have seen it after its demise. Fortunately, another, this time a female or first-winter male, was found on nearby St Mary's on 12th September, where it remained until 20th, allowing those in doubt over the St Agnes bird to revisit the islands and view a live individual! The bird on Bryher's Shipman Down in 1999 was watched quartering the ground in company with a visiting Short-eared Owl *Asio flammeus* on more than one evening.

The death of the 1998 St Agnes Common Nighthawk and the removal of the body by a visiting birder raised important issues concerning the legal and moral ownership of the remains of such nationally important rarities. Dealing first with the legal aspect, it seems beyond argument that, as in the St Agnes case, in cases where a person is granted permission to enter upon land, such authority does not extend to removal of any items discovered, including a dead Common Nighthawk. Coupled with which, very old but still applicable laws impose a right of ownership of wild birds and other animals upon the owner of such land. More importantly, however, as it now stands, the law relating to the possession of wild birds and their parts and derivatives (*Wildlife & Countryside Act 1981*) is extremely inflexible, requiring the possessor to show legal acquisition in all cases. Consequently, the removal of a dead bird from private land without permission may well invalidate its subsequent possession under this statute and in any event it is incumbent upon the possessor to show the bird's death was legal. Taking now the moral point, it seems difficult to argue against the view that the skin of a national rarity belongs either in the national collection, in this case the British Museum (Natural History), or in the appropriate county museum or similar.

*Birds of the Isles of Scilly*

Common Nighthawk arrival dates

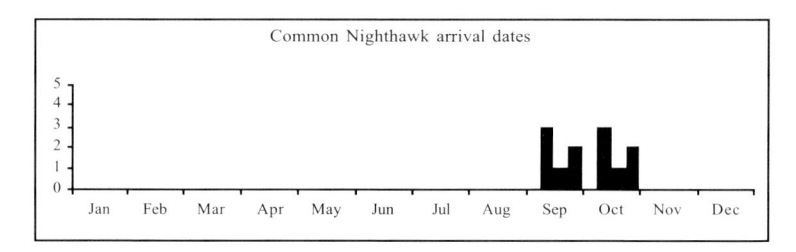

Southward migration of the nominate *minor* from northeast USA occurs during late July to early October, with the bulk of the movement during late August and early September, often in loose flocks of about 20–40 birds. Nevertheless, there is increasing evidence that, like Yellow-billed Cuckoo, an unknown percentage of Common Nighthawks make the non-stop transoceanic crossing from southeast Canada or New England, out over the North Atlantic to Bermuda and the outer West Indies, some perhaps even travelling non-stop to mainland South America. Such flights involve a sea crossing of 2,000 to 3,000 km, or 4,000 km direct to South America and quite clearly put the birds at risk of involuntary eastward displacement in the event of encountering severe weather systems in the mid-Atlantic. Common Nighthawk scored second to last in Robbins' statistical review of anticipated transatlantic vagrancy among 31 Nearctic migrant passerines and near-passerines recorded in Britain or Ireland during the period 1947–76. The six accepted British and Irish autumn records exceed the predicted relative likelihood of no arriving individuals (Robbins 1980). Amazingly, Ireland was without a record until one in Co. Cork in October 1999. For descriptions of some of the birds involved and the circumstances of their stay see B D Harding (1972b) and Wagstaff (1998).

From a European birdwatcher's point of view, surely one of the most magical experiences is to stand with a group of like-minded individuals in rapidly failing light on a remote Atlantic island, whilst one of these extreme rarities races low around and above at great speed snapping up aerial insects, all in complete silence save for the murmur of the sea on the rocks below and the occasional orchestrated gasp of unbounded appreciation.

## Chimney Swift *Chaetura pelagica* A BBRC 20%

**Extremely rare migrant, full written description required by the BBRC.**

1986 One St Mary's & St Martin's 4th to 9th November  *British Birds* 80: 548; *Ibis* 134: 213
1999 One St Mary's 22nd to 25th October  *British Birds* 93: 345, 541
2001 One St Mary's & St Martin's 28th & 29th October  *British Birds* 95: 368, 502

Breeds North America, east of Rocky Mountains from southern Canada south to Florida and Gulf coast. Migratory, wintering South American Amazon basin. Monotypic. Steady recent decline with Canada worst affected (Bryant 1997).

The BBRC accepted a total of just ten British records during the period 1958–99, thus the two Scillonian sightings represent 20% of all records up until that time. The individual found racing around over Lower Moors on St Mary's in November 1986 was then only the third known to have crossed the Atlantic, following two in west Cornwall in 1982. It remained in the same area until disappearing on 6th, only to be relocated next day flying about in the shelter of a hill at Higher Town, St Martin's, and was last seen in deteriorating conditions on the morning of the 9th.

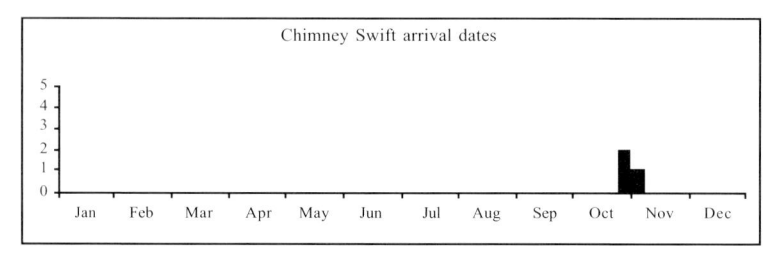

Chimney Swift arrival dates

The archipelago's second Chimney Swift arrived towards the end of a purple patch for Scillonian rarities, following close on the heels of Britain's first-ever Short-toed Eagle *Circaetus gallicus* and Scilly's first Siberian Thrush *Zoothera sibirica*, the islands' first Blue Rock Thrush *Monticola solitarius* and third White's Thrush *Z. dauma* in October 1999. It was discovered doing wide circuits of the St Mary's Higher Moors mid-morning on 22nd, moving to Bant's Carn on the island's north side by the afternoon. It stayed in Scilly until the morning of the 26th, being reported at various sites before settling on St Agnes on 25th. Amazingly, this bird was discovered as news broke of the almost simultaneous arrival of a Chimney Swift in nearby west Cornwall. However, it soon became clear that a major European influx had occurred, with up to 13 reported in Britain and others elsewhere in Europe, e.g. Sweden, Portugal and the Azores. For a photograph of the 1999 individual see *British Birds* 93: plates 322 & 323. A third arrived in Scilly during October 2001 and remained for at least two days, being seen over St Mary's and St Martin's on 28th and 29th. The Chart includes all three arrival dates. Autumn migration takes place from late August through to late October.

## Swift (Common Swift) *Apus apus* A

**Annual spring and autumn migrant, normally in moderate to small numbers but large concentrations may occur. It apparently bred in the past.**

Breeds almost throughout West Palearctic plus central Asia east to Yellow Sea, also fragmentarily southwest Asia. Migratory, all populations winter Africa south of equator. Polytypic: nominate *apus* occurs Europe and North Africa east to Lake Baikal and south to Turkey; *pekinensis* from Iran east to northern China. National 6% increase 1994–99 (Bashford & Noble 2000).

Earliest published mention of Swift in Scilly is probably E H Rodd's autumn 1868 letter to the *Zoologist* pointing out that one appeared among other migrants that autumn (Rodd 1868c), though there are many earlier records for mainland Cornwall. The same author later noted in his appended *List of the Birds Observed on the Scilly Islands* (Rodd 1880) that it occurred as a summer visitor to the islands and indicated that it had been 'ascertained to breed there'. On mainland Cornwall he considered it somewhat local in distribution and seldom arriving before the first week of May. However, by the close of the 19th century, James Clark and E H Rodd's nephew Francis were able to describe it as annually evident on spring passage 'in the last week of July', though they knew of no August sightings and made no specific mention of autumn (Clark & Rodd 1906). They concluded with the interesting comment that despite the resemblance of Scilly's granite rocks to those of the Cornish moors, unlike the Cornish moors there was no record of Swift having bred in Scilly.

These last remarks both conflict with what the elder Rodd had to say about this species breeding in the islands and throw up the perhaps surprising prospect of Swifts nesting on Cornish granite outcrops during the late 19th century. In fact, Penhallurick (1978) listed a large number of reported cases of Swifts nesting either on rocky outcrops in Cornwall, on nearby Dartmoor in Devon, or on Cornwall's coastal cliffs. In particular, he quoted from a Francis Rodd manuscript describing how it bred 'in some numbers under granite ledges' at a site known as Hawk's Tor in east Cornwall, though probably the only active site other than buildings that Penhallurick knew of in the county by the mid-1970s involved Sharp Tor, near North Hill in east Cornwall, close to where Francis Rodd lived. Penhallurick also detailed breeding in an old mill on Peninnis Head, St Mary's, from 1943, possibly even from 1938, this continuing until the structure was demolished around 1957. The same authority drew attention to a report in the *IOSBR* for 1974 to the effect that Swifts may have bred in Hugh Town, St Mary's and on Tresco Abbey. At the same time, however, Penhallurick quoted David Hunt, who stated that whilst breeding had been widely suspected at these two locations it had never been proved (*IOSBR* 1980), the latter taking the view that birds involved were merely prospecting. Certainly that seemed the most likely explanation for the bird seen by the author briefly entering a hole in a building opposite Hugh Town's Godolphin Hotel during summer 2000. Interestingly, the 2000 Breeding Bird Atlas (Chown & Lock 2002) recorded an estimated three pairs in three (4.4%) of the 67 surveyed 1-km squares, two on St Mary's and one on St Martin's, though again breeding was not proved.

Penhallurick (1978) gave the earliest reported Scillonian arrival date as 10th April, on St Agnes in 1961, and the latest annual sighting as 23rd October 1960, but gave no counts for the islands. Taking the ten years from 1990, there was a measure of predictability about spring arrival and autumn departure dates, first of the year being observed between 1st and 28th April, though with a probable bias towards the

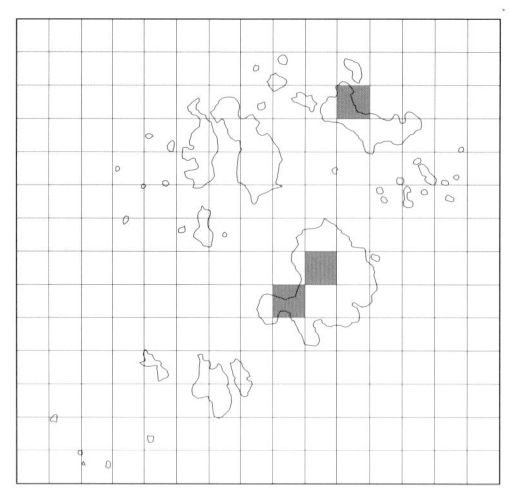

**1-km Swift Summer Distribution – 2000–01 (data Chown & Lock 2002)**

later half of the month. Final departures were equally regular, dates for the nine quoted years falling in the range 17th September to 22nd October, although seven of these occurred after 11th. More difficult to assess, however, was the annual cutoff between spring and autumn passage, mainly owing to the at least intermittent presence of a few birds throughout June and July, though most June sightings appeared to be related to continued spring movement. But as expected with such a mobile species, there are few detailed flock counts and though the highest recorded spring concentration was just 120, birds were generally far more evident throughout this period, unlike autumn when counts varied from none to 'hundreds'. The autumn situation is ably described in the *IOSBR* for 1999, when by early July 'birds began to gather over the islands at altitude, but were forced down to lower levels on various dates, such as July 5th when there were over 100 around St Mary's and 8th August with over 50 over Higher Moors'. The Report goes on to point out that numbers rapidly dropped away during mid-August, with just three September reports and one in October. Undoubtedly, at least some of these mid-year congregations involved feeding flocks from mainland Cornwall or beyond, but this conclusion is perhaps only safely applied during July.

Swift is an undoubted long-range migrant, some *pekinensis* from China wintering in southwest Africa, an annual journey of near equal proportions to the much-publicised pole-to-pole Arctic Tern *Sterna paradisaea* movements. British and Irish birds also winter in southern Africa, apparently crossing the Mediterranean at its western end (Wernham *et al.* 2002). Swift is notable too for the brief period of time spent on the breeding grounds, autumn departure commencing from late July or early August, soon after the young have fledged, only a minority remaining in Europe by September, though October or even November stragglers are not unusual (Cramp *et al.* 1977–94). Returning birds reach southern Europe by late March and continued movement is evident well into June throughout the breeding range. Particularly pale birds have been noted about the islands from time to time, e.g. 1982, usually in autumn. It has been suggested these may be the eastern form *pekinensis* (Gantlett 1998) and although the presence of this form in Britain may be difficult to establish from just field sightings, certainly *pekinensis* mixes with the nominate *apus* in parts of the wintering area and the possibility of it arriving in Scilly in either spring or autumn must be very real.

## Pallid Swift *Apus pallidus* A   BBRC 4.0%

**Extremely rare vagrant, full written description required by the BBRC.**

1998   One St Agnes 17th May   *British Birds* 91: 454, 585
2002   One (photographed) Bryher 25th & 26th March   *British Birds* 96: 155

Breeds northwest Africa and Iberia, east to southern Iran. Migratory, wintering Africa north of equator. Polytypic: *brehmorum* occurs southern France, Iberia, Italy, Greece, Cyprus, Canary Islands, Madeira, coastal North Africa east to northwest Egypt; *illyricus* eastern Adriatic; nominate *pallidus* Saharan Africa, Egypt and Middle East.

The first of two BBRC-accepted records involved a bird watched feeding over St Agnes on 17th May and as recently as 1998. There had been previous claims or suspicions but this was the first bird to stand the full rigors of the examination process, ably supported by colour photographs. During preparation of this text, two others were claimed: one briefly on Bryher and Tresco on 3rd June 2001 (rejected by BBRC), and another on Bryher for two days during late March 2002. The latter was also photographed and gained the approval of BBRC.

Records of vagrant Pallid Swifts in Britain probably involve *brehmorum*, which breeds throughout much of the range, but Gantlett (1998) drew attention to the possibility of the slightly larger and darker *illyricus*

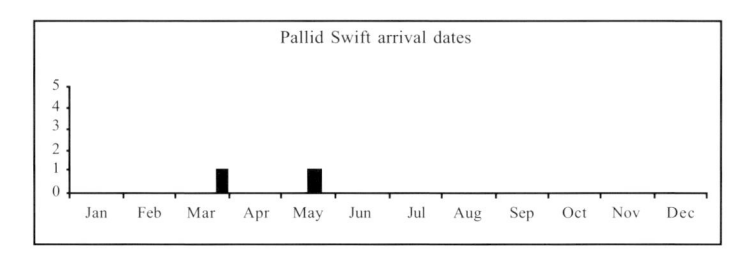

**Pallid Swift arrival dates** (chart showing bars at Mar: 1, May: 1)

from the coastal Adriatic also occurring. The first British and Irish record involved a bird found dead at St John's Point, Co. Dublin, Ireland, on 30th October 1913 and the first British record came from Stodmarsh, Kent as recently as May 1978 (Palmer 2000). Of the only two British or Irish records available for inspection, a bird found moribund on Orkney during late October 1996 (the first Scottish record) showed features consistent with *brehmorum*, but the earlier Irish skin has still to be examined (McGowan 2002).

# [Pacific Swift *Apus pacificus*]

**Two previous British records.**

[1997   One Salakee Farm, St Mary's 23rd September]

Breeds central Russia east to Pacific Ocean. Polytypic: nominate *pacificus* occurs Russia from Altay to Kamchatka, Mongolia, northern China and Japan; *kanoi* Tibet, southern China and Taiwan; *leuconyx* outer Himalayas and Assam; *cooki* Southeast Asia. Long- and short-distance migrant, many from north of range reaching southern Australia or even Tasmania.

Two previous British records, but only one on the mainland: a bird captured on an oil platform 45 km off the Norfolk coast on 19th June 1981 (*British Birds* 83: 43–46; *Ibis* 134: 212) was followed by one seen and photographed at Cley, Norfolk, on 30th May 1993 (*British Birds* 87: 538–539). A sighting of a swift over Salakee Farm, St Mary's, on 23rd September 1997 was believed by the observer to have involved this species but the record was rejected by the BBRC. The BBRC pointed out that the two acceptable earlier records conformed to the expected spring vagrancy pattern also self-evident in records of White-throated Needletail *Hirundapus caudacutus*. This feature perhaps aided rejection of the September St Mary's claim.

# Alpine Swift *Apus melba*  A  BBRC 3.2%

**Scarce migrant or vagrant, full written description required by the BBRC.**

| | | |
|---|---|---|
| 1957 | One Porth Hellick, St Mary's 19th September |
| 1959 | One St Agnes 6th October |
| 1968 | One St Agnes 24th July |
| 1968 | One St Agnes 21st October |
| 1969 | One St Agnes 24th September (found dead – ringed) |
| 1970 | One Tresco 21st September |
| 1972 | One St Agnes 27th October |
| 1979 | One St Agnes & St Mary's 9th May |
| 1981 | One St Martin's 31st May |
| 1986 | One St Mary's & St Agnes 2nd & 3rd May |
| 1986 | One St Mary's 1st July |
| 1988 | One St Agnes & Gugh 22nd May |
| 1991 | One Tresco & St Martin's 7th & 8th July |
| 1991 | One St Mary's 10th October |
| 1995 | One St Mary's, Gugh & St Agnes 8th October |
| 2000 | One Tresco 1st to 3rd July |
| 2000 | One St Mary's 23rd & 24th July |
| 2002 | One Tresco & Bryher 23rd March |
| 2002 | One St Mary's & Tresco 1st to 7th April |

Breeds northwest Africa and Iberia east through southern Europe and southwest Asia to Turkistan and India, north to Alps, Crimea and Caucasus and south to East and southern Africa, Madagascar, Sinai and Sri Lanka. Northern populations migratory, those from West Palearctic wintering Africa. Polytypic: nominate *melba* occurs northern Morocco, southern Europe, Asia Minor and Iran; *tuneti* central and eastern Morocco, Algeria east to Dead Sea; other forms further south in Africa and in India.

There were 17 Scillonian records of this impressive large swift up until the end of year 2000 and two further records in 2002. As elsewhere in Britain, the pattern is very much one of a protracted period of summer arrivals and a more pronounced autumn peak. The earliest arrival date was 22nd March 2002 and the last bird was seen on 27th October 1972. Thirteen birds (68.4%) were seen on only one day and a further three were present only until the following day. The average length of stay for all 19 birds was just 1.8 days.

The first recorded presence in the islands involved a bird watched for five minutes feeding low over Porth Hellick Pool, St Mary's, on 19th September 1957 (*CBWPSAR* 27). The October 1991 individual was seen to strike an overhead cable in Hugh Town, St Mary's, during bad weather and was temporarily taken into care, being released once its situation improved, apparently none the worse for the experience.

No Alpine Swifts have been trapped and ringed in Scilly but the bird found dead on St Agnes during September 1969 had been ringed as a nestling in Solothurn, Switzerland on 26th July the same year, just 60 days earlier. This would appear to be a classic case of reverse migration. However, according to Cramp *et al.* (1977–94) autumn migration through the south Palearctic is mainly concentrated from September through to mid-October, though some juveniles are moving south by August. They mention birds ringed in Switzerland having been recovered on passage in France (29), Spain (8) and Italy (6), but none further north. Nevertheless, the same authors point out that weather-related movements comparable to those undertaken by Common Swift *A. apus* are also know to affect Alpine Swift and as such are likely to be a major cause of northwards vagrancy. The same authors quote recoveries of Swiss-ringed birds in the former Czechoslovakia (2), Austria, Germany (6), Denmark and England, the last presumably involving the St Agnes individual.

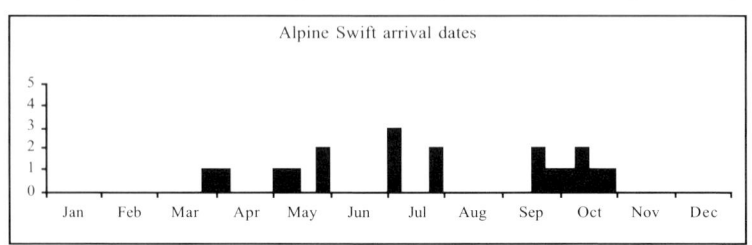

## Little Swift *Apus affinis* A BBRC 0%

**Extremely rare migrant, full written description required by the BBRC.**

*2002 One St Mary's 17th May Birding World 15: 185*

Breeds mainly Africa south of Sahara, Middle East, Iran and adjoining countries, India and Southeast Asia; in West Palearctic confined to northwest Africa and Turkey. Most populations resident, those in the north migratory or partially migratory, wintering within remainder of range. Polytypic: *galilejensis* occurs northwest Africa east to Pakistan; *aerobates* central and West Africa; nominate *affinis* most of India plus East Africa; eight additional forms in Africa and southern Asia.

The first for Scilly was discovered on St Mary's as recently as 17th May 2002, by birders visiting the islands to see the Lesser Kestrel *F. naumanni* discovered the previous day. What was very probably the same bird was reported over the Saltee Islands off southeast Ireland on the 16th. We can only guess at the origin of such a mobile species, especially as only 16 records were accepted by the BBRC for Britain during the period 1958–99. However, given the time of year, one possible answer is that this was an overshooting individual attempting to return to its breeding area, though the closest migratory populations to Scilly may be those in the Middle East and Turkey (Cramp *et al.* 1977–94).

## Kingfisher (Common Kingfisher) *Alcedo atthis* A

Regular and perhaps annual winter visitor in small numbers, also possible migrant. An old report of it having bred is unsubstantiated.

Breeds West Palearctic, central and eastern Asia, Indian subcontinent and Southeast Asia. Polytypic: nominate *atthis* occurs southern Europe; *aspida* north and west of *atthis*; five or six additional forms elsewhere. Dispersive or sedentary in western and central Europe, migratory in east. Included on Annex I of 1979 EEC 'Birds Directive'. Amber-listed in UK: unfavourable world conservation status (Gregory *et al.* 2002), BTO Waterways Bird Survey showed 8% decline 1975–2000.

Gilbert White (in Jesse 1887) considered it resident in the islands, but E H Rodd's knowledge of 19th century Scilly was far more reliable and he viewed it as occasional, and then only during winter (Rodd 1880). However, the early 20th century account by James Clark and Rodd's nephew Francis sounds a lot like a description of the present day, pointing out that at the turn of the century it occurred as a casual autumn and winter visitor, usually singly (Clark & Rodd 1906). They continued by describing how it usually appeared near freshwater pools on St Mary's, Tresco and Bryher 'and especially beside the old well, or rather sloping hollow on the island of Tean', but added that it was occasionally seen at Newford Pond on St Mary's and had been twice encountered among the Western Isles.

Penhallurick (1978) mentioned large numbers killed in winter in Cornwall during the 19th century to supply taxidermists, but found no evidence of it ever having been a common breeder, particularly in the west. He was also of the opinion that its status had changed little during at least the first half of the 20th century. For Scilly, Penhallurick noted its presence from about mid-August through to mid-October, sometimes from early November, and drew attention to a bird seen on the Bishop Rock on 8th September 1966. Analysis of records for the ten years from 1990 shows a pattern of near annual overwintering by at least one individual, last 'spring' sightings ranging from 22nd January to 31st March. A bird on 9th May 1991 had probably not wintered and none were recorded during spring 1995. Autumn returns were surprisingly regular and involved first dates between 10th July (two years) and 27th August, though singles on 6th and 16th June are perhaps difficult to explain. Deciding on the numbers of Kingfishers present in the islands is complicated at any time by their high mobility plus a tendency to wander between coastal sites, but in most years perhaps no more than 2–3 individuals are involved and the possibility of some level of 'roll-over' of migrant birds cannot be entirely discounted. In this last respect, numbers recorded during autumn 1999 are enlightening, with no fewer than 89 reported sightings during October alone, most involving singles apart from two records of two together (*IOSBR* 1999). Kingfishers are still seen at sites described by Clark and Rodd nearly 100 years ago and although the Tean well may no longer attract them, an equally favourite site is the Porth Hellick outlet sluice at the southeast corner of Higher Moors on St Mary's, near the Sir Cloudsley Shovel's memorial.

Penhallurick addressed earlier claims of Kingfishers breeding on Scilly, concluding that they could not be substantiated. Apparently, W P Kennedy had been told of a nest in a bank adjoining Tresco's Great Pool during the three years 1950–52, and although he saw a bird there in 1952, positive proof of breeding was lacking. Importantly, there is apparently no description of the supposed nest site, though Penhallurick quoted from veteran Tresco gamekeeper Frank Wardle, who suggested there were no suitable Kingfisher nest sites on Tresco other than the low sea cliffs. Although this statement may not be entirely true, given the lack of information it seems unwise to accept these records. Meanwhile, the unexplained 1957 statement by Peter MacKenzie 'I feel sure these birds no longer breed on St Mary's' (*CBWPSAR* 27) seems not to have been commented upon by Penhallurick, and certainly since the 1950s there has been no suggestion of breeding in Scilly.

Although Kingfishers from Britain, France and Iberia east to Hungary and Bulgaria are largely sedentary, those from Poland and the former Czechoslovakia eastwards move mainly south or southwest during winter. Some of these birds travel nearly 2000 km to reach mainly France and Spain (Cramp *et al.* 1977–94), though ringing recoveries show some from much nearer, e.g. the Netherlands, also reach Britain at this time (Wernham *et al.* 2002). But regardless of any lack of migratory behaviour, young western European Kingfishers undergo a random post-fledging dispersal, which in Britain involves movements of up to 100 km, with 5% moving greater distances. Nonetheless, the regularity with which Kingfishers appear on Scilly, plus between-year consistencies in numbers involved perhaps argues for something other than purely random dispersal.

A total of 17 Kingfishers had been ringed on Scilly up until the end of 1999 but the only recapture involved a bird ringed on St Agnes and found stuck to a newly painted boat on St Martin's the same year. Two trapped and ringed together in Higher Moors, St Mary's, on the southern edge of the Lunnon Farm study plot had been noted chasing each other around Porth Hellick Pool for several days beforehand. Two mounted and cased skins in the Isles of Scilly Museum on St Mary's form part of the on-loan Tresco Abbey collection and were presumably collected in the islands during the 19th or early 20th centuries.

## Blue-cheeked Bee-eater          *Merops persicus*  **A**  BBRC 25%

**Extremely rare migrant or vagrant, full written description required by the BBRC.**

1921  One (adult *persicus*) shot St Mary's 13th July
   *British Birds* 74: 347; *Ibis* 114: 446; *Bull. BOC* 92: 57–59
1951  One (suggested *persicus*) St Agnes 22nd June   *British Birds* 45: 225–227; *Ibis* 98: 145

Breeds northern Egypt, western Asia, West and northwest Africa. Polytypic: nominate *persicus* occurs Nile Valley east to Kazakhstan and northwest India; *chrysocercus* West and northwest Africa. Mainly migratory, at least in north of range, wintering West and East Africa. Some authorities still treat Blue-tailed Bee-eater *M. superciliosus* as part of Blue-cheeked group but, increasingly, this seems to be accepted as a separate species, including previous Blue-cheeked forms *superciliosus* (East Africa and Madagascar), *alternans* (Angola and Namibia) and *phillippinus* (northern India, New Guinea and Southeast Asia) (Fry *et al.* 1988; Cramp *et al.* 1977–94; S Harrop 1991; Ebels & van der Laan 1994).

Two records of this unlikely visitor to Scilly, the first of which only came to light after examination of an old mounted bee-eater skin in the Tresco Abbey collection, and after a subsequent Scillonian bird had already been accepted as the first for Britain and Ireland. Thus Scilly has the unique distinction of having twice legitimately claimed credit for the first British and Irish record of the same species.

Unfortunately, the period 1900–30 is notable for the lack of published ornithological information, but we are able to piece together the facts surrounding the 1921 individual, partly from the Tresco Abbey records. These show that three bee-eaters were shot during that period, the first being an immature Bee-

*Bee-cheeked Bee-eater arrival dates* chart

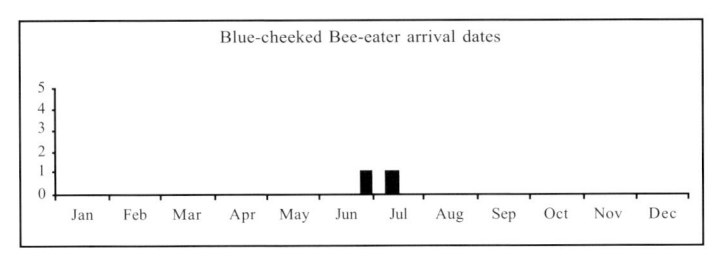

eater *M. apiaster* in September 1901 (Clark & Rodd 1906), plus another *M. apiaster* in October 1906 (Ogilvie-Grant 1906). The third was killed as an adult *M. apiaster* on St Mary's on 13th July 1921, 'on the instructions of A A Dorrien-Smith' (Penhallurick 1978) and subsequently mounted and cased by Pratt and Sons of Brighton (Palmer 2000). The mounted skin then resided in the Tresco Abbey collection labelled 'Bee-eater *M. apiaster*' for forty years, until examined by John Parslow in June 1962, who identified it as a Blue-cheeked Bee-eater of the form *persicus* (Parslow 1972).

By the time Parslow had corrected the earlier error, another Blue-cheeked Bee-eater had already been recorded on St Agnes on 22nd June 1951 (*CBWPSAR* 21; Anon 1952; Quick 1982) and accepted as the first record for Britain and Ireland (BOURC 1956). Interestingly, this bird too was attributed by the observer to the eastern form *persicus* (*CBWPSAR* 21). The subsequent discovery and acceptance of the earlier St Mary's skin downgraded the St Agnes bird's position to second for Britain and Ireland and this was later corrected officially (BOURC 1972).

In suggesting that no British Blue-cheeked Bee-eater records had been identified racially, Gantlett overlooked Parslow's strong claim regarding the earlier individual (Gantlett 1998). Gantlett also pointed out that the African form *chrysocercus* seems likely to occur in Britain as an overshooting spring migrant. More recently, in 2002, the BOURC finally considered Parslow's 1972 paper and accepted the 1921 individual as *persicus* on the strength of Parslow's earlier examination (BOURC 2003), whilst also taking the view that all other British records involved the same form (BOURC 2003).

The BBRC accepted just six records during the period 1958–99, making a total of eight individuals since records commenced, in which case Scilly accounts for 25% of all known sightings up until 1999. A third mounted Blue-cheeked Bee-eater skin, an apparent male, resides in the Isles of Scilly Museum but is apparently not part of the Tresco Abbey collection and though its source remains obscure there is no evidence to suggest it was obtained on Scilly. Neither of these two accepted Blue-cheeked Bee-eaters was trapped and neither is reported to have been carrying a ring.

## Bee-eater (European Bee-eater) *Merops apiaster* A

**Rare migrant. Treated by the BBRC as a national Scarce Migrant, full written description required by the SRP.**

| | | |
|---|---|---|
| 1841 | Three (probable immature female shot) St Agnes 9th May   Clark & Rodd 1906 | |
| 1878 | One Tresco June   Clark & Rodd 1906 | |
| 1901 | Two to three Holy Vale, St Mary's (one shot) October   Clark & Rodd 1906 | |
| 1906 | One (immature male) shot Tresco 8th October   Ogilvie-Grant 1906 | |
| 1953 | Three, Tresco Abbey Gardens & St Martin's 13th to 20th April | |
| 1955 | Four, Tresco Abbey Gardens 18th & 19th May | |
| 1956 | 'Party' Tresco Gardens 14th May for half an hour only | |
| [1982 | One St Martin's June] | |
| 1983 | Up to seven St Agnes & Tresco 4th to 14th May | |
| 1985 | One (first-year) Bryher, Tresco, St Mary's & St Agnes 23rd September to 1st November | |
| 1988 | Two St Mary's 22nd June | |
| 1989 | Up to four St Mary's, Tresco & St Agnes 17th to 19th May | |
| 1990 | One St Mary's 22nd May | |
| 1990 | One St Mary's 27th May | |
| 1990 | One Bryher, Tresco, St Mary's & St Agnes 23rd October to 9th November | |
| 1999 | One (juvenile) various sites St Mary's 29th September to 5th October | |

Breeds Iberia and North Africa east to Kazakhstan and extreme western Himalayas, north to southern France, central Russia and the Caspian Sea and south to Israel and Arabian Peninsula, also southern Africa. Northern populations migratory, wintering Africa. Monotypic. Removed from BBRC Rarities List January 1991 (Lansdown and the Rarities Committee 1990).

Over half the Scillonian records (eight out of 15) of this attractive visitor involved multiple arrivals, with two-thirds of all records coming from the early part of the year. The earliest known recorded is contained in an anonymous handwritten note appended to a copy of Carew's *Survey of Cornwall* (Carew 1602) to the effect that three were seen on St Agnes on 9th May 1841 (Clark & Rodd 1906). One of these, a probable immature female, was shot by a boatman named Hicks (of which there have been many in Scilly), but it fell into the sea and was too damaged to be preserved. The next record was seen on several occasions by Tresco gamekeeper David Smith in June 1878, and a first-year male was shot out of a party of two or three in Holy Vale, St Mary's, in October 1901 (Clark & Rodd 1906). Next to fall to the gun was a first-year male on Tresco in either late September or early October 1906 (Ogilvie-Grant 1906), Penhallurick later giving the date as 8th October (Penhallurick 1978).

Early publications may list a Bee-eater killed on St Mary's on 13th July 1921, although in 1962 the skin of this particular individual was examined by John Parslow and found to be that of Blue-cheeked Bee-eater *M. persicus*, the belated first for Britain and Ireland (see previous species).

The largest number of individuals involved in any arrival was seven, on St Agnes and Tresco during May 1983 (*IOSBR* 1983), though unfortunately we have no record of the exact number involved amongst a 'party' noted by Tresco's head gardener on 14th May 1956 (*CBWPSAR* 26). The 1982 report was apparently never submitted to the BBRC. Known arrival and departure dates for the 11 records give an average stay of 5.6 days, with the shortest just one day or less (four records) and the longest 18 days. The Chart includes all known arrival dates and reveals a predictable pattern of spring arrivals with a smaller group of records around late September and October.

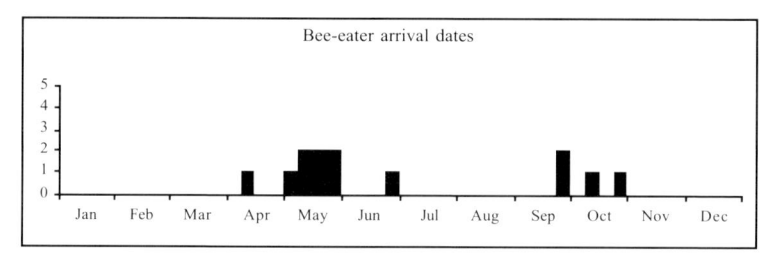

Bee-eater arrival dates

Spring migration commences mid-April and extends through to late May, overshooting individuals regularly reaching northwest Europe, this presumably accounting for birds on Scilly, which supposedly belong to Iberian, French or Mediterranean populations. Return passage begins from late July with the bulk of the population moving south from mid-August to October, and with birds routinely moving in what appear to be family groups (Cramp *et al*. 1977–94).

## Roller (European Roller) *Coracias garrulus* A BBRC 3.1%

**Very rare migrant, full written description required by the BBRC.**

    1928   One Tresco 27th May   Penhallurick 1978
    1958   One (female) St Mary's 6th May, found dead 11th   British Birds 53: 167
    [1958  One Pelistry, St Mary's 22nd September]   CBWPSAR 28
    1959   One St Agnes 22nd & 23rd October   British Birds 54: 178
    1981   One St Agnes 20th May to 9th June   British Birds 75: 513

Breeds Iberia and North Africa east to Kazakhstan and western China, north to Gulf of Finland and south to Israel and Iran. Migratory, wintering tropical East and southeast Africa. Polytypic: nominate *garrulus* occurs throughout except for Iraq, Iran east and south Kazakhstan and China, where replaced by *semenowi*.

The only early reference to Roller on Scilly is a comment by A A Dorrien-Smith to the effect that Francis Rodd saw one prior to 1872 (Penhallurick 1978). But noticeably, Francis Rodd and co-author

James Clark make no mention of such a sighting in their end-of century review (Clark & Rodd 1906). This being the case, there are just four acceptable Scillonian records of this charismatic species, plus one other seemingly worthy of at least some consideration.

Penhallurick referred to a bird killed by Tresco gamekeeper F Wardle on that island on 27th May 1928, which was followed 30 years later by a bird seen alive at Porth Hellick, St Mary's, on 6th May 1958 but found dead by Ron Symons on 11th (*CBWPSAR* 28). A G Parsons skinned the specimen and sexed it as a female, and as it appeared never to have bred we may reasonably assume it was a first-year. On 22nd September the same year, Peter MacKenzie flushed what he was sure was another Roller from a telegraph pole at Pelistry, again on St Mary's. The bird flew away strongly to the west but was not reported subsequently (*CBWPSAR* 28). This sighting does not appear in the list of accepted BBRC rarities and it is difficult to explain why, although the fact that it is also missing from the BBRC list of rejected records suggests that it was not submitted to that committee. The fact that the bird was seen during the Committee's first year of operation may help to explain the reason for its non-submission. Certainly, anyone who has had the pleasure of seeing Roller at any time will attest to the difficulty of confusing it with any other species, except perhaps with other African or Asian rollers.

Interestingly, another Roller arrived in Scilly the following year, remaining viewable around the St Agnes pool for two days from 22nd October. Brian Milne's description ably demonstrated the ease with which particularly characteristic species may be described with just a few well-chosen words, i.e. 'A large Jay-like bird with very striking turquoise-blue plumage clearly visible at quite long range. The wings were turquoise-blue with darker edges and the back was pale chestnut, suggesting it was a bird of the year' (*CBWPSAR* 29). Last of the four accepted records concerned another on St Agnes, appearing on 20th May and staying until 9th June (*IOSBR* 1981).

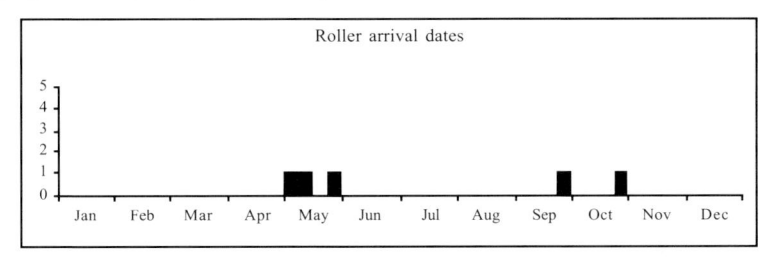

Roller arrival dates

Arrivals in the islands during the early part of the year seem perhaps likely to involve overshoots from the Iberian or Mediterranean populations, whereas autumn arrivals perhaps relate to birds from the extreme northwest part of its breeding range, e.g. northeast Russia or the eastern Baltic states. There are a small number of autumn sightings from Norway and presumably some then make their way down the eastern side of the North Sea, perhaps explaining the bulk of the British sightings from southeast England, and could then reach Scilly. The Chart includes all arrival dates. Average length of stay was 6.2 days, but just 2.5 if the long-staying St Agnes individual is discounted. A total of 95 Roller records accepted by the BBRC during the period 1958–99 compares with 135 records prior to that period; Cramp *et al.* (1977–94) quote a European 19th century decline. The three BBRC-accepted records amount to just 3.1% of the national total for that period. None of the Scillonian Rollers were trapped and none were reportedly carrying rings.

# Hoopoe *Upupa epops* A

**Scarce but nevertheless annual spring migrant, usually singly but sometimes in small groups, occasional in autumn. Typically found feeding in short-grass areas during March or April and often quite approachable. Treated by the BBRC as a national Scarce Migrant.**

Breeds southern Eurasia including India and Southeast Asia, also Africa. Northern populations migratory, most European migrants winter Africa south of Sahara. Polytypic: nominate *epops* occurs northwest Africa and Europe east to northwest India, northwest China and western Siberia; *major* Egypt and northeast Africa; *senegalensis* south of Sahara from Senegal to Ethiopia; *saturata* Asia east of *epops* and south to central China; five or more additional forms south and east.

It would have been surprising indeed had such an obvious species been overlooked by early observers in Scilly. First mention then is E H Rodd's lengthy 1845 letter to the *Zoologist* headed *Occurrence of the Hoopoe at Land's End and the Scilly Isles* (Rodd 1845), in which Rodd described having received first a male then a female from Augustus Smith, these having been obtained on Tresco during early to mid-April that year. He went on to mention how a third specimen was obtained on St Mary's that year, whilst in the Eastern Isles two more were seen on one of the two Ganillys. Various subsequent references to this species by the elder Rodd include mention of birds in Tresco Gardens on 14th May 1865 and more than one seen during spring 1866, one of which was 'captured' (Rodd 1865e, 1866d). Later still the same author noted that Hoopoes had been 'observed at Scilly every year since 1843' (Rodd 1880). By the end of the 19th century, James Clark and E H Rodd's nephew Francis felt able to describe Hoopoe as a regular spring migrant to the islands, either singly or in small parties, pointing out too that in spring 1905 five were together on Tresco's Castle Down. However, up until that time it had not been recorded during autumn (Clark & Rodd 1906).

Penhallurick analysed 367 Cornish and Scillonian Hoopoe records for the period 1926–72, expressing the results in terms of annual percentage presence during fortnightly periods (Penhallurick 1978). Twenty-one percent of all records occurred during mid-April, with 18% during late April and early May and 17% during late March and early April. Less than 1% arrived during late February and spring records continued until mid-June (1%). Autumn records occurred from early July through to late November, though with never more than 6% of the overall total involved.

Gantlett gave the earliest arrival date for Scilly up until 1991 as 21st February 1988 and the latest sighting as 19th October 1987 (Gantlett 1991). Both were exceeded during the late 1990s, the earliest now being a bird on St Agnes on 20th February 1998, whereas the new record of 28th October was held briefly by a bird at Borough Farm, St Mary's, in 1995, until one was seen on 29th on St Agnes the following year. Interestingly, five or six of the birds recorded during spring 1998 arrived in February, along with five on mainland Cornwall (*IOSBR* 1998). Plotting arrival dates is often confounded by the inter-site movement of newly arrived birds, but the Chart includes annual spring and autumn distribution for 210 records for the 23 years from 1977. Of these, 195 (92.8%) arrived during spring, autumn arrivals occurring at a rate of 1.6 per arrival year, or 0.65 for the 23 years.

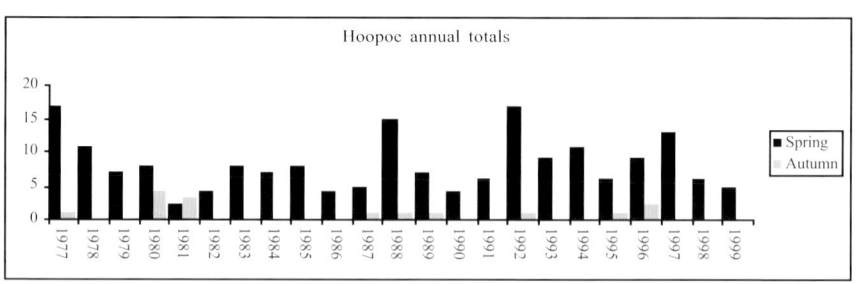

Hoopoe annual totals

Penhallurick (1978) provided brief details of seven or so breeding records for mainland Cornwall between 1878 and 1969 but there is no suggestion of it having bred in Scilly. No Hoopoes breed north of Scilly regularly and the pattern of spring arrivals fits the theory of overshooting migrants returning to breeding areas in Iberia, France or Germany. Return movement is evident in North Africa from early February, peaking during mid-March and April (Cramp *et al.* 1977–94). According to Cramp *et al.*, autumn Hoopoes from west-central Europe (Germany, Switzerland, Austria) move mainly south or southwest between mid-July and late October, ringed birds being recovered in France and Spain, among other countries. Thus it seems possible that the small numbers of Scillonian autumn records may originate from that direction. Most if not all Scillonian records are thought likely to involve the widespread nominate *epops*, though Gantlett (1998) drew attention to the possibility of the duller, eastern Eurasian *saturata* occurring in Britain. Interestingly, in a recent Swedish study at least two early records were found to have involved *saturata*, the same study showing that most Swedish spring records showed a distribution consistent with overshooting from southeast Europe, whereas autumn arrivals had a distribution consistent with an easterly origin (*Birding World* 10: 282). A total of five Hoopoes had been ringed in Scilly up until the end of 1999 but there are no recaptures.

# Wryneck (Eurasian Wryneck) *Jynx torquilla* A

Annual migrant in small numbers, mostly in autumn. Treated by the BBRC as a national Scarce Migrant.

Breeds Europe, northwest Africa and central Asia east to Sakhalin and south to eastern China. Migratory, wintering Africa between Sahara and equator, Indian subcontinent and Southeast Asia. Polytypic: nominate *torquilla* occurs Europe to Ural Mountains and south to Pyrenees and Bulgaria, possibly Iberia and Balearic Islands; *sarudnyi* western Siberia east to Yenisey River; *tschusii* Italy, Corsica and western former Yugoslavia, possibly Greece; *mauretanica* northwest Africa. Red-listed in UK: historical population decline; rapid, greater than 50% decline in breeding population over past 25 years, with 50% or greater range contraction over same timescale; five-year mean of 3.2 breeding pairs; unfavourable world conservation status (Gregory *et al.* 2002).

First mention of Wryneck on Scilly seems to be E H Rodd's account in a letter to the *Zoologist* of one or more on migration during September 1849, plus one shot by Augustus Pechell in October that year (Rodd 1849a, 1878b), though Penhallurick (1978) gives this last as September. Rodd also makes various additional references to its presence in the islands only on autumn migration (Rodd 1880), whilst the normally outgoing James Clark and Francis Rodd had little to say regarding this particular species mentioning only the Pechell individual, plus one picked up dead on Middle Downs, Tresco, in October 1852, one shot in 1882 and one shot by A A Dorrien-Smith during April 1894 (Clark & Rodd 1906).

There are few other early reports and probably the next concerned an individual somewhere in the islands, probably at one of the lighthouses, on 8th May 1911 (Ogilvie-Grant 1912c), followed by one on Tresco on 30th April 1944 (*CBWPSAR* 14). Penhallurick (1978) made the point that early to mid-20th century accounts suggested an annual autumn passage in Cornwall and Scilly as well as a light spring movement. He pointed out too that though less frequently observed, the latter was nevertheless probably annual during April and May and gave 3rd April, on St Agnes, as the earliest date. The latest spring record he knew of involved one taken by a cat in Cornwall on 3rd June. According to Penhallurick's researches, autumn passage was at its height during September with most first-sightings during that same month, with a few during late August. Most, too, involved singles or two together, four on St Agnes in September 1966 being unusual, Penhallurick also considering records at the end of October as late and one on St Agnes on 19th November as exceptional.

Records for the 23 years 1977–99 show 36 birds arriving during spring in only 14 years (60%), at an average of 2.59 per bird-year, or 1.5 overall. The earliest obvious migrant by far was the individual on Bryher on 30th March 1989. One on The Garrison, St Mary's, on 2nd February had apparently overwintered (most unusually), having been seen at nearby Little Porth during November–December. The latest spring sighting was 29th May. Overwintering by Wryneck seems to be extremely unusual north of the Mediterranean (Cramp *et al.* 1977–94) and the above individual, plus one referred to by Penhallurick (1978) at Porthgwarra on mainland Cornwall during winter 1966–67 appear to be the only such records west of the River Tamar.

Reducing all autumn sightings to a reasonably acceptable number is a far less simple task and for several years a known bird-day total plus an estimate of how many birds were actually involved seems the easiest approach. For example, in 1984 on St Mary's, a 53 bird-day autumn total was thought to have involved seven to nine individuals. But for some years the data are more precise, particularly prior to 1990, during which period perhaps between five and 22 were believed to have passed through. There is also a suggestion in the data of rather greater numbers arriving during the 1990s, up to a maximum of 40 per autumn, but the effects, if any, of recent increased birdwatcher coverage are difficult to quantify. Published annual first autumn sightings fell in the range 15th August to 24th September but, interestingly, all published last sightings except two (15 years) fell in the narrow 14-day period 16th and 29th October. The two exceptions were 1st and 9th November, leaving Penhallurick's bird for the 19th as the latest ever.

Typically for Scilly, Wrynecks are encountered in scrubby coastal and heathland areas, though this perhaps reflects the extent to which much of the farmland goes unrecorded, particularly on St Mary's. Main autumn passage is evident within the West Palearctic from mid-August through to early October, though some are still moving into November or later (Cramp *et al.* 1977–94). The general direction of travel within Europe is either south or southwest (Wernham *et al.* 2002) and there is evidence that most in western Europe cross the Mediterranean at the Strait of Gibraltar, at least some from northern Fennoscandia also taking this route. In addition, there is ringing evidence of regular Scandinavian autumn drift migration into at least eastern Britain (Wernham *et al.* 2002). Return spring passage begins from early March and lasts until late April or early May. Gantlett (1998) highlighted the possibility of forms other than nominate *torquilla* occurring in Britain and suggested that the darker, greyer and shorter-winged *tschusii* from Italy and the former Yugoslavia and the paler Siberian *sarudnyi* might both reach Britain. And whilst field identification of these two might prove particularly challenging, the likelihood should certainly be borne in mind by anyone handling live individuals. Six Wrynecks had been ringed on Scilly up until the end of 1999, three in each period. There are no recaptures.

## Green Woodpecker *Picus viridis* A

**Extremely rare vagrant, full written description required by the SRP.**

   1872   One reported killed Tresco   Clark & Rodd 1906
   1901   One killed St Mary's September   Clark & Rodd 1906
  [1962   One Bryher 12th & 13th October – lacks supporting information]   *CBWPSAR* 32

Confined almost exclusively to West Palearctic, breeding mainland western Europe north of Mediterranean from Iberia, France and Britain east to Iran and western Russia and north to central coastal Norway and Sweden. Resident western and central Europe, some local redistribution in winter though rarely over 20 km. Polytypic: nominate *viridus* occurs western Europe south to France, Alps, Romania and former Yugoslavia; *karelini* Italy, southeast Europe, Asia Minor, Iran and western Russia; *sharpei* Iberia; *innominatus* southwest and southern Iran. Amber-listed in UK: unfavourable European conservation status (Gregory *et al.* 2002). National 14% increase 1994–99 (Bashford & Noble 2000).

There are two old records of this extremely unlikely visitor to Scilly, plus a more recent and less certain sighting. It has been said of Scilly that if you thought you saw a Green Woodpecker it was probably a Golden Oriole *Oriolus oriolus* and this is true often enough to cast reasonable doubt on any single-observer sighting by people unfamiliar with the islands. E H Rodd's comments about its status in west Cornwall during the mid-19th century are interesting and seem to imply an increase in numbers and distribution in the Land's End area by 1880, though Holloway (1996) showed it as rare throughout the southwest prior to 1900. Certainly by the 1970s, it was breeding in all Cornish 10-km squares (Sharrock 1976) and though there seems to have been a subsequent decline in the number of squares involved, it still breeds to the tip of the Land's End peninsula (Gibbons *et al.* 1993). It also breeds in France as far north as the Brittany coast (Guermeur & Monnet 1980) but remains totally absent from Ireland.

In their early 20th century review of *The Birds of Scilly*, James Clark and E H Rodd's nephew Francis mentioned the reported killing of a bird on the north end of Tresco in 1872. However, they pointed out that both the authority for that statement and the specimen were by then untraceable (Clark & Rodd 1906). Additionally, in the same paper they referred to a bird killed on St Mary's in September 1901, and though they too gave no authority for this record they clearly accepted it, leaving us to believe they investigated it and found it fully acceptable. The last of the three listed records was reportedly present on Bryher for two days during mid-October 1962 and though it lacks supporting information, it seems difficult to accept that someone might mistake a Green Woodpecker for Golden Oriole for two days in succession. Nonetheless, doubts must remain regarding this particular claim, which emphasises the importance of properly documented sightings. Ringing recoveries suggest that British Green Woodpeckers are entirely sedentary, the mean adult recovery distance of 1 km comparing with just 3 km for juveniles (Wernham *et al.* 2002). No woodpeckers have been trapped and ringed on Scilly and there are no recaptures from elsewhere.

## Yellow-bellied Sapsucker *Sphyrapicus varius* A BBRC 100%

**Extremely rare migrant, full written description required by the BBRC.**

   1975   One Tresco 26th September to 6th October   *British Birds* 69: 343, 72: 410–414; *Ibis* 120: 409

Breeds North America, from south Alaska and Canada east to Newfoundland and south in USA to Montana, Iowa and eastern states as far as Carolinas. Northern populations mainly migratory, wintering central and southern USA to Central America and Greater Antilles. Monotypic. Overall downward trend disguises recent marked swings, increasing in last 15 years, but with recovery mainly confined to south (Bryant 1997). Formerly treated as conspecific with Red-naped Sapsucker *S. nuchalis*.

There are just three European records, two of which involve Britain and Ireland. The first for Britain and Ireland was a first-winter male discovered by David Hunt alongside Tresco's Great Pool in late September 1975 (BOURC 1978; Hunt 1979, 1982). The bird remained in that general area from 26th September to 6th October and, in the absence of Lesser Spotted Woodpecker *Dendrocopos minor*, became Scilly's third woodpecker species. It mainly frequented elm *Ulmus* trees surrounding the pool, typically drilling small neat holes in the bark, which were reportedly still discernible up to five years later (Evans 1994). Such was the state of Scillonian birding at that time that during its 11-day stay it was allegedly seen by just 400 people. Within its home range, Yellow-bellied Sapsucker also regularly feeds on insects in the manner of other woodpeckers.

A gap of 13 years followed before the discovery of Europe's third and Ireland's first: a first-year female on Cape Clear Island, Co.Cork, from 16th to 19th October 1988 (Watmough 1988). The only other European record involved a bird found dead in Iceland in June 1961 (Evans 1994). Unsurprisingly, there was considerable debate surrounding the possible means of this species crossing the North Atlantic, and clearly ship-assisted passage cannot be entirely ruled out, even though Yellow-bellied Sapsucker regularly makes the comparatively brief sea crossing from mainland North or Central America to the Caribbean islands. However, the timing of arrival of the British and Irish individuals fits that of other more likely transatlantic autumn vagrants.

Chandler Robbins examined migration patterns for 104 North American migrant passerines and near passerines, based on accepted records for Britain and Ireland during the years 1947–76 (Robbins 1980). He found that for 31 species there was a significant correlation between the number of British and Irish records and the west-to-east component of normal migration, standard deviation of body weight, migratory distance, and abundance on the west coast of the North Atlantic. Robbins ranked species in order of likelihood of successful transatlantic autumn arrival, finding that, for a few, the observed level of occurrence greatly exceeded the forecast, e.g. 18 Yellow-billed Cuckoos *Coccyzus americanus* against a forecast of 6.26. Yellow-bellied Sapsucker came 24th in the list of 31 previously recorded species, with a forecast expectancy of 1.25 against the observed frequency of one (Robbins 1980). Autumn passage is evident along Atlantic coastal USA from late August to late October but it occurs only infrequently on Bermuda and the Lesser Antilles, with peak movements in northern USA occurring during late September to mid-October (Cramp *et al.* 1977–94). The Tresco individual was not reported to be carrying a ring.

## Great Spotted Woodpecker *Dendrocopos major* A

Scarce migrant or winter visitor from mainland Britain or continental Europe.

1943   One Tresco early November to mid-March 1944   *CBWPSAR* 14
1959   One Parsonage Woods, St Agnes 12th to 14th September
1962   One Bryher 12th & 13th October
1964   One Tresco 27th September and into January 1965
1967   One St Agnes 21st October
1972   One St Agnes 17th October
1989   One (female) Tresco 6th September to at least end of year
1990   One Maypole, St Mary's 16th October
1993   One Middle Down, Tresco 2nd February
1994   One Middle Down, Tresco 22nd April
1997   One (male) St Agnes   Tresco 27th September to 20th April 1998

Breeds West Palearctic except Iceland but including northern Morocco, north to tree-line and east through central and northern Eurasia to Pacific. Mainly resident, northern populations liable to periodic food-related eruptions. Polytypic: nominate *major* occurs northern Europe, Norway, Sweden east to Siberia and south to Poland; *pinetorum* central Europe south to France and east to Romania; *anglicus* British Isles; additional forms further east. National 42% increase 1994–99 (Bashford & Noble 2000).

Eleven arrivals in eleven different years means that what elsewhere in most of Britain would be considered a common bird is less likely to be encountered in Scilly than Bobolink *Dolichonyx oryzivorus* or Blackpoll Warbler *Dendroica striata*, and about as likely as Rose-breasted Grosbeak *Pheucticus ludovicianus*. Neither Rodd (1880), Clark & Rodd (1906), or Ryves & Quick (1946) made mention of it in relation to Scilly, though the latter talked of a small increase and spread into west Cornwall, including the Land's End peninsula. The results of the most recent national breeding survey confirm that it is found to the tip of Cornwall, although more thinly than further east (Gibbons *et al.* 1994).

An obvious feature of Scillonian records is the number of single or two-day sightings of a bird that might be expected to linger once it reached the islands, though at least four appear to have overwintered, the suggestion being that these short-stay individuals were on the move. The presence of the 1964 individual into the following year is not mentioned in the annual bird reports, but it was recorded during the one-off winter survey of Tresco during late January 1965 (B King 1965).

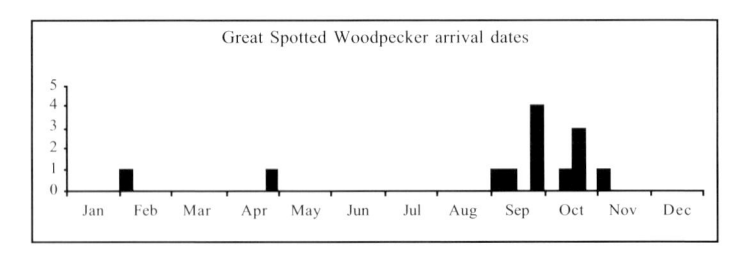

Northern birds of the larger and migratory *major* allegedly reach Britain from Norway and Poland, whilst the central European *pinetorum* may also occur (Gantlett 1998). However, with the exception of one British-ringed individual that reached the Netherlands such movements are unsupported by ringing data, only 18% of British juveniles moving more than 20 km (Wernham *et al.* 2002). Nonetheless, the autumn appearance of birds along Scotland's east coast suggests a northern European origin. Certainly, T A Dorrien-Smith attributed the earliest record to the form *major*, though unfortunately without explanation (T A Dorrien-Smith 1951). However, in the opinion of some, an element of doubt surrounds the 1962 single-observer Bryher individual; interestingly, though, 1962 was a significant irruption year with greater numbers than usual reaching Britain from continental Europe. Following irruption years return spring migration is mainly confined to the period late February to mid-April (Cramp *et al.* 1977–94), which also fits with the two short-stay spring individuals. No woodpeckers have been ringed on Scilly and there have been no recaptures of birds ringed elsewhere.

## Calandra Lark  *Melanocorypha calandra*  **A**  BBRC 22.2%

**Extremely rare migrant or vagrant, full written description required by the BBRC.**

    1985   One St Mary's 26th to 29th April  *British Birds* 79: 560, 80: 382
    1996   One St Agnes 17th & 18th (19th) April  *British Birds* 90: 490

Occurs Spain, North Africa and east around Black and Caspian Seas to Afghanistan, Turkmenistan (former Turkmeniya) and eastern Kazakhstan. Polytypic: nominate *calandra* breeds southern Europe and North Africa east to Ural steppes, though eastern birds resemble forms from far southeast of range.

Just two Scillonian records, the first of which involved a bird found on St Mary's Airfield on 26th April 1985, remaining there and in adjacent fields in the Salakee Lane area until 29th April (Wagstaff 1987). This was the third acceptable record for Britain and Ireland, following birds at Portland Bill, Dorset, on 2nd April 1961 and on Fair Isle, Shetland, on 28th April 1978.

The second for the islands was discovered in the vicinity of the St Agnes Pool on 17th April 1996, where it remained for two days. However, what was almost certainly the same bird was seen near the St Martin's Daymark on the 19th, although not reported until later, it then being seen flying off northeast from St Martin's. Thus it seems that April is the month in which to anticipate this species appearing in the British Isles, or certainly in Scilly.

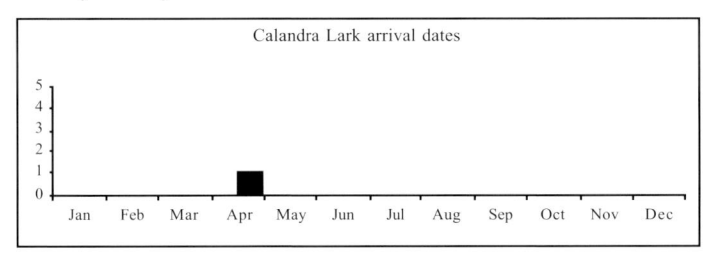

*Calandra Lark arrival dates*

An earlier British claim, involving a bird said to have been shot on Fair Isle in October 1928 was never confirmed, principally because the specimen was mislaid en route to Glasgow's Paisley Museum (Palmer 2000). All British records are thought likely to refer to nominate *calandra*.

## Bimaculated Lark  *Melanocorypha bimaculata*  **A**  BBRC 33.3%

**Extremely rare migrant or vagrant, full written description required by the BBRC.**

    1975   One Peninnis Head, St Mary's 24th to 27th October  *British Birds* 69: 343, 70: 298–300

Breeds Turkey, Transcaucasia, Iran, Syria and Lebanon eastwards to Turkmenistan (former Turkmeniya). Polytypic: nominate *bimaculata* occurs northeast Turkey to Iran, eastwards perhaps to Urals; *rufescens* Iraq to central Turkey and Lebanon; paler *torquata* eastwards from northeast Iran and Turkmenistan.

There is just one Scillonian record, involving a bird on Peninnis Head, St Mary's, from 24th to 27th October 1975. It appeared to dwarf the Skylarks *Alauda arvensis* with which it fed, hugging the ground and occasionally running with a mouse-like action. It was also easily picked out in flight by its shorter tail with very obvious white tips, plus its shorter and broader wings. Obvious in flight too was the lack of any white trailing edge to the wings (Flumm 1977). As an indication of how autumn Scillonian birding was still in its infancy, this bird was seen by perhaps just 65 people during its four-day stay. This was the second British record following one on Lundy Island, Devon, in May 1962. As Gantlett (1998) suggested, British records could relate to any of the three forms.

## Short-toed Lark
## (Greater Short-toed Lark) *Calandrella brachydactyla* A

Scarce but near annual migrant, formerly mostly in autumn but recently occurring mainly in spring. Treated by the BBRC as a national Scarce Migrant, full written description required by the SRP.

Breeds Spain and North Africa east through Mediterranean and around Black Sea to central southern Asia. Polytypic: *brachydactyla* occurs Europe north to former Yugoslavia and probably North African coast; *hungarica* Hungary; *rubiginosa* North Africa; *hermonensis* Sinai north to Syria and southern Turkey; *waltersi* northwest Syria and part of southern Turkey; *artemisiana* Asia Minor and northern Iran; *longipennis* Caucasus, Ukraine east to northern Mongolia and northeast China; one additional form further east. Removed from BBRC Rarities List January 1994 (Lansdown and the Rarities Committee 1993).

The sole early presence of this species in Scilly concerns several references to two at Skirt Point, Tresco, during late September 1854, one of which was shot by Augustus Pechell (Rodd 1854d, 1878b, 1880; Clark & Rodd 1906). The precise date seems unclear, E H Rodd quoting it in different sources as 20th or 23rd, whereas Clark and E H Rodd's nephew Francis later gave it as 28th. The birds were feeding just inland from the beach and according to the observer 'appeared rather wild'.

We then hear no more of this species until exactly 100 years later, when one frequented the shoreline at Porth Mellon, St Mary's, for three days during October 1954 (*CBWPSAR* 24). A description of this individual was submitted to Kenneth Williamson on Fair Isle, who considered it likely to have been of the southern European form *brachydactyla*. This was followed by one on St Agnes on 10th May 1958 and then two more on the same island for two days during mid-May 1959 (Penhallurick 1978), though this last record seems not to have been submitted to the newly formed BBRC. The first for mainland Cornwall also appeared during1959, near Tintagel on 10th August.

Included in the annual totals Chart are 153 records for Scilly from 1960 through to the end of 1999, 65% of these (100) during autumn. This Chart reveals a clear shift from a situation where most records up until the mid-1980s occurred during autumn, to one where most now apparently arrive during spring. It is difficult to say, however, whether this reflects a true shift in the seasonal pattern, or merely increased observer awareness during the early part of the year, or even an increase in the number of observers present at that time. Dymond *et al.* (1989) examined 253 British and Irish Short-toed Lark records for the period 1958–85, finding that autumn records increased greatly from 1966, whilst spring records increased only slightly. However, they also compared records for Scilly and Shetland, finding that Shetland produced 34% of all autumn records, whereas Scilly, which they considered more intensively watched during autumn, had 36%. Importantly, though, up until 1985 Shetland was responsible for 45% of all spring records, with, by inference, under-watched Scilly producing a mere 14%. Thus it seems that the data probably reflect a change in observer coverage and not numbers of birds reaching the islands.

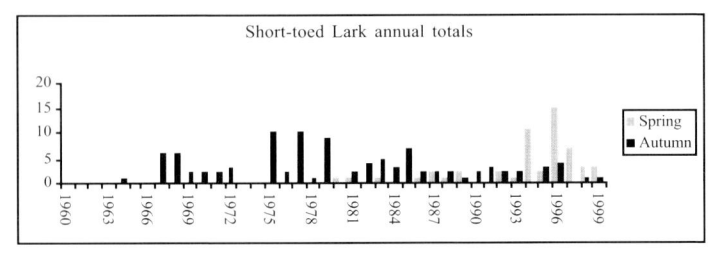

Also charted are Short-toed Lark arrival dates for the 23 years 1977–99, the well-defined early May and late September national peaks found by Dymond *et al.* being readily apparent here. The earliest any individual arrived during spring was 9th April and the latest spring sighting was 7th June, equivalent autumn dates being 8th July and 3rd November.

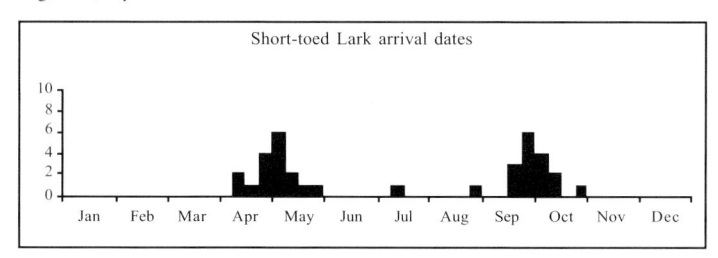

*Short-toed Lark arrival dates*

Two separate racial types of Short-toed Larks occurred in Britain, namely a reddish 'western' type as represented by the forms *brachydactyla*, *rubiginosa* and *hermonensis* and a greyish 'eastern' type, as represented by *artemisiana* and *longipennis* (Snow 1971). But although the exact subspecific status of birds reaching Britain remains uncertain, Gantlett (1998) took the view that both southern European and eastern forms may be involved. Nevertheless, as Snow & Perrins (1998) point out, substantial individual variation and the marked effects of abrasion and bleaching currently present insurmountable difficulties in deciding which of the eight generally recognised forms are involved, though it seems likely that both European and eastern forms occur with regularity. Several authorities have noted the greater number of grey 'eastern' birds involved in Britain during autumn, e.g. Dymond *et al.* (1989), Penhallurick (1978) noting the same in relation to Scilly. The clear implication is that spring Short-toed Larks reaching Scilly are typical overshoots from populations further south in Europe, whereas those in autumn are drift migrants from further east.

Autumn passage commences from mid-August and peaks during late August and early September, with few still evident into October and with the general direction of travel in western Europe being towards the southwest (Cramp *et al.* 1977–94). Return spring passage of northern and eastern European populations is evident from early March and continues into April. Interestingly, Henty (1975 in Cramp *et al.* 1977–94) found that birds reaching Iberia arrived from the west or southwest, implying a longer sea crossing from Atlantic-coastal North Africa than for other passerines. Consequently, the possibility of overshooting Short-toed Larks reaching northwest France and Scilly may be substantially increased. Two Short-toed Larks had been trapped and ringed in Scilly up until 1999 but there are no recaptures.

# Woodlark (Wood Lark) *Lullula arborea* A

**Scarce and irregular migrant occurring in two out of three years, full written description required by the SRP. Allegedly bred during the 1930s.**

Breeds almost exclusively West Palearctic, from Iberia and coastal northwest Africa east to Kazakhstan and southwest Russia, also southeast into Iran. Migratory in north and east wintering mainly within southern range or just beyond. Polytypic: nominate *arborea* occurs Europe south to northern Spain and across to Ukraine; *pallida* remainder of southern Europe and northwest Africa east to Iran. Included on Annex I of 1979 EEC 'Birds Directive'. Red-listed in UK: rapid, 54% contraction of breeding range over past 30 years; 50% or more of breeding population at ten or fewer sites; unfavourable European breeding range (Gregory *et al.* 2002).

During the 19th century, it was considered a rare casual winter visitor. Augustus Pechell shot two by Tresco's Great Rock, south of Abbey Pool, on 5th December 1859 and Francis Rodd shot two at the same spot on 29th December 1870, having discovered them there the previous day (Rodd 1880; Clark & Rodd 1906). Still on Tresco, gamekeeper David Smith shot Scilly's fifth record sometime during 1891 and the sixth was obtained near Peninnis Head, St Mary's, on 28th December 1904 (Clark & Rodd 1906). E H Rodd considered it rare in west Cornwall and much more local than Skylark throughout the county (Rodd 1880).

According to Ryves & Quick (1946) there is an acceptable breeding record from St Mary's for 1933, though further details were not provided and A A Dorrien-Smith is given as the only reference. Penhallurick (1978) was less than enthusiastic about this record and about claims it may have bred in preceding years, but helps by attributing the claim to the Tresco Abbey records. Nevertheless, such a record would have been in keeping with a general increase noted in mainland Cornwall around that time (see below) and so it should perhaps not be dismissed absolutely. The *CBWPSAR* (3) for 1933 listed it as 'Resident on St Mary's but thought not to breed on Tresco', adding that it was almost plentiful on Tresco during December 1932, at which time there were more Skylarks *Alauda arvensis* than for many years. Again, the source is given as A A Dorrien-Smith.

By the mid-1940s, Ryves & Quick (1946) thought there was evidence it had increased as a breeding species on the Cornish mainland, where it occurred throughout the county but was 'liable to be overlooked'. They noted, too, that this increase contrasted with marked declines elsewhere in southern England. Penhallurick (1978) pointed out that almost nothing was published on Woodlark's status in Cornwall during the years of its decline elsewhere in Britain and that it had been inadequately recorded in the country in any case. However, certainly up until 1999 it was still thought to breed at least occasionally (*CBWPSAR* 69). The first island mention of it after 1933 concerned two on separate dates on St Agnes during 1964, from which time onwards it was recorded in 20 out of the 31 years up to and including 1999. A total of 65 birds were involved at an annual average of two a year, or 3.2 per bird-year. The most in any year involved 14 during 1993, followed by 11 in 1980, with the next highest being eight in 1994; singles were noted in seven years (20%). As with many other species in Scilly, ascertaining precise annual Woodlark totals is complicated by an unknown level of inter-site movement and the possibility exists that some higher totals involved duplicate counts.

Apart from two, all records back as far as 1964 occurred during autumn. The exceptions both occurred in 1977 and involved a single near St Mary's Hospital on the surprising date of 27th January and one on Peninnis Head on 24th May. All autumn dates fell between 31st August and 13th November, most during the period mid-September to late October.

One in the vicinity of Normandy, St Mary's, from 20th to 22nd October, during the busy autumn 1993, had been colour-ringed as a nestling in Thetford Forest, Norfolk, that same summer (*IOSBR* 1993); sightings of other Thetford Woodlarks outside the breeding season coming from the Netherlands, Kent (2) and Devon. Certainly in eastern England, breeding areas are deserted by September or October and there are limited, mostly coastal records, from mainly southern England from September through to mid-November and from December to mid-January. Ringing recoveries show Woodlarks from Fennoscandia and the Baltic countries south to Germany regularly move southwest in winter as far as France, some even to Spain (Cramp *et al.* 1977–94). All of this very much fits the pattern of autumn arrivals in Scilly, these same birds presumably returning north further east in England, or along the eastern side of the North Sea. No Woodlarks had been ringed on Scilly up until the end of 1999 and there are no recaptures from elsewhere.

**Controls**

| ? | Pul Thetford, Norfolk spring 1993 | FR Normandy, St Mary's 20th to 22nd October 1993 |

**Woodlark Ringing Recaptures**

# Skylark (Sky Lark) *Alauda arvensis* A

**Annual spring and autumn migrant and winter visitor. Now occurs in quite moderate numbers but at one time appeared in almost unbelievable concentrations. Bred until quite recently.**

Widely distributed throughout most of West Palearctic and northern Asia, plus coastal North Africa. Northern birds move south in winter. Polytypic, situation complex with about twelve recognised forms: *scotica* (not recognised by BOURC) Ireland, northwest England, Scotland and Faeroes; nominate *arvensis* Wales, England, Norway east to Urals and south to central France, Alps, former Yugoslavia and east to European Russia. Various additional forms southern Europe and eastwards. Red-listed in UK: rapid, 55% breeding decline over past 25 years; unfavourable world conservation status (Gregory *et al.* 2002). National 58% decline during 25 years to 1996 and 16% 1994–99 (Bashford & Noble 2000).

By far the earliest probable evidence of Skylark presence on Scilly is contained among results of the archaeological investigation of prehistoric layers from the site on Nornour in the Eastern Isles and takes the form of bone remains tentatively identified as of this species (Turk 1971). However, there is a great deal of 19th century information, much of which refers to migrants and huge autumn and winter concentrations. Robert Heath (1750) reported that it was found on the islands year-round, but over 100 years later E H Rodd considered it only a periodic migrant, suggesting it varied in numbers and time of appearance 'according to circumstances' (Rodd 1878b). However, just two years later this last author thought it both bred and appeared in 'immense flocks in winter' (Rodd 1880).

So descriptive is the classic early 20th century *Zoologist* account by James Clark and Francis Rodd (Clark & Rodd 1906), that it would be remiss not to include it here in full, particularly in view of the change in status undergone by this species in Britain generally over the intervening period.

> During the period of autumn migration, and occasionally in winter during the prevalence of hard frosts on the mainland, it arrives in large flocks, and sometimes in immense numbers. Not infrequently in October and early November, flocks pass over the islands in a westerly or north-westerly direction without landing at all, and on two occasions large scattered flights have been observed coming in from the east, and after some indecision, continuing their journey in a north-westerly direction. The flocks that land usually resume their passage in the course of a day, but large numbers continue on the islands throughout the winter. In the second week in October 1903, the arrival of an almost continuous stream of Larks and Starlings, in flocks of a dozen to fifty or a hundred, was observed through the whole of two days and part of a third. The Larks flew with a steady easy flight, and showed no sign of exhaustion, but hesitated every now and then, as if uncertain whether they should settle or continue their journey. The flocks would come in rapid succession for several hours at a stretch, frequently only a few hundred yards apart, and rarely with an intervening interval of more than two to three minutes. Then would come a lull, and for half an hour or more they would arrive at irregular intervals of three to ten minutes, after which the rush would be again resumed. From twelve to three on the second day the flocks must have averaged about a hundred, and followed each other so closely that at a distance they looked like a dusky band rising out of the sea. The birds apparently came in by night as well as day, and left during the night or in the early morning. On the fourth day several hundred Larks were still about, but were evidently settling in for a prolonged stay.

Clark and Rodd's figures of around 100 birds every two to three minutes produces a likely 6,000 to 9,000 passing Skylarks during the three hours from midday on the second day of their observation. But the likely number involved over the whole three to four days can only be guessed at. The same authorities make mention of a similar mass Skylark movement during 1863, at which time Augustus Pechell, Francis Rodd and one unnamed gunman shot 300 Skylarks in three days, 'nearly all single flying shots'. Helpful too is A A Dorrien-Smith's comment that in December 1933 Woodlark *Lullula arborea* were plentiful on Tresco and that there were more Skylarks than had been seen for many years (*CBWPSAR* 3).

Far less easy to ascertain, though, is Skylark's early 20th century breeding status, especially as several contemporary observers viewed the situation rather differently. However, the fact that in spring 1903 nests were found on at least seven islands, i.e. St Mary's, Tresco, Bryher, Samson, St Martin's, Great Ganilly and St Helen's (Clark & Rodd 1906), goes some considerable way towards demonstrating how numerous and widespread it was at that time. Nonetheless, reports of an apparent decline by the mid-1920s (Wallis 1924; Ryves & Quick 1946) contrast with the 1931 suggestion that it occurred in practically the same numbers on St Mary's as ten years earlier (Boyd 1931), or that in 1938 it was 'Abundant in all suitable localities – more plentiful than on the mainland' (*CBWPSAR* 8), which presumably refers to summer rather than winter. In addition, by 1923 one observer found it 'fairly plentiful, but not breeding as freely as in 1914' (Ryves & Quick 1946).

Quite remarkably, next mention of this species in the annual reports after Ryves and Quick's early century review is when five pairs reportedly bred on St Agnes in 1958 (*SABOAR* 1958), with up to 100 being reported on passage on that same island during late March and up to 130 from mid-September through to late October. Similarly, seven or eight pairs bred on St Agnes in 1961–62, but although marked passage was absent, as many as 500 were present during hard weather in late December 1962. Regrettably, regular annual Skylark reports ended with the transition from the *SABOAR* to the annual *IOSBR*, next mention being the 1973 reference to it 'breeding in rough grassland on major islands', plus what was described as a 'massive' mid-October influx of 200–300 on each of three main islands. This was followed in 1974 by an estimate of 15 pairs breeding on St Mary's and 13 on St Agnes, whilst by 1978 perhaps 20 pairs bred on St Mary's, three to five on St Martin's, three on St Agnes and one on St Helen's.

Various reports of limited breeding pairs during the 1980s and 90s probably referred to singing males, which by 1976 were down to just three on St Mary's – two on the Golf Course and one on Peninnis Head – with none anywhere in the islands from 1997. Of equal or perhaps even greater concern, however, is the decline in numbers of migrant and wintering Skylarks, which in 1999 involved just one late winter and nine spring records of up to 12 birds, and although in autumn Skylarks were noted daily from late September through to mid-November, the peak count was just 150, including flocks of 40 at two separate St Mary's locations (*IOSBR* 1999). Although reported at the time as significant, these figures appear not at all dissimilar to those of the mid-1970s. All of this leads to the inevitable conclusion that a slow decline in numbers of breeding pairs throughout at least the last two decades of the 20th century may now have culminated in Skylark's disappearance from the islands as a breeding species. In addition, and perhaps over a greater period of time, there has been a substantial reduction in the volume of migrant and wintering Skylarks using the islands. This is all broadly in keeping with the situation in mainland Britain and elsewhere in western Europe over much the same timescale, and although local causes have been sought, the driving mechanism behind these Scillonian changes undoubtedly lies elsewhere.

There are several late 19th- and early 20th century autumn Skylark records from the Bishop Rock Lighthouse, from between 1881 and 1910. Some involve what appear to have been substantial diurnal or nocturnal movements, birds moving mostly east but also some in the opposite direction. Greatest numbers involved seem to have been 'thousands' on the night of 22nd–23rd October 1908 (Ogilve-Grant 1910) and 'great numbers' during the nights of 5th–6th and 6th–7th November 1907 and moving west during daylight on the 6th, 7th and 8th of that month (Ogilvie-Grant 1909). Skylarks in the northern and eastern West Palearctic are mainly or largely migratory, moving mainly west or southwest into the Low Countries, Britain and Ireland and south into France and Iberia (Cramp *et al.* 1977–94). Ringing data show that these include many individuals from northern and central European Russia. In contrast, British and Irish Skylarks are largely sedentary and although northern upland populations leave the breeding grounds they seldom move far. However, given the tendency for eastern populations of several species to be involved in big October or November movements in Scilly, it seems likely that Skylarks from quite far east could reach the islands, or at least in some years. Nonetheless, it may be impossible to know the origin of large numbers of birds involved in any cold-weather movements, as seems the likely explanation for the spectacular movements described by Clark and Rodd (Wernham *et al.* 2002).

## Shore Lark (Horned Lark) *Eremophila alpestris* A

**Rare migrant. Treated by the BBRC as a national Scarce Migrant, full written description required by the SRP.**

| | |
|---|---|
| 1958 | One (female) Bryher 4th June |
| 1969 | One St Agnes 6th October |
| 1972 | Two St Agnes 25th October |
| 1974 | One St Mary's Airport 17th to 23rd April |
| 1980 | One St Agnes 29th October |
| 1984 | One St Mary's Airport 5th November |
| 1990 | One (male) St Agnes 9th April |
| 1991 | One Bryher 7th June |
| 1998 | One (probable female) Carn Friars and Airport, St Mary's 12th to 18th May |
| 2001 | One St Agnes & Tresco 2nd October for at least remainder of month |

Unusual arctic and southern uplands distribution, breeds North America, arctic Eurasia, northwest Africa, southeast Europe, Asia Minor and central-southern Asia. Migratory in north, wintering mainly within southern half of range, some altitudinal movement in south. Polytypic: *flava* occurs western arctic Eurasia; *brandti* eastern arctic Asia; *balcanica* Balkans and Greece; *atlas* Morocco; *pencillata* Asia Minor to northern Iran; *bicornis* Lebanon; nominate *alpestris*, or 'Horned Lark' arctic North America; possible 40 or so forms in all, some 25 in Americas.

E H Rodd (1880) mentioned two Shore Larks shot near Padstow, west Cornwall, in November 1879 but there appears to be no 19th century reference to this species in Scilly, though there are eight or nine 20th century records plus one from the 21st century. The first for the islands, possibly a female and found on Bryher on 4th June 1958, was seen well and watched down to a range of 30 metres for half an hour (*CBWPSAR* 28). The 1969 individual gets no mention in the annual reports and Penhallurick referred to it as 'not authenticated' (Penhallurick 1978). However, given that this was not a BBRC species, it seems difficult to know now what authentication might have been required in the absence of a formal Scillonian records committee.

The Chart incorporates all arrival dates, including the reported 1969 individual, and reveals a clear separation between spring and autumn movements. Seven out of ten birds were present for one day or less and two more for just seven days each; mean length of stay was 2.3 days. The clear inference from this is that these were birds on the move. The bird commuting between St Agnes and Tresco from 2nd October 2001 for at least the remainder of that month was considered by many observers to have been nominate *alpestris* or one of the similar North American forms (*Birding World* 14: 405). Judgement was based at least partly on flank coloration and upperpart streaking, plus plain cinnamon-rufous median and lesser coverts, but later on comparison with museum skins (Small 2002). It is interesting, too, that out of the ten records this individual remained in the islands for so long.

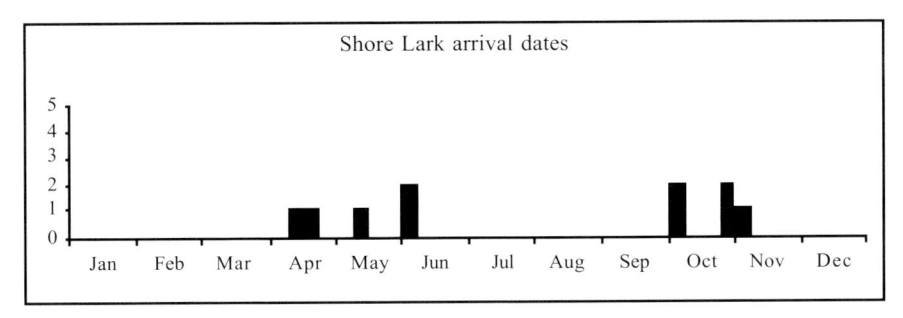

Shore Lark arrival dates

Some *flava* from northern Eurasia winter coastally around the Baltic and southern North Sea, including eastern England (Cramp *et al.* 1977–94), those reaching the southern North Sea doing so by way of continental Europe, rather than mainland Britain. Finnish Shore Larks begin leaving from late September, though those further east depart earlier and birds commence arriving around the North Sea from mid-October or November. In severe weather, some will move further south, even penetrating beyond the species' normal range. Although the presumed origin of British-wintering birds is towards the western end of the range, e.g. Scandinavia, or Russia, the eastern limit of birds reaching Britain remains unknown (Wernham *et al.* 2002). Return passage is evident from March, with the Finnish population reoccupying the breeding grounds from late April. Northern North American forms show the same migration patterns as those in the Palearctic.

## Tree Swallow *Tachycineta bicolor* A BBRC 100%

**Extremely rare migrant, full written description required by the BBRC.**

1990   Adult male St Mary's 6th to 10th June

*British Birds* 84: 490, 85: 534, 88: 381–384; *Ibis* 134: 380

Nearctic species, breeds Alaska to Newfoundland and south to California and eastern southern states. Monotypic. Winters southern USA, e.g. California, Texas and east coast south of New York, to Greater Antilles and Costa Rica. Population apparently static (Bryant 1997).

The sole acceptable West Palearctic record up until summer 2002 involved a bird found by local birder Jeremy Hickman in the area of Porth Hellick, St Mary's, around 7 am on Wednesday 6th June 1990 (Wagstaff 1990; Hickman 1995). The bird remained twitchable in the Porth Hellick and Higher Moors areas until mid-morning on Sunday 10th of June and was seen by a large number of birders. The RMV *Scillonian III* brought about 400 day-tripping birders from the mainland on Saturday 9th. The bird was aged and sexed as an adult male and the record was accepted onto Category A by the BOURC in May 1992 (BOURC 1992b).

In eastern North America, Tree Swallows begin leaving their breeding areas from July and are mostly gone by August, returning from mid-March or April. Thus the St Mary's individual does not easily fit either spring or autumn migration patterns. Although still to be accepted by the BBRC at the time of writing, a bird seen and photographed on the island of Unst, Shetland, on 29th May 2002 was not too dissimilar in arrival date (*Birdwatch* 121: 52). A far earlier Tree Swallow claim concerned a bird allegedly obtained in Derbyshire in or around 1850. In 1893, the skin was said to have been in the Norwich Museum but a more recent search of the collection revealed no skin and no documentation to show that it was ever there. Consequently, the BOURC felt obligated to ignore the claim and treat the Porth Hellick individual as the first for Britain and Ireland (*British Birds* 86: 188).

## Sand Martin *Riparia riparia* A

**Annual spring and autumn migrant, formerly in greater numbers than at present. Allegations that it bred in very small numbers during the 1930s, 1940s and 1970s appear doubtful.**

Breeds Eurasia, from Iberia, Britain and Ireland east to Pacific and south to Nile delta, Iran, northern India and eastern China, also North America. All except northern Indian population migratory, West Palearctic plus Siberian populations winter sub-Saharan Africa. Polytypic: nominate *riparia* occurs northern and southwest Eurasia and North America; *diluta* southern and southeast Asia; *shelleyi* Nile Valley; *ijimae* Sakhalin to southeast Siberia. In North America, known as Bank Swallow. Amber-listed in UK: unfavourable world conservation status (Gregory *et al.* 2002). National 15% increase 1994–99 (Bashford & Noble 2000).

E H Rodd described Sand Martin as a common and generally distributed summer visitor to mainland Cornwall during the late 19th century, noting its favourite nest sites as old sandpits and quarries, which he said were often 'riddled' with nest holes. However, the only two direct early references to Sand Martin on Scilly were E H Rodd's *Zoologist* mention of its arrival during early September 1868 (Rodd 1868c) and the comment by his nephew Francis that one or more appeared for a few days during October 1870 (Rodd 1880). However, 26 years later, Francis and co-author James Clark thought it 'for the most part a casual bird of passage in spring and autumn, but sometimes – as in 1848, 1863, 1867, 1894 and 1901 – flocks of several hundred birds may pause in their southward journey' (Clark & Rodd 1906).

Although no precise figures seem available for the early period, certainly by the mid-1970s Penhallurick thought the total Cornish breeding population in the region of just 250 pairs. The same author quoted Couch (1838), who thought numbers in the county may always have been limited by a shortage of nest sites. However, Penhallurick (1978) suggested that additional sites should have been released by the abandonment of tin mines and china clay workings. The same author pointed out that Sand Martin arrival dates at Cornish breeding sites were largely unknown but that passage birds were normally evident during the last ten days of March, it being rare before that time. The early date Penhallurick gave for Scilly of 15th March was at the early end of the mainland scale and the full spring passage period for the islands extended from late March to mid-May, occasionally into June. Locally, though, the 24th March was considered a reliable first date for Scilly; nevertheless, one over Old Town, St Mary's, on 28th January 1958 was presumably a very early spring migrant (*CBWPSAR* 28). Autumn dates provided by Penhallurick were mostly for mainland Cornwall and ran from 18th July through to 28th November, daily autumn St Agnes counts varying between 50 and an extreme of 100.

Somewhat doubtful still are 20th-century claims of Sand Martins breeding on Scilly. Penhallurick listed some 40 known mainland Cornish sites but included three for Scilly, namely Porthloo and Porth Wreck (the latter near Deep Point) on St Mary's, plus one unnamed site on Bryher. The same source quoted unconfirmed reports for Porthloo for the 1930s and 40s, a single occupied hole at Porth Wreck during 1969 and three holes on Bryher in 1970. The last two sites were allegedly reported by the normally reliable Peter Mackenzie, but only the latter incident appears in the annual reports, and even then without supporting information for a 'probable' three pairs (*IOSBR* 1970). Earlier, Wallis (1923) found none breeding in the islands and several other early to mid-20th century visiting ornithologists made no mention of it as a breeding species. Unsurprisingly, then, it apparently gets no mention in the annual reports until the 1946 comment by Turk that 'many of their nesting holes are to be seen at various places on the eastern side of St Mary's'. From this, Turk concluded that Sand Martins once nested there in 'considerable numbers'. Such a suggestion, however, is not compatible with the lack of other published information and is further undermined by Turk's comment that 'in every case the burrow had been taken over by rats' (*CBWPSAR* 16). It is difficult at best to know what size the holes would have been before being taken over by the rats, if indeed they were not dug by the rats themselves. Noticeably, Ryves & Quick (1946) made no mention of breeding on Scilly in their mid-20th-century review of breeding birds, and in the absence of even a partially documented account the possibility of breeding having occurred in Scilly remains doubtful, particularly as the species gets no further mention after Turk's remarks until the clear statement in the 1974 *IOSBR* that it 'does not breed'.

Figures for the ten years to 1999 show annual Sand Martin numbers varying between years, from a daily trickle of two to three per island to an all-island spring count of 150 and a single-site count over Tresco's Great Pool of 154 on 13th May 1996, though with few annual maximum counts exceeding 50. Most normally pass through during spring, though in some years largest peak counts came in the second half of the year, perhaps due to condensed weather-related movements. The earliest spring arrival was 13th March (two years) and the latest any bird was seen in the islands was on the extreme date of 4th November, the last two weeks of October being more normal. In most years, singles or sometimes two, occasionally more, were recorded during late June or July, creating difficulties deciding where spring passage ceased and the autumn return commenced. As might be expected, main concentrations occurred over open fresh water, e.g. Tresco's Great and Abbey Pools, Porth Hellick and Lower Moors pools in St Mary's and the St Agnes and Bryher pools. In early July 1984, David Hunt watched about 50, a goodly number for that time of year, catching feathers blown into the air, before settling again on the shores of Tresco Great Pool (*IOSBR* 1984), but with no suggestion of breeding.

Nominate *riparia* from the West Palearctic and Siberia east to the North Pacific winters within the African Sahel region, birds from western populations crossing the Mediterranean into Morocco through France and Iberia (Wernham *et al.* 2002), whilst those from northern Asia move through the Nile Valley. Within Britain and Ireland, southward movement becomes obvious by August, birds reaching their African wintering areas by October or early November, adults travelling more rapidly than juveniles (Cramp *et al.* 1977–94). Normal first spring arrival dates in Britain occur around or before the end of March. Sand Martin breeds extensively throughout Britain and Ireland and it seems reasonable to assume that at least some from Ireland use Scilly as a staging post en route to and from Africa. Surprisingly, just 16 Sand Martins had been ringed in Scilly up until the end of 1999 and only two of those after 1970; there are no recaptures.

# Swallow (Barn Swallow) *Hirundo rustica* A

**A common and very obvious annual spring and autumn migrant, also breeds in moderate numbers. It has been recorded in all months of the year.**

Breeds most of Eurasia, including North Africa and Nile Valley, plus North America. Long-distance migrant, all West Palearctic populations except southern Spain and Nile Valley winter sub-Saharan Africa south to the Antarctic Ocean. Polytypic: nominate *rustica* occurs Europe, Asia Minor east to China, also North Africa; *tytleri* southern Siberia and northern Mongolia; *transitiva* Middle East; *savignii* Egypt; *gutturalis* eastern Asia; *erythrogaster*, or 'Barn Swallow', North America. Amber-listed in UK: unfavourable world conservation status (Gregory *et al.* 2002). National 38% decline during 25 years to 1996, then increase of 10% 1994–99 (Bashford & Noble 2000).

There is surprisingly little reference to what was very obviously a common migrant even during the 19th century. E H Rodd described it simply as a 'summer visitor – breeds', but at the same time quoted his nephew Francis, who pointed out that a November frost of 1870 'took away the last of the Swallows' (Rodd 1880). Earlier, the elder Rodd wrote of a large arrival in the Land's End area during early April, which he described as 'several troops of 40 or 50' that arrived from the southwest, between Scilly and the Wolf Rock (Rodd 1872). By the turn of the 20th century, however, Francis Rodd and co-author James Clark felt able to describe it as common in Scilly throughout the summer, although even by then it was recorded in every month of the year (Clark & Rodd 1906). They noted too that the 'sunny side' of Tresco Abbey (presumably the southern side) and that island's Broad Walk were favourite Swallow resorts during winter. As if by way of confirmation, they pointed out that on 10th December 1903 five were feeding beside the Abbey for the whole morning, adding that although most left by 20th October that autumn, they returned to the islands in 'considerable numbers' on or about the 29th November.

A feature of Swallow migration on Scilly is the normally steady daytime movement of birds heading either north or south through the islands, punctuated by the occasionally impressive build-up in numbers during periods of unsettled weather, as on 28th September 1989 when an estimated 800 were present on St Mary's. Taking the ten years from 1990, annual first sightings occurred between 7th February and 23rd March, with recorded latest sightings in the range 4th November to 17th December. Although large gatherings occurred during both migration periods, slightly greater numbers during autumn included 670 on St Mary's on 7th October 1999 and 400+ at Porth Hellick and 200–300 elsewhere on St Mary's in early October 1990. However, numbers involved were usually less impressive, and during periods of normal migration most people on the islands would have been unaware any movement was occurring, as individual birds arrived from out at sea and passed quietly on through the archipelago. Most annual Bird Reports refer to the apparent commencement of return autumn passage around August or even September, the suggestion being that July gatherings of up to 100 may perhaps involve mainly local birds. Also noticeable to visiting birders and 'normal' tourists alike is the frequency with which Swallows are observed at sea between the islands, even out amongst the more remote islands and rocks.

What was probably the greatest recorded concentration in Scilly was described by A A Dorrien-Smith in 1938, when an abnormally large concentration for 2nd June 'increased from hundreds to thousands' next day (A A Dorrien-Smith 1938b). This followed very heavy rain on 1st, the wind strengthening to gale force and moving from the northeast through the southeast and ending up in the northwest. At noon on the 3rd, Dorrien-Smith steamed out to sea north of the islands and encountered several small groups of Swallows moving south in an apparently normal manner. But on return to Tresco at 5 pm he found the freshwater pools 'black with birds, chiefly Swallows and House Martins *Delichon urbica* and there were several thousands of them'. By the 5th, many had departed and by the 8th only normal numbers were in evidence, the air temperature having increased substantially on the 6th. The only early 20th-century report from the lighthouses concerned some noted on 17th April 1911, with what were described as unusual numbers on 1st May. The location is not given but was presumably the Bishop Rock or St Agnes, though the latter was decommissioned some time that year (Ogilvie-Grant 1912c).

As long ago as 1946, Ryves and Quick noted no change in the Swallow's status as a regular breeder in Scilly since H M Wallis visited earlier (Wallis 1923). Although no all-island survey of breeding Swallows has since been carried out, they are known to breed on all five inhabited islands. Most nests are within farm buildings but unusual sites include ten feet down the old brick ventilation shaft on the southwest corner of The Garrison, St Mary's, or the Second World War concrete bunker on the west side of Porth Hellick Bay, also on St Mary's. Up to ten pairs were recorded on St Agnes during recent years, but totals for other islands involve estimates rather than firm figures. Nevertheless, perhaps as many as 25 pairs each are to be found on St Mary's and Tresco with fewer on Bryher and St Martin's, a combined total in the region perhaps of 90 pairs for the entire island group. In most years, many, if not most pairs apparently raise at least two broods. Wallis recorded three breeding pairs on Tean in 1923 and although no suitable site remains it is assumed they were utilising the remains of former known habitation. So presumably abandoned buildings have been in use on other islands, e.g. Samson, from time to time. The 2000 Breeding Bird Atlas's estimated total of 81 pairs, in the range 50–100 (Chown & Lock 2002), is broadly in keeping with the above. The survey recorded birds in 26 (38.3%) of the 67 surveyed 1-km squares, though breeding was thought probable in just 15 (22.3%).

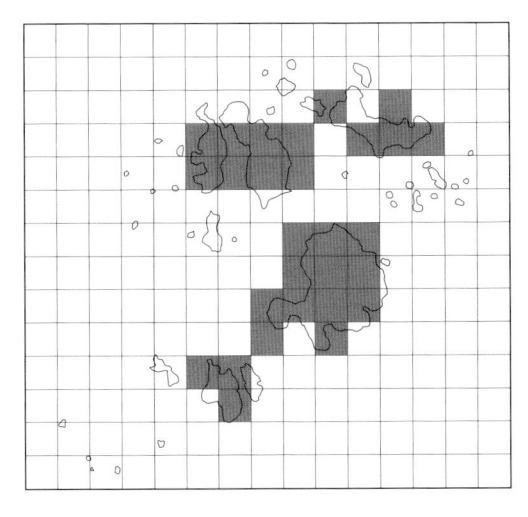

| Island | Pairs |
|---|---|
| Bryher | 7 |
| St Agnes | 8 |
| St Martin's | 12 |
| St Mary's | 42 |
| Tresco | 12 |
| Tean | 1 |

**2000 Breeding Bird Atlas – Swallow (Chown & Lock 2002)**

**1-km Swallow Breeding Distribution – 2000–01 (data Chown & Lock 2002)**

As shown by large-scale ringing, most Swallows from Europe and northwest Asia, i.e. *rustica*, winter in Africa south of the Sahara, most British and Irish birds going as far as South Africa (Cramp *et al.* 1977–94; Wernham *et al.* 2002). Juvenile dispersal commences from July and becomes increasingly directed southwards with the start of full migration during August. Peak passage in northwest Europe occurs during September and early October, although some may remain until forced to move by the onset of cold weather, typically during November. Return spring passage from Africa commences from February with most birds moving through Europe from mid-April to mid-May, some northern Russia birds not reaching the breeding grounds until early June. A small number may winter in Britain or Ireland in some years; King & Penhallurick (1977) recounted one such incident for mainland Cornwall but, interestingly, no obvious overwintering, as different from casual movement, is recorded for Scilly. Passage through Africa, including across the Sahara, is largely a broad-front movement.

Given the location of Scilly and its proven ability to attract migrants from both sides of the North Atlantic, we should at least be alive to the possibility of the North American *erythrogaster* arriving in the islands (Gantlett 1998). Subtle plumage differences might hopefully make it stand out from any accompanying *rustica*, but perhaps our strongest chance of proving a transatlantic crossing is the future control of an individual ringed on the opposite side of the North America. The occasional particularly colourful bird has given rise to a debate over the possibility of the North African form *savignii* reaching the islands, but the point has yet to be proved. Interestingly, then, E H Rodd drew attention to a bird seen in west Cornwall by Penzance taxidermist Vingoe, probably in late summer 1851, which Vingoe later identified as 'Rufous Swallow' from a Gould plate. Perhaps correctly, Penhallurick assumed this to have been Red-rumped Swallow *H. daurica*, but as no specific Gould painting is referred to by Rodd it seems equally likely this may have been either of the two rufous-coloured Swallow forms *transitiva* or *savignii*. There are at least three recent records of birds displaying features of apparent hybrid Swallow x House Martin. One such individual was on St Martin's and then St Mary's between 15th and 21st October 1988, with another at Porth Hellick, St Mary's, for two days during mid-October 1990, whilst a third was present on St Mary's for two days during mid-October 1996, before relocating to Tresco for one day. Other unusually plumaged Swallows included what was described as a grey-and-white bird on Tresco on 24th–25th October 1991 and a melanistic individual, all dark but with whitish wing linings and undertail, for two days during mid-September 1986.

## Control

| | | | | | |
|---|---|---|---|---|---|
| ? | Pul | Penrith, Cumbria July 1931 | AS | 64 km west-northwest of Scilly 20th May 1932 |
| ? | Pul | Mullion, Cornwall 22nd August 1966 | CT | Tresco 11th September 1967 |
| ? | Ad | Bedworth, Warwickshire 2nd September 1979 | FI | Scilly 3rd May 1980 |

## Recoveries

| | | | | | |
|---|---|---|---|---|---|
| J7924 | Ad | Tresco 6th July 1952 | FD | Gouex, Vienne, France 29th April 1956 |
| K91308 | 1stY | St Agnes 3rd October 1963 | CT | Ushant, Finistere, France 4th October 1963 |

**Swallow Ringing Recaptures**

# Red-rumped Swallow *Hirundo daurica* A  BBRC 8.5%

**Scarce migrant, full written description required by the BBRC.**

[1964  One St Mary's 16th & 17th May]
1964  One St Agnes 10th & 11th November
1976  One St Mary's 30th May to 1st June
1979  One Bryher & Tresco 14th April to 5th May
1980  One Bryher & St Mary's 16th May
1980  One (juvenile) St Mary's 23rd October to 3rd November
1984  One St Mary's 24th to 29th April
1984  One St Mary's 13th to 19th October
1984  One Tresco 15th & 16th October
1985  One St Mary's 1st May
1987  Three to four Bryher & Tresco 19th to 21st October
1987  Up to seven St Mary's 21st to 28th October
1987  One St Martin's 23rd & 28th October
1987  One Gugh 23rd & 24th October
1987  One St Agnes 23rd October
1988  Two St Mary's & Tresco 23rd to 27th October
1991  One Bryher 24th April
1991  One Tresco 28th May to 1st June
1994  One Tresco 28th February to 28th March
1996  One Tresco, Bryher & St Mary's 24th April to 15th May
1998  One St Mary's 15th & 16th February
2000  One St Mary's & St Agnes 1st to 14th May
2001  One St Mary's 21st to 23rd May
*2002  One St Agnes & St Mary's 22nd October to 7th November*

Unusual fragmentary distribution, breeds mainly eastern Asia and Indian subcontinent, westwards in narrow band to Iberia and North Africa; numerous isolated sedentary populations central-southern Africa. Northern populations strongly migratory but winter destination of West Palearctic birds unclear. Polytypic: *rufula* occurs Europe, Middle East and North Africa; nominate *daurica* east from Kazakhstan to Mongolia and central China; *japonica* extreme east.

If Red-rumped Swallow occurred in Scilly and Cornwall up until the end of the 19th century, which presumably it did, then it was missed entirely by the otherwise observant early ornithologists. E H Rodd, for example, made no reference to it whatsoever. However, the same authority (Rodd 1880) referred to a swallow seen in west Cornwall by Penzance taxidermist Vingoe, probably during late summer 1851 and which Rodd described as 'Rufous Swallow', allegedly as depicted by Gould. Penhallurick (1978) assumed this to have been Red-rumped Swallow. But as no specific Gould plate is mentioned in Rodd's text, and as Vingoe allegedly referred to a 'uniform copper tint over the whole of the under parts', it seems equally likely this could have been one of two Middle Eastern forms of Swallow *H. rustica*.

First then for Scilly may to have been the bird watched feeding over St Mary's on 16th–17th May 1964, although this record seems never to have been accepted by the BBRC and is referred to in the *SABOAR* for that year as 'an unconfirmed report'. However, there was no doubt about the individual that arrived with House Martins *Delichon urbica* on 10th November that same year and was trapped the following day, this being only the second British autumn record. Interestingly, 10 records (45%) occurred during autumn, with five records (six birds) on 23rd October. The Chart includes all 22 recorded annual arrival dates up until 2000 and shows a clear pattern of spring and autumn migration, though much more protracted during the early period. During spring the mean length of stay was 9 days, whereas autumn individuals remained only 4.8 days. Taking both seasons, only four birds remained for just one day. Dymond *et al.* (1989) analysed all records between 1958 and 1985, concluding that there had been a dramatic increase as the species spread northwards from Spain into France.

The BBRC accepted 341 Red-rumped Swallow records during the period 1958–99, compared with just seven prior to that time. Therefore, the total of up to 30 Scillonian birds up until the end of 1999 represents at least 8.5% of the post-1958 total. There is also a recognisable national trend towards late-winter records (Rogers 2000), which is evident even in this small Scillonian sample. The larger and more streaked nominate *daurica* has already occurred as a vagrant in Norway and Finland and must be expected to occur in Britain at some stage (Gantlett 1998).

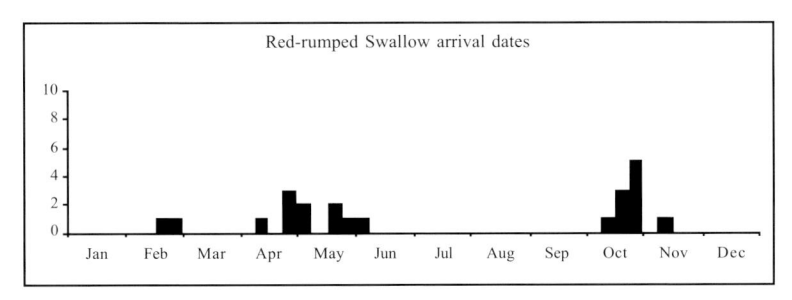

Red-rumped Swallow arrival dates

Red-rumped Swallow now breeds at least as close to Scilly as southern France, where there were 60–70 pairs by year 2000 (Davies 2001). Therefore, the arrival of Scillonian spring records can perhaps best be explained by overshooting migrants. However, this would not account for their presence during autumn, particularly as none breed in the West Palearctic north of southern France, Italy and the former Yugoslavia (Hagemeijer & Blair 1997). Cramp *et al.* (1977–94) raised the possibility of a few European sightings of migrant birds from eastern populations being attributable to more long-range overflying, which perhaps accounts for Finnish and Norwegian *daurica* records, but so far no Scillonian arrivals appear to have been attributed to this form. The fact that spring passage through the Strait of Gibraltar commences as early as February gives additional weight to the overshooting theory. One Red-rumped Swallow was trapped and ringed on Scilly up until the end of 1999 but it was not recaptured.

## Cliff Swallow *Petrochelidon pyrrhonota* A BBRC 33.3%

**Extremely rare migrant, full written description required by the BBRC.**

 1983 One (first-winter) St Agnes & St Mary's 10th to 27th October
                        *British Birds* 77: 37, 80: 550, 81: 440–452
 1995 One (first-winter) Tresco 4th & 5th December *British Birds* 89: 512
 2000 One St Mary's 28th to 30th September *British Birds* 94: 483
 2001 One St Agnes, St Mary's & St Martin's 26th to 30th October *British Birds* 95: 212, 504

Nearctic species, breeds central Alaska east to Nova Scotia and south through most of USA to southern Mexico. Migratory, wintering Central and South America south to Chile. Polytypic: nominate *pyrrhonota* occurs throughout North America except southwest. Population increasing (Bryant 1997).

Up until the end of 2001 there were four Scillonian records of this much sought-after North American rarity, the two earliest accounting for 33% of the six British and Irish records for the period 1958–1999. The Chart shows a clear pattern of late autumn or early winter arrivals. The individual on St Agnes, Gugh and St Mary's during October 1983 was the first for the West Palearctic (BOURC 1988; Crosby 1988), others occurring subsequently in Britain, Ireland, France, Iceland, Canary Islands and the Azores. The 2000 individual was only the fifth for Britain and the bird in 2001 arrived the day before a Cliff Swallow appeared in Madeira, with one in the Azores on 28th September (*Birding World* 14: 421). The particular form involved in Scilly was not ascertained, but seems unlikely to have been other than *pyrrhonota* (BOURC 1991b). At least two of the four records were aged as first-winters.

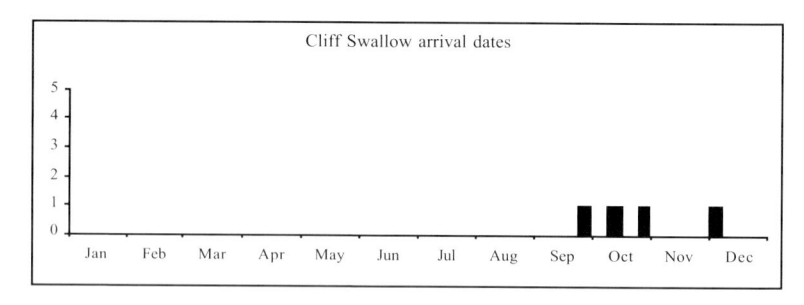

*Cliff Swallow arrival dates* (chart showing records in Sep, Oct, Nov)

Care should be taken with all apparent European Cliff Swallow sightings in order to eliminate the possibility of the closely similar Cave Swallow *P. fulva*, from southern USA and the Caribbean, being involved. Increasing numbers of Cave Swallow records from northeast USA during the late 1990s raise the possibility of this species reaching Europe in the near future. For a review of this situation and for an overview of the criteria involved in separating Cave from Cliff Swallow see Hough (2000).

## House Martin *Delichon urbica* A

**Annual spring and autumn migrant, sometimes in large numbers, a few pairs breed.**

Breeds Eurasia, from North Africa, Iberia, British Isles and Fennoscandia east to Sea of Okhotsk and south to Iran, Himalayas and China. Migratory, West Palearctic and west Asian populations winter Africa south of Sahara. Polytypic: nominate *urbica* occurs Europe and North Africa east to western Siberia and northern India; *lagapoda* central and eastern Asia; three additional forms further southeast. Upgraded from Green- to Amber-listed in UK 2002: moderate population decline over past 25 years (Gregory *et al.* 2002). National 29% increase 1994–99 (Bashford & Noble 2000).

Apart from a lengthy pre-20th-century account by James Clark and Francis Rodd, the only early observations are Gilbert White's comment that it arrived in April or May (in Jesse 1887) and a 1911 note that it was seen on 11th and 24th April (Ogilvie-Grant 1912c). However, in their inimitable style, Clark and Rodd said all that was necessary to convey the full picture of House Martin's presence in Scilly up until the early 20th century, noting that although it did not then breed it was common throughout the summer and like Swallow *Hirundo rustica* was 'not infrequently' seen during winter (Clark & Rodd 1906). They also described how, although in autumn 1903 all had left St Mary's by 20th October, considerable numbers returned around 29th and for over a week it was more numerous than was usual during summer. One was also picked up dead on St Mary's on 20th January 1881 having been shot through the beak.

During the ten years 1990–99 the earliest recorded arrival date was 21st February, though early to mid-March was more usual. By far the largest concentrations occurred during the early half of the year, 810 being recorded at Tresco's Great Pool on 13th May 1996. Similarly, 300 were on Tresco on 24th May 1991 and 350 at Porth Hellick, St Mary's, two days later, though highs of 50–60 were more usual. Establishing cut-off dates for spring migration was confused by the presence of breeding birds, which also clouded the start of the early autumn migration period, though in most years migrants appeared to be moving through again by August or early September. Autumn migration was a far more protracted affair, which perhaps helped explain lower peak numbers, of up to 50, though an earlier high of 400 during early September 1976 proved the exception. In general, last sighting dates fell between 23rd October and 5th November, one in Hugh Town from 30th November until 2nd December being very much the exception for the period under review, although in 1968 a dead juvenile was picked up on 16th December and three were at Porth Cressa, St Mary's, on 8th–9th December 1979.

Penhallurick (1978) summarised the Scillonian breeding situation up until the mid-1970s, noting that first mention came from C J King, who recorded nests in Hugh Town by at least 1927, with birds still feeding young into September. Penhallurick also made the important point that because several visiting naturalists of that period, e.g. Wallis 1923, failed to mention breeding House Martins, this activity was probably sporadic in nature. However, the same author pointed out that nests were found in Hugh Town in 1943, whilst in 1947 A A Dorrien-Smith knew of two nests, presumably on Tresco, where it still breeds in small numbers. Penhallurick also mentioned occupation, by a single pair, of the new water pumping station in Higher Moors, St Mary's, from about 1968, although in the ten years from 1990 there was just one unsuccessful attempt (pers. obs.). During the 1970s and into the early 1990s a small number of pairs bred on St Mary's, Tresco, St Agnes and, less often, St Martin's, although the St Agnes breeding survey (1957–1974) made no mention of it.

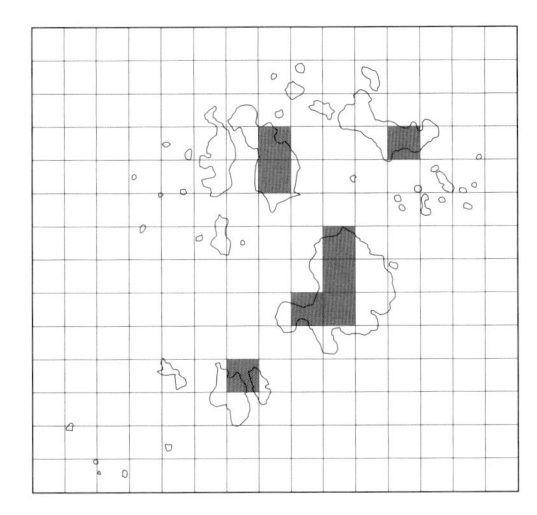

| Island | Pairs |
| --- | --- |
| St Agnes | 1 |
| St Martin's | 1 |
| St Mary's | 9 |
| Tresco | 7 |

**2000 Breeding Bird Atlas – House Martin (Chown & Lock 2002)**

**1-km House Martin Breeding Distribution – 2000–01 (data Chown & Lock 2002)**

More recently, regular breeding appears to be largely confined to Tresco and St Mary's, mainly in Hugh Town on the latter island, though with perhaps no more than 20 pairs involved throughout the islands. Interestingly, this was confirmed by the 2000 Breeding Bird Atlas, which recorded up to 18 pairs in eight (7.4%) of the 67 1-km squares surveyed (Chown & Lock 2002). Cliff nesting occurred regularly in mainland Cornwall up until at least the mid-1970s (Penhallurick 1978) and a few pairs may still do so (*CBWPSAR* 68). However, this behaviour seems never to have been recorded in Scilly.

House Martin is a broad-front migrant and, at least within Europe, autumn passage is mainly directed southwards, rather than towards the southwest as with so many passerines. Consequently, more birds from North Sea countries are recovered in France than Iberia, and most recoveries of birds from Finland and the eastern Baltic states come from Greece, though a few Fennoscandian birds do pass through Britain (Cramp *et al.* 1977–94; Wernham *et al.* 2002). Importantly, there are few European reports of House Martins at passage hirundine roosts and even fewer from African roost sites (Wernham *et al.* 2002). Therefore, the reported 300 roosting at Porth Hellick, St Mary's, on 26th May 1991 (*IOSBR* 1991) is both noteworthy and perhaps questionable, this being the only apparent published claim of roosting migrant House Martins on Scilly. Although ringing data show that many European House Martins move south in winter as far as Southern Africa, there is just one British or Irish recovery south of the Sahara (Wernham *et al.* 2002). Main southerly movement through Europe occurs from September to the end of October, with return passage mainly from late March to late April or early May. There are at least three recent records of birds displaying features of apparent hybrid House Martin x Swallow *Hirundo rustica*: one was on St Martin's and then St Mary's between 15th and 21st October 1988; another was at Porth Hellick, St Mary's, for two days during mid-October 1990; whilst a third was present on St Mary's for two days during mid-October 1996, before relocating to Tresco for one day. A total of just 32 House Martins were ringed in Scilly up until the end of 1999, almost equal numbers before and after 1970; there are no recaptures.

# Richard's Pipit *Anthus novaeseelandiae* A

Scarce but now annual migrant, up to 27 annually, largely in autumn, full written description required by the SRP.

Breeds central Asia north to Sea of Okhotsk and south to southeast China, also southern Africa, Indian subcontinent and southeast to New Zealand. Central Asian populations migratory, remainder sedentary or dispersive; a few may winter African Sahel and southern Spain. Polytypic: *richardi* occurs southwest Siberia east to Lake Baikal; *dauricus* east of *richardi* to Sea of Okhotsk; *centralasiae* central Asia to western China; *ussuriensis* southeast Russia, eastern China and Korea; *sinensis* remaining China; four additional forms further south. Removed from BBRC Rarities List January 1983 (Grant 1982b).

The normally reliable E H Rodd tells of examining one in the flesh after it was shot by Augustus Pechell on Tresco during October 1851 (Rodd 1880), although 25 years later Rodd's nephew Francis and co-author James Clark gave the year as 1849 (Clark & Rodd 1906). however, all agreed that Pechell obtained three more specimens on that same island on 19th September 1868, plus a Tawny Pipit *A. campestris*. The only other 19th-century reference to this species was the elder Rodd's description of it as among the rarer visitors to Cornwall (Rodd 1880). Clark and Rodd's observation that 'a pair' were watched flying backwards and forwards over the marshes at Porth Hellick on 16th May 1903 is interesting, if only because it describes the first spring record for the islands.

Following Clark and Rodd's early publication, Richard's Pipit apparently gets no further 20th-century mention until three were recorded in the islands during 1963. The Chart shows all recorded annual totals since that time, but note that an unknown number were present during 1972. In most years deciding precisely how many individuals were involved was frustrated by the extent of inter-site and even inter-island movements, and for several yearly totals a mean figure is employed. Twenty-seven during 1994 was the highest annual appearance, followed closely by 25 in 1975, compared with a national total of 108 during 1999. Penhallurick (1978) noted a fall-off in numbers in both Scilly and Cornwall during the mid-1970s, and it seems clear from the Chart that low numbers persisted into the early 1980s, though there appears to have been a recent recovery. Most arrival dates fell within the period mid-September to late October, though rare stragglers occurred into November or even mid-December. Since the 1980s there have been about four spring sightings, involving five individuals.

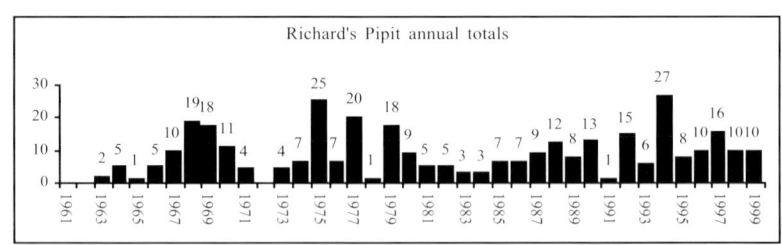

Richard's Pipit is a long-distance migrant and none breed within perhaps 5,000 km of Britain, whilst almost the entire population is believed to winter in the Indian subcontinent and further east. Nevertheless, a marked feature of this species is the number of individuals now annually reaching British shores (Cramp *et al.* 1977–94; Wernham *et al.* 2002). Most reaching Scilly, and indeed Britain, are thought to be the form *richardi*, which breeds as close as southwest Siberia and Lake Baikal, so this is perhaps hardly surprising, though the western breeding limit has still to be fully defined. However, Gantlett (1998) sensibly drew attention to the possibility of birds reaching Britain from even further east, e.g. individuals of the slightly larger and darker *ussuriensis* or the paler *centralasiae*. Earlier Sharrock (1974) suggested that post-breeding dispersal rather than reverse migration might account for the presence of Richard's Pipits in western Europe during autumn and that its spring presence might best be explained by the existence of an as yet undocumented wintering area in southern Europe or Africa. Interestingly, then, Cramp *et al.* drew attention to the possibility of migrant Asian Richard's Pipits wintering in both the African Sahel region and southwest Europe (southern Spain), whilst also noting the frequency with which this species occurs in autumn well to the west of its normal breeding range, enough in fact for it to have been removed from the BBRC Rarities List from January 1983 (Grant 1982b). Dymond *et al.* (1989) noted an 'extraordinary' upsurge in the annual number of British arrivals, of what was previously considered a rare vagrant, from around the mid-1960s, records for the seven years 1976–82 averaging just 48 per year. Up until the end of year 2000, the total for mainland Cornwall stood at 347, the first of which was in 1947 (*CBWPSAR* 70). Two Richard's Pipits were trapped and ringed on Scilly up until the end of 1999, but there are no recaptures, as indeed is the case for Britain and Ireland.

## Blyth's Pipit *Anthus godlewskii* A BBRC 12.5–14.2%

**Extremely rare migrant, full written description required by the BBRC.**

1993   One (first-year) St Mary's 20th to 22nd October   *British Birds* 90: 492

Breeds southern Siberia, China and northeast India. Migratory, wintering India and Sri Lanka. Monotypic.

There is just one accepted Scillonian Blyth's Pipit record, involving a bird that frequented St Mary's golf course for three days from 20th October 1993. This individual was of interest for its particularly pale, Tawny Pipit *A. campestris*-like plumage, and until it was heard to call and good views were obtained of its unmarked pale lores, initially posed identification problems (Evans 1993; D Page 1997).

This bird represented probably the fourth record for Britain and Ireland, though only two of the three previous individuals have thus far been accepted by the BBRC: a bird reportedly shot in what is now East Sussex on 23rd October 1882 (BOURC 1998) and one at Skewjack, west Cornwall, from 22nd October to 1st November 1990 (*CBWPSAR* 60). As of October 2001, a well-documented claim of one on Fair Isle during mid-October 1988 was still under consideration by the BBRC (*British Birds* 94: 504).

Subsequently accepted British records include a bird on Fair Isle eleven days after the St Mary's individual; one in Suffolk during November 1994; Kent in November–December 1994; Dorset November 1998; and Norfolk late September 1999. A claim of a presumed Blyth's Pipit in the vicinity of St Mary's Airport on 9th–10th October 1995 was subsequently rejected by the BBRC in October 2002 (*British Birds* 95: 527). It will be noted, then, that all British records so far have occurred in autumn. Given the number of past sightings of large pipits on Scilly showing features inconsistent with either Tawny or Richard's Pipit *A. novaeseelandiae* it is interesting to speculate on the extent to which this present species may have been overlooked in the islands in the past.

Southward movement from the breeding grounds commences from around July, with some present in the wintering areas from early September (Cramp *et al.* 1977–94). Cramp *et al.* make mention of a possible Blyth's Pipit in Africa's Lake Chad region, though the possibility of Richard's Pipit could not be ruled out. Nonetheless, given the similarity of their normal wintering range it is interesting to note that the presence in Africa of wintering Richard's Pipits believed to originate from northern Asia seems well established (see that species). The Scillonian individual was not trapped and ringed.

## Tawny Pipit *Anthus campestris* A

**Scarce migrant, up to 13 annually, mainly in autumn. Treated by the BBRC as a national Scarce Migrant, full written description required by the SRP.**

Breeds central and southern Europe and coastal North Africa, east to central-southern Siberia, Mongolia and central China. Mainly migratory, West Palearctic population winters Africa and Arabian Peninsula, remainder Indian subcontinent, with some *griseus* Arabia. Polytypic: nominate *campestris* occurs West Palearctic through Iran and southwest Siberia to Omsk; *kastchenkoi* southern Siberia and northern Mongolia to upper Yenisey; *griseus* remainder. Removed from BBRC Rarities List January 1983 (Grant 1982b)

The only early mention of this species involved one shot by Augustus Pechell near Old Grimsby, Tresco, on 19th September 1868, the same day that he shot three Richard's Pipits *A. novaeseelandiae* on the same island (Rodd 1868e; Nicoll 1904; Clark & Rodd 1906). E H Rodd's description of this bird as a male was presumably based on the taxidermist's findings.

The first for mainland Cornwall was captured in 1899 and was followed by additional mainland records from 1949, though Scilly had to wait for its first 20th-century sighting until May 1955 when Hilda Quick discovered one on the Gugh. During the 45 years 1955–99, a total of 194 Tawny Pipits arrived on Scilly, at an annual mean of 4.3, or 4.9 per bird-year. The Chart shows annual totals for this same period, the most being ten in 1977 and 1983. There are a number of similarities between this graph and the national

*Birds of the Isles of Scilly*

Tawny Pipit data analysed by Fraser & Rogers (2001), who also noted a clear increase in numbers up until the late 1970s, plus an exceptional influx during 1983. However, even higher numbers noted by Fraser and Rogers during the 1980s and early 1990s are not apparent among the Scillonian data. Over the period 1980–99, spring arrivals occurred at a rate of one to five in 12 of the 20 years, within a 58-day window from 22nd April to 5th June. Autumn arrivals were evident from mid-September through to mid- or late October, though dates varied between years.

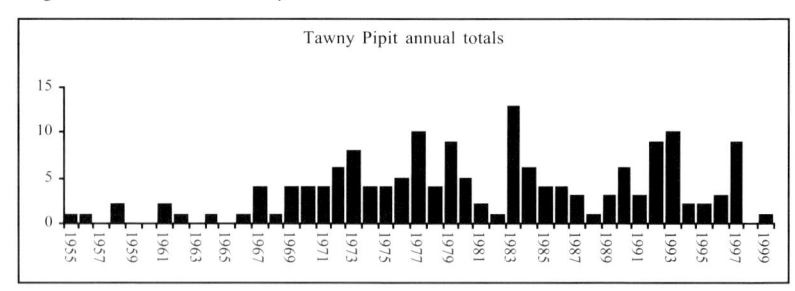

Tawny Pipit annual totals

Within Africa, nominate *campestris* winters in the Sahel region south of the equator, although further south in East Africa, birds leaving Europe on a broad front from late July through to October (Cramp *et al.* 1977–94). Those moving through Egypt perhaps include some *griseus* from Iran or further north or east. Return spring migration commences in Africa as early as February, birds passing through mid-Europe by late April to mid-May. Sharrock (1974) concluded that the disparity in numbers of spring British Tawny Pipit records, compared to southern European species with similar breeding ranges, e.g. Hoopoe *Upupa epops*, was perhaps explained by it being 'better equipped' to determine distance during migration, whereas fewer autumn arrivals, compared to Richard's Pipit, for example, was perhaps due to it being less liable to lateral displacement during adverse weather. Although individuals reaching Britain can normally be expected to be *campestris*, both *griseus* and *kastchenko* remain potential vagrants (Gantlett 1998). Two Tawny Pipits were trapped and ringed in Scilly up until the end of 1999 but there are no recaptures.

## Olive-backed Pipit *Anthus hodgsoni* A BBRC 14.7%

**A scarce autumn migrant, full written description required by the BBRC.**

| | |
|---|---|
| 1976 | One Tresco 20th & 21st October |
| 1977 | One St Mary's 16th to 18th October |
| 1978 | One Tresco 22nd & 23rd October |
| 1979 | One St Mary's 10th November |
| 1980 | One Tresco 21st to 23rd October |
| 1980 | One St Mary's 28th & 29th October |
| 1981 | One St Mary's 21st October to 4th November |
| 1982 | One St Mary's & St Agnes 25th to 31st October |
| 1983 | One Tresco 21st October |
| 1985 | One Tresco 14th October |
| 1987 | One St Martin's 20th & 21st October |
| 1987 | One St Mary's 23rd & 24th October |
| 1988 | One St Mary's 3rd October |
| 1988 | One trapped St Agnes 28th October to 3rd November |
| 1989 | One St Agnes 16th to 23rd October |
| 1990 | One Tresco 13th October |
| 1990 | One St Mary's 15th October |
| 1990 | One St Agnes 19th October |
| 1990 | Two St Mary's 24th October |
| 1990 | One St Mary's 26th October |
| 1990 | One St Agnes 24th & 25th October |
| 1990 | One St Martin's 1st & 2nd November |

1990 One St Mary's 2nd to 5th November
1993 One Tresco 16th October
1993 One St Agnes 23rd to 25th October
1994 One St Mary's 14th October
1994 One St Martin's 24th October
1996 One St Mary's 23rd October
1997 One St Mary's 29th & 30th September
1998 One St Mary's & Tresco 20th to 23rd October
1998 One St Agnes 5th to 7th October
2000 One St Mary's 1st November   *British Birds* 94: 483
2001 One St Agnes 12th to 17th October   *British Birds* 95: 504
2002 *One St Mary's 20th October   British Birds 95: 668*

Breeds central, southern and northeast Asia to Kamchatka, wintering India and southeast Asia. Polytypic: nominate *hodgsoni* occurs southern Asia from Himalayas east to central China and Japan; *yunnanensis* remainder.

This is one of just a few species which, if they occurred in Scilly and Cornwall during the 19th century, were missed by those otherwise extremely observant Victorian naturalists. Indeed, even by the time of Penhallurick's landmark publication (Penhallurick 1978), there had been just five British records and the first Scillonian record, on Tresco for two days during October 1976, was still under consideration by the BBRC. Thirty-two Olive-backed Pipits arrived in Scilly in 18 of the 24 years until 1999, all during the 43-day period between 29th September and 10th November. The Chart includes all arrival or first-sighting dates and shows an obvious late October concentration. The most in any year was nine, in 1990, and mean length of stay was 2.7 days, in the range 1–16. These 31 individuals represent 14.7% of the 210 records accepted by the BBRC during the period 1958–99.

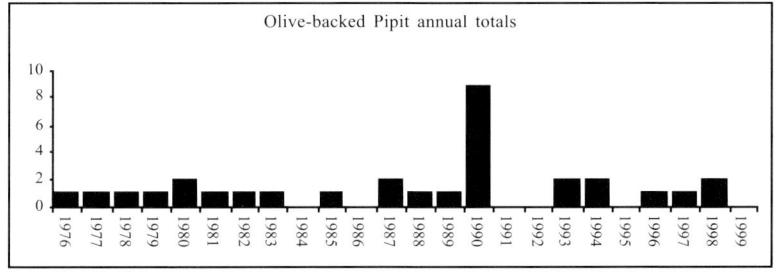

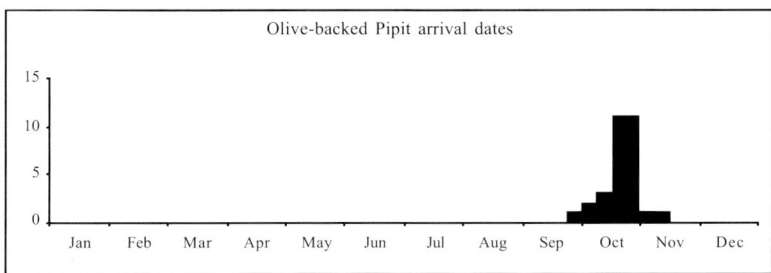

Dymond *et al.* (1989) noted that at least up until 1985 almost all Olive-backed Pipit records originated from locations intensively searched for migrants, e.g. Shetland and Scilly, these two accounting for 46% and 31% respectively of all autumn sightings. Olive-backed Pipit is a long-distance migrant and its presence in western Europe is thought attributable to strong anticyclonic activity over central Asia. And though the precise origin of birds reaching western Europe remains unknown, all breed outside the West Palearctic (Cramp *et al.* 1977–94). The first British or Irish Olive-backed Pipit record was originally thought to involve a bird on Fair Isle on 17th Oct 1964, followed by a second there on 29th September the following year (*British Birds* 60: 161). However, a bird trapped and photographed on Skokholm Island, Pembrokeshire, on 14th April 1948 was later submitted to the BOURC and accepted as the first (*Ibis* 1980: 565; Palmer 2000). One Olive-backed Pipit had been trapped and ringed on Scilly up until the end of 1999 but was not recaptured.

## Tree Pipit *Anthus trivialis* A

**Annual spring and autumn migrant in small numbers, one old breeding record.**

Breeds central and northern Europe and central Asia east to northeast Mongolia and southeast Siberia. Migratory, wintering Africa and Indian subcontinent. Polytypic: nominate *trivialis* occurs Europe and Asia east to Lake Baikal and Caspian Sea; *schlueteri* central Asia east to southwest Siberia; *haringtoni* Himalayas and surrounding region. Upgraded from Green- to Amber-listed in UK 2002: moderate to high (75%) breeding decline over past 25 years (Gregory *et al.* 2002). National 21% increase 1994–99 (Bashford & Noble 2000).

The earliest traceable reference appears to be E H Rodd's mention of two in his collection that were shot at Old Grimsby, Tresco, on 19th September 1868, presumably by Augustus Pechell, who also shot a Tawny *A. campestris* and three Richards's Pipits *A. novaeseelandiae* on Tresco the same day (Rodd 1868e, 1880). Early in the 20th century James Clark and E H Rodd's nephew Francis provided a brief but helpful review of its status in the islands, describing it as occasionally observed during autumn on both St Mary's and Tresco, though twice only on Bryher and once on St Martin's. They further suggested that it may have been frequently overlooked and therefore possibly regular during autumn, and concluded with the information that an apparent adult male was found dead on St Agnes in early June 1902.

Early speculation that Tree Pipit may have bred on St Agnes appears to have been based on the presence of the previously mentioned individual, but in the absence of additional evidence the possibility of it having been just a late spring migrant cannot be discounted, single out-of-range breeding records being always problematical. However, a nest with four eggs found by A W H Robinson near Old Town, St Mary's, during 1914 was later predated, probably by a cat *Felis catus* (*British Birds* 8: 145). Although he considered Tree Pipit common in east Cornwall during the late 19th century, E H Rodd thought it rare in the west of the county and he never heard it singing in the Land's End district (Rodd 1880). Holloway (1996) recorded Tree Pipit as rare throughout Cornwall up until 1900, and by the mid-1940s it was still considered rare in mainland Cornwall as a whole and remained absent from the Land's End peninsula (Ryves & Quick 1946), as indeed it still did by the mid-1970s (Sharrock 1976).

Penhallurick (1978) noted that up until the mid-1970s, spring passage on Scilly normally commenced around mid-April and ended by mid-May, return autumn movement commencing from as early as late July though more usually mid-August, with few present after early October. Spring totals rarely exceeded two to three, with birds not necessarily present daily, whereas autumn daily totals peaked at 30. Taking the data for the period 1990–99, Tree Pipit occurred in all ten years during both periods of the year. Dates involved were surprisingly consistent, most spring arrivals being noted in April up until 21st, though twice in late March, all having moved on before the end of May. All recorded autumn first arrivals fell between 15th and 28th August and in all except one year birds had left between 12th and 30th October, the exception being one in mid-November 1996. Maximum same-island or all-island counts rarely squeezed into double figures and rarely were more than two or three seen to be closely associated. However, as pointed out by Clark and Rodd nearly 100 years ago, this is probably an under-recorded species in Scilly.

All populations migrate, very few individuals wintering in the Mediterranean islands, otherwise all wholly in Africa south of the Sahara, or in India, nominate *trivialis* wintering within both areas. Ringing data show that most Tree Pipits west of a line through central Sweden and southern Italy, plus those from Finland and Russia east to Moscow move south or southwest into the western Mediterranean and Iberia en route to Africa, it being common in Britain on migration. However, those breeding in Britain apparently cross the Bay of Biscay to Portugal, a few of these, or those from further north, moving southwards via Ireland (Cramp *et al.* 1977–94). Fifty-two Tree Pipits had been ringed in Scilly up to the end of 1999, 38 since 1970 and there are no recaptures.

## Pechora Pipit *Anthus gustavi* A BBRC 1.8%

**Extremely rare migrant, full written description required by the BBRC.**

1994   One Borough Farm, Tresco 27th & 28th October   *British Birds* 88: 529

Limited distribution, breeding from northwest Russia east to North Pacific and south to Kamchatka. Migratory, wintering East Indies. Polytypic: nominate *gustavi* occurs northwest Russia; *commandorensis* and *menzbieri* further east.

The single Scillonian record involved a bird at Tresco's Borough Farm during autumn 1994 (*IOSBR* 1994). It was discovered in weedy fields on the 27th October and remained feeding with Meadow Pipits *A. pratensis* in the same area until the following day. Whilst feeding on the ground in low vegetation, it predictably gave only brief views to the assembled crowd, but thankfully spent short periods perched in the open on surrounding hedgerows. It was not heard to call throughout its stay. Slight plumage and structural variation between forms may be detectable in the hand but do not help in this case.

Little is known about the timing of Pechora Pipit migration, but autumn passage is believed to occur from August through to early October, birds arriving back on the breeding grounds during late May or early June (Cramp *et al.* 1977–94). In western Alaska it is recorded as a vagrant during May and June. Given that the entire population is believed to winter in southeast Asia, its presence in Britain during late September and October is difficult to explain with certainty. Dymond *et al.* (1989) analysed all 15 Pechora Pipit records from the period 1958–85, finding that none arrived after mid-October. Combining these with a further 13 records prior to 1958 revealed that 86% of all British records occurred on Shetland or Fair Isle. The Tresco individual was not captured and was not seen to be carrying a ring.

# Meadow Pipit *Anthus pratensis* A

**Spring and autumn migrant and winter visitor, bred until very recently.**

Breeds central and northern West Palearctic including Iceland and adjoining areas of northern Russia and coastal east Greenland. Mainly sedentary in western Europe, migratory Iceland and elsewhere. Polytypic: *whistleri* or 'Hebridean Meadow Pipit' occurs Ireland and western Scotland; nominate *pratensis* remainder of range, including Iceland and Greenland. Some authorities recognise birds from western Ireland as third form *theresea*. Upgraded from Green- to Amber-listed in UK 2002: moderate (43%) breeding decline over past 25 years (Gregory *et al.* 2002). National 7% decline 1994–99 (Bashford & Noble 2000).

Meadow Pipit underwent a marked change of status in Scilly during the 20th century, from that of 'abundant resident' (Clark & Rodd 1906), still 'in all suitable localities' by the late 1930s (*CBWPSAR* 8), to just one to two breeding pairs annually by the late 1990s. Nevertheless, the number of likely pairs formerly involved remains unknown, though from these early accounts we may perhaps safely assume that it was substantial, as indeed was the case on nearby mainland Cornwall at that time. However, by the mid-1940s Ryves & Quick (1946) were confident enough to describe its status as 'still a common breeder', and although Penhallurick (1978) points to the lack of mention of Meadow Pipit by some early to mid-20th-century visiting ornithologists, e.g. Wallis (1923), such accounts were largely unstructured and often tended to ignore abundant species. The truth is perhaps that, regardless of what Ryves and Quick had to say on the subject, as the century progressed Meadow Pipit did in fact become less numerous as a breeding species within the islands, to the point where, although Hilda Quick watched young being fed on St Agnes in 1971, a subsequent search for additional nests 'proved fruitless on all islands' (Penhallurick 1978). Interestingly, a similar breeding decline occurred on Lundy Island in North Devon over much the same timescale, with more than 270 pairs in 1930 decreasing to around 30 by 1965 (Moore 1969).

However, regardless of its breeding status it seems always to have been a regular migrant and sometimes in large numbers, Clark and Rodd making reference to passing large flocks in 1899 and 1904. Penhallurick reviewed Scillonian spring migrant records up until the mid-1970s, quoting first and last dates of 18th March and 28th May respectively, whereas autumn sightings commenced from 11th August, with late migrants becoming indistinguishable from wintering flocks. The same author also noted daily totals of between 100 and 300, but up to an extreme of 1,000 during mid-October 1971.

Bringing the picture up to date, during the ten years 1990–99 most commenced with flocks of ten or fewer about the islands, followed by obvious evidence of spring passage during mid-March, increasing to 50 or so before numbers reduced once more, usually by April or early May. Return migrants were normally in evidence from early to mid-September, as in 1990 when 150 plus were on St Agnes, numbers then building until 400 an hour were thought to be arriving on that island. However, on this occasion, a steady reduction followed, until just 500 were being reported from individual islands. This was then followed by a further, smaller, influx before only a few were noted by the month's end. Subsequently, from November through into the second half of winter, normally only 'small scattered groups' were in evidence about the archipelago.

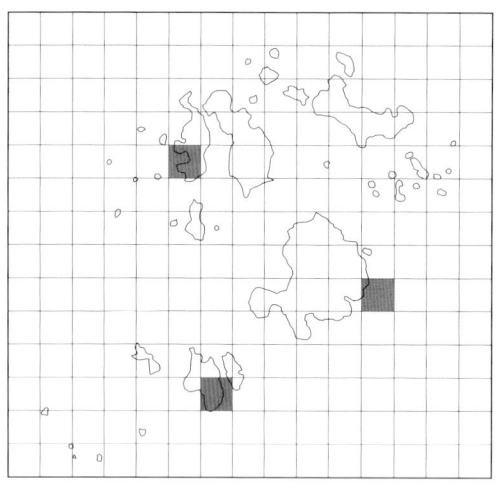

**1-km Meadow Pipit Breeding Distribution – 2000–01 (data Chown & Lock 2002)**

In perhaps a little over half of the years since 1990, a pair, sometimes two, were suspected of breeding, with the occasional summer visitor also apparent. This was confirmed by the 2000 Breeding Bird Atlas (Chown & Lock 2002), which recorded just two to three pairs in three (4.4%) of the 67 surveyed 1-km squares, on St Mary's, St Agnes and Bryher. Some years, as in 1994, any wintering groups appeared to desert the islands during February or March. More than with most species, attempting to gain accurate all-island Meadow Pipit counts are frustrated by the sheer volume of the task involved, especially during large falls, and the possibility exists that numbers have been seriously under-estimated on many occasions. The only reports from the local lighthouses concern two or three 'titlarks' at the Bishop Rock on 20th October 1885, a 'few' there on the night of 21st–22nd October 1908 (Ogilvie-Grant 1910) and 'many' among a large movement of mixed species on 5th–6th November 1909 (Ogilvie-Grant 1911). Obviously, though, these isolated site reports give no idea of the scale of movement involved during peak periods and, interestingly, Penhallurick commented that this was the commonest migrant passerine encountered during sea crossings to and from mainland Cornwall.

As Cramp *et al.* (1977–94) point out, annual northern limits of European wintering are largely dictated by between-year differences in weather conditions, although as far as Britain and Ireland are concerned birds from further north are normally present throughout lowland areas during winter, with much the same holding true for central lowland Europe. However, the majority of Meadow Pipits from northwest Europe and further east move southwest through France as far as Iberia and Morocco (P Lack 1986), birds from Greenland and Iceland mainly moving through Britain and Ireland, where they join other populations heading south. There are few recoveries of British- or Irish-ringed Meadow Pipits south of the Mediterranean (Wernham *et al.* 2002). According to Cramp *et al.* and Gantlett (1998) the more brightly marked *whistleri* from Ireland and western Scotland can be expected to overwinter within their breeding areas, but nonetheless may move during severe winters, in which case some individuals of this form may reach Scilly. Occasionally during autumn on Scilly, pale-grey individuals are encountered which presumably originate from populations east perhaps into western Russia (Cramp *et al.* 1977–94; pers. obs.). An unusually plumaged individual at Watermill, St Mary's, on 12th October 1996 was described as yellow with white wings. Up until the end of 1999, 519 Meadow Pipits had been ringed in Scilly, but the following are the only recaptures.

**Recoveries**

| | | | |
|---|---|---|---|
| AK91195 | Ad St Agnes 28th September 1963 | SH | Las Cabezas de San Juan, Seville, Spain 28th October 1963 |
| F617497 | Ad St Agnes 25th October 1990 | FD | Lezardrieux, Cote-du-Nord, France 18th February 1991 |

Meadow Pipit Ringing Recaptures

## Red-throated Pipit *Anthus cervinus* A BBRC 14.7%

**Scarce migrant, mainly in autumn, full written description required by the BBRC.**

Breeds arctic Eurasia, from northern Norway east to Bering Sea and Kamchatka. Migratory, wintering Africa south of Sahara and India. Monotypic.

This was another passerine species missed by 19th-century ornithologists on Scilly and mainland Cornwall, assuming of course it occurred then, first for the islands being the bird on St Agnes for two days during May 1961. Interestingly, up until the mid-1970s Penhallurick (1978) was able to quote just 15 records, none of which involved mainland Cornwall. During the period 1961–99, there was a total of 53 BBRC-accepted Scillonian records involving 55 birds, seven of which arrived in spring. Earliest spring sighting was 18th April and the latest 19th May, whilst during the second half of the year the earliest was 20th September and the latest an exceptional 12th December, late October being more normal.

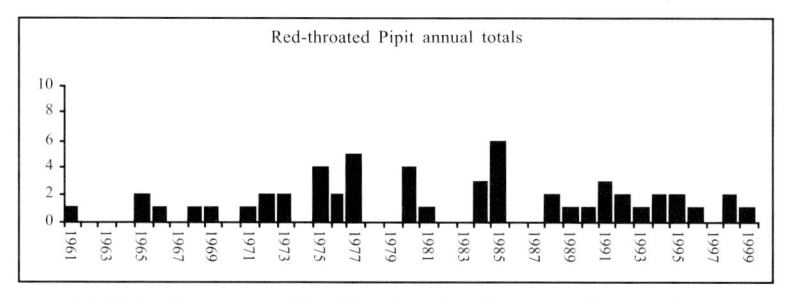

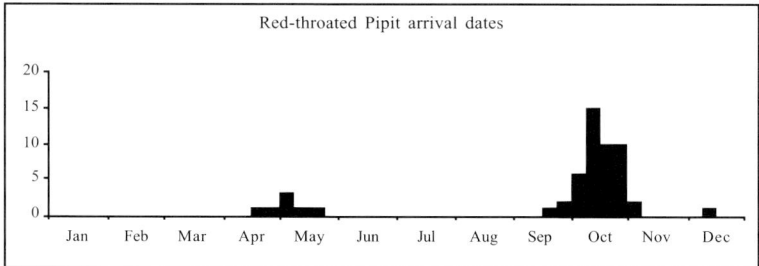

**Red-throated Pipit annual totals**

**Red-throated Pipit arrival dates**

The first of the two Charts shows annual totals up to and including 1999 and the other arrival dates for all but three individuals in 2000, revealing an impressive October concentration plus a clear but far smaller spring peak. However, the apparent increase in numbers of records during the mid-1970s to mid-1980s is difficult to explain. Mean duration of stay for spring migrants was 1.5 days and in autumn 2.8 days. The 55 birds arriving in the islands up until the end of 1999 represent 14.7% of the 374 records accepted by the BBRC for the period 1958–99. Within the breeding grounds, the division between birds wintering in Africa and southeast Asia remains poorly understood, though even the most westerly populations are believed to move mainly east or south during autumn. This presumably accounts for its predominantly East African distribution (Cramp *et al.* 1977–94), though the presence and frequency of so many individuals as far west as Scilly perhaps suggests a rather more complex situation. Cramp *et al.* also point out that it leaves its Russian breeding grounds between late August and early October and suggest the pattern of records in Britain and Ireland fits this known timing. Return spring passage appears to be a more protracted affair, birds passing through the southern West Palearctic from early February through to mid- or late May. Up to and including year 2000 there had been just 12 records from mainland Cornwall (*CBWPSAR* 69). One Red-throated Pipit had been ringed in Scilly up until the end of 1999 but was not recaptured.

# Rock Pipit *Anthus petrosus* A

**A common and obvious breeding resident in many coastal sections of the five inhabited islands and on many smaller islands.**

Primarily coastal, breeds British Isles, western France, Channel Isles, Faeroes and Fennoscandia, including Denmark and northwest Russia. Polytypic: nominate *petrosus* occurs British Isles (except Outer Hebrides and St Kilda) north and northwest France, Channel Isles; *meinertzhageni* or 'Hebridean Rock Pipit' Outer Herbrides; *kleinschmidti* or 'Shetland Rock Pipit' Faeroes, Shetland, Orkney, St Kilda; *littoralis* or 'Scandinavian Rock Pipit' Fennoscandia and northwest Russia. Not normally migratory, northern birds may withdraw south, at least in severe winters. Formerly considered conspecific with Water Pipit *A. spinoletta* and Buff-bellied Pipit *A. rubescens*, as *A. spinoletta*.

Rock Pipit gets scant mention in some of the historical literature, for example E H Rodd (1880) makes no reference to it at all on Scilly. James Clark and Francis Rodd, though, did rather better, describing it as 'an abundant resident, very much in evidence during the summer months'. They went on to say that it nested in 'considerable numbers on nearly all available islands, including Guthers and Round Island' (Clark & Rodd 1906). By comparison, Ryves & Quick (1946) are far less helpful, merely suggesting no change since 1906.

Today, even on inhabited islands, it frequently occupies areas of dry heath well inland, as on Tresco and St Martin's. Sadly, though, little information is available still on numbers of pairs involved, or on productivity. Neither is much known concerning local or larger-scale movements, if any, though it is believed that birds may withdraw from some of the more remote rocks, e.g. Rosevear, during winter to the relative protection of larger islands. Occasional reported counts from various islands appear in the literature but invariably lack qualifying information on extent, duration or method, or even whether they involved pairs, adults or just singing males, thereby greatly reducing their value. Examples of this are a suggested ten pairs for St Mary's in 1980, which seems extremely low, as does four pairs for Gugh in 1986. In comparison, the suggested figure of 80 individuals on Annet on 28th April 1989 is in keeping with our current level of knowledge. More recent and apparently acceptable counts involve three pairs on Rosevear in 1993 and 28 pairs on Samson in 1997, although equally unhelpful of course is the absence during some years of any mention of this species in the published reports.

Assistance on the question of both past abundance and distribution comes in particular from a 1974 English Nature all-island seabird survey (Allen 1974; H P K Robinson 1974b), which confirmed Rock Pipit's presence on 31 islands and a possible presence on ten more. Even more important, however, was the 1974 all-island estimate of 200–250 pairs, plus pair totals for 15 individual islands. On St Agnes, breeding season counts or estimates for five years between 1958 and 1974 gave totals of between 30 (four years) and 52 pairs (one year), suggesting a mean 15-year annual population for that island of 34.4 pairs (H P K Robinson 1974a). It should be noted than Allen's 1974 St Agnes total of 41 pairs differed from the 1974 St Agnes Breeding Bird Survey's total of 52 pairs (H P K Robinson 1974a), though the discrepancy was not explained at the time.

The 2000 Breeding Bird Atlas (Chown & Lock 2002) broadly confirmed Allen's 1974 Rock Pipit findings and showed that within the exposed Western and Northern Isles only precipitous Men-a-Vaur and the unvegetated Maiden Bower apparently lacked birds. The apparent gap in the extreme Eastern Isles had more to do with recording effort than with any real absence, except perhaps for isolated Hanjague. In total, an estimated 366 pairs were recorded, in the likely range 350–380 pairs, with birds present in 56 (83.5%) of the 67 1-km squares surveyed, though breeding was confirmed in only 31 (46.2%) (Table). Based on that assessment, we might be forgiven for thinking that vegetation, or the lack of it, is the key to presence or absence. However, that is clearly not the case, with birds apparently holding territory on Great Creba-wethan, Rosevean and Scilly Rock, all three of which lack any growth above the high-tide line other than lichens, as well as being exposed to the very worst that sea and weather have to offer. Rock Pipits numbers have still to be assessed on the more vegetated and more sheltered Eastern Isles, but they nevertheless appear to hold significantly greater numbers than their more exposed counterparts in the west and north.

However, breeding Rock Pipit density has yet to be fully re-examined anywhere in Scilly, though some areas seem capable of holding quite large numbers, as on Annet, where something in the order of one hundred apparent adults counted during the 2000 Atlas fieldwork suggests a possible density in the order of 2.33 pairs per hectare. On Samson, the same survey suggested at least 30 pairs, giving 0.76 pairs per hectare. The 2000 survey also offers some help with the thorny question of numbers of breeding pairs on St Mary's, proving presence in 11 (78%) of the 14 1-km coastal squares. Participants were asked to score abundance according to a simple scale, results of which suggest a mean of 31 pairs for St Mary's as a whole, in the range 19–43 pairs.

| Island | 1974* | 2000** |
|---|---|---|
| St Mary's | 8 | 31 |
| St Agnes | 41 | 43 |
| Gugh | 11 | |
| Bryher | 25 | 6 |
| St Martin's | | 15 |
| Tresco | | 10 |
| Samson | | 33 |
| Annet | 26 | 100 |
| Tean | | 5 |
| White Is, St Martin's | | 25 |
| St Helen's | | 19 |
| Great Ganilly | | 4 |
| Melledgan | 11 | |
| Rosevear | 2 | |
| Mincarlo | 1 | |
| Illiswilgig | 1 | |
| Scilly Rock | 1 | |
| Gweal | 2 | 8 |
| Samson | 27 | |
| Tean | 10 | |
| Little Innisvouls | 1 | |
| Menawethan | 4 | |
| Arthurs | | 6 |
| Great Ganninic | | 1 |
| Other | | 60 |

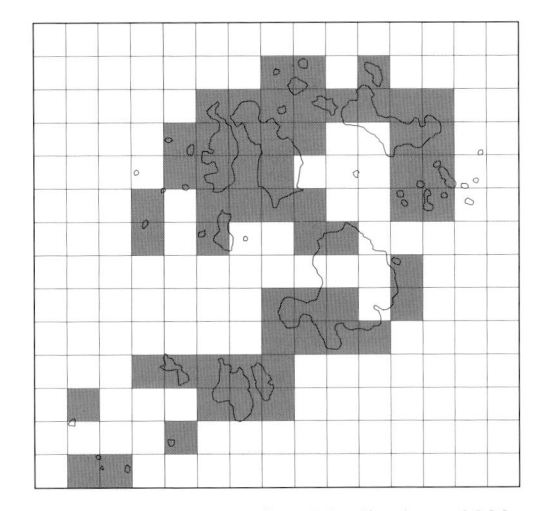

Rock Pipit Pair Counts – Scilly (*Allen 1974, **Chown & Lock 2002)

| Year | Pairs |
|---|---|
| 1958 | 30 |
| 1962 | 30 |
| 1963 | 30 |
| 1964 | 30 |
| 1974 | 52 |

Rock Pipit Pair Counts St Agnes (data for 1958, 62, 63 & 64 SABO records, 1974 data from full count)

1-km Rock Pipit Breeding Distribution – 2000–01 (data Chown & Lock 2002)

The relative lack of small breeding passerines compared with mainland Britain means that Rock Pipits are the Cuckoo's *Cuculus canorus* primary host species in Scilly, approximately 20% of nests found by the author during 1991–99 having been parasitised. In 1969 on Round Island, three out of eight (37%) of nests found contained Cuckoo eggs or young (Beswetherick 1969). On vegetated islands nests are normally well hidden beneath plant debris from previous years, which in turn is often overgrown by the current year's growth, and finding a nest can be quite difficult, even when a bird has just emerged from beneath the observer's feet. On islands with less ground cover, nests are usually concealed in whatever protection is available, e.g. rock crevices, or where Hottentot Fig *Carpobrotus edulis* overhangs a rock or low cliff.

Ringing data suggest that among British birds those in the north, e.g. Orkney, are more inclined to move south in winter, though remaining within Britain, whereas exchanges of Continental birds tend to involve mostly southern Britain and the southern Baltic countries, e.g. Sweden (Wernham *et al.* 2002). Although any of the three forms other than *petrosus* might be expected to reach Scilly during winter, there is little by way of confirmation, though any Baltic individuals presumably involve *littoralis*. One certain record involves a colour-ringed *littoralis* from Sweden being present on St Mary's (see below), but others reported by observers as *littoralis* were at Porth Hellick, St Mary's, in October 1984 and on Tresco during May 1990.

A total of 309 Rock Pipits were ringed in Scilly up until the end of year 2000: 206 prior to 1970 and exactly half that number since. None of these were recovered on Scilly or elsewhere, though a bird colour-ringed in Sweden in July 1991 was on St Mary's during October the same year. In their invaluable 1906

*Zoologist* review of *The Birds of Scilly* Clark and Rodd refer to a bird of 'the Scandinavian form (*A. rupestris*)' shot by a J G Millais on 11th May 1903, though they omit the location. The name *rupestris* is no longer employed but was used by Saunders for 'Scandinavian Rock Pipit' in his 1835–1907 *Manual of British Birds*, as well as in the BOU's 1915 list. According to both Clark & Rodd and W Page (1906) another '*rupestris*' was obtained near Land's End, west Cornwall, some time before 1906.

**Controls**

?     Ad    Onsala Halland, Sweden 11th July 1991      FR   St Mary's 18th October 1991

**Rock Pipit Ringing Recaptures**

# Water Pipit *Anthus spinoletta* A

A scarce, regular but not annual migrant with up to 23 records annually, a full written description is required by the SRP.

Apparent Migrant Water Pipit Records
- 1903   One shot Porth Hellick 17th May   Clark & Rodd 1906
- 1971   One St Agnes 25th October
- 1972   One St Mary's 29th September
- 1974   One St Agnes 26th April
- 1976   One St Agnes 14th September
- 1976   One St Mary's 5th November
- 1977   One Tresco 14th October
- 1977   Up to five Trenoweth, St Mary's 18th to 21st October
- 1977   Three Tresco 20th October
- 1977   One Watermill, St Mary's 24th October
- 1977   One Lower Moors, St Mary's 24th October
- 1977   Two Peninnis Head, St Mary's 25th October
- 1977   One Tresco 25th October
- 1978   One St Agnes Pool 6th April
- 1978   One St Agnes 14th October
- 1980   One Peninnis Head, St Mary's 31st October
- 1981   One St Agnes 9th April
- 1982   One St Agnes 31st October
- 1984   Two Holy Vale, St Mary's 22nd October
- 1984   One Tresco 26th & 27th October
- 1984   One Porth Hellick, St Mary's 28th October
- 1984   One Borough Farm, St Mary's 4th & 5th November
- 1985   One Porth Hellick, St Mary's 26th October
- 1985   One Tresco 28th October
- 1988   One St Agnes 27th April
- 1988   One Lower Moors, St Mary's 25th October
- 1988   One Old Grimsby, Tresco 28th & 29th October
- 1989   c. 7 on Scilly in autumn
- 1990   One Tresco 5th March
- 1990   c. 22 St Mary's & Tresco in autumn, with one remaining at Porth Hellick until 7th January 1991
- 1991   One St Agnes 24th October
- 1993   One St Mary's Camp Site 27th October to 6th November
- 1994   One Troy Town, St Agnes 14th May
- 1996   One Porth Cressa, St Mary's 8th March
- 1997   One Great Pool, Tresco 19th to 28th October
- 1999   One Porthloo Beach, St Mary's 1st to 4th December

Apparent Wintering or Part-wintering Water Pipits
- 1969   Two Porth Hellick, St Mary's 9th February to 23rd March

| | |
|---|---|
| 1977 | One Old Town Beach, St Mary's 28th October to at least 20th December |
| 1983–84 | One November to 12th February |
| 1984–85 | One Little Porth, St Mary's during winter – dates unrecorded |
| 1985–86 | One Little Porth, St Mary's 6th November to 8th April |
| 1986–87 | One Little Porth, St Mary's 2nd November to 4th April |
| 1987–88 | One Little Porth, St Mary's 27th November to 5th April |
| 1988–89 | One Little Porth, St Mary's 31st October to 12th April |

Breeds uplands of southern Eurasia, from Iberia east to Iran, Afghanistan and western China. Mainly migratory with some altitudinal movements, winters south and west as far as Iberia and North Africa. Polytypic: nominate *spinoletta* occurs central southern Europe from Iberia to Balkans and perhaps west Turkey; *coutellii* eastern Turkey and Caucasus to northern Iran; *blackistoni* central Asia from northeast Afghanistan eastwards. Formerly treated as conspecific with Rock *A. petrosus* and Buff-bellied Pipits *A. rubescens*, as *A. spinoletta* (BOURC 1986).

Although only officially split from Rock and Buff-bellied Pipits in April 1986, first record for the islands involved one shot by Clark (presumably James Clark), at Porth Hellick, St Mary's, on 17th May 1903 (Clark & Rodd 1906). There was subsequently a gap of 63 years before it was next recorded, though prior to the split it is unclear if all records of what was then a subspecies would have been reported to the Scilly Records Panel. In summary, a total of up to 80 individuals were recorded in twenty of the 31 years 1969–99. Of those records where the island involved is given, 23 occurred on St Mary's, eight on Tresco and ten on St Agnes, with none on St Martin's or Bryher. The Chart shows all recorded 20th-century arrival or first sighting dates and there is a pronounced late October peak, with no corresponding spring concentration, which very much fits the national picture. Disregarding eight apparent wintering or part-wintering records, mean recorded length of stay for migrants was one day during spring and two days during autumn, or 1.8 days overall; the mean wintering period was 110 days, in the range 43–164.

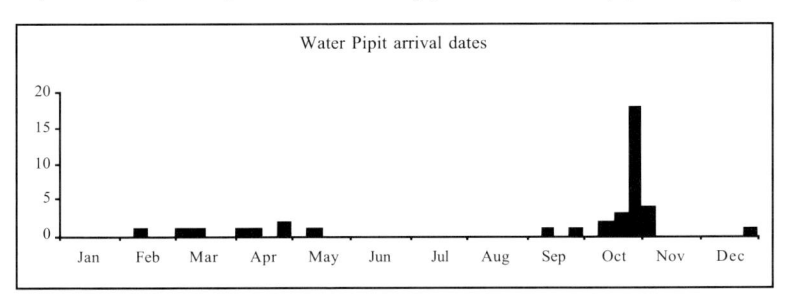

Although *spinoletta* populations from central southern Europe move north and west in winter as far as the Low Countries, few reach the coasts, yet many from further east are long-distance migrants, some even reaching Iberia. Interestingly, according to Cramp *et al.* (1977–94) there are many examples of between-year site faithfulness for wintering *spinoletta*. Worthy of note is what was believed to be the same individual frequenting the Little Porth area of St Mary's for the six successive winters 1983–84 to 1988–89, though precise dates are unavailable for 1984–85 (*IOSBR*). The similarity in dates involved for four of these winters was obvious, though the bird was not individually identifiable, or if so this is not recorded. There are few, if any, records of birds from the two more eastern forms *coutellii* and *blackistoni* reaching western Europe during winter. For an authoritative explanation of the reasoning behind the separation of Water, Rock and Buff-bellied Pipits, see Knox (1988). No pipits identified as this species were trapped and ringed on Scilly up until the end of 1999.

## Buff-bellied Pipit *Anthus rubescens* A BBRC 66.6%

**Very rare migrant with just two records, full written description required by the BBRC.**

1988   One St Mary's 9th to 19th October   *British Birds* 82: 130, 82: 539
1996   One (first-year) various islands 30th September to 28th October   *British Birds* 90: 494

Mainly Nearctic species, also breeds Greenland and northeast Asia. Polytypic: nominate *rubescens* or

## Birds of the Isles of Scilly

'American Buff-bellied Pipit' occurs North America east to western Greenland and northeast Siberia south to Baikal area and east to Sea of Okhotsk; *japonicus*, or 'Siberian Buff-bellied Pipit', eastern Siberia south of *rubescens*. North American populations winter USA and south to Guatemala. Formerly treated as conspecific with Rock Pipit *A. petrosus* and Water Pipit *A. spinoletta*, as *Anthus spinoletta* (BOURC 1968).

Scilly's first and Britain and Ireland's fifth involved an interesting 'plain-backed' pipit seen feeding among Meadow Pipits *A. pratensis* in the Salakee area of St Mary's mid-morning on 9th October 1988, it being eventually identified as this species (Heard 1988). The bird remained in the same general area but was not seen after the 19th. However, the second record for the islands (Britain and Ireland's 6th Buff-bellied Pipit and Scilly's 9th pipit species for the year) proved far more active, being first found at Periglis on St Agnes on 30th September 1996, where it remained until 3rd October. On 7th it was refound at Tresco's Borough Farm where it remained until 13th, following which it was rediscovered at Borough Farm's namesake on St Mary's on 23rd October, and then rediscovered once again, this time in the Maypole–Watermill area of St Mary's from 26th to 28th October (Holt 1996).

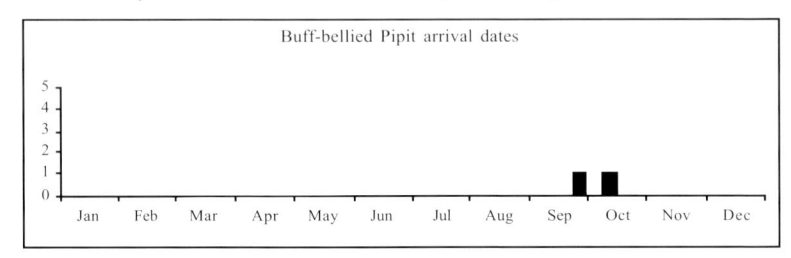

[Chart: Buff-bellied Pipit arrival dates]

Birds arriving in Britain are expected to be *rubescens*, as indeed were the two Scillonian individuals. There are no spring records. However, the more boldly marked and darker *japonicus* has occurred at least once in Europe. It has a similar plumage and call but is darker and has pinkish legs and feet and the possibility of this form must be borne in mind when considering any Buff-bellied Pipit encountered, especially in Scilly. The earliest record apparently involved one obtained on St Kilda in 1910, and prior to the 1988 Scillonian individual one was in Co. Wicklow, Ireland, in 1967 and before that on Fair Isle in 1953. There are also reports from other European countries, including Iceland, Germany and Italy. At least one Italian individual was identified as *japonicus* (Snow & Perrins 1998). Neither of these two birds was trapped and neither was seen to be carrying a ring.

# Yellow Wagtail *Motacilla flava* A

Increasingly scarce migrant as Yellow Wagtail with fewer records of some of the more distinctive European forms, notably *flava*. It has bred at least once.

Breeds throughout Eurasia plus northwest and northeast Africa and extreme northwest North America. Migratory, wintering Africa south of Sahara, India and southeast Asia. Polytypic with extremely complex racial structure, details of which vary between authorities, but general agreement on several distinct groups or sub-groups: *lutea* group – *flavissima* or Yellow Wagtail occurs Britain and coastal continental northwest Europe; *lutea* or 'Yellow-headed Wagtail' Volga River east to Kazakhstan; *flava* group – nominate *flava* or 'Blue-headed Wagtail' continental Europe from France east to Urals and north to Sweden and European Russia; *iberiae* or 'Spanish Wagtail' southwest France, Iberia and northwest Africa; *feldegg* sub-group (treated by some authorities as full species) – *feldegg* or 'Black-headed Wagtail' Yugoslavia east to Afghanistan and south to Iraq; *thunbergi* sub-group – *thunbergi* or 'Grey-headed Wagtail' Norway east to northern Siberia. Additional forms south and east. Upgraded from Green- to Amber-listed in UK 2002: moderate (36%) breeding decline over past 25 years (Gregory *et al.* 2002). National 29% decline 1994–99 (Bashford & Noble 2000), BTO Waterways Bird Survey showed 81% decline 1975–98 (Marchant & Beaven 2000).

First mention of this species on Scilly appears to be E H Rodd's 1868 *Zoologist* letter recording that a large number arrived immediately prior to 5th September that year (Rodd 1868c). This was followed closely by an anonymous letter to the same journal the following year entitled *Ray's Wagtail in Scilly* (Anon 1869), the writer describing large numbers arriving during August that year. Unusually for James Clark and Francis Rodd they had little to say on this species, noting merely that it occurred uncertainly on passage, although in some autumns, as in 1900, 1903 and 1904, it could be 'fairly plentiful' (Clark & Rodd 1906). The only other early reference concerns a report of birds present in the islands on 16th May 1911 (Ogilvie-Grant 1912c).

Penhallurick (1978) described Yellow Wagtail as an occasional spring migrant on the Cornish mainland from mid-April through to mid-May, the earliest sighting up until then being 21st March. Autumn passage was more substantial and Penhallurick thought it might even have increased during the 25 years prior to the mid-1970s. Few arrived in Cornwall before 20th August, numbers peaking during early to mid-September with few evident after mid-October. Largest numbers recorded in Cornwall appear to be up to 200 observed going to roost on various occasions. Nonetheless, it seems always to have been a rare breeder in Cornwall, at the rate of one to two pairs annually, Penhallurick knowing of no nests after 1965.

Scilly too experiences a small spring passage, though with seldom more than ten birds involved at any one site and in some years no more than that number throughout the whole early period. The majority of 'Blue-headed Wagtail' sightings also occur during this period. Occasional summer, rather than summering, records give way to early returning migrants from late August or early September, numbers building until ten or more are to be seen at suitable sites. But whilst single-day, all-island counts of that same magnitude or less are achieved, occasional concentrations of up to 30 are on recent record, though single-day all-island totals of 20–30 are more normal. However, 55 on St Mary's on 20th September 1996 was exceptional. Small roosting flocks in the Porth Hellick or Lower Moors reedbeds on St Mary's also seem to be a quite regular feature.

There is a single reported 1966 St Agnes breeding record involving a *flavissima* male and an apparent *flava* female (*CBWPSAR* 36) but, unfortunately, details of this event are not provided, although Penhallurick (1978) suggested that the attempt was successful. What makes this record equally interesting, however, is the presence of a similar breeding pair of *flavissima* male and *flava* female at Marazion Marsh in nearby west Cornwall during the three years 1963–65. The St Agnes breeding record was the last on record for either Cornwall or Scilly. All West Palearctic Yellow Wagtail populations winter in Africa and reach both wintering and summering areas via a broad-front movement, which is not hindered by short to moderate sea crossings (Cramp *et al.* 1977–94). Western European populations move west-southwest to south-southwest during autumn (Wernham *et al.* 2002), though British *flavissima* initially move south into France. Further east, however, the direction of travel quickly orientates towards the south, presumably helping to explain the absence of British *lutea* records. The presence of at least some spring *flava* individuals could perhaps be attributable to overshooting French birds. Just eleven Yellow Wagtails were ringed in Scilly up until the end of 1999 and there are no recaptures. As of January 2002, the BOURC were debating *Motacilla* relationships, with the possibility that some subspecies occurring in Britain may warrant upgrading to full species (BOURC 2002a).

## 'Blue-headed Wagtail' *M. f. flava*

Referring to it under its old name of 'Grey-headed Wagtail', E H Rodd (1880) pointed out that this form was occasionally observed on mainland Cornwall during spring, together with *flavissima*, though he considered it a rarity throughout the county. According to James Clark and Francis Rodd, Augustus Pechell shot two at an unnamed location in Scilly during September 1871, though they provided no additional information. The Chart shows annual totals since what seems to be the first 20th-century record for the islands, in 1950. However, birds of this form probably occurred in other years as Yellow Wagtail often gets no mention at all in early annual reports, whilst in other years references to forms other than *flavissima*

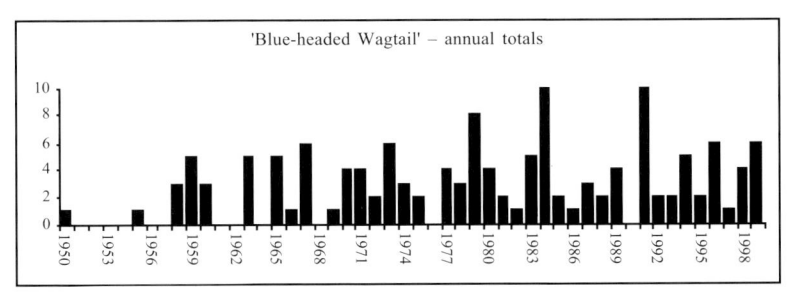

being present lack necessary details. It is possible that the suggestion of recent increased annual numbers apparent in the Chart merely reflects increased observer coverage, in addition to which, as with other non-*flavissima* forms, there is a probable bias towards the identification of spring individuals.

## 'Grey-headed Wagtail'     *M. f. thunbergi*

   1871   One Scilly   Tresco Abbey records; Penhallurick 1978
   1959   One (male) St Agnes 15th May
   1971   One (female) Tresco 7th October
   1980   One (male) this form or *cinerocapilla* Rosehill, St Mary's 13th October
   1982   One St Mary's 7th May
   1983   One (male) this form or *thunbergi* St Mary's 28th April
   1984   One (male) St Mary's 13th to 18th October
   1986   One (male) St Mary's 4th May
   1990   One St Agnes, St Mary's and Bryher 4th to 7th May
   1990   One St Agnes 22nd May
   1991   One Bryher 19th to 21st September
   1994   One St Mary's 5th & 6th October
   1996   One Great Pool, Tresco 3rd & 4th July
   1997   Two (male & female) St Martin's 16th May
   1999   One Tresco 28th May

Interestingly, A A Dorrien-Smith included this form in his *List of Birds Recorded at Tresco Abbey* (T A Dorrien-Smith 1951), presumably on the strength of the 1871 individual. Up until the end of 1999 there were fourteen 20th-century records involving 15 individuals, nine of which occurred in spring (Table). The longest any bird remained was six days and nine were present for one day only. The sole multiple arrival involved a male and female on St Martin's on 16th May 1997. On at least two occasions, observers were unable to discount the possibility that a similar *M. flava* form may have been involved.

## 'Ashy-headed Wagtail'     *M. f. cinereocapilla*

   1967   One (male) this form or *iberiae* St Agnes 11th to 13th May
   1977   One Tresco 17th April
   1984   One (male) Lower Moors, St Mary's 8th June

The Table shows all three recorded arrivals, one of which could have been *iberiae*. All three were in spring, two staying just one day.

## 'Spanish Wagtail'     *M. f. iberiae*

   1981   One (male) St Agnes 9th & 10th May

The sole recorded arrival involved a male on St Agnes for two days during May 1981, though one of the presumed *cinereocapilla* could have been this form.

## ['Black-headed Wagtail'     *M. f. feldegg*]

   [1976   One (immature) Tresco 12th October]
   [1978   One (male) Tresco 26th June]

Descriptions of two individuals, on Tresco in 1976 and 1978, were submitted to the BBRC, that for 1976 being rejected (*British Birds* 70: 451) though the 1978 individual was accepted (*British Birds* 73: 518, 88: 530). However, this form was removed from the British List by the BOURC in 1984 amidst fears that some dark-headed *thunbergi* may give rise to confusion between the two forms (BOURC 1993b), the 1978 record was thus automatically rejected. However, in 1993 the BOURC reinstated *feldegg* to category A on the strength of previous singles on Fair Isle, Shetland, in May 1970 and at Skateraw, Lothian, in April 1984 (BOURC 1993b). Inexplicably, the 1978 record does not appear among the list of previously accepted sightings quoted by the BOURC, although one on the nearby Cornish mainland on June 5th that same year does. The 1978 individual therefore appears to remain rejected.

## ['Yellow-headed Wagtail'] *M. f. lutea*]

[1997 One Tresco 18th to 21st April]

An adult male Yellow Wagtail seen well on Simpson's Field, Tresco, and nearby for four days during mid-April 1997 was believed by observers to have been this form. However, the description was rejected by the BBRC (*IOSBR* 1997; Hathway *et al.* 1997; *British Birds* 92: 608). The record was a potential 'first' for Britain and Ireland and would thus have been additionally liable to scrutiny by the BOURC.

## Citrine Wagtail *Motacilla citreola* A BBRC 11.4%

Rare autumn migrant, full written description required by the BBRC.

| | | |
|---|---|---|
| 1978 | One (first-year) St Agnes 12th October | *British Birds* 90: 494 |
| 1981 | One (first-year) St Mary's 25th & 26th September | *British Birds* 75: 516 |
| 1986 | One (first-year) St Mary's 31st August to 4th September | *British Birds* 81: 578 |
| 1989 | One (first-year) Tresco & Bryher 3rd to 6th September | *British Birds* 83: 475, 479 |
| 1989 | One (first-year) Tresco 2nd to 5th October | *British Birds* 83: 475, 479 |
| 1992 | One (first-year) St Mary's 13th to 16th September | *British Birds* 86: 499, 505 |
| 1993 | One (first-year) Tresco 19th to 21st August | *British Birds* 87: 543 |
| 1995 | One (first-year) Tresco 27th & 28th August | *British Birds* 89: 513, 587 |
| 1995 | One (first-year) Tresco 12th to 15th September | *British Birds* 89: 513, 587 |
| 1996 | One (first-year) Tresco 17th to 20th August | *British Birds* 90: 494 |
| 1996 | One (first-year) St Mary's 29th August to 3rd September | *British Birds* 90: 494 |
| 1996 | One (first-year) St Mary's 1st to 3rd September | *British Birds* 90: 494 |
| 1997 | One (first-year) St Mary's & St Agnes 4th to 8th September | *British Birds* 91: 500 |
| 1999 | One (first-year) Peninnis, St Mary's 26th September & 3rd October | *British Birds* 93: 548 |
| 2002 | One (first-year) Tresco & St Martin's 2nd to 7th October | *British Birds* 95: 604 |

Breeds central Asia, from north of Black Sea to eastern Mongolia and south to Himalayas. Migratory, wintering Indian subcontinent and southeast Asia. Polytypic: *werae* occurs central European Russia east to Altai; nominate *citreola* northern Russia east to Lake Baikal and south to Mongolia; *calcarata* south and east.

A total of 14 Citrine Wagtails arrived in Scilly in 10 of the 22 years since the first was recorded in 1978, all being aged as first-years. The Chart includes all arrival dates, the earliest of which was 17th August and the latest 12th October, which was also the latest any bird was present. Average length of stay was 3.9 days, in the range one to eight days. The Chart compares well with the findings of Dymond *et al.* (1989), who examined 37 British and Irish records for the 28-year period 1958–85, though Scillonian arrivals were perhaps a week or so behind the national average. These 14 arrivals represent 11.4% of all records accepted by the BBRC during the period 1958–99. Seven birds arrived on St Mary's, six on Tresco and just one on St Agnes. More recently, one was on various islands during autumn 2002.

The closest regular wintering area to Britain is perhaps southern Iran, though it is a scarce winter visitor to the nearby Arabian Peninsula (Cramp *et al.* 1977–94). Little information is available on the timing of migration and apparently even less on post-fledging dispersal, although departure from Russian

Citrine Wagtail arrival dates

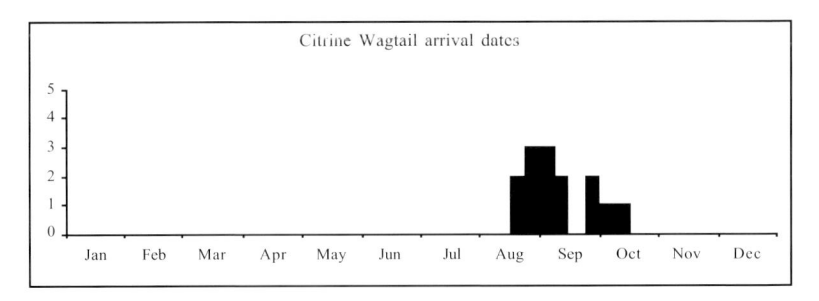

breeding grounds is thought to commence from early September. Nevertheless, the absence of any adults among the Scillonian records is noteworthy. Note, too, that there are recent breeding records from Finland and the former Czechoslovakia, at least. No British records have been identified racially but they seem likely to have involved either the nominate *citreola* or *werae*. Millington (*Birding World* 4: 205–206) drew attention to the known presence in Europe of a small number of hybrid Citrine x Yellow Wagtail *M. flava* individuals and quite obviously this possibility requires consideration when examining any potential Citrine Wagtail, in Scilly as elsewhere. No Citrine Wagtails have been trapped and ringed in Scilly.

# Grey Wagtail *Motacilla cinerea* A

**Annual migrant and winter visitor in small numbers.**

Breeds western and southern Europe and central Asia. Western and most southern populations sedentary or dispersive, migratory in north and east, wintering within southern half of range and south into Africa, Arabia, India and southeast Asia. Polytypic: nominate *cinerea* occurs northwest Africa and Europe east to Iran; *canariensis* Canary Islands; *schmitzi* Madeira; *patriciae* Azores; *robusta* eastern Asia from Kamchatka south to eastern China and Japan; *melanope* remainder of middle Asia. Upgraded from Green- to Amber-listed in UK 2002: moderate population decline over past 25 years (Gregory *et al.* 2002). National 40% increase 1994–99 (Bashford & Noble 2000), BTO Waterways Bird Survey showed 42% decline 1975–2000.

E H Rodd's only comment referred to Grey Wagtail's status in Cornwall generally, suggesting that it was common in winter and that a few pairs bred (Rodd 1880). Therefore, first specific reference to Scilly comes from James Clark and E H Rodd's nephew Francis, who at the start of the 20th century described it as a regular autumn visitor to the islands (Clark & Rodd 1906). These two also pointed out that sometimes, as in October 1903, 'large flocks' were involved, though sadly they failed to explain just how many individuals might have been involved. They concluded with the statement that although it had formerly been regarded as a purely autumn migrant, in 1903 it was allegedly common in the Hugh Town area of St Mary's from 10th to 18th April.

Penhallurick (1978) made the point that up until that time regular spring passage had still to be proved, birds appearing on the then mostly watched St Agnes during late March being possibly nothing more than departing wintering individuals from elsewhere in the islands. Up until the mid-1970s, the earliest autumn appearance was 6th August with main passage apparent from late September through to mid-October. Even so, few individuals were recorded annually, seven on St Mary's on the same day in mid-September and five on St Agnes during October being maximum counts. Bringing the situation up to date, during the ten years from 1990 it was recorded in all years but only once in spring outside the normal end-of-winter period. This last involved a bird at Porth Hellick, St Mary's, on 5th May 1991, wintering birds – usually two to three each on the five main islands – having departed in all years by 31st March. First autumn arrival dates were surprisingly concentrated, within the 14-day period 24th August to 6th September, all-island estimates peaking at around 25 during mid-October, although the majority moved on by the month's end. Often none were apparent during the early winter period though the extent to which this may reflect lack of observer coverage remains unclear.

As might be expected, Grey Wagtails often frequent freshwater areas such as Higher and Lower Moors on St Mary's or the Tresco pools, but their characteristic call can nevertheless often be heard as they fly overheard, even in Hugh Town. Whilst it seems clear that populations from central-western Europe undertake a somewhat random, relatively short-distance autumn or winter dispersal, most movements over 200 km are apparently directed towards the southwest, as far as Iberia, Italy or North Africa (Cramp *et al.* 1977–94). Cramp *et al.* also draw attention to a limited southward movement by British and Irish birds, though few cross the English Channel (Wernham *et al.* 2002) and movement appears largely synchronised around the mid-September period – somewhat later than Scillonian arrivals. Gantlett (1998) drew attention to the possibility of the slightly smaller Asian *melanope* occurring in Britain. Five Grey Wagtails had been ringed in the islands up until the end of 1999, all after 1970, and there were no recaptures.

# Pied/White Wagtail *Motacilla alba* A

Annual spring and autumn migrant in small to moderate numbers, most involved are White Wagtails. Allegedly bred in some numbers during the 19th century (though the form involved is not stated) and less frequently thereafter; a pair of White Wagtails bred in 1975 but it is now largely absent as a breeding species.

Breeds Eurasia, from extreme eastern Greenland, Iceland, Britain, Ireland, France and Iberia east to Bering Strait and extreme western Alaska. Northern and eastern populations migratory, those in the south and west largely sedentary, winters south into Africa north of equator, Arabian Peninsula, India and southeast Asia. Polytypic: nominate *alba* or White Wagtail occurs Greenland, Iceland, Faeroes, continental Europe and Asia Minor; *yarrellii* or Pied Wagtail Britain, Ireland adjacent coasts of western continental Europe; *dukhunensis* southeast Russia and central Siberia east to Altai mountains and south to Iran; at least ten additional White Wagtail forms further east and south. National 18% Pied Wagtail increase 1994–99 (Bashford & Noble 2000), BTO Waterways Bird Survey showed 48% decline 1975–2000.

Nineteenth-century accounts are limited to E H Rodd's comment that it occurred in Scilly during spring and autumn and his nephew Francis's observation that there seemed to be more 'Wagtails' than normal during early January 1865, though this last remark lacked explanation. At the turn of the century, Francis and co-author James Clark thought it common year-round with large flocks arriving during autumn, noting too that it nested on all the larger islands (Clark & Rodd 1906).

Penhallurick's (1978) summary recorded that most identifiable autumn birds were White Wagtails and further suggested that perhaps most of the remainder were of this form, though certainly nowadays a marked proportion of Pied also move through. Penhallurick also found that autumn numbers peaked during late August or early September, the highest count up until the mid-1970s being 1,130 on St Agnes during late August 1960. The same author quoted extreme autumn dates of 5th August and 5th November. As with Yellow Wagtail *M. flava*, spring passage was less pronounced, one to three between 16th March and 24th May being normal, but up to a maximum of 20, and, as in autumn, White's predominate.

Broadly speaking, that situation persists to the present day, though with autumn single-site counts of up to 60 or more, e.g. at Porth Hellick Down on 16th September, and the occasional maximum single-island count of up to 100, as on St Agnes in September 1995. White's predominate during early to mid-autumn but by October the proportion can be nearly equal, though with fewer birds involved overall by that time; perhaps 20% of autumn 1999 records involved Pieds. A small number of Pieds, perhaps less than five in total, were often present throughout the winter period. During the early period, 60 on Tresco on 17th March 1998 was exceptional and 70 in the Normandy area of St Mary's on 9th March the following year was by far the greatest spring count recorded. Referring to Clark and Rodd's suggestion of regular breeding on all islands during the 19th century, Penhallurick (1978) thought this may have been pure fantasy and certainly no acceptable breeding description is now available. However, Penhallurick also drew attention to the island

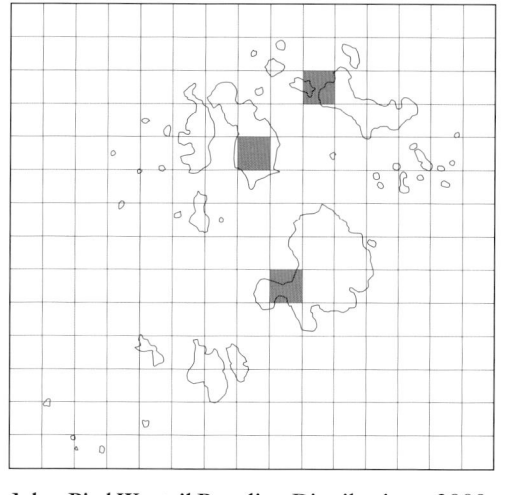

1-km Pied Wagtail Breeding Distribution – 2000–01 (data Chown & Lock 2002)

phenomenon of Pied Wagtail breeding fluctuations, as on Lundy Island, Devon, which provided an excellent example of 'sporadic nesting interspersed with short periods of regular breeding'. Therefore, it is important to note that following the successful pair of Tresco White Wagtails in 1975, at least five pairs of Pieds bred on St Mary's and one on St Agnes during 1980. These were followed by at least one successful pair on St Mary's in 1998 and one on Tresco in 1999 (*IOSBR* 1980, 1998, 1999). The 2000 Breeding Bird Atlas located two breeding pairs plus one individual in three 1-km squares, on St Mary's, Tresco and St Martin's, though breeding was confirmed only in the first two. Breeding occurred again on both islands in 2001, this time involving White Wagtails (Chown & Lock 2002).

Although a few White Wagtails winter within southern Europe, none apparently remain in Scilly, most originating from Iceland (Wernham *et al.* 2002), and although many Pied Wagtails from northern Britain winter in Ireland and southern Britain, many also move on south as far as southern France and Iberia (Cramp *et al.* 1977–94; Wernham *et al.* 2002). The possibility of the slightly paler and whiter-winged *dukhunensis* from southeast Russia and central Siberia occurring in the islands should be kept in mind, southward and perhaps weather-related movements of this form continuing well into October or even November (Cramp *et al.* 1977–94).

## Waxwing (Bohemian Waxwing) *Bombycilla garrulus* A

**Scarce migrant or winter visitor, full written description required by the SRP.**

Pre-1849  One (shot or found dead) Scilly   Clark & Rodd 1906
1937   One presumably Tresco 2nd March (shot)   Penhallurick 1978
1946   Several Tresco 14th November for remainder of year
1947   Several Tresco 25th to 28th February
1949   One Tresco Abbey Gardens 7th to 9th January
1963   Four St Martin's 15th November
1963   One St Mary's & St Agnes 16th & 17th November
1965   Up to four Tresco, St Agnes, St Mary's 2nd to 5th November
1965   Few St Martin's 5th November
1965   Small party Tresco 23rd November
1967   One Tresco 2nd & 9th December
1970   One St Agnes 7th November
1971   One St Mary's 25th November
1974   One St Mary's 9th October
1975   One St Agnes 5th November
1978   One Hugh Town, St Mary's 23rd December
1989   Four Tresco 16th February
1990   Two St Martin's, St Agnes & St Mary's 31st October to 3rd November
1996   One Hugh Town, St Mary's 23rd to 25th April

Breeds northern Eurasia, from Fennoscandia to Kamchatka plus northwest North America. Partial migrant, more so in north, irruptive some years. In West Palearctic winters regularly south to Black Sea and west to Low Countries and eastern France. Polytypic: nominate *garrulus* occurs Fennoscandia to western Siberia; *centralasiae* further east to Kamchatka; *pallidiceps* North America.

The sole early mention of Waxwing in Scilly is James Clark and Francis Rodd's reference to a watercolour painting of a bird killed on Scilly some time prior to 1849 (Clark & Rodd 1906). This and other paintings by Frances Isabella Smith, sister of Augustus Smith, are contained in a book in Tresco Abbey. Interestingly, winter 1849–50 witnessed a massive Waxwing invasion into Britain, at least three of which reached Cornwall (Penhallurick 1978), though the alleged timing of the Tresco acquisition apparently rules out this particular invasion as the source of that individual.

Penhallurick (1978) mentioned one that, according to the Tresco Abbey records, was shot on that island in 1937, the mounted skin being retained in the Abbey collection. Waxwings arrived in Scilly in 15 (24%) of the 63 years from 1937 to 1999, involving at least 40 individuals. In determining this figure, references in the records to 'a few', or 'several' were taken to imply at least four, the longest interval between arrivals being the 14 years 1949–63. The Chart incorporates all 20th-century arrival dates and shows a fairly obvious late autumn peak followed by single casual arrivals through to mid-spring. Interestingly, of the five main islands none were recorded on Bryher, whilst on mainland Cornwall the pattern of arrivals and arrival years was broadly similar to Scilly. The winters of 1946–47 (Gibb 1948) and 1965–66 saw unusually large numbers reaching Britain and certainly in the latter case this is clearly reflected in numbers recorded within the islands. The 1996 individual remained the latest of any recorded in Scilly and was probably present for a few days beforehand, the owner of the garden mistaking it for a Jay *Garrulus glandarius* and therefore not bothering to report its presence; this same person failing to appreciate that Jay is even more of a rarity in Scilly than Waxwing. The possibility of the slightly paler Nearctic *pallidiceps* reaching the islands during autumn should be kept in mind (Gantlett 1989), or even of the closely similar Nearctic Cedar Waxwing *B. cedrorum* doing so. The pattern of Scillonian arrivals very much fits the national situation. No Waxwings have been trapped and ringed in Scilly.

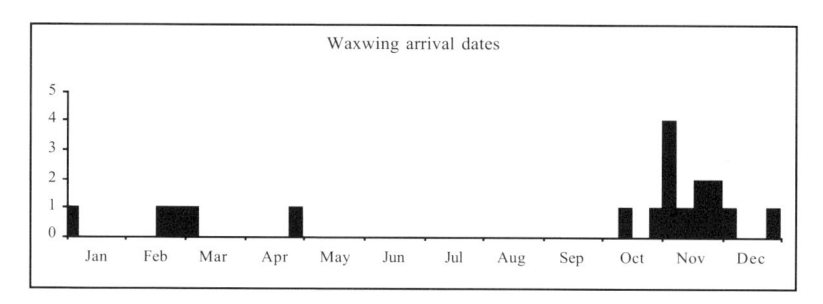

# Wren (Winter Wren) *Troglodytes troglodytes* A

Most abundant and widely distributed breeding landbird, including on most uninhabited islands, it is also a probable migrant and winter visitor.

Breeds Europe, North Africa, eastern and central-southern Asia and North America. In Western Palearctic, from near tree limit southwards to Iberia, North Africa, east to Turkey and Caspian Sea. Extreme northern populations migratory or partially so. Polytypic with complex racial structure: nominate *troglodytes* occurs continental Europe from Fennoscandia and Ural Mountains south to Iberia and North Africa and east to Greece; *indigenus* Britain and Ireland northwards to Orkneys and Inner Hebrides; distinct forms Fair Isle, St Kilda, Outer Hebrides, Shetland, Faeroes and Iceland with 30 or more additional forms elsewhere. National 17% increase 1994–99 (Bashford & Noble 2000).

Very obvious and confiding, often surprising visitors to the islands by its approachability. It is perhaps only absent from some exposed western and northern islands, e.g. Rosevean, or Maiden Bower, probably withdrawing from smaller islands during winter. Coastal pairs spend a considerable amount of time foraging within boulder beaches and on some islands, e.g. Annet; it consequently exists in close proximity to breeding Storm Petrels *Hydrobates pelagicus*. Clark & Rodd (1906) described it as abundant and much in evidence on 'almost every island', including Mincarlo and Castle Bryher. But it has evidently been present far longer as Wren bone remains were tentatively identified among other items removed from prehistoric excavations on Nornour in the Eastern Isles (Turk 1984b).

Annual BTO CBC pair-totals for the 16 hectare Lunnon Farm study plot for the eight years 1991–98 varied in the range 33–66 (Table), at an average of 48, or 3 pairs per hectare. Therefore, assuming all available habitat on the plot was suitable, which appeared to be the case, average territory size was about 0.33 of a hectare, in the range 0.24 to 0.48. These figures are consistent with, but slight lower than territory sizes given by Cramp *et al.* (1977–94) for 'man-modified' habitats in southern England, e.g. 0.37–0.85 for Oxfordshire and 0.48–1.6 for Cambridgeshire. Interestingly, however, Cody & Cody (in Cramp *et al.* 1977–94) quote comparably low territory size for island races, giving 0.37 for *hebridensis* (n = 4), 0.20 for *zetlandicus* (n = 6), and 0.23 for *islandicus* (n = 4), all of which presumably lack the relatively lush habitats provided by Scilly.

As with other numerous Scillonian breeding passerines, e.g. Song Thrush *Turdus philomelos*, or Blackbird *Turdus merula*, Wrens are widely distributed in available habitats: through farmland, reed-scrub, woodland, coastal heath and even seabird islands, to what in Scilly passes for urban development. Assuming Lunnon Farm densities are broadly representative, by extrapolating the plot's average Wren CBC data in combination with known land areas, but excluding a few unvegetated islands, we might perhaps anticipate an all-island average of 4,763 pairs, extremes ranging between 3,275 and 6,550 pairs. However, it cannot be overemphasised that these figures are based on conjecture and much additional work is still required.

In particular, this expectation was not borne out by the more recent all-island 2000 Breeding Bird Atlas (Chown & Lock 2002), which recorded up to 943 pairs in 55 (82%) of the 67 1-km squares surveyed. However, the survey also highlighted known weakness in the concept of ascertaining population size using this type of survey, which relies heavily upon 'guesstimates' and which by necessity employs some fieldworkers inexperienced in this type of evaluation. Thus the authors of the report thought a figure in the range 1,650–3,300 pairs far more likely, based on an estimated 100–200 pairs per km$^2$ (Chown & Lock 2002). If true, this exceeds average mainland CBC farmland totals by a factor of three to six, and is much nearer the figure for woodland CBC plots. As with Rock Pipit *Anthus petrosus*, any apparent absence from the outer islands implied by the 2000 Breeding Atlas perhaps has more to do with recording effort than with reality.

| 1958 | 1961 | 1962 | 1964 | 1974 | 1978 |
|---|---|---|---|---|---|
| 50 | 50 | 50 | 62 | 113 | 67 |

**St Agnes & Gugh Breeding Bird Survey Data – Wren (*IOSBR* 1979)**

| 1991 | 1992 | 1993 | 1994 | 1995 | 1996 | 1997 | 1998 |
|---|---|---|---|---|---|---|---|
| 40 | 44 | 66 | 49 | 58 | 58 | 37 | 33 |

**Wren CBC Data – 16-ha Lunnon Farm, St Mary's 1991–98 (P J Robinson – unpublished data)**

Marked between-year fluctuations are a feature of British mainland Wren populations (Cramp *et al.* 1977–94) and seem largely related to extremes in winter weather, which normally Scilly lacks. Hawthorn & Mead (*British Birds* 68: 349–358) gave an annual overall mortality of 63% for England, whereas on Lunnon Farm three out of seven years witnessed overall increases of 10%, 18.3% and 50%, whilst in one the population remained unchanged. The three remaining years saw declines, of 25.7%, 36.2% and 10.8%. Therefore, on the study plot, average between-year population variation was just 5.6% and the greatest recorded annual mortality 36.2%. Unfortunately, annual ringing has not been carried out long enough on the plot to allow an assessment of long-term survival.

As with other breeding passerines, there is no evidence that Scilly's mild winters induce earlier breeding activity than on mainland Britain. As normal with this species, most nests are positioned low down and are usually difficult to locate, a situation made worse once the particularly pronounced Scillonian vegetation growth takes hold during May. On smaller uninhabited islands where low vegetation is the norm, e.g. Gweal, nests are frequently positioned beneath overhanging growth at the top of low earth cliffs (above boulder beaches), or even concealed within tufts of grass (pers. obs.). Interestingly, during a visit to Annet, Blair (1945) found few Wren nests and recorded few sites he considered suitable. He noted, however, that he saw Wrens disappearing down Rabbit *Oryctolagus cuniculus* and Puffin *Fratercula arctica* burrows and suspected they might be breeding underground. Nonetheless, the author found no evidence of this during eleven years of fieldwork.

| Island | Pairs |
| --- | --- |
| Bryher | 141 |
| St Agne | 122 |
| St Martin's | 132 |
| St Mary's | 235 |
| Tresco | 166 |
| Samson | 50 |
| Tean | 12 |
| White Island, St Martin's | 8 |
| Great Ganilly | 7 |
| St Helen's | 8 |
| Annet | 41 |
| Gweal | 8 |
| The Arthurs | 5 |
| Toll's Island | 1 |
| Others | 7 |

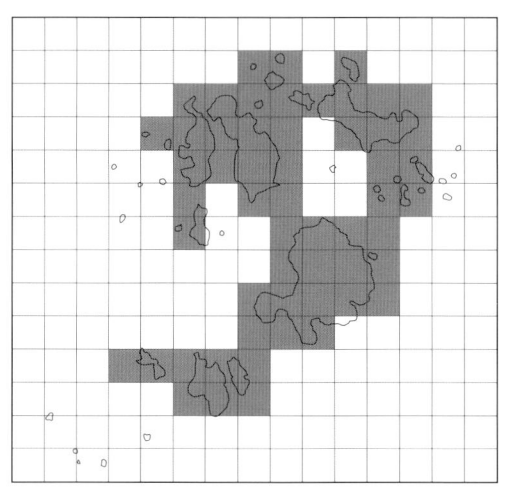

1-km Wren Breeding Distribution – 2000–01 (data Chown & Lock 2002)

2000 Breeding Bird Atlas – Wren (Chown & Lock 2002)

Laying commences mid- to late April and clutch sizes are small by British standards: four to five appearing the norm, with just the occasional six (P J Robinson – unpublished data). In comparison, according to Cramp *et al.* (1977–94), only 9% of British pairs laid 4 eggs, 25% laid 5 and 43% laid 6, mean clutch size being 5.7 (n = 1,115). By mid- to late May, the characteristic 'squeaking' of newly fledged Wren broods becomes a common feature, broods of young frequently erupting away through the low vegetation in front of walkers.

A total of 1,493 Wrens had been ringed on Scilly up until the end of 1999: 214 during the period 1957–69 and 1,279 from 1970. Over 400 Wrens were ringed on the Lunnon Farm plot between June 1994 and the end of 1999, with 112 subsequent recaptures within the study area (some birds were recaptured more than once). However, the capture–recapture rate would undoubtedly have been higher but for the conscious decision not to place nets in areas of high Wren density, as in some Holy Vale sections of the plot. Recaptures show a marked level of site fidelity, with few movements above c. 50 m and with just five recaptures up to 300 m and one of 400 m. Nonetheless, it seems abundantly clear that Wrens know their way about areas occupied by neighbouring pairs, as evident from the rapidity with which trapped individuals are back on territory following release from the ringing station (P J Robinson – unpublished ringing data). As with nearly all resident Scillonian passerines except tits *Parus*, there are no recorded inter-island movements and neither is there any recent evidence of migration to or from Scilly. However, Rodd (1866g) described a passage of migrant passerines at the Wolf Rock Lighthouse, off the southwest tip of Cornwall, during November 1864, when clear views were had of Wrens passing close to the lantern and even landing briefly, all arriving from the direction of Scilly and heading towards mainland Britain. In addition, Harvie-Brown *et al.* (1887) described a September night with a great many Wheatears *Oenanthe* and several 'Wrens' striking the lantern between midnight and 3 am.

Cramp *et al.* (1977–94) described a mainly nocturnal south to southwest autumn movement of nominate *troglodytes* (Fennoscandia and Urals southwards) into western France, plus a similar southward movement of *indigenus* from mainland Britain. And though the latter is masked by more random, shorter movements, plus arrivals of birds from further north, three birds ringed at Dungeness, Kent, were later recovered in southern France (Wernham *et al.* 2002). There is, too, equal evidence of return spring passage and therefore the probability of migration to or through Scilly seems real enough. Within Britain and Ireland, just 21% of ringed breeding adults moved greater than 20 km and the mean travel distance was less than 1 km (Wernham *et al.* 2002).

According to Cramp *et al.* (1977–94), there is much overlap in size and coloration between *troglodytes* and the form *indigenus*, particularly in southern Britain. Although wing lengths of birds trapped in the islands fall broadly within the range for both forms, several knowledgeable individuals have drawn attention to subtle plumage variations between Scillonian Wrens and those from mainland Britain and this too has been the author's experience. In general, adults may have a more 'ginger' appearance and lack the strength of flank and wing-barring apparent on mainland Britain, though caution is advised in view of the known bleaching effect of the Scillonian sunlight on some species. Regardless of this, however, the general view is that this particular island population has not yet strayed as far from the standard form as on various islands in northern Britain. After mainland Cornwall, the next nearest breeding populations are in France, Belgium and the Netherlands.

## Dunnock (Hedge Accentor) *Prunella modularis* A

**Common breeding resident and possible migrant and winter visitor. Occurs on main vegetated islands.**

Breeds western and southern Europe east to Asia Minor and southeast around southern Baltic as far as western Siberia. Migratory in north and east, sedentary or dispersive in west and south. Polytypic: *hebridium*, or 'Hebridean Dunnock' occurs Ireland and Outer Hebrides; *occidentalis* mainland Scotland, Wales and England; nominate *modularis*, or 'Continental Dunnock' central and southern Europe from France east to Ural Mountains, Romania and Alps; *mabbotti* Iberia and Pyrenees east to Greece; four additional forms further east. Amber-listed in UK: moderate (43%) breeding decline over past 25 years (Gregory *et al.* 2002). National 29% decline during 25 years to 1996, but 7% increase 1994–99 (Bashford & Noble 2000).

As with several other species that were apparently common in Scilly during the 19th and early 20th centuries, we hear little of Dunnock from early writers. The only worthwhile account suggests that it was common in every suitable locality year-round, numbers apparently remaining stable throughout autumn and winter, i.e. no evidence of migration or winter arrival (Clark & Rodd 1906).

Dunnock is one of the five commonest breeding Scillonian passerines, being less numerous than Wren, Song Thrush and Blackbird and about equal to Robin. On the Lunnon Farm study plot on St Mary's, a total of 142 pairs were recorded by the annual CBC during the eight years 1991–98, at an average of 17.7 per year (P J Robinson – unpublished data), giving an average pair-density for the 16-hectare plot of one every 0.9 hectares – high of 0.72 per hectare, low 1.06 per hectare. Comparable data comes from two past surveys. One of these was on St Agnes and Gugh, where between 50 and 104 pairs were recorded in four of eight survey years between 1957 and 1978 (*IOSBR* 1979). The average of 81.5 pairs gives a density of one pair per 1.81 hectares and although this is lower than on Lunnon Farm, survey methods are not stated. The report's authors were also unable to account for the increase from 50+ pairs in 1958 and 70 in 1962, to the substantially greater figure of 104 pairs in 1974. The other survey, for which little information now appears available, involved a partial 1980 count of St Mary's, when 115 singing males were recorded in 140 hectares (*IOSBR* 1980). This gives a supposed pair-density of 1.2 per hectare, not far removed from the Lunnon Farm findings. In June 1981, at least 100 pairs were estimated for St Martin's, but methods are again omitted. In addition, during the following year up to 15 pairs were estimated for Bryher, which seems low. The St Mary's survey was repeated in 1986 on The Garrison, where 30 males in 37 hectares gave a density of 1.2 birds per hectare. Three singing males were also noted on Samson in 1997.

| 1958 | 1962 | 1974 | 1978 |
|------|------|------|------|
| 50+  | 70   | 104  | 102  |

St Agnes & Gugh Breeding Bird Survey Data – Dunnock (*IOSBR* 1979)

| 1991 | 1992 | 1993 | 1994 | 1995 | 1996 | 1997 | 1998 |
|------|------|------|------|------|------|------|------|
| 17   | 16   | 22   | 16   | 16   | 19   | 15   | 21   |

Dunnock CBC Data – 16-ha Lunnon Farm, St Mary's 1991–98 (P J Robinson – unpublished data)

Breeding pairs are widely distributed wherever suitable habitat occurs, which apart from the five main islands and attachments includes Samson, St Helen's, Tean and the innermost of the Eastern Isles, though not Annet. Fieldwork for the 2000 Breeding Bird Atlas (Chown & Lock 2002) detected an estimated 378 pairs in 38 (56.7%) of the 67 1-km squares surveyed, though breeding was confirmed in just 21 squares. However, the same survey exposed the limitation of such studies, totals for some islands being surely far too low and with Samson's two isolated squares reportedly holding as many pairs as the whole of St Martin's in 1999. The authors concluded that the true Scillonian breeding total lies in the range 450–750 pairs.

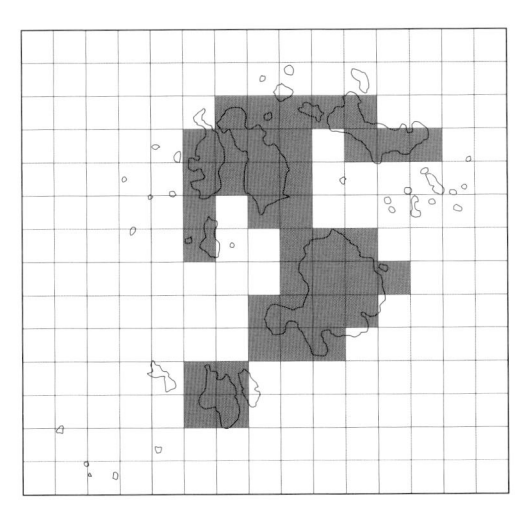

| Island | Pairs |
|---|---|
| Bryher | 51 |
| St Agnes | 34 |
| St Martin's | 31 |
| St Mary's | 185 |
| Tresco | 60 |
| Samson | 12 |
| Tean | 4 |
| St Helen's | 1 |

**2000 Breeding Bird Atlas – Dunnock (Chown & Lock 2002)**

**1-km Dunnock Breeding Distribution – 2000–01 (data Chown & Lock 2002)**

Interestingly, Penhallurick (1978) thought Dunnock numbers second only to those of Wren *Troglodytes troglodytes* by the 1970s, also highlighting the 40% increase in St Agnes counts between 1958–62 and 1974–78. In light of recent Lunnon Farm CBC data, this earlier suggestion that Dunnock totals outnumbered those of Song Thrush *Turdus philomelos* and Blackbird *T. merula* seems unsupportable. However, it is understood that Penhallurick was talking about just the St Agnes surveys up until 1974, at which time Wren and Dunnock were the two most abundant passerines on that island. A very different situation existed on St Mary's, where the two thrushes were apparently increasing. Chown & Lock suggested that Scillonian densities are up to ten times greater than on mainland Britain, Lunnon Farm's suggested 200 pairs per km$^2$ comparing with national CBC figures of 16 pairs per km$^2$ on farmland and 27 per km$^2$ in woodland.

Like other common Scillonian passerines, mean clutch size appears small by mainland standards and early nesting seems to have been unrecorded. During the mid-1990s, the author watched a female Cuckoo eject a newly hatched Dunnock brood from a nest in a *Pittosporum crassifolium* hedge on the Lunnon Farm plot. The female Cuckoo had been observed watching the area long enough to have seen the adult Dunnocks taking food to their nestlings.

Penhallurick (1978) also highlighted distinctive plumage differences among Cornish Dunnocks compared with those from Devon eastwards, pointing out that skins examined by a Mr Hazelwood of Bolton Museum were considered 'closest to the extremely red birds from southern Ireland' i.e. *hebridium*, whilst at the same time differing from skins from Devon and Somerset. Although Penhallurick makes no specific reference to Scilly, it would be illogical to expect island birds to more closely resemble those to the east of the Cornish mainland, rather than Cornwall itself. And in fact, others have subsequently commented on the distinctive features of Scillonian Dunnock plumage compared with birds in mainland Britain, e.g. Mike Rogers and Peter Colston (pers. comm.) and the subject would appear right for further investigation.

Earlier observations at southwest lighthouses produced no evidence of seasonal movements, and Penhallurick thought there was limited evidence from lighthouses or land-based observers for the subsequent period. On Scilly up until the 1970s, there were no recorded Dunnock movements, although in 1964 an apparent September increase on St Agnes was mirrored on St Martin's, a small flock also being seen arriving on St Agnes, before moving away northwards. Forty on Peninnis Head and two on Annet in October 1973 were also considered to suggest some form of movement. Similarly, in 1970 a moderate passage was noted at the Eddystone Lighthouse off southeast Cornwall (Penhallurick 1978). Penhallurick thought dispersal of British birds, i.e. *occidentalis* the most likely explanation for any apparent movements through the islands, whilst pointing out that individuals of nominate *modularis* from continental Europe had been recorded on St Agnes during October 1959 and 1971. However, since the 1970s none of the annual reports makes mention of any annual fluctuation in numbers and in most years the species gets only cursory acknowledgement.

Irish and Scottish west-coast birds, i.e. *hebridium*, are mainly sedentary, *occidentalis* from eastern

Scotland, England and western France moving only short distances. In contrast, *modularis* from Fennoscandia south through the eastern Baltic states to Germany, moves southwest in autumn towards Iberia or the western Mediterranean, with smaller percentages of *modularis* west as far as central France also moving in the same direction. Therefore, the presence or absence of migrants in Scilly is presumably influenced by the extent, if any, of annual westerly drift migration, though it seems likely that small-scale arrivals go unnoticed. Ringing data show a mix of birds from Norway and the Low Countries reaching Britain, most movements of British birds involving those from Scotland, some of which moved southeast into nearby continental Europe. A bird ringed in Portland, Dorset and recovered in western France (Wernham *et al.* 2002) presumably originated from further north. A total of 1,190 Dunnocks have been ringed on Scilly, 801 (67%) since 1970. There are no recaptures away from the islands and few recorded inter-islands movements, a bird found dead on Tresco in March 1980 and ringed at Lower Town, St Martin's, the previous autumn being exceptional. An apparent albino individual, probably a male, was present on St Mary's 1983–85.

## Alpine Accentor *Prunella collaris* A BBRC 9%

**Extremely rare migrant or vagrant, full written description required by the BBRC.**

1977   One St Mary's 30th October to 9th November   *British Birds* 71: 515

Breeds sporadically southern Europe and northwest Africa east to Iran, then more abundantly eastern Asia, from Tibet north and east to Mongolia and Japan. Mainly resident but subject to local altitudinal movements, sometimes covering longer distances. Polytypic: nominate *collaris* occurs northwest Africa and central and western Europe, east to Carpathian mountains; *subalpina* southeast Europe and southern Asia Minor; up to nine additional forms east and south.

The only Scillonian record involved a bird found on Peninnis Head, St Mary's, on 30th October 1977. It later moved to nearby Giant's Castle on 31st, where it remained until 9th November (*IOSBR* 1977). This was the only autumn arrival out of six that occurred in Britain up until 1985, the others arriving between early April and late June (Dymond *et al.* 1989). The BBRC accepted just eleven records during the period 1958–99, the Scillonian individual representing 9% of the total, though prior to 1958 there were a further 29 records. Snow & Perrins (1998) analysed all 40 records, surprisingly finding that most had occurred between August and January, with few during March–June. Snow and Perrins described a 'weak but distinct southerly movement' through Alpine passes during October, upland areas being reoccupied from mid-March or April. However, no Alpine Accentors breed further north in western Europe than the Alps. Gantlett (1998) suggested the possibility of the slightly paler southeast European *subalpina* reaching Britain as a vagrant.

## [Rufous Bush Robin (Rufous-tailed Scrub Robin) *Cercotrichas galactotes*] A

[1883   One Tresco late September to early October]   Clark & Rodd 1906

Breeds southwest Europe and North Africa through Middle East and Turkey, south to Iraq and east to Kazakhstan. Eurasian and North African populations migratory to Afrotropics, sub-Saharan population resident. Polytypic: nominate *galactotes* occurs southwest Europe, North Africa and Middle East; *syriacus* southeast Europe and Turkey south to Lebanon; *familiaris* Iraq and Iran east to Afghanistan and Kazakhstan, some intergrading with *syriacus* and *minor* in northern and sub-Saharan Africa; *minor* southern Sahara and Senegal. One further form (*hamertoni*) northeast Africa. Nearest breeding population southern Spain.

A bird observed from a Tresco Abbey window during late September and early October 1883, as it moved about in a 'reedbed' below the Abbey Road, was considered by the observer, gamekeeper David Smith, to have been this rather distinctive species. Although not accepted at the time (for want of the body), the record is perhaps arguably as acceptable now as some others within the contemporary literature and Penhallurick (1978) appears to have acknowledged the record. According to Clark & Rodd (1906), a 'conspicuous Warbler' was watched for a fortnight by Mr Smith, who, unfortunately for us now, was too ill at the time to handle a gun, and the bird was not seen by any other observer.

In considering this record we must bear in mind several points. Firstly, at that time, it was normal to obtain the specimen as proof of identity and the submission of just a field observation, especially of such an unlikely species, would have been subject to very critical analysis. Also, the presence of such a scrub-loving species in such apparently unlikely habitat as a reedbed might too seem improbable. However, without knowing the exact state of the alleged reedbed it may be difficult to comment constructively at this distance, though we do know from other Abbey records that reeds had not long been introduced to the island (Clark & Rodd 1906). However, much the same doubt concerning reedbeds could be levelled at other species, yet the writer has himself trapped such unlikely species as Wheatear *Oenanthe oenanthe* in a Scillonian reedbed, and over a substantial depth of water.

As always with single-observer sightings, much reliance must be placed upon the experience and credibility of the individual concerned. And whilst Clark & Rodd provide no assistance on this point, we do have a substantial body of evidence showing that the minority element of collectors among the small Tresco community, including David Smith, had extreme hands-on experience in the identification of both common and rare birds. In addition, the unhappy Mr Smith had a full two weeks in which to become familiar with the bird's important features.

According to Evans (1994–97) there were around eleven accepted records of Rufous Bush Robin in Britain and Ireland up to 1994, four of which involved birds shot during roughly the period under discussion here: one near Brighton on 16th September 1854; another at Start Point, Devon, on 25th September 1859; the third at Slapton, Devon, on 12th October 1876; and the last at Old Head of Kinsale, Co. Cork, in September 1876. All were of the western race *galactotes*, all fell within or (in one case) close to the dates of the Tresco sighting and three were from southwest England, or from southern Ireland. Additionally, two of the subsequent British records came from Devon. Witherby *et al.* (1940) list a total of five *galactotes* records up until publication of *The Handbook*, including the above-mentioned four and one other of the same form, plus four *syriacus*. Interestingly, T A Dorrien-Smith included the Tresco Abbey record in his list of *Birds of Scilly as Recorded at the Tresco Abbey*, even attributing it to *galactotes* (T A Dorrien-Smith 1951).

# Robin (European Robin) *Erithacus rubecula* A

**Common breeding resident, sometimes abundant migrant and winter visitor in small numbers.**

Breeds Europe, North Africa and Asia Minor into central-western Asia. Sedentary or dispersive in west and south, migratory in east and north, wintering in southwest portion of range plus North Africa east through Mediterranean to Iran. Polytypic: nominate *rubecula* occurs continental Europe, including some Atlantic Islands, east to Urals and south to Mediterranean and northwest North Africa; *melophilus* Britain, Ireland, grading into *rubecula*, or 'Continental Robin' western France, Netherlands, Denmark and northern Spain; *witherbyi* central coastal North Africa; *superbus* some Canary Islands; *tataricus* western Siberia; three or more additional forms east and south. National 12% increase 1994–99 (Bashford & Noble 2000).

One glance at the dearth of early information tells us this was probably a common species during the late 19th and early 20th centuries, virtually the only reference to it within the islands being James Clark and Francis Rodd's *Zoologist* account in their *Birds of Scilly* (Clark & Rodd 1906). From this we learn that it was present year-round and bred on all five inhabited islands. These two authors also revealed how Robins apparently treated migrant Redstarts *Phoenicurus phoenicurus* as particularly unwelcome autumn intruders, describing 'fierce combats on the rocks'. However, see under Redstart for possible early confusion between that species and Black Redstart *P. ochruros*, particularly as the reference to rocks occurs here again.

Surprisingly for such an abundant migrant or winter visitor, there are just two lighthouse reports. The earlier of these involved the Wolf Rock off Land's End during what was obviously a busy November week for nocturnal migrants, many passing the light from the direction of Scilly (Rodd 1865b). Included among them were an unspecified number of Robins. Equally worth noting, though, is the sole recorded contact with the Bishop Rock Lighthouse, on the night of 2nd September 1910, when one was at the light between 02.30 and 03.30 (Ogilvie-Grant 1912a). However, surely this largely nocturnal migrant occurred far more frequently than these accounts suggest.

The 2000 Breeding Bird Atlas (Chown & Lock 2002) recorded up to 216 Robin pairs in just 25 (37.3%) of the 67 1-km squares surveyed, it being rather surprisingly absent from St Agnes and with breeding confirmed in just 20 squares (29.8%). Birds were neither recorded from lesser islands such as

Samson, St Helen's or Tean, St Mary's apparently representing the species' stronghold in Scilly. If, as seems likely, its numbers were under-recorded during 2000, its scarcity on St Agnes, and presumably elsewhere away from St Mary's, is nevertheless confirmed by the eight St Agnes surveys between 1957 and 1978, during which time a maximum of ten pairs declined to just one or two (see tables). In addressing the possibility of under-recording, Chown and Lock estimated a likely all-island breeding total in the range 250–300, up to a possible 450 pairs.

Island Robin nests are rarely found, due mainly it seems to the vast range of available sites, plus, probably, the density of low vegetation. The total for the 16-hectare Lunnon Farm study plot was in the region of three to four nests in ten years, in contrast to several hundred Blackbird *Turdus merula* and Song Thrush *T. philomelos* nests. Lunnon Farm CBC totals for the eight years 1991–98 varied between nine and 21 pairs, at an average of 17.1, slightly less than Dunnock *Prunella modularis*, giving a figure of 0.93 pairs per hectare, with a low of 0.76 and a high of 1.77 (P J Robinson – unpublished data).

Penhallurick (1978) examined the frequency of Robin migration through Scilly, concluding that it occurred annually, or almost annually, that it largely went unrecorded and was mostly confined to autumn. He further concluded that most if not all birds involved were Continental *rubecula*, partly in support of which he quoted early 20th-century correspondence between James Clark and C J King regarding two apparent Continental birds breeding on Tresco around 1923, plus a claim of one from St Mary's during early December 1967. Numbers of migrant Robins reportedly involved in arrivals up until the 1970s ranged upwards through hundreds during several autumns to an estimated 1,200 Continental birds on St Agnes on 9th October 1959. Most of the latter left within a few days. However, a much earlier record concerned 'many thousands' said to have been present during the enforced arrival in October 1637 of one John Bastwick. This unfortunate had been fined £5,000, had had his ears cut off and been sentenced to 'perpetual imprisonment' in southwest England for seriously satirising an Archbishop (Penhallurick 1978). Allegedly, the Robins welcomed Bastwick with their singing, though he was presumably no longer best equipped to receive such a welcome.

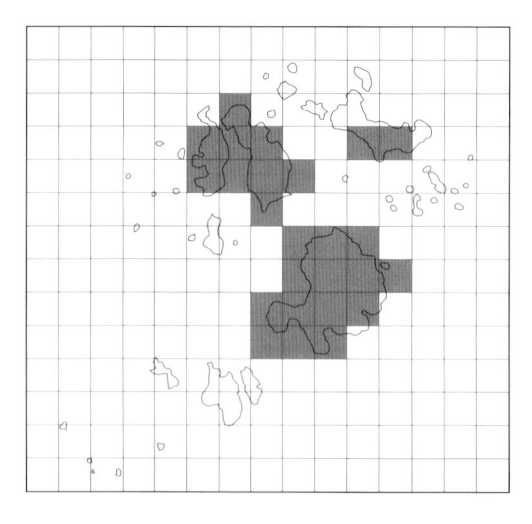

| Island | Pairs |
|---|---|
| Bryher | 7 |
| St Martin's | 7 |
| St Mary's | 151 |
| Tresco | 52 |

2000 Breeding Bird Atlas – Robin (Chown & Lock 2002)

1-km Robin Breeding Distribution – 2000–01 (data Chown & Lock 2002)

Subsequently, there seems to have been far more evidence of a strong autumn passage, with moderate to heavy falls on record most years since the mid-1970s. Usually this involved quite small numbers, e.g. 12 on remote and rocky Rosevear on 1st October 1990 was not an exceptional number, but quite obviously involved migrants. In contrast, 200 on Tresco on 29th October 1987 and 300 the next day, including 150 in one field, was matched by 'thousands' on St Mary's, though most had moved on by the month's end (*IOSBR* 1987). Similarly, 400 on St Agnes and 40 on nearby Gugh on 19th October 1988 had disappeared by November. In 1985, numbers involved in the islands were such that they 'could only be guessed at', this being followed by the interesting comment that on Scilly migrant Robin numbers peak earlier than they do on the English east coast (*IOSBR* 1985). However, not all autumns witness large movements, the 1998 report suggesting that a lack of easterly winds precluded any large arrivals. And on St Agnes, where few if any bred in recent years, 25 in late October reduced to five by the year's end. Far less seems to have been recorded on wintering numbers, however, perhaps owing to the difficulty of separating residents and visitors, comments such as 'Most soon moved on leaving a greater than usual wintering population' being none too helpful. However, there seem to have been agreement recently that in most years most, if not all, autumn arrivals departed the islands by the year's end.

| 1957 | 1958 | 1961 | 1962 | 1963 | 1964 | 1974 | 1978 |
|---|---|---|---|---|---|---|---|
| 10 | 8 | 6 | 2 | 1 | 1–2 | 1 | 2 |

St Agnes & Gugh Breeding Survey Data – Robin (*IOSBR* 1979)

| 1991 | 1992 | 1993 | 1994 | 1995 | 1996 | 1997 | 1998 |
|---|---|---|---|---|---|---|---|
| 19 | 19 | 21 | 18 | 20 | 18 | 9 | 13 |

Robin CBC Data – 16-ha Lunnon Farm, St Mary's 1991–98 (P J Robinson – unpublished data)

Britain and Ireland are situated on the northwest edge of the area occupied by wintering Robins from north and northeast Europe, and on the western edge of the main migration route down to Iberia and Morocco (Wernham *et al.* 2002). Therefore, Scilly seems likely to mainly receive that small proportion of British and Irish birds that move southwest towards Iberia, or larger falls during periods of westerly migrational drift involving birds from further north or east. A total of 1,258 Robins had been ringed in Scilly up until 1999, 968 (77%) since 1970. Although there are surprisingly few recaptures, the following three fit the above theory.

### Recoveries

| ? | Ad | Tresco 13th September 1967 | FD | Shrewsbury, Shropshire 17th May 1968 |
| A037712 | 1stY | St Martin's 1st October 1978 | FD | Ardross, Highland, Scotland 9th September 1979 |
| F617483 | 1stY | St Agnes 24th October 1990 | FD | Portsmouth, Hampshire 16th November 1991 |

Robin Ringing Recaptures

## Thrush Nightingale *Luscinia luscinia* A BBRC 1.48%

**Very rare autumn migrant, full written description required by the BBRC.**

1979 One (first-winter) St Mary's 28th September to at least 2nd October  *British Birds* 73: 519
1983 One (first-winter) St Mary's 26th September to 7th October  *British Birds* 77: 547

Breeds central and northern Europe east to central western China. Migratory, wintering entirely within east and southeast Africa. Monotypic.

There are just two accepted Scillonian records, the earliest not until 1979 and involving a bird frequenting the Holy Vale area of St Mary's for five days from 28th September (*British Birds* 73: 519). Typically, the bird kept within dense vegetation but was eventually seen well over a period of six hours (*IOSBR* 1979: 50). Among observers involved was Mike Rogers, who obtained views of creamy-white tips to the greater coverts, from which the bird was aged as first-winter. The second for the islands skulked around the Rocky Hill area of St Mary's, although eventually giving excellent views to many observers and this time remaining for 12 days (*British Birds* 77: 547). A claim of one on St Martin's 13th–14th October 2000 seems not to have been submitted to the BBRC.

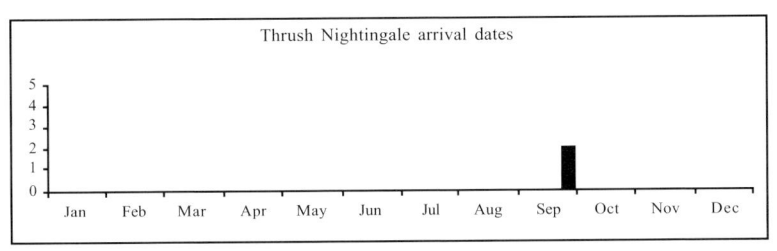

A total of 135 Thrush Nightingale records were accepted by the BBRC during the period 1958–99, therefore these two records represent less than 2% of the national total. Migration to and from Africa appears to be a somewhat direct affair, Thrush Nightingale remaining something of a rarity further west. Neither of these birds was trapped and ringed.

## Nightingale (Common Nightingale) *Luscinia megarhynchos* A

**Scarce migrant, does not breed.**

Breeds discontinuously through southern Europe and North Africa to central-western Asia, from England, France, Iberia and northwest Africa to southern Afghanistan and Mongolia. Migratory, all populations wintering Africa south of Sahara. Polytypic: nominate *megarhynchos* occurs Europe, northwest Africa and western Russia east to Crimea and south to Middle East and Levant; *africana* Caucasus and Turkey east to Iran; *hafizi*, or 'Eastern Nightingale' Aral Sea east to Mongolia. Amber-listed in UK: moderate contraction of breeding range over past 25 years (Gregory *et al.* 2002).

Either this species hardly occurred in Cornwall or Scilly during the 19th and early 20th centuries or it was overlooked. Penhallurick drew attention to the apparently only 19th-century mainland report, involving a bird reliably heard in song over several nights during 1837 (Penhallurick 1978). First mention of Nightingale in a Scillonian context concerned one killed at the Bishop Rock Lighthouse on the night of 17th September 1912 (Ogilvie-Grant 1914). Birds commenced being recorded annually in Scilly from the mid-1950s, with a small but noticeable concentration during early September (Penhallurick 1978). Numbers though were low, with about 20 autumn records over 20 years and less than half that figure during spring. It remained equally, if not more, scarce in the islands during the period 1990–99, being recorded in only seven of the ten years, four years during spring and six in autumn. Records totalled eight in spring and 18 in the latter part of the year, at the rate of two and three respectively per year of presence. All spring arrivals occurred between 3rd and 26th May, though in autumn they were more random, between 20th August and 20th October.

Two records during the 1990s were memorable in their own way. The first, a bird on St Martin's on 12th October 1998, because it was at one time suggested to be a possible Veery *Catharus fuscescens*, which certainly until that time had not been recorded in the islands. The other skulked on St Agnes from at least the 2nd October 1999 and the subsequent search for it allegedly resulted in the discovery of Scilly's first Siberian Thrush *Zoothera sibirica*.

The eastern form *hafizi* has reportedly occurred more than once in Britain, the first of which was found dead on Fair Isle in October 1971 (*British Birds* 65: 341, 73: 519, 94: 47), and this form has been recently added to the British List on the strength of that particular record (BOURC 2002a). However, most similar records remain attributed to either *megarhynchos* or *africana*, although recent new information on Nightingale separation may enable others to be assigned to a particular form. Interestingly, then, a 'strikingly pale' Nightingale with contrasting rufous rump and tail on St Agnes on 23rd October 1987 (Bradshaw 1996; Dukes 1996) was subsequently attributed by at least some observers to the form *hafizi*, though this view has yet to be accepted by the BBRC. For further reading on the identification of Nightingale forms see King & Lewington (1996). The possibility of confusion with the closely similar Thrush Nightingale *L. luscinia* also needs keeping in mind and Heard (1989) drew attention to some of the pitfalls. In particular, he highlighted a Nightingale at Old Town, St Mary's on 9th–11th October 1983, this bird also having been suggested as a possible Veery at one stage; plus a bird at Porthloo, St Mary's, 10th–19th October 1987, this individual starting its stay on the islands as both Veery and Thrush Nightingale, before being correctly identified by Chris Heard as the present species.

In western Europe, autumn passage commences from late July, peaking in Britain during late August, with most having passed by the end of September (Cramp *et al.* 1977–94). Therefore, the preponderance of Scillonian October records and the scarcity of earlier arrivals is interesting, particularly as dates of autumn passage from southern Europe and the Mediterranean extend well into October. Return passage through southern Britain peaks during late April, south-coast late May arrivals being largely attributable to spring overshoots from populations further south in Europe, e.g. France. Just six Nightingales have been ringed in Scilly, five of these prior to 1970. There are no recaptures.

*Chats and Thrushes*

# Bluethroat *Luscinia svecica* A

**Scarce and not always annual migrant, mainly in autumn, does not breed. Treated by the BBRC as a national Scarce Migrant.**

Breeds Europe and northern Asia, from Iberia, France and Norway east through Bering Sea to coastal Alaska, then south through central Asia west of Lake Baikal to China and Himalayas. All populations migratory, wintering Iberia, Africa south of Sahara, and Arabian Peninsula to southeast Asia. Polytypic with complex racial structure: nominate *svecica*, or 'Red-spotted Bluethroat' occurs Scandinavia east to Alaska and south to Altai and Sayan mountains; *cyanecula*, or 'White-spotted Bluethroat' central Europe from northern France and Spain east to southwest Russia; *namnetum* western France; *volgae* central European Russia; at least six additional forms further east. Included on Annex I of 1979 EEC 'Birds Directive'. Upgraded from Green- to Amber-listed in UK 2002: five-year mean of 1.4 breeding pairs (Gregory *et al.* 2002).

Most surprisingly, Bluethroat gets no mention in the early literature, though this is an easily overlooked species. Nonetheless, its 19th-century absence from the islands cannot be blamed entirely on a lack of awareness, at least two being identified on the Cornish mainland during this time: in 1836 and some time before 1851 (Penhallurick 1978). The records show that birds were identified regularly in both Scilly and Cornwall from about 1956, though, unlike the mainland, Scilly hosted surprisingly large numbers from the outset. Twelve or more occurred during some years up until the mid-1970s, all except one of these arriving in autumn. Penhallurick's examination of autumn arrival and departure dates for Scilly and Cornwall showed that numbers peaked between mid-September and mid-October. And as Penhallurick pointed out, White-spotted individuals predominate on Scilly, with most arrivals being aged as first-years in any event.

During the years 1990–99, Bluethroat arrived in eight out of the ten years, but only once in spring: a male Red-spotted on 6th–7th May 1994. In autumn it arrived between 6th September and 12th November, this last being the apparent latest record for Scilly. Nineteen arrivals during eight autumns gave an average of 2.3 individuals per autumn of arrival, the most in any year being three (four years). Most reports failed to make mention of either the age or form of the birds involved, though three in autumn 1996 were said to have been Red-spotted *svecica*.

Bluethroats commence leaving their breeding grounds from late August, numbers in both southern Sweden and Britain peaking during early September, with some evidence of a southwest orientation in western Europe (Cramp *et al.* 1977–94). Many also linger at suitable locations en route, ringing data showing a high level of between-year fidelity at autumn stopover sites. Return spring migration of the Red-spotted *svecica* is by a more easterly route, no doubt explaining the relative absence of birds in Scilly at this time. The possibility of *namnetum* from western France reaching Britain as spring overshoots seems realistic, whereas the preponderance of the more easterly or southerly White-spotted *cyanecula* in autumn is less easily explained. However, Sharrock (1974) noted that this last situation is not identical to that of most southern migrants reaching Britain during autumn, pointing out that Bluethroats include a higher proportion of adults, plus the breeding distribution of *cyanecula* is such that 'relatively little westward displacement is necessary to explain vagrancy of *cyanecula* on the English south coast in autumn'.

Just seven Bluethroats have been ringed in Scilly, six of these prior to 1970. The last bird was a male Red-throated trapped in Higher Moors early on the morning of 6th September 1996 and viewable in the same area until 14th.

# [Red-flanked Bluetail *Tarsiger cyanurus*] A

**No acceptable record, full written description required by the BBRC.**

[1971   One (first-year or female) claimed St Agnes 15th & 16th October]   *British Birds* 66: 360

Breeds northern Asia, from western Russia east to Kamchatka and Japan, smaller population Himalayas. Mainland populations migratory, wintering southeast Asia. Monotypic.

A claim by D I M Wallace of a first-winter or female on St Agnes on 15th–16th October 1971 was rejected by the BBRC (*IOSBR* 1971; *British Birds* 66: 360). The bird was seen briefly on the 15th and 'glimpsed' again on 16th, but according to the observer all essential features were noted, though the *IOSBR* editors noted the lack of any descriptive information of comparative size.

# Black Redstart *Phoenicurus ochruros* A

Annual spring and autumn migrant, small numbers winter but it does not breed. Full written description required by the BBRC for all races except *gibraltariensis*.

Breeds central and southwest Europe, plus North Africa and central-southern and southwest Asia. All populations migratory except southwest Europe, wintering northwest and northeast Africa, plus Arabian Peninsula east to Burma. Polytypic with complex racial structure: *gibraltariensis* occurs central and southwest Europe east to Crimea and Greece, Sicily, northern Spain, northwest Africa; nominate *ochruros*, or 'Eastern Black Redstart', Turkey south and east to Iran; *semirufus* Levant; *phoenicuroides* and *rufiventris* central southern Asia as far as Mongolia and China; one additional form. Amber-listed in UK: five-year mean of 77.4 breeding pairs (Gregory *et al.* 2002).

As remarked under Redstart *P. phoenicurus*, the possibility arises of some 19th-century confusion between that and the present species, at least as far as their use of Scilly's rocky shoreline is concerned (Clark & Rodd 1906). Clark and Rodd took the view that Black Redstart occurred regularly in small numbers in autumn and frequently during winter, pointing out, too, that it demonstrated a particular preference for the large granite boulders scattered around Scilly's coastline, which of course it still does today. The controversy in Clark and Rodd's account is that they attributed the same behaviour to Redstart, which on present-day evidence is difficult to sustain.

Most early references to Black Redstart come from E H Rodd, who at various times wrote to the *Zoologist* or commented elsewhere on its arrival in the islands. He was in full agreement that it appeared every, or most years during autumn and that it was to be seen in winter, though being less clear whether this was annual (Rodd 1867a, 1878b, 1880). The same author suggested that this species was more common in the islands than Redstart (Rodd 1880) and that most arrived in 'the grey state of plumage, only one or two in the black plumage' (Rodd 1867a). However, regardless of claims that it occurred during winter, the latest reports of a bird in the islands before the mid-20th century appears to be 5th January 1865 (Rodd 1880). However, it seems to have been more regular in winter across the water in west Cornwall.

As he did for many species, Penhallurick (1978) examined 20th-century Black Redstart records for Cornwall and Scilly up until the mid-1970s, finding that spring passage was lighter than in autumn and occurred between mid-March and mid-April, though on Scilly passage was sometimes inconspicuous at this time. In general, birds appeared on the islands in ones and twos but single-day, single-island spring counts of up to 100 are on record. Clearly, though, spring passage was sometimes a protracted affair, the latest record being 1st June. During autumn, returning birds were apparent in the islands from late September or even October, late August being exceptionally early. Most though had moved on by early November and mid-month sightings were unusual, 28th November being exceptional. Numbers involved during autumn were less easily assessed, though the impression gained was one of a slow trickle of birds, up to a daily maximum in the low 20s. Nonetheless, greater concentrations did occur, as in October 1975 when between 1,000 and 1,500 arrived in company with fewer Redstarts. Importantly, Penhallurick found no evidence of overwintering in Scilly.

Examining records from Scilly for the years 1990–99 we find a broadly similar situation to that found by Penhallurick. In most years determining the start of spring passage was hampered by the presence of overwintering individuals, though movement through the islands apparently occurred from mid-March through to late May, but with two June records. Numbers involved were mostly small, 50 in 1995 being the highest all-island count. Autumn passage began in late September or early October and, as in the 1970s, lasted well into November. Most years witnessed small numbers passing through but 1995 and 1996 proved the exceptions. In October 1995 'hundreds' were present in the islands on 29th, Peninnis headland on St Mary's alone holding 100. The 1996 arrival also occurred in late October, 150 being counted on just four of the main islands. Unlike Penhallurick's earlier findings, birds were present in small numbers in at least nine of the ten winters, the most recorded being 12 in 1998–99. In several years, numbers present at the end of December were less than recorded in the early part of the following year, leaving uncertainties over whether birds moved between islands during winter, or even away from the islands. There are no reported breeding records from the islands, though the 2000 Breeding Bird Atlas (Chown & Lock 2002) recorded the presence of a male on the north end of Bryher for several weeks during summer. Black Redstarts breed no closer to Scilly than southeast England, though it is numerous in northern France.

As in the 19th century, most Black Redstarts arriving in Scilly are females or first-years, well-marked males being still decidedly scarce. Forms other than the European *gibraltariensis* also occasionally reach Britain, as in October 1975 when an immature described by D I M Wallace on Bryher on 13th October was accepted by the BBRC as the first British record of one or other of the intergrading eastern orange-bellied group *ochruros/semirufus/phoenicuroides* (BOURC 1980; *British Birds* 73: 519, 77: 547). Recently, however, the BOURC decided it was currently impossible to eliminate the likelihood of the three eastern forms described above being confused with possible Black Redstart x Redstart *P. phoenicurus* hybrids and thus removed the group from the British List and deleted the Bryher record (BOURC 2002a). Southern Britain is near the northern limit of Black Redstart's winter range, which in any event varies from year to year, the bulk of European birds wintering in the Mediterranean region. Birds also occur on passage through the Mediterranean from mid-October to early November. However, *gibraltariensis* is the commonest form in winter east through the Mediterranean as far as the Middle East, where the *ochruros/semirufus/phoenicuroides* complex reaches it western limit (Cramp *et al.* 1977–94).

Just 34 Black Redstarts have been ringed in Scilly, about half of these before 1970, the two recaptures being strongly suggestive of a winter movement between southeast England and Scilly.

## Controls
A012510  1stY  Beachy Head, Sussex
                17th October 1985                    FD  St Mary's 25th October 1985

## Recoveries
C99600   Ad   St Agnes 26th March 1958              CT  Dungeness, Kent 19th April 1958

**Black Redstart Ringing Recaptures**

# Redstart (Common Redstart) *Phoenicurus phoenicurus* A

**Annual migrant in moderate numbers, mostly in autumn, does not breed.**

With the obvious exception of Ireland, breeds Europe and central-western Asia, from Britain, France and Spain east to Lake Baikal, outlying populations Iran. Migratory, all populations winter Africa south of Sahara. Polytypic: nominate *phoenicurus* occurs Europe, northwest Africa and Asia east to Lake Baikal and south to Balkans and Ukraine; *samamisicus*, or 'Ehrenberg's Redstart' remainder. Amber-listed in UK: unfavourable European conservation status (Gregory *et al.* 2002). National 37% increase 1994–99 (Bashford & Noble 2000).

There are various 19th-century references to this species, most of which come from the pen of E H Rodd in west Cornwall but originated from his nephew Francis during visits to Tresco. The earliest of these is a description of Redstart's appearance in the islands in 1849, along with 'a host of the migratory warblers', Redstart being named among several that were 'captured' (Rodd 1849b, 1880). Others were reported as arriving in the islands during a 'heavy gale' in the second week of October 1863. The elder Rodd then wrote to the *Zoologist* a few years later describing a noticeable fall of Redstarts and other species, pointing out that Redstart 'scarcely if ever visits the western parts of Cornwall, but is generally found in and about the autumnal migration at Scilly with Pied Flycatchers (*Ficedula hypoleuca*), which are seldom seen in southern and western counties' (Rodd 1871c).

However, the full situation was summarised by Francis and James Clark, who by the turn of the century thought it observed annually in 'pairs' or small flocks in autumn, 'usually perched on granite blocks by the seashore' (Clark & Rodd 1906). This last remark leaves more than a little room for confusion with Black Redstart *P. ochruros*, which, as Clark and Rodd agreed, also spends much of its time frequenting the rocky foreshore. Few if any current-day reports involve Redstarts seen down by the rocky shore and this most certainly cannot be described as 'usual' behaviour. So we can only wonder at the basis for such a comment, unless it was just a simple case of confusion, though just possibly the early lack of trees in Scilly may have played some part. The sole early report of Redstart from the local lighthouses concerned 'one or two' seen along with several species of thrush *Turdus* and others at the Bishop Rock light on the night of 4th November 1909 (Ogilvie-Grant 1911).

In the early to mid-1970s, Penhallurick (1978) noted that both in Cornwall and on Scilly spring Redstart migration was always light, sometimes passing almost without notice, the highest spring total up until that time being 30 on St Agnes on 9th April 1966, birds becoming apparent from as early as 3rd March but with stragglers evident until mid-June. During the later half of the year, birds began arriving in late August and had mostly left by late October, numbers peaking on both islands and the mainland from mid-September through to early or mid-November. The highest single-day autumn count was 50 on Tresco in late October 1975.

Taking now the ten years 1990–99, Redstarts occurred on Scilly in both halves of the year in all ten years. All recorded spring arrivals fell in the narrow 13-day window between 12th and 24th April, the latest spring sighting being 28th May. Overall recorded spring totals fell in the range one to 15. Autumn arrivals, which were slightly more protracted than in spring, occurred between 8th August and 2nd September, the latest any bird remained in the islands being 2nd November, though in six years birds remained into the last week of October. Although overall autumn totals were difficult to assess, highest single-day counts of between eleven and 18 are on record. Perhaps typical was 1999, when most of the 12 spring sightings occurred during late April, whilst in what was described as a 'standard year', 65+ birds overall peaked at ten on St Mary's on 15th October (*IOSBR* 1999). There are years, though, with greater numbers, as in 1975 when 50 were estimated for Tresco and St Mary's alone, or 1987 when an all-island total of 42 was recorded on 4th October.

The overall majority of reports make no mention of the form involved, in which case all are assumed to have been *phoenicurus*. And neither is there mention of the habitat type involved, though had many individuals of this mainly woodland species been seen on coastal rocks, as Clark and Rodd earlier suggested, this would presumably have been mentioned by observers. Indeed, the only recent such report involved a Redstart seen briefly on the Bishop Rock itself on 22nd August 1994. Regardless of the lack of any mention so far, likelihood of an appearance of the recognisable southeast European and southwest Asian *phoenicurus*, otherwise known as 'Ehrenberg's Redstart', remains a clear possibility (Gantlett 1998) and should be kept in mind whenever Redstarts are present in Scilly. On mainland Britain, Redstart breeds no closer to Scilly than east Cornwall, the next closest breeding area being northern France.

Redstart is a broad-front African migrant, northern European populations departing their breeding grounds from late August, peak passage in northwest Europe occurring during early September, most having passed through by late October. Returning spring migrants arrive back in northern Europe by early April, most having returned by late May. Forty-two Redstarts had been ringed in Scilly up until 1999, 32 (76%) before 1970; there are just two recaptures.

### Recoveries

| | | | | |
|---|---|---|---|---|
| C99546 | Ad | St Agnes 14th October 1957 | FD | Boscastle, Cornwall 25th October 1957 |
| K41929 | Ad | St Agnes 18th August 1959 | CT | Beirro Litoral, Portugal 12th September 1959 |

**Redstart Ringing Recaptures**

# Whinchat *Saxicola rubetra* A

**Annual spring and autumn migrant in small numbers, does not breed.**

Breeds Europe and central-western Asia, from England, Ireland, France and Spain north to Fennoscandia, south to the Mediterranean and east to western Siberia. Migratory, all populations wintering Africa south of Sahara. Monotypic. National 9% decline 1994–99 (Bashford & Noble 2000).

When researching their early 20th-century *Zoologist* review of *The Birds of Scilly* James Clark and E H Rodd's nephew Francis could find just 12 or so records of Whinchat (Clark & Rodd 1906). These all occurred between early August and early October, and the authors pointed out that as it apparently occurred singly it may have been overlooked in the past. The elder Rodd earlier noted that the first specimens known to him had been acquired in 1851 (probably shot by Augustus Pechell), though it was first recorded in 1850 (Rodd 1851c, 1880). Notable though is the apparent disparity between Clark and Francis Rodd's description of Whinchat as 'an autumn migratory casual' and the elder Rodd's reference to it as 'a summer visitant', though without stating it bred in the islands (Rodd 1880). The only remaining early mention concerned a report of several 'Furze-chats' at the Bishop Rock Lighthouse on the night of 24th September 1886 (Harvie-Brown *et al.* 1887).

Penhallurick (1978) reviewed Whinchat's status in Scilly and Cornwall up until the 1970s, finding more moved through during autumn than in spring. The latter passage occurred mainly between mid-April to mid-May, with an earliest date on St Agnes of 18th March. Like Clark and Rodd, Penhallurick found most moved through singly, though counts of up to five were on record. Autumn passage became apparent from mid-July, though more normally from mid-August, most appearing during September with few into October, though there was at least one mainland November sighting. Autumn daily island counts normally peaked at about 15, with an upper limit of 35. Examining the ten years 1990–99, earliest recorded arrival dates for eight of the ten years fell within the period 20th to 30th April, the single exception being 1994, when just one individual was recorded on 21st May. Last spring sightings were slightly less compressed, being between 14th May and 13th June. Autumn dates were even more predictable, however, arrivals falling between 11th and 31st August and final departures within an impressive 27th October to 3rd November. The maximum recorded spring count was 10, the autumn equivalent being 35 (two years).

Penhallurick referred to an 1870 claim by Francis Rodd that Whinchat occasionally remained through the winter, apparently on the mainland, though Penhallurick suggested such claims be treated with scepticism. Certainly, there seems to have been no suggestion of overwintering in respect of Scilly. Birds commence moving south from late August, numbers in western Europe peaking during early September. Ringing shows that at least some birds from Finland and areas in between move southwest through Britain and Iberia (Wernham *et al.* 2002). Forty-one Whinchats were ringed on Scilly up until 1999, virtually half in each period, and there are no recaptures.

# Stonechat *Saxicola torquata* A

**Formerly bred commonly but now does so sparingly on the five inhabited islands, plus Samson, Gugh, St Helen's, Tean and perhaps the Eastern Isles. Small numbers occur as migrants or eastern vagrants.**

'Siberian Stonechat' Records
- 1978 One (female or first-year) St Mary's 18th to 31st October *British Birds* 72: 533
- 1979 One (male) St Mary's 14th to 20th October *British Birds* 73: 519, 74: 483
- 1979 One (female or first-year) St Mary's 22nd to 28th October *British Birds* 73: 519, 74: 483
- 1980 One (male) St Mary's & Bryher 29th & 30th October *British Birds* 74: 843
- 1984 One (male) Bryher 13th to 26th October *British Birds* 78: 66, 571
- 1985 One (female or first-year) St Mary's 13th to 18th October *British Birds* 79: 569
- 1987 One (female or first-year) St Mary's 29th September to 1st October *British Birds* 81: 578
- 1987 One (female or first-year) Tresco 3rd November *British Birds* 81: 578
- 1991 One (female or first-year) St Mary's 13th to 18th October *British Birds* 85: 205, 89: 515
- 1991 One (female or first-year) Tresco 16th to 23rd October *British Birds* 85: 205, 89: 515
- 1992 One (female or first-year) St Martin's 7th October *British Birds* 86: 507
- 1993 One (male) St Agnes 13th to 15th May *British Birds* 88: 531
- 1996 One (first-year male) St Mary's 21st to 24th September *British Birds* 90: 495
- 1999 One (female or first-year) Covean, St Agnes 7th to 12th October *British Birds* 93: 549

Breeds mainly eastern Asia, from north of Kamchatka south to China and Himalayas and west just into West Palearctic; also southern and southwest Europe, including Britain, Ireland, France, Iberia and countries bordering Mediterranean, including North Africa; plus discontinuous distribution in southern and eastern Africa. Asian, British, Irish and eastern Mediterranean populations migratory, wintering southeast Asia, India, Arabian Peninsula, Iraq and Iran, northwest and eastern Africa. Polytypic, with complex racial structure: *hibernans* occurs Britain, Ireland, northwest France and western Iberia; *rubicola* North Africa and western and southern Europe from Iberia, France and Belgium east to Caucasus; *variegata*, or 'Caucasian Stonechat' western Russia to Caucasus; *armenica* Turkey east to Iran; *maura*, or 'Siberian Stonechat' eastern European Russia east to Lake Baikal and northwest Mongolia south to Afghanistan and Iran; *stejnegeri* eastern Siberia from Lake Baikal though Mongolia east to Korea and Japan; three or more additional forms. Some authorities (e.g. Wink *et al.*) recommend treating *maura* and the 'African Stonechat' *axillaris* as full species, along with *torquata*. National 80% increase 1994–99 (Bashford & Noble 2000). Amber-listed in UK: unfavourable world conservation status (Gregory *et al.* 2002).

The only early mention of this species seems to be that of James Clark and Francis Rodd, who thought it common in all gorse *Ulex* areas and most 'waste land' throughout the summer (Clark & Rodd 1906). However, interestingly, they found it far less conspicuous during winter and quite remarkable by present-day standards is their reported 30 apparent breeding pairs on St Helen's. Following that we read nothing further until the 1938 comment that Stonechat was 'well established in all suitable localities (*CBWPSAR* 8).

In many parts of Britain, Stonechat populations were reduced by as much as 90% during winter 1962–63. However, Penhallurick thought many Cornish populations had fully recovered by 1965, birds reappearing on main Scillonian islands by 1964 (Penhallurick 1978). Penhallurick also thought there had been a further increase in Scilly (and Cornwall) following mild winters during the 1970s, quoting a 1974 all-island total of up to 80 pairs (*IOSBR* 1974), which for St Agnes represented a 100% increase over 15 years – though the report gave figures for just four islands (Table). Today, Stonechat breeds relatively sparingly on the five inhabited islands, plus Samson, Gugh, St Helen's, Tean and perhaps one or two of the Eastern Isles, e.g. Northwethel, Great Ganilly and Great Arthur, though not on all of these islands in all years. All 56 pairs located during the 2000 Breeding Bird Atlas (Chown & Lock 2002) are incorporated into the Table, though the absence of some 1970's data makes direct comparison difficult. Breeding pairs were recorded in 36 (53.7%) of the 67 1-km squares surveyed, the pair total being somewhat below Penhallurick's 1974 estimate of 80. Between-year fluctuations in Scillonian pair numbers probably result from annual variations in winter weather, though Chown and Lock suggested that the apparent recent island decline may be real. However, even at the 80-pair level, the Scillonian Stonechat population fails to reach the threshold of European importance.

Penhallurick also doubted the occurrence in Cornwall or Scilly of migrants from continental Europe, despite anything earlier writers said to the contrary, though the existence of an autumn passage from further north in Britain seemed to be well accepted. On Scilly, this passage was apparent in most springs and all autumn, though more obvious in the latter part of the year, 55 on St Agnes on 13th October being the largest single-day count. In spring, birds moved through between mid-March and May, whilst in most autumns passage occurred between late August and November, peaking during October. Examination of annual records for the ten years 1990–99 reveals no reference to even a suspected spring passage and although birds are thought to have moved through the islands each autumn, numbers involved were small. These movements were described either as slight in most years or gradual, and only in 1995 were they considered to be at all obvious. Maximum annual daily counts fell in the range 15–32.

The distinctive eastern forms *maura* and *stejnegeri*, described collectively as 'Siberian Stonechat', breed from western Russia across Siberia as far as the Pacific Ocean, wintering from Iraq to southeast Asia. A number of birds showing features of these and perhaps other eastern Stonechat forms have been recorded in Scilly, all of which are tabled above. In addition, the BOURC recently added *variegata*, or 'Caucasian Stonechat' to the British List on the strength of a bird at Porthgwarra, west Cornwall on 1st–4th October 1985 (*BOURC* 1993b). Unlike the other two eastern forms referred to here, *variegata* winters in northeast Africa. For advice on the separation of 'Siberian Stonechats' see Stoddart (1992). Among others, Wink *et al.* (2002) recommend separation of *maura* as a full species *S. maura*.

Importantly, however, evidence has recently been presented demonstrating the existence in Scilly, and elsewhere in southern England, of Stonechats displaying plumage features consistent with European *rubicola*

## Chats and Thrushes

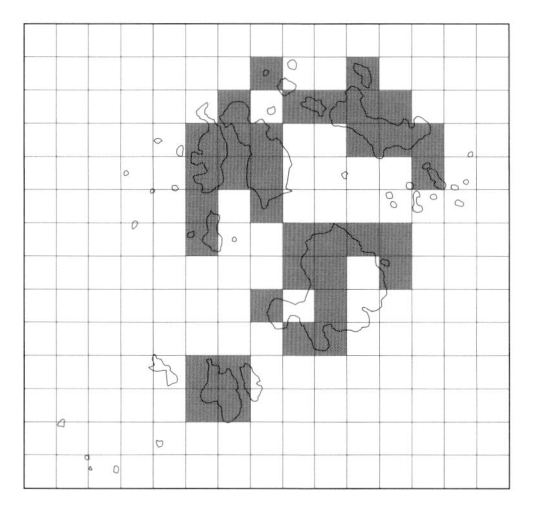

| Island | 1974 | 2000 |
|---|---|---|
| St Mary's | 19 | 13 |
| Tresco | | 13 |
| St Agnes | 12 | 6 |
| St Martin's | | 8 |
| Bryher | | 8 |
| St Helen's | 2 | 1 |
| Tean | | 1 |
| Samson | 3 | 3 |
| White Island, St Martin's | | 1 |
| Great Ganilly | | 1 |
| Toll's Island | | 1 |

**All-island Breeding Stonechat Pairs (1974 Survey\* and 2000 Breeding Bird Atlas\*\*)**
(\**IOSBR* 1974 \*\*Chown & Lock 2002)

1-km Stonechat Breeding Distribution – 2000–01 (data Chown & Lock 2002)

(e.g. Siddle 2001, D Walker 2001). Intergrading between the western *hibernans* and the Continental *rubicola* occurs in nearby areas of Europe and it remains unclear whether birds seen in Britain, including Scilly, are Continental migrants, or merely British individuals showing unusual features. The alternative solution is that hitherto undetected small concentrations of *hibernans* breed in eastern, southern and southwest England. Either way, the exposure of these possibly resident Continental-type individuals, some of which show extreme features, casts at least slight shadows over the former identification of 'Eastern Stonechats' as shown in the Table.

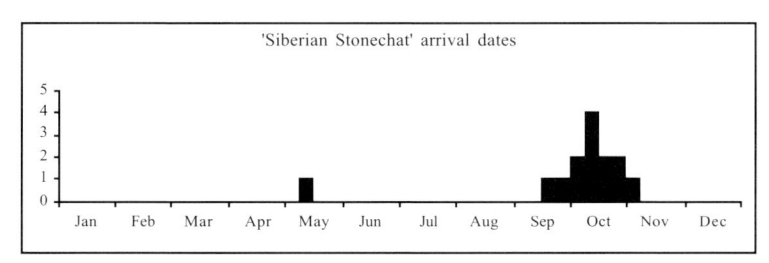

'Siberian Stonechat' arrival dates

Many individuals of the form *hibernans*, including some from Britain and all from Ireland, plus the Continental *rubicola* winter south of their breeding range, concentrations occurring, among other countries, in Spain, the Balearic Islands and northwest Africa (Wernham *et al.* 2002). Autumn passage occurs between September and early November, most moving north again by late March (Cramp *et al.* 1977–94) but whether or not numbers of Continental *rubicola* pass through Britain still seems unclear.

## Isabelline Wheatear  *Oenanthe isabellina*  A  BBRC 18.7%

**Very rare migrant, full written description required by the BBRC.**

1988 One St Mary's 2nd & 3rd October
  *British Birds* 82: 134, 541, 83: 553, *Birding World* 1: 357–358
1990 One St Mary's 18th October to 2nd November  *British Birds* 84: 143, 85: 537, 86: 3–5
1991 One St Agnes & Gugh 15th to 26th October  *British Birds* 85: 537, 542–543, 86: 509)

Breeds southeast West Palearctic and central Asia, east to Mongolia and southern China, wintering West Africa south of Sahara east though Arabian Peninsula to northern India. Monotypic.

There are three records of this much sought-after British rarity, the first of which, and the fifth for Britain and Ireland, was discovered by Pete Dunn in flower fields adjoining St Mary's golf course for two days from 2nd October 1988 (Dunn 1988, 1990). This bird was very confiding, often allowing an approach down to five metres. The second was discovered on the golf course very close to the site of the earlier individual, where it remained from mid-October to early November 1990. Against all odds, a third for the islands was found on St Agnes in mid-October the following year, before transferring to nearby Gugh until 26th (Dean 1993).

A potential fourth Isabelline Wheatear involved a bird reportedly seen well near Bryher Pool on 29th–30th October 1998 (*IOSBR* 1998) but rejected by the BBRC (*British Birds* 95: 527). The only other references to this species in Scilly concern a rejected D I M Wallace claim of a bird on St Mary's on 1st November 1971 (*IOSBR* 1971; BOURC 1978), plus an unacceptable report of two together on St Martin's for one day in August 1971 (*IOSBR* 1972). The Chart includes the three accepted arrival dates. Mean length of stay was ten days.

Earlier accepted British records involved birds at Winterton, Norfolk, in May 1977, Grampian, Scotland in October–November 1979, Northumberland in September 1980 and Cumbria in November 1987, the species having been returned to category A on the strength of the Winterton individual. The BBRC accepted just 16 records during the period 1958–99, in which case the three Scillonian individuals represent 18.7% of the national total.

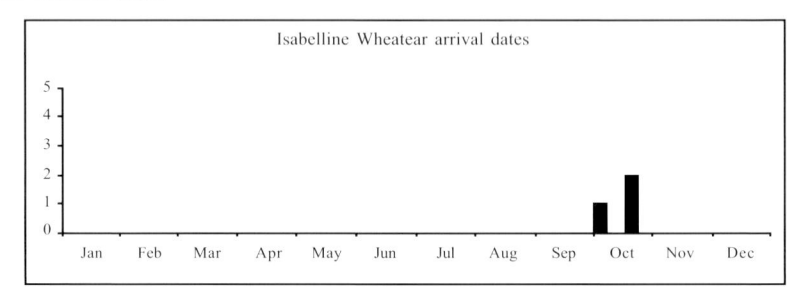

Isabelline Wheatear arrival dates

Autumn passage to the African wintering grounds is primarily orientated towards the southwest but the presence of wintering individuals on a point of longitude west of Ireland makes it less than surprising that at least a few Isabelline Wheatears reach Britain. Birds commence departing their breeding grounds from as early as August or September, although in the east individuals remain well into October. None of these birds were trapped and ringed on Scilly.

# Wheatear (Northern Wheatear) *Oenanthe oenanthe* A

**Common spring and autumn migrant in moderate to large numbers. An apparent former annual breeding visitor, one or two pairs still occasionally remain to do so.**

Breeds Europe and northern Asia, from Iceland, Britain, Ireland, France and Spain east to Bering Sea, also Alaska, northeast Canada and Greenland. Migratory, all populations winter Africa south of Sahara. Polytypic: nominate *oenanthe* occurs Europe east from Faeroes through western and northern Siberia and Alaska, south to Pyrenees, Alps, former Yugoslavia and Urals; *leucorhoa*, or 'Greenland Wheatear' Iceland, Greenland and northeast Canada; *libanotica* Spain, Balearic Islands, Romania, Greece, Turkey and east through Iran, Kazakhstan, Afghanistan to Mongolia. National 3% increase 1994–99 (Bashford & Noble 2000).

A long-range migrant, birds passing though Scilly probably originate mostly from western Europe, Iceland, Greenland and northeast Canada.

It would have been surprising indeed had such an obvious migrant as Wheatear been missed by early observers and, in particular, there are a number of late 19th- and early 20th-century reports from the Bishop Rock Lighthouse. First mention probably comes from William Borlase, who described 'a small Bird here scarce so big as a Lark, of a cinereous and white colour, called Hedge-Chicker, thought by many equal food to Ortolan' (Borlase 1756). E H Rodd (1880) thought this likely to have been Wheatear and most seem subsequently to have accepted that view. Borlase's account suggests Wheatear may have been breeding and this is confirmed in the early 20th-century *Zoologist* review of Scilly's birds (Clark & Rodd 1906). Clark and Rodd suggested that it bred sparingly but was common during autumn migration. However, it was clearly also frequent on passage during the early part of the year, Clark and Rodd recounting how several hundred arrived in three successive 'flocks' above Old Town, St Mary's (presumably on Peninnis), on 9th April, most either remaining or being constantly replaced by further arrivals. In addition, E H Rodd's nephew Francis described how by 30th September 1870 Wheatears were becoming scarce in the islands, later reporting the last on 8th November (Rodd 1880). However, E H Rodd rather contradicted part of James Clark and his nephew Francis's 1906 account by suggesting it bred in 'considerable' numbers during summer.

There are some 12 reports of Wheatears seen at the Bishop Rock Lighthouse between 1880 and 1910. Most concern small numbers, up to 50, attracted to the light, some of which were killed striking the lantern. All reports concern night-time attractions, mostly from midnight through to 4 am but a few involved all-night attractions. The three latest, in autumn 1910, are of interest if only because they make some attempt at defining Wheatear forms involved, i.e. 'small race' or 'large race', small birds passing through on 1st and 5th September, large birds on 29th September (Ogilvie-Grant 1912b). Of the remaining reports, perhaps the most interesting is that for the night of 3rd September 1886, when about 100 Wheatears passed from 11 pm through to daylight, some 20 of which struck (Harvie-Brown *et al.* 1887).

Wheatears still pass through the islands in substantial numbers, the smaller *oenanthe* preceding and outnumbering the larger *leucorhoa* in spring. A bird on Peninnis, St Mary's, on 22nd February 1998 was most exceptional, first birds more normally arriving by the second week of March. Numbers then increase from late March or early April through to May, same-island counts in the range 30–80 normally being reported, with a recent exceptional high of 155 on St Mary's. Most years there is little evidence of spring passage after the end of May and by the end of June first returning birds are becoming apparent. Autumn daily same-island and all-island counts often appear less impressive than those in spring, perhaps because autumn passage is a far more protracted affair; nonetheless recent all-island counts of up to 110 are on record, and in 1981 over 300 were on St Mary's on 18th September. Few are evident about the islands after late October or the first week of November, a bird on 21st November 1998 being most exceptional.

In most years, odd birds remain about the islands throughout June, some of which are shown or thought to have bred, though usually just a single pair and rarely more than two or three pairs. Taking the ten years from 1990, on Bryher a pair bred in 1990–91, fledging at least one young by 7th June 1991 and being last seen on 11th July, whilst in 1997 single pairs reportedly bred on St Mary's and St Martin's. As long ago as 1940, A A Dorrien-Smith's gamekeeper reported seeing a pair, the female of which was carrying nest material to a site on Tresco's northern end. The ten pairs recorded by the 2000 Breeding Bird Atlas (Chown & Lock 2002) in six (8.9%) of the 67 surveyed 1-km squares were probably more perceived than real and were almost certainly attributable to lingering spring migrants. The same authors concluded that 'one or more pairs' was a safer interpretation of the survey's findings.

Surprisingly few Wheatear sightings are attributed racially, though even back in the 1940s it seemed accepted that the larger *leucorhoa*, or 'Greenland Wheatear', moved through the islands on passage (T A Dorrien-Smith 1951). During the ten years 1990–99, only in the last of these is there any mention of this supposedly recognisable form.

Occasionally, Wheatears are discovered showing confusing plumage features, giving rise to the possibility that rarer species may be involved. This was the case in 1997 when a first-year Wheatear in the area of St Mary's golf course showed just enough dark on the underwing to make Pied Wheatear a possibility. This situation was important enough in any event but doubly so since it involved the possibility of a new species for the islands. Of equal interest was an aberrant Wheatear with an all-black tail found on St Mary's in 1976, which for a short time seemed liable to misidentification as Desert Wheatear *O. deserti.* (Norman 1978). That apart, the ever-present possibility of the closely similar Isabelline Wheatear *O. isabellina*, which has already occurred three or four times in Scilly, means that any 'unusual' Wheatear must be examined with care.

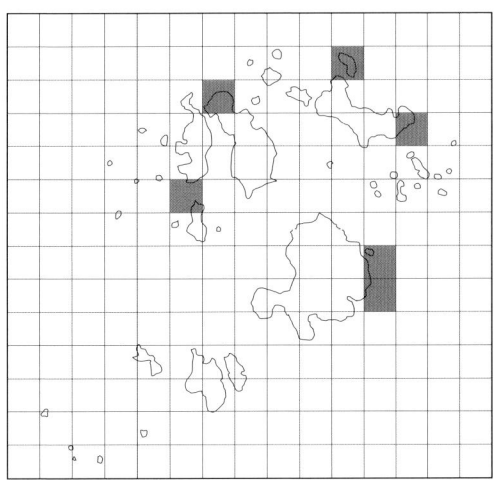

1-km Wheatear Summer Distribution – 2000–01 (data Chown & Lock 2002)

In autumn, most western European Wheatears move south or southwest, birds from Norway and Britain moving through France and Iberia down into Africa. Nevertheless, the equal abundance of birds along the North African coast at this time also indicates a 'strong westerly component in [the] route of populations furthest east' (Cramp *et al.* 1977–94). The larger *leucorhoa* from Iceland, Greenland and northeast Canada winters in West Africa, ringing and other evidence indicating large numbers fly direct from Greenland to western Europe. These last populations vacate the breeding grounds by August or September and also head southwest once reaching Europe. Ringing data suggest that most Wheatears, other than *leucorhoa*, passing though southern Britain originate from within Britain, as far north as Shetland (Wernham *et al.* 2002). In spring, *leucorhoa* returns by much the same route, birds becoming evident in western Europe from April, rather later than nominate *oenanthe*. Ninety-four Wheatears had been ringed on Scilly up until 1999, 63 (67%) since 1970. None were recorded as *leucorhoa*, though some very probably were of that form. There are no recaptures.

## Pied Wheatear *Oenanthe pleschanka* A BBRC 0%

**Extremely rare migrant, full written description required by the BBRC.**

[1933 One Tresco 16th September] Penhallurick 1978
2001 One St Mary's 14th to 18th October *British Birds* 95: 368, 507

Breeds central eastern West Palearctic and central Asia through to eastern China, wintering East and northeast Africa. Polytypic: nominate *pleschanka* occurs throughout, except Cyprus where replaced by *cypriaca*.

Interestingly, T A Dorrien-Smith (1951) had this species in his list of *Birds of Scilly as recorded at Tresco Abbey*, under its old scientific name of '*O. leucomela*'. Although it does not apparently figure in any of the annual reports prior to that year, Penhallurick (1978) mentioned an A A Dorrien-Smith manuscript regarding a female allegedly seen on Tresco on 16th September 1933.

An unusual wheatear at Porth Hellick, St Mary's, for five days during October 2001 was initially though likely to be an 'Eastern' Black-eared Wheatear *O. hispanica melanoleuca*. However, this possibility was eventually ruled out on the strength of broad pale fringes to the scapular and mantle feathers, plus the long primary projection, which at least equalled the exposed tertials and extended well towards the tip of the tail (*Birding World* 14: 407–409). A total of 41 Pied Wheatear records were accepted by the BBRC during the period 1958–99. The Porth Hellick bird was not trapped.

Most Pied Wheatears reach their African wintering grounds via a southwest direction of travel, departing the breeding grounds from August, though with birds still present into October further east (Cramp *et al.* 1977–94).

## Black-eared Wheatear *Oenanthe hispanica* A BBRC 11.1%

**Very rare spring and autumn migrant, full written description required by the BBRC.**

1971 One (adult male) St Agnes 24th September *British Birds* 65: 341
1977 One (male *hispanica*) Samson 22nd to 26th April *British Birds* 71: 516
1987 One (female or first-year male) Bryher 20th September
 *British Birds* 82: 541; *Twitching* 1: 263–264
1997 One (male *hispanica*) Wingletang, St Agnes 5th & 6th May *British Birds* 91: 502
1998 One (male *melanoleuca*) Tresco 18th to 23rd May *British Birds* 93: 549

Breeds northwest North Africa and countries bordering northern and eastern Mediterranean, east to Iran. Migratory, wintering semi-desert south of Sahara. Polytypic: nominate *hispanica*, or 'Western Black-eared Wheatear' occurs northwest Africa and Iberia east to northwest former Yugoslavia; *melanoleuca*, or 'Eastern Black-eared Wheatear' southern Italy and eastern former Yugoslavia to Iran.

Five records, all involving single birds, the first not until 1971 and the most recent in 1998. The earliest arrival, an adult male on St Agnes on 24th September, coincided with two first-years on mainland Cornwall earlier that month. The 1977 male on Samson was described as the black-throated form and, like that in 1997, was attributed to the nominate *hispanica*. In comparison, the bird on Castle Down, Tresco, from 18th to 23rd May 1998 was considered by observers to have been the eastern *melanoleuca*.

The Chart includes all five arrival dates. The overall mean length of stay was 3 days, though removal of the two single-day autumn observations gives a mean spring stay of 4.3 days. A total of 45 Black-eared Wheatear records were accepted by the BBRC for the period 1958–99, these five comprising 11.1%. None of these birds were trapped and ringed on Scilly.

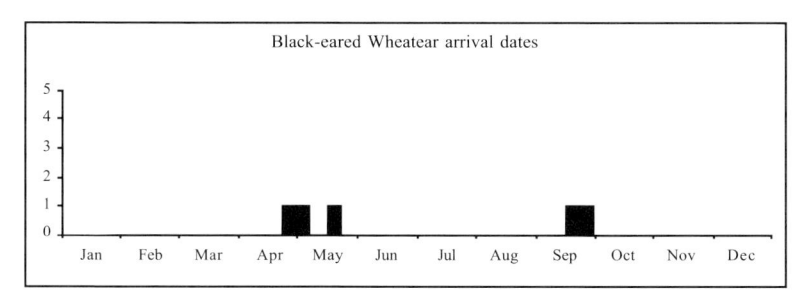

Black-eared Wheatears commence leaving the breeding grounds from August, main passage through Morocco occurring September–October, some into November. Return passage commences from February through to April. During winter, nominate *hispanica* predominates in northwest Africa, being largely replaced by *melanoleuca* east of Mali, the later perhaps being slower to depart in spring (Cramp *et al.* 1977–94).

## Desert Wheatear *Oenanthe deserti* A BBRC 1.5%

**Extremely rare vagrant, full written description required by the BBRC.**

1976   One (male) St Agnes 23rd to 30th March   *British Birds* 70: 431

Breeds coastal North Africa and northwest Arabia eastwards to Mongolia, wintering in Saharan Africa, Arabian Peninsula and Pakistan. Polytypic: *homochroa*, or 'Western Desert Wheatear', occurs North Africa; nominate *deserti*, or 'Levant Desert Wheatear,' northwest Arabian Peninsula; *atrogularis*, or Eastern Desert Wheatear', Iran east through Afghanistan to Mongolia; *oreophila* further south and east.

The sole Scillonian record involved an adult male at Horse Point, St Agnes, from 23rd to 30th March 1976 (*British Birds* 70: 431). Birds reaching elsewhere in Britain have been attributed to nominate *deserti* and the more eastern *atrogularis*, though separation in the field may be difficult (Cramp *et al.* 1977–94). The St Agnes individual was not attributed racially and it was not trapped and ringed.

This single individual represents 1.5% of the 66 records accepted by the BBRC for the period 1958–99. Autumn passage occurs from August through to November, return movement becoming evident from as early as mid-January.

## Rock Thrush
## (Rufous-tailed Rock Thrush)  *Monticola saxatilis*  A  BBRC 19%

Extremely rare spring and autumn migrant, full written description required by the BBRC.

1968 One (male) Samson 21st April  *British Birds* 78: 572
1979 One (female) Peninnis, St Mary's 19th May  *British Birds* 73: 520
1984 One (probable first-year male) St Mary's 16th to 18th October  *British Birds* 78: 572
1996 One Shipman Head Down, Bryher 28th September to 2nd October  *British Birds* 90: 496

Breeds southern Europe and coastal North Africa, east through central Asia to eastern-central China. Migratory, all populations winter Africa south of Sahara. Monotypic.

Earliest evidence of this species in Scilly concerned a belated report of a male seen on Samson by a Mrs Lacey on 21st April 1968 (*IOSBR* 1984). This was followed by details of a female seen frequenting Peninnis Head, St Mary's, on 19th May 1979 and then a probable first-year male, again on the St Mary's southern headlands, this time for three days from 16th October 1984. The most recent record was a bird of the year on Bryher's Shipman Head Down from 28th September to 2nd October 1996. Typically for Scilly, despite this last individual being seen by many observers, no written description was submitted, though fortunately an acceptable set of photographs had been obtained (*IOSBR* 1997). Two out of the four arrivals remained for just one day and the mean length of stay was 2.5 days. The Chart includes all four arrival dates. These four individuals represent 19% of the 21 records accepted by the BBRC for the period 1958–99. None of these four was trapped and ringed on Scilly.

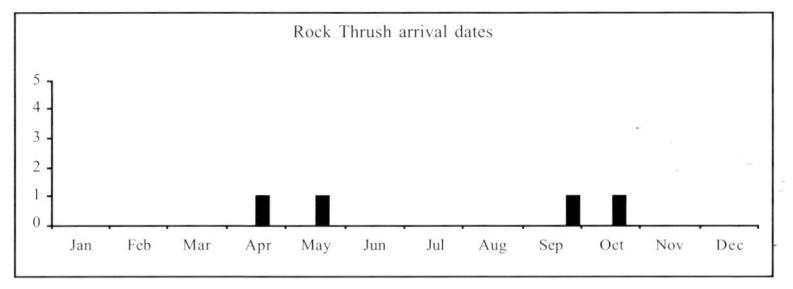

Rock Thrush arrival dates

Most, if not all, Rock Thrushes winter in the Afrotropics north and east of the of the central forests, and as Cramp *et al.* (1977–94) point out, those from eastern China travel a minimum of 7,500 km. Southern European birds are believed to make a broad-front crossing of the Sahara, though the scarcity of records from the western Sahara suggests birds from the west Mediterranean may move southeast. Spring records in northern Europe may be attributable to overshooting, whereas autumn records could be accounted for by the considerable westerly component involved in any migration from extreme eastern Asia.

## Blue Rock Thrush  *Monticola solitarius*  A  BBRC 33.3%

An extremely rare vagrant, full written description required by the BBRC.

1999 One (male) Porthloo, St Mary's 14th & 15th October  *British Birds* 93: 551

Breeds northwest Africa and southern Europe east through Mediterranean to Turkey and across southern Asia to Japan. Populations partially migratory, more so in the far-eastern forms, with most populations wintering in Africa. There is also some seasonal altitudinal movement. Polytypic: nominate *solitarius* occurs throughout the western part of its range eastwards as far as Turkey; *longirostris* in northeast Iraq, Afghanistan and Iran; three other forms further east.

The sole record for Scilly involved an individual discovered during a check for Black Redstarts *Phoenicurus ochruros* among boulders at the northeast end of Porthloo Beach, St Mary's, on 14th October 1999 (M Scott 1999b). It was identified as a first-winter male and not only represented the third record for Britain, but also the third extremely rare thrush species present on Scilly within the space of six days (the others being White's Thrush *Zoothera dauma* and Siberian Thrush *Zoothera sibirica*). Britain's first Short-toed Eagle *Circaetus gallicus* was also present at the same time. Needless to say, with so many observers on the islands already and with so much adrenaline already flowing, a crowd of some 500 birders very soon assembled along the Porthloo shoreline. The bird stayed for just two days but was seen and photographed by many more people before its departure.

The two previous British records involved a first-summer male at Skerryvore Lighthouse, Strathclyde, from 4th to 7th June 1985 and a male near Portmadoc, North Wales, in 1997, also on 4th June. Interestingly, neither of these two was seen by more than two people, making the Porthloo bird even more of a celebrity. According to Evans (1994), a Blue Rock Thrush was seen by David Hunt on St Martin's on 18th May 1972 but the record was not fully documented by the time of David's tragic death.

Although another male Blue Rock Thrush was found in Cot Valley, west Cornwall, on 25th October, just ten days after the Porthloo bird departed, this was not thought to involve the same individual. This was largely because the Cornish bird was very obviously newly arrived when found and apparently very tired, which would not be expected had it been the Scillonian bird, though the possibility of them being one and the same cannot be ruled out entirely.

The Porthloo bird could not be attributed to a particular form, but the 1985 Strathclyde individual was thought likely to have been the more migratory and more easterly *longirostris* (M Scott 1999b). Apart from the David Hunt record, there are two further British sightings, both of which were thought likely to have involved escapes from captivity (BOURC 1993a; Evans 1994). Blue Rock Thrush is quite widely kept in captivity in Britain and as such the possibility of escape is always a reality. More recently, another for mainland Cornwall, a first-summer female, was present at Pendeen from 14th to 18th May 2000 (*Birding World* 13: 181). The single Scillonian record amounts to one third of the records accepted by the BBRC for the period 1958–99. It was not trapped and ringed on Scilly.

The extent of Blue Rock Thrush migration increases further east into Asia, though the main wintering area is perhaps North Africa. West and central European plus North African populations are only partially migratory, with short-distance random dispersal and some high altitude sites abandoned completely (Cramp *et al*. 1977-99). Cramp *et al*. draw attention to a few west European autumn and spring records north to Sweden, suggesting the former may be due to reverse migration, although it is unclear whether this might involve birds from southern Europe, or central Asian populations normally migrating to southeast Asia. The assumption is, nevertheless, that spring records north of the main breeding range may be attributable to overshooting returning migrants. European departure from the breeding grounds occurs from August and is perhaps protracted, whilst return passage is rapid and commences from mid-March. Little seems to be known about the winter movements of the easterly *longirostris*, though it is known to mix with nominate *solitarius* in East Africa.

## White's Thrush *Zoothera dauma* A BBRC 8.6%

**Very rare vagrant, full written description required by the BBRC in all cases.**

    1886   One (shot) Tresco 2nd December   Gurney 1889; Clark & Rodd 1906
    1965   One Tresco 3rd & 4th November   *British Birds* 59: 303, 76: 507
    1999   One St Agnes 6th October to 9th November   *British Birds* 93: 345, 551

Main breeding area central-eastern Siberia east to China, with outlying populations central-western Russia, Japan, Himalayas, India and southeast Asia. Winters India and southeast Asia. Polytypic: *aurea* occurs Russia and southeast China; *toratugumi* southeast Siberia and south of *aurea*; nominate *dauma* Himalayas, southern China and adjacent southeast Asia; at least nine further forms south and east.

E H Rodd made no mention of this species in relation to Scilly, referring only to a bird shot by a gamekeeper at Trewithen on the Cornish mainland in January 1874 (Rodd 1880). Consequently, the first we hear of it in the islands is brief mention of one killed by A A Dorrien-Smith's butler, George Britton, in the Tresco Abbey Gardens on 2nd December 1886, after it had been seen in the area for some three weeks. The incident is described by Gurney (1889) and mentioned by J Clark and Rodd's nephew Francis in their later review of *The Birds of Scilly* (Clark & Rodd 1906). Gurney commented on this being the eighteenth British specimen. Britton apparently misidentified the bird as a Mistle Thrush *Turdus viscivorus* and it was correctly identified only once it passed into the hands of Penzance taxidermist Vingoe, and the product of Vingoe's work still resides in the Tresco Abbey skin collection. Interestingly, Evans (1994) ignored the 1886 bird, despite it being well documented and the skin being available still.

The 1965 individual was seen by the extremely reliable David Hunt, but the BBRC initially rejected his description. This was reconsidered and finally accepted 17 years later in what committee members described as a 'generous change of heart', but apparently without providing a public explanation for their reversal. Penhallurick (1978) gave the year as 1966 but presumably this is an error.

Resident birder Ren Hathway discovered Scilly's third White's Thrush, on St Agnes, on the morning of 6th October 1999. He had crossed from Tresco the previous evening specifically to see the Siberian Thrush *Z. sibirica* found on Gugh on 5th and stumbled across the White's Thrush beside the path as he headed in the direction of a reported Subalpine Warbler *Sylvia cantillans*. With two newly found, extremely rare, eastern thrushes now quite literally within metres of each other on St Agnes, the island quickly came to life, as launches laden with expectant birders began arriving from St Mary's and other islands. A busy and exciting few hours by any standards! Throughout its stay the White's Thrush remained typically elusive, frequenting the island's western side mainly in the areas of Covean, Barnaby Lane, Troy Town and Lower Town Farm, before finally settling at the latter. It fed in the typical White's Thrush manner, scratching away in the leaf litter and with the characteristic bobbing and swaying so reminiscent of Jack Snipe *Lymnocryptes minimus*, perceptively, and rather aptly being described by one island farmer as a cross between Mistle Thrush *Turdus viscivorus* and European Golden Plover *Pluvialis apricaria*. It is also said to have only just escaped the attentions of one of the island cats (*IOSBR* 1999). For a photograph of the 1999 bird see *British Birds* 93: plate 274. None of these birds was trapped and ringed on Scilly.

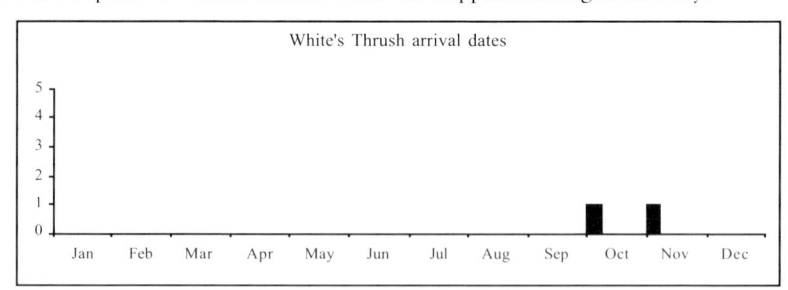

White's Thrush arrival dates

The Chart excludes the initial Tresco record, for which the original finding date remains unknown. The two most recent individuals represent 8.6% of the 23 records accepted by the BBRC for the period 1958–99. Understandably, most British records have so far been confined to Fair Isle, Shetland and the eastern side of England and Scotland, and White's Thrush looks destined to remain an extreme rarity within Scilly. Birds from the northern part of its range are wholly migratory and winter in southern China and southeast Asia, departing the breeding grounds from late August (Cramp *et al.* 1977–94). Logic suggests that European vagrants originate from the small isolated population in southwest Russia, though other migrant species breeding in eastern Asia, e.g. Richard's Pipit *Anthus novaeseelandiae*, regularly reach Britain during autumn.

## Siberian Thrush *Zoothera sibirica* A BBRC 16.6%

1999   One (first-year male) Gugh 5th to 8th October   *British Birds* 93: 551

Breeds central Siberia east to Japan, wintering India, Southeast Asia and Indonesia. Polytypic: nominate *sibericus* occurs Siberia east to Pacific; *davisoni* Sakhalin, Japan and neighbouring islands.

Typically a difficult species to see, Scilly's first Siberian Thrush (and thirteenth thrush species for the islands) will linger long in the memory of many birders. Not just for its own sake but because, at one point, it was possible to stand among the assembled crowd looking for the Siberian Thrush and at the same time watch Britain and Ireland's first Short-toed Eagle *Circaetus gallicus* fly low overhead, knowing too that skulking close by was a White's Thrush *Z. dauma*, itself only the third record for the islands. The bird spent much of its short stay hidden in the thick evergreen hedgerows that are so much a feature of Scillonian flower fields, a situation made worse on Gugh by the lack of any recent cultivation. This was so much so that most birders eventually left having gained only a flight view, albeit of a very distinctive bird. This single individual represents 16.6% of the six records accepted by the BBRC for the period 1958–99. It was not trapped and ringed on Scilly.

Nominate *sibericus* migrates from its northern breeding grounds south and southeast into India and Southeast Asia, moving mainly through Mongolia or further east and departing the breeding grounds from early September. Eastern European records include flocks of up to 18 birds in January and 25 in mid-February (Cramp *et al.* 1977–94).

## Wood Thrush *Hylocichla mustelina* A BBRC 100%

**Extremely rare migrant, full written description required by the BBRC.**

1987   One (first-year) St Agnes 7th October   *British Birds* 84: 485, 88: 133–135; *Ibis* 133: 440

Nearctic species, breeds North Dakota to Nova Scotia and south to Gulf of Mexico and Florida. Migratory, wintering mainly Central America. Monotypic. Population consistently falling, Canadian situation most serious (Bryant 1997).

The only British and Irish record of this exciting Nearctic thrush involved a first-year found on St Agnes by Paul Dukes following heavy rain and strong winds on the morning of 7th October 1987 (Dukes 1987, 1995). This was just three days before the discovery of the Western Palearctic's second Philadelphia Vireo *Vireo philadelphicus* on nearby Tresco and seven days before Britain's third Hermit Thrush *Catharus guttatus* on the same island. Present for just one day and always difficult to see well, the Wood Thrush did eventually provide brief, mainly flight, views to an assembled crown of up to 80 birders. Strong winds on the 8th prevented further searches and it was not rediscovered on the 9th, to the great disappointment of a substantial gathering. The bird was not trapped and ringed on Scilly.

Autumn movement away from the breeding grounds is mainly southwest, perhaps helping to explain this single British and Irish record. Birds begin leaving the breeding grounds from July or August, few remaining after September (Snow & Perrins 1998). Other West Palearctic records involve individuals in Iceland in October 1967 and Madeira in January 1986, plus an undated 19th-century record from the Azores identified some time after 1962

(Snow & Perrins 1998). Wood Thrush scored highly in Robbins's statistical review of expected transatlantic vagrancy among 38 Nearctic migrant passerines and near-passerines unrecorded in Britain or Ireland during 1947–76, coming tenth in the list with a predicted relative likelihood of 2.42 individuals for the period (Robbins 1980).

## Hermit Thrush *Catharus guttatus* A  BBRC 50.0%

**Extremely rare migrant, full written description required by the BBRC.**

1984    One St Mary's 28th October    *British Birds* 78: 573, 79: 297–298
1987    One St Agnes 15th & 16th October    *British Birds* 81: 579
1993    One Tresco 11th to 18th October    *British Birds* 87: 550–551

Nearctic species, breeds central Alaska east to Newfoundland and south to Maryland, Wisconsin, New Mexico and California, though largely absent from central states. Migratory, wintering central and southern USA south to Mexico, Guatemala, El Salvador and Bahamas. Polytypic: nominate *guttatus* occurs southern Alaska and southern Yukon south to southern British Columbia; *faxoni* southern Canada and northeast USA from central Nova Scotia west to Yukon; *crymophilus* Newfoundland and southern Labrador to northern Nova Scotia; up to seven additional forms western North America.

The first for Scilly and the second British and Irish record involved a bird seen by just a few observers in unpleasant weather on Peninnis, St Mary's, for one day only on 28th October 1984. Scilly's second and Britain's third was discovered at Chapel Fields, St Agnes, in mid-October three years later and the most recent appeared on Tresco in October 1993. This last was initially found on the north side of Tresco's Great Pool on the 11th, before being rediscovered near the island Monument on the 18th.

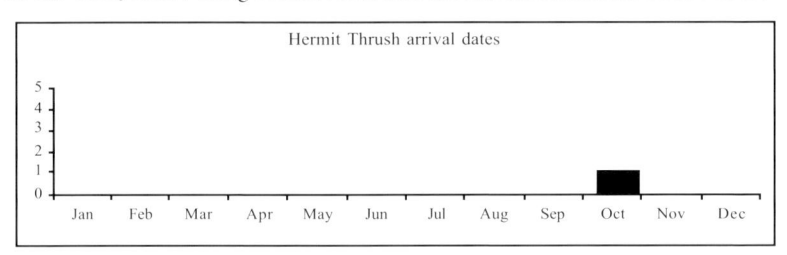

Hermit Thrush arrival dates

The Chart includes all three arrival dates. The mean length of stay was 3.6 days. These three individuals comprise 50% of the six records accepted by the BBRC during the period 1958–99. These were thought likely to have involved either *faxoni*, from southern Canada and northeast USA, or the slightly darker *cymophilus* from Nova Scotia and Newfoundland. However, according to Nisbet's findings (1963) the possibility of nominate *guttatus* should not be discounted. None of the three was trapped and ringed on Scilly. The first British and Irish record involved a one-day individual on Shetland during June 1975. Birds commence leaving the breeding grounds from late September, southward movement peaking by mid-October. Hermit Thrush scored badly in Robbins's statistical review of expected transatlantic vagrancy among 31 Nearctic migrant passerines and near-passerines recorded in Britain or Ireland during the period 1947–76. The single spring record fell short of the predicted relative likelihood of 1.33 individuals (Robbins 1980).

## Swainson's Thrush *Catharus ustulatus* A  BBRC 40%

**Rare autumn migrant, full written description required by the BBRC.**

1979    At least one St Mary's 20th to 28th October    *British Birds* 73: 521
1979    One Tresco 23rd to 28th October    *British Birds* 73: 521
1983    One St Mary's 17th to 19th October    *British Birds* 77: 542, 550,; 78: 573
1984    One St Agnes 30th September to 11th October    *British Birds* 78: 64, 569, 573
1987    One St Mary's 12th & 13th October    *British Birds* 81: 579
1990    Up to two St Mary's 10th to 23rd October    *British Birds* 84: 485, 490
1991    One St Mary's 7th & 8th October    *British Birds* 85: 538
2000    One (first-winter) St Mary's 12th to 19th October    *British Birds* 94: 488

Nearctic species, breeds central Alaska east to Newfoundland and south to line from California to New Hampshire and Main, though largely absent from central northern USA. Migratory, wintering Mexico south to Argentina. Polytypic: nominate *ustulatus* occurs coastal northwest North America from Alaska to Oregon; *swainsonii* Newfoundland and northwest USA west to Alberta; *oedica* western USA from Washington to California; *almae* central western Canada south to Colorado. Slow overall decline, eastern population by over 30% in last 15 years (Bryant 1997).

There are eight island records involving at least nine Swainson's Thrushes in seven years since the first two on St Mary's and Tresco in October 1979, this species having become something of a Scillonian speciality. With the exception of the 1984 individual, all arrived during October, the former missing this month by just one day but remaining until 11th October. Birds typically arrived during bad weather associated with Atlantic depressions, often accompanied by other North America species, e.g. Grey-cheeked Thrush *C. minimus*, or Red-eyed Vireo *Vireo olivaceus*. Also typical were initial doubts over exactly how many individuals were involved, as in 1979 when two sightings each on St Mary's and Tresco were eventually adjudged to have involved just two individuals. This was despite the fact that the St Mary's sightings came from the golf course (three days) and The Garrison (six days) and were separated by a day; and the bird on Tresco was seen at Old Grimsby from 23rd to 25th and then at Borough Farm from 26th to 28th. Swainson's Thrush clearly moves between sites more readily than might be expected by such a skulking species.

These eight or so individuals comprise some 40% of the 20 records accepted by the BBRC during the period 1958–99. The bird at Lunnon, St Mary's, in October 1983 was observed eating the berries of coprosma *Coprosma repens*, a commonly planted Scillonian hedgerow species from the Southern Hemisphere, whilst the 1987 individual arrived three days before one on Lundy Island in North Devon. Particularly interesting were two together at wooded Trenoweth on St Mary's in 1990, the first evident from 10th to 24th October and being joined by the second from 15th to 23rd. These two were often heard calling to each other (*IOSBR* 1990). The Chart includes all nine arrival dates and the mean length of stay was 7.4 days. None of these birds were trapped and ringed on Scilly.

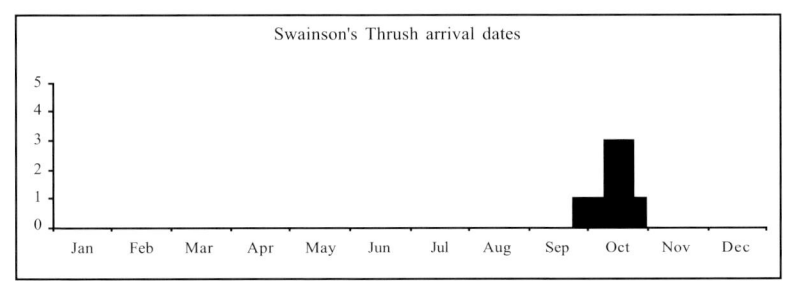

Birds commence moving south from late August, through to October and become regular in remote Bermuda by early October. Interestingly, it is less frequent at this time closer to the USA, in the Bahamas and the west Caribbean islands, suggesting that many take the transoceanic route out over the North Atlantic from Canada and northeast USA direct to South America. The species is thereby subjected to the dangers of involuntary North Atlantic crossings when encountering severe weather systems. On the face of it, the eastern *swainsonii* seems most likely to occur in Britain, but the more westerly *ustulatus* cannot be entirely discounted. Swainson's Thrush scored highly in Robbins's statistical review of anticipated transatlantic vagrancy among 31 Nearctic migrant passerines and near-passerines recorded in Britain or Ireland during the period 1947–76. The four accepted British and Irish records (one spring, three autumn) slightly exceeding the predicted relative likelihood of 3.96 individuals (Robbins 1980).

## Grey-cheeked Thrush        *Catharus minimus*   A   BBRC 46.5%

**Rare to scarce autumn migrant, full written description required by the BBRC.**

    1976   One St Mary's 14th to 23rd October   *British Birds* 70: 430–431
    1976   One St Mary's 15th to 19th October   *British Birds* 70: 430–431
    1976   One St Mary's 15th to 17th October   *British Birds* 70: 430–431
    1976   One Tresco 21st October   *British Birds* 70: 430–431

1979   One (first-year) St Mary's 27th October to 15th November   *British Birds* 73: 521
1983   One (first-year) St Mary's 13th to 19th October   *British Birds* 77: 550
1984   One Tresco 21st October   *British Birds* 78: 573
1986   One (killed by cat) St Mary's 20th & 21st October
                                                 *British Birds* 80: 558, 81: 579; *Ibis* 139, 198
1986   One Tresco 20th to 23rd October   *British Birds* 80: 558, 81: 579; *Ibis* 139, 198
1986   At least two Tresco 20th to 23rd October   *British Birds* 80: 558, 81: 579; *Ibis* 139, 198
1986   One drowned on shore St Mary's 22nd October   *British Birds* 80: 558, 81: 579; *Ibis* 139, 198
1986   One St Mary's 22nd to 25th October   *British Birds* 80: 558, 81: 579; *Ibis* 139, 198
1986   One St Agnes 24th October   *British Birds* 80: 558, 81: 579; *Ibis* 139, 198
1986   One St Mary's 24th October to 16th November   *British Birds* 80: 558, 81: 579; *Ibis* 139, 198
1986   One Bryher 27th & 28th October   *British Birds* 80: 558, 81: 579; *Ibis* 139, 198
1990   One St Agnes 7th & 8th October   *British Birds* 84: 485
1990   One St Mary's 19th to 25th October   *British Birds* 84: 485
1991   One (first-year) St Agnes 16th & 17th October   *British Birds* 85: 538, 542–543, 568, 86: 511
1991   One (first-year) St Mary's 17th to 20th October   *British Birds* 85: 538, 542–543, 568, 86: 511
1991   One (first-year) trapped St Agnes 22nd to 26th September
                                                 *British Birds* 85: 538, 542–543, 568, 86: 511
2002   One (first-year) St Agnes 28th to 30th October   *Birding World* 15: 398

Mainly Nearctic species, breeds Newfoundland west across northern Canada and Alaska to eastern Siberia. Migratory, wintering Central and South America. Formerly treated in Britain as conspecific with Bicknell's Thrush *C. bicknelli* but separated by BOURC July 1996 (BOURC 1997). Polytypic: nominate *minimus* occurs Newfoundland, southern Labrador and eastern Quebec; *aliciae* (not recognised by Cramp *et al.* 1977–94) Labrador west to Alaska and northeast Siberia. Recent 'drastic' population decline (Bryant 1997); note, though, that this last comment was made prior to the recent separation of Grey-cheeked and Bicknell's Thrushes and seems likely to apply mainly to Grey-cheeked, given its greater range.

Twenty Grey-cheeked Thrushes arrived in seven years up until 2001, all but one during October. The Chart includes all arrival dates, except the 2002 individual and those birds killed by a cat or drowned on the foreshore, and reveals an obvious late October peak. Obvious too is the tendency towards multiple arrivals, nine in 1986 being the highest number, followed by four in 1976, three in 1991 and two in 1990. There was also a clear tendency for this species to occur in the same autumn as Swainson's Thrush *C. ustulatus*, the very notable exception being the nine in 1986, in which year no Swainson's were recorded. The 1986 arrival was described at the time as 'unprecedented in the annals of transatlantic vagrancy' and was thought to have involved 'a sizeable disintegrated flock' (*IOSBR* 1986), being accompanied elsewhere in Britain by just three in west Cornwall.

Like Swainson's Thrush, Grey-cheeked has become something of a Scillonian speciality, these 20 individuals comprising 46.5% of the 43 records accepted by the BBRC during the period 1958–99. Autumn migration occurs mainly through eastern North America, the Bahamas and Caribbean islands, but includes Bermuda. Birds commence their departure from early September, peak during late September or early October, and an apparent substantially greater proportion of first-years use coastal routes. The presence of birds on outlying Bermuda suggests that some birds opt for at least a partial transoceanic route, heading out over the North Atlantic and direct to the Caribbean, or even South America, as do various other species. Such a route makes them liable to an involuntary Atlantic crossing when encountering severe weather systems.

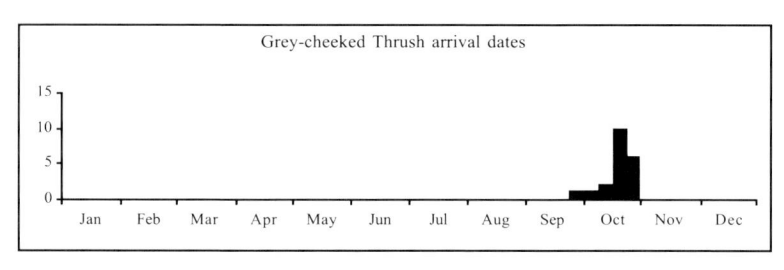

Grey-cheeked Thrush arrival dates

The geographical origin of British records seems not to have been determined, although, given the reported similarity between *aliciae* and Bicknell's Thrush, the drowned St Mary's individual of 22nd October 1986 seems likely to have involved that form. Predominance of this form would fit the theory that populations breeding furthest west in North America are often most likely to succumb to involuntary transatlantic crossings (Nisbet 1963). One Grey-cheeked Thrush had been ringed on Scilly up until the end of 1999 but was not recaptured. Grey-cheeked Thrush scored highly in Robbins's statistical review of anticipated transatlantic vagrancy among 31 Nearctic migrant passerines and near-passerines recorded in Britain or Ireland during the period 1947–76, with the 13 accepted records (all autumn) greatly exceeding the predicted relative likelihood of 5.27 individuals (Robbins 1980). Note, though, that this calculation will have included an unknown percentage of Bicknell's Thrushes *C. bicknelli*.

## [Bicknell's Thrush *Catharus bicknelli*]

Nearctic species, breeds southern Quebec, Canadian Maritime Provinces and New England. Migratory, wintering perhaps exclusively West Indies. Monotypic. Formerly treated as conspecific with Grey-cheeked Thrush *C. minimus*, separated by BOURC July 1996 (BOURC 1997).

As of January 2002, there were no acceptable records of Bicknell's Thrush for Britain and Ireland. However, the species is included here on the basis that a bird found dead on St Mary's on 22nd October 1986 was one of four skins compared by the BOURC with North American material from this species and Grey-cheeked Thrush. None of the four were thought to be Bicknell's but the St Mary's specimen and two of the other three were thought to be close, whereas the fourth was clearly Grey-cheeked (BOURC 1997). If nothing else, this demonstrates the size of the problem involved in now getting a field description accepted, perhaps for either species. For further reading see Curson & Lewington (1994), Anon (1995), Knox (1996) and Anon (1996).

## Ring Ouzel *Turdus torquatus* A

**Annual spring and autumn migrant, in small numbers. Does not breed.**

Limited and incomplete breeding range, from Finland, Norway, Britain and Ireland east through upland southern Europe from northern Spain to Turkey and Iran. Migratory to resident, wintering mainly Mediterranean and Middle East. Polytypic: nominate *torquatus* occurs Britain, Ireland and Scandinavia; *alpestris*, or 'Alpine Ring Ouzel' central and southern Europe; *amicorum* Turkey and Iran. Red-listed in UK: rapid, greater than 50% decline in breeding population over past 25 years and moderate contraction of breeding range over same timescale (Gregory *et al.* 2002).

A fairly obvious species and one clearly not missed by 19th-century ornithologists on Scilly. Earliest mention was probably Francis Rodd's letter to his uncle E H Rodd of Penzance to the effect that one was killed on or soon after 4th October 1870 (Rodd 1880). The same source noted that during a visit from Tresco to nearby Tean on 9th December the same year, three Ring Ouzels were keeping company with Starlings *Sturnus vulgaris* in a rocky hill, a particularly late date for this species. However, most interesting is James Clark and Francis Rodd's account in their *Zoologist* paper, in which they describe it as a frequently seen migrant with a preference for 'rocky eminences' on St Mary's, Tresco and Bryher (Clark & Rodd 1906). They continued by recounting how a fall of over 100 occurred at Old Town, St Mary's, on 12th April 1903 during a southeasterly wind. Several were also noted on 19th April the following year, from which the authors concluded it was probably regular in spring.

Ring Ouzels were also noted at local lighthouses during the late 19th and early 20th centuries, as on the night of 21st April 1884, when many were noted at the Bishop Rock between midnight and 4 am in a misty, force 2, easterly wind (Harvie-Brown *et al.* 1885); or the night of 22nd October 1908, when a few were present amongst large numbers of thrushes *Turdus* that arrived at Bishop Rock from midnight onwards (Ogilvie-Grant 1910). But the most descriptive of such accounts comes from the Bishop Rock on the night of 25th October 1886, when, during a huge fall of thrushes and Bramblings *Fringilla montifringilla*, three Ring Ouzels were killed striking the lantern; also killed were 60 Redwings *T. iliacus* and five Fieldfares *T. pilaris*.

*Birds of the Isles of Scilly*

Birds occur annually, though very occasionally, as in 1983, they fail to appear during spring. Spring passage normally commences from about late March with the majority passing though during April, most if not all having moved on by early to mid-May. Return movement becomes apparent from late September, numbers usually peaking towards mid-October and with few apparent after the first week of November, although late-staying birds do occur and in extreme cases remain through the winter. Such a case involved a female frequenting Tresco from late December 1968 through to mid-February 1969, whilst a male appeared briefly on that island on 17th December 1995. Numbers involved in either season are normally small, with up to a few individuals at one or two sites, but this can be exceeded; an estimated 200 that arrived on St Mary's and St Agnes in autumn 1973 was unprecedented, however. And, of course, 100 were recorded by Clark and Rodd in 1903. Taking the ten years from 1990 as representative, spring sightings occurred between 14th March and 21st June, though early to mid-May was a more normal last date. During autumn, birds arrived between 5th September and 29th November, though again late October was more the norm for last sightings. Single-day spring counts rarely exceeded one or two, whilst autumn daily totals ranged between six and 18.

A few pairs still breed on Dartmoor in nearby Devon but none do so now in west Cornwall (Penhallurick 1978) and there are no records from Scilly. Clearly, the majority of Ring Ouzels passing through the islands must be nominate *torquatus* from populations in either Britain, Ireland or Scandinavia. Nonetheless, birds showing characteristics of populations elsewhere have occurred, including a strikingly pale immature on St Agnes on 6th–7th October 1973. In considering this particular record, the BOURC acknowledged a west to east cline of increasing paleness (due to the amount of white in the wing and body feather edging), and that strikingly pale birds probably originate from central/southern Europe or further southeast. They thought, nevertheless, that the use of subspecific names, i.e. *torquatus, alpestris, amicorum* in relation to British records seemed inadvisable, especially in the absence of a specimen (BOURC 1980). More recently, a further claim of what may well prove to be *alpestris*, and concerning a bird on St Agnes during 21st–23rd May 2001, was submitted to the BBRC (J Gale pers. comm.).

Ringing records show that nominate *torquatus* winters south in the West Palearctic as far as Spain, northwest Africa and Greece. In northwest Africa it winters alongside *alpestris*, particularly in the Atlas mountains (Cramp *et al.* 1977–94). *Torquatus* begins leaving the breeding grounds during September, Scandinavian birds adopting a southwesterly route, mostly down the eastern side of the North Sea, though some pass through Britain (Wernham *et al.* 2002). Return spring migration becomes apparent in southern England from mid-March, passage through Fair Isle peaking during May, and with males preceding females by up to two weeks. If accepted, the recent St Agnes *alpestris* record bears the hallmark of a spring overshoot, though any autumn record would be less easily explained. Five Ring Ouzels have been ringed in Scilly but there are no recaptures.

## Blackbird (Common Blackbird) *Turdus merula* A

**Common breeding resident, passage migrant and probable winter visitor. One of the three most abundant resident landbirds, along with Wren *Troglodytes troglodytes* and Song Thrush *T. philomelos*.**

Breeds most of West Palearctic north of Mediterranean, isolated populations northwest Africa, Canaries, Madeira and Azores. Fragmentary populations southern Asia, introduced New Zealand and southeast Australia. Migratory populations in north and east move south or west to winter in western or southern Europe. Polytypic with complex racial structure: nominate *merula* occurs Europe except in southeast and southern Russia; *aterrimus* southeast Europe south to Crete, Turkey and Iran; *syriacus* Turkey east through Iraq and Iran; at least twelve additional forms. Downgraded from Amber- to Green-listed in UK 2002 (Gregory *et al.* 2002). National 33% decline during 25 years to 1996, but 12% increase 1994–99 (Bashford & Noble 2000).

The earliest reference to Blackbird in Scilly involves bone remains unearthed from the archaeological site on Nornour in the Eastern Isles, these probably coming from the later Bronze Age or Romano-British periods (Turk 1971, 1984b). Next though seems to be Robert Heath's comment that it was found in the islands year-round (Heath 1750). E H Rodd later referred to it as a periodic migrant in varying numbers, according to 'circumstances' (Rodd 1880). In their landmark *Zoologist* paper, James Clark and E H Rodd's nephew Francis described Blackbird as commoner in Scilly than anywhere else in Cornwall (Clark & Rodd 1906). However, their additional comments perhaps seem rather less acceptable now but must of course be viewed in context. For one thing, it was said to breed almost exclusively in furze-brakes (gorse *Ulex*), 'to which they always flew for shelter'. But of course Scilly had still to experience the active tree planting programme of the 1920s and so perhaps Blackbirds were somewhat limited in nest choice, unlike the situation today. Blackbirds were also considered 'remarkably wild and wary' and outside Tresco's Abbey Gardens were allegedly 'rarely heard to sing'. By 1938, it was said to have been abundant 'wherever there is any cover of any sort' (*CBWPSAR* 8).

There is also a wealth of early information from the Bishop Rock Lighthouse, most of which involved autumn movements. Perhaps most descriptive of these concerns the night of 25th October 1886, when Blackbirds figured among hundreds of passing thrushes *Turdus* and Bramblings *Fringilla montifringilla* attracted to the lantern. Sixty Redwings *T. iliacus*, five Fieldfares *T. pilaris* and three Ring Ouzels *T. torquatus* were killed along with one Brambling (Harvie-Brown *et al.* 1887). Then on the night on 5th November 1909, Blackbirds were present at the Bishop Rock along with Song Thrushes *T. philomelos*, Skylarks *Alauda arvensis*, Meadow Pipits *Anthus pratensis* and Starlings *Sturnus vulgaris*, plus four Woodcock *Scolopax rusticola* (Ogilvie-Grant 1911).

Most birds seen are resident in the islands but there are some obvious autumn arrivals. The latter is perhaps even more apparent to anyone handling Blackbirds, with a sudden very noticeable increase in average wing length and body weight, plus an increase in birds with 'frosted' edging to the body feathers. Ringing data show birds involved may have come from as far away as Norway or Sweden, though many arrive in association with weather pattern suggestive of an origin even further east. Whether or not Blackbirds winter in Scilly in any appreciable numbers has still to be determined, but undoubtedly the majority of autumn arrivals have moved on south by mid-November. Interestingly Clark and Rodd thought there was no noticeable increase during severe winter weather, and only small parties reportedly arriving during autumn (Clark & Rodd 1906).

Blackbird breeds on all five inhabited islands plus several that are uninhabited, which certainly includes Samson, St Helen's, Tean and Annet, but probably also Gweal, Great and Little Ganilly, Great Ganinick, the Arthurs and Great Innisvouls, though perhaps not annually on all of these. Breeding numbers involved are difficult to assess, in part due to its sheer abundance, but past counts from St Agnes and Gugh and the more recent Lunnon Farm CBC data from St Mary's assist any estimates. On St Agnes, breeding counts were obtained in eight of the years 1957–78. Pair estimates ranging from 30 to 82, with an average of 54. On the 16-hectare Lunnon Farm study plot, pair totals for the eight years 1991–98 fell in the range 21–33, average 27.3, suggesting a territory size of about 0.6 of a hectare, or between 106–206 pairs per km$^2$. If representative of the islands as a whole, this indicates Scillonian densities may be five to ten times greater than on farmland CBC plots in mainland Britain.

| 1957 | 1958 | 1962 | 1964 | 1974 | 1978 |
|---|---|---|---|---|---|
| 50 | 50 | 40 | 30 | 82 | 72 |

**St Agnes & Gugh Breeding Survey Data – Blackbird Pairs (IOSBR 1979)**

| 1991 | 1992 | 1993 | 1994 | 1995 | 1996 | 1997 | 1998 |
|---|---|---|---|---|---|---|---|
| 21 | 25 | 33 | 27 | 28 | 29 | 28 | 28 |

**Blackbird CBC Pair Totals – 16-ha Lunnon Farm, St Mary's 1991–98 (P J Robinson – unpublished data)**

Application of the Lunnon Farm figures to the known St Mary's land area of 628 hectares suggests a total of 1,046 Blackbird pairs for the island. However, the 2000 Breeding Bird Atlas (Chown & Lock 2002) located an estimated 499 pairs in 47 (70.1%) of the 67 surveyed squares throughout the islands, though the report's authors thought the true figure fell in the range 600–1,000 pairs. Birds were found breeding on 14 islands (Table) and breeding was confirmed in 35 (52.2%) of the surveyed squares. Penhallurick (1978) suggested a 1970's Blackbird-Song Thrush ratio for mainland Cornwall of between 8:1 and 13:4 in both farmland and open country and 23:19 in woodland. Again, the only comparable figures for Scilly involve the St Agnes and Gugh breeding surveys and the Lunnon Farm CBC data. The first of these produces an averaged ratio of almost exactly 1:1, though with evidence of Song Thrush

*Birds of the Isles of Scilly*

increase towards the end of the period, whilst the Lunnon Farm data also suggested a near equal situation, with a Blackbird-Song Thrush ratio of 9:10.

A feature of Scillonian Blackbirds difficult to ignore during spring and summer is bill and orbital ring coloration, which, unlike that of mainland birds, is a rich orange-red. It has been suggested that this difference in colour is related to diet, though with few suggestions as to what the link might be. However, in truth, this is clearly related to breeding condition, the soft-part colour intensifying with the onset of the breeding season, at which time if birds are handled, it will be seen that the red extends into the gap and throat, much in the manner of Kittiwake *Rissa tridactyla*, or even Black Guillemot *Cepphus grylle*. Some older females also show a tendency towards more brightly coloured bills. Equally interesting, but perhaps less easily explained, is the presence of particularly 'pink' pigmented broods among the Scillonian population (pers. obs.). This feature is only noticeable for the few days after hatching, for obvious reasons, but is possibly linked in some way to bill colour. Unlike Song Thrush, more than 70% of Blackbirds breed in the natal area and a further 20% within eight kilometres (Werth 1947), which, particularly in island populations, seems likely to result in a high level in inbreeding.

Like Song Thrush, many Scillonian Blackbirds build low down, probably mainly in response to the prevalence of high winds, particularly early in the season. Clutch size appears small by mainland standards and, as with Song Thrush, clutches of five are extremely rare, as indeed are early nests, few if any Scillonian Blackbirds laying before late March. One interesting feature of the Lunnon Farm study was the small percentage of ground-nesting pairs among early potatoes; Ron Symons noted the same behaviour in both potatoes and bulb flowers on the same island in 1968 (*CBWPSAR* 38). However, this behaviour is recorded elsewhere (N F Ticehurst 1910). Another noticeable feature of this species is the extent to which some pairs with nestlings, particularly on the off-islands, feed on the beaches, noticeably digging for sand hoppers which they then carry away (Quick 1956).

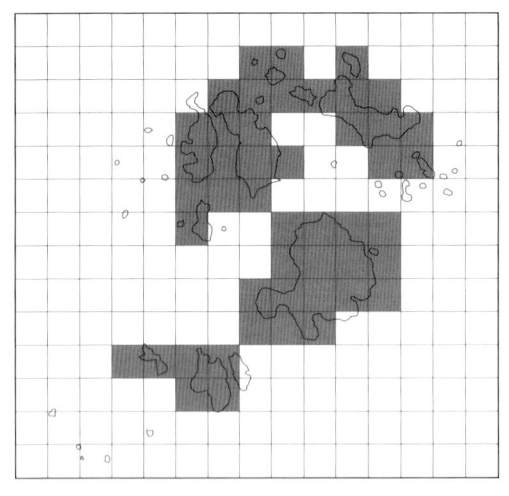

| Island | Pairs |
| --- | --- |
| St Mary's | 211 |
| Tresco | 77 |
| Bryher | 42 |
| St Martin's | 78 |
| St Agnes & Gugh | 54 |
| Samson | 8 |
| Puffin Island | 1 |
| Annet | 7 |
| St Helen's | 7 |
| Tean | 7 |
| White Island, St Martin's | 4 |
| Great Ganilly | 2 |
| Toll's Island | 1 |

**2000 Breeding Bird Atlas (Chown & Lock 2002)**

**1-km Blackbird Breeding Distribution – 2000–01 (data Chown & Lock 2002)**

According to Cramp *et al.* (1977–94) there is something of a divide among wintering European Blackbirds, those from Scandinavia, Britain, Ireland, Germany and Denmark moving mainly west and those from further south wintering in southern Europe. This situation is apparently borne out by Scillonian ringing data (Table). In addition, Penhallurick (1978) listed three birds recovered in mainland Cornwall between November and February, all of which were ringed in Germany during May. However, overlaying this situation is the southwest movement of many Blackbirds from northern Britain, some of which reach northwest France (Wernham *et al.* 2002). And as the breeding bird that hit a window in Bridport during April shows, some Blackbirds from as far south in Britain as Dorset apparently feel the need to move even further west during winter. A total of 2,578 Blackbirds had been ringed on Scilly up until the end of 1999, 77% since 1970.

**Controls**

| | | |
|---|---|---|
| K797906 | 1stY | Ijsselmeerpolders, Netherlands 28th October 1992 |
| RJ70534 | 1stY | Wells-next-the-Sea, Norfolk 16th September 1992 |

CT  St Agnes 30th October 1993
LO  Peninnis, St Mary's 19th September 1995

**Recoveries**

| | | |
|---|---|---|
| RB67785 | Ad | St Agnes 29th October 1988 |
| RB67325 | Ad | St Agnes 22nd October 1990 |
| RR64104 | Ad | Lunnon Farm, St Mary's 21st November 1995 |
| RR00234 | 1stY | Watermill, St Mary's 25th November 1994 |
| RJ21348 | 1stY | St Agnes 30th October 1993 |
| RP31937 | 1stY | St Agnes 25th October 1997 |

CT  Hummelstad, Kalmer, Sweden 28th November 1989
CT  Epwell, Banbury, Oxfordshire 15th February 1995
FD  Bridport, Dorset 8th April 1996
CT  Jomfrudland, Kragero, Telemark, Norway 28th May 1996
KC  Yeoford, Crediton, Devon 28th February 1999
FD  Pas de Calais, France 25th October 1999

**Blackbird Ringing Recaptures**

## Eye-browed Thrush *Turdus obscurus* A  BBRC 41.1%

**Very rare mainly autumn migrant and perhaps winter visitor, full written description required by the BBRC.**

1964  One St Agnes 5th December  *British Birds* 58: 364, 61: 218–223
1984  One (male) St Mary's 20th October  *British Birds* 78: 573
1987  One (first-year) St Mary's 12th October  *British Birds* 81: 580; *Twitching* 1: 378
1987  One (first-year) St Agnes 27th October  *British Birds* 81: 580; *Twitching* 1: 378
1990  One (first-year male) Tresco 21st October  *British Birds* 84: 485
1991  One (first-year) St Mary's & Tresco 12th to 18th October  *British Birds* 85: 538, 89: 516
1993  One (first-year) St Mary's & St Agnes 7th to 16th October  *British Birds* 87: 551–552

Breeds Siberia and eastern Asia to Sea of Okhotsk and south to Lake Baikal and Mongolia. Migratory, wintering southern Japan, southern China, Taiwan, southeast Asia, India and Bangladesh. Monotypic.

The earliest Eye-browed Thrush presence on Scilly involved a bird discovered feeding in a field along Barnaby Lane, St Agnes, on 5th December 1964 (Parslow 1968b, 1982b). Field identification was later confirmed by examination of the skin collection at the British Museum (Natural History) (*SABOAR* 1963–64). Two further Eye-browed Thrushes were recorded elsewhere in Britain that same autumn, these three being the first British and Irish records; the first in Northamptonshire and the second in the Western Isles, followed by the St Agnes individual (Palmer 2000).

Seven Eye-browed Thrushes arrived in Scilly in six years, five of these aged as first-years. The Chart incorporates all arrival dates and shows an obvious mid-October preference. The mean length of stay was 3.1 days, though five were seen for one day or less. This failure to relocate birds after their initial discovery is perhaps surprising, but perhaps reflects a high degree of individual mobility, plus the difficulty of locating a lookalike species among so many passage or wintering Redwings *Turdus iliacus*. In addition, Holman & Walsh (1992) drew attention to either an aberrant Redwing or hybrid Eye-browed Thrush x Redwing, seen on two separate occasions on St Mary's the day prior to the discovery of the 1987 Eye-browed Thrush on nearby St Agnes, the authors emphasising the possibility of confusion and drawing attention the overlap in breeding ranges of these two species.

The 1984 adult male at Salakee, St Mary's was later described as a 'breathtaking beauty' (*IOSBR* 1984), whereas 1987 produced two October arrivals: first-winters at Four Lanes, St Mary's and Barnaby Lane, St Agnes (Shaw 1987). The first Tresco presence involved the fifth Scilly record in 1990 and the only two individuals recorded moving between islands were those on St Mary's and Tresco in 1991, and St Mary's and St Agnes in 1993.

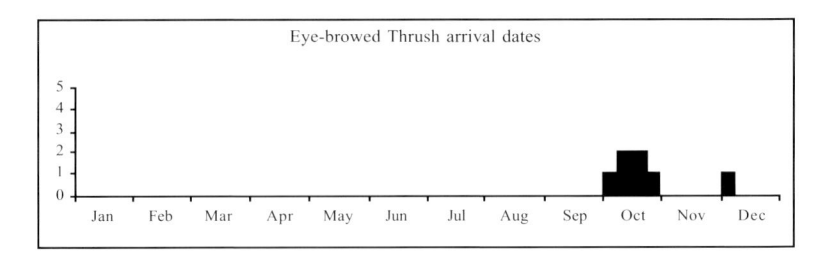

*Birds of the Isles of Scilly*

[Chart: Eye-browed Thrush arrival dates — bars in October and December]

These seven birds represent 41.1% of the 17 Eye-browed Thrush records accepted by the BBRC during the period 1958–99. No Eye-browed Thrushes have been trapped and ringed on Scilly. Departure from the breeding grounds occurs from September and despite its distinctly southeast Asian wintering distribution, Eye-browed Thrush occurs regularly within the West Palearctic and northwest North America (Alaska) (Cramp *et al.* 1977–94). On the face of it, the presence of this species so far to the west of its breeding and wintering range seems difficult to interpret, although the obvious October pattern of Scillonian arrivals apparently demonstrates a high degree of intent.

## Black/Red-throated Thrush (Dark-throated Thrush) *Turdus ruficollis* A BBRC 9.3%

**Vary rare autumn migrant, full written description required by the BBRC.**

    1982   One (*atrogularis* – female or first-year) St Mary's 7th to 14th October   *British Birds* 76: 508
    1987   One (*atrogularis* – male) St Mary's 23rd to 24th October   *British Birds* 81: 580
    1992   One (*atrogularis* – first-year female) St Mary's 22nd October   *British Birds* 86: 511
    1993   One (*atrogularis* – first-year female) St Martin's 13th & 14th October   *British Birds* 87: 552
    2002   One (*atrogularis* – first-year male) St Mary's & Tresco 19th to 24th October   *British Birds* 95: 668

Breeds eastern Europe and central Asia, south to southwest China. Migratory, wintering mainly Iran to western China, northern India and southeast Asia. Polytypic, two distinct forms: *atrogularis* or 'Black-throated Thrush' occurs eastern European Russia through central Siberia to Altai; *ruficollis* or 'Red-throated Thrush' south and east of *atrogularis*.

Just four accepted records of this western European rarity, the first of which was an elusive female or first-winter individual discovered in Holy Vale, St Mary's, in early October 1982, before settling at nearby Mount Pleasant until 14th. During its stay it frequently fed on wild blackberries *Rubus*. It was followed by a fine male in October 1987, again in the Holy Vale area, just seven days before another arrived on Fair Isle. The first-winter female near Seaways Flower Farm in October 1992 immediately enlivened what had been a quiet mid-October for birds, keeping the crowds on the move by rapidly relocating to Borough on the other side of the island. Finally, a first-winter female discovered on St Martin's for two days in mid-October 1993 was then reported in rapid succession from St Mary's and Tresco (*IOSBR* 1993), though only the first of these sightings gained acceptance from the BBRC.

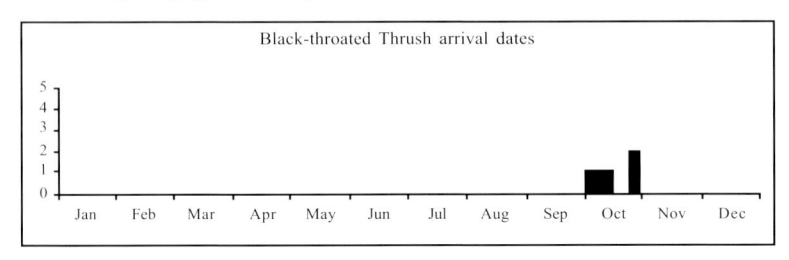

[Chart: Black-throated Thrush arrival dates — bars in October]

All four arrival dates are incorporated in the Chart. The mean length of stay was just 3.25 days. These four individuals comprise 9.3% of the 43 records accepted by the BBRC during the period 1958–99. Most British records have come from Shetland, Fair Isle and central and eastern England and thus far all Scillonian records involved the more westerly black-throated *atrogularis*. The extent of autumn migration varies between years, depending on the success or failure of the annual Siberian berry crop. *Atrogularis* begins leaving the breeding grounds from the end of August, some still moving south into October. It winters 'abundantly' from Iran east through Arabia, Himalayas, India and southwest China, north to southern Kazakhstan (Cramp *et al.* 1977–94). Cramp *et al.* suggest that British records may involve birds delaying southward movement until the onset of severe weather, though the Chart is perhaps suggestive of regular migration. No Black-throated Thrushes have been ringed on Scilly.

## Fieldfare *Turdus pilaris* A

**Annual, mainly autumn migrant or winter visitor, often in substantial numbers.**

Breeds central and northern Europe and Asia east to Lake Baikal and southeast Siberia. Migratory, strongly so in north and east, less so or dispersive in west and south, wintering mainly southern Europe. Monotypic. Amber-listed in UK: moderate breeding decline over past 25 years; five-year mean of 4.0 breeding pairs (Gregory *et al.* 2002).

Rather less early information is available than for Redwing *T. iliacus*, though nevertheless substantial. James Clark and Francis Rodd described it as usually less plentiful than Redwing, whilst E H Rodd thought it a 'periodical migrant, varying, according to circumstances, in numbers and time of appearance' (Rodd 1878b). And it is clear from these early reports how rapidly the situation could change, Francis Rodd describing how on 22nd December the high ground of St Mary's was 'alive with Fieldfares', whereas on 25th he saw only 'a stray Fieldfare or two' during a tour of the Tresco pools (Rodd 1880). Clark and Rodd mentioned a large, apparent cold-weather arrival of Lapwings *Vanellus vanellus* and other species on 13th February 1900, which included many Fieldfares. The Lapwing flock was reportedly three miles (5 km) long and arrived from the northwest. Included amongst this flock were many Fieldfares and Redwings and although they quickly moved on, many dead remained.

Like other thrushes, Fieldfares were also recorded at the Scillonian lighthouses during the 19th and early 20th centuries. In 1880, birds were seen heading west past the Bishop Rock mid-morning on 13th October (Harvie-Brown *et al.* 1881) and between 5th and 12th November 1907 'many' were 'recorded and taken' at the same site (Ogilvie-Grant 1909). Good numbers also arrived at the Bishop with other thrushes on the night of 19th November 1908 (Ogilvie-Grant 1910), whilst on the night of 25th October 1886 five Fieldfares were killed striking the lantern amongst a movement of several hundred thrushes *Turdus* and Bramblings *Fringilla montifringilla* (Harvie-Brown *et al.* 1887).

Birds mostly arrive during October but without the large flocks sometimes evident on mainland Britain, though concentrations do occur, as in winter 1961 when 700 were reportedly on St Agnes. Like Redwing, large arrivals are not necessarily associated with cold weather movements and, also like Redwing, few arrived in the islands during the particularly severe winter of 1963. In an average year few are about the islands during late winter or spring, early autumn migrants becoming apparent from perhaps late September with numbers building towards the end of October. Subsequently, there is a noticeable reduction in count totals and most have departed by late November. Average peak autumn numbers normally hover around the 200–400 mark but in some years struggle to reach even three figures.

Birds from the northern West Palearctic winter mainly in southwest Europe, moving lesser or greater distances depending upon the severity of northern winters (Wernham *et al.* 2002), whilst birds from the Eastern Palearctic winter mostly in the Caspian and Black Sea area. Six Fieldfares have been ringed in Scilly, all since 1970 and there are no recaptures.

## Song Thrush *Turdus philomelos* A

**Abundant breeding resident, particularly on St Mary's, probable annual migrant in unknown numbers and possible winter visitor.**

Breeds Europe and western Asia, from Britain, Ireland, France and Spain east to Lake Baikal and south to Mediterranean and northern Iran. Migratory in north and east, sedentary or dispersive in west and south. Polytypic; nominate *philomelos*, or 'Continental Song Thrush', occurs most of Europe; *hebridensis*, or 'Hebridean Song Thrush', Outer Hebrides and Isle of Skye; *clarkei*, or 'British Song Thrush' remainder of Britain, Ireland and adjacent central Europe; *nataliae* central Siberia. Red-listed in UK: rapid, 53% breeding decline over past 25 years (Gregory *et al.* 2002). National 60% decline during 25 years to 1996, but 7% increase 1994–99 (Bashford & Noble 2000).

The undoubted earliest evidence of Song Thrush presence in Scilly comes from prehistoric sites on Nornour in the Eastern Isles and from May's Hill, St Martin's, bone remains of at least two individuals being recovered at each site (Turk 1984a, 1984b). However, the earliest published record seems to be credited to Robert Heath (1750), who noted it was found in the islands year-round. E H Rodd later commented that it was a periodic migrant 'varying, according to circumstances, in numbers and time of appearance' (Rodd 1880). This observation is not easily interpreted but was presumably intended to denote it occurred as a migrant in some but not all years, numbers also varying between years. Neither are we helped by the occasional 19th- or early 20th-century reference to 'thrush' movements, without clear indication of the species involved. However, such movements today involve mostly Redwings *Turdus iliacus*, Blackbirds *T. merula* and Fieldfares *T. pilaris*, with the number of Song Thrushes not easily defined. As usual, the most informative early comment comes from James Clark and E H Rodd's nephew Francis, who by the start of the 20th century thought it a common breeding resident on all five inhabited islands plus a few others, including Samson, St Helen's, Great Ganilly and (at least in 1903) Annet (Clark & Rodd 1906). They suggested that there was no winter increase but noted that it had been observed arriving on Tresco from the northeast in autumn, not in flocks but in ones and twos, following each other closely 'for hours at a time'. On at least one such occasion (e.g. February 1900), the movement was clearly exceptional and associated with unusually large numbers of other species, e.g. Lapwing *Vanellus vanellus*.

Among early 20th century observations appears the comment that by 1938 it was to be found in 'all suitable localities' (*CBWPSAR* 8). A A Dorrien-Smith also noted that birds breeding in Scilly belonged to the form *ericetorum* (T A Dorrien-Smith 1951), the old name for what we now know as *clarkei* (Witherby *et al.* 1940; Cramp *et al.* 1977–94), although the basis for this remark remains uncertain. There are also a number of early migration reports involving Song Thrushes at the Bishop Rock Lighthouse. Such an example refers to the year 1884, when 'good numbers' were reportedly present from 11 pm until daylight on the night of 19th October (Harvie-Brown *et al.* 1885). Similarly, several hundreds of this and other species were recorded on the night of 14th November that year (Harvie-Brown *et al.* 1985). However, most such reports concern early November rather than October, the only spring account involving its appearance at the Bishop Rock 'in numbers' from midnight to 4 am on the night of 21st–22nd April 1884 (Harvie-Brown *et al.* 1885).

In his mid-1970's review of the birds of Scilly and Cornwall, Penhallurick (1978) thought Song Thrush absent from both Samson and Annet, though it certainly breeds on Samson today, albeit in small numbers. However, as noted by Clark and Rodd, its hold on Annet is less secure and though breeding appears not to have been reported recently, it probably occurs at least occasionally; as may also be true of some of the lesser Eastern Isles. Most writers commented on Song Thrush's abundance in Scilly, from Clark and Rodd in 1906 through to the present day. Penhallurick drew attention to the equal abundance of this species and Blackbird on St Agnes up until the mid-1970s, whilst also suggesting that Song Thrush may have been more numerous on St Mary's.

| 1957 | 1958 | 1962 | 1963 | 1964 | 1974 | 1978 |
|------|------|------|------|------|------|------|
| 40   | 40   | 25   | 20   | 40   | 95   | 83   |

St Agnes & Gugh Breeding Survey Data – Song Thrush Pairs (*IOSBR* 1979)

| 1991 | 1992 | 1993 | 1994 | 1995 | 1996 | 1997 | 1998 |
|------|------|------|------|------|------|------|------|
| 27   | 23   | 33   | 25   | 42   | 48   | 24   | 23   |

Song Thrush CBC Data (pairs) – 16-ha Lunnon Farm, St Mary's 1991–98 (P J Robinson – unpublished data)

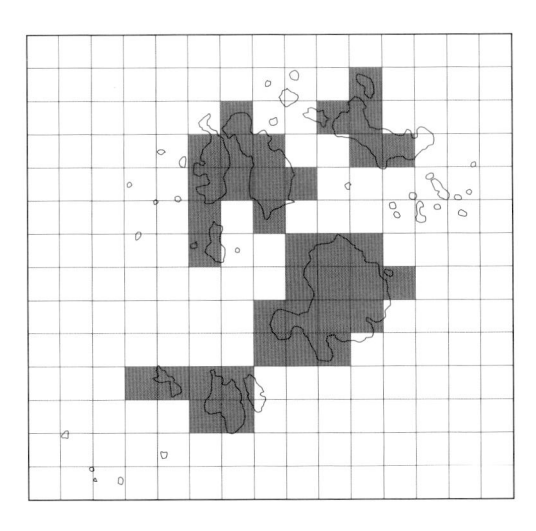

| Island | Pairs |
|--------|-------|
| St Mary's | 221 |
| Tresco | 55 |
| Bryher | 39 |
| St Martin's | 52 |
| St Agnes & Gugh | 42 |
| Samson | 7 |
| Annet | 2 |
| Tean | 1 |
| White Island, St Martin's | 1 |

**2000 Breeding Bird Atlas (Chown & Lock 2002)**

1-km Song Thrush Breeding Distribution – 2000–01 (data Chown & Lock 2002)

The recent 2000 Breeding Bird Atlas (Chown & Lock 2002) located an estimated 420 pairs in 36 (53.7%) of the 67 surveyed 1-km squares (Table), though in addressing the possibility of under-recording, the report's authors thought the likely true figure in the range 525–1,050 pairs.

Examination of St Mary's Lunnon Farm CBC data for the period 1991–98 shows these two occur in near equal numbers now on St Mary's, average annual pair-totals being Song Thrush 30.6 and Blackbird 27.3 (P J Robinson – unpublished data), giving an average Song Thrush density for the 16-hectare study plot of 0.52 pairs per hectare, with a low of 0.33, and a high of 0.69. The Table also shows Song Thrush pair counts from breeding surveys conducted on St Agnes and Gugh during seven of the years 1957–1978, though survey methods and reasons for the later, substantial increase are not explained (*IOSBR* 1979). Nevertheless, an assumed annual average of 89 pairs for the 1970s on St Agnes gives an annual overall density of one pair per 1.66 hectares, in the order of three times less numerous than on St Mary's during the 1990s.

On St Agnes and Gugh, the presence now of 42 pairs in four 1-km squares is down from the high of the 1970s. On Lunnon Farm, fewer pairs occupied the comparatively dry, cultivated centre of the plot, highest concentrations occurring in the damp woodland edge and marshland sections within Higher Moors and Holy Vale. Doubtless, much the same would prove true of Tresco were the situation examined to the same degree, with drier islands like Bryher and St Agnes perhaps holding lesser concentrations.

During the ten years 1991–2000, the author worked extensively on Scillonian Song Thrushes (P J Robinson – unpublished data). In this time, several obvious differences between the physiology of island and mainland populations became apparent, including some presumed similarities with *hebridensis*. However, reasons for these similarities have yet to be examined.

On Scilly, average nest height is low, under one metre on Lunnon Farm and adjacent Higher Moors, perhaps in response to high winds early in the season. The need to protect commercial flower crops from these same high winds gives rise to the planting of *Pittosporum crassifolium* and similar evergreen windbreak hedgerows often used by nesting thrushes. However, although nest height remains unchanged throughout the season, nest-site elevation shows an obvious increase during late April or early May – the Chart includes all Lunnon Farm data for the three years 1998–2000. Lunnon Farm and perhaps other island Blackbirds occasionally nest on the ground among the early potato crop, but although Song Thrushes spend much time on, and often sing from, the ground, no ground nests were recorded, although such behaviour has been recorded elsewhere (N F Ticehurst 1910).

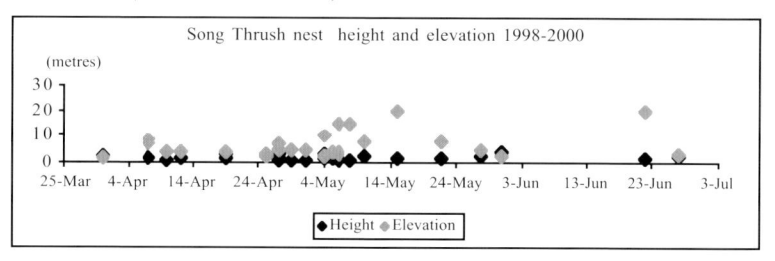

*Song Thrush nest height and elevation 1998-2000*

Nests also lack the base of moss and small twigs characteristic in mainland Britain and instead are composed wholly of dry grasses. And, like *hebridensis* (Cramp *et al.* 1977–94), up to 6% of nests annually lack the mud or wood-chip lining, though this can occasionally occur on mainland Britain (Whitaker 1887). First eggs are laid from about the last week of March, normal clutch size being four with, unlike mainland Britain, a near absence of early season three-egg clutches and no peak of five-egg clutches mid-season. Out of approximately 350 clutches recorded on Lunnon Farm and elsewhere in Scilly during the ten-year study, less than 3% contained five-egg clutches, whereas for Britain generally Cramp *et al.* suggested 13% three-egg clutches, 57% with four eggs and 26% with five eggs, with a seasonal mean of 4.7. Ignoring incomplete clutches, mean clutch size on Lunnon Farm during 1995 was 3.91, commencing almost invariably with four and declining thereafter. The Chart shows data for 1995 arranged into three-week periods; lumping the two late four-egg clutches with those for the preceding period gives a combined mean for these six weeks of 3.83.

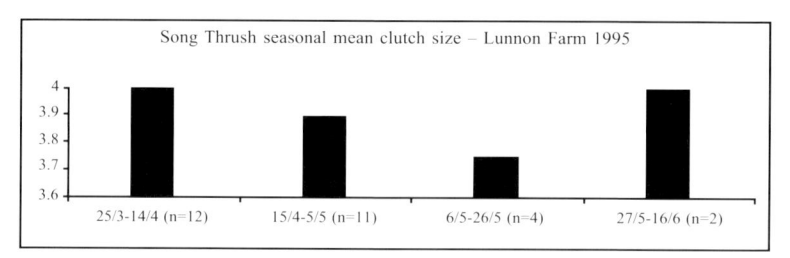

*Song Thrush seasonal mean clutch size – Lunnon Farm 1995*

On Lunnon Farm, and on Scilly generally, potential passerine nest predators are limited to Carrion Crow *Corvus corone*, Brown Rat *Rattus norvegicus* and, less numerous and less active, domestic and feral cats *Felis catus*. However, there is the added possibility of predation by the recently introduced Hedgehog *Erinaceus europaeus* (so far on St Mary's only), although Magpie *Pica pica* and Jay *Garrulus glandarius* are noticeably absent. Nevertheless, annual levels of nest predation are remarkably similar to those in mainland Britain. For example, in 1995 predation accounted for 47.6% of all nests built, or 71.4% of all failed nests, equivalent figures for a comparable 1995 Sussex study being 47.2% and 69.1% (R Taylor pers. comm.). This offers compelling evidence that Magpies may not be the outstanding threat to songbird populations they are so often perceived to be. But is proof also that nest predation will account for up to 80% of all nest failures however many, or few, the number of predator species involved (Cote & Sutherland 1995).

The high Scillonian Song Thrush density was reflected on Lunnon Farm by up to five pairs around a single 0.2 hectare field, plus a total of 49 nests found in a possible 33–38 territories during 1995. There was also a progressive seasonal reduction in both fledging success and chick quality, though early nests are often more exposed and therefore more liable to predation. Successful early nests tend to produce four good quality young, the seasonal decline in chick quality and quantity being apparently related to food availability. There is little evidence of double brooding, though most pairs seem prepared to replace failed nests, at least during the early part of the season. In 1995, of 42 nests with eggs 14 (33%) fledged young, giving a mean fledging successes of 2.92 fledged young per successful nest. Hatching success appeared normal, 104 eggs in 27 nests where incubation commenced producing 78 young during 1995 (75% hatching success). The apparent terrestrial nature of Scillonian Song Thrushes is very noticeable, a feature even more evident during CBC work, when birds are frequently encountered singing on the ground.

Although the presence in Scilly of unknown numbers of migrant Song Thrushes seems established, especially during autumn, there is nonetheless substantial between-year variation. In some years there is little or no evidence of movement, whereas in others numbers involved can be impressive, as in late October 1971 when 'an unusually strong passage' involved up to 600 on St Agnes alone. Less easy to interpret, however, is a report involving up to 200 on St Agnes and 250 on St Mary's on 16th October1973, bearing in mind the likely presence of at least that many resident breeding birds and progeny of the year, and remembering that many autumn counts are compiled by visiting birders unfamiliar with Scilly's high resident Song Thrush density. Based on Lunnon Farm data alone, the islands appear theoretically capable of holding up to 3,500 pairs, which with annual productivity could cause the population to peak at twice that number. Penhallurick (1978) made the same point when he suggested that migration may not always be detectable whilst the resident population is high. Stone *et al.* (1997) suggested a best-estimate of 990,000 British pairs (territories) for the period 1988–91, the present Scillonian population seemingly representing up to about 0.5% of that figure.

Observers have commented on apparent plumage differences between Scillonian and mainland Song Thrushes, in particular the rich brown colour of the crown, the intensity of spotting and a perhaps paler underside, similar in fact to *hebridensis*, which Scillonian birds also resemble behaviourally. Therefore, it is important to note that Song Thrushes in southern Ireland are sometimes considered intermediate between British *clarkei* and *hebridensis* (Kennedy *et al.* 1954) and Penhallurick mentioned a report of birds in west Cornwall resembling *hebridensis*.

The case for overwintering seems less well understood and the possibility of hard-weather movements from mainland Cornwall and beyond further confuses the issue. The reality is that if any Song Thrushes from northern or eastern in Europe do winter in the islands then their presence seems unlikely to be detected in the absence of ringing evidence. Interestingly, Lack examined early ringing data and concluded there was an absence of evidence showing birds from further north in Britain wintered intermediately in southern England, most of those that did move in winter reaching Ireland or France/Spain (D Lack 1943–44). The same author finding that among first-years from southern England ringed as nestlings, a far greater proportion, 84%, reached France or Spain, compared with just over 40% recovered in Ireland or where ringed.

Up to 1999, a total of 2,241 Song Thrushes had been ringed on Scilly, 68% since 1970, making it the second most frequently ringed landbird in Scilly after Blackbird and the fifth most frequently ringed species in the islands overall. Even so, the apparent disinclination of local birds to wander even between islands means there are just two recaptures from outside the archipelago, both ringed on St Martin's and both shot in France, one as recently as 1990. The October ringing date of RV45718 offers the possibility that it may have been a passage migrant, leaving NX88456 as the only known recovery of an apparent Scillonian Song Thrush away from the islands. Also listed is a nine-year recovery on St Mary's of a bird ringed on that island in 1914. In addition to the two French recoveries there are a small number of inter-island recaptures, perhaps no more than ten. Most of these apparently involve movements, in either direction, between St Mary's and St Agnes. The obvious exceptions to this are individuals regularly seen commuting between closely adjacent islands, e.g. St Agnes and Gugh, or Tresco and Bryher. In the latter case, at least one was observed carrying food from Bryher across half a kilometre of tidal water to Tresco (pers. obs.). A large number of Song Thrushes were colour-ringed during the ten-year Lunnon Farm study but with few subsequent field sightings, what little data there are suggesting that young leave the immediate natal area by October. No work has been carried out on the likely effects of this high density on recruitment, though a healthy productivity and lack of subsequent colour-ring reports suggest this is low and that most mortality occurs during the first winter.

Northern European populations migrate either southeast or southwest, the latter wintering from southern England through western France and Iberia into the Mediterranean basin and North Africa. A proportion of British birds also move south or southwest into Ireland, France and Iberia, those from further north moving the greatest distance (D Lack 1943), and although birds of the form *hebridensis* are largely sedentary, at least a few winter in Ireland (Cramp *et al.* 1977–94). Within the southern half of Britain, Song Thrushes from eastern England tend to move greater distances south, as far as southern Spain, than those from the west and southwest (Wernham *et al.* 2002)

*Birds of the Isles of Scilly*

Britain and Ireland are situated on the western fringe of the main migration path from northern Europe, westerly drift migration presumably accounting for the periodic nature of autumn arrivals in Scilly and perhaps explaining the comparative lack of return spring passage through the islands. The possibility that at least a small proportion of Scillonian Song Thrushes follow the example of others in southern England and winter in France or Iberia cannot be dismissed and if true might help explain the June-ringed St Martin's individual shot in France in mid-November, plus the apparent reduction in numbers on the Lunnon Farm plot during winter months.

There are two published records of Song Thrushes falling victim to larger species, the first involving at least two individuals taken by an immature male Hen Harrier *Circus cyaneus* on St Agnes during mid-October 1970 (*IOSBR* 1970), whilst in April 1995 a Purple Heron *Ardea purpurea* was seen to take and swallow an incautious Song Thrush that wandered too close to the motionless bird (*IOSBR* 1995). There are records of Song Thrushes feeding on shoreline periwinkles *Littorina* but this behaviour appears not to have been widely observed in Scilly and, as with most mainland reports, seems largely associated with unusually cold weather (Quick 1956; Milne 1963). Much the same is perhaps true of Song Thrushes reportedly taking lugworms *Arenicola* at low tide on St Agnes (Quick 1956; *British Birds* 86: 630–631).

Recoveries

| | | | | | |
|---|---|---|---|---|---|
| G243 | Pul | St Mary's 27th April 1914 | ? | | St Mary's 23rd June 1923 |
| NX88456 | Ad | St Martin's 13th June 1981 | SH | | Ille D' Oleron, Charente Maritime, France 17th November 1981 |
| RV45718 | 1stY | St Martin's 22nd October 1990 | SH | | Prechacq Les Bains, Landes, France 2nd December 1990 |

**Song Thrush Ringing Recaptures**

# Redwing *Turdus iliacus* A

**Annual, mainly autumn migrant or winter visitor, often in substantial numbers.**

Breeds northern Eurasia, from Iceland, northern Britain, Scandinavia and Baltic east to Lake Baikal and East Siberian Sea. Migratory or partially so, wintering mainly central-southern Europe. Polytypic: nominate *iliacus* occurs throughout, except in Iceland and Faeroes, where replaced by *coburni*, or 'Icelandic Redwing'. Amber-listed in UK: five-year mean of 23.3 breeding pairs (Gregory *et al.* 2002).

There is a great deal of early information about what was clearly an obvious annual visitor to the islands (e.g. Rodd 1864c, 1868d, 1880). James Clark and Francis Rodd considered it more numerous than Fieldfare *T. pilaris* during most winters, though it arrived earlier, usually from early to mid-October. They described how large flocks occasionally passed the islands without landing, usually at night during late autumn or winter (Clark & Rodd 1906), and usefully pointed out how flocks were commonly seen arriving from the northwest over Tresco or Bryher and continuing towards the southeast, 'even in the teeth of a south-easterly wind'. Francis Rodd noted in a letter to his uncle E H Rodd that the direction of travel was 'As if from Ireland to the French coast' (Rodd 1880). In another letter he described how, during early November 1870, and in an easterly gale 'with dark weather', a stream of migratory birds seemed to come from the east every night, graphically describing how he heard them passing 'night after night' as they apparently followed a course straight out into the Atlantic, but being unable to identify any except Redwing and Fieldfare. Later that same year, he recounted to his uncle how Redwings and Starlings *Sturnus vulgaris* were now dying everywhere, having crept into holes and corners of windows for shelter, thousands having roosted in gorse bushes on Tresco's Abbey Hill, with over 200 seen by Francis where they had died on an island road.

Similarly, it was commonly noted at Scillonian lighthouses, including among several hundred thrushes *Turdus* at the Bishop Rock from 10 pm until dawn on the night of 13th November 1984 (Harvie-Brown *et al.* 1885). Whilst on 6th November 1907, flocks were observed heading west past the same location (Ogilvie-Grant 1909). However, most interesting were events at the Bishop Rock on the night of 25th October 1886, when 60 Redwings were killed striking the lantern out of a movement of several hundred thrushes and Bramblings *Fringilla montifringilla*. Other fatalities involved included five Fieldfares *T. pilaris*, three Ring Ouzels *T. torquatus* and a single Brambling. The lighthouse keeper, a Mr Troth, recorded that this was the largest such movement he had witnessed in five years at the Bishop Rock (Harvie-Brown *et al.* 1887).

Generally speaking, the situation remains much as described, birds normally appearing with the October rush of late autumn or early winter arrivals and becoming somewhat less evident into the winter period. Numbers involved vary between years and not necessarily according to weather conditions, or at least not those within western Europe. For example, few arrived in the particularly severe winter of 1963, whilst during the apparently normal conditions of mid-October 1973 an estimated 10,000 were present on St Mary's and 5,000 on nearby St Agnes. Usually, though, about 100–150 might be present about the islands, with periodic increases up to 500, sometimes thousands, per island and with overflying flocks also in evidence during any notable arrivals, but with end-of-year totals usually in the region of 100 or less. There is little published discussion on the racial composition of passage flocks, but as the Icelandic and Faeroes *coburni* winters in Britain and Ireland south into France it would be surprising indeed if it did not pass through Scilly, or even winter, although there is evidence that some reach Iberia directly across the Bay of Biscay (Cramp *et al.* 1977–94). However, nominate *iliacus* also winters in western Europe, with limited evidence that birds from quite far east also reach Britain and Ireland.

Redwings passing through Britain originate from Iceland and northwest Europe as far east as at least northwest Russia (Wernham *et al.* 2002). A total of 185 Redwings had been ringed in Scilly up until 1999, interestingly only four before 1970, and there are no recaptures, though birds ringed in Norway and Finland have been recovered in mainland Cornwall. A bird ringed in Cornwall in January 1939 was recovered in Italy the following November, with an October Cornish-ringed individual shot in Spain a month later. Several unusually plumaged individuals including the following are on record. On St Mary's on 26th October 1987, prolonged views were obtained of a Redwing showing more than a little similarity to Eye-browed Thrush *T. obscurus* (Holman & Walsh 1992), whilst a bird described as leucistic was present at Borough Farm, St Mary's, on 16th December 1996.

# Mistle Thrush *Turdus viscivorus* A

**Scarce migrant or winter visitor and the rarest of the native thrushes. There are breeding records for perhaps three years during the 1930s.**

Breeds Europe east to central Asia, from Britain, Ireland, France and Iberia east to Lake Baikal and south to North Africa, Turkey and western Himalayas. Migratory in east and north, sedentary or dispersive in west and south. Polytypic: nominate *viscivorus* occurs West Palearctic east to western Siberia; *bonapartei* central Siberia and central Asia; *deichleri* Corsica, Sardinia and northwest Africa. Upgraded from Green- to Amber-listed in UK 2002: moderate (38%) breeding decline over past 25 years (Gregory *et al.* 2002). National 4% decline 1994–99 (Bashford & Noble 2000).

First mention of Mistle Thrush on Scilly involved Francis Rodd's report to his uncle E H Rodd of Penzance that one had been seen on St Agnes during January 1865 (Rodd 1880). This was followed by information from the same source stating that 'a few' had arrived in the islands on 11th October 1870, and again the following year to the effect that several seen on Tresco on 3rd January 1871 had probably arrived on 31st December. These records presumably prompted the elder Rodd to comment that it was a 'Periodical migrant, varying according to circumstances, in numbers and time of appearance' (Rodd 1878b), and later that it occurred 'in winter, especially after continental frost' (Rodd 1880). By the early 20th century, however, James Clark and Francis Rodd were describing it as a 'fairly regular winter visitor, usually in small parties, but at long intervals in flocks' (Clark & Rodd 1906). These same two suggested that first birds arrived with Redwings, i.e. from October, though others appeared periodically up until the beginning of March. The only other early reference involved unspecified numbers with 'several hundreds' of other birds, presumably mostly thrushes, at the Bishop Rock Lighthouse from 10 pm until daylight on 14th November 1884 (Harvie-Brown *et al.* 1885).

The earliest 20th-century mention concerned reports of Mistle Thrush having bred in Tresco's Abbey Gardens in 1939, and perhaps the years either side (A A Dorrien-Smith 1939a). Penhallurick (1978) viewed early breeding records with suspicion, though it is unclear if he was referring specifically to the Dorrien-Smith claim or some other record. Admittedly, there appears to be no written description of these 1930s nests, but much the same can be said for a number of more recent breeding claims involving equally unlikely species. At the time of the claimed Tresco nesting, birds were reportedly also present on St Mary's. The apparent haphazard approach towards early recording leaves doubts now over whether any lack of mention equates with a lack of presence. Nonetheless, birds were recorded intermittently from the mid-20th century through to the present day. Most accounts involve few individuals per year, usually singles, for example in 1977, when 15 were reported between 8th October and 13th November, with one each on St Mary's, St Agnes and Tresco on 14th October the best single-day showing. However, larger arrivals are on record, as in winter 1961–62 when 'unusually large numbers' of this species arrived as part of an impressive influx of thrushes, including groups of ten or more in fields on St Agnes and with up to six viewable there daily into late March.

Taking the ten years from 1990, most still arrived during October and departed by November, though in three years singles remained throughout all or most of the winter. Also notable were June singles in 1991, 1994 and 1999, interestingly on the 2nd, 4th and 1st respectively. Birds clearly appeared during both spring and autumn and perhaps further research would reveal clearer movement periods; nevertheless there seems little doubt that birds involved are engaged in some form of regular annual movement. Many Mistle Thrushes passing though or remaining in Scilly during autumn and winter seem likely to be nominate *viscivorus*, perhaps from central Europe, e.g. Estonia or Scandinavia, which winter in southern Europe west as far as France and Spain (Cramp *et al.* 1977–94). However, birds from the mostly sedentary British and Irish population may also travel substantial distances during autumn, at least up to 300 km and even into France (Wernham *et al.* 2002). In addition, there seems to be little reason why the central Siberian *bonapartei* might not also reach western Europe (Gantlett 1998).

Most movement occurs during August–November and with many heading towards the southwest. The early breeding cycle means most birds will be back on their breeding grounds by February. It appears far more common on the nearby Cornish mainland, where of course it also breeds, Penhallurick mentioning a flock of up to 200 moving south near Penzance during October, although this seems far from usual. One Mistle Thrush has been ringed on Scilly and there are no recaptures.

## American Robin *Turdus migratorius* A BBRC 19.0%

**Extremely rare migrant, full written description required by the BBRC.**

1963 Two St Agnes c. 18th to at least 20th December (one trapped 20th)
*British Birds* 58: 371, 59: 41–42
1976 One St Agnes 17th to 30th October  *British Birds* 70: 430
1998 One (first-year male) St Agnes & Gugh 26th to 28th October  *British Birds* 92: 594

Nearctic species, breeds Alaska east to Newfoundland and south to northern Florida, California and Mexico. Migratory, withdrawing from Canadian portion of range as far as Guatemala. Polytypic: nominate *migratorius* occurs Alaska, Canada and northeast USA; *nigrideus* northern Quebec, Labrador and Newfoundland; *achrusterus* southeast USA; *caurinus* west-coast North America from southeast Alaska to northwest Oregon; three additional forms USA and Mexico. Population increasing (Bryant 1997).

Three records of this impressive large North American thrush, all on St Agnes or Gugh and involving perhaps four individuals, though as of late 2001 the 1963 events were under review, presumably to test whether two individuals were in fact involved. Around the first week of December that year an American Robin was identified on Gugh by Jack Hick and identified by Donald Hicks. From perhaps the 18th, two American Robins were allegedly present on the Gugh side of the sand bar joining Gugh and St Agnes at low tide. One or other was trapped and ringed by Fran Hicks on 20th, though it died soon after (*SABOAR* 1963–64). However, subsequent descriptions leave room for doubt whether two birds were involved, and if true, these two represented the sixth and seventh records for Britain and Ireland. The first involved a bird in Dublin, Ireland, in May 1891, and the first for Britain was discovered on Lundy Island, Devon, in October 1952 (Palmer 2000).

The 1976 St Agnes individual was discovered by Nigel Redman and was present for 14 days from mid-October. A gap or 22 years then followed before the next arrival, during a period of extremely unpleasant weather on 26th October 1998. Identified as a first-winter male, it was first discovered on Gugh but soon moved to nearby St Agnes, frequenting fields off Barnaby Lane until the 28th. By the time of its arrival most visiting birders had already left the islands, those that returned to see it experiencing an extremely unpleasant crossing to and from St Agnes.

Given the recent suggested population increase (Bryant 1997) the dearth of Scillonian records is perhaps surprising. It also remains scarce throughout the rest of Britain, these three or four individuals representing 14.2–19.0% of the 21 records accepted by the BBRC during the period 1958–99. Like the Eurasian Black/Red-throated Thrush *T. ruficollis*, the extent of autumn migration is dictated by the success or failure of the annual berry crop plus the severity of the weather (Cramp *et al.* 1977–94), features also doubtless reflected in numbers reaching western Europe. Birds from the most northern population commence moving south from August, those from central Canada perhaps remaining until September and in northern USA until October. Nonetheless, some northern populations may not arrive in southern USA until late December.

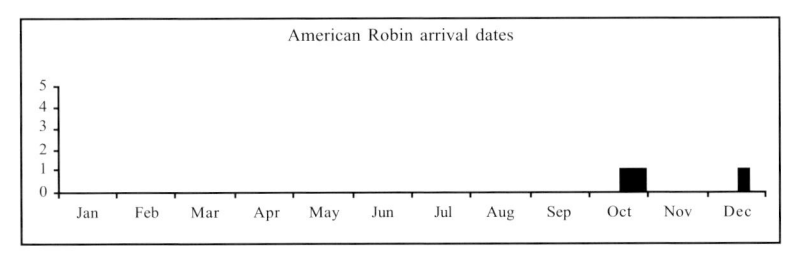

American Robin arrival dates

None of the Scillonian records was identified as to form, though nominate *migratorius* seems most likely. American Robin scored midway in Robbins's statistical review of anticipated transatlantic vagrancy among 31 Nearctic migrant passerines and near-passerines recorded in Britain or Ireland during the period 1947–76, the 15 accepted British and Irish records (two spring, 13 autumn) greatly exceeding the predicted relative likelihood of 2.85 individuals (Robbins 1980).

## Cetti's Warbler *Cettia cetti* A

**Extremely rare migrant or vagrant, full written description required by the SRP.**

  1980   One Porth Hellick, St Mary's 2nd February
  1996   One Harry's Walls, St Mary's 10th May
  1996   One (female – trapped) Higher Moors, St Mary's 10th October
  *2001   One St Mary's 9th to at least 20th October*

Breeds southern Eurasia, from Iberia, France and North Africa east through Mediterranean to southern Kazakhstan. Largely sedentary in west, migratory in east, wintering North Africa and Pakistan. Polytypic: nominate *cetti* occurs North Africa and Europe east to western Russia, western Turkey and Crete; *orientalis* Asia Minor, Levant and Caucasus east to Caspian Sea and northern Kazakhstan; *albiventris* Iran east along southern range. Downgraded from Amber- to Green-listed in UK 2002 (Gregory *et al.* 2002).

Four records of this secretive species make it scarcer in Scilly than many Nearctic migrants. The first, described by David Hunt at Porth Hellick in early February 1980, was presumably a wintering individual, whilst the second of two 1996 individuals, a female, was unexpectedly extracted by the author from a mistnet in Higher Moors, adjacent to Porth Hellick, being unseen and unheard before and after. More recently, a bird was reportedly present on St Mary's for at least 12 days in mid-October 2001. The odd-one-out was a presumed male in song in the Harry's Walls area of St Mary's on 10th May 1996.

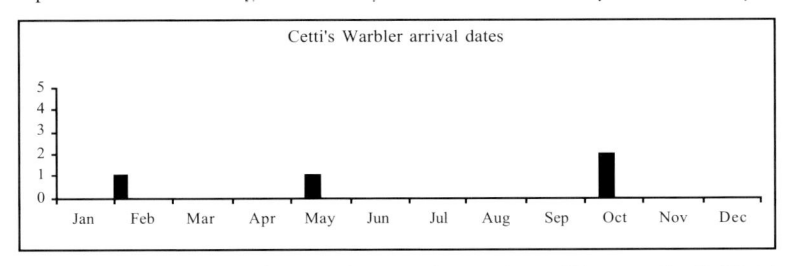

Cetti's Warbler arrival dates

Since its early 1960s colonisation of Britain from nearby continental Europe, Cetti's Warbler has spread west and now breeds as close to Scilly as Marazion in west Cornwall (ten singing males in 2000), it having first reached the county in 1973 (*CBWPSAR* 70). In 1996, a countywide survey of mainland Cornwall recorded a total of 32 males at 26 sites, representing some 6% of the national total. Birds trapped during winter on the Land's End peninsula indicate a measure of October and November dispersal away from the breeding grounds, apparently mostly involving females. This last perhaps explains these October Scillonian sightings, though the possibility of colonisation of areas such as the outwardly suitable Porth Hellick and Tresco pools must be real, in which case the singing male in May could be encouraging. The only Cetti's Warbler ringed on Scilly involved the October 1996 female trapped by the author; there are no recaptures.

## [Pallas's Grasshopper Warbler *Locustella certhiola*] A

**Full written description required by the BBRC. No acceptable Scillonian record.**

[1961   One St Agnes 7th October]   *SABOAR* 1961–62: 31; Wallace 1963

Breeds central and eastern Palearctic, from western Siberia and Turkestan east to Kamchatka and south to China and Japan. Migratory, wintering India, southeast China and Philippines. Polytypic, with complex racial structure: *rubescens* occurs north of range from western Siberia to Amur basin; five further forms south and east.

A detailed written description of a bird matching the characteristics of this species and identified on St Agnes on 7th October 1961 by D I M Wallace and R E Emmett was rejected by the BBRC. The bird was found in a sheltered patch of kale at Per Killier following an abrupt change of wind, from easterly to a northwest gale. It was one of a mixed small group of passerines that included Reed Warbler *Acrocephalus scirpaceus*, Sedge Warbler *A. schoenobaenus*, probably Aquatic Warbler *A. paludicola* and what seems at first to have been thought of as an unidentified *Phylloscopus* warbler. However, the last was eventually seen to be a *Locustella* warbler and in the opinion of experienced observers equally clearly not a Grasshopper Warbler *L. naevia*. The mystery bird was seen well on only about 10 occasions over the space of several hours, at distances from a few to 70 metres, always during organised drives through the kale patch. Three out of four observers obtained glimpses of an apparent incomplete greyish-white tail rim.

On 14th October the four observers carried out an independent examination of skins in the collection of the British Museum (Natural History), all but one agreeing with the earlier identification of Pallas's Grasshopper Warbler. Had the record been accepted it would have been the fourth for Britain. A total of 22 British Pallas's Grasshopper records were accepted by the BBRC during the period 1958–99, all but three since the above sighting. Determining racial characteristics in such a retiring species is no easy matter and most records were considered indeterminate, though the three earliest were thought likely to have been *rubescens*.

## Lanceolated Warbler *Locustella lanceolata*  A   BBRC 0.0%

**Extremely rare migrant, full written description required by the BBRC.**

2002   One Annet 22nd & 23rd September   *British Birds* 95: 604; *British Birds* 96: 155

Breeds from Urals east through Siberia to Kamchatka and from central Siberia south to Kazakhstan in west and northern China, wintering southeast Asia. Monotypic.

A report of a bird found on unoccupied Annet on the afternoon of 22nd September 2002 was accepted by the BBRC in December 2002 and is only the second record ever for southern England, the first involving a bird trapped and ringed well inland in Hampshire during late September 1979 (*British Birds* 74: 484).

## Grasshopper Warbler
## (Common Grasshopper Warbler) *Locustella naevia*  A

**Annual spring and autumn migrant, one old breeding record plus a very recent claim. Because birds tend to sing on spring passage, it is perhaps more evident at that time than in autumn.**

Breeds central Europe and central Asia, from Britain, Ireland, France and Spain east to Mongolia, China and southern Siberia. Migratory, wintering mainly India, plus probable small areas of North, West and East Africa. Polytypic: nominate *naevia* occurs Europe east to European Russia; *straminea* west-central

Asia and Siberia east to northwest China; *mongolica* western Mongolia and adjacent Russia; *obscurior* Turkey and Caucasus. Red-listed in UK: rapid, 79% breeding decline over past 25 years and moderate (37%) contraction of breeding range over past 30 years (Gregory *et al.* 2002). National 3% decline 1994–99 (Bashford & Noble 2000).

There is limited early evidence of this species on Scilly, though it was almost certainly overlooked. Earliest mention is James Clark and Francis Rodd's account of how the Reverend H D Astley heard one on Tresco on 12th May 1901, two more being watched for an hour on Samson on 13th April 1903 (Clark & Rodd 1906). The same authors pointed out that as neither Augustus Pechell, Rodd (presumably Francis, rather than his uncle E H Rodd), or the Reverend J H Jenkinson recorded it during the 1800s, it was evidently uncommon in the islands at that time. These records are followed by one aboard ship 35 km south of the islands on 8th May 1936 (*CBWPSAR* 6).

Penhallurick (1978) summarised the situation on Scilly up until the mid-1970s, noting that migrants were recorded regularly from about 1959, spring passage commencing during late April and ending by about mid-May, it being mostly reported singly. Understandably, Penhallurick experienced difficulty assessing the timing and volume of autumn migration and that situation persists through to the present day. Examination of records for the ten years 1990–99 gives a broad view of the present situation. Many spring records involved singing individuals, the earliest date being 14th April (two years) and the latest 2nd June, with an average of about mid-May. By far the majority of annual reports came from the early part of the year, with as many as four present per island during peak passage. In contrast, autumn numbers were lower, down to only one or two in 1991 and 1993, early and late dates being 13th August and 15th October. Fairly average was 1998, with singles on St Agnes on six dates between 14th April and 19th May, plus 13 on St Mary's, two on Tresco and singles on Bryher and St Martin's, all on 3rd May. Autumn 1998 produced four field sightings plus two birds ringed in Higher Moors on St Mary's.

There are occasional reports of birds present during early summer in suitable breeding habitat, e.g. 8th June 1920 on St Mary's, but until recently the only confirmed breeding report involved a pair reportedly feeding young on St Agnes in 1969 (Penhallurick 1978). Breeding may also have occurred in 1971 but could not be proved – unfortunately Penhallurick gives no references for these two records. During fieldwork for the 2000 Breeding Bird Atlas, a pair reportedly bred on St Agnes, though details of the event were not provided (Chown & Lock 2002).

Cramp *et al.* (1977–94) emphasised the inconspicuous nature of Grasshopper Warbler migration and the species' apparent scarcity even in well-studied areas. Western populations move almost directly south during autumn and eastern populations progressively more southwest, British arrivals and departures being concentrated mainly in the southwest. In southern Europe during autumn, many leave via southwest Iberia and the heaviest Africa passage is down the west coast. The main influx of returning birds reaches Britain by late April and early May, whereas autumn passage occurs mostly throughout August and September. Most if not all Grasshopper Warblers moving through Scilly seem likely to be nominate *naevia* and too little may be known to speculate on other likely forms involved, though the western Asian *straminea* might be expected to occur in western Europe on occasions (Gantlett 1998).

## [River Warbler     *Locustella fluviatilis*]   A

**Full written description required by the BBRC. No acceptable Scillonian record.**

[1992   One Tresco 28th September]   *British Birds* 87: 569

Breeds central and southern Europe and extreme central-western Asia, from Poland and Hungary east to northern Kazakhstan. Migratory, wintering central East Africa. Monotypic.

A claim by Will Wagstaff of a bird seen briefly on Tresco's southern end on 28th September 1992 was subsequently rejected by the BBRC.

## Savi's Warbler     *Locustella luscinioides*   A

**Very rare migrant, full written description required by the BBRC.**

2003   *One St Marys 9th April to 23rd May*   Birding World 16: 188

Breeds central and southern Europe and northwest Africa east to central western Asia, from coastal North

Africa, Iberia and France through Mediterranean to northwest China. Migratory, wintering Africa north of equator. Polytypic: nominate *luscinioides* occurs northwest Africa and eastern Europe east to Balkans; *sarmatica* European Russia to Urals and Caucasus; *fusca* further east. Red-listed in UK: rapid, greater than 50% decline over past 25 years; five-year mean of 4.4 breeding pairs (Gregory *et al.* 2002).

One reported at Port Hellich, St Marys, for six weeks in spring 2003 seems likely to be accepted by the BBRC, though a 1974 St Agnes report was not submitted (*IOSBR* 1974).

## Aquatic Warbler *Acrocephalus paludicola* A

Scarce autumn migrant. Treated by the BBRC as a national Scarce Migrant, full written description required by the SRP.

| | |
|---|---|
| 1959 | One St Agnes 27th August |
| 1959 | One St Agnes 30th August |
| 1959 | One trapped St Agnes 6th September |
| 1959 | One trapped St Agnes 8th September |
| 1959 | One trapped St Agnes 16th to 18th September |
| 1960 | One trapped St Agnes 9th October |
| 1966 | One trapped St Agnes 30th September to 5th October |
| 1967 | One Tresco 15th August |
| 1968 | One Tresco 9th September |
| 1971 | One (first-year) St Mary's 22nd to 28th September |
| 1971 | One (adult) Tresco 13th October |
| 1972 | One (first-year) St Mary's 8th & 9th October |
| 1974 | One St Agnes 14th September |
| 1975 | One St Mary's 26th September |
| 1976 | One Tresco 30th September to 2nd October, two 1st October |
| 1979 | One St Mary's 1st to 9th October |
| 1981 | One St Mary's 12th October |
| 1989 | One Lower Moors, St Mary's 2nd to 5th October |
| 1990 | One St Agnes 8th to 17th October |
| *2002* | *One Tresco 9th October* |

Breeds West Palearctic portion of western Russia, with small outlying populations central-eastern Europe and Kazakhstan. Migratory, wintering areas poorly understood, though most are thought to winter in Africa south of Sahara. Monotypic. Included on Annex I of 1979 EEC 'Birds Directive'. Red-listed in UK: globally threatened; 50% or more of UK passage birds at ten or fewer sites (Gregory *et al.* 2002). Removed from BBRC Rarities List January 1983 (Grant 1982b).

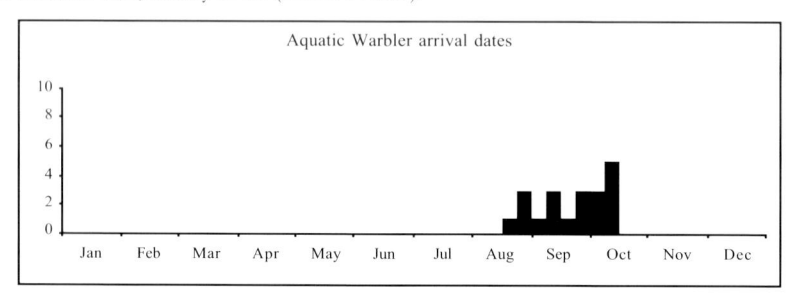

Aquatic Warbler arrival dates

Nineteen records involving 20 birds in 14 different years, all between mid-August and mid-October. One only arrived most years, five in 1959 being something of an exception, with two in 1971. Away from Scilly, migrant Aquatic Warbler sightings appear to be mainly restricted to sedge or reedbeds but several reaching the islands spent time feeding in the open, sometimes on the ground, as in the case of the 1990 St Agnes individual that spent a good deal of its time feeding on the bank separating St Agnes Pool from the nearby sea. The Chart incorporates all 20 arrival dates and shows a clear pattern of early autumn appearances. The clear mid-October cut-off is interesting and seems unlikely to be explained by observer coverage, many birders remaining in the islands until at least the end of the month. The mean length of stay was just 2.8 days. A serious contender for favourite mis-print among the various annual reports concerns the 1967 Aquatic Warbler watched 'pruning in a Tamarisk [*Tamarix gallica*] hedge' (*CBWPSAR* 37).

Departure from the breeding grounds may commence as early as July, though most passage in the west of its range occurs August–September and into October (Cramp *et al.* 1977–94). Information, largely from ringing, suggests a mainly west to southwest initial orientation, many (most) then entering Africa via Iberia, though return passage perhaps involves a more direct easterly route. In addition, Aquatic Warbler appears to have opted for a strategy of long non-stop flights interspersed with equally long stopovers at 'traditional' sites; highest recorded autumn numbers occurring in northwest Europe, including Britain. Cramp *et al.* suggest birds straying furthest north and west in autumn may be 'drift migrants'; however, the migration strategy described here seems bound to deposit a percentage of individuals along Europe's western seaboard.

## Sedge Warbler *Acrocephalus schoenobaenus* A

**Common spring and autumn migrant, occasionally remains during summer and a few pairs probably breed annually, though this is not often confirmed.**

Breeds central and northern Europe and central western Asia, from Britain, Ireland and France east to Kazakhstan. Migratory, wintering Africa south of Sahara as far as South Africa. Monotypic. National 14% increase 1994–99 (Bashford & Noble 2000).

There is surprisingly little information available for what was described in Scilly at the start of the 20th century as a common summer migrant (Clark & Rodd 1906). Even the normally informative E H Rodd noted only that as a summer visitor it was generally distributed in Cornwall and frequented 'wet ditches, willow plots and river banks'. However, he made no specific mention of Scilly (Rodd 1880).

Clark and Rodd referred to it breeding freely on Tresco, and in 1938 several were in song on St Mary's (*CBWPSAR* 8), whilst H W Robinson (1923) recorded five or six pairs by a small pool on St Mary's, and Boyd (1924) reported a nest with four eggs on St Mary's on 2nd July the following year, many other pairs being present. Indeed, the presence of territorial males seems well established right through to the 1990s, with singing birds present during summer 1998 at Tresco Great Pool, Lower Moors, St Mary's and Lawrence's Pool, St Martin's. All of these were assumed to have bred. Numbers also seem to have remained reasonably stable, in the range four to nine apparent pairs. For many years the suggestion is that breeding was successful, but few if any published reports offer conclusive evidence, regardless of statements such as 'breeding took place', or 'breeding proved at Lower Moors and Porth Hellick'. The most recently published probable proven breeding record involved a bird seen carrying food on St Mary's in 1981. Penhallurick (1978) thought there was evidence of a decline in mainland Cornwall by the 1970s, a suggestion borne out by the most recent national survey (Gibbons *et al.* 1993), though, regrettably, a lack of precise early data prevents us knowing whether this decline was reflected in Scilly. More recently, the 2000 Breeding Bird Atlas recorded a possible nine pairs in four (5.9%) of the 67 1-km squares surveyed, though breeding was reportedly confirmed in only one square (Chown & Lock 2002).

Like Reed Warbler *A. scirpaceus*, numbers of birds recorded annually in the past presented a misleading picture of the volume passing through the islands, simply because Sedge Warblers mainly utilise reedbeds and wet scrub areas, most of which are inaccessible and therefore not always well covered by birders. The Table shows annual trapping totals for the Higher Moors reedbed for the years 1994–98, the highest daily total of new birds from this

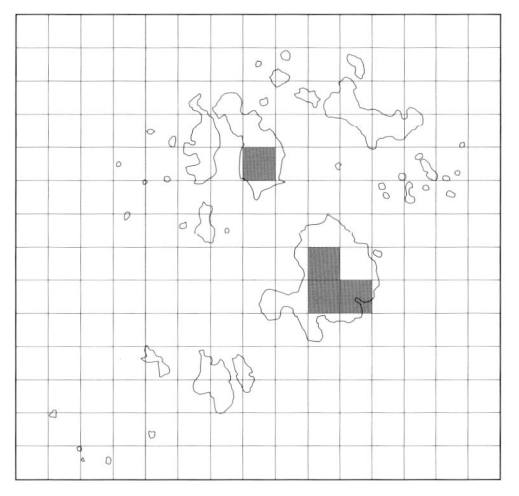

1-km Sedge Warbler Breeding Distribution – 2000–01 (data Chown & Lock 2002)

*Birds of the Isles of Scilly*

one net site being 61. And again, like Reed Warbler, numbers of birds annually involved must be increased by whatever volume also pass through the very similar Lower Moors and the much larger Tresco reedbeds.

| Year | Adult |
|------|-------|
| 1994 | 50 |
| 1995 | 159 |
| 1996 | 285 |
| 1997 | 191 |
| 1998 | 266 |

**Annual Sedge Warbler Trapping Totals, Higher Moors, St Mary's 1994–98 (P J Robinson – unpublished data)**

The Chart includes all Higher Moors autumn trapping totals for the three years 1996–98, in monthly four-week periods. This shows that, although passage commenced at the same time as Reed Warbler the volume of birds involved quickly decreased, with few evident after mid-September and none after the end of that month, though away from the reedbed birds continued to be reported into mid-October. In spring, birds begin arriving in Scilly from mid- to late April, most having passed through by late May with any still present by the end of that month likely to remain through the summer. Very occasional late individuals included one on 4th–6th November 1986.

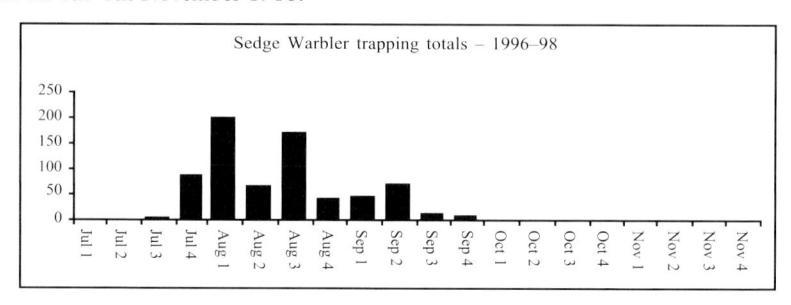

Like Reed Warbler, Sedge Warblers from northwest Europe head mainly southwest or south in autumn, the direction of travel shifting progressively southeast from Scandinavia eastwards. Adults mainly precede juveniles on autumn passage, northern birds leaving the breeding areas from July onwards, slightly later in Britain and Ireland. Sedge Warblers acquire large fat reserves at the commencement of both spring and autumn migration, which during autumn are capable of permitting unbroken flight from southern Britain to sub-Saharan Africa (Cramp *et al.* 1977–94). The length of stay at feeding sites between summer and wintering grounds is dictated by the abundance of Plum-reed Aphids *Hyalopterus pruni*, with evidence of short-distance movements east or west between feeding sites in southern England, or across the English Channel. In addition, the annual early failure of Portuguese aphid stocks causes most British and French Sedge Warblers to overfly southwest Europe. Understandably perhaps, there is a tendency for birds arriving in Scilly in good weather to be low on fat deposits, whereas those arriving in bad weather often have substantial reserves (P J Robinson – unpublished data). At the lower end of the scale, autumn Sedge Warbler weights are about 10–12 grams, but with an upper limit of nearly 21 grams, heavier individuals tending on average to be adults.

A total of 1,207 Sedge Warblers were ringed on Scilly up until 1999, 1,147 (95%) since 1970 and the majority since 1994. The following Table lists the more informative recaptures. The two individuals moving between Slapton and Scilly could perhaps be examples of the lateral feeding movements referred to. In addition, the two Irish-ringed individuals suggest that at least some Sedge Warblers originate from northwest of Scilly, as we might expect with this being the most numerous breeding Irish warbler and the most numerous migrant departing the Wexford coastline during early August and September, few still moving by October (Kennedy *et al.* 1954).

**Controls**

H003179  1stY Slapton Ley, Devon 16th August 1991    CT  Higher Moors, St Mary's
                                                         12th August 1994

| | | | |
|---|---|---|---|
| J902880 | 1stY | Shannon Airport, Ireland 28th June 1995 | CT Lower Moors, St Mary's 21st July 1995 |
| K444889 | 1stY | Youghal, Cork, Ireland 27th August 1996 | CT Higher Moors, St Mary's 6th September 1996 |

**Recoveries**

| | | | |
|---|---|---|---|
| J690600 | 1stY | Higher Moors, St Mary's 5th August 1994 | FD Caceres, Spain 21st April 1995 |
| K443498 | 1stY | Higher Moors, St Mary's 14th August 1996 | CT Treogat, Finistere, France 22nd August 1996 |
| K904694 | 1stY | Higher Moors, St Mary's 12th September 1996 | CT Slapton Ley, Devon 15th September 1996 |
| K640725 | Ad | St Agnes 21st April 1997 | CT Radipole Lake, Weymouth, Dorset 7th August 1997 |
| N202284 | 1stY | Higher Moors, St Mary's 2nd August 1998 | CT Ploven, Finistere, France 6th August 1998 |
| N397714 | 1stY | Higher Moors, St Mary's 16th August 1998 | CT Trunvel, Finistere, France 24th August 1998 |
| N397722 | 1stY | Higher Moors, St Mary's 16th August 1998 | CT Baixo Alentejo, Portugal 27th August 1998 |
| N788055 | 1stY | Higher Moors, St Mary's 11th August 1999 | CT Trundvel, Finistere, France 15th August 1999 |

Sedge Warbler Ringing Recaptures

## Paddyfield Warbler  *Acrocephalus agricola*  A  BBRC 6.6%

**Very rare migrant, full written description required by the BBRC.**

 1974 One St Mary's 30th September to 15th October  *British Birds* 69: 364, 71: 95–101
 1983 One St Mary's 26th & 27th September  *British Birds* 77: 551
 1988 One Tresco 27th & 28th October  *British Birds* 88: 538
 [1997 One St Mary's 9th to 11th June]  *British Birds* 91: 505
 [2001 One St Mary's 13th & 14th October]  *British Birds* 94: plate 350, 95: 511
 *2002 One Gugh 1st to 6th November  British Birds 95: 668*

Breeds extreme central-eastern Europe and central Asia east to Mongolia and western China. Migratory, wintering Indian subcontinent. Monotypic (BOURC 2002b).

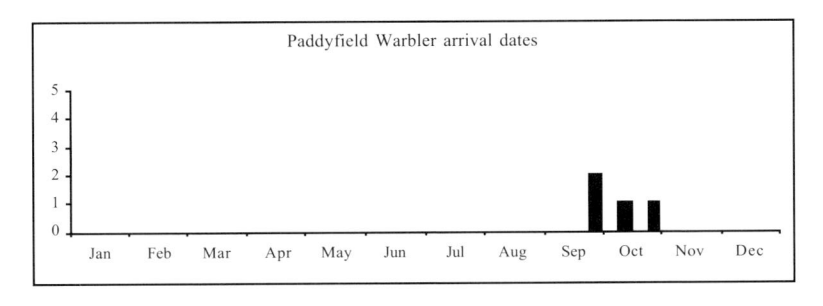

Just three BBRC-accepted records up until 2001 of this scarce species within the West Palearctic, the first as recently as 1974. Found by Dave Flumm and N Lord frequenting the Porth Hellick area of St Mary's for 16 days from late September, though no other individual remained for more than three days. The only spring arrival frequented this same area for three days during June 1997, though more recently the BBRC overturned that record on the grounds that it was 'inadequately documented' (*British Birds* 95: 511). A well-watched bird on St Mary's for at least two days during mid-October 2001 had still to be submitted to BBRC by October 2002 (*British Birds* 95: 511). The Chart omits the 1997 individual. Excluding the 1997 bird, mean length of stay was 5.5 days, though this reduces to two days if the long-staying 1974 individual is discounted. The more recent and still to be accepted (early 2003) 2002 record is also omitted from the analysis.

Again omitting the 1997 record, the three earliest arrivals represent 6.6% of all records accepted by the BBRC for the period 1958–99. Main autumn passage occurs August–September, western populations initially moving east, with adults departing earlier than juveniles (Cramp *et al.* 1977–94). Cramp *et al.* subscribed to the view that birds west of the normal breeding range during autumn are reverse migrants, whereas June records are believed attributable to overshooting. The forms *septima* and *capisrtata* seem almost equally likely to occur in Britain.

## Blyth's Reed Warbler *Acrocephalus dumetorum* A BBRC 0%

**One unacceptable 1970s claim plus what may prove to be a more creditable record during autumn 2002; full written description required by the BBRC.**

   [1977   One Bryher 29th October to at least 4th November]   IOSBR 1977
   2002   *One St Mary's 30th October to 12th November*   British Birds 95: 669; Birding World 15: 451

Breeds central Eurasia, from the Baltic east to Lake Baikal and south to southern Kazakhstan. Migratory, wintering Indian subcontinent and Burma. Monotypic.

A claimed Blyth's Reed Warbler on Bryher from 29th October to at least 4th November 1977 was identified by Ron Johns and described by Chris Heard, though the observers were later said to consider the record unsafe (*IOSBR* 1982) and it was reportedly rejected by BBRC in any event.

More recently, a bird identified as this species and seen by several observers was present on St Mary's from late October 2002 into the following month, although when this text was prepared the record had still to be accepted by the BBRC as the first for Scilly. The similarity between these dates and those for the 1977 claim are notable. The presence of the 2002 individual closely followed Blyth's Reed Warbler arrivals in Northumberland, North Yorkshire and Shetland.

## Marsh Warbler *Acrocepahlus palustris* A

**A scarce migrant, its true status is confused by frequent claims that are difficult to substantiate. Treated by the BBRC as a national Scarce Migrant, full written description required by the SRP.**

   1959   One (trapped) St Agnes 7th to 25th October
   1959   One St Agnes 9th October
   1961   One (in song) St Mary's 28th September
   1961   One (trapped) St Agnes 8th to 11th October
   1961   One (trapped) St Agnes 13th October
   1962   One St Agnes 31st October to 3rd November
   1972   One St Mary's 28th to 31st October
   1973   One St Agnes 14th & 15th October
   1979   One Newford, St Mary's 5th to 13th October
   1979   One Lower Town, St Agnes 13th to 23rd October
   1980   One Lower Moors, St Mary's 20th to 24th September
   1980   One Porth Hellick, St Mary's 23rd & 24th September
   1981   One (in song) St Agnes 27th to 31st May
   1981   Up to two Porth Hellick, St Mary's 16th to 26th September
   1981   One Salakee, St Mary's 18th October
   1987   One St Mary's 1st & 2nd November
   1989   One Porth Hellick & Salakee, St Mary's 12th & 13th October
   1994   One Porth Hellick, St Mary's 24th August to 7th September
   1996   One (trapped) Higher Moors, St Mary's 6th September
   1996   One Tresco 16th & 17th October
   1996   One Watermill, St Mary's 23rd to 30th October
   1997   One (in song) St Agnes 30th May to 1st June
   1997   One St Agnes & St Mary's 22nd August to 1st September

1997    One Newford Pond, St Mary's 22nd October
1999    One Porth Hellick, St Mary's 24th October

Breeds central and southern Europe, from southern England and France south to Mediterranean and east to Caspian Sea and western Afghanistan. Migratory, wintering southeast Africa. Monotypic. Removed from BBRC Rarities List January 1963 (Harber & Swaine 1963). Red-listed in UK: rapid, greater than 50% decline over past 25 years and moderate contraction of breeding range over same timescale; five-year mean of 27.6 breeding pairs (Gregory *et al.* 2002).

Given the doubts surrounding many present-day records, it comes as no surprise to find Marsh Warbler gets no mention in the 19th- and early 20th-century Scillonian literature. The first British account involved a bird or birds in Hampshire in 1863, though the species failed to gain recognition until 1903 (Palmer 2000), E H Rodd making no reference to it in his late 19th-century work on *The Birds of Cornwall and The Scilly Isles* (Rodd 1880).

First documented record for the islands concerned one trapped and ringed on St Agnes during October 1959, this being following by a further 25 individuals during the 41 years to 1999, at the rate of 0.6 per year. The Chart incorporates all known arrival dates and reveals an obvious October concentration, with smaller numbers of occurrences during late May and late August to early September. The two spring arrivals were both heard in song. The earliest autumn arrival was on 22nd August, whereas the latest sighting was 2nd November. The mean length of stay was five days, in the range one (seven records) to 19 days.

Scillonian Marsh Warbler reports are subject to much scrutiny, opinions still differing on the ability to identify this species in the field without risk of confusion with the closely similar, and far more numerous Reed Warbler *A. scirpaceus*, or even with other species, e.g. Melodious Warbler *Hippolais polyglotta* (at least initially), or the more closely related Blyth's Reed Warbler *A. dumetorum* (Harrop & Quinn 1989). However, a number of reports were unsupported by a written description and were therefore discounted. In addition, one obvious problem associated with the task of examining any Marsh Warbler claim is the apparent extent of plumage variation in both this species and Reed Warbler, many birders still apparently convinced that any unusual *Acrocephalus* must be Marsh Warbler. The relevant plumage and other features of the bird on St Mary's during October 1989 were discussed by Harrop (*Birding World* 2: 369–370), this individual actually being initially misidentified as Melodious, whilst ten years earlier Peter Grant discussed the problems of identifying two first-winter individuals on St Mary's and St Agnes during October 1979 (*IOSBR* 1979: 54–57).

Just four birds had been trapped on Scilly up until 1999, only one recently. Prior to the 1990s, most *Acrocephalus* warblers trapped on Scilly were caught away from the main reedbeds, e.g. on St Agnes, and only during the 1990s have they been annually caught in substantial numbers. So it is interesting to note that out of 1,511 *Acrocephalus* warblers trapped in or around the Higher Moors reedbed during the seven years 1994–2000, only one Marsh Warbler was identified, compared with 469 Reed Warblers.

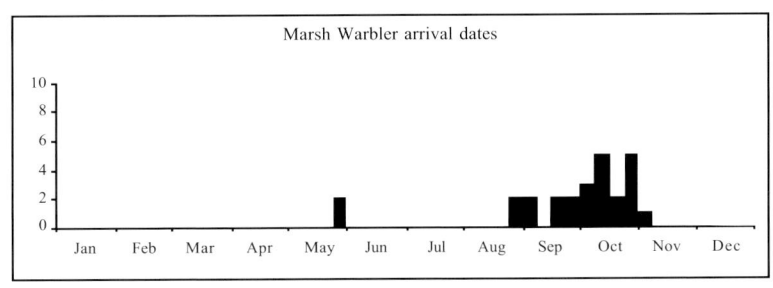

Marsh Warbler arrival dates

Most autumn migrants apparently move south into Africa via the Middle East and the Arabian Peninsula, those from western Europe initially adopting a southeast route. Departure commences from July or August, heaviest passage in central Europe occurring mid-July to mid-August, but with birds still moving through the Middle East into mid-October or early November (Cramp *et al.* 1977–94). Spring Scillonian arrivals could presumably be attributable to a measure of overshooting by western European birds, but the same does not hold true for any autumn records, these perhaps being at least partly accounted for by westerly drift migration involving birds from either the central-northern or eastern portions of Marsh Warbler's breeding range. There are no Marsh Warbler recaptures.

# Reed Warbler                                           *Acrocephalus scirpaceus*  A

**Breeding summer visitor in small numbers, many more pass through on migration.**

Breeds central and southern Europe east into central Asia as far as western Mongolia. Migratory, wintering Africa south of Sahara. Polytypic: nominate *scirpaceus* occurs Europe and northwest Africa east to Asia Minor and Caspian area; *fuscus*, or 'Eastern Reed Warbler' (recognised by some authorities as a full species) further east and south. National 15% increase 1994–99 (Bashford & Noble 2000), BTO Waterways Bird Survey showed 79% increase 1975–2000.

Earliest mention of this species in Scilly, under the old name of 'Reed Wren', involved E H Rodd's account of one, perhaps several, shot by Augustus Pechell during September 1849 (Rodd 1849d, 1880), others being obtained during the autumns of 1852, 1864, 1868 and 1871. James Clark and Rodd's nephew Francis later blamed the lack of subsequent records on a shortage of observers, there being no further autumn reports until October 1903 (Clark & Rodd 1906).

The first suggestion that Reed Warbler might summer in Scilly was probably Clark and Rodd's observation of several in song by Tresco's Great Pool on 11th April 1904 (Clark & Rodd 1906). These two authors also correctly identified the fact that the species passed through the islands during spring. Interestingly, back in 1880 the elder Rodd described its Cornish status as 'met with occasionally during the summer months' (Rodd 1880). Somewhat surprisingly, however, breeding was not proved on Scilly until juveniles were observed in 1970, birds having been reportedly heard in song only since 1962 (Penhallurick 1978); and although it was suspected of breeding in mainland Cornwall from as early as 1899, this was not proved until 1945. Penhallurick (1978) took the view that this and subsequent reports represented a genuine expansion of range into Cornwall. Even so, no nest was reported in the islands until the present writer commenced survey and ringing work in the Higher Moors reedbed on St Mary's in 1991. Subsequently, at least fours pairs were noted annually, with at least one proven case of double-brooding. Very little, though, seems to be known still about the Tresco population, except for the annual reports of up to ten singing birds. Nonetheless, the size of Tresco's reedbeds, compared to those of St Mary's Higher and Lower Moors, suggests many more pairs could be involved. Interestingly, then, the 2000 Breeding Bird Atlas located up to 17 pairs in five (7.4%) of the 67 squares surveyed: two on Tresco and three on St Mary's (Chown & Lock 2002). This figure was presumably based largely on the presence of singing males.

Annual reports through to the 1990s give an apparently misleading picture of small numbers of Reed Warblers passing through the islands during autumn, with even fewer during spring, a typical comment being that for 1979: 'No information on breeding this year. No records received which indicate spring passage. In autumn peaks of 15 on Tresco on Sept. 12th and Oct. 13th, four on St Agnes and 13 on St Mary's. Numbers then decreased, last seen on Oct. 29th.' The main reason for this image of low Reed Warbler numbers is that recorded totals were understandably based primarily on birds seen away from reedbeds, i.e. in scrub. However, average daily autumn captures in the Higher Moors reedbed for each of the five years 1994–98 were c. 15 birds and annual captures (Table) probably equalled previously published annual all-island totals. Importantly, too, trapping occurred less than daily and there were few between-session recaptures. The latter suggests a quite rapid turnover of migrants, in which case the total numbers of birds annually using this site was substantially greater than trapping figures suggest, with whatever figure was actually involved increased by whatever number of birds passed through nearby Lower Moors, plus the more extensive Tresco reedbeds. The Chart includes all Higher Moors autumn trapping totals for

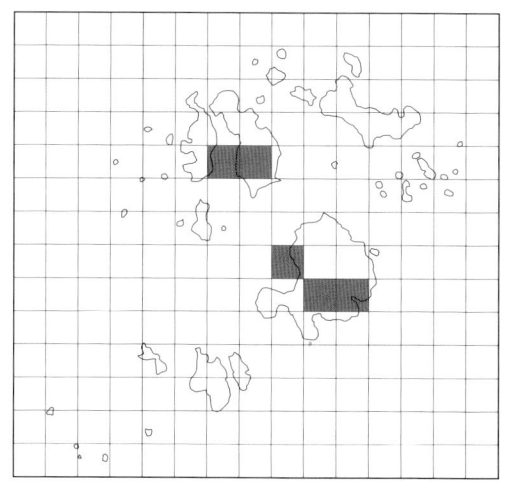

1996–98, in monthly four-week periods, showing that although Reed Warbler passage commenced about the same time as that for Sedge Warbler, it peaked three weeks later than in that species, with occasional individuals still passing through into November, six weeks after the last Sedge Warbler. Captures prior to 20th July involved at least some of the local breeding population.

Scillonian recapture data mainly suggest a pattern of east-west movement between a limited number of Scillonian and Cornish sites and those in Belgium and the Netherlands, the bulk of any British and Continental migration presumably passing east of Scilly (Wernham *et al.* 2002). With the exception of a locally reared individual hatched by a Portuguese-ringed female, there are only two records suggestive of any north-south involvement (Table). The exception referred to was a nestling ringed in a Higher Moors nest in 1995, controlled in the Channel Isles during May 1996 and retrapped as a breeding female in Higher Moors in late July 1996. Unlike the closely related Sedge Warbler *A. schoenobaenus*, Reed Warbler is almost absent from Ireland during summer (Kennedy *et al.* 1954) and is only thinly distributed throughout Wales and southwest England.

**1-km Reed Warbler Breeding Distribution – 2000–01 (data Chown & Lock 2002)**

| Year | Adult | Pulli |
|------|-------|-------|
| 1994 | 37    |       |
| 1995 | 101   | 12    |
| 1996 | 125   |       |
| 1997 | 100   |       |
| 1998 | 93    |       |

**Annual Reed Warbler Trapping Totals, Higher Moors, St Mary's 1994–98 (P J Robinson – unpublished data)**

The eastern, normally greyer and whiter *fuscus* or 'Eastern (Caspian) Reed Warbler' breeds from Cyprus and the Levant eastwards through Turkey and the Caspian area. Gantlett (1998) drew attention to at least seven reported *fuscus* on mainland Britain and there have been several claimed on Scilly, the most recent involving a bird at Porth Hellick 24th–26th October 1999 (*IOSBR* 1999). However, Pearson *et al.* (2002) took the view that no western European claim of *fuscus* had been sufficiently convincing to merit acceptance, though they singled out a bird at Lower Town, St Agnes, during October 1979 as a prime contender. After much debate, this last individual was trapped, but identified in the hand at the time as Marsh Warbler *A. palustris* (*IOSBR* 1979; Grant 1979), though Pearson and colleagues considered the detailed description highlighted features closer to *fuscus* than first-winter Marsh Warbler.

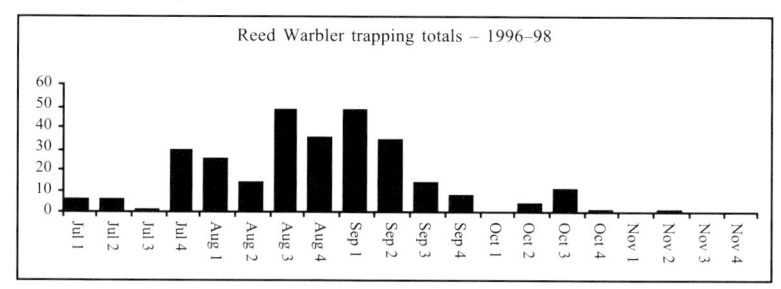

Nominate *scirpaceus* Reed Warblers from northwest Europe head mainly southwest in autumn towards Iberia, the preferred direction of travel shifting progressively southeast from Scandinavia eastwards, this

*Birds of the Isles of Scilly*

situation being reversed in spring (Cramp *et al.* 1977–94). Although the not-so-recognisable *fuscus* also moves either southwest or south, its more southeastern origin takes it mainly through the Middle East and down into East Africa, where it mixes with more northerly and eastern European *scirpaceus* populations. Of the 510 Reed Warblers ringed on Scilly up until 1999, 475 (93%) were ringed after 1970 and the majority since 1994. The following are the more informative recaptures.

## Controls

| | | | | |
|---|---|---|---|---|
| J137031 | 1stY | Marloes, Dyfed 3rd August 1993 | CT | Higher Moors, St Mary's 22nd July 1994 |
| 4941437 | 1stY | West Vlaanderen, Belgium 22nd September 1994 | CT | Higher Moors, St Mary's 11th October 1994 |
| A087914 | 1stY | Baixo Alentejo, Portugal 29th August 1993 | CT | Higher Moors, St Mary's 5th July 1995 |
| F478502 | 1stY | Marazion, west Cornwall 19th August 1993 | CT | Higher Moors, St Mary's 14th August 1995 |
| F693008 | 1stY | Ijsselmeerpolders, Netherlands 15th July 1995 | CT | Higher Moors, St Mary's 16th August 1995 |
| 5808630 | 1stY | Muizen, Antwerp, Belgium 17th September 1995 | CT | Higher Town, St Martin's 21st October 1995 |
| J492172 | 1stY | Marazion, west Cornwall 2nd August 1995 | CT | Higher Moors, St Mary's 9th August 1996 |
| K741127 | 1stY | Par Beach, west Cornwall 1st September 1996 | CT | Higher Moors, St Mary's 14th September 1996 |
| F879787 | 1stY | Castricum, Netherlands 22nd October 1997 | CT | Higher Moors, St Mary's 7th November 1997 |

## Recoveries

| | | | | |
|---|---|---|---|---|
| J965626 | Pul | Higher Moors, St Mary's 8th June 1995 | CT | St Ouen, Jersey, Channel Isles 25th May 1996 |
| | | | CT | Higher Moors, St Mary's 31st July 1996 |
| K904751 | 1stY | Higher Moors, St Mary's 5th July 1997 | CT | Nanjizal, Land's End, west Cornwall 16th May 1998 |
| K904721 | 1stY | Higher Moors, St Mary's 16th September 1996 | CT | Nanjizal, Land's End, west Cornwall 25th June 1998 |
| N202059 | 1stY | Higher Moors, St Mary's 6th August 1997 | CT | Nanjizal, Land's End, west Cornwall 18th July 1998 |

Reed Warbler Ringing Recaptures

## Great Reed Warbler    *Acrocephalus arundinaceus*  **A**  BBRC 3.2%

**Rare spring and autumn migrant, full written description required by the BBRC.**

  1884   One (shot) Tresco late September   Clark & Rodd 1906
  1962   One (in song – trapped) St Agnes 6th to 8th June   *British Birds* 56: 403
  1978   One Porth Hellick, St Mary's 12th October   *British Birds* 72: 536
  1985   One (in song) St Agnes 16th May (found dead 4th June)   *British Birds* 79: 571
  1989   One (in song) St Agnes 8th May   *British Birds* 83: 482
  1997   One (in song) Watermill, St Mary's 19th to 23rd May   *British Birds* 91: 506

Breeds central and southern Europe and central Asia, from Iberia and North Africa east to Sakhalin, Japan, northern Philippines. Migratory, two widely separate wintering ranges in Afrotropics and southeast Asia. Polytypic: nominate *arundinaceus* occurs northwest Africa and Europe east to Volga basin; *zarudnyi* northern Iraq, Iran east to western China; *orientalis* western China and Mongolia east to Japan; *griseldis* Iraq. *Arundinaceus*, *zarudyni*, and *griseldis* all winter in Africa, *orientalis* southeast Asia.

Just six arrivals in Scilly of a species that produced 285 British and Irish records during the period 1958–99 demonstrates its scarcity so far west in Britain. The five birds within this period represented just 3.2% of the national total. The earliest was a bird shot on Tresco during late September 1884 although, as so often in Scilly, events were complicated. Tresco gamekeeper David Smith shot 'what was evidently a Great Reed Warbler' in the Tresco reedbeds. He then held the bird in his hand admiring it as it 'lay quietly for a moment spreading out its tail like a fan, but before he could kill it, it suddenly slipped over and went away like a mouse'. However, although 'His description of the bird left no reasonable doubt of its identity' (Clark & Rodd 1906), Witherby & Ticehurst (1907) later square bracketed the record.

St Agnes accounted for three out of five modern records. First of these concerned a male in song in Tamarisk *Tamarix* bushes along St Agnes's Barnaby Lane for three days during June 1962, being audible from a goodly proportion of the island. Also on St Agnes, one heard in song on 16th May was presumed the same as that found dead on 4th June, though details of the likely timing are lacking. Finally, one at Watermill on the eastern end of St Mary's proved somewhat elusive throughout its four-day stay, though it was heard to sing occasionally.

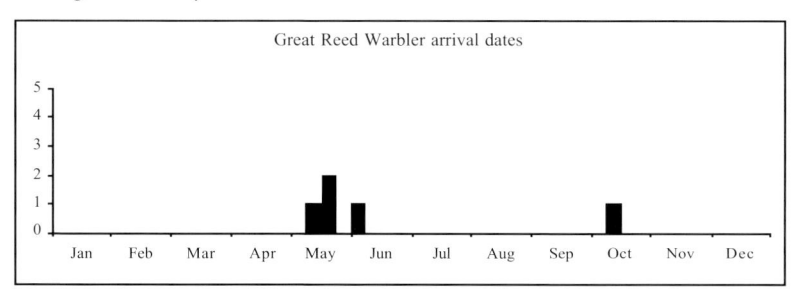

*Great Reed Warbler arrival dates* (bar chart showing counts by month)

Disregarding the shot bird and the 1985 individual, for which the date of death remains unknown, the mean length of stay was just 2.6 days. The Chart includes the five apparent 20th-century arrival dates and shows a pattern of mid- to late spring and mid-autumn presence. The former presumably involves overshooting birds from southern European populations, e.g. France or Iberia (Cramp *et al.* 1977–94) and as seems normal with this species, all five on Scilly were heard in song. The general southwest heading of many eastern European (or closer) migrants perhaps explains any autumn presence in Scilly, as elsewhere in Britain, though there are two or more West Palearctic records of the far-eastern *orientalis*. Sight records do not normally exclude the possibility of the closely similar Clamorous Reed Warbler *A. stentoreus* (BOURC 2002b). One Great Reed Warbler had been ringed on Scilly up until 1999 – prior to 1970. There are no recaptures and although the 1997 individual was carrying a metal ring, dates involved apparently discount any possibility that this was the 1970 bird.

## Eastern Olivaceous Warbler *Hippolais pallida* A  BBRC 35.7%

**Very rare autumn migrant, full written description required by the BBRC.**

 [1961   One St Agnes 3rd & 4th October]   *British Birds* 55: 579, 59: 195–197, 93: 567
 [1962   One St Agnes 30th September to 2nd October]   *British Birds* 56: 405, 59: 195–197, 93: 567
  1984   One St Mary's 16th to 26th October   *British Birds* 78: 65, 575
  1985   One St Mary's 17th to 27th October   *British Birds* 79: 571
  1998   One St Agnes 24th September to 8th October   *British Birds* 92: 170, 595

Breeds Africa and southwest Asia, from central-northern Africa east through Balkans and Asia Minor to southern Kazakhstan. Migratory away from central Africa, all populations winter Africa south of Sahara. Polytypic, racial distribution still not fully understood: *reiseri* central northern Sahara and perhaps Morocco; *laeneni* Chad, Niger, western Sudan; nominate *pallida* Egypt; *elaeica* southeast Europe and southwest Asia. Separated from Western Olivaceous Warbler *H. opaca* by BOURC September 2002 (BOURC 2002b).

The first 'Olivaceous Warbler' record for Scilly, and at the time the 4th for Britain and Ireland, involved a bird on St Agnes for two days during early October 1961, with another on the same island for three days from 30th September the following year (Wallace 1966). However, rejection of two earlier British records by the BOURC during 1999 (BOURC 2000) apparently promoted the 1961–62 records to second and fourth for Britain and Ireland, although, importantly, these two St Agnes records were also both under review by the BBRC as at October 2002 (*British Birds* 94: 504, 95: 528).

A bird recorded on St Agnes on 16th September 1963 (*CBWPSAR* 33) was allegedly reported by the St Agnes Bird Observatory, but does not appear in the *SABOAR* and is not listed among accepted BBRC records. Nevertheless, Penhallurick (1978) appeared to find it acceptable. Third confirmed record for the islands, a bird at Watermill, St Mary's, for eleven days during October 1984, was later described as 'almost ostentatious in revealing to all-comers the characters of this species' (*IOSBR* 1984). This was followed by an equally showy individual at Lunnon on the same island in 1985, also for eleven days during mid-October. Last of the five so far acceptable records involved one on St Agnes, this time for 15 days, from 24th September 1998, this individual favouring the area known as 'the fruit cage' to the northwest of the Lighthouse. The Chart shows all five arrival dates and mean length of stay was 8.4 days.

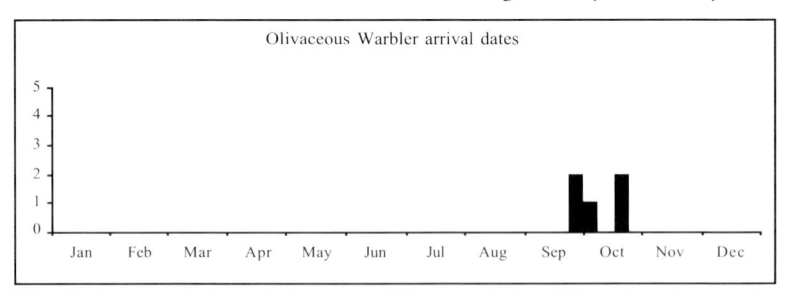

Olivaceous Warbler arrival dates

These five 'Olivaceous Warbler' records represent 35.7% of the 14 records accepted by the BBRC during the period 1958–99 and are believed to have involved the form now known as Eastern Olivaceous Warbler. The 1998 arrival was thought by at least initial observers to have involved the slightly smaller and paler form *elaeica*, which occurs in southeast Europe and southwest Asia and winters in East and northeast Africa, but confirmation of this is difficult in the field. Any British spring record might seem a prime contender for overshooting Western Olivaceous Warbler but that is not an issue in Scilly, where all five occurred during autumn. Explanations for these autumn arrivals are not obvious but presumably involve either reverse or drift migration, though the limited 'window' involved suggests something more regular, perhaps the most obvious suggestion being the involvement of long-distance migrant *elaeica* from southwest Asia, at least one of the 14 national records being attributed to this form. No Eastern Olivaceous Warblers have been trapped and ringed on Scilly and there are no recaptures.

## Booted Warbler *Hippolais caligata* A BBRC 12.5%

Rare autumn migrant, full written description required by the BBRC.

1966  One St Agnes 23rd October  *British Birds* 60: 325, 65: 170–172
1980  One (*caligata*) St Agnes 13th to 24th October  *British Birds* 74: 485
1981  One St Agnes 28th September to 8th October  *British Birds* 75: 521, Plate 211, 77: 366, 89: 126
1981  One St Mary's 15th October to 1st November  *British Birds* 75: 521, Plate 211, 77: 366, 89: 126
1985  One St Mary's 15th to 19th October  *British Birds* 79: 13, 572
1987  One St Mary's 18th to 21st October  *British Birds* 81: 582
1987  One St Agnes 23rd to 27th October  *British Birds* 81: 582
1993  One St Agnes 27th September  *British Birds* 87: 553–554
1993  One (first-year – trapped) St Martin's 19th to 27th October  *British Birds* 87: 533–554
1999  One Popplestone Bay, Bryher 4th October  *British Birds* 93: 555
2001  One St Agnes 26th to 29th August  *British Birds* 95: 512
2001  One Tresco 19th October  *British Bird* 95: 512

Breeds central Eurasia south to Aral Sea and east to western China, wintering India. Monotypic. Split from Sykes's Warbler *H. rama* by BOURC September 2002 (BOURC 2002b).

A total of 12 acceptable records involving 12 birds in eight years, earliest of which was an individual that spent four hours in a St Agnes kale patch on 23rd October 1966 (Wallace 1972b). Not included among these 12 is a bird seen in a kale patch and described by Brian Bland at Content, St Mary's, on 8th October 1974, the record failing to gain acceptance by the BBRC (*IOSBR* 1975; Penhallurick 1978). Other records failing to gain acceptance included a claim of one on St Martin's during October 1992

Average length of stay was 6.75 days. The Chart includes all twelve accepted arrival dates up until 2001 and shows an obvious late September–October preference, the one exception being the early individual on St Mary's and St Agnes during August 2001. Two birds arrived in four of the years involved. Although St Mary's and St Agnes received the lion's share, records were nonetheless well distributed between the five main islands. The ten records during the period 1958–99 constitute 12.5% of the 80 records accepted by the BBRC during that same period.

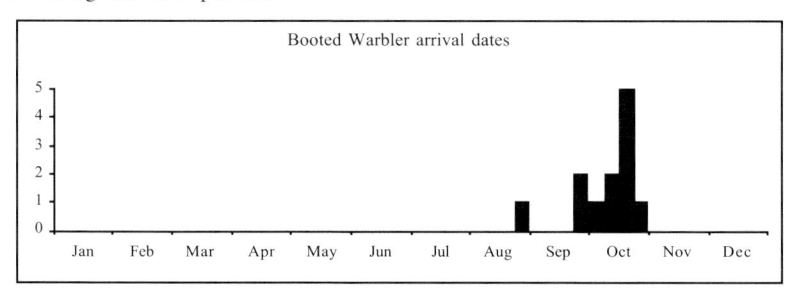

Booted Warbler arrival dates

Given the species' exclusive Indian wintering grounds plus its breeding presence in eastern Europe, the possibility of spring overshoots seems plausible, as has already happened elsewhere, e.g. Finland (Cramp *et al.* 1977–94). Nonetheless, all Scillonian records occurred in autumn. The simplistic explanation is reverse migration but, as with Eastern Olivaceous Warbler *H. pallida*, the consistency and volume of records suggests something rather more established. The possibility of the presence in Scilly of the newly separated Sykes's Warbler from south-central Asia seems real enough; the first such British record occurred in Shetland as recently as 1993. The bird adjacent to the St Martin's cricket pitch for nine days during October 1993 was trapped and ringed, but there are no recaptures.

# Icterine Warbler *Hippolais icterina* A

Scarce autumn migrant, plus one very recent spring arrival. Treated by the BBRC as a national Scarce Migrant, full written description of all spring individuals required by the SRP.

The northern European counterpart of Melodious Warbler *H. polyglotta*. Breeds central Europe and central-western Asia, from northern France, Netherlands, Germany and Hungary north and east to Norway, western Siberia and Kazakhstan. Migratory, wintering southern Africa. Monotypic. Downgraded from Amber- to Green-listed in UK 2002 (Gregory *et al.* 2002). Removed from BBRC Rarities List January 1963 (Harber & Swaine 1963).

If it occurred at all in southwest England then, like the closely related Melodious Warbler, this species was overlooked by the 19th-century ornithologists. The first for Britain was obtained in Kent in 1848 (Palmer 2000). The first for Scilly involved a first-year found and described by Hilda Quick on St Agnes on 25th September 1953, with some 15 records between then and 1975, it being reported annually from the mid-1960s. Nonetheless, it comprised only 29% of specifically identified *Hippolais* warblers in Cornwall and Scilly up until at least the 1970s (Penhallurick 1978) and in spring was absent from the islands until 1999.

Taking the ten years 1990–99, it occurred during all autumns, and 1999 witnessed the first ever Scillonian spring arrival, involving a bird on St Agnes on 26th–27th May. During the ten years, 104 birds were recorded at an average of 10.4 per year, in the range two to 22, the latter in 1997 and with the previous highest total 15 in 1994. Autumn arrival dates fell in the range 6th August to 24th September and the latest any bird was seen was 27th October. Thus, Icterine Warbler arrivals for the ten-year period outnumbered Melodious by a ratio of just over 5:4. A rather dramatic reversal of the earlier 29% Icterine presence found by Penhallurick, though the discrepancy may partly be explained by the 25% or more previously unidentified *Hippolais* warbler sightings (Penhallurick 1978).

Icterine Warbler is a broad-front migrant leaving its breeding areas from late July and having abandoned sites in western Siberia from the second week of August. The standard travel direction is slightly east of south. Understandably, most British autumn reports come from English east-coast counties, though with significant numbers also in Kent, Dorset, Scilly and, surprisingly, Co. Cork, Ireland (Sharrock 1974). The latter is believed attributable to birds having filtered south and west (Dymond *et al.* 1989). Sharrock offered a somewhat complicated explanation for the presence of autumn Icterine and Melodious Warblers in southwest England and southern Ireland, suggesting a combination of factors, random post-juvenile dispersal during anticyclonic conditions being the primary influence, but with reverse migration perhaps also involved. However, this failed to address the question of exactly why so many individuals reached Co. Cork, or perhaps Scilly, but were absent or in far lower numbers in adjacent areas, the Cornish mainland, for example, receiving just 53 Icterine Warblers up until year 2000 (*CBWPSAR* 67; 70). Such a theory also fails to address the near total absence of this species from Scilly during spring migration. But if it is true and drift migration is a contributing factor, then perhaps at least some autumn Scillonian arrivals originate from populations in the extreme east of its range. Dymond *et al.* attributed the national increase in numbers of records to an increase in observers, which may also be true of Scilly. A total of nine Icterine Warblers have been ringed in Scilly. The sole recapture, very interestingly on an apparent course for Co. Cork, was reportedly the first recovery of a British-ringed individual (*SABOAR* 1963–64)

Recoveries
AK91738  Ad  St Agnes 2nd September 1964            AS  136 km WNW of Scilly 3rd September 1964
**Icterine Warbler Ringing Recaptures**

## Melodious Warbler                                                 *Hippolais polyglotta* A

**Scarce but annual migrant. Treated by the BBRC as a national Scarce Migrant, full written description of all spring individuals required by the SRP.**

Breeds southwest Europe and North Africa, from northern France south to Iberia, Italy and northwest Morocco. Migratory, wintering West Africa between Sahara and equator. Monotypic. Removed from BBRC Rarities List January 1963 (Harber & Swaine 1963).

Melodious Warbler is a rare example of a species that escaped the attentions of the 19th-century Cornish, and indeed British, ornithologists. The first national record involved a bird shot near Looe, Cornwall, on 12th May 1905, although Penhallurick (1978) gives the date as 1907. The previous first and second records were lost with the discrediting of the 'Hastings Rarities' (Palmer 2000). Quite remarkably, Ireland's first arrival also occurred during 1905. None were then recorded in Britain until 1951, though it appears to have been annual in Cornwall and Scilly since 1960 and intermittently a few years before that. Mid-20th-century difficulties over the field separation of Melodious and Icterine Warblers *H. icterina* are reflected in the number of reports involving unspecified *Hippolais* warblers, whereas most subsequent sightings are attributed to one or other. Penhallurick charted all Cornish and Scillonian arrival and departure dates for this and Icterine Warbler, concluding that no Melodious arrived before 31st August and that, with the exception of one in late November, all had left by the third week of October (Penhallurick 1978). However, the first Scillonian spring record involved a singing individual discovered on St Agnes during 9th–11th May 1981, since when there have been just two more, in May 1987 and May 1992.

Birds arrived in all years during 1990–99, though only once in spring (1992). First autumn arrival dates ranged from 5th August to 5th October (two years), whereas annual last sightings occurred between 15th October (two years) and 1st November. Annual totals ranged between one and 19, average eight, but with sometimes substantial gaps between arrivals, as in 1996 when one on 11th August was followed on 18th October by the first of four subsequent arrivals.

From all of the above it is apparent that Melodious Warbler remains a scarcity in Scilly during autumn and a positive rarity in spring, making it imperative that all necessary care is taken with the separation of this and the previous species. Sharrock (1974) concluded that the majority of all of British spring records involved non-breeding individuals, though the timing of Scillonian arrivals is compatible with over-shooting and a known late arrival on the southern European breeding grounds (Cramp *et al.* 1977–94). However, autumn arrivals require a different explanation, most authorities opting for a combination of random post-juvenile dispersal, probably during anticyclonic conditions, and reverse migration (Sharrock 1974; Cramp *et al.* 1977–94). A total of 14 Melodious Warblers have been ringed in Scilly and there are no recaptures.

## [Olive-tree Warbler                              *Hippolais olivetorum*]

**Full written description required by the BBRC. No acceptable Scillonian record.**

[1972   One St Agnes 27th September]   *British Birds* 71: 532

Breeds former Yugoslavia south to Crete and east to southwest Russia and coastal southern Turkey, migratory wintering southern Africa. Monotypic. No acceptable British or Irish records.

A multiple observer claim of an Olive Tree Warbler on St Agnes on 27th September 1972, the potential first for Britain and Ireland, failed to gain acceptance. Nevertheless, Wallace (1980) included it among is list of predicted future British vagrants.

## Dartford Warbler                                 *Sylvia undata*   A

**Extremely scarce vagrant, full written description required by the SRP.**

1960   One Deep Point, St Mary's, 13th October to 19th November
1964   One Gugh 24th October
1966   One St Agnes 24thOctober to 28th November
1975   One St Martin's & St Mary's 30th & 31st October
1993   One Castella Down, St Agnes 11th & 12th April
1993   One Chapel Down, St Martin's 18th to 22nd October
1993   One Wingletang, St Agnes 10th to 28th October
1993   One Wingletang, St Agnes 28th October
1994   One Abbey Woods, Tresco 10th to 12th October 1994
1996   One St Agnes, 16th to 21st October

Breeds southern England, France, Iberia, coastal North Africa, Corsica, Sardinia, Sicily and Italian mainland. Mainly sedentary, dispersive. Polytypic: *dartfordiensis* England, western France, northwest Spain and northern Portugal; nominate *undata* southern France, northeast Spain, Corsica, Sardinia, Sicily, Balearic Islands, Italian mainland; *toni* southern Portugal, southern Spain, northwest Africa. Included on Annex I of 1979 EEC 'Birds Directive'. Downgraded from Red- to Amber-listed in UK 2002: historical population decline but population more than doubled over past 25 years; 50% or more of breeding population at ten or fewer sites; unfavourable European conservation status (Gregory *et al.* 2002). Removed from BBRC Rarities List January 1963 (Harber & Swaine 1963).

First mention of Dartford Warbler on Scilly appears to be the description by Ron Simmons of a bird he and Peter MacKenzie saw at Deep Point on St Mary's in October–November 1960 (*CBWPSAR* 30). Since that time there have been just nine further arrivals, though there seems to have been an increase since the mid-1990s. The Chart includes all ten arrival dates, just one of which occurred in spring. The nine autumn arrivals were squeezed into the narrow 21-day window between 10th and 30th October, the latest annual sighting involving the bird on St Agnes on 28th November 1966. The mean length of stay was 8.2 days, though this drops to around five days if the long-staying 1966 individual is discounted.

E H Rodd considered Dartford Warbler rare in Cornwall until the 1880s or thereabouts, the first he saw in forty years in west Cornwall being one shown him by Penzance taxidermist Vingoe in January 1869 (Rodd 1880). Penhallurick (1978) thought the Cornish population probably peaked around 1870, following which it suffered from a series of cold winters, though by the very early 1900s it had made something of a recovery, although it still occurred only in small numbers. However, from that point on, the county, including Scilly, entered into what Penhallurick described as 'the Dark Age of Cornish ornithology'. As far as the Dartford Warbler was concerned this situation endured at least until publication of Penhallurick's work, with just scattered records involving probable vagrants, and with the last mainland breeding record in 1943 (*CBWPSAR* 70). Since 1980, there is a mainland history of sporadic small, short-term breeding groups, the most recent of which involved the Lizard peninsula in west Cornwall, and the timing of these matches the increase in Scillonian records.

Certainly the Chart gives no impression of random or vagrant arrival and is strongly suggestive of a more structured autumn movement, with a complete absence of winter records. Surprisingly, none of the published records makes reference to the likely age or sex of the individual concerned, making it impossible

*Birds of the Isles of Scilly*

Dartford Warbler arrival dates

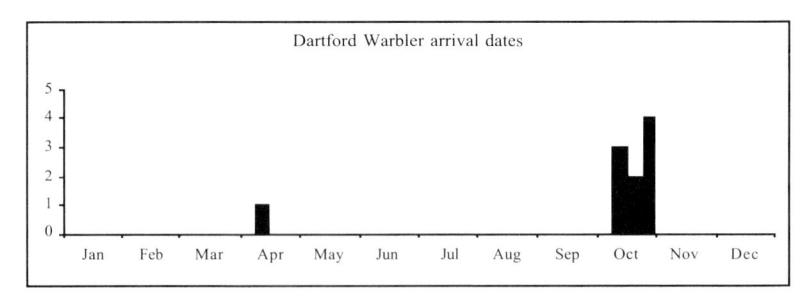

to say whether the to-be-expected dispersing first-years were involved in the nine autumn arrivals. Interestingly, Cramp *et al.* (1977–94) point out that British autumn sightings away from the breeding areas occur mainly along the coast, perhaps entirely involving first-years. None, however, remained for long and none through the winter, the suggestion being that at least some Dartford Warblers leave the country, being possibly involved in southward migration, though proof is lacking (Wernham *et al.* 2002). Most occurred from early October to early November, with smaller numbers from early February to mid-April, a situation that exactly fits these Scillonian records.

## Spectacled Warbler *Sylvia conspicillata* A BBRC 0%

2000   One Tresco 15th to 21st October   *British Birds* 94: 489

Breeds central and southeast Spain, northwest North Africa (including Madeira, Canary and Cape Verde Islands), southern France, Sardinia, southern Italy, Sicily, Cyprus and Israel. Polytypic: nominate *conspicillata* occurs North Africa and Mediterranean Basin; *orbitalis* Madeira, Cape Verde Islands and Canary Islands.

One very recent record, Scilly's first and Britain's fourth. A first-year bird was found by a visiting birder at Middle Down, Tresco, on 15th October 2000. It remained, frequenting an area of gorse, until 21st and was seen by several hundred birders in the process (Broyd 2000). It arrived on a southeasterly breeze, but Scilly in October being what it is, not too much should perhaps be attached to that, other birds present on the islands including Pallas's Warbler *Phylloscopus proregulus* and Common Nighthawk *Chordeiles minor*!

All populations breeding in and north of the Mediterranean region migrate to North Africa in autumn, so exactly why this species should turn up in Scilly in October is an interesting question and a difficult one to answer. According to Cramp *et al.* (1977–94), a few remain to winter in southern France, southeast Spain, Sicily, etc. However, those from populations north of the Mediterranean that do migrate do so between late August and early October, in which case a late and disoriented first-winter migrant from somewhere as far north even as the Camargue seems a distinct possibility, although it might equally have originated from one of the more easterly populations.

## Subalpine Warbler *Sylvia cantillans* A BBRC 9.7%

**Scarce spring and autumn migrant, full written description required by the BBRC.**

Breeds North Africa, Iberia and southern France east through northern Mediterranean to former Yugoslavia and Turkey. In northwest Africa partially migratory, remainder wholly migratory, wintering African Sahel zone. Polytypic: nominate *cantillans*, or 'Western Subalpine Warbler' occurs southern Europe east to perhaps mainland Italy; *inornata* northwest Africa; *moltonii* (not recognised by all authorities, e.g. Cramp *et al.* 1977–94), Balearic Islands, Sardinia and Corsica; *albistriata*, or 'Eastern Subalpine Warbler' Italy east to former Yugoslavia and Turkey.

Since Hilda Quick described a fine male on St Agnes for five days during early May 1958, a total of 44 Subalpine Warblers have arrived in the islands up until the end of year 2000. The Charts include all records and show both annual totals and arrival dates. It is obvious from the latter that records divide clearly into spring and autumn concentrations, with slightly more in the former period. The tendency towards more records in more years since the 1970s seems certain to partly reflect increased observer coverage within the islands, though Dymond *et al.* (1989) found evidence among national data of a recent steady increase over much the same period. These same authors also found far greater disparity between spring and autumn totals than seems apparent in Scilly, with 76% of all arrivals during the early period.

The sex and/or age was determined for 34 individuals, 22 (65%) of which were described as adult or subadult males, thus male-plumaged individuals outnumber females and first-years by almost 2:1. Several spring males were heard in song. Earliest arrival was 30th March, on St Agnes in 1996 and the latest any bird was present in the islands was 8th November 1999, exceeding the previous latest (1984) by five days. One or more Subalpine Warblers arrived in 23 (53%) of the 43 years since 1958, multiple arrivals being a feature of 11 years (48%).

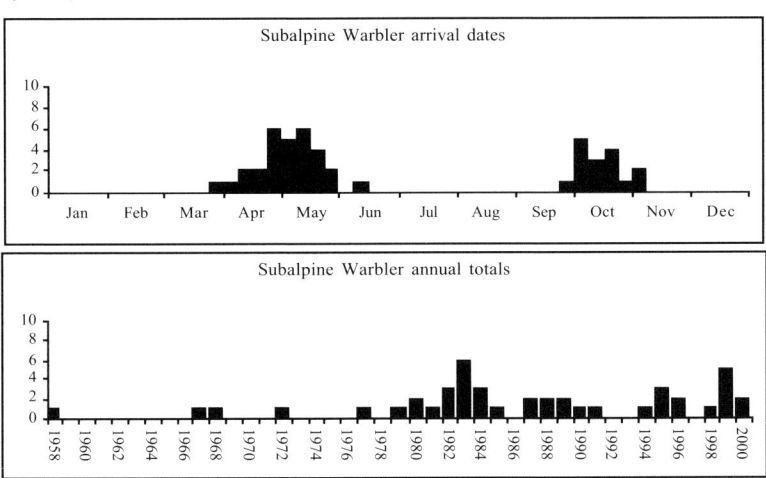

Most authorities agree that overshooting seems likely to account for most spring northern European records, though eastern *albistriata* has also been identified in Britain at this time (Cramp *et al.* 1977–94). Far less seems to have been published on British autumn arrivals, though Dymond *et al.* (1989) found evidence among national data of a southeast, i.e. *albistriata*, origin for birds reaching Britain in autumn. The form *moltonii* recently reached central Europe (Belgium) for the first time. Unfortunately, racial identification seems rarely to have been attempted in Scilly, though spring males should pose no particular problem if seen well.

## Sardinian Warbler     *Sylvia melanocephala*  A  BBRC 10.7%

**Rare spring and autumn migrant, full written description required by the BBRC.**

    1980  One (first-year) Tresco 25th September to 30th October    *British Birds* 74: 486
    1981  One (male) St Agnes 16th April    *British Birds* 75: 521
    1985  One (male) St Mary's 23rd & 24th October    *British Birds* 79: 565, 573
    1988  One (female) St Agnes 10th & 11th May    *British Birds* 82: 548
    1996  One (female) St Agnes 29th & 30th March    *British Birds* 90: 501
    1999  One (singing male) Porth Hellick and Salakee, St Mary's 17th to 23rd April    *British Birds* 93: 557
    *2002  One (singing male) St Agnes 29th March to 1st April*
    *2002  One (first-summer male) St Martin's 21st to 25th April*

Almost exclusively confined to West Palearctic in both summer and winter, breeding southern Europe, Mediterranean and North Africa. Mainly sedentary or partially migratory in west, migratory in east, wintering Middle East and North Africa south to Sahel zone.

At least eight records in seven different years. The Chart incorporates all arrival dates and shows a typically scattered pattern, though recognisably separable into spring and autumn periods. These six individuals constitute 10.7% of the 80 records accepted by the BBRC for the period 1958–99. First was a difficult-to-see first-winter male on Tresco's Beacon Hill from 25th September to 30th October 1980. This was followed by a male on St Agnes for one day in mid-April 1981 which was considered by some as possibly the same as the 1980 individual. Whatever criticisms may have been aimed at previous skulkers were forgotten following the splendid showing by the male in Higher Moors for two days during October 1985. However, even this showy individual was overshadowed by the superbly plumaged singing male in the Porth Hellick and Salakee area of St Mary's from 17th to 23rd April. Typical of Scilly, it was sometimes possible, whilst watching this last bird and without moving position, to also see Terek Sandpiper *Xenus cinereus* and Night Heron *Nycticorax nycticorax*. The presence of this 1999 individual coincided with that of another male in East Sussex from 19th to 23rd.

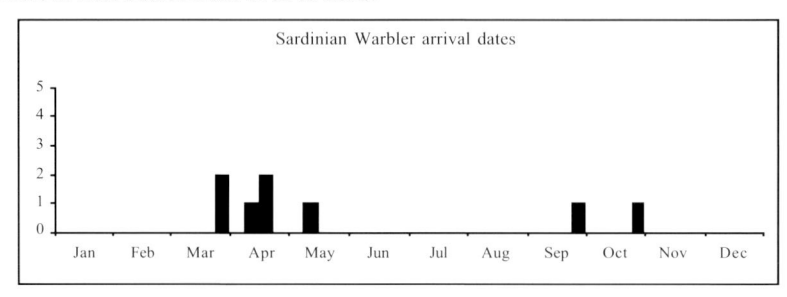

Sardinian Warbler arrival dates

Like several other warbler species, spring Sardinian Warblers on Scilly seem likely to involve overshooting individuals from further south, although the nearest fully migratory populations may be those in the Italian Alps and the former Yugoslavia. However, autumn records of this mainly southern European species are less easily explained. No Sardinian Warblers have been trapped and ringed on Scilly and there are no recaptures.

## Orphean Warbler *Sylvia hortensis*  A  BBRC 25%

**Extremely rare migrant, full written description required by the BBRC.**

1981   One (male) St Mary's 16th to 22nd October   *British Birds* 75: 522, 78: 150

Breeds North Africa, southern Europe and Mediterranean east to Kazakhstan, Afghanistan and Pakistan. Migratory, wintering African Sahel, Arabian Peninsula and Indian subcontinent. Polytypic: nominate *hortensis*, or 'Western Orphean Warbler' occurs southwest Europe and North Africa east to Italy and Libya; *crassirostris* east of *hortensis*, as far as Iran and Turkmenistan (formerly Turkmeniya), where replaced by *jerdoni*.

The first and only Scillonian record of this southern European and south-central Asian species involved a male frequenting the Higher Moors area of St Mary's for seven days from 16th October 1981 (Turton & Greaves 1985). A description of the bird, by Rupert Hastings, also appeared in the annual report for that year (*IOSBR* 1981: 54). However, the distinction of first record for Cornwall and Scilly went to a bird trapped and ringed at Porthgwarra, west Cornwall, on 22nd October 1967, it being the third for Britain and Ireland (Penhallurick 1978). The similarity of the dates involved in these two records is noteworthy. Just four Orphean Warbler records were accepted by the BBRC during 1958–99, the Scillonian individual representing 25% of the national total.

Like Sardinian *S. melanocephala* and other southern European warblers, agreeing on the driving mechanisms behind these northwest European autumn arrivals is no easy matter and no British records have been identified to form. However, for Scilly, the suggestion of Cramp *et al.* (1977–94) that the eastern *jerdoni* perhaps migrates through the West Palearctic may perhaps provide the answer, even though Gantlett (1998) considered nominate *hortensis* or the east Asian *crassirostris* equally probable.

# Barred Warbler *Sylvia nisoria* A

**Scarce autumn migrant. Treated by the BBRC as a national Scarce Migrant, full written description required by the SRP.**

Breeds central Europe east to central southern Siberia and northern Mongolia, and south to Black Sea and southern Kazakhstan. Migratory, wintering East Africa. Polytypic: nominate *nisoria* occurs Europe and southeast Asia east to northern Iran and Ural Mountains; *merzbacheri* elsewhere.

This is another warbler species missed in Scilly by 19th- and early 20th-century ornithologists. First reference to this species involved two on St Agnes during October 1961, one of which was trapped and ringed. Since then it has occurred almost annually, and certainly so during the 20 years from 1980 to 1999. The Chart includes 119 arrivals for these 20 years, the most being 16 in 1992, followed by 13 in 1981, and eleven and ten in 1994 and 1991 respectively. The lowest numbers recorded were the single bird in 1998 and two in 1995, the late 1990s witnessing something of a low patch for this species in Scilly. Interestingly, the first record for mainland Cornwall came in 1963, just two years after that for Scilly (Penhallurick 1978), though here it was less regular during the early years than on the islands. The Chart shows a clear peak in numbers during the early to mid-1990s, followed by an equally obvious reduction from 1995. Numbers in mainland Cornwall do not appear to have kept pace with those in Scilly, the total since the first in 1963 being just 53 (*CBWPSAR* 70). It is also worth noting that the species seems to have been rare generally in western Europe until the 1960s, the first for Belgium only occurring in 1964 (Sharrock 1974).

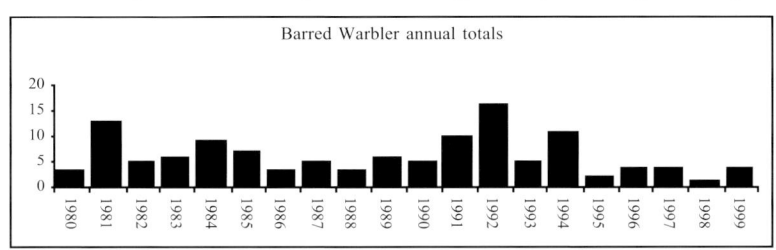

Barred Warbler annual totals

During the ten years 1990–99, birds were present in the islands from late August to late October, the earliest arrival being 22nd August and the last any bird was present 27th October. However, there was considerable between-year variation, the latest first sighting being 18th October and the earliest last sighing 24th August. Western European Barred Warblers winter in East Africa along with the eastern *merzbacheri*. Birds from all breeding areas mostly pass through the Middle East and central European birds thus head southeast. Generally, acceptable explanations for the appearance of this species in autumn west of its breeding grounds include a combination of further westward displacement of that part of the population already migrating in a southwesterly direction, plus random post juvenile dispersal. With the possibility, also, of reverse autumn migration, birds seen in southern Britain during late autumn are believed to be these same individuals moving southwards (Sharrock 1974). Two Barred Warblers have been ringed in Scilly but there are no recaptures.

# Lesser Whitethroat *Sylvia curruca* A

**Annual autumn migrant in small numbers, less frequent in spring. There are two confirmed breeding records, both from 1965.**

Breeds central Eurasia, from England, Scandinavia and France east to Mongolia and central Siberia. Migratory, wintering African Sahel zone east through Arabian Peninsula to India. Polytypic with complex racial structure, normally separated into *curruca* group and *althaea* group. Within *curruca* group, nominate *curruca* occurs western and central Europe south to northern Italy and east to western Siberia; *blythi*, or 'Siberian Lesser Whitethroat', Siberia east of *curruca*; *halimodendri* southern Russia; *minula*, or 'Desert Lesser Whitethroat', western China. Several more forms east and south. National 31% decline 1994–99 (Bashford & Noble 2000).

James Clark and Francis Rodd's 19th-century *Zoologist* review of *The Birds of Scilly* described just one Lesser Whitethroat obtained in early October 1857, plus a possible pair on Tresco's Castle Down in 1863 (Clark & Rodd 1906) although no precise date was given. Penhallurick (1978) thought the 1857 individual was the sole 19th-century record for both Scilly and the Cornish mainland. However, in 1869, Francis's uncle E H Rodd referred to it among the common warblers observed in Scilly during autumn (Rodd 1880), later writing that it was occasionally seen on migration during autumn (Rodd 1870a). Similarly, in his review of 19th-century English Lesser Whitethroat distribution, Mathew (1891) queried whether E H Rodd's statement that 'this warbler never visits Cornwall and is only met with at Scilly occasionally in the autumn' was correct.

The only confirmed record of Scillonian breeding concerns two pairs on Tresco in 1965, the same year that four pairs of Whitethroat *S. communis* also bred in the islands for the first time (*CBWPSAR* 35). Both Lesser Whitethroat pairs fledged young, one at Old Grimsby, the other on Middle Downs. Penhallurick's analysis of Scillonian and Cornish records up until the mid-1970s showed that Lesser Whitethroat became regular in Scilly from about 1957 and that some 85% occurred during autumn. In comparison, Cornwall had only one-third as many migrant sightings as Scilly, but twice as many were in spring as in autumn.

Examining records for the ten years from 1990, birds passed through the islands in autumn in all ten years but only nine during spring, the earliest arrival being 23rd April and the first autumn migrants occurring during the last week of August. Last autumn sightings ranged from late October through to an exceptional 7th December in 1990. However, whilst overall spring totals were quite easily calculated, mostly hovering around four to five birds, the volume of autumn passage was more difficult to calculate, though seldom were more than seven or so present in the islands, with the daily total more usually one to two and with October bringing the main movement. Even during this period, however, numbers can be low, as in autumn 1997 when there were just three in September and two in October, giving an annual maximum of eleven individuals.

Like most other migrant species in Scilly, little seems to have been published on the racial origin of Lesser Whitethroats passing through the islands. Most, though, seem likely to be nominate *curruca* from mainland Britain or nearby continental Europe, which winters mainly in East Africa and Egypt. The fact that, unlike most migrant passerine species, most western European Lesser Whitethroat populations move southeast in autumn (Cramp *et al.* 1977–94; Wernham *et al.* 2002) doubtless helps explain the species' scarcity in Scilly compared to some other European warblers, it being most likely to occur, in theory, as a spring overshoot. Within Britain, birds mostly leave the breeding grounds from mid-July, peaking about the end of August or early September and being more narrowly concentrated than in spring. Cramp *et al.* attribute British autumn west-coast and northern records to reverse migration of western European birds, whilst also acknowledging the presence of some *blythi*. Apart from *blythi*, autumn migrants on Scilly could also possibly include the paler and recognisable *minula*, which has been recorded elsewhere in Britain. Just 13 Lesser Whitethroats had been ringed in Scilly up until the end of 1999, nine after 1970, and there are no recaptures.

## Whitethroat (Common Whitethroat) *Sylvia communis* A

**Annual migrant in moderate numbers, several recent sporadic breeding records or attempts with the possibility that it is becoming more regular.**

Breeds central and southern Europe, North Africa and central-western Asia, from northwest Morocco, Mediterranean, Iberia, France, Britain, Ireland and Scandinavia east to Lake Baikal and western China. Migratory, all populations winter Africa south of Sahara. Polytypic: nominate *communis* occurs western Europe and northwest Africa, east to Greece, Austria and Scandinavia; *volgensis* eastern Europe and western Siberia; *icterops*, or 'Eastern Whitethroat' Levant, Turkey and into Iran; *rubicola* further south and east. National 6% increase 1994–99 (Bashford & Noble 2000).

Any lack of early information generally suggests a species was either extremely scarce in Scilly, or that it occurred in such numbers as to make any comment unnecessary. And in the case of Whitethroat, we can perhaps safely assume the former. The only apparent 19th-century reference to this species is James Clark and Francis Rodd's observation that it had 'been noted in Autumn. It occurs irregularly, and is probably a frequent migratory casual' (Clark & Rodd 1906). However, it is unclear whether Penhallurick's comment that it was 'almost unknown' as a breeding bird on Scilly (Penhallurick 1978) was based solely on this lack of any evidence to the contrary, the same authority admitting that it was common on the Cornish mainland from the early 1800s. The only other early information from Scilly involved 'many' seen at the Bishop Rock Lighthouse on the night of 27th September 1907 (Ogilvie-Grant 1909), plus 'a few' at the same location on the night of 5th September 1910 (Ogilvie-Grant 1912b).

The first recorded breeding on Scilly occurred in 1965, when a nest was found in Lower Moors, St Mary's, whilst on the same island a pair were seen carrying food, and a third male apparently held territory. Meanwhile, a pair reared young on Tresco that year and on St Agnes a fourth nest apparently failed, this last pair and three additional males all leaving St Agnes by 22nd June. Allegedly, the Tresco male disappeared and the female successfully fledged three young. Since then, singing males or nest building behaviour have been evident in several years, e.g. in 1991 one of two singing birds was seen carrying nest material but both soon moved on. In only one year, though, do the records suggest fledged young: a St Martin's pair raising two in 1993. Comments such as 'On St Mary's a pair bred near Mount Todden' may have involved a successful attempt, but lack adequate descriptive detail. The most recent and most comprehensive survey involved the 2000 Breeding Bird Atlas of 2000–2001 (Chown & Lock 2002), which located an estimated eleven pairs in seven (10.4%) of the 67 1-km squares surveyed – Bryher and Tresco being particularly favoured. However, the presence of singing passage birds probably confused the picture and the report's authors thought two pairs a more realistic interpretation.

Penhallurick gave normal arrival dates for both Scilly and Cornwall up until the 1970s as between 10th and 25th April, with birds on 21st and 30th the only March arrivals. On Scilly, the earliest autumn arrival was 24th July, birds continuing to pass through until mid-October. Spring daily totals on St Agnes usually peaked at about 50, with occasional highs in the region of 100–150, whereas in autumn, daily totals on the same islands rarely exceeded 20, less than ten being more the norm. By way of comparison, Penhallurick quoted a maximum of 1,000 on Lundy on 16th September 1968. Arrival and departure dates for the ten years 1990–99 were broadly in keeping with earlier findings, though one on Tresco 8th–15th November was the latest on record by five days. There was also a slight tendency towards records later than Penhallurick's mid-October, perhaps in response to increased observer coverage. Daily all-island counts were perhaps frustrated by inter-site or inter-island movement, but in most years were in the range five to 20. The obvious major reduction in the volume of spring passage since the 1970s reflects the known national situation (Cramp *et al*. 1977–94), with just 21 records in 1998 and 36 the following year.

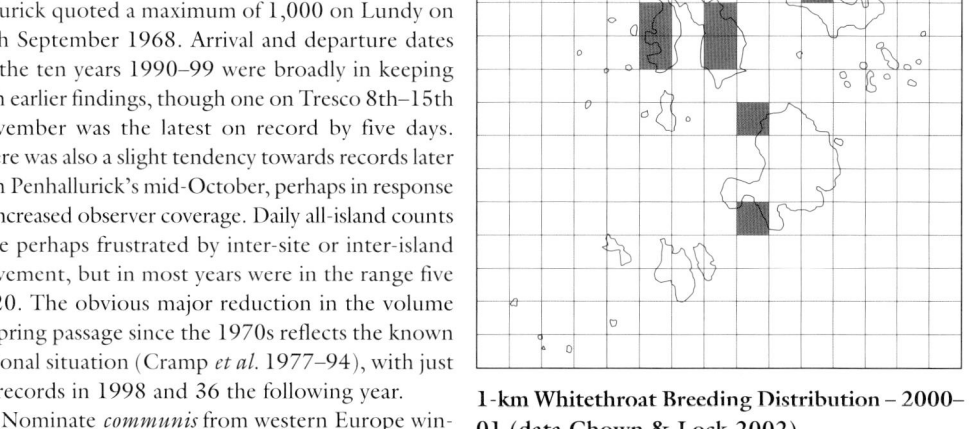

**1-km Whitethroat Breeding Distribution – 2000–01 (data Chown & Lock 2002)**

Nominate *communis* from western Europe winters mainly in West Africa, whilst eastern *communis* populations and other eastern forms, e.g. *volgensis, icterops*, winter in East Africa. Birds west of a line from approximately Oslo to Rome move largely west towards Iberia in autumn, those to the east of it heading southeast (Cramp *et al*. 1977–94). However, Scandinavian birds have the reputation for ranging more widely than birds from elsewhere, with ringing recoveries from Italy to southwest France and Swedish birds from Morocco to Lebanon. In addition, the possibility of the greyer *icterops*, or 'Eastern Whitethroat' from southwest Asia reaching Scilly must be real, and, indeed, individuals showing characteristics of this form have already been claimed from various English locations (Gantlett 1998). The west Siberian and eastern European *volgensis* must be equally likely as a drift migrant during late autumn.

Whitethroats commence moving south from late July, numbers in Britain peaking by late August. The broad-front return spring passage through southern England occurs from early to mid-April, peaking in mid-May in southwest England, which is slightly earlier than elsewhere. A total of 113 Whitethroats had been ringed in Scilly up until 1999, 89 (78.7%) prior to 1970. The only recapture involved a colour-ringed first-year ringed in Bedfordshire two years earlier.

## Controls
J030—    1stY Everton, Bedfordshire 3rd August 1993    FR  St Agnes 1st May 1995

**Whitethroat Ringing Recaptures**

## Garden Warbler *Sylvia borin* A

**Annual spring and autumn migrant in moderate numbers, two old and extremely suspect breeding records.**

Breeds western and central Europe east to western Asia. Migratory, wintering Africa south of Sahara. Polytypic: nominate *borin* occurs northern, western and central Europe east to Finland, Poland, Hungary and former Yugoslavia; *woodwardi* remainder of range. National 13% increase 1994–99 (Bashford & Noble 2000).

Garden Warbler was considered a rare autumn migrant during the 19th century, and the first published account involved a bird shot by the Reverend J H Jenkinson in September 1849 (Rodd 1849a, 1849b). E H Rodd later claimed that several had been obtained in Scilly by the 1880s (Rodd 1880), though his nephew Francis and James Clark could name only three records up until the end of the 19th century (Clark & Rodd 1906). One of these involved the Jenkinson bird, another 'seemingly came over with a flight of Redwings' (*Turdus iliacus*) in October 1874, and two were seen during late September 1900, one of which was shot. From this Clark and Rodd concluded it was evidently rare and casual during autumn.

Like Blackcap *S. atricapilla*, Garden Warbler seems always to have been scarce in west Cornwall, Penhallurick (1978) pointing out that even by the 1970s it was scarce west of the Camel Valley. Penhallurick also referred to entries in the Tresco Abbey records stating that three pairs nested on that island during 1932 and one pair in 1943, perhaps rightly describing these as 'unsubstantiated and generally viewed with incredulity'. Certainly, there has been no subsequent suggestion of breeding having even been attempted in the islands and it was not detected during the 2000 Breeding Bird Atlas (Chown & Lock 2002).

The pattern and timing of migration is much the same as for Blackcap, though slightly later in spring and like that species far fewer pass through during spring than in autumn. However, unlike Blackcap there is no scope for confusion with wintering individuals. During the ten years 1990–99, first birds arrived in spring within the narrow window of 25th April to 7th May, whilst recorded annual last spring sightings occurred between 20th May and 20th June, up to a month later than for Blackcap. Autumn first arrivals were noted between 4th July and 18th September, whereas last sighting dates ranged between 27th October and early November, with 15th November the extreme. Overall numbers involved in spring were generally around ten to 15, whereas autumn daily sightings involved at best ones and twos, with daily same-island counts of ten or less. During 1998, 54 autumn records were believed to have involved 35 individuals, seven on St Agnes on 9th October being viewed as a respectable island total.

Within western Europe, Garden Warblers, i.e. the form *borin*, migrate mainly south or southwest in autumn, heading for Iberia and West Africa (Wernham *et al.* 2002). In contrast, those from northeast Europe, including possibly some *woodwardi* and an unknown percentage of intergrades between the two forms, cross the Mediterranean at the Italian peninsula (Cramp *et al.* 1977–94). Most birds involved even further east are presumably of the recognisably larger and paler *woodwardi*. In western Europe, southward movement commences from mid-July, many more moving during mid-August and with numbers peaking later towards the west, e.g. Scilly and Ireland. Spring records in southeast England peak during early May, though there is evidence that the largest numbers in the southwest occur during April. There is occasional evidence too of overwintering in Britain, though apparently not from Scilly. The recognisably paler *woodwardi* ought to occur as an extralimital migrant in Britain (Gantlett 1998) and should be looked for in Scilly during October. A total of 201 Garden Warblers had been ringed on Scilly up until 1999, 128 prior to 1970, but there are no recaptures.

## Blackcap *Sylvia atricapilla* A

**Annual spring and autumn migrant in moderate to sometimes large numbers, a few pairs probably breed most years.**

Breeds central and southern Europe east into western Asia. Migratory in north and east, southern and western populations less migratory. Winters western Europe, Mediterranean, including North Africa, central West Africa and East Africa. Polytypic: nominate *atricapilla* occurs Europe and western Siberia south to Pyrenees, Italy, Balkans and Crimea; *pauluccii* northern Mediterranean from Balearic Islands to Italy, including Tunisia; *heineken* Portugal, western Spain, Canary Islands and Madeira, perhaps also Morocco,

Algeria and remainder of Spain; *gularis* Azores and Cape Verde Islands, Morocco, Algeria and remainder of Spain. National 50% increase 1994–99 (Bashford & Noble 2000).

Earliest published mention of Blackcap appears to be Francis Rodd's letter to his uncle E H Rodd in Penzance, in which he reported it figured among considerable numbers of the 'smaller species of warblers' appearing on Scilly during September 1849 (Rodd 1880). In subsequent letters he mentioned the possibility of finding it in Tresco's Abbey Gardens at the end of October 1863 (Rodd 1863a), a male in the Abbey Gardens on 17th December 1870 (Rodd 1871a) and one, presumably on Tresco, from autumn into the following January.

Francis and James Clark later summarised the situation, stating it occurred in autumn and winter and was obtained by Augustus Pechell in September 1850 and October 1854 (Clark & Rodd 1906). They pointed out, too, that since 1854 it had been noted over 12 times, including twice in December and twice in January. Interestingly Clark and Rodd made no mention of it having been seen in the islands during spring, though chances are it was overlooked, especially as most early information for all species comes from the latter half of the year. There is an early 20th-century mention from the Bishop Rock Lighthouse involving one killed on the night of 21st October 1908 (Ogilvie-Grant 1910).

Penhallurick summarised the situation for Scilly and Cornwall up until the 1970s, finding it thinly represented during spring in ones and twos, normally from early April to mid-May, the most on any day on St Agnes being six, although at that time few totals were being reported from other islands in the group. Autumn passage occurred between early September and mid-November, most appearing during October; the latest apparent migrant being a bird on Cornwall's Eddystone Rock on 22nd October. Maximum daily autumn totals on St Agnes were 22 in early October.

Little seems to have changed since, spring daily totals remaining in the region of five to 15 birds and with apparent passage occurring between late March or early April through to mid-May. Similarly, birds arrive in autumn from late August or early September and have mostly passed through by late October or early November. Same-island counts are frequently as low as ten but can increase substantially during October, as in 1997 when 80 were estimated for St Martin's alone. However, on 14th October 1999 just 50 were believed present on all islands. The presence of apparent annually varying numbers of wintering individuals creates difficulties determining precise dates for the onset and finish of spring and autumn passage. In addition, reported winter totals may not accurately reflect numbers present, numbers of observers being much reduced at this time. Nonetheless, a report of eight birds at Salakee, St Mary's, on 29th December 1992 suggests that numbers involved can be quite high.

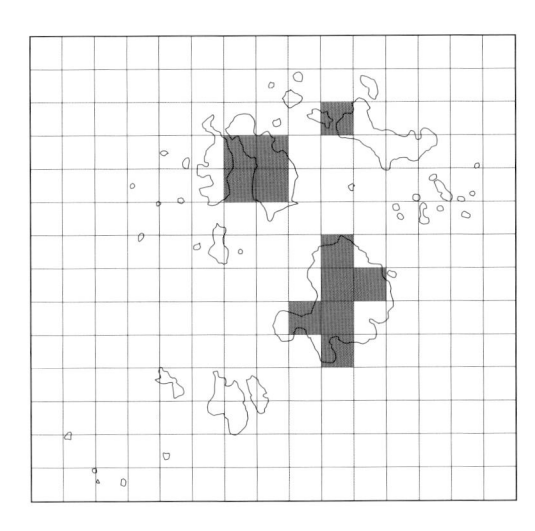

| Island | Pairs |
| --- | --- |
| Bryher | 1 |
| St Martin's | 1 |
| St Mary's | 9 |
| Tresco | 7 |

**2000 Breeding Bird Atlas – Blackcap (Chown & Lock 2002)**

**1-km Blackcap Breeding Distribution – 2000-01 (data Chown & Lock 2002)**

Penhallurick (1978) made the point that Blackcap was always considered scarce in west Cornwall, the first Scillonian nest being described from Holy Vale, St Mary's, in 1972, though birds were present in summer and believed to be breeding for some years beforehand. During the 1990s, pairs were believed to have bred, or in one case reported to have done so, in six of the ten years, the most being a possible four pairs in 1991. Nevertheless, no details of a nest were described, the most informative accounts for the islands apparently involving a pair with young in 1977 and a female with young in 1983, both on Tresco (*IOSBR* 1977, 1983). On the Lunnon Farm study plot on St Mary's, a singing male held territory in five of the eight years 1991–98, though no active nest was found. More recently, the 2000 Breeding Bird Atlas recorded a possible 18 pairs in eleven (16.4%) of the 67 1-km squares surveyed, though the report's authors thought a more likely figure fell in the range three to ten pairs (Chown & Lock 2002). During the survey, breeding was confirmed in just two St Mary's squares, though once again details were omitted.

Although nominate *atricapilla* occurs in all wintering areas, those west of a line from Oslo to Rome head mainly southwest in autumn towards southern France, Iberia and North Africa (Cramp *et al.* 1977–94). Within Britain, most head initially southeast, before altering course to the south or southwest and crossing France to northeast Spain (Wernham *et al.* 2002). Although most Blackcaps reaching Scilly should be nominate *atricapilla*, Gantlett (1998) drew attention to the possibility of the slightly darker and shorter-winged Iberian *heineken* also occurring as a vagrant.

According to Cramp *et al.*, numbers of wintering birds in Britain increased from an average of 22 during 1945–54, to 380 during 1970–77 and an estimated 3,000 individuals by the early 1990s, including small numbers in Scilly. The source of these increases is traced to a shift in the wintering range of birds from continental Europe. A total of 1,139 Blackcaps had been ringed on Scilly up until 1999, 976 since 1970. All known recaptures are shown below, the four controls and the bird killed by a cat in Co. Cork in late January ably demonstrate the autumn movement of Continental birds already referred to, whereas the two recoveries further south in Europe presumably involved migrants from north of the islands.

**Controls**

| | | | | | |
|---|---|---|---|---|---|
| E791218 | 1stY | Spurn Point, Humberside 11th October 1988 | CT | St Agnes 29th October 1988 |
| 3812656 | ? | West Vlaanderen, Belgium 7th October 1991 | CT | St Martin's 24th October 1991 |
| 5832828 | 1stY | Awirs, Liege, Belgium 7th October 1995 | CT | St Agnes 26th October 1995 |
| 5722343 | 1stY | Oost Vlaanderen, Belgium 5th October 1995 | CT | St Martin's 26th October 1995 |

**Recoveries**

| | | | | | |
|---|---|---|---|---|---|
| AK13673 | Ad | St Agnes 23rd October 1962 | ? | Puebla de los Infantes, Seville, Spain 22nd December 1962 |
| KS81737 | Ad | St Agnes 30th April 1978 | FD | Cherbourg, Manche, France 10th May 1979 |
| K483092 | 1stY | Higher Town, St Martin's 28th October 1995 | KC | Fermoy, Co. Cork, Ireland 29th January 1996 |

**Blackcap Ringing Recaptures**

# Greenish Warbler *Phylloscopus trochiloides* A BBRC 3.3%

**Rare migrant or vagrant, full written description required by the BBRC.**

- 1962 Two trapped St Agnes 15th to 21st September  *British Birds* 56: 405, 78: 450
- 1965 One St Agnes 7th to 14th October  *British Birds* 59: 294, 78: 450
- 1976 One St Lower Moors, St Mary's 9th to 14th October  *British Birds* 71: 521
- 1977 One Great Pool, Tresco 8th October  *British Birds* 71: 521
- 1978 One Parsonage, St Agnes 20th October to 3rd November  *British Birds* 72: 537
- 1983 One (*nitidus*) St Mary's 26th September to 4th October
  *British Birds* 94: 278–283, 284–288; *Ibis* 128: 602, 135: 221
- 1987 One (*plumbeitarsus*) Gugh 22nd to 27th October
  *British Birds* 94: 278–283, 284–288; *Ibis* 135: 221
- 1988 One St Mary's 11th to 15th October  *British Birds* 82: 549
- 1990 One Tresco 9th October  *British Birds* 87: 556
- 1998 One in song St Agnes 1st to 5th June  *British Birds* 92: 597

Formerly acceptable Greenish Warbler Records, now rejected
  [1963   One St Agnes 26th & 27th November]   Dean 1985
  [1964   One St Agnes 20th December to 15th January 1985]   Dean 1985
  [1967   One St Agnes 21st September]   Dean 1985
  [1967   One St Agnes 29th & 30th October]   Dean 1985

Breeds central-eastern West Palearctic and central-western Asia south and east to China. Polytypic: *viridanus* occurs eastern Europe through western Asia to Afghanistan; *ludlowi* southeast Afghanistan and western Himalayas; nominate *trochiloides* central and eastern Himalayas; *obscuratus* central China (Cramp *et al.* 1977–94). Now considered by BOURC as conspecific with widely separated former species, 'Bright Green Warbler' ('Green Warbler') *P. nitidus*, now *P. t. nitidus*, and 'Two-barred Greenish Warbler' *P. plumbeitarsus*, now *P. t. plumbeitarsus* (BOURC 1986, 1993a, 2002a; Collinson 2001a), although some authorities still treat these as full species. *Nitidus* occurs mainly between Black and Caspian Seas; *plumbeitarsus* eastern Russia. All populations migratory, apparently wintering mainly India and Sri Lanka, though little has been published in western Europe on wintering *plumbeitarsus*.

There are just eleven currently acceptable Greenish Warbler records for the islands, although a further four individuals were previously accepted as this species. Two of the still acceptable records were originally treated by the BBRC as 'Green Warbler' *P. nitidus* and 'Two-barred Greenish Warbler' *P. plumbeitarsus*. The Chart includes all eleven still acceptable records and shows a clear preference for late September–October, all of which, with the obvious exception of the June individual, arrived within the 38-day window 15th September to 22nd October. First for Scilly involved the quite remarkable two on St Agnes during September 1962, one 15th–21st (trapped on 19th) and a second, reportedly greyer individual, present on 16th (*SABOAR* 1962–63). This was followed by a report that failed to gain acceptance, involving a wing-barred *Phylloscopus* on St Agnes from 20th December 1964 through to mid-January 1965. More creditable was the bird on that same island in mid-October 1965.

The 1983 arrival involved an individual of the former 'Green Warbler' *P. nitidus*, which was followed in 1987 by the much-discussed and greatly admired 'Two-barred Greenish Warbler' *P. plumbeitarsus* (Grant 1987; Bradshaw 2001). Both were considered to have been first-years and both represented first British records of these two species/forms. Other Greenish Warblers arriving in Scilly may have been heard in song, but the only recorded occasions involved individuals in Lower Moors, St Mary's, in October 1988 and, more understandably, in the St Agnes Parsonage garden during early June 1998. The Table lists four bracketed entries, all of which were originally found acceptable by the BBRC but which have since been rejected (Dean 1985). The eleven still acceptable Scillonian records represent 3.3% of the 330 accepted by the BBRC during the period 1958–99.

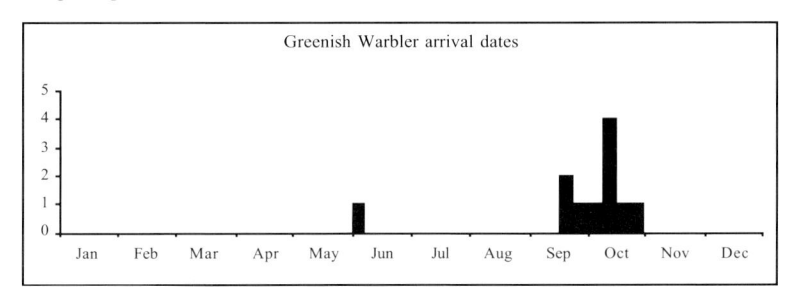

Greenish Warbler arrival dates

There is evidence of a fluctuating westward spread of *viridanus* since the second half of the 19th century and it now breeds as close to Britain as Poland (Hagemeijer & Blair 1997). Like other Asian warbler species wintering in India or southeast Asia, most authorities, e.g. Cramp *et al.* (1977–94), consider western European autumn vagrancy attributable to either reverse migration or westerly drift during anticyclonic conditions. However, as the last authors point out, any recent increased occurrence could also be allied to recent westerly range extensions, which perhaps involve changes to wintering areas and migration routes. The single Scillonian June record is presumably most likely to be explained by overshooting. The only Greenish Warbler ringed in Scilly involved one of the first two arrivals and there are no recaptures.

## Arctic Warbler *Phylloscopus borealis* A BBRC 7.3%

**Scarce autumn migrant, full written description required by the BBRC.**

| | |
|---|---|
| 1960 | One trapped St Agnes 10th October |
| 1971 | One St Agnes 30th October |
| 1975 | One St Agnes 23rd to 27th September |
| 1975 | One St Agnes 24th to 27th September |
| 1976 | One St Agnes 17th September |
| 1981 | One (trapped) St Martin's 29th September |
| 1981 | One St Mary's 2nd to 5th October |
| 1981 | One St Mary's 11th to 14th October |
| 1983 | One Tresco 25th & 26th September |
| 1986 | Two St Mary's 30th September to 2nd October |
| 1988 | One St Agnes 11th to 19th October |
| 1988 | One Tresco 17th to 19th October |
| 1992 | One St Agnes 20th September |
| 1992 | One St Agnes 28th September |
| 1996 | One St Agnes 7th to 14th October |
| 2000 | One Garrison, St Mary's 6th to 11th October |

Breeds northern Eurasia, from northern Fennoscandia east across Bering Strait to northwest Alaska and south to northern Mongolia. Migratory, wintering southeast Asia. Polytypic: nominate *borealis* occurs northern Europe east to Bering Sea and south to Mongolia; *xanthodryas* Kamchatka, Sakhalin and Japan; *kennicotti* Alaska (BOURC 2002b).

There were 16 records involving 17 birds in eleven years up to and including an individual on The Garrison, St Mary's, during October 2000. The Chart includes all arrival dates and shows an obvious pattern of late autumn arrivals, within the 44-day window 17th September to 30th October, mean length of stay being just 3.1 days. Two or more were recorded in four years, the most being three in 1981. Not included among the totals shown are two claims of birds in 1975, one on St Mary's on 3rd October, the same or another on St Agnes on 5th–6th October. Both are mentioned in the annual report (*IOSBR* 1975) but neither appears to have been accepted by the BBRC.

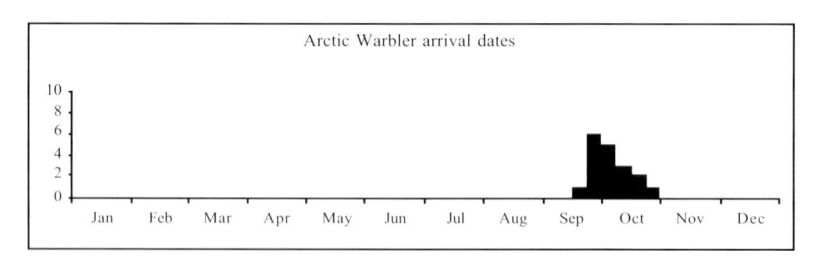

Arctic Warbler is a long-distance migrant, northern European populations moving east across Russia and south through Mongolia and China to reach wintering grounds in southeast Asia (Cramp *et al.* 1977–94). Northwest European birds mainly depart their breeding areas during August and travel some 13,000 km. The majority of European records away from breeding areas come from Britain and those in autumn are believed attributable to reverse migration. However, there is evidence of a recent increase in European records generally, some authorities suggesting western birds may be in the process of seeking a new, and closer, wintering area (Cramp *et al.* 1977–94). The BBRC accepted 219 records during the period 1958–99, all or most of which were believed attributable to the nominate form (BOURC 2002b), the 16 Scillonian arrivals during this same period representing 7.3% of the national total. Two Arctic Warblers had been ringed in Scilly up to and including 1999, one during each period. There are no recaptures.

## Pallas's Warbler (Pallas's Leaf Warbler)     *Phylloscopus proregulus*    A

**Scarce autumn migrant. Treated by the BBRC as a national Scarce Migrant, full written description required by the SRP.**

Breeds northeast Asia, from Altai region of Siberia east to Sakhalin and south to Afghanistan, Himalayas and central China. Migratory, wintering southern China, India and southeast Asia. Polytypic: nominate *proregulus* occurs from Altai east and south to northern Mongolia; *cholonotus* northwest China south and west to Himalayas; *simlaensis* northwest Himalayas eastwards. Removed from BBRC Rarities List January 1991 (Lansdown and the Rarities Committee 1990).

    An estimated 71 Pallas's Warblers arrived in 25 of the 37 years since the first in 1963, at an average of 1.7 a year, or 2.8 per arrival year, the greatest annual total, by far, involving 16 in 1997. All arrival dates are plotted up until Pallas's Warbler's removal from the BBRC's rarity list in 1991, showing a very concentrated 28-day window between 12th October and 13th November. Interestingly, Cramp *et al.* (1977–94) emphasised an increase in northwest European records since the 1960s. Various authors catalogued periodic autumn influxes of Pallas's Warblers into eastern Britain, not all of which were reflected by numbers arriving in Scilly. The phenomenal east-coast passerines fall during mid-October 1985 (Howey & Bell 1985) resulted in five Scillonian arrivals, whilst the far less impressive national 1963 autumn total of just six (R E Scott 1964) produced one Scillonian arrival.

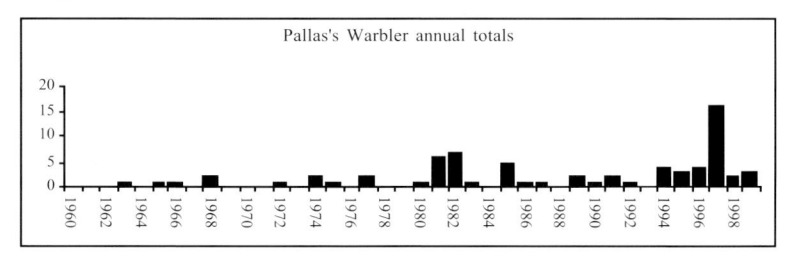

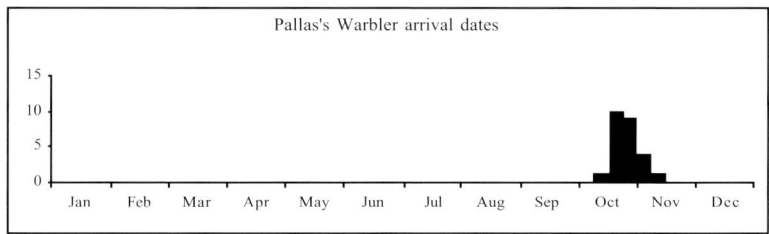

    Pallas's Warblers leave their breeding grounds from late August to September, western populations heading towards wintering quarters in India or further east, in which case it is surprising that so many arrive in northwest Europe at this time. Most authorities attribute this to a combination of reverse migration and westward displacement during anticyclonic conditions. One Pallas's Warbler had been ringed in Scilly up until 1999; there are no recaptures.

## Yellow-browed Warbler     *Phylloscopus inornatus*    A

**Scarce autumn migrant but in increasing numbers, occasional in winter. Treated by the BBRC as a national Scarce Migrant.**

Breeds Siberia, from Ural Mountains east to Sea of Okhotsk and south to Sayan mountains. Migratory, wintering Nepal and Bangladesh east to southern China and southeast Asia. Monotypic: until recently treated as conspecific with Hume's Warbler *P. humei* (BOURC 1997). Removed from BBRC Rarities List January 1963 (Harber & Swaine 1963).

    Augustus Pechell shot two small warblers on St Martin's during October 1867, one of which (unsurprisingly) was too badly damaged for it to be preserved. The other was mounted and retained in the Tresco Collection as an 'immature' Firecrest *Regulus ignicapilla*. However, when the latter was examined by an unspecified authority in 1890, its true identity was revealed as the present species (Clark & Rodd 1906). Equally interesting are the facts surrounding Scilly's third Yellow-browed Warbler, which was obtained by Tresco gamekeeper David Smith, 'who knocked it down with a stick as it flew out of a hedge' (Clark & Rodd 1906; Witherby & Ticehurst 1907). David Smith having more success with a stick this time than with a gun and several other rarities (e.g. Sooty Tern *Sterna fuscata*, or Great Reed Warbler *Acrocephalus arundinaceus*)

An unexplained lack of records then followed from both Scilly and Cornwall up until the 1950s, the species being an almost annual visitor to eastern Britain during the same period (Baker & Catley 1987). The first 20th-century record for the islands was found and identified by Hilda Quick on St Agnes in October 1951, followed by her description of one on the same island the following January. Next mention involved a bird brought to A A Dorrien-Smith on 22nd November 1953 (presumably shot), Dorrien-Smith concluding that the species was probably not rare in Scilly and might even winter. During the remainder of the 1950s, birds were recorded only in 1957, when five visited St Agnes, but from 1961 it became annual, the only subsequent year of absence being 1966. Gantlett (1991) listed annual numbers for the 18 years 1973–90, the most in any year being 92 in 1986. These figures are repeated here with his kind permission (Chart). However, from the early 1990s the number of annual arrivals and, more importantly, the volume of reported sightings from an increasing number of observers, made the compilation of meaningful totals a near impossibility. This was certainly the case for those years when the species was represented in good numbers, as in 1996, when 169 October sightings were reported from five islands on 29 days during October, plus 94 sightings from three islands on 22 days in November.

Penhallurick (1978) plotted arrival dates in weekly periods for all Scillonian and Cornish records up until 1974, all but two occurring between the last week of September and the third week of November. The exceptions were individuals in mid-September and early January. During the ten years 1990–99, all first arrivals occurred within the 24-day period 11th September to 4th October, and annual last sightings fell within the slightly greater period 26th October to 25th November.

Yellow-browed Warbler is one of the commonest breeding Siberian birds and one of the most regular and numerous Siberian vagrants reaching western Europe, occurring mostly between September and December and being first documented in 1846 (Baker & Catley 1987). Baker & Catley also commented on the influence upon the number and distribution of British records of the continuing growth in the number of observers, 24% of the national total being reported from Scilly by 1987. They noted too that northern records occurred earlier than in the south and west and that the annual timing and distribution varied substantially in any event, though all areas received early and late records.

Baker & Catley also found that, on average, the timing of national records was one week later than for a previous study (Sharrock 1974), much of that difference being accounted for by a large increase in Scillonian records. They were forced to concede, nonetheless, that the mid-20th century had seen 'an unprecedented increase' in the number of Yellow-browed Warblers (and Pallas's Warblers *P. proregulus*) reaching Britain, and concluded that although this could be partly accounted for by weather patterns in the northwest approaches, it failed to explain what appear to be mass departures of birds from breeding areas in western or central Asia. However, ringing data showed that the majority of birds involved are first-years, perhaps still involved in post juvenile dispersal and taking the line of least resistance by 'drifting' in the direction of the prevailing wind.

Yellow-browed Warblers leave their Siberian breeding grounds during August–September, peak movement in north and west Siberia occurring during mid-August, most having left by early September

**Yellow-browed Warbler annual totals**

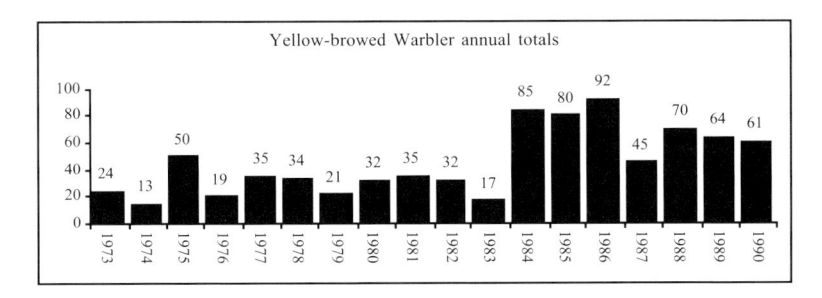

| Year | Total |
|------|-------|
| 1973 | 24 |
| 1974 | 13 |
| 1975 | 50 |
| 1976 | 19 |
| 1977 | 35 |
| 1978 | 34 |
| 1979 | 21 |
| 1980 | 32 |
| 1981 | 35 |
| 1982 | 32 |
| 1983 | 17 |
| 1984 | 85 |
| 1985 | 80 |
| 1986 | 92 |
| 1987 | 45 |
| 1988 | 70 |
| 1989 | 64 |
| 1990 | 61 |

(Cramp et al. 1977–94). Further east, e.g. Mongolia, birds are sometimes still present on the breeding grounds into mid-September and in southeast Russia it is the most numerous migrant *Phylloscopus*, peaking late September or early October. The arrival dates of Scillonian birds perhaps suggests that they originate from rather far east, unless of course they are birds that arrived in northern or eastern Britain and took time gravitating towards the southwest. It has been suggested (Wernham et al. 2002) that increasing numbers of Yellow-browed Warblers annually reaching Britain and Ireland may be contributing genetically to this population and are thus helping pioneer new wintering areas. Thirteen Yellow-browed Warblers had been ringed in Scilly up until 1999, ten since 1970. Although there are no recaptures, a bird in 1995 was seen to be wearing a ring. As none were trapped in the islands that year, it was perhaps a returning individual from a previous year.

## Hume's Warbler
## (Hume's Leaf Warbler)      *Phylloscopus humei*   A   BBRC 2.9%

**Extremely rare migrant, full written description required by the BBRC.**

    1996    One Higher Moors, St Mary's 4th to 7th October – possibly from 1st

*British Birds* 91: 507–508, 94: 493

    2002    One St Mary's 12th to 15th November  *Birding World* 15: 451

Breeds Sayan and Altai mountains south to northwest Himalayas, mainly wintering Indian subcontinent from Pakistan to Bangladesh. Polytypic; formerly treated as conspecific with Yellow-browed Warbler *P. inornatus* but separated by BOURC in 1997 into at least two forms: nominate *humei* and *mandellii* (BOURC 1997). *Humei* occurs Sayan and Altai mountains southwards to northwest Himalayas, wintering mainly Indian subcontinent from Pakistan to Bangladesh (Cramp et al. 1977–94). British records thus far involve only *humei*.

Just one accepted Scillonian record up until the end of 2001, involving a bird in Higher Moors, St Mary's, from at least 4th to 7th October 1996, though probably present at the same site since 1st. The first British record considered acceptable by BBRC following the split involved an individual at Beachy Head, Sussex, in November 1966 (BOURC 1998). The BBRC accepted 34 Hume's Warbler records up until the end of 1999, this individual representing 2.9% of the national total.

With no UK records before 13th October and with the majority falling during November, its occurrence pattern differs markedly from that of Yellow-browed Warbler and more closely mirrors that of Pallas's *P. proregulus* and Dusky Warblers *P. fuscatus*, though with a greater tendency towards overwintering (Madge & Quinn 1997). For a useful discussion on plumage differences between this species and Yellow-browed Warbler see Shirihai & Madge (1993). The reported 2002 individual fits the required timescale well but at the time of writing had still to be accepted by the BBRC.

## Radde's Warbler      *Phylloscopus schwarzi*   A   BBRC 21.2%

**Scarce autumn migrant, full written description required by the BBRC.**

    1971    One (first-year) St Agnes 24th October
    1973    One St Agnes 13th October
    1973    One St Agnes 22nd to 26th October

| | |
|---|---|
| 1977 | One St Agnes 26th & 27th October |
| 1979 | One St Agnes 20th October |
| 1981 | One Tresco 22nd October |
| 1982 | One St Agnes 12th & 13th October |
| 1982 | One St Mary's 23rd October |
| 1982 | One St Mary's 28th October |
| 1984 | One St Agnes 25th October |
| 1985 | One Tresco 19th & 20th October |
| 1985 | One Gugh 24th & 25th October |
| 1986 | One St Agnes 8th to 10th October |
| 1987 | One St Mary's 16th to 18th October |
| 1987 | One St Mary's 20th October |
| 1988 | One St Mary's 23rd October |
| 1988 | One St Mary's 23rd to 28th October |
| 1988 | One St Mary's 24th & 25th October |
| 1988 | One Tresco 28th October |
| 1989 | One St Mary's 4th October |
| 1989 | One St Martin's 16th October |
| 1989 | One St Agnes 25th to 27th October |
| 1990 | One Tresco 8th October |
| 1990 | One Tresco 26th to 28th October |
| 1991 | One St Mary's 21st to 23rd October |
| 1993 | One St Agnes 3rd October |
| 1994 | One St Mary's 14th to 19th October |
| 1997 | One St Mary's 14th to 19th October |
| 1997 | One St Agnes 18th & 19th October |
| 1998 | One St Agnes 1st November |
| 1999 | One Tresco 6th October |
| 1999 | One Troytown, St Agnes 6th to 10th October |
| 1999 | One Troytown, St Agnes 15th October |
| 1999 | One Rosevear 15th October |
| 1999 | Five St Mary's 15th October |
| 1999 | One Watermill, St Mary's 16th October |
| 1999 | One St Martin's 17th October |
| 2000 | One St Mary's 25th & 27th October |

Breeds northeast Asia, from Altai east to Sakhalin, eastern China and northern Korea. Migratory, wintering Burma and Indonesia. Monotypic.

Since the first in 1971, a total of 42 Radde's Warblers arrived in the islands in 21 (70%) of the 30 years up to and including 2000. The 41 up until 1999 represented 21.2% of the 193 records accepted by the BBRC during the period 1958–99. The Chart incorporates all arrival dates, all of which fell within the 30-day arrival window of 3rd October to 1st November. Multiple arrivals occurred in eight years, by far the largest number being 11 in 1999. Mean length of stay was just 1.9 days.

The 1999 fall was exceptional even by national standards and the discovery of one even on small and exposed Rosevear in the Western Isles suggests that more than the 11 recorded may have been associated with that particular arrival. Also included among the listed records is a St Mary's individual watched by numerous observers at Rosehill, although up until mid-2000 no description had been submitted to the BBRC, a not unusual problem associated with Scillonian rarity records. The sharp drop-off in records in late October is difficult to explain, but seems unlikely to be associated with observer coverage, even though the majority of visiting autumn birders normally vacate the islands by the end of that month. Given the volume of Radde's Warblers reaching the islands, at least a small percentage of any November arrivals might be expected to show themselves to resident birders.

Like other Asiatic warblers with outlying populations in or close to the West Palearctic, western Radde's Warbler populations move east or southeast in autumn. Birds depart the breeding grounds from late

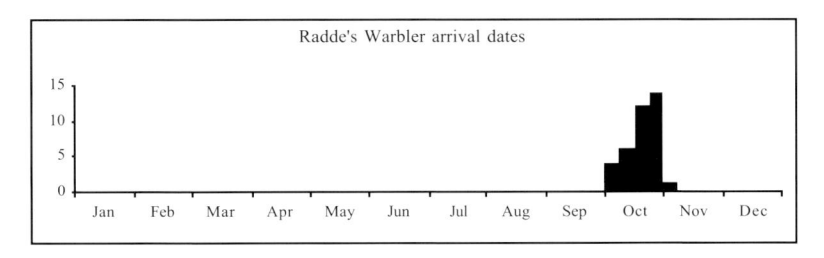

*Radde's Warbler arrival dates* [chart showing arrivals peaking in October]

August to mid-September and are most evident on passage in central Asia until the beginning of October (Cramp *et al.* 1977–94). As with similar species, e. g. Dusky Warbler *P. fuscatus*, most authorities attribute any western European autumn vagrancy to either reverse migration or westward displacement during anticyclonic conditions. However, such a solution seems somewhat simplistic given the obvious regularity of Scillonian arrivals and their equally obvious concentration during late October.

## Dusky Warbler                             *Phylloscopus fuscatus*  **A**  BBRC 7.1%

**Rare autumn migrant, full written description required by the BBRC.**

| | | |
|---|---|---|
| 1964 | One trapped St Agnes 19th October |
| 1968 | One Tresco 25th October |
| 1969 | One dead Seven Stones Lightship 20th October |
| 1976 | One St Agnes 11th to 16th October |
| 1979 | One St Agnes 23rd to 25th October |
| 1982 | One Gugh 23rd October |
| 1984 | One Tresco 15th to 20th October |
| 1984 | One St Mary's 23rd & 24th October |
| 1985 | One St Mary's 19th & 20th October |
| 1987 | One St Mary's 2nd to 6th November |
| 1994 | One St Agnes 18th to 22nd October |
| 1996 | One Tresco 14th October |
| 1997 | One St Mary's 22nd October |
| 1997 | One St Mary's 5th & 6th November |
| 1999 | One Troytown, St Agnes 12th & 13th November |
| 2000 | One Tresco & St Mary's 19th & 20th October |
| 2001 | One Bryher 13th & 14th October |
| 2001 | One Tresco 3rd November |
| *2002* | *One St Mary's 6th to 27th November   Birding World 15: 451* |

Breeds central Siberia to Sea of Okhotsk and south to Mongolia, Manchuria and Sakhalin, and from Mongolia to Himalayas. Migratory, wintering northern India and Himalayan foothills east to southern China, Taiwan, Thailand, Indochina. Polytypic: nominate *fuscatus* occurs Siberia south to Mongolia and China; *weigoldi* at higher altitudes than *fuscatus* in southeast of range.

A total of 16 birds were recorded in 14 of the 37 years since the first in 1964 and up until year 2000; the claimed November 2002 individual is omitted from this analysis. The Chart includes all arrival dates and shows a narrow 33-day preference window from 11th October to 12th November, similar to the situation for Pallas's Warbler *P. proregulus*. Excluding the dead bird on the Seven Stones Lightship, mean length of stay was 2.6 days.

Typical of the confusion that can surround rarity reports on Scilly during October, a Dusky Warbler reportedly seen well on Tresco early on 22nd October 1997 failed to gain acceptance, whilst one, possibly the same bird as that on Tresco, seen on St Mary's for four days from 22nd was accepted by the BBRC for just the initial day. In addition, a bird shown in the annual bird report (*IOSBR* 1997) as present on St Mary's for only the 5th November was accepted by the BBRC for the 5th and 6th. The BBRC accepted 211 Dusky Warbler records during the period 1958–99, the 15 Scillonian arrivals during this same period amounting to 7.1% of the national total.

*Birds of the Isles of Scilly*

Dusky Warbler arrival dates

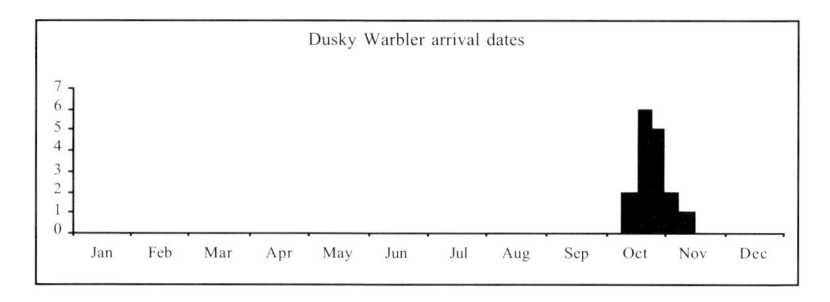

Dusky Warbler is a long-distance migrant, leaving its breeding grounds in western Siberia during August–September and moving southeast towards it wintering grounds in India and further east (Cramp *et al.* 1977–94). Most authorities, e.g. Cramp *et al.*, attribute the widespread western European autumn vagrancy to a combination of reverse migration and westward displacement during anticyclonic conditions. However, this fails to address the absence of arrivals during the heaviest period of migration in August and September. One Dusky Warbler was trapped and ringed on Scilly during the early period and there are no recaptures.

## Eastern Bonelli's Warbler  *Phylloscopus orientalis*  A  BBRC 33.3%

**Extremely rare autumn migrant, full written description required by the BBRC.**

1987   One (first-year) St Mary's 30th September and 8th to 10th October
    *British Birds* 81: 585, 91: 509, 92: 519–523; *Ibis* 139: 182–183, 200, 140: 182

Breeds Greece and former Yugoslavia east to Levant. Monotypic. Migratory, wintering Africa along southern edge of Sahara. Until recently treated as conspecific with Western Bonelli's Warbler *P. bonelli* (as Bonelli's Warbler *P. bonelli*) but split by BOURC July 1996 (BOURC 1997). Probably Britain's rarest *Phylloscopus* warbler.

There was just the single record prior to the split, involving a bird on St Mary's from late September to early October 1987. Initial doubts and confusion surrounding the racial identity of this individual stemmed from the failure of the original finders on 30th September to pay particular attention to the call. However, when it was rediscovered at the same site a week latter the new finders were immediately impressed by the typical *orientalis* 'chip' call, not at all dissimilar to that of Crossbill *Loxia curvirostra*. However, for a time, the true picture was clouded by a *Phylloscopus*-type 'hooeet' call heard from the bird's general proximity, though the originator of the call was not seen and in hindsight the call could not be attributed to the Bonelli's Warbler with certainty (BOURC 1998; Wilson & Fentiman 1999). When out of view, the bird could often be located by this distinctive call, which, according to the observers, bore a close similarity to that of the North American wood warblers (Parulidae) (Palmer 2000). Despite the gap of seven days between the first observation and the bird's rediscovery, on 8th October, it is generally accepted that just one individual was involved.

This was the first acceptable record for Britain and Ireland following a review of all past Bonelli's Warbler records by BOURC. It was followed by a bird found at Whitley Bay, Tyne and Wear, on 20th September 1995, whilst the BOURC were still considering separation of the two species. This bird too was noticeable by its distinctive 'chip' call. The BBRC accepted one additional record up to and including 1999; thus the Salakee record represents one-third of the British total. Given the present level of knowledge and understanding, any claimed sighting of this or the following species seem far more likely to be accepted by the BBRC if accompanied by a field recording of the bird's calls.

## Western Bonelli's Warbler  *Phylloscopus bonelli*  A  BBRC 13.2%

**Very rare spring and autumn migrant, full written description required by the BBRC.**

1965   One trapped St Agnes 4th & 5th October   *British Birds* 59: 295
1971   One trapped St Agnes 4th to 24th October   *British Birds* 65: 209–210, 433; *IOSBR* 1971
1973   One St Agnes 12th to 15th September   *British Birds* 67: 333

1975   One St Mary's 7th May   *British Birds* 69: 350
1975   One St Agnes 2nd September   *British Birds* 69: 350
1976   One St Mary's 2nd to 25th October   *British Birds* 70: 435
1977   One St Mary's 2nd to 8th October   *British Birds* 71: 522
2000   One St Agnes 30th April to 5th May   *British Birds* 94: 494
*2002   One St Martin's 4th to 6th October   Birding World 15: 409*

Breeds northwest Africa, Iberia, France and south-central Europe, east and south to Italy. Monotypic. Migratory, wintering Africa along southern edge of Sahara. Until recently treated as conspecific with Eastern Bonelli's Warbler *P. orientalis* (as Bonelli's Warbler *P. bonelli*) but split by BOURC July 1996 (BOURC 1997).

Following the 1996 BOURC split of the former 'Bonelli's Warbler' a review of all previously accepted British Bonelli's Warbler records was carried out by the BBRC (Rogers 1998), examining mainly in-hand descriptions of trapped birds or call descriptions provided by observers. As a consequence, seven earliest Scillonian records shown here were assigned to Western Bonelli's, but this left 21 best treated as 'either Western or Eastern' (see following section).

Up to and including the year 2000 there were 30 accepted Scillonian 'Bonelli's Warbler' records. The Chart incorporates all Western Bonelli's arrival/discovery dates except the 2000 and claimed 2002 individuals and reveals no difference in the pattern of occurrence between Western Bonelli's and records classified as Western/Eastern Bonelli's Warbler, or indeed the single Eastern Bonelli's. The earliest autumn arrival for a 'Bonelli's Warbler' in Britain and Ireland was 21st August and the latest one was present on 4th November. The average length of stay for all 'Bonelli's Warbler' records was 6.46 days: Eastern 10 (n=1), Western 8.2 (n=7) and Eastern/Western 5.3 (n=21); again, the 2000 Western was excluded from these calculations.

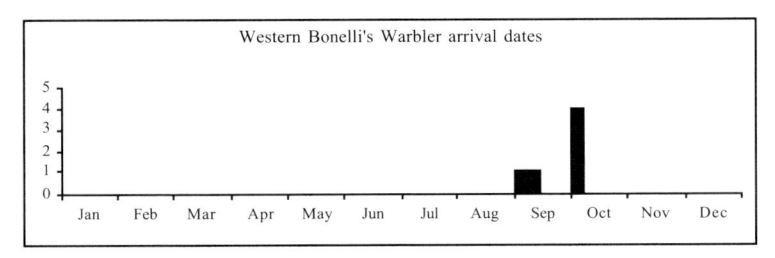

Typically, birds are found feeding high in the elm *Ulmus* canopy and are very active. Twenty-four (83%) of all records occurred on St Mary's and St Agnes (14 and 10 respectively), though reasons for this are unclear. The BBRC review plus subsequent sightings means there were a total of 53 accepted national Western Bonelli's records up to and including 1999, with Scilly accounting for 13.2% of these. A bird trapped and ringed prior to 1970 was recorded as 'Bonelli's Warbler' but it is not now possible to know which of the two species was involved. There are no recaptures. Given the present level of knowledge and understanding, any claimed sighting of this or the previous species seem far more likely to be accepted by the BBRC if accompanied by a field recording of the bird's calls.

## Western/Eastern Bonelli's Warbler
### *Phylloscopus bonelli/orientalis*  A  BBRC 15%

Rare migrant, full written description required by the BBRC.

Western or Eastern Bonelli's Warbler Records
   1974   One St Agnes 11th September   *British Birds* 68: 327
   1976   One St Mary's 4th September   *British Birds* 70: 435
   1977   One St Mary's 26th October   *British Birds* 71: 522
   1980   One St Mary's 2nd to 4th November   *British Birds* 74: 487
   1981   One in song St Agnes 8th to 13th May   *British Birds* 75: 524
   1981   One in song St Mary's 14th & 15th May   *British Birds* 75: 524
   1982   One St Martin's 10th to 13th October   *British Birds* 76: 518

1983    One St Mary's 21st & 22nd August    *British Birds* 77: 553, 78: 578
1983    One St Agnes 22nd September    *British Birds* 77: 553, 78: 578
1983    One St Mary's 1st to 4th October    *British Birds* 77: 553, 78: 578
1986    One St Agnes 1st September    *British Birds* 80: 562, 81: 585
1986    One (first-year) Bryher 10th to 14th October    *British Birds* 80: 562, 81: 585
1986    One (first-year) St Mary's 17th October to at least 1st November    *British Birds* 80: 562, 81: 585
1990    One St Agnes 19th October    *British Birds* 84: 495
1991    One (first-year) Bryher 22nd September to 6th October    *British Birds* 85: 545
1992    One St Martin's 24th September to 10th October    *British Birds* 87: 559
1993    One St Mary's 25th to 30th September    *British Birds* 87: 559
1994    One St Mary's 25th August to 7th September    *British Birds* 88: 542
1995    One Bryher 18th to 26th October    *British Birds* 89: 520
1996    One St Mary's 22nd to 31st August    *British Birds* 90: 503
1997    One St Agnes & St Mary's 15th May    *British Birds* 91: 509

The former Bonelli's Warbler *P. bonelli* was split into two species, Eastern Bonelli's Warbler *P. orientalis* and Western Bonelli's Warbler *P. bonelli*, by the BOURC in July 1996 (BOURC 1997). Following the split, the BBRC reviewed all past records and decided a lack of adequate information meant many could not safely be ascribed to either of the two new species.

The above 21 Scillonian records comprise all those considered by the BBRC as possibly involving either species. A total of 143 records thought likely to have involved either species were accepted by the BBRC for the period 1958–99, therefore the following list represents 15% of the national total. Given the present level of knowledge and understanding, any claimed sighting of these two species seem far more likely to be accepted by the BBRC if accompanied by a field recording of the bird's calls.

## Wood Warbler *Phylloscopus sibilatrix* A

**Scarce spring and autumn migrant, does not breed.**

Breeds western and central Europe and central western Asia, from Britain, Ireland and France north to Norway and south to Italy, east as far as Kazakhstan and southern west Siberia. Migratory, wintering equatorial Africa. Monotypic. Upgraded from Green- to Amber-listed in UK 2002: moderate breeding decline over past 25 years (Gregory *et al.* 2002). National 45% decline 1994–99 (Bashford & Noble 2000).

Gilbert White is generally attributed with separating this species from Willow Warbler *P. trochilus* in 1768, during what has been described as 'a period of great discovery among common species found in Britain' (Palmer 2000). Earliest mention of it in Scilly seems to have been by North (1850), followed by a report of one or more present during severe weather in October 1863. It being also noted among migrant warblers during autumn 1869 and again in 1870 (Rodd 1863b, 1880). Inevitably, though, James Clark and Francis Rodd provided the most informative early account (Clark & Rodd 1906), pointing out that it has been occasionally seen in autumn, mostly in September but once in early November, though it appeared to have been overlooked throughout the last 30 years of the 19th century. Their assumption that it was also a spring migrant was based on a single record of one 'seen and heard' in trees near Tresco's 'duck pond' (presumably Abbey Pool) in May 1903.

Following Clark and Rodd's publication, Wood Warbler seems to have entered a further substantial period of ornithological neglect, the apparent earliest 20th-century report involving a bird on St Mary's on 14th September 1958 (*CBWPSAR* 28). It was subsequently recorded as present on St Agnes on 11th September 1963 and 25th September to 9th October the same year (*CBWPSAR* 33). All of this is in stark contrast to Yellow-browed Warbler *P. inornatus*, which received almost annual mention in the same publication from as early as 1952. And tempting as it may be to suggest that Wood Warbler was overlooked during this period, separation of Yellow-browed from numerous other small *Phylloscopus* warblers seems equally problematical.

Penhallurick (1978) summarised spring and autumn arrival and departure dates for Cornwall and Scilly up until the 1970s. He found 18th March on St Agnes to be the earliest arrival date, though most Scillonian records occurred between mid-April and early May. He also found it less than annual in the islands during spring. Autumn sightings occurred between late July and late September, the latest being 31st October on St Martin's. However, by the 1970s it was being mentioned annually, with most during autumn still.

Examining published records for the ten years 1990–99, it occurred in all years in both spring and autumn. Spring arrivals were confined within the 12-day window 22nd April to 3rd May, recorded last dates generally being equally compressed, between 12th and 23rd May, though with one exceptionally late individual on 16th June. Less easy to categorise, however, were birds on 23rd and 27th July 1990. Autumn arrivals were more protracted, the earliest on 23rd July and the latest 7th September, though mostly in August. During the four years 1996–99, birds occurred at an annual average of 21, about 33% during spring. Out of 26 recorded during autumn 1996, only five apparently remained more than one day and of all published records few spring individuals were mentioned as in song.

Most European Wood Warblers apparently cross the Mediterranean via the Italian peninsula, those from western Europe heading initially south or southeast (Wernham *et al.* 2002), although there is also evidence that many overfly North Africa directly from southern Europe (Cramp *et al.* 1977–94). The general southeast movement raises the possibility that some at least of the birds passing through Scilly originate from the small Irish population. European return spring migration occurs mainly through April and into mid-May, birds reaching western and central Europe by mid- to late April. Eight Wood Warblers had been ringed in Scilly up until 1999, all since 1990; there are no recaptures.

## Chiffchaff (Common Chiffchaff) *Phylloscopus collybita* A

**Numerous spring and autumn migrant, also winters in significant numbers. Since at least the 1960s it has bred in small numbers on main islands.**

Breeds Europe and northern Asia, from Britain, Ireland and France east to north of Sea of Okhotsk; also coastal North Africa. Most populations migratory, wintering Africa north of equator and Arabian Peninsula to northern India. Presence of northern birds within western breeding range during winter clouds full extent of migration. Polytypic: nominate *collybita* occurs western Europe north perhaps to southern Sweden, south to Mediterranean and east to Hungary and Poland; *abietinus*, or 'Scandinavian Chiffchaff' northern Sweden and Norway east to Urals, Caucasus and northern Iran; *tristis*, or 'Siberian Chiffchaff' east of *abietinus* to limit of range and south to northern Iran. Canary Island Chiffchaff *P. canariensis* and Iberian Chiffchaff *P. ibericus* were formerly considered conspecific with Chiffchaff, until recently separated by BOURC (BOURC 1999). National 7% decline 1994–99 (Bashford & Noble 2000).

As seems often to be the case with species that were common in Scilly during the 19th century, there are few early references to Chiffchaff. There is mention of it occurring in small numbers on Tresco in 1863, 1864 and 1865 (Rodd 1863a, 1878b, 1880) but James Clark and E H Rodd's nephew Francis provided the only detailed account. These two described it as a common autumn migrant on Tresco and St Mary's, though only occasionally on the equally large island of St Martin's (Clark & Rodd 1906). This last comment is typical of the somewhat unreliable nature of early reports, in this case almost certainly reflecting the little time observers spent on that island, rather than any real autumn Chiffchaff absence. Clark and Rodd also described how it had been noted 'several times' on Tresco during November and December and frequently heard in song during January and February; from this they assumed that a few probably remained during most winters.

There are two early 20th-century records worth recounting. The first involved 'great numbers' seen and killed during an attraction at the Bishop Rock Lighthouse on the night of 27th September 1907 (Ogilvie-Grant 1909), the sole apparent reference to this species at Scillonian lighthouses. The other concerns one or two heard in song in the Tresco woods during June 1938, none being heard elsewhere in the islands, this possibly being the earliest reference to probable breeding in Scilly.

Penhallurick (1978) examined Chiffchaff arrival and departure dates for Scilly and the Cornish mainland up until the 1970s, pointing out that these were often confused by the presence of wintering individuals. He found, nonetheless, that in most years apparent migrants arrived during the first half of March and became widespread by the last week. By this time large falls were sometimes recorded, as on St Agnes on 24th and 26th March 1958 when an estimated 150 were present. The same author estimated that spring passage ended by mid-May, with few in evidence to the month's end. On Scilly, return passage commenced at the end of August and peaked during early October, late migrants and potential wintering individuals presumably then confusing the situation as numbers declined. Penhallurick also explored the level of Cornish overwintering, quoting records of up to 25 individuals from 16 localities during winter 1972, with fewer numbers allegedly evident on Scilly, including some of the more exposed islands, e.g. Round Island. Whilst in Tresco's Abbey Gardens David Hunt described the enthusiasm with which Chiffchaffs exploited insects attracted to winter-flowering exotics, such as *Banksia* or *Eucalyptus* (Penhallurick 1978).

Apart from an obvious increase in wintering numbers during most years, the situation on Scilly today seems little changed, except perhaps that greater observer coverage, both in numbers and annual duration, has resulted in an apparent increase in numbers of birds recorded each year. Nonetheless, birds still arrive and depart within much the same timescale and at both ends of the year it becomes difficult separating birds moving through Scilly from those wintering in the islands. If anything, initial arrivals are rather later than Penhallurick suggested, mid- to late March seemingly more typical, whilst at the other end of the year most passage birds have moved on by mid-November. Sheer numbers involved during both passage periods render same-island or all-islands counts problematical. Nevertheless, published same-island counts during the ten years 1990–99 seldom exceed 50, even for the larger islands, which surely misrepresents the true situation. The single obvious exception was in late October 1997, when an estimated 200 were on St Martin's on 31st, and 60 on St Agnes. Wintering numbers can be impressive, particularly at favourable sites, e.g. the St Mary's Higher and Lower Moors, or around the Tresco Pools.

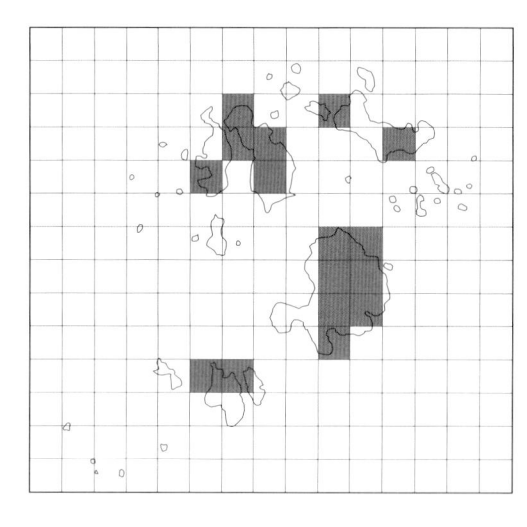

| Island | Pairs |
| --- | --- |
| Bryher | 2 |
| St Agnes | 2 |
| St Martin's | 2 |
| St Mary's | 28 |
| Tresco | 13 |

**2000 Breeding Bird Atlas – Chiffchaff (Chown & Lock 2002)**

1-km Chiffchaff Breeding Distribution – 2000–01 (data Chown & Lock 2002)

Breeding in the islands was first reported in 1968, when a pair allegedly did so in St Mary's Lower Moors, though details of the event were not published (*CBWPSAR* 38). However, this was followed by a 1972 David Hunt account of a pair feeding young on St Agnes and during subsequent years reports of breeding became more numerous. During the 1990s, 'a few pairs' reportedly bred on most if not all main islands but the only indication of likely numbers involved comes from the St Mary's Lunnon Farm study plot, where the annual CBC recorded between one (three years) and five territorial males on the 16-hectare farmland, woodland and marshland plot during the eight years 1991–98, at an average of 2.3 per year. Although breeding was not proved with certainty, these figures suggest that Chiffchaff may be more numerous in summer than the annual reports indicate. In confirmation of this, the 2000 Breeding Bird Atlas recorded up to 46 possible pairs in 17 (25.3%) of the 67 1-km squares surveyed (Chown & Lock 2002). However, the report's authors thought a figure in the range ten to 30 pairs more realistic, also pointing out that breeding was confirmed in just one square.

The racial make-up of Chiffchaff numbers seen in Scilly gets little mention, the notable exception being autumn and winter reports of birds showing characteristics of the extreme eastern form *tristis*, or the so-called '*fulvescens*' intergrades. These often occur in some numbers, up to 28 being present in the islands during October–November 1996 (*IOSBR* 1996). Caution, though, is necessary as some dull-plumaged *abietinus* may closely resemble *tristis* or '*fulvescens*' (Pennington 1997; Svensson 1992). Understandably, the less easily distinguished *abietinus* was reported less often in the field, though ringers should be able to separate a few on wing length, or perhaps on call (pers. obs.), as in October 1994, when greyish individuals appearing in the islands were confirmed in-hand as likely to have been *abietinus*. The reality surely being, however, that the latter is a frequent if not common passage migrant through the islands and perhaps the source of many wintering individuals. Interestingly T A Dorrien-Smith (1951) attributed all early records to *collybita*, though this was probably based on assumption rather than fact.

Ringing recoveries show Chiffchaffs from extreme western Europe, including Norway, Sweden and the Netherlands, head southwest into western Iberia en route to North and West Africa (Wernham *et al.* 2002). In comparison, those immediately to the east, e.g. Germany are mainly recovered in eastern Iberia (Cramp *et al.* 1977–94). However, this presumably relates to normal migration conditions, birds from further east being likely to appear in Britain, Ireland or elsewhere in western Europe during appropriate weather conditions. European autumn passage commences from August and is protracted, early and late periods confused by overwintering within the breeding range. Returning spring migrants reach southern Britain by early March, greatest numbers occurring in the west of the country, where it also peaks earlier than in eastern Britain. A total of 1,895 Chiffchaffs were ringed in Scilly up until 1999, 1,670 (80%) since 1970 and there are five recaptures. Both birds ringed on St Agnes surprisingly moved east or southeast after release, though this fits the statement (Wernham *et al.* 2002) that birds present in Britain during winter originate from many parts of the Palearctic. Apart from anything else, the last two recaptures indicate the extent to which wintering Chiffchaffs are vulnerable to the local cats *Felis catus*, or at least on St Mary's.

**Controls**
PA7450　　Ad　　Arraincourt, Moselle, France
　　　　　　　　1st April 1986　　　　　　　　　　　　　　CT　St Martin's 17th October 1987

**Recoveries**
1J6841　　Ad　　St Agnes 27th April 1987　　　　　　　CT　Vale Marais, Guernsey, Channel Islands
　　　　　　　　　　　　　　　　　　　　　　　　　　　　　　27th May 1987
8X2069　　Ad　　St Agnes 10th May 1993　　　　　　　 CT　Sandwich Bay, Kent 19th May 1993
0L8616　　Ad　　Lower Moors, St Mary's 1st June 1994　KC　Old Town, St Mary's 27th February 1995
7Y0753　　1stY　Lower Moors, St Mary's
　　　　　　　　7th December 1995　　　　　　　　　　 KC　Old Town, St Mary's 21st January 1996

**Chiffchaff Ringing Recaptures**

## Iberian Chiffchaff　　　　　　　　　　　*Phylloscopus ibericus*　**A**　BBRC 50%

　　1992　One in song Higher Moors, St Mary's 14th April to 21st May　*British Birds* 93: 560

Breeds Iberian Peninsula, southwest France and northwest Africa, wintering mainly Iberia but also Africa south to Mali and Bukina Faso. Formerly treated as conspecific with Chiffchaff *P. collybita* but split by BOURC October 1998 (Helbig *et al.* 1996; BOURC 1999, 2002a). Monotypic.

An unusual sounding *Phylloscopus* warbler singing in Higher Moors, St Mary's, for over a month during spring 1992 was later accepted by BBRC as the second British record of the newly split Iberian Chiffchaff. This followed their earlier acceptance as the first for Britain and Ireland of a bird at Brent Reservoir, Greater London, in June 1972 (*British Birds* 93: 560). Both records were accepted in retrospect, being based on sound recording made at the time. They were followed, in 1999, by claims of birds in south Devon and south Dorset. Thus the St Mary's individual represented 50% of the accepted national total up until the end of 1999.

For a comprehensive review of the logic behind the separation of this species from Chiffchaff see Helbig *et al.* (1996). Lars Svensson recently put forward the argument for renaming this species from *P. brehmii* to *P. ibericus*, pointing out that the alleged type specimen was an undoubted Chiffchaff and that the next creditable specimen was collected by Ticehurst in Portugal during 1937 and described by him as *P. ibericus* (Svensson 2002; BOURC 2002b).

# Willow Warbler *Phylloscopus trochilus* A

**Abundant spring and autumn migrant, breeds in very small numbers on some main islands.**

Breeds central and northern Europe and northern Asia, from Britain, Ireland and France east almost to Kamchatka. All populations migratory, wintering solely equatorial Africa south to Cape of Good Hope. Polytypic: nominate *trochilus* occurs western Europe north to southern Sweden and east to Poland and northern Romania; *acredula*, or 'Northern Willow Warbler' Norway, Sweden and eastern Europe east to Yenisey River; *yakutensis* Siberia east of *acredula* as far as Kamchatka. Upgraded from Green- to Amber-listed in UK 2002: moderate (31%) breeding decline over past 25 years (Gregory *et al.* 2002). National 14% increase 1994–99, though 9% decline 1998–99 (Bashford & Noble 2000).

Early information on Willow Warbler in Scilly fits the pattern for many other species, in particular it was described almost exclusively as an autumn migrant (Clark & Rodd 1906). Clark and Rodd took the view that it was 'Occasionally noticed on autumn migration, for the most part singly', though they conceded that during early October 1903 it was fairly common in the area of Holy Vale, St Mary's, whilst two were also seen and heard in Tresco's Abbey Gardens on 22nd November 1904. However, as early as October 1849 E H Rodd wrote to the *Zoologist* noting that this species had been acquired from amongst 'a host of migratory warblers' appearing in the islands that September (Rodd 1849b, 1880).

Two early 20th-century reports are of interest. One involved 'several' seen at one of the lighthouses on 11th March 1911 and was the first mention of Willow Warbler on Scilly in spring (Ogilvie-Grant 1912c). The other recorded one aboard ship 22 miles (35 km) south of the islands mid-morning on 8th May 1936, before eventually flying away towards the north (*CBWPSAR* 6). Somewhat earlier than this, E H Rodd recounted information from the Wolf Rock Lighthouse, immediately southwest of Land's End, west Cornwall (Rodd 1865b). His informant described the movement of migrating birds past the light – apparently at night – during early November 1864, 'which at different times, and in twos and threes, passed the rock'. Included among the list were both Wren *Troglodytes troglodytes* and 'Willow Wren', all of which flew close enough to make identification possible and all moved from southwest to northeast.

Penhallurick's mid-1970s review of Cornish and Scillonian data is extremely useful. In this he pointed out that spring migration commenced during late March or early April and ended by mid-May, with up to 100 per day on St Agnes, though the highest daily total was 500 during mid-April. Autumn migration on Scilly commenced during late July and had finished normally by mid-October, 2nd November being extreme. The same author considered the possibility of Willow Warblers overwintering, pointing out that there is no evidence to support A A Dorrien-Smith's earlier claim of birds doing so on Tresco, whilst also drawing attention to the predicament whereby any *Phylloscopus* warbler in the islands during winter is liable to be labelled as a Chiffchaff *P. collybita*.

Willow Warbler is one of only a few Scillonian migrants whose numbers on spring passage are liable to exceed autumn totals, 700 to 1,000 believed to have been on St Agnes alone on 13th April 1991, whilst 25–30 were recorded on the comparatively small island of Annet on 9th May that same year. In contrast, in autumn few if any single-island, or even sometimes all-island counts exceeded ten. An exception to the rule was 1997, when 30 were on Annet on 9th August and 170 on St Agnes on 20th. More recently, one at Carn Gwarvel, St Mary's, on 4th December 1992 was allegedly the latest ever.

First apparent mention of breeding in Scilly came in 1974, with a report of a pair at Porth Hellick, St Mary's and a further four singing males on the same island that year (*IOSBR* 1972), although, once more, details of such an important event were not published. However, and as Penhallurick pointed out, sporadic breeding had probably occurred previously, although it was clearly unknown during the 19th century and may have been a quite recent development. Certainly, there is no mention of Willow Warbler having bred on St Agnes among the results of breeding surveys carried out on that island between 1957 and 1974. Next mention is of a bird seen feeding young at Porth Hellick Down, St Mary's, in 1981, following which the volume of reports increased, though probably not annually, until CBC work commenced on the Lunnon Farm study plot in 1991. Numbers of territorial males on the plot varied between one and four (average 1.6), with none present in 1997. Nests were found on the plot in two years, in both of which young were fledged, one nest being located in the top of one of Higher Moors' impressive Tussock Sedges *Carex paniculata*. Looking at the islands as a whole, the 2000 Breeding Bird Atlas recorded a possible 23 pairs in 10 (14.9%) of the 67 1-km surveyed squares, though the report's editors thought a more realistic figure was in the range ten to 20 pairs (Chown & Lock 2002). Even so, breeding was not proved during the two-year survey.

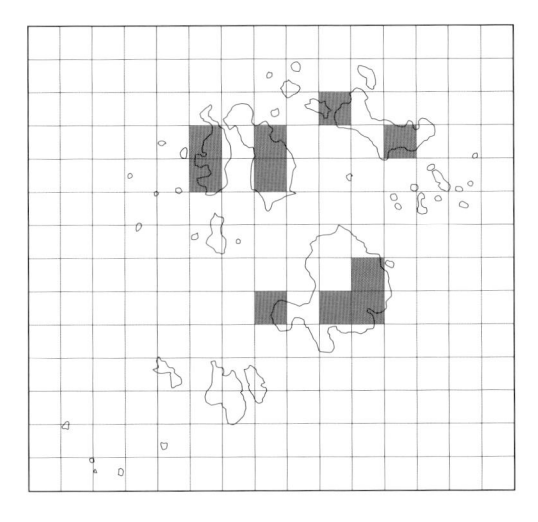

| Island | Pairs |
|---|---|
| Bryher | 4 |
| St Martin's | 2 |
| St Mary's | 9 |
| Tresco | 8 |

2000 Breeding Bird Atlas – Willow Warbler (Chown & Lock 2002)

1-km Willow Warbler Breeding Distribution – 2000–01 (data Chown & Lock 2002)

Published accounts of birds identified to form are few. Recent reports involved a possible *acredula* on St Agnes for eight days in late October 1996, three on Tresco on 1st November and another on Tresco on 12th November. A further likely *acredula* was identified on St Agnes in early October 1997 and a possible *acredula* or *yakutensis* during late October 1999. Willow Warbler migrates later than Chiffchaff in spring and earlier in autumn, at least as far into Africa as the Gulf of Guinea, autumn movement commencing from the end of July or early August, with numbers peaking in Britain by mid-August and most having past through by late September. Ringing records show that a mix of British and Continental birds are involved in Britain during autumn (Wernham *et al.* 2002). Return passage through western Europe peaks around mid- to late April or early May, birds progressing north more slowly than those further east. There is no evidence that the more northerly *acredula* migrates any earlier in autumn than nominate *trochilus* breeding further south (Cramp *et al.* 1977–94).

### Recoveries

| | | | | | |
|---|---|---|---|---|---|
| 3B0420 | Ad | St Agnes 6th April 1980 | CT | Bardsey Island, Gwynedd 21st April 1980 |
| 6E3403 | Ad | St Agnes 25th April 1985 | CT | Hook Head, Wexford. Ireland 2nd May 1986 |
| 6E3422 | Ad | St Agnes 27th April 1985 | CT | Lundy Island, Devon 30th April 1985 |
| 6K2250 | Ad | St Agnes 29th April 1987 | CT | Emmedsbo Platage, Jylland, Denmark 12th May 1987 |

Willow Warbler Ringing Recaptures

# Goldcrest  *Regulus regulus*  A

**Annual spring and autumn migrant, sometimes in large numbers, a small number of pairs apparently breed.**

Discontinuous breeding range, mainly in Europe and central-western Asia, south into southern Afghanistan and east along the Himalayas to China, with outlying population Japan, Sakhalin and adjacent mainland Asia. Migratory in north, dispersive or sedentary in south. Polytypic: nominate *regulus* occurs Europe east to western Russia; *coatsi* central Asia east of *regulus*; *buturlini* Caucasus and Crimea; *azoricus*, *sanctae-mariae* and *inermis* Azores; *teneriffae* Canary Islands; five or more forms further east or south. Upgraded from Green- to Amber-listed in UK 2002: moderate to high (55%) breeding decline over past 25 years (Gregory *et al.* 2002). National 61% increase 1994–99 (Bashford & Noble 2000).

The consensus of 19th-century opinion seems to have been that this was a common spring and autumn migrant, often arriving in large flocks during the latter period and sometimes also in spring. Great numbers reportedly sometimes spent 'a considerable portion of the winter' in conifers by Tresco Abbey (Clark & Rodd 1906). Clark and Rodd described how, in January 1904, the trees were 'literally alive with them', whilst also pointing out that flocks appeared to be composed entirely of first-year individuals, though adults occasionally arrived in small numbers, reportedly almost always with Chiffchaffs *Phylloscopus collybita*, Siskins *Carduelis spinus*, or Redstarts *Phoenicurus phoenicurus*.

Early 20th-century reports are equally limited, one though involved the island of St Agnes allegedly 'swarming' with Goldcrests, on 1st November 1910, most of which apparently left a day or two later (N F Ticehurst 1911; Ogilvie-Grant 1912a). Surprisingly, the only lighthouse observations involved two at the Bishop Rock at 2 am on 23rd October 1908 (Ogilvie-Grant 1910), plus an unspecified number amongst a large attraction at the same light on the night of 4th November 1909 (Ogilvie-Grant 1911).

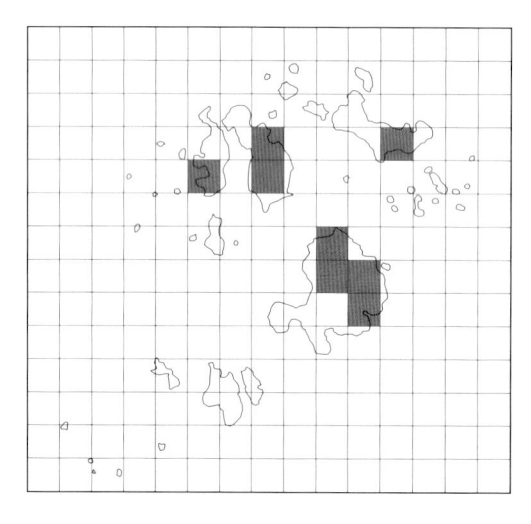

| Island | Pairs |
|---|---|
| Bryher | 1 |
| St Martin's | 1 |
| St Mary's | 14 |
| Tresco | 7 |

**2000 Breeding Bird Atlas – Goldcrest (Chown & Lock 2002)**

**1-km Goldcrest Breeding Distribution – 2000–01 (data Chown & Lock 2002)**

Bringing the situation up to date, during the ten years 1990–99 most years saw large, sometimes very large, numbers during autumn. For example, on 1st October 1990 reportedly hundreds arrived overnight on all islands. Most of these were thought to have remained in Scilly, with no obvious change in numbers, at least 200 being counted around Tresco's Great Pool during the month. However, most were believed to have left the islands by the month's end. Mid-November counts later produced just 20 in the normally favoured Higher Moors on St Mary's. By comparison, 1996 produced no reports of major influxes. Meanwhile, at the other end of the year, records for 1991, 1992 and 1997 suggest little or no spring migration, spring migrants in 1994 being noted on just 6th April and 23rd May, with few more in 1995. Penhallurick (1978) made mention of a huge arrival on St Agnes (at least) during autumn 1912, when there were so many that 'boys caught them in their caps like butterflies'. The same source quoted 'uncountable numbers' arriving on St Mary's on 26th October 1971. In spring, apparent migrants arrive from about late March through to early May, equivalent autumn dates being mid-September to early November.

Breeding is reported to have taken place annually on St Mary's and Tresco, and perhaps other islands, since at least the 1980s, though likely numbers involved have been rarely discussed. However, on the 16-hectare Lunnon Farm study plot on St Mary's, the annual CBC recorded one to two territorial males in seven of the eight years 1991–98 at an average of 1.25 per total number of years (P J Robinson –unpublished data). The more recent 2000 Breeding Bird Atlas located a possible 23 pairs in eight (11.9%) of the 67 1-km squares surveyed, the report's editors suggesting 20 pairs was a more realistic expectation (Chown & Lock 2002). However, breeding was confirmed in just two squares. Past observers suggested more pairs may have been present on Tresco than on the larger St Mary's, so the finding of 14 pairs on the latter island and seven on Tresco was unexpected.

Two-thirds of winter recoveries of British and Irish-ringed breeding Goldcrests involve movements of less than 20 km, those in southern England being even less inclined to wander, any longer movements being noticeably inclined towards the south or southeast (Wernham *et al.* 2002). Scandinavian birds probably mostly move on through Britain and winter further south, whereas ringing data show that at least some Goldcrests from further east, e.g. northwest Russia, do winter in Britain and Ireland. There is little or no evidence to indicate where all these autumn Goldcrests passing through Scilly originate, though a fall of 'hundreds' in misty rain on 15th October 1999 arrived in the islands in company with up to eight Radde's Warblers *Phylloscopus schwarzi*, a species that breeds only in eastern Asia (*IOSBR* 1999). Consequently, some arriving Goldcrests might be expected to be the central Asian *coatsi*, or even *buturlini* from the Caucasus or Crimea.

A total of 1,182 Goldcrests were ringed in Scilly up until 1999, 1,045 (88%) since 1970. Even so there are just two recaptures, the second of which involved a bird moving northwest the day after ringing in mid-October.

**Controls**
2X2091    Ad    Nanquidno, Cornwall
                 15th October 1989                            CT  St Martin's 17th October 1989
**Recoveries**
9P6305    1stY  St Martin's 22nd October 1989                 CT  Lundy Island, Devon 23rd October 1989

**Goldcrest Ringing Recaptures**

# Firecrest                                    *Regulus ignicapilla*  **A**

Annual migrant, mostly in autumn and usually in small numbers, though very occasionally equalling Goldcrest. A few sometimes also winter.

Breeds central and southern Europe, from southern England, France and Iberia north to Denmark and east to extreme western Russia, also coastal North Africa. Migratory in northeast, resident, dispersive or partial migrant elsewhere. Polytypic: nominate *ignicapilla* occurs Europe, including Sardinia and Corsica; *balearicus* Balearic Islands and North Africa; *madeirensis* Madeira. Amber-listed in UK: five-year mean of 65.8 breeding pairs (Gregory *et al.* 2002).

As with several other species, first mention of Firecrest in Scilly involved a bird shot by Augustus Pechell during the mid-19th century, this time in mid-November 1851 (Rodd 1880; Clark & Rodd 1906). E H Rodd, his nephew Francis and James Clark agreed that birds occurred during the autumn or winter months, from October or November through to March, according to the last two authors arriving with Goldcrest *R. regulus*, Chiffchaffs *Phylloscopus collybita* and Redstarts *Phoenicurus phoenicurus*. The elder Rodd added that it sometimes equalled Goldcrest in numbers, as indeed still happens occasionally. Interestingly, E H Rodd thought that most specimens were obtained during February and as this seems unlikely to reflect any increase in observers, we must assume numbers in the islands actually increased at that time. Nevertheless, this seems not to be the situation now and Rodd's other writings all apparently involve only birds obtained during autumn (Rodd 1867d, 1880). It is noticeable, too, that even by 1870 E H Rodd was describing it as 'now very often obtained at Scilly' (Rodd 1970a). E H Rodd was also familiar with Firecrest in the Land's End area of west Cornwall during the same period of the year.

Summarising the situation for Scilly and the Cornish mainland up until the 1970s, Penhallurick (1978) found spring passage normally much lighter than in autumn and, like Chiffchaff, the timing of migration was often confused by the presence of wintering individuals. Birds passed through in spring from late March to early April, late dates on Scilly being 27th April and 14th May. During the latter part of the year, birds became evident on Scilly from the second half of September through to late October or mid-November, the earliest date being 10th September and the latest 3rd November, numbers peaking on 21st October. The maximum recorded all-island count up until then was 20. Penhallurick's researches also confirmed that Firecrest wintered in the islands, though not necessarily every year. The same author pointed out that although wintering birds may be discovered in conifer woodlands, their preferred habitat appeared to be low-lying damp woods, which certainly seems to be the case in Scilly still.

The situation today seems unchanged, birds still arriving broadly within the earlier timescale. In general, though, the impression is of greater numbers, though doubtless this largely, if not entirely, reflects the increased volume of observers, and improved means of communication and publication. Numbers involved are often difficult to interpret, though of the ten years 1990–99, 1993 seemed fairly representative, the maximum all-island October total peaking at 58 on the 9th, with more than ten birds on at least 16 days, more than 20 on eight days and birds on every day throughout the month, though obviously the extent of any daily rollover remains unknown. Winter numbers, however, seem rarely to have exceeded 15–20 during the ten-year period. Within the same ten years, 1997 demonstrated how this species can apparently outnumber the normally far more numerous Goldcrest, though part of the explanation is perhaps that far fewer of the latter species were present than usual. However, in Loire-Atlantique in western France, where it does not breed but is common in winter, numbers regularly exceed those of Goldcrest by a factor of 10:1 (Cramp et al. 1977–94).

Firecrest is extremely scarce in the islands during summer, one on St Agnes from 16th June to 1st July 1992 being described as the first summer record. It has never bred in Scilly, the nearest regular breeding areas being central-southern England and northwest France (Hagemeijer & Blair 1997; Guermeur & Monnat 1980). The timing of western European migration is clouded by short-distance, more local movements, though birds moving around the Baltic during September–November seem likely to be migrants from further north or east. Locally, the very obvious autumn arrival and departure, plus the small number of wintering individuals point to most Firecrests reaching Scilly being true migrants, rather than dispersing central and southern European birds, as indeed seems the case for the closely related Goldcrest. In southern England, ringing data suggest a mainly east-west movement, though in part this probably reflects Firecrest's preference for crossing the North Sea at its narrowest point. Ringing data also reveal a later wave of birds from continental Europe during late October, which has been attributed to the onset of cold weather in central Europe (Wernham et al. 2002). A total of 160 Firecrests had been ringed in Scilly up until 1999, 142 (89%) since 1970, it being not too unusual to trap five or six at one site on one day, or on one island during the same day. The single known Scillonian recapture away from the islands was in west Cornwall nine days after being ringed on St Martin's in late October and not further south as might be expected. In addition, a bird ringed in Belgium in late April 1970 was recaptured near Penzance, west Cornwall, in mid-October the same year. However, the presence in April still of a bird trapped and ringed by the author in the Higher Moors–Holy Vale complex the previous December shows that not all Firecrests reaching Scilly in autumn move on south.

### Recoveries

4X7480    1stY St Martin's 26th October 1993      CT Treveal, Zennor, Cornwall 4th November 1993

5Y1077    Ad Holy Vale, St Mary's 16th December 1995      RT Higher Moors, St Mary's 6th April 1996

### Firecrest Ringing Recaptures

## [Brown Flycatcher  *Muscicapa dauurica*]  D

**Full written description required by the BBRC. No acceptable Scillonian record.**

[1971   One St Agnes 5th October]   *British Birds* 68: 337; Penhallurick 1978

Breeds central Asia east to Japan, and from India to Southeast Asia. Northern populations migratory, wintering India to Southeast Asia. Polytypic: nominate *dauurica* occurs central Asia to Japan and south to India; perhaps five additional forms Southeast Asia.

Included here (in square brackets) on the basis of a bird seen and described on St Agnes on 5th October 1971. Along with various other records from other parts of Britain, it was rejected owing to the probability of escaped individuals of other similar flycatcher species perhaps being involved (*British Birds* 67: 19, 68: 337).

## Spotted Flycatcher  *Muscicapa striata*  A

**Former common spring and autumn migrant and summer resident in small numbers, recently somewhat reduced on passage with perhaps one breeding pair but no longer annually.**

Breeds most of Eurasia, from northwest Africa, Iberia, France, British Isles and northern Scandinavia north to northern Russia, east to western Siberia and south to Persian Gulf and west Himalayas. Winters northwest India, Arabia and tropical and southern Africa. Polytypic: nominate *striata* occurs Europe east to the Urals, including northwest Africa but excluding some Mediterranean islands and Balkans; *neumanni* Siberia, Asia Minor and eastern Mediterranean islands east to Iran; *balearica* Balearic Islands; *tyrrhenica* Corsica and Sardinia; two to three additional forms further east and south. Red-listed in UK: rapid, 75% breeding decline over past 25 years; unfavourable world conservation status (Gregory *et al.* 2002). National 68% decline during 25 years to 1996 and 11% 1994–99 (Bashford & Noble 2000).

Considering E H Rodd was able to document the acquisition of both Pied *Ficedula hypoleuca* and Red-breasted Flycatcher *F. parva*, his failure to mention Spotted Flycatcher in either his systematic list or his supplementary *List of the Birds Observed on The Scilly Islands* appears significant (Rodd 1880). However, the omission merely highlights one of several inconsistencies in this otherwise extremely useful volume, for in Rodd's own account of *Notes From Scilly*, we see that first-year Pied and Spotted Flycatchers were noted by his nephew Francis on 22nd September 1870, whilst on 8th November that same year Francis saw a first-year Spotted Flycatcher on St Mary's – apparently the first recorded instances of this species on Scilly. So it is interesting that in their later *Zoologist* review James Clark and Francis Rodd felt able to say only that it was 'probably a regular autumn visitor in immature plumage', though clearly they were unsure (Clark & Rodd 1906). Nonetheless, Clark provides us with the first proven breeding record for the islands – a nest with young in an outhouse on the west side of Bryher on 7th July 1903 – plus details of a female caught near Holy Vale on 28th May 1905. The reference to the bird being a female rather suggests that it was collected and skinned. Next mention comes from the Bishop Rock Lighthouse on the night of 27th–28th September 1907, when 'many were taken' (Ogilvie-Grant 1909) and again on 16th May 1911 when one or more was present (Ogilvie-Grant 1912a). However, despite Clark's earlier Bryher observation, Ryves and Quick failed to make mention of it in their later review of species breeding on Scilly (Ryves & Quick 1946).

Information-wise the first half of the 20th century was the ornithological equivalent of the Dark Ages for this species, with perhaps just three references to it between 1912 and 1956. In 1947 it allegedly occurred 'in numbers' and 1951 saw the 'heaviest autumn passage for years', whereas the only sighting in 1948 involved just one on 2nd October (*CBWPSAR*). However, it seems reasonably clear from more recent reports that it was passing through the islands in considerable numbers by the mid-1950s, leading us to the tempting conclusion that an increase in spring and autumn passage occurred during the early part of the 20th century. Certainly, by 1961–62 the St Agnes Bird Observatory was recording a spring passage commencing around 10th May, with up to seven birds per day and up to 170 'bird-days' in autumn. That same situation continues through to the present day with the earliest spring arrivals around 28th April and the last of the year well into November. There is a clear pattern of 'good and bad' years, probably related to differences in annual weather patterns, but always with greater numbers in the second half of the year. One or two single-day spring counts of 40 birds are on record but this increases to 50–60 during autumn, with exceptional counts of up to 100 some years, e.g. 1986. Nevertheless, since the mid-1990s there has been some suggestion of a reduction in annual numbers.

Breeding has been recorded almost annually since at least the mid-1970s, involving one to five pairs but with a recent decrease to just one pair. Particularly favoured breeding sites are in Holy Vale on St Mary's and in Tresco's Abbey Gardens. The greatest recorded number of breeding pairs occurred in 1987, when birds bred at Watermill, Holy Vale and Carn Friars on St Mary's plus two pairs on Tresco. In 1994, the Holy Vale pair, or a perhaps a second pair for that area, reared four young in an open-fronted nestbox in woodland on the northwest corner of the Lunnon Farm study plot. The most recent breeding involved a single pair in the much-favoured Holy Vale on St Mary's during the 2000 Breeding Bird Atlas (Chown & Lock 2002).

A total of 132 Spotted Flycatchers have been ringed on Scilly, 78 prior to 1970 and 54 since then, including the 1994 brood of four young in a Lunnon Farm nestbox. No birds ringed on Scilly have been recovered elsewhere, but a first-year ringed on Great Saltee Island, Wexford, Ireland, on 24th May 1993 was controlled by Will Wagstaff in Lower Moors, St Mary's, on 22nd May 1995. This perhaps provides a clue to where at least some Spotted Flycatchers using Scilly originate; indeed, we might reasonably expect Irish birds to move through Scilly on annual migration. However, whether the bulk of Scillonian migrant Spotted Flycatchers originate from Ireland is difficult to know and it may be that migrants comprise a mix of *striata* from Ireland and west-coast Britain, plus some *striata* from continental Europe or further east. Gantlett (1998) drew attention to the possibility of the paler *neumanni* reaching Britain from Siberia, plus the browner, less streaked and shorter-winged *balearica* and perhaps even the recognisably different *tyrrhenica* from Corsica and Sardinia. In addition, bearing in mind Scilly's well-earned reputation for attracting extralimital migrants from far away eastern Eurasia, the possibility of the similar but much rarer and slightly smaller Brown Flycatcher *M. dauurica* turning up in a row of elms *Ulmus* along the edge of a weedy flower field one autumn morning must be kept constantly in mind. Brown Flycatcher has already occurred in Britain, but other possible confusion species yet to do so include the similarly sized Sooty Flycatcher *M. sibirica* and the more robust looking Grey-streaked Flycatcher *M. griseisticta*, both of which show a restricted frontal collar (Cramp *et al.* 1977–94).

### Controls
J059712    1stY  Great Saltee, Wexford, Ireland
                      24th May 1993                                                    CT  Lower Moors, St Mary's 22nd May 1995

**Spotted Flycatcher Ringing Recaptures**

## Red-breasted Flycatcher                                                  *Ficedula parva*  A

**Scarce migrant, mainly in autumn. Treated by the BBRC as a national Scarce Migrant.**

Breeds central Europe, north to southern Finland and east through central northern Asia to Pacific, south to Austria, Balkans, Iran and northern Mongolia. Winters southern and Southeast Asia. Recent evidence of range extension into western Europe includes Norway, Sweden, Denmark and Greece (Cramp *et al.* 1977–94). Polytypic: nominate *parva* occurs Europe east to western Siberia, Turkey, northern Iran; *albicilla*, or 'Red-throated (Taiga) Flycatcher' remaining areas.

Considering that about 30 individuals have been recorded on Scilly in recent years, it is hard to accept that although the second and third British records of Red-breasted Flycatcher came from the islands in 1863 and 1865, it then went unrecorded until two were seen on St Agnes in 1951. E H Rodd's account of early Red-breasted Flycatchers in Cornwall and Scilly makes interesting reading (Rodd 1880), particularly his description of the first British record, involving a bird shot in 1963 by Horace Copeland near Falmouth on the surprising date of 24th January. The record came close to being lost as the specimen was placed 'in some insecure place, and the head was eaten by mice or rats, so that the body alone could be preserved'. By letter Copeland informed Rodd 'There is another in the neighbourhood, for which a vigilant watch will be kept. I saw it a few days back in the plantation which is 400 yards from my house. Should I be fortunate to capture it, you shall have due notice.'

E H Rodd also described events surrounding the second British record, shot by Augustus Pechell and Rodd's nephew Francis Rodd in Tresco Abbey gardens on 16th October 1963, just nine months after the above incident (Rodd 1863f). When found it was in company with Pied Flycatchers *F. hypoleuca* and E H Rodd referred to the specimen being 'sent over to me, with others, for my inspection'. What the 'others' were is unclear, but probably included two Pied Flycatchers shot at the same time. Rodd must quickly have passed the body to Penzance taxidermist Vingoe, who confirmed Pechell's view that it was a first-year male, presumably by internal examination. Rodd next sent the skin to Gould at the Natural History Museum for confirmation but made it clear that it was back in his possession by the time the second Tresco bird was shot, in November 1865 (Rodd 1866h). This time the collector was the Reverend John Jenkinson. Rodd made no mention of the whereabouts subsequently of this second Tresco skin, though it is clear from his writings that he saw it at some stage and was able to compare it with the first from that island, which he confirmed was in his own collection.

At this point the possibility arises of a fourth, undocumented, bird having been acquired from Scilly in the 1860s–70s. Norfolk naturalist J H Gurney described visiting Penzance taxidermist Vingoe on return from Scilly during mid-May 1887 and purchasing a Red-breasted Flycatcher skin – 12 years after Jenkinson shot the second Tresco bird. He pointed out that only after he returned home to Norfolk did he learn the skin was 'unrecorded' (Gurney 1889). Vingoe told Gurney (either at the time of the purchase or later by letter) that he received the specimen from Scilly 'in the same parcel as Mr Rodd's, both in the flesh'. Penhallurick (1978) dismisses this discrepancy by suggesting Gurney purchased the bird Jenkinson shot 12 years earlier. Interestingly, Rodd gives the Jenkinson specimen scant mention in his *Annual Summaries to the Royal Institution for Cornwall* (Rodd 1880), even though the two were friends, and makes no reference to it at all in the body of his main text. As that particular record was never in contention, it seems possible he may have failed to mention a subsequent bird. We know Rodd's papers to the *Zoologist* ceased in 1879 and that he died in January 1880 (shortly before publication of his book) and that James Harting did the final editing, so perhaps Harting overlooked another record.

Gurney's reputation as a reliable and competent naturalist was no less than E H Rodd's and if correct in his statement that the skin purchased from Vingoe was unrecorded, then we must search for explanations. According to Gurney, Rodd suggested confusion on Vingoe's part but it is not impossible that another skin was acquired by some unknown, who saw the chance to make a small profit by offering it to Vingoe, particularly at a time when any gentleman naturalist might be expected to carry a gun. Unfortunately, though, Vingoe apparently did have a reputation for bad record keeping.

Whatever the truth of this last matter, no further Red-breasted Flycatchers were recorded in either Cornwall or Scilly until a bird was discovered at Morvah Hill, Cornwall, in September 1944. This was followed by two on Scilly in 1951, one each on St Mary's and St Agnes, plus one on the latter island in 1953. By 1964, St Agnes Bird Observatory was recording around seven per year on that island alone and over the 12-year period 1973–84 an average of 26 per year were noted over all islands (*IOSBR* 1985). Examination of the same reports for the 15 years 1985–99 shows an average of slightly more than 17 per year, with a high of 32 (1985) and a low of six (1995 and 1999). Nonetheless, there is a strong suggestion that numbers may now be in decline on Scilly, as, looked at in five-yearly blocks, average annual totals for the same period are 1985–89 (22.8), 1990–94 (18.8) and 1995–99 (9.8).

There have been just two spring records of Red-breasted Flycatcher on Scilly: an unsexed individual on St Agnes on 9th May 1994 and a male on St Martin's and Great Arthur, Eastern Isles, on 2nd May 1979. Earliest autumn arrival date for the period since 1985 was 9th September and the latest recorded bird was on 17th November, both of which are close to equivalent dates given by Penhallurick (1978) for earlier years in Scilly. On September 24th 1968, a bird flew aboard-ship midway between Land's End and Brest, northern France (*CBWPSAR* 38). An examination of the circumstances surrounding Red-breasted Flycatcher

**Red-breasted Flycatcher annual totals**

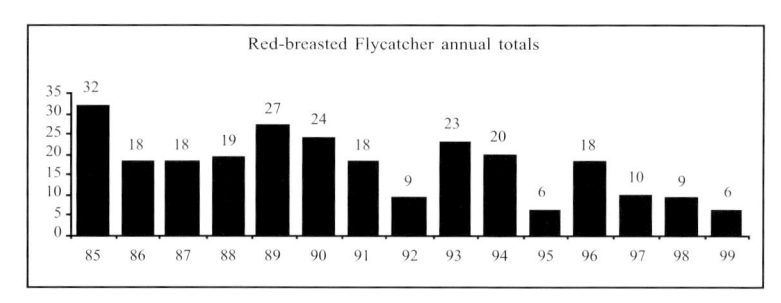

| Year | 85 | 86 | 87 | 88 | 89 | 90 | 91 | 92 | 93 | 94 | 95 | 96 | 97 | 98 | 99 |
|------|----|----|----|----|----|----|----|----|----|----|----|----|----|----|----|
| Total | 32 | 18 | 18 | 19 | 27 | 24 | 18 | 9 | 23 | 20 | 6 | 18 | 10 | 9 | 6 |

vagrancy in Britain concluded that spring arrivals were conducive with overshooting in anticyclonic conditions, whereas autumn arrivals were attributable to reverse migration (Sharrock 1974). However, more recently it was suggested that some birds involved may be heading southwest in autumn to so far unidentified wintering grounds (Wernham *et al.* 2002).

Both Snow (1971) and Gantlett (1998) referred to the possibility of individuals of the paler, eastern form *albicilla* occurring in Britain as vagrants. A bird on St Agnes from 6th to 10th October 1999 was initially thought to meet the necessary criteria, though that view was later reversed (*IOSBR* 1999). More recently, one was claimed for nearby Finistere, France, on 5th October 2000 (Davies 2001). Nineteen Red-breasted Flycatchers had been ringed on Scilly up until 1999, 13 prior to 1970 and six subsequently. Although there have been no recaptures, a newly ringed individual on St Agnes in October 2000 was thought to have been trapped days earlier near Land's End (G Avery & K Wilson pers. comm.). A bird on St Agnes on 16th October was killed by a cat.

## Collared Flycatcher *Ficedula albicollis* A BBRC 5.0%

**Extremely rare migrant, full written description required by BBRC.**

1984   One (male) St Martin's 20th & 21st May   *British Birds* 78: 578

Outlying breeding populations France, Germany, Italy, with main concentration central and southeast Europe from Baltic east to central Russia, south into Ukraine and Asia Minor, eastwards to Iran. Winters east-central Africa south of equator, from Tanzania south to Zimbabwe. Monotypic.

Just the single, spring record of this attractive little flycatcher, a male which spent two days feeding and resting in the vicinity of the St Martin's camp site. There were 20 records in Britain from 1958 until the end of 1999, so this single bird on Scilly represents 5% of the national total. Prior to 1958 there were just two records nationally, the first of which involved an adult male shot on Whalsay Island, Shetland, in May 1947. Cramp *et al.* (1977–94) make the point that in Britain, and elsewhere away from the breeding grounds, most records involve males, presumably emphasising the difficulty of separating this species in anything other than the conspicuous spring-male plumage from the closely related Pied Flycatcher *F. hypoleuca*. In view of the fact that it now breeds as close to Britain as France and Germany, we might perhaps be forgiven for expecting rather more than have so far been identified in Britain. The St Martin's bird was not trapped.

## Pied Flycatcher *Ficedula hypoleuca* A

**Annual spring and autumn migrant, does not breed.**

Breeds mainly West Palearctic but extends into Eurasia via central Siberia. Polytypic: nominate *hypoleuca* occurs Europe east to the Urals; *sibirica* in eastern Urals and Siberia; *iberiae* in Iberia. The North African form of Pied Flycatcher *speculigera* awaits acceptance as a full species, Atlas Flycatcher *Ficedula speculigera* (Saetre *et al.* 2001). Long-distance migrant, winters West Africa south of Sahara. National 13% decline 1994–99 (Bashford & Noble 2000).

There are various 19th-century references to this species in Scilly, earliest of which seems to be more than one account by E H Rodd of a bird shot by Augustus Pechell in 1849. On September 29th that year Rodd wrote to the *Zoologist* pointing out that 'an example of this species was procured during the past week and has hitherto been unknown to our fauna. It appears to be a young bird of the year' (Rodd

1849d). However, on 24th October he wrote again to say that 'a host of the migratory warblers still hangs about the islands', proceeding then to include Pied Flycatcher in a list of species mentioned (Rodd 1849b), and to enforce the point he later referred to this same incident in his landmark publication *Birds of Cornwall and the Scilly Islands*, pointing out that since that time others had been seen in autumn, e.g. 1857 (Rodd 1880).

More birds were recorded in 1863, including two shot in company with a Red-breasted Flycatcher *F. parva* (Rodd 1863e, 1863f) and again in 1869 (Rodd 1880). Surprisingly perhaps, James Clark and E H Rodd's nephew Francis Rodd found little to add in their later review of Scilly's bird life, merely commenting that Pied Flycatcher occurred not infrequently in twos and threes and that a single bird had been seen near Hugh Town, St Mary's, on 16th April 1903 (Clark & Rodd 1906). Yet in the same year the *Victoria History of Cornwall* felt able to describe it as 'A not infrequent autumn and spring visitor to Scilly, but on the mainland seldom seen' (W Page 1906).

Next mention of this species comes in 1948 via a reference to one on St Martin's for eight days in October (*CBWPSAR* 18), followed by a report of one on board the RMV *Scillonian* somewhere between the Wolf Rock Lighthouse and Scilly in September 1951. Subsequently, there is mention of one on St Agnes in spring plus 'some' on Tresco and two to three elsewhere in autumn 1952. But from around this time annual reports become more frequent and the number of birds increases; for example, even by 1964 we find reference to 'autumn peak passage on 3rd September' when 70 were present on St Agnes.

During the last 30 years, the pattern of seasonal occurrence has been very much one of a small spring passage of perhaps less than 20 birds in total, though there were exceptions. Autumn movement has been far more substantial, sometimes involving all-island single-day counts of 100 or more birds, as in 1997. As might be expected, spring migration is invariably a more hurried affair, usually commencing in late April and ending by mid-May, unlike the return movement, which in some years commences in early August and often lasts into early November.

Most Pied Flycatchers passing though Scilly seem likely to be British birds, though the ringing data show that birds also reach Britain on autumn passage from Scandinavia and western Russia (Wernham *et al.* 2002). A total of 257 Pied Flycatchers were ringed in Scilly up to 1999, 184 prior to 1970. A bird ringed as a first-year on Great Saltee Island, Wexford, Ireland, on 29th August 1962 and trapped on St Agnes three days later was the only recapture. Nonetheless, Pied Flycatcher remains a scarce bird on Irish soil regardless of recent increases in numbers of migrants recorded at Irish observatories (Andrews 1964; Gibbons *et al.* 1993). There is also a quite recent Scillonian control of a Spotted Flycatcher *Muscicapa striata* ringed on Great Saltee, but that species is far more abundant in Ireland. As Gantlett (1998) pointed out, other forms of Pied Flycatcher might be expected to reach Britain and therefore Scilly, including the larger and greyer *sibirica* from western Russia and the distinctive *iberiae* from southwest Europe.

## Controls
AC40530   1stY  Great Saltee, Wexford, Ireland
                29th August 1962                          CT  St Agnes 1st–3rd September 1962

**Pied Flycatcher Ringing Recaptures**

# Bearded Tit                                                    *Panurus biarmicus*   A

**Very rare vagrant or migrant, a full written description required by the SRP.**

Pre-1863   Clark & Rodd 1906; Witherby & Ticehurst 1907
    1965   At least nine Tresco & St Agnes October
    1972   Up to 25 various islands 18th October to 15th November
    1980   At least four St Mary's & Tresco 19th October to 12th November
    1981   One Tresco 23rd to 26th October
    1993   One Great Pool, Tresco 24th to 27th October

Breeds western Europe through central Eurasia to Pacific. West European population fragmented, reflecting reliance on reedbeds. Polytypic: nominate *biarmicus* occurs Spain, France, Britain (England), Sweden, Poland, Switzerland, Italy, former Yugoslavia, Albania, Greece; *kosswigi* southern Turkey (though possibly extinct); *russicus* central Europe east through central Asia to China. Populations mainly sedentary but subject to periodic eruptive movements, with tendency to wander during winter. Amber-listed in UK: 50% or more of breeding population at ten or fewer sites (Gregory *et al.* 2002). Removed from BBRC Rarities List January 1963 (Harber & Swaine 1963).

Slight doubt surrounds the timing of the earliest known record, mention of which Clark & Rodd (1906) credited to an 1863 manuscript note by E H Rodd, stating Bearded Tit 'has occurred once on St Mary's Moors'. In the *Victoria History of Cornwall* Clark attributed the record to the 1850s (in W Page 1906) and if a skin was obtained it seems not to have been preserved. Penhallurick queries this record's authenticity on the grounds that Rodd failed to published it, and whilst this omission appears inexplicable, there is evidence that Rodd may not always have been as meticulous with his records as we might wish. Certainly, no lesser authorities than Witherby and Ticehurst felt the record reliable enough to later repeat it (Witherby & Ticehurst 1907).

The October 1965 arrivals were presumably part of the much larger national irruption that autumn, with birds also reaching Northumberland and Anglesey (Axel 1966; Snow 1971; Cramp *et al.* 1977–94). At least 22 individuals figured in seven sightings on mainland Cornwall that year, mostly along the north coast from 13th October until late December, with at least two remaining until April 1966. A party of nine was in the Tresco reedbeds, and though no date is given it was presumably during October, otherwise it pre-dates the mainland arrivals. We do know, though, that on 16th October seven were on St Agnes, three remaining on that island on 26th. The 1972 arrivals were also part of a larger irruption noticeable elsewhere in Britain, being first noted on Scilly four days after birds arrived in west Cornwall. First to reach Scilly were seen on St Martin's on 18th October and a total of at least 25 were then reported at various sites around the islands, until the last on 15th November. These included a party of 13 on St Agnes. According to David Hunt, when they first arrived Bearded Tits were seen in all sorts of unlikely habitats, including bracken slopes and *Pittosporum crassifolium* hedges. By the end of October, however, most had found their way to the Tresco reedbeds, where up to 25 were together (Penhallurick 1978). On mainland Cornwall, as in 1965–66, most birds ended up in the extensive Marazion reedbed west of Penzance, where 42 was the largest count and where birds remained until mid-March 1973. This emphasises, incidentally, how the Marazion, Tresco and St Mary's reedbeds probably represent the largest areas of this habitat in west Cornwall.

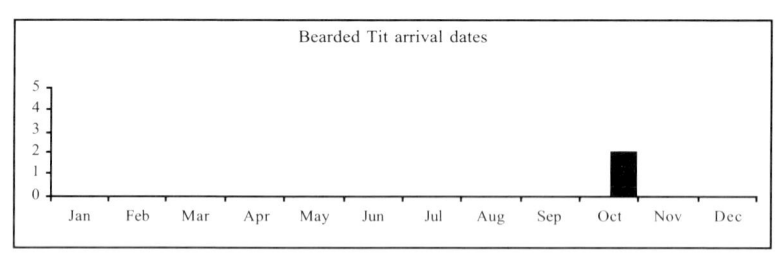

Bearded Tit arrival dates

First indication of Bearded Tits on Scilly during 1980 came with a bird in Lower Moors, St Mary's, on 19th October, followed quickly by four at nearby Porth Hellick next day. By 22nd two were on Tresco, where they remained until at least 4th November and a lone individual was back at Lower Moors for just one day on 12th November. Since then there have been no multiple arrivals in Scilly and the only records involve a bird on Tresco from 23rd to 26th October 1981 and one there from 24th to 27th October 1993. The erratic and eruptive dispersal in this species results in a certain amount of random exchange between populations, coupled with some colonisation of new sites. Birds have been recorded moving between Britain and continental Europe but the overall picture is confused and it seems possible that birds reaching Cornwall and Scilly may come either from sites elsewhere in Britain or from continental Europe (Wernham *et al.* 2002). However, there is a measure of uniformity in arrival and departure dates on Scilly suggestive perhaps of migration or at least regular dispersal, rather than cold-weather movement. The 1965 arrivals fall within the well-documented period of irruptive autumn dispersal from breeding sites in East Anglia and the Netherlands, which commenced in 1959 and were attributed to increasing numbers within local populations (Axel 1966). Axel also described a huge build-up of birds in the Netherlands in 1965, which resulted in an irruption within that population and the first recoveries in Britain of birds ringed in that country.

# Long-tailed Tit *Aegithalos caudatus* A

Scarce migrant or vagrant, full written description required by SRP.

  1876  Seven (three shot) Tresco October   Clark & Rodd 1906
  1903  Five Tresco   Clark & Rodd 1906; W Page 1906
  1905  Several Tresco   Clark & Rodd 1906; W Page 1906
  1952  One Tresco 10th March
  1961  One Covean, St Agnes 22nd March
  1961  Five Normandy Farm, St Mary's 18th November (one freshly dead 26th)
  1974  One Porth Cressa, St Mary's 17th October
  1975  Twelve to 32 birds St Mary's, Tresco & St Agnes 21st October to 26th December
  [1984  One reported Watermill, St Mary's 26th]
  1995  One Lower Moors, St Mary's & Tresco 1st November to 1st September 1997
  1999  Up to seven St Mary's (various sites) 10th November to 18th March 2000

Breeds from North Atlantic to the North Pacific. Within West Palearctic occurs commonly westwards from Spain, Portugal, France and British Isles, south into Italy, Greece, Turkey as far as Caspian Sea and north to near Arctic Circle, even extending as far as the coastal Barents Sea. Polytypic, with complex racial structure: nominate *caudatus*, or 'Northern Long-tailed Tit', in north, e.g. Fennoscandia; intergrading to *europaeus*, or 'Continental Long-tailed Tit', Denmark, western and central Europe; *aremoricus* western France; *taiti* southwest France; *rosaceus* Britain and Ireland. Inter-racial differences a combination of size and plumage, but most northerly populations distinguishable by wholly white head. Populations mainly sedentary but irregular and sometimes massive irruptions associated with high population levels. Migration apparently more usual further east. National 15% increase 1994–99 (Bashford & Noble 2000).

Typically, birds arrive in autumn, singly or in small groups, usually remaining for extended periods, sometimes apparently overwintering. There is no positive account of breeding, though it is rumoured to have occurred. No sightings thus far have involved white-headed individuals, e.g. *caudatus*, from northern Europe. E H Rodd (1880) made no mention of it in relation to Scilly though he acknowledged it was resident locally on mainland Cornwall.

Clark & Rodd (1906) were of course concerned specifically with Scilly, recording that in October 1876 Tresco gamekeeper David Smith shot three Long-tailed Tits out of a 'family' of seven, whilst on 28th September 1903 he also saw a 'family' of five. They added that in autumn 1905 Long-tailed Tits were 'fairly common at Tresco', thereby implying it was not normally so common. However, given the known difficulty of ageing Long-tailed Tits after post-juvenile moult, even in the hand, we must treat any references to autumn 'families' with considerable caution and there is certainly insufficient detail in these early records to establish breeding.

Scillonian photographer C J King included Long-tailed Tit in his 'Full List of the Birds of Scilly' (in C J King 1924) but did not help resolve the breeding question. Boyd visited Scilly in September 1920, June and July 1924 and again in September 1931 (Boyd 1924, 1931) but mentions only Great Tit *Parus major*. However, Wallis (1923) perhaps does help, by pointing out that during two spring visits he saw no species of tit except Great Tit. But we can be confident that Long-tailed Tits were absent from Scilly by 1946, through their omission from the authoritative list of breeding island birds (Ryves & Quick 1946). The authors of this list informed us it had increased in the Land's End area of Cornwall. Holloway too makes no mention of it breeding in Scilly in his Historical Atlas (Holloway 1996).

The current situation is much clearer, with birds arriving in Scilly in just seven years since commencement of the *CBWPSAR* in 1931. However, one further record, for 1984, was never confirmed in writing to the SRP and therefore remains questionable. Four of the remaining records involved single individuals, three of which were recorded on one day only. The 1995 bird remained in the islands for 22 months, being seen first on St Mary's and then Tresco, though it presumably also accounted for a claimed brief sighting back on St Mary's. The other three years involved multiple autumn sightings, but because small groups of Long-tailed Tits typically wander extensively after arrival in Scilly it is difficult to be certain how many were involved in each case. This was especially so in 1975, when a total of 15 sightings on three different islands could have involved from 12 to 32 individuals, though more probably the former.

*Birds of the Isles of Scilly*

Long-tailed Tit arrival dates

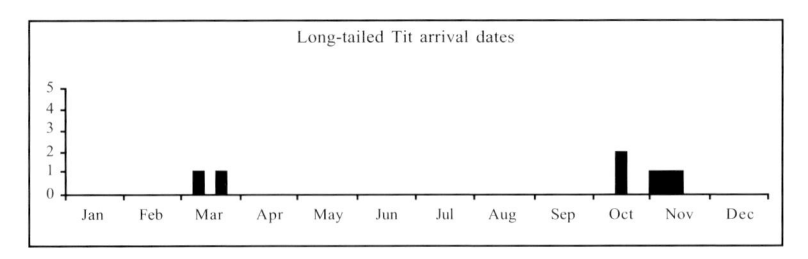

    The pattern of periodic irruptions, particularly from central and northern European populations, is well understood, birds tending to travel and remain in family groups. Although British and Irish birds are mainly sedentary, short-distance movements are common, and can be more substantial. Nonetheless, 95% of recoveries involved distances of less than 60 km, the mean distance of birds found dead being 2 km (Wernham *et al.* 2002). Cramp *et al.* (1977–94) mention that 10% of 233 recoveries in the 1980s were over 100 km, up to a limit of 142 km. Cramp *et al.* also make no direct reference to British Long-tailed Tits crossing water, though in western Ireland birds often wander to offshore islands during winter; the only foreign recovery of a British-ringed Long Tailed Tit involved a bird ringed in Norfolk in October 1983 and recovered in Belgium the following September (Wernham *et al.* 2002). Regardless of any tendency towards periodic irruptions, there is little evidence of birds from continental Europe reaching Britain, and no ringing recoveries, Long-tailed Tit being hardly represented in the massive 1957 invasion of various tit species into the British Isles (Cramp *et al.* 1960; Perrins 1979). There are also few sightings of the white-headed European forms in Britain. The nearest breeding Long-tailed Tits to Scilly are in west Cornwall, southern Ireland, the Channel Islands and northern Brittany (Guermeur & Monnat 1980; Gibbons *et al.* 1993). Nonetheless, colonisation of Scilly remains a possibility; birds recolonised the Channel Islands in 1997 following an absence of 13 years (Davies 2001). In his useful booklet *Birds of Scilly as Recorded at Tresco Abbey* T A Dorrien-Smith attributed all birds prior to the 1950s to the British and Irish form *rosaceus*, though grounds for this are not stated (Dorrien-Smith 1951). The 1996 bird was trapped and ringed in Lower Moors but was not recovered subsequently and there are no other recaptures.

## Marsh Tit *Parus palustris* A

**Former rare vagrant, not reported with certainty since about 1863. Full written description required by the SRP.**

    1851   Or 'thereabouts', one 'obtained' Scilly October   Clark & Rodd 1906
    1863   One to two seen by F R Rodd November   Clark & Rodd 1906; W Page 1906
    1946   'Several' seen among reeds Porth Hellick, St Mary's   *CBWPSAR* 16

Two discrete populations, one restricted to the West Palearctic, the other Asia. In West Palearctic breeds England, Wales and southern Scotland, southern Scandinavia, France and northern Spain east to Urals and south to Italy and Turkey. Polytypic: nominate *palustris*, or 'Continental Marsh Tit' occurs southern Scandinavia and central Europe east to Poland and Greece, including northern France and northern England and southern Scotland; *dresseri* England and Wales south from Lancashire and Yorkshire and in western France. Sedentary, undergoing short-distance post-breeding dispersal, with tendency towards nomadic wandering in winter in north of range. Reclassified from Amber- to Red-listed in UK 2002: rapid, 50% breeding decline over past 25 years (Gregory *et al.* 2002). National 37% decline during 25 years to 1996 but increase of 23% 1994–99 (Bashford & Noble 2000).

    The obvious difficulty associated with treating all early records of this species is the possibility of at least some having involved the now Red-listed Willow Tit *P. montanus*, which of course was not separated from Marsh Tit until 1897 (Perrins 1979; Palmer 2000). In addition, although Willow Tit is now rare in Cornwall west of the river Tamar (Sharrock 1976; Gibbons *et al.* 1993), that may not always have been entirely so. Considering E H Rodd (1880) made no reference to Marsh Tit in relation to Scilly, his nephew Francis Rodd and James Clark had quite a lot to say on the subject (Clark & Rodd 1906). According to these two authors A A Dorrien-Smith once told Rodd (presumably Francis, who spent much time on Tresco) that Marsh Tit was once the commonest of all tits on Scilly. However, not too much should perhaps be attached to that statement as all tit species seem to have been something of a rarity on the islands in the late 19th century. Clark and Rodd also quote a record of a Marsh Tit obtained in the islands about the same time that Augustus Pechell acquired a Coal Tit *P. ater* specimen (1851), also stating the species was seen twice more by 'Rodd' around 1863. As E H Rodd apparently visited Scilly only occasionally, we must assume that this last remark refers to Francis Rodd, who would have been familiar with Marsh Tit in the woods around his house on the upper Tamar in east Cornwall.

Nevertheless, whilst it seems to be accepted that Marsh Tit (or Willow Tit) occurred occasionally on Scilly in the late 19th century, sole evidence for its presence in the 20th century rests on the undated 1946 claim of 'several' seen by a single observer in reeds *Phragmites communis* at Porth Hellick on St Mary's. As with many earlier Scillonian records, this one lacks important detail and whilst it is not unusual to encounter tit flocks in reed scrub, the possibility of this record actually referring to Bearded Tit *Panurus biarmicus* cannot be discounted, particularly as it is the sole claim of Marsh or Willow Tit in Scilly throughout the entire 20th century. In addition, Marsh Tits pair for life and are disinclined to wander far outside their territories, even when bad weather has forced most other tit species to move. This occurs to the extent that even if they do attach themselves to passing tit flocks they will disengage once the edge of their territory is reached. In addition, of course, Marsh Tits do not seem to be irruptive and there are few ringing recoveries of any distance (Perrins 1979); Sellers (in Wernham *et al.* 2002) points out that, typically, birds in a Gloucestershire study moved from 800 to 1,000 metres between hatching and breeding. More likely perhaps to reach Scilly is the northern form of Willow Tit, *P. m. borealis* or 'Boreal Willow Tit', several of which have already occurred elsewhere in Britain (Palmer 2000). No Marsh Tits have been trapped and ringed on Scilly and there are no recaptures.

# Crested Tit *Parus cristatus* A

**Extremely rare vagrant, full written description required by the SRP.**

1947   One St Mary's 15th September   *CBWPSAR* 17
1971   One St Mary's 11th November

Within West Palearctic, distributed from Iberia and France through central Europe and Fennoscandia, northeast through southern Finland, northern Ukraine and Romania, with outlying populations former Yugoslavia into Greece and Romania. Polytypic: *scoticus*, or 'Scottish Crested Tit', occurs Scotland; *weigoldi* Brittany; *mitratus*, or 'Continental Crested Tit' remainder of France, northwest and central Spain, Pyrenees and Alps through to former East Germany; nominate *cristatus*, or 'Northern Crested Tit', further north and east, including Fennoscandia. Removed from the BBRC Rarities List January 1963 (Harber & Swaine 1963). Downgraded from Amber- to Green-listed in UK 2002 (Gregory *et al.* 2002).

Neither E H Rodd (1880) nor Clark & F R Rodd (1906) make reference to this species, from which we must assume it went unrecorded in Scilly or Cornwall until at least the latter date, though the possibility of a very occasional vagrant having being overlooked must exist. Clark & Rodd made mention of a Coal Tit *P. ater* having been obtained on Scilly in 1851 and we now know that Crested Tits probably arrive in Scilly in company with Coal Tits. The first, questionable, record for the Cornish mainland involved two Crested Tits allegedly seen in woodland near Liskeard in 1899 (Penhallurick 1978).

The two documented Scillonian records both lack the level of accountability nowadays required, but both were accompanied by quite compelling descriptions nonetheless. On 15th September 1947, there was an arrival of exhausted Coal Tits on St Mary's, including in the area of a Mr Kennedy's house at Harry's Walls, overlooking Lower Moors. He was able to approach some of these birds closely and, according to his account, obtained excellent views of a 'rather battered' Crested Tit. The arrival on Scilly of this 1947 bird coincided with what by current standards could only be described as an exceptional influx of Coal Tits, 'large flocks (40–50)' following 'a spell of westerly weather'. We know from more recent events that Scilly does receive periodic influxes of Coal and other tit species from continental Europe, in varying numbers. But although the weather in winter 1947 was of course exceptionally severe, this record was perhaps too early to have been affected by that.

According to Cramp *et al.* (1977–94) the more northerly Coal Tit populations are both eruptive and irregular short-distance migrants, tending to move in a southwest direction. Regardless of the fact that Crested Tits do not normally share this desire to wander, European distribution maps of the two species bear a remarkable similarity and it perhaps seems not at all unreasonable that an occasional Crested Tit might get caught up in a large Coal Tit movement. Records of Crested Tits found in Morocco and the Caucasus have been taken to represent just such wandering, but could possibly involve as yet unknown local breeding populations (Cramp *et al.* 1977–94). Importantly, perhaps, another bird (or just possibly the Harry's Walls individual) was seen in south Devon on 28th December that same year (Moore 1969 in Penhallurick 1978).

The subsequent record, again from a single observer and again on St Mary's, occurred during the morning of 11th November 1971. This bird too was extremely approachable, allowing the observer, R. Symons, to obtain a detailed description and make a sketch that was later seen and accepted by the editors of the *IOSBR* (1971). Indeed the editors went as far as reproducing part of the description, which appears to stand the test of time: 'erectile crest … upperparts mousy brown, breast and belly off-white tinged brown. Black beak and legs.' The bird was under observation for 2–3 minutes before flying off into conifer trees.

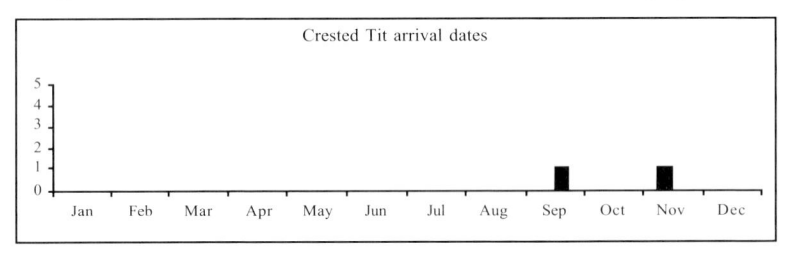

Crested Tit arrival dates

The nearest breeding populations to Scilly are in France, Belgium and the Netherlands, but northern birds may be more prone to southward cold-weather movements. Birds belonging to both *cristatus* from Scandinavia and *mitratus* from the Netherlands, Belgium and France, were recorded in Britain up to at least the 1870s (Wernham *et al.* 2002). There is limited information too that Crested Tits do become involved in large movements of other tit species, as in the Netherlands in 1957. However, there are no ringing data showing the extent of such movement and the shortage of observations at migration stations suggests it is small in any event (Cramp *et al.* 1977–94). Neither of the above two birds was trapped and ringed.

# Coal Tit *Parus ater* A

**Until very recently a breeding resident in small numbers. Now a scarce migrant with usually just a few birds involved, large influxes occasionally occur. Full written description required by the SRP.**

Breeds Eurasia, from Britain, Iberia, North Africa and southern Fennoscandia east to Pacific and Southeast Asia. Polytypic, divided into five distinct groups. The *ater* group occupies northern West Palearctic eastwards; *britannicus*, or 'British Coal Tit', occurs Britain; *hibernicus* Ireland; *vieirae* Iberia; *sardus* Corsica and Sardinia; nominate *ater*, or 'Continental Coal Tit', remaining areas, east to Mongolia. In North Africa, *atlas* occurs Morocco; *ledouci* northern Algeria and Tunisia. Mainly sedentary in south and west of range but eruptive over most of remainder, most heading west or southwest and avoiding long sea crossings (Cramp *et al.* 1977–94). National 2% increase 1994–99 (Bashford & Noble 2000).

Up until 1947 there was just one recorded instance of this species in Scilly. James Clark and Francis Rodd referring to it briefly in their useful 1906 *Zoologist* paper, attributed a shot bird to Augustus Pechell in autumn 1851; Pechell also obtained a Marsh Tit *P. palustris* around the same time (Clark & Rodd 1906). It is difficult to understand why E H Rodd (1880) never mentioned the record, but Clark and E H Rodd's nephew Francis Rodd were much closer in time than we are and it is clear from their review that they researched the elder Rodd's papers thoroughly. In addition, much of what E H Rodd learnt and subsequently wrote about Scilly came initially from Francis and his close companion Augustus Pechell, or from the equally well-informed Augustus Smith. However, considering Coal Tit bred as close in the mid- to late 1800s as mainland Cornwall, albeit uncommonly (Holloway 1996), its absence is all the more surprising and the occasional wanderer from there or continental Europe may well have been overlooked.

Nevertheless, any doubts surrounding the likelihood of Coal Tits reaching Scilly were dispelled with the appearance of a flock of 40–50 evidently exhausted birds on St Mary's in westerly winds early on 15th September 1947 (*CBWPSAR* 17). No suggestion is given for the possible origin of these birds, but the presence among them of a Crested Tit *P. cristatus* perhaps indicates a Continental source and of course 1947 turned out to be a particularly severe winter in Europe. These birds were followed ten years later by a flock of 60 on St Agnes mid-morning on 6th October 1957. Most left the islands the same day but subsequent smaller influxes occurred over the next four days, a few remaining until at least early November. One trapped on 1st November was identified as the Continental form *ater*. By 13th October birds were also on St Mary's, with 'very many' from 20th to 27th and with a few still present into December. The 1957 influx was accompanied by up to 70 Great Tits *P. major* and 200+ Blue Tits *P. caeruleus*, all presumably part of the exceptionally large irruption of *Parus* species into Britain that autumn (Cramp *et al.* 1960). None were recorded in 1958 but up to four about the islands in 1959 presumably formed part of a further smaller invasion into Britain that year (*CBWPSAR* 27, 28; Cramp *et al.* 1960; Cramp 1963).

From the late 1960s onwards, the overall picture was one of a continued presence, of from one to perhaps six birds on various islands and with a suggestion of at least the majority having a Continental origin. However, the situation was confused by small-scale invasions during autumns 1969, 1972, 1975, 1993 and 1996, with the establishment of up to four possible breeding pairs on Tresco from around 1976; the latter were also attributed to the form *ater*. Throughout the 1970s and into the early 1990s it became difficult differentiating between likely wandering Tresco 'residents' and genuine vagrants, though there does seem to have been a tendency towards autumn arrivals. We are therefore left to speculate whether this reflects a real increase in the number of annual arrivals compared with the 19th and early 20th centuries, or is simply a reflection of increased observer coverage.

Birds were recorded apparently holding territory on Tresco from the mid-1970s until perhaps 1982, following which it becomes unclear whether birds seen were residents or new arrivals. Up to four pairs allegedly bred during this period, with the first claim of success involving a pair that allegedly raised two young in 1976 (*IOSBR* 1976). Sadly no supporting information is published and thus a question mark hangs over the acceptability of all these breeding reports. Certainly no details are given of any nest found and allegations of successful breeding are apparently based solely on claimed sightings of young, plus the presence of singing males; the latter is not necessarily acceptable proof of breeding.

The recent situation is more easily described. The last small influx occurred in 1996, when parties of up to five Coal Tits were to be seen about the islands from mid-October through to early November. In 1997 there were just three sightings, one in January and two in autumn, with singles only during 1998 and 1999, the last accompanying a party of Long-tailed Tits *Aegithalos caudatus* on St Mary's during mid-November.

Unlike many other autumn migrants, we have an idea of where at least some Scillonian Coal Tits originate, all subspecific identification appearing to involve the Continental *ater*. For whilst this form occurs from Scandinavia south to France, the Low Countries, Italy and eastwards and birds could originate from any part of that area, we know irruptions often show a westerly bias and so might expect those reaching Scilly to come from France, Germany or the Low Countries. Indeed, this is exactly what recoveries of birds involved in the big 1957 invasion of Britain show for Coal Tit, Blue Tit and Great Tit (Cramp *et al.* 1960; Cramp *et al.* 1977–94). Only a small proportion of recoveries of British Coal Tits ringed in the breeding season were of birds which had moved greater than 20 km (Wernham *et al.* 2002). As might be expected, sight records of Coal Tits came from the inhabited islands only, the single exception being a bird on Round Island in October 1969 (Beswetherick 1969). Five Coal Tits have been ringed on Scilly, all prior to 1970, one of which was the bird already referred to and identified as belonging to the Continental form *ater*.

# Blue Tit *Parus caeruleus* A

**Breeding resident and occasional irruptive migrant or winter visitor.**

Confined almost exclusively to West Palearctic, breeding central and southern Europe and extreme northwest Africa, with outlying population Iran. Mainly resident, irruptive in north and centre of range. Polytypic with complex racial structure, usually divided into *caeruleus* and *teneriffae* groups. Within *caeruleus* group, *obscurus*, or 'British Blue Tit', occurs Britain, Ireland and Channel Islands; nominate *caeruleus*, or 'Continental Blue Tit' continental Europe from Fennoscandia and western Russia south to Mediterranean and east to Volga River, merging with *obscurus* in western France. Fourteen or so additional forms further south and east. National 7% increase 1994–99 (Bashford & Noble 2000).

Much the same comments apply as for Great Tit *P. major* regarding any early accounts. Clark and

Rodd described it as seen only occasionally during autumn or winter, either singly or in 'pairs', suggesting these had probably been blown over from mainland Britain during storms (Clark & Rodd 1906), Blue Tit being a widely distributed and common breeding species in Cornwall during the 19th century (Rodd 1880). Clark and Rodd also suggested a storm-driven arrival may have accounted for all tit species recorded in Scilly up until then. E H Rodd thought it only occasional during winter but gained his information mainly from his nephew Francis Rodd, James Clark's co-author in the above paper, who spent much time on Tresco during the mid-19th century. Francis also commented on the fresh arrival of a Blue Tit in the Abbey Gardens on 19th December 1864 and the presence there of five Blue Tits and a Great Tit throughout winter 1870 (Rodd 1880).

In his mid-20th-century review, Penhallurick (1978) found no evidence of breeding in Scilly prior to 1953, though birds had been noted as 'resident' from around 1946. The eight St Agnes and Gugh breeding bird surveys conducted between 1957 and 1978 recorded it in only 1961, 1962, 1974 and 1978, respective pair totals being one, one, two and three. Unknown but nonetheless small numbers were also present on St Mary's and Tresco during the mid-1970s, plus one pair on St Martin's. Annual CBC pair totals recorded on the 16-hectare Lunnon Farm study plot on St Mary's for the eight years 1991–98 varied between eleven and three, average of 6.75, and like Great Tit the data suggest a decline over this period. Average pair density on the plot was 2.3 per hectare, low of 1.45, high of 5.3. Interestingly, Penhallurick thought it less numerous in Scilly than Great Tit and that seems still to be the case, with St Mary's still its undoubted stronghold. Meanwhile, the 2000 Breeding Bird Atlas (Chown & Lock 2002) recorded a total of up to 54 breeding pairs in 16 (23.8%) of the 67 1-km squares surveyed, birds being confined to three main islands, with 44 (81%) on St Mary's (Table). However, addressing the possibility of under-recording, the report's authors thought a figure in the range 50–75 pairs a more realistic proposition. A pair also bred on St Martin's in 2001, following completion of the Atlas survey (Chown & Lock 2002).

| 1991 | 1992 | 1993 | 1994 | 1995 | 1996 | 1997 | 1998 |
|---|---|---|---|---|---|---|---|
| 11 | 7 | 9 | 7 | 7 | 5 | 5 | 3 |

**Blue Tit CBC Pair Totals – 16-ha Lunnon Farm, St Mary's 1991–98 (P J Robinson – unpublished data)**

There seems rather more evidence in support of occasional migration, or more frequent irruption, among the mid-20th-century data than for Great Tit, flocks of up to 50 being recorded on St Mary's (Penhallurick 1978). However, the size of the resident population was poorly understood at that time and it would not have taken many pairs to produce a winter flock of that magnitude. A report of 25–30 seen coming in off the sea at Deep Point on the eastern side of St Mary's on 15th April 1958 was perhaps connected with the exceptional European irruption the previous autumn, many birds reaching Scilly and Ireland (Cramp *et al.* 1960). Interestingly, Parslow (1967a) was unable to identify any national increase during the period that Blue Tits spread to Scilly in the mid-20th century and as with Great Tit, the answer probably lies at least partly in those European irruptions.

As with Great Tit, recent observations of quite small numbers of Blue Tits were frequently viewed as indicative of passage. This was the case in 1981 when a flock of 20 on St Mary's during mid-October were thought to have been migrants, despite an estimated 28 pairs on that island the previous summer. And even as recently as 1991, October flocks no greater than 14 were reportedly on passage. In reality, however, apart from the 1957 irruption the only other suggestion of either passage or irruption involved two seen

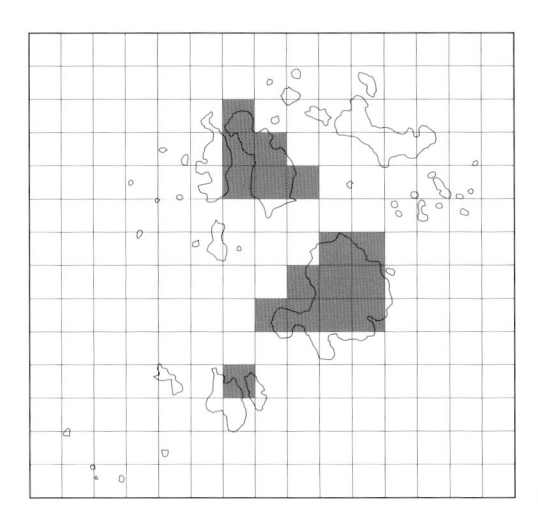

| Island | Pairs |
|---|---|
| St Mary's | 44 |
| Tresco | 9 |
| St Agnes & Gugh | 1 |

**2000 Breeding Bird Atlas – Blue Tit (Chown & Lock 2002)**

**1-km Blue Tit Breeding Distribution – 2000–01 (data Chown & Lock 2002)**

apparently arriving on the eastern end of St Mary's during late October 1996. Indeed, with up to 90 pairs resident in the islands it seems likely that the presence of birds from elsewhere would now only become obvious during large European irruption years. On St Mary's the 1997 annual CBC detected five breeding pairs on the Lunnon Farm study plot, yet over 120 individual Blue Tits were captured on the 16-hectare plot, in addition to 19 pulli ringed that year. These included birds recaptured from St Agnes, St Martin's and elsewhere on St Mary's but none from further afield. This inter-island movement of Blue and Great Tits has only recently become apparent and very probably accounted for the flock of 15 supposed 'migrants' on Bryher during October 1998.

Like Great Tit, few British or Irish Blue Tits move far, over 80% of ringed birds being recovered within 10 km; short-distance post-fledging dispersal occurs from late June to mid-August (Cramp *et al.* 1977–94). Continental birds of the form *caeruleus* show a slightly greater tendency than their Great Tit equivalent to reach Britain other than during irruption years, though this nevertheless occurs uncommonly (Wernham *et al.* 2002), the last notable invasion of Scilly being 1957. A total of 521 Blue Tits were ringed in Scilly up until 1999, 84% since 1970. The only recaptures away from Scilly are shown in the Table, the birds recovered on St Agnes and St Martin's in 1957 are included to show that not all involved in that year's irruption moved on. Ringing evidence during invasion years (at least) reveals a tendency towards onward westerly or northerly movement of birds ringed in southern England, a feature apparent in E14546, though where E14537 spent the winter months is unknown. Quite exceptional is the bird ringed in Dorset in winter 1995 and found breeding on the Lunnon Farm plot on St Mary's the following June; only 1.2% (n=657) of ringed Blue Tits move more than 20 km within a winter, though this figure increases to 9% during subsequent winters (Wernham *et al.* 2002).

**Recoveries**

| | | | | |
|---|---|---|---|---|
| E14546 | Ad | St Agnes 8th September 1957 | AS | off Tuskar Rock, Ireland 12th September 1957 |
| E14537 | Ad | St Agnes 8th September 1957 | FD | Marazion, Cornwall 22nd March 1958 |
| J960661 | Ad | Sherborne, Dorset 15th January 1995 | CT/BR | Kitty Down, St Mary's 3rd June 1995 |

**Local**

| | | | | |
|---|---|---|---|---|
| E14529 | ? | St Agnes 8th September 1957 | CT | St Martin's 13th November 1957 |
| C99455 | ? | St Agnes 8th October 1957 | KC | St Agnes 26th October 1957 |
| AK13660 | 1stY | St Agnes 23rd October 1962 | FD | Tresco 11th January 1963 |

**Blue Tit Ringing Recaptures**

# Great Tit
*Parus major* A

**Breeding resident and occasional irruptive migrant or winter visitor.**

Breeds central and southern Eurasia, from British Isles and Iberia east to Sakhalin and Japan, south into India and Southeast Asia. Resident or irruptive. Polytypic with complex racial structure, normally divided into *major*, *cinereus* and *minor* group. Within *major* group, *newtoni* occurs Britain and Ireland; nominate *major*, or 'Continental Great Tit', France, central Spain and Scandinavia east to Iran and Altai mountains, grading into *newtoni* in southeast England, northwest France, Belgium and Netherlands; *corsus* southern Spain, Portugal and Sardinia grading into *major* in northern Portugal and central Spain. Twenty or more additional forms further south and east. National 12% increase 1994–99 (Bashford & Noble 2000).

This is clearly a species that underwent a substantial change of status in Scilly during the 20th century. E H Rodd recorded as unusual one that appeared in the Tresco Abbey gardens during October 1870, where it remained together with five Blue Tits *P. caeruleus* throughout the following winter, allegedly 'feeding on the scale blight on the *Acacia* trees' (Rodd 1880). By the early 20th century it was still considered only occasional during autumn, usually singly but twice in small parties, plus twice during January, despite breeding commonly on the nearby mainland (Clark & Rodd 1906). Clark and Rodd also pointed out that singles occasionally lingered for two to three weeks during autumn. More importantly, they recorded that it was wrongly listed by E H Rodd as breeding in Scilly, where, up to then, it had not been recorded during spring.

Ticehurst documented the considerable tit *Parus* invasion of 1910, when large numbers of Great Tits arrived on St Agnes on 1st November, the island being described as 'swarming' with them. However, all were in the process of leaving the islands by the last week of November. At least one examined by Ticehurst was believed to be the Continental form *major* (N F Ticehurst 1911; Ogilvie-Grant 1912a).

| 1991 | 1992 | 1993 | 1994 | 1995 | 1996 | 1997 | 1998 |
|------|------|------|------|------|------|------|------|
| 8    | 10   | 9    | 8    | 7    | 6    | 6    | 5    |

Great Tit CBC Pair Totals – 16-ha Lunnon Farm, St Mary's 1991–98 (P J Robinson – unpublished data)

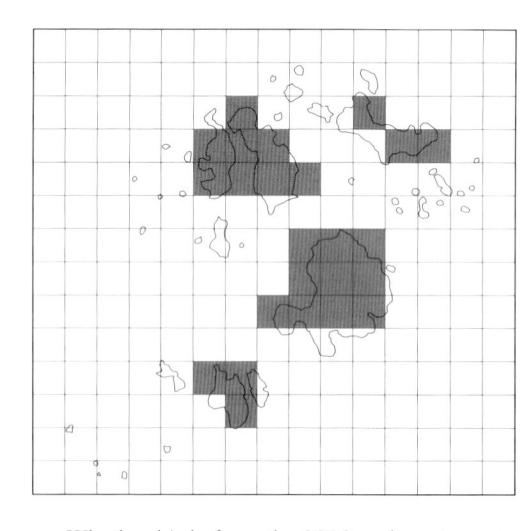

| Island | Pairs |
|--------|-------|
| St Mary's | 55 |
| Tresco | 13 |
| Bryher | 4 |
| St Martin's | 6 |
| St Agnes & Gugh | 3 |

2000 Breeding Bird Atlas – Great Tit (Chown & Lock 2002)

1-km Great Tit Breeding Distribution – 2000–01 (data Chown & Lock 2002)

Whether birds from the 1910 or later irruptions remained behind in Scilly is unclear, but breeding seems to have commenced between then and the 1940s. As early as 1924 it was considered 'not uncommon' on St Mary's, Tresco and Bryher (Boyd 1924). The year before H W Robinson (1923) had reported three pairs with young on St Mary's, and Wallis (1923) had heard and seen it on St Mary's, Tresco and Tean. In 1938 there came a report of several seen on St Mary's during June, including a family party, others being seen on Tresco and St Martin's (*CBWPSAR* 8). By 1946 it was thought to be breeding regularly, including abundantly in drystone walls on St Mary's (Ryves & Quick 1946). That aside, the continued occasional mass arrival doubtless had the potential to boost the breeding population, as in the irruption year of 1957, when up to 70 daily were present on St Agnes during early October (Cramp *et al.* 1960).

Today, Great Tit clearly breeds in substantial numbers on the five main islands, though estimating totals has proved difficult. Great Tit numbers recorded on the 16-hectare Lunnon Farm study plot during the ten years 1991–98 (Table) varied between ten and five pairs, mean of 7.3, with some suggestion of a decline during that same period. Maximum pair density was one every 1.6 hectares, with a low of one per 3.2 hectares. Although nestboxes were erected on the plot from about 1993, this was not thought to affect numbers overall, even though most boxes were occupied from year one, birds presumably moving from natural sites to the more secure boxes. Average clutch size varied somewhat between years, but on average seemed comparable with populations in southern England (Cramp *et al.* 1977–94).

During eight breeding surveys on St Agnes between 1957 and 1978, a maximum of 12 and a minimum of two pairs were recorded, and a mean of 5.6. In comparison, the recent 2000 Breeding Bird Atlas (Chown & Lock 2002) recorded an estimated 81 possible pairs in 24 (35.8%) of the 67 1-km squares surveyed, all confined to the five inhabited islands. Addressing the possibility of under-recording, the authors thought a figure of 100 pairs a more realistic proposition. However, breeding was proved in just 12 squares and the 55 pairs on St Mary's represented 70% of the total, perhaps reflecting the close relationship between this species and urbanisation, or what passes for urbanisation on Scilly.

Even more difficult than assessing the breeding population is measuring the extent, if any, of seasonal movement through the islands, any such movements perhaps being limited, or mainly limited to irruption years. Many *IOSBR*s include comments such as those for 1977 and 1979, i.e. 'No indication of passage this year', whereas in 1978 there was 'Indication of a small passage in October'. This last was based largely on an increase on St Agnes from eight to 25 birds between 7th and 15th of that month and took no account of any increase in the Scillonian population through local productivity, or the species' inclination to flock at the end of the breeding season. Even less helpful are comments such as 'a small influx' noted on such and such a date, but without supporting data, though for 1991 this was based partly on up to eight seen flying from Gugh to St Mary's. Similarly, the suggestion of an influx during October 1992 was based on 20+ seen on the St Mary's Garrison.

Examination of all annual reports for the 25 years from 1975 shows no obvious evidence of passage and no evidence of an invasion. The only possibility of either concerns the report of 120–150 daily on St Mary's during late September 1976, with about 30 present daily on St Agnes (*IOSBR* 1976). On the Lunnon Farm plot all Great and Blue Tit pulli and all trapped adults were ringed during the eight-year study, during which time the only birds recaptured from elsewhere originated from other ringing sites within the islands. During 1997, 85 Great Tits were either newly ringed or recaptured on the plot from previous years, mostly during the two winter periods, during which time feeding stations were maintained.

Great Tit is resident over much of its southern and central European range and is an irregular irruptive migrant elsewhere. British and Irish *newtoni* seldom move far, post-fledging dispersal being normally measured in hundreds of metres rather than kilometres (Cramp *et al.* 1977–94); post-fledging recovery distance varies with age but at its greatest 95% were within 52 km (Wernham *et al.* 2002). Over 80% of British and Irish ringing recoveries moved under 10 km, though the remainder included birds moving as far as the Netherlands and Lithuania, the latter perhaps a returning individual from a past irruption. The last major irruption involving Britain and Ireland was that of 1957 referred to above. There is also evidence to suggest that most birds involved in irruptions may be first-years. A total of 641 Great Tits were ringed in Scilly up until 1999, 500 (78%) since 1970 and the only recaptures involve locally ringed individuals.

## Treecreeper (Eurasian Treecreeper) *Certhia familiaris* A

**Very rare migrant, full written description required by the SRP.**

 1961 One Parsonage, St Agnes 8th October
 1975 One St Mary's & St Martin's 11th to 14th October
 1986 One St Mary's 20th October
 1987 One Tresco 14th to 18th October
 1988 Two Tresco 30th September, one 10th to 17th October

Surprisingly widespread west European breeding range encompassing almost all countries north of

Mediterranean and Black Sea, through eastern Europe and Asia to Pacific, marginally north into Arctic coastlands and south to Himalayas. Northerly populations at least partially migratory. Polytypic: nominate *familiaris*, or 'Northern Treecreeper', occurs northern Europe east to central Russia; *britannica* Britain and Ireland; *macrodactyla* continental western Europe, including France and east to the former Czechoslovakia. Additional forms further east and on Corsica. National 41% increase 1994–99 (Bashford & Noble 2000).

Treecreeper has apparently never been anything but a rarity on Scilly, regardless of the fact that it always seems to have bred commonly on the Cornish mainland. E H Rodd (1880) described it as a hardy little bird, apparently generally distributed, though not on Scilly, and Clark & Rodd (1906) confirmed its absence from the islands, stating there had been 'no certain record'. Therefore, it is not surprising that Ryves & Quick (1946) failed to mention it in their 1946 summary of breeding birds, though they too confirmed its widespread but somewhat scarce distribution in Cornwall.

Therefore, the entire history of this species on Scilly is confined to six individuals in five different years since 1961, with none present outside a narrow 20-day window commencing 30th September and with a mean arrival date of 10th October. This all points to involvement in some regular autumn movement of birds from an as yet unknown origin. Penhallurick (1978) referred to additional sightings of the 1961 bird on St Agnes and St Mary's and suggested that it was trapped, but provided no further information and no Treecreepers appear to have been ringed on Scilly. Nevertheless, it is interesting that on Scilly Treecreeper is much less frequent than Short-toed Lark *Calandrella brachydactyla*, Subalpine Warbler *Sylvia cantillans* or Woodchat Shrike *Lanius senator*, among others; and far less frequent even than several extreme British rarities, e.g. Common Nighthawk *Chordeiles minor*, Blackpoll Warbler *Dendroica striata*, Penduline Tit *Remiz pendulinus* and Bobolink *Dolichonyx oryzivorus*.

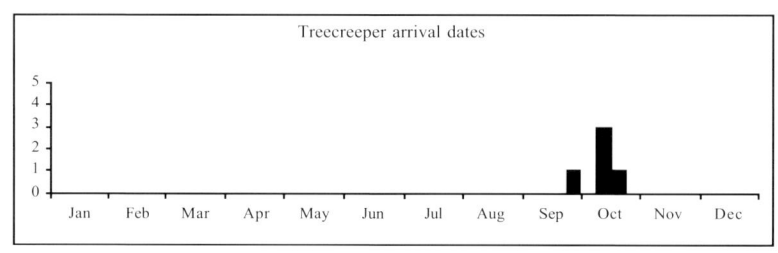

Treecreeper arrival dates

The Chart incorporates all five arrival dates. Assuming that observers involved took all necessary steps to eliminate the possibility of Short-toed Treecreeper *C. brachydactyla*, we are left with three probable choices to explain the presence of Treecreepers on Scilly: they could be *britannica* from Britain or Ireland, true *familiaris* migrants from perhaps Norway or Sweden, or short-distance *macrodactyla* migrants from nearby continental Europe. According to both Cramp *et al.* (1977–94) and Wernham *et al.* (2002), British birds are unlikely to move far, though occasional exceptional movements of up to 200 km are on record, but visitors to Britain mostly involve *familiaris*, especially in Scotland. Continental birds appear to move even less, though again there are exceptions. However, the arrival of Treecreepers in Scilly only during late September or October must be viewed against the frequent arrival during this same period of extralimital vagrants from very much further east than might be expected. Wernham *et al.* also draw attention to evidence suggestive of eastern European Treecreepers (or birds from even further away) arriving in association with other more obvious migrants, though up until 1997 there had been no ringing recoveries. Gantlett (1998) too drew attention to the possibility of the nearest two Continental forms reaching Britain. In addition, of course, the possibility of Short-toed Treecreeper reaching Scilly must be kept constantly in mind. There are no recaptures from elsewhere.

# Penduline Tit
## (Eurasian Penduline Tit) *Remiz pendulinus* A BBRC 11.7%

Rare migrant, full written description required by the BBRC.

    1977    One (first-year) St Agnes 25th October    British Birds 72: 483–484, 539
    1988    One (first-year) St Agnes & St Mary's 17th & 18th October    British Birds 82: 553, 90: 503
    1988    One (first-year) St Mary's 18th October    British Birds 82: 553, 90: 503

1989  Two (adult & first-year) St Mary's 24th October, adult to 27th  *British Birds* 83: 485
1990  Three (male, female & first-year) Tresco 17th & 18th October  *British Birds* 85: 546
1993  Two (male & first-year) Tresco 15th to 28th October  *British Birds* 87: 559–560
1994  Three (first-years) Tresco 20th August to 21st October  *British Birds* 88: 542–543
1995  Two (first-year plus one) Tresco 8th to 15th November  *British Birds* 90: 503
1997  One (first-year) Tresco 28th October  *British Birds* 91: 510
1997  One St Mary's 7th & 8th November  *British Birds* 91: 510

Breeds locally Spain, France, Italy, Denmark east across central Eurasia into China, south to Iran and Afghanistan. Currently increasing in north of range but decreasing in south. Migratory in north of range, with West Palearctic birds moving mainly south or southwest in winter, whereas those further east winter south to Iraq and northwest India. Polytypic with complex racial structure: split into three distinct groups, most westerly of which is *pendulinus* group, for which Cramp *et al.* (1977–94) recognise four forms, including nominate *pendulinus* from western and southern Europe east to central European Russia and western Asia Minor.

This is one of those species that commenced its appearances in Britain quite recently and so gets no mention in earlier Scillonian literature, the first record coming from Spurn, Humberside, in October 1966, but becoming annual since 1980 (Palmer 2000). The first Scillonian record involved a first-year individual on St Agnes on 25th October 1977, representing only the second in Britain and Ireland (Dukes 1979; *British Birds* 72: 539). In total there have been 17 birds in eight different years and of the 15 that were aged by their observers, 11 (73%) were in their first-year. Tresco accounted for 11 (61%) individuals plus three out of four multiple visits. Only one individual visited two islands. Earliest arrival date was 20th August and no bird remained beyond 15th November, the August arrival being exceptionally early by comparison and involving particularly long-staying individuals. A total of 145 Penduline Tits were recorded in Britain and Ireland from 1966 to the end of 1999, Scilly accounting for 11.7% of these. Evans (1994) analysed the minimum of 55 records up to 1990, showing that some 50% occurred in southeast England, around 20% in East Anglia and around 14% in southwest England. Group arrivals were an obvious feature and, as expected, numbers dropped significantly towards the north and northwest.

It may be no coincidence that most Penduline Tits chose either Tresco or St Mary's, both of which contain areas of habitat typical of that occupied elsewhere. Therefore, should we perhaps be looking ahead in anticipation to the addition of a new breeding species for both the islands and for Britain? There has been at least one published breeding attempt already, involving a male that took up territory at a site in Kent in 1990 and built two nests, though it failed to attract a female (Evans 1994).

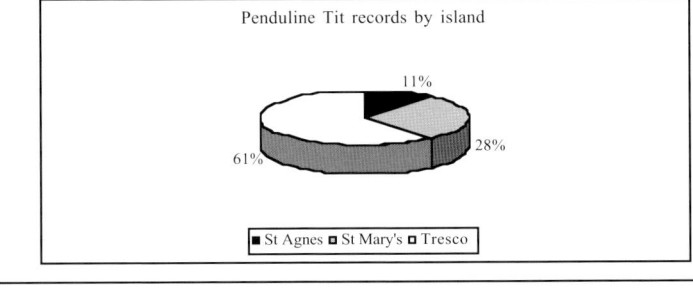

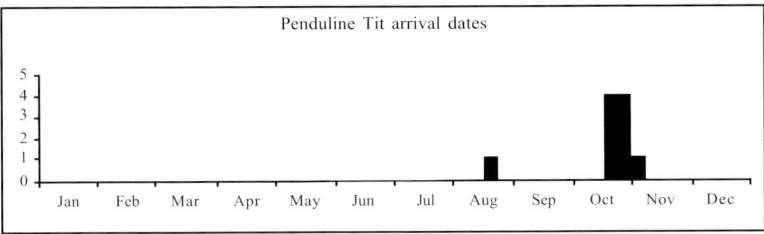

Penduline Tit records by island
St Agnes 11%
St Mary's 28%
Tresco 61%

Penduline Tit arrival dates

The recent noticeable westwards range extension has resulted in marked changes to migration patterns. Ringing data show that most birds from central European populations winter in southwest Europe, including western France and southern Portugal, east to southern Italy; reportedly with 'large numbers' in Atlantic coastal France. Birds normally migrate in small groups of around three to ten but occasionally up to 40. Specific ringing movements cited include birds ringed in the Camargue in southern France in winter and recovered northeast to Poland, but with large numbers also recorded moving between northeast Spain and eastern Germany (Cramp *et al.* 1977–94). Cramp *et al.* also mention 'invasion-like' movements into western Europe being first recorded in 1961. In Scandinavia, dispersal of young birds commences mid-July with adults moving south from September, most having left Sweden by mid-October. Most if not all arrivals on Scilly can be expected to involve the nominate form *pendulinus* but the possibility of other forms from much further east also reaching the islands presumably cannot be dismissed. No Penduline Tits have been trapped on Scilly.

## Golden Oriole (Eurasian Golden Oriole) *Oriolus oriolus* A

Annual migrant in small numbers, largely in spring. Treated by the BBRC as a national Scarce Migrant.

Breeds central and southern Europe and extreme northwest Africa, from Morocco, Iberia, France and eastern England east into central Asia and then south to Himalayas and northern India. Polytypic: nominate *oriolus* occurs Europe and North Africa east to central Asia; *kundoo* central Asia south through Afghanistan to India. *Oriolus* migratory, wintering tropical and southern Africa, *kundoo* partially migratory, wintering India. Amber-listed in UK: five-year mean of 25.5 breeding pairs (Gregory *et al.* 2002).

Probably more 19th-century ink was expended on this species than on any other visiting the islands, the volume of reports amounting to a minor obsession among some early writers, undoubtedly due to the combination of Golden Oriole's rarity as a British species and its flamboyant plumage. Earliest mention of it in Scilly seems to be North's record of singing males obtained on Tresco in 1848 and 1849 (North 1850). James Clark and E H Rodd's nephew Francis considered it an almost annual spring migrant to the islands, mostly to Tresco but also in the Holy Vale area of St Mary's (Clark & Rodd 1906). These two authors pointed out that towards the end of the 1800s a Rev. F D Astley heard up to five singing birds in the area of Tresco Abbey, though they thought it usually occurred singly. However, they were unclear on its autumn frequency, noting only that Francis and Augustus Pechell once unsuccessfully pursued a bird on St Martin's at that time of year. The first of many letters by the elder Rodd to the *Zoologist* came a few years after North's account (Rodd 1861b), several regrettably referring to 'specimens' having been obtained (e.g. Rodd 1869b, 1870f, 1871b, 1875), as in spring 1865, when several were reported in Tresco's Abbey gardens, three of which were 'obtained' (Rodd 1880).

The frequency with which Golden Oriole occurred during spring, its regularity in Tresco's Abbey gardens and the regular appearance of apparent pairs led E H Rodd to the view it might have nested, had in been 'left unmolested', even though he was a main recipient of Scillonian specimens. Nonetheless, there is no evidence that it ever even attempted to breed. Although Golden Oriole was not unknown on mainland Cornwall, E H Rodd considered Scilly the favoured southwest locality, birds normally appearing around the end of April or the first week of May and occurring less frequently in early June (Rodd 1880). Perhaps correctly, E H Rodd attributed the concentration of records on Tresco to the presence there or a mixture of evergreen plantations and exotic shrubs, the remainder of the islands being mostly treeless at that time. The first dated occurrence on mainland Cornwall involved a bird obtained near St Austell during March 1824 (Penhallurick 1978), the same author mentioning one taken aboard a fishing boat during late May 1835.

During his mid-20th century review Penhallurick found no convincing autumn records for either Scilly or the Cornish mainland, at least some of the claimed early winter mainland reports being attributed to Green Woodpecker *Picus viridis*. Penhallurick also noted a shortage of early 20th-century records from Scilly. He pointed out, however, that comments by A A Dorrien-Smith during the 1940s made it clear that there had been no change in the regularity of its appearance in the islands since Clark and Rodd's summary. He also made the comment that, with the exception of 1959, it had been recorded annually since 1954, most arriving in May but also commonly during April. Extreme dates were 31st March and 19th June, the exception being an out-of-season individual singing on Tresco during July 1971.

During the ten years 1990–99, it occurred in every year during spring, four times during July or August and once in autumn. Average annual spring totals were around 30, though in good years deciding an overall figure proved difficult. This was the case in 1992, when there were two ten-bird days (16th and 22nd May) and 99 sightings during the 19 days 13th to 31st May. Although there were the expected exceptions, first arrival dates fell into the clear pattern of the last week of April to the first week of May, last sighting dates falling largely between 3rd and 23rd June. More difficult to explain were birds on 2nd, 17th and 28th July plus one on 10th August. A bird on St Mary's from 7th to 21st October 1991 provided the latest date ever recorded for Scilly. Previous autumn records involve two in October 1977, one in September 1980 and one in October 1981.

Spring passage extends further west than in autumn, males preceding females by several days. Spring passage also occurs later than for many species, birds returning to their breeding grounds from late April or May, numbers peaking in southern and central Europe during early May (Cramp *et al.* 1977–94). There has been a dramatic increase in spring records since 1964 and the pattern of south- and east-coast bias to spring sightings is indicative of overshooting Continental migrants, Kent and Scilly receiving the lion's share (Dymond *et al.* 1989). Four Golden Orioles have been ringed in Scilly, three of these since 1970 but there are no recaptures from elsewhere.

# Brown Shrike *Lanius cristatus* A  BBRC 0.0%

**Extremely rare migrant, full written description required by the BBRC.**

2001   One (first-winter) Bryher 24th to 28th September   *British Birds* 94: plate 345, 95: 516

Breeds northeast Asia, from Ob River east to Sea of Okhotsk and Japan. Long-distance migrant; nominate *cristatus* winters Indian subcontinent, remaining three forms Southeast Asia. Polytypic: *cristatus* occurs northeast Asia and northern Mongolia; *confusus* southeast Russia northern Manchuria and eastern Mongolia; *lucionensis* Korea and China; *superciliosus* Sakhalin to Japan. Formerly considered conspecific with Red-backed Shrike *L. collurio*.

A first-winter *Lanius* on Bryher for five days during September 2001 was initially identified as a Red-backed Shrike *L. collurio*, but later correctly attributed to the present species using colour photographs and video footage pasted onto the Internet after the bird had departed (Lawson 2001). This was the first English record and the fourth for Britain and Ireland, previous individuals occurring at Grutness, Shetland, in September–October 1985; Ballyferriter, Co. Kerry, Ireland, in November 1999; and Fair Isle, Shetland, on 21st October 2000.

The bird was discovered in fields alongside the road leading from the town towards Hell Bay Hotel, initially affording only brief views but being well photographed nevertheless, before moving about the island and coming to rest near Fraggle Rock Café. During the period following its discovery on 24th and its departure on 28th September, it was seen by a number of local and visiting birders, none of which apparently questioned its identity as Red-backed Shrike. The photographs first appeared on the Internet on 1st October, but it was probably not until 5th October that the decision was made to announce it as Britain and Ireland's fourth Brown Shrike, and therefore a new species for Scilly. The bird's somewhat pale underside but warmly toned upperparts, particularly the crown, are all thought suggestive of it being nominate *cristatus*.

## Isabelline Shrike *Lanius isabellinus* A BBRC 5.66%

**Extremely rare migrant, a full written description required by the BBRC.**

1978 One St Agnes & Gugh 26th to 28th October  *British Birds* 73: 525, 82: 553
1980 One (probable *isabellinus*) St Mary's & Gugh 3rd October to 8th November
*British Birds* 82: 553
1991 One St Mary's 12th October  *British Birds* 85: 547
2002 *One (first-winter isabellinus) St Mary's 18th to 22nd October  British Birds 95: 669*

Taxonomic complexities surrounding *isabellinus* shrikes have still to be resolved, some authorities favouring treating the different forms as full species. But as that view has not yet been adopted by the BOURC, they are treated here as a single species, Isabelline Shrike, following Worfolk (2000). In general, Isabelline Shrike occurs to the south of both Red-backed *L. collurio* and Brown Shrike *L. cristatus*. Polytypic: *phoenicuroides*, or 'Turkestan Shrike' (treated by some authorities as a full species) occurs Kazakhstan to Iran (wintering Arabian Peninsula and Africa south of Sahara); nominate *isabellinus*, or 'Daurian Shrike' Mongolia and northwest China (wintering with *phoenicuroides*); *arenarius* northwest Mongolia (wintering northwest India, Pakistan and Iran); *tsaidamensis* northern China (wintering range unclear).

There have been just three Scillonian records of what even by mainland standards remains a very rare bird. The BBRC accepted only 53 sightings during the period 1953 to the end of 1999 and therefore the three Scillonian records represent not quite 6% of the British total. There was just a single British and Irish sighting prior to 1953 involving a bird on the Isle of May, Fife, in September 1950 (Palmer 2000).

The 1978 bird was initially discovered on St Agnes and described by its finders as an 'odd-looking pale shrike', before being refound on Gugh the same day and tentatively identified as perhaps Red-backed Shrike. By the time the *IOSBR* for 1978 went to press, BBRC were still awaiting a written description and for reasons that are unclear now, the record did not finally appear in print until publication of the 1988 report, together with brief details of the individual on St Mary's in 1980. Sadly, the report describing the appearance of Scilly's third Isabelline Shrike, in October 1991, is equally lacking in detail (*IOSBR* 1988, 1991). The Chart includes only the first three of the tabled records.

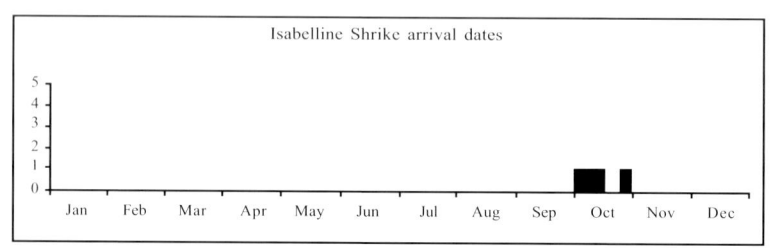

Isabelline Shrike arrival dates

According to Gantlett (1998), in most cases where the origin of British adult Isabelline Shrikes was determined, they were attributed to the form *phoenicuroides*. However, Evans (1994) suggested that subspecific identification may also involve *isabellinus* or 'Daurian Shrike' and at least one Scillonian bird was thought to be of this form, with another, still to be accepted,s on St Agnes and Gugh during autumn 2002 being even more likely. The form *phoenicuroides* breeds Kazakhstan to Iran, whereas *isabellinus* breeds further north and east, in Mongolia and northwest China, though both move southwest to winter in the southern Arabian Peninsula and Africa south of the Sahara (Worfolk 2000). Birds migrating west or southwest in autumn from east Asian populations, e.g. *isabellinus*, might perhaps have the greatest chance of reaching Britain. Dymond *et al.* (1989) considered the pattern of British autumn arrivals typical of that for eastern vagrants as a whole, suggesting that birds arrive across the North Sea and then perhaps move southwest, rather than arriving in Scilly or Cornwall by a direct route.

## Red-backed Shrike *Lanius collurio* A

Scarce spring and autumn migrant. Treated by the BBRC as a national Scarce Migrant.

Breeds Eurasia, from northern Spain and France north to southern Norway and Sweden, east to central Siberia and south to the northern Mediterranean, Turkey and Caspian Sea. Long-distance migrant, wintering Africa south from Angola and southern Tanzania (Worfolk 2000). Monotypic or polytypic: nominate *collurio* occurs Europe to western Siberia and south to Mediterranean, former Yugoslavia and northern Caucasus; some authorities also recognise *kobylini* Caucasus south to Cyprus, Asia Minor and Iran; with *pallidifrons* further east. Included on Annex I of 1979 EEC 'Birds Directive'. Red-listed in UK: historical population decline; rapid, 90% breeding decline over past 25 years and 86% contraction of breeding range over past 30 years; five-year mean of 4.8 breeding pairs; unfavourable world conservation status (Gregory *et al.* 2002).

Earliest reference to this species in Scilly is probably E H Rodd's letter to the *Zoologist* describing one present during late October or early November 1867 (Rodd 1868d). This was followed by a similar letter three years later regarding an immature seen in Tresco's Abbey Gardens on 22nd September (Rodd 1870l). Clearly, though, it was far from common in the islands during the 19th century, James Clark and E H Rodd's nephew Francis describing it as a rare autumn visitor by the early 1900s (Clark & Rodd 1906). These two also pointed out that it had occasionally been shot by Augustus Pechell and reported about six timed by Francis Rodd and other observers, 'probably always in immature plumage'. The most recent individual Clark and Rodd knew of had been shot in Holy Vale, St Mary's, in November 1905. However, it is interesting that in his important work on *The Birds of Cornwall and The Scilly Islands* (Rodd 1880) the elder Rodd described it as occurring in summer, though he did not think it bred. This was despite it appearing to be clear that Red-backed Shrike was something of a rarity as a breeding species in Cornwall, or at least in west Cornwall (Penhallurick 1978) at this time.

Penhallurick's mid-1970's review of Scillonian and Cornish records highlighted the shortage of early 20th-century information from Scilly, though it had been regularly reported since 1951 and annually since 1961. Spring records, however, were few. The earliest autumn record quoted by Penhallurick involved one at Lelant, mainland Cornwall, on 4th August, with the latest on St Agnes on 28th October 1970. The same author made the point that surprisingly few published reports provided details of the age or sex involved, though most appeared to have been juveniles.

The Chart shows spring and autumn Scillonian Red-backed Shrike totals for the 25 years since 1975, these apparently reflecting the decrease in numbers throughout western Europe during this same period (Cramp *et al.* 1977–94), whilst also suggesting an increase in spring records, though this last may at least partly reflect recent increased spring observer coverage. The highest autumn total was 13 in 1978, this also equalling the highest annual total in 1991 (two in spring and eleven in autumn). Birds arrived during spring in only 15 years (60%), though in all but one since 1991, the highest spring total being four in 1992, followed by three each in 1998–99. Taking the ten years from 1990, spring birds were present during the period 12th April to 1st June, but most frequently during the second half of May. During autumn, birds were to be seen between the third week of August and early November, first arrival dates varied between 16th August and 26th September. The latest any bird remained over the 25 years was 11th November in 1991.

Red-backed Shrike is a classic 'loop' migrant, returning spring birds following a more easterly route than in autumn, with few crossing the Mediterranean at its western end in any event (Cramp *et al.* 1977–94). Birds commence leaving their European breeding grounds from late July, mid-August seeing the bulk of any movement in central European latitudes, though in western and northern England records peak during September. Some authorities attribute early British autumn records to random post-fledging dispersal and later arrivals to reverse migration. The suggestion is, therefore, that most late migrant Red-backed Shrikes reaching Scilly do so from populations to the south or southeast of Britain. In early spring most northward

*Birds of the Isles of Scilly*

*Red-backed Shrike annual totals*

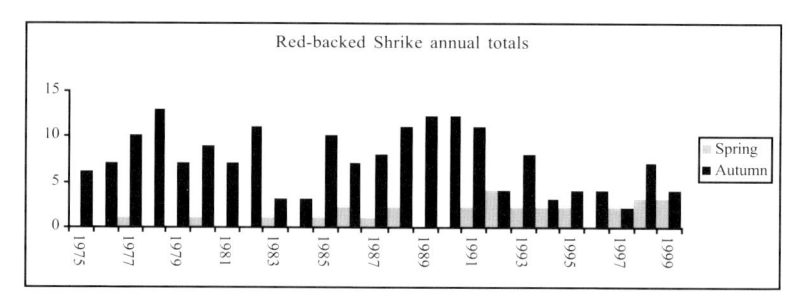

movement occurs through East Africa, most Red-backed Shrikes entering Europe through the Middle East. Early birds reach northern Europe by mid-May, some at least of any British spring records being attributable to overshooting. Two Red-backed Shrikes were ringed in Scilly prior to 1970; there are no recaptures.

## Lesser Grey Shrike *Lanius minor* A BBRC 0.78%

**Very rare migrant, full written description required by the BBRC.**

- 1851   One (female) shot St Mary's 16th November   Rodd 1851e, 1867e
- 1925   One shot Tresco 15th September   Penhallurick 1978; Abbey Records
- 1951   One found injured and released Tresco 20th August   Penhallurick 1978; Abbey Records
- 1955   One St Agnes 28th September   *CBWPSAR* 25
- 1956   One (first-year) Bryher 25th September   *CBWPSAR* 26
- 1956   One (female) St Mary's 29th & 30th September   *CBWPSAR* 26
- 1976   One St Mary's 28th May   *British Birds* 70: 439

Main breeding population central Europe east to western Siberia and south to Italy, Balkans and Afghanistan, with small scattered isolated populations further west into northern Spain, France, Germany, etc. Winters tropical Africa south of equator. Monotypic.

There has been a total of seven records in Scilly. The first was thought at the time to be the first for Britain and Ireland – a bird shot by Augustus Pechell on St Mary's in 1851 (Rodd 1867e). This record was later upstaged following the discovery in Lord Malmesbury's collection of a skin obtained in Dorset in 1842 (Palmer 2000). There were subsequently 32 recorded in Britain up until 1957, with Scilly accounting for 18.7% of these, and 128 in the period 1958 to the end of 1999, with the single Scillonian record accounting for less than one percent.

E H Rodd gave a detailed summary of the circumstances surrounding his identification of the 1851 individual, which he originally recorded in the *Zoologist* as Great Grey Shrike *L. excubitor* (Rodd 1851e). He later realised his mistake and forwarded the skin to Gould at the British Museum, who identified it as a first-year Lesser Grey Shrike, it having previously been confirmed as a female by dissection (Rodd 1880). For a while, however, Rodd and his friend the Reverend John Jenkinson entertained the idea it might have been Loggerhead Shrike *L. ludovicianus* from North America, a surprisingly adventurous line of thinking for the mid-1880s. The 1951 individual also occurred in unusual circumstances, being found in distress in a Tresco water butt on 20th August and released apparently none the worse for the experience.

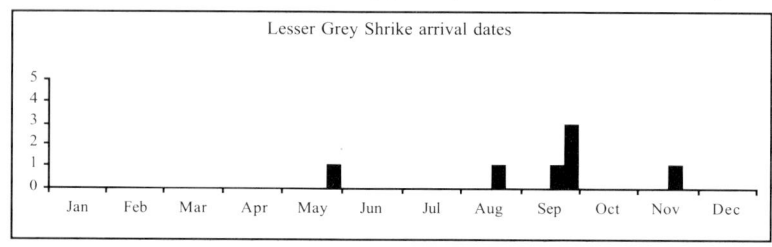

*Lesser Grey Shrike arrival dates*

Apart from the autumn 1925 individual, which was shot on Tresco, and the previously mentioned individual, all remaining records involved field sightings, including an amazing two just four days apart, but clearly separable from each other by distinctive plumage features.

By 1989, annual Lesser Grey Shrike records had declined nationally from a peak during the late 1960s and early 1970s, and that situation seems to be reflected in the lack of records in the islands since the last in 1976. Most British records come from Shetland, coastal Scotland and the English east and south coasts and the suggestion is that birds arriving in Britain originate from eastern Europe, rather than from closer populations (Dymond *et al.* 1989). The species went unrecorded on the Cornish mainland until one near Mevagissey on 8th September 1958 (Penhallurick 1978).

## Great Grey Shrike *Lanius excubitor* A

**Very rare migrant. Treated by the BBRC as a national Scarce Migrant, full written description required by the SRP.**

    1966   One Tresco 20th & 21st October
    1969   One Porth Hellick, St Mary's 8th to 13th February
    1972   One St Agnes 20th & 21st October
    1974   One Garrison, St Mary's 9th October
    1975   One Bryher 31st October
    1976   One Peninnis, St Mary's 28th May
    1978   One Wingletang, St Agnes 19th October
    1998   One Porthloo Lane, Airport and Porth Hellick, St Mary's 5th & 6th October

Widespread, including North America. Until recently recognised as comprising two groups, with *excubitor* group northern Eurasia and North America; *meridionalis* group southern Europe, southwest Asia and North Africa. Since 1997, BOURC have treated the latter group as a separate species, Southern Grey Shrike *L. meridionalis* (BOURC 1997). Great Grey Shrike breeds northwest Europe except British Isles, France and southern Scandinavia east to Pacific and south to Kazakhstan and Mongolia, but some overlap with Southern Grey Shrike. Northerly populations entirely migratory, birds from West Palearctic perhaps reaching Mediterranean. Polytypic: nominate *excubitor* occurs Europe and west Siberia; *homeyeri* southeast Europe and west Asia; *leucopterus* central Siberia; *sibiricus* east Siberia and Mongolia. At least three additional forms further east, plus two in arctic Canada and Alaska that winter in central North America from Atlantic to Pacific (Clement 1995).

A total of eight documented records make this species almost as rare in Scilly as Lesser Grey Shrike *L. minor*, though unlike that species all confirmed Great Grey Shrike records occurred since 1960 and all involved field sightings. As with so many apparent 'vagrant' species in Scilly, there is a clear pattern to arrival dates, only one individual giving the appearance of being a winter wanderer and just one in the early part of the year. All six autumn arrival dates fell within the 26-day window 5th to 31st October, with an average stay of just 1.5 days enforcing the view they were on the move, even the late winter individual remaining only five days.

Unfortunately the historical position is far from clear, with no record of a specimen having been obtained but with a clear inference in the literature to Great Grey Shrike having been a scarce but regular 19th-century visitor. This mainly takes the form of a comment by the experienced collector of Scillonian rarities, Francis Rodd, who in his *Notes from Scilly for 1870–71* (Rodd 1880) remarked that (among various other passerines) 'Red-backed and Grey Shrikes, seem either to have avoided the islands altogether, or have appeared only in solitary instances'. However, he refers to grey shrikes in the plural and by that time E H Rodd had succeeded in identifying the only 'grey' shrike thus far seen on Scilly as Lesser Grey Shrike *L. minor*. But in their *Zoologist* review of *The Birds of Scilly*, Clark and Francis Rodd (1906) refer to an 1871 manuscript note by E H Rodd stating that Great Grey Shrike had been both observed and shot by Augustus Pechell 'generally as birds of the year'.

However, we know that Great Grey Shrike occurred far more commonly on the Cornish mainland than its smaller relative: Penhallurick (1978) listed some ten records up until 1960, the earliest in 1828, with just one Lesser Grey Shrike on the mainland during the same period. In total, Penhallurick lists some 28 Great Grey Shrike records for the Cornish mainland up to 1976, compared with just six on Scilly. He also found that, unlike Scilly, only half the dates involved fell within October or November, the remainder occurring mostly in winter, though a bird near Mullion on 2nd June 1928 is noteworthy.

According to Cramp *et al.* (1977–94) most Scandinavian *excubitor* move southwest to winter in central and west-central Europe, with from 30 to 140 evenly distributed individuals (many from Norway) within the British Isles annually (Wernham *et al.* 2002). Apart from those birds coming from Norway, there is ringing evidence linking Britain with Denmark, Belgium and the German Bight (Wernham *et al.* 2002). The slightly less migratory *homeyeri* withdraws inwards to winter in the centre and south of its breeding range, south to Iran, and there is little evidence thus far of it occurring in extreme western Europe (Clement 1995).

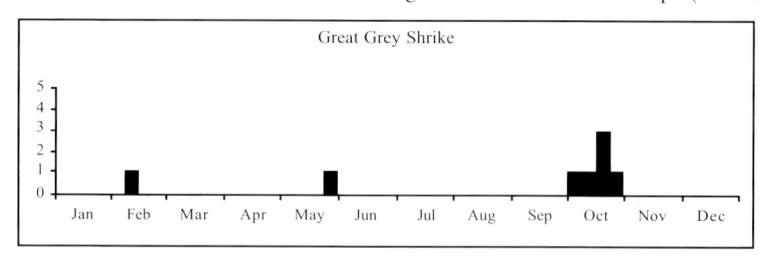

Great Grey Shrike

Of considerable relevance to any debate on the origin of large grey shrikes in Scilly in autumn is the northeastern form of Southern Grey Shrike *pallidirostris*, or 'Steppe Grey Shrike'. This is a long-distance migrant which almost completely deserts its southern-Eurasian breeding grounds in autumn and winters west to northeast Africa, which as Clement points out, places it within the winter range of Isabelline Shrike *L. isabellinus*, which has already reached Scilly. A number of Southern Grey Shrikes have already been recorded in Britain, at sites as widely separated as Fair Isle, Suffolk, Wiltshire, Dorset and, more importantly, Cornwall. In addition, it has occurred in the Netherlands, Germany, Norway and Sweden. Presumably, then, the message is to pay careful attention to any large grey shrike putting in an appearance in Scilly and be prepared to move swiftly, as it may not stay long. On balance it is likely to be the *excubitor* form of Great Grey Shrike, but there is the possibility of *pallidirostris* or even *homeyeri* forms of Southern Grey Shrike. We should perhaps also not close our minds entirely to the possibility of wandering individuals of the *meridionalis* form of Southern Grey Shrike also reaching Scilly from southern France or Iberia. Spring arrivals, such as the 1976 individual, perhaps deserve special scrutiny. No Great Grey Shrikes have been trapped on Scilly. A dried wing found on Tresco in spring 1967 could have represented the remains of the October 1966 individual (*CBWPSAR* 36).

# Woodchat Shrike *Lanius senator* A

**Scarce annual migrant in about equal proportions during spring and autumn. Treated by the BBRC as a national Scarce Migrant, full written description required by the SRP. Scilly is probably the most likely site in Britain at which to see this species.**

Mainly confined to southern half of West Palearctic, all populations winter sub-Saharan Africa north of equator. Polytypic: nominate *senator* occurs south to Pyrenees, Italy, Greece and western Turkey; *rutilans* Iberia and northwest Africa; *badius*, or 'Balearic Woodchat Shrike', Balearic Islands, Corsica and Sardinia; *niloticus* Cyprus, Levant and eastern Asia Minor to Iran. Removed from BBRC Rarities List January 1991 (Lansdown & the Rarities Committee 1990).

This is another species that, if records are to be believed, ceased visiting Scilly for 30 or 40 years around the late 19th and early 20th centuries, for after two good autumns for Woodchat Shrikes in the 1840s, it was not recorded again until the report of a possible pair on St Helen's in May 1946, from which time it became an almost annual visitor. From 1958 the species was included in the list of national rarities considered by BBRC, but was removed from January 1991 owing to the increased volume of reports.

Earliest reference to this species on Scilly is E H Rodd's 1840 mention of it, in his annual *Communication to the Royal Institution of Cornwall*, as having been taken aboard a fishing boat (Rodd 1880), confirmation of this record appearing in a letter to the *Zoologist* (Rodd 1843c). Second mention came in Rodd's account of the September 1849 shooting, by Augustus Pechell, of 'several in immature plumage' (Rodd 1849a, 1880), describing how birds were apparently driven to the islands by a strong easterly wind 'which intercepted their migratory movement southwards, there being good ground for supposing from their condition and plumage that they may have bred somewhere in Great Britain'. In support of this last remark he cited a note by A G More in the *Zoologist* of 1856 describing Woodchat Shrikes breeding on the Isle of Wight in two different years – later to be repeated in *The Handbook* (Witherby *et al.* 1940).

James Clark and Francis Rodd's 1906 *Zoologist* summary of *The Birds of Scilly* described it as a 'very rare accidental visitor', stating it had not been reported in the islands since the Pechell shooting incident of 1849 (Clark & Rodd 1906). The start of a long-running series of records began with a report of two on St Helen's during May 1946 up to the present day. Regrettably, the St Helen's record remains in doubt, in respect both of the species involved and the claim of attempted breeding, though obviously more so on the latter count. According to the observer, identification of the male was certain but the other individual 'might have been a female'. However, any doubts surrounding Woodchat Shrike's occurrence in Scilly were subsequently dispelled with its regular appearance from 1952 onwards, leaving just the identity of the second 1946 bird and the possibility of their attempted breeding at issue. According to the original observer, the male was 'constantly' carrying pieces of grass into a dense bramble bush on the island but, unfortunately, the bush was not examined at the time. Nevertheless, when a more experienced observer visited in June (three or more weeks later) the birds could not be found (*CBWPSAR* 16). Both sexes are known to participate in nest building so presumably the observation cannot be ruled out purely on the basis that the male only was seen carrying what appeared to be nest material (Cramp *et al.* 1977–94). One other possibility, of course, is that the observer mistook prey items for nest material, or even that scraps of grass were carried along with prey items. Regrettably, we will probably never know the truth.

The annual totals Table includes all spring and autumn records for the second half of the 20th century, birds arriving in 43 (86%) of these years, with a spring–autumn ratio of 60:50, unlike mainland Cornwall where spring sightings outnumber those in autumn by 4:1. Individual arrival dates are charted for the years up to and during which Woodchat Shrike was included on the BBRC list (ignoring 19th-century records). During the ten years 1991–99, birds continued to occur at around two to five per year, with a clear tendency towards increased spring numbers and with recognisable peaks in arrival dates in both seasons. Again ignoring the 19th-century records, 86% of all autumn sightings up to and including 1990, where age was determined, involved first-year individuals (75% of all autumn records).

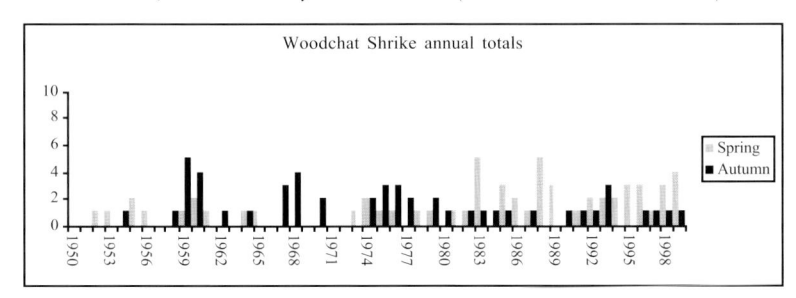

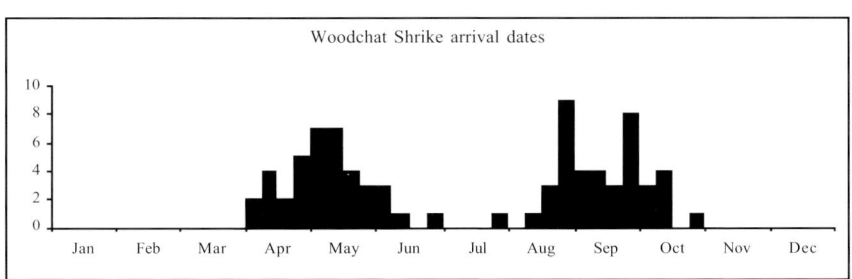

Sharrock (1974) examined all British and Irish Woodchat Shrike records for the ten years 1958–67, pointing out that although he too found roughly equal numbers during both seasons, this conflicted with an earlier finding of greater numbers during spring (Witherby *et al.* 1940). He suggested that the change demonstrated an increased observer ability to separate first-winter Woodchat Shrikes from other closely related species. In an exercise aimed at determining causes of British arrivals, Sharrock attributed spring Woodchat Shrike records to overshooting in anticyclonic conditions, whereas he thought autumn arrivals mainly resulted from random post-breeding dispersal. Certainly, the absence of any single pronounced peak in the spread of autumn arrival dates, such as occurs with some classic long-distance eastern migrants, is suggestive of a more protracted movement. But it remains unclear why so many presumably move north or northwest to reach Britain, as opposed to the broad-front south to southwest heading described by Cramp *et al.* (1977–94). Most birds occurring in Britain or Ireland might be expected to belong to the nominate form *senator*, but with the perhaps obvious likelihood of the form *badius*, or 'Balearic Woodchat Shrike', occurring as overshoots in spring. Unsurprisingly, then, a number of photographs of Woodchat Shrikes taken in Britain have since been examined and the birds identified as *badius*, including those taken in Kent and Norfolk in July and in Gwent in August (Corso 1997). The broad spread of spring arrival dates fits the protracted spring departure from its African winter quarters described by Cramp *et al*. Its earliest presence on mainland Cornwall preceded that on Scilly by some 25 years, the first being shot near Penzance in 1815, to be followed by several seen near Helston in 1928 (Penhallurick 1978).

## Jay (Eurasian Jay) *Garrulus gladarius* A

**Very rare vagrant or migrant, full written description required by the SRP.**

    1961   One St Agnes 29th December
    1964   Three (flying northeast and calling) St Agnes 2nd December
    1991   One Abbey Gardens, Tresco 23rd April
    1993   One Abbey Drive, Tresco 17th May
    1993   One Abbey Woods, Tresco 19th to 25th October

Breeds West Palearctic east through northern Asia to Pacific, including Kamchatka and Japan, with separate population China and Himalayas. Sedentary in west and south of range but migratory or irruptive in north and east. Polytypic, with complex racial structure, divided into several groups with *glandarius* group in west. Nominate *glandarius*, or 'Continental Jay', occurs Fennoscandia and European Russia south to Pyrenees, Alps and Balkans; *rufitergum* Britain and Brittany; *hibernicus* Ireland. Scottish birds show some similarity to *glandarius*. National 15% decline 1994–99 (Bashford & Noble 2000).

Considering this species was common in southwest England in the latter half of the 19th century and breeds now as far west as Land's End, as well as in Ireland and the Channel Islands (Holloway 1996; Gibbons *et al.* 1993), it seems incongruous that there should be just five records from Scilly. This is even more so, of course, once we consider the tendency for northern European populations to periodically irrupt into Britain and central Europe. For though Scilly may lack adequate woodland for Jays to breed in any numbers, the islands have more than proved their ability to attract winter flocks of other corvid species. In addition, of course, any habitat deficiencies would not necessarily explain why they do not reach Scilly, but merely why they might choose not to remain.

E H Rodd was obviously familiar with it in woodlands in both east and west Cornwall, but thought it unknown west of Penzance and made no mention of it in Scilly. At the same time, he pointed out that, like Magpie *Pica pica*, it was 'shot or trapped at every opportunity' (Rodd 1880). In addition, James Clark and Francis Rodd could find no reference to it having occurred in Scilly during their own extensive search of the literature (Clark & Rodd 1906). So, unsurprisingly, it gets no mention either in the 1946 review of the breeding birds of Scilly (Ryves & Quick 1946). However, the authors of the 1946 review refer to a large invasion of Jays into west Cornwall during winter 1923–24 (*British Birds* 18: 164), making the point that this did not 'materially affect resident stock', but then apparently contradicting that statement by suggesting an increase later in breeding pairs in the north of the county, plus a 'spread to the west, where it now breeds thinly'. This presumably means a spread west of Penzance, where Rodd previously knew it to be absent and where of course it still breeds today (Gibbons *et al.* 1993). Well might we wonder, though, why birds from that early invasion, and indeed others, more recently failed to reach Scilly even briefly. There was always the possibility that any Jay arriving in Scilly would have been shot or trapped, especially as it would most probably gravitate to Tresco's wooded areas, which also contain the local Pheasant *Phasianus colchicus* population. But we know from numerous shooting instances involving other species, e.g. Magpie, that we would have read about it in the literature had it occurred.

The British form *rufitergum* is primarily sedentary, some 98% of recoveries involving distances of less than 50 km and much the same applies to *hibernicus* in Ireland, though it inclines towards a southwestern dispersal in winter (Cramp *et al.* 1977–94). Only 5% of British- or Irish-ringed Jays move further than 40 km,

*Crows and Jays*

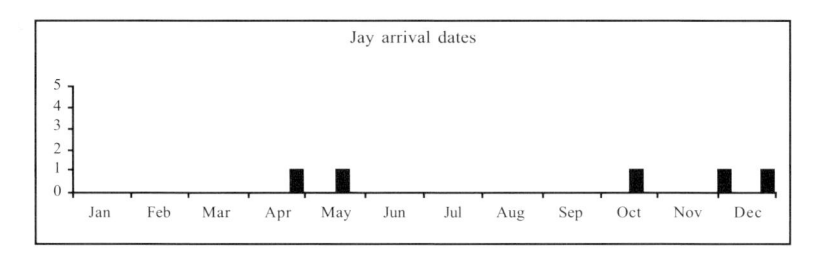

[Chart: Jay arrival dates — bars in May, Oct, Nov, Dec]

the overall mean being less than 1 km (Wernham *et al.* 2002). The northern *glandarius* is prone to large periodic, eruptive, diurnal migrations, very probably influenced by failure of the acorn *Quercus* crop and normally in a west to southwest direction, birds from eastern populations showing a greater westerly orientation. However, a marked feature of these movements is a reluctance to cross water, thus there are few records of sea crossings from Norway or Finland and Swedish records mainly involve 'island-hopping' to Denmark, with sightings on record of birds abandoning attempted sea crossings. Passage birds also rarely reach Heligoland off the coast of northern Germany. Nevertheless there are records of Continental birds reaching Britain and Gantlett (1998) considered it a regular winter visitor. Particularly large *glandarius* irruptions occurred during 1955, 1977 and 1983, none of which coincide with birds reaching Scilly, even though flocks of hundreds were present in Cornwall during the 1983 autumn. None of the Jays seen on Scilly were trapped and ringed.

## Magpie (Black-billed Magpie)                                *Pica pica* A

**Rare migrant or vagrant, regardless of recent mainland range extensions, full written description required by the SRP.**

    1859    One (shot) St Agnes October    Clark & Rodd 1906
    1859    One (shot) St Helen's October    Clark & Rodd 1906
    1937    One 'obtained' Tresco 1st December    Penhallurick 1978
    1970    One Tresco 27th March then St Mary's from 4th April 'for a few days'
    1992    One Holy Vale St Mary's 11th October
    2001    One St Martin's 28th March until at least October 2002

Breeds most of western, northern and eastern Europe, from Atlantic to Pacific and south of Black Sea. Polytypic with complex racial structure. Birds in northwest USA and Canada previously treated as form *hudsonia*, but American Ornithologists' Union recently elevated them to full species status, as Black-billed Magpie *P. hudsonia*, recommending *P. pica* be renamed Eurasian Magpie (Anon 2000c). However, recent authors used American Magpie, e.g. *Field Guide to the Birds of North America*, National Geographic, Third Edition. Nominate *pica* occurs southern Norway south through western Europe to southern France, including British Isles and east to Asia Minor; numerous additional forms further south and east. Even in northern extremities surprisingly sedentary, a common breeding bird throughout much of Britain. Recent substantial British range extensions through 1980s and early 1990s now slowed; national 4% increase 1994–99 (Bashford & Noble 2000).

    There have been just six accepted occurrences of this unmistakable species (including one very recent), the fifth resting somewhat insecurely. Clark & Rodd (1906) mentioned two blown over from mainland Cornwall with Rooks *Corvus frugilegus* in an October gale of 1859. Both were subsequently shot, at least one by the redoubtable Augustus Pechell, with another on Tresco on 1st December 1937. In addition, a single was to be seen about the latter island on 27th March 1970 and what was presumably the same bird on St Mary's from the 4th April for a 'few days'.

    Mixed or single-species, either migrant or vagrant, corvid flocks are a not infrequent autumn feature of Scilly, though few individuals remain long and the first four records fit comfortably within that picture. Plus of course three skins involved were subsequently available for closer examination. Less easy to explain, but nevertheless accepted by the Scilly Records Panel, is a single-observer, single-sighting record of a bird in the Holy Vale area of St Mary's on 11th October 1992, which remained unseen by several hundred other birders present about that island. This lack of additional sightings is particularly puzzling, given the distinct improbability of a Magpie making just a brief touchdown in the islands, as does happen with some other species. Indeed, one would expect such a bird to remain and to be well watched, particularly as most birders still 'need' Magpie for their Scilly list. And as if to enforce this point, the most recent bird, on St Martin's from late March 2001, was present there and seen by many birdwatchers until at least October 2002. The Chart shows the four known arrival dates.

There seems little reason to doubt that the 45 km of open sea between Cornwall and Scilly primarily accounts for the absence of Magpies from the islands and Cramp *et al.* (1977–94) confirm that the species is 'reluctant to cross sea'. According to Penhallurick (1978), the species has been common in Cornwall since at least 1800, with numerous recorded examples of Parish bounties paid for their destruction. Further confirmation of its past mainland status comes from a Major Williams, who in 1913 counted a gathering of at least 227 near Redruth (Penhallurick 1978). In addition, both the 1968–72 *Atlas of Breeding Birds in Britain and Ireland* (Sharrock 1976) and its 1988–91 successor (Gibbons *et al.* 1993) established that they nest as close to Scilly as Land's End.

Interestingly, Taylor *et al.* (1981) drew attention to claims of September–October influxes of Magpies into Kent (presumably from France), plus sightings of birds flying out to sea at Dungeness on several dates during late March or early April, which if true would have involved a sea crossing of some 32 km, though with numerous opportunities for a ship-assisted passage. Also, Fairless (1997) watched seven apparent migrant Magpies fly out to sea from Waxham, east Norfolk, at a height of c. 60m and for c. 5 km, on a heading that would take them to the Netherlands 190 km away.

Most dispersal occurs in the north of the Magpie's range, i.e. Scandinavia (Cramp *et al.* 1974–99), British birds being markedly sedentary, with a median first-winter dispersal of just 5 km (n=25) and the subsequent age-group figure being just 1 km (Wernham *et al.* 2002). Cramp *et al.* quote observers at Falsterbo, southern Sweden, watching 'incipient' Magpie migratory behaviour associated with movements of Jay *Garrulus glandarius* and Nutcracker *Nucifraga caryocatactes*. Birds were seen to leave the coast, rise to a height and head off in the direction of Denmark 24 km to the west, but always returned in 'full panic' and with no successful departures recorded. Nonetheless, in northern Britain vagrant Magpies have also occurred on the islands of Islay and North Ronaldsay and clearly long-distance dispersal does occur, as evident from a Finish recovery of 450 km and a French recovery of 330 km, plus a small number of long-distance North American movements (Wernham *et al.* 2002). Given that Scandinavian Jackdaws *Corvus monedula* are already known to cross the North Sea to Britain mainly via Denmark we might expect Continental Magpies to do likewise, in which case it is interesting to note ten Danish ringing recoveries over 100 km, including one 470 km north into Norway (Wernham *et al.* 2002). In the absence of any ringing recoveries, the presence of Continental birds in Britain or Ireland during winter doubtless goes undetected and might only become apparent once birds reach areas where they are normally absent, e.g. Scilly.

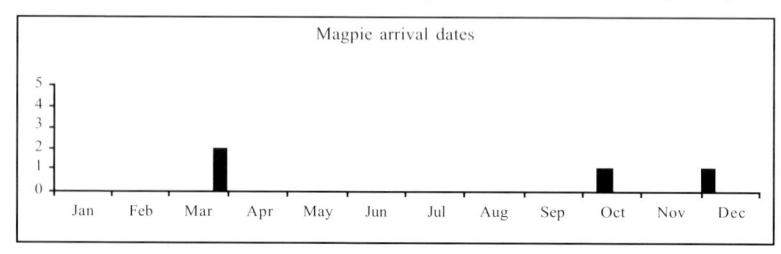

Magpie arrival dates

The nearest breeding populations are in west Cornwall, Brittany and southern Ireland. Given the Magpie's reluctance to cross even small areas of open sea, we can perhaps assume that birds reaching Scilly originate from mainland Cornwall. No Magpies have been trapped and ringed in Scilly.

# Nutcracker
# (Spotted Nutcracker) *Nucifraga caryocatactes* A BBRC 0.5%

**Extremely rare vagrant, full written description required by the BBRC.**

   1966   One St Martin's 5th October   *British Birds* 61: 363
   1968   At least one Tresco 17th to 20th September   *British Birds* 62: 476, 63: 371

Breeds as close to Britain as southwest Norway and eastwards to Pacific. Polytypic, being divided into three racial groups, with *caryocatactes* group in north of range. Within this group, nominate and sedentary *caryocatactes*, or 'Thick-billed Nutcracker', occurs northern, central and southeast Europe east to east European Russia; irruptive *macrorhynchos*, or 'Slender-Billed Nutcracker', Mongolia and Manchuria; *rothschildi* and *japonicus* further east. Scare vagrant in Britain generally, with around one record per year during the second half of 20th century (Dymond *et al.* 1989).

Just two confirmed sightings with none since 1968. A forty-minute sighting down to a few metres on St Martin's on 5th October 1966 was the first record for the islands and second for Cornwall and Scilly combined (*CBWPSAR* 36). One, perhaps two, individuals involved in the unprecedented 1968 invasion of Britain travelled as far as Tresco, when just after midday on 17th September 1968 David Hunt watched a bird at close range by Old Grimsby beach. Three days later he relocated what he thought was the same individual at Middle Down in the late afternoon, where he watched it tearing away rotten wood from a fallen pine tree and feeding on exposed insects. He later heard that two Nutcrackers had reportedly been seen together by visitors near Abbey Pool but was unable to confirm that two birds had been involved (*CBWPSAR* 38). In referring to the Tresco record, Penhallurick (1978) noted 'a pair frequented the Abbey Pool, Tresco 16th September', but omits where this information originated.

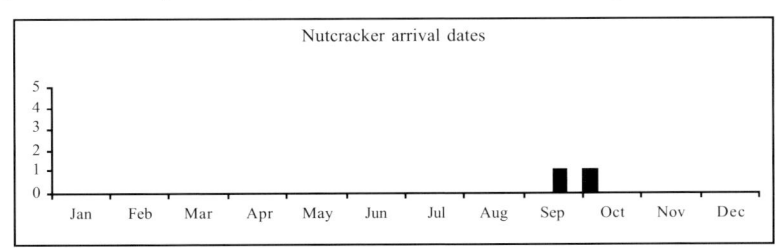

Nutcracker arrival dates

Most Nutcrackers reaching Britain make landfall in the eastern counties, from Norfolk southwards to Kent (Dymond *et al.* 1989), perhaps suggesting they leave from Germany or the Netherlands, rather than making the longer sea crossing from Scandinavia. First birds in the 1968 invasion reached Kent by 7th to 9th August, with a second, larger wave between 22nd August and 11th September. Many birds then moved west, as far even as the Welsh border counties, but with perhaps five remaining in Kent into December (Taylor *et al.* 1981). However, we can only guess why the Tresco bird moved as far as Scilly, or by what route. Of the 315 Nutcrackers involved in the 1968 invasion of Britain, those where racial origin was determined were all attributed to the irruptive and migratory *macrorhynchos* (Snow 1971), so although no mention of likely origin is made in *CBWPSAR*, we may safely assume that the Tresco arrival was also *macrorhynchos*, as very probably was the bird on St Martin's two years earlier.

The St Martin's individual was preceded in mainland Cornwall by a report of one presumably shot, supposedly in 1908 and probably on the Lizard peninsula or nearby (Penhallurick 1978). No Nutcrackers have been trapped on Scilly.

## Chough (Red-billed Chough) *Pyrrhocorax pyrrhocorax* A

**Very rare migrant or vagrant, full written description required by the SRP.**

    1870   One St Martin's November   Clark & Rodd 1906
    1876   One (shot) St Martin's November   Penhallurick 1978
    1899   One (shot) St Mary's December 1899   Clark & Rodd 1906
    1901   One (shot) (presumably Tresco) December   Penhallurick 1978
    1937   Six Tresco November   Penhallurick 1978
    1992   One Garrison, St Mary's 11th October   *IOSBR* 1992
    2001   One St Agnes 28th February to at least 5th March
    2002   One St Martin's 13th August

Fragmentary distribution, mainly associated with mountainous areas. Within West Palearctic, occurs western Britain and Ireland, Iberia, northwest Africa eastwards through Alps, Italy, Balkans, Greece and Turkey, with outlying populations in, for example, Brittany. Mainly sedentary but with seasonal altitudinal movements, not inclined to wander far from breeding areas (Cramp *et al.* 1977–94). Polytypic: nominate *pyrrhocorax* occurs Britain and Ireland; *erythrorhamphus* Iberia, southern France and Alps east to Yugoslavia, Italy and Sardinia; *barbarus* Canary Islands and northwest Africa. Birds in northwest France intermediate between *pyrrhocorax* and *erythrorhamphus*. After former range contraction, British population now stable. Until recently, the last known successful Cornish breeding attempt occurred in 1947, with the last reported sighting in 1973 (Penhallurick 1973). However, a pair that fledged three young on the Lizard peninsula in 2002 possibly made obsolete the much-talked-about plan for a Cornish reintroduction scheme. Included on Annex I of 1979 EEC 'Birds Directive'. Amber-listed in UK: 50% or more of breeding population at ten or fewer sites; unfavourable world conservation status (Gregory *et al.* 2002).

There is no indication among what few records there are of Chough ever having bred in Scilly. Neither E H Rodd (1880), Ryves & Quick (1948) nor any earlier writers made mention of it having done so, and Clark & Rodd (1906) referred only to the 1870 and 1899 birds, though there is a remote possibility that eggs may have been laid on Annet in the late 19th century (see below).

As early as 1662, 'great flocks' were reported near Padstow on the north Cornwall coast (Ray 1676), whilst Christopher Merrett reported that by 1666 it occurred on all southern cliffs from Cornwall to Dover (in Penhallurick 1978). And whilst it seems clear a Cornish decline followed, it was still found 'in tolerable abundance' by 1856 (S W Jenkins in Penhallurick 1978), the last recorded breeding on the Lizard peninsula occurring some time before 1865 (Rev. A G L'Estrange in Penhallurick 1978). Reasons behind any decline appear reasonably clear, for according to Bullmore (1866 in Penhallurick 1978) much 'fatal trapping' of adults took place in Cornwall and by 1870 a pair of dead birds allegedly fetched up to £3 10s. Inevitably, as Chough numbers declined, so the desire for and thus the commercial value of their eggs and skins increased.

Cramp *et al.* (1977–94) mention feeding movements of several kilometres, whereas limited, mainly winter, ringing recoveries suggest a post-fledging dispersal of less than 10 km, though not infrequently up to 45 km from natal areas in Wales, the Isle of Man and Ireland. However, the same authors detail a limited number of sea crossings, including Bardsey Island to Liverpool and Isle of Man to Northern Ireland. Nevertheless, considering the species' reluctance to stray far from its breeding areas, we should perhaps not be too surprised by the dearth of Scillonian records.

According to Clark & Rodd (1906), the earliest known Scillonian record involved one seen by Augustus Smith on St Martin's in November 1870 (Penhallurick gives the site as St Mary's), though they provided no additional information. Penhallurick quoted from personal communication with J L F Parslow relating to the Tresco Abbey game books and a bird shot on St Martin's in 1876. According to Clark & Rodd (1906) the 1899 bird was shot by a fisherman on St Mary's during Christmas week and afterwards 'secured' by L R George of Holy Vale on St Mary's. The fourth record also comes from the Tresco Abbey records and refers to a bird shot (presumably on Tresco) during Christmas 1901.

Two of the remaining three records are perhaps not entirely understandable. In the first, according to the Tresco Abbey records (Penhallurick 1978), a party of six were seen on that island during November 1937, but without the provision of additional detail it is difficult to comment on what might seem a most unlikely event.

Until just prior to completion of this account, the only modern record accepted by the Scilly Records Panel involved a reported brief sighting of a lone bird on The Garrison, St Mary's, on 11th October 1992. Apart from the various issues already discussed, what made this record noteworthy was the failure of so many other visiting birders to see (or hear) the bird, either on The Garrison or elsewhere in the islands. The bird's apparent failure to remain more than a few minutes after such a long sea crossing is surprising, though it could possibly have moved to a more remote area of Scilly. The Recorder for the islands at the time could find no evidence of any recent mainland escapees; a Chough previously known to have escaped from Hayle Bird Gardens, west Cornwall, had drowned during the April prior to the above sighting (*CBWPSAR* 62). However, a bird on St Agnes from 28th February 2001 was seen and photographed by several resident birders, having been first found on a snowy morning (only the third Scillonian snowfall in ten years) following two to three days of cold and extremely wet weather, with gale-force northerly winds. Its arrival preceded that of other Choughs on headlands along the southwest coast of England that spring, i.e. Portland in Dorset, Prawle Point and Plymouth in Devon, and west Cornwall's Lizard and Land's End peninsulas. At least three birds remained on the Lizard into 2002, with three young fledged there during May that year. Although the bird seen briefly on St Martin's during summer 2002 was somehow associated with this general increased southwest activity, it was not one of the Lizard family group.

One final point of interest involves a sternum found among bones from excavations at May's Hill, near Higher Town, St Martin's and provisionally identified as Chough (Turk 1884). The excavation level involved was either Romano-British or between the second and seventh centuries AD. But whatever the truth, the find leaves us wondering if the species did in fact have a secure foothold in the islands at some time past, particularly as the presence of a species' remains at an ancient midden usually indicates a former presence in sufficiently exploitable numbers, for whatever purpose (Turk 1884). Turk also pointed out that in 19th century Cornwall, Choughs were caught on baited hooks and sold by poulterers and therefore were a likely former food source on Scilly (Penhallurick 1978).

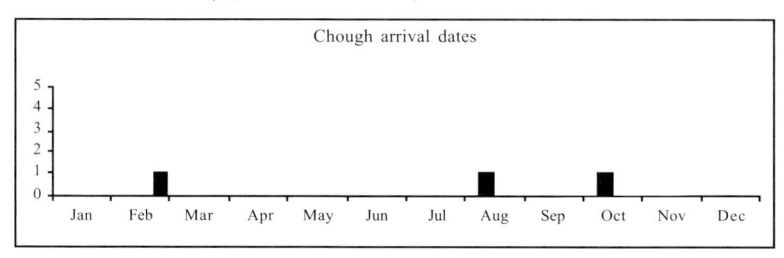

**Chough arrival dates**

The nearest breeding Choughs to Scilly are in southwest Wales, southern Ireland and Brittany. Choughs formerly reaching Scilly most probably originated from either mainland Cornwall or Ireland and therefore would have involved the form *pyrrhocorax*, though the possibility of birds intermediate between *pyrrhocorax* and *erythrorhamphus* from Brittany also doing so seems equally possible. Acceptable British or Irish ringing recoveries of up to 143 km are on record and sightings of unringed birds as far south as Cornwall may have involved birds from the same source (Wernham *et al*. 2002). Certainly, T A Dorrien-Smith attributed the pre-1950s individuals to *pyrrhocorax* (Dorrien-Smith 1951), though the distribution of 2001–02 sightings in Scilly and elsewhere in southwest England perhaps more pointedly suggests Brittany as the source, even though there appear to be no previous such records. The remote possibility of a breeding attempt referred to above involved a nest and two eggs of an unknown corvid species found on Annet's northern end in 1889. The eggs were shown to A E Newton, who 'thought they belonged to the Jackdaw' (Clark & Rodd 1906). Nevertheless, eggs of Jackdaw and Chough are sufficiently similar for an inexperienced person to perhaps confuse the two and we are given no information on Newton's expertise. However, it seems probable that had Choughs been present on Annet long enough to build a nest and lay eggs, the fact would have been recorded, in which case we can only wonder why the same was not true of the pair of Jackdaws involved.

## Jackdaw (Eurasian Jackdaw) *Corvus monedula* A

**Occasional migrant or vagrant, it may have unsuccessfully attempted to breed in 1905 and was similarly unsuccessful in 1992, though a pair apparently fledged young in 2000.**

Breeds West Palearctic north of Mediterranean and east to northwest China. In west of range breeds south to Sicily, Cyprus and Turkey, with outlying populations north Africa. Polytypic: nominate *monedula*, or 'Nordic Jackdaw', occurs Scandinavia, southern Finland, Denmark, eastern Germany, Poland, Czechoslovakia, Austria, Hungary, northern Romania and former Yugoslavia, *spermologus*, or 'Western Jackdaw', British Isles, France, Iberia, Morocco, Netherlands, western Germany, western Switzerland, Italy; *soemmerringii*, or 'Eastern Jackdaw', eastern Europe and western Asia, including southeast Finland, central former Yugoslavia and eastern Romania east to Mongolia and northwest China; *cirtensis* Algeria. Resident to migratory, wintering almost entirely within breeding range. National 21% increase 1994–99 (Bashford & Noble 2000).

Jackdaw seems always to have been something of a rarity in Scilly, showing a pattern of periodic arrival perhaps more aptly described as invasions, usually in autumn and typically accompanied by Rooks *C. frugilegus*. Most birds involved normally leave the islands quickly but occasionally a few remain through the winter, sometimes longer. Earliest reference to this species is contained in E H Rodd's *The Birds of Cornwall and The Scilly Islands* (1880), in a letter from his nephew Francis describing the arrival of a large flock of Rooks and Jackdaws during November 1870. Typical of their behaviour still today, most departed with the first change of weather, leaving just a few individuals behind. Somewhat confusingly, in his supplementary *List of Birds Observed in The Scilly Islands*, towards the end of his 1880 publication, Rodd said merely that it bred in numbers in the Land's End district and made no specific mention of it reaching Scilly. However, this was an obvious oversight on his part, or on that of his posthumous editor, James Harting. In their post-19th-century review of the birds of Scilly, James Clark and Francis Rodd made mention of the 1870 arrival and gave details of similar influxes during January 1885 and November 1901. They also mentioned a flock of 400 that arrived on Tresco on 1st November 1905, this event probably accounting for four seen on St Martin's on 8th and seven near Giant's Castle, St Mary's, on 15th November that year.

Particularly interesting is Clark & Rodd's account of either T A or A A Dorrien-Smith finding a nest with two eggs on the north end of Annet in 1889. Clearly the identity of the nest's occupant was in question as the eggs were later shown to A E Newton, 'who thought they belonged to the Jackdaw'. However, without knowing Newton's level of expertise regarding the eggs of Jackdaw and any likely confusion species, e.g. Chough *Pyrrhocorax pyrrhocorax*, it is difficult to either accept or reject this record after so much time. Certainly, Annet Head, the location given by Clark and Rodd, seems as likely as any on Scilly for either Jackdaw or Chough to breed, though Ryves & Quick (1946) made no mention of any previous breeding attempt.

Jackdaws are recorded on Scilly in only about 30 years throughout the whole of the 20th century, seven of which can be described as invasion years, with the pattern one of lingering individuals or small groups from recent arrivals, numbers gradually declining in subsequent years until none remain. However, there also appear to have been random arrivals of less than ten birds, involving an apparently obvious spring and autumn bias, with roughly equal numbers in both halves of the year. Invasions can sometimes be spectacular, as was the case when 1,000 arrived on St Mary's Airfield early on 23rd October 1983, most of which had returned to the mainland by the end of the day. These were followed by 4,000, seen flying in over Peninnis early next morning, but though having arrived on St Mary's by 7.30 am, one-third had returned to the mainland by 10 am, the remainder following soon after. Another 100 arrived on the 25th and on 28th a further 250, following which numbers slowly declined until none were thought present after late November. However, presumably not all left as up to 15 were present about the islands from January until at least the following June. In addition, 1976 seems to have been exceptional for the numbers left at the year's end following an earlier influx, with around 30 wintering but all allegedly departing by April 1977.

Other invasion years were 1947, 1957, 1976, 1981, 1990 and 1993. None of these were quite as impressive as 1983, however, and in 1957 perhaps only 200 individuals were involved. A notable feature of some large movements was the arrival of birds from the west or southwest, coming in off the sea over St Agnes and towards St Mary's. Or, alternatively, the arrival of birds over St Mary's from the east and on over St Agnes, heading west or southwest out to sea. In the latter case, large groups were sometimes watched departing to the west, only to come straggling back later in smaller but presumably much wiser groups.

These residual, post-invasion populations always offer the prospect of colonisation, but only in three years did this come close to happening and only once did it succeed. In 1992, two out of up to four birds present on Tresco for all or most of the year built a nest inside a chimney, but sadly the construction was removed and the pair abandoned the attempt. In 1995, two out of up to 12 birds present in the islands were seen carrying nest material, again on Tresco, but this attempt too was abandoned. Then in 2000, a pair fledged young from a nest on Tresco, though this first breeding report lacks a full description (IOSBG 2000).

As with most migrants or vagrants only occasionally reaching Scilly, determining where these Jackdaws originate from is no simple matter. For although logic suggests they arrive either from mainland Britain, Ireland or northern France, their true origin could lie much further afield. And although anything resembling true migration probably involves birds from northern or eastern European populations, some British Jackdaws undertake medium-distance winter movements, especially away from upland areas. The average winter displacement of British Jackdaws is about 30 km south and 10 km west, whereas post-fledging dispersal averages 30 km or less (Wernham *et al.* 2002). Most large west-European movements involve a west or southwest element of *monedula* from Scandinavia and Denmark, or *spermologus* from the Low Countries, all of which are known to reach western Britain and northern France (Cramp *et al.* 1977–94). Nevertheless, British sightings of the eastern-European *soemmerringii* have been claimed, though there is much variation in plumage characteristics (Palmer 2000; Wernham *et al.* 2002). In his useful booklet *Birds of Scilly as Recorded at Tresco Abbey* T A Dorrien-Smith (1951) attributed all island Jackdaw sightings up until then to *spermologus*, although without providing details. No Jackdaws have been trapped and ringed on Scilly and there are no controls.

# Rook *Corvus frugilegus* A

**In most years a scarce migrant or vagrant, occasional large invasions occur during autumn, some then perhaps remain into the following spring. It has occasionally attempted to breed but never successfully. There was also at least one attempt to introduce the species to Scilly.**

Breeds southern and central Europe east through central Asia to Japan, outlying populations eastern Kazakhstan and China. Migratory in north and east, wintering south to Mediterranean, Iran and China. Polytypic: nominate *frugilegus* occurs Europe and Asia Minor east to Altai and northwest China; *pastinator* from Altai to eastern Siberia, Japan and eastern China. National 8% increase 1994–99 (Bashford & Noble 2000).

Although Rook breeds as close to Scilly as the Land's End peninsula it remains something of a rarity in Scilly, regardless of infrequent autumn or winter invasions of several hundreds. The only worthwhile early published account is James Clark and Francis Rodd's lengthy description of a few 19th-century mass arrivals, with small groups appearing at other times (Clark & Rodd 1906). The same authors noted that birds from these end-of-year invasions often remained into the following spring, as in the 1850s when what Augustus Smith described as 'a whole rookery' arrived in Scilly during an autumn gale. At least some of these attempted to nest in conifers *Pinus pinaster* near Tresco Abbey the following spring but gradually disappeared before building had been completed. This last was perhaps the mass arrival of 1859, which was accompanied by two Magpies *Pica pica* (Clark & Rodd 1906). Clark and Rodd also suggested that birds remained and built nests on at least three other occasions up until 1906, although as far as they knew no egg was ever laid in the islands. There is also a suggestion in Clark and Rodd's account of birds arriving in Scilly from further north or west, as in 1845 and 1905 when birds arrived on Bryher and the north end of Tresco during bad weather. However, they also recount elsewhere how corvid flocks were seen leaving Scilly and heading west, only to return after some time.

This same account described Augustus Smith's 1865 attempt to introduce Rooks, presumably to Tresco, all of which 'flew off to the mainland, leaving only some half-built nests behind'. Some time during the early 1900's, Tresco gamekeeper David Smith reported a flock of 800 Rooks arriving from the east, which after flying around Tresco flew out to sea in a northwesterly direction. A similar flock landed aboard a ship inward bound for Bristol on the same date (Clark & Rodd 1906). Another first-hand description of a mass arrival comes from Francis Rodd himself in a letter to his uncle E H Rodd in Penzance (Rodd 1880). This involved 'a great flock' which left the islands with the first change of weather, leaving just a few immatures, 'one of which was seen eating a Redwing *Turdus iliacus* alive'.

Many of these corvid flocks arriving in Scilly are today made up of more than one species, though one usually predominates and doubtless this was always the case. However, the situation remains as already described, with one to perhaps ten birds arriving during most years, occasional mass autumn arrivals, rare years of total absence, e.g. 1982, and equally rare summering individuals, as in 1969 when one remained on St Mary's. In normal years, one or two in spring possibly involve dispersing juveniles and most autumns see a similar or slightly greater number of arrivals, some of which remain into the winter. Nevertheless, mass arrivals are scarce, with just two in the 25 years to year 2000. Autumn 1976 saw the arrival of large numbers, 100 of which remained into March 1977 with at least one nest being built, though all had departed by early June. In 1983, 80–100 Rooks accompanied the brief but nonetheless huge arrival of 4,000 Jackdaws. More recently, four and five Rooks respectively accompanied large movements of Jackdaws *C. monedula* in 1990 and 1993. There seems no doubt, though, that despite frequent attempts by Rook to breed in Scilly, it has repeatedly failed to grasp the opportunity, presumably because the islands lack suitably large feeding areas.

British and Irish birds are almost wholly resident and movements of ringed birds beyond 50 km are exceptional, the extent of any true migration increasing further north and east and with birds often travelling in company with Jackdaws. Western European birds move mainly west or southwest and whilst further east the direction of migration is more variable (Cramp *et al.* 1977–94) the overall tendency is for birds from central Europe to winter in Britain and Ireland and be replaced in their home range by those from Scandinavia, though a few of the latter also reach Britain along with even greater numbers from the Baltic region (Wernham *et al.* 2002).

## Carrion Crow *Corvus corone* A

**Resident and breeds in small numbers, perhaps with temporary or even permanent additions during some years. Individual wintering or migrant Hooded Crows *C. cornix* occasionally remain in the islands and produce hybrid offspring.**

Breeds western Europe, east through central-southern Europe to central and eastern Asia. Migratory in north, wintering mainly within remainder of range. Polytypic, nominate *corone* occurs England, Wales and southern Scotland south to Iberia and Alps and east to northern Germany, Austria and former Czechoslovakia; *orientalis*, or 'Black Crow' further east as far as Korea and Japan. National 12% increase 1994–99 (Bashford & Noble 2000). Split from Hooded Crow *C. cornix* by BOURC September 2002 (BOURC 2002b).

James Clark and Francis Rodd's early 20th-century summary was brief, these two describing Carrion Crow as breeding regularly on all outer uninhabited islands. However, 'in spite of repressive measures, and the apparent absence of immigrant recruits' it was sufficiently numerous 'to be a serious menace to young poultry and broods of game'. This last was the typical comment directed towards any predatory bird species during the 19th and early 20th centuries, though sadly that situation has still not altogether left us. However, the even more brief comment of Francis's uncle E H Rodd is no less important, alleging as he did that it bred entirely, or at least mainly, on Scilly's cliffs, in obvious contrast to the situation now (Rodd 1880).

Regardless of what Clark and Rodd had to say concerning early 20th-century abundance, that situation clearly changed rapidly, C J King reporting (in Wallace 1923) that none were present in the islands 20 years later. Therefore, the next published mention of Carrion Crow was not until 1943, when according to A A Dorrien-Smith a pair were 'deterred from reproducing' (*CBWPSAR* 14). Following this a small number of birds, perhaps no more than four, were about the islands annually and although successful breeding was not recorded until 1966, by 1979 four pairs were present on St Mary's and one on Tresco. By the 1990s, this had increased to five pairs on St Mary's, two on Tresco and one each on St Agnes and St Martin's, all of which were traditional tree nesters. The 2000 Breeding Bird Atlas (Chown & Lock 2002) recorded up to 25 pairs, mostly on the main islands (Table) though the report's authors thought this a substantial overestimate and suggested 10 to 15 pairs as a more likely expectation. Birds were recorded in 24 (35.8%) of the 67 1-km squares surveyed. The two suggested pairs on Samson and one on Annet probably involved visiting birds from nearby islands; the author has no knowledge of this species breeding on these two islands during 12 years of fieldwork. A major surprise in recent years was a brood of four nestlings among breeding seabirds on a rocky pinnacle on treeless Great Innisvouls in the Eastern Isles during May 1999 (pers. obs.). This was the first nest recorded in circumstances anything like those described by E H Rodd for over 100 years and although this behaviour may have been overlooked in Scilly recently, it cannot have been widespread.

Interesting also are occasional references to a small-scale passage of Carrion Crows at both ends of the year, as in 1977, when 16 were counted on three islands on 7th October, or 1978 when what was described as 'a marked passage' occurred during October. However, such claims were unsupported by co-ordinated all-island counts and were apparently based on assumptions that inter-island movement was uncommon. We now realise this is untrue, a recent feature being the apparent ease with which individuals or groups commute between islands, not just to Annet and Samson but even out to the most remote seabird colonies. Certainly, during the 1990s groups or small flocks of up to 30 or so birds were recorded on various islands, most evident perhaps being a summering flock of about 12 birds on St Mary's (Wernham *et al.* 2002). There may be little reason to suppose these were other than the product of local pairs though the possibility that migrant group do pass through Scilly cannot be dismissed, but has yet to be proved.

Another feature difficult to ignore has been the occasional hybrid Carrion x Hooded Crow pair, including on St Mary's during the late 1970s and on Tresco in the 1990s. The product of these liaisons has been a succession of individuals showing varying hybrid features. Elsewhere, e.g. northeast England, coastal Carrion

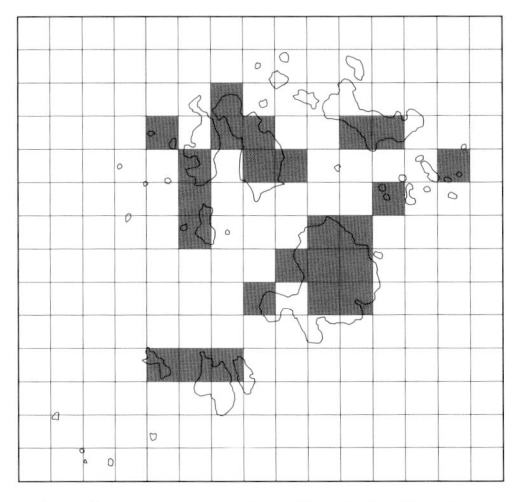

| Island | Pairs |
| --- | --- |
| St Mary's | 8 C |
| Tresco | 6 P |
| Bryher | 1 P |
| St Martin's | 2 P |
| St Agnes & Gugh | 2 P |
| Samson | 2 P |
| Annet | 1 P |
| Gweal | 1 P |
| Great Ganninick | 1 P |
| Others | 1 C |

**2000 Breeding Bird Atlas – Carrion Crow (Chown & Lock 2002)**

P = possible breeding, C = confirmed breeding

1-km Carrion Crow Breeding Distribution – 2000–01 (data Chown & Lock 2002)

Crows have been recorded feeding extensively along the shoreline (Dunn 1985) and whilst this behaviour is known in Scilly (pers. obs.) it seems to have been little reported. Individuals are also occasionally observed dropping shellfish.

British Carrion Crows are largely sedentary, few recoveries exceeding 20 km, with the greatest distances involving first and second-year individuals and more northerly populations. At least up until 1997 there were no overseas recoveries of Carrion Crows ringed in Britain and no evidence of birds reaching Britain from other countries (Cramp *et al.* 1977–94; Wernham *et al.* 2002). Similarly, there is little evidence of migratory movement in France, though juveniles disperse up to several hundred kilometres, any overseas recoveries involving birds from Belgium, Switzerland or Germany. The only Carrion Crows ringed in Scilly were the brood of four found by the author in the ground nest on Great Innisvouls in 1999 and there are no recaptures from elsewhere. The recent spread of House Crow *C. splendens* in western Europe, e.g. northern France in 2000 (Davies 2001) and at least once in Ireland, raises the possibility of this species reaching Scilly and perhaps being overlooked.

## Hooded Crow *Corvus cornix* A

Breeds northwest Europe east through southern Russia and central Eurasia, eastern Mediterranean and Balkans to Kazakhstan, in places intergrading and hybridising with Carrion Crow *C. corone*. Polytypic: nominate *cornix* occurs Ireland, northern Scotland, Isle of Man, Faeroes, Fennoscandia and Denmark east to Yenisey valley and south to western Russia, eastern Germany, Czechoslovakia, northern Romania, former Yugoslavia, Italy and Corsica; *sharpii* Sardinia, Sicily and southern Italy and southern Yugoslavia east through Bulgaria, Turkey, southern Ukraine to northern Kazakhstan and central Turkmenistan (formerly known as Turkmeniya); at least two additional forms in south of range. Split from Carrion Crow by BOURC September 2002 (BOURC 2002b).

Clark and Rodd (1906) treated this as a separate species from Carrion Crow, noting it as occasional between November and May, a few at a time wintering on Tresco. On St Mary's a Mr George obtained one in what would then have been a far less wooded Holy Vale during May 1900 and five spent several days at the last location in spring 1901, whilst in April 1903 one was on St Martin's. From all of this, the authors concluded there was a probable regular but small spring passage. Further support for this came in the form of two by Tresco's ponds during May 1871 (Rodd 1880), whereas five present throughout winter 1870–71 were seen feeding on a dead horse on 8th November. Earliest modern reference to Hooded Crow may have involved A A Dorrien-Smith's mention of singles during 1943 and 1944 (*CBWPSAR* 13; 14). Since then, singles have been about the islands during various winters, Penhallurick (1978) locating records for ten of the 34 years since 1938. Occasional individuals still winter and more rarely remain into the following summer, occasionally breeding with resident Carrion Crows; one full-blooded or near full-blooded individual present from about 1987 and throughout most of the 1990s producing several offspring.

Although, like Carrion Crow, most Hooded Crows from Scotland and Ireland move hardly at all, many Continental populations are fully or partially migratory, most birds reaching the Low Countries, France and southern England are believed to originate mainly from western Fennoscandia (Wernham *et al.* 2002); populations further east head mainly south or southeast. Recent reductions in the number of Hooded Crows wintering in England, and therefore Scilly, are believed attributable to a change in the migratory behaviour of Scandinavian birds (Wernham *et al.* 2002). No Hooded Crows have been ringed in Scilly and there are no recoveries from elsewhere.

## Raven (Common Raven) *Corvus corax* A

One recent resident breeding pair; it is perhaps also a scarce visitor. Raven also bred at least occasionally in the 19th century.

Huge breeding range encompassing North and Central America and Eurasia from the Atlantic to the Pacific, north to the Arctic and south to North Africa, Nepal and China. Mainly sedentary. Polytypic: nominate *corax* occurs British Isles and France through Scandinavia east to Yenisey basin; numerous additional forms eastwards and in Americas. National 15% increase 1994–99 (Bashford & Noble 2000).

With one resident breeding pair in what appears to be ideal Raven breeding habitat we might be forgiven for thinking it has always been so, but that is not the case, Ravens having only recently become a permanent feature. By the early 1900s, it was still considered a scarce wanderer to the islands, although in all seasons (Clark & Rodd 1906). Clark and Rodd also pointed out that it appeared to have bred on isolated Gorregan in the Western Isles about 1840, noting too that in May and June 1893 two birds frequented the Western Isles generally, although no nest was discovered. Interestingly, E H Rodd thought it had not bred in the islands up until at least the 1880s (Rodd 1880).

It seems clear from the various records that Ravens were absent from Scilly from 1974 to 1978 inclusive, but that in 1979 two wide-ranging birds were present from 6th April to 11th May, with one equally active individual from mid-July to the year's end. According to the following year's *IOSBR*, two had reportedly taken up residence on St Martin's, but made daily visits to other islands, particularly in autumn, and were seen feeding on a stranded dead Pilot Whale *Globicephala melas* on Tean. There was no reported evidence of breeding in 1980, but they were present about the islands, and again in 1981. In 1982, the pair reportedly hatched three young at an unspecified site in the Eastern Isles, with three birds seen about the islands until the end of October.

From then on the pattern has been fairly predictable, with a pair breeding annually, usually on the southwest corner of Great Innisvouls in the Eastern Isles, but with an alternative nest site on the eastern face of Men-a-Vaur to the west of Round Island. Although young are known or thought to have hatched most years, none were shown to have fledged successfully until two were seen, still with the adults, in November 1990, from which time the pair became more productive. Suggested reasons for earlier post-fledging failures include 'oiling' of the young by Fulmars *Fulmarus glacialis* but there seems to be no evidence of this and few Fulmars would then have been involved. An equally likely explanation could be that the adults were inexperienced breeders. In about half the years when young were fledged, one to two additional full-grown birds were present about the islands, though it is unclear whether these might have been young from the current or even previous years.

What does seem clear, though, is that despite regularly fledged young, the island population remains at one breeding pair, plus one to three additional birds in some years. The very clear suggestion is that Scilly is capable of sustaining only one breeding pair, be that for reasons of periodic food shortage or simply territorial requirements. In one or more years, small groups of what were believed to be vagrants or migrants were present, as in 1988 when four were observed arriving from the northeast on 21st May, these remaining mostly on Tresco until the year's end. Fieldwork for the 2000 Breeding Bird Atlas recorded a possible one to four pairs but this was very probably accounted for by the high mobility of the resident pair, the report's authors conceding that just the single pair were probably involved (Chown & Lock 2002).

The earlier 20th-century picture is far less clear, though certainly Ryves & Quick (1946) made no mention of it having bred on Scilly since Clark and Rodd's earlier review. The species subsequently gets mentioned in only 12 of the 47 years from 1931 to 1978, most sightings apparently involving casual wanders. The probable exception was 1969, when two birds noted about Round Island in March by lighthouse keepers coincided with reports of birds about Tresco and Bryher then and to the end of April. Particularly interesting, though, was one keeper's account of seeing a bird enter a 'dark recess' on nearby Men-a-Vaur on 29th March (*IOSBR* 1969): a site sometimes used by the recent resident pair. Unfortunately, there is nothing in the literature to suggest breeding was successful, or indeed that it actually occurred, but it remains an important observation.

There is archaeological evidence indicating Ravens inhabited Scilly well before the period under discussion, bone remains believed to be from this species being found at sites on Nornour in the Eastern Isles and at May's Hill on St Martin's. In the latter case, leg bones involved were believed to date from between the second and seventh centuries AD (Turk 1971, 1984b). It is possible Ravens could have been acquired for food but it seems more likely they would have been kept alive, either as pets or for some functional requirement.

Although there is no evidence that Fulmars were responsible for the demise of young Raven broods in Scilly, Fulmars have been and still are increasing their breeding numbers within the islands. Therefore, the possibility of site competition between Ravens and Fulmars, or between Fulmars and other coastal nesting species may be real enough (Robertson 1975). Wherever their ranges coincide, Ravens frequently share their breeding cliff with Peregrine Falcons *Falco peregrinus*. Therefore, it is worth recording that since the return of a breeding pair of these large falcons to Scilly in 1994, two of the nest sites they have occupied are also Raven sites, i.e. Great Innisvouls and Men-a-Vaur. Both though are small areas of cliff and it seems well understood these two species have difficulty breeding together successfully if forced to nest closer than about 50 m (Ratcliffe 1980).

The closest breeding Ravens to Scilly are on Cornwall's Land's End and Lizard peninsulas, southern Ireland and Brittany. However, British Ravens are extremely sedentary, the average dispersal distance from fledging being 27 km, adults moving even less between years. Interestingly, although the regular presence of Continental birds in Britain was not hitherto suspected, a recent build up of isolated wintering individuals in southeast England is thought at least partly attributable to a successful Netherlands reintroduction programme (Wernham *et al.* 2002). Three nestling Ravens were ringed in a nest on Great Innisvouls on 18th April 1994, but there are no recaptures.

# Starling (Common Starling)            *Sturnus vulgaris* A

**Common and widespread breeding resident, migrant and winter visitor.**

Breeds throughout Europe except Iberia, north to Fennoscandia and east through central Asia almost to Sea of Okhotsk. Migratory in north and east, resident or partial migrant in south and west. Polytypic with complex racial structure: nominate *vulgaris* occurs most of Europe from Iceland south to Pyrenees and Bulgaria and east to European Russia; *zetlandicus*, or 'Shetland Starling' Shetland and Outer Hebrides; *faroensis* Faroes; *poltaratskyi* western Urals east to Lake Baikal and through Kazakhstan to Mongolia; eight or more additional forms further south and east. Reclassified from Amber- to Red-listed in UK 2002: rapid, 66% breeding decline over past 25 years (Gregory *et al.* 2002).

There is much early writing concerning this species in Scilly, most of which can be summed up by describing it as a late autumn or winter visitor appearing in large and visible flocks but with numbers fluctuating considerably, both between years and within particular winters and few but the local breeding population evident after mid-April (Clark & Rodd 1906). It is perhaps important to note that it did not breed in Scilly during the 19th century and was not known to do so on mainland Cornwall until the middle of that century (Rodd 1880). Clark and Rodd mentioned a large and exceptionally late flock of c. 400 that arrived in the islands from the west during May, in company with Lapwings *Vanellus vanellus*, all birds departing the islands the following day. The same authors also described how on some winter evenings on Tresco 'a veritable cloud' of Starlings would wheel over a reedbed or plantation before going to roost. The timing of these autumn Starling arrivals can be more clearly judged from Francis Rodd's letter to his uncle E H Rodd in which he mentioned seeing the first of the year on 24th September (Rodd 1880), and from James Clark and Francis Rodd's reference to the second week of October, 'when the Larks and Starlings make their great movement to the islands'.

No account of this species would be complete without inclusion of Francis Rodd's graphic tale of Starlings aboard ship during early November (Rodd 1880). On 5th November 1870, a ship put into St Mary's and reported that whilst still 300 miles (480 km) west of the islands a large flock came aboard, a number of which were killed by the crew, presumably to eat. A 'considerable number' remained aboard, however, until the ship reached Scilly, Francis concluded his story with the comment that autumn migration that year had been later than usual. Not unexpectedly, there are also a number of accounts from the Bishop Rock Lighthouse between the years 1880 and 1911, most of which support the above observations on numbers and timing.

As with most species, there is little information from the early part of the 20th century. Therefore, Blair's statement that by 1938 it was probably breeding on St Martin's, Tresco, Bryher and St Agnes and that breeding had been proved for St Mary's comes as something of a surprise (*CBWPSAR* 8). However, its presence as a breeding species had been noted earlier, in 1923, though the author omitted the location (Wallis 1923); but according to C J King they did not breed prior to 1911–1913. But by 1910 they were reported to have reached the Penzance area of west Cornwall 15 years beforehand, many nests by then blocking rain-water pipes (A W Harvey 1910). D'Urban (1910) assisted by suggesting that none bred in Cornwall prior to 1855 but that by 1892 it was resident throughout the county. By 1959 there were a recorded 15 pairs on St Agnes, the total remaining between 10 and 15 pairs through to at least 1978 (*IOSBR* 1979).

A feature seemingly only recently recorded is the number of pairs utilising natural cliff sites on both inhabited and uninhabited islands, some of which are not much above sea level. One to two pairs used cliff recesses in the Gugh Kittiwake colony throughout most of the 1990s and single pairs bred in old seabird burrows on Samson's southern end from 1998 and on Annet more recently, whilst in the late 1990s up to four pairs bred in the rocky cliff face by the *Turk's Head* public house on St Agnes, though this cliff-nesting behaviour may have occurred beforehand.

Pairs also still regularly utilise tree sites in Scilly, in contrast to mainland Britain where this no longer occurs commonly. More interestingly, perhaps, is that the trees involved are mainly elm *Ulmus*, Scilly escaping the recent ravages of Dutch Elm Disease. This being the case, the few hectares of stunted Holy Vale elm woodland bordering the Lunnon Farm study plot on St Mary's may currently be of national importance. The Table shows the Lunnon Farm plot totals for the eight years from 1991. The 2000 Breeding Bird Atlas recorded a possible 333 pairs in 31 (46.2%) of the 67 1-km squares surveyed throughout the islands. The subsequent report fixed the likely expectation in the range 250–500 pairs (Chown & Lock 2002).

The situation during autumn and winter remains broadly as described by Clark and Rodd nearly one hundred years ago, birds normally arriving mostly from October onwards and with many reports in the thousands. This was the case in October 1990, when 1,000-plus roosted on Tresco and although these were replaced by further arrivals over subsequent weeks, most had reportedly left the islands by mid-November, leaving only the 'usual wintering population'. Most reports, though, talk of hundreds or less, the only specific St Mary's roost site mentioned being in trees on The Garrison, where over 1,000 were present in mid-October 1994, whilst on nearby St Agnes 4,000–5,000 were roosting during November the same year. One of the largest recently recorded arrivals involved flocks of 'some thousands' seen arriving from the southeast on 19th November 1964, with further big arrivals from the same direction next day.

| 1991 | 1992 | 1993 | 1994 | 1995 | 1996 | 1997 | 1998 |
|---|---|---|---|---|---|---|---|
| 9 | 11 | 6 | 8 | 8 | 6 | 7 | 11 |

**Starling CBC Pair Totals – 16-hectare Lunnon Farm, St Mary's 1991–98 (P J Robinson unpublished data)**

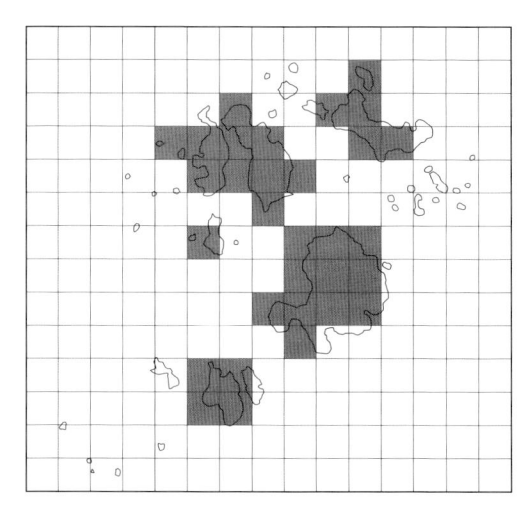

| Island | Pairs |
|---|---|
| St Mary's | 186 |
| Tresco | 53 |
| Bryher | 28 |
| St Martin's | 29 |
| St Agnes & Gugh | 29 |
| Samson | 4 |
| Tean | 1 |
| White Island, St Martin's | 1 |
| Annet | 1 |
| Gweal | 1 |

**2000 Breeding Bird Atlas – Starling (Chown & Lock 2002)**

**1-km Starling Breeding Distribution – 2000–01 (data Chown & Lock 2002)**

Occasional reports of unusually plumaged Starlings attract little interest, as in the case of a white-rumped individual on St Mary's for at least two years from 1994. Nonetheless, the discovery, in Hugh Town during late January 1998, of a starling showing features apparently consistent with Spotless Starling *S. unicolor* instantly enlivened a typically quiet winter on St Mary's, attracting as it did numerous mainland birders and causing the transport companies to provide extra aircraft unusually early in the year. However, after several days, even weeks, of debate, the bird was considered by most observers to be an aberrant nominate *vulgaris* Starling (Gantlett & Millington 1998). Alternative suggestions included one of the less well-known eastern forms, or perhaps even a hybrid Starling x Spotless Starling (Caton 1998; Gantlett & Millington 1998). The latter was thought to possibly explain, among other features, the Hugh Town individual's noticeably pink legs. Perhaps surprisingly, this individual or one showing identical features reappeared in Hugh Town in November 2002 (*Birding World* 15: 455). Wallace (1980) had previously predicted the likely arrival of vagrant Spotless Starling in Britain but this has yet to be fulfilled. That aside, one of the most bizarre reports from Scilly involving any species is that of 15 Starlings roosting nightly beneath a domestic chicken during the cold weather of early 1963 (*CBWPSAR* 33).

The main autumn direction of travel for the bulk of the migratory Starling population of Europe and Asia is towards the southwest, most wintering from Britain and Ireland south through France to Iberia, where they winter alongside resident local birds. Ringing data show that although birds from northwest Europe cross the North Sea to Britain and Ireland, those from further east also migrate through the Low Countries (Wernham *et al.* 2002), passage occurring during September–November. A total of 653 Starlings were ringed in Scilly up to and including 1999, 403 (62%) since 1970. What few recaptures there are strongly support the view that most Starlings reaching Scilly do so via the southern North Sea route, having originated in eastern Europe or central Asia. Penhallurick (1978) lists eight birds ringed in Russia or Poland and recovered in mainland Cornwall up until the 1970s, all of which may also help explain the annual autumn arrival in Scilly of first-year Rose-coloured Starlings *S. roseus*.

## Controls

| | | | | |
|---|---|---|---|---|
| F150329 | ? | Klaipeda (Memel), Lithuania 2nd August 1933 | ? | Scilly 8th December 1933 |
| Z6065 | 1stY | Westkapelle, Belgium 21st October 1962 | FD | St Agnes January 1963 |
| M105748 | Ad | Rybachi, USSR 15th April 1962 | FD | St Agnes 5th February 1963 |
| ? | 1stY | Wargem, West Flanders, Belgium 9th August 1964 | CT | Bryher 31st January 1965 |
| 77178S | Ad | Barnsley, West Yorkshire 16th June 1962 | CT | St Agnes 3rd February 1965 |
| 12286417 | 1stY | Anzegum, West Vlaanderen, Belgium 19th August 1991 | KC | Bryher 1st February 1992 |

**Recoveries**
XH97812  Ad   St Agnes 2nd November 1990        FD  Dusseldorf, Germany 15th April 1993

**Starling Ringing Recaptures**

## Rose-coloured Starling
## (Rosy Starling)                    *Sturnus roseus*  **A**  BBRC 10.2%

Scarce but regular and now almost annual migrant, full written descriptions required by the SRP.
Pre-BBRC Rose-coloured Starling Records
Pre-1848   One (adult) shot Scilly   Clark & Rodd 1906
   1850s   Two (one shot) Scilly   Clark & Rodd 1906
   1899   One (shot) Tresco 1st June   Clark & Rodd 1906; Witherby & Ticehurst 1907
   1937   One (male) Bryher 13th June   *CBWPSAR* 7
   1944   One (first-year) Scilly November   *CBWPSAR* 14

Breeds central-eastern Europe and central-western Asia. Migratory, wintering India and Arabian Peninsula, erratic and irruptive visitor to central and western Europe. Sporadic breeding records from countries west of normal range, as far as Hungary, Greece and Italy, more regularly Bulgaria and former Yugoslavia. Monotypic. Removed from BBRC Rarities List January 2002 (*British Birds* 94: 290, 497).

Scillonian Rose-coloured Starling records were scarce in the second half of the 19th and early 20th centuries but became noticeably more frequent during the 1970s, from which time it arrived almost annually. According to James Clark and Francis Rodd (1906), the first record for Scilly was shot prior to 1848. However, Penhallurick (1978) quoted this record as a 'fine male' reportedly shot by Pechell prior to 1841, and in the *Victoria County History* James Clark apparently attributed the shooting to Tresco gamekeeper David Smith (W Page 1906).

Whatever the truth, this was followed some time in the 1850s by two more, one of which was killed and the other seen by Augustus Pechell (Clark & Rodd 1906). The third island record, involving one shot by David Smith on 1st June 1899 (Clark & Rodd 1906), was followed by a substantial gap before the next, a male on Bryher on 13th June 1937 (*CBWPSAR* 7). Clark, however (in W Page 1906), gave the date of the first of these two as June 1892. Further time passed before one was observed by a Tresco gamekeeper in November 1944, to be followed by the first of the modern records, a bird on Bryher on 12th October 1964.

The Table shows only pre-BBRC records, subsequent records being summarised in the Charts. During the 36 years 1964–2000, 44 Rose-coloured Starlings arrived in Scilly at an average of 1.2 per year. Of these, just seven (15.9%) were aged by observers as adult or first-summer birds and, as the Charts show, all adults occurred in the 1990s, though two early records also involved adults. The most arrivals in any single year was six in 1991, a record perhaps unmatched by any other county. The Charts also show how concentrated were first-year arrivals compared with adults, the majority of which occurred during summer. Among first-years, the average length of stay was 16.6 days, the longest being 65 days and only one remained for one day. In comparison, adults stayed only 3.1 days, or 1.2 days if the 13-day individual is discounted, and four remained only one day.

British Rose-coloured Starling records are a mix of first-summer or adult birds and first-years but this is clearly not so in Scilly, 37 (84%) out of 44 records where age was determined involving first-years. This high proportion of first-years (or low occurrence of adults) is substantially against the national trend, most

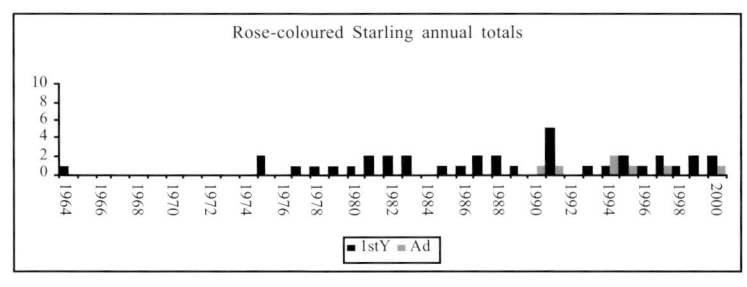

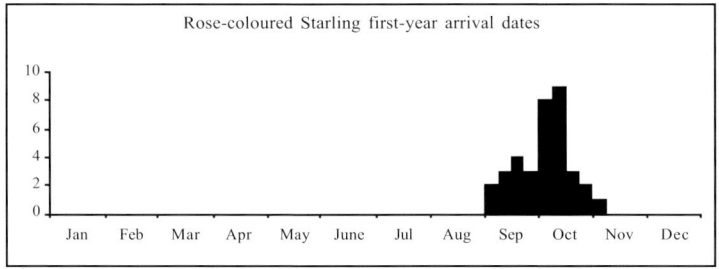

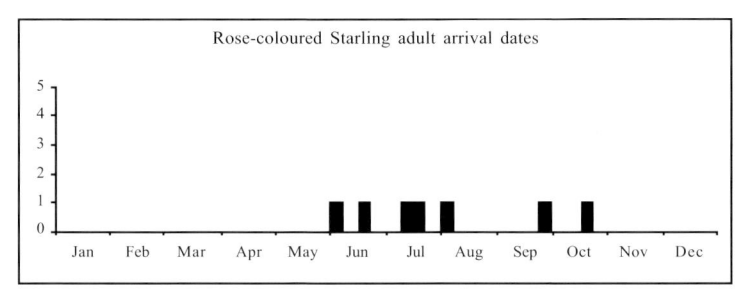

### Rose-coloured Starling annual totals

### Rose-coloured Starling first-year arrival dates

### Rose-coloured Starling adult arrival dates

mainland arrivals involving adults or first-summer individuals during late May to late August, with peak numbers during June (Dymond *et al.* 1989). But this may be at least partly explained by annual autumn concentrations in Scilly of numerous experienced birdwatchers, plus the knowledge that such birds are probably there to be found. Therefore, the shortage of sightings elsewhere might perhaps be due to a lack of large-scale birdwatcher interest in autumn Starling *S. vulgaris* flocks. The same reason may, of course, account for the relative scarcity of Scillonian sightings prior to the 1970s. Earlier concerns over the likely increased involvement of escaped imported birds among sightings, e.g. BBRC Annual Report for 1960, appear not to have been borne out, particularly in view of the greatly increased involvement of juvenile and first-winter individuals. Nationally, the marked occurrence of records from May to October suggests that most individuals are genuine vagrants, with juveniles predominating during September–October. Penhallurick gives 1829 as the first recorded date for the Cornish mainland, from a Lostwithiel garden, and, inevitably, it was shot.

Rose-coloured Starlings move east or southeast from their breeding grounds during autumn, mostly to India and adjoining countries. Thus the spring appearance in western Europe of adults and first-summer individuals (Dymond *et al.* 1989) is perhaps largely explained by overshooting migrants. This being one of the latest migrants to reach its Eurasian breeding grounds, these westward adult arrivals often take the form of an invasion perhaps because they travel in large flocks (Cramp *et al.* 1977–94). However, the annual presence of so many first-years as far west of its range as Scilly seems less easily explained, though it is also one of the earliest migrants to leave the breeding grounds. Birds rapidly desert the colonies after fledging, flocks soon separating into adults and juveniles, with adults migrating first. Cramp *et al.* make no mention of long-distance random juvenile dispersal and so one likely explanation for these first-year birds in extreme western Europe is that they arrived in company with migrant Starlings from eastern Europe, or even further afield, an association often apparent in Scilly. No Rose-coloured Starlings have been ringed in Scilly and there are no recaptures.

# House Sparrow *Passer domesticus* A

**Common breeding species on the five inhabited islands, with most pairs nesting in buildings or tree cavities but a small number utilise holes in coastal cliffs. Reports of free-standing hedgerow nests largely refer to former behaviour.**

Widespread but fragmentary world range, in part due to escapes and introductions. Highly adaptable. Main concentrations Eurasia, southern Africa, Australia and New Zealand, plus North and South America. Within West Palearctic, occurs throughout European landmass plus North Africa and the Nile Valley, with outlying population even in Iceland. Largely sedentary with sporadic large-scale movements mostly involving northern populations. Polytypic, within Eurasia separated into two groups, with *domesticus* group in the north and west and *indicus* group in the south and east. Within *domesticus* group, nominate *domesticus* occurs northern Eurasia including British Isles, western and northern France and Scandinavia east to Ukraine, Crimea, Kazakhstan and northern Mongolia; *balearoibericus* southern France, Spain and Mediterranean islands east to Greece, Balkans and western-central Asia. Red-listed in UK from 2002: rapid, 62% breeding decline over past 22 years. National 7% decline 1994–99 (Bashford & Noble 2000).

As is probably true throughout much of its range, House Sparrow is greatly under-recorded in Scilly, many 20th-century reports either ignoring it or describing it merely as 'widely distributed'. Only on St Agnes and the St Mary's Lunnon Farm study plot do we have any precise counts of breeding number. Lunnon Farm also provided a run of up-to-date breeding data from its small nestbox population. We have also become increasingly aware in recent years of the extent to which House Sparrows utilise natural nest sites in Scilly's low sea-cliffs, though we have no clear information on how long this may have been occurring. Also something of a puzzle are earlier reports of the widespread construction of free-standing tree nests, behaviour which is now extremely uncommon in the islands.

Unfortunately, E H Rodd (1880) proved to be no more productive than later sources, stating only that House Sparrow was common and generally distributed throughout the Cornish mainland, though he did include it in his supplementary list of birds known to occur and breed on Scilly. We also know it occurred on Tresco in 1864, from an otherwise insignificant comment by Rodd's nephew Francis Rodd, who after morning church on an unusually cold Christmas Day took a walk around Tresco Pools, noting a 'singular dearth of little birds in the gardens, nothing to be seen but Sparrows' (Rodd 1880). Twenty-six years after E H Rodd's publication, James Clark and Francis Rodd did slightly better, describing it as a common resident on inhabited islands, adding intriguingly that in July 1903 it was 'abundant between the two hills of Samson' (Clark & Rodd 1906). Certainly, the presence of even a single House Sparrow on Samson now would be notable (pers. obs.) and we can only wonder how anyone had cause to make such a comment early in the 20th century. Unless, of course, it was in some way connected with the even earlier human occupation of Samson. By 1938 it was still being described as common in all suitable habitats, though one visitor noted 'tree nesting seemed more prevalent than on the mainland' (G H Harvey 1938) and a few years on the situation had changed little (Ryves & Quick 1946).

These reports of House Sparrows building free-standing nests are particularly interesting. It seems generally accepted that the growth of the Scillonian flower industry and the associated need for windbreak hedges commenced around the mid-1800s but that the islands remained largely treeless well into the early 20th-century (W Page 1906; Penhallurick 1993). It also seems generally agreed that a substantial tree-planting programme occurred during the 1920s and that this largely accounts for existing shelterbelts of mature Monterrey Pine *Pinus radiata*. The perhaps logical conclusion is that the earlier lack of hedges or trees left buildings as the probable sole option for breeding House Sparrows, but with the added choice of constructing free-standing nests in the newly arrived evergreen hedges from around 1850. The options were perhaps later extended by the appearance of natural tree cavities with the increasing maturity of larger tree species, and by the addition of more buildings. Interestingly, free-standing nests may predominate in areas where enclosed sites are in short supply, with females showing a tendency to select males advertising hole sites (Summers-Smith 1988).

Certainly there is no reason to doubt reports of free-standing hedge nests, as the activity was also formerly more common on mainland Britain. Nonetheless, such nests are now extremely rare in Scilly, just two examples being recorded in ten years of fieldwork between 1991 and 2000 (pers. obs.). Most Scillonian nests nowadays are either in buildings or natural tree cavities, with no shortage of pairs willing to occupy nestboxes, both close to and away from buildings. Most cavity tree nests are in elms *Ulmus*, probably because they provide most cavities, though around Tresco Abbey House Sparrows have been noted excavating holes in the trunks of palm trees *Palmaceae* (*CBWPSAR* 35). Difficult to explain, though, are observations of free-standing nests being common as recently as the mid-1980s and that evidence of this was apparent after the frost of winter 1986–87 killed *Pittosporum* hedges and revealed numerous old nests. But if this was the case, then there seems to have been a rather marked and rapid change in a fundamental aspect of House Sparrow ecology in Scilly.

With the exception of St Agnes, the lack of detail on House Sparrow distribution and numbers continued into the 1980s, what information there was mainly concerning a minority of cliff-nesting pairs. For example, in 1945 a visiting ornithologist listed House Sparrow among the species recorded, but only for St Mary's, with no birds noted on Gugh or St Agnes (Blair 1945). In contrast, a 1957 survey of breeding birds recorded 100+ pairs on these last two islands, with similar numbers in 1958, 1963 and 1964; a similar count on the same islands ten years later again recorded 100 breeding pairs (H P K Robinson 1974a). But importantly, the 1963 count established that out of the 100 nests, 68 on St Agnes and three on Gugh were free-standing structures in *Pittosporum* hedges, whilst eleven were in Tamarisk *Tamarix gallica* bushes, with just one in a building (*SABOAR* 1963–64). However, free-standing House Sparrow nests are bulky, rather obvious affairs and there is likely to have been a clear bias towards recording these, compared with nests in tree cavities, buildings or cliffs.

Regular use of Scillonian cliff sites by House Sparrows became apparent from the early 1980s (Penhallurick 1993) but could have been a feature long before then and may help explain where House Sparrows nested prior to the introduction of trees and evergreen hedgerows. Cliff sites known to have been used, or to be used still, include Lawrences Bay and Wine Cove on St Martin's; Pelistry Bay, Porth Cressa Bay, Porthloo, Old Town Bay, Normandy Sand Pit and Carreg Dhu Gardens, all on St Mary's; plus Gull Point on Gugh and others on Bryher. The Gugh site contains three to four nests and is within one of the largest Kittiwake *Rissa tridactyla* colonies and above an active Herring Gull *Larus argentatus* site. It also contains a pair or two of both Starling *Sturnus vulgaris* and Wren *Troglodytes troglodytes* (pers. obs.). Penhallurick suggested that nests are 'invariably' placed in the soft, black, sandy soil near the clifftop and are possibly excavated by the birds themselves. But whilst this may be true at certain sites, at least some nests on Gugh were in existing holes on the lower and harder strata, perhaps excavated by Brown Rats *Rattus norvegicus*, as is also the case with a high proportion of Starling *Sturnus vulgaris* cliff nests (pers. obs.).

Penhallurick suggested that this tendency for House Sparrows to nest in cliffs above the sea may be unique in Britain, but it was recorded earlier from Shetland (Campbell & Ferguson-Lees 1972) and doubtless occurs elsewhere. But as most cliffs involved in Scilly may be above stretches of beach only reached by the sea during severe weather, this perhaps slightly misrepresents the true situation in any event. One point not made by Penhallurick is that most cliffs involved are quite low (as indeed are the majority of cliffs in Scilly) with the result that House Sparrow nests are frequently only two to three metres from the base. But because Scilly's cliffs face in all directions, not all sites are similarly affected by weather conditions.

Considering the timescale involved, Scillonian flock counts are minimal, being limited to 234 and 308 on St Mary's on 17th and 18th October 1987 and 110 on 13th October 1999. On nearby St Agnes, in 1994 there were 77 in October and 80–100 in November–December, 156 in October 1995 and 300 in mid-October 1999. The only spring count on St Agnes involved 60 in May 1994. There is just one count for Tresco, of 150 in early November 1987. In truth, though, flocks of this size are not unusual, particularly near suitable food supplies during autumn and winter, as around poultry pens in Holy Vale and Normandy on St Mary's, or around New Grimsby on Tresco.

One additional count of 450 for St Agnes (the largest count recorded in the islands) is interesting not just for the number of birds involved but also for the editor's accompanying note 'suggested influx' (*IOSBR* 1973). There is in fact no evidence of House Sparrow movements to or from Scilly or, for that matter, between islands within the archipelago. This is despite a total of 1,757 House Sparrows ringed in Scilly, and even at regular ringing sites local recaptures are unusual. Equally, there is little evidence of large-scale movements between populations within Britain or between Britain and continental Europe. Nevertheless, a small number of birds ringed in Britain and recovered in Belgium and France show there is some exchange, plus autumn passage is known to occur along coastal Brittany, though no information is provided on the source of these birds (Cramp *et al.* 1977–94). Nowadays, House Sparrows are rarely seen away from the five inhabited islands and are largely absent even as winter feeding parties from other islands, e.g. Annet, Samson, St Helen's, Tean or the Eastern Isles; a female on Round Island in November 1983 was the only recent record.

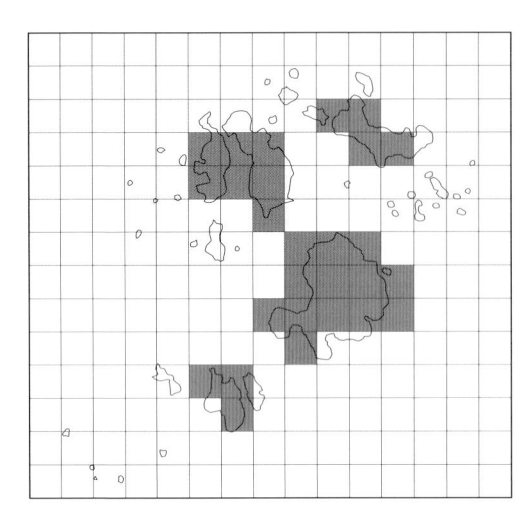

| Island | Pairs |
| --- | --- |
| St Mary's | 190 |
| Tresco | 57 |
| Bryher | 54 |
| St Martin's | 23 |
| St Agnes & Gugh | 21 |

**2000 Breeding Bird Atlas – House Sparrow (Chown & Lock 2002)**

**1-km House Sparrow Breeding Distribution – 2000–01 (data Chown & Lock 2002)**

Until very recently, the only detailed breeding information came from nests on Lunnon Farm, St Mary's and adjoining farmland between 1991 and 2000, mostly in nestboxes but also in farm buildings (P J Robinson unpublished data). Boxes were originally erected for Blue Tits *Parus caeruleus* and Great Tits *Parus major*, their substantial use by House Sparrows being unexpected. About 50% of the ten boxes in use on the plot were annually utilised by tits, House Sparrows occupying the remainder. In general, once a box was occupied by either of these three there was a clear tendency for it to remain in the same occupation. In every year but one there was little indication that House Sparrows attempted to nest in a box once tit broods fledged. The notable exception being 1998, when all boxes vacated by tit broods were taken over by additional sparrow pairs, most of which then raised one or more broods. In this particular year, Starlings too had a high success rate and for both species causes were thought to be weather related. Mean House Sparrow clutch size for 21 Lunnon Farm nests for the three years 1998–2000 was 4.66 (near the upper limit quoted by Cramp *et al.* 1977–94), mean brood size at fledging being 3.05. An attempted annual three broods appears normal for this population (again near the upper limit quoted by Cramp *et al.*) but with a progressive seasonal reduction in clutch size. There was a single recorded instance of predation to a nestbox clutch, presumably by a small mammal, which, owing to the scarcity of small mammalian predators in Scilly, is likely to have involved either House Mouse *Mus domesticus* or Wood Mouse *Apodemus sylvaticus*. Although there has been no past co-ordinated all-island count of House Sparrow pairs, we can nevertheless gain a broad idea of likely numbers involved by reference to three sets of data, namely the former St Agnes and Gugh counts, the annual Lunnon Farm CBC for the eight years 1991–98 and now the 2000 Breeding Bird Atlas (Chown & Lock 2002). Counts of 100 pairs in five out of six survey years on St Agnes and Gugh produce a density in the region 1.48 pairs per hectare for these two islands. However, because House Sparrows are largely absent from large areas, e.g. open heathland, true density where they do occur will be higher. Lunnon Farm annual CBC pair totals for the 16-hectare plot ranged from a low of three to a high of 14, with a mean of 8.8, producing a mean density of 1.8 pairs per hectare. Primitive extrapolation of the St Agnes and Lunnon Farm data to the five main islands suggests a possible figure of anything up to 880 pairs for Scilly, though too much reliance cannot be placed on this. However, the 2000 Breeding Bird Atlas located an estimated 345 pairs in 27 (40.2%) of the 67 1-km squares surveyed, understandably 50% or more of these on St Mary's. Nonetheless, survey methods employed may have seriously underestimated numbers involved and the report's authors thought an upper limit of 600 pairs was possible (Chown & Lock 2002).

Ringing data show that once they have bred House Sparrows remain faithful to the colony for life, any dispersal therefore involving juveniles or non-breeders, only 3% of which nevertheless move more than 20 km (Wernham *et al.* 2002). There have been just three overseas recoveries of British-ringed House Sparrows, from France (2) and Belgium. Seton Gordon & Seton Gordon (1930) saw 'large flocks' on Tresco on 17th March 1929, noting that they 'were chatting in the woods … away from any houses and were apparently on the move'. From this he assumed that they were migrating, though surely he was mistaken. However, there is some suggestion of substantial English east-coast migratory movements prior to the 1950s, though the source or destination of such birds remains obscure (Wernham *et al.* 2002). A total of 1,757 House Sparrows had been ringed on Scilly up until 1999, 1,157 prior to 1970. There are no inter-island recaptures and none away from the islands.

## Spanish Sparrow *Passer hispaniolensis* A BBRC 33.3%

**Extremely rare migrant, full written description required by the BBRC.**

   1972   One (male) St Mary's 21st October   *British Birds* 66: 355, 74: 150
   1977   One (male) Bryher 22nd to 24th October   *British Birds* 71: 524, 74: 150–151

Fragmentary distribution, breeds northwest Africa and Iberia, and from Balkans east through Asia Minor to Turkestan and south into Israel and Egypt, plus Cape Verde Islands, Canary Islands and Sardinia. Complex migration pattern, being more pronounced in east and mainly sedentary in west, in North Africa both sedentary and migratory. Polytypic: nominate *hispaniolensis* occurs in west; *transcaspicus* in Iran and Transcaspia east to Afghanistan. Hybridises with House Sparrow *P. domesticus* in Mediterranean region.

The first record for Britain and Ireland came from Lundy Island, North Devon, on 9th June 1966, to be followed six years later by the first of two on Scilly. The latter was discovered on St Mary's by two fortunate observers on 21st October 1972, as it fed on the ground among a large mixed flock of House Sparrows and Linnets *Carduelis cannabina* in a typical weedy Scillonian flower field. They watched it at close range for half an hour, establishing that it was a male, but it could not be relocated subsequently (Charlwood 1981). The second for Scilly and third for Britain and Ireland, again a male, was found on Bryher in very similar circumstances on 22nd October 1977. An observer searching a weedy field for an Arctic Redpoll *Carduelis hornemanni* present the previous day was distracted by a brief view of a well-marked male among a flock of House Sparrows feeding in the same field. Soon identified as Spanish Sparrow by the original finder plus two inquisitive passing birders, it was subsequently seen by just one other observer before it disappeared for the day. This was to the great consternation of several boatloads of birders en route from St Mary's following release of the information, though it was rediscovered next day and at times provided the unique spectacle of feeding together with the Arctic Redpoll. It was last seen on 24th (Britton 1981).

There were just six records of Spanish Sparrow in Britain from 1958 to the end of 1999, with these two representing one-third of the total. Given reasonable views males should be easily identified from among a flock of House Sparrows but the same is not true of females, in which case we ought not to assume extralimital wandering is confined to males. In this respect, it is interesting to note that two Spanish Sparrows found in Norway prior to 1992 and four in the Camargue, southern France, within the same timescale were all males (Evans 1994). The first for mainland Cornwall, another male, was associating with House Sparrows at Rame Head in November 2000.

The fragmented breeding range and complex movements both among and within populations makes speculation on where these Scillonian records originated extremely difficult, though we must not forget just how many individuals of species with Asiatic or east European breeding ranges do annually reach Scilly. In addition, it may not be unreasonable to suggest that there is more chance of birds from the migratory eastern Spanish Sparrow populations becoming involved in extralimital sightings than the more

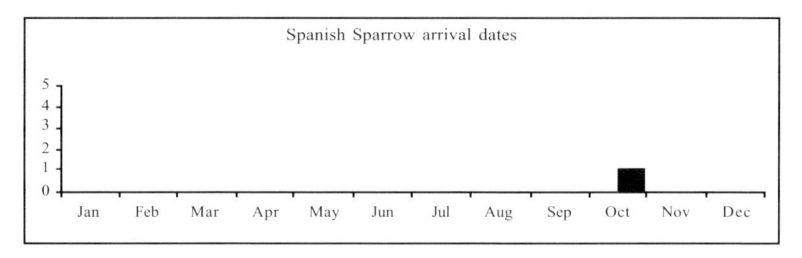

[Chart: Spanish Sparrow arrival dates — single bar in October]

sedentary western birds. Nevertheless, recent substantial Spanish population increases and range extensions (Davies 2001) mean the possibility of birds originating from much closer to the islands cannot be totally dismissed. Neither of these two birds was trapped and ringed.

## Tree Sparrow (Eurasian Tree Sparrow) *Passer montanus* A

**Former regular migrant in small numbers, one to two pairs may have bred during the mid- to late 1960s. Full written description required by the SRP.**

Breeds most of Eurasia apart from Arctic zone, as far as Pacific, including Japan and south into western Indonesia. Various introduced populations, e.g. North America, Australia, Philippines and eastern Indonesia. Mainly sedentary, particularly in west of range. Polytypic: nominate *montanus* occurs Europe from Norway south to Portugal and east to Siberia in north but only Greece in south; *transcaucasicus* Turkey and Caucasus east to Iran; additional forms further east. Red-listed in UK: rapid, 95% breeding decline over past 25 years (Gregory *et al.* 2002). National 92% decline during 25 years to 1996, but 11% increase 1994–99 (Bashford & Noble 2000).

Any preconceptions that Tree Sparrow was formerly common in southwest England are quickly dispelled by a glance at its distribution throughout Britain at the end of the 19th century (Holloway 1996). And the point is further enforced by reference to what E H Rodd had to say about it in Cornwall, describing just two specimens: one he obtained near Penzance and one in Falmouth Museum (Rodd 1880). Of particular interest, however, is Rodd's detailed account of six Tree Sparrows obtained from a Norwegian ship arriving at Penzance on 8th November 1860, having passed through the North Sea. Rodd described how an immense flock of several thousands reportedly came aboard midway between Norway and Britain. The ship's master kept the six as evidence of the event and as further proof of the numbers involved drew attention the 'extent of the droppings on board'. If for no other reason, this account is valuable for what it has to say about the volume of Tree Sparrow movement that might have occurred between Britain and Europe at that time, especially as this report seems not to be referred to by Cramp *et al.* (1977–94).

Nevertheless, Rodd's only mention of Tree Sparrow in relation to Scilly is to include it in his *List of Birds Observed in The Scilly Islands*, against the brief comment 'occasionally met with' (Rodd 1880). James Clark and Francis Rodd's *Zoologist* account repeated that comment, adding that in their own researches they had been unable to locate any authentic specimen or record (Clark & Rodd 1906). A similar statement appeared in the *Victoria County History* (W Page 1906). Therefore, it is not surprising that Ryves & Quick made no mention of Tree Sparrow in their later summary of the status of breeding birds in the islands (Ryves & Quick 1946).

Examination of published reports for the 69 years 1931 to 2000 confirms its scarcity and shows an obvious pattern, with comparatively more in spring than autumn in earlier years and none at all in spring since 1991, except that is for one on Tresco on 6th June 2000. There were a total of 16 years when no birds were recorded on the islands, with none since five were seen coming in off the sea on St Agnes on 15th October 1993 until the 2000 surprise individual. The majority of sightings involved single birds, though twos and threes were recorded more than once, the highest numbers seen together being 15 on St Agnes on 17th May 1961 and then seven on 1st June 1967. Autumn arrivals occurred from the second week of September, with the bulk during October and with just two in early November. Spring arrivals were mostly in May, with one in April and three in early June.

A claim that Tree Sparrows were 'common in outlying parts of St Mary's' in 1946 (*CBWPSAR* 16) is entirely against the evidence of other years and therefore must be treated with caution. More interesting though are David Hunt's descriptions of birds visiting his bird table on Tresco around 1965–69 and one seen there among House Sparrows *P. domesticus* from March to the end of 1966. In 1967 two individuals visited the bird table and in June were seen carrying away food. On 17th June one was watched feeding newly fledged young nearby while the other continued to take food away 'to some distance'. All of this appears to be reasonable proof of breeding in Scilly. However, neither adult was seen again after 17th.

Although in western Europe Tree Sparrow is mainly sedentary, a small proportion undertaking short-distance migration, mostly in a south or southwest direction and periodic large-scale eruptive movements are also known, mostly involving northern populations. In addition, some post-breeding juvenile dispersal takes place and there is evidence of small-scale migration from Fennoscandia down the North Sea coast of Britain from September to November. There is ringing evidence too of movement between England and adjacent coasts of continental Europe (Wernham *et al.* 2002), lending support to a previous theory of east to west movement of Continental birds via southeast England, as formerly suggested from observations at lightships (Cramp *et al.* 1977–94). In this last respect Rodd's account of the birds coming aboard the Norwegian ship, referred to above, may be particularly relevant.

One difficulty in trying to interpret any Tree Sparrow movements through Scilly involves the recent dramatic and well-documented decline in the British population, in common with a number of agriculturally related species, e.g. Corn Bunting *Miliaria calandra*, or Skylark *Alauda arvensis*. However, the drop-off in numbers nationally appears not to be reflected in the pattern of appearances on Scilly up until 1993. Looked at over time, arrivals appear randomly distributed between years, though some earlier reports fail to mention either Tree Sparrow or House Sparrow and it is not always clear if this indicates absence.

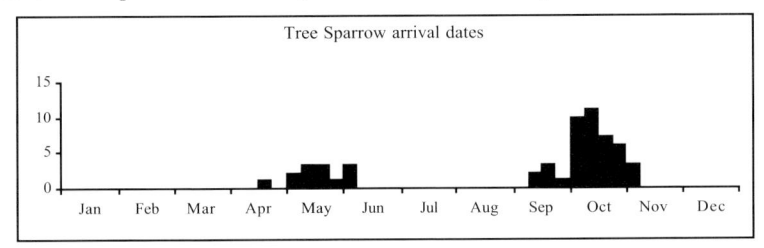

One isolated comment in the 1975 *IOSBR* is particularly difficult to explain, alleging as it does that 'Care is needed with this species as there have been hybrid House x Tree Sparrows in Scilly'. Other than David Hunt's 1967 observations of two birds carrying away food, there appears to be nothing in any of the literature remotely capable of supporting this statement and even were these hybrids coming from elsewhere, we might justifiably expect them to get a mention. In any event, instances of Tree Sparrow x House Sparrow pairs are rare, 'though widely reported' and *BWP* quotes just two cases, both from Malta (Cramp *et al.* 1977–94). It is clear, too, from both Cramp *et al.* and Summers-Smith (1988) that both species normally live sympatrically where their ranges overlap.

## Philadelphia Vireo    *Vireo philadelphicus*  A  BBRC 50%

**Extremely rare migrant, full written description required by the BBRC.**

1987   One Tresco 10th to 13th October
*British Birds* 81: 588, 84: 449, 572–574; *Twitching* 1: 301–302

Nearctic species, breeds mainly Canada, from the Atlantic coast, including Newfoundland, west to British Columbia and south to North Dakota, Michigan and Maine. Migratory, wintering Mexico, Central America and Colombia. Monotypic. Population increasing (Bryant 1997).

One island record, the first for Britain and second for Europe, involved a bird found on Tresco on 10th October 1987. It was first located about 16.00 hours feeding in a hedge by fields on Borough Farm on the island's eastern side. It stayed in the same area until late afternoon on 13th, during which time it was seen by an estimated 1,000 birders (Filby & Good 1987; Good 1991). The bird's discovery followed the arrival on Britain's west coast the previous week of fast-moving weather systems from the opposite side of the North Atlantic, with the associated arrival of other Nearctic migrants in western Britain. The bird's general condition seemed good when found and it had apparently already settled into something of a routine, leading to the belief that it may have arrived prior to the finding date, though not necessarily where first found and perhaps not directly from across the Atlantic. The original observers were of the opinion that the bird could not be aged safely on plumage features, given that no reliable criteria were currently available for this or indeed for a number of other Nearctic passerines, to the extent that BBRC no longer publish ages for these species (*British Birds* 84: 449). For further information on the identification of American vireos in Britain and Europe see Bradshaw (1992).

Philadelphia Vireo rated low in Robbins's statistical review of anticipated transatlantic vagrancy among 38 migrant Nearctic passerines and near-passerines unrecorded in Britain or Ireland during 1947–76, coming thirty-second in the list with a predicted relative likelihood of 0.91 individuals within this period (Robbins 1980). The earliest British, Irish or European presence involved a bird at Galley Head, Co. Cork, Ireland, on the remarkably similar dates of 12th to 17th October 1985 (*Irish Birds* 3: 327). In North America, autumn migration takes place mainly through central USA east of the Rocky Mountains and west of the Appalachians. Southward movement commences in August, most birds passing through interior USA in September and across the Gulf of Mexico mainly in October. The closely related Red-eyed Vireo *V. olivaceus* is the commonest transatlantic North American landbird migrant, but Philadelphia Vireo has a far more restricted breeding range and is far less common than the larger species. This no doubt helps to account for its infrequent appearances on the eastern side of the Atlantic.

# Red-eyed Vireo *Vireo olivaceus* A  BBRC 30.0%

**Rare, regular but not annual autumn migrant. Full written description required by the BBRC.**

1962   One St Agnes 4th to 10th October   *British Birds* 56: 406
1962   One St Agnes 4th to 17th October   *British Birds* 56: 406
1966   One trapped St Agnes 6th October   *British Birds* 60: 329, 61: 176–180
1968   One St Agnes 6th & 7th October   *British Birds* 62: 485
1978   One St Mary's 11th October   *British Birds* 72: 540
1980   One St Mary's 11th to 16th October   *British Birds* 75: 488
1981   One St Mary's 27th Sep to at least 5th October   *British Birds* 72: 527, 78: 514
1981   One St Mary's 29th September to 10th October   *British Birds* 72: 527, 78: 514
1981   One Tresco 11th to 13th October   *British Birds* 72: 527, 78: 514
1982   One St Mary's 21st to 29th September   *British Birds* 76: 521
1983   One Tresco 12th & 13th October   *British Birds* 77: 556
1985   One St Agnes 3rd to 11th October   *British Birds* 79: 8, 578, 82: 555, 83: 488
1985   One St Mary's 4th to 17th October   *British Birds* 79: 8, 578, 82: 555, 83: 488
1985   One St Mary's 7th to 20th October   *British Birds* 79: 8, 578, 82: 555, 83: 488
1985   One Bryher 18th October   *British Birds* 79: 8, 578, 82: 555, 83: 488
1985   One St Martin's 27th October   *British Birds* 79: 8, 578, 82: 555, 83: 488
1986   One St Agnes 19th October to at least 2nd November   *British Birds* 80: 564
1987   One St Mary's 9th to 11th October   *British Birds* 81: 588
1987   One St Agnes 9th to 16th October   *British Birds* 81: 588

| | | |
|---|---|---|
| 1988 | One St Mary's 10th to 15th October | *British Birds* 82: 133, 555 |
| 1988 | One St Mary's 10th to 19th October | *British Birds* 82: 133, 555 |
| 1989 | One St Mary's 20th to 22nd September | *British Birds* 83: 153, 488, 87: 561 |
| 1989 | One St Martin's 11th to 17th October | *British Birds* 83: 153, 488; 87: 561 |
| 1990 | One Tresco 29th September | *British Birds* 84: 487, 499 |
| [1990 | One St Mary's 25th & 26th September] | *IOSBR* 1990 |
| 1993 | One Bryher 1st & 2nd October | *British Birds* 87: 561 |
| 1993 | One Gugh 6th & 7th October | *British Birds* 87: 561 |
| 1995 | One Tresco 3rd to 10th October | *British Birds* 89: 522, 90: 505 |
| 1995 | One St Mary's 7th to 14th October | *British Birds* 89: 522, 90: 505 |
| 1995 | One St Mary's 9th October | *British Birds* 89: 522, 90: 505 |
| 1995 | One St Mary's 10th October | *British Birds* 89: 522, 90: 505 |
| 1995 | One St Agnes 15th to at least 21st October | *British Birds* 89: 522, 90: 505 |
| 1996 | One Tresco 28th September to 2nd October | *British Birds* 90: 505 |
| 1996 | One St Mary's 11th to 20th October | *British Birds* 90: 505 |
| 1996 | One Tresco 13th & 14th October | *British Birds* 90: 505 |
| 2000 | One St Mary's 28th September | *British Birds* 94: 497 |
| 2000 | One Bryher 28th September to 8th October | *British Birds* 94: 497 |
| 2000 | One Tresco 1st October | *British Birds* 94: 497 |
| 2000 | One St Mary's 5th to 12th October | *British Birds* 94: 497 |
| 2000 | One Gugh 15th to 20th October | *British Birds* 94: 497 |
| *2002* | *One St Mary's 26th September* | |

Nearctic species, breeding central Canada south in east to Gulf coast, in west to Oregon and Idaho. Polytypic, comprising two groups: *olivaceus* group occurs North America; *chiva* group South America. Within *olivaceus* group, nominate *olivaceus* occurs throughout North America except interior northwest USA, where replaced by *carniviridis*. North American populations migratory, wintering northern South America. Population increasing (Bryant 1997).

Forty Red-eyed Vireos arrived in Scilly during the 39 years from the first appearance in 1962 and up to year 2000, at an average of just over one per year. Five each in 1995 and 2000 were the most in any year. The Chart includes all arrival dates, including that of a bird seen by numerous observers in Lower Moors, St Mary's, on 25th–26th September 1990 but nonetheless not submitted in writing to the BBRC. Similarly, the 1990 Tresco individual was first noted on 25th September (*IOSBR* 1990) but was accepted by the BBRC only for 29th. Such omissions are hardly unusual among Scillonian rarities and are partly the product of multiple observers assuming others will complete the documentation. Griffiths (1982) also mentioned a bird on St Mary's during 1979 that failed to make the literature and the reader may well know of others. The pattern of arrivals shows this is a classic autumn Nearctic migrant, numbers in Scilly peaking during the first half of October, similar to the national pattern. Birds remained in the islands an average of 6.1 days, the shortest stay being one day (nine individuals) and the longest 24 days.

The BBRC have become uncertain of the safety of attempting to age Red-eyed Vireos based on field reports and now withhold such information (*British Birds* 84: 499); therefore, ages have been omitted from Scillonian records pre-dating that decision. Red-eyed Vireo came ninth in Robbins's statistical review of expected transatlantic vagrancy among 31 migrant Nearctic passerines and near-passerines recorded in Britain or Ireland during 1947–76. However, the eight accepted autumn records greatly exceeded the predicted 4.32 individuals (Robbins 1980). Red-eyed Vireo is a broad-front migrant leaving the breeding areas from mid-August, earliest birds passing the West Indies and Central America by the month's end. Most have left northwest states by early September and few remain in North America by the end of October (Cramp *et al.* 1977–94).

That some birds take the transoceanic route out over the North Atlantic seems self-evident from the fact that it is common in Bermuda at this time. Most if not all of the 113 records accepted by the BBRC up to and including 1999, along with several other Nearctic species, were presumably birds encountering severe westerly winds whilst attempting to reach South America. Differences in Atlantic weather patterns during the early part of the year presumably account for the lack of European spring records, any that are discovered seeming likely to be transatlantic migrants from a previous autumn. The 34 Scillonian records

[Red-eyed Vireo arrival dates chart]

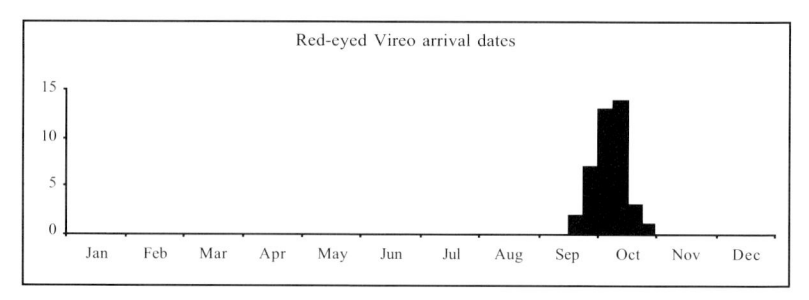

accepted by the BBRC during the period 1958–99 represent 30% of the national total. Two birds on St Agnes in October 1962 represented the first and second records for Britain, being preceded in the British Isles only by a bird killed at the Tuskar Rock Lighthouse, Co. Wexford, Ireland, on 4th October 1951 (Palmer 2000). One Red-eyed Vireo has been ringed in Scilly but there are no recaptures.

# Chaffinch                                                                                                    *Fringilla coelebs*  A

**Breeding resident, migrant and winter visitor.**

Breeds throughout most of Europe, central western Asia and extreme northwest Africa. Resident or dispersive in south and west, migratory in north and east, wintering within remainder of range. Polytypic with complex racial structure, normally separated into *coelebs*, *spodiogenys* and *canariensis* groups. Within *coelebs* group, *gengleri* occurs Britain and Ireland; nominate *coelebs*, or 'Continental Chaffinch', France, Netherlands and Scandinavia east to central Siberia and south to Pyrenees and Mediterranean; sixteen or so additional forms elsewhere. National 3% increase 1994–99 (Bashford & Noble 2000).

James Clark and Francis Rodd viewed this species as a non-breeding frequent autumn migrant, arriving in small flocks often in company with Linnet *C. cannabina*, following which it generally remained through the winter (Clark & Rodd 1906). Occasional larger autumn flocks normally left again within a day or so, with late winter (or early spring) flocks during March mostly comprising females. The latter commonly arrived on a southerly wind, again in company with Linnets.

Several other reports support this description, not least from the Bishop Rock lighthouse, where Chaffinches were noted passing the light from midnight to daybreak on the night of 20th October 1885 (Harvie-Brown *et al.* 1886). Others were reported on the night of 5th November 1907 (Ogilvie-Grant 1909) and the morning of 23rd October 1908 (Ogilvie-Grant 1910). Similarly, E H Rodd reported Chaffinches seen from the deck of the Scilly packet en route from Scilly to Penzance, as they too headed east directly into the wind (Rodd 1866g).

Like most other species, we hear little more of Chaffinch until the 1930s, by which time it was being encountered in the Tresco woodlands during June, though not elsewhere (*CBWPSAR* 8), breeding having been suspected since 1923 (Penhallurick 1978). By 1945 it was being seen on St Mary's during June and A A Dorrien-Smith thought it bred regularly, presumably on both Tresco and St Mary's. In addition, two pairs bred on St Agnes in 1947, where as Penhallurick pointed out, they would hardly have been overlooked had they done so previously. The 2000 Breeding Bird Atlas (Chown & Lock 2002) recorded up to 52 pairs in 13 (19.4%) of the 67 1-km squares surveyed. Birds were confined to just the three islands, St Mary's, Tresco and Bryher. The report's authors suggested that the true figure is probably in the range 40–60 pairs and doubtless a few pairs went unrecorded, as suggested by CBC totals from the Lunnon Farm study plot on St Mary's for the ten years 1991–98 (Table). The ten-year average for the plot was 1.8 pairs, at a density of one pair per 8.8 hectares, though the highest density was a pair every four hectares.

Penhallurick drew attention to mid-20th-century interest in Chaffinch migration through southern England. From this it became clear that westward autumn passage mainly involved Continental birds, which moved through central-southern England as far as the north Devon coast, before heading north towards Ireland, comparatively few continuing west along the northern or southern Cornish coasts as far as Land's End, where they too then headed northwest towards Ireland. Very few apparently flew south towards France. Much Chaffinch migration takes place during darkness, however, and, as we have seen, there is comparatively little information on this species from the Bishop Rock and other local lighthouses.

Nonetheless, birds have been noted passing the Eddystone Rock light at night off southeast Devon between late September and early November, apparently on a southerly heading.

| 1991 | 1992 | 1993 | 1994 | 1995 | 1996 | 1997 | 1998 |
|------|------|------|------|------|------|------|------|
| 2 | 1 | 3 | 0 | 4 | 2 | 3 | 3 |

Chaffinch CBC Pair Totals– 16-ha Lunnon Farm, St Mary's 1991–98 (P J Robinson – unpublished data)

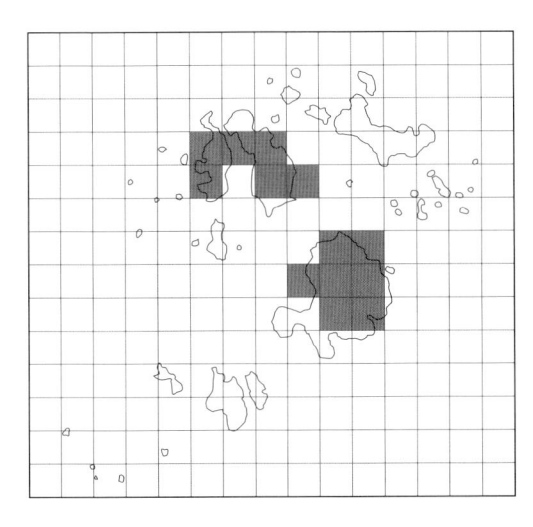

| Island | Pairs |
|--------|-------|
| St Mary's | 20 |
| Tresco | 30 |
| Bryher | 2 |

2000 Breeding Bird Atlas – Chaffinch (Chown & Lock 2002)

1-km Chaffinch Breeding Distribution – 2000–01 (data Chown & Lock 2002)

During the ten years to 1999 large numbers were recorded during autumn and winter, still from around late September, but with falls during mid-October 1990 raising the all-island total to around 2,500, although 200–300 or less was more normal, with Tresco attracting the bulk of any arrivals. Most usually leave the islands by mid-November, those remaining through normal winters seldom exceeding 150. If it occurred at all during the period, then spring passage went largely unnoticed, partly due perhaps to the possibility of confusion with late-staying wintering individuals and residents. The exception was 1999, when peak counts of up to 70 were recorded during mid- to late March, a 'few' only having been reported at the end of 1998.

A largely diurnal migrant, northern European Chaffinch populations move mainly southwest in autumn, western populations wintering furthest west (Cramp *et al.* 1977–94). Most British birds are mainly sedentary, 90% moving no further than 5 km from the natal site, the remainder less than 50 km. However, large numbers of nominate *coelebs* from continental Europe winter in central and southern Britain and Ireland, most of which arrive from Scandinavia via the Low Countries (Wernham *et al.* 2002). A total of 333 Chaffinches had been ringed on Scilly up until the end of 1999, 292 (88%) since 1970 and there are no recaptures.

# Brambling *Fringilla montifringilla* A

Annual, mostly autumn migrant, small numbers may occasionally winter.

Breeds northern Eurasia, from Norway east to Kamchatka. Migratory, wintering south in Europe and western Asia to Mediterranean and Iran, also central eastern Asia. Monotypic. Downgraded from Amber- to Green-listed in UK 2002 (Gregory *et al.* 2002).

James Clark and Francis Rodd considered Brambling an occasional autumn or winter visitor to the islands, being usually rare but occasionally occurring in much greater numbers (Clark & Rodd 1906). They also quoted autumn 1863 and winter 1890–91 as examples of when it was more numerous. However, earliest mention seems to have been E H Rodd's letter to the *Zoologist* describing birds seen in December 1859 (Rodd 1860b). The same authority described how during one winter a youth shot 50 in one morning in west Cornwall (Rodd 1880).

*Birds of the Isles of Scilly*

The apparent lack of early reports from Scillonian lighthouses may perhaps be explained by it being more often referred to by lighthouse keepers as 'Copper Finch', many of which passed the Bishop Rock on the night of 24th October 1886. One dead bird also figured among 70 thrushes *Turdus* killed striking the lantern (Harvie-Brown *et al.* 1887). Penhallurick (1978) perhaps rightly attributed the shortage of early 20th-century Cornish and Scillonian sightings to a lack of observers, though the situation improved post-1949. The last author's mid-1970's review of Scillonian and Cornish records suggested a sharp increase in autumn records in the islands from early October followed by a decrease from mid-November. During the earlier period there was a suggestion of passage between mid-March and the third week of April.

Examination of records for the ten years 1990–99 proves enlightening, earliest autumn arrival dates for the eight recorded years all falling between 3rd and 16th October, whilst seven of the last-sighting dates fell within November, the exceptions being birds on 7th and 15th December. As anticipated, overall numbers involved were difficult to assess but the maximum recorded single-day, all-island count was 49 on 24th October 1997. However, it seems clear a measure of daily, or at least weekly roll-over was involved, in which case numbers of birds passing though the islands may have been greater than records suggest. The highest recent same-day count was 400 on St Mary's on 3rd November 1986, all but 70 of which left by the 5th. Birds were recorded in all ten years during spring, at the rate of over three per year, dates involved falling between 13th March and 14th May, slightly later than Penhallurick's earlier findings. Evidence of overwintering was sparse during the ten years 1990–99, involving birds seen on 1st January 1995, 2nd January 1998 and five during late February 1998. A male on St Martin's on 29th March was in song.

European populations move mainly southwest in autumn, the extent of movement being largely food related, birds favouring areas where beech *Fagus* predominates. Wintering numbers vary substantially between years and additional hard-weather movements may occur. Ringing data show that females and first-years move further than adult males, and whilst some birds reached Britain via the Low Countries, others cross the North Sea direct (Wernham *et al.* 2002). In western Europe, Bramblings winter south of breeding range, mainly as far as France, which perhaps helps explain the bulk of any movement though Scilly, ringing showing that most wintering in Britain originate from Fennoscandia (Cramp *et al.* 1977–94; Wernham *et al.* 2002). Within France, the distribution of Fennoscandian birds shows clear areas of separation, those from Norway in the northwest, from Sweden in the centre and south, and from Finland and western Russia in eastern France. Just seven Bramblings have been ringed in Scilly, all since 1970 and there are no recaptures.

## Serin (European Serin) *Serinus serinus* A

Scarce migrant or vagrant. Treated by the BBRC as a national Scarce Migrant, full written description required by the SRP.

Breeds southern and southwest Europe, from northwest Africa, Iberia, France and (recently) southern and eastern England, east along northern Mediterranean to southern Black Sea and north to southern Baltic coast. Migratory, wintering within southern breeding range. Monotypic. Amber-listed in UK: five-year mean of 1.8 breeding pairs (Gregory *et al.* 2002). Removed from BBRC Rarities List January 1983 (Grant 1982b).

Apparently one of only a few species overlooked by early observers in Scilly and Cornwall, if indeed it occurred at all. The first British record came from Hampshire in 1852 (Palmer 2000), but E H Rodd makes no mention of this species in his epic late 19th-century work (Rodd 1880). Therefore, the first record for the islands involved a male discovered on St Agnes as recently as 9th May 1962, to be followed later the same year by two, a male plus one other, on the same island on 13th October.

The Charts incorporate all arrival dates and show all birds recorded in Scilly, regardless of the species' removal from the BBRC Rarities List in 1983. The recent increase in spring sightings is in line with the recent British increase generally; Dymond *et al.* (1989) found a 'dramatic' increase in spring and summer records nationally from 1967, at which time breeding commenced in southern England. The arrival dates show a clear separation into spring and autumn, though with greater numbers during the latter period. There is little doubt that the majority, if not all birds were involved in some form of regular movement. Several sightings involved two or more individuals, up to a maximum of eight being present in the islands at any time. The first sightings for mainland Cornwall occurred during winter 1966–67, when up to eleven were present in the county between late October and mid-March (Penhallurick 1978).

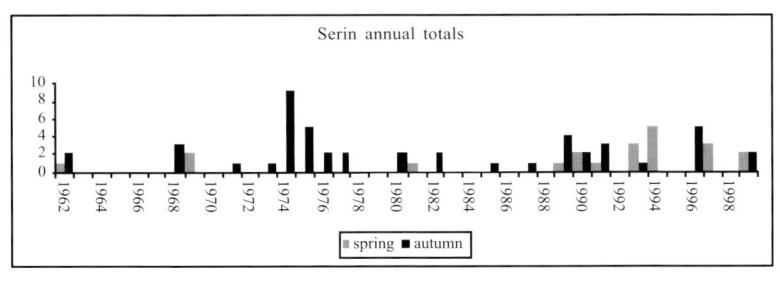

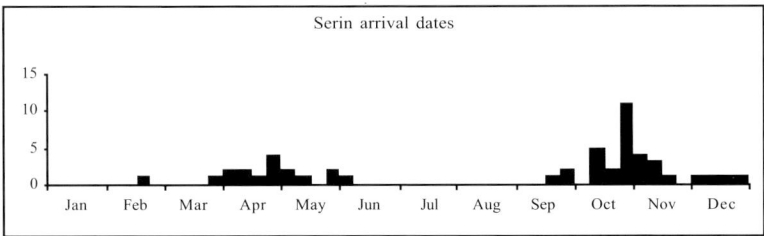

*Serin annual totals* chart (spring/autumn bars, 1962–1998)

*Serin arrival dates* chart (Jan–Dec)

Spring arrivals are perhaps mainly attributable to overshooting by populations returning to breeding grounds in central Europe, although birds are increasingly present in winter as far north as France. Autumn passage commences from September, a few birds moving earlier, peaks during October and continues through into November, birds from western Europe heading mainly southwest towards Iberia. Nevertheless, the fact that few breed further north in Europe than Denmark or Poland fails to explain the autumn movement of birds though Scilly, unless of course they are from the small English population. Return spring passage commences from late February or March, most reaching central Europe by April, though the timing varies considerably between years (Cramp *et al.* 1977–94).

## Greenfinch (European Greenfinch)                   *Carduelis chloris* A

**Breeding resident and spring and autumn migrant, both the source and destination of which are unclear.**

Largely confined to West Palearctic, with outlying population southern Kazakhstan and introduced populations elsewhere, e.g. Australia. Partial migrant, some southern populations resident or dispersive. Polytypic, with complex racial structure: *harrisoni* (not recognised by BOURC) occurs England, Wales, Ireland and southern Scotland; nominate *chloris* northern Europe, from northern Scotland, Scandinavia, Belgium and Netherlands east to Ural Mountains and south to Alps and European Russia; *aurantiiventris* France, Spain, Balearic Islands east to Greece; *vanmarli* northwest Spain, Portugal and northwest Morocco; six or so additional forms south and east. National 20% increase 1994–99 (Bashford & Noble 2000).

It is clear that even as long ago as the mid-19th century, Greenfinch was recognised as a regular migrant through the islands. Clark and Rodd, however, thought it more a winter visitor, despite describing how a flock of 400 in October 1904 rested only two or three days before moving on (Clark & Rodd 1906). They also thought it usual in small parties during most years, or even singly, though in 1849, 1894 and 1904 it arrived in 'large flocks'. These two also saw fit to mention twelve or so in Holy Vale, St Mary's, in late April 1903, none of which, according to them, remained to breed. Equally descriptive is Francis Rodd's account to his uncle E H Rodd of large flocks present on all main islands during October 1870, two barrels of a shotgun fired into a flock 'of some hundreds' producing 33 birds (Rodd 1870h).

Actual accounts of visible migration are few, one of interest involving a flock seen from the Scilly packet as they passed the ship flying directly into an easterly wind en route for mainland Cornwall (Rodd 1966g). Another is the description of large flocks arriving in Scilly after 1st September 1870, along with similar or greater numbers of other finches Fringillidae (Rodd 1870h).

Clark and Rodd's observation that none in spring 1903 remained to breed perhaps suggests they may have done so in other years, but the first recorded evidence came in 1923, with one singing on Tresco

*Birds of the Isles of Scilly*

(Wallis 1923), whilst in the following year Boyd (1924) reported 'many' in Tresco Gardens on 30th June, which he thought were 'doubtless family parties'.

| 1991 | 1992 | 1993 | 1994 | 1995 | 1996 | 1997 | 1998 |
|------|------|------|------|------|------|------|------|
| 6 | 8 | 8 | 6 | 5 | 5 | 10 | 6 |

Greenfinch CBC Pair Totals– 16-ha Lunnon Farm, St Mary's 1991–98 (P J Robinson – unpublished data)

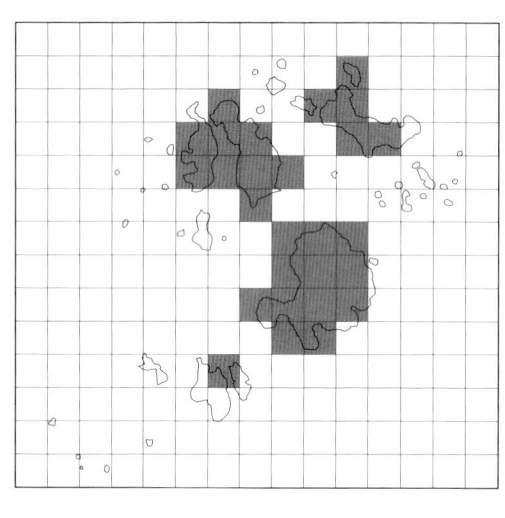

| Island | Pairs |
|--------|-------|
| St Mary's | 97 |
| Tresco | 18 |
| Bryher | 2 |
| St Martin's | 14 |
| St Agnes & Gugh | 1 |
| White Island, St Martin's | 1 |

2000 Breeding Bird Atlas – Greenfinch (Chown & Lock 2002)

1-km Greenfinch Breeding Distribution – 2000–01 (data Chown & Lock 2002)

By 1946, small numbers were breeding on both Tresco and St Mary's, the first breeding record for St Agnes coming in 1974, though even by this last date an all-island figure remained elusive (Penhallurick 1978). On the 16-hectare Lunnon Farm study plot on St Mary's during the eight years 1991–98, an average of 6.75 pairs was recorded by the annual CBC, giving an average density of one pair per 2.3 hectares, high of 1.6 hectares, low of 3.2. On the five main islands, the 2000 Breeding Bird Atlas (Chown & Lock 2002) located an estimated 133 pairs in 27 (40.2%) of the 67 1-km squares surveyed, 73% of these on St Mary's (Table). The report's authors fixed the possible upper limit at 150 pairs.

Penhallurick also commented on the lack of information indicating either the source or destination of Greenfinches moving through both Scilly and Cornwall (Penhallurick 1978). And for Scilly, that rather surprisingly remains the situation still, regardless of the fact that 892 have been ringed in the islands, 761 (85%) since 1970. Furthermore, 62% of that overall total (556 birds) were ringed on the Lunnon Farm plot during the four years 1997–2000: 99 in 1997, 244 in 1998, 130 in 1999 and 83 in 2000. In an attempt to establish both source and destination, birds have been targeted using feeder stations, a centrally placed feeder on an island the size of St Mary's being likely to attract most birds present. However, at the end of the four years, it was still not possible to say with certainty what the movement patterns were, though it seems increasingly likely, as suggested by the few recaptures (Table), that these were mainly Scillonian Greenfinches. This is evident from the apparent spring return of birds ringed in mainland Britain and the winter controls on mainland Britain of birds ringed in Scilly, plus a high between-year recapture rate and the absence of many recaptures elsewhere. It is also interesting that observations on St Agnes prior to the 1970s, and before the recent population growth, suggested only a light spring passage.

The annual spring movement (return) becomes evident from as early as late February and peaks during early April. A population of up to 175 pairs plus any non-breeders is seemingly likely to support the kind of numbers involved in recent annual captures. The two obvious anomalies are the Essex control three weeks after being ringed on St Agnes in April and the bird ringed in Dorset the previous June. Of significance, too, is the lack of mainland winter recaptures of birds ringed in Scilly, bearing in mind the number of garden trapping stations targeting this and similar species.

Nevertheless, the possibility that Greenfinches do annually pass though the islands during spring and autumn, perhaps en route to and from France or further south, cannot be discounted. The source of such movements could be either mainland Britain or Ireland. And certainly any suggestion of local breeding birds now being involved fails to explain 19th- and early 20th-century reports of large autumn and winter arrivals. Reports for the ten years from 1990 contain frequent reference to apparent autumn influxes, mainly based on the presence of small flocks, though up to 210 were involved in 1997. Most reports made it clear that few remained in the islands by the year's end. However, an earlier report, for 1976, recorded a peak of 350 on St Agnes on 22nd October.

Within western Europe, the general direction of autumn migration or winter dispersal is towards the southwest, birds nonetheless remaining within the limit of the breeding range. Within Britain, birds from central and eastern England are more likely to move greater distances than those from the southwest, recoveries of birds ringed in the southwest during winter coming mainly from southeast England (Cramp et al. 1977–94), which perhaps explains the Essex individual from St Agnes. Most overseas recoveries of British-ringed Greenfinches come from coastal France and Belgium, with evidence of a small movement between Britain and Ireland (Wernham et al. 2002). In addition, some birds from northern Europe winter in or pass through Britain on passage, though none apparently from east of Norway.

## Controls

| | | | | |
|---|---|---|---|---|
| VR99534 | Ad | Nanjizal, Land's End, Cornwall 9th March 1997 | CT | Lunnon Farm, St Mary's 29th March 1997 |
| VX48916 | Ad | Lundy Island, Devon 31st October 1997 | CT | Lunnon Farm, St Mary's 30th March 1999 |
| VX47956 | 2ndY | Portland Bird Observatory, Dorset 6th June 1998 | CT | Lunnon Farm, St Mary's 4th April 1999 |
| VX68329 | Ad | Nanjizal, Land's End, Cornwall 30th October 1999 | CT | Lunnon Farm, St Mary's 5th April 1999 |

## Recoveries

| | | | | |
|---|---|---|---|---|
| NK07981 | Ad | St Agnes 16th April 1986 | CT | Epping, Essex 7th May 1986 |
| VC73931 | ? | St Martin's, 30th October 1990 | CT | Timsbury, Avon 9th December 1990 |
| VC73945 | 1stY | St Martin's 19th October 1991 | KW | Drift, west Cornwall 9th November 1991 |
| VP22800 | Ad | Lunnon Farm, St Mary's 29th March 1997 | CT | Plymouth, Devon 23rd January 2000 |

**Greenfinch Ringing Recaptures**

# Goldfinch (European Goldfinch) *Carduelis carduelis* A

**Widespread but not abundant breeding species, autumn flocks may include birds from elsewhere.**

Breeds southern and central Europe east though central Asia to Mongolia, outlying population Himalayas. Migratory in north and eastern Turkey, wintering within remainder of range. Polytypic with complex racial structure, normally divided into *carduelis* group and *caniceps* group. Within *carduelis* group, *britannica* occurs Britain, Ireland, northwest France and coastal Low Countries; nominate *carduelis* central France and Denmark east to central European Russia; *volgensis* European Russia; *major* central and western Siberia and further east and south. Additional forms further west, south and east. Downgraded from Amber- to Green-listed in UK 2002 (Gregory et al. 2002). National 28% decline during 25 years to 1996, then 1% increase 1994–99 (Bashford & Noble 2000).

The apparent earliest reference to Goldfinch was Heath's observation that it was found in the islands year-round (Heath 1750). E H Rodd later described it as a periodic migrant, varying in numbers and time of appearance, his only mention of flocks involving the winter months (Rodd 1880). James Clark and Francis Rodd's early 20th-century account mentioned the prominence of autumn family parties, as is still the case, but made mention only of spring flocks, mainly in the region of 12–20 birds (Clark & Rodd 1906). In comparison, nowadays late summer or autumn flocks of 100 or more are a prominent feature. However, again in 1906, in the *Victoria History of Cornwall*, James Clark mentioned family parties occurring both in autumn and winter (in W Page 1906).

By the mid-20th century, Goldfinch was being described as having recently spread to the islands and by 1938 was presumed to breed only on Tresco (Ryves & Quick 1946). The first confirmed breeding occurred in 1940, according to Penhallurick (1978) in a pear tree in the Tresco orchard. Ryves and Quick also quoted a family party on St Mary's in August 1943 as the first summer record for that island. Penhallurick thought Heath's mid-18th-century comment could not be considered proof of breeding, but it is difficult to see why else Goldfinch would remain in Scilly 'year-round'. In addition, from Clark and Rodd's reference to family parties, we can perhaps assume it bred also during the 19th century, though Penhallurick was again doubtful, perhaps because it was considered rare in southwest England at that time (Holloway 1996). Nonetheless, the case for a summer absence from the islands prior to the 1940s seems not fully proved, particularly as so little information has found its way to us from the early 20th century and the possibility exists that it was overlooked. However, that is not quite the same as denying an increase took place in Scilly from the 1940s, which would have been in line with the national situation (Parslow 1968a). On St Agnes, two pairs were recorded in six of the eight survey years between 1957 and 1978, the exceptions being 1963 and 1964, when none and a single pair were recorded respectively. Annual pair totals on the 16-hectare Lunnon Farm study plot during the eight years 1991–98 ranged between two and six, at an average of 3.87, giving a mean density of 4.1 hectares per pair, maximum 2.6, minimum 8.0. The 2000 Breeding Bird Atlas (Chown & Lock 2002) located an estimated 82 pairs in 21 (31.3%) of the 67 1-km squares, birds being limited to the five main islands (Table). However, the report's authors thought the upper limit could be as high as 100 pairs.

Although Goldfinch migration through the islands does possibly occur, there is little direct evidence. Numbers of pairs recorded during the most recent breeding survey were perhaps enough to account for two or three late summer or autumn flocks of several hundred birds. The largest reported flock in the ten years to 1999 was 250 on St Mary's in late October. In addition, a feature of this species in Scilly are the late summer, e.g. August or September, family parties of quite recently fledged young, the majority of which are too young to have reached the islands from mainland Cornwall, much as described by Clark and Rodd in 1906. But although there appears to be no mention of this species at Scillonian lighthouses, Penhallurick referred to an 'undeniable' pre-1912 mid-October peak at the Eddystone light off south Devon. Several 19th-century comments also seem to indicate migration, e.g. Francis Rodd wrote to his uncle E H Rodd in Penzance in 1870 suggesting that there had been more Goldfinches than usual since 1st September (Rodd 1870h).

| 1991 | 1992 | 1993 | 1994 | 1995 | 1996 | 1997 | 1998 |
|---|---|---|---|---|---|---|---|
| 4 | 4 | 3 | 2 | 6 | 4 | 6 | 2 |

Goldfinch CBC Pair Totals – 16-ha Lunnon Farm, St Mary's 1991–98 (P J Robinson – unpublished data)

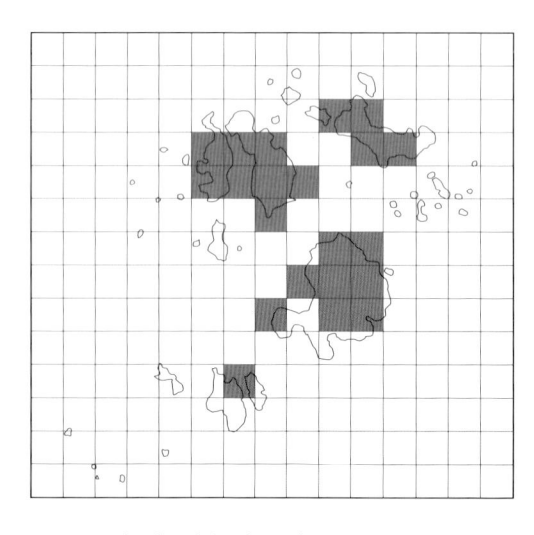

| Island | Pairs |
|---|---|
| St Mary's | 48 |
| Tresco | 18 |
| Bryher | 9 |
| St Martin's | 6 |
| St Agnes & Gugh | 1 |

**2000 Breeding Bird Atlas – Goldfinch (Chown & Lock 2002)**

**1-km Goldfinch Breeding Distribution – 2000–01 (data Chown & Lock 2002)**

Most birds of the form *britannica* breeding in Britain migrate, most moving initially southeast into central Europe, where they may be joined by nominate *carduelis*, before then migrating southwest into France and Iberia, more rarely North Africa (Wernham *et al.* 2002). Some 95% of Goldfinches wintering in

Iberia originate from western Europe. However, different individuals may leave Britain in different years and the extent of migration may similarly vary between years. Importantly perhaps for Scilly, there is some evidence of passage between south and southeast Ireland and Britain, and if migrants do pass through Scilly then this seems a likely source. Some early reports of winter arrivals were doubtless attributable to hard-weather movements. A total of 285 Goldfinches had been ringed in Scilly up until 1999, 200 of those since 1970 and there are no recaptures.

## Siskin (Eurasian Siskin) *Carduelis spinus* A

**Annual migrant in moderate numbers, mostly in autumn and occasional winter visitor.**

Breeds central Eurasia, from Norway, Britain and Pyrenees east to Sakhalin and Japan. Populations from northern Europe east to Pacific migratory, in the west wintering southern Europe and extreme northwest Africa east to Kazakhstan, in the east wintering Japan and southeast China. Monotypic.

James Clark and Francis Rodd considered Siskin a regular visitor to the islands both in autumn and winter, sometimes singly but more often in parties of from four to seven (Clark & Rodd 1906). However, the only examples they gave involved a confiding but restless party of five along Tresco's Abbey Drive for several days during January 1904, plus six or so separate parties that arrived on Tresco in company with Goldcrests *Regulus regulus* and Chiffchaffs *Phylloscopus collybita* during early November 1905. Earlier, Francis's uncle E H Rodd noted it appearing in flocks chiefly during winter (Rodd 1880), and that it occurred in 'considerable numbers during the latter half of November 1867, (Rodd 1868d). Similarly, Francis recorded birds present in gorse *Ulex* bushes on St Martin's during early November 1870 (Rodd 1880). The picture that emerges until at least the start of the 20th century is one of a late autumn or early winter appearance.

Siskin underwent an expansion in England and Wales during the mid-20th century (Parslow 1968a), to the point where it now breeds commonly in Devon, though still scarcely in Cornwall. Penhallurick (1978) examined records for Scilly and Cornwall up until the mid-1970s, finding a recognisable autumn passage both sides of the water, peaking in the islands during the latter half of October with fewer sightings after early November. The only Scillonian winter records involved singles on the 1st December 1955 and 1961, plus one caught by a cat *Felis catus* on St Mary's on 10th January 1965. Autumn parties normally numbered less than ten, though six daily counts of 100 or more during late October were on record. The highest count for the period involved 200 in late October 1975, at which time 'unprecedented' numbers were present in Cornwall. The only presence Penhallurick could trace during the early part of the year concerned one heard in song from February up until 12th March 1973.

Examining the ten years 1990–99, numbers varied substantially between years, the least in any one year were perhaps the 12 during October 1995. At the other extreme, single flocks of 300 or more were present on both St Mary's and Tresco during early to mid-October 1990, which together with other islands suggests at least 1,000 may have been present at one time. In autumn, first arrivals occurred most frequently during late September, with most final sighting dates during November, though in a few years birds remained to the year's end or later. There were also a surprising number of late spring sightings, mostly involving singles between mid-April and mid-May, though no more than one per year. Also surprising was the presence of singles during mid- to late June 1990 and 1992, the earlier of these representing the first recorded summer presence in the islands. Despite several references to Siskins remaining into the following year, the only record for the latter half of the winter period involved one on 17th and three on 29th January 1992.

Most Siskins are nomadic during winter, numbers migrating varying between years. During years of ample food availability, many in Britain, Ireland and southern Scandinavia either remain within or close to the breeding areas, or delay movement until the winter (Cramp *et al.* 1977–94). Routes to and from breeding and wintering areas are complex, with much between-year variation. Nonetheless, British-ringed birds have been recovered in both western Russia and Algeria (Wernham *et al.* 2002). In northern Europe, autumn migration commences as early as August, peaking September or October, though again the timing and numbers of birds involved varies from year to year.

A total of 135 Siskins had been ringed in Scilly up until the end of 1999, 128 (95%) of these since 1970. The only recapture involved a bird ringed on St Martin's on 27th October 1993 and controlled on

St Agnes the following day. The capture of four Siskins (one male and three females) out of a slightly larger group on the Lunnon Farm study plot on 29th October 1996 involved birds clearly attracted to the taped song of Yellow-browed Warbler *Phylloscopus inornatus*. All four were concentrated in a tight group in the bottom shelf of the mistnet adjacent to the tape recorder (pers. obs.).

## Linnet (Common Linnet) *Carduelis cannabina* A

**A mainly summer visitor, breeding on all main and some smaller islands. Also an annual spring and autumn migrant, it reportedly occurred previously in wintering flocks.**

Breeds Europe except extreme north, plus North Africa and central Asia east to western Siberia and Kazakhstan. Northern populations migratory, wintering within or just south of breeding range. Polytypic with complex racial structure: nominate *cannabina* occurs Europe and western Siberia south to Pyrenees, former Yugoslavia and Kazakhstan; *autochthona*, or 'Scottish Linnet', Scotland; *mediterranea* Iberia east through Mediterranean to Bulgaria; three or more additional forms Atlantic islands; North African form unclear. Red-listed in UK: rapid, 55% breeding decline over past 25 years (Gregory *et al.* 2002). National 53% decline during 25 years to 1996 and 14% decline 1994–99 (Bashford & Noble 2000).

As long ago as the 18th century, Robert Heath noted the year-round presence of Linnets in the islands (Heath 1750), though by the 1800s its seasonal status seemed less clear. E H Rodd thought it a periodic migrant, 'varying according to circumstances, in numbers and time of appearance' (Rodd 1878b). Nonetheless, the apparent 19th-century assumption that it was mainly an autumn or early winter visitor perhaps largely reflected a scarcity of observers at other times, there being few spring or summer reports from the islands during the 1800s. Writing to his uncle E H Rodd in both December 1864 and January 1865, Francis Rodd commented on new arrivals of Linnets on Tresco. However, only just into the 20th century, Francis and co-author James Clark felt able to describe it as a regular migrant in both spring and autumn, when it frequently occurred together with Chaffinches *Fringilla coelebs*, whilst it also sometimes appeared during winter (Clark & Rodd 1906).

Importantly, Clark and Rodd noted that although it had not previously been recorded breeding in the islands, nests were nevertheless found on the St Mary's Garrison and on St Martin's in 1903, and on Tresco the following year. One possible explanation is that it may previously have been overlooked, support for this view perhaps coming from the casual discovery of three nests on St Mary's in 1914, with additional family parties in evidence (H W Robinson 1914). However, Penhallurick (1978) was of the opinion that all this pointed to an increase in breeding activity in the islands, whilst acknowledging that it may have been overlooked at the end of the 19th century. Most certainly, in the 1938 publication of *CBWPSAR* G H Harvey felt able to describe it as 'Common in June – abundant in all suitable localities – more plentiful than on the Mainland'. Thirty years on, Parslow found evidence of a national 19th-century decrease, and a subsequent 20th-century increase involving parts of central and southern England. Although it is unclear exactly what the effects of all this might have been on southwest England, by the mid-1900s the national trend appeared mostly downwards, driven mainly, it seems, by habitat loss. This was most notably loss of 'waste land' to agricultural improvement, but also through reductions in gorse (Parslow 1968a). Neither of these changes would have been particularly marked in either Scilly or west Cornwall. Interestingly, Holloway (1996) thought it common throughout Cornwall during the late 19th century and though he did not show Linnet as occurring in Scilly, it is difficult to believe it would not have crossed from the mainland. More recently, there appears to have been some reduction in both range and numbers breeding in mainland Cornwall between the 1970s (Sharrock 1976) and the early 1990s (Gibbons *et al.* 1993).

The most useful past survey was probably the series of counts on St Agnes and Gugh during eight of the 22 years 1957–78. Linnet numbers on this pair of connected islands was recorded in six of those years, with a 50% increase between the two extremes (Table). Importantly, Penhallurick drew attention to an earlier survey on the same islands by Buxton, who found just 20 pairs in 1948.

| 1957 | 1958 | 1962 | 1964 | 1974 | 1978 |
|---|---|---|---|---|---|
| 40 | 40 | 40 | 50 | 80 | 65 |

St Agnes & Gugh Breeding Survey Data – Linnet Pairs (*IOSBR* 1979)

| 1991 | 1992 | 1993 | 1994 | 1995 | 1996 | 1997 | 1998 |
|---|---|---|---|---|---|---|---|
| 10 | 6 | 9 | 9 | 3 | 4 | 5 | 8 |

Linnet CBC Data – 16-ha Lunnon Farm, St Mary's 1991–98 (P J Robinson – unpublished data)

| Island | Pairs |
|---|---|
| St Mary's | 101 |
| Tresco | 111 |
| Bryher | 90 |
| St Martin's | 99 |
| St Agnes & Gugh | 30 |
| Samson | 5 |
| St Helen's | 6 |
| Tean | 7 |
| White Island, St Martin's | 1 |
| Great Ganilly | 2 |
| Others | 2 |

2000 Breeding Bird Atlas – Linnet (Chown & Lock 2002)

1-km Linnet Breeding Distribution – 2000–01 (data Chown & Lock 2002)

Regrettably, we have little information on survey methods employed on St Agnes, for what is acknowledged as a difficult species to census in any event. On the 16-hectare Lunnon Farm study plot during the eight years 1991–98 recorded totals ranged between three and ten pairs. If true, this would give an annual mean of 6.7 pairs, or a pair every 2.3 hectares. However, there was considerable doubt over the validity of CBC counts involving this species on the plot, which for the most part recorded females that fed on the ground accompanied by attentive males, both of which then rapidly moved elsewhere. Resorting to counts based on numbers of nests found produced a substantially smaller figure, though this is an even less effective census method. In addition, the mainly farmland and low wetland plot contains little of what can be considered typical Linnet breeding habitat, e.g. gorse *Ulex*. Penhallurick quoted an unnamed source as suggesting that Song Thrush *Turdus philomelos* outnumbered Linnet on St Mary's (presumably during the breeding season), though such a suggestion nowadays would be difficult to substantiate.

More recently, the 2000 Breeding Bird Atlas (Chown & Lock 2002) recorded a possible 454 pairs in 41 (61.1%) of the 67 1-km squares surveyed. Birds were located on at least eleven islands and breeding was reportedly confirmed in 14 squares, though details of what constituted confirmation were not provided. The report's estimate of the overall likely pair total fell in the range 300–600. If true, then figures of this magnitude probable give the Scillonian Linnet population at least regional importance.

*Birds of the Isles of Scilly*

Penhallurick thought that on Scilly Linnet was mostly seen on migration, quoting 1960 flocks of up to 600 on St Agnes as exceptional, although by 1974 up to 3,000 were being recorded in the autumn Tresco fields. The same author drew attention to difficulties involved in distinguishing between lingering winter 'residents' and spring migrants, though he thought April the main migration period during the early part of the year. Although most autumn migration apparently occurred during October, he was unclear to what extent this also reflected the increased presence of birdwatchers at this time. Examination of the *IOSBRs* for the 1990s reveals a pattern of small-scale spring arrivals from about early to mid-March, though rarely with flocks of more than 100 involved. Autumn passage commenced from late July to early September, flock counts usually remaining around 250 or less, though a St Mary's island count produced 800 during mid-September 1991. Very noticeable is the shortage of Linnets after November and through to the commencement of any spring influx, 25 being evident still by the end of 1991, whilst in 1993 two on 17th December were the last of the year. This situation conflicts markedly with Penhallurick's and earlier observers' suggestions of wintering flocks, though perhaps these more properly referred to late autumn numbers. Autumn flocks can be widely distributed, these being frequently encountered feeding on Annet's seeding Thrift *Armeria maritima*, or similarly on the summit and slopes of Round Island (Beswetherick 1969).

The Table shows all except local ringing recaptures and reveals a somewhat confused situation. For whilst there is a clear pattern of movement between Lundy Island to the north and France and northern Spain to the south, the timing of these movements is not always so easily understood. As in the case of the bird ringed on St Agnes in early May and recaptured in northern France the following July. Some though, like AA43810, were presumably on autumn migration from further north or, like KC09559, perhaps on return migration. Penhallurick drew attention to A858260, pointing out that it may have been breeding locally, thus making its subsequent recovery in France somewhat surprising. A total of 1,956 Linnets have been ringed in the islands, 1,216 (62%) prior to 1970, this last figure perhaps demonstrating a recent fall-off in the volume of Linnet passage.

Of those European Linnet populations that migrate, most ultimately move south or southwest in autumn, remaining within or immediately south of the breeding range, which in southern Europe takes them no further than coastal North Africa (Cramp *et al.* 1977–94); this last area and the Mediterranean basin hold notable wintering concentrations. There is no obvious logic to any British migration, different individuals moving south in different years and with the proportion of the population involved also varying between years. Birds move mainly by day, most crossing the English Channel at its eastern end, before altering direction and heading in a narrow band towards western France and central Spain (Wernham *et al.* 2002). Ringing data also reveal individual variation in the distance travelled.

Few winter in Ireland and despite a lack of ringing data most are thought to head southeast towards France and Spain, a route that would presumably bring a proportion to Scilly, some British birds perhaps also taking the Irish route. Within Britain, hard-weather movements occur during some winters though direction of travel and destination remain unclear, but could perhaps account for at least some Scillonian winter records. Positive evidence perhaps for the autumn presence in Britain of Continental birds includes a very small number of British-ringed individuals recovered in the Low Countries (Wernham *et al.* 2002). Presumably some individuals of the closely similar *autochthona* or 'Scottish Linnet' reach Scilly.

**Controls**
KC09559  1stY  Lundy Island, Devon
              20th September 1976           CT  St Agnes 20th April 1977

**Recoveries**
J69332    Ad    St Agnes 2nd May 1960       ?   Quimper, Finistere, France 11th July 1960
AA43810   1stY  St Agnes 13th September 1960 CT  Lundy Island, Devon 21st October 1960
AA43855   1stY  St Agnes 14th September 1960 FD  Plouhinec, Finistere, France
                                                 2nd February 1963
?         1stY  Gugh 10th July 1972         ?   Suances, Santander, Spain
                                                 23rd February 1973
A858260   Ad    St Martin's 9th June 1982   FI  Pleyben, Finistere, France 9th March 1983

**Linnet Ringing Recaptures**

# Twite                                                    *Carduelis flavirostris*  **A**

**Extremely rare vagrant, full written description required by the SRP.**
  1965   One St Agnes 2nd October
  1990   One St Agnes 23rd October

Discontinuous European and Asian breeding distribution, restricted mainly to upland or tundra, with isolated northwest European population in western Ireland, northern Britain, Norway, Sweden and Arctic coast east to Murmansk. Eastern populations from southeast of Black Sea to central Eurasia and south to the Himalayas. Northwest European populations other than British Isles wholly or partially migratory, wintering central Europe. Polytypic, with complex racial structure: nominate *flavirostris*, or 'Northern Twite', occurs Norway, Sweden and northwest Russia; *pipilans* Britain and Ireland except Outer Hebrides: *bensonorum*, or 'Hebridean Twite', Outer Hebrides; many additional forms further east and south. Red-listed in UK: historical population decline (Gregory *et al.* 2002).

There are just two confirmed reports from the islands, both on St Agnes and both involving single birds. Both reports lack detail, however, the earlier one merely giving the date as 2nd October 1965 (*CBWPSAR* 35), though it seems to have been a multiple-observer record. The second report appears in *IOSBR* 1990 and is equally brief, just recording the place as Wingletang Down and the date as 23rd October. There were at least two further, unsubstantiated, claims, involving birds thought to have been present on St Agnes on 14th October 1993 and at Old Grimsby, Tresco, on 13th and perhaps 14th October 1995.

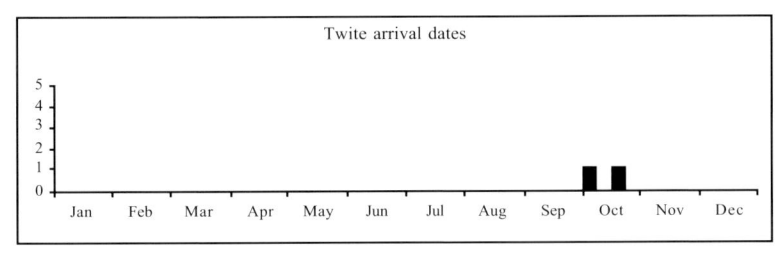

Twite arrival dates

Twite is another British species with its population currently in decline (Gibbons *et al.* 1996). Clearly it was far more widely distributed at the end of the 19th century, but even so was absent from much of the southern half of England, including the southwest peninsula, though it seems to have been abundant in southwest Ireland (Holloway 1996). By the late 1980s, it had withdrawn from much of its former range, with the closest breeding populations to Scilly being North Wales and the Pennines, plus a few scattered sites in western Ireland (Parslow 1968a; Gibbons *et al.* 1993). In general, British populations are either sedentary or inclined to move only to the coast in winter, whereas northern European populations are short- to long-distance migrants, though some overwinter. Twite breeding in the Pennines move mainly southeast to winter around the shores of the southern North Sea (Wernham *et al.* 2002), whereas Scottish birds probably do not come far south. Northern European migrants head mainly southeast, e.g. Germany, and winter mainly within towns, though there is visual evidence that some reach Britain, though unsupported by ringing data (Cramp *et al.* 1977–94). All of this perhaps explains why there are so few sightings on Scilly.

# Lesser Redpoll                                              *Carduelis cabaret*  **A**

**Annual, mainly autumn migrant in small numbers, perhaps also infrequent winter visitor.**

Formerly treated as conspecific with Common Redpoll *C. flammea* but split by BOURC October 2000 (Knox *et al.* 2001; BOURC 2001). Breeds central Europe, from Britain and Ireland east to Poland, Romania and Bulgaria and from southern Norway and Sweden south to Alps. Migratory or partially so, wintering south to Mediterranean and Black Sea. Monotypic. Upgraded from Green- to Amber-listed in UK 2002: possible greater than 50% breeding decline over past 25 years; 20% or more of European breeding population in UK (Gregory *et al.* 2002). National 18% decline 1994–99 (Bashford & Noble 2000).

No early Scillonian records (see Common Redpoll), though according to Penhallurick (1978), James Clark mentioned one on Scilly some time between 1906 and 1923 in a letter to C J King. The first published record of any of the three redpoll species now recognised concerned several small flocks, of what was presumably the present species, about the islands during January 1956 (*CBWPSAR* 26). Following this, it increasingly figured among the reports until by the 1980s it had became an annual feature.

Penhallurick examined Scillonian and mainland records up until the mid-1970s, detecting a small spring passage through the islands between late April and early May, whereas autumn passage commenced from mid-September and peaked during late October, being mainly evident between 3rd September and 5th November. During the ten years 1990–99, birds appeared annually but in only six years during spring, the latter between 19th April and 28th May, the most in any year being seven, though in four years there was just one. First autumn sightings occurred between 19th September and 29th October, the last a particularly late date, whereas final autumn sightings occurred between 18th October and 7th December. Assessing autumn numbers is difficult but in at least six years the upper limit was about 30 birds and the highest recorded daily count seems to have been 22 during late October. Nevertheless, this represents a substantial improvement over earlier years, as in 1983 when the only records involved one on 16th October and eight more on the 20th, all of which had left by 27th; or the following year, when one on Tresco in late September and two on St Mary's in October were the only reports.

Evidence of overwintering is slight, five on St Mary's on 24th January 1994 being the only suggestion during the 1990s. Most northern European Lesser Redpolls move mainly southeast in autumn (Wernham *et al.* 2002), periodic irruptions affecting numbers involved. British populations winter mainly within Britain but in years of food shortage may move further south or east, into Iberia or central Europe. The relative scarcity of all redpoll species in Scilly is reflected by the fact that just 15 have been ringed, 13 since 1970 and all except two presumably of the present species. There are no recaptures.

## Common Redpoll *Carduelis flammea* A

**Rare migrant, full written description not currently required by the SRP, but perhaps should be.**

Pre-1923  At least one Scilly
[1966  One (*rostrata*) St Agnes 27th & 28th October]
1971  One (*rostrata*) St Agnes 25th October
1976  One (*flammea*) St Mary's 10th October
1980  Three (*flammea*) Peninnis, St Mary's 5th November
1982  One (*flammea*) St Agnes 10th October
1985  One (*flammea*) Tresco 6th & 9th October
1985  Two (*flammea*) St Martin's 10th to 16th October
1985  One (*rostrata*) Normandy, St Mary's 14th to 18th October
1985  Two (*flammea*) St Mary's 18th October
1985  One (*flammea*) St Martin's 22nd October
1986  Three (*flammea*) Scilly, dates uncertain
1986  Two (*flammea*) St Mary's 7th December

Previously treated as conspecific with Lesser Redpoll *C. cabaret* but split by BOURC October 2000 (Knox *et al.* 2001; BOURC 2001). Circumpolar, breeds low Arctic in northern Europe and northern North America. Polytypic: nominate *flammea*, or 'Mealy Redpoll', occurs Norway east to Kamchatka plus North America from Alaska east to Newfoundland; *rostrata* or 'Greater (Greenland) Redpoll', Greenland and Canadian Arctic islands; some authorities recognise a third form *islandica*, occurring Iceland but resembling *rostrata* (Cramp *et al.* 1977–94; Knox *et al.* 2001).

Until recently treated as part of a wider 'redpoll' complex, including Arctic *C. hornemanni* and Lesser Redpoll *C. cabaret*, thus often no attempt was made to distinguish between various forms involved and there are perhaps eleven acceptable reports (involving 18 individuals), nine of which occurred during October or early November and most of which appear in the records as showing the characteristics of *flammea*. However, singles on Wingletang Down, St Agnes, in late October 1971 and at Normandy, St Mary's, in mid-October 1985 were thought by observers to have been *rostrata* (*IOSBR* 1971, 1985). Noticeably, five of these reports (seven birds) are from 1985. Penhallurick (1978) mentions an earlier *rostrata* on St Agnes in late October 1966 but gives no details and as the record does not appear in the *CBWPSAR* it is included here in square brackets. However, Wallace's description of the 1971 individual, as the second for Scilly, appears to support the earlier record. Penhallurick also referred to a *flammea* specimen mentioned by James Clark in a letter to C J King and obtained some time after Clark and Rodd's 1906 review, but before 1923. The same letter mentioned others seen subsequently, i.e. pre-1923.

Early publications are surprisingly silent on the subject of any redpoll presence on Scilly, Clark and Rodd (1906) making no reference to it whatsoever, whilst E H Rodd said only that redpolls were almost as rare in mainland Cornwall as Twite *C. flavirostris* and that he was unaware of 'Mealy Redpoll' having occurred (Rodd 1880). Clearly, any *rostrata* arriving in Scilly originate from no closer to Scilly than Greenland, though there seems room for confusion in the field between this and the closely similar birds breeding in Iceland. Autumn orientation of northern European populations is also primarily towards the southeast, in addition to which the species is sometimes irruptive (Cramp *et al.* 1977–94). Greenland Common Redpolls leave the breeding grounds from August, in northern Britain any irruption usually revealing itself by September. Riddington *et al.* (2000) documented the irruption of winter 1995–96, none of which reached Cornwall or Devon, though two Arctic Redpolls reached Scilly. The Chart shows all arrivals except the first two in the Table, and suggests, like many other species reaching Scilly in autumn, that most were involved in some form of migration. Average length of stay was 2.4 days – shortest one day (eleven birds), longest seven days. As Penhallurick suggested, these records perhaps represent the southern limit of this species' European range, though if they were on migration they perhaps went even further south. The lack of spring sightings is also interesting. In addition to those listed, a 'very light-coloured bird' on St Agnes on 30th October 1957 could have been this species. In addition, David Hunt described a 'very pallid' individual on Tresco in October 1970, which he thought may have been Arctic Redpoll, though *flammea* seems equally likely.

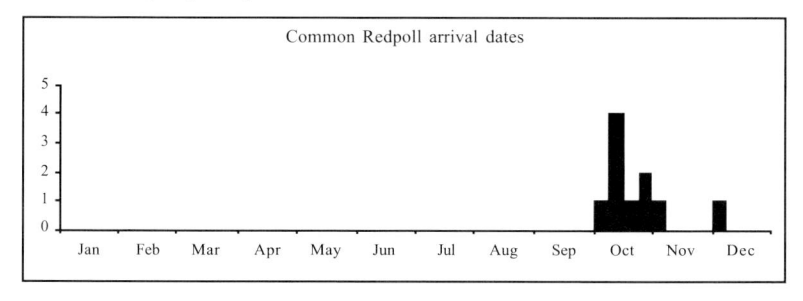

Common Redpoll arrival dates

A few Common Redpolls reach Britain each winter, and some years, as in 1972, there are large-scale European eruptions, though comparatively few reach Britain. Nonetheless, there are a few recoveries of British-ringed birds from Scandinavia, and vice versa (Wernham *et al.* 2002). Of the 15 'redpolls' ringed in Scilly, two only may have involved this species; these were trapped together by the author in the Higher Moors section of the Lunnon Farm study plot on 7th December 1998 and had wing lengths of 70 and 77 millimetres. These measurements suggest they were probably the present species rather than Lesser Redpoll, though this was difficult to establish based on in-hand plumage features (Svensson 1992).

## Arctic Redpoll                                          *Carduelis hornemanni*  A  BBRC 0.42%

**Very rare vagrant, full written description required by the BBRC.**

   [1970   One Tresco 26th October]
   [1971   One St Agnes 25th October]
   1977    One Bryher 19th October to 5th November
   1995    One (male – probable *hornemanni*) Shag Point, Samson 5th December
   1996    One (probable *exilipes*) Popplestone Bay, Bryher 10th May

Circumpolar, breeds low Arctic from Iceland and northern Norway east through North America to Greenland. Polytypic: nominate *hornemanni*, or 'Hornemann's Redpoll' occurs northern Greenland plus Ellesmere, Baffin and associated islands; *exilipes*, or 'Coues' Redpoll' northern Eurasia and northern North America away from range of *hornemanni*; identity of form breeding Iceland unclear (Cramp *et al.* 1977–94). Erratic, southward winter dispersal, *hornemanni* only occasionally reaching northwest Europe.

Uncertainty surrounds the first two of five island records. The Tresco individual was seen by David Hunt, who described it as a 'very pallid bird', believing it may have been this species; Penhallurick (1978) quoted the record as authentic but gives no explanation. The St Agnes bird was described by D I M Wallace, who appeared in no doubt as to its identity. It is not known if either of these two individuals was submitted to the BBRC, though neither apparently figures under the relevant rejected records list.

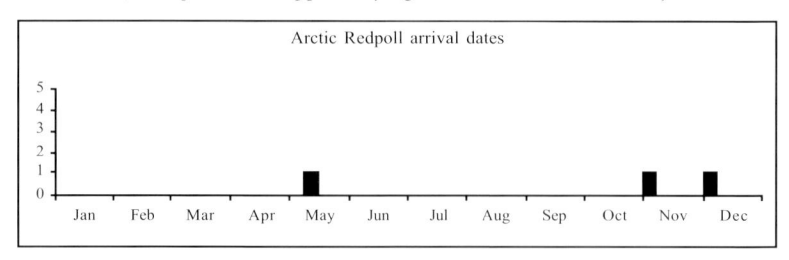

Arctic Redpoll arrival dates

Even now the Committee is likely to turn down all but in-hand descriptions of Arctic Redpoll and are even more cautious about attributing individuals to either form. Indeed, the author described the 1995 Samson bird as a classic *hornemanni* and supported this with an examination of skins, particularly from Canada and northern USA, in the British Museum (Natural History) (P J Robinson 1995b). Nevertheless, the Committee erred on the side of caution and decided not to assign the record to subspecific level. Although the Committee took into account the substantial influx of *exilipes* into eastern Britain that autumn, it failed to address the simultaneous appearance in December 1995 of Cliff Swallow *Hirundo pyrrhonota* and Green-winged Teal *Anas carolinensis* about 1 km away on Tresco. For further reading on separation of Arctic Redpoll from the two related species see Stoddart 1991, and for details of the 1995–96 influx of redpolls into western Europe see Riddingtin *et al.* 2000.

## [Two-barred Crossbill *Loxia leucoptera*] A

**One very old and questionable record. Full written description required by the BBRC.**

Breeds northeast Europe through northern Asia to Pacific Ocean, plus northern North America from Alaska east to Newfoundland. Sedentary, dispersive or irruptive. Polytypic: *bifasciata* occurs Eurasia; nominate *leucoptera* North America; extralimital *megaplaga* Hispaniola.

The undated 19th-century *Besley's Handbook* refers to 'White-winged Crossbills' occurring near Penzance, west Cornwall and 'in the Scilly Islands'. In addition, the Appendix to *A Guide to Penzance and its Neighbours, including The Islands of Scilly* (Courtney 1845) contains the statement 'The White-winged Crossbill, *Loxia leucoptera*, a native of North America, has been procured from the Islands of Scilly, and has also been noticed in the Minney (Lariggan Valley), near Penzance.' Shortly after, Blight also mentioned the species in his *A Week at the Land's End*, listing it among the 'numerous interesting birds of the (Land's End) district' (Blight 1861). However, this last is perhaps misleading as Blight included Scilly within the scope of this title. Later still, in *An Illustrated Manual of British Birds*, Saunders stated that 'A few years prior to 1843 one was killed in Cornwall' (Saunders 1889).

However, the noted authorities on Cornish birds, James Clark and co-author Francis Rodd, made no mention of this species in their comprehensive *Zoologist* review of *The Birds of Scilly* (Clark & Rodd 1906). This is despite the fact that even in his review of Cornish birds in the *Victoria History of Cornwall*, Clark acknowledged the shot 1843 individual from west Cornwall (W Page 1906). Additional support for the one-bird theory in 19th-century southwest England is found in E H Rodd's masterly work on the birds of Cornwall and Scilly (Rodd 1880) in which he mentions only the 1843 individual. The skin of this bird was in Rodd's collection and attributed by him to *bifasciata*. Interestingly, Penhallurick (1978) put the date of the Lariggan bird as pre-1840 and pointed out that prior to Rodd acquiring the skin it had been identified and preserved as a Chaffinch *Fringilla coelebs*.

# Crossbill (Common Crossbill) *Loxia curvirostra* A

**Scarce, mainly autumn migrant and occasional winter visitor. An old report of breeding may not be sustainable.**

Breeds Europe and northern Asia from Britain east to Japan with isolated populations further south, also North America from Alaska east to Newfoundland. Resident, dispersive and irruptive, largely remaining within normal range. Polytypic with complex racial structure: nominate *curvirostra* occurs Britain to Sea of Okhotsk and south to northern Spain and east to Balkans, European Russia and Siberia; *japonica* Lake Baikal east to Japan; perhaps ten additional forms south and east.

Nineteenth-century reports concentrated mainly on obvious irruption years, as in 1868 when large flocks on Tresco during June and July were accompanied by Greenfinches *Carduelis chloris* and Hawfinches *Coccothraustes coccothraustes* (Rodd 1868a; Clark & Rodd 1906), E H Rodd receiving several specimens from Tresco over several weeks, including seven on 28th July (Rodd 1868a). However, most must soon have left the islands as Rodd later recorded the arrival of just two along with other autumn migrants during mid-September (Rodd 1868c). Otherwise, Rodd was of the opinion it occurred in small flocks at uncertain times (Rodd 1880). James Clark and E H Rodd's nephew Francis recording several seen during 1901 (Clark & Rodd 1906).

Reports of irruptions into southwest England stretch back beyond the 19th century, one alleging that in autumn 1602 invading flocks in Cornwall caused substantial damage to the apple crop (Carew 1602). Penhallurick (1978) quoted similar but more recent accounts from Cornwall for the late 1890s. He also listed invasion into Scilly up until the mid-1970s, involving years 1930, 1938, 1949–50, 1953, 1958, 1959, 1962, 1963, 1966–67 and 1972–73. The largest recorded group Penhallurick could trace involved 200 feeding on thistles on Tresco in September 1930, though fewer than 20 was more normal, birds mostly arriving during July or August.

The pattern for the 1990s was one of invasion in greater or lesser numbers, interspersed with years of near absence. Dealing first with the latter, singles only were recorded during 1992, 1994 and 1995, whilst 1996 and 1998 each saw just five arrivals. Probable inter-site movements made accurate recording difficult during years of greater abundance, as in 1990 when seven in mid-June were followed by peak counts of up to 36 into early November, with daily counts in the range three to 20. Consequently, anything between 36 and perhaps a hundred individuals may have been involved throughout the autumn, though the true figure seems likely to have been nearer 50. However, small and apparently mobile groups (many seen only in flight) were also evident throughout Cornwall at this time (*CBWPSAR* 60) and so the possibility of new arrivals in Scilly cannot be ignored.

During the two recent years of greatest numbers, 1990 and 1997, first birds arrived on 16th and 23rd June respectively, somewhat earlier than normal. Disregarding these two years, birds were recorded in spring in five years. In four of these, six birds (five records) occurred between 25th April and 18th May, dates suggestive of passage. In the fifth year, up to three birds were noted between 25th May and 30th June, though breeding was not suspected. The only evidence of possible overwintering during the 1990s involved eight on St Mary's on 17th January 1991 and then two on 8th February 1998, following the big influx of autumn 1997. Penhallurick also mentioned birds present in Scilly during winter 1972 through to 20th March 1973, again following an invasion autumn.

Penhallurick also referred to an earlier claim by A A Dorrien-Smith that Crossbills bred on Tresco following the large 1930 influx. But this was latter questioned by his gamekeeper and there remains no authenticated claim of breeding from the islands. The nearest breeding birds are in Devon.

Penhallurick quoted a report by Couch (1838) of Crossbills aboard ship 'a few leagues from our shores' as proof that it arrives in Cornwall directly from northwest France, though this may not be the only interpretation placed upon such a sighting. The same author also mentioned birds seen arriving on the Lizard peninsula from out at sea in July 1927. In most year in western Europe, Crossbills disperse randomly but only over short distances, most remaining within the normal range. However, in irruption years they may move up to 4,000 km, though usually all in the same direction, such movements mostly commencing earlier than normal and ending later, birds involved in western Europe mainly originating west of the Urals (Wernham *et al.* 2002). Birds involved are mainly *curvirostra* from either Fennoscandia or northwest Russia (Cramp *et al.* 1977–94), though the suggested maximum of 4,000 km could bring birds to Scilly from within the range of the east-Asian *japonica*. Southern European populations move very little by comparison and thus seem unlikely to reach Britain. No Crossbills have been ringed in Scilly and there are no recaptures.

## Common Rosefinch *Carpodacus erythrinus* A

**Scarce annual migrant, mainly in autumn. Treated by the BBRC as a national Scarce Migrant, full written description required by the SRP.**

Breeds central-northern Europe east through northern Asia to Pacific and south through Himalayas to central China. Migratory, wintering mainly India and Southeast Asia. Polytypic: nominate *erythrinus* occurs Europe east through northern Asia to Altai and northern Mongolia; *ferghanensis* central Asia through Himalayas to Mongolia; *grebnitskii* northeast Asia; *kubanensis* Caucasus and northern Turkey through Iran and Turkmenistan (former Turkmeniya); at least one additional form. Amber-listed in UK: five-year mean of 7.2 breeding pairs (Gregory *et al.* 2002). Removed from BBRC Rarities List January 1983 (Grant 1982b).

Another species either overlooked by early ornithologists or absent until the mid-20th century, first record for the islands coming with one on St Agnes on 8th October 1962. Birds occurred in 30 of the 38 years since 1962 and in every year since 1974. The Charts show arrival dates and annual totals, numbers remaining reasonably constant since an increase around 1988, with an obvious rise in the number and frequency of spring sightings. This spring increase follows a westward European range expansion and the first British breeding record in 1982. Southwest England and particularly Scilly share with Shetland and Orkney the distinction in Britain of receiving the greatest number of autumn Common Rosefinch records, which, as Dymond *et al.* (1989) pointed out, is suggestive of an east-coast arrival across the North Sea and a subsequent southwest movement. Spring arrivals are a quite recent phenomenon on Scilly, with the exception of a singing male on Tresco in 1968, and are less easy to explain, although they too coincide with the recent westward spread.

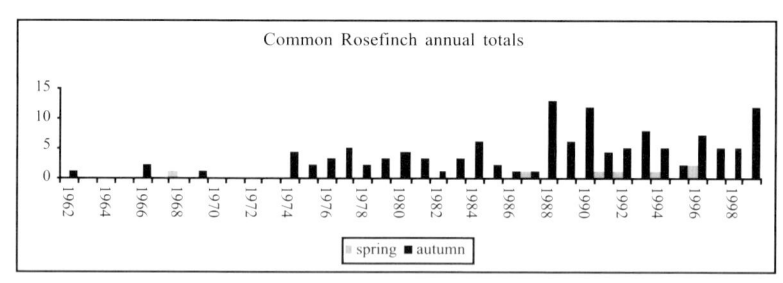

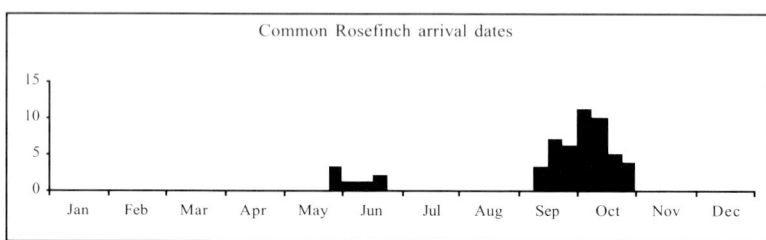

Western populations are long-distance migrants heading east or southeast in autumn, initially perhaps even northeast around the Caspian Sea (Wernham *et al.* 2002). Most British records involve autumn first-years, perhaps as part of the range expansion, the recent increase in spring arrivals in Scilly being mirrored in Germany (Cramp *et al.* 1977–94), perhaps as spring overshoots. The likelihood of confusion with the Nearctic House Finch *Carpodacus mexicanus* is real, should that species occur in Britain, and should be kept in mind when examining any Common Rosefinch, especially in Scilly. For further reading see Wallace (1999).

# Bullfinch (Common Bullfinch) *Pyrrhula pyrrhula* A

**Currently a scarce but almost annual migrant or vagrant in small numbers but more common and perhaps even resident during the 1970s and 1980s, when it may have bred.**

Breeds northern Eurasia from the Atlantic to Pacific, north to the tree-line and south in West Palearctic to northern Spain, Italy, Balkans and Iran. Most populations wholly or partially migratory, with most movement in north. Winters within or just south of breeding range, sometimes irruptive. Polytypic: nominate *pyrrhula*, or 'Northern Bullfinch', occurs northern Eurasia from Scandinavia to eastern Siberia south to central and southeast Europe; *pileata* British Isles; *europoea* Germany, Netherlands, France; other forms further east and south, with a degree of intergrading. Red-listed in UK: rapid, 57% breeding decline over past 25 years (Gregory *et al.* 2002). National 51% decline during 25 years to 1996 and 28% 1994–99 (Bashford & Noble 2000).

This is one of those species for which our knowledge of past events is clouded, with a surprising number of reports failing to mention even the sex of the bird involved and with a run of claimed breeding reports from Tresco. Several of these look probable but none is supported by an acceptable level of published information. And the situation seems never to have been very different. Whilst E H Rodd (1880) made no mention of it on Scilly during the 19th century, early in the 20th century Francis Rodd and James Clark thought it had been absent from the islands until the previous four years (Clark & Rodd 1906). These two authors went on to report that it was first recorded (by Clark) in 1902, but by the following spring 'they were plentiful on St Mary's, Samson and Bryher; and in April 1904 a flock of twenty-five spent several days in the churchyard at Old Town, St Mary's'. However, Clark and Rodd concluded by pointing out that no nest had so far been discovered. Further confirmation for this last observation comes from the mid-20th-century review of the breeding birds of Scilly, the authors of which quote Tresco's A A Dorrien-Smith in saying the species had never been known to nest in the islands (Ryves & Quick 1946).

The obvious question that arises is was Bullfinch really absent from Scilly until 1902 or was it simply overlooked? Yet E H Rodd leaves us in no doubt that it was reasonably common on the Cornish mainland up until at least 1880 and we know enough about the vigilance of men like Francis Rodd and Augustus Pechell to be confident they would have noticed Bullfinch, had it occurred. On the other hand, it is difficult to think of any obvious reason why the species might quite suddenly become a regular visitor around the turn of the 20th century and after an absence of at least several decades.

Interestingly, Bullfinch receives no coverage at all in the *CBWPSAR* from its commencement in 1931 until mention of a female on Tresco in April 1965, followed by just one or two in most years until around the mid-1970s. Throughout the 1970s and 1980s, however, numbers of annual sightings increased two- or three-fold, though the true situation may have been distorted by a small number of 'resident' birds on Tresco. On the latter island, one to two pairs of adults reportedly remained throughout the period of increase and were allegedly accompanied by birds variously described as 'immatures' or 'juveniles' in at least four of those years. However, as a cautionary note and as with one or two other species, frequent references to a 'pair' perhaps involved just two unattached individuals, further confusing the issue, as indeed do unqualified statements like 'The resident pair on Tresco reared at least one young' (*IOSBR* 1984) for what was, if correct, a first breeding record for the islands!

But whatever the truth concerning Tresco, it seems likely, but is by no means proven, that a pair or two of Bullfinches did raise young there during the 1980s, though elsewhere the pattern appeared to be one of spring and autumn arrivals, presumably involving birds on passage. A small number of overwintering individuals on other islands occurred mainly during the period of Tresco 'residency' and could presumably have involved wanderers from that island. However, one further possible complication is the fact that, like some other cardueline finches, e.g. Redpoll *Carduelis flammea*, adult Bullfinches occasionally move substantial distances during the breeding season, sometimes even between broods and particularly from June to August, with no apparent directional preference and sometimes up to 30 km; perhaps even accompanied by their previous brood (Newton 2000). In addition, of course, the nearest resident breeding population to Scilly is as close as west Cornwall (Gibbons *et al.* 1993) and even during the last quarter of the 19th century it occurred there uncommonly (Holloway 1996).

Examination of spring and autumn arrival dates is especially illuminating, particularly once all Tresco records are ignored, revealing as it does a pattern similar to several other species, with an obvious peak around mid-October and a lesser, more protracted spring concentration. Outside those two periods small

*Birds of the Isles of Scilly*

**Bullfinch arrival dates**

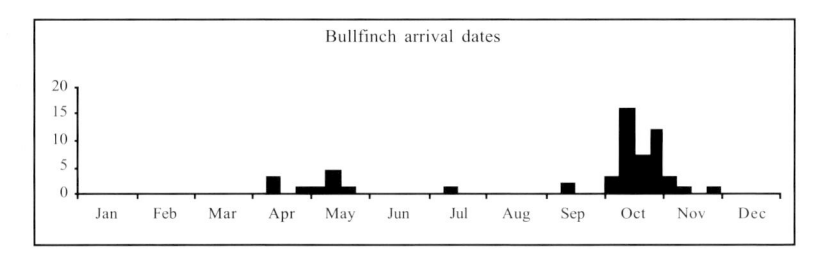

numbers of birds arrived during winter, or some that arrived in autumn were then to be seen about the islands until the following spring, though as already stated, the winter picture may be confused by birds from Tresco. However, in the context of both passage birds and winter arrivals, the records are silent on the possibility of individuals of the normally recognisably larger *pyrrhula* from more northern Europe being involved. From this we presumably must accept that they were not, and there are few records of this form from southern Britain in any event (Cramp *et al.* 1977–94). Ringing recoveries show most British Bullfinches (75%) move less than 5 km, a few up to 20 km and even less, 3% to 12%, up to 50 km (Wernham *et al.* 2002). Although the extent of autumn or winter arrival in Britain of Continental Bullfinches remains unclear, there is evidence of the central European *europoea* moving southwest in winter, some of which reach northwest France and Spain, and this seems a far more likely explanation for these Scillonian seasonal Bullfinch movements. Six Bullfinches have been trapped and ringed on Scilly, five since 1970, but there have been no recaptures.

# Hawfinch *Coccothraustes coccothraustes* A

**Occasional though not annual migrant, mostly in autumn. Full written description required by the SRP.**

Breeds central and southern Europe east through central Asia to Kamchatka and northern Japan. Sedentary in western and central Europe, migratory elsewhere, in Europe wintering south to Mediterranean. Polytypic: nominate *coccothraustes* occurs Eurasia to Mongolia and south to Iberia, Italy, Bulgaria and Caucasus; *nigricans* Caucasus east through Asia Minor and Iran; at least four additional forms further south and east. Amber-listed in UK: moderate (31%) contraction of breeding range over past 30 years (Gregory *et al.* 2002).

James Clark and Francis Rodd viewed Hawfinch as an occasional autumn visitor in immature plumage, though it had several times been recorded in April and once, 1868, in June (Clark & Rodd 1906). This last referred to mention under Crossbill *Loxia curvirostra* in the same paper of a large arrival of Greenfinches *Carduelis chloris*, Hawfinches and Crossbills during June and July 1868. E H Rodd also pointed out that an 'immense irruption' of Crossbills occurred in Cornwall during these two months, many of which reached Scilly (Rodd 1880). Apart from the above, there are a few scattered observations involving a further four or so years (e.g. Cornish 1883), two of which, seen by the Reverend J H Jenkinson in October 1854, are the earliest published records for Scilly. Interesting, too, is the arrival of yet more Hawfinches in 1868, this time following a gale during the second week of October (Rodd 1863b).

Although Clark and Rodd's early description stands the test of time, Penhallurick (1978) found only 50 or so records for Cornwall and Scilly attributable to a particular month, 40% being during October or November. He also discovered slight evidence of an autumn passage through Scilly, but not Cornwall, and only seven records from the islands for the thirteen years 1950–73. More recently, birds arrived in 16 of the 23 years 1977–99, 13 years in autumn and seven in spring. The Charts show spring and autumn first-arrival dates and annual totals for the same period. No birds are recorded as remaining later than 8th December, though the subsequent shortage of observers means wintering individuals may have been overlooked, although most birds departed the islands by early November. Particularly impressive arrivals occurred in 1978 (up to 40 birds), 1988 and 1993, all other years involving single figures. The area on St Mary's from Holy Vale south into upper Higher Moors apparently holds a particular attraction for this species.

Most European Hawfinches, i.e. *coccothraustes*, winter north of the Mediterranean and within the species' normal range, northerly populations moving furthest (the whole of the Russian population is migratory), but with comparatively little movement of British birds, 20 km is apparently a substantial British movement (Wernham *et al.* 2002). The heading of European autumn passage is largely between south and west, numbers involved fluctuating substantially between years (Cramp *et al.* 1977–94). Cramp *et al.* suggested that most movements into southern England involve British birds, though they also acknowledged the possibility of east-west Continental migrants occasionally reaching Britain; birds ringed in northern Norway and Czechoslovakia were recovered in northern Scotland (Wernham *et al.* 2002). Certainly, the timing of autumn arrivals in Scilly is suggestive of regular migration, between-year differences in numbers perhaps attributable to the presence or absence of suitable drift migration conditions. There is some suggestion in the Scillonian data that spring arrivals are perhaps becoming more frequent, though still lacking the periodic exceptional numbers of autumn. The only Hawfinch ringed in Scilly involved a female trapped by the author in the Holy Vale section of the Lunnon Farm study plot on 9th April 1997, interestingly during a marked Greenfinch movement.

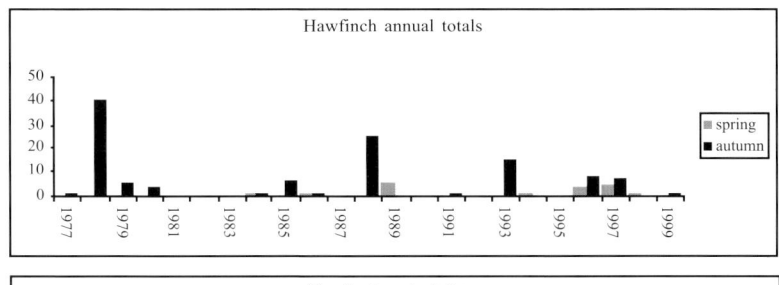

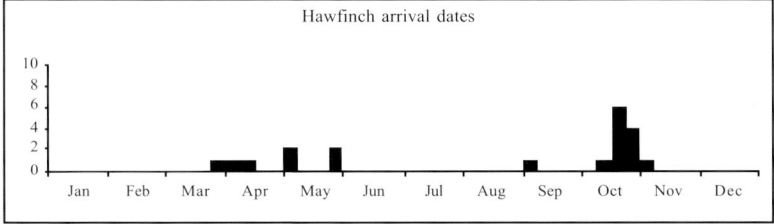

## Black-and-white Warbler *Mniotilta varia* **A** BBRC 28.5%

**Very rare migrant, full written description required by the BBRC.**

1975   One (first-winter) Garrison, St Mary's 27th to 30th September  *British Birds* 69: 345
1977   One Lower Moors, St Mary's 29th September to 1st October  *British Birds* 71: 526, 541–542
1996   One (first-year male) Garrison, St Mary's 5th to 14th October  *British Birds* 90: 509
1996   One (first-year female) Pool Road, Tresco 20th to 25th October  *British Birds* 90: 509

Nearctic species, breeds British Columbia east to Newfoundland, south to Texas and Georgia. Winters northern Mexico and southeast USA south through Central America and West Indies to northern South America. Monotypic. Recent steady but slow population increase (Bryant 1997).

Just four records of this virtually unmistakable and strikingly attractive North American warbler with Treecreeper *Certhia familiaris* habits. The first, on St Mary's in 1975, was preceded in Europe by one found dead on Shetland in 1936 (Evans 1994). This species shows a slightly broader spread of dates than for most other transatlantic warblers reaching Scilly, with two individuals arriving within two days of each other at the end of September. The 1977 bird (Grant 1978) was initially thought by the BBRC to be possibly the same as one seen in Tavistock, Devon, on 3rd March 1978, but the two were eventually treated as separate records (*British Birds* 73: 528). There was no doubt though that two different individuals were involved in the 1996 sightings, regardless of the gap in dates, both being photographed; at least two other birds reached Britain during the same autumn. Fourteen records were accepted by the BBRC between 1958 and the end of 1999, thus Scilly's apparent small showing represents over 28% of the national total (BBRC 2000).

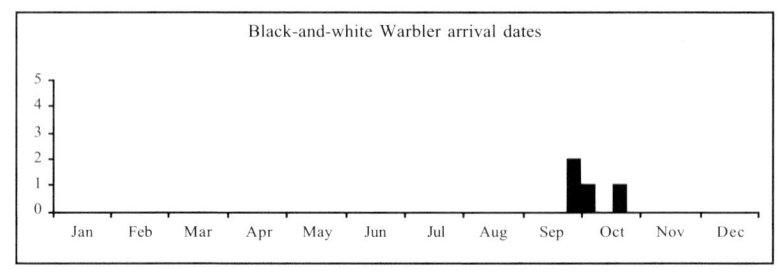

Black-and-white Warbler arrival dates

Main southward movement commences late August in the north of the breeding range, but with migrants lingering throughout October all over the northeast. Birds move south on a broad front, including through Bermuda, and with migration continuing through Central America in October (Cramp *et al.* 1977–94). Black-and-white Warbler scored twenty-second in Robbins's statistical review of expected transatlantic vagrancy among 31 migrant Nearctic passerines and near-passerines recorded in Britain or Ireland during 1947–76. The single accepted autumn record fell short of Robbins's predicted relative likelihood of 1.96 individuals (Robbins 1980). None of these Black-and-white Warblers was trapped and ringed and there are no recaptures.

## Northern Parula *Parula americana* A BBRC 37.5%

**Very rare migrant, full written description required by the BBRC.**

1966   One Tresco 16th & 17th October   *British Birds* 60: 329, 63: 149–151; *Ibis* 113: 144
1983   One (first-year) Borough Farm, Tresco 1st October   *British Birds* 77: 557; 79: 432–433, 434
1983   One (first-year) Parsonage, St Agnes 10th to 13th October
                                          *British Birds* 77: 557; 79: 432–433, 434
1985   One (male) Hugh Town, St Mary's & St Agnes 3rd to 21st October
                                          *British Birds* 79: 9, 564, 580
1992   One Garrison, St Mary's 8th to 10th October   *British Birds* 86: 530
1995   One (first-year male) Parsonage, St Agnes 10th October   *British Birds* 89: 524, 528

Nearctic species, breeds southeast Canada south to Gulf of Mexico, being scarce except in northeast and southeast states. Winters Central America, from southern Mexico to Costa Rica and from Florida to Bahamas then south to West Indies. Monotypic. Population static (Bryant 1997).

There are six records for the islands, with the species added to the British and Irish List on the strength of a bird on Tresco in October 1966 (BOURC 1968; King & Hunt 1970, 1982). However, there were just 16 accepted British records of Northern Parula between 1958 and the end of 1999, the six on Scilly therefore representing over 37% of the total (BBRC 2000). Like most other Scillonian records of Nearctic warblers, all six birds arrived during October and only one remained for more than three days. Dates of arrival fell within a 16-day window, from 1st to 16th with no birds present after 21st. Interestingly, four of the six were identified as males, though only one, in 1985, was thought to be adult. Details of the two 1983 individuals appear in Chittenden (1986) for Tresco and Gravet (1986) for St Agnes. The 1985 bird was discovered by the entrance to Tregarthens Hotel in Hugh Town, St Mary's, feeding in elm *Ulmus glabra/procera* trees leading up to The Garrison Arch, remaining in that general area until 17th, before relocating to St Agnes and being last seen on 21st.

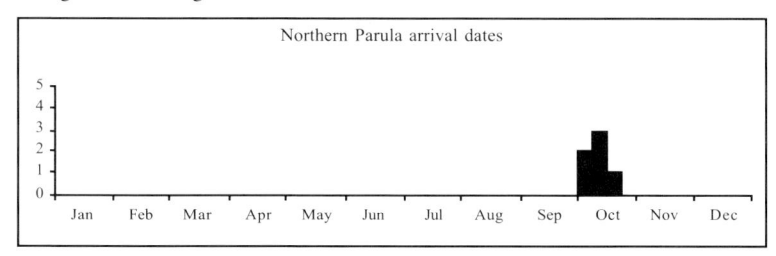

Peak movement south from the breeding range commences mid-September with large-scale passage through Florida into mid-October (Cramp *et al*. 1977–94), which fits arrival dates for the islands. Northern Parula scored twenty-third in Robbins's statistical review of expected transatlantic vagrancy among 31 migrant Nearctic passerines and near-passerines recorded in Britain or Ireland during 1947–76, with the three accepted autumn records exceeding the predicted relative likelihood of 1.33 individuals (Robbins 1980). The 1966 individual was preceded in Europe by one in Iceland, in 1913 (Evans 1994). None of the Northern Parulas arriving in Scilly were trapped and ringed and there are no recaptures.

## Magnolia Warbler          *Dendroica magnolia*  A  BBRC 100%

**Extremely rare migrant, full written description required by the BBRC.**

1981   One Barnaby Lane, St Agnes 27th & 28th September
                                                    *British Birds* 75: 529, 88: 107–108; *Ibis* 126: 441

Nearctic species, breeds British Columbia and south Mackenzie east to Newfoundland, plus northeast USA. Migratory, wintering Central America and Greater Antilles. Monotypic. Population increasing (Bryant 1997).

An adult male on St Agnes on 27th and 28th September 1981 represented the first and only occurrence of this species in Britain and Europe (BOURC 1978; Enright 1995), though a 'mummified' first-winter corpse was found mid-November 1993 on an oil tanker at Sullom Voe, Shetland, the ship having left Delaware in the USA and travelled via Mexico and Venezuela. Autumn migration commences gradually, with only stragglers remaining in the breeding areas by late September and with the first birds reaching southern USA by early September, though few remain after October (Cramp *et al*. 1977–94). Although migration is east of the Rocky Mountains, mostly along or west of the Appalachians, few appear in Florida or southern Georgia, perhaps explaining why there is just the single European record. The arrival of the St Agnes individual coincided with that of Red-eyed Vireo *Vireo olivaceus* on St Mary's and at Prawle Point, Devon, with another Red-eyed Vireo on Scilly on 29th. Just a little earlier, on 23rd, a Yellow-billed Cuckoo *Coccyzus americanus* had been discovered on St Mary's, where the arrival of Booted Warbler *Hippolais caligata* on 28th demonstrated the archipelago's ability to simultaneously attract rare migrants from opposing directions of the compass.

Magnolia Warbler scored just below midway in Robbins's statistical review of expected transatlantic vagrancy among 38 migrant Nearctic passerines and near-passerines unrecorded in Britain during 1947–76, coming twentieth in the list with a predicted relative likelihood of 1.33 individuals within the period (Robbins 1980). The St Agnes individual was not trapped and ringed and was reportedly seen by just 58 observers.

## Yellow-rumped Warbler          *Dendroica coronata*  A  BBRC 21.7%

**Very rare migrant, full written description required by the BBRC.**

1968   One (first-year) St Mary's 22nd to 27th October   *British Birds* 62: 486, 69: 359, 71: 186
1973   One Tresco 16th to 24th October   *British Birds* 67: 336, 71: 526
1985   One Peninnis, St Mary's 7th to 22nd October   *British Birds* 79: 11, 566, 580
1985   One Pelistry, St Mary's 10th October   *British Birds* 79: 11, 556, 580
1995   One Pool Road, Tresco 4th to 15th October   *British Birds* 89: 525

Nearctic species comprising two distinct groups (formerly treated as two species); monotypic *coronata* group, or 'Myrtle Warbler', and polytypic *auduboni* group, or 'Audubon's Warbler', with 'Myrtle Warbler' occurring in the north and east and 'Audubon's Warbler' in west. *Coronata* breeds Alaska and Canada south to British Columbia and east to Labrador and Newfoundland. Within *auduboni* group, *auduboni* occurs western North America from British Columbia, Alberta and Saskatchewan south to northeast Baja California and other southwest states; two additional forms Mexico and Guatemala. *Coronata* and northern *auduboni* populations fully migratory, southern *auduboni* partially so. Population increasing (Bryant 1997).

Five Scillonian records of this attractive warbler all relate to nominate *coronata*, or 'Myrtle Warbler', accounting for over 21% of the British total of 23 Yellow-rumped Warblers between 1958 and the end of 1999 (BBRC 2000). All five occurred within a 24-day window in October, from 4th to 27th, with a total of 44 bird-days at an average of 8.8 days per bird. The 1968 individual was the third record for Britain and Ireland and was found feeding in Tree Mallows *Lavatera arborea* just above the beach on St Mary's, where it remained for the duration of its stay (Jobson 1978a). The 1973 Tresco bird was found near Cromwell's Castle on the island's exposed northwest corner, later moving to the more sheltered Great Pool area. Towards the end of its stay, it was seen to defend a feeding territory (which included several trees) against Great Tits *Parus major*, Blue Tits *Parus caeruleus* and Chiffchaffs *Phylloscopus collybita* (Hunt 1973).

The 1985 Peninnis individual wandered to Old Town and Carn Gwavel but could often be located by its call as it fed among the elms (pers. obs.). This was a distinctive 'tick' or 'chip' call more than a little reminiscent of Great Spotted Woodpecker *Dendrocopos major*, which of course is normally absent from Scilly. In comparison, the other 1985 individual was more poorly marked, and the 1995 bird, thought to be a first-year, performed to literally hundreds of birders as it fed along Tresco's Pool Road throughout is stay.

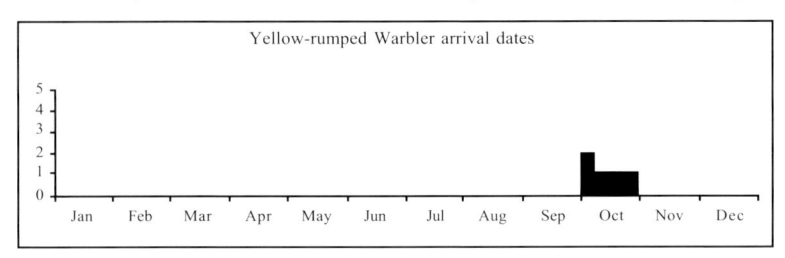

The first and second British and Irish records both came from Devon, in 1955 and 1960. Yellow-rumped is the sole short-range migrant among northern paruline warblers and the most hardy, regularly wintering into the snow zone where food and cover exist. Passage south is broad-front, being prolonged and commencing during early August in the northwest, with the main movement throughout October in the east. Yellow-rumped Warbler migration strategy does not seem as conducive to transatlantic vagrancy as that of Blackpoll Warbler *D. striata* and there is evidence suggesting it may not always do so unaided, with known examples of ship-assisted passage (Margeson 1959; Tousey 1959). Yellow-rumped Warbler scored highest in Robbins's statistical review of expected transatlantic vagrancy among 31 migrant Nearctic passerines and near-passerines recorded in Britain or Ireland during 1947–76. However, the seven accepted autumn records fell short of the predicted relative likelihood of 8.18 individuals (Robbins 1980). As with other North American passerines reaching Scilly in autumn, the appearance of Yellow-rumped Warbler has been associated with the simultaneous arrival of fast-moving severe weather systems originating off the eastern seaboard of North America. Nonetheless, ship-assisted passage remains a possibility. No Yellow-rumped Warblers have been ringed on Scilly and there are no recaptures.

## Blackpoll Warbler *Dendroica striata*  A  BBRC 55.5%

Rare migrant, full written description required by the BBRC.

1968  One St Agnes 12th to 25th October  *British Birds* 62: 486, 63: 129, 153–157; *Ibis*: 133, 144
1970  One trapped St Agnes 20th to 26th October  *British Birds* 64: 365
1975  One St Agnes 19th October to 1st November  *British Birds* 69: 355, 71: 186–187
1976  Up to two St Mary's 4th to 23rd October  *British Birds* 70: 440, 76: 525
1976  Two to three St Agnes 7th to 20th October  *British Birds* 70: 440, 76: 525

| | | |
|---|---|---|
| 1976 | One St Martin's 9th October | *British Birds* 70: 440, 76: 525 |
| 1976 | One St Mary's 14th October | *British Birds* 70: 440, 76: 525 |
| 1976 | One Tresco 20th Oct & 2nd & 3rd November | *British Birds* 70: 440, 76: 525 |
| 1977 | One Bryher 29th October | *British Birds* 71: 526 |
| 1982 | One Old Town, St Mary's 17th to 23rd October | *British Birds* 76: 49, 525 |
| 1983 | One Bryher & Tresco 22nd October to 2nd November | *British Birds* 77: 558, 78: 581 |
| 1984 | One St Agnes 2nd to 16th October | *British Birds* 78: 63, 581, 79: 580 |
| 1984 | One St Mary's 25th October to 4th November | *British Birds* 78: 63, 581, 79: 580 |
| 1987 | One Borough Farm, Tresco 12th to 22nd October | *British Birds* 81: 590 |
| 1990 | One Bant's Carn, St Mary's 22nd to 25th October | *British Birds* 84: 487, 500 |
| 1995 | One St Agnes 27th October to 6th November | *British Birds* 89: 523 |
| 1997 | One Tresco 12th October to 1st November | *British Birds* 91: 494, 513 |

Nearctic species, breeds Alaska around Hudson Bay and east to Newfoundland, south to eastern New York state. Average migration is the longest among paruline warblers, wintering South America from Panama south to Chile and Argentina. Monotypic. 'Devastating' population decline during last 15 years (Bryant 1997).

The recent population decline may help explain why this is no longer the commonest Nearctic migrant reaching Scilly. The species was admitted to the British List on the strength of the 1968 St Agnes individual (BOURC 1968; Grant 1970, 1982a). Due to uncertainty over the validity of ageing in the field during the period August to March, the BBRC now withhold such information from published records for this species. Therefore, ages are similarly withheld from records shown here. The 20 records for Scilly represent over 50% of the British total of 36 recorded between 1958 and the end of 1999 (BBRC 2000). Details of the 1975 bird are written up in Jobson (1978b). All records fall within the autumn period, with the earliest 2nd October and the latest 6th November: a period of just 36 days involving a maximum of 18 to 20 individuals over 29 years. First arrival or finding dates span a period of just 27 days, all during October. Autumn departure from the northern breeding ground is believed to commence from early August, with last records during late August to late September. However, main passage in the northeast is mostly late September to mid-October, suggesting birds reaching Britain, or at least Scilly, originate from northeast USA, rather than from further north and west (Cramp *et al.* 1977–94)

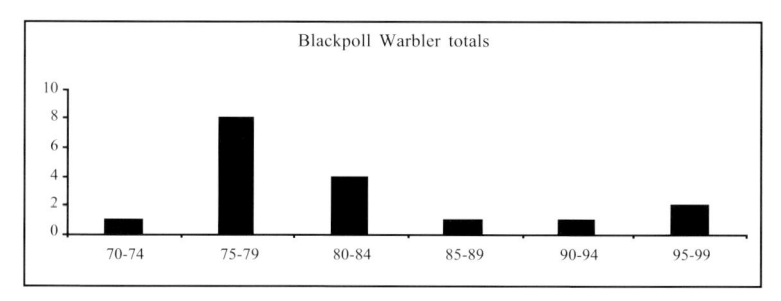

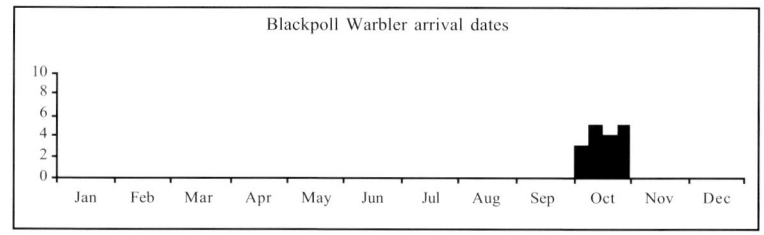

Blackpoll Warbler totals

Blackpoll Warbler arrival dates

This last view finds support in records from its normal Atlantic stopover sites, Blackpoll Warbler being very common in Bermuda throughout October but diminishing by mid-November, with peak movements in the Caribbean during October also. Southward migration is almost exclusively through eastern North America, even for birds breeding in Alaska, and there is indecision still over whether or not this species uses a non-stop southward strategy out over the western Atlantic, or moves mainly through the southeast states (Cramp *et al.* 1977–94). If the former route is taken, then that greatly increases the possibility of transatlantic vagrancy. Interestingly then, Blackpoll Warbler came fourth in Robbins's statistical review of expected transatlantic vagrancy among 31 migrant Nearctic passerines and near-passerines recorded in Britain during 1947–76, the 14 accepted autumn records exceeding the predicted relative likelihood of 6.02 individuals by more than 100% (Robbins 1980). Elsewhere in Europe, there are records from Iceland, France and the Channel Isles (Evans 1994). Numbers of birds recorded in Scilly during five-year periods commencing 1970 are charted, revealing a level of decline in line with the recent sharp population decline (Bryant 1997). No Blackpoll Warblers have been ringed on Scilly and there are no recaptures.

## American Wood Warbler *Parulidae*

Unspecified American wood warbler Records
    1979   One, possibly Blackpoll Warbler *Dendroica striata* Rocky Hill, St Mary's 10th October
    1981   One, possibly Blackpoll Warbler *Dendroica striata* St Mary's 10th October
    1995   One, possibly Blackpoll Warbler *Dendroica striata* 'Dump Clump', St Mary's 19th October

Nearctic family *Parulidae* comprising 126 species in 29 genera, of which 19 species of 8 genera have occurred in Europe. In general, they are highly active, insect-eating species with the more northerly being migratory.

Just three individuals so far have not been attributable specifically, but in each case were thought likely to have involved Blackpoll Warbler *Dendroica striata*. This view is clearly supported by the spread of dates involved. Presumably uncertainties over positive identification of Blackpoll Warbler unless seen well reflect the likelihood of confusion with other streaked *Dendroica* warblers. It may also be relevant that all three involved one-day sightings. None of the birds involved were trapped and ringed.

## Northern Waterthrush *Seiurus noveboracensis* A BBRC 57.1%

**Very rare migrant, full written description required by the BBRC.**

    1958   One trapped St Agnes 30th September to 12th October
                                           *British Birds* 53: 172, 373, 513–518; 56: 205; *Ibis* 102: 629
    1968   One Tresco 3rd to 7th October   *British Birds* 62: 486, 65: 484–485, 69: 27–33
    1982   One Bryher 29th September to 4th October   *British Birds* 76: 526, 77: 368–371
    1989   One Porth Killear, St Agnes 29th & 30th August   *British Birds* 83: 152, 489

Nearctic species, breeds central Alaska east to Newfoundland and south to Canadian-USA border, including west Montana, Great Lakes and southeast to New Jersey. Winters West Indies, Central and South America to northern Ecuador, northern Peru, Venezuela and Guianas. Monotypic. Long-distance migrant, all individuals move over 1,000 km from breeding to wintering areas (Cramp *et al.* 1977–94). Signs of recent slight decline (Bryant 1997).

There are four Scillonian records of this extremely distinctive warbler, including the first for Britain and Ireland and second for Europe: on St Agnes on 30th September 1958 (BOURC 1960; Harris *et al.* 1960, 1982). The 1958 individual was first found in sheltered Cove Vean on the island's western side, remaining in that area until last seen on 12th October. It was trapped and ringed shortly after being found. The remaining records involved one each on St Agnes, Tresco and Bryher with the most recent at the end of August 1989 (Wallace 1972d, 1976a; Woodcock 1984). These four individuals represent nearly 60% of the British total of seven recorded between 1958 and the end of 1999 (BBRC 2000).

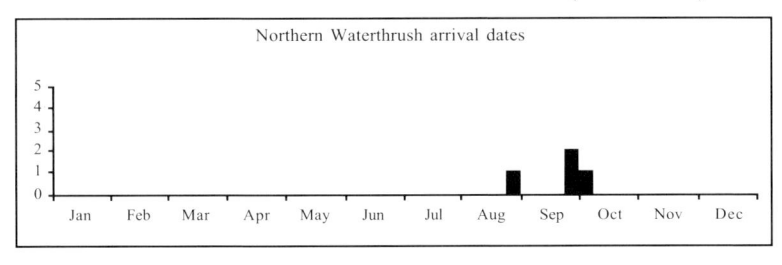

Other European records involved birds in Ireland, northern France and the Channel Islands, with this species or Louisiana Waterthrush *S. motacilla* in the Canary Islands (Snow & Perrins 1998). Autumn migration is compressed, birds leaving the breeding grounds from late July and with a few individuals reaching California, Arkansas and even Costa Rica by mid-August. Peak movement in west and mid-Canada commences early August but main passage further south is from September (Cramp *et al.* 1977–94). This timescale fits the arrival dates of bird on Scilly.

Northern Waterthrush came fourteenth in Robbins's statistical review of expected transatlantic vagrancy among 31 migrant Nearctic passerines and near-passerines recorded in Britain or Ireland during 1947–76. The two accepted autumn records fell short of the predicted 3.22 individuals (Robbins 1980). The only Northern Waterthrush ringed in Scilly involved the 1958 record; there are no recaptures.

## Yellowthroat
## (Common Yellowthroat)         *Geothlypis trichas*  A  BBRC 33.3%

**Extremely rare migrant, full written description required by the BBRC.**

1984   One (first-year male) Bryher 2nd to at least 17th October 1984
*British Birds* 78: 582, 79: 434–435
1997   One (first-year male) St Mary's 9th October to 2nd November   *British Birds* 91: 494, 513

Nearctic species, breeds Alaska and southern Yukon east to Newfoundland and south to southern Mexico. Winters southern USA, Mexico and Central America south to Colombia and Venezuela; northern populations more migratory. At least five recognised forms; with *campicola* occupying south-central Canada and northern Great Plains area of USA; nominate *trichas* central New Jersey, southeast Pennsylvania into Maryland, Delaware, southwest into Texas, Louisiana and Oklahoma; *brachidactylus* eastern USA and Canada north from New Jersey, New York and Connecticut to Newfoundland, and west to Nebraska and Kansas (Cramp *et al.* 1977–94). Ten or more additional forms occur further west or south but are presumably less inclined towards vagrancy. Steady decline, particularly in central and eastern populations, with high upward and downward Canadian swings (Bryant 1997).

Just two autumn records, one on Bryher in 1984 and the other on St Mary's in 1997. The first of these, the third British and Irish record, was first located late morning on 2nd October in a small apple tree on the eastern side of Bryher's Samson Hill. It was eventually identified as a first-winter male and remained in the same area until at least the 17th. The discovery of this bird followed close on the heels of one on Fetlar, Shetland, in June the same year, though the first British record was on Lundy Island, Devon, back in November 1954 (Kolodziejski & Skinner 1986).

Unlike the 1984 individual, which came in the midst of a typical rarity-filled October, Scilly's second arrival gave temporary relief to a period devoid of migrants. First found on 9th October in low brambles at Rose Hill, St Mary's, it relocated to nearby Harry's Walls on 11th and remained in that area until last seen on 2nd November. This too proved to be a first-winter male. Neither individual was attributed to a particular form and though, simplistically, we might perhaps guess at *trichas* or *brachidactylus*, being the closest, there is evidence that westerly populations of some North American migrants are more prone to eastward vagrancy (Nisbet 1959).

Six birds were recorded in Britain from 1958 to the end of 1999 and therefore Scilly accounts for one-third of the total (BBRC 2000). Yellowthroat scored midway in Robbins's statistical review of expected transatlantic vagrancy among 31 migrant Nearctic passerines and near-passerines recorded in Britain or Ireland during 1947–76. The single accepted autumn record fell below the predicted 3.04 individuals (Robbins 1980). Neither of these two birds was trapped and ringed.

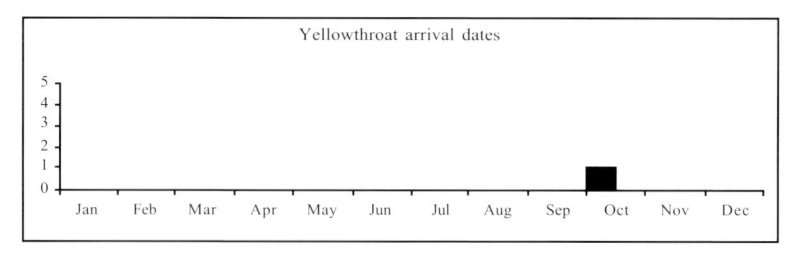

## Hooded Warbler *Wilsonia citrina*  A  BBRC 50.0%

**Extremely rare migrant, full written description required by the BBRC.**

1970   One (female or first-winter) St Agnes 20th to 23rd September
*British Birds* 65: 203–205, 351; *Ibis* 144: 446

Nearctic species, breeds Rhode Island to Nebraska and south of Gulf of Mexico and northern Florida. Winters northeast Mexico south to Panama. Monotypic. Slight population increase overall, more so in east (Bryant 1997).

The first for Britain and Europe (Edwards & Osborne 1972, 1982) was discovered beside St Agnes Big Pool late afternoon on 20th September 1970, giving only brief and inadequate views before disappearing for the night. It was relocated about the same time next day but again gave only brief views, preferring to remain within poolside vegetation, though it did eventually provide a clear view to three observers. Bad weather meant the bird was not seen on 22nd but on the morning of 23rd it was again present in vegetation surrounding the pool, proving much more amenable and giving excellent but again only brief views to six observers over several minutes. All observers subsequently agreed it was a female or first-winter Hooded Warbler, a common North American east-coast autumn migrant departing the breeding grounds from late July to early September (Cramp *et al.* 1977–94).

Given that this was a potential first European record, four of the observers made subsequent independent visits to skin collections, three to the British Museum (Natural History) and one to Liverpool Museum. All four independently confirmed the original identification, following which the record was submitted and accepted (BOURC 1972; *British Birds* 65: 351).

A later British record and the second for Europe involved a bird seen, again only briefly, by two observers in severe weather on St Kilda, Western Isles, on 10th September 1992. Evans (1994) did not acknowledge the St Agnes bird but did include details of the St Kilda individual. Hooded Warbler scored third from last in Robbins's statistical review of expected transatlantic vagrancy among 31 Nearctic migrant passerines and near-passerines recorded in Britain or Ireland during 1947–76. The single accepted autumn record exceeded the predicted 0.15 individuals (Robbins 1980). The St Agnes bird was not trapped and ringed.

## Scarlet Tanager *Piranga olivacea*  A  BBRC 42.8%

**Extremely rare migrant, full written description required by the BBRC.**

1970   One (first-year male) St Mary's 4th October   *British Birds* 65: 155–158, 352; *Ibis* 114: 446
1975   One (first-year male) Tresco 28th September to 3rd October   *British Birds* 68: 357, 70: 300–301
1982   One (female) St Mary's 12th to 18th October   *British Birds* 76: 52, 77: 490–491

Nearctic species, breeds eastern North America, from North Dakota and Manitoba east to Nova Scotia and south to Kansas and Arkansas. Migratory, wintering mainly northwest South America. Monotypic. Evidence of slight population decline, though up to 40% decline in Canada (Bryant 1997).

A first-year male found in the Porth Hellick area of St Mary's on 4th October 1970 was the second British and Irish record of this much-sought-after species (B D Harding 1972a, 1982; BOURC 1972).

The bird was seen briefly by about ten fortunate observers around midday, its arrival coinciding with that of Yellow-billed Cuckoo *Coccyzus americanus* on St Mary's the same day and being followed by Europe's first Veery *Catharus fuscescens* in west Cornwall on 6th. The St Mary's bird was followed five years later by another first-year male at Gimble Porth, Tresco, during late September, this individual remaining viewable for six days. The third for the islands, a female, was again in the Porth Hellick area of St Mary's, this time for seven days during mid-October 1982 (Goodwin 1984).

The Chart includes all three arrival dates and shows a perhaps somewhat earlier arrival pattern than for most Nearctic migrants on Scilly. The average length of stay was 4.6 days. The earlier record involved a female tanager trapped on Copeland Island, Northern Ireland, on 12th October 1966 and initially identified as either the present species or Summer Tanager *P. rubra*. However, after further review it was accepted as Scarlet Tanager (BOURC 1988), the species by then already having been added to the British List on the strength of the initial St Mary's individual. The BBRC accepted just seven British Scarlet Tanager records during the period 1958–99, Scilly accounting for 43%.

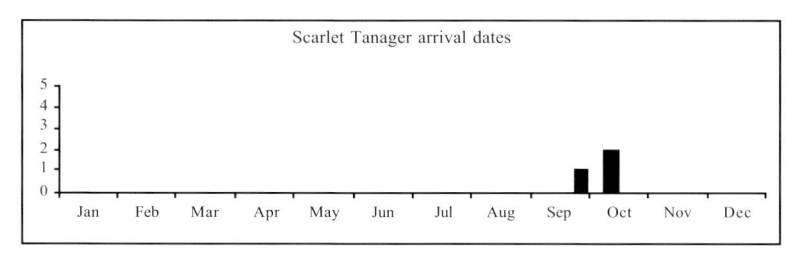

Scarlet Tanager is a long-distance migrant, autumn migration in northern North America peaking from mid-August to late September and extending into October at lower latitudes (Cramp *et al.* 1977–94). Most birds apparently cross the Gulf of Mexico en route to South America, it being scarce on passage in Mexico, Central America and the West Indies. However, the presence of up to seven autumn individuals in Britain, and others in Ireland and Iceland, suggests that some may take the transoceanic route out over the North Atlantic from northern North America direct to northwest South America.

## [White-throated Sparrow                                   *Zonotrichia albicollis*]  A

**Unrecorded in Scilly so far, full written description required by the BBRC.**

[1980   One (probable) 25th April leaving *QE2*   *IOSBR* 1980: 50, 1982: 48; Griffiths 1982

Nearctic species, breeds Yukon to Newfoundland and south to British Columbia and east to Ohio, northern Pennsylvania and northern New Jersey. Wintering Iowa, Ohio, Pennsylvania and Massachusetts south to California, northern Mexico, Texas, Gulf of Mexico and Florida. Migratory with small percentage of population wintering in southeast portion of breeding range. Monotypic. Most regularly recorded Nearctic seed-eater in Western Palearctic with, apart from Britain, records in Iceland, Netherlands, Denmark, Sweden, Finland and Gibraltar.

Along with other North American sparrows, White-throated is notable in southwest England, by its absence. In fact, British records of White-throated Sparrow have a distinctly northwest bias, some 70% occurring in Scotland and northern England, but with a few at least making it as far as Humberside, Suffolk and Hampshire, plus of course those continental European records. One explanation for the northern predominance is the species' tendency to overshoot its breeding range in spring (Cramp *et al.* 1977–94). This does seem a likely explanation, with the majority of Shetland and Fair Isle records occurring in spring, in obvious contrast to the marked Scillonian tendency towards autumn arrivals of other Nearctic species. Records were accepted by the BBRC for a total of 21 White-throated Sparrows in Britain between 1958 and the end of 1999 (BBRC 2000).

The one claimed record involving the islands concerned a bird seen leaving the liner *QE2* as she passed Scilly on 25th April 1980 inbound from North America (*IOSBR* 1980: 50, 1982: 48). However, identification was not certain. As with the Red-shouldered Hawk *Buteo lineatus* seen leaving a ship in similar circumstances, it is assumed the vessel was within sight of the islands, which might, however, still place it outside the then 25-km limit of British territorial waters. Consequently, the bird could only have been claimed as a British record if seen arriving on the islands – disregarding of course the additional issue of ship-assisted passage. Evans (1994) made the point that a number of White-throated Sparrow records involve ports handling large ships, e.g. Southampton (six or more individuals) and Felixstowe. It has also been recorded aboard ship throughout voyages from New York to Southampton (Frankland 1989) and northeast North America to the Baltic (Cook 1998). White-throated Sparrow came twelfth in Robbins's statistical review of expected transatlantic vagrancy among 31 Nearctic migrant passerines and near-passerines recorded in Britain or Ireland during 1947–76. The ten accepted records (six spring, four autumn) exceeded the predicted relative likelihood of 3.56 individuals (Robbins 1980). Surely it can only be a matter of time before Scilly plays host to this or some other species of American sparrow.

## Lapland Bunting (Lapland Longspur) *Calcarius lapponicus* A

Scarce, largely autumn migrant and rare winter visitor.

Circumpolar, breeds edge of Arctic tundra region, from Norway through northern Asia, Bering Sea, Alaska, northern Canada to western and southern Greenland. Migratory, Eurasian populations winter mainly central Eurasia, from Poland east to northeast Mongolia. Polytypic: nominate *lapponicus* occurs arctic Eurasia east to Sea of Okhotsk; *kamtschaticus* north of Sea of Okhotsk; *alascensis* northeast of *lapponicus* through Bering Sea to northwest Canada; *subcalcaratus* Greenland west to northwest Canada; one additional form North Pacific islands.

This is another of that minority of species escaping the attentions of early visitors to Scilly. First records for the islands came as recently as 1956, though it was surely overlooked earlier, a distinction Lapland Bunting shares with both Rustic *E. rustica* and Little Bunting *E. pusilla*. E H Rodd's only reference to it was as an occasional visitor to eastern Cornwall (Rodd 1880). However, its first recorded appearance in Scilly was somewhat memorable, involving as it did a substantial movement of up to 50 individuals daily during the second half of September. First were two on Bryher's northern end from 15th to 19th, these increasing to perhaps 50 by 25th, with an apparent daily rollover of birds (*CBWPSAR* 26). Meanwhile, one was at Porth Hellick, St Mary's, on 30th September, with up to six on Peninnis Head on the same island on 3rd to 5th November. The mass arrival that year coincided with exceptional numbers in western Europe of what were believed to have been mainly Scandinavian migrants (Cramp *et al.* 1977–94). However, whilst the view that it was overlooked on Scilly beforehand is tempting, first records for mainland Cornwall were not until 1960. Cramp *et al.* point out that it remains unclear whether changes in observer coverage or migration patterns are responsible for the increase in European passage and wintering records since the 1950s.

Penhallurick's mid-1970s review of mainland Cornwall and Scilly established that up to five or six per day occurred at some time during most autumns, but found no evidence of subsequent movements on the scale of those in 1956 (Penhallurick 1978), the closest being 1973, when up to 35 were noted throughout the autumn period. The earliest record Penhallurick could find involved one on St Agnes on 23rd August 1969, whereas the latest was on Cornwall's Hayle estuary on 26th November. Most autumn passage was evident on Scilly between mid-August and the third week of November, weekly totals never exceeding 20 for Cornwall and Scilly combined. The sole winter record for the islands concerned a bird at Porth Hellick, St Mary's, on 19th January 1969 and the only spring record a male moulting into summer plumage on St Mary's on 5th May 1972.

Little seems to have changed since then, birds normally arriving in Scilly from around mid-September and remaining evident in singles or small groups through to late October, punctuated by the occasional individual remaining into early or mid-November. During the ten years 1990–99, all autumn first arrival dates fell within the 14-day window of 9th–22nd September, whereas final sightings dates ranged between 14th October and 3rd November (21 days), though with one exceptional individual on 14th November. The only spring record within the ten-year period involved a bird on St Agnes and, presumably, the same over St Mary's, on 25th April 1997.

The extent, if at all, of any daily rollover is difficult to assess and this is not helped by the normal spread of birds between main islands. Deciding annual totals involved is equally problematical but in 1998 perhaps as few as 12 were believed to have passed through the islands, whilst in 1993, from one to 22 were present daily on up to five islands between 1st and 28th October alone.

In autumn, Lapland Buntings commence leaving the breeding areas from August or September, those from northern Europe heading between southwest and southeast (mainly the latter), whilst a proportion of the Greenland population heads southeast towards northwest Europe. Although explaining the obvious and regular autumn passage through Scilly is not easy, strong indications of Greenland birds on Britain's northwest coast, a regular passage through western Ireland and the arrival of birds in northwest France before those in the east all suggest the Nearctic *subcalcaratus* may perhaps be involved (Wernham *et al.* 2002). Although the possibility of birds reaching Scilly from Scandinavia (most of which move southeast) cannot be discounted, the regularity of the Scillonian passage perhaps argues against that region as the primary source, in which case the lack of anything other than the occasional spring records remains to be explained. Just one Lapland Bunting has been ringed on Scilly and there are no recaptures.

## Snow Bunting *Plectrophenax nivalis* A

**Annual, mainly autumn migrant in small numbers and rare winter visitor.**

Circumpolar, breeding mainly north of tree-line but including some high ground to south, plus Arctic islands, e.g. Iceland, Greenland and Spitsbergen, with small population in northern Scotland. Partially or wholly migratory, more so in the extreme north, wintering south to central Eurasia and northern USA. Polytypic: *insulae*, or 'Icelandic Snow Bunting', occurs Iceland and Scotland; nominate *nivalis* arctic North America, Greenland, Svarlbard, Fennoscandia, Faeroes, Kola peninsula, with some intergrading into *insulae* in Iceland. Additional forms further east. Amber-listed in UK: five-year mean of 25.4 breeding pairs (Gregory *et al.* 2002).

Unlike at least three other bunting species now occurring regularly in Scilly, Snow Bunting was well known in the late 19th century, the earliest reference being E H Rodd's comment in a letter to the *Zoologist* that 'Snow Buntings have made their appearance' (Rodd 1866e). In his *Birds of Cornwall and The Isles of Scilly* (1880), E H Rodd quoted his nephew Francis Rodd's observations on autumn migration in Scilly during 1870, Francis having pointed out that even though autumn had been marked by a larger number than usual of some rarer waders and seed-eating passerines, Snow Buntings 'which often appear in considerable flocks' were very scarce. However, Francis Rodd and James Clark (1906) later provided a valuable insight into just how detailed the level of knowledge obtained was for some species, even by 1906, such that it is difficult to avoid quoting them in full, if only to support the view that early observers would have noticed Little Bunting, Rustic Bunting and Lapland Bunting had they occurred, either in Scilly or on the Cornish mainland.

> The Snow Bunting is a regular bird of passage in the early autumn, sometimes in pairs, usually in small flocks of six to twelve, and on some three occasions in parties of twenty-five to thirty. Stray birds and small parties are not infrequent during the winter months, and are occasionally noticed in March, April and the first week of May. The birds, as a rule, settle on the barest and most exposed headlands, and their arrival appears to be independent both of wind and weather. They are, as a rule, remarkably tame, and show little restlessness or uneasiness on being approached. About four-fifths of the birds are young, and, with the exception of a splendid adult male in full breeding plumage, shot by Dorrien-Smith on April 29th, 1890, have all, so far as observed, been in autumn plumage. In this condition the 'snowflake' is strikingly descriptive, for when a flock pitches on an exposed headland on a dull grey day it looks exactly like a scud of snow.

So good is this early account that it exceeds much of what can reliably be said about Snow Buntings in Scilly today, with, for example, few recent observers attempting to categorise flocks or groups in terms of age and sex. Few reports appeared at all in the early *CBWPSAR*s and after mention of a dead bird on St Mary's golf course in November 1933 we hear nothing further until a party of three females and a male were noted on St Martin's in October 1948. However, a 1951 comment 'First noticed rather later than usual' suggests they may actually have been more regular than published records show.

Certainly this last view gains support from the *IOSBR* from 1977 onwards, with birds appearing annually in some numbers and with a very obvious pattern of arrival and onward movement, from September through into November and with only one to two in some springs and even less frequent wintering individuals or small groups. Autumn first-arrival dates for the 23 years 1977–99 show a marked concentration within a 22-day period, from 11th September to 2nd October – though one late arrival on 10th October is omitted from this calculation. Calculating departure dates is more difficult owing to the extent of inter-island movement thought to be involved, but the final date on which birds were recorded over the 23 years ranged between 6th October and 30th November. In other words, no birds were recorded in autumn outside the period 11th September to 30th November.

During the same 23-year period, fifteen birds arrived in the early part of the year, from mid-February to mid-May, 10 (66.6%) of these in April. The only winter arrival involved a party of 12 on Round Island from 4th to 7th January 1986, with two to three remaining until 10th March. Consequently, it seems difficult to resist the view that, as with so many non-resident species in Scilly, Snow Bunting arrivals and departures form part of a regular seasonal movement. However, deciding origins and destinations is more difficult.

Estimating numbers of birds annually involved is frustrated by a combination of single-day sightings and an unknown amount of inter-island movement, but the total seems likely to vary, up to a limit of around 30 or 40 individuals, though it could be higher. The majority of records comprise from one to five birds but flocks of up to 20 or 30 can occur.

Most northern European Snow Buntings winter around the sea coasts, and Britain and Ireland annually holds 10,000–15,000 individuals, mostly in Scotland and comprising 70–85% *insulae* and 15–30% *nivalis*. However, small numbers also winter in coastal France and even reach northwest Spain, though most winter further east. Icelandic *insulae* winter mainly in Britain and the Netherlands but some also reach France, even the Azores (Wernham *et al.* 2002). Although the wintering range of Fennoscandian *nivalis* remains largely unknown, it probably lies within the Scandinavian and Baltic regions, though some authorities believe most wintering British *nivalis* originate from Scandinavia. In addition, although there is as yet no direct evidence, it is believed that some Snow Buntings move between Greenland and central Europe, and perhaps Britain and Ireland. Unsurprisingly, Scottish birds are thought to move shorter distances than those further north (Cramp *et al.* 1977–94).

From the above, it seems probable that birds seen on passage in Scilly are either *insulae* or *nivalis* from Iceland (or perhaps even *nivalis* from Greenland), *nivalis* from Fennoscandia or possibly *insulae* from Scotland, all on passage to wintering grounds in France or further south in western Europe. The pattern of arrival and departure rules out the possibility of random winter movements and is matched by that for mainland Cornwall, which is equally lacking in evidence of regular wintering.

## Pine Bunting *Emberiza leucocephalos* A BBRC 5.7%

**Extremely rare migrant or vagrant, full written description required by the BBRC.**

1983 One (female or first-year) Porth Mellon, St Mary's 16th to 18th November
*British Birds* 82: 557
1985 One (male) Telegraph, St Mary's 19th to 23rd April  *British Birds* 78: 367, 79: 565, 581

Breeds Asia north to tree-line, from western Russia across Siberia to Pacific and Sakhalin, south to central Asia, western China and Turkestan. Winters south of breeding range in China, central Asia and India, west to Iraq. Polytypic: nominate *leucocephalos* occurs throughout except western China, where replaced by *fronto*. Migrants move mainly south; some overlap in range and inter-breeding with Yellowhammer *E. citrinella* in western Siberia.

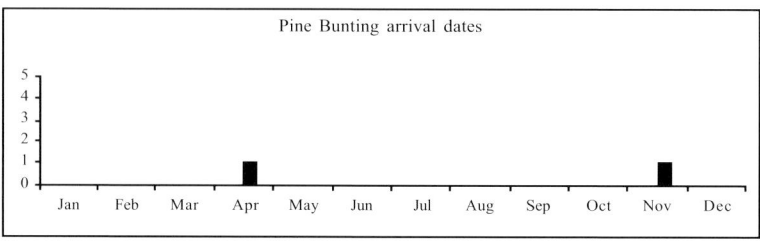

There have been just two accepted Scillonian records of this exciting bunting, and a total of 35 British records during the period 1958–99 mean the islands accounted for 5.7% of these. One was a pristine spring male on the eastern end of St Mary's golf course for five days in April 1985, the other a female or first-winter individual at Porth Mellon, St Mary's, for three days in November 1983. What was initially identified as Rustic Bunting *E. rustica* and then Lapland Bunting *Calcarius lapponicus* at Borough Farm, Tresco, for one day only during October 1995 was eventually thought to be a first-year male Pine Bunting, but the record was not accepted by the BBRC (*IOSBR* 1995). All apparent or suspect Pine Buntings must be scrutinised carefully in order to eliminate the possibility of any hybrid Yellowhammer features, with birds showing even a trace of yellow in their plumage being immediately suspect (Evans 1994; Byers *et al.* 1995). The likelihood of the eastern form *fronto* appearing in the British Isles seems remote but cannot be entirely discounted; however, relevant plumage features are often extremely subtle and care must be taken in examining suspect individuals.

## Yellowhammer *Emberiza citrinella* A

**Scarce but regular and almost annual migrant, mainly in autumn, a full written description required by the SRP.**

Breeds Europe and western Asia, from northern Fennoscandia, British Isles and northern Spain eastwards to Siberia and northern Russia, south to Mediterranean and Black Seas. Northern populations migratory, wintering south to Mediterranean, Middle East, Iran and Kazakhstan. Polytypic: nominate *citrinella* occurs western Europe from Norway, southeast England and northern Spain east to European Russia, Poland, Hungary and former Yugoslavia; intergrading with *caliginosa*, or 'Western Yellowhammer', in western England and with *erythrogenys* in west European Russia, Baltic states, Ukraine, etc.; *caliginosa* in Scotland, Ireland, Isle of Man and Wales and *erythrogenys* reappearing in eastern Europe and Asia. Red-listed in UK: rapid, 54% breeding decline over past 25 years (Gregory *et al.* 2002). National 16% decline 1994–99 (Bashford & Noble 2000).

Yellowhammer was a common and familiar bird in Britain and Ireland throughout the 19th century, breeding in a variety of agricultural and open habitats, the situation remaining almost unchanged throughout the first half of the 20th century (Holloway 1996). As with many common species, E H Rodd merely noted it as found generally throughout Cornwall, without particular reference to Scilly. However, in their later *Zoologist* review of *The Birds of Scilly* James Clark and Francis Rodd described it as a 'very rare autumn casual', recording that Augustus Pechell shot one in October 1849 and noting another some years later (Clark & Rodd 1906). This sounds not too far removed from the situation today.

Interestingly, in their otherwise informative mid-20th-century review of the breeding birds of Cornwall and Scilly, Ryves & Quick (1946) made no specific mention of it in relation to the islands, and from this we may assume that Yellowhammer remained uncommon on Scilly up to that time. However, examination of published reports from 1957 to the end of 1999 shows a total of 88 individuals recorded on Scilly during that time, 30 (34%) in spring and 58 (66%) during autumn. Autumn birds appeared mainly in October, with lesser numbers during September and November. Spring arrivals commenced from March, but with the majority in April and with a reasonable showing still in May. Three singing males recorded included one on St Martin's in March 1961, one on Gugh in May 1971, and one in October 1971 on St Mary's Airport. There were no records in at least seven years and no obvious trend in the overall pattern of occurrence. Slightly higher annual numbers recorded on St Agnes in the late 1950s and early 1960s perhaps reflect increased levels of observer coverage on that island, though seven to eight in 1958 and 15 in autumn 1976 may have reflected a genuine increase between those years.

British Yellowhammers are largely sedentary and although there is some withdrawal from the uplands, ringing data show that most adults winter within 5 km of their breeding territories – 95% of all ringing recoveries were within 25 km, mean dispersal distance being 1 km and random (Wernham *et al.* 2002). However, Ireland may be an exception to this as the difference between summer and winter distribution is said to be more marked. Northern populations are more inclined to migrate, heading mainly southwest but seldom more than 500 km from northern Europe, whereas birds from more southerly populations move only 250 km on average. Birds from elsewhere within the British Isles are not expected to reach Scilly on passage, except perhaps dispersing Cornish birds and, as with Corn Bunting *Miliaria calandra*, those that do appear are perhaps more likely to originate from populations east or northeast of Britain. However, differences between forms are slight and not necessarily detectable in the field. Interestingly, a Norwegian-ringed Yellowhammer was recovered in Kent in winter and British-ringed birds were recovered in winter in France (1) and the Netherlands (2) (Wernham *et al.* 2002). Recorded dates of autumn and spring arrival on Scilly fit normal movement patterns for European migrants quoted by Byers *et al.* (1995). Four Yellowhammers have been trapped and ringed on Scilly but there are no recaptures.

## Cirl Bunting *Emberiza cirlus* A

**Rare migrant or winter visitor, full written description required by the SRP.**

  1857   One shot Scilly November   Clark & Rodd 1906
  1859   One shot Scilly December, plus probably several others
                                                   Clark & Rodd 1906; Penhallurick 1978
  1905   One shot St Mary's 16th November   Clark & Rodd 1906
  [1908  Allegedly bred Gugh]   Penhallurick 1978
  1937   One St Mary's   Penhallurick 1978
  1976   Up to 12 St Mary's November to January 1977

Breeds northwest Africa and southwest Europe, north through France and including southwest England, then east through the northern Mediterranean to Turkey and southern Black Sea area. Resident, any movements limited to post-breeding or cold-weather dispersal. Monotypic (BOURC 2002b). Red-listed in UK: national 83% decline during 20 years to 1996, rapid, 88% contraction of breeding range over past 30 years (Gregory *et al.* 2002).

Up until the end of the 19th century and even beyond, the Cirl Bunting was common over the greater part of southern England, with its stronghold very much in Devon and Cornwall (Aplin 1892a; Holloway 1996). Confirmation of this comes from E H Rodd's enthusiastic account of its status throughout Cornwall during the late 19th century, describing it as generally common and particularly so in the vicinity of Penzance. In fact so great was his familiarity with Cirl Bunting that he was able to describe subtle differences in markings between its eggs and those of Yellowhammer *E. citrinella*, whilst also drawing comparisons between its song and that of both Yellowhammer and Wood Warbler *Phylloscopus sibilatrix* (Rodd 1880). However, his only direct reference to Scilly involved the 1859 bird mentioned above (Rodd 1860b). Moving forward in time, we soon find confirmation it was indeed a rarity in the islands during the 19th and early 20th centuries, only three being 'obtained' by 1906: in November 1857, December 1859 and November 1905 (Clark & Rodd 1906). And a summary of breeding birds in Cornwall and Scilly during the first half of the 20th century helps clarify Cirl Bunting's status, noting as it does an increase in Cornwall after 1906 but 'no great change recently', and the fact that it was thinly distributed in woody pastures and occurred in the greatest concentration in mid-Cornwall (Ryves & Quick 1946). The failure of these authorities to mention Scilly confirms Cirl Bunting's absence as a breeding species.

The much publicised national decline in both breeding range and numbers seems to have commenced around the mid-1930s (Holloway 1996). This had developed into wide-scale collapse by the late 1950s and early 1960s, with the main national Cirl Bunting breeding concentration centred on southwest Devon, but with pairs present at some 15 Cornish sites west as far as the Lizard peninsula until at least 1975 (*CBWPSAR*).

There are, in fact, probably only five reliable Cirl Bunting records for Scilly. Penhallurick (1978) mentioned 'several' in November 1859, which presumably includes the shot bird mentioned by Clark & Rodd in their 1906 paper, plus one in November 1905, which presumably is another of those mentioned by Clark & Rodd. However, Penhallurick also quoted a Tresco Abbey record of one allegedly found breeding on Gugh in 1908, but then dismisses it for want of evidence, and as it was not referred to by Ryves & Quick (1946) we too should ignore it – though a breeding bunting of any other species would be an equally important record. The only additional claims involve an individual discovered by an E W Hendy on St Mary's in 1937 (Penhallurick 1978) and a more recent record involving perhaps twice as many birds as previously seen on the islands. This was a quite astounding occurrence of up to 12 individuals frequenting St Mary's from around mid-November 1976 to late January 1977 (*IOSBR* 1977; Penhallurick 1978).

Cirl Buntings are normally sedentary though many in continental Europe leave the colder parts of their range during winter and head south or west, the longest such movement involving a Belgian individual that travel 725 km to southwest France (Wernham *et al.* 2002). Almost all Continental populations occur south of Britain, the nearest being those in northern France (Dontchev & Magyar, in Hagemeijer & Blair

1997). In England, although disinclined to move far, birds may wander in autumn, but normally keep within 100 km of the breeding area. According to ringing data, in Devon at least up until 1994 most birds wintered within a few kilometres of the nest site, some less than 1 km, though two moved south 40 km. One notable exception involved a bird ringed in Sussex prior to 1960 and recovered on the Isle of May in Scotland the following June (Cramp *et al.* 1977–94). Most birds are said to vacate northeast France during winter and it was perhaps from there or Belgium, and not Britain, that the 1966–67 birds originated.

## Ortolan Bunting *Emberiza hortulana* A

Scarce annual migrant, mainly in autumn. Treated by the BBRC as a national Scarce Migrant, full written description required by the SRP.

| | |
|---|---|
| 1944 | One 'Scilly' 25th April |
| 1958 | One (male) St Agnes 4th May |
| 1959 | Up to two St Agnes 22nd to 27th April |
| 1964 | One St Agnes 3rd May |
| 1974 | One Bryher 10th May |
| 1978 | One Tresco 30th April to 1st May |
| 1984 | One Gugh 21st April |
| 1985 | One St Mary's 18th April |
| 1986 | One St Agnes 2nd May |
| 1988 | One St Agnes 20th April |
| 1988 | One St Agnes 8th May |
| 1989 | One St Mary's 12th May |
| 1990 | One St Martin's 1st May |
| 1994 | One St Agnes 26th to 28th April |
| 1996 | One St Martin's 6th to 10th May |
| 1997 | One Bryher 3rd May |
| 1999 | One St Mary's 3rd May |

Breeds most of Europe, from Sweden south to France, Iberia and Mediterranean and east into central-western Asia, as far almost as Lake Baikal. Migratory, wintering sub-Saharan Africa. Monotypic.

The only 19th-century record involved a female or first-winter individual shot off a wall near Tresco Abbey by Augustus Pechell on 7th October 1851 (Rodd 1851b; Clark & Rodd 1906). Penhallurick examined all records for Scilly and mainland Cornwall up until the mid-1970s, finding that most occurred during autumn, between late August and the third week of October. Scilly received the bulk of these records, with spring sightings confined to the three weeks between late April and mid-May. Normal annual totals on Scilly rarely exceeded five, but by far the largest movement ever recorded in the islands was that of 25th September 1956, when 100 were noted on St Agnes alone, along with a movement of Meadow Pipits. All involved were reportedly either females or first-years and none remained by the following day, the only other reports that month involving singles on 15th and 23rd (*CBWPSAR* 26).

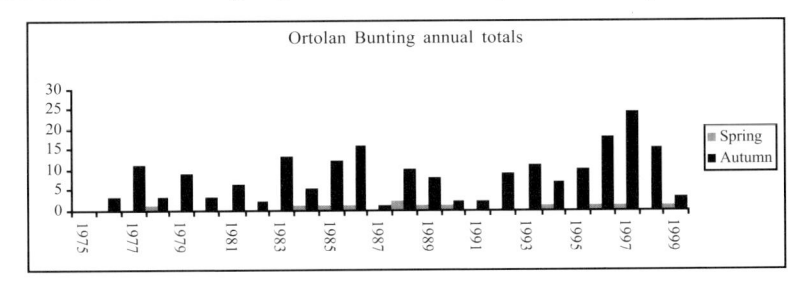

The Chart shows annual spring and autumn totals for the 25 years 1975–99, whilst the Table provides details of all spring records. There is the suggestion of a slight increase in recent years, though this could be attributable to greater observer coverage; Dymond *et al.* (1989) actually suggested evidence of a recent national decline in numbers. Twenty-four in 1997 was the highest autumn total, whereas two in 1988 was the highest spring number. Autumn arrival dates ranged between late August and mid-October, early to mid-September being most frequent, whereas final sighting dates ranged throughout October and in two years extended into early November.

In Sweden and Denmark, southward migration commences from mid-August or September, birds moving mainly southwest. Ortolan Bunting is scarce on passage in Britain, occurring mostly on the east coast in spring and along the south coast during autumn (Cramp *et al.* 1977–94). Consequently, Sharrock (1974) concluded that most Ortolan Buntings in western Britain and Ireland in autumn arrive from the south and are either from southern populations or are Scandinavian birds that previously moved south through continental Europe. Certainly, the presumed suggestion of random pre-migration dispersal would help explain the comparative lack of recorded autumn adults in Scilly. Four Ortolan Buntings were ringed in Scilly prior to 1970; there are no recaptures.

## Yellow-browed Bunting *Emberiza chrysophrys* A BBRC 20.0%

**Extremely rare migrant, full written description required by the BBRC.**

1994   One (probable first-winter) St Agnes 19th to 22nd October
*British Birds* 88: 551; *Birding World* 7: 410–411

Breeds Asia, from southeast Siberia east to Barguzin and Stanovoy Mountains. Winters central and southeast China. Monotypic.

One record, a probable first-winter individual, in the Lower Town area of St Agnes from 19th to 22nd October 1994 (Wright 1994). First found mid- to late afternoon and identified simply as a 'funny little bunting' it soon became apparent this was Britain and Ireland's fourth record of this extreme eastern rarity. The previous three occurred in Norfolk in October 1975, Shetland in October 1980 and Orkney in September 1992, whereas the fifth was on Orkney again, on 4th–5th May 1998.

Surprisingly, there were, at least until 1998, just three other acceptable European records, involving Belgium in October 1966, an island off the Netherlands in October 1982 and the Ukraine in January 1983 (Snow & Perrins 1998). Consequently, it seems that if we wish to add further European sightings of this species, our best chance of doing so may be on an island in October. Not surprisingly, this was yet another Scillonian arrival that managed to attract a substantial crowd throughout its brief stay.

The population normally migrates in a southeast direction in autumn, to winter in eastern China (Cramp *et al.* 1977–94).

## Rustic Bunting *Emberiza rustica* A BBRC 9.41%

**Scarce but regular migrant, mainly in autumn, full written description required by the BBRC.**

1960   One (male) St Agnes 7th October
1962   One (male) St Agnes 26th & 27th October
1962   One (male) St Agnes 4th November
1965   One (male) St Agnes 21st to 28th October
1968   One (first-year male) Tresco 24th to 27th October
1968   One Tresco 7th & 8th November
1972   One (first-year male) Tresco 2nd to 5th November
1975   One St Martin's 5th October

1975  One (first-year male) St Mary's 31st October
1976  One Tresco 1st November
1977  One (first-year male) St Mary's 11th to 16th October
1977  One (first-year male) St Agnes 12th October
1979  One (female or first-year) St Agnes, Bryher & St Mary's 10th to 19th October
1979  One (male) St Mary's 14th October
1981  One St Mary's 4th to 7th October
1982  One (first-year) Tresco 22nd to 26th October
1982  One (male) St Martin's 27th October
1984  One St Mary's 14th & 15th October
1984  One Tresco 16th to 25th October
1985  One Tresco 13th October
1985  One St Mary's 13th to 19th October
1985  One St Martin's 16th & 17th October
1986  One St Mary's 7th to 12th October
1988  One St Mary's 15th October
1988  One St Mary's 17th to 19th October
1990  One Tresco 19th October
1990  One Tresco 20th to 22nd October
1993  One St Agnes 6th to 9th October
1993  One St Mary's 9th to 12th October
1993  One Tresco 11th October
1994  One Tresco 11th to 14th October
1995  One St Mary's 23rd to 27th October
1996  One Tresco 20th to 28th October
1996  One Tresco 21st to 28th October
1997  One Tresco 19th to 24th October
1998  One St Mary's 11th to 14th October
1999  One St Mary's 18th & 19th March
2000  One St Agnes 10th October

Breeds Eurasia, from northern Fennoscandia through Russia and Siberia to Kamchatka, north to tree-line and south to mountains of southern Siberia. Long-range migrant, wintering Turkestan east to China and Japan. Polytypic: nominate *rustica* occupies most of breeding range; *latifascia* further east.

Occurring in about half the years since 1960, this and Little Bunting *E. pusilla* help our understanding of ornithological perspectives in Scilly. For although BBRC listed and extreme rarities over much of Britain, on Scilly both occur more frequently than Corn Bunting *Miliaria calandra* or Yellowhammer *E. citrinella* and about as regularly as Ortolan *E. hortulana* and Reed Buntings *E. schoeniclus*.

If Rustic Bunting occurred in Scilly as an autumn migrant prior to the 20th century, then it appears to have been overlooked by those otherwise vigilant men with their eager guns, for nobody, including E H Rodd (1880) and Clark & F R Rodd (1906), made mention of it. Indeed, the earliest written record seems to be that of the 1960 bird on St Agnes, which was accompanied by a detailed description (but see remarks under Little Bunting).

As with several other species, numbers of claimed sightings often exceed the number of records finally accepted by the BBRC. This was the case in 1990, when up to four different Rustic Buntings were reportedly present and seen by many birders on Tresco between 3rd and 21st October, though only two appeared in the BBRC's acceptance list for that year. Often it is difficult to tell whether individual birds moving between sites gave the impression more were present. However, concern remains that, because so many observers are often involved, some birds remain unrecorded, observers assuming that others will write up the necessary descriptions. This is a common but nonetheless unfortunate theme evident in any examination of Scillonian rarity reports. Often, too, minor points of individual behaviour may have led observers to conclude that different birds were present at different sites, but such subtleties may not always become evident to distant committees via subsequent written descriptions.

All 37 autumn individuals were squeezed into a narrow 35-day window, between 5th October and 8th

November, with one additional two-day record in mid-March, 11 of the 12 sightings where the sex was determined involving males. However, it is difficult to know if this last accurately represents the true situation, or merely reflects difficulties in separating females and first-year birds, which, given the overall level of autumn observer competence on Scilly, seems unlikely. However, from the mid-1980s, BBRC ceased publishing individual assessments of sex or age for Rustic Buntings, following doubts whether these can be relied upon in autumn. The average length of stay was just 3.6 days, the longest being ten days (two individuals) and the shortest one day (13 individuals, or 34% of arrivals).

As with several other eastern migrants, there were years with greater numbers of accepted Rustic Bunting records, 1985 and 1993 topping the list with three each. The species' preference for particular islands was evenly divided between Tresco and St Mary's, with 14 records each and with eight on St Agnes, three on St Martin's and one on Bryher (one bird visited more than one island). These 37 Scillonian records represent 9.41% of the 393 sightings accepted by BBRC from 1958 to the end of 1999 (BBRC 2000). For an insight into the problems of separating Rustic and Little Bunting see Bradshaw (1991).

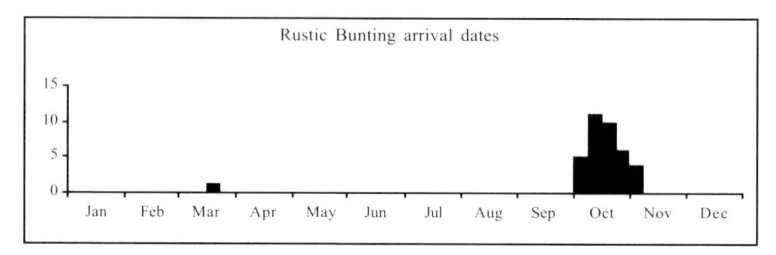

*Rustic Bunting arrival dates chart (bar chart showing arrivals by month, with small bar in March and larger bars from September to November peaking in October)*

Despite the bulk of the population wintering in China and Japan, Rustic Bunting breeds as close to Britain as southern Norway (Ukkonen & Vaisanen, in Hagemeijer & Blair 1997). European autumn migration commences August or September, with western birds first heading east, then south (Cramp *et al.* 1977–94). The Chart shows all 38 arrival dates and reveals a typical migrant pattern, in this case presumably involving reverse migration. The presence of just one apparent spring overshoot is noteworthy.

## Little Bunting *Emberiza pusilla* A

**Scarce but regular migrant, mainly in autumn. Treated by the BBRC as a national Scarce Migrant, full written description required by the SRP.**

Breeds northern Eurasia, from Lapland east to Pacific and south to central Siberia. Long-range migrant, wintering tropical Asia from northeast India to China. Monotypic. Removed from BBRC Rarities List January 1994 (Lansdown and the Rarities Committee 1993).

This is one of the two most frequent former BBRC rarities on Scilly (together with Richard's Pipit *Anthus novaeseelandiae*), with a total of 81 individuals between 1956 and the end of 1999, two together on St Agnes in 1956 representing the earliest record for the islands (*CBWPSAR* 26). Little Bunting is one of three or more bunting species presently known to occur in Scilly but which the 19th-century collectors apparently failed to identify, the other obvious examples being Rustic *E. rustica* and Lapland Buntings *Calcarius lapponicus*. Of course, all three are not dissimilar in winter plumage and typically keep very low, so could just conceivably have been confused with each other, though that would not explain all three being overlooked completely. It is also difficult to accept that people of the ability of Augustus Pechell and Francis Rodd failed to record any of these three, whilst correctly identifying Ortolan Bunting *E. hortulana* and successfully separating Cirl Bunting *E. cirlus* from Yellowhammer *E. citrinella*. Unless, of course, they confused them with Reed Bunting *E. schoeniclus*, which James Clark and Francis Rodd noted as 'an occasional visitor from October to January, sometimes singly, sometimes in small parties' (Clark & Rodd 1906). Otherwise the only sensible answer is that Little, Rustic and Lapland Buntings all occurred far less commonly on Scilly prior to the 1950s, if indeed they occurred at all. Significantly, 274 (75%) out of 367 Little Buntings recorded in Britain and Ireland up until 1985 occurred after 1958 (Dymond *et al.* 1989), Dymond *et al.* attributing this increase to a general growth in observer activity. Interestingly, much the same holds true for Rustic Bunting, 200 (86%) out of 233 recorded in Britain up until 1990 occurring after 1958, with an obvious marked increase in number and frequency after 1971 (Evans 1994).

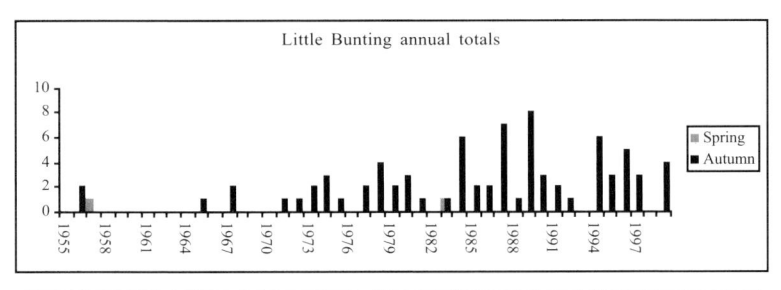

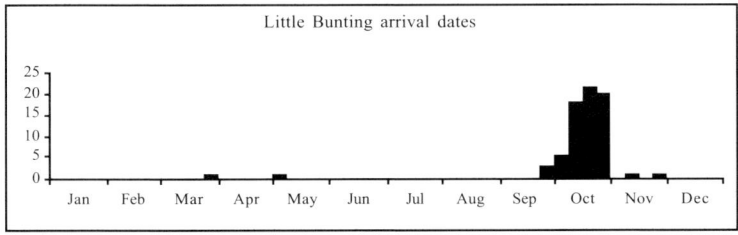

The Charts include annual Little Bunting totals for the 44 years 1956–99, only two of which involved single spring records, plus all 69 known arrival dates for the same period, the latter revealing a clear mid- to late October peak. As with some other autumn migrants on Scilly, the possibility of at least some degree of autumn observer bias cannot be discounted. This most probably accounts for any sharp drop-off in sightings at the end of October following the annual bulk departure of visiting birders. However, the apparent sharp drop-off in Little Bunting records at the end of October involves only arrival dates, though it is true few remained into November. Mean duration of stay was 4.05 days with the longest 24 days. However, 45% of all birds were recorded on one day only. The earliest autumn Little Bunting arrival date was 25th September (two on St Agnes in 1956 and one at Borough Farm, Tresco in 1994) and the latest any remained was 25th November 1997, giving an arrival–departure window of 62 days.

The nearest Little Bunting breeding populations to Scilly are in Norway and Finland (Koskimies, in Hagemeijer & Blair 1997) and in order to reach their wintering grounds birds from western Europe normally move southeast, although small numbers head southwest (Cramp *et al.* 1977–94), presumably eventually correcting their direction of travel. Bradshaw (1991) gave a comprehensive insight into the separation of Little and Rustic Buntings.

## Yellow-breasted Bunting        *Emberiza aureola*  A  BBRC 1.54%

Very rare migrant, full written description required by the BBRC.

  1974   One (first-year) St Mary's 25th to 27th September   British Birds 68: 332
  1993   One (first-year or adult male) St Agnes 14th & 15th September   British Birds 87: 565
  1993   One (first-year or adult male) St Mary's 1st October   British Birds 87: 565
  2000   One (female or first-year) Tresco 24th to 26th September   British Birds 94: 499
  2001   One St Agnes 5th to 9th October   British Birds 94: plate 353, 95: 521–522

Breeds Eurasia, from Finland east through Russia and Siberia to Kamchatka and Kurile Islands, north to tree-line and south to central Russia, Mongolia and Manchuria. Long-range migrant, wintering northeast India to southern China and south to Malay Peninsula. Polytypic: nominate *aureola* occurs throughout except for extreme east, where replaced by *ornata*.

Just five Scillonian records of this easily overlooked bunting: two on St Mary', two on St Agnes and one on Tresco. With 194 British records accepted by the BBRC during the period 1958–99, the three island records up until 1999 accounted for just 1.5% of the national total, perhaps demonstrating how much of a northeast bias is attached to this species in Britain. It is clearly less frequent in the islands than most visiting Nearctic and several other Eurasian rarities, which perhaps seems puzzling, given how closely it breeds to Scilly compared with, for example, Richard's Pipit *Anthus novaeseelandiae* or Olive-backed Pipit *A. hodgsoni*.

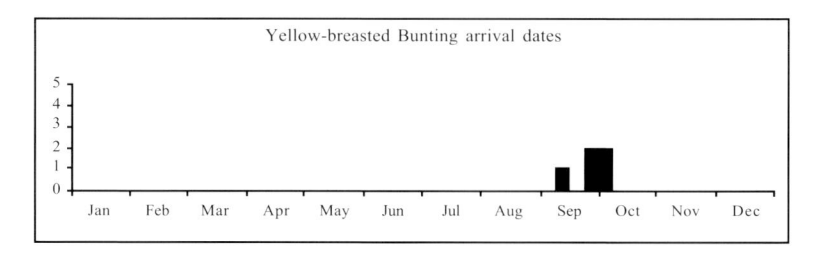

*Yellow-breasted Bunting arrival dates chart (bars in Sep and Oct)*

Until the early 1980s, Yellow-breasted Bunting increased in its closest breeding area of Finland, since when it has shown a decline (Ojanen, in Hagemeijer & Blair 1997). For useful information on identification of female and juvenile Yellow-breasted Buntings see H Harrop (1993). Ojanen also made the point that for long-distance migrants such as this, populations breeding in western Europe are seriously restricted in terms of available breeding time, particularly during prolonged periods of severe weather.

# Reed Bunting *Emberiza schoeniclus* A

**Scarce migrant, full written description required by the SRP.**

Breeds much of Eurasia, from Atlantic to Pacific north to tree-line and south to Mediterranean, though fragmentarily in south. Polytypic, with hugely complex racial structure, divided into northern *schoeniclus* group and southern *pyrrhuloides* group. Nominate *schoeniclus* of northern group occurs western Europe, including Britain, western France, east to the Urals; *witherbyi* of southern group Iberia, the Balearic Islands, southern France and perhaps northwest Africa. Cramp *et al.* (1977–94) recognise more than 20 additional forms. Northern populations migratory, wintering within breeding range and beyond, which in West Palearctic includes countries north of Mediterranean, coastal northwest Africa and Turkey. Red-listed in UK: rapid, 62% breeding decline over past 25 years (Gregory *et al.* 2002); BTO Waterways Bird Survey showed 68% decline 1975–2000.

First mention of Reed Bunting in Scilly comes from Francis Rodd's account of a walk around Tresco on 27th December 1870, in his uncle E H Rodd's milestone work *Birds of Cornwall and The Scilly Isles* (Rodd 1880). This gives his description of how a 'shy dark bird' among a flock of Brambling *Fringilla montifringilla* turned out to be this species, and uses the name we now know it by and not the 'Black-headed Bunting' preferred by his elder relative. Although E H Rodd gave no further information, Francis and co-author James Clark later felt able to describe Reed Bunting as an occasional visitor to the islands from October to January, sometimes singly and sometimes in small parties (Clark & Rodd 1906), having last been seen near Tresco Abbey on 8th January 1904. By the mid-20th century, Ryves & Quick (1946) made no mention of it breeding on Scilly, though they did consider it sparsely distributed in all suitable habitats in Cornwall, as indeed had the senior Rodd earlier. The sole remaining old record involved a bird recorded aboard a boat 32 km southwest of Scilly on 8th May 1936 (*CBWPSAR* 6).

Penhallurick (1978) felt confident enough to suggest Reed Bunting had been overlooked in Scilly prior to 1952, quoting records for all months except February, August and December. He pointed out that 66% of sightings fell within the period 24th September to 12th November, with a marked peak during mid-October, whilst also detecting a less well-defined return passage during March and April. A reported sighting by Hilda Quick of a 'pair' on Samson on 14th June 1959 (*CBWPSAR* 29) lacks supporting information of the kind normally expected for a first breeding record, though admittedly the date is unusual for Reed Buntings on Scilly.

A deterioration in the level of recorded information for this species since the 1960s unfortunately makes it impossible to draw comparisons with Penhallurick's earlier analysis. However, much of this loss of detail may be attributable to an increase in the annual number of records, which may now total to up to 40 birds a year. Nevertheless, spring sightings still appear limited to less than ten, with none at all in two or so years, though dates involved still broadly match earlier findings.

Although the British population is principally sedentary, with 40% of females and 80% of males moving no more than 5 km during winter, some 20% move over 100 km and head mainly southwest, though only exceptionally leaving Britain (Cramp *et al.* 1977–94). Origins of birds wintering in Britain from elsewhere involve western Scandinavia and, to a lesser extent, the Low Countries (Wernham *et al.* 2002). The former populations are almost entirely migratory and winter mainly in southern France, with fewer in Britain, northern France and the Low Countries, as far south as Iberia. Birds ringed in Gloucester and Suffolk in early spring were recovered in Sweden later the same spring and a bird ringed on Fair Isle, Shetland, in October was recovered in southwest France the same winter.

Thus it seems that birds recorded on Scilly in both autumn and spring could involve British individuals that moved southwest or, perhaps more likely, western Scandinavian migrants en route to and from France or further south, or perhaps even short-distance winter migrants from the Low Countries (Wernham *et al.* 2002). Consequently, only the nominate *schoeniclus* should be involved, but with the presumed outside chance of a *witherbyi* individual moving north with them, though this last might be difficult to establish in the field. Gantlett (1998) drew attention to the possibility of the slightly paler northwest Siberian *passerina*, or even the eastern Siberian *parvirostra* reaching Britain as vagrants, plus various other forms from the eastern extremities of Reed Bunting's breeding range. Reed Buntings reaching Scilly should also be examined carefully for any possibility of the closely similar Pallas's Reed Bunting *E. pallasi*, which breeds within the range of Reed Bunting and in the north is a long-distance migrant. Its appearance would seem quite possible given Scilly's record for attracting extralimital migrants from eastern Europe and beyond, but it should be bourne in mind that some of the paler eastern forms of Reed Bunting are more liable to confusion with Pallas's Reed Bunting (Byers *et al.* 1995). Indeed, a 'strikingly pale' Reed Bunting on Scilly on 30th October 1987 was thought to be one of the eastern forms, possibly *pallidior* (*Birding World* 15: 85). Four Reed Buntings have been trapped on Scilly, two prior to 1970 and two since, but there are no recaptures.

## Black-headed Bunting *Emberiza melanocephala* A BBRC 7.14%

**Rare migrant, full written description required by the BBRC.**

   1958   One (male) St Agnes 31st August to 5th September   *British Birds* 53: 172
   1973   One (male) St Agnes & Gugh 16th to 19th May   *British Birds* 67: 339
   1977   One (female or first-year) St Mary's 14th October   *British Birds* 72: 544
   1979   One (male) trapped St Agnes 15th to at least 26th April   *British Birds* 73: 529
   1979   One (male) Bryher 9th to 11th May   *British Birds* 73: 529
   1986   One (male) trapped St Agnes 13th & 14th June   *British Birds* 80: 568
   1987   One (male) Tresco 7th to 12th September   *British Birds* 81: 593
   1989   One (male) St Mary's 25th May   *British Birds* 83: 492
   1992   One (male) St Martin's 18th to 23rd May   *British Birds* 86: 536
   1997   One (male) St Agnes 3rd & 4th June   *British Birds* 91: 514
   *2002   One (first-year male) Tresco 29th September to 3rd October   Birding World 15: 368, 415*

Breeds southern West Palearctic, from northern Italy to Iran, north to lower Danube and lower Volga and south to Balkans, Asia Minor and Levant, with recent northwards spread along Black Sea coast (Cramp *et al.* 1977–94). Long-distance migrant, wintering western and central India. Monotypic.

Not to be confused with earlier reports of 'Black-headed Bunting', which in the 19th century was commonly used to describe Reed Bunting *E. schoeniclus* (e.g. Rodd 1880). However, the latter individual made no mention of *E. melanocephala* in Scilly or Cornwall and we can perhaps safely assume that had anything as obvious as a male Black-headed Bunting occurred during the 1880s, it would have been the immediate focus of attention among the many experienced collectors. Clark & Rodd (1906) also omitted any reference to it in their well-researched *Zoologist* paper on *The Birds of Scilly*, which means the first record for the islands probably involved a male on St Agnes in late summer 1958, since when there have been a further nine accepted sightings to the end of 2000. All but one of the ten involved adult males, leading Penhallurick (1978), among others, to suggest most individuals originate from captivity, it being not uncommonly imported, though perhaps less now than formerly.

What makes these Scillonian Black-headed Bunting records particularly interesting, however, is the obvious bias towards spring arrival, with seven reaching the islands within a 59-day window from 15th April to 13th June and over a period of 24 years. Autumn arrivals, too, seem quite compressed, involving as they do a 45-day period from 31st August to 14th October. These ten individuals represent just over 7% of the 140 British records accepted by the BBRC during the period 1958–99. The Chart incorporates all ten arrival dates up until 1997. On average, birds remained in the islands 4.2 days in spring, 4.3 in autumn, the longest being 12 days (spring) and the shortest one day (one each in spring and autumn).

It seems generally accepted now that most, if not all British Black-headed Bunting sightings involve genuine wild migrants, though considering most of their breeding range lies within the West Palearctic its annual migration to India and back seems more than a little surprising. Birds leave their wintering grounds during March or April, males preceding females. They sometimes arrive as far west as Cyprus by early March, though usually not until early to mid-April. In the former Yugoslavia it is noted as arriving 'very suddenly' at the end of April or the beginning of May. And as most vagrancy to the west of its breeding grounds occurs in spring and involves males, the evidence points perhaps convincingly to overshooting being involved. Also noteworthy is the fact that only nine were recorded in Britain or Ireland prior to 1958, even though the volume of imported birds would almost certainly have been higher prior to that date. Equally important in any discussion on a captive origin is the spread of extralimital spring arrivals in other countries northwest of its breeding range, e.g. Iceland, Norway, Denmark, Finland, Poland, or to the southwest, e.g. Morocco, Algeria and Tunisia (Byers *et al.* 1995). And whilst autumn arrivals are less easily explained, they are perhaps attributable to reverse migration, only one of the three Scillonian individuals involving a first-year.

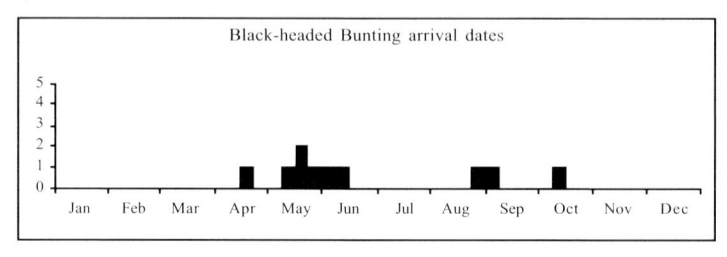

It seems difficult to avoid speculating on how long it might be before this species comes to appreciate that Africa is substantially closer to most of its breeding areas than India, though perhaps there are habitat preferences in India that Africa fails to accommodate. One Black-headed Bunting was trapped and ringed in Scilly since 1970 but not recaptured. For an informed view on separation of female Black-headed from Red-headed Bunting *E. bruniceps* see Shirihai & Gantlett (1993), or M Scott (1998).

# Red-headed Bunting *Emberiza bruniceps* D

Rare migrant, vagrant or perhaps escape from captivity, full written description required by SRP.

- 1952 Two (male and female) St Agnes 2nd to 6th September
- 1961 One (male) trapped St Martin's 28th May
- 1962 One (male) trapped St Agnes 13th to 15th June
- 1964 One (male) Old Grimsby, Tresco 6th to 10th September
- 1965 One (male) in song St Agnes 28th June
- 1965 One (male) in song St Agnes 26th & 27th September
- 1965 One (male) St Agnes 6th & 7th October
- 1966 One St Mary's 16th to 21st May
- 1966 One St Martin's 6th to 20th September
- 1969 One St Agnes 12th May
- 1969 One (adult male) St Mary's 5th September
- 1970 One (adult male) in song St Martin's 28th March
- 1970 One (male) Samson 28th May
- 1980 One (adult male) St Agnes 22nd September to 2nd October
- 1990 One (male) Bryher 3rd May
- 1994 One (first-year male) Tresco, St Martin's & St Mary's 21st October to 4th November
- 1996 One (male) St Agnes 2nd to 14th July

Breeds central western Asia, from southwest Russia and Kazakhstan south to Iran and Afghanistan. Migratory, wintering northern and western India. Monotypic. British status currently under review by the BOURC, presumably with a view to reassessing suitability for inclusion in Category A (BOURC 2000). Up until at least December 2002, Red-headed Bunting remained in Category D of the British List – species that would otherwise appear in categories A or B except that there is reasonable doubt they have ever occurred in a natural state – the BOURC persisting with the view that the possibility of escape from captivity tainted all records similarly.

There have been 17 accepted records involving 18 individuals of this attractive bunting since a male and female were present together on St Agnes for five days during early September 1952 (*CBWPSAR* 22). These two having been noted from 2nd but not identified until seen by Hilda Quick on the 4th. All but three, at least, of the remaining 16 records involved males.

The Chart includes all 17 Scillonian Red-headed Bunting arrival dates and reveals a pattern extremely similar to that of Black-headed Bunting *E. melanocephala*, which is listed in category A and which occurs rather closer to Britain but winters in the same area. Of the 15 Red-headed Bunting individuals for which the sex is recorded, only one (6.6%) was female and, similarly, out of ten Black-headed Bunting records one (10%) was female. Thus the two situations are very similar and it apparently makes little sense to reject these Red-headed Buntings on the basis that the overwhelming majority were males, unless the same logic is followed for Black-headed, the females of which are presumably far less evident in the field than males. The overall average length of stay for Red-headed Bunting was 4.3 days, though in spring it was just 3.1 days, compared with 5.8 in autumn. In both cases this was about one day less than for Black-headed Bunting. However, the adult male on St Agnes during September 1969 lacked a tail and therefore did seem a likely candidate for escape.

An incident during October 1998 suggests one reason why there may be fewer female records of these two species, involving as it did a mystery bird found on Tresco on 3rd and rediscovered on St Mary's on 4th–5th. During its stay it was variously thought to be both Black-headed and Red-headed Bunting, the majority view being in favour of the latter, though other (brief) suggested possibilities included Common Rosefinch *Carpodacus erythrinus* and Indigo *Passerina cyanea* and Cinereous Buntings *E. cineracea*. But in the final analysis it was considered too borderline for certain identification and so does not figure among official statistics for either this or the previous species (*IOSBR* 1978: 62–63).

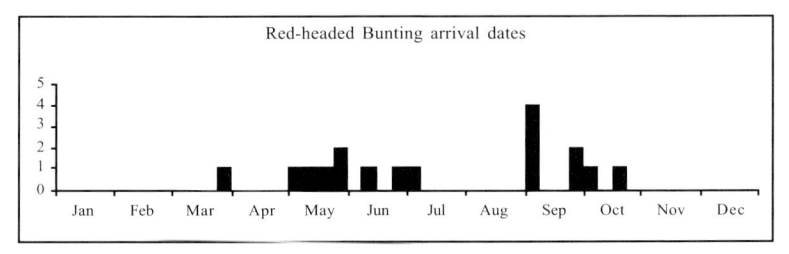

Much the same arguments and logic can be advanced for the presence of this species in western Europe during spring and autumn as are outlined for Black-headed Bunting. Suggestions of a mainly escaped origin for British records increasingly fail along with falling numbers of imported individuals, plus the absence of any birds in Scilly outside the two main migration periods (*British Birds* 60: 344–347, 423–426, 529, 61: 41–43; Tomlinson 1991). Dymond *et al.* (1989) were also of the opinion that despite the escape likelihood, 'some birds may be occurring naturally'. Two Red-headed Buntings were ringed in Scilly prior to 1970 but there are no recaptures.

# Corn Bunting *Miliaria calandra* A

**Occasional spring or autumn migrant in very small numbers, may have bred formerly but not adequately documented. Full written description required by the SRP.**

Breeds Eurasia, from Britain, southern Sweden, Baltic States and Russia, east to Turkestan and south to northern Sahara, Middle East and Iraq. Northern population fully or partially migratory, wintering within breeding area or just beyond in Egypt, southwest Asia and northwest India. Polytypic: nominate *calandra* occurs North Africa and Europe, including Canary Islands and most of Great Britain east to Asia Minor and coastal Levant; *clanceyi* (not recognised by the BOURC) western Ireland and western Scotland; *buturlini* remainder of range. Red-listed in UK: historical population decline; rapid, 89% breeding decline over past 25 years and moderate (33%) contraction of breeding range over past 30 years; (Gregory *et al.* 2002). National 26% decline 1994–99 (Bashford & Noble 2000).

This is one of those species afforded scarce mention in the historical literature, from which we normally assume a species was common. E H Rodd referred to it under its old name of 'Common Bunting', describing it as 'generally distributed throughout the county, frequenting both open and enclosed ground, and is far from uncommon' (Rodd 1880). His remarks on this occasion referred principally to the Cornish mainland and he made no specific reference to Scilly. More helpful were James Clark and E H Rodd's nephew Francis, who point out that although it bred in Scilly it was 'very much commoner as a visitor late in the autumn, when it occurs in flocks' (Clark & Rodd 1906).

Forty years on, the picture becomes clearer, as evident first from the comments of Ryves & Quick in their mid-20th-century review of breeding birds in Cornwall and Scilly (Ryves & Quick 1946). They reported H W Robinson as having seen none in 1914, though he found it breeding 'not uncommonly' on St Mary's in 1923. In contrast, Wallis, who also visited in spring 1923, described it as 'present but few' (Wallis 1923), though a year later it was viewed as common in 'almost all parts' of St Mary's (Boyd 1924). But by 1930, and again in 1938, G H Harvey heard only one to two and by 1946 A A Dorrien-Smith was doubtful that it continued to breed (Ryves & Quick 1946; *CBWPSAR*s). However, a late report talked of seeing and hearing several in song on St Agnes during 1930 (Lloyd 1946). Certainly, there are no reports of breeding post-1923, and up to the 1960s it was only reported occasionally, e.g. one to three on St Agnes in four different years, with birds evenly divided between spring and autumn.

Thus the picture is of a once perhaps common 19th-century breeder with an obvious passage movement, at least during autumn, followed by a marked decline by the 1920s or 1930s, to the point where it became a scarce migrant or vagrant. This was a situation reflected to a greater or lesser extent throughout southwest England, and indeed much of Britain and Ireland, and over much the same timescale, with population numbers highest, and its range greatest, in the later half of the 19th century (Parslow 1968a; Holloway 1996).

Sadly the situation has not improved during the last 40 years, against the background of a continuing and well-documented national decline resulting from the vastly altered agricultural situation (Donald *et al.* 1994). As a consequence, this and a number of other, mainly farmland species now have the unenviable distinction of being Red-listed as in need of serious conservation assistance (Gibbons *et al.* 1996), a situation apparently reflected in many parts of western, northern and central Europe (Cramp *et al.* 1977–94). On Scilly since 1960, one to three (mostly the former) birds were recorded in some 12 different years, with perhaps most in spring. The one very obvious exception was 1992, for on 16th April that year a single bird was noted on St Martin's with four there from 17th to 20th, all in song. On 21st, one had moved to St Agnes and one to Tresco, with the remaining two on St Mary's and from then until the end of May up to seven individuals were known to be on the islands, with several continuing to sing and in one or two cases apparently hold territory. The greatest concentration was in the sheltered Holy Vale–Sunnyside area of St Mary's, where one male even distorted long-running CBC data on the Lunnon Farm study plot by being recorded singing there during several visits. However, by 23rd May only one remained in the islands, continuing to sing on St Mary's until 30th June.

There is also an interesting prehistoric dimension to this species, Corn Bunting bones identified from the archaeological site at May's Hill, St Martin's, dating from possibly the Romano-British period but certainly no later than around the 7th century AD (Turk 1884a). Presumably this individual had been obtained for food.

According to Cramp *et al.* (1977–94), few British Corn Buntings move far from their breeding grounds during winter, with only eight ringing recoveries of 15 km or more and a mean of 2.4 km (Wernham *et al.* 2002). Almost all long-distance ringing recoveries in Europe involve birds from central European populations moving southwest, or south-southwest, mainly into southeast France or northeast Spain (Cramp *et al.* 1977–94). Given the lack of normal migration through Britain of birds from populations further north, it perhaps seems not unreasonable to suggest that birds involved in the spring 1992 influx may have been in the process of returning to somewhere in central Europe. Or even that this is the source of most spring or autumn Corn Buntings that occasionally visit the islands. No Corn Buntings have been ringed in Scilly and there are no recaptures from elsewhere.

# Rose-breasted Grosbeak     *Pheucticus ludovicianus*   **A**   BBRC 40.0%

**Rare autumn migrant, full written description required by the BBRC.**

   1966   One (female) trapped St Agnes 6th to 11th October    *British Birds* 60: 330, 61: 176–180
   1976   One (female) St Mary's 16th to 31st October    *British Birds* 70: 443
   1976   One (first-year or female) Tresco 20th to 26th October    *British Birds* 70: 443
   1979   One (first-year male) St Mary's 12th to 29th October    *British Birds* 73: 529
   1983   One (first-year male) St Agnes 10th to 19th October (perhaps taken by cat)
                                                                                           *British Birds* 77: 550
   1985   One (first-year male) Longstone Lane, St Mary's 9th to 28th October
                                                                                          *British Birds* 79: 10, 583
   1986   One (first-year male) Borough Farm, Tresco 10th to 25th October    *British Birds* 80: 568
   1987   One (first-year female) Tresco 9th to 21st October    *British Birds* 81: 593
   1993   One (first-year male) Vane Hill, Tresco 12th to 14th October    *British Birds* 87: 566
   1998   One (first-year male) Bryher 30th October to 1st November    *British Birds* 92: 220, 606
   2001   One (first-year female) St Martin's 13th & 14th October    *British Birds* 95: 368, 523

Nearctic species, breeding British Columbia east to Nova Scotia and south to Alberta, North Dakota, Nebraska, Kansas, Oklahoma, Tennessee and Maryland. Migratory, wintering central Mexico south through Central America to northwest South America. Monotypic. Recent population decline with Canada worst aeffected, populations there having halved since 1979 (Bryant 1997).

    A total of eleven individuals on Scilly in ten different years, with one each finally on Bryher, in 1998, and one on St Martin's during 2001. The first, a female trapped on St Agnes and present from 6th to 11th October 1966, was also the first British record, following birds in Co. Antrim in November 1957 and on Cape Clear Island, Co. Cork, in October 1962 (Dick & Tree, Fogden & Sharrock, in Sharrock & Grant 1982). Nine out of the eleven were aged as first-years, six of which were males. Rose-breasted Grosbeak is a classic October Scillonian migrant, with all birds arriving during that month and only one staying on into November, by one day. Arrival dates up until 1999 spanned a 25-day window from 6th to 30th October, with an average stay of 11.3 days (ignoring one believed to have been taken by a cat), shortest two days, longest 20 days. Typically, a newly arrived bird might be found feeding on brambles, often with the telltale signs adhering to feathering around the bill. One or two birds were extremely active throughout all or part of their stay, like the 1979 individual, which after being discovered on The Garrison, St Mary's, was for the next 18 days variously to be seen at Carn Warvel, Porth Hellick, Holy Vale, Maypole and back on The Garrison. Others though were distinctly sedentary. The 1983 St Agnes individual was possibly taken by a cat.

    Rose-breasted Grosbeak scored eighth in Robbins's statistical review of expected transatlantic vagrancy among 31 Nearctic migrant passerines and near-passerines recorded in Britain or Ireland during 1947–76. The seven accepted autumn records exceeded the expected relative likelihood of 4.33 individuals (Robbins 1980). A total of 25 British records were accepted by the BBRC for the period 1958–99, with the islands providing 40% of these (BBRC 2000). Autumn migration begins from early August and main movement is underway by the end of the month, the peak occurring early to mid-September in the north and mid- to late September in mid latitudes. Most arrivals in the wintering range occur mid-October to December (Cramp *et al.* 1977–94).

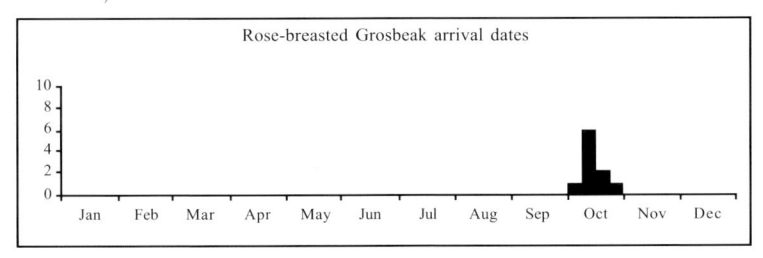

    Away from Britain, European records have come from at least the former Yugoslavia, Malta, Norway, Sweden, Spain, France and the Channel Islands. One Rose-breasted Grosbeak was trapped and ringed on Scilly prior to 1970 but there are no recaptures.

## Bobolink  *Dolichonyx oryzivorus*  **A**  BBRC 59.09%

Rare autumn migrant, full written description required by the BBRC.

1962   One (first-year male) trapped St Agnes 19th & 20th September
British Birds 56: 205, 58: 208–214; Ibis 113: 144
1968   One St Mary's 10th October   British Birds 62: 486
1975   One St Mary's 9th October   British Birds 69: 355, 70: 223–224
1976   One Tresco 28th & 29th September   British Birds 70: 440
1979   One St Agnes 7th October   British Birds 73: 530
1981   One between Tremelethan & Parting Carn, St Mary's 7th October   British Birds 75: 531
1983   One St Mary's 22nd September to 4th October   British Birds 77: 37, 544, 560
1983   One St Mary's 8th to 14th October   British Birds 77: 37, 544, 560
1985   One (female or first-year) Longstone, St Mary's 9th to 21st October   British Birds 79: 566, 584
1991   One Old Town & Airport Lane, St Mary's 11th to 15th October   British Birds 85: 552
1995   One St Mary's 20th October   British Birds 89: 526
1996   One Longstone & Carn Friars, St Mary's 6th to 8th October   British Birds 90: 517
1996   One Tresco & Bryher 8th to 15th October   British Birds 90: 517, 94: 500

Nearctic species, breeding British Columbia east to Nova Scotia and south to northern California, northern Utah and east to West Virginia and New Jersey. Long-distance migrant, wintering south to Bolivia and northern Argentina. Monotypic. Undulating population levels but with overall trend severely downwards since 1979, greatest declines in Canada and eastern USA (Bryant 1997).

This species was added to the British and Irish List on the strength of the 1962 individual on St Agnes (Parslow 1965b; BOURC 1968; Parslow & Carter 1982). Given the number that have since occurred it is interesting to realise that identification of the first St Agnes bird was by no means straightforward, it only being confirmed as Bobolink after skins had later been consulted at the British Museum (Natural History).

Thirteen individuals arrived in eleven different years, arrival dates falling within the 32-day window of 19th September to 20th October, dates during which birds were present within the islands being 33 days, one day greater. Inexplicably, there are no records for St Martin's, though birds can be extremely difficult to locate when feeding on the ground in weedy fields, though that problem is no more or no less applicable between islands. The 1975 record is written up in Holman (1977). Griffiths (1982) gives the date of the 1981 individual as 10th October.

Bobolink came third in Robbins's statistical review of expected transatlantic vagrancy among 31 Nearctic migrant passerines and near-passerines recorded in Britain or Ireland during 1947–76. The six accepted autumn records as good as equalled the expected relative likelihood of 6.11 individuals (Robbins 1980). Twenty-two British records were accepted by the BBRC during the period 1958–99, with Scilly providing almost 60% of these. Migration becomes general along the Atlantic coast of North America after mid-August, with thousands per day reported locally and with most having left northern USA by late September. Only stragglers remain in USA after mid-October, this pattern of movement being largely reflected in arrival dates of Scillonian records. Furthermore, most populations exit North America through the southeast states, but notably Florida, bypassing Mexico and with some probably taking the transoceanic route out over the western Atlantic and Caribbean directly to South America. The bird on St Agnes in 1962 was trapped and ringed but there are no recaptures.

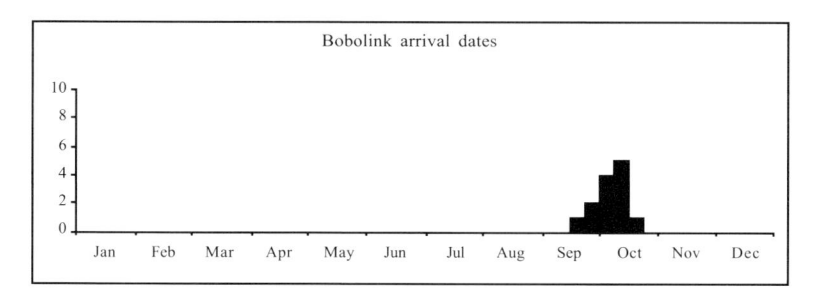

## Baltimore Oriole *Icterus galbula* A  BBRC 31.5%

**Very rare migrant, full written description required by the BBRC.**

1967 One St Agnes trapped 18th to 26th October  *British Birds* 61: 356
1968 One St Agnes 29th September to 3rd October  *British Birds* 62: 487
1983 One (female or first-year) St Agnes 23rd September to 4th October
 *British Birds* 77: 544, 560, plate 227
1988 One (first-winter male) St Agnes 4th to 12th October  *British Birds* 82: 559
1996 One Popplestone Bay, Bryher 30th September  *British Birds* 90: 517
1999 One (first-year male) Popplestone, Bryher 27th & 28th September  *British Birds* 93: 565

Nearctic species, previously treated as conspecific with Bullock's Oriole *I. bullockii* and one other, as Northern Oriole *I. galbula*, but split by AOU in March 1996 (*Auk* 112: 827). Breeds central Canada east to Nova Scotia, to northern limit of Great Lakes, east of a line from central Alberta to northeast Texas and south to the Gulf of Mexico, excluding southeast states. Migratory, wintering south to northwest South America. Most north of 35°N are long-distance migrants but more southerly populations mainly sedentary. Monotypic. Some hybridisation with Bullock's Oriole in southwest. Marked population increase early to mid-80s but now in decline (Bryant 1997).

There are six records from six different years with the first on St Agnes in 1967. All four pre-1986 records appear in the literature as 'Northern Oriole' without mention of the form involved. Only the last two individuals, in 1996 and 1999, post-dated the AOU's decision and underwent scrutiny to ensure they were the species under discussion here. However, most reaching Europe are thought to have involved what is now known as Baltimore Oriole, e.g. Cramp *et al.* (1977–94) refer only to *galbula* in discussing birds reaching the Atlantic seaboard of the West Palearctic. Therefore, all six records shown below are assumed to have involved this present species.

The spread of dates involved appears quite similar to that of Bobolink *Dolichonyx oryzivorus*, with the earliest present from 23rd September and the latest 26th October. Arrivals were squeezed into a 26-day window, with an average arrival date of 5th October and an average stay of 6.5 days. Interestingly, no birds were recorded on St Mary's, Tresco or St Martin's. As with Bobolink, most Baltimore Orioles breeding north of 35°N are long-distance migrants, southerly populations being more sedentary. Some migrants leave their breeding areas by mid-July but main migration occurs from mid-August and last northern records around early September, most having vacated mid-latitude states by mid-September. Therefore, the Chart shows a later pattern of arrival dates than might be expected. Southward migration occurs on a broad front but mainly west of Florida and extreme eastern Mexico.

The former 'Northern Oriole' came eighteenth in Robbins's statistical review of expected transatlantic vagrancy among 31 Nearctic migrant passerines and near-passerines recorded in Britain or Ireland during

## Birds of the Isles of Scilly

**Baltimore Oriole arrival dates**

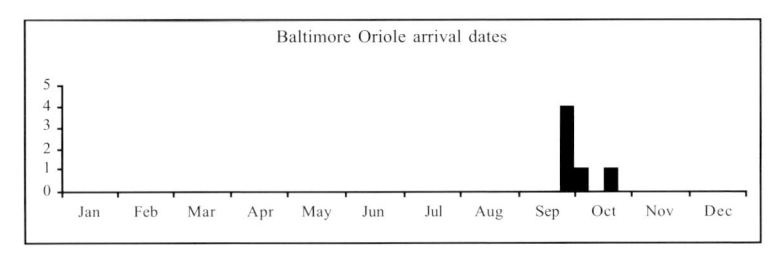

1947–76. The 12 accepted records (two spring, ten autumn) exceeded the predicted relative likelihood of 2.77 individuals (Robbins 1980). The 1967 St Agnes bird, the 8th for Britain and Ireland, was trapped and ringed but not recaptured subsequently. The BBRC accepted 19 records during the period 1958–99, with the result that these six individuals represent 31.5% of the national total. A record of a bird on Unst, Shetland, in September 1890 was previously rejected by the BOURC but is currently under reconsideration (BOURC 2002a); there were no other pre-1958 British arrivals. Within western Europe, birds have also occurred in Iceland, Norway and the Netherlands.

# RECORDS OF INTRODUCED OR ESCAPED BIRDS

## Dalmatian Pelican *Pelecanus crispus*

Confined to wetlands across southern Eurasia, from Balkans, Greece and Romania east to Mongolia. Monotypic. Widely kept in captivity.

One record, involving a bird believed to have escaped from an Essex zoological garden. It first appeared on St Agnes during January 1968 and could often be seen on the Big Pool, before transferring its affections to Tresco for a few days and then departing the islands. It was widely believed to be the bird first seen in Colchester, Essex, the previous October and then subsequently in Sussex and at Falmouth and Hayle across the water in west Cornwall (*CBWPSAR* 38; BOURC 1972).

## Flamingo *Phoenicopterus*

Seven species belonging to three different genera (BOURC 2002a), originating from Africa/Europe, the Caribbean and South America, at least four of which are widely encountered in captivity.

An unidentified flamingo, presumed at the time to be an escape from captivity, was seen in the Penzance area in 1912 and later shot in Scilly (Penhallurick 1969). Similarly, an unknown flamingo species escaped from an aviary on Tresco in either 1938 or 1939 and lived wild in the islands until perhaps the winter of 1948–49. It was often seen feeding in the area of Samson Flats, to the east of that island, and apparently became something of a celebrity (Quick 1949). Most likely to have been involved perhaps were Greater Flamingo *Phoenicopterus roseus*, Chilean Flamingo *P. chilensis* or Caribbean Flamingo *P. ruber*.

## Black Swan *Cygnus atratus*

Confined to Australia, where widespread and common, though absent from central desert area. Introduced New Zealand. First imported into Britain around 1791, feral breeding pairs were evident in mainland Britain by the mid-1850s and some persist to the present day, though organised attempts at introduction have been unsuccessful (Fitter 1959).

A full-winged Black Swan of unknown origin arrived on Tresco's Great Pool on 8th October 1991, where it remained until 24th February the following year. Apart that is from a week's absence around 12th January, which coincided with the presence of a bird on 17th at Newlyn Harbour, west Cornwall.

What must surely have been the same bird returned to Tresco from 5th October 1992, before moving to Porth Hellick, St Mary's and being last recorded on 15th of that month, two days before a bird appeared at Hayle, west Cornwall. After giving Scilly a miss for one winter it was back again on Tresco from 10th November to 5th December 1995 and then on Tresco again for about two weeks during mid-February 1996.

Its earliest arrival date on Scilly was 5th October and the latest recorded sighting 24th February. Throughout most of the above four or five years, a Black Swan, presumably the same bird, frequented Cornwall intermittently. It initially appeared there in 1991 and was subsequently reported from numerous, widely scattered locations from Saltash in the east to Cape Cornwall in the west, and from Marazion in the south to the Camel Estuary in the north. It remained in Cornwall well into 1998, with two together on two occasions and three at Drift Reservoir on 24th August that same year.

## Chinese Goose *Anser cygnoides*

Original wild ancestor, Swan Goose *A. cygnoides*, breeds central eastern Asia, from southern Siberia to northern China. Migratory, wintering south into China. No established feral populations in West Palearctic but occurs widely in captivity as Chinese Goose.

A very small semi-captive population occurs on Tresco, though they normally get no mention in the annual bird reports. Penhallurick drew attention to an interesting story concerning the possible origin of the Tresco Chinese Geese. The ancestors of these birds allegedly swam ashore from the wreck of the Liverpool-registered China tea-clipper *Friar Tuck*, bound for London out of Foochow in 1863. Having put in at St Mary's harbour on 2nd December, she dragged her anchor during a gale and went ashore on

Taylor's Island at the eastern end of Porthloo, opposite what is now the St Mary's Quay (Penhallurick 1978).

One of the few published records concerns 18 noted on Tresco on 23rd January 1965 (B King 1965b), though there may be fewer now. Penhallurick also mentioned their being killed annually for the table and also that new blood was introduced on one occasion since 1924. The existence of the Tresco population is not mentioned by Delany in his paper on 'Introduced and escaped geese in Britain in summer 1991' (*British Birds* 86: 591–599), though he was more concerned with individuals showing the characteristics of Swan Goose. Concealed away in the vast skin collection of the British Museum (Natural History) is that of a hybrid Chinese x Canada Goose *Branta canadensis* (Ref 1953.74). It was contributed by A A Dorrien-Smith as one of two hatched on Tresco during 1953.

## Egyptian Goose *Alopochen aegyptiacus*

Breeds Africa south of equator, an introduced and self-sustaining population of currently 900 individuals breeds mainly East Anglia. Monotypic. Although J L Long (1981) made no specific reference to birds being introduced in Scilly, he pointed out that 'considerable numbers of free-flying breeding colonies were established on estates in southern and eastern England as well as other parts of Britain during the mid-nineteenth century'. The earliest British record he quoted involved a bird shot in Berkshire in 1795, with others killed in the same county during 1803–04. He further noted that a great many were either shot or recorded during the period 1808–49.

According to E H Rodd (1880, Appendix, p. 311), Courtney stated that this species had 'been naturalised in the islands of Scilly' as elsewhere, though unfortunately no additional information is provided.

## Chestnut Teal *Anas castanea*

Australian species occurring in Tasmania and southeast and southwest mainland Australia. Commonly kept in captivity in Britain and elsewhere. Birds present among the small mixed pinioned waterfowl collection at Porthloo, St Mary's.

One or two birds about St Mary's from the late 1990s were thought to originate from pinioned adults in the Porthloo collection. A pair of these same birds also probably bred at Porth Hellick, St Mary's, during 2000.

## Mandarin Duck *Aix galericulata*

Breeds eastern Asia, from Sea of Okhotsk south through eastern China, Korea and Japan to Taiwan. Widespread and prolific in captivity in Britain and elsewhere.

A small captive and mainly pinioned population at Porthloo, St Mary's, from perhaps the late 1980s. Perhaps no more than two to three pairs at present but the species could spread to other parts of the islands if young are not pinioned.

## Muscovy Duck *Cairina moschata*

Breeds Central and South America as far as Peru and Uruguay. Widespread in captivity.

Small numbers are kept semi-captive on Tresco from time to time, mostly involving white individuals. There are no published records of them appearing elsewhere in the islands.

## Common Ground-dove *Columbina passerina*

Nearctic species occurring Florida, southern Texas, southern Arizona and southern California. Widespread in Mexico, occurring southwards into northern South America. Formerly known as *Columbigallina passerina*, there are eighteen currently recognised forms and although *C. p. terrestris* is not one of these, Ridgeway (1916) uses that name for the nominate form occurring in the USA. There are no acceptable European records.

Four birds described as 'Northern Ground Doves *Columbigallina passerina terrestris*' were among a consignment of 29 live birds liberated from the stricken *Minnehaha* on 18th April 1910, whilst in transit from the New York Zoological Society to the London Zoological Society. Their liberation was publicised

*Introduced or Escaped Species*

in the *Zoologist* of that year 'so if any reports of their being shot should come to hand ornithologists will know their origin' (Seth-Smith 1910). The 13,500-ton *Minnehaha* ran aground in fog on the north end of Bryher in the early hours, carry 66 passengers, 160 cattlemen and crew and some 250 head of cattle. The passengers and crew were rescued and the cattle thrown over and towed ashore alive, mostly on nearby Samson. The ship was refloated three weeks later.

## Inca Dove *Scardafella inca*

Nearctic species, occurs Texas, southern New Mexico, southern Arizona and Colorado valley, south into most of Mexico except the Yucatan. No acceptable European records.

Six 'Inca Doves *Scardafella inca*' were released from the stricken *Minnehaha* in the Bryher area on 18th April 1910 – see Common Ground-Dove *Columbina passerina* for details.

## Barbary Dove *'Streptopelia risoria'*

Domesticated form of African Collared Dove *S. roseogrisea* but widely treated as a species in its own right. Widely encountered in captivity from which it frequently escapes.

One on St Mary's from 22nd to 31st October 1985 was believed to have arrived in company with Collared Doves *S. decaocto* (IOSBR 1985).

## Spot-bellied Bobwhite *Colinus leucopogon*

Neotropical species, formerly known as Columba Crested Quail *Eupsychortex leucopogon* and lumped with what is now know as the Crested Bobwhite *Colinus cristatus* of northern South America. As might be expected, there are no accepted European records; though see Northern Bobwhite *Colinus virginianus* for details of the former introduced population of that species on Tresco.

Six 'Columba Crested Quails *Eupsychortex leucopogon*' were released from the stricken *Minnehaha* in the Bryher area on 18th April 1910 – see Common Ground-Dove *Columbina passerina* for details. Just which of the above two bobwhites was involved may be impossible to say now, but in view of other species included in the consignment it seems likely to have been the more northerly *cristatus*.

## Green-rumped Parrotlet *Forpus passerinus*

Neotropical species, formerly know as Guiana Parrotlet *Psittacula guianensis* but now known more commonly as Green-rumped Parrotlet, with the new scientific name *Forpus passerinus* (Peters 1937). There are a number of recognised forms occupying the lower Amazon basin northwards across Venezuela, with more recent introductions on some Caribbean islands (Foreshaw & Cooper 1973).

Three birds described as 'Guiana Parrotlets *Psittacula guianensis*' were released from the stricken *Minnehaha* in the Bryher area on 18th April 1910 – see Common Ground-Dove *Columbina passerina* for details.

## Red-winged Blackbird *Agelaius phoeniceus*

Nearctic species, occurs central and southern Canada and USA south to the Gulf states, plus much of Mexico, Bahamas, Cuba and Costa Rica. Partial migrant, northern birds withdrawing south in winter (Cramp *et al.* 1977–94). *A. p. sonoriensis* was one of 23 forms recognised by Peters (1937) and is still acknowledged today (Jaramillo & Burke 1999), being restricted to southwest USA and northwest Mexico. Both Evans (1994) and Cramp *et al.* referred to a number of 19th-century British records of Red-winged Blackbirds and Evans suggested captive birds were intentionally released, though J L Long (1981) made no mention of this. Evans documented eighteen records of apparent escaped birds at widespread locations in Britain between 1824 and 1885, one of which, a male in South Glamorgan in October 1866, is thought by some to have been a contender for genuine vagrancy. However, Cramp *et al.* point out that all British records involve males and suggest that there are no acceptable European records.

Four birds described by Seth-Smith (1910) as 'Sonoran Redwings *Ageloeus phoeniceus sonoriensis*' were released from the stricken *Minnehaha* in the Bryher area on 18th April 1910 – see Common Ground-Dove *Columbina passerina* for details.

In the *Victory History of Cornwall* (W Page 1906), James Clark mentioned one shot on the Cornish mainland at Swanpool, Falmouth, during August 1881, which of course substantially pre-dates the above account. Penhallurick latter added that it was shot by taxidermist Gill after the bird had been seen for about two weeks (Penhallurick 1978).

## Silvereye *Zosterops lateralis* E

Breeds commonly in eastern and southern coastal Australia, also occurring in nearby Indonesia. Long-standing prohibitions on export of Australian wildlife mean it is uncommon in captivity, though birds may still be obtainable from other parts of range. Polytypic, six or more forms, some, e.g. *lateralis*, show varying degrees of buff on flanks. Infrequently encountered in captivity in Britain, Europe or elsewhere.

A bird of this species, originally identified as Chestnut-flanked White-eye *Z. erythropleura*, frequented Barnaby Lane orchard, St Agnes, from 15th to 31st October 1990. Under its initial identification the possibility of genuine vagrancy was given early and enthusiastic consideration, with the result that the bird attracted many admirers, though the debate became redundant once the bird's true identity was established. As with all likely escapes from captivity, we can only guess at where this individual may have originated, though certainly up until 1988 this particular white-eye species was not at all common in captivity in Britain (S Harrop 1990).

Against all odds, two extremely attractive little birds frequenting the proximity of Tresco's Borough Farm from 23rd to 31st October 1995 were initially identified as either Chestnut-flanked or Japanese White-eye *Z. japonica*, but were again eventually attributed to the present species. The dates of occurrence of these two records are impressively similar. Other white-eye sightings in recent years involve birds in Hampshire, Cornwall and Devon, at least one of which was identified as Oriental White-eye *Z. palpebrosa*. Interestingly, the recent, early 21st-century decision to utilise Silvereyes as insect control agents inside the Eden Project now presents the very real possibility of an escaped population becoming established in Cornwall.

## Common Grackle *Quiscalus quiscala*

Nearctic species, occurs Alberta to Quebec, south through USA east of Rocky Mountains to New Mexico, Texas and Florida; casual to Alaska, Pacific states and Mexico. Partial migrant, withdrawing southeast in winter. Jaramillo & Burke (1999) recognised three subspecies: 'Bronzed' *Q. q. versicolor* (formerly *aeneus*), 'Purple' *Q. q. stonei* and 'Florida' *Q. q. quiscalus*, with Purple Grackle primarily occurring in the southeast and Bronzed Grackle in the north and west. No acceptable British or Irish records but Cramp *et al.* (1977–94) mention one in Denmark in 1970.

Twelve birds, described as six 'Purple Grackle *Quiscalus quiscalus*' and six 'Bronze Grackles *Quiscalus quiscalus aeneus*' were released from the stricken *Minnehaha* in the Bryher area on 18th April 1910 – see Common Ground-Dove *Columbina passerina* for details.

More recently, Mike Rogers described a reported long-tailed 'starling' with a glossy-blue head seen by island resident John Thompson feeding with Starlings *Sturnus vulgaris* on St Mary's on 2nd June 1984. Regrettably, the news was late reaching local birders and despite extensive searching the bird could not be refound. Thus its identity remains unknown, although, as Mike Rogers pointed out, the present species seems a likely contender (Rogers 1995).

## White-cheeked Starling *Sturnus sinensis/cineraceus*

White-shouldered Starling *S. sinensis* breeds southern China through Southeast Asia to Borneo and is a partial migrant, whilst what is normally referred to as White-cheeked Starling *S. cineraceus* occurs broadly within the same geographical area. Both seem likely to be encountered in captivity.

A starling present on St Agnes from 30th August to 1st September 1996 was described in the annual *IOSBR* as 'White-cheeked Starling *S. sinensis*' (*IOSBR* 1996)

## Chinese Grosbeak *Eophona (Coccothraustes) migratoria*

Breeds Southeast Asia, from Mongolia southeast to Northern Korea. Sedentary or migratory, wintering east to Japan and south to North Vietnam. Polytypic: nominate *migratoria* occurs throughout, except in eastern China, where replaced by larger-billed *sowerbyi*.

A presumed escaped female, apparently not from Scilly, was discovered on a nut-feeder in Hugh Town, St Mary's, on 30th May 1997, before wandering around that island until 31st October, with a brief visit to St Agnes from 1st to 3rd June.

## Canary *Serinus canaria*

Confined to the Atlantic islands of Madeira, Canary Islands and Azores. Widely and abundantly bred and kept in captivity worldwide. Although monotypic in the wild, occurs in captivity in a number of varieties and colour variations.

Two published records involving individuals on Tresco and St Mary's. The first of these, in apparent 'natural' plumage, occurred during October 1977 and although seen by perhaps 250 birders over a period of about one week, was initially identified and widely accepted as Serin *S. serinus* (*IOSBR* 1977: 53). Plumage features were not reported for the second, which appeared on St Mary's golf course on 24th April 1991.

## Zebra Finch *Poephila guttata*

Confined to Australia, where widespread and numerous, though absent from some coastal areas. Common in captivity worldwide, both in normal plumage and numerous colour variations.

One record, involving a bird present briefly during October 1990, first in Lower Moors on St Mary's on the 7th, before being refound on The Garrison the following day and then on St Agnes on 9th.

## Chestnut Munia *Lonchura malacca*

Breeds India to southern China and Taiwan, south into Southeast Asia. Widely imported from the wild and kept in captivity.

A bird present on Bryher for five days during mid-September 1993 was identified as this species. It was not known to have escaped from within the islands but other than that its origin remains unknown.

## Painted Bunting *Passerina ciris*

Nearctic species, breeding southeast USA to northeast Mexico, wintering south to Florida, Bahamas, Greater Antilles and Central America (Cramp *et al*. 1977–94). Casual vagrant to coastal northeast America as far as New York State. Polytypic: nominate *ciris* occurs coastal southeast USA, from Carolinas south to northern Florida; *pallidior* from Arkansas south to Gulf coast and from Mississippi west into northeast Mexico. Allegedly common in captivity in Britain, but although formerly the case this may no longer be true.

An adult male on St Mary's was viewable in the area of Porth Hellick on 25th June 1978. The record was submitted to BBRC/BOURC as the fourth for Britain, following one on Skokholm in 1971, one trapped in Shetland in 1972 and one in Lancashire in 1974. But none of these four has so far been accepted by BOURC as genuine migrants/vagrants. This is regardless of the fact that further birds occurred as follows: Shetland (trapped) also 1978, Fair Isle (again trapped) 1979 and 1981.

On the strength of the 1972 bird on Shetland, the BOURC placed Painted Bunting onto its Category D, believing it was an 'unlikely natural vagrant to Britain and was in any case common in captivity'. However, by 1994 the BOURC had reviewed its position and removed the species from category D. Thus it presumably now resides on the new category E, 'species that have been recorded as introductions, transportees or escapees from captivity, and whose breeding populations (if any) are thought not to be self-sustaining' (BOURC 1994).

# BIBLIOGRAPHY

ALEXANDER, H. G. 1946. Great Shearwaters in the English Channel. *British Birds* 39: 55–56.

ALEXANDER, W. B. & FITTER, R. S. R. 1955. American land birds in Western Europe. *British Birds* 48: 1–14.

ALLEN, R. 1974–77. *Gulls and other Sea-birds in the Isles of Scilly, April to August 1974–77.* Unpublished reports to Nature Conservancy Council.

ALSTRÖM, P. 1991. Identification of Double-crested Cormorant. *Birding World* 4: 9–16.

AMENGUAL, J. F., GARGALLO, G., SUAREZ, M., BONNIN, J., GONZALES, J. M., BEBASSA, M. & McMinn. M. 1999. The Mediterranean Storm Petrel *Hybrobates pelagicus melitensis* at Cabrera archipelago (Balearic Islands, Spain): breeding moult, biometry and evaluation of the population size by mark and recapture techniques. *Ringing and Migration* 19: 181–190.

ANDREWS, D. G. 1964. Birds in Ireland during 1960–62. *British Birds* 57: 1–10.

ANON. (undated). *The Hand Book of Western Cornwall, Penzance, Falmouth, and Neighbourhoods.* Besley, Exeter.

ANON. 1869a. Ray's Wagtail at Scilly. *Zoologist* 27: 1847.

ANON. 1869b. Spoonbill at Scilly. *Zoologist* 27: 1848.

ANON. 1910. White-tailed Eagle in the Scilly Islands. *British Birds* 8: 341.

ANON. 1936. American Goshawk in the Scilly Isles. *British Birds* 30: 197.

ANON. 1942. Kittiwakes not breeding in Scilly Islands. *British Birds* 36: 78.

ANON. 1952. Blue-cheeked Bee-eater in Scilly: a new British bird. *British Birds* 45: 225–227.

ANON. 1960. American Purple Gallinule in the Isles of Scilly: a bird new to Britain and Europe. *British Birds* 53: 145–146.

ANON. 1994. Twenty-five years ago. *British Birds* 87: 473.

ANON. 1995. Pigeonhole: Bicknell's Thrush Split. *Birding World* 8: 360.

ANON. 1996. New American splits. *Birding World* 9: 122.

ANON. 2000a. New bird for the Scilly List. *British Birds* 93: 294.

ANON. 2000b. Ringed birds reveal extent of *Erika* devastation. *British Birds* 93: 352.

ANON. 2000c. Forty-second supplement to the American Ornithologists' Union Check List of North American birds. *The Auk* 117: 847–858.

ANON. 2000d. The BOU British List. *Birding World* 13: 342.

ANON. 2002. Snowy Owls offered wizard new homes. *British Birds* 95: 28.

APLIN, O. V. 1890: On the distribution and period of sojourn in the British Islands of the Spotted Crake. *Zoologist* 48: 411.

APLIN, O. V. 1892a. On the distribution of the Cirl Bunting in Great Britain. *Zoologist* 16: 121–128.

APLIN, O. V. 1892b. The status of the Woodchat, Lanius Rufus, in Great Britain. *Zoologist* 16: 352.

ASHBEE, P. 1999. Halangy Down, St Mary's, Isles of Scilly, excavations 1964–1977. *Cornish Archaeology* 35: 113–116.

AXEL, H. E. 1966. Eruptions of Bearded Tits during 1959–65. *British Birds* 59: 513–543.

BAILLIE, S. R., CRICK, H. Q. P., BALMER, D. E., BASHFORD, R. I., BEAVAN, L. P., FREEMAN, S. N., MARCHANT, J. H., NOBLE, D. G., RAVEN, M. J., SIRIWARDENA, G. M., THEWLIS, R. & WERNHAM, C. V. 2001. *Breeding Birds in the Wider Countryside: their conservation status 2000.* BTO Research Report No. 252. BTO, Thetford.

BAKER, J. K. & CATLEY, G. P. 1987. Yellow-browed Warblers in Britain and Ireland, 1968–85. *British Birds* 80: 93–109.

BALANCE, D. 2000. *Birds in Counties: An Ornithological Bibliography for the Counties of England, Wales, Scotland and the Isle of Man.* Imperial College Press, London.

BASHFORD, R. & NOBLE, D. 2000. The Breeding Bird Survey: 1994–1999. *BTO News* 230: 12–14.

BATTEN, L. A., BIBBY, J., CLEMENT, P., ELLIOTT, G. D. & PORTER, R. F. 1990. *Red Data Birds in Britain: action for rare, threatened and important species.* Poyser, London.

BATTY, C. & LOW, T. 2001. Vagrant Canada Geese in Britain and Ireland. *Birding World* 14: 57–61.

BBRC 1997. From the Rarities Committee's Files: Problems presented by a pale Blyth's Pipit. *British Birds* 90: 404–409.

BBRC 2000. *British Birds Rarities Committee: Species statistics summary.* BBRC 30th November 2000.

BESWETHERICK, A. 1959. Bird life on and about the Wolf Rock. *Cornwall Birdwatching and Preservation Society Annual Report* 29: 54–55.

BESWETHERICK, A. T. 1961. Bird notes from Round Island. *Cornwall Birdwatching and Preservation Society Annual Report* 31: 62–64.

BESWETHERICK, A. T. 1968. Birds of Round Island. *Cornwall Birdwatching and Preservation Society Annual Report* 38: 72–73.

BESWETHERICK, A. T. 1969. Birds of Round Island. *Isles of Scilly Bird Report* 1969: 19–20.

BIDWELL, E. 1889. A visit to the Isles of Scilly during the nesting season. *Transactions of the Norfolk and Norwich Naturalists' Society* 4: 201–214.

BIRKIN, M. & SMITH, A. 1987. *Breeding Seabirds: Isles of Scilly.* Unpublished Report for the Nature Conservancy Council.

BLAIR, R. H. 1945. Visit to the Isles of Scilly, June 2nd–9th, 1945. *Cornwall Birdwatching and Preservation Society Annual Bird Report* 15: 57–58.

BLAIR, R. H. 1950. Roseate Tern in the Isles of Scilly. *Cornwall Birdwatching and Preservation Society Annual Bird Report* 20: 15.

BLAND, B. 1998. The Wilson's Snipe on the Isles of Scilly. *Birding World* 11: 382–385.

BLAND, B. 1999. The Wilson's Snipe on Scilly revisited. *Birding World* 12: 56–61.

BLIGHT, J. T. 1861. *A Week at the Land's End*. Longman, Truro and London.

BORLASE, W. 1756. *Observations on the Ancient and Present State of the Islands of Scilly, and their Importance to the Trade of Great Britain*. Jackson, Oxford.

BOSANQUET, S. 2000. The Hudsonian Whimbrel in Gwent. *Birding World* 13: 190–193.

BOSWELL, J. H. 1947. Herring Gulls nesting on buildings. *British Birds* 40: 255–256.

BOTONER, W. 1478 (published 1778). *Itinerary of William of Worcester*. Jacob Nasmith, Cambridge.

BOTTOMLEY. J. B. 1972. Danish White Storks in south-west England. *British Birds* 65: 4–5.

BOURC 1956. British Ornithologists' Union Records Committee: First Report. *Ibis* 98: 154–157.

BOURC 1958. British Ornithologists' Union Records Committee: Second Report. *Ibis* 100: 299–300.

BOURC 1960. British Ornithologists' Union Records Committee: Third Report. *Ibis* 102: 629–630.

BOURC 1968. British Ornithologists' Union Records Committee: Fifth Report. *Ibis* 113: 142–145.

BOURC 1972. British Ornithologists' Union Records Committee: Seventh Report. *Ibis* 114: 446–447.

BOURC 1974. British Ornithologists' Union Records Committee: Eighth Report. *Ibis* 116: 578–579.

BOURC 1978. British Ornithologists' Union Records Committee: Ninth Report. *Ibis* 120: 409–411.

BOURC 1980. British Ornithologists' Union Records Committee: Tenth Report. *Ibis* 122: 564–568.

BOURC 1984. British Ornithologists' Union Records Committee: Eleventh Report. *Ibis* 126: 440–444.

BOURC 1986. British Ornithologists' Union Records Committee: Twelfth Report. *Ibis* 128: 601–603.

BOURC 1988. British Ornithologists' Union Records Committee: Thirteenth Report. *Ibis* 130: 334–337.

BOURC 1991a. British Ornithologists' Union Records Committee: Fourteenth Report. *Ibis* 133: 218–222.

BOURC 1991b. British Ornithologists' Union Records Committee: Fifteenth Report. *Ibis* 133: 438–441.

BOURC 1992a. British Ornithologists' Union Records Committee: Sixteenth Report. *Ibis* 134: 211–214.

BOURC 1992b. British Ornithologists' Union Records Committee: Seventeenth Report. *Ibis* 134: 380–381.

BOURC 1993a. British Ornithologists' Union Records Committee: Eighteenth Report. *Ibis* 135: 220–222.

BOURC 1993b. British Ornithologists' Union Records Committee: Nineteenth Report. *Ibis* 135: 493–499.

BOURC 1994. British Ornithologists' Union Records Committee: Twentieth Report. *Ibis* 136: 253–255.

BOURC 1995. British Ornithologists' Union Records Committee: Twenty-second Report. *Ibis* 137: 590–591.

BOURC 1997. British Ornithologists' Union Records Committee: Twenty-third Report. *Ibis* 139: 197–201.

BOURC 1998. British Ornithologists' Union Records Committee: Twenty-fourth Report. *Ibis* 140: 182–184.

BOURC 1999. British Ornithologists' Union Records Committee: Twenty-fifth Report. *Ibis* 141: 175–180.

BOURC 2000. British Ornithologists' Union Records Committee: Twenty-sixth Report. *Ibis* 142: 177–179.

BOURC 2001. British Ornithologists' Union Records Committee: Twenty-seventh Report. *Ibis* 143: 171–175.

BOURC 2002a. British Ornithologists' Union Records Committee: Twenty-eighth Report. *Ibis* 144: 181–184.

BOURC 2002b *Taxonomic recommendations for British Birds*. *Ibis* 144: 707–710.

BOURC 2003. British Ornithologists' Union Records Committee: Twenty-ninth Report. *Ibis* 145: 179.

BOWEY, K. 1995. European Storm-petrels without their toes. *British Birds* 88: 111.

BOYD, A. W. 1924. Notes on the birds of Scilly. *British Birds* 18: 106–108.

BOYD, A. W. 1931. Notes on the birds of Scilly. *British Birds* 24: 208–210.

BRADSHAW, C. 1991. Identification of Little and Rustic Buntings. *Birding World* 4: 309–313.

BRADSHAW, C. 1992. The identification of vireos in Britain and Europe. *Birding World* 5: 308–311.

BRADSHAW, C. 1996. The Scilly eastern Nightingale. *Birding World* 9: 197.

BRADSHAW, C. 2001. 'Two-barred Greenish Warbler' on Scilly: new to Britain and Ireland. *British Birds* 94: 284–288.

BREWER, D., DIAMOND, A., WOODSWORTH, E. J., COLLINS, B. T. & DUNN, E. H. 2000. *Canadian Atlas of Bird Banding*. Canadian Wildlife Service.

BRINKLEY, E. S. & PATTERSON, B. 1998. Gadfly petrels in the western North Atlantic. *Birding World* 11: 341–354.

BRITTON, D. 1980. Identification of Sharp-tailed Sandpiper. *British Birds* 73: 333–345.

BRITTON, D. 1981. Spanish Sparrows in the Isles of Scilly. *British Birds* 74: 150–151.

BROYD, S. 2000. The Spectacled Warbler on the Isles of Scilly. *Birding World* 13: 418–419.

BRUUN, B. 1971. North American waterfowl in Europe. *British Birds* 64: 385–408.

BRYANT, J. 1997. Population trends of American vagrants. *Birding World* 10: 340–349.

BURN, D. M & MATHER. R. J. 1974. The White-billed Diver in Britain. *British Birds* 67: 257–296.

BURTON, J. F. & FRENCH, R. A. 1970. Monarch butterflies coinciding with American passerines in Britain and Ireland in 1968. *British Birds* 63: 493–494.

BUTLER, C. 2002. Breeding parrots in Britain. *British Birds* 95: 345–348.

BYERS, C., CURSON, J. & OLSSON, U. 1995. *Sparrows and Buntings: a guide to the Sparrows and Buntings of North America and the World.* Pica Press, Robertsbridge.

CAMDEN, W. 1610. *Britain, or a Chorographical Description of the most flourishing Kingdoms, England, Scotland, and Ireland, and the Islands adjoining, out of the depths of the Antiquitie: Beautified with mappes of the Severall Shires of England.* Philemon Holland, London.

CAMPBELL, B. & FERGUSON-LEES, J. 1972. *A Field Guide to Birds' Nests.* Constable, London.

CAREW, R. 1602. *The Survey of Cornwall.* Jaggard, London.

CATON, R. 1998. Hybridisation of Starling and Spotless Starling in captivity. *Birding World* 11: 474–476.

CHANDLER, R. J. 1981. Influxes into Britain and Ireland of Red-necked Grebes and other waterbirds during winter 1978–79. *British Birds* 74: 55–81.

CHARLWOOD, R. H. 1981. Spanish Sparrows in the Isles of Scilly. *British Birds* 74: 150–151.

CHATFIELD, J. 1987. *F. W. Frohawk: His Life and Work.* Crowood Press, Marlborough.

CHITTENDEN, R. 1986. Northern Parula in Scilly. *British Birds* 79: 432–433.

CHOWN, D. & LOCK, L. 2002. *Breeding Birds in the Isles of Scilly, Incorporating the Results of the Breeding Bird Atlas (2000–2001) and Seabird 2000 (1999–2000).* RSPB, Sandy.

CHUDLEIGH, D. (undated). *Bridge over Lyonesse.* New Headland Printers, Penzance.

CLARK, J. 1902. The Birds of Cornwall. *Journal of the Royal Institution of Cornwall.*

CLARK, J. & RODD, F. R. 1906. The Birds of Scilly. *Zoologist* 10: 241–246.

CLEEVES, T. 1999. The Short-toed Eagle on the Isles of Scilly: a new British Bird. *Birding World* 12: 408–411.

CLEGG, D. 2000. Birds new to Britain found in Cornwall and the Isles of Scilly. *CBWPS Newsletter April 2000*: 27–30.

CLEMENT, P. 1995. Southern and eastern Great Grey Shrikes in northwest Europe. *Birding World* 8: 300–309.

CLEMENT, P., HARRIS, A. & DAVIS, J. 1993. *Finches & Sparrows.* Christopher Helm, London.

COLE, A. C. & TROBE, W. M. 2000. *The Egg Collectors of Great Britain and Ireland.* Peregrine Books, Leeds.

COLLINSON, M. 2001a. Greenish Warbler, 'Two-barred Greenish Warbler', and the speciation process. *British Birds* 94: 278–283.

COLLINSON, M. 2001b. Genetic relationships among the different races of Herring Gull, Yellow-legged Gull and Lesser Black-backed Gull. *British Birds* 94: 523–528.

COMBRIDGE, P. & PARR, C. 1992. Influx of Little Egrets in Britain and Ireland in 1989. *British Birds* 85: 16–21.

COOK, S. 1998. White-throated Sparrow at sea. *Birding World* 11: 269–270.

CORDAUX, J. 1880. Migration of Redbreasts. *Zoologist* 38: 363–364.

CORNISH, T. 1882a. Eider Duck at Scilly. *Zoologist* 40: 189.

CORNISH, T. 1882b. White-winged Black Tern at Scilly. *Zoologist* 40: 235.

CORNISH, T. 1882c. Totanus solitarius at Scilly. *Zoologist* 40: 432.

CORNISH, T. 1883. Rare birds in Cornwall and Scilly. *Zoologist* 41: 495.

CORNISH, T. 1885. Killdeer Plover in Cornwall. *Zoologist* 43: 113.

CORNISH, T. 1887. Esquimaux Curlew at Scilly. *Zoologist* 45: 388

*Cornwall Birdwatching and Preservation Society Annual Reports* 1931–1997 (eds.). 1931–36 RYVES, B. H. & HARVEY, G. H.; 1937–41 RYVES, B. H. & VALENTINE, D.; 1942–46 RYVES, B. H., VALENTINE, D. & QUICK, H. M.; 1947–49 RYVES, B. H. & QUICK, H. M.; 1950–55 RYVES, B. H., PARSONS, A. G. & QUICK, H. M.; 1956–57 RYVES, B. M., QUICK, H. M. & BECKERLEGGE, J. E.; 1958 ALLSOP, G., BECKERLEGGE, J. E., BLAIR, R. H., PARSONS, A. G., QUICK, H. M. & RYVES, B. H.; 1959 RYVES, B. H., BECKERLEGGE, J. E. & ALLSOP, G.; 1960 BECKERLEGGE, J. E. & ALLSOP, G.; 1961 BECKERLEGGE, J. E., PHILLIPS, N. R., ALMOND, W. E. & QUICK, H. M.; 1962 BECKERLEGGE, J. E., PARSONS, A. G., PHILLIPS, N. R. & QUICK, H. M.; 1963–64 BECKERLEGGE, J. E. & PHILLIPS, N. R.; 1965 BECKERLEGGE, J. E., PARSONS, A. G. & PHILLIPS, N. R.; 1966–67 BECKERLEGGE, J. E., BOTTOMLEY, S., PARSONS, A. G. & PHILLIPS, N. R.; 1968 BECKERLEGGE, J. E. & PHILLIPS, N. R.; 1969 BECKERLEGGE, J. E. & BOTTOMLEY, J. B.; 1970–72 BECKERLEGGE, J. B.; 1973–74 PHILLIPS, N. R.; 1975–80 BAKER, D. J.; 1981–93 CHRISTOPHERS, S. M.; 1994–97 CONWAY, G; 1998–99 WILSON, K. A. *Cornwall Birdwatching and Preservation Society.*

CORSO, A. 1997. Balearic Woodchat Shrikes in Britain. *Birding World* 10: 152–153.

COTE, I. M. & SUTHERLAND, W. J. 1995. *The scientific basis for predator control for bird conservation.* English Nature Research Report No. 144, Peterborough.

COUCH, J. 1878. *The Cornish Fauna: a compendium of the Natural History of the County, intended to form a companion to the Collection in the Museum of the Royal Institute of Cornwall; with revisions and large additions by J. B. Rowe (Mammalia), T. Cornish*

(Reptilia and Pisces), E. H. Rodd (Aves), and C. S. Bate (Crustaceans). – Part 1. *The Vertebrate Animals and Crustaceans*. Royal Institute of Cornwall, Truro.

COULSON, J. C. & BRAZENDALE, M. G. 1968. Movements of Cormorants ringed in the British Isles and evidence of colony-specific dispersal. *British Birds* 61: 1–21.

COULSON, J. C. & WHITE, E. 1958. Observations of the breeding of the Kittiwake. *Bird Study* 5: 74–83.

COUNCIL OF THE EUROPEAN COMMUNITY 1979. Directive of the Council of the European Community on the Conservation of Wild Birds (Birds Directive). Council Directive 79/409/EEC: *O. J. Eur. Comm.* No. L 103 (25th April 1979).

COURTNEY, J. S. 1845. *A Guide to Penzance and its Neighbours, including The Islands of Scilly*. P. 28 (of appendix). Penzance.

CRAMP. S. 1963. Movements of tits in Europe in 1959 and after. *British Birds* 56: 237–263.

CRAMP, S. 1971. Gulls nesting on buildings in Britain and Ireland. *British Birds* 64: 476–487.

CRAMP. S., PETTET, A. & SHARROCK, J. T. R. 1960. The irruption of tits in autumn 1957. *British Birds* 53: 49–77.

CRAMP, S., SIMMONS, K. E. L. & PERRINS, C. M. (eds.) 1977–1994. *Handbook of the Birds of Europe, the Middle East and North Africa: The Birds of the Western Palearctic*. Vols. 1–9. Oxford University Press, Oxford.

CROSBY, M. J. 1988. Cliff Swallow: new to Britain and Ireland. *British Birds* 81: 449–452.

CURSON, L. & LEWINGTON, I. 1994. Identification forum: separation of Bicknell's and Grey-cheeked Thrushes. *Birding World* 7: 359–365.

DAVIES, C. 2001. The European Bird Report: Passerines. *British Birds* 94: 419–430.

DAVIS, P. 1964. Crossbills in Britain and Ireland in 1963. *British Birds* 57: 477–501.

DEAN, A. R. 1984. Origins and distribution of British Glaucous Gulls. *British Birds* 77: 165–166.

DEAN, A. R. 1985. Review of British status and identification of Greenish Warbler. *British Birds* 78: 437–451.

DEAN, A. R. 1993. From the Rarities Committee's files: Isabelline Wheatear in Scilly. *British Birds* 86: 3–5.

del HOYO, J. & ELLIOTT, A. (eds.) 1974. *Handbook of the Birds of the World*. Vol. 4. Lynx Edicions, Barcelona.

DOBSON, R. 1952. *The Birds of the Channel Islands*. Stopes Press, London.

DONALD, P. F., WILSON, J. D. & SHEPHERD, M. 1994. The decline of the Corn Bunting. *British Birds* 87: 106–132.

DORRIEN-SMITH, A. A. 1938a. Black Kite in the Isles of Scilly. *British Birds* 32: 237.

DORRIEN-SMITH, A. A. 1938b. Abnormal southward movement of Swallows in June. *British Birds* 32: 45–46.

DORRIEN-SMITH, A. A. 1939a. Mistle-Thrush, Kittiwake and Quail breeding in Scilly Islands. *British Birds* 33: 110.

DORRIEN-SMITH, A. A. 1939b. Greater Yellowshank seen in Scilly Islands. *British Birds* 33: 113.

DORRIEN-SMITH, A. A. 1941. Scarce Birds in the Scilly Isles. *British Birds* 34: 181.

DORRIEN-SMITH, A. A. 1942. Black Kite and Reeves in Scilly Islands. *British Birds* 36: 74.

DORRIEN-SMITH, T. A. 1951. *Birds of Scilly as recorded at Tresco Abbey*.

DUBOIS, P. J. 1991. Identification forum: Royal, Lesser Crested and Elegant Terns. *Birding World* 4: 120–123.

DUKES, P. 1979. Penduline Tit in the Isles of Scilly. *British Birds* 72: 483–484.

DUKES, P. 1980. Semipalmated Plover: new to Britain and Ireland. *British Birds* 73: 458–464.

DUKES, P. 1982. Semipalmated Plover in Scilly. In SHARROCK, J. T. R. & GRANT, P. J. 1982. *Birds New to Britain and Ireland*: pp. 235–239. Poyser, Calton.

DUKES, P. 1987. Wood Thrush on St Agnes. *Twitching* 1: 299–300.

DUKES, P. 1995. Wood Thrush in Scilly: new to Britain and Ireland. *British Birds* 88: 133–135.

DUKES, P. 1996. A possible eastern Nightingale on Scilly. *Birding World* 9: 62.

DUNN, P. 1988. Isabelline Wheatear on Scilly. *Birding World* 1: 357–358.

DUNN, P. J. 1985. Feeding methods of coastal Carrion Crows. *British Birds* 78: 151–152.

DUNN, P. J. 1990. Isabelline Wheatear in Scilly. *British Birds* 83: 553–554.

DURAND, A. L. 1972. Landbirds over the North Atlantic: unpublished records 1961–65 and thoughts a decade later. *British Birds* 65: 428–442.

D'URBAN, W. S. M. 1910. Increase of Starlings in Cornwall and Devon. *British Birds* 4: 213.

DYMOND, J. N, FRASER, P. A. & GANTLETT, S. J. M. 1989. *Rare Birds in Britain and Ireland*. Poyser, Calton.

EBELS, E. B. & VAN DER LANN, J. 1994. Occurrence of Blue-cheeked Bee-eater in Europe. *Dutch Birding* 16: 95–101.

EDWARDS, K. D. & OSBORNE, K. C. 1972. Hooded Warbler in the Isles of Scilly: a species new to Britain and Ireland. *British Birds*: 203–205.

EDWARDS, K. D. & OSBORNE, K. C. 1982. Hooded Warbler in Scilly. In SHARROCK, J. T. R. & GRANT, P. J. *Birds New to Britain and Ireland*: pp. 169–172. Poyser, Calton.

ELKINS, N. 1977. Falls of Nearctic passerines in Britain and Ireland. *British Birds* 70: 399–400.

ELKINS, N. 1979. Nearctic landbirds in Britain and Ireland: a meteorological analysis. *British Birds* 71: 417–433.

ELKINS, N. 1999. Recent records of Nearctic landbirds in Britain. *British Birds* 92: 83–95.

ELVY, R. J., CORD, J. F., CORD, R. A. & CROOK, P. H. 1960. Rufous Turtle Dove in the Isles of Scilly. *British Birds* 53: 445–446.

ENRIGHT, S. D. 1995. Magnolia Warbler in Scilly: new to Britain and Ireland. *British Birds* 88: 107–108.

EVANS, L. 1993. The Isles of Scilly Blyth's Pipit. *Birding World* 6: 398–400.

EVANS, L. 1994. Killdeers in Britain and Ireland. *Birding World* 7: 57–60.

EVANS, L. G. R. 1992. *Rare Birds in Britain 1991*. L. G. R. Evans, Little Chalfont.

EVANS, L. G. R. 1993. *Rare Birds in Britain 1992*. L. G. R. Evans, Little Chalfont.

EVANS, L. G. R. 1994. *Rare Birds in Britain 1880–1990*. L. G. R. E. Publications, Little Chalfont.

EVANS, L. G. R. 1995. *Rare Birds in Britain 1993*. L. G. R. E. Publications, Little Chalfont.

EVANS, L. G. R. 1997. *Rare Vagrants, Scarce Migrants and Rare Breeding Birds in Britain 1994*. L. G. R. E. Publications, Little Chalfont.

EVANS, L. G. R. & TURNER, D. 1998. *Rare and Scarce Migrant Birds of the Isles of Scilly – up to and including 1998*. L. G. R. E. Publications, Little Chalfont.

FAIRLESS, T. W. 1997. Magpies flying out to sea apparently to migrate. *British Birds* 90: 149.

FARRANT, A. 1938. Probable North Atlantic Great Shearwaters off Cornwall. *British Birds* 32: 197–198.

FEFELOV, I. V. 2001. Comparative breeding ecology and hybridisation of Eastern and Western Marsh Harriers *Circus spilonotus* and *C. aeruginosus* in the Baikal region of Eastern Siberia. *Ibis* 143: 587–592.

FERNANDEZ-CORDEIRO, A, & COSTAS, R. 1991. Sandwich Terns *Sterna sandvicensis* feeding juveniles during autumn migration around the NW Iberian Peninsula. *Seabird* 13: 70–71.

FILBY, R. A. & GOOD, J. B. 1987. Philadelphia Vireo on Tresco. *Twitching* 1: 301–302.

FISHER, A. & FLOOD, B. 2001. The Fea's Petrel off the Isles of Scilly. *Birding World* 14: 289–292.

FISHER, J. & LOCKLEY, R. M. 1954. *Sea-Birds*. Collins, London.

FITTER, R. S. R. 1939. North Atlantic (or Mediterranean) Great Shearwater in Cornish Seas. *British Birds* 32: 371–372.

FITTER, R. S. R. 1959. *The Ark in our Midst*. Collins, London.

FLUMM, D. S. 1974. Sharp-tailed Sandpiper *Calidris acuminata* Porthellick, St Mary's, September 25th 1974. *Isles of Scilly Bird Report* 1974.

FLUMM, D. S. 1977. Bimaculated Lark in the Isles of Scilly. *British Birds* 70: 298–300.

FLUMM, D. S. 1993. Do Mediterranean Shags occur in southwest England? *British Birds* 86: 166–173.

FOGDEN, S. & GREENWOOD, D. 1965. Guillemots nesting in deep cavity. *British Birds*: 470.

FORESHAW, J. M. & COOPER, W. T. 1973. *Parrots of the World*. David & Charles, Newton Abbot.

FOWLER, J. A. & HOUNSOME, M. V. 1998. Migration and arrival of immature Storm Petrels *Hydrobates pelagicus* in Shetland. *Ringing and Migration* 1998 19: 91–94.

FOX, A. D. 1988. Breeding status of the Gadwall in Britain and Ireland. *British Birds* 81: 51–66.

FRANKLAND, J. B. 1989: North American landbirds on the QE2. *British Birds* 82: 568–569.

FRASER, P. A. & ROGERS, M. J. 2001. Report on scarce migrant birds in Britain in 1999. *British Birds* 94: 560–589.

FRASER, P. 1997. How many rarities are we missing? Weekend bias and length of stay revisited. *British Birds* 90: 94–101.

FROHAWK, F. W. 1908. Habits of the Manx Shearwater. *The Field* 1908: 1021.

FROHAWK, F. W. 1909. White-tailed Sea Eagle in the Scilly Islands. *The Field* 114: 1100.

FROHAWK, F. W. 1910a. On a white-breasted variety of the Common Cormorant. *British Birds* 3: 385–390.

FROHAWK, F. W. 1910b. Exhibition of female white-breasted Cormorant shot on 30th June 1909 off the Scilly Isles. *Bulletin of the British Ornithologists' Club* 25: 88–89.

FROHAWK, F. W. 1915–16. The Bird-life of the Scilly Isles: The Manx Shearwater. *Proceedings of the South London Entomological and Natural History Society* 1915–16: 70–72.

FROHAWK, F. W. 1936. American Goshawk in the Scilly Isles. *The Field* 30th May 1936: 1318.

FRY, H., STUART, K. & URBAN, E. K. 1988. *The Birds of Africa*. Academic Press, London.

FULLER, E. 1999. *The Great Auk*. Southborough, Kent.

GANTLETT, S. 1988. Matsudaira's Storm-Petrel off Cornwall: a new British Bird. *Birding World* 1: 285.

GANTLETT, S. 1991. *The Birds of the Isles of Scilly*. S. J. M. Gantlett, Norfolk.

GANTLETT, S. 1998. Bird forms in Britain. *Birding World* 11: 222–239.

GANTLETT, S. 1999. The 1999 Scillonian pelagic. *Birding World* 12: 315.

GANTLETT, S. 2001. A Checklist of the Bird Forms of Britain and Ireland. *Birding World* 14: 19–26.

GANTLETT, S. & HARROP, S. 1992. Identification forum: South Polar Skua. *Birding World* 5: 256–270.

GANTLETT, S. & MILLINGTON, R. 1998. The Scilly Starling. *Birding World* 11: 53–57.

GARNER, M. & MILLINGTON, R. 2001. Grey-bellied Brant and the Dundrum conundrum. *Birding World* 14: 151–155.

GARNER, M., KOLBEINSSON, Y. & MACTAVISH, B. 2000. Identification of first-winter Kumlien's Gull and the 'Whitby Gull'. *Birding World* 13: 116–119.

GARNER, M., QUINN, D. & GLOVER, B. 1997. Identification of Yellow-legged Gulls in Britain. *British Birds* 90: 369–383.

GEARY, S. & LOCK, L. 2001. *Winter Nearshore Seabird Survey of South Cornwall Coast Important Bird Area (1999/2000)*. RSPB unpublished report.

GIBB, J. 1948. Report on the immigration of Waxwings, winter 1946–7. *British Birds* 41: 34–40.

GIBBONS, D., AVERY, M., BAILLIE, S., GREGORY, R., KIRBY, J., PORTER, R. F., TUCKER, G. & WILLIAMS, G. 1996. *Bird Species of Conservation Concern in the United Kingdom, Channel Islands and Isle of Man: revising the Red Data List.* RSPB Conservation Review. RSPB, Sandy.

GIBBONS, D. W., REID, J. B. & CHAPMAN, R. A. 1993: *The New Atlas of Breeding Birds in Britain and Ireland: 1988–1991.* Poyser, London.

GILL, C., BOOKER, F. & SOPER, T. 1967. *The Wreck of the Torrey Canyon.* David and Charles, Newton Abbot.

GLEGG, W. E. 1920. Some Notes from the Scilly Isles. *British Birds* 14: 59–60.

GOLLEY, M. & STODDART, M. 1991. Identification of American and Pacific Golden Plovers. *Birding World* 4: 195–204.

GOOD, J. B. 1991. Philadelphia Vireo in Scilly: new to Britain. *British Birds* 84: 572–574.

GOODBODY, I. M. 1947. Early nesting of Cormorant. *British Birds* 40: 119.

GOODWIN, A. G. 1984. Scarlet Tanager in Scilly. *British Birds* 77: 490–491.

GORMAN, G. 1994. The Rose-coloured Starling invasion, and breeding in Hungary. *Birding World* 7: 316–318.

GRANT, P. 1987. Two-barred Greenish Warbler on Scilly – a new British bird. *Twitching* 1: 333–336.

GRANT, P. J. 1970. Four American passerines new to the British and Irish List – Blackpoll Warbler in the Isles of Scilly. *British Birds* 63: 153–155.

GRANT, P. J. 1978. Black-and-white Warbler in the Isles of Scilly. *British Birds* 71: 541–542.

GRANT, P. J. 1979. Identification of two first-winter Marsh Warblers. *Isles of Scilly Bird Report* 1979: 54–57.

GRANT, P. J. 1982a. Blackpoll Warbler in Scilly. In SHARROCK, J. T. R. & GRANT, P. J. *Birds New to Britain and Ireland*: pp. 156–159. Poyser, Calton.

GRANT, P. J. 1982b. Removal of species from Rarities Committee list. *British Birds* 75: 338.

GRAVET, T. 1986. Northern Parula in Scilly. *British Birds* 79: 434.

GREENWOOD, A. 1843: Note on the occurrence of the Squacco Heron near Penzance. *Zoologist* 1: 143–144.

GREENWOOD, J. 1963. Variation in leg-colour of Kittiwakes. *British Birds* 56: 110.

GREGORY, R. D., WILKINSON, N. I., NOBLE, D. G., ROBINSON, J. A., BROWN, A. F., HUGHES, J., PROCTER, D., GIBBONS, D. W. & GALBRAITH, C. A. 2002. The population status of birds in the United Kingdom, Channel Islands and Isle of Man: an analysis of conservation concern 2002–2007. *British Birds* 95: 410–448.

GRIFFITH, A. F. 1906. Exhibition of Greater Yellowshanks (*Totanus melanoleucus*), shot by Capt. Arthur Dorrien-Smith at Tresco Abbey, Isles of Scilly on September 16th 1906. *Bulletin of the British Ornithologists' Club* 19: 7.

GRIFFITHS, E. 1982. American vagrants in Cornwall and the Isles of Scilly 1830–1982. *CBWPSAR* 52: 97–111.

GUERMEUR, Y. & MONNAT, J-Y. 1980. *Histoire et Geographie des Oiseaux Nicheures de Bretagne.* Sociætæ Pour L'ætude et la Protection de la Nature en Bretagne, Brest.

GUILLEMETTE, R. 1992. Status of breeding seabirds on the north coast of Brittany. In *Report of Seminar to Consider the Status of Breeding Seabirds in the Gulf of St Malo.* La Societe Guerneisaise, Guernsey, Channel Islands.

GURNEY, J. H., Jr. 1868. Departure and arrival of migratory birds observed in Cornwall and Devonshire during August and September 1868. *Zoologist* 26: 1454.

GURNEY, J. H., Jr. 1871. Wholesale destruction of Manx Shearwater. *Zoologist* 29: 2646.

GURNEY, J. H., Jr. 1889. Notes on the Isles of Scilly and the Manx Shearwater (*Puffinus angorum*). *Transactions of the Norfolk and Norwich Naturalists' Society* 4: 447–454.

GURNEY, J. H. 1921. *Early Annals of Ornithology.* Witherby, London.

HAGEMEIJER, W. J. M. & BLAIR, M. J. 1997. *The EBCC Atlas of European Breeding Birds: Their Distribution and Abundance.* T & A D Poyser, London.

HALE, J. H. 1994. An analysis of waders roosting on St Agnes October 1994–April 1995. *Isles of Scilly Bird Report* 1994.

HALLE, L. J. 1960. Birds crossing the Atlantic on ships. *British Birds* 53: 39–41.

HARBER, D. D. & SWAINE, C. M. 1963. Report on rare birds in Great Britain 1962. *British Birds* 56: 393–395.

HARDING, B. D. 1972a. Scarlet Tanager in the Isles of Scilly: a species new to Britain and Ireland. *British Birds* 65: 155–158.

HARDING, B. D. 1972b. Nighthawk in the Isles of Scilly. *British Birds* 65: 301–302.

HARDING, B. D. 1982. Scarlet Tanager in Scilly. In SHARROCK, J. T. R. & GRANT, P. J. *Birds New to Britain and Ireland*: pp. 172–174. Poyser, Calton.

HARDING, R. 1959. Kittiwakes attacking Grey Seals carrying fish. *British Birds* 52: 96–97.

HARRIS, G. J., PARSLOW, J. L. F. & SCOTT, R. E. 1960. Northern Waterthrush in the Isles of Scilly. *British Birds* 53: 513–518.

HARRIS, G. J., PARSLOW, J. L. F. & SCOTT, R. E. 1982. Northern Waterthrush in Scilly. In SHARROCK, J. T. R. & GRANT, P. J. *Birds New to Britain and Ireland*: pp. 95–98. Poyser, Calton.

HARRIS, P. 1988. Seabirding aboard the *Chalice* in 1988. *Birding World* 1: 345–348.

HARRIS, P., FOWLEY, J. A. & OKILL, J. D. 1993. Initial results of Storm Petrel *Hydrobates pelagicus* ringing in Portugal. *Ringing and Migration* 14: 133–134.

HARRISON, T. H. & HOLLOM, P. A. D. 1932. The Great Crested Grebe Enquiry, 1931. *British Birds* 26: 62–92.

HARROP, H. 1993. Identification of female and juvenile Yellow-breasted Bunting. *Birding World* 6: 317–319.

HARROP, S. 1990. Chestnut-flanked White-eye: a new British bird? *Birding World* 3: 383–384.

HARROP, S. 1991. The Blue-cheeked Bee-eater by any other name. *Birding World* 4: 127–129.

HARROP, S. & QUINN, D. 1989. The difficulties of Reed, Marsh and Blyth's Reed Warbler identification. *Birding World* 2: 318–323.

HARTING, J. E. 1890. Black Stork in the Scilly Islands. *Zoologist* 48: 353.

HARVEY, A. W. 1910. Increase of the Starling in Cornwall. *British Birds* 4: 122.

HARVEY, G. H. 1938. Notes on birds at Scilly. *CBWPSAR* 8: 92–99.

HARVEY, P. 1983. *Breeding Seabird Populations, Isles of Scilly 1983.* Unpublished Report for the Nature Conservancy Council.

HARVIE-BROWN, J. A., CORDEAUX, J., KERMODE, P. M. C., BARRINGTON, R. M., & MORE, G. A. 1881. Report on the Migration of Birds in the Spring and Autumn of 1880. *Bulletin of the British Ornithologists' Club* 1881.

HARVIE-BROWN, J. A., CORDEAUX, J., KERMODE, P. M. C., BARRINGTON, R. M., & MORE, G. A. 1882. Report on the migration of birds in the spring and autumn of 1881. *Bulletin of the British Ornithologists' Club* 1982.

HARVIE-BROWN, J. A., CORDEAUX, J., BARRINGTON, R. M., MORE, G. A. & EAGLE CLARKE, W. 1885. Report on the migration of birds in the spring and autumn of 1884. *Bulletin of the British Ornithologists' Club* 1885.

HARVIE-BROWN, J. A., CORDEAUX, J., BARRINGTON, R. M., MORE, G. A. & EAGLE CLARKE, W. 1886. Report on the Migration of Birds in the Spring and Autumn of 1885. *Bulletin of the British Ornithologists' Club* 1886.

HARVIE-BROWN, J. A., CORDEAUX, J., BARRINGTON, R. M., MORE, G. A. & EAGLE CLARKE, W. 1887. Report on the migration of birds in the spring and autumn of 1886. *Bulletin of the British Ornithologists' Club* 1987.

HATHWAY, R., SCOTT, M. & WAGSTAFF, W. 1997. The Yellow-headed Wagtail on Scilly: a new British Bird? *Birding World* 10: 136–137.

HAWTHORN, I. & MEAD, C. J. 1975. Wren movements and survival. *British Birds* 68: 349–358.

HEANEY, V., RATCLIFFE, N., BROWN, A., ROBINSON, P. & LOCK, L. 2002. The status and distribution of Storm Petrels and Manx Shearwaters on the Isles of Scilly. *Atlantic Seabirds* 4: 1–16.

HEARD, C. 1988. American Pipit on Scilly. *Birding World* 1: 383–384.

HEARD, C. 1989. Problem Nightingales. *Birding World* 2: 91–94.

HEARNE, T. 1710. *The Itinerary of John Leland, the Antiquary.* Bodelian Library, Oxford.

HEATH, M., BORGGREVE, C. & PEET, N. 2000. *European Bird Populations Estimated and Trends.* BirdLife International, Cambridge.

HEATH, R. 1750. *A Natural and Historical Account of the Islands of Scilly, with a Description of Cornwall.* London.

HEATHERLY, F. 1913. *The Peregrine Falcon at the Eyrie.* George Newnes, London.

HEATON, W. H. 1876. Does the Common Gull breed in the Scilly Islands? *Zoologist* 34: 5126.

HELBIG, A. J., MARTENS, J., SEIBOLD, I., HENNING, F., SCHOTTLER, B. & WINK, W. 1996. Phylogeny and species limits in the Palearctic chiffchaff *Phylloscopus collybita* complex: mitochondrial genetic differentiation and bioacoustic evidence. *Ibis* 138: 650–666.

HICKMAN, J. 1995. Tree Swallow in Scilly: new to the Western Palearctic. *British Birds* 88: 381–384.

HIRSCHFELD, E. 1992. Identification of Rufous Turtle Dove. *Birding World* 5: 52–57.

HOLLOM, P. A. D. 1940. Report of the 1938 survey of Black-headed Gull colonies. *British Birds* 33: 202–221.

HOLLOM, P. A. D. 1960. *The Popular Handbook of Rarer British Birds.* Witherby, London.

HOLLOWAY, S. (ed.) 1996. *The Historical Atlas of Breeding Birds in Britain and Ireland 1875–1900.* Poyser, London.

HOLMAN, D. J. 1977. Bobolink in the Isles of Scilly. *British Birds* 70: 223–224.

HOLMAN, D. J. & WALSH, D. 1992. Presumed aberrant Redwing showing characters of Eye-browed Thrush. *British Birds* 85: 135–136.

HOLT, P. 1996. The Buff-bellied Pipit on Scilly. *Birding World* 9: 390–391.

HOUGH, J. 2000. Identification of Cliff Swallow and Cave Swallow. *Birding World* 13: 368–374.

HOWELL, S. G. 1985. Ship-assisted passage. *British Birds* 78: 52–53.

HOWEY, D. H. & BELL, M. 1985. Pallas's Warblers and other migrants in Britain and Ireland in October 1982. *British Birds* 78: 381–392.

HUDSON, R. 1965. The spread of the Collared Dove in Britain and Ireland. *British Birds* 58: 105–139.

HUDSON, R. 1972. Collared Doves in Britain and Ireland during 1965–70. *British Birds* 65: 139–154.

HUME, R. A., HARRISON, P., WALLIS, H. W., CUTTING, K., YOUNG, S. A., CHARLES, P.,

ENGLAND, T. M. & WARD, J. R. 1997. From the Rarities Committee's Files: 'The *Chalice* Petrel'. *British Birds* 90: 305–313.

HUNT, D. B. 1969. Scilly Honeyseekers. *Isles of Scilly Bird Report* 1969: 21–22.

HUNT, D. B. 1973. Myrtle Warbler *Dendroica coronata* Tresco 16th to 23rd October 1973. *Isles of Scilly Bird Report* 1973: 23.

HUNT, D. B. 1979. Yellow-bellied Sapsucker: new to Britain and Ireland. *British Birds* 72: 410–414.

HUNT, D. B. 1982. Yellow-bellied Sapsucker in Scilly. In SHARROCK, J. T. R. & GRANT, P. J. *Birds New to Britain and Ireland*: pp. 202–205. Poyser, Calton.

HUTCHINSON, C. D. 1989. *Birds in Ireland*. Poyser, London.

INGLIS-JONES, E. 1969. *Augustus Smith of Scilly*. Faber & Faber, London.

IRISH RARE BIRDS COMMITTEE 1998. *Checklist of the Birds of Ireland*. BirdWatch, Dublin.

ISLES OF SCILLY BIRD GROUP 2000. *Isles of Scilly Bird and Natural History Review 2000*. Isles of Scilly Bird Group, Isles of Scilly.

*ISLES OF SCILLY ANNUAL BIRD REPORTS* 1969–1999 (eds.). PARSONS, G. 1969; PARSONS, A. G. & QUICK, H. M. 1970–71; QUICK, H. M. 1972; HUNT, D. B. & ROBINSON, P. K. 1973–77; ROBINSON, P. K. & HUNT, D. B. 1978–80; HUNT, D. B. & ROGERS, M. J. 1981–83; ROGERS, M. J. 1984–87; ROGERS, M. J. & WAGSTAFF, W. H. 1988–89; ROBINSON, P. J. 1990–97; SCOTT, M. S. 1998–99. *Cornwall Birdwatching and Preservation Society*.

JACKSON, D. B. & GREEN, R. E. 2000. The importance of the introduced Hedgehog (*Erinaceus europaeus*) as a predator of the eggs of seven waders in machair in South Uist. *Biological Conservation* 93: 333–348.

JAMES, P. (ed.) 1996. *Birds of Sussex*. Sussex Ornithological Society.

JARAMILLO, A. & BURKE, P. 1999. *New World Blackbirds: the Icterids*. Christopher Helm, London.

JENKINSON, J. H. 1891. Lesser Kestrel at Scilly. *Zoologist* 39: 153.

JESSE, E. 1887. *Gleanings in Natural History*. John Murray, London.

JIGUET, F. 1997. Identification of South Polar Skua: the Brown Skua pitfall. *Birding World* 10: 306–310.

JOBSON, G. J. 1978a. Yellow-rumped Warbler in the Isles of Scilly. *British Birds* 71: 186.

JOBSON, G. J. 1978b. Blackpoll Warbler in the Isles of Scilly. *British Birds* 71: 186–187.

JONES, W. E. 1975. Kittiwakes associating with feeding Razorbills. *British Birds* 68: 296.

JONSSON, L. 1998. Yellow-legged gulls and yellow-legged Herring Gulls in the Baltic. *Alula* 3: 74–100.

JOY, N. H. 1912. Observations on the Manx Shearwaters and Storm-Petrels at the Scilly Islands. *British Birds* 6: 118–120.

KENNEDY, P. G., RUTTLEDGE, R. F. & SCROOPE, C. F. 1954. *The Birds of Ireland*. Oliver and Boyd, London.

KING, C. J. 1924. *Some Notes on the Wild Nature of Scillonia – Particularly of Sea-birds and Seals*. C J King & Son, St Mary's, Isles of Scilly.

KING, B. 1965a. Peregrine attacking Manx Shearwater. *British Birds* 58: 297.

KING, B. 1965b. *Bird Census, Tresco, Isles of Scilly* January–February 1965. *CBWPSAR* 35: 91–95.

KING, B. 1974. Aerial plung-diving by Shags and Manx Shearwaters. *British Birds* 67: 77.

KING, B. 1978. Free-winged Budgerigars in the Isles of Scilly. *British Birds* 71: 82–83.

KING, B. & CURBER, R. M. 1972. Great Blue Heron coming on board ship in mid-Atlantic. *British Birds* 65: 442–443.

KING, B. & HUNT, D. B. 1970. Four American passerines new to the British and Irish list: Parula Warbler in the Isles of Scilly. *British Birds* 63: 149–151.

KING, B. & HUNT, D. B. 1982. Parula Warbler in Scilly. In SHARROCK, J. T. R. & GRANT, P. J. *Birds New to Britain and Ireland*: pp. 142–144. Poyser, Calton.

KING, B. & LADHAMS, D. E. 1967. Crossbills feeding on pine cones on the ground. *British Birds* 60: 524–525.

KING, B. & PENHALLURICK, R. D. 1977. Swallows wintering in Cornwall. *British Birds* 70: 341.

KING, J. & LEWINGTON, I. 1996. Identification of nightingales. *Birding World* 9: 179–189.

KING, J. & PARKIN, D. 1997. Great skua upheavals. *Birding World* 10: 362–363.

KING, J. R. 1999. Taxonomy of *Anas* ducks: Green-winged Teal *is* a separate species. *Birding World* 12: 344.

KINNEAR, N. B. 1922. Exhibition of Bartram's Sandpiper (Bartrarmi longicauda) shot at Tresco, Scilly Isles on 22nd September 1922. *Bulletin of the British Ornithologists' Club* 43: 76.

KIRBY, J. S. 1988. *Winter Wader Populations on the Isles of Scilly in 1984/85*. Unpublished report.

KNOX, A. 1988. Taxonomy of the Rock/Water Pipit superspecies *Anthus petrosus, spinoletta* and *rubescens*. *British Birds* 81: 206–211.

KNOX, A. 1994. Claimed occurrences of Red-billed Tropicbird in Britain. *British Birds* 87: 480–487.

KNOX, A. 1996. Grey-cheeked and Bicknell's Thrushes: taxonomy, identification and British and Irish records. *British Birds* 89: 1–9.

KNOX, A. G. 1992. *Checklist of the Birds of Britain and Ireland*. 6th edn. BOURC, Tring.

KNOX, A. G., HELBIG, A. J., PARKIN, D. T. & SANGSTER, G. 2001. The taxonomic status of Lesser Redpoll. *British Birds* 94: 260–267.

KOLODZIEJSKI, S. & SKINNER, P. C. J. 1986. Common Yellowthroat in Scilly. *British Birds* 79: 434.

LACK, D. 1943–1944. The problem of partial migration. *British Birds* 37: 122–130, 142–150.

LACK, D. & LACK, E. 1952. Visible migration at Land's End. *British Birds* 45: 81–96.

LACK, P. 1986. *The Atlas of Wintering Birds in Britain and Ireland.* Poyser, Calton.

LANDSBOROUGH THOMSON, A. 1958. The migrations of British falcons (Falconidae) as shown by ringing results. *British Birds* 51: 179–188.

LANGTON, H. 1920. Record of the shooting of a female Buffleheaded Duck by Miss Dorrien-Smith on Great Pool, Tresco, Isles of Scilly, January 17, 1920. *Bulletin of the British Ornithologists' Club* 40: 155.

LANSDOWN, P. G. 1995. Ages of Great Spotted Cuckoos in Britain and Ireland. *British Birds* 88: 141–149.

LANSDOWN, P. G. & THE RARITIES COMMITTEE. 1987. Rarities Committee news and announcements. *British Birds* 80: 421–423.

LANSDOWN, P. G. & THE RARITIES COMMITTEE. 1990. Rarities Committee news and announcements. *British Birds* 83: 411–414.

LANSDOWN, P. G. & THE RARITIES COMMITTEE. 1992. Rarities Committee news and announcements. British Birds 85: 330–333.

LANSDOWN, P. G. & THE RARITIES COMMITTEE. 1993. Rarities Committee news and announcements. *British Birds* 86: 415–422.

LAWSON, M. 2001. The Brown Shrike on the Scilly Isles. *Birding World* 14: 428–430.

LEADER, P. 1999. Identification forum: Common Snipe and Wilson's Snipe. *Birding World* 12: 371–374.

LEES, J. 2001. The 14th annual Scillonian pelagic trip. *Birding World* 14: 326–328.

LLOYD, C. S., BIBBY, C. J. & EVERETT, M. J. 1975. Breeding terns in Britain and Ireland. *British Birds* 68: 221–237.

LLOYD, C., TASKER, M. L. & PARTRIDGE, K. 1991. *The Status of Seabirds in Britain and Ireland.* Poyser, London.

LLOYD, S. 1946. Corn-Buntings in Scilly. *British Birds* 39: 177.

LOCK, L. 1996. *Isles of Scilly Non-Breeding Wader Survey 1996.* RSPB, Sandy.

LOCK, L. 1999. *Assessment of the Importance of Winter Waterfowl/Wader Populations on the Isles of Scilly.* RSPB, Sandy.

LOCK, L. & COOK, K. 1998. The Little Egret in Britain: a successful colonist. *British Birds* 91: 273–280.

LOCKWOOD, W. B. 1984. *The Oxford Book of British Bird Names.* Oxford University Press, Oxford.

LONG, J. L. 1981. *Introduced Birds of the World.* David & Charles, London.

LONG, R. 1965. Gulls preying on adult Storm Petrels. *British Birds* 58: 219–220.

LOWE, P. R. 1927. American Nighthawk in Scilly. *Bulletin of the British Ornithologists' Club* 48: 41.

MADGE, S. & QUINN, D. 1997. Identification of Hume's Warbler. *British Birds* 90: 571–575.

MARCHANT, J. & BEAVEN, P. 2000. Yellow Wagtails sinking: Waterways Bird Survey's latest population trend. *BTO News* 231: 12–13.

MARCHANT, J. H., HUDSON, R., CARTER, S. P. & WHITTINGTON, P. 1990. *Population Trends in British Breeding Birds.* NCC & BTO, Tring.

MARGESON, J. M. R. 1959. Myrtle Warbler crossing the Atlantic on board ship. *British Birds* 52: 237–238.

MATHEW, M. A. 1891. Distribution of Lesser Whitethroat in the S.W. of England. *Zoologist* 49: 273–274.

McCANCH, N. V. 1981. Predation of Manx Shearwaters by Grey Seals. *British Birds* 74: 348.

McGEEHAN, A. & MILLINGTON, R. 1998. The adult Thayer's Gull in Donegal. *Birding World* 11: 102–108.

McGOWAN, R. Y. 2002. Racial identification of Pallid Swift. *British Birds* 95: 454–455.

McKEE, N. D. 1982. *Factors relevant to the estimation of colony size of the Storm Petrel (*Hydrobates pelagicus*).* Unpublished MSc dissertation, New University of Ulster.

McLEAN, I. & WILLIAMSON, K. 1959. Migration notes from the Western Approaches. *British Birds* 52: 177–185.

MEAD, C. 1993. Auk mortality causes and trends. In *Britain's Birds in 1990–91: the conservation and monitoring review*: pp. 66–67. BTO & JNCC, Thetford.

MEAD, C. 2000. *The State of the Nation's Birds.* Whittet Books, Stowmarket.

MILLINGTON, R. 1991. Spring Citrine and Yellow Wagtails. *Birding World* 4: 205–206.

MILLINGTON, R. 1998. The Green-winged Teal. *Birding World* 11: 430–434.

MILLINGTON, R. 2000. An interesting skua in Dorset. *Birding World* 13: 336–339.

MILLINGTON, R. 2001. A possible Rough-legged Hawk on the Isles of Scilly. *Birding World* 14: 439–440.

MILLINGTON, R. & GARNER, M. 1998. American Herring Gull: in another age. *Birding World* 11: 109–112.

MILNE, B. S. 1960. Huge flock of Grey Phalaropes in the Isles of Scilly. *British Birds* 53: 403.

MILNE, B. S. 1963. Bird life in the cold weather. *St Agnes Bird Observatory Annual Report* 1961–62: 30–31.

MOON, S. & CARRINGTON, D. 2002. A Brown Skua in Glamorgan. *Birding World* 15: 387–389.

MOORE, R. 1969. *The Birds of Devon.* David & Charles, Newton Abbot.

MORRIS, F. O. 1851–57. *A History of British Birds.* Groombridge & Sons, London.

MORRISON, S. 1998. All-dark petrels in the North Atlantic. *British Birds* 91: 540–560.

MOTHERSPLE, J. 1910/1. *The Isles of Scilly: their story their folk and their flowers*. Religious Transactions Society.

MOYLE, W. 1726. *The Works of Walter Moyle Esq.* Darby, London.

MULLARNEY, K. 1991. Identification of Semipalmated Plover: a new feature. *Birding World* 4: 254–258.

NATIONAL GEOGRAPHIC SOCIETY. 1999. *Field Guide to the Birds of North America*. 3rd edn. National Geographic, Washington.

NAYLOR, K. A. 1996. *A Reference Manual of Rare Birds in Great Britain and Ireland*. Vol 1. K. A. Naylor, Nottingham.

NAYLOR, K. A. 1998. *A Reference Manual of Rare Birds in Great Britain and Ireland*. Vol 2. K. A. Naylor, Nottingham.

NELSON, B. 1978. *The Gannet*. Poyser, Berkhamsted.

NEWELL, D., PORTER, R. F. & MARR, T. 1997. South Polar Skua: an overlooked bird in the eastern Atlantic. *Birding World* 10: 229–235.

NEWELL, D., VOTIER, S., BEARHOP, S., FURNESS, B., KENNEDY, M., SCOTT, M., DUKES, P. & MOON, S. 2002. Brown Skuas: new for the Western Palearctic. *British Birds* 95: 538.

NEWTON, A. 1864. On the Irruption of Pallas's Sandgrouse in 1863. *Ibis*: 185–222.

NEWTON, I. 2000. Movements of Bullfinches *Pyrrhula pyrrhula* within the breeding season. *Bird Study* 47: 372–376.

NICOLL, M. J. 1904. The Tawny Pipit (Anthus campestris) as a visitor to England. *Zoologist* 8: 452–454.

NIGHTINGALE, B. & ALLSOP, K. 1994. Invasion of Red-footed Falcons in spring 1992. *British Birds* 87: 223–231.

NISBET, I. C. T. 1959. Wader migration in North America and its relation to transatlantic crossings. *British Birds* 52: 205–215.

NISBET, I. C. T. 1960. Notes on the American Purple Gallinule. *British Birds* 53: 146–149.

NISBET, I. C. T. 1961. Dowitchers in Great Britain and Ireland. *British Birds* 54: 343–357.

NISBET, I. C. T. 1963. American passerines in western Europe, 1951–62. *British Birds* 56: 204–217.

NORMAN, D. 1978. Aberrant Wheatear in the Isles of Scilly. *British Birds* 71: 463–464.

NORTH, I. W. 1850. *A Week in the Isles of Scilly*. 147–160. Rowe, Penzance & Longman, London.

ODDIE, W. E. 1994. American Golden Plover in Scilly. *British Birds* 87: 67–69.

ODIN, N. 1992. Merlins hunting at sea. *British Birds* 85: 497.

OGILVIE-GRANT, W. R. 1906. The Birds of Scilly. *Zoologist* 10: 470.

OGILVIE-GRANT, W. R. (ed.) 1909. Notes on the migratory movements during the autumn of 1907. *Bulletin of the British Ornithologists' Club* 14 – Migration Report 4: 179–205.

OGILVIE-GRANT, W. R. (ed.) 1910. Notes on the migratory movements during the autumn of 1908. *Bulletin of the British Ornithologists' Club* 16 – Migration Report 5: 223–277.

OGILVIE-GRANT, W. R. (ed.) 1911. Details of the chief movements observed at the light-stations during the autumn of 1909. *Bulletin of the British Ornithologists' Club* 28 – Migration Report 6: 261–298.

OGILVIE-GRANT, W. R. (ed.) 1912a. Notes on migratory movements during the autumn of 1910. *Bulletin of the British Ornithologists' Club* 30 – Migration Report 7: 215–267.

OGILVIE-GRANT, W. R. (ed.) 1912b. Details of the chief movements observed at the light stations during autumn of 1910. *Bulletin of the British Ornithologists' Club* 30 – Migration Report 7: 275–315.

OGILVIE-GRANT, W. R. (ed.) 1912c. Report on the immigration of summer residents in the spring of 1911. *Bulletin of the British Ornithologists' Club* 30 – Migration Report 7: 9–188.

OGILVIE-GRANT, W. R. (ed.) 1912d. Details of the chief movements observed at the light stations during the spring of 1911. *Bulletin of the British Ornithologists' Club* 30 – Migration Report 7: 189–214.

OGILVIE-GRANT, W. R. 1914. Report on the immigrations of summer residents in the spring of 1913: isolated records and single observations. *Bulletin of the British Ornithologists' Club* 34 – Migration Report 9: 181

OWEN, M., ATKINSON-WILLES, G. L. & SALMON, D. G. 1986. *Wildfowl in Great Britain*. 2nd edn. Cambridge University Press, Cambridge.

PAGE, D. 1997. Problems presented by a pale Blyth's Pipit. *British Birds* 90: 404–409.

PAGE, W. (ed.) 1906. *Victoria History of Cornwall*. Vol. 1. Archibold Constable, London.

PALMER, P. 2000. First for Britain and Ireland 1600–1999. Arlequin Press, Chelmsford, Essex.

PARKIN, T. D. & KNOX, A. G. 1994. Occurrence patterns of rare passerines in Britain & Ireland. *British Birds* 87: 582–592.

PARNELL, C. 2002. The Grey-cheeked Thrush on the Isles of Scilly. *Birding World* 15: 466–467.

PARSLOW, J. L. F. 1965a. Recoveries of Shags ringed in Scilly, 1957–63. *St Agnes Bird Observatory Report 1963-1964*.

PARSLOW, J. L. F. 1965b. Bobolink on the Isles of Scilly: a bird new to Great Britain and Ireland. *British Birds* 58: 208–214.

PARSLOW, J. L. F. 1965c. Great Black-backed Gulls preying on Storm Petrels. *British Birds* 58: 522–523.

PARSLOW, J. L. F. 1967a. Changes in status among breeding birds in Britain and Ireland. *British Birds* 60: 2–47, 97–123, 177–202, 261–285, 396–404, 493–508.

PARSLOW, J. L. F. 1967b. The *Torrey Canyon* incident and the seabirds of Cornwall. *Cornwall Birdwatching and Preservation Society Annual Report* 37: 78–89.

PARSLOW, J. L. F. 1968a. Changes in status among breeding birds in Britain and Ireland. *British* 61: 49–64, 241–255.

PARSLOW, J. L. F. 1968b. Eye-browed Thrushes in Northamptonshire, Hebrides and Scilly: a species new to Britain and Ireland. *British Birds* 61: 218–223.

PARSLOW, J. L. F. 1972. An early record of a Blue-cheeked Bee-eater *Merops superciliosus* in the Isles of Scilly. *Bulletin of the British Ornithologists' Club* 92: 57–59.

PARSLOW, J. L. F. 1982a. American Purple Gallinule in Scilly. In SHARROCK, J. T. R. & GRANT, P. J. 1982. *Birds New to Britain and Ireland*: 101–102. Poyser, Calton.

PARSLOW, J. L. F. 1982b. Eye-browed Thrushes in Northamptonshire, Western Isles and Scilly. In SHARROCK, J. T. R. & P. J. GRANT 1982. *Birds New to Britain and Ireland*, 129–132. Poyser, Calton.

PARSLOW, J. L. F. & CARTER, M. T. 1982. Bobolink in Scilly. In SHARROCK, J. T. R. & P. J. GRANT 1982. *Birds New to Britain and Ireland*, 120–123. Poyser, Calton.

PATERSON, A. M. & RIDDIFORD, N. J. 1990. Does the Cape Gannet enter European waters? *British Birds* 83: 519–526.

PEARSON, D. J., SMALL, B. J. & KENNERLY, P. R. 2002. Eurasian Reed Warbler: the characters and variation associated with the Asian form *fuscus*. *British Birds* 95: 42–61.

PELLOW, K. 1990. Caspian Plover in Scilly: first British record this century. *British Birds* 83: 549–551.

PEMBERTON, J. E. 2000. *The Birdwatcher's Yearbook*. Buckingham Press, Peterborough.

PENHALLURICK, R. D. 1969. *Birds of the Cornish Coast*. D Bradford Barton Ltd, Truro.

PENHALLURICK, R. D. 1978. *The Birds of Cornwall and the Isles of Scilly*. Headland Publications, Ruthin.

PENHALLURICK, R. D. 1990. *Turtles of Cornwall, The Isles of Scilly and Devonshire*. Dyllansow Pengwella, Truro.

PENHALLURICK, R. D. 1993. House Sparrows nesting in cliffs in Scilly. *British Birds* 86: 435–436.

PENNINGTON, M. 1997. Siberian Chiffchaffs in Britain. *Birding World* 10: 153–154.

PERRINS, C. 1979. *British Tits*. Collins, London.

PETERS, J. L. 1937. *Check-list of birds of the world*. Vol. 3. Harvard University Press. Cambridge, Massachusetts.

PHILLIPS, J. 2000. Autumn vagrancy: 'reverse migration' and migratory orientation. *Ringing and Migration* 20: 35–38.

PHILLIPS, N. R. 1967. After the *Torrey Canyon*. *Cornwall Birdwatching and Preservation Society Annual Report* 37: 90–129.

PHILLIPS, N. R. 1968. *Torrey Canyon* follow-up census. *Cornwall Birdwatching and Preservation Society Annual Report* 38: 75–77.

PIGOTT, D. 1903. Capture of American Bittern on Scilly Islands. *Bulletin of the British Ornithologists' Club* 14: 32.

PRITCHARD, D. E., HOUSDEN, S. D., MUDGE, G. P., GALBRAITH, C. A. & PIENKOWSKI, M. W. 1992. *Important Bird Areas in the United Kingdom, including the Channel Islands and the Isle of Man*. RSPB, Sandy.

PROCTOR, B. & DONALD, C. 2003. Yellow-headed Blackbirds in Britain and Europe. *Birding World* 16: 69-81.

QUICK, H. M. 1947. Fulmars in Cornwall. *Cornwall Birdwatching and Preservation Society Annual Bird Report* 17: 50–51.

QUICK, H. M. 1949. Holidays in Scilly. *Bird Notes* 23: 185–191.

QUICK, H. M. 1955. Little Egret in Scilly Isles. *British Birds* 48: 141.

QUICK, H. M. 1956. St Agnes Shores (Isles of Scilly). *Cornwall Birdwatching and Preservation Society Annual Report* 26: 36–37.

QUICK, H. M. 1964. *Birds of the Isles of Scilly*. Bradford Barton, Truro.

QUICK, H. M. 1982. Blue-cheeked Bee-eater in Scilly. In SHARROCK, J. T. R. & GRANT, P. J. 1982. *Birds New to Britain and Ireland*, 24–25. Poyser, Calton.

RABEL, J. 1970. Reverse migration as the cause of westward vagrancy by four *Phylloscopus* warblers. *British Birds* 63: 89–92.

RATCLIFFE, D 1980. *The Peregrine Falcon*. Poyser, Calton.

RATCLIFFE, N., VAUGHAN, D., WHYTE, C. & SHEPHERD, M. 1998. Development of playback census methods for Storm Petrels *Hydrobates pelagicus*. *Bird Study* 45: 302–312.

RAY, J. 1676. *The Ornithology of Francis Willughby*. London.

REED, T. M. 1984. The numbers of landbird species on the Isles of Scilly. *Biological Journal of the Linnean Society* 21: 431–437.

REDMAN, P. S. & HOOKE, W. D. 1954. Firecrests in Britain, 1952–1953. *British Birds* 47: 234–335.

RICHARDSON, R. A., SEAGER, M. J. & CHURCH, A. C. 1957. Collared Doves in Norfolk: a bird new to the British List. *British Birds* 50: 239–246.

RIDDINGTON, R., VOTIER, S. C. & STEELE, J. 2000. The influx of redpolls into Western Europe, 1995/96. *British Birds* 93: 59–67.

RIDGEWAY, R. 1916. *Birds of North and Middle America*. Part IV. Smithsonian Institute, Washington DC.

ROBBINS, C. S. 1974. Probable interbreeding of Common and Roseate Terns. *British Birds* 67: 168–170.

ROBBINS, C. S. 1980. Predictions of future Nearctic landbird vagrants to Europe. *British Birds* 73: 448–457.

ROBERTS, B. B. 1929. Manx Shearwaters' Departure Flight from Land. *British Birds* 23: 223–224.

ROBERTSON, I. S. 1975. Fulmars occupying Ravens' nest. *British Birds*: 68: 115.

ROBINSON, H. P. K. 1974a. Survey of the breeding birds of St Agnes in 1974. *Isles of Scilly Bird Report* 1974: 28–29.

ROBINSON, H. P. K. 1974b. A survey of seabirds of the Scillies. *Isles of Scilly Bird Report* 1974: 30–33.

ROBINSON, H. P. K. 1975. Passerine Migration in Scilly. *Isles of Scilly Bird Report* 1975: 37–43.

ROBINSON, H. P.K. 1976. Waders in Scilly. *Annual CBWPS Bird Report for the Isles of Scilly* 1976: 43–51.

ROBINSON, H. W. 1911a. Slaughter of Manx Shearwaters by Black-backed Gulls. *British Birds* 5: 55–56.

ROBINSON, H. W. 1911b. Herring Gull's nest with five eggs. *British Birds* 5: 81.

ROBINSON, H. W. 1913. Breeding habits of the Steganopodes. *British Birds* 7: 145–146.

ROBINSON, H. W. 1914. Breeding status of the Linnet in the Scilly Isles. *British Birds* 8: 144–145.

ROBINSON, H. W. 1920. Disappearance of nesting species in the Scilly Isles. *British Birds* 14: 65–66.

ROBINSON, H. W. 1923. Recent changes in the birds of Scilly. *British Birds* 17: 91–92.

ROBINSON, H. W. 1925a. Buffon's Skua in the Scilly Isles. *British Birds* 19: 54.

ROBINSON, H. W. 1925b. Black Terns in Scilly. *British Birds* 19: 54.

ROBINSON, H. W. 1925c. Black-headed Gull nesting in the Scilly Isles. *British Birds* 19: 134.

ROBINSON, H. W. 1926. White-tailed Eagle in the Scilly Isles. *British Birds* 19: 287.

ROBINSON, P. & COLOMBE, S. 2001. *Roseate Tern Species Recovery Programme: Isles of Scilly 2001.* Unpublished report for English Nature.

ROBINSON, P. J. 1991a. Breeding passerines at Lunnon Farm, St Mary's, Isles of Scilly. *Isles of Scilly Bird Report* 1991: 70–76.

ROBINSON, P. J. 1991b. 'Red-legged' Kittiwake on Scilly. *Birding World* 4: 258–259.

ROBINSON, P. J. 1992a. The status of breeding seabirds in the Isles of Scilly. *Isles of Scilly Bird Report* 1992: 67–87.

ROBINSON, P. J. 1992b. *Breeding Seabirds in the Isles of Scilly 1992.* Unpublished report for English Nature.

ROBINSON, P. J. 1992c. *A Review of Seabird Management and Research Activities in 1992.* Unpublished report.

ROBINSON, P. J. 1993. *Breeding Seabirds in the Isles of Scilly 1993.* Unpublished Report for English Nature.

ROBINSON, P. J. 1994. *Terns and Kittiwakes in the Isles of Scilly 1994.* Unpublished Report for English Nature.

ROBINSON, P. J. 1995a. *Breeding Seabirds in Scilly 1995: Terns and Kittiwakes and All Species on Annet.* Unpublished Report for Isles of Scilly Environmental Trust.

ROBINSON, P. J. 1995b. Arctic Redpoll *Carduelis h. hornemanni*, Samson 5th December 1995. *Isles of Scilly Bird Report* 1995.

ROBINSON, P. J. 1998. *Seabird Survey and Monitoring Report, Isles of Scilly 1998.* Unpublished Report for Isles of Scilly Environmental Trust.

ROBINSON, P. J. 1999a. *The Breeding Status of Terns in the Isles of Scilly: current and historical review.* Unpublished Report for English Nature.

ROBINSON, P. J. 1999b. *Distribution of European Storm Petrel* Hydrobates pelagicus *in the Isles of Scilly, with probable abundance.* Unpublished report for English Nature.

ROBINSON, P. J. 1999c. (in prep.) 'Seabird 2000' species status counts for the Isles of Scilly. In *Seabird 2000.*

ROBINSON, P. J. & HAW, J. (in prep). *Storm Petrels* Hydrobates pelagicus *on Annet: diurnal playback and examination of breeding phenology.*

RODD, E. H. 1843a. Note on the early breeding of the Ring Plover. *Zoologist* 1: 190.

RODD, E. H. 1843b. Notes on the occurrence of some rarer British Birds in the County of Cornwall: Pectoral Sandpiper. *Zoologist* 1: 141.

RODD, E. H. 1843c. Notes on the occurrence of some of the rarer British Birds in the County of Cornwall: the Woodchat. *Zoologist* 1: 142.

RODD, E. H. 1843d. Notes on the occurrence of the Squacco Heron near Penzance. *Zoologist* 1: 143–144.

RODD, E. H. 1845. Occurrence of the Hoopoe at Land's End and the Scilly Isles. *Zoologist* 3: 1025.

RODD, E. H. 1846. Late stay of the Swallow at Penzance. *Zoologist* 4: 1247.

RODD, E. H. 1847. Occurrence of the Scops Eared Owl at the Scilly Islands. *Zoologist* 5: 1773.

RODD, E. H. 1849a. Occurrence of the Woodchat (Lanius rufus) at Scilly. *Zoologist* 7: 2620–2621.

RODD, E. H. 1849b. Autumnal migration of birds at Scilly. *Zoologist* 7: 2622.

RODD, E. H. 1849c. Occurrence of the Night Heron at Scilly. *Zoologist* 7: 2498.

RODD, E. H. 1849d. Occurrence of the Osprey, Pied Flycatcher and Reed Wren at Scilly. *Zoologist* 7: 2620.

RODD, E. H. 1850. Occurrence of the Spoonbill on St Mary's, Scilly. *Zoologist* 8: 2853.

RODD, E. H. 1851a. Occurrence of Little Stint (Tringa minuta) at Scilly. *Zoologist* 9: 3279.

RODD, E. H. 1851b. Occurrence of Ortolan Bunting (Emberiza hortulana) at Scilly. *Zoologist* 9: 3277.

RODD, E. H. 1851c. Occurrence of Whinchat at Scilly. *Zoologist* 9: 3276.

RODD, E. H. 1851d. Occurrence of Whiskered Tern at Scilly. *Zoologist* 9: 3280.

RODD, E. H. 1851e. Occurrence of Great Grey Shrike

(Lanius Excubitor) and the Reed Wren (Acrocephalus Scirpaceus) at Scilly. *Zoologist* 9: 3300.

RODD, E. H. 1852a. Occurrence of the Gull-billed Tern (Sterna Anglica) at Scilly. *Zoologist* 10: 3536.

RODD, E. H. 1852b. Occurrence of the Iceland Gull (Larus Icelandicus) at Scilly. *Zoologist* 10: 3536.

RODD, E. H. 1852c. Second Occurrence of Montagu's Harrier at Scilly. *Zoologist* 10: 3475.

RODD, E. H. 1854a. Occurrence of Schinz's Tringa, the Hawfinch and White-fronted Geese at Scilly. *Zoologist* 12: 4512.

RODD, E. H. 1854b. Occurrence of the Goosander (Mergus Merganser) at Scilly. *Zoologist* 12: 4179.

RODD, E. H. 1854c. Occurrence of the Glossy Ibis at Scilly. *Zoologist* 12: 4478.

RODD, E. H. 1854d. Occurrence of the Short-toed Lark (Alauda brachydactyla) at Scilly. *Zoologist* 12: 4477.

RODD, E. H. 1856. Remarkable flight of Woodcocks. *Zoologist* 14: 4946–4947.

RODD, E. H. 1857a. Occurrence of the Brown Snipe (Scolopax grisea) at Scilly. *Zoologist* 15: 5832.

RODD, E. H. 1857b. The Land Rail (Gallinula crex) in Scilly. *Zoologist* 15: 5832.

RODD, E. H. 1857c. Occurrence of Temminck's Stint (Tringa Temminckii) at Scilly. *Zoologist* 15: 5832.

RODD, E. H. 1857d. The Occurrence of Lesser Whitethroat (Sylvia curruca) at Scilly. *Zoologist* 15: 5832.

RODD, E. H. 1860a. Occurrence of the Red Phalarope at Scilly. *Zoologist* 18: 7236.

RODD, E. H. 1860b. Sport at the Scilly Isles. *Zoologist* 18: 6807.

RODD, E. H. 1861a. Large fight of Woodcocks at the Lizard, Land's End and Scilly districts. *Zoologist* 19: 7315.

RODD, E. H. 1861b. The Golden Oriole at Scilly. *Zoologist* 19: 7646.

RODD, E. H. 1863a. Little Ring Plover at Scilly, with a glance at the autumnal visits of migratory birds at the islands. *Zoologist* 21: 8847–8849.

RODD, E. H. 1863b. Marsh Harrier in the Scilly Isles. *Zoologist* 21: 8841.

RODD, E. H. 1863c. Pallas's Sandgrouse at the Scilly Islands. *Zoologist* 21: 8682.

RODD, E. H. 1863d. Occurrence of Temminck's Stint at Scilly. *Zoologist* 21: 8827.

RODD, E. H. 1863e. Pied Flycatcher near Land's End. *Zoologist* 21: 8818–8819.

RODD, E. H. 1863f. The Redbreasted Flycatcher in company with Pied Flycatchers at Scilly. *Zoologist* 21: 8841.

RODD, E. H. 1863g. The Spotted Redshank (Totanus fuscus) in Cornwall. *Zoologist* 21: 8827.

RODD, E. H. 1864a. Greylegged Geese near Penzance. *Zoologist* 22: 8891.

RODD, E. H. 1864b. Long-tailed Duck at Scilly. *Zoologist* 22: 9364.

RODD, E. H. 1864c. The great autumnal migration of birds. *Zoologist* 22: 9364.

RODD, E. H. 1865a. Curlew Tringa: change of plumage. *Zoologist* 23: 9793–9794.

RODD, E. H. 1865b. The autumnal migration at the Land's End, Cornwall. *Zoologist* 23: 9414–9415.

RODD, E. H. 1865c. The Golden Oriole. *Zoologist* 23: 9616–9617.

RODD, E. H. 1865d. Occurrence of the Golden Oriole at Scilly. *Zoologist* 23: 9617.

RODD, E. H. 1865e. Occurrence of the Hoopoe and Golden Oriole at Scilly. *Zoologist* 23: 9617.

RODD, E. H. 1865f. Female Golden Oriole at Scilly. *Zoologist* 23: 9617.

RODD, E. H. 1865g. Surf Scoter at Scilly. *Zoologist* 23: 9794.

RODD, E. H. 1866a. Honey Buzzard at Scilly. *Zoologist* 24: 522.

RODD, E. H. 1866b. Little Bittern at Scilly. *Zoologist* 24: 311.

RODD, E. H. 1866c. Occurrence of the Glossy Ibis at Scilly. *Zoologist* 24: 524.

RODD, E. H. 1866d. Ornithological notes from Scilly. *Zoologist* 24: 227.

RODD, E. H. 1866e. Red Lobefoot [Red-necked Phalarope] at Scilly. *Zoologist* 24: 501.

RODD, E. H. 1866f. The Great Northern Diver: summer and winter plumage. *Zoologist* 24: 99.

RODD, E. H. 1866g. The migration of birds. *Zoologist* 24: 40.

RODD, E. H. 1866h. Third occurrence of the Redbreasted Flycatcher in Cornwall. *Zoologist* 24: 31.

RODD, E. H. 1867a. Autumnal migration at Scilly. *Zoologist* 25: 1014.

RODD, E. H. 1867b. Golden Oriole at Scilly. *Zoologist* 25: 825.

RODD, E. H. 1867c. Occurrence of a Merlin in Scilly. *Zoologist* 25: 555.

RODD, E. H. 1867d. Surf Scoter and Firecrest Regulus (Birds of the Year) at Scilly. *Zoologist* 25: 1017.

RODD, E. H. 1867e. The Lesser Grey Shrike (Lanius minor) a British bird. *Zoologist* 25: 703.

RODD, E. H. 1868a. Crossbills at Scilly. *Zoologist* 26: 1320.

RODD, E. H. 1868b. Flight of Bitterns. *Zoologist* 26: 1059.

RODD, E. H. 1868c. Isles of Scilly: autumnal migration. *Zoologist* 26: 1421.

RODD, E. H. 1868d. Ornithological notes from Scilly. *Zoologist* 26: 1059.

RODD, E. H. 1868e. The Tawny Pipit and Richard's Pipit at Scilly. *Zoologist* 26: 1458.

RODD, E. H. 1869a. *A List of British Birds as a Guide to the Ornithology of Cornwall, especially in the Land's End District: with remarks on the capture, habits etc. of some of the rarer species.* Simpkin, London and Cornish, Penzance.

RODD, E. H. 1869b. Golden Oriole at Scilly. *Zoologist* 27: 1800.
RODD, E. H. 1870a. A list of the birds of Cornwall. *Zoologist* 28: 2193–2204, 2229–2244, 2269–2280, 2321–2326.
RODD, E. H. 1870b. Autumn migration at Scilly. *Zoologist* 28: 2406.
RODD, E. H. 1870c. Blacktailed Godwit in summer plumage at Scilly. *Zoologist* 28: 2181.
RODD, E. H. 1870d. Buffbreasted Sandpiper at Scilly. *Zoologist* 28: 2346.
RODD, E. H. 1870e. British Sandpipers at Scilly. *Zoologist* 28: 2345.
RODD, E. H. 1870f. Golden Oriole at Scilly. *Zoologist* 28: 2139.
RODD, E. H. 1870g. Hooded Crows at Scilly. *Zoologist* 28: 2407.
RODD, E. H. 1870h. Ornithology of Scilly Islands in October. *Zoologist* 28: 2405.
RODD, E. H. 1870i. Pectoral Sandpiper – Scilly. *Zoologist* 28: 2274.
RODD, E. H. 1870j. Pectoral Sandpiper at Scilly. *Zoologist* 28: 2346.
RODD, E. H. 1870k. Pied Flycatcher at Scilly. *Zoologist* 28: 2382.
RODD, E. H. 1870l. Schinz's Stint at Scilly. *Zoologist* 28: 2384–2385.
RODD, E. H. 1871a. Blackcap at Scilly in December. *Zoologist* 29: 2483.
RODD, E. H. 1871b. Golden Oriole at Scilly. *Zoologist* 29: 2639.
RODD, E. H. 1871c. Redstarts at Scilly. *Zoologist* 29: 2849.
RODD, E. H. 1871d. Notes from Scilly. *Zoologist* 29: 2679.
RODD, E. H. 1871e. Marsh Harrier at St Mary's, Scilly. *Zoologist* 29: 2847.
RODD, E. H. 1871f. Snipe-shooting at St Mary's, Scilly. *Zoologist* 29: 2852.
RODD, E. H. 1871g. Spoonbill at Scilly. *Zoologist* 29: 2522.
RODD, E. H. 1872. Arrival of Swallow. *Zoologist* 30: 3064.
RODD, E. H. 1874. Woodcocks in the Scilly Isles. *Zoologist* 32: 4260.
RODD, E. H. 1875. Golden Oriole at Land's End and in Scilly. *Zoologist* 33: 4499.
RODD, E. H. 1876. Our summer migrants in Cornwall. *Zoologist* 34: 5040.
RODD, E. H. 1877. Scaup Duck at Scilly. *Zoologist* 35: 525.
RODD, E. H. 1878a. Purple Heron and Wood Sandpiper at Scilly. *Zoologist* 36: 891.
RODD, E. H. 1878b. A list of some of the rarer and more interesting species of British birds observed and captured at Scilly. In COUCH, J. 1878: *The Cornish Fauna: a compendium of the Natural History of the County, intended to form a companion to the Collection in the Museum of the Royal Institute of Cornwall; with revisions and large additions by J. B. Rowe (Mammalia), T. Cornish (Reptilia and Pisces), E. H. Rodd (Aves), and C. S. Bate (Crustaceans). – Part 1. The Vertebrate Animals and Crustaceans.* Royal Institute of Cornwall, Truro.
RODD, E. H. 1879a. Great Plover or Thick-knee at the Scilly Isles. *Zoologist* 37: 61.
RODD, E. H. 1879b. Hen Harrier at Scilly. *Zoologist* 37: 491.
RODD, E. H. 1879c. Sea birds breeding at Scilly. *Zoologist* 37: 380–381.
RODD, E. H. 1880. (ed. J. E. Harting) *The Birds of Cornwall and The Scilly Islands.* Trubner & Co, London.
ROGERS, M. J. 1995. A possible Common Grackle. *British Birds* 88: 156.
ROGERS, M. J. 1998. Records of Western Bonelli's Warbler in Britain, 1948–96. *British Birds* 91: 122–123.
ROGERS, M. J. 2000. Report on rare birds in Great Britain in 1999. *British Birds* 93: 512–567.
ROWE, S. & JONES, I. L. 2000. The enigma of Razorbill *Alca torda* breeding site selection: adaptation to a variable environment. *Ibis* 142: 324–327.
RUTTLEDGE, R. F. 1966. *Ireland's Birds: Their Distribution and Migrations.* Witherby, London.
RYVES, B. H. 1928. Numbers of eggs laid by various species in Cornwall. *British Birds* 22: 107.
RYVES, B. H. 1948. *Bird Life in Cornwall.* Collins, London.
RYVES, B. H. Lt-Col. & QUICK, H. M. 1946. A survey of the status of birds breeding in Cornwall and Scilly since 1906. *British Birds* 39: 3–11, 34–43.
SAETRE, G-P., BORGE, T. & MOUM, T. (2001). A new bird species? The taxonomic status of the 'Atlas Flycatcher' assessed from DNA sequence analysis. *Ibis* 143: 494–497.
SAGE, B. L. & KING, B. 1959. The influx of phalaropes in autumn 1957. *British Birds* 52: 33–42.
*ST AGNES BIRD OBSERVATORY REPORTS* 1957–1964. (ed. J L F Parslow 1958–64) St Agnes Bird Observatory Committee.
SALTER, F. C. 1986. Egret in mid Atlantic. *British Birds* 79: 500.
SANGSTER, G., COLLINSON, J. M., HELBIG, A. J., KNOX, A. G. & PARKIN, D. T. 2002a. The generic status of Black-browed Albatross and other albatrosses. *British Birds* 95: 583–585.
SANGSTER, G., COLLINSON, J. M., HELBIG, A. J., KNOX, A. G. & PARKIN, D. T. 2002b. The specific status of Balearic and Yelkouan Shearwaters. *British Birds* 95: 636–639.
SAUNDERS, H. 1907. Additions to the list of British Birds since 1890. *British Birds* 1: 4–16.
SAUNDERS, H. 1889. *An Illustrated Manual of British Birds.* Van Voorst, London.

SCOTT, M. 1998. Red-headed Bunting *Emberiza melanocephala*: a hysteria-led record. *Isles of Scilly Bird Report* 1998: 62–63.

SCOTT, M. 1999a. The pelagic trips from Scilly. *Birding World* 12: 316.

SCOTT, M. 1999b. The Blue Rock Thrush on the Isles of Scilly. *Birding World* 12: 412–413.

SCOTT, M. 2002. A Brown Skua on the Isles of Scilly – the first for Europe. *Birding World* 15: 383–386.

SCOTT, M. & WAGSTAFF, W 1999. Scilly in spring. *Birding World* 12: 60–70.

SCOTT, R. E. 1964. Pallas's Warblers in Britain in 1963. *British Birds* 57: 508–513.

SCOTT, R. E. 1972. Little Gulls associating with feeding Razorbills. *British Birds* 65: 259.

SETH-SMITH, D. 1910. American birds liberated on the Scilly Islands. *British Birds* 4: 28–29.

SETON GORDON & SETON GORDON, A. 1930. Some birds observed on the Islands of Scilly. *British Birds* 23: 18–19.

SHARROCK, J. T. R. 1974. *Scarce Migrant Birds in Britain and Ireland*. Poyser, Berkhamsted.

SHARROCK, J. T. R 1976. *The Atlas of Breeding Birds in Britain and Ireland*. Poyser, Calton.

SHARROCK, J. T. R. & GRANT, P. J. 1982. *Birds New to Britain and Ireland*. Poyser, Calton.

SHAW, K. 1987. Eye-browed Thrush on St Agnes, Scilly. *Twitching* 1: 378.

SHIRIHAI, H. & GANTLETT, S. 1993. Identification of female and immature Black-headed Buntings. *Birding World* 5: 195–197.

SHIRIHAI, H. & MADGE, S. 1993. Identification of Hume's Yellow-browed Warbler. *Birding World* 6: 439–443.

SIDDLE, J. 2001. Apparent Continental Stonechats on Scilly. *Birding World* 14: 389.

SILVA, E. T. 1949. Nest Records of the Song Thrush. *British Birds* 42: 97–111.

SMALL, B. 2002. The Horned Lark on the Isles of Scilly. *Birding World* 15: 111–120.

SMART, Rev. R. W. J. 1885–86. List of Birds of the Scillies. *Transactions of the Penzance Natural History and Antiquarian Society for 1885–86*.

SMITH, J. 1980. In praise of birdwatchers. *British Birds* 73: 195.

SNOW, D. W. (ed.) 1971. *The Status of Birds in Britain and Ireland*. Blackwell Scientific Publications, Oxford, London and Edinburgh.

SNOW, D. W. & PERRINS, C. M. 1998. *The Birds of the Western Palearctic*. Concise edition. Oxford University Press, Oxford.

STANLEY, P. I. & MINTON, C. D. T. 1972. The unprecedented westward migration of Curlew Sandpipers in autumn 1969. *British Birds* 65: 365–380.

STEELE, J. & McGUIGAN, C. 1989. Plumage features of a hybrid juvenile Lesser Crested ´ Sandwich Tern. *Birding World* 2: 391–392.

STODDART, A. 1991. Identification forum: Arctic Redpoll. *Birding World* 4: 18–23.

STODDART, A. 1992. Identification of Siberian Stonechat. *Birding World* 5: 348–356.

STONE, B. H., SEARS, S., CRANSWICK, A., GREGORY, R. D., GIBBONS, D. W., REHFISCH, M. M., AEBISCHER, N. J. & REID, J. B. 1997. Population estimates of birds in Britain and the United Kingdom. *British Birds* 90: 1–22.

STONEHOUSE, J. 1996. European Storm-petrels and other seabirds without their toes. *British Birds* 89: 185.

SUFFERN, C. 1939. Earliest references to the Puffin. *British Birds* 32: 376.

SUMMERS-SMITH, J. D. 1988. *The Sparrows*. Poyser, Calton.

SVENSSON, L. 1992. *Identification Guide to European Passerines*. British Trust for Ornithology, Stockholm.

SVENSSON, L. 2002. The correct name of the Iberian Chiffchaff *Phylloscopus ibericus*, Ticehust 1937, its identification and new evidence of its wintering grounds. *Bull. BOC* 121: 281–296.

SWASH, A. 1988. Matsudaira's and Swinhoe's Storm Petrels. *Birding World* 1: 405.

SYMONS, R. 1963. Observation on Rosevear – 22nd September 1963. *Cornwall Birdwatching and Preservation Society Annual Report* 33: 88.

TAPPER, S. (ed.) 1999. *A Question of Balance*. The Game Conservancy Trust, Fordingbridge.

TASKER, M. L. 1991. *Seabird Conservation in Scilly*. Unpublished Report.

TATUM, J. B. 1981. Peregrine fishing at sea. *British Birds* 74: 97.

TAYLOR, D. W., DAVENPORT, D. L. & FLEGG, J. J. M. 1981. *The Birds of Kent: A Review of their Status and Distribution*. Kent Ornithological Society.

THOMAS, C. 1985. *Exploration of a Drowned Landscape: archaeology and history of the Isles of Scilly*. Batsford, London.

THOMSON, K. R., BRINDLEY, E. & HEUBECK, M. 1996. *Seabird numbers and breeding success in Britain and Ireland, 1995*. JNCC, Peterborough.

THOMSON, K. R., BRINDLEY, E. & HEUBECK, M. 1997. *Seabird numbers and breeding success in Britain and Ireland, 1996*. JNCC, Peterborough.

THOMSON, K. R., BRINDLEY, E. & HEUBECK, M. 1998. *Seabird numbers and breeding success in Britain and Ireland, 1997*. JNCC, Peterborough.

THOMSON, K. R., PICKERELL, G. & HEUBECK, M. 1999. *Seabird numbers and breeding success in Britain and Ireland, 1998*. JNCC, Peterborough.

THORPE, W. H. 1935. Remarkable spring migration of Manx Shearwaters and other sea birds off Cape Cornwall. *British Birds* 19: 43–44.

TICEHURST, C. B. 1910. Age of a white-breasted Cormorant. *Bulletin of the British Ornithologists' Club* 17: 26.

TICEHURST, N. F. 1910. Blackbirds and Song Thrushes nesting on the ground. *British Birds* 4: 75–77.

TICEHURST, N. F. 1911. Immigration of Continental Great Tits in Norfolk, Suffolk, Kent and Scilly. *British Birds* 4: 247–248.

TICKLE, W. H. 1965. Oystercatcher killing young Ringed Plover. *British Birds* 58: 298.

TOMLINSON, D. 1991. The status of Red-headed Bunting. *Birding World* 4: 313–314.

TOUSEY, K. 1959. Myrtle Warbler crossing the Atlantic on board ship. *British Birds* 52: 237.

TRAHAIR HARTLEY, P. H. 1935. A contribution to the study of sea-bird movements. *British Birds* 19: 203–210.

TRELEAVAN, R. B. 1981. Peregrine feeding Herring Gull chick to young. *British Birds* 74: 97.

TURK, F. 1973. Notae De Ossibus In Cornubia Inventis: Manipulus 1. *Cornish Studies* 1: 49–52.

TURK, F. A, 1968. Notes on Cornish mammals in prehistoric times, I (Tean, St Agnes). *Cornish Archaeology* 7: 73–79.

TURK, F. A. 1971. Notes on Cornish mammals in prehistoric and historic times: a report on the animal remains from Nornour, Isles of Scilly. *Cornish Archaeology* 10: 79–91.

TURK, F. A. 1973. Distribution patterns of the mammalian fauna of Cornwall (with 73 maps). *Cornish Studies* 1: 5–32.

TURK, F. A. 1984a. A study of the vertebrate remains from May's Hill, St Martin's. *Cornish Studies* 11: 69–80.

TURK, F. A. 1984b. A sub-fossil fauna of Cornwall and the Isles of Scilly. *Cornish Biological Records* 7.

TURTON, J. M. & GREAVES, P. K. 1985. Orphean Warbler in Scilly. *British Birds* 78: 150.

UK BIODIVERSITY STEERING GROUP 1995. *Biodiversity: The Steering Group Report 1995 – Vol. 2: Action Plans.* HMSO, London.

UPTON, A. J., PICKERELL, G. & HEUBECK, M. 2000. *Seabird numbers and breeding success in Britain and Ireland, 1999.* JNCC, Peterborough.

UREN, J. G. 1907: *Scilly and the Scillonians.* Plymouth.

VINGOE, W. H. 1881. Crane at Scilly. *Zoologist* 39: 213.

VINICOMBE, K. E. 1985. Identification of first-winter Sora. *British Birds* 78: 145–146.

VINICOMBE, K. E. 1999. Lesser Scaup on Tresco: a first for Scilly. *Isles of Scilly Bird Report* 1999: 100–101.

VOTIER, S. C., BEARHOP, S., FURNESS, R. W., NEWELL, D. & HARVEY, P. 2002. Ageing and moult in *Catharacta* skuas – some comments. www.surfbirds.com/mb/Features/skuas-identification.html.

VYVYAN, C. C. 1953. *The Isles of Scilly.* Robert Hale, London.

WAGSTAFF, W. H. 1987. Calandra Lark in Scilly. *British Birds* 80: 382.

WAGSTAFF, W. H. 1990. Tree Swallow on Scilly: a new Western Palearctic bird. *Birding World* 3: 199–200.

WAGSTAFF, W. H. 1996. *Breeding Seabirds in Scilly – 1996: Terns, Kittiwakes and all species on Annet, all-island count of Shag nests.* Unpublished Report to The Isles of Scilly Environmental Trust.

WAGSTAFF, W. H. 1997. *Seabirds on the Isles of Scilly.* Unpublished Report to The Isles of Scilly Environmental Trust.

WAGSTAFF, W. H. 1998. The Common Nighthawks on the Isles of Scilly. *Birding World* 11: 338–340.

WALKER, D. 2001. Apparent Continental Stonechats in England. *Birding World* 14: 156–158.

WALKER, F. A. 1871. Notes on the Scilly Isles. *Zoologist* 29: 2839–2844.

WALLACE, D. I. M. 1963. Red-eyed Vireos and other American birds in the Isles of Scilly in early October 1962. *British Birds* 56: 462–464.

WALLACE, D. I. M. 1964. Least Sandpiper in the Isles of Scilly. *British Birds* 57: 124–125.

WALLACE, D. I. M. 1966. Olivaceous Warblers in the Isles of Scilly. *British Birds* 59: 195–197.

WALLACE, D. I. M. 1972a. Laughing Gull in the Isles of Scilly. *British Birds* 65: 79–80.

WALLACE, D. I. M. 1972b. Booted Warbler in the Isles of Scilly. *British Birds* 65: 170–172.

WALLACE, D. I. M. 1972c. An October to remember on St Agnes in 1971. *British Birds* 65: 208–220.

WALLACE, D. I. M. 1972d. Northern Waterthrush in the Isles of Scilly. *British Birds* 65: 484–485.

WALLACE, D. I. M. 1976a. A review of waterthrush identification with particular reference to the 1968 British record. *British Birds* 69: 27–33.

WALLACE, D. I. M. 1976b. Sora Rail in Scilly and the identification of immature small crakes. *British Birds* 69: 443–447.

WALLACE, D. I. M. 1980. Possible future Palearctic passerine vagrants to Britain. *British Birds* 73: 388–397.

WALLACE, D. I. M. 1998. Identification forum: Marsh Hawk – the end of a 41-year hunt? *Birding World* 11: 454–457.

WALLACE, D. I. M. 1999. History of the Common Rosefinch in Britain and Ireland, 1869–1996. *British Birds* 92: 445–471.

WALLIS, H. M. 1923. Recent changes in the birds of Scilly. *British Birds* 17: 55–58.

WALLIS, H. M. 1924. Birds in the Islands of Scilly. *British Birds* 18: 73–74.

WALPOLE BOND, J. 1937. With seabirds in the Scillies. *Oologists' Record* 17: 16–20, 25–29.

WALSH, P. M., BRINDLEY, E. & HEUBECK, M. 1994. *Seabird numbers and breeding success in Britain and Ireland, 1993.* JNCC, Peterborough.

WALSH, P. M., HALLEY, D. J., HARRIS, M. P., del NEVO, A., SIM, I. M. W. & TASKER, M. L. 1995. Seabird monitoring handbook for Britain and Ireland. JNCC, RSPB, ITE and Seabird Group.

WATMOUGH, N. 1988. Yellow-bellied Sapsucker in County Cork. *Birding World* 1: 392–393.

WATSON, D 1977. *The Hen Harrier*. Poyser, Berkhamsted.
WERNHAM, C. V., TOMS, M. P., MARCHANT, J. H., CLARK, J. A., SIRIWARDENA, G. M. & BAILLIE, S. R. (eds.). 2002. *The Migration Atlas: movements of the birds of Britain and Ireland*. Poyser, London.
WERTH, I. 1947. The tendency of Blackbird and Song-Thrush to breed in their birth place. *British Birds* 40: 328–330.
WHITAKER, J. 1887. Thrush's nest without the usual lining. *Zoologist* 45: 268.
WILLIAMSON, K. & FERGUSON-LEES, I. J. 1960. Nearctic birds in Great Britain and Ireland in autumn 1958. *British Birds* 53: 369–378.
WILSON, T. J. & FENTIMAN, C. 1999. Eastern Bonelli's Warbler in Scilly: new to Britain and Ireland. *British Birds* 92: 519–521.
WINK, M., SAUER-GÜRTH, H. & GWINNER, E. 2002. Evolutionary relationships of stonechats and related species inferred from mitochondrial-DNA sequences and genomic fingerprinting. *British Birds* 95: 349–355.
WITHERBY, H. F. 1911. Fulmars breeding in Ireland. *British Birds* 5: 141–142.
WITHERBY, H. F. 1919. A transatlantic passage of Lapwings. *British Birds* 12: 6–16.
WITHERBY, H. F. 1922. American Yellow-billed Cuckoo in the Scilly Islands. *British Birds* 15: 242.
WITHERBY, H. F. 1927a. Greater and Lesser Yellowshanks in the Scilly Isles. *British Birds* 21: 162.
WITHERBY, H. F. 1927b. Snowy Owls in the Atlantic. *British Birds* 20: 228.
WITHERBY, H. F. 1928. Some new British birds and other alterations to the British List: American Nighthawk. *British Birds* 22: 98–102.
WITHERBY, H. F. 1933. American Black-billed Cuckoo in Scilly. *British Birds* 27: 111.
WITHERBY, H. F. 1939. The influx of Bewick's Swans and Whooper Swans, winter 1938–9. *British Birds* 32: 378–381.
WITHERBY, H. F. 1940. The species of Great Shearwaters in the English Channel. *British Birds* 33: 248–249.
WITHERBY, H. F. & TICEHURST, N. F. 1907. On the more important additions to our knowledge of British birds since 1899. *British Birds* 1: 52–56, 81–85, 109–114, 147–152, 178–184, 246–256, 280–284, 314–322, 347–350.
WITHERBY, H. F. & TICEHURST, N. F. 1908. On the more important additions to our knowledge of British birds since 1899. *British Birds* 2: 51.
WITHERBY, H. F., JOURDAIN, F. C. R., TICEHURST, N. F. & TUCKER, B. W. 1940. Witherby's Handbook of British Birds. Witherby, London.
WOODCOCK, M. W. 1984. Northern Waterthrush in Scilly, and notes on waterthrush identification. *British Birds* 77: 368–371.
WORFOLK, T. 2000. Identification of Red-backed, Isabelline and Brown Shrikes. *Dutch Birding* 22: 323–362.
WRIGHT, J. 1994. The Yellow-browed Bunting on Scilly. *Birding World* 7: 410–411.
YARRELL, W. 1837–43. *A History of British Birds* John Van Voorst, London.
YÉSOU, P. 1982. Semipalmated Plover in Western Palearctic. *British Birds* 75: 336–337.
YÉSOU, P., PATERSON, A. M., MACKRILL, E. J. & BOURNE, W. R. P. 1990. Plumage variation and identification of the 'Yelkouan Shearwater'. *British Birds* 83: 299–319.
YOUNG, H. G. 1987. Herring Gull preying on rabbits. *British Birds* 80: 630.
ZINK, R. M. & ELDRIDGE, J. L. 1980. Why does Wilson's Petrel have yellow on the webs of its feet? *British Birds* 73: 385–387.
ZONFRILLO, B. 1996. European Storm-petrels and other seabirds without their toes. *British Birds* 89: 186–187.

# INDEX

**Accentor** Alpine 402, Hedge 400
*Accipiter gentilis* 149
　*nisus* 150
*Acrocepahlus palustris* 446
　*agricola* 445
　*arundinaceus* 450
　*dumetorum* 446
　*paludicola* 442
　*schoenobaenus* 443
　*scirpaceus* 448
*Actitis hypoleucos* 251
　*macularia* 252
*Aegithalos caudatus* 489
*Agelaius phoeniceus* 581
*Aix galericulata* 580
　*sponsa* 109
*Alauda arvensis* 366
**Albatross** Black-browed 44, Wandering 44
*Alca torda* 312
*Alcedo atthis* 353
*Alectoris rufa* 167
*Alle alle* 316
*Alopochen aegyptiacus* 106, 580
*Anas acuta* 118
　*americana* 110
　*carolinensis* 114
　*castanea* 580
　*clypeata* 121
　*crecca* 113
　*discors* 120
　*penelope* 109
　*platyrhynchos* 115
　*querquedula* 119
　*rubripes* 117
　*strepera* 111
*Anser albifrons* 99
　*anser* 101
　*brachyrhynchus* 98
　*cygnoides* 579
　*fabalis* 97
*Anthus campestris* 379
　*cervinus* 384
　*godlewskii* 379
　*gustavi* 382
　*hodgsoni* 380
　*novaeseelandiae* 378
　*petrosus* 385
　*pratensis* 383

　*rubescens* 389
　*spinoletta* 388
　*trivialis* 382
*Apus affinis* 352
　*apus* 349
　*melba* 351
　*pacificus* 351
　*pallidus* 350
*Ardea alba* 85
　*cinerea* 85
　*purpurea* 87
*Ardeola ralloides* 82
*Arenaria interpres* 253
*Asio flammeus* 344
　*otus* 342
*Athene noctua* 340
**Auk** Great 315, Little 316
**Avocet** 190, Pied 190
*Aythya affinis* 127
　*collaris* 124
　*ferina* 122
　*fuligula* 125
　*marila* 126
　*nyroca* 125
*Bartramia longicauda* 240
**Bee-eater** 355, Blue-cheeked 354
**Bittern** 77, American 78, Great 77, Little 79
**Blackbird** 426, Red-winged 581
**Blackcap** 462
**Bluetail** Red-flanked 407
**Bluethroat** 407
**Bobolink** 576
**Bobwhite** Northern 167, Spot-bellied 581
*Bombycilla garrulus* 396
*Botaurus lentiginosus* 78
　*stellaris* 77
**Brambling** 533
*Branta bernicla* 105
　*canadensis* 102
　*leucopsis* 104
*Bubulcus ibis* 83
*Bucephala albeola* 132
　*clangula* 133
**Budgerigar** 331
**Bufflehead** 132
**Bullfinch** 549
*Bulweria bulwerii* 47

**Bunting** Black-headed 571, Cirl 564, Corn 573, Lapland 560, Little 568, Ortolan 565, Painted 583, Pine 562, Red-headed 572, Reed 570, Rustic 566, Snow 561, Yellow-breasted 569, Yellow-browed 566
*Burhinus oedicnemus* 191
**Bustard** Little 185
*Buteo buteo* 152
　*lagopus* 153
　*lineatus* 153
**Buzzard** 152, Honey 137, Rough-legged 153
*Cairina moschata* 580
*Calandrella brachydactyl* 364
*Calcarius lapponicus* 560
*Calidris acuminata* 219
　*alba* 209
　*alpina* 222
　*bairdii* 217
　*canutus* 208
　*ferruginea* 219
　*fuscicollis* 215
　*maritima* 221
　*mauri* 212
　*melanotos* 218
　*minuta* 212
　*minutilla* 214
　*pusilla* 211
　*temminckii* 213
*Calonectris diomedea* 49
**Canary** 583
*Caprimulgus europaeus* 345
*Carduelis cabaret* 543
　*cannabina* 540
　*carduelis* 537
　*chloris* 535
　*flammea* 544
　*flavirostris* 543
　*hornemanni* 545
　*spinus* 539
*Carpodacus erythrinus* 548
*Catharacta antarctica* 264
　*lonnbergi* 264
　*skua* 263
*Catharus bicknelli* 425
　*guttatus* 422
　*minimus* 423
　*ustulatus* 422

# Birds of the Isles of Scilly

*Cepphus grylle* 315
*Cercotrichas galactotes* 402
*Certhia familiaris* 497
*Cettia cetti* 439
*Chaetura pelagica* 348
**Chaffinch** 532
*Charadrius alexandrinus* 199
  *asiaticus* 200
  *dubius* 193
  *hiaticula* 194
  *morinellus* 200
  *semipalmatus* 197
  *vociferus* 198
**Chiffchaff** 475, Iberian 477
*Chlidonias hybrida* 307
  *leucopterus* 308
  *niger* 307
*Chordeiles minor* 346
**Chough** 511, Red-billed 511
*Chrysolophus pictus* 172
*Ciconia ciconia* 89
  *nigra* 88
*Circaetus gallicus* 143
*Circus aeruginosus* 144
  *cyaneus* 145
  *pygargus* 147
*Clamator glandarius* 332
*Clangula hyemalis* 128
*Coccothraustes coccothraustes* 550
  *migratoria* 582
*Coccyzus americanus* 335
  *erythrophthalmus* 334
*Colinus leucopogon* 581
  *virginianus* 167
*Columba oenas* 323
  *palumbus* 325
  *livia* 322
*Columbina passerina* 580
**Coot** 182
*Coracias garrulus* 356
**Cormorant** 70, Double-crested 74, Great 70
**Corncrake** 178
*Corvus corax* 518
  *cornix* 517
  *corone* 516
  *frugilegus* 515
  *monedula* 513
*Coturnix coturnix* 170
**Crake** Baillon's 178, Corn 178, Little 177, Spotted 175

**Crane** 184
*Crex crex* 178
**Crossbill** 547, Two-barred 546
**Crow** Carrion 516, Hooded 517
**Cuckoo** 333, Black-billed 334, Great Spotted 332, Yellow-billed 335
*Cuculus canorus* 333
**Curlew** 239, Eskimo 237, Stone 191
*Cygnus atratus* 579
  *columbianus* 95
  *cygnus* 96
  *olor* 93
*Delichon urbica* 376
*Dendrocopos major* 362
*Dendroica coronata* 553
  *magnolia* 553
  *striata* 554
*Diomedea exulans* 44
**Diver** Black-throated 33, Great Northern 34, Red-throated 33, White-billed 35, Yellow-billed 35
*Dolichonyx oryzivorus* 576
**Dotterel** 200
**Dove** Barbary 581, Collared 327, Eurasian Collared 327, European Turtle 329, Inca 581, Oriental Turtle 330, Rock 322, Rufous Turtle 330, Stock 323, Turtle 329
**Dowitcher** Long-billed 231
**Duck** American Black 117, Black 117, Ferruginous 125, Long-tailed 128, Mandarin 580, Muscovy 580, Ring-necked 124, Ruddy 137, Tufted 125, Wood 109
**Dunlin** 222
**Dunnock** 400
**Eagle** Short-toed 143, White-tailed 141
**Egret** Cattle 83, Great 85, Great White 85, Little 83
*Egretta garzetta* 83
**Eider** 128
*Emberiza aureola* 569
  *bruniceps* 572
  *chrysophrys* 566

  *cirlus* 564
  *citrinella* 563
  *hortulana* 565
  *leucocephalos* 562
  *melanocephala* 571
  *pusilla* 568
  *rustica* 566
  *schoeniclus* 570
*Eophona migratoria* 582
*Eremophila alpestris* 368
*Erithacus rubecula* 403
*Falco columbarius* 160
  *naumanni* 155
  *peregrinus* 164
  *rusticolus* 162
  *subbuteo* 161
  *tinnunculus* 157
  *vespertinus* 159
**Falcon** Gyr 162, Peregrine 164, Red-footed 159
*Ficedula albicollis* 486
  *hypoleuca* 486
  *parva* 484
**Fieldfare** 431
**Finch** Zebra 583
**Firecrest** 481
**Flamingo** 579
**Flycatcher** Brown 483, Collared 486, Pied 486, Red-breasted 484, Spotted 483
*Forpus passerinus* 581
*Fratercula arctica* 317
*Fringilla coelebs* 532
  *montifringilla* 533
*Fulica atra* 182
**Fulmar** 45
*Fulmarus glacialis* 45
**Gadwall** 111
*Gallinago delicata* 230
  *gallinago* 228
  *media* 230
*Gallinula chloropus* 179
**Gallinule** American Purple 181
**Gannet** Northern 69
**Garganey** 119
*Garrulus gladarius* 508
*Gavia adamsii* 35
  *arctica* 33
  *immer* 34
  *stellata* 33
*Geothlypis trichas* 557

# Index

*Glareola pratincola* 192
**Godwit** Bar-tailed 236, Black-tailed 235
**Goldcrest** 479
**Goldeneye** 133
**Goldfinch** 537
**Goosander** 135
**Goose** Barnacle 104, Bean 97, Brent 105, Canada 102, Chinese 579, Egyptian 106, 580, Greater White-fronted 99, Greylag 101, Pink-footed 98, White-fronted 99
**Goshawk** 149
**Grackle** Common 582
**Grebe** Black-necked 42, Great Crested 38, Little 37, Pied-billed 36, Red-necked 39, Slavonian 41
**Greenfinch** 535
**Greenshank** 244
**Grosbeak**, Chinese 582, Rose-breasted 575
**Ground-dove** Common 580
**Grouse** Black 166
*Grus grus* 184
**Guillemot** 309, Black 315
**Gull** Black-headed 269, Bonaparte's 269, Common 272, Glaucous 284, Great Black-backed 285, Herring 277, Iceland 282, Ivory 295, Laughing 266, Lesser Black-backed 273, Little 267, Mediterranean 265, Ring-billed 270, Sabine's 268, Yellow-legged 281
*Haematopus ostralegus* 186
*Haliaeetus albicilla* 141
**Harrier** Eurasian Marsh 144, Hen 145, Marsh 144, Montagu's 147
**Hawfinch** 550
**Hawk** Red-shouldered 153
**Heron** Black-crowned Night 80, Grey 85, Night 80, Purple 87, Squacco 82
*Himantopus himantopus* 189
*Hippolais caligata* 452
  *icterina* 453
  *olivetorum* 455
  *pallida* 451
  *polyglotta* 454
*Hirundo daurica* 374
  *rustica* 371
**Hobby** 161
**Honey-buzzard** European 137
**Hoopoe** 357
*Hydrobates pelagicus* 61
*Hylocichla mustelina* 421
**Ibis** Glossy 91
*Icterus galbula* 577
*Ixobrychus minutus* 79
**Jackdaw** 513
**Jay** 508
*Jynx torquilla* 359
**Kestrel** 157, Lesser 155
**Killdeer** 198
**Kingfisher** 353
**Kite** Black 139, Red 140
**Kittiwake** 289, Black-legged 289
**Knot** 208, Red 208
*Lanius collurio* 503
  *cristatus* 501
  *excubitor* 505
  *isabellinus* 502
  *minor* 504
  *senator* 506
**Lapwing** 207, Northern 207
**Lark** Bimaculated 363, Calandra 363, Greater Short-toed 364, Horned 368, Shore 368, Short-toed 364, Sky 366, Wood 365
*Larus argentatus* 277
  *atricilla* 266
  *canus* 272
  *delawarensis* 270
  *fuscus* 273
  *glaucoides* 282
  *hyperboreus* 284
  *marinus* 285
  *melanocephalus* 265
  *michahellis* 281
  *minutus* 267
  *philadelphia* 269
  *ridibundus* 269
  *sabini* 268
*Limnodromus scolopaceus* 231
*Limosa lapponica* 236
  *limosa* 235
**Linnet** 540
*Locustella certhiola* 440
  *fluviatilis* 441
  *lanceolata* 440
  *luscinioides* 441
  *naevia* 440
*Lonchura malacca* 583
**Longspur** Lapland 560
*Loxia curvirostra* 547
  *leucoptera* 546
*Lullula arborea* 365
*Luscinia luscinia* 405
  *megarhynchos* 406
  *svecica* 407
*Lymnocryptes minimus* 226
**Magpie** 509, Black-billed 509
**Mallard** 115
**Martin** House 376, Sand 370
*Melanitta fusca* 131
  *nigra* 129
  *perspicillata* 130
*Melanocorypha bimaculata* 363
  *calandra* 363
*Melopsittacus undulatus* 331
**Merganser** Red-breasted 135
*Mergus albellus* 134
  *merganser* 135
  *serrator* 135
**Merlin** 160
*Merops apiaster* 355
  *persicus* 354
*Miliaria calandra* 573
*Milvus migrans* 139
  *milvus* 140
*Mniotilta varia* 551
*Monticola saxatili* 418
  *solitarius* 418
**Moorhen** 179
*Morus bassanus* 69
*Motacilla alba* 395
  *cinerea* 394
  *citreola* 393
  *flava* 390
    *cinereocapilla* 392
    *feldegg* 392
    *flava* 391
    *iberiae* 392
    *lutea* 393
    *thunbergi* 392
**Munia** Chestnut 583
*Muscicapa dauurica* 483
  *striata* 483
*Netta rufina* 122
**Nighthawk** Common 346
**Nightingale** 406, Thrush 405

## Birds of the Isles of Scilly

**Nightjar** 345
*Nucifraga caryocatactes* 510
*Numenius arquata* 239
   *borealis* 237
   *phaeopus* 238
**Nutcracker** 510, Spotted 510
*Nyctea scandiaca* 339
*Nycticorax nycticorax* 80
*Oceanites oceanicus* 59
*Oceanodroma leucorhoa* 66
   *matsudairae* 47
   *monorhis* 67
*Oenanthe deserti* 417
   *hispanica* 416
   *isabellina* 413
   *oenanthe* 414
   *pleschanka* 416
**Oriole** Baltimore 577, Golden 500
*Oriolus oriolus* 500
**Osprey** 154
*Otis tetrax* 185
*Otus scops* 338
**Ouzel** Ring 425
**Owl** Barn 337, Eurasian Scops 338, Little 340, Long-eared 342, Scops 338, Short-eared 344, Snowy 339, Tawny 341
*Oxyura jamaicensis* 137
**Oystercatcher** 186
*Pagophila eburnea* 295
*Pandion haliaetus* 154
*Panurus biarmicus* 487
**Parakeet** Rose-ringed 332
**Parrotlet** Green-rumped 581
**Partridge** Grey 168, Red-legged 167
*Parula americana* 552
**Parula** Northern 552
*Parus ater* 492
   *caeruleus* 493
   *cristatus* 491
   *major* 496
   *palustris* 490
*Passer domesticus* 524
   *hispaniolensis* 527
   *montanus* 528
*Passerina ciris* 583
*Pelecanus crispus* 579
**Pelican** Dalmatian 579
*Perdix perdix* 168
*Pernis apivorus* 137

**Petrel** Bulwer's 47, Cape Verde 48, Fea's 48, Leach's 66, Storm 61, Swinhoe's 67, Wilson's 59, Zino's 48
*Petrochelidon pyrrhonota* 375
*Phaethon aethereus* 68
*Phalacrocorax aristotelis* 74
   *auritus* 74
   *carbo* 70
**Phalarope** Grey 258, Red-necked 256, Wilson's 255
*Phalaropus fulicarius* 258
   *lobatus* 256
   *tricolor* 255
*Phasianus colchicus* 171
**Pheasant** 171, Golden 172
*Pheucticus ludovicianus* 575
*Philomachus pugnax* 225
*Phoenicopterus* 579
*Phoenicurus ochruros* 408
   *phoenicurus* 409
*Phylloscopus bonelli* 472
   *borealis* 466
   *collybita* 475
   *fuscatus* 471
   *humei* 469
   *ibericus* 477
   *inornatus* 467
   *orientalis* 472
   *proregulus* 467
   *schwarzi* 469
   *sibilatrix* 474
   *trochiloides* 464
   *trochilus* 478
*Pica pica* 509
*Picus viridis* 360
**Pigeon** Common Wood 325, Stock 323
*Pinguinus impennis* 315
**Pintail** 118
**Pipit** Blyth's 379, Buff-bellied 389, Meadow 383, Olive-backed 380, Pechora 382, Red-throated 384, Richard's 378, Rock 385, Tawny 379, Tree 382, Water 388
*Piranga olivacea* 558
*Platalea leucorodia* 92
*Plectrophenax nivalis* 561
*Plegadis falcinellus* 91
**Plover** American Golden 201, Caspian 200, European

Golden 204, Grey 205, Kentish 199, Little 193, Little Ringed 193, Pacific Golden 203, Ringed 194, Semipalmated 197
*Pluvialis apricaria* 204
   *dominica* 201
   *fulva* 203
   *squatarola* 205
**Pochard** 122, Red-crested 122
*Podiceps auritus* 41
   *cristatus* 38
   *grisegena* 39
   *nigricollis* 42
*Podilymbus podicep* 36
*Poephila guttata* 583
*Porphyrula martinica* 181
*Porzana carolina* 176
   *parva* 177
   *porzana* 175
   *pusilla* 178
**Pratincole** Collared 192
*Prunella collaris* 402
   *modularis* 400
*Psittacula krameri* 332
*Pterodroma feae* 48
   *madeira* 48
**Puffin** 317, Atlantic 317
*Puffinus assimilis* 59
   *gravis* 50
   *griseus* 51
   *mauretanicus* 58
   *puffinus* 52
*Pyrrhocorax pyrrhocorax* 511
*Pyrrhula pyrrhula* 549
**Quail** 170
*Quiscalus quiscala* 582
**Rail** Sora 176, Water 173
*Rallus aquaticus* 173
**Raven** 518
**Razorbill** 312
*Recurvirostra avosetta* 190
**Redpoll** Arctic 545, Common 544, Lesser 543
**Redshank** 243, Spotted 242
**Redstart** 409, Black 408
**Redwing** 436
*Regulus ignicapilla* 481
   *regulus* 479
*Remiz pedulinus* 498
*Riparia riparia* 370
*Rissa tridactyla* 289

# Index

**Robin** 403, American 438, European 403, Rufous Bush 402, Rufous-tailed Scrub 402
**Roller** 356
**Rook** 515
**Rosefinch** Common 548
**Ruff** 225
**Sanderling** 209
**Sandgrouse** Pallas's 321
**Sandpiper** Baird's 217, Buff-breasted 223, Common 251, Curlew 219, Green 249, Least 214, Marsh 244, Pectoral 218, Purple 221, Semipalmated 211, Sharp-tailed 219, Solitary 248, Spotted 252, Terek 250, Upland 240, Western 212, White-rumped 215, Wood 250
**Sapsucker** Yellow-bellied 360
*Saxicola rubetra* 410
  *torquata* 411
*Scardafella inca* 581
**Scaup** 126, Greater 126, Lesser 127
*Scolopax rusticola* 233
**Scoter** Common 129, Surf 130, Velvet 131
*Seiurus noveboracensis* 556
**Serin** 534
*Serinus canaria* 583
  *serinus* 534
**Shag** 74
**Shearwater** Balearic 58, Cory's 49, Great 50, Little 59, Manx 52, Sooty 51
**Shelduck** 107, Ruddy 108
**Shoveler** 121
**Shrike** Brown 501, Great Grey 505, Isabelline 502, Lesser Grey 504, Red-backed 503, Woodchat 506
**Silvereye** 582
**Siskin** 539
**Skua** Arctic 261, Brown 264, Great 263, Long-tailed 262, Pomarine 259, South Polar 264
**Skylark** 366
**Smew** 134
**Snipe** 228, Great 230, Jack 226, Wilson's 230
*Somateria mollissima* 128
**Sora** 176
**Sparrow** Eurasian Tree 528, House 524, Spanish 527, Tree 528, White-throated 559
**Sparrowhawk** 150
*Sphyrapicus varius* 360
**Spoonbill** 92
**Starling** 519, Rose-coloured 522, Rosy 522, White-cheeked 582
*Stercorarius longicaudus* 262
  *parasiticus* 261
  *pomarinus* 259
*Sterna albifrons* 306
  *anaethetus* 305
  *bengalensis* 297
  *caspia* 297
  *dougallii* 299
  *fuscata* 305
  *hirundo* 301
  *maxima* 297
  *nilotica* 296
  *paradisaea* 304
  *sandvicensis* 298
**Stilt** Black-winged 189
**Stint** Little 212, Temminck's 213
**Stone-curlew** 191
**Stonechat** 411
**Stork** Black 88, White 89
**Storm-petrel** European 61, Leach's 68, Matsudaira's 47, Swinhoe's 67, Wilson's 59
*Streptopelia decaocto* 327
  *orientalis* 330
  'risoria' 581
  *turtur* 329
*Strix aluco* 341
*Sturnus cineraceus* 582
  *roseus* 522
  *sinensis* 582
  *vulgaris* 519
**Swallow** 371, Barn 371, Cliff 375, Red-rumped 374, Tree 369
**Swan** Bewick's 95, Black 579, Mute 93, Tundra 95, Whooper 96
**Swift** 349, Alpine 351, Chimney 348, Little 352, Pacific 351, Pallid 350
*Sylvia atricapilla* 462
  *borin* 462
  *cantillans* 456
  *communis* 460
  *conspicillata* 456
  *curruca* 459
  *hortensis* 458
  *melanocephala* 457
  *nisoria* 459
  *undata* 455
*Syrrhaptes paradoxus* 321
*Tachybaptus ruficollis* 37
*Tachycineta bicolor* 369
*Tadorna ferruginea* 108
  *tadorna* 107
**Tanager** Scarlet 558
*Tarsiger cyanurus* 407
**Teal** 113, Blue-winged 120, Chestnut 580, Green-winged 114
**Tern** Arctic 304, Black 307, Bridled 305, Caspian 297, Common 301, Gull-billed 296, Lesser Crested 297, Little 306, Roseate 299, Royal 297, Sandwich 298, Sooty 305, Whiskered 307, White-winged 308, White-winged Black 308
*Tetrao tetrix* 166
*Thalassarche melanophris* 44
**Thrush** Bicknell's 425, Black-throated 430, Blue Rock 418, Dark-throated 430, Eye-browed 429, Grey-cheeked 423, Hermit 422, Mistle 437, Red-throated 430, Rock 418, Rufous-tailed Rock 418, Siberian 420, Song 431, Swainson's 422, White's 419, Wood 421
**Tit** Bearded 487, Blue 493, Coal 492, Crested 491, Eurasian Penduline 499, Great 496, Long-tailed 489, Marsh 490, Penduline 498
**Treecreeper** 497
*Tringa erythropus* 242
  *flavipes* 246

607

*glareola* 250
*melanoleuca* 245
*nebularia* 244
*ochropus* 249
*solitaria* 248
*stagnatilis* 244
*totanus* 243
*Troglodytes troglodytes* 397
**Tropicbird** Red-billed 68
*Tryngites subruficollis* 223
*Turdus iliacus* 436
*merula* 426
*migratorius* 438
*obscurus* 429
*philomelos* 431
*pilaris* 431
*ruficollis* 430
*torquatus* 425
*viscivorus* 437
**Turnstone** 253
**Twite** 543
*Tyto alba* 337
*Upupa epops* 357
*Uria aalge* 309
*Vanellus vanellus* 207
**Vireo** Philadelphia 529, Red-eyed 530
*Vireo olivaceus* 530
*Vireo philadelphicus* 529
**Wagtail** Ashy-headed 392, Black-headed 392, Blue-headed 391, Citrine 393, Grey 394, Grey-headed 392, Pied 395, Spanish 392, White 395, Yellow 390, Yellow-headed 393
**Warbler** American Wood 556, Aquatic 442, Arctic 466, Barred 459, Black-and-white 551, Blackpoll 554, Blyth's Reed 446, Booted 452, Cetti's 439, Dartford 455, Dusky 471, Eastern Bonelli's 472, Eastern Olivaceous 451, Garden 462, Grasshopper 440, Great Reed 450, Greenish 464, Hooded 558, Hume's 469, Hume's Leaf 469, Icterine 453, Lanceolated 440, Magnolia 553, Marsh 446, Melodious 454, Olive-tree 455, Orphean 458, Paddyfield 445, Pallas's 467, Pallas's Grasshopper 440, Pallas's Leaf 467, Radde's 469, Reed 448, River 441, Sardinian 457, Savi's 441, Sedge 443, Spectacled 456, Subalpine 456, Western Bonelli's 472, Willow 478, Wood 474, Yellow-browed 467, Yellow-rumped 553
**Waterthrush** Northern 556
**Waxwing** 396, Bohemian 396
**Wheatear** 414, Black-eared 416, Desert 417, Isabelline 413, Northern 414, Pied 416
**Whimbrel** 238
**Whinchat** 410
**Whitethroat** 460, Lesser 459
**Wigeon** 109, American 110
*Wilsonia citrina* 558
**Woodcock** 233
**Woodlark** 365
**Woodpecker** Great Spotted 362, Green 360
**Woodpigeon** 325
**Wren** 397, Winter 397
**Wryneck** 359
*Xenus cinereus* 250
**Yellowhammer** 563
**Yellowlegs** Greater 245, Lesser 246
**Yellowthroat** 557
*Zonotrichia albicollis* 559
*Zoothera dauma* 419
*Zoothera sibirica* 420
*Zosterops lateralis* 582

# ISLES OF SCILLY

Shipman Head

**BRYHER**

SCILLY ROCK
GWEAL
Gweal Hill
SHIPMAN HEAD DOWN
The Town
Great Pool

MAIDEN BOWER

CASTLE BRYHER

ILLISWILGIG

RUSHY BAY
North Hill
PUFFIN ISLAN

MINCARLO

**SAMSON**

WEST PORTH
EAST PORTH
WHITE ISLAND
Shag Point

South Hill

|—— 1 kilometre ——|

NORTHWEST PORTH
Annet Head
**ANNET**
WEST PORTH

POR KILL
Big Pool
Midd Town

GREAT CREBAWETHAN

MELLEDGAN

ROSEVEAR
ROSEVEAN
GORREGAN
**WESTERN ISLES**